The Essential Jazz Records

Volume 2

Modernism to Postmodernism

The Essential Jazz Records

VOLUME 2

Modernism to Postmodernism

Max Harrison, Eric Thacker and Stuart Nicholson

Mansell Publishing Limited
London and New York

First published 2000 by
Mansell Publishing, *A Cassell imprint*
Wellington House, 125 Strand, London WC2R 0BB
370 Lexington Avenue, New York, NY 10017-6550

http://www.cassell.co.uk

British Library Cataloguing in Publication Data
A catalogue record for this book is available from the British Library.
ISBN 0-7201-1822-0 (hardback)
0-7201-1722-4 (paperback)

Library of Congress Cataloging-in-Publication Data
Harrison, Max.
The essential jazz records/Max Harrison, Charles Fox, and Eric Thacker.
p. cm.
Vol. 2 by Max Harrison, Eric Thacker, and Stuart Nicholson.
Includes bibliographical references and indexes.
Contents: —v. 2. Modernism to postmodernism.
ISBN 0–7201–1822–0 (hardcover).—ISBN 0–7201–1722–4 (paperback)
1. Jazz Discography. I. Fox, Charles, 1921–1991. II. Thacker, Eric, 1923–97. III. Nicholson, Stuart. IV. Title
ML 156.4.J3H33 2000
781.65′0266—dc21 99–40414
CIP

Typeset by SetSystems Ltd, Saffron Walden, Essex
Printed and bound in Great Britain by Biddles Ltd, Guildford and King's Lynn

This book is dedicated to the memories of Charles Fox
(born Weymouth 1921, died Weymouth 1991),
who contributed so much to Volume 1 and Eric Thacker
(born Leeds 1923, died Leeds 1997),
who contributed so much to both.

Contents

Introduction

There is no question in jazz history of a central identity being lost amid a welter of experiment, although proclamations of its death as a result of the latest innovations have been one of the oldest parts of its tradition. While we should be careful not to be hypnotized by metaphors (such is the magic power of words over our minds), the development of a music like jazz may surely be likened to the growth of an oak tree. In its sapling years jazz was naturally limited in its expressive scope and stylistic variety. But slowly, as the tree matured, an increasing number of branches were put out – the technical resources multiplied, the expressive potential increased. The musical diversity by now attained may at first confuse us, yet if we look closely enough we see that all the branches stem from the same trunk, that the roots penetrate further into the soil than before. And it all started from the same acorn.

One way of looking at this is to recognize that jazz has shown an extraordinary capacity for adapting other idioms. Indeed this may in the end prove to be its most remarkable single quality, because it changes, absorbs, enriches borrowed musical resources. *Body and soul* after it has been improvised on by Coleman Hawkins (**192**) or *Embraceable you* after Charlie Parker has done with it (**258**) mark large advances on the initial Tin Pan Alley ballads. Similarly jazz bossa nova has greater musical substance than the original Brazilian bossa nova, and the best jazz-rock, as discussed in these pages, deserves far more attention than rock 'n' roll or later rock.

In short, jazz is an inclusive music and long has been. Which means that it does not merely allow but demands individuality, a fact confirmed by all the recordings cited in the following pages. Having explored – though not necessarily exhausted – any given style and evolved a fresh jazz concept out of it, the music, generation by generation, moves on. Change is not only inevitable but essential for its further development. To define jazz in terms of its past, as certain players have repeatedly tried to do, is to reduce it to a repertoire music and threatens its future growth.

By the time the first of these two volumes was published, in 1984, what had seemed like a fatal blow to jazz delivered by rock had long passed. Jazz activity had resumed and the flow of recordings gradually rose to flood levels. Since then the CD has resulted in a further huge number of issues and particularly reissues. Record buyers have had the unnerving experience of a century's recorded music being reissued in the past ten years. This plethora of discs has gradually been accompanied by a large increase of writing on jazz. Inevitably this takes various forms but really detailed analytical consideration of specific recorded performances receives little space. This book, together with its predecessor, is an attempt to fill the vacuum by providing a critical survey of the whole field of recorded jazz, an attempt to see both the wood and specimens of significant individual trees. As such it is obviously highly selective and this serves a number of purposes in turn.

Chief among these is of course drawing attention to some of the finest jazz that has survived on disc. It should occasion no surprise that while some of our citations are obvious, there is also a lot of music dealt with here which has not been trodden flat by hordes of writers. All too often in deciding what jazz should receive attention the mentality of the auction room prevails, whereby the flimsiest sketch by a big name is valued more highly than the choicest canvas of a minor master. Hence together with familiar classics we have, especially in our book's later pages, included many records that will be unexpected.

These latter are present because originality in art, as perhaps in science too, often consists of a shift of attention to aspects of reality previously hidden, of discovering connections hitherto ignored, of seeing familiar objects or procedures in a new light. And these sometimes occur in places that are by no means obvious. Real music uses notes to convey meanings, and fresh meanings can only be communicated by setting notes in new forms and relationships. Such endeavours may entail increasing the alienation of the audience, hence the limited acceptance of much of the jazz dealt with herein and hence its obscurity, which is to say its lack of fame. So far as recent music of worth is concerned, recordings often appear on small labels which have limited distribution and almost no publicity. Indeed the low cost of a short run of a CD has led to very numerous musicians making it a point of honour to have their work enshrined in that format. The difficulties this puts in the way of the authors of a publication like this are obvious. A vast quantity of evidence has been examined and re-examined during the years of this book's preparation, yet a good deal more has eluded us with a persistence which almost suggests diabolical intervention.

It is true that recordings are simply what chanced to be preserved. It is also true that the recording process acts against romantics' love of impermanence, and all jazz fans are romantics. But with most live performances disappearing into thin air, recordings plainly are all we have left to assess the musician's contribution. This is even true with composers such as Monk (**292**) and ensembles like the Modern Jazz Quartet (**363**) who produced well-defined repertoires of music. Despite the problems just noted, we have tried to locate the best of the evidence and this not least because of the relationship between live and recorded work. We all hear contemporaneous music, which is to say live performances, against the background of the past, which in this case means against recordings, and we hear the past against the background of the present; and as our experience of one changes, so mysteriously does our experience of the other. Historians and, perhaps even more cogently, historically oriented critics have been described as prophets facing backwards.

An important task of criticism should arise out of clear division and classification, this supposedly making the whole subject matter accessible and comprehensible. Yet we decided in such matters to venture beyond the security of convention and routine, which often is nothing more than the frail furniture of an undignified make-believe. In reality, the parameters according to which periods are demarcated are so manifold and overlapping that valid periodization may be almost impossible to achieve. And so we have repeatedly tried to subvert chronology and stylistic unity, this in accord with André Malraux's concept of a museum as a device for abolishing time and confounding space, unsystematically violating the contexts in which and for which given bodies of work were created.

Because this is first a book about music and only second a record guide, we have not been unduly concerned with what is currently obtainable in the shops, or even with availability on CD. Perhaps nearly all the jazz mentioned in these pages will eventually appear on CD, perhaps not. But our planet's huge stock of LPs will survive, even if not listed in any current catalogue; and experience teaches that even the rarest items turn up eventually. A special problem we had, though, was of repeated and different reissues on CD. As an almost random example, take the Getz material dealt with under **368–9**. At the time of going to press the most recent local issue of *Focus* is †Verve (E) 521 419–2, this including additional performances not covered in this book. Likewise *The Steamer* and *West Coast Jazz* have appeared as *Stan Getz East of the Sun – The West Coast Sessions* on †Verve (E) 314 531 935–2. This material has also come out as *West Coast Jazz: Stan Getz and the Cool Sounds*, which further includes 12 hitherto unissued tracks. Other reissues will presumably appear in due course, so where does one stop?

There are some paths, however, which for various reasons we have not pursued. It is too bad there was no room for highly talented, rather isolated, individuals such as Bernie McGann in Australia or the late John Park in the United States. Our representation of European jazz, indeed, is seriously incomplete and, as the case of McGann suggests, we have not covered jazz from other parts of the world such as Japan at all. The truth is that an entire book like this could easily be devoted to non-American jazz.

A matter for considerable offence, at least to some reviewers, was the small section in Volume 1 devoted to classical works influenced by jazz. This, like the matter of Third Stream, touches a hypersensitive nerve of the average jazz commentator's massive sense of inferiority about European (and for that matter American) classical music. That the influence of jazz continues in such spheres has been illustrated by numerous works, such as Stefan Wolpe's Quartet for Trumpet, Saxophone, Piano and Percussion, Tippett's Symphony No. 3, which evidently was prompted by the Davis–Evans *Porgy and Bess* (**382**), Schnittke's Symphony No. 1, Peter Maxwell Davies's *St Thomas Wake*, subtitled 'Foxtrot for Orchestra', and more recent pieces such as Mark-Anthony Turnage's *Blood on the Floor*, which uses actual jazz soloists. Yet although such music continues to proliferate we have not dealt with it here, so as not to offend certain tender sensibilities.

Concepts like Third Stream and the jazz that employs aspects of serial technique dealt with under **456–7** and elsewhere are facilely dismissed as 'theoretical', as *a priori* constructs – as if there ever was a valid theoretical idea that did not first emerge as an intuitive musical practice. The distinctions between description of style and analysis of structure continue to haunt contemporary writing on music although there is interest and value in both approaches. The best music will of course survive without the help of apologist or analyst, but our understanding and enjoyment can be enhanced by both. Much art history is a tale of craft and language, whereas that of jazz is, in its public dimension, all too often a sequence of fashions. And yet in the finest art the audience is never given something for nothing: it has to pay in emotional currency by exerting its imagination. And indeed listening is at best a creative act, involving a continuous exercise of the imagination. But although there are great contemporary musicians, there are few great contemporary listeners. Most of us are too involved in present conflicts, too mesmerized by the dominant falsehoods of our time, too aware of what is currently thought 'right' or 'wrong' often to match the clear-sighted impartiality of the finest music.

We need to be aware that group mimicry is a real force in the world and for guidance we all do well to go outside our own generation. To belong to a particular generation, to be stamped by certain events, developments, even particular phases of art, is a destiny sometimes lucky and sometimes unlucky, but not in itself a merit. Hence it was thought a sensible precaution that the three contributors to this book should each be from a different generation. And we did get help from elsewhere. Useful advice was received from Peter Apfelbaum, Terence Boyd, Todd Coolman, Brian Davis, André Hodeir, Michael James, Sharon Kelly (Sony Jazz), Keith Knox, Bill Laswell, Gunnar Lindqvist, Kerstan

Mackness (New Note Records), Alun Morgan, Malcolm Nicholson, Steven Sanderson (New Note), Maria Schneider, Adam Seif (Sony), Michael Sparke, Becky Stevenson (Polydor), Duane Tatro and Alan Zeffertt. One cannot simply adopt the judgements of others; if we do they cease to be judgements. But Yeats comforts us with the notion that 'truth flourishes where the student's lamp has shone'.

Max Harrison, Stuart Nicholson

Abbreviations

Instrumental and Related Abbreviations

acc	piano accordion
ah	alto horn
alt	alto saxophone
alt clt	alto clarinet
alt fl	alto flute
arr	arranger
bar	baritone saxophone
bh	baritone horn
bj	banjo
bon	bongos
bs	string bass
bs clt	bass clarinet
bs fl	bass flute
bs g	bass guitar
bsn	bassoon
bs sx	bass saxophone
bs tbn	bass trombone
bs tpt	bass trumpet
cel	cello
cls	celeste
clt	clarinet
clv	claves
clvt	clavinet
cnt	cornet
comp	composer
con	conga drum
cond	conductor
cw bl	cow bell
cym	cymbal
d	drums
el bs	electric bass
el p	electric piano
el g	electric guitar
eng h	english horn
eu	euphonium
fl	flute
fl h	flugel horn
fr h	french horn
g	guitar
glock	glockenspiel
har	harmonium
hpschd	harpsichord
hrp	harp
kybd	keyboard
mar	maraccas
mel	mellophone
mrm	marimba
mus	musette
ob	oboe
org	organ
p	piano
ped-st g	pedal-steel guitar
perc	percussion
picc	piccolo
sop	soprano saxophone
synth	synthesizer
tbn	trombone
ten	tenor saxophone

th	tenor horn	vcl intrjc	vocal interjection(s)
timb	timbales	vib	vibraharp
timp	timpani	vla	viola
tpt	trumpet	vln	violin
tu	tuba	v-tbn	valve trombone
vcl	vocal	wbd	washboard
vcl gr	vocal group	xylo	xylophone

Discographical Abbreviations

After records' label names, the country of origin is indicated as follows:

(A)	United States of America	(G)	Germany
(Ar)	Argentina	(H)	Holland
(Au)	Austria	(Hun)	Hungarian
(B)	Brazil	(It)	Italy
(C)	Canada	(J)	Japan
(Cz)	Czechoslovakia	(P)	Poland
(E)	Great Britain	(Por)	Portugal
(Eu)	Europe	(Sd)	Sweden
(F)	France	(Sp)	Spain
(Fi)	Finland	(Sw)	Switzerland

† before a label, either in the discographical heading or in the main text or in the notes following each chapter, indicates a compact disc. An asterisk (*) in the same position indicates a record whose contents are only in part – though in most cases substantially – the same as those of the record actually discussed, whose number appears first. In such cases no exactly equivalent issue exists elsewhere.

Warning

Although every effort has been made to ensure the correctness of record numbers, neither the publisher nor the authors hold themselves responsible for purchases made with reference to this book.

1

The Swing to Bop

Heralds and Collaborators

Bop, the first wave of modern jazz, was not the abrupt revolution that it still is often claimed to have been. Several of its central characteristics emerged during the 1930s in the work of leading musicians.

Charlie Christian

251 **The Harlem Jazz Scene**
Musidisc (F) 33JA5122, Archive of Folk and Jazz Music (A) 219, †Jazz Anthology (F) 550012

Joe Guy (tpt); Thelonious Monk (p); Christian (g); Nick Fenton (bs); Kenny Clarke (d). Minton's Playhouse, New York City, *c.* May 1941.
Swing to bop · *Stomping at the Savoy*

Vic Coulsen, supposedly 'Hot Lips' Page, unidentified (tpt); Don Byas (ten); Al Tinney (p); Christian (g); Ebenezer Paul (bs); unidentified, perhaps Taps Miller (d). Monroe's Uptown House, New York City, *c.* May 1941.
Guy's got to go · *Up on Teddy's hill* · *Lips flips*

Dizzy Gillespie (tpt); Byas, unidentified (ten); Tinney (p); unidentified bs, d. Same location and approximate date.
Stardust I

Gillespie (tpt); Kenny Kersey (p); unidentified bs, d. Presumably same location and approximate date.
Kerouac · *Stardust II*

Among the indestructible clichés of jazz anecdotage is that as this music shifted from swing to bop, much effort was expended on the stylistic delineation of the latter in New York after-hours venues like Minton's and Monroe's. [1] Such tales were lent apparent substance by Jerry Newman, who ventured into these establishments with two disc-cutters which, by using 12-inch recording blanks, could take down performances much longer than was then possible on commercial discs. Thus was preserved free, demonstrably spontaneous, improvising by young, then mainly obscure jazzmen, some of whose playing departed from standard practice and several of whom offered thoughts that were significantly new. By no means all this music is fully achieved, and some of it, particularly in the roughly jammed ensembles, is inchoate. Whether it overall shows us the emergence of a major new phase in jazz might be questioned, were it not that legend normally gets the better of history because people find more comfort in fantasy than in fact.

What stands far beyond such reservations, however, and makes the above record not just essential but almost the only one with which this volume could begin, is Christian's work. Only he and Byas had established reputations, only they sound quite secure stylistically in everything they do here; and the latter, though masterful in all else, lacks originality. The guitarist's role in some more conventional endeavours is considered in Volume 1, but his output as a whole shows that it is mistaken to regard him solely as an aggressive modernist who was restricted by the disciplines of the Benny Goodman large and small groups of which he was a member (**159**). Musical circumstances changed his responses and a few months before performances like *Swing to bop* Christian recorded, admittedly with an acoustic guitar, a three-chorus solo on Ed Hall's *Profoundly blue* (**187**) that, while making a personal enough statement, employs a notably traditional vocabulary to do so.

Such cases establish how firmly rooted his innovations were, and transitional figures like Christian usually emphasize what was common to both styles. As central to his most representative music as the blues was the electrification of his instrument. There were precedents such as Floyd Smith's *Floyd's guitar blues* with Andy Kirk (**132**) and the Jimmy Lunceford band's *Hittin' the bottle* with Eddie Durham (**138a**). But the point was the consistency with which Christian took advantage of the guitar's new status as a front-line instrument with a voice equal to those of the horns. Electrification gave him a ringing, almost percussive tone, though one also relaxed and without vibrato, seemingly detached beside Django Reinhardt's overt passion (**104–6**). His sound added to the force and precise statement of his ideas on melodic, harmonic and especially rhythmic planes, and the most telling of the above performances, the ones on which his playing is most different from his playing with Goodman, are those with Clarke. Even in 1941 the latter's playing approached modern drumming, and the teaming of Christian with Clarke was an important step towards a bop conception.

Indeed the guitarist was, in a suitably free context, capable of this kind of jazz even earlier, as his two *Tea for two* solos, recorded at a 1939 Minneapolis jam session, indicate (Musica Jazz [It] 2MJP1058, CBS [A] 67233). At such times he produced longer lines, the runs of quavers, or semiquavers at slow tempos, being more conspicuously even than in purely swing settings. In this he followed Lester Young, as he did in a frequent use of the major sixth degree of the scale in both major and minor keys. However, while Christian employed the ninth and higher intervals more often than Young, often accenting them, he was among the first (recorded) players to take on Young's feeling for the beat, dividing the crotchet into two quavers, and doing so still more evenly than Young. At the same time Christian's accents are displaced more freely, with more chromaticism – and less of the blues – in the implied harmonies. Another factor was his use of harmonic anticipations, resulting in a beneficially heightened tension between his improvised lines and the underlying chords. Also heard more frequently in these informal circumstances than elsewhere was a use of tritones to link dominant seventh chords.

Yet there were still plenty of Christian's blues riffs, mainly in the A sections of AABA 32-bar song forms. Into and out of these flowed his strong vein of melodic invention, whose characteristically arching phrases are at their most angular on the middle eights of themes such as *Swing to bop* (alias Basie's *Topsy* **[133]** and first issued as *Charlie's choice*). Despite this particular feature, Christian in such places asserts what perhaps was first demonstrated by Bix Beiderbecke, namely that improvised jazz melody can be a continuous unfolding, which flows independently across the patterned repetitions of the underlying harmonic sequence. It may be significant that, according to Mary Lou Williams, Beiderbecke's *In a mist* (**63**) was an early favourite of Christian's. [2]

The zestful linearity of this music, with its shifting, nearly always satisfying balance between repetition and new material, clearly relates not only to Young but also to the more flexible way of swinging that Charlie Parker would introduce. [3] That there are further links with Parker in the background of such music is implied by pieces by Ornette Coleman (who, like Christian, was from Texas) such as *Ramblin'* – the 1958 version on Improvising Artists (A) IA373852 even more than the one on **400**. Christian's solos on *Swing to bop*, *Stompin' at the Savoy* (his two longest improvised solos on record), *Guy's got to go*, *Up on Teddy's hill* (on the *Honeysuckle rose* chords) and *Lips flips* are the most advanced jazz he left us. But it should be remembered that, although he was now inside the last year of his life, he was very young, born only in 1916. That he could produce in close proximity solos like those on *Profoundly blue* and *Swing to bop*, the Minneapolis *Tea for two* and Goodman's *Seven come eleven* (**159**) suggests that besides being transitional for jazz as a whole this music was also transitional for Christian himself, that further development in his style would have followed, leading, presumably, to a more integrated mode of expression. And if Christian had survived, the guitar might have enjoyed a more secure place in the bop rhythm section, whose internal organization would consequently have been rather different.

There are no such tantalizing questions with Gillespie, whose steady growth towards a mature style of singular individuality is quite well documented on records. He is found here between the sort of playing he did for Calloway (**148**) and his solo on Lucky Millinder's *Little John special* (**123**). That is, although the flow of invention in his three *Kerouac* solos, interspersed with Kersey's many-noted elegance, is impressive, especially in the daring second one, he is crossing a stylistic no-man's-land where the general manner is that of Roy Eldridge-prompted swing trumpeting disrupted by a more personal choice of notes. More satisfying and more advanced is the second *Stardust*, where his muted playing clearly points to some of his later ballad interpretations.

Although they were the same age – both born in October 1917 – Monk was further from his destination than Gillespie. There are some unusual rhythmic displacements in his accompaniments, and it is noteworthy that in *Swing to bop* he improvises on the theme of *Topsy*, not just the chords. But his technique is more conventionally pianistic than it became a few years later, and more fluent in the ordinary sense. On *Stompin' at the Savoy* there are even suggestions of Teddy Wilson.

One item has persistently been omitted from collective reissues of this material, *Down on Teddy's hill*, which up to the time of this book's publication has only appeared on Xanadu (A) X107 and the Musica Jazz LP referred to above. It includes more excellent Christian and is by the *Swing to bop/Stompin' at the Savoy* Minton's personnel with the addition of an unidentified second trumpeter, two tenor saxophonists, and with Monk either absent or inaudible. *Down on Teddy's hill* is in fact an early form of Monk's *Rhythm-a-ning* and was recorded by Al Haig in 1950 as *Opus caprice* (Prestige [A] PRLP7156) and in a thoroughly smoothed-down version by Basie as *Taps Miller* (CBS [F] 54163). Further, *Lips flips* (on the *Stompin' at the Savoy* chords) also appeared as *On with Charlie Christian*. These are two different editings of the same performance, the former including an initial tenor solo that is absent from the latter.

M.H.

Lester Young

252 The Complete Aladdin Sessions

Blue Note (A) BN-LA456-H2 (2 LPs)

Young (ten); Dodo Marmarosa (p); Red Callender (bs); Henry Tucker Green (d). Los Angeles, December 1945.
These foolish things

Vic Dickenson (tbn) added. Same date.
D.B. blues · *Lester blows again* · *Jumpin' at Mesner's*

Young (ten); Wesley Jones (p); Curtis Counce (bs); Johnny Otis (d). Los Angeles, January 1946.
After you've gone

Howard McGhee (tpt), Dickenson (tbn), Willie Smith (alt) added. Same date.
It's only a paper moon · *Lover, come back to me* · *Jammin' with Lester*

Young (ten); Joe Albany (p); Irving Ashby (g); Callender (bs); Chico Hamilton (d). Los Angeles, August 1946.
You're driving me crazy · *The new Lester leaps in* · *Lester's be-bop boogie* · *She's funny that way*

Young (ten); Argonne 'Dense' Thornton (p); Fred Lacey (g); Rodney Richardson (bs); Lyndall Marshall (d). Chicago, 18 February 1947.
Jumpin' with Symphony Sid · *On the sunny side of the street* · *No eyes blues*

Shorty McConnell (tpt) added. Same date.
Sunday · *S.M. blues* · *Sax-o-be-bop*

Young (ten); Thornton (p); Lacey (g); Ted Briscoe (bs); Roy Haynes (d). New York City, 28/30 December 1947.
Jumpin' at the Woodside · *Easy does it* · *I'm confessin'*

McConnell (tpt) added. Same date.
Movin' with Lester · *Just coolin'* · *Lester smooths it out*

Young (ten); Gene DiNovi (p); Chuck Wayne (g); Curly Russell (bs); Tiny Kahn (d). New York City, 29 December 1948.
East of the sun · *Sheik of Araby* · *Something to remember you by*

Careful listening to these and allied recordings ought long ago to have dispelled the myth that Young's postwar years were an unrelieved decline. But, given a prevailingly anecdotal attitude to jazz history, once the notion took root that he was 'broken', psychologically speaking, by his time in the US Army, examination of the musical evidence has seldom been thought necessary. In fact there is a second myth here, to the effect that Young's music had nothing whatever to do with bop, this being a fiction that, during those years when the new style was under ferocious attack, he himself sometimes fostered. Yet on the first two of the above sessions it is Dickenson, a typical swing player, who sounds out of place while the leader accords excellently with Marmarosa and Albany, both pioneer bop pianists, with McConnell, plainly a Gillespie follower, and with McGhee. So he does too with Haynes, wholly a bop drummer, with Hamilton, and with the purely bop rhythm section of the final date.

Faced with Coleman Hawkins's adamantine achievement, Young had taken an entirely different path even though this meant rejection by a pillar of the establishment such as Fletcher Henderson's orchestra, and it is likely that he would sympathize with others who wanted to 'make it new'. More significant, however, is that once the actual detail of his recordings is observed it becomes clear that Young's playing in the decade after World War II included many fresh departures, firmly built, of course, on what he already had achieved. Unlike most of his disciples, he was not tied to any one version of his style, and signs that his music was changing in an entirely positive way are apparent at least as early as the 1943 quartet date for Keynote (Trip [A] 5509). By the time we reach his Aladdin sessions many passages occur that he would not have played, perhaps could not have conceived, in the 1930s, there being for example a much greater degree of rhythmic abstraction. *After you've gone*, with its extreme angularity of phrase and mocking use of clichés such as honks and repeated notes played with alternating fingerings, shows how, when a straightforward swinging performance was expected, he could impose something quite different. That the result might be misunderstood, even accounted a failure, would appeal to Young's sense of humour.

He said that to begin with he 'tried to get the sound of a C melody [saxophone] on a tenor', [4] but he was no longer doing so by the time these recordings were made. Though he still followed Frankie Trumbauer in avoiding vibrato, his tone is larger than in the 1930s, more virile, even combative. The assertion of his beautifully sculpted stop-time passages on *The new Lester leaps in*, the vividness of his best ideas, their sheer communicative force, as on *Movin' with Lester* or *Just coolin'* (based respectively on *Honeysuckle rose* and *Sheik of Araby*), should be obvious. Young's affinities with bop can be heard most clearly, though, in the music of the sextet which did the June 1949 session on **196** and more especially in the many live recordings taken of that band. For instance, their March 1949 Royal Roost version of *D.B. blues* (Affinity [E] AFFD80, Charlie Parker [A] PLP409) is very boppish and is one of a considerable number of such performances which demonstrate that Young was at home amid the new music's turbulence. Such occasions were recreated by the churning excitement of the above *Jammin' with Lester*, with its high-stepping McGhee solo; and he was indeed well suited by the forceful ensemble backing he received on this second Aladdin session.

Much – very much – has been written about how gentle, detached, retiring Young was in person, but performances like the above, and many others, indicate how naïve is the conclusion that his music could only be the same. A very few of these pieces, such as *Lester smooths it out* and *Jumpin' at the Woodside*, are almost unqualified failures, yet until near the end he was perfectly capable of looking after himself in artistic matters. Thornton was a self-taught pianist and sounds it, but Young faced down the harmonic and rhythmic near-chaos of his strumming, Otis's incipient rhythm 'n' blues drumming or Lacey's overly prominent guitar as firmly as Armstrong did the saccharine Lombardo-echoing saxophone section. Also relevant here is his capacity for improvising throughout a performance from first bar to last, examples include *You're driving me crazy* and *Lover, come back to me*.

None of this is to deny that this music has another aspect, resulting in pieces that almost sound like private meditations. Though not much exploited during his years with Basie, Young's powers as a ballad player were shown to be extraordinary in the period under consideration here, his interpretations being uncommonly slow, often of surprising poignancy and at the same time of enhanced rhythmic flexibility. *These foolish things* was a favourite vehicle and the above reading should be compared with the 1944 one on **196**, the 1949 Royal Roost broadcast (Affinity and Charlie Parker issues as above) and the 1952 version (Columbia [E] 33CX10031, Norgran [A] MGN1005); note especially bars 25–32 of this last. It is not quite the point that the original tune is ignored in each case but that, as André Hodeir has said, he produces music that is 'like a negative image of the original, a cleaned-up, retouched and disturbing image'. [5] Further instances of Young's melodic creativity and capacity for sustained linear thought are *I'm confessin'*, *She's funny that way*, making a particular use of the tenor saxophone's lower register, and *On the sunny side of the street*, which recaptures the mood of his performance in the 1944 film *Jamming the Blues*.

A comparable type of sustained intensity is found in Young's blues playing, of which *Jumpin' with Symphony Sid* and *No eyes blues* can serve as contrasting examples. Here, as in the ballads, he is shown to have a kind of strength not always evident in his big-band appearances. And nobody worked this idiom with greater originality than he, especially noteworthy being his avoidance of traditional flattened blue notes without any loss of blues feeling. Significantly, many of Young's own themes during these years were in blues form, although the Symphony Sid piece is supposedly by Thornton. [6]

D.B. (= disciplinary barracks) *blues* is the interesting case of a 'blues with a bridge', the chorus being 12 + 12 + 8 + 12 bars. On it Dickenson's fatuous caperings, besides providing a glaring contrast with Young and Marmarosa, amount to exactly the 'square unswinging phrases' of which bop trombonists were supposedly so often guilty. On the more positive side it may be added that Ashby's *You're driving me crazy* solo implies that he was a link between Charlie Christian and Barney Kessel. The initial tenor saxophone phrase on this track supplied the basis of Cy Touff's *Prez-ence* (**305**).

Despite the sleeve's inevitable claim, this set does not contain Young's complete Aladdin recordings. Missing are his 1942 trio date with Nat Cole and Callender (Spotlite [E] SPJ136, Score [A] SLP4019), a session with Helen Humes which includes a little-known yet outstanding *Riffin' without Helen*, *One o'clock jump* and an alternative take of *Easy does it* from the penultimate date plus *Tea for two* from the last. These are all included on the further †Blue Note 2-CD reissue, CDP832 787–2. The *D.B. blues* session is usually assigned to October 1945, but Young was in the army until 1 December of that year, hence the latter month is the earliest possible. As has happened on several previous reissues, Blue Note has reversed the titles of *No eyes blues* and *Sax-o-be-bop* on both sleeve and label.

M.H.

Coleman Hawkins

253 Bean and the Boys

Prestige (A) PR7824

Hawkins (ten); Thelonious Monk (p); Edward 'Bass' Robinson (bs); Denzil Best (d). New York City, 19 October 1944.
On the Bean · Recollections · Flying Hawk · Drifting on a reed

Fats Navarro (tpt); J. J. Johnson (tbn); Porter Kilbert (alt); Hawkins (ten); Hank Jones (p); Curly Russell (bs); Max Roach (d). New York City, December 1946.
I mean you

Milt Jackson (vib) added. Same date.
Bean and the boys (2 versions)

Navarro, Johnson, Kilbert absent. Same date.
Cocktails for two · You go to my head

Hawkins (ten); Jean-Paul Mengeon (p); Pierre Michelot (bs); Kenny Clarke (d). Paris, 21 December 1949.
Sophisticated lady · I surrender, dear

Nat Peck (tbn), Hubert Fol (alt) added. Same date.
Sih-sah · It's only a paper moon · Bay-u-bah · Bean's talking again

Jazz has all too often confirmed Scott Fitzgerald's dictum that 'American lives have no second act'. With many a jazz musician nothing so becomes his career as the beginning of it, this being succeeded by repetition, self-imitation, perhaps even self-caricature. Hawkins's case could not have been more different. His creative energy was surpassed by that of no other jazz improviser, and he sustained it longer than most of them. Partly this arose from his ambition to remain, as he had been since the later 1920s, a leader in this field. But its deeper, less accessible roots lay in an intense musical curiosity, this being intimately related to a capacity for self-renewal perhaps only paralleled by Miles Davis. Certainly there was never any question of passively reflecting new trends. Rather did Hawkins, an avid listener, identify the most significant features of a fresh jazz development and absorb them into his own playing, thereby extending the scope of a style which, because it was long since fully mature, remained entirely his.

As with Young and Tatum, the main body of Hawkins's recorded work is discussed in Volume 1 and our concern here is the recorded outcome of his encouragement of, and musical relationships with, leading members of the next generation. The harmonic substitutions he employed during the 1930s, not to mention his exploratory 1933 composition *Queer notions* (**126**), suggest that at least some aspects of bop can have held few surprises for Hawkins. The influence of early bop phraseology is already evident in *Stumpy* (**194**) from a 1943 session that also produced his *Voodt*, a notable bop theme. That was the year Gillespie left Hines's band to play with the tenor saxophonist in New York, and February 1944 saw the making under Hawkins's name of what are often regarded as the first bop records. Besides three magnificent ballad interpretations in the master's best vein, these two sessions (Mode [F] 9863, Grand Award [A] 33–316) produced Gillespie's *Woody 'n' you*, Budd Johnson's *Bu-dee-daht*, and *Disorder at the border*, a Hawkins blues arranged by Gillespie that employs a riff from Jay McShann's (Charlie Parker's) *The jumpin' blues* (Affinity [E] AFS1006, *Decca [A] DL5503) and in turn provided an idea for *Cool breeze* (**315**).

Against such a background the music of the above LP was a natural further step, although there is another aspect to the situation. Often in his career Hawkins had been interested solely in fronting a band rather than in putting together and being a member of a true ensemble. But such an attitude would have been inadvisable in the presence of such obviously dangerous young men as Navarro and Johnson: listen to the way Navarro follows him on both versions of *Bean and the boys*! (In 1953 this theme was recorded by Powell as *Burt covers Bud*: see **261**.) Again, what bop drummers like Clarke and Roach were up to would obviously have been of interest, in fact of value, to one whose rhythm at fast tempos had sometimes been on the unduly regular side. Dominant though he is, on the 1946 date Hawkins is very much *in* this band rather than simply in front of it.

But first came the session that accorded Monk his first real chance. Based on the same *Whispering* chord sequence as the above-mentioned *Stumpy*, *On the Bean* gave the pianist eight bars to demonstrate that he was ready. His full chorus on *Flying Hawk* confirms, despite the final gesture on *Recollections*, that he had eliminated many of the standardized procedures heard from him on **251** and was well on the way to a keyboard technique that would exactly match the needs of his unique musical mind.

In *Recollections* and *Drifting on a reed* what is especially memorable is not only the beauty of Hawkins's ideas but the logical way they are connected. So they are too on his next venture in this direction, a February 1946 date with Shelly Manne on which against all the odds another tenor saxophonist, the young Allen Eager, shone, above all in *Allen's alley* (alias *Wee*). The remaining titles from this session, *Say it isn't so*, *Spotlite* and *Low flame* (RCA [F] PM42046, RCA [A] LJM1017), shift intriguingly between swing and bop in feeling, not least when Hawkins is playing.

From December of that year, *I mean you* is a Monk theme and his own 1948 recording of it can be heard on **292**. [7] Here it is effectively, though alas anonymously, scored, particularly the final ensemble passage. The solos are short yet pithy, with Kilbert reminding us of Benny Carter and the other horns sounding like themselves; indeed, sensitive accompanist though he is, only Jones presents solos that are without interest on this date. Jackson, who does have something of his own to offer, joins in with *Bean and the boys*, which is based on the *Lover, come back to me* chords. Here the solos are most impressive in the first version, the ensembles more cleanly executed in the second, which goes the barest fraction slower.

These two performances should be heard in conjunction with Hawkins's *c.* 1950 version (Phoenix [A] LP22), from a session which also preserved another reading of *Disorder at the border*. And it must be added that his association with such material and such players continued. In 1947, for example, he led a session with Miles Davis, Kai Winding and Roach, another with Navarro, Johnson and again Roach. This latter included Tadd Dameron's warmly coloured *Half step down, please*, which has brilliant Navarro. A decade later appeared *The Hawk Flies High* (†Original Jazz Classics [A] OJC027), a splendid record with Johnson, Idrees Sulieman, Barry Galbraith and others, and in 1962 Shelly Manne's *2, 3, 4* in which Hawkins draws quite close to free jazz. This can be read about under **215** in Volume 1.

Before these latter, though, came the Paris 1949 date, evidently a happy occasion. It was in fact among Hawkins's very best, and supported with Michelot's excellent bass playing, driven by Clarke's great drumming, and despite Mengeon's uncertainty at some points what the chords are supposed to be, the leader's improvising was at its most creative. His tone is as rich as ever, yet lither, more precisely defined, than was often the case. And while there is a far more explicit awareness of the harmonies than we find with Young or even Christian, whose lines flow through the chords without needing to state all their notes, the elaborate detail of Hawkins's playing here tumbles out with more relaxation than usual. This is apparent not only in the ballads but also in the blues *Sih-sah* and *Bean's talking again*, authoritative statements in a form he had not much cultivated in his earlier years. The other horns, one French, one American, make for a slightly unusual front-line instrumentation, solo briefly on *It's only a paper moon*, and otherwise provide apt background chords and riffs. *Bay-u-bah* is a fanciful reworking of *Sweet Georgia Brown*, Latin American to Clarke's advantage fore and aft. Alternative takes of this and *Paper moon* are on Swingtime (D) ST1004. [8] M.H.

Art Tatum

254a The Complete Capitol Recordings Vol. 1
†EMI/Capitol (E) CDP792.866–2

Tatum (p). Los Angeles, 13 July 1949.
Willow, weep for me · I cover the waterfront · Aunt Hagar's blues · Nice work if you can get it · Someone to watch over me · Dardanella

Same. Los Angeles, 25 July 1949.
Time on my hands · Sweet Lorraine · Somebody loves me · Don't blame me

Everett Barksdale (g), Slam Stewart (bs) added. New York City, 20 December 1952.
September song · Melody in F · Tea for two · Out of nowhere

254b The Complete Capitol Recordings Vol. 2
†EMI/Capitol (E) CDP792.867–2

Tatum (p). Los Angeles, 29 September 1949.
My heart stood still · You took advantage of me · I gotta right to sing the blues · How high the moon? · Makin' whoopee · Goin' home · Blue skies · It's the talk of the town · Dancin' in the dark · Tenderly

Barksdale (g), Stewart (bs) return. New York City, 20 December 1952.
Just one of those things · Indiana · Lover · Would you like to take a walk?

One clue towards explaining the above recordings' inclusion here lies in statements by a number of later pianists, such as Steve Kuhn, to the effect that it was only after they had learned from Bud Powell that they began to appreciate Tatum. [9] The latter had drawn together virtually everything of significance that had appeared thus far in the musical language of jazz, and it would be surprising if his doing so had not yielded indications of what was going to happen next. This may well account for the fact that, aside from a few instances such as Coleman Hawkins, Tatum's mastery had more influence on the new generation than on his contemporaries. Entries devoted to the pianist in Volume 1 should have made clear the imagination and skill that he brought to the intensification of traditional chord sequences through the interpolation of substitute and passing harmonies, sudden transitions into remote keys etc. Even quite early Tatum solos contain decided thrusts into the future such as the bitonal passage in his 1937 *Gone with the wind* (**181a**), and the interest of these to, say, Parker, a great admirer of his, is obvious, as is the pianist's inexhaustible capacity for rhythmic variation.

All this is communicated through a similarly vast invention of keyboard textures whose elaboration had no precedent in this music. Like other virtuoso pianists, not only in jazz, Tatum had a preoccupation with the left hand and with inner voices (shared between the hands), although his bass lines could be every bit as adventurous, in fact and implication, as the rest. It is in such elements as these that his foreshadowings of bop are often most apparent. The Capitol solos were recorded four years after bop had decisively emerged in 1945, but they essentially are the result of initiatives he had taken up in the 1930s. Besides, something close to bop single-line phrasing can be heard in Tatum's solos on the 1943 Esquire All-Stars session (**191**) and in his two versions of *Exactly like you* dating from a *c.* 1943/4 (Shoestring [A] SS105) and 1944 (Official [D] 83042), where bitonality is again implied. The point is that whereas in Hawkins, Young and latter-day Miles Davis we see established artists changing their music as a result of pressure from styles more recent than their own, Tatum had in some respects quite simply got there first.

Other features of his work that interested the younger men were its concentration, the packing of so much music, not just a lot of notes, into short time lengths and – another aspect of the same thing – his often compositional shaping of each performance as a whole instead of as simply an episode of open-ended improvisation on the chords. It was all done with an ease so extreme as to suggest ironic detachment. Yet Tatum's virtuosity was also a source of inspiration, rather as Paganini's violin playing was to the romantic piano composers of the 19th century. That is to say, virtuosity was shown not to be merely a means of display but a vehicle for emotional and musical exploration. Tatum rather than Coltrane may be said to have introduced 'sheets of sound' into jazz, yet his influence perhaps also worked in quite the opposite direction. Monk can be seen as his reverse image, pianistically at least, answering all that luxuriance with his own brand of asceticism.

Another consequence of Tatum's virtuosity was that he was a master of meaningful ambiguity and could make his music appear to 'say' several things at once. A good example is *Aunt Hagar's blues*, through which he threads a quite different piece, *Black coffee*, doing so from the performance's opening bars, this seemingly prompted by Sarah Vaughan's recording, and Joe Lippman's harmonically rich arrangement, of the previous January. A little-remarked interest of his, indeed, was that of uncovering, or constructing, relationships between seemingly unconnected pieces. Other instances are his demonstration of links between *Dardanella* and *Exactly like you* (Shoestring, as above), or between *Memories of you* and MacDowell's *To a wild rose*. In such things we meet Tatum the illusionist, who at other times makes us believe that a melody is being stated when it is only implied. This side of his playing became ever more subtle, as did the humour that went into it. An aspect of the latter is his brinkmanship, which took several forms, not necessarily used one at a time. In *Sweet Lorraine* he almost quotes a certain Paderewski *morceau* but does not quite do so. Even at such moments the music has an air of inevitability about it, although we know that he might have taken any one of a dozen other routes.

These Capitol solos are as virtuosic as ever, and one is as aware as before of Tatum's absorption of jazz history. Yet the listener also senses not a new discipline, for there are plenty of his earlier solos that are as well ordered as these, but the discipline being applied more consistently. This is so in *I cover the waterfront*, *Nice work if you can get it* and more especially *Dancing in the dark*, *Willow, weep for me*, *Aunt Hagar's blues* and *Blue skies* – in the last of which, in a typical piece of metrical displacement, he goes into the bridge two beats early and then adds two beats at the end so it comes out even. In such performances the blaze of bravura is prompted by the highest poetic impulse, and at a slightly more mundane level one can say that each detail arises out of, and relates back to, the whole. Something more easily pinpointed is that Tatum's actual statement of the beat is still more flexible, having a measure of true *rubato* within a strict tempo. This is partly a matter of stride elements being at a minimum, as with *Dancing in the dark*.

A further point about these 1949 solos is that what had been anticipations of bop here become confirmations of it. Yet at the same time *Aunt Hagar's blues* is a definitive *haute école* statement about piano blues, as likewise is *Dardanella* about some aspects of the post-ragtime novelty piano music that was another of Tatum's sources (hear his 1934 *The shout* on **181a**).

However, whereas these solos are baroque, with everything essential no matter how richly the detail proliferates, the trios are rococo, with nearly everything garish and exhibitionistic. His sole musically successful trio recordings with guitar are the little-known ones employing Les Paul (Shoestring, as above). Despised for his later very successful multi-recorded popular pieces, Paul had more invention and rhythmic suppleness than Tatum's regular guitarists and so the pianist is encouraged to play with better continuity than was usual with him in this format.

So far as the solos are concerned, the extraordinary thing is that he went beyond the level here attained, and the best Capitols represent just one of several kinds of perfection he gave us. As instances of Tatum reaching further heights, listen to **217a/b** and more specifically to his reharmonizations of the July 1955 *Sweet Lorraine* (Official, as above). The trio instrumentation with guitar pared away almost everything that was genuinely progressive in his work but this made no difference to his most representative music: the eagle flies to the sun. M.H.

Red Norvo

255 Fabulous Jam Session

†Spotlite (E) SPJCD127, †Stash (A) STB2514

Dizzy Gillespie (tpt); Charlie Parker (alt); Flip Phillips (ten); Teddy Wilson (p); Slam Stewart (bs); Specs Powell (d); Norvo (vib). New York City, 6 June 1945.

Hallelujah (3 versions) · *Get happy* (2 versions)

J. C. Heard (d) replaces Powell. Same date.
Slam Slam blues (2 versions) · *Congo blues* (5 versions)

Norvo was underrated despite an original and exploratory contribution to jazz that began, on records, in the early 1930s with pieces such as the often atonal *Dance of the octopus* (**199**). Like Coleman Hawkins or Lester Young, and unlike so many established jazzmen, he was always sympathetic to younger people who were doing new things in this music. Typically, the year after this session with Parker and Gillespie he became a member of Herman's First Herd (**312**) and went on to lead a nimble and uncompromising trio with Farlow and Mingus (**247**) in 1950–1. Having made the transition to bop, he ventured considerably further, appearing on the remarkable *Blues and Vanilla* LP of Jack Montrose (RCA [Sp] NL45844, RCA [A] LPM1451) in 1956 and the following year recording **451**. Given his capacity for blending with such diverse players in a variety of styles, it perhaps is not altogether surprising that Norvo's work retained its delicacy, energy and quiet humour well into the 1980s.

He began on the marimba, then xylophone, and these naturally influenced the way he approached the vibraharp, to which he moved permanently only in 1944 on joining Benny Goodman's sextet. Normally he played without vibrato though with discreet tremolos at the ends of some phrases. He was always very fluent so that everything sounds easy – but not too easy – and his clarity of thought at fast tempos, as in *Hallelujah* or *Get happy*, is usually impressive. These four titles also demonstrate Norvo's steady flow of ideas, and that his solos, which are full of surprising turns of phrase, also include sensitive, often unexpected, harmonic nuances. Altogether he is very far from sounding, as has been claimed, 'the most old-fashioned player on the date', [10] being indeed at his most creative nearly throughout.

This justly famous meeting was not at all the confrontation that it usually is represented as having been. In fact there is better stylistic integration here than at a Norvo concert of three days later which lacked the supposedly disruptive presences of Gillespie and Parker but employed Phillips, Wilson, Stewart and Powell (Jazztone [A] J1219). The recording session's fairly unusual premise was that of making two 12-inch 78s, rarely used for jazz, featuring two old standards and two blues, one fast, one slow. After Norvo's crucial decision to invite Parker's and Gillespie's participation, his next most important choice was Wilson. He and the pianist were regular sources of inspiration to one another, borrowing, altering, developing each other's ideas, as on their appearances with Goodman. Phillips was then with Herman, in whose First Herd and attendant small groups he was always heard to best advantage. The two drummers were fruitfully, though rather differently, influenced by Sidney Catlett, but the supposedly amusing banalities of Stewart (really the most old-fashioned player on the date) are mainly humour for people with no sense of humour.

Gillespie offers a thrusting virtuoso display on the first attempt at *Hallelujah* yet one based on a sequence of real musical ideas. The riff behind him, perhaps contributed by Phillips, sounds like something from the First Herd. At this stage Parker has less good continuity than Gillespie, Norvo or Wilson but he is surer of what he wants to do in the next version. On this latter Wilson gives almost bop comping support to the leader's solo. A further take of *Hallelujah*, not on the above compilation, appeared on *Charlie Parker on Dial* Volume 5 (Spotlite [E] 105), and this finds the alto saxophonist still more imaginative, with Phillips doing some effective slipping and sliding. The latter is even better on the final reading, quite properly chosen for 78-rpm release. Gillespie is slightly less intense than on the two preceding performances but still his solo is a bold, even daring, flight. Parker, having built steadily across the three earlier versions – plus several others never issued – presents a splendidly integrated, highly characteristic improvisation. The last chorus unison ending was probably Gillespie's idea, being the kind of passage he and Parker can be heard playing with almost uncanny unanimity in several items on the record discussed below.

The incomplete first essay on *Get happy* includes a finely, even delicately, chiselled trumpet solo and, perhaps in response, we get the cooler side of Parker, sounding rather as he does on, say, *Groovin' high* (**256a**). In the second *Get happy* Gillespie is more decisive, Parker hits an entirely different mood, and there is another unequivocal bop ensemble to close. On the slow *Slam Slam blues* (the first version of which is in some places reissued as *Bird blues*) Gillespie is muted, sinuous, pensive, while Parker's solos speak, in different manners, with the authority of sadness. At the vibraharp, the son of Beardsville, Ohio, offers solos that diverge substantially, yet equally are latter-day vibraharp equivalents to his three xylophone choruses on Wilson's *Just a mood* (**176**). That his instrument lacks the horns' or even the piano's capacity for dramatic impact should not deafen us to the closely packed significant musical detail here.

At the beginning of the first, incomplete, *Congo blues* Gillespie plays muted, then open, while on the second he stays muted and sounds surer of himself. There follows an excellent Parker solo, then another breakdown. He is less poised in the third attempt which, being complete, also gives us solos from Wilson, Phillips, Norvo and, alas, Stewart. On the fourth version Parker starts in an entirely new way and goes on to a much better achieved, and rather more complicated, piece of work. The final account is, however, clearly the best, or the one that points most decisively not so much to the future as to the postwar present. Recalling ideas heard in previous readings but putting them to more integrated use, Gillespie plays with the surging fluency of one whose time has come. Yet Parker, at once blue and exultant, quite simply takes over. M.H.

Charlie Parker and the Emergence of Modern Jazz

Bop, or bebop, originally rebop, was slightly more complex than earlier styles, but the overall movement of jazz, in terms of rhythm, harmony and hence of melody, had for some years been in that direction. These modest enrichments of style were grandly proclaimed a 'revolution' by most commentators, and some of the musicians, alas, believed them.

Dizzy Gillespie

256a **Groovin' High Vol. 1**
Musicraft (A) MV2009, *†Musicraft (A) CDMVSCD53

Gillespie (tpt); Dexter Gordon (ten); Frank Paparelli (p); Chuck Wayne (g); Murray Shipinsky (bs); Shelly Manne (d). New York City, 9 February 1945.
Blue 'n' boogie

Gillespie (tpt); Charlie Parker (alt); Clyde Hart (p); Remo Palmieri (g); Slam Stewart (bs); Cozy Cole (d). New York City, 28 February 1945.
Groovin' high · All the things you are · Dizzy atmosphere

Gillespie (tpt, vcl[1]); Parker (alt); Al Haig (p); Curly Russell (bs); Sidney Catlett (d); Sarah Vaughan (vcl[2]). New York City, 11 May 1945.
Salt peanuts[1] · *Shaw nuff* · *Loverman*[2] · *Hot house*

Gillespie (tpt, vcl[1]); Sonny Stitt (alt); Haig (p); Ray Brown (bs); Kenny Clarke (d); Gil Fuller (arr, vcl[3]); Alice Roberts (vcl[4]). New York City, 15 May 1946.
A hand fulla gimme[4]

Milt Jackson (vib) added. Same date.
Oop-bop-sh'bam[1,3] · *That's Earl, brother*

256b **One Bass Hit Vol. 2**
Musicraft (A) MV2010

Same personnel as above session. Same date.
One bass hit I

Gillespie, Dave Burns, Raymond Orr, Talib Daawud, John Lynch (tpt); Al Moore, Leon Comegeys, Charlie Greenlea (tbn); John Brown, Howard Johnson (alt); Ray Abrams, Warren Lucky (ten); Pee Wee Moore (bar); Jackson (p); Brown (bs); Clarke (d); Tadd Dameron (arr[5]); Fuller (arr[6]); Roberts (vcl[4]). New York City, 10 June 1946.
Our delight[5] · *Good dues blues*[4,6]

Gordon Thomas (tbn) replaces Greenlea, Jackson switches to vib, John Lewis (p) added. New York City, 9 July 1946.
One bass hit II · *Ray's idea* · *Things to come* · *He beeped when he should have bopped*[4] (2 versions)

Matthew McKay (tpt), Taswell Baird (tbn), Scoops Carry (alt), James Moody, Bill Frazier (ten), Joe Harris (d) replace Daawud, Comegeys, Johnson, Abrams, Lucky, Clarke; Kenny Hagood (vcl[7]) added. New York City, 12 November 1946.
I waited for you[7] · *Emanon*

It must be a matter for permanent regret that Gillespie and Parker recorded together so little in the early days of bop. The tiny store of jazz which they produced at that time is so precious that items will be discussed here which are not on the above Musicraft issues. The earlier of these small combo dates mix swing and bop players, as do the foregoing Young, Hawkins and Norvo sessions, but the music is far more decisively shaped by new ideas because Gillespie's, and to a lesser extent Parker's, concepts dominate. In their most representative passages these records define the bop idiom in its primal form, and as such they are something towards which these two musicians, and others, had been working for some years. Consider Gillespie's contributions to **161b**, **148**, **123** (and Parker's to **250**).

The trumpeter had in those recordings with Lionel Hampton, Cab Calloway and Lucky Millinder given increasingly clear indications of what his mature style would be like. It was a highly original mode of utterance and Roy Eldridge's influence, despite the obvious precedents he provided regarding speed and flexibility, has been overemphasized in some commentaries. In the 1940s, having reached the point where musical thought and instrumental technique were as one, Gillespie redefined the jazz trumpet's scope, and in the second half of that decade occasionally made it seem as if all limitations had disappeared. Restless in attack, his style was dramatic, full of sharp contrasts which created a dynamic sense of insecurity in listeners, who felt themselves always being approached from an unexpected angle as Gillespie, nearly always successfully, took one risk after another. The authority of such playing derived most obviously from what for several years remained a fantastic executive skill. This virtuosity enabled him – as a similar accomplishment allowed Parker – to improvise with emotion and constant invention at tempos beyond the reach of most earlier jazzmen. In Gillespie's case the results often conveyed an exhilarating *joie de vivre*, yet behind the seeming abandon there was calculated design even if no very strong sense of structural continuity. There was, indeed, a suggestion of detachment: he was less an instinctive artist than his partner. It was necessary that some of the leaders of this new phase in jazz should be so, for the music was changing its function as well as enriching its language. The best jazz had always been music for listening, yet now it became more insistently so, and this because, within certain limits, it became more complex.

Like each major jazz style, bop undertook a reassessment of each of the music's elements while retaining much from the past. Its harmonic usage, as indicated under **253–4**, was largely known to such men as Hawkins and Tatum, but the more extreme resources were now employed more consistently. Nor was emphasis on the upper intervals of extended chords new, but there was a more frequent melodic use of dissonant leaps made available by these extensions. In fact more chromatic harmony naturally gave rise to a larger melodic vocabulary, and as harmonic density increased, so did harmonic rhythm accelerate. Nobody illustrates better than Gillespie bop's productive tension between the richness of these resources and its usually lean, athletic solo idiom which, even if made possible only by virtuosity, is at its best shorn of all inessential detail. This is paralleled by a further contrast between the enlarged musical vocabulary and the bop combo's ascetic instrumentation, although, again, the tight-lipped thematic passages were not new, having been pioneered by small swing bands in the immediate pre-bop years.

For Gillespie as for bop in general, however, the main changes were rhythmic, and so far as solo playing is concerned, these are hard to define because often they are a matter of small – yet crucial – nuances of pulse, accent, division of beats. Luckily the reorganization of the rhythm team's function can be described quite easily, the essential point being that the homogeneous texture of swing and earlier rhythm sections is broken up. Building perhaps on Jimmy Blanton's liberation of the instrument with Ellington's 1940 band (**153**), the double bass now stated the basic pulse. This was elaborated by the drummer with hi-hat and ride cymbals while a variety of off- and on-beat punctuations were stated by snare drum, bass drum and the piano, the whole providing not an indifferent background but a fully participating commentary on what the soloists, or the horns collectively, were playing. Equally, a good soloist, or inventive writing for the front line, would be a stimulus to the rhythm players. So far as improvisation was concerned, irregular accents by the rhythm section encouraged asymmetrical phrasing from soloists, generating tautness and forward drive. Although its regular pulse is what jazz fans love best, the vitality and specific character of this music has always to some extent depended on the irregularity of its rhythms.

Naturally this was not put together all at once, and though Catlett met bop requirements more completely on the 11 May 1945 session than Cole on 28 February, it was only when Clarke took over in 1946 that everything fell into place. Really this sequence ought to begin with Gillespie's January 1945 date represented by two pieces on **249**. Of these, *I can't get started* may seem an improbable initial statement of the new jazz, yet the trumpeter improvises a beautiful variant of Vernon Duke's melody, full of interesting harmonic touches, a slow-motion demonstration of one facet of bop. Dameron's attractive and individual contributions to Gillespie's repertoire were clearly foreshadowed by his scores for Harlan Leonard's Kansas City band and remained in the swing rather than bop idiom. On *Good bait* Don Byas 'eats up the changes', as they used to say, in his tenor solo, but the most telling feature is Gillespie's counterpoint to the theme restatement. More significantly, this January 1945 session produced *Salt peanuts* and *Bebop* (Queen [It] Q039, Smithsonian [A] R004). The former might seem a pure bop theme, yet its main idea appeared in Millinder's *Little John special* (**123**) and before that in Charlie Shavers's arrangement of *Sweet Georgia Brown* for John Kirby in 1939, not to mention Joe Bushkin's *Pickin' at the Pic* (Mosaic [A] MR23–128, 1944) and Goodman's *Oh, baby* (Columbia, 1946). Likewise the immediate ancestor of *Bebop* was Shavers's *Deuce-a-rini* (Phoenix, 1944), but Gillespie's trumpet solo on *Salt peanuts* is bop full blown, and his three choruses on *Bebop* can, and should, astonish us decades later. This is among the great trumpet solos in recorded jazz and after it there could be no serious question about his status as a major figure.

If these performances be thought to include disparate elements, the reader should hear the date led by Joe Marsala in which Gillespie took part three days later. Seconded by Wayne's excellent guitar though not by Cliff Jackson's stride piano, still less by Buddy Christian's thumping drums, the trumpeter stands defiantly as an exponent of bop at its purest in splendid solos on *My melancholy baby*, *Cherokee*, *On the Alamo* (Phoenix [A] LP2) and *Perdido* (Official [D] 3056–2). Another example of Gillespie coping as well as Armstrong ever did with an incongruous setting is *Red cross*, recorded with Hampton's large band the following April (Official, as above). Here too he offers a long solo crammed with fresh ideas against a leadenly unswinging pulse.

Again companioned by Wayne, Gillespie takes another lucidly organized solo on the first of the Musicraft titles, *Blue 'n' boogie*. Here we must once more look elsewhere for the origin of the piece, the main thematic idea having appeared on some, not all, takes of *No smokes blues* recorded by Sarah Vaughan the previous year. Missing is the session mate, *Groovin' high*, to be found in the Official and Smithsonian collections already noted. This finds the trumpeter considerably more adventurous than on the Musicraft of 20 days later with Parker, tidier though this latter is as a version of the piece despite a chugging rhythm section and bathetic bass solo. Here and in *Dizzy atmosphere* we get the lighter, more airy side of Parker's music, while on the bridge of the first chorus of *All the things you are* he plays an imaginative paraphrase of Kern's original line. (Incidentally, the bridge of the *Dizzy atmosphere* theme bears a considerable resemblance to the equivalent passage in the fifth chorus of Ellington's *Cottontail* [**153**].)

The band that cut the first of the May dates was better integrated and was in fact Gillespie and Parker's regular 52nd Street combo of that time, although with Catlett in place of Stan Levey. It produced a more vigorous *Salt peanuts* with a sequence of solos by Haig, Parker and Gillespie during which excitement steadily mounts, the trumpeter, deft and highly detailed, surpassing his January performance. But one cannot imagine his and Parker's execution of the thematic passages ever being surpassed, this sounding, for instance on *Shaw nuff*, as if one mind were playing both instruments. *Hot house* is another strong, if not at all boppish, Dameron theme and it occasions brilliant use of double time, perfectly fitted into the solo's long line, by Gillespie. *Loverman* was one of several pieces that Sarah Vaughan recorded with Parker and Gillespie that went far to establish her as one of the few genuine jazz singers of this period. [11]

Towards the end of 1945 this band, with Levey restored and Jackson added, visited Los Angeles, and attention should be drawn to further accounts of four of these themes which they recorded there (Spotlite [E] SPJ123). The Californian *Shaw nuff* belongs to the trumpeter, for he improvises on it to stunning effect while Parker makes a fluent use of stock phrases. The latter does much better on *Groovin' high* with a superbly developed solo, longer than his February one and consisting almost entirely of new ideas. Gillespie altogether matches him and this little-known performance is one of the best they ever recorded together. In *Dizzy atmosphere* Parker again presents a variant on, and extension of, his February solo and here it is the trumpeter who resorts to stock ideas – although, as with Parker on *Shaw nuff*, they are his own.

Their other Californian recording was of *Diggin' for Diz* (Spotlite [E] 101), done in February 1946. This theme was by George Handy, the date's pianist, and is in proper bop style; Gillespie's and Parker's solos are restrained rather than spectacular. Next day, under the name of the Tempo Jazzmen, the trumpeter recorded a full session with the band he had taken to Los Angeles, though with Parker regrettably absent. On tenor Lucky Thompson was an entirely compatible replacement and, with sterling contributions from Haig and Jackson, the ensemble displayed a secure collective mastery of what was a very new jazz style. This applies especially to the leader, in *Confirmation*, another *Diggin' for Diz* and two further readings of *Dizzy atmosphere* retitled *Dynamo A* and *Dynamo B* (Spotlite [E] SAJ132). While there is no doubt that his solos on *Bebop*, the May 1945 *Salt peanuts* and *Hot house* or the Los Angeles *Shaw nuff* are magnificent jazz, there is about them an almost frantic, if exuberant, assertion, a rather too apparent tenseness. This now departs, leaving Gillespie's imagination as active, his technical mastery as staggering as before, yet with the invention more finely honed and flowing with a new relaxation.

Back in New York an RCA session dealt with under **315** was followed by the May 1946 one, the first in the Musicraft series to have Clarke, a real bop drummer. This makes a positive difference, to some extent negated by Stitt's sounding enough like Parker to make us regret his absence all the more. Yet this music still has the stylistic homogeneity of the Tempo items, and in *Oop-bop sh'bam* there is another great trumpet improvisation. It is a sign of the music's newly won poise that this almost overwhelming solo is juxtaposed with ostentatiously meaningless scat singing. And humour is driven further in *A hand fulla gimme*, a truly drastic modernization of the sort of blues record that was made in the 1920s. The inimitable Alice Roberts vocalizes as a well-educated blues singer should and Gillespie turns in a wickedly accomplished caricature of the kind of music Armstrong used to play behind Bessie Smith (**94**). The hilariously subversive intent of this outrage has seldom received comment.

This is surprising because it hints at Gillespie's well-known geniality on the bandstand. His acceptance by a broader public than any other modernist of his generation depended, as with Armstrong, on an ability to work on a number of different levels. His first recordings with a small string orchestra, of four Kern melodies, were cut as early as 1946, although not issued until much later (Phoenix [A] LP4). This confirms his willingness to abandon the collective requirements of the newly established style, yet his stinging, elaborately detailed and daringly high-flying phrases are in themselves pure bop and some of the most virtuosic trumpet playing that he, or anyone, can ever have recorded. In fact Gillespie stands off from his grotesquely inappropriate accompaniments with the faintly sinister self-possession of a priceless *objet* placed among fakes.

A less extreme compromise was marked by his return to the large-band instrumentation with which his generation had grown up. This in the mid-1940s was inevitable. It might be contrary to the nature of bop, yet Gillespie's developing career demanded that he front a big band. On *Little John special* (1942) his two solo choruses, surprisingly close to his mature style, occur in a conventional swing-band setting, and the matter was never taken further. A confirmation is Dameron's *Our delight*, a melodious piece in swing style, well written for the ensemble yet quite lacking in the rhythmic features of bop – until the leader solos. Likewise *Emanon* and *Good dues* are simply the blues, with dissonant harmony but without further modernization. However deep its roots in earlier music, bop was in essence a post-swing small-combo style that was adapted to large ensembles only at the cost of so much rhythmic simplification that it lost its point. Fuller's remarkable *Things to come* was a brave attempt at getting a big band to play a piece in full bop style, but it receives an insecure, snatched-at performance except, again, when Gillespie is soloing. Indeed his superlative improvisations on virtually all of these large-band tracks are their main justification.

But not their only one, for on 9 July 1946 Miss Roberts surpassed herself. Singing like a veteran of a thousand elocution lessons, she reproves the miscreant who beeped when he ought to have bopped with the studied detachment of an Edwardian governess shepherding her charges round the Chamber of Horrors at Madame Tussaud's waxworks. And Musicraft have made available a second take that no connoisseur could wish to miss. Less enthusiasm is aroused, though, by *I waited for you*. In fact Hagood's glutinous warbling, unconnected with bop or any sort of jazz, represents a vein that recurs all too often in American black music.

During the latter half of the 1940s, in whatever surroundings, Gillespie played the music of his life. In it an acutely personal concept of jazz was perfected, his virtuosity was unsurpassable, and the drive to innovate could take him no further. Parker remained to challenge him for a few more years, as **265** and the last session on **266a** indicate, but any feeling of constructive adventure thereafter departed from his music. Though he often led small combos, Gillespie repeatedly went back to large bands, as if in reaction against the bop style he had done so much to create. In the end he could not avoid becoming an elder statesman. M.H.

Charlie Parker

257 The Complete Savoy Studio Sessions

†Savoy (A) CD2DS5500 (4 CDs)

Parker (alt); Clyde Hart (p); Tiny Grimes (g, vcl[1]); Jimmy Butts (bs); Doc West (d). New York City, 15 September 1944.

Tiny's tempo (3 versions) · *I'll always love you just the same*[1] (2 versions) · *Romance without finance is a nuisance*[1] (3 versions) · *Red cross* (2 versions)

Miles Davis (tpt[2]); Dizzy Gillespie (tpt[3], p[4]); Parker (alt); Argonne 'Dense' Thornton (p[5]); Curly Russell (bs); Max Roach (d). New York City, 26 November 1945.

Billie's bounce[2,4] (3 versions) · *Warming up a riff*[4] · *Now's the time*[2,4] (2 versions) · *Thriving on a riff*[2,5] (2 versions) · *Koko*[3,4] · *Meandering*[5]

Gillespie (tpt); Parker (alt); Jack McVea (ten); Dodo Marmarosa (p); Slim Gaillard (g, vcl[6], p[7]); Bam Brown (bs, vcl[8]); Zutty Singleton (d). Hollywood, 29 December 1945.

Dizzy boogie[7] (2 versions) · *Flat foot floogie*[6,8] (2 versions) · *Poppity pop*[6,8] · *Slim's jam*[6]

Davis (tpt); Parker (alt); Bud Powell (p); Tommy Potter (bs); Roach (d). New York City, 8 May 1947.

Donna Lee (4 versions) · *Chasin' the Bird* (3 versions) · *Cheryl* (2 versions) · *Buzzy* (5 versions)

Davis (tpt); Parker (ten); John Lewis (p); Nelson Boyd (bs); Roach (d). New York City, 14 August 1947.

Milestones (3 versions) · *Little Willie leaps* (3 versions) · *Half Nelson* (2 versions) · *Sippin' at Bell's* (4 versions)

Davis (tpt); Parker (alt); Duke Jordan (p); Potter (bs); Roach (d). Detroit, 21 December 1947.
Another hair-do (4 versions) · *Blue Bird* (2 versions) · *Klaunstance* · *Bird gets the worm* (2 versions)

Davis (tpt); Parker (alt); Lewis (p); Russell (bs); Roach (d). New York City, 18 September 1948.
Barbados (3 versions) · *Ah-leu-cha* · *Constellation* (4 versions)

Davis absent. Same date.
Parker's mood (3 versions)

Davis returns. New York City, 24 September 1948.
Perhaps (6 versions) · *Marmaduke* (8 versions) · *Steeplechase* (2 versions) · *Merry-go-round* (2 versions)

258 The Complete Dial Sessions

†Spotlite (E) SPJCD101, †Stash (A) STCD567–70 (4 CDs)

Gillespie (tpt); Parker (alt); Lucky Thompson (ten); George Handy (p); Arv Garrison (g); Ray Brown (bs); Stan Levey (d). Los Angeles, 7 February 1946.
Diggin' Diz

Davis (tpt); Parker (alt); Thompson (ten); Marmarosa (p); Vic McMillan (bs); Roy Porter (d). Los Angeles, 28 March 1946.
Moose the mooche (3 versions)

Garrison (g) added. Same date.
Yardbird suite (2 versions) · *Ornithology* (3 versions) · *A night in Tunisia* (2 versions) · *Famous alto break*

Howard McGhee (tpt); Parker (alto); Jimmy Bunn (p); Bob 'Dingbod' Kesterton (bs); Porter (d). Los Angeles, 29 July 1946.
Max is making wax · *Loverman* · *The Gypsy* · *Bebop*

Parker (alt); Russ Freeman (p); Arnold Fishkin (bs); Jimmy Pratt (d). Los Angeles, 1 February 1947.
Lullaby in rhythm · *Home cookin' I* · *Home cookin' II* · *Home cookin' III* · *Blues I* · *Blues II*

McGhee, Shorty Rogers, Melvin Broiles (tpt) added. Same date.
Yardbird suite

Parker (alt); Erroll Garner (p); Red Callender (bs); West (d); Earl Coleman (vcl[9]). Los Angeles, 19 February 1947.
This is always[9] (2 versions) · *Dark shadows*[9] (4 versions) · *Bird's nest* (3 versions) · *Cool blues* (4 versions)

McGhee (tpt); Parker (alt); Wardell Gray (ten); Marmarosa (p); Barney Kessel (g); Callender (bs); Don Lamond (d). Los Angeles, 26 February 1947.
Relaxin' at Camarillo (4 versions) · *Cheers* (4 versions) · *Carvin' the bird* (2 versions) · *Stupendous* (2 versions)

Davis (tpt); Parker (alt); Jordan (p); Potter (bs); Roach (d). New York City, 28 October 1947.
Dexterity (2 versions) · *Bongo bop* (2 versions) · *Dewey Square* (3 versions) · *The hymn* (2 versions) · *Bird of paradise* (3 versions) · *Embraceable you* (2 versions)

Same personnel. New York City, 4 November 1947.
Bird feathers · *Klact-oveeseds-tene* (2 versions) · *Scrapple from the Apple* (2 versions) · *My old flame* · *Out of nowhere* (3 versions) · *Don't blame me*

J. J. Johnson (tbn) added. New York City, 17 December 1947.
Drifting on a reed (3 versions) · *Quasimado* (2 versions) · *Charlie's wig* (3 versions) · *Bongo beep* (2 versions) · *Crazeology* (4 versions) · *How deep is the ocean?* (2 versions)

Although Parker is one of the major figures in jazz, his work essentially is part of an ongoing process in this music, an expression of a seemingly innate tendency that goes back to earlier than the 1920s and continues some way beyond him. That tendency, as noted in the brief introductory remark to this section of the book, was one of continual enrichment of musical resources. However, we should try to avoid a common weakness in discussions of artists' work, that of attributing everything to external causes, because there was much in Parker's music that he invented himself. Surely he was a major contributor, along with Louis Armstrong and, moving in a rather different direction, Ornette Coleman, to a central tradition. The originality of what each of these men did, and the cogency with which they did it, were such that many nonlisteners rejected Parker and Coleman in turn as not being part of jazz. And Armstrong would have been rejected in exactly the same way if there had been any coherent body of commentary on this music during the 1920s.

In the face of such rejections, and notwithstanding the large element of personal invention in his music, it is necessary to insist that Parker, like the other two, though a great innovator, was firmly rooted in tradition, and the simplest indication of this is on the formal level. Indeed his repertoire was limited to just a few models, to the 12-bar blues and various AABA 32-bar popular songs and the chord sequences on which these are based, most prominently alterations of the *I got rhythm* harmonies. Like the Tristano school, he used only a relatively few such chord progressions upon which to base his improvisations, as if to test his ingenuity and powers of invention. These harmonic sequences were the basis of new melodies that were more in keeping with the new style and although this procedure was not new to jazz the boppers employed it more than hitherto and Parker was especially fertile here. Examples include *Thriving from a riff*, also known as *Anthropology*, credited to Parker under the first title and to him and Gillespie under the latter, although Parker always insisted that it was his alone. This is based on the *I got rhythm* chords, whereas *Scrapple from the Apple* is on the

Honeysuckle rose changes but with those of *I got rhythm* on the bridge. Other cases are *Ornithology* on *How high the moon?* and *Klact-oveeseds-tene* based on a variant of *Perdido*'s chords, and *Now's the time*, which is the blues.

The boppers particularly liked the flexibility inherent in the blues changes because they could easily be subjected to a great variety of substitute harmonies, as is demonstrated in *Blues for Alice* (**266b**). In fact the participation of the blues in bop is exactly as one might expect and further instances include Parker's *Au privave*, *Billie's bounce* and *Blue Bird*, Monk's *Mysterioso*, *Straight, no chaser* and *Blue Monk*, John Carisi's *Israel*, Miles Davis's (Richard Carpenter's) *Walkin'* and Milt Jackson's *Bags' groove* among numerous others.

As such names imply and as the previous entry indicates, Parker was far from being solely responsible for the bop idiom. Rather it was the result of work by a number of individuals, at first isolated and then coming together. Yet he was its chief embodiment and the main source of inspiration to musicians taking part in its early growth and establishment. Again like Armstrong before him and Coleman later, he affected players on all instruments, not just his own, and this because he had led a change in the musical language of jazz. From this it follows that he had other ways of dealing with the popular ballad repertoire besides composing new themes, at various tempos, on their chord sequences. This gave rise to interpretations like *Don't blame me* and *Out of nowhere* which, though as inventive as the rest, also express acute sensitivity and can sound nearly ominous in their tranquillity.

Obviously contrasting with this was the stormy restlessness of another side of his music, typified by performances like *Bird's nest* and *Bird gets the worm*. And such themeless vehicles serve to emphasize that no matter what the value of Parker's composing, his main achievement was plainly in his improvisations. These fused many-faceted expression of emotion with a sophisticated organizing of pitch, rhythm and nuance. Tone is as important as the other factors and indeed a central point is that melody, rhythm, harmony and instrumental sound all operated together, each influencing the rest. Understanding has been considerably advanced since the 1970s by the appearance of not hitherto widely available recordings from Parker's developmental years, such as the piece known as *Honey and Body*.

Once thought to have dated from as early as 1937, this apparently belongs to 1940, and on it he is heard improvising for over three minutes on *Honeysuckle rose* and *Body and soul* (†Média 7 [F] MJCD78/79). Parts of his later rhythmic and harmonic practice are already in place and rather than holding to the four-bar phrases so common in jazz and popular music, he departs considerably from these, the fact that he is unaccompanied no doubt aiding this. He also displays an excellent sense of swing. To judge from such performances from late in his apprentice years, Parker's tone was still in transition, although given the poor quality of the recordings we cannot be dogmatic. He made little use of the scoops in pitch which characterized alto saxophonists hitherto, and in comparison with major predecessors like Carter and particularly Hodges, his vibrato, though slightly faster and more extensive in the earlier years, became slower and narrower than theirs during his maturity, occurring chiefly on long notes at slow tempos.

Whatever Parker may later have said to the contrary, there is a notable Lester Young influence on those early performances; in fact his pre-1944 recordings contain more allusions to Young than to anyone else. One parallel between them is that, like so many other jazz musicians of the time, they used no great variety of keys. Mostly Parker employed concert B-flat, F and C, and while this lack of variety is disappointing, we do best to focus on his wide range of tempos and note values.

By the time of his 1941 Dallas recordings with McShann (Affinity [E] AFS1006), Parker's sound appears to have acquired a new richness and depth, although perhaps that is the result of superior Decca recording technique rather than any shift in his concept of saxophone tone. A piece such as *Hootie blues*, the slowest items of it session, confirms his refined control of vibrato, and indeed he is more at ease than anyone else in the band, whatever the tempo. His sense of swing and air of rhythmic authority continue to develop, as is shown by *Swingmatism*, an intelligent arrangement by William Scott of a 16-bar blues in F minor; minor-keyed blues were then rather unusual, yet Parker, despite what is said above about his normally choosing only a few keys, sounds entirely relaxed. *The jumpin' blues*, recorded in New York the following year, is most remarked because of Parker's opening phrase, which Benny Harris adapted in another key for *Ornithology* – although Lester Young had played a comparable passage in his *Shoe shine boy* solo (**135a**).

No matter what anticipations there may have been in other aspects of the music, Parker was by now beginning to displace his accents with an imaginative freedom that had no real precedent, and in the mature work discussed below he even produced polyrhythmic effects with his cross-rhythms. Also his phrases characteristically include notes that are not part of the prevailing harmony; he seemed especially fond of flattened ninths and sharpened elevenths. Pitches outside the stated chords were also produced by passing and auxillary notes, by suspensions, anticipations and prolongations of harmonies; and there are chromatic interpolations implying passing chords etc. Note further that all this is shaped by lucid and usually very fast thinking, the harmonic subtlety informed by melody and rhythm. Often Parker's solos are further shaped by motivic development if not by thematic variation, the example usually cited being take 1 of *Klact-oveeseds-tene*. His first chorus here is based almost entirely on three brief ideas which are extended in a quite unpredictable mixture of sound and silence.

Any comprehensive listening to Parker in due course reveals that he drew on a very large number of brief germinal phrases, arranging them according to circumstances in terms of rhythm, the prevailing harmony etc. Certain of these ideas, however, were specific to particular keys or to certain pieces. Some were adapted from swing music, especially from Lester Young, but most were originated by Parker himself and later became common property to others playing bop and later styles. To refer to such improvising as 'formulaic' is unfortunate, particularly when that term is applied to Parker himself, for there was nothing random, still less formulaic, about his solos, the motivic ideas being subject to constant variation, as just noted.

Savoy's first entry here actually placed its main emphasis on Grimes's inane vocalizing, yet although the verbosely titled *I'll always love you just the same* and *Romance without finance is a nuisance* filled the A sides of the resultant 78-rpm discs, history has decided a different order of importance. This is because Parker played excellently on all four tracks, demonstrating almost the full mastery of his personal idiom. The 16-bar alto solo in the second chorus of *I'll always love you* is an early instance of his mature ballad improvisation, moving on from the *Body and soul* on **250** and almost having arrived at the level of the following year's *Meandering*. *Tiny's tempo* is exactly the kind of swing-oriented blues we should expect from Grimes and Parker takes three fine choruses on the first two versions. These cut off just as Hart begins his solo but the third is complete and on it Parker delivers with real intensity. *Red cross* stands as his earliest traced composition apart from *What price love?*, the original vocal form of *Yardbird suite*. At first *Red cross* was called *The devil in 305* and it was renamed for Bob Redcross, a friend of Billy Eckstine. Basically it is an *I got rhythm* AABA, though with an intriguing twist in bars five and six; the melody even includes a triplet figure which Parker would use a great deal later. As with many another of his 'themes', there is not much composing, the chief idea being in the A section while the B is a sequential repetition of a short riff. At the start of this B section in his solo he is close to what he would play at the same point in *Shaw nuff* (**256a**).

Next came his first date as leader and it naturally goes some way to define his ideas about the nature of jazz in terms of his choice of players and material and the way the music is organized. His employing Davis rather than Gillespie may even now appear surprising in view of the state of Davis's playing at that early stage, yet Gillespie was present and had an important part in the session's main event. Bud Powell was supposedly Parker's first choice as pianist but with him out of town the leader persuaded Gillespie to comp for him, which he did well enough on *Koko* and elsewhere. But the great trumpeter was no piano soloist and Parker instead got Thornton, who turned in a performance of finely tuned mediocrity. Roach was crucial and would remain so for most of the music discussed here.

It seems the material was quickly decided: two blues in F and two bop themes based on standard chord sequences. Of the blues, one, *Now's the time*, was elemental while the other, *Billie's bounce*, was distinctly modern; of the ballad-derived bop themes *Thriving on a riff* has two superb Parker choruses in take 3 and *Koko* is a sophistication of the already sophisticated *Cherokee* (whose notorious bridge moves rapidly through several keys). Besides these, *Warming up a riff* was a trial run for *Koko* which, despite poor intonation and bad recording, vividly catches the spontaneity of Parker's improvising. *Meandering*, from the end of the session, is a solo by the leader, again strikingly unconstrained, on the chords of *Embraceable you*.

Both versions of *Now's the time* include masterly alto solos of three choruses, very blue and very boppish; take 4 was originally issued as a 78 and it contains an improvement of an idea heard in *Hootie blues* with McShann. Five accounts of *Billie's bounce* were attempted, three are complete and takes 4 and 5 have splendid Parker solos, especially take 5. This solo starts with a phrase which later turns up in various places such as Wardell Gray's *Twisted* (**268**); and the fact that he was capable of borrowing from himself is illustrated by the double-time run in his second chorus having already surfaced in his *Salt peanuts* solo (**256a**) and earlier still in the 1943 reading of *Body and soul* (†Stash [A] STCD535). Davis evidently could not manage the trumpet part of the *Koko* theme statement so Gillespie played this as well as serving at the piano during the leader's two central choruses. It follows the ABCD format of *Cherokee* with only A and D predetermined; B is Gillespie improvising over brushes on a snare drum and C is Parker in the same role. A and D find them together and were apparently written out or at least carefully prepared. These sections have rhythmic and harmonic ambiguity and anticipate Ornette Coleman's more boppish themes. Parker's solo marks an extraordinary advance on the *c.* 1942 version of *Cherokee* on **250** and stands as a definitive statement about his status as a musical thinker and about his powers as an instrumentalist, a statement that few were equipped to understand at the time. It is perfectly capped by the nervous brilliance of Roach's following half-chorus (even if Feather, Ulanov and George Simon combined to describe it as 'horrible, utterly beatless' in *Metronome* six months later).

After the purposefulness of that occasion we descend to Slim Gaillard's inconsequentiality. He led the other group at Billy Berg's in Hollywood during the Gillespie–Parker band's stay on the West Coast in late 1945 and early 1946 and somebody had the fruitless notion of recording elements from both ensembles together. *Flat foot floogie* was an attempt to repeat the 'success' of Gaillard's big hit of 1938 and he sings 'Bang, bang!' Parker solos in both versions, the first seeming best, yet both here and on *Poppity pop* the vocal fatuities are such ('Pop, pop!' from Gaillard) that neither he nor Gillespie can do much. *Dizzy boogie* could have been better for both Gillespie and Parker solo well, especially Parker in the second version. But in the first Gaillard bangs away inanely in the piano treble.

With the March 1946 Dial session we find Parker back on his true path and, although major health problems arose later that year, he was now on his way towards the 1947–8 performances which produced an entire series of masterpieces of jazz improvisation. Perhaps nothing from this particular date was at quite the level of *Koko* but the fact that the whole occasion was less frantic benefited the music, as did the presence of Davis, Thompson and Marmarosa. Besides their solos there was an avoidance of extreme tempos which might have suited Gillespie and Roach, yet few others. Gillespie's absence in particular meant that some pressure was off Parker and he was hence less inclined to feats of dramatic virtuosity. Altogether, the circumstances brought out his more thoughtful side.

Parker's own *Moose the mooche* and *Yardbird suite*, Gillespie's *A night in Tunisia* and Benny Harris's *Ornithology* meant that it was jazz themes all the way and the first of these, on the *I got rhythm* changes, is one of the altoist's best in the AABA format, and he did compose the B section instead of just improvising it. Most effective is his use throughout the melody, with variations in pitch and position within the phrase, of the opening motif. Quite fascinating is his solo on take 2 of *Moose the mooche*, where he brings together an apparently contradictory succession of thoughts and draws them into a mysteriously balanced whole. In take 3 he reshapes some of his ideas from 1 and 2, whereas in *Yardbird suite* he makes a new departure each time. There is magnificent work from him on take 4 of *Ornithology* and 5 of *A night in Tunisia*, and his four-bar break from an incomplete version of the latter was issued separately because he said he would never play it again so perfectly. In that he was mistaken for he surpassed it several times, for example at the 1947 Carnegie Hall concert (†Savoy [A] 650 128) and in 1953 at Massey Hall (**265**).

Record companies' widespread issuing of alternative takes started in the late 1950s due to the special concern with Parker's work. In his case these subtly different versions of any given performance give us – to be thoroughly Nabokovian about it – the curious sensation of Narcissus fooling Nemesis by helping his image out of the brook (see *Despair*, Chapter 1).

Alas, the session of July 1946 was a chaotic occasion. Parker was very ill as a result of drug addiction and nearly all that need be said about the music he produced is indicated by his later comment that he 'had to drink a quart of whiskey to get through the date'. One should also note his fully justified resentment that anything recorded by him that day was ever issued; he particularly objected to *Loverman* being circulated. The occasion led to his complete physical and mental breakdown, which resulted in his being confined to California's Camarillo State Hospital for six months. After Parker had left the studio, McGhee and the other musicians recorded two pieces which are dealt with under **262**.

Following his release from Camarillo early in 1947 came the most productive time of Parker's life, which lasted until the breaking-up of his regular working group in the spring of 1950. He headed a band of his own choice that was entirely compatible with him musically and seemingly in most other respects. This was the best-documented period with regard to his artistic intentions and he attained new heights during this time of complete mastery; the finest of his performances have remained quite simply among the best jazz records ever made. A most important aspect of Parker's post-Camarillo playing was an ability accurately to subdivide the beat into a variety of smaller units and at almost any tempo. Equally he could now accent any note falling on any part of the subdivided beat. Presumably arising out of this extended mastery was the fact that during this period the sense of discovery in his music was at its most acute.

This is apparent even in the *Home cookin'* pieces. These were recorded in most informal circumstances in a musician's flat, *Home cookin' I* being on the chords of *'Swonderful* with the *Honeysuckle rose* bridge while *Home cookin' II* is *Cherokee* and *III* is on *I got rhythm*. Parker sounds altogether relaxed and his melodic continuity shows particular imagination in these, with *II* a bit more intense than the others.

Before what may be called the first post-Camarillo Parker session for Dial, there was a diversion a week earlier. This was really a date for Earl Coleman, an Eckstine imitator, and the Garner trio which also produced the earliest performances on **263**. It seems that Parker just happened to turn up and was invited to take part, which at least gives us a chance of hearing him in an accompanimental role. *This is always* has an unusual AAB structure while *Dark shadows* is the normal AABA. Parker solos well on all four versions of the latter, briefly quoting his *Hootie blues* solo in take 1. His take 3 solo is in turn quoted in Herman's *I've got news for you* (**312c**), which is the version originally issued; however, his contribution to take 4 is best in that he modifies and condenses some of his ideas from the previous takes.

Very fast, *Bird's nest* again resorts to the *I got rhythm* sequence and in it Parker and Garner play two choruses apiece, then alternate eight-bar sections with a final chorus for Parker. Takes 1 and 3 find him at his most fluent. Already he had alluded to the *Cool blues* riff in his solo on take 4 of *Yardbird suite* and its ancestry goes further back than that. In these performances he and Garner play two choruses each, then Callender solos before alto and piano return for one chorus each. Garner found the pace of takes 1 and 2 unduly fast whereas 3 is too slow for the theme and 4 is the best compromise for both of them. Although Garner draws fairly close to bop pianism in take 3 of *Bird's nest,* he is not really a suitable partner for Parker and the session was somewhat irrelevant to his real direction. Even so, *Cool blues* and *Bird's nest* both have excellent work from him and he later identified the former as one of the few records of his own that he at all liked.

That first post-Camarillo full-dress session for Parker came a week later and was highly productive. *Relaxin' at Camarillo* is a blues whose initial title was *Past due.* It has a notably tricky theme which the other musicians had considerable trouble in learning although its unexpected accents are typical of his work at this time. On the first take he, Gray and Kessel have two choruses each, McGhee (muted) and Marmarosa one apiece. The final ensemble is rough but there is a polyrhythmic coda from the pianist that is used as both introduction and coda in all the other versions, for example the eight-bar prelude to take 3. Parker's two choruses on this latter form perhaps his finest solo of the date yet it is take 5 that appeared as a 78, presumably because it has the most cleanly executed theme statement. His solo here is very good but not at quite the level of take 3. *Carvin' the Bird* was by Kessel, who recorded it elsewhere as *Swedish pastry.* It is another intriguing theme and the pair of treatments preserved are rather similar. The leader has two choruses and all the others are heard from. *Stupendous,* on *'Swonderful,* was by Melvyn Broiles, a pupil of McGhee, and its first take gives rise to Marmarosa's best solo of the session. *Cheers,* an alteration of the *I got rhythm* chords though with the *Honeysuckle rose* bridge, was by McGhee. Parker throughout sounds nothing if not optimistic, nowhere more so than in the first version of *Cheers.* On this he takes a full chorus, Gray, Marmarosa, Kessel and McGhee half each. Take 2 is quicker, again with fine Parker but with a final ensemble that is untidy, as is that of take 3. The final take 4 is best in this respect yet when he was back in New York Parker described himself as being dissatisfied with this date, or was paraphrased by Feather as being so.

When he got back to New York, his studio activities switched between the Savoy and Dial companies, with three sessions for one and five for the other. When this music was new, some of us thought Davis a most unsuitable partner for Parker, who should, we thought, have had Fats Navarro. He and Navarro did in fact work together and to magnificent effect, on for instance *The street beat, Cool blues* and *Ornithology* (†Savoy [A] 650 126). Yet in place of the virtuoso challenge of Navarro (or Gillespie), Davis brought a different atmosphere to the band's music, another climate of feeling, as is especially apparent in the Dial ballads. It also tells us something about Parker's aims for the group that Powell, who was close to the leader stylistically, was after one session replaced by the cooler Jordan or Lewis. It could be said that in, for example,

Embraceable you three kinds of introversion meet, those of the altoist, the trumpeter and the pianist.

At the next date, for Savoy, two contrasting blues, *Cheryl* and *Buzzy*, one simple and one more complex, are again featured as with *Now's the time* and *Billie's bounce* and *Relaxin' at Camarillo* and *Carvin' the Bird.* (Later pairs would include *Blue Bird* and *Another hair-do*, *Parker's mood* and *Barbados.*) A plain riff tune, *Buzzy* is not exactly typical of Parker but his three choruses on take 1, though not perfect in execution, are splendid in terms of fresh invention. Davis and Powell likewise take three choruses each on this and the latter improvises at a very high level. The leader again has three choruses in *Cheryl*, beginning with the theme's last phrase – as he would do on *Bird feathers*. *Chasin' the Bird* has a strange canonic theme as would the following year's *Ah-leu-cha*. Parker is especially assertive on take 3 of *Chasin' the Bird.* At first *Donna Lee* was credited to Parker, although this theme's lack of syncopation and the fact that it quotes from Navarro's *Ice freezes red* solo suggest that the later idea that it was actually by Davis is probably correct. Everyone sounds uncertain in take 1; Davis is best on 4, Powell and the leader on 5.

Some would say that the next session is part of another story, recorded under Davis's name and with Parker heard on the tenor saxophone. This *Milestones* is different from the piece of that name which the trumpeter set down in 1958 and was surely composed by Lewis; Boyd may also have contributed to *Half Nelson*. But the others were written by Davis, who arranged them all, selected the personnel, presumably asked Parker to play the tenor saxophone, and called two rehearsals. The music is cooler and more mellow than the other performances on these discs and quite surprising for 1947, being Davis's first step towards **376.** The tempos are more sedate than was mostly the case when Parker was in charge, the themes less syncopated than his, their rather dense harmonies strikingly different from Davis's later stress on uncluttered structures. The emphasis on themes and arrangements was again different from a Parker date. *Half Nelson* is related to Dameron's then unrecorded *Ladybird* (see **260**) and *Little Willie leaps* is on the chords of *All God's children got rhythm.*

Back on his real path, and back on the alto saxophone, was Parker at the session he led for Dial in October 1947, which produced, in take 1 of *Embraceable you*, one of his masterpieces, a supreme achievement in jazz improvisation. Both here and in take 2 the original melody is only referred to in a fleeting manner. The former is argued with a closeness that is unusual among improvisations; the latter is rather differently inventive and not conceived quite so much as a whole. Jordan's preludes are exquisitely apt and Davis's are his best solos in this entire series of recordings – no small achievement in view of what Parker had just played. Both readings should be compared with *Meandering*, which may be considered an early draft for these improvisations, and with the later, brisker *Quasimado* (alias *Trade winds*), a piece on the same chords.

Rather in the same way, the solo on *All the things you are* with Gillespie (**256a**) might be taken as a preliminary study for the three accounts of *Bird of paradise*, which even have the same introduction and coda that had earlier still been heard in Eckstine's *Good jelly blues*. On take 1 of *Bird of paradise* Parker decorates Kern's melody whereas in takes 2 and 3 he goes straight from the introduction into his solo, take 3 perhaps being the best; the atmosphere is beautifully maintained in all three cases by Davis and Jordan. In *The hymn* (alias *Superman*) Parker offers four particularly intense blues choruses before a calm theme harmonized by trumpet and alto which had appeared as *Blues* in **250**.

On take 1 of *Dewey Square* also the theme is only heard at the end. Parker sounds relaxed and cool here, takes 64 bars, gets hotter in the 32-bar solo of take 2 and in 3 revises and condenses some of his ideas from takes 1 and 2. Take 1 was also issued as *Prezology*, *Air conditioning* and *Bird feathers*. This last retitling led to confusion because it was the name also given to a blues on the session of the following December, whereas *Dewey Square* is a 32-bar AABA. So also is *Dexterity*, on an altered *I got rhythm* progression, in take 1 of which Parker displays fine continuity across the chorus's section divisions. The second version is faster, hotter. *Bongo bop* (alias *Charlie's blues*) is indeed a blues, with Latin American rhythms – as is December's *Bongo beep*! Parker starts his solos on both takes of *Bongo bop* with the same phrase but extends them differently. Unusually, this theme is stated in octave unison.

Unique in Parker's recorded output is the sequence of three ballads which concluded the next Dial session – five performances, counting the three versions of *Out of nowhere*. All three takes of this can be heard as studies in the use of double time at a slow pace and they offer enlightening comparisons. Thus he shifts between different levels of intensity within each solo,• exploiting contrasts of volume, force of execution, of accentuation, adding further point to his ideas by shading his tone with much variation. The haunted lyricism of his improvisations here and on *My old flame* and *Don't blame me*, if set beside the thrusting yet subtle brilliance of his three choruses on the fast *Bird feathers* (alias *Schnourphology*), gives an impression of this music's diversity of feeling. Different again is the finished elegance of *Scrapple from the Apple*, which has a particularly melodious main thematic phrase; in his solo on the second take he further develops some of his inventions in the first. A quite different case is *Klact-oveeseds-tene*, the first take of which receives comment above. For the second version Parker comes up with an entirely different sequence of ideas, yet the most extraordinary music was made by the softly wreathing arabesques he spins on *Don't blame me*, which, apart from a few trumpet notes fore and aft, is alto saxophone all the way. This is jazz at virtually the level of the first version of *Embraceable you*, a rare feat of spiritual concentration and an apt conclusion to the date.

Obviously the addition of a trombone, usually played with a mute, made a difference to the final Dial occasion, though Johnson fitted into this music extremely well. *Drifting on a reed* is not the Hawkins–Monk theme on **253** but there was confusion because take 2 was issued as *Air conditioning*, take 4 as *Giant swing*, and Parker sometimes announced it as *Big foot*. He solos with indomitable energy on all versions, taking three choruses in each case, Johnson, Davis and Jordan having two each. The final version is best for all of them, as is the last account of *Crazeology*. This is on an interesting alteration of the *I got rhythm* chords and was set down the previous January by Powell as *Bud's bubble* on **261**. Other recordings are titled *Ideology* and *Little Benny* – which last may have been the original name as the composer was Benny Harris. On this December session Parker soloed with blistering assertion which far surpasses Johnson and Davis, good though their contributions are. *Charlie's wig* is unusual, having an ABCD 32-bar format deriving from *When I grow too old to dream* and having a quite unexpected out-of-tempo introduction by all three horns. The melancholy regret of *How deep is the ocean?* made it a suitable postscript to the previous session's three ballads.

Neither *Bird gets the worm* nor *Klaunstance* presents a theme, both offering improvisations on the chords of respectively *Lover, come back to me* and *The way you look tonight*, which convey from Parker a stormy restlessness. Jordan's sparse yet melodious solos are an even more apt counterweight to this than are Davis's passages. *Bird gets the worm* is at crotchet = *c*. 370 about as fast as he ever recorded. (And *Don't blame me* at crotchet = *c*. 65 is the slowest.) As expected, *Blue Bird* has more indelible blues playing. *Another hair-do*, likewise a blues, is unusual in that its theme chorus has a 3-6-3 format: the two groups of three bars are theme while the middle six bars are improvised. This is as surprising as his canonic themes and one regrets that it led nowhere during his short life.

A ban on recording by the American Federation of Musicians was responsible for the last two sessions being delayed for several months. Considering that Parker was at the height of his powers at the time this was singularly unfortunate, yet when it came, the penultimate Savoy date touched a considerable peak. *Barbados*, another blues with Latin American rhythms, is one of his most attractive themes just as *Constellation*, on the *I got rhythm* changes but with the *Honeysuckle rose* bridge, is his dullest. He is superb on take 4 of *Barbados* and likewise on the very rapid *Constellation*. *Ah-leu-cha* is his other canonic theme and like *Chasin' the Bird* it yet again uses the *I got rhythm* chords. Its brief counterpoint is more tidily performed than the 1947 piece. Finally came *Parker's mood*, which leaves no question about the traditional basis of bop. This is one of the great instrumental blues statements in the jazz idiom, an elaboration whose every note is essential. Indeed one is tempted to quote Hans Sachs and say that 'It sounded so old yet was so new' (*The Mastersingers*, Act II scene 3).

Far from being the 1935 Ellington piece, *Merry-go-round* is another themeless venture and yet another on the *I got rhythm* changes, as is *Steeplechase.* During take 1 of *Merry-go-round* Parker quotes a snatch of the *High society* clarinet solo just as he had in *Koko*, and this, like the second take, has superlative improvising by him. As this was the last performance for Savoy, that is appropriate. Here, as in most of these other recordings, Parker's mind searches restlessly but is always in control. Its activity is manifest in the order and concentration of his music, which contrasts with the confusion, and latterly even chaos, of his private circumstances. One's impression of the latter is not so much of a person embracing life with a giant's grasp as of somebody perpetually on the run. It may be that Parker, however inchoately, attempted Rimbaud's '*long, immense et raisonné dérèglement de tous les sens*'. In person he perhaps was something like the central character in Julio Cortázar's story 'The Pursuer' (in a collection of his shorter fiction variously called *End of the Game* and *Blow Up*). But this is no place for biographical speculations.

M.H.

Fats Navarro

259 Fat Girl

Savoy (A) SJL2216 (2 LPs), †Savoy (Eu) 650.115, 650.150

Navarro, Kinny Dorham (tpt); Sonny Stitt (alt); Morris Lane (ten); Eddie de Verteuil (bar); Bud Powell (p); Al Hall (bs); Kenny Clarke (d); Gil Fuller (arr). New York City, 6 September 1946.
Boppin' a riff · *Fat boy* · *Everythin's cool* · *Webb City*

Navarro (tpt); 'Lockjaw' Davis (ten); Al Haig (p); Huey Long (g); Gene Ramey (bs); Denzil Best (d). New York City, 18 December 1946.
Callin' Dr Jazz · *Fracture* · *Maternity* · *Stealin' trash*

Same personnel. New York City, 20 December 1946.
Just a mystery · *Red pepper* · *Spinal* · *Hollerin' and screamin'*

Navarro (tpt); Leo Parker (bar, vcl intrjc[1]); Tadd Dameron (p, comp); Ramey (bs); Best (d). New York City, 16 January 1947.
Fat girl[1] · *Ice freezes red* · *Eb pob* · *Goin' to Minton's*

Navarro (tpt); Ernie Henry (alt); Dameron (p, comp); Curly Russell (bs); Clarke (d); Kay Penton (vcl[2]). New York City, 28 October 1947.
A bebop carol (2 versions) · *The Tadd walk* · *Gone with the wind*[2] · *That someone must be you*[2]

Navarro (tpt); Charlie Rouse (ten); Dameron (p, comp); Nelson Boyd (bs); Art Blakey (d). New York City, 5 December 1947.
Nostalgia (2 versions) · *Barry's bop* (2 versions) · *Bebop romp* (2 versions) · *Fats blows*

260 The Complete Blue Note and Capitol Recordings of Fats Navarro and Tadd Dameron

†EMI/Blue Note (E) CDP7243 8 33373 2 3 (2 CDs)

Navarro (tpt); Henry (alt); Rouse (ten); Dameron (p, comp); Boyd (bs); Shadow Wilson (d). New York City, 26 September 1947.
The chase (2 versions) · *The squirrel* (2 versions) · *Our delight* (2 versions) · *Dameronia* (2 versions)

Navarro (tpt); Benny Goodman (clt); Wardell Gray (ten); Gene DiNovi (p); Mundell Lowe (g); Clyde Lombardi (bs); Mel Zelnick (d). New York City, 9 September 1948.
Stealin' apples

Navarro (tpt); Allen Eager, Gray (ten); Dameron (p, comp); Curly Russell (bs); Clarke (d); Chano Pozo (bon[3]); Kenny Hagood (vcl[4]). New York City, 13 September 1948.
Jahbero[3] (2 versions) · *Ladybird* (2 versions) · *Symphonette* (2 versions) · *I think I'll go away*[4]

Howard McGhee (tpt, p[5]); Navarro (tpt); Henry (alt); Milt Jackson (p, vib[6]); Russell (bs); Clarke (d). New York City, 11 October 1948.
The skunk (2 versions) · *Boperation*[5,6] (2 versions) · *Double talk* (2 versions)

Navarro (tpt); Kai Winding (tbn); Sahib Shihab (alt); Dexter Gordon (ten); Cecil Payne (bar); Dameron (p, comp); Russell (bs); Clarke (d); Diego Ibarra (bon); Vidal Bolado (con); Rae Pearl (vcl[7]). New York City, 18 January 1949.
Sid's delight · *Casbah*[7]

Miles Davis (tpt); J. J. Johnson (tbn); Benjamin Lundy (ten); Payne (bar); Dameron (p, comp); John Collins (g); Russell (bs); Clarke (d); Kay Penton (vcl[2]). New York City, 21 April 1949.
John's delight · *What's new?*[2] · *Heaven's doors are open wide*[2] · *Focus*

Navarro (tpt); Sonny Rollins (ten); Powell (p); Tommy Potter (bs); Roy Haynes (d). New York City, 8 August 1949.
Bouncin' with Bud (3 versions) · *Wail* (2 versions) · *Dance of the infidels* (2 versions) · *52nd Street theme*

Considering that he was among the most imaginative jazz improvisers and demonstrably one of this music's supreme trumpet masters, Navarro's case is unusual in that he thus far has received little attention in the literature. Such comments as have appeared are mostly inaccurate and indeed patronizing, often amounting to outright dismissals for having merely copied Gillespie. [12] Navarro's debt to Gillespie (six years his senior) is as obvious as Gillespie's to Eldridge (six years his senior) or Clifford Brown's to Navarro (seven years his senior), though in each instance the pervasive nature of the influence has been exaggerated. And Navarro, in the few interviews he gave during his short life, usually claimed Howard McGhee, his section mate in Andy Kirk's band, as his chief exemplar, mentioning too Charlie Shavers 'for his trumpet playing, not his jazz'. McGhee was also affected by Gillespie (and Eldridge) of course, and Gillespie once nominated Dud Bascomb as a possible influence on Navarro. Given the sophistication of Bascomb's work, this is an interesting idea, and these several names indicate that the background of Navarro's music will not be accounted for in terms of a simple parroting of Gillespie. Nor will all the praise accorded him by such diverse fellow trumpeters as Joe Newman, Miles Davis, Richard Williams, Don Cherry, Clifford Brown and Gillespie himself.

In fact the differences between Navarro and Gillespie were considerable. As noted under **256**, in his best years the latter's expression was mercurial, his phrases darting across the instrument's entire range, his abrupt switches of register giving rise to boldly angular phrases. Navarro had just as impressive a command of the trumpet and could ascend into its upper register with all the young Gillespie's ease and panache, but if he sounded less volatile it was because of a more explicit commitment to form and continuity. Each of Gillespie's finest solos is a sequence of surpassingly brilliant gestures, with much dependent on their immediate impact and no particularly strong motivic links between them. Those by Navarro have superior musical logic, are extensions of fairly rigorous trains of thought, yet can rise to as great an intensity as the improvisations of anybody then working in the bop style, including Parker and Powell. If Navarro broke fewer barriers than Gillespie it is because he did not have to: free of the burden of linguistic innovation, he could produce statements of greater formal coherence.

What above all separated Navarro from Gillespie was his tone, which is fundamentally different from that of the Eldridge–Gillespie–McGhee succession and is more like Freddie Webster, to judge from the few solos the latter recorded. Even further removed from the nervous harshness then popularly associated with bop, Navarro's sound, largely free of vibrato, was full, warm, soft at the edges. And it never had to be sacrificed to speed, even in the upper register during his most acrobatic passages. Claims such as that 'his tone is usually thin and dry' [13] are inexplicable.

Often Navarro conveys the paradoxical impression of taking risks yet sounding completely secure. Such is the fruit of a comprehensive technical mastery, of course, as is the characteristic feeling of relaxation. The latter is particularly evident in comparison with the worthy but as yet unsettled Dorham on the first of the above sessions. A further result of Navarro's combined virtuosity, relaxation and power of invention is that it allowed him to shepherd collections of extremely diverse phrases into finely balanced improvisations. An especially good instance is the second version of *Symphonette*, although there perhaps is in such cases something of what George Eliot called 'the suppressed transitions that unite all contrasts'. Certainly Navarro's ability to think several moves ahead while playing a solo was important, and this operates not only on studio recording sessions with their repeated takes and with Dameron's regular working band (Milestone [A] M47041, †Carrère [F] 98.196) but also in the somewhat disorganized circumstances of a so-called Saturday Night Swing Session (America [F] 30-AM-6065, 1947). Here, amid excellent work by Allen Eager, Bill Harris and Ralph Burns and abysmal interventions from Charlie Ventura, Navarro, in *High on an open mike* and particularly *Sweet Georgia Brown*, improvises beautifully shaped solos, each tightly packed with an orderly succession of ideas.

One might go further and say that his best statements were conceived as wholes, this often being confirmed by the alternative takes. The details may be different yet the basic concept is usually the same (though not always: hear *Dameronia*). And his musicality was such that the shades of emotion which coloured his solos could change with a speed and subtlety rare in jazz now, let alone in his day. This was not simply an equivocation between exuberance and melancholy but rather between the trumpet's direct power and an oblique refinement of emotion. Assertions that he 'seldom reached any real depth of feeling' [14] can only be a matter for amusement, the more so as despite his executive prowess he seldom played superfluous notes, was never merely facile. Each note pulled its full weight and, at least until we reach Bill Evans, we shall find no jazz virtuoso who was so little tempted by his virtuosity.

Always very swinging, Navarro's phrases are more closely allied to the beat than Gillespie's and this despite his relative independence of four- and eight-bar units which sometimes amounts to a shifting balance between long and short, often double-time, phrases. Certainly within the unity won by his clarity of thought there is constant variety of melodic shape, rhythmic pattern, harmonic inflection. On take 2 of *The squirrel* he piles one climax on another to entirely lucid effect, and something comparable happens in *Barry's bop*. This may appear excessive, but, unlike some other great jazz figures, Navarro had faultless taste, even allowing him to fit in a diversity of quotations and make them sound perfectly apt. Examples are Bonnell's *Turkey in the straw* in *Eb pob*, Verdi's *La donna è mobile* in *Fats blows* and Ellington's *Rockin' in rhythm* during *Nostalgia*. Again, as excitement mounts in the chase passages of *Double talk* it is Navarro's taste that is the surer.

As those who have little time always must, he matured early, and solos like that on Billy Eckstine's *Airmail special* (Musica Jazz [It] 2MJP1080) in early 1945 already have an almost disconcerting authority and are played with a luminous tone. The earliest of the above dates has the advantage of real bop drumming, as do most of those which follow, a little of what Clarke does having been anticipated by Cuba Austin with McKinney's Cotton Pickers etc. (**83–4**). These double-length pieces, originally filling both sides of 10-inch 78s, also present the beginning of Powell's maturity. Though Fuller, a few excellent scores like *Swedish* *suite* (**315**) notwithstanding, was never the composer and organizer that Dameron became, the ensembles here are delivered not just with youthful exuberance but with the proud conviction of men who know they have something important to say. This session had two great soloists in Navarro and Powell, two good ones in Dorham and Stitt, and what is generally the best sequence of improvisations comes in *Webb City*. This has two choruses each by Powell and Navarro, another by Powell, one each by the mediocre Lane, then Dorham, Stitt. Dorham is in fact happier elsewhere (e.g. *Boppin' a riff*), as is emphasized by Navarro's returning for a brilliant final solo after Stitt.

A weakness is that three of these pieces are based on the chords of *I got rhythm* (*Fat boy* is a blues), as are six of the eight titles which Navarro recorded with Davis. By the end of this Savoy series, however, Dameron and the trumpeter had dealt with this problem, the four items recorded in December 1947 using, with modifications, the harmonic sequences of respectively *Out of nowhere*, *What is this thing called love?*, *Fine and dandy* and *Lady, be good*. The dates with 'Lockjaw' Davis, an arch vulgarian who subsequently found his true *métier* as a cog in Basie's ponderous latter-day machine, resulted in performances which juxtapose some of the best and worst qualities that jazz has to offer. Sounding as if impaled on his own indignation, Davis naïvely deploys his armoury of honks and whinnyings as Navarro soars with majestic freedom. The exchange of four-bar phrases in *Hollerin' and screamin'* (alias *Lard pot*) demonstrates all too vividly the divergent ideals of this pair, with the trumpet's dancing melodic fragments answering the tenor's incoherent belches. Note also the perfect calculation and poise of the break with which Navarro begins his solo here, the beautifully choreographed tumble at the end of his *Stealin' trash* solo and the exactly placed trumpet portamentos. The high note with which his solo on *Callin' Dr Jazz* ends, precisely timed and executed, well illustrates his use of the upper register, always to strictly musical ends. *Just a mystery*, just a blues, gives rise to a superb Navarro solo, full of bounding melodic phrases, but Davis, hollering and screaming, returns all too soon. Luckily the solo order is reversed for *Red pepper* and both here and in *Spinal* are found trumpet solos that are pitched daringly high yet flow with untroubled zest.

Several of these groups were assembled just for the recording dates, but the first of them was preceded, only the day before, by a session under Clarke's name and playing other Fuller scores with a closely similar personnel (Pathé [F] C054–16030, †RCA/Bluebird [Eu] ND82177). Again, the ensemble which recorded the October 1947 date was Dameron's regular working band (usually with tenor saxophone or trombone added), and in fact it is this composer-pianist's involvement with most of the remaining music that makes all the difference. A lot of it was first issued under his name and on the first CD of the EMI/Blue Note set 13 of the 14 themes are his. As suggested under **280**, the strongsinewed lyrical melodies and rich harmonizations of his pieces chime excellently with the amplitude of Navarro's expression, as in *Our delight* and perhaps above all the first two 1949 items. He was to remain the most perceptive interpreter Dameron's music ever found, executing the written parts so as to impart a feeling of spontaneity, as in *Jahbero*, making it hard to distinguish between what is written and what improvised. The keyboard accompaniments, too, being free of conventional pianistic formulas, were a stimulus to the trumpeter's solos, as in *Barry's bop*; and the main justifications for the singers' presences are the sensitively enhancing settings that Dameron provided for them.

Ice freezes red is the theme with which Powell had six days before closed his recording of *Indiana* (**261**), and Navarro sounds as if he cannot wait to begin his fully comparable race through that tried and true chord sequence. In fact he almost explodes with a dazzling flow of ideas, as he does again in *Fat girl.* For *Eb pob*, a blues with a bridge, he places the climax early, then relaxes the tension gradually as he moves away from it. This is a beautifully structured improvisation, as is the solo on *Goin' to Minton's*, where he builds a comparable shape though levelling off sooner. He takes two choruses on each of the December 1947 items and where there are two versions it is difficult to choose between them, especially in the case of *Nostalgia* and *Bebop romp*. In fact the consistency of his inspiration is one of the most extraordinary things about Navarro. However, on *Barry's bop*, as in *The squirrel* from the previous September's Blue Note date, the magnificent second take finds him bringing to more complete fulfilment ideas uncovered on the first time round. These two accounts of *Barry's bop* should be heard in conjunction with the version titled *Fats flats* (Spotlite [E] 108), broadcast the previous month with Parker and Tristano, on which Navarro solos almost throughout. In several pieces, like *The Tadd walk* and *Nostalgia*, he uses a cup mute and the resulting delicate, fine-spun lines are the reverse image of the flaring exultance of much of his open playing.

All of Navarro's subsequent front-line partners are superior to 'Lockjaw', even Leo Parker, who is almost on his best behaviour and alludes to *Bebop* (see **256**) in *Ice freezes red* and *Jive at five* (**134**) in *Eb pob*. At some points invention sparks regularly yet at a low voltage, Rouse providing examples on *Bebop romp* and *Barry's bop*. Henry sometimes overcomes his obvious technical limitations, as on *The Tadd walk*, making his effect through phrasing, tone, attack. Taking quite different routes out of Lester Young's territory, Gray and Eager are far most interesting and further comments on them appear under **268** and **297**. Best of Navarro's reed-playing companions, though, was Dexter Gordon, and their 1947 date together appeared on Savoy (A) SJL2211.

A few days before Dameron's *Jahbero/Ladybird* session Gray also took part along with Navarro on a version of *Stealin' apples* with Goodman. This was during the latter's brief flirtation with bop and the result was certainly surprising. Both Navarro and Gray, and the others present, perform excellently yet are surpassed by a leader brilliantly on his mettle. There can be few Goodman solos on record better than this.

While Navarro took part in only the first two 1949 studio titles with Dameron, it is revealing to listen to him moving through these more complex textures. Perhaps there is an indication here of the sort of music they might have made together in the 1950s. Incidentally, *Casbah*, like *Nostalgia*, is on the *Out of nowhere* chords, these two pieces forming a notable illustration of how the same harmonic sequence can be put to altogether different uses. (The remaining 1949 items, for which Miles Davis replaces Navarro, ought to be heard along with **376** and the Mulligan tentette on **300**.)

A few marginal points remain, such as that the two Savoy CDs between them have the same programme as the Savoy 2-LP set, and *That someone must be you* seems to be a mistitling of *For me there must be you.* The August 1949 items, recorded under Powell's name, are dealt with in the next entry.

In the end one returns to Navarro, whose most inspired passages defy us *not* to listen. By the time we reach headlong performances like *The chase,* whose heart is his irresistible surge of invention, there are, or should be, no questions left, and one's response can only be an awestruck acquiescence. Nothing can reconcile us to the cynicism of a tone-deaf Fate which terminated his life so prematurely; yet what a fine use he made of those few years to leave recordings like these! M.H.

Bud Powell

261 The Complete Blue Note and Roost Recordings

†EMI/Blue Note (E) CDP7243 8 30083 2 2

Powell (p); Curly Russell (bs); Max Roach (d). New York City, 10 January 1947.
I'll remember April · *Indiana* · *Somebody loves me* · *I should care* · *Bud's bubble* · *Off minor* · *Nice work if you can get it* · *Everything happens to me*

Fats Navarro (tpt); Sonny Rollins (ten); Powell (p); Tommy Potter (bs); Roy Haynes (d). New York City, 8 August 1949.
Bouncin' with Bud (3 versions) · *Wail* (2 versions) · *Dance of the infidels* (2 versions) · *52nd Street theme*

Navarro, Rollins absent. Same date.
You go to my head · *Ornithology* (2 versions)

Powell (p); Russell (bs); Roach (d). New York City, 1 May 1951.
Un poco loco (3 versions) · *A night in Tunisia* (2 versions) · *Parisian thoroughfare*

Russell, Roach absent. Same date.
Over the rainbow · *It could happen to you* (2 versions)

Powell (p); George Duvivier (bs); Art Taylor (d). New York City, 14 August 1953.
Autumn in New York · *Reets and I* (2 versions) · *Sure thing* · *Collard greens and black-eyed peas* (2 versions) · *Polka dots and moonbeams* · *I want to be happy* · *Audrey* · *Glass enclosure*

Same personnel. New York City, September 1953.
Embraceable you · *Burt covers Bud* · *My heart stood still* · *You'd be so nice to come home to* · *Bags' groove* · *My devotion* · *Woody 'n you*

Duvivier, Taylor absent. Same date.
Stella by starlight

Powell (p); Paul Chambers (bs); Taylor (d). Hackensack, N.J., 3 August 1957.
Blue pearl (2 versions) · *Keepin' in the groove* · *Some soul* · *Frantic fancies*

Curtis Fuller (tbn) added. Same date.
Idaho · *Don't blame me* · *Moose the mooche*

Fuller, Chambers, Taylor absent. Same date.
Bud on Bach

Powell (p); Sam Jones (bs); Philly Joe Jones (d). Hackensack, N.J., 24 May 1958.
John's abbey (2 versions) · *Sub city* (2 versions) · *Buster rides again* · *Dry soul* · *Marmalade* · *Monopoly* · *Time waits*

Powell (p); Chambers (bs); Taylor (d). Hackensack, N.J., 29 December 1958.
The scene changes · *Down with it* · *Comin' up* (2 versions) · *Duid deed* · *Cleopatra's dream* · *Getting there* · *Crossin' the channel* · *Danceland* · *Borderick*

Powell (p); Pierre Michelot (bs); Kenny Clarke (d). Paris, 23 May 1963.
Like someone in love

Powell has been reduced to one who merely transferred Parker's ideas to the keyboard, and whose later work declined, even reached total failure, because he did not go on repeating his initial statements. This indictment's first thrust apes that aimed at Earl Hines, who, 'trumpet style' and all, was supposedly just a pianistic reflection of Armstrong. In fact, and in each case, the two hands evolved textures whose outlines could scarcely be suggested by even the most virtuosic playing of a single horn. Besides, viewing Powell's work as merely a keyboard transcription of Parker's is to ignore its sources and background, not least the study of classical music which had begun in childhood, even if few signs of any apprenticeship survive. Pianist and alto saxophonist first recorded together in 1944 (*The boppers*, Connoisseur Rareties [It] CR522), and on several records with Cootie Williams that same year Powell offers an assured version of early bop pianism, an example being *Blue garden blues* (Big Band Archives [A] LP1208, Affinity [E] AFS1031). True, we tend to hear even a much later recording like *Some soul* as echoing *Parker's mood* (**257**), yet, as Michael James has suggested, 'similarities between the two men may have stemmed as much from the inspiration both drew from Tatum as from any deliberate duplication of style'. [15]

During those early years Powell was less affected by the blues idiom than Parker, just as he was less interested in substitute chords. What we hear on the 1944 records is an intensification of what he had learned from Teddy Wilson, certain aspects of Tatum, and transitional figures such as Clyde Hart, Billy Kyle and in particular Nat Cole. This intensification continued in the light of bop innovations, as is shown, for instance, by Powell's solo on Frank Socolow's 1945 *Reverse the charges* (Duke [A] 112), until we can almost speak of his reaching, on such 1946 dates as those with Dexter Gordon (Savoy [A] SJL2211), J. J. Johnson (SJL2232), the Bebop Boys (SJL2225 and **259**), a startling early maturity.

The basics of Powell's style are detailed in countless texts which hardly need to be paraphrased here, but his 1947 titles, first issued on Roost, must be noted as a first, seemingly definitive, exposition of this. Despite the emergence of so strong a musical personality, some traces of conventional figurations do survive, but these were soon eliminated and from now until the end the individuality of Powell's statements remained virtually complete, whatever may be thought about other aspects of his later work. He never played the piano more efficiently than here, and these eight 1947 performances give a splendid account of his *method*, which is in one sense perfected. Yet he was only 22, and besides his nuances of touch and accentuation later becoming more varied, this early peak hardly suggests the emotional depth and diversity of his subsequent output. The diversity needs to be stressed because an excessive concentration in jazz commentary on the admittedly appalling facts of Powell's life has led to the notion that he could only focus on the darker shades of experience. Had this been so he would of course have been a considerably lesser artist.

Regarding depth of emotion, set *Nice work if you can get it* or *Somebody loves me* from 1947 beside the greater expressive power with which he shaped these pieces in 1953 (Elektra Musician [A] MUS52363). Even the 1949 Blue Note *Ornithology* and *You go to my head* are more relaxed, less patterned, than what he had been doing two years before. With a more flexible delivery of more varied phrases, a stronger feeling of spontaneity is conveyed; and this applies to the theme statements as well as the improvisations. The tone he draws from the piano here, as in the 1951 unaccompanied solos, has a shining, almost luminous quality which, unless the recording deceives us, is rather different from that produced in 1947. Though still indisputable, the brilliance less assertively draws attention to itself, and it would be hard to imagine anything occurring at the 1947 date quite so unpredictable as *You go to my head*'s coda, this being the point at which Powell repeatedly displayed an especially strong sense of fantasy, a further example being the second version of *Wail*. Another advance is implied by the very oblique restatement, or rather suggestion, of the final chorus of the second reading of *Ornithology*, this, too, becoming characteristic. Hear, for instance, the allusions to the melody, with barely a direct statement, in his 1955 *Tenderly* (†Verve [A] 314 521 669–2), and the following year's *Over the rainbow* (RCA [A] LPM1423), so different from the above Blue Note, where the melody is never quite abandoned, never unequivocally stated.

Such playing as was caught at that first Blue Note session, and the musical thinking behind it, were almost enough to establish Powell as the most influential jazz pianist between Tatum and Bill Evans. Tatum was clearly the origin of his approach to slow ballads, and this can be heard in its earliest recorded 'state' on *Sweet Lorraine* and particularly *My old flame* with Cootie Williams (Phoenix [A] LP1). Though Tatum is still a presence in the two unaccompanied pieces from the 1951 Blue Note date, these well demonstrate how strongly personal an adaptation Powell made of his predecessor's method. From the Blue Note occasion of two years later, *Polka dots and moonbeams*, almost the only ballad treatment from that productive session, takes further the slow-moving chordal approach he initiated with 1947's *Somebody loves me*. Such performances certainly did give rise to dark thoughts as the years passed, and their travelling so very far from the emotional climate of the songs receives an almost paradoxical emphasis from Powell in these cases staying close to the original melodies.

Following Hines, Tatum was a major exemplar for bop pianists' freeing the left hand from its regular statement of rhythm (and tempo). They also got valuable lessons from Basie, or rather from the Basie rhythm section as a whole. Occasional reversions to stride bass patterns occur relatively late in Powell, for example *Idaho* and *Monopoly*, but usually the left hand's discontinuity allows more of the rhythm section's pulse to come forward, à la Basie, and hence there is an increased buoyancy. With Powell, virile left-hand chording goes beyond mere harmonic and rhythmic punctuation, even beyond the music's further intensification on those planes. At once subtle and dynamic, the shifting relationships, including the oppositions, between the hands generate the improvisations' up-tempo linear energy in balance with a productive tension between discipline and expressive immediacy.

It is amusing to recall that this method, simultaneously used by such musicians as Al Haig as well as Powell, ushered in that mythical figure, still celebrated by seriously deaf commentators on jazz, the 'one-handed modern pianist'. [16] The bulk of Powell's recordings are trio music in the fullest sense, bass and drums providing no mere accompaniment but integrating completely with the activities of the pianist's two hands. His darting keyboard lines represent a free and rapid flowering of unpredictable melody, from which arises the striking irregularity of phrase lengths already noted, these often surging across the chorus's formal divisions. Several of the September 1953 performances are especially good examples of this, and some of these, like others, are fired by a highly compressed lyricism. This, rather than virtuoso display, is always the point of the speed, so that even quite elaborate passages can sound stark, unadorned. It is another Powell paradox that his improvisations at rapid tempos should make a fairly ascetic impression, and this is heightened by his very precise, exactly centred touch, which at best gives the music a singular clarity. Here the model was Nat Cole, yet, again, Powell made a sound that was resolutely individual.

A classic embodiment of the mature bop style, the 1949 Modernists session was only the third studio date under his own name and remained the only one at which he led a quintet that was apparently of his own choosing. This does not greatly matter, because Powell had few gifts as a combo leader, this presumably relating to his not – except in one circumstance dealt with below – being an interesting accompanist. [17] Though inside the last year of his life, Navarro plays superbly, he and Powell manifestly inspiring each other to solos that are virtually perfect in continuity and variety while obviously having, unlike most cases of perfection, the potential for further growth. There is no loss whatever in the music's inner tension as piano follows trumpet in, say, *Wail*. Rollins shows exactly the promise he displayed on his two sessions with J. J. Johnson that same year. The alternative takes allow us to hear the band working at the improvement of three of these pieces, the third version of *Bouncin' with Bud* (alias *Bebop in pastel*) in particular benefiting from some last revisions.

Another advance is registered by the 1951 date: one cannot imagine the Powell of 1949, let alone 1947, bringing off anything like the magnificent series of three takes of *Un poco loco*, evidently recorded in very rapid succession. The pianist's ideas grow more vivid each time round, and it is equally remarkable that the second version of *A night in Tunisia* likewise improves on the first. Both these pieces are in the Latin American vein, of which Powell made a more fruitful use than many jazzmen. Roach has a crucial role in each, though note should be taken of the free, strikingly resourceful solo piano codas to both accounts of the latter title.

An indication of his range of expression is given by the music of the first 1953 session in particular, which opens several fresh paths. For example *Autumn in New York*, its melody not much departed from, is the kind of performance that is scarcely mentioned in the Powell literature, being, like *Sure thing*, not the kind of thing he is supposed to have done. Neither of them offers hard-driven bop piano nor Tatumesque rhapsody, but their large contrapuntal element – here strengthened by Duvivier's exceptional bass playing – reappears in his other recordings of both items, and these highly 'compositional' treatments point to *Glass enclosure.* Despite its brevity, this last is among the most memorable of all his recordings, its imaginative power taking it sufficiently far across the supposed frontiers of jazz to ensure repeated dismissals as 'pretentious'. [18]

Very different yet palpably from the same mind is *Collard greens and black-eyed peas* (alias *Blues in the closet*), the first blues he recorded in trio format; and his bold accompaniments to Duvivier on both takes were the first of many that helped make bass solos on Powell's records less dull than in most other places. Hear, for instance, *Coscrane* and *Blues for Bessie* from 1956 (RCA, as above) and both takes of *Blue pearl*; in *Some soul, Keepin' in the groove* and *The scene changes* there are virtual duets between keyboard and bass. Different again is 1957's *Bud on Bach.* The person responsible for the very poor booklet which accompanied a previous (Mosaic) reissue seemed to imagine that we were dealing with Johann Sebastian rather than Carl Philipp Emanuel. But what Powell achieved with the latter's *Solfeggietto* was a satirical reminiscence of the drudgery of youthful keyboard practice, for this piece early becomes familiar to all pianistic tyros. Perhaps only those who have such memories can grasp all the humour of this purposeful outrage.

Although some of this music does invoke Wordsworth's 'spontaneous overflow of powerful feeling', its character and variety ought to have been enough to discredit the stereotyping of Powell as a kind of thoughtless, unrestrainable expressionist who put his entire bid on the inspiration of the moment. In fact, of the 43 themes used on the Blue Note dates 27 are by Powell, and a comparable situation prevailed elsewhere, his two RCA LPs of 1956–7, for example, including nine themes by him. A further clue ought to have been his careful and often deeply perceptive accounts of Monk pieces, starting not so much with the 1947 *Off minor* as with his *Round about midnight* of 1954 (Verve, as above). The early relationship between these two musicians is often noted and Monk's influence on Powell's work is quite apparent, an instance being his ability to take considerable rhythmic liberties without impeding the music's flow. It is no small tribute to Powell that he made something out of both Tatum's virtuoso approach and Monk's knowing keyboard primitivism. One of the few able to improvise intelligently on Monk compositions, he played much of the older man's music in later years, yet perhaps because only a few of his themes, such as *Monopoly*, are overtly Monkish, it is never asked who nudged Powell towards his quite prolific composing.

Some of these pieces are doubtless based on ideas that came to him while improvising, but their formal implications were then evidently worked out in a balanced, systematic way, as *Glass enclosure*, *Un poco loco* and many others show. And such themes make statements as decisive as his finest passages of improvisation. It is not without significance that Miles Davis's *Swing spring* (**272**) was based on one of Powell's inventions. Though as much was hinted at as early as 1949 by *Tempus fugit* and

Strictly confidential (Verve, as above), it would seem that in later years the character of his themes became a more potent stimulus to him than the standard chord sequences, even if these remained in the background (the *Strike up the band* harmonies, for example, being the basis of *Frantic fancies*).

Powell's lack of general acceptance as a composer is unsurprising, however, in the light – or darkness – of persistent misunderstanding of his later work, the swift recognition of the fruits of his early maturity leading to an almost unqualified rejection of everything that followed. The diminishment of his at first masterly technique is indisputable, yet claims that as a simple consequence his later music was only an imperfect reflection of his youthful achievements miss all relevant points. The depth and richness of Powell's gifts were such that as virtuosity declined he had plenty upon which to fall back, and slow blues like *Dry soul* prove that his essential characteristics survived all simplifications. Elmo Hope's nonvirtuosic use of some of Powell's basic discoveries underlines the point (**290**), and in the latter's case the elimination of inessentials led to the emergence of something further of his purely melodic powers. In contrast with Hope, Powell's mere imitators conventionalized his method while he went in the opposite direction, his mode of expression remaining sufficiently volatile to escape, even to contradict, the neat formulations of his detractors. Enough to confirm this is a comparison between the two 1958 Blue Note sessions, with their different realizations of his concern with texture, with the interplay of light and shade in terms of harmony, rhythm, space, accent.

The 1957 date was Powell's first in stereo and Fuller's heavy, sometimes fuzzy contributions do not add much, although there is a particularly good piano solo on *Moose the mooche*. The trombonist's presence was the idea of Alfred Lion of Blue Note, not of Powell. There are further lucid and logical improvisations in *Blue pearl* and *Keepin' in the groove*, and *Some soul*, like the subsequent *Dry soul*, is a superb slow blues. This is not the sort of music with which Powell would have been much associated in his youth but, like Parker's work of some years before in this idiom, it asserts the fundamentally traditional nature of bop.

These sessions were highly productive, and further points to notice include the way both readings of *John's abbey* slow down near the close, lessening tension just when it might be expected to increase, the entirely different endings to the two versions of *Sub city*, the purposeful concentration of Powell's solos on *Buster rides again* and the second accounts of *John's abbey* and *Sub city*. He was still more creative at his final Blue Note trio date and, excepting the very fast *Crossin' the channel*, most of these performances are classic statements of latter-day bop piano, an especial vitality being apparent from the opening bars of *The scene changes* onwards. This title is perhaps a reference to his imminent departure for

Paris (though no coded message need be read into his covert allusion to *Santa Claus is coming to town*). In *Comin' up* – which, like *Buster rides again*, is a return to the sphere of *Un poco loco* – bass and drum repetitions throw into relief Powell's exceptionally well-contrasted flow of invention rather as the unadorned beat preferred by Tristano heightened the linear freedom and rhythmic variety of his improvising: these are both highly musical uses of paradox. Finally, as a curious postlude to a great session, comes *Borderick*, which has something of Satie's defiant simplicity.

After so conclusive a demonstration of the fertility of Powell's themes the point hardly needs making that they would bear fruit elsewhere. There has indeed been some proof of this, particularly Mike Mellilo's *Alternate Changes* (Red [It] NS211), Herb Robertson's *Shades of Bud Powell* (JMT [F] LP834.420). In the latter, pieces like *Hallucinations* (alias *Budo*) and *Glass enclosure* are scored for a sextet of brass and percussion, and they well survive the transfer to an utterly different medium. They also survive considerable transformations, *I'll keep loving you*, for example, becoming a sombre processional chorale, monochrome yet very beautiful. Earlier precedents for such treatments of Powell themes include the John Dankworth Seven's 1951 recording of *Strictly confidential* (†Esquire [E] CDESQ100–4) and Tubby Hayes's of *Parisian thoroughfare* (Fontana [E] TL5221) of 1964. A later one is Shorty Rogers's further extension of some of Powell's *Un poco loco* ideas in *Like it is* (†Candid [A] CCD79521) of 1992. M.H.

Howard McGhee

262 **Trumpet at Tempo**

Spotlite (E) SPJ131

McGhee (tpt); Jimmy Bunn (p); Bob 'Dingbod' Kesteton (bs); Roy Porter (d). Hollywood, 29 July 1946.

Trumpet at tempo · *Thermodynamics*

McGhee (tpt); Teddy Edwards (ten); Dodo Marmarosa (p); Arv Garrison (g); Kesterton (bs); Porter (d). Hollywood, 18 October 1946.

Dilated pupils (2 versions) · *Midnight at Minton's* · *Up in Dodo's room* (2 versions) · *High wind in Hollywood*

McGhee (tpt); James Moody (ten); Hank Jones (p); Ray Brown (bs); J. C. Heard (d); Milt Jackson (vib). New York City, 3 December 1947.

Night music · *Dorothy* · *Night mist* (2 versions) · *Coolerini* · *Turnip blood* (2 versions) · *Surrender* · *Sleepwalker boogie* · *Stoptime blues* · *You*

Although it was Armstrong who prompted McGhee to switch from clarinet and tenor saxophone to trumpet in 1935, Eldridge, then an avant-gardist, provided the basis for his work on the latter instrument. Part of the special character and success of the above music arises in fact from McGhee's being, along with two of his main partners here, Edwards and Moody, committed to bop yet with roots in swing. The latter were, indeed, two of the earliest tenor saxophonists to sound quite natural when playing the new music of the mid-1940s, and Edwards, with a background in territory bands, had a typical Southwestern leaning to the blues, as evident in his tone as in his phrasing. Like McGhee, he was an important pioneer of bop in California.

The trumpeter's *McGhee special*, recorded with Andy Kirk's band in 1942 (**132**), shows that, like a number of its major figures, he was moving towards bop some years before the style actually emerged. This is evident in some of the piece's harmonic moves, [19] in the duly emphasized chromatic alterations of his solo part, and these factors are taken further in his 1945 rerecording on JCB (Sw) JCB20. [20] That was the year he went to Los Angeles with Hawkins, with whom he can be heard doing some excellent if rather conservative work on **195**. It was the beginning of two very active years in California for McGhee during which he performed extensively with Parker, recording with him (**258**) and many others. It might be a helpful simplification to say that his rhythmic feeling is basically that of the swing period, other aspects of his music more fully according with bop. His status as an overt modernist had in any case been established by a 1945 *Northwest passage* recorded with a contingent from Woody Herman's First Herd before leaving New York (Mercury [E] SMWL21038). Also dating from 1945 and particularly relevant to the second of the sessions detailed above is a very boppish reading of *Mop mop* with Edwards, Kesterton and Porter (Spotlite [E] SPJ133).

This last especially includes superbly accomplished upper-register passages of strongly melodic content that were always a McGhee hallmark. *Trumpet at tempo* and even the less frantically paced *Thermodynamics* offer furious cascades of notes played with a seeming lack of effort and purposefully shaped into concise melodic variations. He maintained that this high-flying and very agile playing owed something to his early experience with the clarinet, and its occasional relentlessness is mitigated by a hot, expressive and personal tone.

These last two items came at the end of a date with Parker which resulted in the disastrous *Max is making wax*, *Loverman*, *Bebop* and *The Gypsy*, briefly dealt with under **258**. The first of these sessions led by McGhee produced some beautifully shaped open and muted solos from him, notably in *Midnight at Minton's*, forthright Edwards, lucid and elegant piano work by Marmarosa. There also are good post-Christian contributions from Garrison, particularly on the second version of *Up in Dodo's room*. Here and on *Dilated pupils* the second take is a considerable improvement, each man surer of what he wants to do, yet also more venturesome. No doubt is left, especially by *High wind in Hollywood*, *Midnight at Minton's* or the second version of *Up in Dodo's room*, of Marmarosa's position as one of the early masters of bop piano. And this was further demonstrated by his 1946 trio recordings (Phoenix [A]

LP20) and 1947 solos (Spotlite [E] SPJ128). What little there is of his later output is discussed under **345**.

Although attributed to McGhee, *Trumpet at tempo* is an undisguised *Indiana* and ought not to have been titled otherwise. The New York *Surrender* is plainly *I surrender, dear*, and there is no doubt of the relationship between *High wind in Hollywood* and *52nd Street theme.* But all the other items on this well-filled LP are his, have real melodic substance and are most attractive; several deserved to become part of the standard jazz repertoire. Instances from the New York date include *Dorothy*, *Coolerini* and *Turnip blood.* As *McGhee special* early proved, the trumpeter had a real potential for composition and arranging that was never to be completely fulfilled, though he provided a stream of excellent originals on many sessions, including for Parker. An idea of his ambitions is given by *Lifestream* (Spotlite [E] SPJ133) and the two-part *Cool fantasy* (JCB, as above), both of 1945. And it is confirmed by the above New York date, which covers a wider range of expression than might have been expected of a comparatively new idiom like bop. Clearly *Night mist* is largely written out, and it features an almost concertolike keyboard part. There is virtually nothing to choose between the two versions, although they should be compared with the 1946 recording on IAJRC (A) 25. *Night music*, elsewhere issued as *Fantasy for piano and jazz band*, is similar, and like *Night mist* is not well served by Jones's efficient but faceless playing.

Speaking for a quite different ambition, namely the desire to have a hit on the jukeboxes, is the crude *Sleepwalker boogie*, even more an indiscretion than the introduction to *Dilated pupils.* But several of these performances, like *Dorothy*, contain virtually definitive examples of McGhee's version of bop trumpet playing. This never pretended to the overwhelming power and seemingly infallible virtuosity of Gillespie or Navarro during those years, but it was at best a distinguished and individual contribution to jazz, one that nobody else could have made. The 1947 occasion is also noteworthy for some fine instances of Jackson's early work, perhaps above all on the two versions of *Turnip blood.*

It is instructive, even reassuring, to turn from this music to a reunion between McGhee and Edwards of 15 years later, the 1961 *Together Again!* (Contemporary [E] LAC12291, Contemporary [A] S7588, †Original Jazz Classics [A] OJCCD693–2). Both had considerably refined their improvising with any loss of inner strength, and McGhee presents solos that are at once striking and thoughtful. This is also one of the few records on which the virtuoso pianist Phineas Newborn ever showed signs of fulfilling his vast potential. M.H.

Erroll Garner

263 Play, Piano, Play
Spotlite (E) SPJ129

Garner (p); Red Callender (bs); Doc West (d). Hollywood, 19 February 1947.
Pastel · *Trio* (2 versions)

Callender, West absent. Hollywood, 10 June 1947.
Play, piano, play · *Love is the strangest game* (2 versions) · *Blues Garni* · *Don't worry about me* (3 versions) · *Loose nut* · *Love for sale* · *Fantasy on Frankie and Johnny* · *Sloe gin fizz*

During the last quarter-century and more of his life, Garner's output showed scant awareness of anything at all new that was going forward in jazz, and his inclusion here may appear surprising. Yet his acceptance by a public far broader than any that can be expected by any genuinely adventurous musician should not obscure the fact that he might have taken a different path entirely. He is one of only two performers represented in this work by music selected precisely because it is untypical (see **470**). The above recordings are among the few to find Garner even slightly engaged with a significant jazz movement, in fact with bop. More importantly, certain of these improvisations prove that his music had, for a while, the makings of a potentially major new style of modern piano jazz. All too soon any further growth in that direction, like his involvement in the continuing evolution of jazz, was submerged by his populist tendencies.

The two most revealing items are *Play, piano, play* and the *Fantasy on Frankie and Johnny*. This latter is aptly named because it remains, particularly in harmonic and rhythmic terms, a daringly modern structure raised on what after all is a folk melody; in fact it is remarkably successful as an application of relatively advanced procedures to such material. *Play, piano, play* is another sort of expansion, based on a 16-bar solo Garner had contributed to Slam Stewart's otherwise inconsequential 1945 *Play, fiddle, play* (Savoy [A] SJL1118). Here, as in *Frankie and Johnny*, a vital artistic imagination operates with just sufficient aggressiveness, manifest in all kinds of unexpected details of melody, rhythm, harmony and keyboard texture, each finely integrated with the whole. This is also true, if to a noticeably lesser extent, in *Sloe gin fizz* (not to be confused with Buster Bailey's 1938 *Sloe jam fizz*) and *Blues Garni*, although in the latter, in a genre he did not much use, he fails properly to extend his ideas, striking though some of them are. The guitarlike strumming left-hand chords of the later performances that brought Garner such wide success had not yet emerged, and what we find here is a potentially most interesting modernization of the basic stride approach (rather than Tatum's sublimation of it). *Loose nut* gives further indications of the route he might have taken.

Partly original jazz on the above lines, the two takes of *Love is the strangest game* also admit to a rather blowsy romanticism which resurfaces in the three readings of *Don't worry about me.* Garner's seeking to draw the fullest possible sound from the piano in such performances is praiseworthy, and his ballads are, at least potentially, the necessary reverse image of his hard-hit bouncing pieces. Also here is the beginning of what might also be called the desynchronization of his hands, with the wayward right eventually lagging as much as a full quaver behind the strict left. But decadence, in the forms of soft-centred lushness and overtly ornate eccentricity, was soon to assume control.

As much is broadly hinted by *Pastel,* though bass and drums participate with more independence than they would do on his countless later sessions. This is from the date with Parker, and *Bird's nest* (**258**), especially take 3, like the above *Trio,* finds Garner at times fairly close to bop piano, hinting at how valuable a contributor he could have been to the mainstream of piano jazz. This potentiality survived as late as 1955, as a few passages of *I'll remember April* and *It's alright with me* on the vastly overrated *Concert by the Sea* programme (†CBS [A] 451 042–2) suggest. It should be added, however, that the meeting with Parker, though subject to much uncomprehending praise, only worked partially, and this because they felt the music's basic pulse rather differently.

Garner's subsequent career was no doubt rewarding in its own way, but he stands as the entertainer who could have been an artist, probably a great one. He had enormous gifts, musical and pianistic, but chose, or was led, to develop only one side of them. Garner had an influence, musical rather than pianistic, on a few minor players such as Jimmy Rowles and Jaki Byard, but his excessively mannered and all too recognizable later work, relating, as noted, to little then happening in jazz and to still less that happened in the past, is a negative yet conclusive illustration of the importance of tradition in this music.

It is usually claimed that *Pastel,* supposedly written by Garner, was turned into a song, *Please let me forget,* credited to Welsh and Armstrong, this being taken as another example of Tin Pan Alley tunesmiths plagiarizing jazz. But the song was recorded by David Allyn with Boyd Raeburn's band in 1946, Garner being present. He solos briefly, plays an *obbligato* to Allyn's singing, and also solos on this date's *C jam clues* and *Caravan* (all on Hep [E] 22). As this was his one period of involvement in general jazz activity, his presence on at least one other big-band performance should be noted. This was Georgie Auld's 1945 *In the middle* (Smithsonian [A] R004), on which Garner solos twice. There were also two sessions under Byas's name in 1945 and to these may be added Garner's contribution to the 1949 Teddy Edwards–Dave Lambert *Cherokee* (Queen [It] Q039). Further takes of *Love is the strangest game* and *Loose nut* are on Hall of Fame (A) JG604, and a much

inferior trio version of *Play, piano, play* from 1951 appeared on CBS (A) 62914.
M.H.

Bop Takes Over

As it became clear that bop was one of the major styles in jazz history, it gained the allegiance of an increasing diversity of players. Hence the language of this music was greatly enriched, most crucially in polyrhythmic terms.

Charlie Parker

264 The Apartment Sessions
Spotlite (E) SPJ146

Parker (alt); John Williams (p); Buddy Jones (bs); Phil Brown[1], Frank Isola[2], Buddy Bridgeford[3] (d); others present and heard briefly include Norma Carson, Jon Eardley (tpt), Jimmy Knepper (tbn), Joe Maini (alt), Bob Newman, Gers Yowell (ten). New York City, 4, 11, 18, 25 June 1950.
Little Willie leaps[1] · *All the things you are*[2] · *Bernie's tune*[3] · *Donna Lee*[1] · *Out of nowhere*[2] · *Half Nelson*[1] · *Fine and dandy*[1]

Parker (alt); unidentified p, bs; probably Isola (d); others present and heard briefly include Jon Neilsen (tpt), Knepper (tbn), Maini (alt), Don Lanphere (ten). New York City, *c.* 1950.
Half Nelson · *Cherokee* · *Scrapple from the Apple* · *Star eyes*

Charlie Parker

265 Quintessential Jazz at Massey Hall
†Original Jazz Classics (A) OJCCD044–2

Dizzy Gillespie (tpt); Parker (alt); Bud Powell (p); Charles Mingus (bs); Max Roach (d). Massey Hall, Toronto, 15 May 1953.
Perdido · *Salt peanuts* · *All the things you are* · *Wee* · *Hot house* · *A night in Tunisia*

Many a one of those recorded sessions that are bizarrely called 'live' has been hailed critically as demonstrating inspirations of which its participants had fallen short under the restrictions of scheduled studio engagements. The two 'location' items considered below are unlikely to prompt confident judgements about Parker and his companions, though there are here some exciting achievements to be taken account of.

Certainly the Manhattan apartment, on 136th Street, was one place where Parker could jettison customary patterns of performance. 'You'd give up a night's work,' the pianist Bob Dorough declared, 'when word came round that Bird was playing at the William Henry . . . We'd all crowd into this basement pad . . . and sometimes you'd get to play two or three times with Bird! And it was taped.' [21] Not surprisingly, the tapes have been edited to omit all but a few snatches of the solos by Parker's supporters, described by one writer as his 'white acolytes'. [22]

In several of these extracts Parker is in superb form. The exuberant continuum of invention which he threads through 15 or so choruses of a fast *Little Willie leaps* should not, for the intent ear, hide the sheer thoughtfulness, the unaccountable hovering of concentration that contradicts any impression of wild fervour. This improvisation is daunting in length and astounding in inspiration. Never at any point is the pace forced by the soloist. *Donna Lee* draws close to such brilliance, the altoist magisterially scattering dazzling multiplications and etched-out indications of the tune's harmonic possibilities; but an overenthusiastic rhythm section does force an accelerando, and the celebrating ensemble comes in like a boppers' convention. Something of that conviviality touches *Out of nowhere*, yet Parker contrives to sound lively and serious at once, savouring the tune while the other participants gird themselves for a shapeless 'all in'. On the 100-miles-per-hour *Fine and dandy* – a solo of 11 choruses, the first four of which are woven seamlessly into each other – the overriding impression is still not of immense stamina or dominance but of a miraculous ease of intellectual strategy.

All the things you are was turned by Gillespie into a standard bop number though a 1945 recording (**256**) allowed Parker only a few bars of solo. Another version will be referred to below and there are other preserved examples, some under Parker's title, *Bird of paradise* (**258**). The apartment treatment must have fair claim to being one of the best. This keeps six choruses of Parker, and there may have been others because an initial four have been spliced to two more.

The two shots at *Half Nelson*, taped on separate occasions, while they contain fascinating alto pronouncements, are spoiled by rather chaotic accompaniment, and, particularly in the second of them, Parker's vitality flags. He does not really get going in *Cherokee* as he duels with savage cymbal-bashing, and *Scrapple from the Apple* blunders into riffs and quotations. Shapeliness struggles back into *Star eyes* but here, suddenly, Parker sounds solitary. The pianist comps doggedly along but the poorly tuned enthusiasts leave their hero in the lurch. 'Provisions and contributions' perhaps had something to do with such moments of laxity, but relaxation was a provision too, and contributed to the stimulus of some of Parker's most beautiful recorded work, music that was hidden from the public ear for 27 years before the commercial issue of this remarkable jazz document.

In its personnel the Massey Hall group is the bop quintet *par excellence*. It may be that Mingus had been slightly towards the edges of the mid-1940s movement, yet he supports these companions congenially, with an aptitude and an enterprising initiative which extended, as will be explained, beyond the temporal occasion itself.

This concert recording has long been held in high regard. Its items hew closely enough to the presentation pattern of many a studio meeting, to the extent of setting roughly determined length, order of solos and balance of individual contribution. Naturally the response of an expectant audience is a telling factor, as is the choice of music intimately associated with the leading participants and their movement. Only *Perdido* falls a little outside the expected bop repertoire. As noted above, *All the things you are* was claimed for the Gillespie–Parker canon by the former's addition of a proprietorial vamp. This record preserves some of Gillespie's most arresting work of the time. The incisive aerobatic flights in *Salt peanuts* and *Wee*, along with the contrasting thoughtfulness of *All the things you are*, would be sufficient evidence of his pre-eminence; but all that he plays is excellent. If, as seems likely, Roach's momentous drum solos meant little more than loud excitement to crowing Toronto fans, we can be grateful for this opportunity to savour the fantastically skilful display of colourful polyrhythms achieving genuine jazz impressiveness, again in *Salt peanuts* and *Wee*.

Parker, playing a plastic alto on this date, improvises with a beauty and relaxation equal to his later years' work. In every item his inspirations are instant and, it appears, effortless. Each solo possesses spontaneous integrity; and one marvels even more that the same sort of overarching craft and artistic imagination can be made to encompass long strings of choruses like those on **264**. Gillespie's vivacity of expression issues from a different brand of artistic sustenance, one more readily stimulated by the kind of popular excitation displayed by this audience than Parker's demon could have been.

It is Powell's solos with the quintet (and the longer ones taped in a protracted interlude during the concert (Original Jazz Classics [A] OJC111) that move most interestingly within the great altoist's creative ambit. The better bop pianists drew linear lessons from Parker, rather than from Gillespie's trumpet style; and, without doubt, Powell was the best of them all.

Addendum: A report that for *All the things you are* Powell and Roach were replaced by Billy Taylor and Art Taylor can be dismissed on aural evidence. Conclusive evidence for the long-lurking theory that Mingus had to overdub his bass parts after the concert [23] – an in-action photograph suggests that the microphone placing was rather casual – is provided by a boxed set of CDs (†Debut [A] 12DCD4402) which recently appeared and allows comparison of the initial tapes (Mingus was both overseer of the recording and first issuer on his Debut label) with the tapes bearing the bass dubbing. The latter have long been the familiar versions. Only an occasional patch of tonal prominence might have suggested the subterfuge, if, indeed, that is what it has to be called. There should be admiration for the fine balance which Mingus contrived to restore. The original registrations preserve some excellent bass solos for which, presumably, Mingus drew closer to the piano microphone. E.T.

Charlie Parker

266a The Complete Charlie Parker on Verve Vol. 4

†Verve (A) 837146–2

Parker (alt); Mitch Miller (ob, possibly eng h); Bronislaw Gimpel, Max Hollander, Milt Lomask (vln); Frank Brieff (vla); Frank Miller (cel); Myor Rosen (hrp); Stan Freeman (p); Ray Brown (bs); Buddy Rich (d); Jimmy Carroll (cond, arr). New York City, 30 November 1949.

Just friends · *Everything happens to me* · *April in Paris* · *Summertime* · *I didn't know what time it was* · *If I should lose you*

Parker (alt); Hank Jones (p); Ray Brown (bs); Buddy Rich (d). New York City, Early April 1950.

Star eyes · *Blues (fast)* · *I'm in the mood for love*

Dizzy Gillespie (tpt); Parker (alt); Thelonious Monk (p); Curly Russell (bs); Buddy Rich (d). New York City, 6 June 1950.

Bloomdido · *An Oscar for Treadwell* (2 versions) · *Mohawk* (3 versions) · *My melancholy baby* (3 versions) · *Leapfrog* (5 versions) · *Relaxin' with Lee* (3 versions)

266b The Complete Charlie Parker on Verve Vol. 6

†Verve (A) 837149–2

Miles Davis (tpt); Parker (alt); Walter Bishop Jr (p); Teddy Kotick (bs); Max Roach (d). New York City, 17 January 1951.

Au privave (2 versions) · *She rote* (2 versions) · *K.C. blues* · *Star eyes*

Parker (as); Walter Bishop Jr (p); Teddy Kotick (bs); Roy Haynes (d); Jose Mangual (bgos); Luis Miranda (cga). New York City, 12 March 1951.

My little suede shoes · *Un poquito de tu amor* · *Tico tico* · *Fiesta* · *Why do I love you?* (3 versions)

Red Rodney (tpt); Parker (alt); John Lewis (p); Ray Brown (bs); Kenny Clarke (d). New York City, 8 August 1951.

Blues for Alice · *Si si* · *Swedish schnapps* (2 versions) · *Back home blues* (2 versions) · *Loverman*

The first six titles of **266a** with a small string section appeared as three 78s in a binder which became a hit album for Parker, with *Just friends* going on to become his best-selling single. Such commercial success was quickly branded as 'selling-out' and the critical opprobrium with which they were greeted in the 1950s has influenced subsequent generations of fans to the extent that the 'with strings' sides are often dismissed when his work is considered in the round. However, these recordings, along with the subsequent 'with strings' sessions from the summer of 1950 and January 1952, by no means deserve such a fate; on the contrary, they are an important documentation of Parker's great talent.

With his quartet, quintet and sextets it is fair to say that much of Parker's repertoire boiled down to probably no more than a dozen basic chord structures played in standard keys, with the blues representing the basis for a sizeable number of his compositions. Further, the emotional climate of these small groups was biased towards a hard-blowing format which in turn tended to follow a predictable rotation of solos within the head-solos-head format. In contrast, the strings concept allowed Parker to express a romantic sensibility that struggled to find an outlet with his various small groups. With his 'strings' ensemble he addressed a variety of compositions from the American popular songbook with their sophisticated chord progressions set in a range of keys against an emotional backdrop quite different to his other work.

There is a parallel to be made here with the Lester Young–Billie Holiday sides (**204–5**). Just as Young was constrained within Basie's big band to arrangements that were similarly set in standard keys based on less than half a dozen basic chord structures, his work with Miss Holiday (often, of course, under Teddy Wilson's leadership) similarly took him through a variety of popular songs with their differing chord progressions, often in unusual keys, and in addition he found himself in a quite different musical climate to that of a hard-blowing big band, enabling him to express himself across a far broader emotional spectrum.

It is a measure of Parker's desire to expand his artistic horizons that the strings concept was his own and was not, as conventional wisdom would have it, foisted upon him by his record producer Norman Granz. In his liner notes to *The Complete Charlie Parker on Verve*, Phil Schaap quotes Parker twice: 'When I recorded with strings, some of my friends said, "Oh, Bird is getting commercial." That wasn't it at all. I was looking for new ways of saying things musically. New sound combinations' and 'Why, I asked for strings as far back as 1941 and then years later, when I went with Norman, he okayed it.' [24] Doris Parker too in a letter to Robert Reisner says: 'Norman Granz did not conceive the idea of Charlie working with strings. This was Charlie's dream . . . Norman did it only to please Charlie.' [25]

While on the West Coast with Gillespie in 1946, Parker had seen the trumpeter make four sides using strings with an orchestra directed by Johnny Richards (Phoenix [A] LP4), and throughout the 1940s popular bandleaders had taken to adding a desk or two of strings to their ensembles. It was a concept very much of the times; certainly Earl Hines was considering adding them to his own big band when Parker played for him in 1943. Parker was also a great lover of the European tradition of classical music, citing works by Stravinsky, Bartók, Prokofiev, Hindemith, Ravel and Debussy that clearly impressed him; indeed at the Royal Roost he would play the opening phrases of Hindemith's *Kleine Kammermusik* Op. 24 No. 2 to recall his sidemen to the bandstand. Strings, with their connotations of classical music, seemed to represent a step towards conferring the kind of artistic respectability Parker sought for his art.

Parker's efforts to deal with this static and sometimes uncomplimentary setting were often highly successful. Perhaps the best example is *Just Friends*, which includes one of his finest solos that even the saxophonist himself, notoriously self-deprecatory, acknowledged as one of his favourites. The song is a 32-bar ABAB[1] form and from the scheme alone it can be seen that Parker's role is far more extensive here than with his small groups:

[*Rubato* inst prelude] [4-bar intro: Parker] (Parker: 8 + 8 + inst: 8 + Parker: 8) [oboe: 4] (Parker: 8 + 8 + 8 + 8) [inst: 2] (pno: 8 + 8 + Parker: 8 + 6) [coda Parker: 8]

This is not the Parker of the head-solo-head format that dominates his discography. Here the whole performance is built around him to an extent that there are only 30 bars where his alto is not heard. His entry is literally Bird-like as he flies through the four-bar introduction in a squall of semiquavers and it is immediately clear that in contrast to small group performances, he has adopted a softer, more expressive tone, which he manipulates fluidly throughout. The chord sequence makes extensive use of the II-V-I progression, and Parker's handling of it provided a reference source for generations of aspiring jazz instrumentalists. During the first AB section, he embellishes and paraphrases the melody, but does not allow it to emerge as written, creating a subtle tension since we expect to hear the theme presented at the beginning of the song and not in variation. Although he teases us with fragments of melody, it is not until the second AB[1] section that this tension is resolved when the theme emerges, revealed first by the ensemble and then Parker, an effective touch by the arranger Jimmy Carroll.

The centrepiece of this performance, and one of the highlights of Parker's discography, is his 32-bar solo after Miller's four-bar modulation. Played with a double-time feel, it sparkles with rhythmic vitality and variety. Interspersed with wide interval leaps and frequent semiquaver triplets, it has a headlong, tumbling feel throughout, almost as if he could not get his ideas out quickly enough. Yet his solo is impeccably constructed and makes use of chord substitutions and rhythmic complexity; his ease of execution makes the listener feel as if his improvisations on the repeated coda vamp continue long after the recording finished, an endless stream of ideas offered into space.

On *Everything happens to me*, *If I should lose you* and *Summertime* Parker largely restricts himself to melodic statement and embellishment, although on *April in Paris* and *I didn't know what time it was* he offers short but effective partial choruses. On subsequent sessions with strings Parker would contribute some absorbing improvisations, such as *Dancing in the dark* and the overlooked *Out of nowhere*, which, together with *Just friends*, remain important exhibits from this period of experimentation. A detailed examination of the strings ensemble in concert is provided by *The Complete Legendary Rockland Palace Concert 1952* (†Jazz Classics [A] CD-JZCL5014), a 2-CD set of some 106 minutes that documents Parker's concert at Harlem's Rockland Palace on 26 September 1952. The fidelity is surprisingly good and reveals two arrangements that Parker did not record for Verve, *Stardust* and Gerry Mulligan's *Gold rush*, also known as *Turnstile*, plus *Ornithology* and *My little suede shoes* adapted for the larger ensemble. Here, Parker is the bardic voice unable to stop storytelling. He sounds relaxed and his level of invention never flags over the whole concert, but, perhaps more important, he was totally at home in the strings environment to the extent that when he occasionally returned for a blow with his bebop rhythm section without the strings – Walter Bishop (p); Mundell Lowe (g); Teddy Kotick (bs) and Max Roach (d) – the familiarity of the standard bebop ensemble appears limiting. In contrast, it is the string ensemble that today seems to be posing the greater creative challenge to Parker who, in order to make such an unusual liaison work, responds with improvisations of soaring majesty.

The early 1950 session with Hank Jones was shelved by Granz, who did not like it. Yet the interplay between Rich and Parker on *Blues (fast)* is tight, particularly on the abrupt two-bar tag that ends the song, despite its being worked up through 12 takes. The arrangement of *Star eyes* is less effective than the January 1951 version and, despite an elegant 24 bars by Jones and a full chorus by Parker, seems to lack the rhythmic poise of the latter, largely because of the stylistic divide between saxophonist and drummer. Although *I'm in the mood for love* is another example of Parker's exemplary handling of a ballad, he restricts his improvisation to a somewhat desultory 16 bars, entering hesitantly and going off mike once or twice, as if he was expecting the take to be ended at any moment, bearing out the producer Norman Granz's notes on the files for this session: 'not very good'. [26]

Rich again appears on Parker's next studio date, this time to some controversy. The occasion was Parker's first reunion with Gillespie in a recording studio since 1945 and it simultaneously provided the only opportunity to hear Parker perform with Monk. The pianist was not among the most helpful accompanists in jazz; he was lean and often obtuse (his use of dissonance behind Parker's solo on *Mohawk*, for example) and posed something of a puzzle to Rich, often prompting him to greater and greater but ultimately superfluous industry. Although his swing-era style had undergone changes that acknowledged some of the conventions of bop drumming (as exemplified by his solo in *Bloomdido*), he nevertheless displays a lack of sympathy on many numbers. Granz has stated that Rich was not his first-choice drummer for this particular session, but the best available at the time. [27] However, he is certainly not the most inappropriate drummer to work with Parker, and today these sessions do not sound quite as marred by his efforts as was felt at the time of their original release. Indeed, the emergence of countless airchecks with all manner of drummers bashing away behind the saxophonist without appearing to trouble him in the slightest has positively inured all but Parker purists to rhythmic imperfections of this date. [28]

Parker and Gillespie were such secure players that they remained untroubled by any imperfections in the rhythm section. Parker's four choruses on *Bloomdido* are bright and fresh, and contain a phrase at the end of the second chorus that would again fall under his fingers in the July 1953 *Now's the time* solo, although most of the second and third choruses emerge as fine, cliché-free examples of Parker's creativity within the blues idiom. Take 3 of *An Oscar for Treadwell*, an *I got rhythm* contrafact, is marred by a fluffed ending; on the following take (the master) Gillespie, removing the cup mute he uses in ensemble, contributes two well-executed choruses that are a reminder of how his very real contribution to jazz was overshadowed by Parker's subsequent martyrdom. *Mohawk*, another blues line, contains Monk's somewhat puzzling accompaniment behind both the head and Parker's solo, although such moments are more than compensated by his highly individual introductions which give this date a quite specific character. Even so, *Melancholy baby* emerges as either parody or mediocre, depending what day of the week you listen to it.

The themeless *Leapfrog*, despite an exciting exchange between saxophonist and trumpeter, more than any other number exposes Rich's shortcomings within the bop idiom, particularly during his exchange of fours. While his drumming often reverted to swing-era type, it was ironic that the final number of the session, *Relaxin' with Lee*, should have been based on the chords of the old swing-era warhorse *Stompin' at the Savoy*. Although this session has its flaws, with Rich and to a lesser extent Monk the culprits, Parker, with a perversity that was not an entirely unknown personality trait, shone. It is in such circumstances, where lesser men might falter or be deflected from their path by others, true genius reveals itself.

At the time of the 17 January 1951 session, Parker had only recently been discharged from New York Medical Arts Hospital. Without a set working group, he put together an *ad hoc* ensemble that is interesting because of Davis, who had left Parker's employ in high dudgeon on 24 December 1948. Now back in New York after a brush with the law on the West Coast, he was due to make his debut on Bob Weinstock's Prestige label later the same day. Once the gauche straight man to Parker's flights of fantasy, he had matured considerably in his playing since the 1945 *Koko* session (**257**) when he was forced to give best to Gillespie. Here, his tone is better centred and his technique somewhat closer to bridging the gap between aspiration and execution, although on both takes of *Au privave* he experiences problems articulating the theme. On the more assertive master take he stays well behind Parker in the mix, so as to camouflage any botches, but emerges to produce a well-constructed solo, even borrowing a descending arpeggiated phrase at the end of his first chorus patented by Clark Terry, with whom he was close during his upbringing in St Louis. He uses a cup mute for *She rote*, which combines chord sequences from *Out of nowhere* and *Slow boat to China*, and it is interesting to note that parts of his solo are subservient to scales, rather than the specific harmonic logic offered by the underlying chords, a harbinger of the modal-based lyricism that would absorb him as the decade closed.

Parker himself is splendidly assured throughout. A strikingly aggressive player, he handles the theme of *Au privave* with great aplomb and intensity. His solo on the master take produces a motif at the beginning of chorus three that would return in fuller form as the much-quoted entry to his 1953 *Now's the time* solo. It has often been said that his compositions were like one of his solos that had been written down, but, like all sweeping generalizations, this was only partly true. Whereas it might be the case for some compositions, such as a *Donna Lee*, a *Cheryl* or a *Barbados*, such numbers as *Chasin' the Bird, Billie's bounce* (all **257**) and, here, *Au privave* and *She rote* are full of complex and often abrupt syncopation and stabbing staccato phrases, contrasting with the forward momentum of his solos, which created a tension and release effect between theme and improvisation.

K.C. blues is a superb example of Parker's mature style. With longer performance lengths about to be made available on record through the growing popularity of the LP, recorded jazz solos would grow to fill the space available, their profundity, however, not always directly proportionate to their length. But Parker, even in live performance, seldom played more than two or three choruses. It was almost certainly a result of his formative experience in big bands, where solo length was strictly rationed to fit arrangements. To make ideas count, the finest big band musicians became remarkably focused in their solos, a trait Parker inherited. Even today, his playing remains a valuable lesson in getting to the point quickly and making every note count.

Just how effective he could be in just two 12-bar choruses is illustrated perfectly on *K.C. blues*. He enters after Bishop's four-bar introduction and states the theme, following it with two powerful, cogently constructed choruses, a relentless flow of dramatic, yet interlocking ideas that grows into one of his most enduring statements in the blues form. In the 1970s it was harmonized across the brass and saxophone sections of the Don Ellis big band (*Autumn*, Columbia [A] 63503), his poetic eloquence standing firm even when revealed in that very different light. Such was the emotional force of this solo that it completely eclipsed those that followed by Davis and Bishop before Parker returns with another improvised chorus, this time alluding to the 1947 Savoy *Bluebird* (**257**), with Roach anticipating the finish at the end of 12 bars. However, Parker continues for a final chorus, this time paraphrasing the *K.C.* theme and ending with a slight *ritenuto* in the final bar.

Parker's expansive version of *Star eyes* which follows demonstrates how riveting he could be, even in a straightforward exposition of the theme (a 36-bar AABA[1] song, where his only improvisation is on the final middle eight). After a four-bar *ostinato* played by Bishop and Kotick against a cup-muted *obbligato* played by Davis, Parker imperiously launches into the melody in an even four and, although keeping embellishment to a minimum (he holds back in bars two and three of the second A section, there is a slight decorative figure in the release but the final A[1] section is again straight), he nevertheless remains commanding. Davis follows with an open-horn chorus, played with almost Zen-like concentration but leaning towards the articulation of a Clark Terry or a Clifford Brown. Bishop enters for half a chorus, with Parker streaking through the middle eight in double time before recapitulating the melody on the final A[1] section, tagged by the reappearance of the four-bar *ostinato*. Yet as in *K.C. blues* it is Parker's contribution that remains in the memory, even though all he had done here was, to all intents and purposes, present the melody.

The 17 January session was the first for some little while that placed him in a straight-ahead jazz environment after a series of dates with strings (see *The Complete Charlie Parker on Verve* Vol. 5 [†Verve (A) 837148–2]). Granz has pointed out that the job of a record producer was to try to ensure 'every record did not end up sounding the same', [29] and clearly his intention was to introduce variety to the quartet, quintet and sextets of the Savoy and Dial discography, which he and countless fans knew well. Consequently the next session was with two Latin percussion players from Machito's orchestra (see **316**). Parker knew both of them well from sitting in with Machito's band and they were present on the sides he cut with him in 1948, 1949 and the previous month, on 21 December 1950, the date that produced Chico O'Farrill's overlooked large-scale work *Afro-Cuban jazz suite*. However, here the feel that Mangual and Miranda evoke reflects, as Phil Schaap has noted, more a Caribbean influence than a Hispanic one, [30] and this is nowhere clearer than on *Un poquito de tu amor*, with Bishop laying down a calypso vamp. *My little suede shoes*, using a rhythm that is close to a tango, is based almost entirely on a series of II-V-I progressions. It became Parker's most requested number in the final years of his life and his second most popular single.

Perhaps surprisingly, the samba *Tico tico* had been a favourite of Parker's since at least 1944 when he asked bandleader Andy Kirk if he could be featured on the number. [31] Bright and cheerful, it is played with seriousness and affection by Parker to a samba rhythm. His lively solo is followed by a chorus by the percussionists who manage to sustain interest and momentum before another improvised chorus by the saxophonist and a return to the theme to complete an off-the-wall, but nevertheless fascinating, item in his discography. [32] In contrast, none of the three takes of *Why do I love you?* are wholly satisfactory; on each confusion reigns of the who-does-what-when variety, which Parker seems unable to resolve satisfactorily on any of the three takes.

The August 1951 session is perhaps Parker's finest for Verve label; indeed, it ranks among his best recorded work. Although it was not made with his regular rhythm section, their playing is nevertheless tight and in the pocket, contributing significantly to the proceedings. Rodney, at the time recuperating in Allen Eager's mother's hotel in the Catskills, journeyed into New York specially for the date. His playing is fresh, but utilizes a surprisingly broad tone more characteristic of the preceding generation of swing-era musicians. However, he blends surprisingly well with the saxophonist's hard tone, and their statements together achieve a unity of expression that Davis often failed to achieve. *Blues for Alice* opened the session and is a Parker composition that sounds close to an improvisation; like all his themes, it combines melodic integrity with structural unity, despite its complexity. Free-flowing, his three choruses appear a logical continuation of the ensemble passage that precedes them and are followed by two choruses by Rodney that suggest he never got the credit he deserved as an able and interesting bop trumpeter.

Si si sees Parker locking in on Brown's driving bass line, something that is a feature of these sessions. So often the saxophonist seemed to suck rhythm sections into his vortex – he led, they followed – but in contrast Brown's forceful playing adds significantly to the rhythmic excitement of these performances. The climax of *Si si*, a 12-bar blues variant that uses the *Rhythm* changes in bars 1–4, is an exchange of two-bar phrases among the members of the quintet. Here the challenge Parker sets for his band is one of continuity of line rather than one of contrast, something exchanges of longer duration often become with their inherent tendency towards competition. It provides textural contrast without fragmenting what is usually the climax of a performance with, as all too often happens, displays of the 'anything-you-can-do-I-can-do-better' kind.

In contrast to *Blues for Alice*, *Swedish schnapps* is one of those themes full of short, syncopated phrases that throw into sharp relief the headlong rush of Parker's ideas as he emerges from the ensemble. Particularly effective on this *I got rhythm* variant, his soaring improvisation in the middle eight makes it a 'release' in the literal sense. *Back home blues* contains some elegant playing by Parker, particularly on take 1, the version that appeared on LP, where he is in splendid form, taking an extended solo of four choruses. Even at the bright medium tempo,

Parker manages to imply double time at the end of his first chorus, highlighting the ease, speed and clarity of ideas that characterized his work.

Perhaps the most controversial number from this session was his version of *Loverman*, a 32-bar AABA song. Lewis has said this was done as a personal favour for Granz, whereas Rodney said Parker had always been angry with the version put out by Ross Russell in 1946 (**258**) and wanted to do it again. [33] Whatever the situation, there is none of the subjective angst that so endeared the Dial to fans, but, even so, this later version almost manages to step out of the shadow of the earlier version with its focus and emotional directness. Lewis traces the pianist Jimmy Bunn's original introduction and once again it is Parker's imperious way of presenting a melody that instantly grips the listener. For the first 16 bars he liberally embellishes the theme, often using chromatic neighbour tones, but in bar three of the middle eight he tosses in two successive semiquaver triplets that presages a dazzling double-time sequence in demisemiquavers (or 32nd notes), in other words eight notes per beat, capping with a stunning flourish in the last bar where he crams in an incredible 14 notes in a grouping of 5 and 9 in the second beat followed by two groups of 6 on the penultimate beat, an incredible 26 notes in just two beats, and all perfectly articulated. He then returns to the melody for the final A section, in turn followed by two A sections, one by piano and one by trumpet with a Parker *obbligato* before an abrupt ending with Parker's overused, and by now tedious, quotation from Percy Grainger's *Country gardens*. With the exception of the double-time passage in the middle eight, his performance stayed close to the melody as written, yet changes its meaning utterly, something all the great jazz musicians succeed in doing even when playing a melody more or less straight. [34] S.N.

Sonny Stitt

267 Sonny Stitt – Bud Powell – J. J. Johnson

†Original Jazz Classics (A) OJCD 009–2

Stitt (ten); J. J. Johnson (tbn); John Lewis (p); Nelson Boyd (bs); Max Roach (d). New York City, 17 October 1949.
Afternoon in Paris (2 versions) · *Elora* (2 versions) · *Blue mode* (2 versions) · *Teapot* (2 versions).

Stitt (ten); Bud Powell (p); Curly Russell (bs); Max Roach (d). New York City, 11 December 1949.
All God's children got rhythm · *Sonnyside* · *Bud's blues* · *Sunset*

Same personnel. New York City, 26 January 1950.
Strike up the band · *I want to be happy* · *Taking a chance on love* · *Fine and dandy* (2 versions)

In 1943 Stitt was playing second alto in the Tiny Bradshaw band. By 1947 he had been voted 'New Star' on the instrument by the readers of *Esquire* magazine. However, he was not around to receive any acclaim; a victim of drug addiction, he had been sent to the Federal Narcotics Hospital in Lexington. When he was released in 1949, his first recordings were those with Johnson where he decided to switch to tenor saxophone, bringing a remarkable technical facility to the instrument that on alto had branded him a Bird copyist, a charge he refuted throughout his life. 'I was playing my thing and he was playing his and it came out real close,' he asserted in 1981. 'It wasn't Charlie [Parker] that made me do it. I had experience playing the tenor before. I had a great fondness for Lester Young. One gets a different perspective on tenor.' [35]

Although he later went on to form a two-tenor alliance with Gene Ammons, immortalizing their union with the exciting *Blues up 'n' down* and *Stringin' the Jug*, his most important recordings during this period, and indeed of his career, were with Bud Powell in December 1949 and January 1950 that presented 'some of the most highly charged, dually inspirational collaborations ever recorded'. [36] Stitt's approach to the tenor was extremely influential in smoothing out the angular contours of bop through his use of pattern-running that helped unlock the complexities of the 'new music'. There are two methods of pattern-running, or 'sequencing' as it is sometimes known. 'Melodic sequencing' is that of preserving the relationship of a group of notes, one to another, through a new sequence of chords so that, for example, the tonic, the mediant and the dominant in one chord are played as the tonic, mediant and dominant in another. 'Rhythmic sequencing' is the repetition of a rhythmic figure in which the notes don't necessarily retain their melodic relationship to one another but their rhythmic relationship is preserved. Either form of sequencing was hardly new to jazz at the time of these recordings – one of the best examples of melodic sequencing (and one of the oldest clichés in popular music) is moving a complete A section of an AABA popular song up a fourth to make the B section. Examples of this include Bob Haggart's *What's new?*, Billy Strayhorn's *Take the A train* and Victor Schertzinger's *I remember you.* And in 1927, Louis Armstrong employed an amazingly modern-sounding nine bars of sequencing during his vocal on *Hotter than that* (**48**).

However, the less predictable and rhythmically complex figures of bop – exemplified by the playing of Charlie Parker – seemed beyond the ken of mere mortals. Stitt helped unravel such complexities by systematically applying patterns to negotiate his way through the complex, extended chord progressions of bop, a methodology that became widely influential. Players such as Sonny Rollins, Dexter Gordon, Wardell Gray, Joe Henderson, George Coleman and Frank Foster, for example, have all cited Stitt as an influence on their style in this respect. This method of improvisation would reach its apotheosis in John Coltrane's *Giant steps*, where Coltrane used the scale fragment 1-2-3-5 approximately 35 times during his solo (**421**).

All God's children got rhythm, which also provided the harmonic base for a number of jazz classics including Denzil Best's *Move*, Parker's *Little Willie leaps*, Ike Quebec's *Suburban eyes* and Stitt's own *Never felt that way before*, is here in its original incarnation and presents a full exposition of Stitt's command of his instrument. What is especially notable is the ease with which he could power through the chord changes at the fastest tempos of bebop. [37] His playing still sounds fresh and modern today and there is no suggestion that he is performing at the limit of his abilities, rather he suggests controlled abandon as he spins one idea after another with precision and fire. During his solo, it is obvious that certain thematic elements recur regularly, and these motifs or patterns give a sense of cohesion and logic as his solo unfolds. This feeling of logical construction and continuity is sustained by Powell, whose solo follows Stitt's, although he is a bit slow on the uptake on the first of the two four-bar exchanges when Stitt re-enters, but nevertheless this performance is one of the classics of jazz.

While Stitt's sides with Powell are characterized by thrusting power, the saxophonist's debt to Lester Young is at its most apparent on *Bud's blues*. Constrained by the playing time of the 10-inch 78-rpm record, Stitt makes every note count with a graceful horizontal melodicism that contrasts his more vertical approach on *God's children*. But however different Stitt claimed to be from Parker, the fact remains that *Sonnyside*, a 32-bar AABA *I got rhythm* contrafact, is Bird's *Dexterity* (**258**). Here, he returns to a more vertical approach and with it the application of little motifs which are spun through the changes with Stitt's hallmark care in phrasing and accenting. Stitt mixes phrase groups of differing character that nevertheless respect the underlying harmonies of the song, and although they move rapidly, it is clear that motivic thought is taking place. Stitt's solos on *I want to be happy, Taking a chance on love, Fine and dandy* (both versions) and *Strike up the band* continue to impress with the cogency and internal logic of his ideas as much as the powerful momentum his solos generate, a model for any aspiring young players.

With the exception of *Teapot*, a *Sweet Georgia Brown* contrafact, Stitt's sides with J. J. Johnson are a more congenial affair. The easy swing of *Afternoon in Paris, Elora* and *Blue mode* with, on take 2, Lewis's introduction amusingly parodying that of Ellington's to *I'm just a lucky so-and-so*, are, surprisingly for Stitt, noncombative affairs. But Stitt was one of the most competitive musicians in jazz and he could not resist laying down the gauntlet on *Teapot*. Johnson battles gamely, but Stitt leaves him for dead with an imperious solo that seems to take wings at such a bright tempo. [38] It simply served to underline that these sides moved Stitt into the very top rank of tenor saxophonists in jazz, something that has been blurred over the years with his bilateral affinity to the alto saxophone (and for a while, the baritone sax). However, to musicians, including some of the top names of jazz, from a Gillespie to a Getz, nothing was more daunting than the sight of Stitt arriving unannounced at their bandstand demanding to sit in. They were all well aware that on song he was one of the most formidable improvising talents in jazz, as these sides show. S.N.

Wardell Gray

268 Easy Swing

Swingtime (D) STD1032 (2 LPs), †*Swingtime (D) STCD1

Gray (ten); Dodo Marmarosa (p); Red Callender (bs); Doc West (d). Hollywood, 23 November 1946.
Dells' bells · *One for Prez* · *The man I love* · *Easy swing*

Chuck Thompson (d) replaces West. Same date.
The great lie

Ernie Royal, unidentified (tpt); unidentified (tbn); Gray (ten); Ivory Joe Hunter (p, vcl); unidentified g, bs; Chuck Walker (d). San Francisco, 1947.
We're gonna boogie

Gray (ten); Al Haig (p); Jimmy Raney (g); Tommy Potter (bs); Charlie Perry (d); Terry Swope (vcl[1]). New York City, April 1949.
In a pinch · *It's the talk of the town* · *Five star*[1] · *Sugar Hill bop*[1]

Roy Haynes (d) replaces Perry; Raney absent. New York City, 11 November 1949.
Twisted · *Southside* (5 versions)

Gray (ten); Phil Hill (p); John Richardson (bs); Art Mardigan (d). Detroit, 25 April 1950.
Blue Gray (2 versions) · *Grayhound* (2 versions) · *Treadin' with Treadwell* (2 versions)

Gray (ten); Little Willie Littlefield (p, vcl); Jesse Irvin (g); Mario Delgarde (bs); Bill Douglass (d). Los Angeles, 30 October 1953.
Goofy dust blues

Gene Phipps (tpt); Gray (ten); Tate Houston (bar); Norman Simmons (p); Victor Sproles (bs); Vernell Fournier (d). Chicago, 19 January 1955.
Sweet mouth · *Blues in the closet* · *Dat's it* · *Hey there*

Like others of his generation, Gray, born in 1921, was influenced first by Lester Young and then by Charlie Parker. That he assimilated aspects of their music so thoroughly was partly due to a fine instrumental technique, but more especially because of really exceptional powers of melodic invention; he appeared able to sustain an improvisation almost indefinitely. The point was not that he imitated Young's or Parker's actual phrases, although some borrowings, especially from the latter, can be found in Gray's work even quite late, but that he put some of their general principles to fresh uses. One instance was his adoption of Young's flowing, seemingly effortless swing, though at the same time his tone, consistent throughout the tenor saxophone's range, was markedly warmer than that of early Young, smoother than that of late. There was little place, the essential virility of Gray's expression notwithstanding, for Parker's sometimes fiercely displaced accents and when elements of his vocabulary appear we find them used in a quite different way, partly because of Gray's more symmetrical, and indeed more traditional, sense of construction. The divergences between Parker and Gray are in any case obvious when the latter repeatedly follows the former on the *Relaxin' at Camarillo* date (**258**).

At the same time Gray's capacity for swinging seemed positively to thrive on the complexity of some of his lines, this being well demonstrated by the Detroit session, particularly by *Grayhound*, a blues. This is a beautiful example of how he makes one idea appear to arise out of another, an achievement all the more creditable in so cliché-ridden an idiom. Everything unfolds easily yet each phrase is expressive, never facile, and it is no surprise, no matter how recognizable his points of departure, that Gray soon arrived at statements that were altogether his own. One musically so well adjusted grew into the new style without effort, as is shown by some of the above performances with aggressively bop-slanted rhythm sections led by Marmarosa and Haig. Gray sounded at his most modern in such circumstances, yet had it both ways in that he was equally at home in large bands led by Basie or Goodman. Indeed nothing seemed to put him off, be it competition from the clamorous brass of Earl Hines's *Let's get started* (Official [D] 3029) or the galumphing Hunter or Littlefield rhythm sections.

From this it virtually follows that the sentiment of Gray's music is optimistic rather than anxious, not just vigorous but often exhilarating. Marmarosa's eagerly participating accompaniments and sometimes ebullient solos therefore appear wholly apt on the 1946 date. Indeed to fill both sides of a 10-inch 78-rpm disc, *The great lie* (on the chords of *Fine and dandy*) is an early instance of Gray's sustained inventive ability, although the pianist makes almost equally good use of the extra space. Gershwin's *The man I love* is paraphrased in a resourceful demonstration of Gray's melodic sense. *Easy swing* employs the line that Parker recorded two years later as *Steeplechase* (**257**) and in fact provides a chance of studying the Parker influence early at work in Gray. Marking a real advance on the above session, and mandatory listening at this point, is a 1948 session (Spotlite [E] SPJ139) on which the tenor lines are often both more complex and more decisive. On *Light Gray* and particularly the two versions of *Stoned* Gray's drive is more overt, the animation more explicit, while at the piano Haig – too much having been made of his elegance, urbanity etc. – plays with a matching fire, as does Tiny Kahn behind the drums. In fact they all sound incapable of going wrong.

Two further sizzling Haig-led rhythm sections preside at the 1949 dates, from the second of which *Twisted* remains Gray's most famous title, chiefly because of the pseudosophisticated words of Annie Ross's later vocal adaptation. Admirable though the original *Twisted* is, *Southside* really is more typical in its straight-ahead impetus. Such improvisations seldom rise to a climax, their effect, rather, being cumulative, a point made with no little thoroughness by the five versions included on the 2-LP set. Although Perry was no West, Haynes or Kahn, the earlier 1949 session was surely one of Gray's finest hours, and he never much surpassed *Five star, Sugar Hill bop, In a pinch* or, in a quite different mood, *It's the talk of the town*. Improvised music this undoubtedly is, yet it all sounds inevitable, as the work of the finest artists often does. Not even Swope's scatting in the ensembles of the first two items unsettles Gray. No wonder he always has seemed so much more interesting than Dexter Gordon.

If Gray sounds even better on the sextet date, this is simply because the other horns are undistinguished. Coming from the year of his premature and mysterious death, these performances do show him to have attained greater poise, but there is no advance beyond the boundaries of his established range of expression, no hint of further development. Yet even more than *It's the talk of the town* is *Hey there* a classic bending of a popular song to jazz ends. *Dat's it*, too, contains memorable late instances of his complicated phrasing, but the ultimate point of these virtually definitive statements is that there is never a note too many. From such heights it is a steep descent to the two rhythm 'n' blues charades to which Gray, no doubt for purely financial reasons, submitted himself. All that can be said of Littlefield and Hunter is that they do not fear the obvious, least of all on the rhythmic plane.

Although they were the best available selections at the time of this book's publication, neither of the above issues is entirely satisfactory. For example, the LP set unnecessarily includes five versions of *Southside* yet omits this session's *Easy living, Sweet Lorraine* and, from Detroit, *A sinner kissed an angel.* Only in part overlapping with the LPs, the CD offers some alternative versions from the 1946 date but misses the *Twisted* session altogether. The complete 1946 material, with many alternative takes including several never before obtainable, is on Black Lion (E) 60106. To all of which may be added that elsewhere *Blues in the closet* has sometimes appeared as *Oscar's blues.* M.H.

J. J. Johnson

269a The Eminent J. J. Johnson Vol. 1

Blue Note (A) BST81505, †*Blue Note (Eu) CDP781 505–2

Clifford Brown (tpt); Johnson (tbn); Jimmy Heath (alt, bar); John Lewis (p); Percy Heath (bs); Kenny Clarke (d). New York City, 22 June 1953.
Capri (2 versions) · *Turnpike* (2 versions) · *Loverman* · *Get happy* (2 versions) · *Sketch 1* · *It could happen to you*

J. J. Johnson

269b The Eminent J. J. Johnson Vol. 2

Blue Note (A) BST81506, †*Blue Note (Eu) CDP781 506–2

Johnson (tbn); Wynton Kelly (p); Charles Mingus (bs); Clarke (d); Sabu Martinez (con). New York City, 24 September 1954.
That old devil moon · *Jay* · *Time after time* · *Too marvellous for words* · *It's you or no one* · *Coffee pot*

Johnson (tbn); Hank Mobley (ten); Horace Silver (p); Paul Chambers (bs); Clarke (d). New York City, 6 June 1955.
Daylie double (2 versions) · *You're mine you* · *Pennies from heaven* (2 versions) · *Groovin'* · *Viscosity* (2 versions) · *Portrait of Jennie*

When he first received attention in the late 1940s there were many who, on listening to his records without yet having seen him play, insisted that Johnson must be using a valve trombone. His swiftness of execution and in particular his speed of articulation were thought to be impossible on the slide instrument, and this betrays the lack of historical perspective which frequently operates when fresh developments are going forward in jazz, leading to the extent of the innovations being exaggerated. Several performers offered precedents for Johnson's ability to manoeuvre so rapidly and to such expressive purpose, the obvious names being Charlie Green, Miff Mole, Jimmy Harrison, Jack Teagarden and Lawrence Brown. Less prominent but still having a role in extending the trombone's jazz capabilities were Fred Beckett with Harlan Leonard and Lionel Hampton, Bobby Byrne with Jimmy Dorsey, Jack Jenney with Artie Shaw, and this is quite apart from pre-jazz concert band virtuosos like Arthur Pryor.

Despite this considerable background to his achievements, which in no way detracts from his originality, Johnson mentioned only Beckett as having pointed to the instrument's still further scope. When he said years later that he had 'wanted to make the trombone more articulate' [39] he was referring to goals set by Eldridge and Lester Young, and then more especially by Parker and Gillespie. It is these latter names, invoking the bop style, which signal the double nature of Johnson's contribution. His earliest recorded solo, on Benny Carter's *Love for sale* (**248**), was followed by others which already hint at the direction he was to take, such as those in Basie's *Rambo* (alias *Bambo*, †Smithsonian [A] RC/RD108), *Stay cool* of 1946 (CBS [F] 54165) and particularly in Karl George's quite boppish *Grand slam* and *Peek-a-boo* from 1945 (Xanadu [A] 124). But a systematic study of his large output can only begin with the three Savoy dates recorded under Johnson's own name in 1946, 1947 and 1949 (†Savoy [Eu] 650 119, with interesting alternative versions on the 2-LP Savoy [A] SJL2232), the two Prestige sessions also from 1949 (Prestige [A] LP7253, **267** respectively).

These performances chronicle Johnson's steady, almost relentless, advance and show an increasing mastery of the trombone and of the bop style, the former being put entirely at the service of the latter. Indeed, as with other leading exponents of this idiom, his commitment to bop evidently was total, and he worked very hard at reconciling its characteristic ideas with the particular strengths of the trombone without losing their musical point. From the beginning Johnson's skills were such that he scarcely ever made a bad record, although during this period he did produce a certain number of solos that were rather too formulaic, for example the three versions of *Charlie's wig* with Parker (**258**). Yet by the end of the 1940s he had brought about a reorientation of the instrument in respect of jazz improvisation, this accounting for his eventual widespread influence, for the long-enduring opposition to his work in the public prints, and perhaps for his seeming indifference to most of his predecessors on the trombone.

Even the most skilled of these made liberal use of the slurs and tonal variations to which the instrument so easily lends itself, whereas Johnson turned aside from such effects in the light of bop's fierce demands for a phraseology that was complex in terms of melody, rhythm, harmonic inflection; in short, not just for speed but for accuracy. Despite such amazing episodes as the double-timing in his 1947 *Boneology*, the point was less rapidity of movement than the ends to which that facility was directed. A few others were by then working in comparable ways, as scattered solos by Kai Winding prove, [40] yet Johnson's arriving at his results through the effects of line, and with consistent tonal purity, led his listeners' attention to strictly musical considerations instead of to instrumental, which is to say colouristic, devices. His achievement was a double one in that he redefined both the capabilities and the character of the trombone.

All this implies a degree of abstraction, but Johnson's bypassing traditional attitudes to no degree lessened the emotional depth of his music, this being especially obvious in blues such as the two versions of *Blue mode* from Prestige (**267**). His ballads had an equivalent expressive force, however, and worthy precursors of the powerful lyricism of the finest Blue Notes are items like the Savoy *Yesterdays* and *Don't blame me* of 1947 and 1949 respectively. So far as we can tell from records, it was in the former year that the lighter, clearer tone emerged, and from now on vibrato was reserved for special effects. The rhythmic variety of these slow performances was almost as pronounced as that of the fast, and in fact the subtleties of timing and accent upon which jazz so much depends were in no way restricted by Johnson's approach. There was evidence, too, of a dry sense of humour.

While the leader's playing is the main interest of the 1946–9 Savoy and Prestige sessions, they do contain much else of value, in particular early instances of the remarkable early maturity of Powell and Roach. The two earlier 1949 occasions likewise emphasize the young Rollins's exceptional promise, and from Johnson's last date of that year came not only *Blue mode* but also *Afternoon in Paris*. The latter is a small masterpiece in terms both of Lewis's composing and of the performance by him, the leader, Roach and Stitt, and of all these early recordings it is the one that points most directly to the Blue Notes.

By the time we are a few bars into *Capri*, an excellent Gigi Gryce theme, it is clear that enlightening though Johnson's previous sessions have remained, they essentially dealt with preliminaries. Everything he had been working for comes together even at the unforgiving pace of *Turnpike*, every note in his solos being precisely articulated in a seamless flow of invention. These three Blue Note dates constitute the first comprehensive statement of mature trombone bop, yet in playing which is as elegant as it is urgently communicative, he transcends the bop idiom as such and appears as one of the greatest jazz musicians of his generation, on any instrument.

Aside from Jimmy Heath, almost the only weak link on these sessions, who heightens even the least adept listener's powers of prediction, Johnson is fully matched by his companions. Powered by a rhythm section consisting of three-quarters of the original Modern Jazz Quartet, the fire and conviction informing every note on the quick items, plus their intense swing, lead one yet again to wonder at bop ever being thought cool. And despite all the space for improvisation, these performances rarely submit to the lazy theme-solos-theme pattern, plenty of activity being undertaken by the horns during solos and in links between them.

Nor do slow tempos bring any musical relaxation. In *It could happen to you*, from which Brown and Jimmy Heath are absent, Johnson most imaginatively rephrases the melody, then reshapes the new phrases, the effect being one of subdued restlessness. This also applies to the next date's *Time after time*, and in both these pieces, as in *Sketch 1* and *You're mine you*, he produces a tone of the most acute expressive resonance. The impact of this is heightened on *Loverman* by the simple yet unusually telling score by Lewis, who also provides an entirely apt piano interlude. Even at this leisurely pace Johnson still articulates most notes separately, so that when he at last employs a pronounced slide from one pitch to another, in the middle eight of the first chorus, its effect is all the greater.

Form should be the result of process, the best pieces grow into their own form, and that is what happens with *Sketch 1*, the real 'work' of this first Blue Note session. Despite fine trumpet, trombone and piano solos, the ensemble dominates, or rather enfolds, the whole, Lewis's writing for it being splendidly proportioned – the magic power of exactitude! – in melodic development and tonal and textural contrasts. Many details contribute to the larger unity. Note for example how the chords grouped in twos and threes which urge on Brown's stop-time solo are echoed by the piano during the following solo from Johnson. This, deeply embedded in the enhancing commentaries of the rhythm section and the other horns, is an especially beautiful passage. Fairly similar in atmosphere to Dameron's later *Fontainebleau* (**280**), *Sketch 1* suggests a line of development in Lewis's composing that goes back to such little-known works as his *Period Suite* (†Jazz Time [F] 251 288–2), recorded in Paris during 1950, and to *Afternoon in Paris*, recorded at that same date in an alternative version as *Pierre*, and which continued in a few items such as his contribution to **482**. It is unfortunate that the international and very long-term success of the MJQ prevented Lewis exploring this path more fully.

The first Blue Note session also appears on **270** and Brown's part in it is dealt with there. It also looks forward to his sextet dates of 1959–60, especially to the band with Freddie Hubbard and Clifford Jordan which he at one stage referred to as 'the best I ever had. I'd always wanted three horns.' [41] This group made the outstanding *J.J. Inc.* LP in 1960 (Columbia [A] PC36808), where all compositions and arrangements are by Johnson himself and which reaches towards the writing he would later do for larger ensembles.

Meanwhile at his second Blue Note session he submitted himself to the severe test of sustaining an entire date without relief from any other horns. This he does unfalteringly through six performances because of the sheer quality of his invention and the virtual perfection with which it is delivered. In *Jay*, a blues, Johnson's improvising, as in *Coffee pot*, is if anything even freer and more flexible than on the previous session's quick pieces, the music's dramatic impetus arising from the ideas being so tightly packed, from their density, rather than from his virtuosity, astonishing though the latter is. Clarke's usual, but still remarkable, consistency is an important factor in the success of this as of the other sessions, as is the bass playing of Heath, Mingus and Chambers in turn. The drumming is intricate yet unfussy, the swing insistent but nearly unobtrusive. And luckily Martinez gets in nobody's way.

On the last Blue Note date under his own name, Johnson used the trombone and tenor saxophone instrumentation which has so often been productive. Mobley, though not yet a mature soloist, responds well, but Silver, alas, hits on all the clichés that Lewis and Kelly had so successfully avoided. Rising above such discouragements, the leader presents superb improvisations on both versions of the inaptly named *Viscosity*, one phrase flowing out of another with seeming inevitability. Earlier we had wondered at his apparently infallible articulation, whereas now that is almost taken for granted and a stronger impression is made by the variety of expressive nuances with which he is able to shade the music, even at the optimistically bouncing tempo of this piece or *Daylie double*. Comparable refinements are even more noticeable amid his cogent elaborations on *Portrait of Jennie* (from which Mobley is absent), *Groovin'* and *Pennies from heaven*. In fact by now everything he plays is, as James Boswell wrote in a slightly different connection, 'thoroughly impregnated with the Johnsonian aether'.

This material is distributed haphazardly across the LPs, systematically on the CDs. Vol. 1 in the latter format has everything from the 1953 date including some alternative versions never issued on LP; Vol. 2 likewise carries everything from the remaining sessions. On all copies of CD Vol. 2 examined during the preparation of this book, *Too marvellous for words* is labelled as *That old devil moon*, *That old devil moon* as *Time after time*, *Time after time* as *It's you or no one*, *It's you or no one* as *Too marvellous for words*. Nor have the LP sleeve notes been revised for CD reissue: Basie's record of *Pennies from heaven* was still, it seems, made 'some 19 years ago'. M.H.

Clifford Brown

270 The Complete Blue Note and Pacific Jazz Recordings

Mosaic (A) MR5–104 (5 LPs)

Brown (tpt); Lou Donaldson (alt); Elmo Hope (p); Percy Heath (bs); Philly Joe Jones (d). New York City, 9 June 1953.
Bellarosa · *Carvin' the Rock* (3 versions) · *Cookin'* (2 versions) · *Brownie speaks* · *De-dah* · *You go to my head*

Brown (tpt); J. J. Johnson (tbn); Jimmy Heath (alt, bar); John Lewis (p); Percy Heath (bs); Kenny Clarke (d). New York City, 22 June 1953.
Capri (2 versions) · *Loverman* · *Turnpike* (2 versions) · *Sketch 1* · *It could happen to you* · *Get happy* (2 versions)

Brown (tpt); Gigi Gryce (alt, fl); Charlie Rouse (ten); Lewis (p); Percy Heath (bs); Art Blakey (d). New York City, 28 August 1953.
Wail bait (2 versions) · *Hymn to the Orient* (2 versions) · *Brownie eyes* · *Cherokee* (2 versions) · *Easy living* · *Minor mood*

Brown (tpt); Donaldson (alt); Horace Silver (p); Curly Russell (bs); Blakey (d). Birdland, New York City, 20 February 1954.
Split kick · *Once in a while* · *Quicksilver* (2 versions) · *Wee dot* (2 versions) · *Blues* · *A night in Tunisia* · *Mayreh* · *If I had you* · *Lou's blues* · *The way you look tonight* · *Now's the time* · *Confirmation*

Brown (tpt); Stu Williamson (v-tbn); Zoot Sims (ten); Bob Gordon (bar); Russ Freeman (p); Joe Mondragon (bs); Shelly Manne (d); Jack Montrose (arr). Los Angeles, 11–12 July 1954.
Daahoud · *Finders keepers* · *Joy spring*

Carson Smith (bs) replaces Mondragon. Los Angeles, 12–13 August 1954.
Gone with the wind · *Bones for Jones* · *Blueberry Hill* · *Tiny's capers* (2 versions)

There may be some point to the suggestion that the wide popularity achieved by Brown before his violent death in June 1956 had its initial boost from his compact with Max Roach early in 1954. 'He owed much to this decision,' claimed a writer who felt that Roach's establishment on the West Coast and his 'important connections' spelled success for Brown more surely than his own 'excellent musicianship and strong jazz powers'. [42] A rather more than incidental virtue of this Mosaic compilation is its evidence of the trumpeter's recording activity during the year preceding his joining Roach, including a very significant session almost on the eve of his departure westwards, and adding a Los Angeles assembly conceptually quite different from the new Roach–Brown enterprise. 'His gifts would have counted for nothing without public exposure'. [43] Maybe, yet at least equally important had been exposure to the stimulus of his peers and masters. Too much can be made of his supposed occultation in the Chris Powell rhythm-'n'-blues outfit wherein he also played the piano (1952–3); Ira Gitler's Mosaic notes suggest a fair jazz colouring for that band, and for a young man recovering from an extended stay in hospital it may have seemed about right. His first recorded solos were made with Powell. Later in 1953 he was with Tadd Dameron, and then in Europe with the Lionel Hampton band. His solo work, backed by Hampton associates and Parisian musicians in Gigi Gryce's telling orchestration of *Brown skins* (September 1953), and his playing the following month with Henri Renaud and Pierre Michelot (Vogue [F] VG304–416008), reveal an artist who has regained his feet. In 1949–50 student encounters with the music and the personal encouragement of, among others, Gillespie, Parker and Navarro gave him essential impetus. The things considered below help to fill out the story of 1953 and carry us a little beyond that.

The first three sessions, all for Blue Note between early June and late August 1953, happened before Brown joined Hampton. On 9 June he was still a Chris Powell employee, Donaldson, already recorded by Blue Note, co-led the quintet and Hope, just about to record a trio session with Heath and Jones, brought a questing style nourished at the first springs of bop.

Unison horns delineate the swaying *Bellarosa* theme. Donaldson, here as in the bulk of his contributions, sounds a not quite fully committed Parkerite. Brown enters firmly, yet his phrases are rather circumspect;

better notions shape the bridge of the theme which returns after Hope's edgy statement. In the three versions of *Carvin' the Rock* (a Hope–Rollins theme referring to a penal settlement on Riker's Island) Brown achieves expression in varying ways, while Donaldson duplicates ideas from version to version. Brown's first improvisation is flowing yet emphatically stressed; the second, on the issued master, is surer in terms of inner contrast and investigates new ideas; his third essay is probably the most certain of purpose, and this take's demotion may be due to uncertainties on the part of Donaldson and Hope. Considering the vigour of Hope's work in this forceful minor-keyed number, it is interesting to find his trio version of 18 June (†Blue Note [Eu] CDP784 438–2) sounding much more sombre, and his lines lacking some of the grace gained in response to the tensions of front-line cooperation.

Cookin', Donaldson's augmented blues theme, is led in, staccato, by Jones. Again there is progression through Brown's two solos; in the alternative version he hints at multiplications, veering towards cliché; in the master he finds variation, surer of his flashing intentions. The swiftly coursing *Brownie speaks* is aptly named, for here are the confident accents of a man conscious of staging an arrival. He enters aggressively and, through three choruses, realizes some powerful strategies, splendidly accompanied by Hope. At *De-dah*'s calmer pace his extended solo, though leisured in the main, is introduced at high register with a touch of Navarro's clarion peremptoriness. The early part of *You go to my head* consists of hastily uttered episodes fashioned by the altoist. Brown, when he enters, and as he collaborates with Donaldson in a sort of closing duet, gleams like a flambeau in a twilit landscape.

The group gathering on 22 June 1953 has as leader Johnson, who was at the time working outside professional music. Despite respectable jazz experience going back to the early 1940s, this was the trombonist's first recording date as leader for Blue Note and the stamp of his musical personality is set upon the proceedings (**269a**). *Capri* is a 32-bar Gryce theme. In both versions Johnson is assured, rethinking his two-chorus solo in the second. Brown is similarly progressional, expanding, in the master take, his earlier brilliantly toned minor-key witticisms. There is praiseworthy assistance from most of the others throughout the session. Percy Heath's brother Jimmy plays a light-toned solo between Johnson's and Brown's in *Capri* which exemplifies his somewhat vaguely focused aspiration to the bop style. *Loverman* is chiefly Johnson's, Brown's only role being in an atmospheric introduction and a heraldic group valediction. Two versions of Johnson's *Turnpike* – a Monkish riff, fast and simple in basis – invite two choruses of crackling invention from the trumpeter and, while Jimmy Heath may seem a bit awed by the speed, Johnson, spitting staccato clauses, is almost as agile as Brown. Heath's baritone helps to establish a mood for Lewis's stately *Sketch 1* which colours the combination of horns over which delightful piano figures climb and dip; then, at the heart of the piece, Brown produces a bluesy rococo conceit. The best of the soloists in the two versions of *Get happy*, Brown shows his gifts for wedding precision to vivacity in constantly surprising twists and turns of melodic adventure. In the alternative (second) account the excitement generated almost, yet not quite, threatens the precision.

Two versions of *Wail bait* introduce the sextet recordings under the trumpeter's leadership at a point of transition between the bands of Dameron and Hampton. The lucid Lewis, perhaps the best pianist Brown worked with, offers the first solo interpretation of Quincy Jones's mid-tempo rocking subject. He does this with typical acumen. Both of Brown's solos have genuine bop eloquence, and one hears a little more of Navarro's inflectional influence than this disciple was normally wont to admit. The second solo – on the issued master – confirms and enhances the earlier statement.

Gryce and Rouse both acknowledge debt to Parker. The altoist's voice and his linear assurance may be closer than Donaldson's to the venerated source most of the time; but in any case Gryce, who was about to make the same migration as Brown, was to become more honoured for his composing than for his instrumental activity. It was he who produced *Hymn to the Orient* (used less than a year earlier by Getz on **299**). There are two versions of this number also, the first in this Mosaic sequence being the issued master. The conception is altogether pleasing, and Brown, excellently backed, plays with fine distinction, the alternative solo being differently thought through. He evidently relishes a tennis rally of slick phrases with Blakey.

In addition to two standard themes – *Cherokee*, in the serially placed versions of which Brown initially pits his dazzling variations against Lewis's dogged rehearsal of Ray Noble's tune, and *Easy living*, in which Brown's contention with an awkward melody is poorly complemented by a lugubrious flute duet from Gryce and Rouse. And there is Brown's own *Minor mood*, for which Lewis offers an MJQ-ish introduction plus a short solo which, unassuming as it is, wins imaginative edge over the admittedly authoritative exposition of the composer.

Brown's personal style, which would not now alter or develop significantly, can be examined confidently enough within a subchapter devoted to bop in the ascendant. Where the group settings, and some of Brown's companions, in the range of this anthology are concerned, music is encountered which is priming its guns for other campaigns. Freelancing in New York into early 1954, Brown took part in a celebrated club session which has long been thought of as clearly prophetic of that further bop consolidation dealt with in this chapter's next section – 'Bop Hardens'. The prototypical Jazz Messengers group, inseparable in its emergence from the enterprise of Horace Silver and Art Blakey, was not quite at the threshold of formation. The very year of this 20 February gig would see the arrival of a band and a style which would maintain fame and influence through many personnel shifts – Blakey himself being the sole constant – and over almost four decades. Issued first as *A Night at Birdland* on two Blue Note LPs, this item involved a quintet the explosive underlying power of which is generated by Silver and Blakey. *Split kick* is Blakeian hard bop, without doubt, and although Brown is in highly confident temper, inserting more extraneous quotations than usual, one immediately asks whether this could possibly have been his true métier. He receives appropriate support from Silver and, notwithstanding what was said earlier about Lewis, a telling expressive relationship springs up between the trumpeter and this pianist which affects most of the session. *Quicksilver*, Silver's waggish transmogrification of *Lover, come back to me*, posits the Silver–Brown consideration with plain emphasis. Brown may have taken some hints from Silver regarding linear rhythm, or they may both, in this respect, being echoing some mutual influence. At all events it is Brown who is quicksilver itself in his insouciant multiple chorus in both master and alternative versions. In the second of these Silver starts to sound merely busy.

There are two takes of *Wee dot*, the second in this sequence being the master. It is a fairly fast blues with aggressive high-note work from Brown which Silver urges forward with simple figures. In the steadier *Blues*, which gives Donaldson an opportunity to shine, Brown may be thought to commit himself unduly to the hubris of a growing reputation. During *A night in Tunisia*, pitting intricacies against a merciless rhythm, he sounds almost vulnerable. *Lou's blues*, Donaldson's fleet bop idea, spurs Brown into rapid lines which sound curiously dark-stained. He does not quite hit the straight, and tongues carelessly, in *The way you look tonight*; but *Now's the time* finds him in rich-voiced, meditative form, tackling outré urgencies and oblique tangents of several kinds. In *Confirmation*, Silver-paced, he does serious tune-building, edging towards fervent altitude before peeling off sardonically to admit a vigorous Donaldson.

This context seems to suit Donaldson better than the June 1953 date; and to write that here he 'seemed uncertain of what he wanted to do other than raising Charlie Parker's ghost', [44] leaving aside the fact that Parker was still around and making music, strikes one, on the evidence, as unjust.

Brown's stamina seems equal to this often relentless hard-bop assault course, yet one feels grateful, in retrospect, that he did not get embroiled in it for too long. To that extent at least Roach's long-distance call from the West Coast might be regarded as fortunate. Nevertheless, the importance for Brown of the short liaison with Blakey and Silver must not be underestimated.

Before the Roach–Brown quintet reached a recording studio, Brown took part in the summer 1954 sessions for Pacific Jazz that produced music which also slants off from the bop context. Williamson, Gordon,

Freeman, Mondragon and Manne all were habitués of the Western jazz scene, and Sims, a wider-roving Californian, had just come back from freelancing in New York. No doubt these fellows had absorbed influences similar to those in Brown's formation as a jazzman. What gives an intriguing cast to the enterprise is the involvement of Montrose (whose 1955 collaboration with Gordon is assessed at **303**) as arranger for the group. Brown, who came at Richard Bock's invitation, and for whom this combination of players and writers appears to have been specifically conceived, sounds quite at home. For the July meeting two Brown compositions fell under Montrose's pen. Harmonically and contrapuntally these arrangements of *Daahoud* and *Joy spring* are colourfully textured and are lent proper assurance by the performers. Brown's *Daahoud* solo might stand as one of his most relaxed and tuneful pronouncements, yet he matches it in *Joy spring*, his distinguished theme of stepped sections, for which Montrose so orders affairs that the trumpeter-composer has good elbow room to determine the spirit of the performance. Montrose's *Finders keepers* is no great subject but the contributions of Brown and Sims, unsensational though they be, redeem its shortcomings.

Early in August the Brown–Roach five were recording in Los Angeles. *Joy spring* and *Daahoud* were included in a session of 6 August and *Daahoud* is tough and driving hot bop (†EmArcy [A] 842 933–2). The Brown–Roach *Joy spring* exhibits a different kind of relaxation; this is Brown breathing his native air and his solo is full of subtle contrasts of emphasis.

At the second date for Pacific Jazz, Smith's bass replaces Mondragon's and the rhythm support at each of these gatherings is all that might be expected from such participants. Freeman's tough whimsy is set loose to steer the unusual introduction to *Gone with the wind*. Sims's and Brown's solos, though quite differently sparked, have a shapeliness formed to the occasion. Two further Brown originals are given the Montrose treatment and *Bones for Jones* (Brown's enigmatic title) has a long exploratory trumpet solo followed by shorter essays by Gordon, Sims and Freeman. *Tiny's capers* (named for Tiny Kahn) is included here in the sequence of master and alternative. Freeman leads into the glancing, rather quaint counterpoint, slipping in snatches of mock-Oriental funk for the second version. Brown is beautifully poised through his two choruses and Sims is calmly, elegantly inventive . . . philosophical, almost. The insertions of 3/4 time in the arrangement of *Blueberry Hill* are negotiated by the players in skilful instrumental distribution. Brown's early solo is as carefree as the song.

After the frenetic marathons he had to run with Blakey, Brown's accommodation to this characteristically even-tempered West Coast cooperative affirms his artistic flexibility, and remains as a rather rare example of his response to an enterprise significantly conditioned by careful writing for the ensemble. The earlier sessions in this collection, and the many recordings with Roach yet to come, emphasize the interaction of soloists in combo situations where the minimum of formal arrangement is normally sufficient. There were other encounters, including a sequence with Neal Hefti and strings in January 1955 (EmArcy [A] MG636005). One quite brilliant example of formality and freedom miraculously fused is the Brown–Roach group realization of Bud Powell's *Parisian thoroughfare* (EmArcy, as above).

The trumpeter's own composed themes all are admirable, and Benny Golson's posthumous tribute, *I remember Clifford*, distills something of their and Brown's spirit. Perhaps the most wistful of the threnodies for this brilliant jazz ephemerid is Gil Evans's strangely austere orchestration of *Joy spring* (**460**). E.T.

Miles Davis

271 Walkin'

†Original Jazz Classics (A) OJCCD296–2, †Prestige (Eu) CDRIVM004

Davis (tpt); Davey Schildkraut (alt); Horace Silver (p); Percy Heath (bs); Kenny Clarke (d). New York City, 3 April 1954.

Solar · *Love me or leave me*

Schildkraut absent. Same date.

You don't know what love is

Davis (tpt); J. J. Johnson (tbn); Lucky Thompson (ten); Silver (p); Heath (bs); Clarke (d). Hackensack, N.J., 29 April 1954.

Blue 'n' boogie · *Walkin'*

272 The Modern Jazz Giants

Prestige (A) PR7650, *†Original Jazz Classics (A) OJCCD347–2

Davis (tpt); Thelonious Monk (p); Heath (bs); Clarke (d); Milt Jackson (vib). Hackensack, N.J., 24 December 1954.

Bags' groove (2 versions) · *Bemsha swing* · *Swing spring* · *The man I love* (2 versions)

In his autobiography Davis says that 1954 was an important year for him [45] and these recordings amply confirm it. What he attempted on earlier Prestige dates with mixed success came resoundingly into focus on 29 April and some useful hints of why this happened are given by the 3 April session. Lacking the cutting edge, let alone the seemingly effortless mobility, cultivated by such trumpeters as Gillespie or Navarro, Davis, never a virtuoso in any conventional sense, needed to hit upon a completely different yet still viable approach.

Throughout the 3 April titles he plays with a cup mute, and always close to the microphone. This seemingly dubious stratagem yielded a new sound, an important aspect of which is the humanizing of the electronic component in the formula. It proves a considerable stimulus to his thinking and some memorable phrases emerge, especially in *You don't know what love is* and *Solar*, an excellent theme that is said to have been written by Chuck Wayne though persistently credited to Davis. Of 12 bars, it does not follow the blues changes but is based on part of *How high the moon?* The other crucial element comes from Clarke, who matches his leader's consistent use of a mute by confining himself to brushes, and to model effect throughout.

While clearly misplaced on this date, Schildkraut, particularly in *Solar* and *I'll remember April* (the track from this session not included here), is neither so tentative nor so completely in Parker's shadow as commentaries on this music have usually insisted. [46] But there is no doubt that he had done himself more credit on slightly earlier dates with Kenton and did so again at sessions led by Ralph Burns, Chuck Wayne, Sam Most and others.

The key to this music is Davis's seeking a fresh sound, this being the most obvious sign of his bringing a new sensibility to jazz. It had earlier led to the so-called *Birth of the Cool* recordings (**376**), but his career was for some years afterwards in decline and so another, and different, beginning was necessary, the initiatives of the Capitol scores being taken up again later (**382**). Such was Davis's boldness and imaginative power meanwhile that he took his obvious technical limitations as a starting point.

That purity of tone heard in his best moments with Parker (**257–8**, **266b**) was our first glimpse of a larger purity, musical rather than just instrumental. In, say, his seven-chorus *Walkin'* solo there is virtually nothing redundant and every note possesses expressive meaning. If at a given point he does not have an idea he displays, in Gil Evans's words, 'the courage to wait' [47] until one comes rather than playing a conventional flourish. His solos from this time onwards thus make a positive use of space, the first on the initial version of *Bags' groove*, for example, being strikingly aired out with rests. The impact of this procedure is naturally heightened in *Walkin'* and *Blue 'n' boogie* by Silver, Heath and Clarke, the first of a series of powerfully swinging rhythm sections that would feature prominently in Davis's music. And just as his playing appears spontaneous despite the choice of notes obviously being made with extreme care, so the rhythm section's insistent propulsion does not lessen the music's relaxation. This latter feeling was of course by no means unfamiliar in jazz (Lester Young etc.), but it had never been articulated in this way before. Davis's basic tone is soft, round, the trumpet, though mostly unmuted, still often held rather close to the microphone.

Presumably because he was employing three horns, Davis asked Thompson to provide four arrangements for the 29 April date. For reasons never explained the musicians could make little of these and so they instead recorded head arrangements of two blues. With everyone no doubt on his mettle as a result of their failure with Thompson's scores, the result was a pair of classic performances, Davis's first major sustained and nearly flawless achievements on disc.

Its title describes the tempo of Richard Carpenter's *Walkin'* and this piece is a blues whose vocabulary is extended, as the theme's flattened fifths suggest, by a distillation of early modern jazz; indeed it is a fine illustration of how bop revitalized, rather than broke with, an older tradition. The heart of both this performance and of Gillespie's *Blue 'n' boogie* (see also **256a**) is a sequence of long solos by trumpet, trombone and tenor that conveys a quite unusual feeling of rapt concentration. In each case Davis sets the tone of the proceedings but what he does would have counted for much less if Johnson, Thompson, Heath and Clarke had not responded from the full depth of their talents. Trumpet and trombone dialogue with the rhythm section only but part of Thompson's solo is backed with brass riffs and it is while these are maintained that his improvisation and the whole performance attains its climax. This having passed, the riffs stop but Thompson runs hard for another two choruses, losing none of the music's impetus. Much of it escapes during the piano solo, however. Silver meshes finely with Heath and Clarke, proving himself a perceptive accompanist on both these April sessions, but as a soloist he merely strings together clichés in statements which can only be superfluous after the horns' sustained intensity. Davis returns for another couple of choruses to raise the music to its former level, leads into an ensemble riff that dialogues with the drums, and then Carpenter's theme is heard again in the three horns' sonorous unison, lazily yet exactly timed as in the beginning.

Blue 'n' boogie follows the same routine except that there is no riff to reintroduce the theme. Davis sounds less introverted at this faster tempo and, rather than merely playing more notes, subjects his ideas to greater elaboration, balancing diatonic phrases with chromatic, stepwise motion with large intervals. He plays indeed with energetic melancholy and, like Johnson and Thompson, uses traditional devices to make indelibly personal statements. In fact it was at this session that his mature style emerged in its first version.

In terms of such basics as tone production and articulation, the *Walkin'* and *Blue 'n' boogie* solos are still not impressive as trumpet playing by the extremely high standards that have usually prevailed in jazz. Yet besides making an entirely individual sound, Davis shows in almost every nuance and accent a much improved mastery of the means of musical expression. Marianne Moore's phrase 'circumspectly audacious' exactly suits his output at this stage. It is often claimed that this session discredited cool jazz and cleared the way for the glories of hard bop, yet there are plenty of records in this book which disprove appealing simplifications of that kind. There is no question, however, that with his 29 April 1954 music Davis began a series of recordings which has few rivals for its length, variety of contents or breadth of influence.

And the next major event followed on Christmas Eve of the same year, when he assembled with three-quarters of the original Modern Jazz Quartet plus – reportedly not his choice – Thelonious Monk. The clash between trumpeter and pianist has been detailed in too many texts to need repeating here. [48] Both their styles are based on the elimination of inessentials but judging from his response to Silver on earlier sessions (and to Red Garland on **334**), Davis needed the security of a more conventional manner of accompaniment from pianists. His difficulties with Monk arose more specifically from their quite divergent rhythmic and particularly harmonic senses. The practical result is that there is no piano accompaniment to Davis's improvisations except in *Bemsha swing* and his second solo on the first version of *The man I love*. This produces an entirely acceptable variation of texture that is by no means without precedent. Indeed, when Jackson and Monk enter together after Davis's main solos on both takes of *Bags' groove* the effect is notable.

Take 2 of *The man I love* is the *cause célèbre*, Monk's idea for his solo being to spread the first two statements of the main eight-bar phrase of Gershwin's melody over twice the usual distance, to revert to normal metre for the bridge, then to stretch the return of the main phrase over 16 bars again. As the bridge approaches he apparently gets lost and is reduced to silence until an angry-sounding trumpet interjection prompts his busy return. It was not an especially inspired notion, as his successful completion of the manoeuvre in take 1 indicates, and the rewards of this session lie elsewhere. There is more significant trouble, though, with Monk's theme, *Bemsha swing*, which, whatever the master numbers of these recordings suggest, was perhaps undertaken first. Davis is obviously uncomfortable with Monk's support, sounding stiff, and his continuity is less good than elsewhere on the date. However, he ends his solo with some distinctly Monkish ideas which the pianist – after Jackson has demonstrated his complete understanding of the piece's melody and chords – takes up in his own solo and makes considerably more of. [49]

As Davis pointed out later, his *Swing spring*, evidently prompted by an idea of Bud Powell's, is based on a scale rather than chords [50] and hence gives a hint of what was to happen on **393**. Jackson and Monk again fire each other's invention: note the productive rhythmic contrasts between them during both vibraharp solos. The leader is also heard from twice, again quoting a favourite Monk phrase which the latter duly seizes upon in variant form.

Bags' groove, another blues in F like *Walkin'*, is by Jackson and is the kind of melody that sounds both ancient and modern. Davis takes two solos, a long one after the theme and a shorter one near the end, as on *Blue 'n' boogie* and *Walkin'*, but these mark an advance on those earlier achievements. At least on take 1, the tone is purer yet more vocal, the nuances more subtle but more sharply expressive, the melodic ideas and their rhythmic placement a degree more personal. Most important, although each of his choruses is complete in itself, they together form a genuinely larger whole. As the solo unfolds there is little increase in volume, the climax being reached via tone and phrasing – and with improved trumpet execution.

Monk's solo likewise is a peak of the session, up to the level of his finest Blue Note work (**292**), a piece of sustained musical thinking that is punctuated with daringly long rests, frugal in gesture yet eloquent. Jackson's virtuoso fluency is a perfect foil to both Davis and Monk, and he is as solidly inventive as either. He is just as good in the second version of *Bags' groove*, Davis rather less so. As for Monk, he comes up with an almost completely different improvisation, less austere, more pianistic.

Both the above CDs have short playing times, and the Prestige could easily have accommodated the early April date's *I'll remember April.* The second OJC CD lacks both accounts of *Bags' groove* and has instead an irrelevant *Round about midnight* by an entirely different 1956 Davis band with Coltrane. Extensive work by that group is discussed under **334** but mention can be made here of the handy 8-CD *Complete Prestige Recordings of Miles Davis* (†Prestige [A] PCD012). Noticeably more oblique comments on *Bags' groove* occur in Chapter 6, 'Outside the Capsule', of Hodeir's *The Worlds of Jazz* (see Bibliography). M.H.

Conte Candoli

273 Groovin' Higher

Affinity (E) AFF92, Bethlehem (A) BCP30

Candoli (tpt); Bill Holman (ten); Lou Levy (p); Leroy Vinnegar (bs); Stan Levey (d). Los Angeles, 26 July 1955.

Four · I'm getting sentimental over you · Full Count · Groovin' higher · Jazz city blues · My old flame · Toot suite

Although *Four* was composed by Eddie Vinson, it is usually attributed to Miles Davis, but Candoli was not among those many who followed his example as a result of the impact of the *Blue 'n' boogie/Walkin'* session (**271**). His teenage solo on Herman's *Put that ring on my finger* (**312a**) suggest Roy Eldridge's influence, perhaps with a touch of Sonny Berman, yet his best music was founded on Gillespie's innovations. This is obvious from the records made in Sweden under Chubby Jackson's leadership when Candoli was just 20, especially of his own themes *Crown pilots* and *Boomsie* (Esquire [E] 323). Even in later years he seemed always to improvise with particular incisiveness on Gillespie material, instances being *A night in Tunisia* with Getz (**368**) and *The champ* with Howard Rumsey–Charlie Persip (Liberty [A] LRP3045, 1957).

But too much should not be made of this, for although rooted in Gillespie's style, he was not confined by it. A comparison between the older man's justly celebrated *I can't get started* (**249**) and Candoli's later reading (Affinity [E] AFF173, Bethlehem [A] BCP1016, 1954) shows some positive differences. Even as early as the Swedish dates there were signs, for example on *Crying sands*, of a more personal sensibility, and this is heard fully grown in performances such as the above *My old flame*. Candoli is in truth our old friend the musician who turned in high-class work not for years but for decades, yet is either ignored or subject to offhand dismissals in the histories and reference books. There is so much fine improvisation by him scattered around, sometimes in unlikely places, that the case would be met best with some kind of annotated discography. Random selections from this might include *Fine and dandy* with Charlie Ventura for its triumph over an adverse setting (Vogue [E] LDE107, Gene Norman Presents [A] GNP1, 1949), Shelly Manne's *Deep people* (Savoy [A] SJL22254, 1952) for the exultant lead playing as much as for the solo, the tightly packed yet well-varied phrases of his contribution to *Quicksilver* on the Rumsey–Persip issue referred to above, Candoli's own *Mambo Diane* with Buddy Collette (Eros [E] ERL50028, Crown [A] CLP5162, 1960) and his account of Thelonious Monk's *Ruby, my dear* with Stan Levey (Affinity [E] AFF93, Bethlehem [A] BCP37, 1955).

This last is especially impressive, and is enough to make one regret that Candoli did not tackle more of Monk's themes. It is from one of those occasions – and the Getz session dealt with under **368** came from another – when right through a recording date the trumpeter improvised one sustained and excellently developed solo after another. Such consistency is fully apparent on the session detailed in the heading, which, if a label be insisted upon, produced what might be termed Californian hard bop. The title piece, *Groovin' higher*, is the leader's sensible variant of the theme Gillespie recorded on **256a** and *Full Count* is also Candoli's ('Count' being his nickname). These are well-crafted themes, as, predictably enough, are Holman's *Jazz city blues* and *Toot suite*, but this music's emphasis is on improvisation.

Candoli seems never to have an indecisive moment, his every idea being absolutely clear-cut. The phrases are sometimes fairly complex but his attack, while constantly varying in emphasis, is direct, with few inflections. Although this date was spearheaded by his aggressive virtuosity, the trumpet tone is full and quite warm, most noticeably in the pair of ballads. The occasion serves, too, as a useful reminder of Holman's prowess on the tenor saxophone, this having been obscured by his prolific arranging and composing activities. Just as Candoli was affected first by Eldridge, then Gillespie, so Holman's exemplars, like most tenor saxophonists of his generation, were Lester Young followed by Charlie Parker. His sound is rather dry, but this accords satisfyingly with the strong rhythmic current of his solos. Certainly Holman's playing sheds an interestingly different light on his musical personality from that offered by his writing. To hear the two at their most fruitful, reference should be made to the 1954 octet sessions under Holman's own name (Affinity [E] AFF65).

An important aspect of this 1955 date is the unrelentingly intense dialogue between the horns and the rhythm section on the fast and medium-paced items. So far as this dimension of the music is concerned, Candoli's, Holman's and Vinson's themes give rise to strikingly heated discourses. Having always been a perceptive accompanist, Levy in particular shines, seeming always to contribute the right thought at the right place and time in these intently detailed commentaries; he is a fine soloist also. Yet while these seven performances make up a thoroughly rewarding example of their sort of jazz, the truth is that the above LP is another of this book's arbitrary selections. Which is to say that there was no way, logical or otherwise, of choosing between it and *West Coast Wailers* (Atlantic [A] 1268). Recorded less than a month later by the same personnel, this latter maintains the same consistently high level of musical invention and communicative fire. Of especial note in the Atlantic issue's account of *Flamingo*, one of the most telling expressions on record of Candoli's little-regarded lyricism. M.H.

George Wallington

274 George Wallington Trios

Prestige (A) PR7587, †Original Jazz Classics (A) OJCCD1754–2

Wallington (p); Chuck Wayne (mandola[1]); Charles Mingus (bs); Max Roach (d). New York City, 4 September 1952.

Love beat[1] · *Summer rain* · *Escalating* · *Laura*

Oscar Pettiford (bs) replaces Mingus. Same date.

Tenderly · *When your old wedding ring was new* · *Red, white and blue* · *Arrivederci*

Curly Russell (bs) replaces Pettiford. New York City, 25 May 1953.

Squeezer's breezer · *Among friends* · *Variations* · *My nephew and I* · *Ours* · *I married an angel* · *Cuckoo around the clock*

Wallington made a lively contribution to the styles which emerged through the mid-to-late 1940s. He entered the ferment of bop experiment, joining Gillespie's 1944 group while Bud Powell was in Cootie Williams's band. There are few clues to the shapes of the Wallington style at that stage, and the question still is asked regarding his degree of indebtedness to Powell. There are undeniable similarities. One guesses that, as bop assumed a recognizable style, both Wallington and Powell were pursuing their own formation. In his recorded work for Williams, Powell was required to echo 'appropriate' figurations from Teddy Wilson, Ellington, Basie and so on; but *Honeysuckle rose* (Big Band Archives [A] LP1208, Affinity [E] AFS1031) contains one of a few tantalizing evidences of the growing of one of the most influential of jazz voices. We miss clear coeval evidence of how men like Al Haig and Wallington were shaping up.

By the time of these recordings, styles are fully formed, and Wallington's admiration for Powell is plain. But other inspirations and influences show themselves, and there are emphases which are decidedly individual. Powell's most boppish stylistic suit (he had other garments) is adapted by Wallington to a rather squarer cut, and maybe a bristlier texture. The treatment of *When your old wedding ring was new* gives one opportunity for comparison. More similarities might have shown themselves – or possibly more divergences – if this pianist had been more given to extending himself. But he seems to have had an instinct for the miniature, and he did fall some way short of Powell's remarkable imaginative stamina.

His own creative gift formed smaller, shapelier things, and he is remembered for themes (*Godchild* is a famous example: **376**) which attracted arrangers. He was himself no arranger, yet his typical compositions are spontaneously organized by a kind of ensemble instinct. *Polka dot* is one such, and it is the focus of *Variations.* In a 1951 session with the same companions (†Savoy [A] SV0136) he presented this piece jauntily; here it prompts a threefold variation. The first phase narrowly evades McDowellish pastoral to become a well-steered slow treatment of the tune, and this gives way to a fast canter showing Wallington's whirling boppery near its most dazzling. After that things lurch into sombre self-caricature, out-of-tempo runs and affective plungings into the bass notes, grand gestures asking little imagination.

Elsewhere, when he resorts to the romantic mode, as he does in his *Summer rain*, in *Laura*, *I married an angel* and the wholly atemporal *Tenderly*, there are, among the traceries and arpeggiations, wry asides and chordal refractions which call airy affectation seriously in question. Acidly clashing intervals interposed during *Laura* have suggested to some a borrowing from Monk. In fact, they echo a prophetic interjection by Ellington in 1940, *Mr J.B. Blues* (**153**).

Escalating seems an exercise in pianistics, and would dispel any doubts that Wallington had thoroughly absorbed Powell's procedures; and the simple excitement of it is, like much else here, enhanced by the superb drumming of Roach. Even here, though, there is a more personal ambience; a characteristic that one has noticed elsewhere. *Twins* (from the *Polka dot* Savoy date) began with a snatch of contrary motion, exhilarating yet utterly formal; and even in the whirling bop lines of *Escalating* the sense can be of a pianist exercising his great technical virtuosity in a manner which might, in jazz-piano terms, be called 'professorial'. That feeling is there also in *Red, white and blue*, which has comic patriotic interjections, and parts of *Cuckoo around the clock*, where the weaving, intricate, speedy improvisation tends to fall into quasi-automated patterns – formal affecting to sound like free. This does not prevent such pieces from being splendid examples of a style of which Wallington was an undoubted pioneer, and which he was edging towards further discovery.

Love beat is a singularity in the 4 September programme – as well as being the only expansion of the record's trio instrumentation – since it includes Wayne, a team-mate of Wallington in Joe Marsala's band. Wayne was a mandolinist before taking up the guitar. Wallington evidently wished to include the muscular-toned mandola (a type of electrified tenor mandolin) to suit the character of this theme. *Love beat*'s improvised section is an attractive *moderato* duet of rarely (in jazz) combined voices.

Squeezer's breezer is joyous exhibitionism, more fluid than some other of the fast things, less indebted to Powell, and as good an example of a newly established style as can be found. *My nephew and I* is yet another to add to the list of delightful, often quaintly entitled (*Hyacinth*, *Lemon drop*, *Joy bell*, *High score*, the lucky *Godchild*) and half-forgotten miniatures; a theme of skipping, tripping rhythms, dancing chords, staccato ligatures, and an unerring sense of natural integrality.

Short or incomplete careers were not unusual among the bop pianists. Wallington withdrew in 1957 chiefly out of professional disillusionment, and it is a tribute to his strengths that his exuberant jazz still leaps fresh from the record today. However, in the 1980s he after a long interval returned to musical activity (e.g. Interface [J] YF7092, 1984). E.T.

Frank Rosolino

275 Frank Rosolino

Affinity (E) AFF61, *Capitol (A) T6507

Sam Noto (tpt); Rosolino (tbn, vcl[1]); Charlie Mariano (alt); Claude Williamson (p); Curtis Counce (bs); Stan Levey (d); Bill Holman (arr). Los Angeles, 12, 16 March 1954.

Boo boo be bop · *Yo yo* · *Freckles* · *The carioca* · *Pennies from Heaven*[1] · *That old black magic*[1]

Pete Jolly (p), Max Bennett (bs), Mel Lewis (d) replace Williamson, Counce, Levey. New York City, 6 November 1954.

I'm gonna sit right down and write myself a letter · *Linda* · *Embraceable you* · *Ragamuffin* · *Besame mucho* · *Frank 'n' earnest*

The Capitol issue, titled *Stan Kenton Presents: Frank Rosolino Sextet*, lacks the two vocal performances.

It says much for the inherent richness of jazz that when faced with J. J. Johnson's major achievement, Rosolino was able to arrive at a way of improvising on the trombone that was quite different yet just as firmly rooted in the bop idiom. Although there are solos by him, like the one on Benny Carter's 1958 *Blue Lou* (†Original Jazz Classics [A] OJCCD167–2), which show that he could adopt a more traditional stance, Rosolino can usually be placed between the suavity of Johnson and the more rough-edged music of Kai Winding. As with Johnson and Winding, precedents for his extreme mobility were set by several earlier masters of trombone jazz, as noted under **269**, but he used this, and every other aspect of his formidable technique, very much for his own ends.

Listening to Rosolino pile one elaboration of melody and rhythm on another, as in *Besame mucho* or *The carioca*, is rather like watching an implausibly complex juggling act: something must soon go wrong – yet it seldom does. Indeed this music contains an 'advanced games' element such as Richard Hadlock identified in Earl Hines. [51] Rosolino's speed can seem to go against his instrument's character, but it would be more accurate to say that it represents an extension of its capabilities; as such it is very much in the tradition of jazz, which has always discovered new potentialities in instruments. Beyond extreme ease of movement Rosolino had flexibility in the larger sense, and it is important to recognize that his elaborations are seldom merely decorative, the result of squeezing in more notes for their own sake and because he had the executive capacity to do so.

Sheer virtuoso exuberance is a factor, yet if this music had no more to offer it would be one-sided and unsatisfying. Stronger emotions flow beneath its highly detailed surface and though his ideas have an intrinsic complexity, this never subverts, for example, the expressive accents of *Embraceable you*. If the listener is never left at rest, this is partly because of the music's incessant invention but partly also because, to the attentive hearer, darker shades of experience are hinted at, these representing tendencies that finally broke out in the ghastly circumstances of Rosolino's suicide in 1978. Even the humour, the one thing for which he attained real fame, is ambiguous, as when he dispatches the rigmarole of the *Old black magic* lyrics as if he did not believe a single word; and hear the eldritch goblin snicker of that laugh in *Pennies from heaven*!

Playing with an almost unrelenting drive, all participants were notably consistent throughout both of these 1954 sessions. The original themes are all Holman's and are pieces of real substance despite their often silly titles (*Boo boo be bop* should not be confused with Sal Salvador's *Boo boo be doop*). Scored bridges and backgrounds break up the sequences of solos and heighten their effect. *Frank 'n' earnest* and *Ragamuffin* in particular deserve the extended workouts they receive, and they give rise to excellent solos from Noto and Mariano and masterly ones from the leader. Normally associated with Fats Waller, even *I'm gonna sit right down and write myself a letter* is transformed into bop via Holman's unobtrusive arrangement, and it has an especially fine Noto solo. He and Mariano are true bop players, who took Gillespie and Parker respectively as their initial points of reference but arrived at manners of their own. Mariano's phrases are clean, precise, yet always thrusting and he is quite memorable, for instance, on *Linda*. Virtually all trumpet and alto solos here possess a beautiful overall shape, yet they are more conventional than those of Rosolino, who never sounds as if he was influenced by anyone.

As with other items in this book, the choice of the above to represent him was somewhat arbitrary. The 1955 *Frankly Speaking* (Affinity [E] AFF69, Capitol [A] T6509) and *The Rosolino Connection* of 1956 (†Affinity [E] CDAFF761, retitled *Trombomania!*) contain improvisations just as powerfully individual as any of those here, plus imaginative contributions from such men as Mariano on the former LP and Sonny Clark on the latter CD. That Rosolino maintained the same levels of expression, inventiveness and virtuosity over a long period of years is demonstrated by his *Thinking About You*, recorded with the Ed Bickert Trio in Toronto during 1976 (Sackville [C] 2014). M.H.

Herb Geller

276 The Herb Geller Sextet

Trip (A) TLP5539

Conte Candoli (tpt); Geller (alt); Ziggy Vines (ten); Lorraine Geller (p); Red Mitchell (bs); Eldridge Freeman (d). Los Angeles, 19 August 1955.
Outpost incident · Crazy, he calls me · Rockin' chair · You'd be so nice to come home to

Leroy Vinnegar (bs) replaces Mitchell. Los Angeles, 22 August 1955.
Vone mae · Gin for fuguelhorns · Owl eyes · Tardi for Zardi's

West Coast modernism was given an added stimulus by the 1946 visit of Parker and Gillespie. Geller showed more Parker influence than other West Coast saxophonists; even so, his prior influence was Benny Carter. Born in Los Angeles in 1928, he found his first professional job with Joe Venuti in 1946. Several bands later, he was in New York with Claude Thornhill in 1950 and met the pianist Lorraine Welsh, who became his wife. The next year the Gellers returned to California, where Herb joined Billy May for a while before a period with Howard Rumsey's Lighthouse band at Hermosa Beach. Lorraine had been with the clarinettist Jerry Wald when Herb met her. Before she and Herb formed their own quartet in 1954, she gained appropriate experience in gigs with Shorty Rogers, Maynard Ferguson and Zoot Sims. This album was one of a number which the Gellers recorded for EmArcy in 1954–5, the fine and similarly manned *Herb Geller Plays* (EmArcy [A] MG36040) carrying four numbers recorded only a few days earlier than the two sessions preserved here.

The altoist's companions are lively and competent – the little-known Vines bringing useful tonal enrichment to ensemble timbres and soloing in a manner which bespeaks his allegiance to the fellowship of Lester

Young admirers. His voice adds the deeper shades which the contrapuntal writing in *Outpost incident* and *Gin for fuguelhorns* sometimes calls for. Geller's alto solo in the latter piece mixes laconicism and prolixity in balanced measure, his important emphases sounding a Parkerish acidity. The older influences upon him show in gliding linkages and in a subtle ease in tempo doubling.

Rockin' chair receives a whimsical jump-band handling with a good ensemble lead by Candoli. Herb rather pensively restrings Birdlike fragments of melody, following which Lorraine finds, in a close examination of the tune, other fragments closer to the riffs of swing. Vinnegar takes a good *pizzicato* solo and the mood is generally convivial. *Gin for fuguelhorns* conjures the style of the Mulligan quartet (**300**), a virtually unavoidable contemporary exemplar. The fugueing is competently negotiated. Lorraine's solo, full-toned and two-handed, sets a contrast to Herb's lively stylistic ambivalences.

A Hollywood club where the Gellers were playing regularly figures in the title of *Tardi for Zardi's*, an exploitation of the chord sequence of *All God's children got rhythm* which is the exact opposite to tardy. Herb's vigour is sprightly enough here, but Candoli, who is variable elsewhere, seems to relish the dangerous pace even more than does his leader.

Freeman, who solos as the *Tardi* number rushes towards its unison reprise, composed the minor riff *Vone mae*, which he ushers in and out with enfilades learned at the Art Blakey school of gunmanship; yet he has no desire to overwhelm. Along the way the flow of Herb's ideas sounds a bit restricted, and Lorraine too seems relatively under restraint; but the performance is not short on interest. Vinnegar's support is rich and rhythmically subtle. *Owl eyes* is a boppish blues with Latin appendages which finds Herb in prodding mood – tentative it may be, but he does not, as Candoli does, lapse into routine comment. Vines aims at, yet cannot quite hit, rhythmic heroism.

The beauty of Herb's ballad style in *Crazy, he calls me* springs out of a marvellous relaxation in the shape and timing of pivotal melodic phrases which lend the tune a surprising elasticity. With similar skill, he goes directly into an improvisation on *You'd be so nice to come home to* which clearly finds the minor emphasis of the tune far less inhibiting than *Vone mae* seemed to be. There is sombre *pizzicato* from Mitchell in his ample and satisfying solo passage. The unstated theme is eventually led in by Candoli, more or less straightly quoted and with some ensemble harmonies leading to a tricksy, peremptory goodbye coda.

Other fine jazz was recorded by the Gellers round this time, but in October 1958 Lorraine died, and by the early 1960s Herb had moved to Europe, where he long remained. E.T.

Lucky Thompson

277 **Dancing Sunbeam**

Impulse (A) AS9307–2, *HMV (E) CLP1237

Thompson (ten); Skeeter Best (g); Oscar Pettiford (bs). New York City, 27 January 1956.
Tricotism · O.P. meets L.T. · Bo-bi my boy · Dancing sunbeam · Little tenderfoot · The plain and simple truth · Mister Mann · Body and soul

Hank Jones (p), Osie Johnson (d) added; Best absent. New York City, 30 January 1956.
A lady's vanity

Jimmy Cleveland (tbn) added. Same date.
Tom-cattin' · Translation · Old reliable

Don Abney (p) replaces Jones. Same date.
N.R.1 · N.R.2 · Good luck

Cleveland and Johnson absent. Same date.
Once there was

Thompson relished his control over these sessions, and his success in setting his stamp upon them is one of the best available answers to the nagging question of this swing survivor's true relation to bop and its aftereffects. For these are minor classics of the modern era, one of the chief tokens of their success being a relaxed kinship between players of differing formation, in particular the key partnership between Thompson and Pettiford.

Thompson's involvement with the initiators of bop would, of itself, have been no guarantee of his establishment as a modernist. His romantic accents, sharply contrasted in the Dial session of 28 March 1946 (**258**) with Parker's bop coinage fresh-minted, may make his ready choice as a sideman by both Gillespie and Parker for their West Coast sessions seem as curious as the engagement of numerous other swing survivors in nascent bop recordings through the winter and spring of 1944–5 and beyond. But, at one short step aside, the 1947 'Lucky Seven' date for RCA-Victor reveals sufficient evidence of the flair which put Thompson, at least in the brisker vehicles, markedly closer than Benny Carter to the spirit of their companions Marmarosa and Kessel.

Skilfully exploiting his own range of expression, increasingly as sensitive to the genius of Parker as it had been to that of Young, Hawkins or Byas, the tenorist sounds as natural a participant in Miles Davis's *Walkin'* and *Blue 'n' boogie* (**271**), in Monk's *Carolina moon* session of 1952 (**292**), and in Milt Jackson's *Plenty, Plenty Soul* (†Atlantic [A] 1269–2) as any other present. Those may have been occasions on which he had to stand and deliver in modernist terms, and he did that to exceptional effect as a sideman. Here, in 1956, he proves himself more comprehensively, for he can be assessed not simply as one man among several but as the master of the entire conception. 'I felt the freedom to express myself,' he would recall, '. . . and [had] the men I desired.' [52]

Most of the desired men are successful men of transition, similar to Thompson in formation. In addition, Jones, Best, Thompson himself and Cleveland (the nontransitional, new-generation man) had played under Pettiford's leadership at one time or another. Pettiford, who had ventured beyond Blanton's enhancement of the double bass's ensemble role to make the instrument even more subtle in solo expression, may be regarded as Thompson's first lieutenant in much of what happens here.

A matching of fine imagination makes every one of the eight trio pieces brim with freshness. And there is variety of mode and mood. In *O.P. meets L.T.* it is Best who harmonizes the simple rising and falling theme line with Thompson as Pettiford adds his own supple commentary. *Tricotism, Dancing sunbeam, The plain and simple truth* and *Mister Mann* each has tenor and bass in unison, and both arrangement and improvising express a range of feelings, whimsical, sombre, conspiratorial and so on. *Bo-bi my boy* is set forth by Thompson, spacing out and shoving ahead his rhythmic shapes. Pettiford's inventions here and in *The plain and simple truth* surely count among his finest work. Best takes a lovely solo in the number just mentioned; and in each of the trio's creations his varied supporting and enhancing techniques are sounded with satisfying vividness.

Body and soul (retitled *Deep passion* for the occasion) unsurprisingly wires Thompson into his earliest musical sources, but the thought, the accent, the communicative intention are of his own alchemy. Pettiford and Best are equally personal in support.

The music from the sessions that added trombone, piano and drums reflects contemporary instincts, and in a number of ways expands the cooperative methods of the trio to utilize the added voices. An unsigned 1960 review of these items referred to Cleveland as 'a frustrated trumpet playing trombone'. [53] Notwithstanding the fact that the trombonist's ensemble parts are often designedly trumpetlike (e.g. in *Old reliable*), this was a measly judgement in respect of a young star whose light-hearted skill was as apposite to the needs of Thompson's ensemble as it was to be several weeks later to the demands of George Russell's scores for the McKusick octet (**379**).

Stylistic hardihood is Jones's evident qualification for this kind of enterprise. Having already established himself in bop company, he has no call to be ashamed of a little eclecticism. Even Abney, a more rugged, more bop-sparked player, nods to Tristano in *Good luck*. Concert-grand expansiveness out of tempo from Jones sees *A lady's vanity* in and out, framing a Thompson *adagio* which is as good an example as any of how genuine jazz romanticism is to be distinguished from romanticized jazz. Pettiford, Jones and Johnson nourish the mood quietly; Cleveland retires to the sidelines.

E.T.

Curtis Counce

278 **Counceltation**
†Original Jazz Classics (A) OJCCD159–2, Vogue (E) LAE12133

Jack Sheldon (tpt); Harold Land (ten); Carl Perkins (p); Counce (bs); Frank Butler (d). Los Angeles, 8 October 1956.
Big foot

Same personnel. Los Angeles, 15 October 1956.
Stranger in paradise

Same personnel. Los Angeles, 22 April 1957.
Too close for comfort · *Counceltation*

Same personnel. Los Angeles, 13 May 1957.
Complete · *How deep is the ocean?*

Same personnel. Los Angeles, 3 September 1957.
Mean to me

Although there has been a growing number of bassists whose musicianship has transcended the expected supportive role, the number of those who have won persisting honour as the leaders of distinctive groups is small. The name and example of Counce are little mentioned four decades and more after his series of mid-1950s sessions for Contemporary, and have virtually disappeared from jazz literature. [54] Even in the years following the issue of his records, the music he had made and overseen was not infrequently praised in particular because of the admittedly fetching skills of his ill-fated pianist Carl Perkins; and insufficient attention may have been paid to the effect upon the internal musical commerce of this quintet of a mind whose sense of the less-expected strategies of bop development was heightened by encounters with the experimental teaching of the arranger Lyle 'Spud' Murphy, as well as by membership of Shorty Rogers and Stan Kenton groups.

The title of the leader's composition *Counceltation* might be indicative of the 'conciliar' character of much of this music: of the way in which statements are exchanged and in which tasks of interpretation overlap. *Complete* is an impressive interaction of wayfaring and restfulness, gentle, reflective, and yet full of reassuring strengths. The blues vigour of Perkins has assistance of high-register lines from Counce, acknowledging the influence of his favourite, Jimmy Blanton. When Counce himself plays solo here, the mock uncertainty of fluttering tenor-trumpet unisons serves merely to emphasize his full-toned confidence.

Land, not long past more famous liaisons with Max Roach and Clifford Brown, is frequently heard working out the language of Charlie Parker in his own less penetrating manner. In *How deep is the ocean?* and *Stranger in paradise*, beautifully considered tenor lines find suitable contrast in spiky statements from Perkins and in deceptively polite comments from Sheldon. Land had joined Roach and Brown in Los Angeles, and he, along with other local figures, would play his part in bop's 'hardening' process; yet although *Big foot* (alias *Giant swing*, *Drifting on a reed* and *Air conditioning*), as a celebration of Parker, might have seemed an invitation to toughness, the tenorist gives the impression of holding the lineaments of his bop demon under fairly cool control. Indeed, Land and Sheldon seem sometimes, as in the interestingly apportioned *Too close for comfort*, to be set in a conspiracy of moderation against the vivid exuberance of Perkins. There is musical effectiveness in this, and the inventive support from Counce and Butler adapts itself to the game with some wit. *Mean to me* moves with uncommon rapidity, giving Sheldon and Land opportunity for dazzling unisons and punctuating breaks which give them better equality with the pianist's dancing improvisation. Perkins, hauling the melody of *Stranger in paradise* back out of variation and exchange, for a moment overweights the balance of dynamics; and it is fair comment that his style of pianism veers towards a different amalgam of bop and the blues spirit and towards different jazz departures.

But it is also fair comment to admit that the character of Counce's ensemble owes a great deal to Perkins, who died shortly after a January 1958 recording session (long ago available on Vogue-Contemporary [E] LAC12263) at which Sheldon was replaced by Gerald Wilson. Counce evidently regarded his pianist highly.

Counce's *Complete* and *Counceltation* display his vision of cohesion in freedom to good advantage. The elasticity of *Complete* has been indicated already. In certain ways, *Counceltation* – described on the LP sleeve as 'Curtis's first composition in the Lyle Murphy 12-tone system' – contradicts the idea of deliberation which its name implies. It is an airy piece with swaying, wavelike phrases, sonorous alliances of bass and piano, and ruminative solos. Haunting music. The excellent Butler, who made his recording debut with this group, shows here how precise and unobtrusive his gift for imaginative accompaniment can be rendered.

This record was originally issued on Contemporary (A) as *You Get More Bounce with Curtis Counce*, reissued, e.g. on Vogue (E), as *Counceltation*, then reissued again on Original Jazz Classics (A) as *You Get More Bounce with Curtis Counce.* E.T.

Art Farmer

279 Portrait of Art Farmer

†Contemporary (A) VDJ 1627

Farmer (tpt); Hank Jones (p); Addison Farmer (bs); Roy Haynes (d). New York City, 19 April and 1 May 1958.

Back in the cage · *Stablemates* · *The very thought of you* · *And now . . .* · *Nita* · *By myself* · *Too late now* · *Earth*

Although Farmer emerged at a time when bop was the lingua franca of jazz, he developed a style of playing that moved away from the dominant influence of the extrovert Gillespie school towards an elegance and precision that made virtues out of control and calculation. That he would depart from the prevailing orthodoxy was by no means clear on *Bright boy*, recorded with Wardell Gray in January 1952 when he was 23, on *Central Avenue* (Prestige [A] PR24062). Here, much of what he played could be traced back to Gillespie's influence, although he has said he was a great admirer of the playing of Clark Terry after hearing him play in the Jeter–Pillars band in 1946. [55] In the autumn of 1952 he joined Lionel Hampton's big band, where he found himself among the kindred spirits of Gigi Gryce, Quincy Jones and Clifford Brown. However, it was playing alongside Brown that forced him to confront the extent of his own instrumental horizons, prompting the realization that his own voice might lie in a different direction to that being staked out by the new young standard-bearer of bop trumpet.

Farmer's career in music began when he hitch-hiked with Addison, his bass-playing twin, from their home town of Phoenix to Los Angeles when they were just 15. They completed their high school education in LA; the trumpet-playing sibling then found work in local bands led by Floyd Gray, Horace Henderson, Benny Carter and Gerald Wilson (when the reed section included Eric Dolphy and Buddy Collette) and after travelling to New York with Johnny Otis in 1946 he joined Jay McShann. It was an association with big bands that continued throughout his life. After moving to Austria in 1968 he could be heard in the bands of Kenny Clarke–Francy Boland and in the more commercial surroundings of the Vienna Radio Big Band, the Peter Herbolzheimer orchestra and the big band of the Österreichischer Rundfunk. However, after leaving Hampton in 1953 his involvement was primarily with small groups. He formed an association with Bob Weinstock and appeared on the Prestige label in a variety of combinations alongside the likes of Sonny Rollins, Jackie McLean, Wynton Kelly and Gene Ammons and in a band he co-led with Gigi Gryce that made three albums for the label. He also worked with Gil Evans, George Russell (**379–80**) and Teddy Charles (**378**). It was with Charles's New Directions band alongside Teo Marceo and Charles Mingus that led to rehearsing for a short period under the baton of Edgard Varèse. A two-year tenure with Horace Silver was then followed by a stint with Gerry Mulligan which brought him international recognition.

Farmer recorded two albums with Silver, *The Stylings of Silver* (Blue Note [A] BST1562) from 1957 and *Further Explorations by the Horace Silver Quintet* (BST81589) from 1958. *Stylings* sees him sharing the front line with Hank Mobley during the tenor saxophonist's brief spell with the quintet before leaving to join Max Roach. On *No smokin'*, a brisk up-tempo swinger, Farmer is clearly working towards a greater use of space in his line than would customarily be associated with playing of a

Gillespie, Navarro or a Clifford Brown at such a tempo. It is interesting to note that this was a quite specific characteristic of the playing of the Chicago pianist Ahmad Jamal, whom both Farmer and Miles Davis admired. 'Sometimes that space is very scary,' Farmer observed. 'I think Ahmad was a very brave man because he would use space more than anyone else, just let the time go by and set up a tension by not playing.' [56] Farmer's playing also revealed a desire to move away from the quaver as the basic unit of his solos, making greater use of larger note values, such as his solo on *Soulville.* A year later, on *Further Explorations* from January 1958, his solo on *Ill wind* suggests his style was finding greater focus, beginning with a motif that is repeated, inverted, extended and varied, producing a solo of great clarity of thought and structural unity.

During 1958, Farmer was offered some dates by Gerry Mulligan when a planned reunion tour with Chet Baker failed to work out. According to Silver, Mulligan was able to offer Farmer more money [57] and by the spring of that year he had left. The new Mulligan group went into the recording studios in December that year to cut *What Is There to Say?* (Columbia [A] JCS 8116), but their appearance at the Newport Jazz Festival on 5 July provides an earlier examination of how Farmer was responding to the quite different environment on Mulligan's quartet. 'When playing with Horace,' he once explained, 'you had to stay on top of it, you couldn't lay back. Horace is very compelling, driving and forceful . . . With Mulligan I felt I would have to be harmonically more defined. I would have to create harmonic form more clearly in the improvisation than I would with Horace, where you have the piano to rely on.' [58] Although just a portion of *As catch can* showing Farmer with Mulligan (bar), Bill Crow (bs) and Dave Bailey (d) appears in the film *Jazz on a Summer's Day* directed by Bert Stern, [59] Mulligan's complete set can be heard on *Newport Jazz Festival 1958, July 3rd–6th* Vol. 2 (†Phontastic [Sd] NCD8814). Here, Farmer's playing had not quite acquired the poise of the studio session later in the year and sounds rushed on *As catch can*, for example, although it is interesting to hear motifs within his solo that would be developed and expanded in his later version.

A Portrait of Art Farmer was recorded at a time when he was making the transition from the extremely proactive rhythmic support of Silver to the minimalistic environs of Mulligan's pianoless quartet. Farmer bridges these polarities by opting for extremely passive rhythmic support from Jones, his brother and Haynes. This subdued rhythmic interaction would also characterize the quartet he would later co-lead with Jim Hall between 1962 and 1964. *Back in the cage* is a 12-bar blues that begins with Farmer's a cappella introduction which appears to lead straight into his improvisation. However, it is only his re-entry after Jones's piano solo later in the piece, when he freely restates the first 12 bars of his solo, which announces that the piece is not themeless. His tone is warm and round and is given greater emphasis by being recorded forward in the mix. It has a slightly breathy quality and on long tones he favours a carefully controlled terminal vibrato. His style is thoughtful, rarely using obvious phrases or cliché, and is consistently clear and unhurried, giving the impression of great self-restraint in the construction of his lines. His use of silence often invests his phrases with gravity, rather like an orator pausing to give dramatic impact to his pronouncements, particularly his final choruses after Jones's solo on piano, where the rhythm switches from *alla breve* to a straight-ahead four.

Within a year, Farmer would form the Jazztet, a sextet he co-led with Benny Golson. Here he plays Golson's *Stablemates*, a sophisticated 36-bar ABA tune with the A sections of 14 bars and the B section an orthodox eight bars. The tune makes extensive use of the ii-V-1 progression, which, other than the blues, is the most commonly recurring progression in contemporary jazz. After the theme statement by Farmer, Jones enters with a solo of elegance, and, like Farmer, is a musician determined to exile cliché from his playing. The trumpeter follows and although he would not switch to flugelhorn until 1962, his tone is so close to the larger-bored instrument that it is difficult to tell he had not already made transition. *The very thought of you* is a slow ballad performance using a cup mute, and reveals perhaps the deepest aspect of Farmer's art. By picking perfect notes and playing them with a burnished elegance, he distills hard bop down to a purely lyrical state. He is unsentimental yet moving, creating a powerful duality that is at the heart of any great ballad performance in jazz. *And now . . .* returns to the blues, this time a simple up-tempo riff leading into several choruses where he leans against the rhythm section using scalar runs and repeated motifs that scrupulously avoid public-domain blues licks. Haynes respects Farmer's air of subdued excitement during his exchanges of fours with tactful restraint; though he is normally an exuberant drummer, his solos are not a celebration of the self in the Max Roach mode, but tailored to suit the needs of this quietly introverted little quartet.

The genial swing of George Russell's *Nita* prompts an engagingly cautious Farmer to investigate a more expansive mood before retreating into well-crafted circumspection with a cup-muted treatment of the standard *By myself* with Jones echoing his mood of restraint. *Too late now*, a ballad performance played *largamente*, exploits his sumptuous tone in the lower and middle registers of his instrument, and only on the final notes does he actually invoke the brassier tone of the trumpet in contrast to the flugel-like breathiness he maintains throughout the album. *Earth* returns to the blues, a series of choruses in search of the economy of construction and melodic logic that in combination represented the kind of craftsmanship Farmer demanded of himself. The centre of his harmonic and rhythmic gravity always remained firmly within the grip of his intellect so that he was able to create a discrete, self-sufficient world of manageable emotions that did not trespass in the extremes of the human condition wherein lay life's dramas. The sober dignity of his playing thus remained on a level emotional keel so that any small fluctuation to port or starboard was felt more keenly than most improvisers – the subdued exuberance of *Nita* or his love for Miles Davis's playing on *Too late now* or the pleasure of swinging, pure and simple, on *Earth.* Yet these were exceptions. Farmer's search for perfection always remained within the self-imposed discipline of a style that strove for poetic understatement rather than flaunting bebop's inherent athleticism. That he managed to develop such a strong voice within such carefully proscribed parameters was no mean achievement. S.N.

Tadd Dameron

280 Fontainebleau

†Original Jazz Classics (A) OJCCD055–2, Esquire (E) 32–034

Kinny Dorham (tpt); Henry Coker (tbn); Sahib Shihab (alt); Joe Alexander (ten); Cecil Payne (bar); Dameron (p, comp); John Simmons (bs); Shadow Wilson (d). Hackensack, N.J., 9 March 1956.

Fontainebleau · *Delirium* · *Clean is the scene* · *Flossie Lou* · *Bulla-babe*

After writing for several lesser bands, Dameron began to attract attention, in his early 20s, with pieces for Harlan Leonard's Rockets. Several of these scores, like *A la Bridges* and *Dameron stomp* (RCA [F] PM43263, RCA [A] LPV531) of 1940, offer hints, particularly in their harmony, of the direction taken by music he recorded years later, as do the two versions of *Poor little plaything* on **196**. He gained real prominence, however, with contributions to the repertoire of Gillespie's large band, and some of these are discussed under **256b** and **315.** They contain certain bop characteristics, as, no more decisively, does Dameron's *Hot house* on **256a,** but he maintained that several of these pieces, including *Hot house,* were composed as early as 1939, before there were many general signs of the new style later to emerge.

This is to an extent plausible because, although he was to be much involved at one stage with the leading proponents of bop, it could later be seen that, like Monk, Dameron always followed a path of his own. Not only did the rhythmic dimension remain closer to swing than to the new music but, more positively, his beautiful melodies and sensitive instrumental textures, clothed in warm, unobtrusively personal tone colours embodied an older, more settled kind of lyricism. Perhaps it would be fairest to say that Dameron's path and that of bop crossed, or ran parallel, at a certain stage, but the marked individuality of nearly all his mature output had implications beyond this.

Averse to writing arrangements, even of his own pieces, he saw himself entirely as a jazz composer; that is to say, as one of those relatively few who, like Jelly Roll Morton or George Russell, have sought to fuse written and improvised elements. This was Dameron's gift and misfortune, for such a musician needs a nucleus of players who can serve as idiomatic interpreters while producing improvisations of their own which relate organically to the frameworks, and more, that he provides. This Dameron was scarcely able to do, although a rare, if substantial, exception was the band he led for 39 weeks in 1948 at the Royal Roost, New York; a selection of superlative performances from their broadcasts may be heard on Milestone (A) M47041, †Carrère (F) 98.196, the studio sessions being dealt with under **259–60**. Navarro aside, there were several other fairly obvious *in potentia* members of the band that he should have led over a period of years, notably Shihab on this 1956 date. Dameron's failure to maintain a vehicle for his continued musical thinking means that his gifts reached only partial fulfilment, that all we have are fragments, and the weightiest of these, even if the performances are by no means immaculate, are probably on the record detailed above.

In fact, the most accurate set of readings Dameron ever received on disc make up *The Magic Touch* (†Original Jazz Classics [A] OJCCD143–2), yet despite the presence of such musicians as Bill Evans and Johnny Griffin these often suffer from a kind of session-man glibness. That the 1956 interpretations are on the contrary full of the spirit of this music can be checked by comparing the two versions of *Fontainebleau*.

A long blues, *Bulla-babe* unites Dameron's writing, the contributions of his sidemen – with Shihab outstanding – and indeed his own keyboard work to exceptionally fine effect. *Delirium* is a solo vehicle mainly for Alexander, *Flossie Lou* exclusively for Coker, no doubt the best they ever had, though neither quite rises to the occasion despite the glowing ensembles in which they are set. Alexander's playing, while very capable, is simply not personal enough to justify his prominence here and he is completely surpassed by Dorham, whose splendid solo is the highlight. In *Flossie Lou* Coker's tone is rather fruity and even if Dameron was an essentially conservative stylist this piece would have been better suited to one of the bop trombonists. Coker's opening quotation from *The continental* suggests that he did not have much sense of occasion, but he fared better in the more 'basic' format of *Bulla-babe*.

As a soloist himself, Dameron was often accused, on something like the following lines, of perpetrating what is called 'arranger's piano' in which 'not much happens except chords are stated and perhaps slightly embellished or a theme gets stated without really being reinterpreted'. [60] Quite apart from what happens in *Bulla-babe*, *Clean is the scene*, along with *Dial 'B' for beauty* on his 1953 Prestige session (Prestige [A] 16008), might almost have been recorded to refute such charges. In Dameron's playing as in his writing, melody arising out of rich harmony is always the main point, but he makes a quite daring use of space in *Clean is the scene*. His improvising is framed with beautifully composed ensembles which, as on the other tracks, are strongly coloured though never to excess, the instrumental lines being closely woven yet each of interest in itself. Though admittedly of modest accomplishment, Dameron's playing has occasionally been influential. Hear, for instance, Freddy Jefferson in Lester Young's 1948 Royal Roost broadcast of *I cover the waterfront* (Affinity [E] AFF80, Sessions Disc [A] 103).

Like Ellington, who began with such ventures as *Creole rhapsody* (**88, 90**) and *Reminiscing in tempo* (**131b**), and some other jazz composers, Dameron occasionally attempted to escape the normal limitations of this music, as in his *Soulphony*, recorded by Gillespie's big band in 1948 (Queen Disc [It] 003, Ozone [A] LP17). In this present case the other tracks' emphasis on solo improvisation is balanced with *Fontainebleau*, a work that is both completely written out and played with much jazz feeling. Again like some of Ellington's longer pieces, it is programmatic to an extent, and undertakes to suggest, rather than overtly to portray, the palace referred to in the title and the surrounding forest. Of course, it is Dameron's way to seek his results though suggestion, not direct statement.

The score cannot be analysed here, [61] but thematic cross-references between the three linked sections result in a fairly satisfying overall structure. And there is genuine variety of thematic invention, the main ideas of 'Le forêt' and 'Les cygnes', for instance, being quite different from each other yet both typical of their composer. The writing for the ensemble is also characteristically effective, the two above themes, for example, being introduced in low register and reappearing in high. These and similar changes of emphasis work via a slowly increasing tempo to produce an impression of increasing brightness as *Fontainebleau* moves from a sombre opening to a positive, almost optimistic, conclusion.

Dameron was given opportunities for very few such achievements, and so attention should be drawn to the recordings of Philly Joe Jones's Dameronia band. Its repertoire was almost entirely made up of Dameron's compositions in his orchestrations or adaptations thereof. *To Tadd with Love* (Uptown [A] UP2711) dates from 1982, *Look, Stop and Listen* (UP2715) from the following year. Again the performances are untidy, but they demonstrate that Dameron's music was still viable in the 1980s, perhaps beyond. The record discussed above first appeared as *Fontainebleau* but was misleadingly renamed *Dameronia* (Prestige [A] 16007) and *The Memorial Album* (Prestige [A] 7842), only to have its original name restored on Original Jazz Classics. M.H.

Bop Hardens

Certain aspects of bop were intensified at the expense of others and in general the music became darker, earthier, more overtly hard-driving, with a more explicit emphasis on blues.

Thad Jones

281 The Magnificent Thad Jones

†Blue Note (Eu) CDP746 814–2

Jones (tpt); Billy Mitchell (ten); Barry Harris (p); Percy Heath (bs); Max Roach (d). Hackensack, N.J., 14 July 1956.

April in Paris · Billie-doo · If I love again · Thedia

As above, minus Mitchell. Same date.

If someone had told me · I've got a crush on you

Jones (tpt); Kenny Burrell (g). Hackensack, N.J., 9 July 1956.

Something to remember you by

Big bands loomed large in the life of Thad Jones, obscuring his credentials as a trumpeter (and later cornetist) of consummate improvising skills. His first important job was in Detroit in the latter part of 1950 in a band that was led by Billy Mitchell and also included the pianist Tommy Flanagan, the bassist James Richardson and Thad's brother, the drummer Elvin Jones. The band lasted into 1953 and recorded a few sides that year for Dee Gee, [62] although the date has been given incorrectly as 1948. When Jones decided to try his luck in New York, his advanced ideas and remarkable technique quickly impressed musicians, not least Charles Mingus, who on hearing him wrote: 'I've just heard the greatest trumpet player that I have ever heard in this life.' [63] Jones quickly moved into Mingus's orbit, recording *The Fabulous Thad Jones* (Debut [A] DLP12) on the bassist's independently produced label in August 1954 and following it with a quartet album in March 1955 that included the bassist himself and Max Roach (Debut [A] DLP17). However, although he seemed poised to make a name for himself at the cutting edge of jazz, two months later, in May 1955, he took up an offer to join Count Basie's orchestra, where he remained until late February 1963.

Jones soon made an indelible mark with the Basie band when in July 1955 they recorded an arrangement by the organist Wild Bill Davis of *April in Paris.* Jones's solo began with a cheeky *Pop goes the weasel* quotation that wrote itself into the history books. Subsequently, the number was never played without reproducing Jones's solo note for note. Two years after leaving Basie, in December 1965, Jones formed the Thad Jones/Mel Lewis Jazz Orchestra and in the last year of his life conducted the Basie ghost band. Effectively, his association with big bands since the mid-1950s as much as his reputation as a composer and arranger of great distinction for the Jazz Orchestra detracted from his reputation as an improvising musician. In fact, once the Basie band claimed him, his appearances with small bands on record were few and far between, further obscuring his reputation as an instrumentalist, something that the valuable reissue *The Complete Blue Note/United Artists/Roulette recordings of Thad Jones* (†Mosaic [A] MD3–172) sought to rectify in 1997. The first of only three albums for the Blue Note label was *Detroit–New York Junction* (Blue Note [J] K18P–9124), recorded in March 1956, which all but reconvened the old Billy Mitchell band from the beginning of the decade. Mitchell, who would later also be inducted into Basie's ranks, again shared the line-up for *The Magnificent Thad Jones*, which initially had difficulty in living up to its hyperbolic title.

The session was originally called for 9 July, but four of the five titles recorded that day were rejected; only the duet with Burrell was useable. A further session was scheduled for five days later which delivered the goods. With *April in Paris* selling well for Basie on the Verve label, it was decided to cover the number for a single release and as a part of the album. It opens with a haunting vamp played by unison piano and bass against Roach's brushes. Jones and Mitchell share the theme before Jones's solo, beginning – of course – with his *Pop goes the weasel* quote as he claims the number as his own, showing just what he *could* do with it after Basie's request that he play his solo exactly as recorded night after night. Perhaps the most striking aspect of his playing was a highly refined melodic sense of construction and a big round tone that remained even throughout every register of his instrument. His solo emerges as a logical flow of interconnecting ideas assembled with clarity of construction and originality of execution. Throughout Jones employs subtle rhythmic variety in his phrases and flashes of harmonic daring that suggest, despite relatively few recording opportunities under his own name, a player of maturity and originality.

Billie-doo is a 12-bar blues with a cut-time feel to the theme and a secondary theme inspired by Richard Carpenter's *Walkin'*. Mitchell is a sound, resolute soloist comfortable in the hard-bop idiom; Harris is neat, economical if uncontroversial. *If I love again* is a number associated with Clifford Brown, appearing on *Study in Brown* (EmArcy [E] 6336708) with Max Roach from February 1955. Here it serves to show how different the two trumpeters were; the unusual construction of Jones's often angular melodic shapes, the variation of his rhythmic line and his use of space in particular were quite unlike Brown's approach to improvisation.

Perhaps it was the sudden and unexpected death of Brown on 26 June 1956, some two weeks before the first of these sessions, that explains Roach's singularly detached drumming. On *Thedia*, for example, an easy-swinging Jones original, he is boorishly metronomic, plugging away with a basic ride pattern near the cup of his cymbal throughout Jones's long solo. He maintains the same volume level throughout, taking no account of light and shade or rhythmic variety and failing to respond in any way to Jones's wholly original lines. This unyielding and unsupportive aspect of his ensemble playing is the one weak feature of this album and indeed is a criticism that can be levelled at Roach's drumming in general. For all the technical expertise and innovation he brought to his solos, his ensemble playing often emphasized the purely mechanical aspects of time-keeping to the exclusion of emotional involvement.

The final tracks deal with Jones's impressive handling of ballads. *If someone had told me* begins with a *rubato* statement of the melody, with just Harris's accompaniment before Roach and Heath enter in tempo. Here, as in *I've got a crush on you* and *Something to remember you by*, Jones is both sensitive and lyrical in the construction of his solos; there is variety in his use of original melodic motifs, use of tension and release in his skilful use of double time, all allied to a secure rhythmic feel, despite the very slow tempos. Jones's decision to join Basie, a move which removed him from the burgeoning hard-bop movement that was just beginning to gather momentum, robbed this period of jazz of a particularly distinctive voice. However, the financial security, after a year of scuffling on the highly competitive New York music scene, enabled him to raise two children; such mundane tasks also come the way of jazz musicians.

His work with the Jazz Orchestra, the big band he co-led with the drummer Mel Lewis, equally placed him apart from the main thrust of jazz during the 1960s, 1970s and early 1980s. Yet as albums by the band (not to mention **462**) reveal, Jones continued to develop as a brass musician, turning more and more frequently to the bigger-bored, broader-toned cornet, producing an even more resoundingly full tone than that he obtained from the trumpet. His solo work with the band could often be breathtaking, and albums by the band are well worth seeking out. [64] They underline what a remarkable, yet sadly underrated, soloist Thad Jones was. S.N.

Sonny Rollins

282 Saxophone Colossus and More

Prestige (A) HB6013 (2 LPs), *†Prestige (A) VDJ1501

Clifford Brown (tpt); Rollins (ten); Richie Powell (p); George Morrow (bs); Max Roach (d). Hackensack, N.J., 22 March 1956.

I feel a song coming on · Pent-up house · Kiss and run

Rollins (ten); Tommy Flanagan (p); Doug Watkins (bs); Roach (d). Hackensack, N.J., 22 June 1956.

You don't know what love is · St Thomas · Strode rode · Blue seven · Moritat

Kinny Dorham (tpt); Rollins (ten); Wade Legge (p); Morrow (bs); Roach (d). Hackensack, N.J., 5 October 1956.

I've grown accustomed to her face · Kids know · The house I live in · Star eyes

The imperfections of Rollins's earliest recorded playing – the 1949 date on **260** and **261**, for example – are obvious, and it is rewarding to follow his growing mastery of both improvisation and the tenor saxophone on his sessions of 1949–54. The 1951 *I know* (†Original Jazz Classics [A] OJCCD011–2) was the first performance to point at all clearly in the direction that he would follow, this being succeeded by landmarks such as *Friday the 13th* with Monk in 1953 (†OJCCD059–2), *Doxy* with Miles Davis (†OJCCD245–2) and his own *Solid* with Dorham (†OJCCD058–2) in 1954. By the following year forces were gathering in Rollins for an outburst, and this came with an extraordinary sequence of records beginning with *Worktime* (†OJCCD007–2) and ending only in the summer of 1958 with the *Big Brass* LP (MGM [E] C776, Metrojazz [A] E1002). During this period he contributed at a similar level to dates led by Monk and Davis, and was from November 1955 until May 1957 a regular member of the band that Roach led, at first jointly with Clifford Brown.

This was a sustained creative effort such as few in the history of jazz could hope to match and it is not surprising that Rollins so much dominated his own sessions. Starting with the 1957 *Way Out West* (†Original Jazz Classics [A] OJCCD337–2), the piano was sometimes not used, and later that year he set down *It could happen to you*, his first entirely unaccompanied improvisation (†OJCCD029–2). Others followed, such as *Body and soul* in the *Big Brass* collection, and decades later he recorded an entire disc in this format. Yet on the sessions detailed above Roach has almost as vital a role as his leader. The drummer's partnership with Brown caught the imagination of such audience as jazz has, but his involvement with Rollins broke more new ground and was scarcely less significant that his earlier teaming with Parker. The enhancing richness of, say, Roach's commentary on several passages in the tenor improvisation on *Pent-up house* is the fruit of his working alongside Rollins in a regular band.

Parker, acting in part through Roach, was the most crucial of several influences on the young Rollins, especially in terms of rhythmic variation. He also prompted a flexible interpretation of the underlying chord sequence and, if less directly, a striking freedom of phrase structure. To this expressive armoury Rollins added what for the 1950s were uncommonly diverse inflections of instrumental tone, but there were two more fundamental rejections of earlier methods, one arising out of the other. Firstly, the best statements of a Parker, or indeed of an Armstrong, sound definitive, nearly inevitable, whereas Rollins's seem more open-ended, even suggesting at full flood, as in *Strode rode*, the 'stream of consciousness' approach of some modern literature. Almost anything might happen next. Certain of his more extravagant rhythmic departures, both with and against Roach, his ironic use of the clichés of lesser men, and his most outrageous tonal distortions should obviously be seen as outbreaks of what was, with Monk's, the sharpest sense of humour ever to reach expression in jazz. Yet beyond all that lies a considerable paradox.

As during those years Rollins became more expansive, so he evidently grew more concerned with musical order, formal discipline. This presumably arose out of greater freedom entailing larger risks, a bigger chance of coherence being lost. As a result – and this was his second departure from bop orthodoxy – Rollins became more consciously interested in improvising on melodies rather than just on their chords. In the second chorus of *You don't know what love is* new ideas are interspersed with echoes of the original tune; in *Moritat* references to Weill's melody in the improvisation are usually clear; and again in *The house I live in*. Sometimes he broke a tune down into separate motives and worked on these individually, as in *Wagon wheels* in the *Way out West* collection. He tried other methods, as the modified rondo layout of *Blues for Philly Joe* (**286**) suggests, but a motivic approach was resorted to most often and the finest, or at least the most clearly demonstrated, instance is *Blue seven*.

Rollins had undertaken something comparable with *Vierd blues* with Davis three months earlier (†OJCCD071–2), but this second attempt received a detailed analysis by Gunther Schuller. [65] Indeed, to an extent that never occurred before or since in jazz commentary, *Blue seven* and Schuller's dissection of it became forever joined, like a planet and its orbiting moon, one scarcely mentioned without the other. There will be no present attempt at summarizing the findings of that essay, which is still required reading, beyond objecting to its assertion that Rollins with *Blue seven* introduced a new dimension to jazz. Cases like *Vierd blues* notwithstanding, he did not often use the rather exact variation technique employed here, and although such music offers almost infinite scope for hermetic interpretation, Schuller's analysis by no means accounts for everything played in the three *Blue seven* tenor solos, for there is other material that can be traced in his earlier work. Further, Monk and Morton should be enough to remind us that motivic development, or 'thematic improvisation' as Schuller terms it, was not unknown in jazz.

But even if *Blue seven* did not match all the claims made for it and certainly did not institute a new method for jazz improvisation, there can be no doubt that Rollins's solos demand to be heard as complete entities to an extent that Parker's, and most others', rarely had. And in his last three *Blue seven* choruses almost everything does arise from the performance's opening motif, and the result is music of absolutely exceptional intensity – up to and including the quiet ending. There could be no better confirmation of Rollins's status as the most important jazz saxophonist between Parker and Ornette Coleman, the most important, though not the most influential, tenor between Lester Young and Albert Ayler.

It should be remembered that Morton and Monk were used to working in a compositional situation whereas Rollins did it all while improvising, and without sacrificing swing or rhythmic drive. An admirable solo like Oliver's in *Dippermouth blues* (**44**), based on two motifs, is rather obviously a set piece; and Rollins had to venture far beyond the time limits of a 10-inch 78-rpm disc. Nor did the spontaneity preclude the musical intelligence that enabled him, for example, to take good advantage of the opening *Blue seven* idea's tonal ambiguity: only when Flanagan enters are we sure what key the piece is in. Among the most telling points made by this classic of jazz improvisation is that what matters is not Rollins's prodigal invention or magnificent saxophone technique but the original thinking that so exhilaratingly directs these. Not that masterpieces ever give away all their secrets.

The earliest performances here are by an edition of the Roach–Brown band, an overrated group despite the talents involved. There is no point in denying the bombast of the ending to *I feel a song coming on*, which does not stem from Rollins. He on the contrary shows an almost Olympian ability not merely to think coherently at this unforgiving tempo but to do so constructively in the long term. The June session needed a ballad, and *You don't know what love is* stands as a conclusive answer to the once current notion that Rollins's clarity of thought had been won at the cost of undue detachment, even coldness. Here especially the dynamic level shifts according to the character of the phrases, all too much jazz being played at an unvarying volume. Rollins's sound was caught with particular realism at the Hackensack studios, and his tone, above all in pieces like *You don't know*, is shown to have an acutely expressive resonance.

Moritat, *The house I live in* and most notably *Strode rode* are climaxed with superb exchanges of four-bar phrases between Rollins and Roach. The last of these items especially has the leader going at full tilt from the first bar of the second chorus. Several of these pieces, including *Blue seven*, show Flanagan to have been an apt foil to the greater intensity of Roach and Rollins. The ¾ *Kids know* and *St Thomas* include drum solos that are phenomenal, even for Roach. The latter 16-bar theme, though credited to Rollins on the label, is actually a traditional melody called *Fire down there* which he may have picked up from Randy Weston's recording of the previous year (Riverside [A] RLP12–203). Rollins's 1956 performance should be compared with the 1959 version on **349**. The entire body of his Prestige recordings will be found on the seven CDs of †Prestige (A) 7PCD4407–2. M.H.

Johnny Griffin

283 Introducing Johnny Griffin

†Blue Note (A) B21Y46536, Blue Note (A) BST81533

Griffin (ten); Wynton Kelly (p); Curly Russell (bs); Max Roach (d). New York City, 17 April 1956.

Mil dew · *Chicago calling* · *These foolish things* · *The boy next door* · *Nice and easy* · *It's all right with me* · *Loverman*

Leaping out of *Mil dew*'s thunderous drum opening, Griffin comes at us full tilt, lines rearing and dipping over a simple accompaniment. The tone is tough but there is lyricism, a singing sense. The fearless vigour was no doubt encouraged by early postwar membership of the Lionel Hampton band alongside Arnett Cobb; but to identify the main source of the vocabulary (and the lyricism) one need not follow Alun Morgan's old advice to play 'any Griffin LP . . . at 45 rpm' in order to recognize 'the indebtedness to Bird'. [66] Griffin is sometimes linked, rather too glibly, to a strand of hard-bop saxophone playing that made positive truce between the styles of Coleman Hawkins and Lester Young. Even at a period so redolent of change as the mid-1950s, it is clear that this 28-year-old is very much under Parker's spell. When he attempts a personal extension of Parker's language, as, say, in the mid-tempo *Chicago calling*, it becomes clear that his debt to the great pioneer is less a rhythmic than a melodic one, and it is not always easy to decide whether he sometimes loses the rhythmic tension which is part and parcel of Parker's style because he has not grasped the rhythmic secret, or whether he is forging a rhythmic tension of his own. The best object for studying that rather subtle question is the very fast *It's all right with me*. Parker himself seldom recorded at such a speed, and whatever of his subtleties of rhythmic emphasis Griffin may have learned seem here to be going by the board. Yet the quickness of thought is impressive.

In the number just referred to, Kelly, whose light control in *Mil dew* makes him sound rather ill at ease, copes better with the headlong scamper by adopting a narrower range of melodic invention. He is more confident with easy-going things like *Chicago calling* and *Nice and easy*. His wry opening to *These foolish things* heralds a solo in which Griffin gets closer to sounding a diction of his own, a broader vibrato, idiosyncracies of tonguing and keying, extended notes probing for drama. This is not the only kind of improvisation on the record that asks for more rhythmic enterprise in accompaniment; though Griffin gets it unfailingly from Roach, and usually from Kelly, he seldom receives it from a generally rather wooden Russell. Witness the contrast between the tenorist's spry multiplications towards the end of *These foolish things* and the bassist's stolid plucking. Conversely, Griffin's challenges do sometimes touch upon awkwardness; and Russell, responding to Kelly's neatly turned figures in *The boy next door*, shows the mettle of a bop veteran. With Griffin any awkwardness may be taken as betokening a keenness for fresh discoveries. In later times he would develop further expressive skills, and if he came, however unfairly, to be regarded as a hard-bop 'epithet' rather than as an individual stylist, that may be less to do with the nature of his gifts than with the inconclusive character of the 'school' he is taken to represent. There is evidence of his example having had its effect upon the young lions of later jazz periods. [67]

Loverman might be heard with some reference to a famous 1945 recording which had Parker as one of Sarah Vaughan's accompanists, and at which Russell was present and playing. Griffin's tribute to Parker has a fine variety of interest, and his companions share an admirable sense of occasion which really has nothing whatever to do with nostalgia. E.T.

Hampton Hawes

284 **Four!**

†Original Jazz Classics (A) OJCCD165–2, Boplicity (E) COP22

Hawes (p); Barney Kessel (g); Red Mitchell (bs); Shelly Manne (d). Los Angeles, 27 January 1958.

Yardbird suite · There will never be another you · Bow jest · Sweet Sue · Love is just around the corner · Like someone in love · Up blues

Six months almost to the day before the above session, it was suggested that 'The basic task facing [Hawes] is to rebuild completely the [Bud] Powell tradition of jazz piano from the rhythmic shambles to which it has descended; furthermore to place the "horn" line in its proper context in relation to the larger concept of really "playing the piano".' [68] By 'playing the piano' John Mehegan, from one of whose articles the above quotation comes, meant utilizing the instrument's full resources, but Hawes, though an accomplished pianist, was never a virtuoso and repeatedly stated that his main source of inspiration was Parker (rather than Powell). As a youth he performed with the great alto saxophonist during his 1945–7 stay on the American West Coast and this indeed was a formative experience. (They can be heard together on *Dee Dee's dance* [Spotlite (E) 107, Jazz Anthology (A) JA5108].) In fact the ancestry of his music in Parker's innovations and – at least by implication – in Powell's approach to the keyboard is obvious, yet the oft-repeated simplification that he offered merely piano transcriptions of Parker's lines misses several important points. Hawes's voice soon became his own.

Though not always evident in his later output of the 1960s and particularly the 1970s, a driving exuberance characterized his improvising at the time the above record was made. His phrases at fast tempos are busy yet nearly always with real musical purpose, the lines precisely executed, the rhythm exact but relentlessly flowing. As this implies, Hawes's touch, while sprightly, is percussive, and his often fierce accents give further point to his phrases' melodic content. All this decisiveness is, in his best moments, the vehicle of an irresistible succession of ideas. *Love is just around the corner*, for example, includes an especially lucid solo in which one idea arises directly out of another with seeming inevitability.

Hawes is always praised above all for his blues playing, yet *Up blues*, evidently recorded at the end of the session, is the weakest track here. His playing presents an obvious series of rapid-fire formulas, and there is more real invention in Kessel's solo. Perhaps the indisputable blues element in Hawes's work acts most beneficially when he is not playing the blues. Indeed, there sometimes is a productive tension between blues feeling and the relative sophistication of ballads with their larger harmonic vocabulary. At the same time parallels with Horace Silver are obvious, in his touch and particularly his timing, although Hawes is more boppish and, for some listeners, far more engaging.

Among the 13 LPs he made for the Contemporary label, *Four!* comes halfway, seventh in the succession. The inclusion of a guitar, besides bringing the slightly underrated Kessel into the picture, breaks the monotony of Hawes's (and countless other pianists') normal trio instrumentation. In fact he had employed a guitarist before – the excellent Jim Hall – on his three 1956 *All-Night Session* discs (†Original Jazz Classics [A] OJCCD638–40), but to less integrated purpose. *Yardbird suite* probably best demonstrates Kessel's value as an additional voice, in the theme statement, his solo after Hawes's, and in the fours. Such exchanges of four-bar phrases are a stale device on all too many dates, yet here the pianist and guitarist strike sparks off each other on track after track, the sequence in *Sweet Sue* being especially good. There is something of the blues in Kessel's boppish, post-Christian style and this of course chimes tellingly with certain aspects of Hawes's work.

Often the listener feels rather than hears Manne's contribution to this music, which, for all the pianist's aggressive leadership, is quite largely a matter of interplay between keyboard, guitar and bass. Though not inspiring as a soloist, especially with a bow, Mitchell functions superbly as a member of the ensemble and can be heard to particular advantage during Kessel's solos, for instance on *Bow jest*. Hawes also accompanies exceptionally well and this performance displays the teamwork at its absolute best. Elsewhere, too, the keyboard punctuations of Mitchell's solos show unusual imagination, *Yardbird suite* again being a good example. Note how Kessel's distant accompaniment lends a further dimension to the *Sweet Sue* bass solo.

Like many West Coast pianists at that time, Hawes had a marked preference for quick tempos, *Like someone in love* being the only piece taken slowly here. It embodies a good feeling for keyboard texture as he by this time had eliminated most of the mechanical arpeggios and scales that had spoiled many of his earlier attempts of this kind; and most of the other ascending cocktail-piano figurations have gone too. This is indeed a satisfying instance of the post-Powell rhapsodic vein, and worth any number of fast, frantic and mechanical blues. M.H.

Sonny Clark

285 Cool Struttin'

†Blue Note (E) CDP746 513–2, Blue Note (A) BST81588

Art Farmer (tpt); Jackie McLean (alt); Clark (p); Paul Chambers (bs); Philly Joe Jones (d). New York City, 5 January 1958.

Cool struttin' · Blue minor · Sippin' at Bell's · Deep night

Here is a session providing revealing indications of how hard bop was progressing by the late 1950s and also of how it was able to reinterpret material closely associated with bop pioneers, in this case with Parker and Powell. The paradox in the album title is apposite, and the proof of its aptness is heard in the eponymous number, in the one that follows it, and in much of the improvisation throughout the record. A splendid relaxation merges with exultation in the almost neoclassical firming-up of melodic shapes which in hard bop grew in counteraction to the more fevered expressions of early bop. The solos of Farmer and McLean in *Cool struttin'* are rhythmically laggard yet certainly not hesitant in imagination. Clark's piano lines are sprightly but firm. It is instructive to hear how the group draws its feeling from elements inherent in Clark's style. Critics, when they have remembered him at all, have often and too glibly bracketed his name with hard-bop heroes like Horace Silver (**350**) and Hampton Hawes (**284**); but he may be seen in retrospect as a rather more eclectic thinker, frequently capable of originality. In the *Cool struttin'* solo there is a small hint of an avowed admiration for Lennie Tristano (**294**).

As with McLean, there is a good deal in Clark's vocabulary which derived from a stylized interpretation of the blues, though neither with pianist nor altoist did this ever become obsessional, as it did with other contemporary musicians. *Blue minor* (not to be confused with Coltrane's *Blues minor* on **422**) is composed by Clark in 16-bar song form. There is a lot of the blues in McLean's long solo, and also in Clark's chordal support. Farmer sounds more interested in exploiting the minor mode's invitations to phrasal angularities of more personal motivation. Clark in solo is again relaxed and committed at once, receiving well-nigh perfect support from Chambers and Jones. The bassist plucks a terse solo against Clark's high-register tone clusters.

The leaping agitation of bop is brought back with Miles Davis's *Sippin' at Bell's*. Clark prances in, revealing a distinct debt to Powell, who was probably his most admired influence. Homage is paid with a personal touch, both digital and intellectual. A tough, writhing essay from McLean pays equally unslavish tribute to Parker. Farmer's vividly coloured phrases are complemented by a bright commentary from the pianist. Altoist and trumpeter each solos a second time. Clark is quietly dry in accompaniment, but exuberantly gleeful in his additional solo.

The mid-tempo *Deep night* is clear Powell reminiscence. Closely recorded brushwork from Jones abets Clark's first solo, emphasizing lightness. Farmer would have darker timbre, more serious architectures; yet he too swings back, as complement rather than paradox, to optimistic gestures. McLean utters poignant complaints, Oriental phrases here and there, drawing out the character of the tune. Clark adds some delicately formed observations, before Jones, a drummer both responsive and thoughtful, contributes a totally appropriate brief monologue. The piano coda is Powell undiluted.

Clark's great merits as an accompanist (he was Dinah Washington's pianist when he reached New York from the West Coast in 1957) can be sampled in items by two very different saxophonists, Serge Chaloff (**310**) and Dexter Gordon (**348**). Bill Evans was one of several pianists who admired Clark for his achievements; achievements that would, considering his patent openness to the new, have led to further stylistic developments had he not died in 1963 at the age of 31. E.T.

Sonny Rollins

286 Newk's Time

†Blue Note (E) CDP784 001–2, Blue Note (A) BST84001

Rollins (ten); Wynton Kelly (p); Doug Watkins (bs); Philly Joe Jones (d). New York City, 28 September 1958.

Tune up · *Asiatic raes* · *Wonderful wonderful* · *The surrey with the fringe on top* · *Blues for Philly Joe* · *Namely you*

Commenting favourably upon an Ornette Coleman track played to him in a 1962 blindfold test, Rollins remarked: 'Rhythm is the most necessary part, the prerequisite for the jazz musician – the positive element. But, of course, harmony is the negative through which the positive must exert itself.' [69] How would this powerfully influential saxophonist have applied these rather enigmatic words to the musical self-disclosures which he was achieving during the later 1950s? *Newk's Time* (highlighting a Rollins nickname) was one of several albums recorded not long before his sabbatical period of now famous nocturnal visits to the Williamsburg Bridge for solitary practising, celebrated in February 1963 by *The Bridge* (RCA/Bluebird [A] ND824696). A month before *Newk's Time* there had been the Music Inn session with the MJQ (†Atlantic [A] SD1299); earlier still he had chosen for *The Freedom Suite* (†Original Jazz Classics [A] OJCCD067–2) a pianoless trio format like that used for the 1957 *Way Out West* (†Original Jazz Classics [A] OJCCD337). For *The surrey with the fringe on top* Kelly withdraws, but although Rollins's liking for that set-up was to be re-emphasized by the fine trios he recorded in Sweden in March 1959 (**349**), it seems to have applied in the present case for the sake of the presentation of a particular number; and it should not be taken as comment upon the nature of the other pieces. Rollins is not noticeably less at liberty when improvising with the complete rhythm section.

In general the saxophonist seems to be one for whom the deliberate pursuit of musical freedom within order and the exercise of a richly humorous instinct are of leading importance. As his idiosyncracies developed over this period, critics divided. Those who would have preferred him to develop further the Parker-based style they had heard from him in the earlier 1950s disliked the rhythmic curiosities and the cavalier approach to both beat and harmony. Portents of such things were already sounding, though, in Rollins's *Pent-up house* solo back in the Roach–Brown quintet (**282**). Others, particularly in the wake of the *Blue seven* session (also **282**), produced enthusiastically admiring analyses of his procedures and improvising methods which appear to have caused the man some degree of alarm. Perhaps he began to feel rather like the centipede effectively immobilized when asked which set of legs moved first. He vowed to disregard his further record reviews.

Newk's Time finds this increasingly self-contained jazz master with natural insouciance unthreatened, and playing some of his best music along with the admirable Kelly, Watkins – a hard-bop bassist who was to die short of suitable fame – and Jones, whose drumming scarcely suffers in comparison with that of Roach, Rollins's best-remembered colleague.

As the speedy *Tune up* (composed by Eddie Vinson, though usually credited to Miles Davis) gets under way the influences of Parker and Dexter Gordon peer through from the tenor statement. At first there is less staccato emphasis and tonal distortion, but a more radical variation of phrase lengths becomes evident before very long, and dissevered figures appear like mocking codes which only half conceal Rollins's impish messages. Kelly, with spurting figures and beautifully sustained threads, presents the first of several solos in the session which more than prove his worth as a pianist both strong and sensitive. (He was soon to join Davis.)

Asiatic raes, an ambiguous 3/4, finds Rollins sticking closer to his theme, but swirling his temporal multiplications a little recklessly against the beat. In *Wonderful, wonderful* there are those running passages of extemporization which, in Rollins as in Kelly, do acknowledge recent proving grounds. There is also much that is regardant of bop, in both theme and variations, during *Blues for Philly Joe*: yet here, as in the previous piece, there are brief and enigmatically related tenor signals heightening a sense that the overall conception aimed for is an achievement of greater rhythmic freedom. Those critics who were anxious for Rollins's jazz soul might have wanted to regard the daring means by which he sought better elbow room as a series of blunders masquerading as inspiration; but most of the time Rollins knew exactly what he was up to.

Much of his freedom is due to his uncanny ability to hold entire the basic material of any piece at any given point within it. This has often enabled him to recharacterize well-known themes in ways that (as, for example, *How high the moon?* on **349**) can be distinctly unnerving for the listener familiar with the tune. The mutual attentiveness of his two team-mates in *The surrey with the fringe on top* assists his daring in inventing, mostly within small compass, successions of variously shaped motifs, some of them inverted and partially reversed. In addition, the tune itself has simple, repetitive elements which he can use for the sake of his rhythmic and sonic game. Here, with the pianist absent, he is able the better to work out his variations *in extenso*, taking more liberties in his attitudes to the harmonic sequence, referring to this as often in retrospect or in prospect as in direct respect. Thus the relaxed mixture of the negative and the positive which his style was becoming may be recognized the more vividly.

The style adopted for slow numbers like the song *Namely you*, deep-toned and closely involved, is not a wholehearted identification with the more rhapsodic players of an earlier jazz generation, yet it abuts upon their territory. Kelly is given the first variation here, and Jones is allowed a little of the playfulness of which he has had better rations in other parts of the session. E.T.

J. R. Monterose

287 Straight Ahead

†Xanadu (A) 32DIW303CD, †Fresh Sounds (Sp) FSRCD201

J. R. Monterose (ten); Tommy Flanagan (p); Jimmy Garrison (bs); Pete La Roca (d). Englewood Cliffs, N.J., 24 November 1959.

Straight ahead · Violets for your furs · Chafic · I remember Clifford · Green Street scene · You know that · Short bridge

The staccato opening of *Straight ahead* is not the only thing here that shows Monterose's admiration for Rollins, yet there is in addition a healthy number of things which prove this imaginative tenorist's personal gift. At the fast tempo of the first number, as the glancing, lightly executed, and almost *duettino* lines of Monterose and Garrison proceed, it is clear that the tenorist is less dependent upon staccato execution than he had been in the 1956 *J. R. Monterose* album (Blue Note [A] BLP1536). When his tone differs most from hard-bop toughness – there is breathiness and increased vibrato in *Violets for your furs* and *I remember Clifford* – there are admittedly phrasal echoes of Rollins and, in the second piece here cited, a ranging scope of melody-building which honours the same influence.

Clarity of tonguing and light sound in the waltzlike *Chafic* go with subtle control of minute contrasts within Monterose's melodic syntax: a sense of interior dialogue and of a passion which increases, though with a wry deceptiveness. In the lively *Green Street scene*, too, the phraseology is cunning, the clauses used repetitively, twisted, spun out, incidental challenges being answered by La Roca, who here, in contrast to the reverberant close of *Straight ahead*, sounds a bit distant. The drummer engages in exchange also with Flanagan and Garrison, the latter drawing wine-dark bowed 'brushstrokes' and scattering lightly plucked notes.

It is Garrison who abets Monterose in a rocking ¾ illusion to usher in *You know that*, wherein variations of tenor tone plus a great deal of break-swapping build a feeling of pleasing enigma. Both Monterose and Flanagan exhibit much skill in reconciling the mocking riddles within a basic continuum.

In terms of improvising distinction this is as much Flanagan's record as it is the leader's. The piano solos in *Straight ahead* and *Short bridge* are beautifully eloquent and shapely, and the pianist's supportive enterprise can hardly be lauded too highly. Where judicious economy or quiet lack of presumption are called for, Flanagan still can tickle the ears. Garrison is consistently pleasing, too. His skills make his early semi-obscurity puzzling, and his imminent discovery by Coleman and Coltrane easy to understand.

Early in the year of his notable Blue Note record Monterose played with Charles Mingus and also with Teddy Charles (**378**). He reacted unfavourably to the experimentations of Mingus and sidestepped back into the hard-bop milieu under Kinny Dorham's leadership in the Jazz Prophets. That he was quite capable of achieving a striking variety of thought in such a context is evident; but he was unable to sustain a prominent musical career although he did record again in 1979 (Uptown [A] 2702).

When the above record first appeared it was titled *The Message* and was on Jaro (A) JAM5004. Michael James's assessment in *Modern Jazz: The Essential Records 1945–70* (see Bibliography) gives it a different date from the above, namely October 1960. E.T.

Duke Jordan

288 Flight to Jordan

†Savoy (A) 650 118, Savoy (A) MG12149

Jordan (p). New York City, 10 October 1955.
Summertime

Percy Heath (bs); Art Blakey (d) added. Same date.
Forecast · *Sultry eve* · *They can't take that away from me* · *A night in Tunisia*

Eddie Bert (tbn); Cecil Payne (bar) added. New York City, 20 November 1955.
Cu-ba · *Two loves* · *Flight to Jordan* · *Scotch blues* · *Yesterdays*

Listening to Jordan's work with Parker (1947–8: **257–8**) and Getz (1952: **299**), it is hard to give credit to the information that Miles Davis and Max Roach had a low opinion of the pianist's musical abilities. Davis recreates, with routine obscenities, old conflicts in his *Autobiography*; [70] but the evidence of the records is that Jordan's contributions were more than apt. He ran into difficulties with Getz too, it seems, [71] yet his playing with the tenorist's quintet is consistently pleasing and inventive. Clearly, though, whether the reason lay in the attitudes of colleagues, in the unusual prompting of his own aspiration, or in some extra-musical impediment, something was amiss. His jazz career has been discontinuous, and for periods he followed nonmusical employment.

This album, titled *The Street Swingers* when it first appeared, features Jordan in the context of quintet and trio. All his recorded essays outside the trio format have been notable; but trio recordings form the most substantial part of his preserved body of work. The first of those was in January 1954 for the Swing label, Gene Ramey and Lee Abrams being his supporters then (†Vogue [F] 655010). In March 1955, with Oscar Pettiford and Kenny Clarke, he played his first session for Savoy (MG12145) which included a version of *Jordu*, his best-known composition, which, as *Minor escamp*, had already graced the Swing (Vogue) LP. Twice, in fact, for on that date Gigi Gryce was added for an exact rerun of the trio's programme. During the 1970s Jordan was able to record many of his compositions for the Danish SteepleChase label (e.g. †SteepleChase [D] SCCD31011 and 31135). In all those later sessions the freshness found in these 1955 performances is quite undiminished.

Forecast runs at mid-tempo, the piano's confident dance, its bop turns and ranging melody brightly concelebrating the rhythmic interplay with Heath and Blakey. (He produced an even better, slightly quicker solo when, 11 days later, he repeated *Forecast* with Art Farmer's quintet [†Original Jazz Classics (A) OJCCD241–2].) *Sultry eve* is, despite a clarion introduction, songlike, and the improvisation contrives to intensify the ballad feeling; for running through all Jordan's inventions there is a strikingly lyrical instinct. Here, as again in *Summertime*, his enterprise in registral contrast is displayed vividly. Brilliant doublings of tempo, utilizing fragments of the tune in *They can't take that away from me* have their faultlessness matched by a gentle drummer and a sensitive bassist. *A night in Tunisia* is a reinterpretation by a pioneer of bop whose established style had already penetrated to the hardly explored interior of the bop ideophony. Atmospheric stickwork matches Jordan's succinct comments upon the mock-exotic 'idea' of the theme.

Starting with dusky cadences, he recreates *Summertime* in his own image, journeying through his landscape of variational contrasts to arrive at what can surely be regarded as one of the loveliest pianistic tributes, exquisite and haunting, of Gershwin's famous lullaby.

Trombone and baritone stab out the ascending theme of *Flight to Jordan*, sounding a congress of unusual voices. First the piano is scarcely in evidence: suddenly it is there, managing to sound appropriately gruff before it writhes into a midregister courtship dance. *Two loves*, another Jordan tune, starts with an example of his liking for occasionally fashioning an introduction in a tempo differing from that of the theme. (Anyone who knows Jordan at all will know that his piano introductions can be distinguished inventions in their own right.) The piano solo in *Yesterdays* does not quite attain melodic liberty, though it proceeds with a bright logic. Payne's best playing is in this piece; Jordan leads it out, and the sturdy Bert is not heard.

Early in 1954 Henri Renaud sought out a workless Jordan in a wintry Brooklyn. 'I was much impressed,' Renaud was to write many years later, 'by the unostentatious way in which he sat down at his piano in order to play a few of his compositions to me.' [72] That image of modesty and perhaps domesticity chimes with the impression created by Jordan's music, to wit, that a significant strand of its magic is its carelessness of sensation, its almost private concentration of its gathered elements, its sense of an independent alchemy which, if it beguiles a public ear, will have done so, as it were, by accident. Michael James's words of 1968 are worth echoing, for they are as true today: '[Jordan's music] will surely be remembered long after the work of more fashionable pianists has passed into oblivion.' [73]

To avoid confusion it should be noted that the above record's original title, *The Street Swingers*, was also given to a Bob Broomeyer issue (Pacific Jazz [A] WP1239); and that its more recent title, *Flight to Jordan*, also belongs to a later Jordan record, Blue Note (A) BST84046. E.T.

Max Roach

289 Conversations

Milestone (A) M47061 (2 LPs)

Booker Little (tpt); Ray Draper (tu); George Coleman (ten); Art Davis (bs); Roach (d). New York City, 4 September 1958.

You stepped out of a dream · *Filide* · *It's you or no one* · *Jodie's cha cha* · *Deeds, not words* · *Larry Larue* · *Conversations*

Clifford Jordan (ten); Mal Waldron (p); Eddie Kahn (bs); Roach (d). San Francisco, 27 October 1962.

Speak, brother, speak · *A variation*

The October 1962 session happened just a few weeks after the encounter of Roach and Mingus with Ellington chronicled under **223** where the drummer is described as 'a major innovator and master improviser' in the field of jazz drumming. Of course, by that year Roach had been 20 years involved in the music, having sat in with Parker as a teenager already soundly affected by the example of Kenny Clarke in the experimental prelude to bop (**251**). The music of 1958 belongs to a varied sequence following upon the death of Clifford Brown and the consequent demise of an influential quintet partially dealt with under **282**.

Conversations, a combination of former Riverside and Debut LPs, to wit, *Deeds, Not Words* and *Speak, Brother, Speak*, provides ample evidence of Roach's solo mastery, and in ways that may be more instructive in terms of his sense of the jazz ensemble than were his culminatory rodomontades with the Brown–Roach group which might be judged more obligatory than properly integral. At all events, if proof were needed that Roach was and is one of the truly inventive geniuses of modern jazz music, irrespective of instrument, the testimony of this aural document ought to suffice.

In 1957 Kinny Dorham and Hank Mobley were fairly frequent Roach associates. Little and Coleman were with the drummer in the spring of 1958, and the September session was preceded by an appearance at the Newport Jazz Festival in July. The line-up is unusual for a group clearly loyal to the spirit of hard bop: no pianist, and a tuba player who often assumes a front-line role. A virtuosic musician, Draper was to tour with this quintet for several months more. Little, as a hopeful from Memphis, had been introduced to Roach by Sonny Rollins. It is a bit too easy to assess his questing notions in the light of the posthumously still influential Brown or of the similarly questing Freddie Hubbard – contemporary and acquaintance. Hubbard would soon be shuttling between hard bop and free jazz (**346**, **400**, **426**, **428**). Little's 1961 work with Roach and Eric Dolphy (†Impulse [A] GRP11222, †Candid [A] CCD79033), in addition to its close relation to what happens here, is revelatory of the excitement currently in the air. A month or so after *Victory and Sorrow* (**339**) Little was dead, aged 23. Coleman, also Memphis-born and Little's sidekick, came to Roach after work in blues bands. He was, and remains, a less enigmatic character, but he was one of the finest and most arresting tenorists around at the time (see **354**).

You stepped out of a dream begins and ends slow, but is fast in between. After Coleman's solo combination of force and sensitivity, and Little's post-Brown obliqueness, there is an amount of break-swapping of which the agile Draper takes his share. The Latin *Filide* is Draper's composition and he solos early with a not unengaging galumphing sprightliness. The estimable Davis improvises with bent tones and split effects before Roach, drumming gently throughout the number, closes with leisurely contrasts of timbre. Little, who injects a brilliant racing exuberance into the theme of *It's you or no one*, is composer of the *moderato Larry Larue*; but it is Draper who looms large there, improvising within the ensemble with lines that are not always well judged in terms of contrast. The tuba tends to muddy things a bit in the slowly interwoven sections of *Deeds, not words*, passages which sandwich splendid solos by tenor and trumpet buoyed additionally by Roach's double-time drumming.

Some stylistic tensions were made likely by the furore of the times, but are less evident than on the 1961 discs alluded to above. Free-jazz dreams were implicit in some hard-bop expressions, just as bop aspirations lurked in late swing. The consistency of this quintet's achievement and its testimony to Roach's musical vision is remarkable, and seems largely so 'natural' that it has not been customary to regard the group as experimental despite its unusual manning. Much of its liveliness and colour can be attributed to the variety and the constant aptness of Roach's playing. Davis's role is always a telling one, and it is a pity, considering later liaisons with Ornette Coleman and Coltrane, that he was often inactive and is not well known. Though himself practised in tuba technique, he does not altogether avoid clashes with Draper, but, all in all, he is a considerable asset to the realizing of the quintet's aim.

The two lengthy (25 minutes and 22 minutes 30 seconds) numbers from October 1962 utter a different and, in some ways, perhaps a simpler message. Jordan is a tenorist of wider artistic ambition than might appear on the evidence of this date, wherein his closeness to such fellow Chicagoans as Johnny Griffin (**283**) and Gene Ammons is evident. Waldron seems, on surface judgement, an obsessive pianist, and on some of his earlier work, with Mingus, tended to hammer down his rhythmic references like a man putting up fences. He does sound extra powerful if heard immediately after the pianoless quintet. But in fact, even at his quirkiest, he is a genuinely thoughtful and constructive musician following in the wake of Monk and Powell. His restless re-evaluation of bop ideas in *Wheeling and dealing* with Coltrane and others in 1957 is just about the best feature of that record, Trane's aspirations notwithstanding, and not typical of hard-bop piano conventions (†Original Jazz Classics [A] OJCCD127–2).

The form of *Speak, brother, speak* is the blues; the feeling is set by a $^6/_8$ 'gospel' signature. Jordan's tough phrases extend upon staccato riffs, and as the bold sequences proceed through slight shifts of tempo, the affinity of tenorist and pianist becomes more evident. As might be expected, Roach's accompaniments constantly 'monitor' the intensely controlled build-up of excitement as Waldron, starting from a simple, worriting, bluesy phrase behind Jordan, conducts a darkly mesmeric procession of increasingly minatory chordal shapes.

Jordan is more expansive, and a little more strident, in *A variation*, which follows a mock-romantic atemporal introduction with a vigorous, rocking harmonically elemental theme which Waldron interprets with simpler melodic piano lines. Jordan develops these with some clarity of purpose. The rise of tension is hardly less relentlessly powerful than that in *Speak, brother, speak*, and a firm community of intention grows between the four participants. Kahn takes his solos as ably as he supports elsewhere, and usually resists the temptation to busyness which tugs at him during the first number.

Roach's great solo perorations – these, and *Conversations* from the first session – brim so richly with polyrhythmic eloquence and dynamic variegation that the best descriptive words are vain. The artistry is marvellous. In the four-minute *Speak, brother, speak* solo, for instance, expression ranges from arch delicacy to fire and brimstone without contrivance or sensationalism. Still, those who know and love this fellow's music will not have needed to be told. E.T.

Elmo Hope

290 Elmo Hope Trio

Contemporary (A) S7620, †Fresh Sounds (Sp) FSRCD74

Hope (p); James Bond (bs); Frank Butler (d). Los Angeles, 8 February 1959.

B's a-plenty · Barfly · Eejah · Boa · Something for Kenny · Like someone in love · Minor Bertha

Butler absent. Same date.

Tranquillity

Harold Land

291 The Fox

Contemporary (A) S7619, †Original Jazz Classics (A) OJCCD343–2

Dupree Bolton (tpt); Land (ten); Hope (p); Herbie Lewis (bs); Butler (d). Los Angeles, August 1959.

The fox · Mirror-minded Rose · One second, please · Sims a-plenty · Little Chris · One down

Eleven of these 14 performances are based on themes by Hope. The trio recordings give us the bare bones of his music, and several tracks on Land's session explore its implications more thoroughly. Monk and Powell are always mentioned as respectively marginal and central influences on Hope, though it might seem that his lack of virtuosity, despite early classical training, would make absorption of the latter's innovations impossible. In fact this apparent weakness was turned to advantage, for instead of attempting directly to copy, or even adapt, any of Powell's up-tempo procedures, he took some of that master's basic musical – rather than pianistic – ideas and developed them in his own way, this resulting in something that is unusually personal. It is also possible that Hope's somewhat limited skill in orthodox keyboard situations kept him independent of many of the standard devices of jazz pianism. Not too much should be made of this, however, because, as a genuine improviser, he took an impressive number of risks, and while there are undeniable botches, such as the ending of *B's a-plenty*, his daring frequently paid off and hence his executive skills were probably greater, in their way, than one tends to assume.

Working through line, accent, keyboard figuration, Hope produces in these trio performances results that, as noted, are strikingly individual both in detail – the surprising variety of the figurations – and in the ways they are put together. For example, in *B's a-plenty* the promptings of Powell obviously affect the music's general aspect, yet at the local level, not least in his imaginative accompaniment to the bass solo, everything is Hope's own. Comparison between this and *Boa*, another fast piece, begins to give a notion of the diversity of expression he achieved, for in the latter, as rather often with this musician, many of the ideas are implied, glanced at, instead of being fully stated. Actively sympathetic listening is required, and this, plus the music's oblique, sometimes fugitive character may largely account for Hope's neglect.

Different again are *Barfly* and *Eejah*, both lyrical yet in different, if equally hard-centred, ways and with the textures growing very active despite the slow tempos, purposefully extending the melodic invention of the themes. Busy and assertive, with just a hint of Monk, *Minor Bertha* follows another line of argument and the almost stark *Tranquillity* is different again, offering the irreducible essence of Hope's ideas. Though exceptional piano music is to be heard in this trio recital, the highly advantageous ensemble developments of his themes at *The Fox* session suggest, as does the more direct communicativeness of his own playing, as on *Sims a-plenty*, that his greatest potentials, alas largely unrealized, were as composer and bandleader. Here the quality of his music is so consistently high that one scarcely notices the extremely conventional instrumentation, employed on thousands of other dates.

Crucial is that it was a meeting, evidently at just the right time, between three independent spirits: Hope, Bolton and Land. Such events are rarer than might be assumed in jazz, a music that prides itself on – or at least is valued by its adherents for – its supposedly dangerous revolutionary status but that normally contains large elements of conformism. The two poles of the session are Hope's organizational capacities and Bolton's expressionism, although it was fortunate that Land had not yet come under the influence of Coltrane. His playing, with its dry tone, melancholy yet warm, remained as unpredictable as during his period with Curtis Counce (**278**). Indeed he makes a further advance and does some of his finest work on record here. Instances are *Mirror-minded Rose* and *One second, please*. Butler's contribution is hardly less important and, as on the trio date, he provides exactly the reconciliation of strength and refinement that Hope's music needs. There are frequent polyrhythmic implications in what the horns and piano do and he follows them through with much zest. This altogether was a singular occasion when everyone understood the requirements of Hope's music – arising, for example, from the unusual structures of *Mirror-minded Rose* and *Sims a-plenty* – and met all its challenges. An indication of how acute the problems set by his compositions are can be gained from the struggle an excellent 1962 Lee Morgan band had with Hope's *Take twelve* (Jazzland [A]

JLP80), a genuinely complicated 12-bar structure that floors everyone except Barry Harris.

Certainly the group Land assembled had little in common with other quintets of that period, such as those led by Art Blakey or Miles Davis, and this is quickly made plain by the agitated catch-as-catch-can of *The fox* itself. Despite his relatively few known professional appearances, [74] Bolton is notably untroubled by the fleet tempo and shines in the sequence of short, furious exchanges between the horns and Butler at the end. When this record first appeared all kinds of influences – Gillespie, Navarro, even Clifford Brown – were heard in this trumpeter's playing, but now, presumably because of the passage of time, they are hard to detect and he sounds almost disconcertingly original, separate. A secretive, in fact convincingly mysterious figure, Bolton appears to have spent much of his time in prisons, yet almost every move he makes here suggests a very considerable, perhaps even major, talent.

As it is his only other significant outing on disc, Bolton's part in *Katanga* (Affinity [E] AFF128, †Pacific Jazz [A] 494 850–2), a bluer, freer 1963 session under Curtis Amy's name, should be mentioned. Like *The Fox,* this presents jazz of rare consistency, in aim as well as quality. Taking the two LPs together, each of Bolton's solos has a stance of its own and there is a kind of largeness about nearly everything he plays. There is less dark anger to his solo on *Mirror-minded Rose,* but at all times he offers rare shadings of tone and accent, their effect at once harsh and subtle. From the *Katanga* set hear in particular the paradoxically intent yet explosive sadness of Bolton's playing on *You don't know what love is.* If his work is more patterned on *The Fox* than on *Katanga* it is mainly because of what may be termed the hard-bop classicism of the former. That near-perfection in itself implied changes, however, and these were duly set in motion by Ornette Coleman (**400** etc.).

Hope's trio LP is best heard in conjunction not only with *The Fox* but also with *Here's Hope!* (Celebrity [A] LP209) and *High Hope!* (Beacon [A] LP401), if copies of these fairly obscure 1961 sessions, each consisting entirely of his compositions, can be located. M.H.

2

Alternatives to Bop

Thelonious Monk

Monk was early involved with the pioneers of bop yet he from the beginning had a path of his own to follow.

Thelonious Monk

292 The Complete Blue Note Recordings of Thelonious Monk

†EMI/Blue Note CDP7243 8 30363 2 5 (4 CDs)

Idrees Sulieman (tpt); Danny Quebec West (alt); Billy Smith (ten); Monk (p); Gene Ramey (bs); Art Blakey (d). New York City, 15 October 1947.
Humph · *Evonce* (2 versions) · *Suburban eyes* (2 versions) · *Thelonious*

Sulieman, West, Smith absent. New York City, 24 October 1947.
Nice work if you can get it (2 versions) · *Ruby, my dear* (2 versions) · *Well, you needn't* (2 versions) · *April in Paris* (2 versions) · *Off minor* · *Introspection*

George Taitt (tpt); Sahib Shihab (alt); Monk (p); Bob Paige (bs); Blakey (d). New York City, 21 November 1947.
In walked Bud · *Monk's mood* · *Who knows?* (2 versions) · *Round about midnight*

Monk (p); John Simmons (bs); Shadow Wilson (d); Milt Jackson (vib); Kenny Hagood (vcl). New York City, 2 July 1948.
All the things you are · *I should care* (2 versions)

Hagood absent. Same date.
Evidence · *Mysterioso* (2 versions) · *Epistrophy* · *I mean you*

Shihab (alt); Monk (p); Al McKibbon (bs); Blakey (d); Jackson (vib). New York City, 23 July 1951.
Four in one (2 versions) · *Criss cross* (2 versions) · *Eronel* · *Straight, no chaser*

Shihab, Jackson absent. Same date.
Ask me now (2 versions)

Jackson returns. Same date.
Willow, weep for me

Kinny Dorham (tpt); Lou Donaldson (alt); Lucky Thompson (ten); Monk (p); Nelson Boyd (bs); Max Roach (d). New York City, 30 August 1952.
Skippy (2 versions) · *Hornin' in* (2 versions) · *Sixteen* (2 versions) · *Carolina moon* · *Let's cool one*

Dorham, Donaldson, Thompson absent. Same date.
I'll follow you

Sonny Rollins (ten); Monk (p); Paul Chambers (bs); Blakey (d). Hackensack, N.J., 14 April 1957.
Reflections

J. J. Johnson (tbn), Horace Silver (p) added. Same date.
Mysterioso

John Coltrane (ten); Monk (p); Ahmed Abdul-Malik (bs); Roy Haynes (d). Five Spot, New York City, 11 September 1958.
Crepuscule with Nellie · *Trinkle tinkle* · *In walked Bud* · *I mean you* · *Epistrophy*

Although it expresses the individuality of all who play it well, jazz is ultimately a musical language that is largely shaped by its major figures, and as such it developed rapidly through much of the 20th century. All Monk's jazz conveys something of his vision, but he made what may be termed his linguistic contributions early, and hence is represented in this book solely by his Blue Note recordings. His later music is a valuable further projection of his unique sensibility but it proposed no further enrichment of the jazz language.

Monk began recording under his own name unusually late for a major figure in this music, the first of the above sessions taking place five days after his 30th birthday. By then he had been performing professionally for well over a decade and was able to present a finished body of music that was his own to a singular degree. We have almost no exact knowledge of when these two dozen themes were written, or in what order, but Monk had presumably had plenty of opportunities of playing them, even if in obscure venues, and knew how he wanted them performed and improvised on. In this last respect he was often to be disappointed, yet few jazzmen have approached the recording studio so well prepared.

As with other first-generation modernists, Monk's roots are taken to be in swing and considerably earlier music, Ellington's 1950 *New piano roll blues* (†Original Jazz Classics [A] OJCCD108) wryly hinting at just one of several unlikely affinities. A certain passage in *Thelonious*, too, is always cited as proof of his descent from the New York stride players, although a more important point about this lucidly organized performance is that the pianist's most personal improvising occurs in the non-stride sections. Much weight is attached also to his having spent part of his teens touring with a sanctified evangelist, many commentators wanting to see the gospel, blues, stride and other elements that undoubtedly formed part of the background to his music as an 'Afro-American continuum' to which Monk's work obligingly contributed in its turn. Similarly his 'I sound like James P. Johnson', a remark allegedly made after his completing a certain 1957 recording, was eagerly applauded by those seeking assurance that this awkward figure had been pigeonholed at last. In fact, and as always, he sounded like Monk. As with any artist of comparable significance, what matters are not his origins but what he makes of them, not where he resembles others but where he differs. Monk is best served not by another assertion of his safely traditionalist status but rather by identifying the nature of his dangerous originality.

This was first evident obliquely. The earliest recordings of themes by Monk were Cootie Williams's of *Epistrophy* (retitled *Fly right*, Columbia [A] C3L38) in 1942 and the same leader's 1944 account of *Round about midnight* (Big Band Archives [A] LP1208, Affinity [E] AFS1031). Apart from Joe Guy's trumpet solo on the former, these show not the slightest comprehension of the music's style. Again, Monk's earliest important public associations were with pioneer boppers, yet he was on none of the sessions which crucially defined the new idiom (**256** etc.). This is amusingly emphasized by certain of his pieces, such as *Humph* with its noticeable flattened fifths caricaturing a well-worn bop cliché, this particular joke being taken much further in *Skippy*. His separateness is more positively signalled by *Mysterioso* adopting such an independent line with our old friend the 12-bar blues in B flat (in the same year as the authoritative *Parker's mood* [**257**]!). The point is that Monk was all along moving in a direction of his own, and hence this book places him in a section by himself.

The lasting impact of the best of these records was not the result simply of an audacious new style. However much improvisation there may be, including by Monk himself, the innovations are those of a composer, and one whose world was that of the piano. Near the heart of this music is what in jazz terms is an exceptionally original concept of piano sound. His particular kind of touch may have developed while playing inferior instruments during formative years spent touring the American backwoods. Yet without denying the plausible claim that his sources were solely Afro-American, it is of more than passing interest that his percussive approach aligns with that adopted in earlier decades by major straight composers such as Bartók and Stravinsky. This essential modernity relates closely to the sorts of musical material Monk chose and the ways that he used them. Although often seeming awkward, much of what he played lies well under the hands on the keyboard, and Monk was in fact an unusual kind of virtuoso.

His music unfolds via motivic development on melodic, rhythmic and harmonic planes, and this may be said to work through various types of distortion – anticipation, delay, extension, condensation, the displacement of notes, chords, accents, a matter of asymmetrical phrases within the symmetry of repeating choruses of (generally) 12, 16 or 32 bars. Monk's themes, motifs and their derivatives are often based on very simple ideas, an example being *Straight, no chaser*, which ultimately is 'about' the alternation of major and minor thirds placed in different positions in relation to the beat and within the phrase. [1] He imparts a remarkably pungent character to these fragments through the variations to which he subjects them, and herein resides his rare sort of virtuosity. Beyond the choice of notes lies his exact placing of them in musical space with precisely the right degree of attack. As Robert Palmer said, each composition has 'its own vocabulary of stress and nuance'. [2] For such an enterprise an accomplished and acutely sensitive drummer was necessary, and this Monk found in Blakey, who perhaps understood him, at every stage of his career, better than any other musician.

Arising out of these dialogues between keyboard and percussion Monk had the ability, like Parker, to produce solos made up of apparent fragments that actually cohere into fully integrated wholes. In the pianist's case this was because instead of following the usual bop procedure of throwing the theme away after the first chorus and improvising only on its chords, he built his solo *on* the theme and expected all who played his music to do the same. This relates to his insistence on his themes being executed just as he wrote them and his being highly critical of those who failed to do so – very much a composer's attitude. In improvisation on them, as Ran Blake has suggested, the theme should be treated like a *cantus firmus*, ideally present in the performance even when not being directly stated. [3] Indeed each theme is so close-knit that, along with its bass line, it cannot be ignored, a sort of 'thematic consciousness' being required, and a grasp of this is the best point of entry into Monk's world.

Given the strongly individual character of these themes on melodic, rhythmic and harmonic levels, this demand is considerable, and even Monk sometimes found his own music hard to deal with in the early years. It seems this was especially so on the 1948 session, to judge from the extra beats he inserted into *Evidence* and *Mysterioso*. But the soloist who ignores the theme and just improvises on its harmonies condemns himself to irrelevance, as is shown by the 1957 *Mysterioso*, which some of the players treat as simply one more blues. The result, despite some fertile invention, is that this luxuriantly extended performance is less memorable than the one of nine years earlier. And even those few, such as Jackson, Thompson and, on sessions elsewhere, Rollins, who do properly link up with the melodic and harmonic substance of Monk's themes only in part reflect the rhythmic subtlety of the composer's own improvisations.

An indication of how central the keyboard is to his thinking is that even when theme statements are transferred to the horns they still sound pianistic, as if he had taken no account of the special characteristics of reed and brass instruments. This remains so even when the orchestrations are for large ensembles and are done by other hands, and it might be accounted a weakness. Really it signifies an uncommon degree of abstraction, for Monk was unconcerned with such resources as contrasts between themes, a wide range of colours, or most of the other elements with which, say, Ellington worked. Although still his most familiar piece, *Round about midnight* is extremely unusual in that it portrays a mood: it is not just the title that tempts one to call this a jazz nocturne for there is a real power of evocation here. But it is, apart from two later 'train' pieces, *Little rootie tootie* (†Original Jazz Classics [A] OJCCD010) and *Locomotive* (OJCCD016), almost unique in his output, which otherwise centres, as noted, with a purity rare in jazz, on strictly musical ideas.

This sort of abstraction is underlined by Monk's unconventional accompaniments – if that is the right term. A further sign of his originality, these help explain why so few musicians have been completely successful in improvising with him on his themes. Clearly Monk's kind of keyboard support would unsettle many, and the harmonic departures, jagged phrases, unpredictable accents and constant attack did not work for Miles Davis (**272**). However, they admirably suit those few such as Jackson or Thompson who were able to improvise not just on but *in* Monk's pieces. Though he dealt with opposing patterns rather than the flow of counterpoint, at best his participation restored jazz polyphony to a degree comparable with the very different happenings in the MJQ (**363**). It scarcely needs adding that his accompaniments derive from the theme, or that they are a significant indication of his ensemble sense and beyond that of his feeling for overall structure. As with predecessors like Jelly Roll Morton, no matter how much improvisation there is by others, the composer's mind always presides in the most representative performances. At best, as was repeatedly said of Ellington's work, most of this music is produced by the sidemen, then shaped by their leader.

Generally this situation was at its most acute on Blue Note, and never again did Monk bring forward anything like so large a body of new music. There are some new, or at least unfamiliar, themes on his subsequent Prestige records, [4] fewer on the later Riversides, very few on the still later CBS series. If in holding to a settled repertoire during his later years Monk composed far less and improvised more, it is the Blue Note dates that offer the most purposeful and complete presentation of him as a composer, arranger, creative bandleader and pianist. Many of the pieces he introduced on this label he recorded several times more, yet hardly ever to such concentrated and intense effect. Naturally there are exceptions, and some of the later versions of *Round about midnight* are superior to this one. Again, the *Evidence* theme is hardly announced in the unequivocal manner expected from Monk, and it is possible to prefer the 1954 Paris solo reading as an account of the piece itself (Mosaic [A] MR4–112). But there are several Blue Note titles that Monk did not feel any need to record again: *Humph*, *Who knows?*, *Skippy*, *Hornin' in* and *Sixteen*. The 1947–52 Blue Notes belong to the days of 78-rpm discs and it may seem implausible to claim that the resulting miniatures are the fullest embodiments of Monk's gifts. True, he was quite often to make cogent use of the extra time available on long-playing records, yet it has been in the 'three-minute form' of these early works that his sense of structure is most acute and all the other facets of his work are most sharply in focus.

All facets, that is, except one. The single aspect of his music that Monk did take further in later years was his use of popular material. Like all real composers, he was self-sufficient in the world he had created and did not really need the challenge of themes produced by others. But he obviously enjoyed assaulting the outpourings of Tin Pan Alley and did so with an acerbity that precluded the survival of their sentimental associations while perhaps also signalling a larger rejection of conventional values. His method was the opposite of Tatum's: simplification, ultimately distillation. The songs are ruthlessly adapted to the nature of the piano and beyond that – and beyond Blue Note – lay such pieces as the 1954 *Smoke gets in your eyes* (OJCCD016), which takes further the 'miniature concerto' format of *Round about midnight*. Monk's other route with these popular ditties was closer to bop orthodoxy and was to ignore the tunes and transform the chord sequences. This produced such results as *Just you, just me* becoming *Evidence* and *Tea for two* re-emerging as the tritone-impregnated *Skippy*.

On the second Blue Note date *April in Paris* and *Nice work if you can get it* were treated less drastically, although the alternative takes make it clear that while Monk was a tireless improviser he had his conception of each piece fully worked out. That he never quite loses the melodies makes these performances useful introductions to his approach as both composer and improviser. Two further popular songs were rendered by Hagood at the 1948 session. He is sufficiently incongruous on **376** and the poor man's comic irrelevance here can well be imagined, especially in view of the sequence of masterpieces that followed. But on *All the things you are* there is an excellent Jackson solo with Monk characteristically at work behind – or beside – him and they move into full polyphony when the vocalist returns.

Earlier the opening date had juxtaposed *Humph* and *Thelonious*, eminently typical Monk themes, with two examples of conventional bop from Ike Quebec. Few listeners would find the comparison uninstructive, although the hornmen perform well throughout – better in the leader's terms than more famous players were to do later. With his trio on the following session Monk was particularly decisive in *Well, you needn't* and *Off minor*, showing how mistaken were the tales of his pianistic incompetence. [5] *Ruby, my dear* is our first sight of Monk's lyrical side, the necessary counterbalance to the toughness and density of most of his music. In *Off minor* he develops his argument with especial lucidity, drawing it entirely from the theme. He does the same, though more obliquely, on *In walked Bud* from the next date. Here the chord sequence's derivation, from *Blue skies*, is clearer than in cases such as *Skippy* or *Evidence*. Regarding *Monk's mood* from this quintet session, considering that Shihab is obviously out of tune it is surprising they recorded only one version.

With Hagood disposed of, definitive Monk was caught on the 1948 occasion, at least in the master take of *Mysterioso*. The varied recapitulation here and on *Evidence* should be noted as something adventurous in the jazz of that time. Jackson was always at his best in the sort of compositional framework set up by Monk and later by John Lewis with the MJQ. Monk and Jackson have a superb duet on *Epistrophy*, there being perfect understanding between them and each complementing the other exactly. Something comparable was brought off by Rollins and Monk on *Reflections* in 1957, and such achievements provide some of the finest moments in jazz.

Plainly the 1951 meeting was a great session. *Criss cross* has repeatedly been commended, and rightly, as a beautiful summation of what Monk brought to jazz in this first and freshest period of creativity. Yet with Shihab far advanced beyond his 1947 showing and Jackson and Blakey almost beyond praise, the purposeful economy of this masterpiece is nearly matched by *Four in one*, *Eronel* and *Straight, no chaser*. Recorded the previous year by Miles Davis as a member of the Birdland All-Stars (Session [A] 102), *Eronel*'s main idea is said to have originated with Sadik Hakim, only the bridge being Monk's. If this is so, then Monk achieved his usual very close relationship between the bridge and the main thematic phrase. He did likewise with *Four in one*, in its twists and turns an archetypal Monk theme. Normally the best take of each title was chosen for the initial release but *Four in one* is an exception, the alternative version, which only appeared later, having superior balance and better solos.

Ask me now shows the more conventional side of Monk – and it is important to recognize that this existed. *I'll follow you* also is more orthodox than any of the other ballads here, let alone ones he recorded later, but it too remains a personal statement even if made by less outré means than usual. Relevant here is the direct melodic appeal of *In walked Bud* and, from the 1952 sextet date, *Let's cool one*. Monk's playing is his absolute best throughout the latter occasion, which also produced the 6/4 *Carolina moon*, one of the pieces that helped establish triple metre in jazz.

That Monk was not acknowledged before the second half of the 1950s remains among the worst failures of jazz commentary. His belated recognition is always linked to his signing with Riverside in 1955, but probably far more relevant was Parker's death that same year, the enormous impact of which on the jazz community has since been forgotten. Monk's Prestige records had gained some small, if partly uncomprehending, attention, this leading a few musicians and other insiders to turn to him. But he offered no ways out of post-bop or post-cool dilemmas, of course, and stood apart, as real jazz composers usually do.

What probably had more effect on Monk attaining at all wide recognition was not any recording contract but what in effect was his first New York nightclub residency, at the old Five Spot in 1957. Cecil Taylor had been there in 1956, Ornette Coleman would be in 1959 (his New York debut), Eric Dolphy and Booker Little in 1961. We tend to forget that Monk's stand with Coltrane was part of that Five Spot sequence. Wilbur Ware played bass and at first Philly Joe Jones was behind the drums, later replaced by Shadow Wilson. Aside from three studio performances first issued on Riverside/Jazzland (A) JLPS946, that group seemed to leave no recordings, though rumours persisted of all kinds of marvels taken down on the Coltrane family tape recorder. When Monk's son in 1993 became contracted with Blue Note, he produced the five items detailed above, on which Ware and Wilson are replaced by Malik and Haynes. These first appeared as *Live at the Five Spot* on Blue Note (A) 99786 and were the following year incorporated into the general run of the elder Monk's Blue Note recordings.

For this further issue the pitch has been 'corrected' and the sound is a trifle more harsh but the main trouble is the balance, Coltrane being off microphone so he is heard best when the piano is silent. His infinite capacity for taking extremely long solos had not bloomed fully, yet the predatory manner and tumbling unstoppability of the natural demagogue were not far over the horizon. Conveying all the strenuousness of a juggernaut changing gear, Coltrane's searchings imply that it is better to travel than to arrive, that the journey itself is the only home for this voyager without a destination.

In the sharpest contrast Monk's various sorts of wry distortion, on the Five Spot performances as much as elsewhere, are enigmatic but profoundly satisfying, his irony sometimes barbed, sometimes elusive. His wit comes from a need to reconcile feeling with intelligence and is a musical equivalent to what Henry James termed 'continuous relevance'. Whereas the humour of, say, Waller is sentimental or at best decorative, Monk's is structural, which is to say it depends on dislocations of musical syntax. The 1948 *Mysterioso* is a particularly good illustration of the fact that its jokes can only be grasped by those who truly understand music, and that was probably of no little satisfaction to one of Monk's temperament.

Although he offered no solutions to current jazz problems, the best of his music has, as noted, made a lasting impact. Bud Powell, one of the most influential pianists in this music, was much affected by Monk early on and returned to his music in later years, producing, in parallel with some later performances by Solal, Bill Evans and Gaslini, a considerable body of authoritative keyboard interpretations of Monk pieces. Nor did Monk's example affect only pianists such as Mal Waldron, Andrew Hill, Jaki Byard, Herbie Nichols and Randy Weston, and this was in due course acknowledged by such musicians as Coltrane, Lacy and Giuffre. Monk's themes also stimulated recompositions, such as those by Hodeir (**455**), Schuller (**400**) and Stadler (**462**), that pursued goals very different from his own.

His later sequences of recordings, for Prestige, Riverside and CBS, may be less complete fulfilments of his gifts than the Blue Notes examined here. But even if he later withered into what is called success and toured internationally, there was a final creative outburst in London during 1971 (Mosaic [A] MR4–112). And he for a long time remained, in Bill Evans's words, 'an exceptionally uncorrupted creative talent'. [6] Monk's finest music and his performance of it were all of a piece, and this reflected the stubbornness with which he conducted most of his career – unswerving through long years of neglect. Great artists in other disciplines have always behaved that way, of course, but in jazz it has been rare. M.H.

Lennie Tristano and His School

Tristano's music and that of his main pupils stands apart from the mainstream of modern jazz as represented by bop and its descendants and marks an alternative shaped by demands of severe intellectual rigour.

Lennie Tristano/Buddy DeFranco

293 **Crosscurrents**
Capitol (H) 5CO52 80 853

Lee Konitz (alt); Warne Marsh (ten); Tristano (p); Billy Bauer (g); Arnold Fishkin (bs); Harold Granowsky (d). New York City, 4 March 1949.
Wow · *Crosscurrent*

Konitz, Marsh absent. New York City, 14 March 1949.
Yesterdays

As for 4 March but Denzil Best (d) replaces Granowsky. New York City, 16 March 1949.
Marionette · *Sax of a kind* · *Intuition* · *Digression*

Bernie Glow, Paul Cohen, James Pupa, Jack Eagle (tpt); Ollie Wilson, Earl Swope, Bart Varsalona (tbn); DeFranco (clt); Konitz, Frank Socolow (alt); Al Cohn, Jerry Sanfino (ten); Serge Chaloff (bar); Gene DiNovi (p); Oscar Pettiford (bs); Irv Kluger (d). New York City, 23 April 1949.
The bird in Igor's yard · *This time the dream's on me*

DeFranco (clt); Teddy Charles (vib); Harvey Leonard (p); Jimmy Raney (g); Bob Carter (bs); Max Roach (d). New York City, 24 August 1949.
Extrovert · *Good-for-nothing Joe* · *Aishe*

Stan Fishelson (tpt); Bill Harris (tbn); Fred Preiffer (fr h); Hal Feldman (ob); Sam Marowitz (clt); Milt Yaner (bs clt); Lou Stein (p); Eddie Safranski (bs); Shelly Manne (d). New York City, 2 November 1949.
Opus 96

'Tristano's music was a departure beyond bop in which the choice of notes involved a subtler and more complex harmonic knowledge.' [7]

How much Tristano thought in terms of 'departures beyond bop' when he arrived in New York may be open to question. Moving from Chicago in 1946 he was in possession of a developed keyboard style which bore out sufficiently his claim that 'in 1944 I had reached the point where I could riffle off anything of Tatum's and with scandalous efficiency'. [8] And he had a musical mind which, though not noticeably touched by encounters with musicians of 'progressive' experience, was by no means inimical to bop's goings-on. His admiration for Gillespie's music is borne out not only by published remarks, but also by a lively recording of *A night in Tunisia* with Bauer and Fishkin in early 1946 (Raretone [It] 5008FC).

Airy and skilfully offhand as the unisons of *Wow* may sound, their Parkerish echoes are fairly distinct. What gives this ensemble its somewhat determined cast is undoubtedly Tristano's unvarying concept, at this time, of the relation of improvised 'lines' to the beat. The two saxophonists and the guitarist shape their solos out of steady strings of notes, affected certainly by 'subtler and more complex harmonic knowledge', phrasing habituated to the leader's liking for contrapuntal ensembles, whether pre-devised or aleatory. *Crosscurrent*, with another boppish unison theme, includes a brilliant chorus by Bauer, who throughout these spring sessions sounds the most robust of the main voices other than Tristano himself, and who remains, in long retrospect, perhaps the freshest in instant ideas.

Tristano recorded *Yesterdays* in several versions, including one entirely solo (Jazz Guild [C] 1008). Here, with Konitz and Marsh silent, he traces new paths round the tune's periphery. Dialogue with Bauer makes this *Yesterdays*, brief as it is, a masterpiece of patient interplay. In *Marionette* Bauer provides a theme that would have suited Miles Davis's Capitol nonet (**376**) admirably. Bauer's lightly riding solo precedes some thoughtfully agile steps by Tristano with a snatch of that block-chords emphasis which became his rather dubious bequest to a modish and mercifully transient style of pseudo-jazz.

This celebrated sextet, inspired by the vigorous wisdom of a leader who, while he was keen to explore both new harmonic avenues and the possibilities of classical procedures, also directed his students to the techniques of earlier jazz and encouraged a 'workshop' approach to jazz-making that was to stimulate other varieties of jazz growth. Konitz and Marsh show something of their independent skill in their *Sax of a kind*, aiming to join their rapidly executed exchanges seamlessly, and succeeding through the closeness of their musical thought. This runs on into an ingenious weaving of unison with glancing minor seconds.

The character of the two aleatory numbers is affected strongly by the group's own character as a didactic discipleship. Undoubtedly, *Intuition* and *Digression* were well ahead of their day. The known bewilderment of Capitol may be understandable, but their erasure of two of Tristano's other free essays remains inexcusable. Some early listeners thought these pieces premeditated; and it is evident enough that Tristano's companions, responding to his pianistic hints, invent as men conditioned to make unusual responses even in usual contexts.

Throughout *Intuition* it is the pianist's work that captures the ear. Unsolemn, he initiates the slide towards conclusion with puckish multiplications, lines trailing the ensemble's atonal reactions like feathery accretions. *Digression* is slow and conjures associations both ancestral and contemporary. Is not Tristano's introduction a younger relative of Bix's *In a mist* (**63**)? And does not the rest of the interchange suggest a first cousin to Gil Evans's *Moondreams* (**376**) rather than a grand-uncle to *Free jazz* (**400**)?

With the first number by the DeFranco orchestra we run into a composer whose links with the Tristano school are traced in **379–80**, where George Russell's workshop creations some years after *The bird in Igor's yard* are considered. DeFranco's serried wind players attack the startling jazz offcuts from Stravinsky's *The Rite of Spring* with admirable gusto, making the clarinettist's solo part sound fragile and, if Parkerish, only spectrally so. This work is from the period of Russell's *Cubana be/bop* (**315**), and while it clearly carries his aspiration further over bop frontiers, it seems not much more than a flexing of his biceps for contests well ahead in time. The group's other offering is warm romanticism, possibly arranged by the leader.

The DeFranco sextet pieces display nicely the post-swing imagination of the clarinettist; but they are more notable for Raney's and Charles's work. Fuller studies of these two latter musicians will be found under **355** and **378**. Finally, Neal Hefti's *Opus 96* is 1940s progressivism as yet unaware that the audience is reaching for its hat.

As Capitol (J) ECJ150076 this anthology was entitled *Cool and Quiet*. **365** reveals Konitz in other company, reviving the challenges of *Intuition*

30 years on. Numerous other outworkings of the Tristano spirit, not always acknowledged as such, will be found elsewhere below. E.T.

Lennie Tristano

294 Requiem

†Atlantic (Eu) 8122715952 (2 CDs), Atlantic (A) SD2–7003 (2 LPs)

Tristano (p). New York City, 1954–5.
Requiem · *Turkish mambo*

Peter Ind (bs); Jeff Morton (d). Same date.
Line up · *East Thirty-second*

Lee Konitz (alt) added; Gene Ramey (bs), Art Taylor (d) replace Ind, Morton. Confucius Restaurant, New York City, 11 June 1955.
These foolish things · *You go to my head* · *If I had you* · *A ghost of a chance* · *All the things you are*

Tristano (p). New York City, 1960–1.
Becoming · *C minor complex* · *You don't know what love is* · *Deliberation* · *Scene and variations: Carol, Tania, Bud* · *Love lines* · *G minor complex*

As the previous entry implies, Tristano's finest recordings belong in that rare category of jazz which has been cleansed of reassuring clichés. Consequently they never aroused the enthusiasm of any large part of the jazz public, and the number of his listeners declined, even substantially. It was the old story of a rapidly evolving artist of great originality who lost part of his audience with each new phase of his growth. Tristano understood this perfectly well, saying in connection with his early bands: 'Instead of consolidating our position, it was always in a state of development; and that's no way to sell something.' [9] Later he turned the tables, abandoning what remained of his public, devoting himself chiefly to teaching, and recording just an occasional session like those detailed above.

No doubt its sheer musical richness was the main reason for his output failing to make a commercially advantageous impression: it was not the first or last time such a thing happened in jazz. That the supposed 'coldness' of Tristano's music was a defensive notion of superficial listeners is suggested, first, by the heated expression of many of the players he most admired, Roy Eldridge, Charlie Parker and Bud Powell among them. This is reflected in the impetuosity of his early work, for example on Earl Swope's 1945 *Tea for two* – with a completely different piano solo on each version – or *Blue Lou* (Jazz Guild [C] JG1008). Second, they sometimes responded in kind, as on the Metronome All-Stars 1949 *Victory ball* (**315**), where Parker improvises brilliantly not just on the chords of *'Swonderful* but also, rather unusually for him, on Tristano's theme. Allegations of rhythmic weakness are especially lacking in substance: if the 1961 solos were beaten out on a single note they would still embody greater rhythmic invention than much better regarded jazz which uses far more elaborate resources. The intensity which runs through his playing from the seemingly effortless elaborations of early times to the stoic decisiveness of the 1961 music and beyond makes the 'cerebral' charge altogether comic.

Its unintended humour does hint, though, at the real problem for inept hearers, particularly those who still imagine jazz to be good-time music. Their difficulty lies not in such features as the rather dizzying ensemble precision of early up-tempo performances like those on **293** but in the intellectual rigour which necessarily lies behind it. Compounding this is the fact that, for all its virtuosity of conception and execution, his music is watchfully pared down to essentials. As the opening paragraph's quotation makes clear, its creation was Tristano's sole concern, never the promotion of his personality.

In case it be supposed that 'intellectual rigour' here inhibits the glories of unthinking spontaneity, it should be noted that Tristano was instantly recognizable even on his first discs, implying that considerable development had taken place before he ever reached a recording studio. There is, indeed, something almost disconcertingly personal about even his earliest solos, made in 1945 (Jazz Records [A] JR1) and 1946 (Jazz Guild, as above). And by the time we reach the 1947 trio performances (Raretone [It] 5008FC, †Mercury [J] 8330 921–2), a style of remarkable independence and self-consistency has emerged, as in *Coolin' off with Ulanov* and in solos from that year such as *Spontaneous combustion* (Musica Jazz [It] 2MJP1065). The 1949 items dealt with above represent a mature and unmistakably original mode of improvisation, and most jazzmen would not have ventured beyond this. The 1954–5 pieces show, however, that Tristano went much further, and then further still.

The entirely individual sound he drew from the piano was of course partly a matter of touch, yet it was much coloured by a very distinctive harmonic idiom. With Ellington and Tatum, Tristano is in fact one of the great harmonists of jazz, and Gunther Schuller claimed for him 'a harmonic ear of genius calibre'. [10] His starting points are the chord sequences of a fairly restricted number of old popular songs, which he subjects to much sophistication. Thus the above *East Thirty-second* and *C minor complex* both use the harmonies of *Pennies from heaven*, as do Konitz's *Movin' around* (**295**) and *Hi, Beck* (**298**). The capacity of Tristano and his best pupils repeatedly to renew themselves on this limited body of material is exceptional, and reminiscent of Beiderbecke doing some of his most daring improvisations on ODJB themes (**63–4**). In each case the aim was apparently to retain a link with the past while moving towards the future. Tristano's harmony is sometimes atonal but even in the most venturesome passages it relates back to the tonal framework of the original song; some of it may be considered bitonal. This densely chromatic harmony is often dissolved into spinning contrapuntal textures, and if there is a Bachian aspect to Tristano's music it is because some of the power of these improvisations derives, as in Johann Sebastian, from tension between the contrapuntal lines and the harmonies through which they pass.

Unusually long phrases, which characterize this music, are necessitated by the density of the lines' content. Tristano aimed at their being shaped by intense rhythmic variation, frequent key changes, and not the shifting time signatures of constant metric variation so much as no time signatures, and no bar lines, at all. Such music can be perplexing, especially when moving rapidly, and the insistence on an unadorned beat from the drummer in ensemble performances is the opposite of the retrogressive eccentricity castigated by the jazz press. If a drummer stressed certain beats he would imply a metre of his own that was not inherent to the music and this would detract from the long sequences of nearly even quavers, full of angularities and subtle deviations of pulse, to which latter, as Konitz once pointed out, the drummer should be able to respond. Although Tristano was sometimes very explicit in his complaints about rhythm sections, [11] this was an ideal, and not always adhered to even on his own sessions, as can be heard from Taylor's playing on the Confucius Restaurant titles. Other factors included his virtuosic use of double time, and occasionally of double double time, to suggest two (or three) tempos and then to fluctuate between them or employ them simultaneously. Note should also be made of his acutely expressive use of block chords, their effect remote from the bombast of most pianists who have resorted to this device.

Although a detailed study of Tristano's style and its development still waits to be written, the above paragraphs may be enough to refute in general terms the charge that he innovated in harmony and melody but not in rhythm. [12] A style and method so complex (by jazz standards) implies activity in several directions and perhaps most explicitly the multiple use of Tristano's own instrument to create textures and forms packed with significant detail. It is no surprise that the 1954–5 solo and trio performances result from manipulations of the recording process described below, and Tristano had begun playing duets with himself some years before. In the earliest, *Pastime* and *Ju-ju* of 1951 (East Wind [J] EW8040, Inner City [A] IC6002), which are in effect music for two pianos recorded by one man, melodic voices strive together in a broad current of song. Two years later came *Descent into the maelstrom* (East Wind, Inner City), which must always stand as one of the most astonishing pieces ever recorded in the name of jazz.

Yet despite Tristano's great emphasis on spontaneity, this sort of multitracking obviously demands considerable forward planning, and one might almost call it a composer's solution to the problem of improvisation. At the same time, the continuation of bass and drum parts in *Line up* and *East Thirty-second* beyond the points at which he stops playing, like the fading-out of *Ju-ju* and *Pastime*, underlines the open-ended nature of these performances. These are among the earliest seriously musical utilizations of overdubbing and in the light of all the electronic manipulation that now goes on in many areas of music, the outrage initially caused by Tristano's initiative seems amusing. His reasoned defence of the simple processes involved here still deserves attention, however. [13]

So far as *Requiem* is concerned, modernism has been here and gone. He laid down a full chordal accompaniment with both hands and over this is placed a blues improvisation recorded at half speed. When the whole was played at normal speed, with a little tape echo added, the 'solo' line, as on the other three tracks of the same date, has a flinty yet still entirely musical tone. Such mixtures of 'natural' and modified sounds later became a commonplace of electronic music, of course. Though possibly conceived as a memorial for Parker, *Requiem* may have been recorded in 1954 and as there is little of the bop vocabulary and none of its pet phrases in Tristano's work here, the great alto saxophonist is never directly evoked. The piece stands as a deeply felt tribute by one great musician to another, though won at the cost of rather too considerable a realignment with tradition. The result is beautiful yet – for once – regressive, and the racing lines of *East Thirty-second* and *Line up*, [14] with their rich patterns of accents and marvellously fluid use of block chords, are more to the point. So are the superimposed rhythms of *Turkish mambo*, even if it is not a mambo and has nothing to do with Turkey.

Konitz is dealt with elsewhere (**293**, **295**, **298**, **365**, **375–6**), but, thanks to early stereo, the Confucius Restaurant performances give us our best-recorded chance of studying Tristano as a singularly perceptive accompanist. His relaxed manner in his own solos can deceive, for each improvisation proves, with sufficient listening, to be an organic whole. Divisions between choruses and between eight-bar segments within a chorus are, if not obliterated, banished to the music's distant background. These pieces are best heard in conjunction with the further items recorded on the same occasion and issued as †Mosaic (A) MD6–174 (6 CDs).

Likewise the 1961 solos ought to be studied with the three items all titled *Rehearsal for a recording date* on the East Wind/Inner City issues. After years of complaining about drummers and bassists, Tristano took the obvious step, this time without the aid of multitracking. Fats Waller was not the only one who could say that his best rhythm section was his own left hand, and Tristano spells out the bass line not in 4/4, which is to say in groups of four beats, so much as in a continuous stream of unmeasured – or unmetred – pulses. The *Bud* movement of *Scene and variations* is a development of the quick 1954–5 trios, but all the other pieces show his thought to have advanced considerably along the ascetic path he essentially had always followed. While this was an extremely individual line of endeavour, several of the 1961 items do suggest that Tristano knew Schoenberg's Piano Pieces Op. 33a and b (1928 and 1931), especially the latter. Not that this affects their status as one of the great sets of recorded jazz piano solos, shaped by a power and cogency of continuous and constructive thought seldom found in such music. The irresistible momentum of *C minor complex* is typical. By this time the tempo switches of *Becoming* or the figures in $^{9}/_{8}$ or $^{13}/_{8}$ can be taken for granted.

Despite the presence of bass and drums, by now completely irrelevant, further developments out of these 1961 pieces are suggested by *Cool boogie* and *It's you or no one* recorded in Berlin in October 1965 (Philology [It] W102) and more especially by the solos *Dream* and *Image* (East Wind/Inner City) taken down in Paris the following month. This might also have been true of *Con con* and *Stretch* (East Wind/Inner City) dating from 1966, had the music not been sabotaged by a drummer who evidently imagined himself to be on a Blue Note blowing date. However, all this later music needs to be heard in the light of *Descent into the maelstrom*, a Gesualdoan thrust into the future which, even decades later, it is hard to credit, impossible to account for. It ought to have caused even more interest than *Intuition* and *Digression* (**293**) but had to wait even longer for issue. If art indeed results from a conspiracy between the clarity of the intellect and the chaos of the unconscious, then *Descent into the maelstrom* is a memorable confirmation of Novalis's dictum that 'chaos has to shine through the veil of order'.

Tristano's bypassing of the trends current in jazz during his life did not, as the anecdotal histories usually insist, consign his music to a backwater but gave it, rather, a timeless quality. It deserves to have exerted a wider influence than it is normally considered to have done. Often he is written off for reasons which have little to do with his music, and the matter of Tristano's long-term effect on jazz needs, like that of Tatum, to be restudied. Such an undertaking would reveal nothing comparable to the crowds who followed Parker, let alone the hordes which fell in behind Coltrane. But consider a record like Peter Ind's *Peter Ind Sextet* (Wave [E] LP13) dating from 1975. This deploys two each of tenor saxophones, guitars and basses in an intriguingly personal application of Tristano's precepts. Much of his influence has in fact been through former pupils such as Ind, as in Konitz's effect on Art Pepper, Bud Shank and Lennie Niehaus, and through their teaching in turn, instances here being Warne Marsh, Sal Mosca and again Konitz. Yet some of Tristano's influence has been direct, for example on Bill Evans (e.g. *Concerto for Billy the Kid*, **380**), who duly had a considerable effect on such influential pianists as Herbie Hancock and Keith Jarrett. Especially if it was larger than at first thought, a stone cast into the sizeable pond of jazz pianism can send ripples in many directions for a long time. M.H.

Lee Konitz

295 Very Cool

Verve (A) MGV8209, Verve (F) 2304 344

Don Ferrara (tpt); Konitz (alt); Sal Mosca (p); Peter Ind (bs); Shadow Wilson (d). New York City, 12 May 1957.

Sunflower · *Stairway to the stars* · *Movin' around* · *Kary's trance* · *Crazy, she calls me* · *Billie's bounce*

Very cool? Surely not the coolness which could have been expected from an earlier Konitz; but the epithet is not really helpful here anyway. What makes this record particularly provocative in its sense of fresh development is the subtlety of the interplay, disclosing itself to careful attention, between Konitz's search for fresh tonal and rhythmic adjustments, and the variously inspired cooperation he receives from his fellows in this satisfying programme.

The theme of *Sunflower* is brightly assertive, and yet Konitz's first solo has something of the old reserve. Yes, the tone is less tenuous, and ideas flow in unexpected ways. Ferrara, a thoughtful, laconic player, follows, enjoying strong support from Ind. Mosca shows both debt and independence where his Tristano conditioning is concerned. It is Ferrara who states the theme of *Stairway to the stars* with Konitz and Mosca devising appropriate melodic support. The *Movin' around* is done lightly and swiftly, a tripping theme interpreted by alto and trumpet ranging purposefully through their notions with a sense of vigorous development which, with Ferrara particularly in mind, prompts not unfamiliar thoughts about deserving skills and critical disregard. The trumpeter sounds quite like the early Miles Davis, only he might be judged a little more sure-footed.

If the ensemble passages of *Movin' around* sound rather like hard bop with a certain loss of candour, *Kary's trance* revives memories of the Tristano mode to some degree. The theme has a bit of the former inevitability, and yet there develops through this number a liberated interaction of ideas which, though it is not the atonal conversation of 1949 (**293**), does call upon the same gifts of responsive perception. Similar things happen towards the close of *Sunflower* and appear almost endemic to *Crazy, she calls me*. Ferrara is silent during the latter, and it is the rhythm team which abets Konitz in his long, probing, celebratory solo improvisation, adapting this also towards mutual exchange.

Shadow Wilson, an immigrant from more assertive jazz zones, is less of a prodder in these circumstances, and both Shelly Manne and Denzil Best may be considered to have been, in earlier Konitz sessions, distinctly more keen to be heard.

The choice of *Billie's bounce* stimulates the bop/cool question again. This version is a little gentler in tone than any of the 1945 Parker Savoy takes (**257**), but that is no comment upon its vigour; and, in fact, it prompts reflections upon both the rhythmic coolness inherent in bop from the start, and the distinctive vivacity which Konitz's kind of jazz had to bring when it chose to reinterpret themes from the bop canon. The arresting composed variations which here precede the reprise of Parker's tune are more than sufficient evidence of an independent brilliance.

Related performances by Konitz and Ferrara recorded in March 1957 have been reissued as part of *The Complete Atlantic Recordings of Tristano, Konitz and Marsh* (†Mosaic [A] MD6–174, 6 CDs). E.T.

Warne Marsh

296 Star Highs

Criss Cross (H) 1002, †Criss Cross (H) 1002CD

Marsh (ten); Hank Jones (p); George Mraz (bs); Mel Lewis (d). Monster, Holland, 14 August 1982.

Switchboard Joe (2 versions) · *Star highs* (2 versions) · *Hank's tune* · *Moose the mooche* · *Victory ball* · *Sometimes* (2 versions) · *One for the band*

Once it seemed that the destiny of Marsh was so closely shaped by the response of Konitz to Tristano's requirements that he became incapable of moving on to the sort of personal freedom in personal development that Konitz was able to discover. There are places during this session where the tenorist echoes the earlier tone and phraseology of the altoist with whom he devised the telepathic *Sax of a kind* (**293**), and also the Tristano-inspired lines which facilitated counterpoint in ensemble. But there is more to this situation than that, and the occasional moments of deliberate recollection may be reckoned within the overall motive of a very engaging sequence of jazz-making.

There is, in the tone and rhythmic language of Marsh's spacious solos in both versions of *Switchboard Joe*, much more than a hint at the influence upon Marsh of a pre-Tristano model. Both Marsh and Konitz were active admirers of Lester Young, Konitz acknowledging his own debt to the Young of the Basie years. Whatever the two men imbibed at the Tristano fountain, they (and particularly, it appears, Konitz) had already drawn expressive wisdoms from the older man's approach. There is a lot of the old master in Marsh's improvising voice during *Switchboard Joe*, *Star highs* and *Sometimes*, and sufficient originality of vocabulary and accent to suggest that his ability to hark back beyond a more rigid early discipline made possible a kind of creative release.

He is also greatly helped towards freshness by his companions, and there is some marvellous playing from Jones, one of the best accompanists and a soloist of genial delicacy, playing here with Marsh for the very first time. Mraz and Lewis were members of Jones's trio at the time. Mraz, very much the junior member, has a singing resonance and a sense of phrasing in solos which also has quasi-vocal marks. He had been a member of the Thad Jones–Mel Lewis big band; and here, too, is Lewis, known as a forceful drummer yet showing great variety and sensitivity in what quite frequently becomes a four-way conversation. Only in the stop-time chorus of *Victory ball* is Lewis expected to be assertive.

Since the alternative takes (all three missing from the LP version of this issue) are of numbers in which Marsh is best discovering an innovative voice, the opportunity of comparison is fruitful. There is only small variation in quality. Jones may be a little less predictable, less prone to bop clichés, in the *Switchboard Joe* alternative, and he touches a wider imaginative range in the alternative version of *Star highs*. In the latter Marsh threatens the balance a little with an uncharacteristic excess of bravura towards the close.

Moose the mooche moves a bit too swiftly for relaxed management, and the most satisfactory solo comes from Mraz. Jones and Marsh dive into rather ill-considered contrapuntal gambolling both here and in Tristano's adaptation of *'Swonderful* as *Victory ball.* (Marsh's old aptitude for that sort of thing diminished during his years of patchy involvement in jazz, and he never quite regained it even when reunited with Konitz.)

In his breathing of semiprivate thoughts in *Sometimes* – following upon Jones's beautiful introductory solo – Marsh discloses a nicer transmuting of the Konitz legacy than the bursts of imitative plaintiveness one hears later in the same piece. There is more of this tenuousness at the start of *One for the band*, but it sounds appropriate over the initial tiptoeing of Mraz and Lewis. After Jones has egged the rhythm to stronger impulses, and beyond some alterations of spurting counterpoint and broader phrasal contrasts between tenor and piano, one hears Marsh playing certain elisions which summon up the spirit not only of Young but also of some of the members of that emulative brotherhood who were the messengers of a once popular strand of cool jazz. It is to the credit of Marsh that the samba rhythm of *Star highs* does nothing to deter him from treading a very individual measure or from sounding an equally individual note. E.T.

Cool Jazz

A misnomer, most so-called cool jazz is hardly cool. Just as bop inevitably grew out of swing, so what is thought of as cool jazz was implicit in bop. These recordings show that as usual music looked both into the past and the future.

Stan Getz, Zoot Sims, Brew Moore, Serge Chaloff, Allen Eager

297 Brothers and Other Mothers

Savoy (A) SJL2210 (2 LPs)

Eager (ten); Ed Finckel (p); Bob Carter (bs); Max Roach (d). New York City, 22 March 1946.

Rampage · *Vot's dot* · *Booby hatch* · *Symphony Sid's idea*

Red Rodney (tpt); Earl Swope (tbn); Chaloff (bar); George Wallington (p); Curly Russell (bs); Tiny Kahn (d). New York City, 5 March 1947.

Pumpernickel (2 versions) · *Gaberdine and Serge* (2 versions) · *Serge's urge* (2 versions) · *A bar a second* (2 versions)

Eager (ten); Duke Jordan (p); Russell (bs); Roach (d); Terry Gibbs (vib). New York City, 15 July 1947.

All night frantic · *Donald Jay* · *Meeskite* · *And that's for sure*

Moore (ten); Gene DiNovi (p); Jimmy Johnson (bs); Stan Levey (d). New York City, 22 October 1948.

Blue Brew (3 versions) · *Brew blue* (2 versions) · *More Brew* (2 versions) · *No more Brew*

Swope (tbn); Getz, Sims (ten); Al Cohn (ten, arr); Jordan (p); Jimmy Raney (g); Russell (bs); Charlie Perry (d). New York City, 2 May 1949.

Stan gets along · *Stan's mood* · *Slow* · *Fast*

Cohn (ten); Wallington (p); Tommy Potter (bs); Kahn (d). New York City, 29 July 1950.

Groovin' with Gus · *Infinity* · *Let's get away from it all*

The important participants here are 'brothers' because of their associations with the 1947 Herman–Giuffre *Four brothers* (**312c**) – Getz, Sims, Chaloff, plus Herbie Steward – and with the 1949 *Five brothers* (†Original Jazz Classics [A] OJCCD008) – Getz, Sims, Cohn, Moore, Eager. (Lester Young, popularly the musical idol of most of them, referred, according to Buddy Tate, to 'those other ladies, my imitators'.) Only the four Getz items here, made a few weeks after *Five brothers*, echo the formative collaborations. This collection gives opportunity for some assessment of individual initiatives and of these men's stylistic interrelationship. The degree of Young-influence varies, and in the case of Chaloff it is scarcely an issue. Eager's performances reveal an unabashed Young devotee, and much the same judgement may be made in respect of Moore. Eager's 1948 work with Navarro (**260**), while it finds him at ease in the bop sphere, does not find him veering far from his chosen master's path; and his long sequence of exchanges with Mulligan during an impressive *Mulligan's too* (†Original Jazz Classics [A] OJCCD003) may have better aural evidence of his well-attested heeding of Charlie Parker.

The presence of Roach and Carter on the March 1946 date and of Roach, Jordan and Russell on the July 1947 one, enhances the 52nd

Street connection for these, the first two recording sessions under Eager's name. The unboppish theme *Rampage* gets a brusque introduction, then is treated by all to a flowing, vivacious development. Finckel, who wrote much for Boyd Raeburn's band (**314**), possesses an authoritative if not original piano style. His abilities shine again in *Booby hatch*, a telling feature of which is Eager's sleight-of-style combination of extremely rapid improvisation with Lesterish coursing calls and bland slitherings. The wryness of the tenorist's approach in the riffy *Symphony Sid's idea* opens a door, possibly, to other saxist promptings, but Lesterism is paramount.

Gibbs, later to be regarded as a West Coaster, had in fact been active on 52nd Street. Strongly attracted to bop, his rhythmic habits may still seem tethered to pre-bop vibraharpists, though he admired Milt Jackson and Teddy Charles. His part in the second Eager session is just right for the occasion, and the boplike unisons and passing harmonies in *All-night frantic* and *Donald Jay* suit the fashions of the day without in any way confounding Eager's instinct for using the Young springboard to modernism. The vibraharpist sounds a little less integrated in *Meeskite*, and against the urgency of this peerless rhythm section, even Eager loses some certainty. But the session, a recording debut for Gibbs, has pleasures in plenty, not the least of which are the solos which Jordan wrests out of conflict with an antagonistic piano.

Thus far the bop motivations are patent – bop was still in its first flush – even though the trends exploited by Herman associates put this music, generally, within what has now long been termed the cool orbit. Many jazz ideas, both distinct and interrelated, were surfacing more or less simultaneously in the later 1940s. Critical categories had not yet stiffened, and musicians have usually paid scant heed to them in any case. The Chaloff sextet's front line has Hermanite links (though Rodney had yet to join Herman); Wallington's composing gifts were, incidentally, part of the as yet inchoate cool movement. His *Godchild* would be arranged for Herman (First Heard [A] FH29) as well as, more significantly, for Claude Thornhill (Hep [E] 17) and then, crucially, for Miles Davis's nonet (**376**). Russell is here again. Kahn, an important modern thinker, is rather less easy to categorize.

Each of the four themes at this March 1947 meeting is cast in a slightly self-conscious bop mould. In *Pumpernickel* Chaloff threads his way masterfully through two choruses brimming with ideas. The other version has him working over similar figurations, the agility even more marked. Here, as in **310**, we listen to the major baritonist of bop. Rodney proves himself an excellent colleague, Swope is dependably forthright, Wallington excites even when made a bit breathless by the rate of *Serge's urge*; Kahn and Russell cannot be faulted. But it is Chaloff who grabs our attention. Hear his tumbling, writhing, somersaulting inventions in both versions of *Gaberdine and Serge*. So stunning is his facility that the question never is prompted, as it would sometimes be by the emergent Mulligan, how suitable the baritone might be to the intricacies of post-Parker techniques and linear possibilities.

Single takes of the Chaloff items and the May 1949 Getz titles appeared also on Realm (E) RM113 and Savoy (A) MG12105, together with four numbers by a septet led by Brew Moore. The latter session was notable for a performance of John Carisi's cyclic blues, *Lestorian mode*. Appropriate as that title may have seemed, the modality of Carisi's idea tended to restrict the customary effervescence of Moore's improvising approach. In the two versions of *Blue Brew* the approach seems a trifle measured at first, the similarity to Young marked through inflection rather more than in structure. The second version is faster, not necessarily more extrovert. Moore's best form surfaces in the engaging *More Brew*, the second take of which also raises tempo. Throughout the entire proceedings DiNovi (who during this period recorded with Young himself – **252**) courts chaos with extravagant attempts at the juggling with rhythms, and practically reaches incoherence during the easy-going *No more Brew* as Moore, with considerable verve, demonstrates how very close his allegiance to Young is. In his day his musicianship was much admired, and his devotion to his idol's style was thoroughly principled, but his prominence effectively came to an end during the 1950s.

The satisfactions of the Getz sextet's 1949 session owe much to the musical supervision of Cohn, the effective shaper of the event. The teaming of the three tenorists draws the production near to the 'brothers' concept. Cohn's arrangements are pleasing in themselves and are skilfully related to individual freedoms. The ensemble sound takes character from the 'vocal' similarity of the saxes and from the fact that Swope is the sole brass player. In *Stan gets along* the soloing roster runs: Getz, Swope, Cohn, Raney, Sims, Jordan. In *Slow* and *Fast* the order is much the same, certainly as far as the tenorists are concerned, Cohn's slight edge of force contrasting with Sims's limpidity in ways not clearly prophetic of their popular partnership started in the late 1950s. Getz sounds less distinctive here than he would soon become, a Young admirer with a personal sound. In 1946, tilting towards bop with Hank Jones, Russell and Roach, he could quite easily be mistaken for Dexter Gordon (Savoy [A] SJL1105); but here, extending himself in *Stan's mood*, he can give a better demonstration of a forming style. Less imitative of Young than Eager or Moore, he still may conjure Young's more rhapsodic work, tempering it with the personal emphases of cadence and rhythm that, reaching cohesion, were to make the music on **299** so memorable. Two companions for the future, Raney and Jordan, play excellently, the pianist having some brief chance to display his penchant for prefatory songs without words.

A good line-up for Cohn's first name session does not enable him to achieve real excellence. A strong but never flamboyant player, he actually sounds unambitious in parts of *Groovin' with Gus*; and Wallington, at mid-tempo, is tentative also. *Infinity* is a fast and intricate theme: Cohn threads it along with some Lester-like upward thrusts, a time-stretching exercise. Yet neither he nor Wallington quite manages to keep up to the urgings of the theme, and there are occasional yawings of impetus. None of this uneasiness is the fault of Potter or Kahn; but in *Let's get away from it all* some muddiness in the recording balance makes the bassist's contribution hard to appreciate properly. Despite these reservations, though, this is jazz which makes its forward-looking message clear enough. E.T.

Lee Konitz, Miles Davis, Teddy Charles, Jimmy Raney

298 **Ezz-thetic**
Prestige (A) PR7827, Xtra (E) 5004

Davis (tpt); Konitz (alt); Sal Mosca (p); Billy Bauer (g); Arnold Fishkin (bs); Max Roach (d). New York City, 8 March 1951.
Odjenar · Ezz-thetic · Hi, Beck · Yesterdays

Konitz, Bauer only. New York City, 13 March 1951.
Indian summer · Duet for saxophone and guitar

Raney (g); Dick Nivison (bs); Ed Shaughnessy (d); Charles (vib). New York City, 23 December 1952.
Edging out · Nocturne · Composition for four pieces · A night in Tunisia

George Russell's rather more than fledgling compositions *Odjenar* and *Ezz-thetic* (the first titled for his painter wife, the second for the boxer Ezzard Charles) already sound provocative in this transitional period. An indication of Konitz's shift to a firmer tone is the interesting contrast his shapely *Odjenar* solo sets against the rather bleak atmospherics of Russell's writing. The tune *Ezz-thetic*, later to become more frequently heard as a sprinting unison, is sounded by Konitz, swiftly, yes, but against a Davis countermelody which seems to have an element of spontaneity. The altoist's dazzling improvising over Roach's equally brilliant brush-strokes gives this version its most exciting moments. Even so, the promise of Russell's innovations is arresting, and these pieces should be heard in comparison with the music of **324**, **379–80** and **405** to understand the musical motives of a musician far more important than inconsistent critical opinion has suggested. Of interest here is that the challenge thrown by Russell to Davis and Konitz in particular differs from that presented by the radically motivated consortium of writers who served the more famous Davis sessions for Capitol in 1949–50 (**376**).

The excellent Bauer picks up the gauntlet too, and copes as skilfully with his *Odjenar* parts as he did in Tristano conceptions formal and free. Elsewhere his role is largely supportive, but it is often rich in tone and rhythmically enterprising, especially during Konitz's beautiful three-chorus variation upon *Pennies from heaven* which is called *Hi, Beck* in dedication to the altoist's daughter, Rebecca. That solo, along with the fine one in *Ezz-thetic*, should be rated among Konitz's finest work from any of his periods.

The second March session's numbers are true duets, with Konitz in generous form on *Indian summer* while Bauer devises eminently appropriate chordal settings. The guitarist contributes linear effects to the brief *Duet for saxophone and guitar* which, with its interweavings and tempo shifts, partially heeds Russellian messages.

Taken down almost contemporaneously with the recording debut of the MJQ (see **363**, also **482**), the Charles group could hardly avoid the obvious comparison. The presence of Raney is the patent textural difference, but the comparison is not, even at this stage, particularly edifying. Charles, whose expression is less touched by the blues than is Milt Jackson's, is not a particularly original stylist on an instrument whose aided resonances easily make it something of a stylistic leveller. A strong interest of his, though, was in developing the relationship between writer and improviser in projects such as the Jazz Composers' Workshop. His abilities as a forward-looking composer and perceptive encourager of others similarly gifted have determined his more enduring contributions to modern music.

Edging out suggests a love of rhythmic drama and of atmospheric colouring not unlike Russell's ideas. Charles's mixture of exaggerated resonance and forceful harmonized patterns backs Raney's designedly tentative introductory phrases, before the piece surges into some fleet and hyper-vigorous improvising from guitar and vibraharp. Atmosphere in *Nocturne* is first achieved by Nivison's murky bowing, cymbal hissing from Shaughnessy, and by Charles, who both augments and alters the mood, yet with less liberal employment of his resonators. Imaginative as *Nocturne* is, its dark adumbrations seem less related to jazz advance than is *Composition for four pieces*, where Russell is again bowed to as exemplar. Brevity makes the *Composition* sound slightly self-justifying; but one is surely right to attend to the intentions and promises even of Charles's inconclusiveness at this stage. The course of such aspirations will be better traced in an assessment of his 1956 *Tentet* recordings on **378**.

Heavy on 'rhythmic drama', *A night in Tunisia* could easily seem an overlong ride to nowhere, but along the clattering way there are good solos from Charles and from the guitarist who, considerably younger than Bauer, will appear more effectively touched by the light phrasing of bop (**355**).

The unwary should be told that at least three other records share, or partially share, the title of this one. They are Konitz's *Ezz-thetic* (Prestige [A] HBS6133), which has the 18 March session but is otherwise quite different; the French reissue of Russell's *The Jazz Workshop* as *Ezz-thetic* (RCA [F] PL42186); and *Ezzthetics* by the Russell sextet, which is dealt with under **405**. E.T.

Stan Getz

299 The Complete Recordings of the Stan Getz Quintet

Mosaic (A) MR4–131 (4 LPs), †MD3–131 (3 CDs)

Getz (ten); Horace Silver (p); Jimmy Raney (g); Leonard Gaskin (bs); Roy Haynes (d). New York City, 15 August 1951.
Melody express · *Yvette* · *Potter's luck* · *The song is you* · *Wildwood*

Getz (ten); Al Haig (p), Teddy Kotick (bs), Tiny Kahn (d) replace Silver, Gaskin, Haynes. Storyville, Boston, 28 October 1951.
Budo · *The song is you* · *Parker 51* · *Mosquito knees* · *Thou swell* · *Yesterdays* · *Jumpin' with Symphony Sid* · *Pennies from heaven* · *Move* · *Rubberneck* · *Hershey bar* · *Signal* · *Everything happens to me*

Getz (ten); Duke Jordan (p), Bill Crow (bs), Frank Isola (d) replace Haig, Kotick, Kahn. New York City, 12 December 1952.
Stella by starlight · *Time on my hands* · *'Tis autumn* · *The way you look tonight* · *Lover, come back to me* · *Body and soul* · *Stars fell on Alabama* · *You turned the tables on me*

Same personnel. New York City, 19 December 1952.
Lullaby of Birdland · *Autumn leaves* (2 versions) · *Fools rush in* (2 versions) · *These foolish things*

Same personnel. New York City, 29 December 1952.
Thanks for the memory · *How deep is the ocean?* · *Hymn to the Orient* · *These foolish things*

Hall Overton (p), Red Mitchell (bs) replace Jordan, Crow. New York City, 23 April 1953.
Signal · *Round about midnight* · *Motion* · *Lee*

There is a critical theory regarding what has been called 'the evolution of the cool sonority' [15] that made Getz the cynosure of the proceedings – the chief accoucheur, it might be said, at 'the birth of the cool'. Within a very few years of the issue of Herman's *Summer sequence*, *Early autumn* and *Four brothers* (**312c**), Barry Ulanov wrote emphatically: 'The change, the new conception, the revolution are all best illustrated by the playing of Stan Getz . . . the highly attractive centre of cool jazz.' [16] During the period preceding the 1947–9 Herman–Getz liaison Getz, on his own testimony, was 'beginning to dig Lester' as an antidote to the pushy vigour demanded of the Benny Goodman reed section he inhabited at that time. The consequences of heeding a great swing-era prophet soon showed themselves, but within more congenial groups. Other tenorists – some to become his 'brotherly' colleagues (see **297** and **370**) – assumed the Lester Young form and spirit in varying degrees. Within the following decade another writer commented that 'The cool musicians . . . ignoring what bop had achieved . . . generally adopted outmoded melodic and rhythmic conceptions. With few exceptions they preferred Lester Young's example to Charlie Parker's.' This kind of 'backtracking' might, he thought, be 'only temporary', but it was 'nonetheless one of the most disquieting signs in the history of jazz'. [17]

Wider perspectives and more varied aural evidence have made for better judgements. In 1946, playing, within the span of about six months, first with a Kai Winding band much in the mould of the Young–Basie Kansas City Six and Seven (**135a**), and then as leader of a quartet with a pristine bop rhythm section, Getz veered from unabashed Young impersonations to a style that took account of the Parker effect through impersonation of the style-straddling voice of Dexter Gordon (**348**). In Herman's saxophone section he was with what someone has called 'the Lester Young Communicant Society', but was rapidly finding himself. In the period of the recordings appraised below he had clearly opted not for Gordon, not for Young, but for Getz. Unquestionably Young had been a powerful mentor, but now the disciple had a voice and a vocabulary recognizable by their own virtues, a style that was to win him extended renown and that altered only minimally over the length of his career.

Through the four changes of personnel in this dedicated Mosaic reproduction of 37 items linking the second half of 1951 with the end of 1952 and the spring of 1953, the uniting thread is the constant presence of Raney. The guitarist is, in fact, the nominal leader of the 1953 ensemble. Four pianists with four affecting styles are involved. The standard of bass/drums support reflects the leaders' choice of distinguished men. The playing of Getz, in his mid-20s, has probably never been surpassed in its brilliant expressiveness.

The virility, even toughness, of the August 1951 studio group owes more than a little to Silver's approach. Three original numbers by Gigi Gryce and one by Silver, plus a Kern–Hammerstein standard, were chosen. (Although newer technology was coming to hand, the length of tracks still was determined by 78-rpm time limits. Only at the 1953 session does modest elasticity invade the studio. For the Storyville live performance, such restrictions are manifestly null.)

Silver's theme *Potter's luck* is an augury of hard-bop messages yet to be. Getz introduces its mock-hesitant pattern with Haynes's collaboration, and his lissome extension of it mixes wiry with gentle effects. He opens Gryce's *Melody express* in fleet unison with Raney, exhibiting an uncool energy which carries through the solos following from Getz, Raney and Silver. Getz was the first leader to feature Gryce compositions, and *Yvette* is another. Close to standard song style, its instrumental lines are similarly marshalled to those of *Melody express* and *The song is you*. The last finds Getz's decisive lead receiving counter-melodies from Raney. Gryce's *Wildwood*, while taken at a brisk pace, has a more leisured feel to its proceedings which are completed by Silver's emphasis of the theme's bop derivation. Some interest may attach to the not infrequent interweavings of melodic strands in some of these numbers. When the

Getz–J. J. Johnson *At the Opera House* recordings appeared around 1957 (†Verve [A] 831 272), much was made of the notion that the leaders' stretches of simultaneous extemporization were retrieving a collective craft common in early jazz but effectively lost during the days of swing and bop. That point, though not without shrewdness, can be overemphasized. New freedoms of interaction followed upon the emancipation of rhythm sections won in further bop developments; but what will be noticed in some of these Getz sessions may instructively be compared with the contemporaneous and subtly achieved free collectivism that will be noted at **363** in reference to the MJQ.

Haig had been a frequent companion of Getz on recordings, and lends his distinctive emphasis and sustenance to the famous Storyville occasion, slipping a snatch of Parker adulation into the breakneck *Budo.* Tenor–guitar unison starts this number off, and Getz poses angular challenges in his solo to which Raney responds with perhaps some lack of colour. As elsewhere, the splendid Kahn lifts the tensions when necessary. There will be a number of passages where Getz and Raney achieve joint improvisation – 'circling each other in mid-air', as Bill Crow has it – e.g. *The song is you*, wherein, with brittle lines, Raney also inserts complementary thought into the piano solo; Gryce's *Mosquito knees*, swift-riding, and ending with Getz–Kahn exchanges; and the dizzyingly rapid *Move*, with Haig and Raney in dialogue, and a front-line echo at the end of the Miles Davis nonet prototype of January 1949 (**376**).

The Getz improvising manner has great ease, fluidity and variety of expression, and the level of inventiveness is pretty constant throughout all these sessions. The immediacy of his creative acumen, and the vigour of its continuity, can leave the hearer breathless; yet it seldom, if ever, touches mere suavity. The undoubted peak at Storyville is his four-chorus *allegretto* treatment of *Pennies from heaven*, a kaleidoscope of fresh ideas and whimsical allusions. Young may still be glancing over the shoulder of his unslavish proselyte, but to transcend example is not necessarily to abandon it wholly. There is little of the master's dryness of timbre, and less still of his sardonicism, but rhythmic influence still shows and also the effects of Young's habits of registral contrast, though when the latter are emulated they avoid the old air of deliberate mischief.

Perhaps it is not chance that Young's forceful one-note staccatos surface during *Jumpin' with Symphony Sid* – it is supposed to be Young's composition, after all (see **252**), and the overall trend of the piece, focused on Haig's firm nods to Parker, is one that airs the relationship to bop of both Getz and the post-1945 Young. Other than that, and bearing in mind Young's singular reputation as a penetrating interpreter of popular songs, the bulk of the material used on the occasions which follow is drawn from a standard repertoire. Whereas in the sessions considered above, five items only out of 18 are standards, of the 16 numbers (two repeated) of the three December 1952 sessions, *Hymn of* *the Orient* and *Lullaby of Birdland* only are jazz originals. According to Crow's Mosaic notes, the emphasis on standards followed a request from Norman Granz, supervisor on 12 and 29 December. Lyricism is a pronounced feature of the group with Jordan, Crow and Isola; and from Getz there is frequently an intricate romanticism and an instinct for swing that allows for several kinds of cross-beat manoeuvre. A lot of this belies the epithet 'cool', and seemingly gave pause to critics whose welcome to the 'cool sonority' was an *ave* to intellectual advance or to 'the search for purity'. [18] Hodeir complained a little later that 'Getz seems to be sacrificing richness of improvisation to an increasingly predominant concern with swing.' [19]

As in the cases of Silver and Haig, the choice of pianist affects the character of his band. Crow writes of the fascination with which he and the other men heard Jordan's 'delicious inventions'; and though this makes odd the report referred to in **288** that Jordan 'ran into difficulties with Getz', of even greater moment is the way in which the music itself bears out Crow's assertion, and incidentally strengthens a suspicion that if there were frictions their cause may not have been directly musical. Definitive as the leader's brilliance may be for the lasting fame of these recordings, such revelations as Jordan's introductions to *Stella by starlight*, *Time on my hands*, *Body and soul*, *Stars fell on Alabama*, *Fools rush in* (different for each take) and *These foolish things* leave their own distinctive impression on the memory.

As for Getz himself, so high is the calibre of his skill that piecemeal comment upon his solos would become tedious by mere adulation. An idea of their expressive diversity may come from indication of the dreamy elaborations of *Stella by starlight*, the immense lift of *The way you look tonight*, the remoulding of the rhythmic cast of *You turned the tables on me*, and the exalted aloofness and stuttered musings in *Autumn leaves.* Then there are the subdued combativeness aimed at the shape of Shearing's *Lullaby of Birdland*, and the manner in which Getz, as if to exorcise Coleman Hawkins firmly from any hearer's memory, coos his way through his *Body and soul* variations like a conspiratorial dove.

After the 12 December meeting, Raney's role changes from the prominently active and interactive to the largely functional. Most of the solo space is Getz's. Both Raney and Jordan, when they solo at all, are allotted half-choruses at most. There are stretches where Raney's participation is not easily discernible, places where Jordan's chordal and other forms of gentle propulsion need little enhancement. There is an arranged counter-melody in the first statement of *The way you look tonight*, and deft tenor–guitar unison closes the same piece. Various guitar delicacies are heard in *Stars fell on Alabama* and *You turned the tables on me*, and Raney's aptitudes assist the calculated theme truncation at the close of *Lullaby of Birdland.* There is a bit more elbow room for him on 29 December, chording an introduction to *Thanks for the memory*, and in solo and ensemble comment sounding strong and lyrical. He had already demonstrated, in the sessions with Silver and Haig, that his lyricism and ingenuity could be a fair match for the leader's.

On the 1953 recording Raney is leader. Getz was still under contract to Granz so the Prestige release identified him as 'Sven Coolson', and the quintet was completed by the jazz-classical amphibian Hall Overton at the piano, bassist Red Mitchell who, according to Ira Gitler, who was there, had just dropped in, and Isola, still a Getz employee. There is some reversal of roles for tenor and guitar. Expectedly, Raney is more prominent, and in the re-emergence of his *Signal* theme, its form minimally adapted, he is able to achieve the same sustenance of conception with marked flexibility. *Lee* is his theme, too, a bow towards Konitz and Tristano, and he honours his own motives for such a composition in a brilliantly fingered solo.

Round about midnight is gently reimagined by Raney and Getz and there is notable collaboration here from Overton and Mitchell. *Motion* has yet more Tristanoan touches, at least in Raney's theme, and, directing it, the guitarist appears to be relishing his liberty and control. (Comparable material can be examined under **297** and on *Jimmy Raney in Three Attitudes* (Jasmine [E] JASM1049.) Overton, a musician justly regarded as magisterial, is, in demonstrating his bop capabilities, unassuming and yet brilliantly clear. Mitchell maintains the pose of an ebullient friend, asserting his enjoyment of the occasion frequently; and Isola serves impeccable and unobtrusive succour, just as he did through a score of earlier pursuits of jazz excellence.

Much of Getz's work in this long sequence might be judged an object lesson, or a whole set of such, in a manner of improvised thematic development, variously influenced, and undoubtedly reaching a stage of fulfilment in this jazz period, especially in this man's craft and vision. In so far as he was able to maintain his relaxed achievement acceptably through three and a half subsequent decades, his style did not become outmoded. His albums *Anniversary* (†EmArcy [H] 838 769) and *Serenity* († EmArcy [H] 838 770), both from the summer of 1987, will bear out the claim. That he came to be taken for granted by his public is, one supposes, some kind of offhand accolade. E.T.

Gerry Mulligan

300 The Complete Pacific Jazz and Capitol Records of the Original Gerry Mulligan Quartet and Tentette with Chet Baker

Mosaic (A) MR5–102 (5 LPs)

Mulligan (bar); Red Mitchell (bs); Chico Hamilton (d). Los Angeles, 9–10 June 1952.

Get happy · 'Swonderful · Godchild · Haig and Haig · She didn't say yes

Baker (tpt); Mulligan (bar); Jimmy Rowles (p). Los Angeles, 9 July 1952.
Bernie's tune · *Lullaby of the leaves* · *Utter chaos*

Baker (tpt); Mulligan (bar); Bobby Whitlock (bs); Hamilton (d). Los Angeles, 15–16 October 1952.
Aren't you glad you're you? · *Frenesi* · *Nights at the turntable* · *Freeway* · *Soft Shoe* · *Walkin' shoes*

Baker, Pete Candoli (tpt); Bob Envoldsen (v-tbn); John Graas (fr h); Ray Seigal (tu); Bud Shank (alt); Mulligan, Don Davidson (bar); Joe Mondragon (bs); Hamilton (d). Los Angeles, 29 January 1953.
A ballad · *Westwood walk* · *Walkin' shoes* · *Rocker*

Baker, Candoli (tpt); Envoldsen (v-tbn); Graas (fr h); Seigal (tu); Shank (alt); Mulligan, Davidson (bar); Mondragon (bs); Larry Bunker (d). Los Angeles, 31 January 1953.
Takin' a chance on love · *Flash* · *Simbah* · *Ontet*

Baker (tpt); Lee Konitz (alt); Mulligan (bar); Carson Smith (bs); Bunker (d). Live at the Haig, Los Angeles. **Note**: The three sessions with Konitz probably took place on 23 January 1953, 30 January 1953 and 1 February 1953 but it has been impossible to attribute any date to a specific session.
Too marvellous for words · *Loverman* · *I'll remember April* · *These foolish things* · *All the things you are* · *Bernie's tune*

Same personnel as above. Los Angeles, see note.
Almost like being in love · *Sextet* · *Broadway*

Same personnel as above, except Mondragon replaces Smith (bs); see note.
I can't believe you're in love with me · *Lady be good* (2 versions)

Baker (tpt); Mulligan (bar); Smith (bs); Bunker (d). Los Angeles, 24 February 1953.
Makin' whopee · *Cherry* · *Motel* · *Carson City stage*

Same personnel. Los Angeles, 27 March 1953.
Festive minor · *My old flame* · *All the things you are*

Same personnel. Los Angeles, 27 April 1953.
Love me or leave me (2 versions) · *Swing house* · *Jeru* · *Utter chaos*

Same personnel. Los Angeles, 29–30 April 1953.
Darn that dream (2 versions) · *I may be wrong* (2 versions) · *I'm beginning to see the light* (2 versions) · *The nearness of you* · *Tea for two*

Same personnel. Los Angeles, 20 May 1953. **Note**: There is some evidence that this session may have taken place in January 1953.
Five Brothers · *I can't get started* · *Ide's idea* · *Haig and Haig* · *My funny Valentine*

Same session, Chico Hamilton replaces Bunker (d).
Aren't you glad you're you? · *Get happy* · *Poinciana* · *Godchild*

Of the five arrangers who contributed to the *Birth of the Cool* sessions (**376**), Mulligan was the most original and the most prolific, responsible for five of the 12 numbers recorded for Capitol. [20] It was an impressive vote of confidence by his peers, including Miles Davis, Gil Evans, George

Russell, John Lewis and Lee Konitz; indeed Russell would later say: 'The most important innovator of 1950s was Gerry Mulligan.' [21] Previously, Mulligan had caused a stir in musicians' circles with his charts of *How high the moon?* and *Disc jockey jump* for the Gene Krupa band of 1946–7 and *Sometimes I'm happy, Godchild* and *Elevation* for Claude Thornhill's orchestra during the summer of 1948. What is interesting about this early work was its gradual move away from the angular contours of bop towards smoother, less frantic forms of expressionism. However, in tandem with his arranging was a fast-developing skill on baritone sax after a spell playing a variety of saxophones in bands led by Tommy Tucker, Elliot Lawrence, Krupa and Thornhill, all of whom had recruited him primarily as an arranger.

Having initially come under the spell of Charlie Parker, Mulligan was absorbing the lessons of Lester Young, rationalizing both his playing and his writing in favour of a conspicuously melodic, linear approach, even naming his music publishing company Pres Music. Several arrangements and originals he wrote during this period reveal this trend, including those for Kai Winding (Wallington's *Godchild* and *Sleepy bop* from April 1949), Brew Moore (the May 1949 *Lestorian mode* session), and his own tentette recordings for Prestige in 1951. When, Kerouac-like, he hitch-hiked to the West Coast in early 1952 he endured a brief, somewhat fraught, relationship with the Kenton orchestra while also sitting in at the Lighthouse, Hermosa Beach, and the Monday-night jam sessions at the Haig, a tiny 85-seater club on Wilshire Boulevard at Kenmore Street. Here, in early July, Mulligan met the trumpeter Chet Baker and just over a month later he approached the club owner John Bennett to fill the Monday-night spot with a group of his own.

The June and July 1952 sessions reveal him evolving a small-group concept, having spent his whole career with large and medium-sized ensembles. Consequently there a clear sense of experimentation, of feeling his way, and at this stage a piano appeared central to his ideas; the fact that there is no piano on the first session, other than Mulligan's 'arranger's piano', is because Jimmy Rowles had promised to appear but failed to do so. Ultimately, however, it seems it was a practical reason rather than a cerebral concept that persuaded Mulligan to go without a keyboard. When the Red Norvo trio opened at the Haig in mid-July for an indefinite engagement, the club's piano was put in temporary storage. Mulligan's hand was forced: if he wanted the job he played *sans* piano.

Their first 'pianoless quartet' session came after playing five successive Monday nights at the club and produced *Bernie's tune* and *Lullaby of the leaves*. They were released in the autumn of 1952 and became a minor hit, putting both Mulligan and Pacific Records on the map. The saxophonist has often said his approach was to simplify rather than complicate [22] and certainly his handling of *Bernie's tune*, a minor-key 32-bar AABA tune then popular with musicians for jamming, could not be simpler with its unisons, Mulligan's improvised backgrounds and a somewhat strained 'baroque' passage before the final chorus. Equally, *Lullaby of the leaves*, with its skeletal background figures and economy of purpose, gives a hint of the exceptional empathy that would develop between Mulligan and Baker, neither of whom at this stage had fully come to terms with the absence of a pianist. Indeed, their treatment of *Bernie's tune* sounds as if they expected one to walk through the door at any moment.

Two months and a hit with *My funny Valentine* for the Fantasy label later, Mulligan's little ensemble was hitting its stride. Every number from the October 1952 session has something to commend it. Three are original Mulligan compositions specially tailored for the group and a fourth, *Freeway*, was by Baker. The group was now beginning to attract large crowds at the Haig and regular performance together was bringing focus and unity in dealing with the 'pianoless' concept. In contrast to the August session, Mulligan and Baker had now come to terms with how their lines stood out in sharp relief with the absence of chordal backing and were taking advantage of how this allowed for greater clarity of expression, whether in a leading or secondary role. This session and those that follow reveal the spirit of the Davis *Birth of the Cool* sessions and Mulligan's own Prestige tentette recordings with their sophisticated contrary voicings and elegant counterpoint, albeit boiled down to their very essence. With his miniature ensemble, Mulligan attempted to duplicate these lines as much through part-writing as through the inspiration of the moment.

The role of the bass is given prominence, calling for greater vertical development of the front line's role. While Mulligan, almost from the start, seemed aware of this, by now Baker too realized what an ideal forum the pianoless concept offered to show off his melodic ideas. 'Chet was one of the best intuitive musicians I've seen,' Mulligan would assert later. [23] And although Baker did not sight-read well, he had an exceptional ear and picked up quickly on things, contributing his own improvised lines that often sounded as if they had been written out in advance. [24] *Nights at the turntable* is typical of the engaging originals Mulligan devised for the group. A 36-bar AABA^1 composition, Mulligan and Baker open in unison, followed by a brief period of open and closed harmony followed by the final four bars in unison. The middle eight and final A^1 section (A+4 bars) introduce quite precise contrapuntal lines, but always the recurring opening motif of four quavers is played in unison. Mulligan and Baker are now more confident of what they are trying to achieve, and this shows when each plays accompanying lines to the other's solo. These are not riffs, but engaging background figures of varying length and complexity that would have lost their impact competing with a piano, which would have directed them towards a more traditional relationship between trumpet and saxophone. *Soft shoe* and

Walkin' shoes, both 32-bar AABA Mulligan compositions, follow *Nights at the turntable* with its engaging mixture of simple part-writing and orderly, rhythmic counterpoint. In contrast, Baker's *Freeway* is all hustle and bustle, which, while providing contrast to Mulligan's love of cut-time medium tempos, muddies the studied interrelationship between saxophone and trumpet with its fast-moving lines.

Mulligan's next session was with a West Coast version of his tentette and formed, like his 1951 East Coast unit with which he made his debut as a leader on records for Prestige, as a rehearsal band. On *Westwood walk* and *Walkin' shoes* Mulligan succeeds in capturing the engaging characteristics of his quartet with a larger ensemble. On the former, a 32-bar AA song with A sections of 16 bars each, the emphasis is on hard swing without decibel excess, exemplified by Mulligan's writing for the ensemble after the solo choruses. However, the latter, while capturing the poise of the smaller group, lacks its intimacy of the earlier version of the song.

The remaining sides appear as a logical continuum of Mulligan's generally overlooked role in helping to midwife the *Birth of the Cool* dates. Both his compositions and arrangements favour the subdued lyricism and similar tone colours favoured by the Davis nonet. Even so, *A ballad*, with its Claude Thornhill-like 'clouds of sound', is wholly convincing in its own right. A 44-bar AA^{1}BA song with the A sections of 12 bars and a B section of eight bars, the whole performance comprises just one chorus of the song (plus a four-bar tag). Mulligan would later say that much of what he wrote in the 1950s was based on what he wrote for Davis, [25] but it was also clear that he was seeking to expand on his past achievements, despite the inclusion of *Rocker* from the *Birth of the Cool* sessions.

On *Simbah* he experiments with a minimum of chord changes over an extended composition of 48 bars, in an unusual AABAA form where the A sections are eight bars and the B section 16 (the basic form excludes the 24-bar introductory passage). The A sections are confined to just one chord throughout, while the B section, except for a couple of passing chords to modulate back to the A section, is effectively based on three chords. This was unusual in jazz at the time and a sharp contrast to bop, which made extensive use of passing chords during periods of static harmony and anticipated the move towards modal harmonies by some five years. Yet Mulligan did not stop there; after the exposition of the AABAA theme he never returns to it. The rest of the composition includes transitional passages, pedal points and *ostinato* figures and is a miniature masterpiece of developmental writing for a small jazz ensemble; this 'second' section, although related to the first, is unmistakably more lyrical in content and more imaginative, particularly the feeling of rhythmic suspension in the coda. A lot happens in a short space of time, yet there is never a feeling of congestion in Mulligan's writing, rather an orderly and logical progression from one idea to another.

In contrast to the static harmonic movement of *Simbah*, there are moments in *Flash*, a 32-bar AABA song, where new chord changes are coming at the rate of one every beat, such as the particularly affecting chromatic ascent of diminished chords at the end of each A section. Here Mulligan plays 'arranger's piano', and, as in *Ontet* (a variation on George Wallington's *Godchild*), introduces the harmonic movement of the songs rather revealing any of its specific melodic contours per se. Flash opens like a small-group performance, with piano, trumpet and alto taking successive choruses. Only at the end of the alto chorus does an ensemble emerge briefly, before a somewhat lumpy Mulligan piano solo and the introduction of the ensemble proper. It is impossible not to think Mulligan's piano style was inspired by Monk's work on numbers such as *I mean you*, *Thelonious* or *Epistrophy* when he came up with this composition. It evokes Monk as much in terms of the minimal melodic line, sharp rhythmic displacements and the essentially pianistic nature of the composition as in Mulligan's own slightly ham-fisted piano technique. *Ontet*, with its melody based around the ii-V-I progression, uses the group more fully, an exercise as much in tone colours as part-writing. Taken together, the tentette recordings, originally issued on one side of the *Modern Sounds* album shared with a Shorty Rogers group (**359**), certainly do not deserve the semi-obscurity to which they have been consigned. Not only are they among the very best of what would become known as West Coast jazz but they stand up today both in terms of compositional form and orchestral ingenuity.

The final three studio sessions show the quartet expanding their repertoire with a variety of originals and sometimes quite unusual standards. *Makin' whoopee*, for example, is customized into the group's carefully prescribed world of gruff melody and tactful counterpoint and emerges as a typically ingratiating performance. *Cherry* does not fare so well; the group's quite stylized delivery did not sit well with the attempted humour of a Dixieland coda. However, as ever it is Mulligan's originals that are the most captivating; *Motel*, a 32-bar AABA composition, is built around a descending figure answered by a motif built around the interval of a fourth, then quite an unusual interval to use as a specific feature of a melody line. Equally, the middle eight is based on the descending cycle of fourths (although his use of the cycle was not so unusual in song construction; the *Walkin' shoes* middle eight, for example, is also based on a cycle, this time descending fifths). Both *Festive minor* and *All the things you are* were not released until this 1983 compilation. The former, not surprisingly in F minor, would appear in versions by subsequent Mulligan ensembles on the Columbia and Mercury labels. Here, however, it does not work quite so well with just the baritone stating the theme, so reducing the group to a trio for a large portion of the performance. Equally, while both Mulligan and Baker contribute good solos to *All the things you are*, a tentative ending was probably the reason it was not selected for release.

With the popularity of the group taking off, Mulligan needed to expand the group's repertoire quickly, so it is hardly surprising that he turned to numbers with which he was familiar. *Darn that dream* and *Jeru* (like *Rocker* and *Godchild*) came from the *Birth of the Cool* sessions, *Swing house*, *Walkin' shoes* and *All the things you are* from arrangements he had contributed to Kenton and *I may be wrong* from a chart he wrote for Chubby Jackson. Somehow, however, this little group seemed at its best with cut-time medium-tempo numbers, a device that succeeds in bringing a quiet integrity to the master take of *I'm beginning to see the light*, Helen Forrest's big hit with the Harry James orchestra. Although making allusions to a larger ensemble with its powerful unisons, both Mulligan and Baker clearly get a kick out of the old warhorse which conveys itself to the listener all these years later. Another cut-time piece, although at a brighter tempo, *Tea for two* provides the chords for an ingenious Mulligan variation that cleverly juxtaposes paraphrase with his witty writing; played with zest by the quartet, it is among the best sides cut by this unique group.

Unquestionably live recordings provide jazz music's most vital life studies, and the inclusion of six previously unissued sides, plus *Five brothers* and *My funny Valentine* restored to their full length, all recorded at the Haig in early 1953, provide an important documentation of this group. Mulligan has spoken of how they developed a remarkable empathy during their performances at the club, [26] and it is interesting to hear how they react away from the confines of a recording studio. Certainly there is more risktaking – Baker's solo on *Haig and Haig*, for example – prompted by a free and easy feeling that permeates the group as a whole. *My funny Valentine* is a reprise of their hit for the Fantasy label, played *andante maestoso*, and *Five brothers* is a Mulligan original dating back to a 1949 Stan Getz date. A straightforward 32-bar AABA song which he would arrange for Claude Thornhill's orchestra a matter of weeks after Getz recorded it, it is a perfect vehicle for the conversational exchanges of the trumpeter and saxophonist. By the time these recordings were made, Mulligan was announcing that he had requests for numbers 'from our new Pacific Jazz album'. Both *Aren't you glad you're you?* and a rampaging *Get happy* immediately distance themselves from the sometimes introspective moods created in the studio and are far removed from the concept of 'cool' jazz. They are the confident and sometimes exuberant (Bunker's drums on *Get happy*, for example) statements of young men at one with their art, palpably playing for their own enjoyment as much as their audience's.

The introduction of Lee Konitz into Mulligan's tightly knit ensemble was not wholly successful, yet it evoked memorable performances from the alto saxophonist. Konitz, a major improviser on his instrument in a way that Mulligan and Baker were not, effectively dominated a group that had previously relied on a careful interrelationship of leading and secondary voices in both ensemble and solo passages. Only Mulligan, with his arranger's skill, seemed secure in improvising accompaniments behind Konitz, who takes centre stage. Mulligan and Baker take a back seat as Konitz works out on *Loverman,* his big feature number with the Kenton orchestra of which he was currently a member, and *All the things you are* and *Too marvellous for words.* That he was sitting in with the Mulligan Quartet is clear only on *I'll remember April* when baritone and trumpet unite in typical catch-as-catch-can counterpoint to announce the theme before stepping back from the microphone to allow Konitz to take the only solo. Although *Bernie's tune* is shown as coming from these live sessions, this seems doubtful; no audience sound is audible and there is a degree of preparation that is not apparent on the previous numbers.

Bernie's tune, like the studio versions of *Almost like being in love, Sextet* and *Broadway* that follow, shows thought had now been given to integrating Konitz into the quartet by his doubling or harmonizing Mulligan's lines an octave higher (easy to do from arrangements since both alto and baritone are E-flat instruments) and, incidentally, providing interesting tonal colour in so doing, or by the altoist occasionally doubling Baker's part in unison or simple harmony. On their final session together Mulligan has clearly taken more trouble with arrangements and it can only be a matter of speculation whether the four recordings at Phil Turetsky's house, like those of a year before that presaged the quartet, might have in turn heralded an expansion of the group. Whatever Mulligan intended, however, became moot when he was arrested for a narcotics offence and was sent to the minimum-security jail at Newhall for six months. As a postscript to this remarkable little unit, Getz – currently in Los Angeles to play the Tiffany Club – filled in for Mulligan at the Haig during June 1953. The 16 June recordings that exist (†Fresh Sounds [Sp] FSCD-1022) reveal the extent to which Mulligan had focused his playing with the specific end of producing a cohesive and integrated group sound, his playing shaped in service of the ensemble, most particularly in accompanying figures that spelled out the harmonic movement of chords that often presented fuguelike effects against Baker's trumpet. In contrast, Getz's accompanying figures are closer to big-band riffing than specific counterpoint, producing instead a rather workaday jam-session feel quite removed from the detailed ensemble characteristics that made the Mulligan's original concept so unique. This is also true of *Stan Meets Chet* (†Verve [A] 837436–2), their 1958 meeting in Chicago for the Verve label.

Mulligan's imprisonment marked the end of his association with Baker. During their year together their uncanny rapport, sometimes mechanical but frequently inspired, would never again be recaptured in subsequent reunion sessions. By dispensing with a piano he had created a group that was unique in jazz, something that even got a mention in *Time* magazine. [27] It respected the primacy of the improviser both in shaping the ensemble sound and in creating an environment for the soloist to flourish. It was a concept later picked up by Ornette Coleman and Albert Ayler and became common in free jazz, but for the moment, Mulligan had found a niche that he would subsequently develop with Bob Brookmeyer (v-tbn) and Jon Eardley (tpt), eventually expanding into a sextet (**362**) before ultimately returning to his first love, a big band.

What is interesting about these sides is that at no point can either Mulligan or Baker be accused of creating a truly great solo. Mulligan's playing was as far removed from the stunning virtuosity of Serge Chaloff in one direction as Chet Baker was from a Fats Navarro or a Dizzy Gillespie in another. Mulligan's role as conceptualist, composer and arranger in ordering the interrelationship of the group's instrumentation actually revealed their strengths – Baker's ingenious, warm lyricism and Mulligan's genial swing – rather than their weaknesses. Simply dispensing with a piano is in itself no guarantee of success, as, for example, various configurations of Max Roach's small groups demonstrated, from his 1957 group with Kinny Dorham and Hank Mobley to his quartet with Cecil Bridgewater and Odean Pope of the late 1970s and 1980s. Here, much of their repertoire was based on the bop/hard-bop methodology of head-solos-head, casting the soloists adrift with the skeletal accompaniment of bass and drums for long periods, which tended to highlight the improvisers' weaknesses rather than their strengths in a way that no amount of resourceful drumming could compensate for. In contrast, Mulligan's organization of the limited tone colours at his disposal through clever part-writing, well-conceived transitional passages and judicious counterpoint created a context where both baritone and trumpet functioned effectively within the clearly prescribed limitations of their respective styles. It is to his credit that both Mulligan and Baker were able to appear profound, exciting and occasionally moving without recourse to artifice or grand gesture. S.N.

Tal Farlow

301 **Autumn in New York**

Verve (A) MGV8184

Farlow (g); Gerry Wiggins (p); Ray Brown (bs); Chico Hamilton (d). Los Angeles, 15 November 1954.

I like to recognize the tune · *Strike up the band* · *Autumn in New York* · *And she'll remember me* · *Little girl blue* · *Have you met Miss Jones?* · *Tal's blues* · *Cherokee*

Jim Hall

302 Jazz Guitar

†EMI/Pacific Jazz (E) CDP746 851–2, Pacific Jazz (A) PJ1227

Hall (g); Carl Perkins (p); Red Mitchell (bs). Los Angeles, 10, 24 January 1957.

Stompin' at the Savoy · *Things ain't what they used to be* · *This is always* · *Thanks for the memory* · *Tangerine* · *Stella by starlight* · *9.20 special* · *Deep in a dream* · *Look for the silver lining* · *Seven come eleven*

Taking to his instrument when the advent of bop was in the offing, Farlow latched on to the rhythmic and melodic characteristics that were adapted from swing styles. The remarkable fluency of technique at speed, which he claimed to have acquired perforce when a member of Red Norvo's 1950–1 trio, is amply exemplified by *I like to recognize the tune*, *Strike up the band*, *Have you met Miss Jones?* and elsewhere here, and that skill is frequently breathtaking. His work with Norvo and Mingus is dealt with under **247** and that entry contains an enlightening paragraph regarding Farlow himself, his early background as a guitarist, and the unorthodox devices he used to enhance the trio's rhythmical resources. The success of the Norvo trio helped him in a number of ways and it involved him in an unusual celebration of parts of the 'cool' repertoire, including items then recently featured by the Miles Davis Capitol nonet (**376**). Together with the Jim Hall item, the *Autumn in New York* collection fits amicably enough into this subsection of our book, yet it will be evident from any review of their careers that neither Farlow nor Hall is as easy to categorize as that.

In the atemporal prologue to *Autumn in New York* itself, Farlow combines strong tonal quality with a flexible approach to incidental stresses; a flexibility which may appear to be sacrificed to some extent at the lickety-split tempos he seems to like. In this number, and in the gentle, almost hesitant *Little girl blue*, Wiggins sounds to be a more suitable pianist for the occasion than he does in the livelier pieces. His spikey chorus in the rapid *Have you met Miss Jones?* is fetching, but in other places his style is a slightly uneasy mixture of elements from hard bop and a certain pianistic hinterland of the cool movement. This approach is one of the things that make *Tal's blues* the least successful track, another being the guitarist's inappropriate frequent resort to double-timing. Brown's contribution here is admirable, as it is in all other numbers. Similarly Hamilton plays along just as though he is enjoying everything famously. In the breakneck tricksiness of *Cherokee* the streaking Farlow might sometimes be offering wry comments upon his own facility.

His tilting at extended improvisation may, in its fluency, occasionally call to mind the contemporary tenor playing of Getz; but the guitar style probably heeded, whether studiously or not, the long lines and bounding intervals of the original bop pianist. Jimmy Raney, a Getz associate at this period, developed what is in some ways a more directly guitaristic mode (**299**, **355**), but several of the guitar modernists tended to follow keyboard models. Hall's relation to such influences may be hinted at by a discernible contrast of his style with that of his pianist on the 1957 session.

A review of the Hall trio's disc – the first under his name – published in the year following its issue found his playing inadequate beside that of his companions Perkins and Mitchell. The calibre of Hall's performance may be variously judged, but it should be judged in the proper context, which in this case is hardly to be understood, as the 1958 commentator understood it, as that of 'pianist with accompanists'. [28] It is much more of a cooperative group. A number recorded at this session but not included here, *Too close for comfort*, was extracted for issue on an album titled *Pianists Galore* as by the Carl Perkins trio (World Pacific [A] JWC506, Vogue [E] LAE12097).

These men are easy collaborators, and although Hall, by no means the weakest partner, often indeed sets the pace in expressive terms, there is a good sharing and balancing of roles. In *Stompin' at the Savoy* a sense of greater thoughtfulness and a more patent concern for form may compensate for any small lessening of sprightliness discerned in a comparison with Farlow. Hall makes a personal use of chordal punctuations, and while he gives the impression of gentle simplicity in *Things ain't what they used to be*, there is real strength in his laying-down of standards, and he shows more originality than does Perkins.

The guitar–piano interplay in *This is always* shows rapport, but still emphasizes the two men's imaginative differences somewhat. Here is no suggestion that the contrast is anything other than stimulating. The warmth of expression in *Thanks for the memory* and the fine relaxation of *Tangerine* owe a great deal to close support of pianist and bassist. Perkins's absorbed influences are not so very different from those of Wiggins, but he makes more coherent use of them. The strength of his personal style is a feature of a mid-tempo *Stella by starlight* during which statements closer to hard bop subtend the precise, though never laggard, cool phraseology of Hall. The short-lived swing hit *9.20 special*, for which Mitchell handles the theme-statement fore and aft, has what may be judged Perkins's nicest solo of the session.

Hall is a fairly self-effacing musician, but he is impressive in both technical control and artistic inspiration, sounding rather more firmly rooted than Farlow in a guitar succession reaching back through Charlie Christian. (In fairness, Christian was a catalyst for the emergent Farlow; and Hall has named Farlow among his personal favourites.)

Hall vis-à-vis pianistic styles? Work with the pianoless groups of Hamilton and Giuffre and with the almost pianoless *Traditionalism Revisited* band of Bob Brookmeyer (**458**) was congenial to him. His approach in such settings was distinctly guitaristic; the very quality which, given his open responsiveness, made his encounters with John Lewis (**307**) and Bill Evans (†EMI/Blue Note [E] CDP790 583–2), pianists close to him in temperament and aim, so very satisfying. However, critical speculation of this sort must seem idle to a musician whose long and distinguished career has stretched well into the 1990s, and has touched associations many and various along the way.

N.B. Beware of a version of the Hall record on an LP called *The Winner* (Fontana [E] FJL121, Pacific Jazz [A] PJST79). Six tracks were edited down and *This is always* disappeared, so that more than nine minutes' playing time was stolen. Worse still, and most misguided, Larry Bunker's drums were dubbed to change a trio patently adequate to its jazz aims into a quartet. Another reissue claimed to offer alternative takes which in fact were simply repeats of the original performances. The only issues that are as they should be are those whose labels and catalogue numbers appear in the above heading. E.T.

Jack Montrose

303 Jack Montrose with Bob Gordon

London (E) LTZ-K15043, *Atlantic (A) LP1223

Montrose (ten); Gordon (bar); Paul Moer (p); Red Mitchell (bs); Shelly Manne (d). Los Angeles, 11 May 1955.

A little duet · Paradox · When you wish upon a star · Have you met Miss Jones? · Dot's groovy

Same personnel. Los Angeles, 12 May 1955.

I'm gonna move to the outskirts of town · Cecilia · April's fool · The news and the weather

Montrose first attracted serious attention with his 1954 *Etude de concert* (*Shelly Manne and His Men* Vol. 2, Contemporary [A] C2511, Vogue [E] LDC143), an unusually free composition for the period and in some respects the most satisfying piece on that always absorbing record. Indeed there was a time when it seemed that his powers as a composer and arranger would completely overshadow his tenor-saxophone playing. Several items on *The Jack Montrose Sextet* (Pacific Jazz [A] PJ1208, Vogue [E] LAE12042), such as the fugal *Listen, hear*, enterprisingly follow up on *Etude de concert*; there is excellent work too by Conte Candoli, Montrose himself and particularly Gordon. But in fact the greatest virtues of the sessions detailed above arise out of his notable improvising partnership with Gordon.

They met in 1948 and besides working briefly in a few bands, such as John Kirby's last group, they played together in private at every opportunity. Thus developed the exceptional rapport that is evident on the few

* This appeared in the USA as *Arranged/Played/Composed by Jack Montrose.*

sessions they were able to record. Montrose's and Gordon's melodic ideas and rhythmic invention were significantly different yet fruitfully complemented each other. Among the above issue's best illustrations of this are the close-woven non-imitative counterpoint of the *Little duet* and *News and the weather* theme-statements and their exchanges of four-bar phrases both here and on *Dot's groovy*, a fast, vigorous piece like the *Duet*. Passages such as these latter are all too often an occasion for mere exhibitionism but here provide some of the performances' most intense moments, because there is a real meeting of minds.

Montrose arranged every piece, the five original themes are all his, and the ballads and blues from other sources are with a single exception transformed in his image. Many of the specific antiphonal and contrapuntal procedures in his writing appear to have arisen from his informal playing with Gordon, this being a good example of how initiatives in jazz composition arise out of discoveries made in jazz improvisation. The moody, even sombre, *April's fool* makes what might be termed Parisian references, but Montrose's pieces are usually his own rather than just new lines over other people's chord sequences. In fact *Paradox*, a blues, is the most individual theme here, and is presented in a novel way. The blues idiom is hardly thought of as the strongest suit of West Coast jazz, yet both Gordon and Montrose wax eloquent on *I'm gonna move to the outskirts of town*, propelled here as in *Cecilia* and *Dot's groovy* by superlative teamwork from Moer, Mitchell and Manne. *Cecilia*, which has especially good Moer, is quite abrasive and ends with a deftly managed recapitulation of the melody, quite different from the initial statement. *When you wish upon a star* is too easy-going, but it is brief.

Gordon had a zest and fluency on his instrument that were still uncommon decades later, and this without any sacrifice of tonal fullness. Having a distinct musical personality of his own, he was a potentially formidable rival to Mulligan, even to Chaloff, and his death in a motoring accident three months after the above dates was a serious loss, the more so as the baritone saxophone can boast few outstanding exponents. He had time to record only a single LP under his own name, *Meet Mr Gordon* (Pacific Jazz [A] PJLP12, †Fresh Sounds [Sp] FSRCD180, 1954), which also has Montrose and Moer and compositions by the former. The music is similar in character and quality to that on these 1955 sessions.

Productive though his alliance with Gordon was, however, the suggestion that after the accident Montrose lost creative momentum [29] is unfounded. He soon made further advances with such works as *Blues and vanilla*, a 20-minute piece that evolves with exceptional buoyancy in terms of both composition and improvisation, recorded with Red Norvo in 1956 (†RCA [A] 74321–18521). This disc has other achievements such as a particularly independent treatment of Ellington's *Don't get around much any more*, and further notable efforts by Montrose can be found elsewhere, such as his *Poème* on Norvo's **451**. Indeed he might have been more advantageously represented in this volume by the above RCA recording, were it not for the need to accommodate Gordon also.

Both Montrose and Gordon were unfortunate. Pointedly ignored by writers on jazz, they have gone unmentioned in histories, have been dealt with perfunctorily in works of reference or omitted altogether, and their records have not been much reissued (except in Japan). Hence they were both long since forgotten. Montrose played for many years in non-jazz situations where there was no call for his composing or arranging. He was on Frank Butler's *The Stepper* (Xanadu [A] 152) in 1977 but did not make another record under his own name until *Better Late Than Never* (Slingshot [A] 1001), done in 1986, 30 years after *Blues and vanilla*. And musicians pretend that the good or bad opinions of writers on jazz make no difference! M.H.

Al Cohn

304 The Jazz Workshop – Four Brass, One Tenor

RCA-Victor (A) LPM1161, RCA (F) PM45164

Joe Newman, Thad Jones, Joe Wilder (tpt); Nick Travis (tpt, tbn); Cohn (ten, comp[1], arr[2]); Dick Katz (p); Freddy Greene (g); Buddy Jones (bs); Osie Johnson (d); Manny Albam (comp[3], arr[4]). New York City, 9 May 1955.

Rosetta[2] · *Every time*[2] · *Just plain Sam*[3,4] · *Alone together*[4]

Bernie Glow (tpt) replaces Wilder. New York City, 14 May 1955.

The song is ended[4] · *Cohn, not Cohen*[1,2] · *A little song*[1,2] · *Foggy water*[3,2]

Phil Sunkel (tpt) replaces Glow. New York City, 18 May 1955.

Sugar Cohn[3,4] · *Linger awhile*[4] · *Haroosh*[1,2] · *I'm coming, Virginia*[2]

Although it differs in general character from the Russell and McKusick issues (**379**, **380**), which also were made possible by the Victor 'workshop' policy of the mid-1950s, this fine record seems an equally important document of its time, evident of other aims, other demarcations, other fulfilments. Among other things, it celebrates the twin aspects of Cohn's jazz ability. Developing simultaneously his improvising and his writing gifts, he submitted his bop-shaped swing score, *The goof and I*, to Woody Herman a year before he, Cohn, replaced Herbie Steward in the famous Herman saxophone team, Herman having recorded Cohn's piece in 1947, three days before the original Giuffre *Four brothers* (both **312c**).

Diction and artistic purpose were established at that time, and Cohn apparently saw little need to alter them significantly over later years. A 1981 Herman octet recording of *The goof and I* found him hardly changed in either role, except for a toughening of tenor tone (Concord Jazz [A] CJ-180).

Rosetta is Cohn's arrangement, its closing chorus a brilliant written improvisation for the brass. Cohn's tenor presents the theme, with his tone and phrasal emphasis sounding less close than they had been to Lester Young – certainly somewhat warmer of voice; and from then on the Hines classic becomes a playground for the trumpeters, who play tag with a boppish enthusiasm which touches Newman less than the others. The solo rota and chase in *Linger awhile* bring in the insufficiently known Sunkel, who modifies modernism with hints of Bix; Cohn dips and circles, and the Albam score has stimulating brass accompaniments. Albam directed a workshop of his own (RCA-Victor [A] LPM1211, RCA [F] PM43551) and his work for these Cohn sessions matches the leader's in quality most of the time. A mild lapse occurs with the rather trite dance-band clichés for muted trumpets in *The song is ended*; yet the latter has a laggard Cohn improvisation which shows excellently how Young accents had been adapted to a personal style. And there are moments during Katz's solo where Greene's full-toned strum emphasizes, as does the presence of Thad Jones and Newman, the Basie link that is a motivating factor in this workshop's programme. A few Neal Hefti echoes ring in *Cohn, not Cohen*, tumbling phrases which Cohn appropriates to launch his solo. Albam's chart steers the moderately paced *Sugar Cohn* in further celebrations of the contemporary Basie manner, utilizing the relaxed assurance of a splendid rhythm team, and allowing Travis his longest trombone excursion.

Cohn's respect for the Basie mode, linked to his filial allegiance to Young, was proved by other essays, less on **297** than in an affectionate recapturing of the sound of the Kansas City Seven on *The Natural Seven* (RCA-Victor [A] LPM1116). But the fact that other influences surface here is not surprising, considering the group's web of associations – Herman, Sauter-Finnegan, Getz, Jay and Kai, in addition to the Count . . . And there are firmly personal things as well. The rhythmically leisurely but harmonically astringent *Haroosh* is Cohn's most interesting score here. A double-tempo insertion and an out-of-tempo coda help Cohn to vary his soloing moods, and Thad Jones's full-toned, lyrical reflection strengthens a wish that this trumpeter had been given some of the solo chances so liberally handed to Newman elsewhere. The excellent Wilder, whose chief opportunity is *Every time*, might have been heard more. A modest Cohn arrangement of *Foggy water* suits well Albam's Benny Carter-like tune. Newman proves an apt foil to Cohn in *Alone together* during a freely developed duet, anticipating Albam's brass counter-melody to the theme's reprise.

The unpretentiousness of this music might easily conceal the fact that by such means as these the best genius of swing was being carried forward with due regard to newer insights. It maintains freshness of thought at a time when Herman and Basie were about to abandon pace-setting for self-preservation. Like all the best jazz combinations, this Workshop honours its stylistic sources by accepting them as stimuli to musical advance. As an example of how the spirit of Lester Young prompted a new generation of responsive groups, writers and soloists, this record can hardly be bettered. There is also an adventitious link with the high days of swing, a happy if unintentional reminder of a 1940 band in which the French tenorist Alix Combelle aired his stylistic amalgam of Coleman Hawkins and Pete Brown, with a quartet of trumpets plus one trombone, and a rhythm section graced by the participation of Django Reinhardt, in arrangements of Basie standards and originals of similar provenance (Pathé [F] C054–16009, 16024 etc.). E.T.

Cy Touff

305 Octet and Quintet

Pacific Jazz (A) PJ1211, Fresh Sounds (Sp) 240265–1

Conrad Gozzo, Harry Edison (tpt); Touff (bs tpt); Matt Utal (alt, bar); Richie Kamuca (ten); Russ Freeman (p); Leroy Vinnegar (bs); Chuck Flores (d); Johnny Mandel (arr[1]); Ernie Wilkins (arr[2]). Los Angeles, 4 December 1955.

Keester parade[1] · *TNT*[1] · *What am I here for?*[2] · *Groover wailing*[1]

Gozzo, Edison, Utal absent; Pete Jolly (p) replaces Freeman. Los Angeles, 5 December 1955.

Prez-ence · *Half-past jumping time* · *A smo-o-oth one* · *Primitive cats*

Unlike so many jazz recording dates, these, as explained in detail in Woody Woodward's sleeve notes, were planned over a long period. It started in 1953 with Pacific Jazz considering possible musicians one by one and the kinds of material they might play, but that was also the year that Touff joined Woody Herman and it was he who began to put the project into focus, especially as Kamuca also joined the Herd in 1954. For part of the following year Herman appeared with a reduced ensemble, in fact with an octet including Touff, Kamuca and Flores using an instrumentation close to that of the first of the above sessions. Herman's band, indeed, recorded only days before, and the two sets of performances are best heard together, preferably in conjunction with another similarly composed group, the Nat Pierce–Dick Collins nonet, with which Touff had recorded the previous year. Herman's disc in particular carries several excellent Touff and Kamuca solos, but the main points are the similarities and differences between these three related units and the fact that this kind of instrumentation brought out the best in Touff and, at this stage of his career, in Kamuca.

The benefits of careful planning are quite evident on Touff and Kamuca's own dates but they are not the ones originally anticipated. For Pacific Jazz the starting point had been scores by Mandel, and his unambitious idea had been to produce a small-combo version of Basie's kind of music. Luckily the modernistic tendencies of the players – Touff, for example, had been a pupil of Tristano's and had worked for Raeburn, Russo and others – resulted in something far more interesting. In fact it is no paradox to say that the main consequence of long-term preparation was jazz of uncommon fire and spontaneity, above all from the octet. This, indeed, was a band with obvious further potential which, like Mulligan's Tentet (**300**), ought to have been recorded again.

In the event, Mandel (a sometime bass trumpeter himself with Basie et al.) wrote only three of the octet scores, thereby letting in Wilkins, whose bland diminishment of Ellington's *What am I here for?* is the record's only weak feature. Yet even if his ideas became rather incidental to the enterprise, Mandel still drew a sound strikingly close to that of a big band from the complete ensemble in parts of *Keester parade*, *Groover wailing* and Tiny Kahn's *TNT*. This contrasts tellingly with the intimacy of other passages, as when Touff and Kamuca's unusual two-voiced introduction to *Keester parade* is followed by the full band playing the theme. It is a blues, and Edison solos first, using rather familiar phrases, to be followed by Kamuca and Touff with fresher ideas. The two latter exchange four-bar inventions as ensemble riffs build in support; a sample of Freeman's bop pianism follows and Mandel's theme returns, this time with keyboard interjections. In short, the outline could not be simpler and the music's impact arises from the intentness of its performance and the quality of most of its ideas.

Combining the mobility of the trumpet with the weight of the trombone, Touff's instrument ought to have been used more often in jazz. Its larger bore gives it a fuller, more mellow sound than that of the standard trumpet and Touff makes good use of this here and in the other recordings mentioned. The motivic basis of *Prez-ence* was provided by the opening phrase of Lester Young's *You're driving me crazy* (**252**) – and, unusually for such cases, he receives composer credit on the sleeve and label. Kamuca's own work is founded on earlier Young than this, although he had arrived at an attractively personal variant of it by the time of these sessions. (Hence his phrases are nowhere stale as Edison's are on *Keester parade*.) In fact Kamuca's most individual playing lay some years ahead, but it was always highly melodious and his technique was such that his improvisations are engagingly relaxed in delivery.

Edison is more inventive on *TNT* and it is noticeable both that when Freeman succeeds him he lets none of the tension escape as piano solos so often do and that he brings off the same feat in *Groover wailing*. There is detailed interplay between Kamuca and the ensemble on *TNT*, Touff is near his finest, and because of the faster tempo this performance builds most impressively. Here as elsewhere no little credit is due to Gozzo and Utal, who are heard only in the ensembles. The precipitate *Groover wailing* also packs a punch and the backgrounds urge the soloists forward to splendid effect. Touff's and Kamuca's ideas interlock beautifully in the chase which separates the solos, and this passage relates to the head arrangements they worked out during their time with Herman, which are the basis of the following day's quintet performances.

Altogether worthy of the great man, the *Prez-ence* theme is an extension of a Lester Young idea, as noted above, and is further extended in Kamuca's solo. This is perhaps his best here, lyrically sustained, with one phrase arising out of another beautifully. Touff and Jolly attain a similar level. True, the bass solo is dull, but Vinnegar is magnificent in accompaniment, as is Flores. Hear them propelling Jolly's solo through *Primitive cats*, a piece which prompts what is probably the finest of Touff's improvisations. *A smo-o-o-oth one*, done in a single take like *Keester parade*, receives an entirely un-Goodman-like reading which includes more outstanding tenor. Despite solos of comparable quality from both horns, *Half-past jumping time*, a Neal Hefti theme, belongs to Jolly, who offers a piano improvisation that is developed with an almost rigorous logic.

Recorded on 1 and 2 December 1955, the Herman disc noted above, *Woody Herman and the Las Vegas Herd*, appeared on Capitol (A and E) T748 and was reissued as *Jackpot*. The Pierce–Collins nonet was on Fantasy (A) LP3224. *Keester parade* has been included in various anthologies, often edited down, but it is complete on the issues shown in the heading. One reissue, retitled *Having a Ball!* (World Pacific [A] PJM410), omits *Primitive cats*. It was bad luck for Jolly that the remaining quintet track, *It's sand, man*, was never included on the LP because in it he if anything surpasses his *Half-past jumping time* effort. This fugitive piece only appeared in the *West Coast Jazz* Vol. 2 anthology (Pacific Jazz [A] JWC501, Vogue [E] LAE12061). In 1958 Edison recorded *Keester parade* in a somewhat different form as *Centerpiece* (Roulette [A] R52023). M.H.

Lars Gullin

306 Danny's Dream and Manchester Fog

Dragon (Sd) DRLP181

Gullin (bar); Rolf Berg (g); Georg Riedel (bs); Robert Edman (d). Stockholm, 25 May 1954.

Danny's dream · *Be careful* · *Igloo* · *Circus*

Gullin (bar, p[1]); Berg (g); Riedel (bs); Bo Stoor (d). Stockholm, 26 January 1955.

Manchester fog (2 versions) · *Lars meets Jeff*[1] · *A la carte*[1] · *Soho*[1]

The point about Gullin's – as it then appeared – sudden emergence at the start of the 1950s was that it suggested Django Reinhardt might not be a fluke after all. At least for a couple of generations, European jazz was necessarily imitative of US models, and Reinhardt (**104–6**) was seen as the music's sole outstanding non-American participant. In fact, his justified pre-eminence led to several other excellent European jazzmen of the 1930s and 1940s being undervalued, but it did seem at the time that Reinhardt was the exception proving an apparent rule of permanent

US dominance. The arrival of Gullin, an indisputable major figure as an improviser, as an instrumentalist and eventually as a composer, implied, however, that non-American jazz might have a greater potential for originality than had been assumed hitherto. And so it proved. In the year of the first of the two above sessions he became the first European to share with many American masters the ignominy of winning a *down beat* popularity poll.

Gullin became a professional musician in 1947, as a pianist, going on to play alto and clarinet, then settling for the baritone in 1949. Mulligan's contributions to **376** had suggested considerable potentialities, and it may be that the international impact of Mulligan's subsequent quartet (**300**) prompted Gullin to leave Arne Domnerus's famous band and form a group of his own. There was no particular resemblance, however, between his improvising and that of Mulligan, or anyone else. Indeed, Gullin's position reflects a strikingly individual mind, first apparent in a personal vein of melodic invention. This soon came to operate on other musical levels through his writing many durable themes and later through his creating more or less large-scale settings for other soloists as well as himself, as jazz composers usually do.

Yet melodic power came first, this seeming to be effortless while also full of drive. He could during personal appearances – though such an occasion was never caught in the recording studio – solo on a favourite ballad for upwards of half an hour, these improvisations giving the impression both that they were parts of a larger, concealed whole of a work in progress, and also, paradoxically, of their being distillations of something larger. [30] Related here is Gullin's sense of the overall shape and structure of a performance, which later became apparent in his larger works, and what can only be called his capacity for self-editing. His music is manifestly improvised, and this is apparent from comparing the two above accounts of *Manchester fog*, and from setting these versions of *Danny's dream*, *Igloo* and *Lars meets Jeff* beside the slightly later concert readings. [31] Yet whatever the differences between these pairs of performances, they have in common with each other and with most of Gullin's solos elsewhere an absence of decorative flourishes: there is seldom a note too many, and that is a great achievement for an improviser.

This seamless flow, very evident on all titles of these 1950s sessions, can deceive us, masking the quantity of invention going on. Relevant are the distinctive ways Gullin's ideas are developed and related to one another; and these are as elusive of analysis as his self-editing processes. However, jazz improvisation being the art of performance it is, we cannot separate Gullin's sheer fluency of musical thought from his sovereign executive mastery. In particular his early manner was not surpassed, especially the delicacy with which he handled an unwieldy instrument. He was affected in this by such Tristano pupils as Konitz and Marsh, and Konitz admired Gullin in turn. [32] Though technique is normally the last thing one thinks of while listening to such music, his flexibility on the baritone suggested an alto. Indeed he was a highly competent altoist early on and although he displayed the same melodic fertility, continuing acquaintance with his work soon makes it evident that his thinking was better suited to the larger instrument.

His sound on the baritone was as direct an expression of Gullin's musical personality as his melodic gift, and it led to the acute sense of ensemble colours and textures evident in his many scores for small and medium-sized combos [33] and then to the highly personal orchestration of his later and larger compositions (**360**).

In Paris 10 and 20 years earlier Reinhardt had been lucky in finding companions who, though not approaching his stature, were entirely sympathetic and musically compatible. It was rather the same with Gullin in Stockholm in the 1950s, and it says much for Swedish jazz that the men with whom he recorded were able to keep pace with him in his more complex and ambitious projects of the 1970s. The item chosen for this chapter is vol. 5 of a Dragon series bringing together most of his early recordings, and these are best heard in chronological sequence. On the sessions detailed above, the instrumentation allows him extensive freedom of movement while leaving him no chance of concealment. And Gullin faces this sustained and unsparing test in such a way that his every note can bear the closest attention.

The title *Manchester fog* (later this piece was renamed *Prima vera*) is a reference to the cheerless climate of northern England and the sombre mood is ardently and differently sustained in both performances by the leader, who improvises right through each version. Even if both came to sadly premature ends, Gullin's world scarcely was so dark as Serge Chaloff's (**310**), but *Danny's dream*, the longest track, further explores sombre feelings, and here as elsewhere Berg's solo beautifully continues the line of thought set up by his leader. In fact Berg keeps doing this, perhaps aided by Gullin's switching to the piano during some of the guitar-led passages. *Soho* is another local reference, to a particularly sordid area of central London, but Gullin adds value to the proceedings, as he does in *Lars meets Jeff*, by returning after guitar and bass outings for a second, extended solo. He and Berg are sprightly in *Igloo*, and there is deft interplay between them during the theme statements of *Be careful* and *A la carte*. All the themes are by the leader except this last, contributed by Riedel, who on most tracks solos briefly and with greater melodic distinction than most bassists. Apart from a brief chase with Riedel during *Circus*, Stoor takes no solos at all: such restraint! M.H.

John Lewis

307 **The John Lewis Piano**
Atlantic (A) 1272

Lewis (p); Barry Galbraith (g[1]); Percy Heath (bs[2]); Connie Kay (d[3]). New York City, 30 July 1956.
D & E[2,3] · *The bad and the beautiful*[1] · *It never entered my mind*[1] · *Little girl blue*[2,3]

Lewis (p); Jim Hall (g[4]); Kay (d[3]). New York City, 24 August 1957.
Wärmland[4] · *Two lyric pieces (Pierrot, Colombine)*[4] · *Harlequin*[3]

In *D & E* we find Lewis demonstrating a personal interpretation of the blues which grew through (a) his solos in the three versions of *Parker's mood* (**257**), where the pianist's expression sounds like calm piety alongside Parker's searing passion, and (b) his *True blues* with a 1952 Milt Jackson group about to become the MJQ (Savoy [A] SJL1106). If there is a brisker impetus to *D & E*, some of this is due to the patterns of Kay's drumming, though there is a naïve touch to this which, happily, is countered by subtle reactions from Lewis and Heath. The austere simplicity of pianistic approach invites comparison with Basie's old blues-shaped trios from the late 1930s (†Classics [A] 503, 504), because Nat Pierce's remark that Basie's speciality was space [34] applies equally to Lewis's style. And this may be discerned more clearly in *Little girl blue*, not only in the musing atemporal introduction but also, and more pointedly, in measured sections where bass and drums cease and Lewis's ability to calculate his silences as precisely as his notes seems like a response to some sense of inaudible wit. The audible acumen – melodic, rhythmic, harmonic – is another wayfaring re-evaluation of bop, for though, not only in the blues, emphasis is gained by crushed notes not dissimilar to Basie's, the shapes and accents of his lines are enlivened much more by delicate bop 'turns' and doublings of time.

While the interactions between Lewis, Heath and Kay do indicate a stage in the development of shared improvising in the MJQ, it is in the duets with Galbraith, at this first session, that ingenious interplay predominates; and in *The bad and the beautiful* and *It never entered my mind*, there is great richness of contrast, and the liberal use of out-of-tempo extemporization is forward-looking in enterprise.

Galbraith has a mellower tone than Hall, who, in *Wärmland* and the *Lyric pieces*, fulfils a differing role, contributing fine solos and quietly strummed support, but not being required to act as adventurously as the other guitarist. *Pierrot* and *Colombine* (with *Harlequin*) are early tokens of Lewis's long affair with *commedia dell'arte* – in its French derivation here. A taste for such stylized pantomime (though the *Lyric pieces* are meditative) may explain partly the pianist's liking for the nursery-song themes included in some MJQ programmes. But Lewis is never quite the seeker after artlessness, the doodler of sketches, some critics have made him out to be. The feline ways by which he extracts simplicity from others' complexities, the studied nonconformity of his attenuations of the bop manner, and his perfection of touch which magically combines fragility with interior vigour, are consistently displayed. *Harlequin* – a more whimsical portrait – evinces some of these characteristics, and adds brusque chordal punctuations. Kay alone assists here, his brushwork faultless, as elsewhere.

N.B. Nat Hentoff's prolix notes to this record misspell *Wärmland*, and mistakenly aver that Galbraith is the guitarist for this number. E.T.

John Graas

308 Coup de Graas

EmArcy (A) MG36117

Pete Candoli (tpt); Graas (fr h); Red Callender (tu); Art Pepper (alt); Bob Cooper (ten, ob[1]); Buddy Collette (bar, fl[2]); Paul Moer (p); Buddy Clarke (bs); Larry Bunker (d, timp, vib). Los Angeles, 13 August 1957.
Development
Pete Candoli absent; Bunker plays d only. Same date.
Swing nicely[1,2]
Conte Candoli (tpt) added. Same date.
Land of broken toys[1,2] · *Block sounds*[2] · *Van Nuys indeed* · *Blues street*[2]
Graas (fr h); Pepper (ten); Moer (p); Clark (bs); Bunker (d). Los Angeles, 15 August 1957.
Rogeresque · *Walkin' shoes*

Almost inevitably, the french horn came into jazz as an ensemble voice, offering new resources of tone colour, sonority, texture. Its earliest intelligent musical use in this field was by Claude Thornhill's band (**375**), of which Graas was a member in 1941–2. He also worked for Gerry Mulligan (**300**) and Stan Kenton (**477**) before taking a leading role in the instrument's emergence as a vehicle for solo improvisation. This was a hazardous undertaking because there was absolutely no jazz french-horn tradition on which to build. The other chief adventurer in this direction was Julius Watkins, who may, in a strictly jazz sense, have been potentially Graas's superior, but who, even in Les Jazz Modes (1956–9), never found an entirely apt setting for his work. This Graas did repeatedly, aided by the exploratory tenor of West Coast jazz, not least in terms of instrumentation.

Coming in 1953, the same year as Watkins's session with Monk (†Original Jazz Classics [A] OJCCD016–2), Graas's first showings were two dates for the Trend label, reissued on Kapp (A) KL1046 and preserving early instances of the West Coast style. As was to be usual with him, these strongly featured original compositions and arrangements, by himself and others. From his viewpoint, the best items are *Pyramid*, *Not exactly* and in particular *Be my guest*, which, regarding both solo and ensemble performance, contains the most convincing jazz that anyone had thus far drawn from the french horn in a recording studio. But improved Graas solos, with a freer flow of more varied ideas, were achieved on *Westchester Workshop* (Coral [G] 6.22188, Decca [A] DL8343) of 1955–6, examples being *Canon ball* and *Lighthouse 6/4*. The instrument's traditional capacity for evoking romantic melancholy is turned to jazz ends in *Softly the horn blows*; and *Friar Tuck* offers deft contrapuntal wit. There are further compositions here by the leader, such as *Minor call*, but so far as solos are concerned the star of the *Westchester* dates is Herb Geller, some of whose finest work is hidden in unexpected places.

Graas's most fruitful adaptation of the french horn to jazz and his most imaginative composing in this context come together in the *Coup de Graas* collection, although this is closely followed by the *Jazzmantics* set, made up from sessions recorded on either side of those detailed above (Fresh Sounds [Sp] 252283–1, Decca [A] DL8677). He takes several notable solos here, as in *Flip-tip* and *Id*, in which latter there are an interlude and coda based not on a chord sequence but on a scale over a pedal point. Obviously Graas neglected to read the histories of jazz, otherwise he would have known that this kind of thing was never done in such music until **393** was recorded two years later. Similarly, as *Coup de Graas* and *Jazzmantics* deploy tuba as well as french horn, conventional wisdom dictates that they must be pale carbon copies of **376**, although in reality there is scarcely the faintest resemblance.

A striking aspect of both records, though especially the former, is the full-toned mobility of Callender's admirable tuba work, this enabling him to participate not in a supporting role but as an equal-voiced member of the ensemble. This has a considerable influence on the character of the first six items, which, bringing five other horns into play, have the advantage of a rich and constantly varied instrumental palette, their lines crossing and recrossing, juxtaposing and dividing, contrasting and fusing. Superbly performed, as was usual with the West Coast school, and having abundant rhythmic vitality, this music has retained its ability to surprise. Six of the themes and all eight arrangements are by Graas, and in the best cases the ensemble passages contribute to the ongoing development of the subject matter rather than just linking the improvisations. Shifts between solo and ensemble dominance are well judged yet unpredictable, and in some improvisations a response to the challenges of the scores is explicit.

Although there is no reference to the fact in the notably offhand sleeve notes, *Development* is derived from the first movement of Graas's *Jazz Symphony No. 1*, recorded in full on Andex (A) A3003. (Two further movements, similarly reduced for a small instrumentation, can be found in the *Westchester Workshop* collection.) Quite polyphonic in concept, *Development* is the most original composition here, and far from being a mere decoration, the use of timpani is well integrated into the fabric of the piece. It at the same time gives rise to a fine sequence of solos, as does the much simpler *Van Nuys*. Indeed, Pepper is on top form virtually throughout, with both alto and tenor, though it is always possible to prefer his more volatile work on the smaller horn. Cooper's tenor playing is also his best, particularly on *Development* and *Swing nicely*, while Moer is his usual aggressive self in solos on *Walkin' shoes*, *Rogeresque* and, again, *Swing nicely*. This last and *Land of broken toys* take up initiatives of Cooper and Bud Shank on Howard Rumsey's **388**, and here, as in *Block sounds* and *Blues street*, Collette once more shows himself to be among the few to get fully persuasive jazz from the flute.

As to Graas, he presents an outstanding solo in *Walkin' shoes*, possibly his best on record, closely followed by the one in *Blues street*. This latter melancholy piece is by Dick Grove, who contributed an intriguing *Jazz chorale* to *Jazzmantics*, and makes beautiful use of the french horn in its ensembles. In fact there is some especially inventive writing in this score and one wonders how much credit is due to Grove and how much to Graas. That the former deserves more attention is confirmed by his LP-long *Little Bird Suite* (Pacific Jazz [A] PJ74), a distinguished if almost unknown essay in orchestral jazz dating from 1963. The year before that, Graas's premature death had precluded his extending the achievement embodied in this and the other records mentioned here. His is not particularly cool jazz and we have placed it in this section for the lack of any more obvious home. As good music should, it ultimately defies classification. M.H.

Lennie Niehaus

309 Vol. 1: The Quintets

Contemporary (A) C3518

Niehaus (alt); Jack Montrose (ten); Bob Gordon (bar); Monty Budwig (bs); Shelly Manne (d). Los Angeles, 2 July 1954.

I'll take romance · Prime rib · Inside out · Bottoms up

Same personnel. Los Angeles, 9 July 1954.

You stepped out of a dream · Whose blues · I remember you · Day by day

Stu Williamson (tpt, v-tbn); Niehaus (alt); Hampton Hawes (p); Red Mitchell (bs); Shelly Manne (d). Los Angeles, 20 January 1956.

I can't believe that you're in love with me · Poinciana · Happy times · I should care

Niehaus was one of the many West Coast jazz musicians who were highly active during the 1950s but were ultimately claimed by the big Hollywood movie sound stages. In his case he had almost completely withdrawn from jazz by 1960, working as an arranger for both television and motion pictures. This work culminated in a long association with the actor, producer and director Clint Eastwood, whose production company Malpaso hired him as musical director on over ten films. Not least of these was Eastwood's controversial film *Bird*, the life story of Charlie Parker released in 1988, where, under Niehaus's supervision, Parker's solos were separated from the original recordings by selective EQing (equalization), dynamic noise-filtering and other hi-tech skulduggery and rerecorded accompanied by a contemporary rhythm section. [35] In the furore that followed, Niehaus was by all accounts left somewhat bemused. By then his role in West Coast jazz in the 1950s and a series of fine albums he made for the Contemporary label were long forgotten.

Niehaus was an exceptionally rounded musician who gravitated towards Kenton's big band in 1952, where, except for a two-year period of military service, he was something of a fixture for most of the 1950s. One of the band's major soloists and the finest lead saxophonist Kenton ever hired, he also contributed several arrangements to the band's library, beginning with *Pennies from heaven* recorded by Kenton in 1953 (*Sketches on Standards*, Creative World [A] ST1041). In it, the saxophone section plays an important role in the exposition of the theme. The writing is deft and light, and includes skilful embellishments and interesting detail in inner voice movement before disappearing into the shadows cast by the ubiquitous halls of brass. Niehaus's writing for the greater portion of *Vol. 1: The Quintets* is a logical continuum of this fluid yet subtle approach to the saxophone section, albeit developed to a point that would be impossible to contemplate within Kenton's big band. The pianoless rhythm section is light and airy and permits greater transparency of the voicings while lending an uncluttered feel to Niehaus's writing which reveals a wealth of contrapuntal devices, inversions, sequential development and contrary motion. Frequently the ensemble appears to sound fuller than just three voices through his well-crafted arranging. As the main featured soloist, his charts allow him to stretch out to an extent that was impossible with a big band; it perhaps goes without saying that Niehaus was doing everything here that he was unable to do in Kenton's band in terms of both writing and playing.

The July 1954 sessions were originally issued on a 10-inch LP (Contemporary [A] C2513) and are of a piece, a big-band saxophone section out of school. Nevertheless, there was a tight degree of organization imposed by Niehaus's writing that was characteristic of the so-called West Coast school that placed greater emphasis on written arrangements and counterpoint than the then prevalent hard-bop school of the East Coast. It is interesting that although much of the West Coast style was dubbed 'cool', in reality many of the musicians were bop musicians who took their inspiration from the unruffled calm of a Lester Young or a Miles Davis. This, however, was not the case with Niehaus, a fluent virtuoso who had taken account of Parker on the way to developing a very fluid, mobile style that was wholly his own. 'He had little to learn about playing a saxophone,' Max Harrison wrote in 1958, 'his ease and fluency conveyed a feeling of relaxation and security that is always rare and his attack and swing were almost equally striking.' [36]

These elements are clearly apparent on *Whose blues*, the major exhibit from these sessions. Niehaus opens with a declamatory unaccompanied four-bar introduction that leads into an improvised blues chorus of 12 bars with the bass and drums. Manne's rimshot announces another unaccompanied four bars before a further 12-bar chorus and another four-bar tag, accompanied this time, making a 4 + 12 + 4 + 12 + 4 combination of 36 bars that Niehaus refers to as 'three choruses' in the liner notes. [37] This sequence leads into the 12-bar theme, the first time it is revealed, which is played twice, with the final two bars pinched as an unaccompanied pick-up leading into two further improvised choruses by Niehaus. Then follows an unaccompanied four-bar saxophone choral with the tenor and baritone before he sweeps on to the end of the chorus, topping it with a final 12 bars of further improvisation against some sleek accompanying figures from Montrose and Gordon. He seems to be taking a fifth chorus when Montrose abruptly enters on bar five to begin an exchange of fours between the saxophones, each trying to develop a logical continuum of the four bars that preceded it. Their amiable discourse ends with two choruses of congenially improvised counterpoint between all three saxophones before Manne enters with one of his typically appropriate solos, leading into a recapitulation of the 12-bar theme. Despite the high degree of organization in the performance which presents the blues in an interesting and resourceful way, Niehaus created enough latitude to reveal himself as a lithe, highly accomplished soloist with a technique that few players in jazz, even to this day, could match. While *Whose blues* is the complete antithesis of hard bop it is nevertheless a highly animated performance and is a fine example of 'West Coast jazz' at its best.

If *Whose blues* is the finest cut of the album, then *You stepped out of a dream* follows closely behind, both in terms of conceptualization and execution. Niehaus begins with a two-bar unaccompanied introduction and then launches straight into an unaccompanied improvisation for eight bars. The rhythm section enters underneath him and as he develops his solo, the tenor and baritone outline the beginning of each section with fragments of the theme which are gradually expanded until a full exposition appears as the final chorus. It was an unusual touch, reversing the time-honoured practice in jazz of theme first, then variation; here it is variation and theme. Again there are flashes of his superlative saxophone technique; both here and on *Prime rib* Niehaus plays phrases that can only be described, to use Ira Gitler's later phrase, as 'sheets of sound', but significantly they appear here four years before Coltrane first employed the device on his 1957 album *Traneing In* (Prestige [A] PR7426).

On such numbers as *I'll take romance* or *You stepped out of a dream*, Niehaus creates the illusion of a larger ensemble by adding additional comments to the melody statement that in a larger ensemble would come from the brass section, creating an allusion of antiphony. In contrast, *Prime rib* is treated as a sax solo, with a solo from Niehaus that reveals his quite staggering technique, albeit this time at the expense of content. He is back on the money on both *Inside out* and *Bottoms up*, each a 32-bar AABA swinger, where he takes the unusual step of having the rhythm section lay out on the initial AA section on both compositions, joining proceedings on the middle eight, the B section.

The standard *I remember you* is perhaps less adventurous in comparison but an absorbing performance nonetheless; a saxophone solo reveals the melody with Niehaus contributing a compelling solo against the wonderful, easy swing of Budwig and Manne. Niehaus as a ballad interpreter is sure-footed on *Day by day*, a much neglected 32-bar ABAC songform with a pleasing resolution of the ii-V-1 sequence in the first half of the A sections and at *fine*. Niehaus plays with an elegance that belies his image as an intense swinger, implying double time with ease and grace at the outset of his solo and then going the whole hog at the end, culminating in a rounded *rallentando* ending. Equally, his arrangement frames his playing to maximum effect, his lines fingering the contours of the song behind his improvisation without stating the obvious, with resonances of the *Birth of the Cool* nonet's static calm on *Moondreams*.

On the 1956 sessions a standard piano-bass-drums rhythm section lends an easy informality against the unusual tonal dimension provided by Williamson's use of the valve trombone in tandem with the leader's alto on three numbers, returning to bebop orthodoxy with a trumpet–sax front line on *I can't believe you're in love with me*. The emphasis is on counterpoint, tightly voiced lines of contrary motion and punching unisons that in their neat, orderly way have the poise of a chamber group combined with the swing of the 1938–9 Basie band. It is a testament to Niehaus's playing that the role of the piano in the rhythm section on the later tracks by no means appears as essential. Niehaus's very agile facility favoured a vertical approach to chords and the speed of his execution allowed him to spell out the chordal movement of songs so succinctly that Hawes actually appears to be muddying the waters behind the saxophonist's cleanly executed lines. Ultimately, however, these 1956 tracks lack the richness and diversity of the 1954 dates; as a postscript to the latter it is interesting to note that when Kenton heard the original 10-inch Contemporary, he commissioned Niehaus to contribute a small library of standards for his band, several of which were featured on Kenton's successful *Adventures in Standards* (Creative World [A] ST1025). On it, Niehaus produced some of the most ingenious writing for saxophones to be heard in Kenton's discography, no mean achievement in a band dominated by a well-stocked brass section. S.N.

Serge Chaloff

310 Blue Serge

Capitol (A) T742, †Capitol (E) 494 505–2 and disc 4 of †Mosaic (A) MD4–147

Chaloff (bar); Sonny Clark (p); Leroy Vinnegar (bs); Philly Joe Jones (d). Los Angeles, 14 March 1956.

A handful of stars · *The goof and I* · *Thanks for the memory* · *All the things you are* · *I've got the world on a string* · *Susie's blues* · *Stairway to the stars* · *How about you?* (on CD only)

Drug addiction, or, to use that well-worn euphemism, 'personal problems', loomed large in the career of Serge Chaloff. It disrupted his brilliant potential and was largely responsible for his premature death at the age of 33 in 1957. Although he was once a key member of Woody Herman's Second Herd, his reputation, seemingly so secure after topping the *down beat* (1949–51) and *Metronome* (1949–53) readers' polls, was quickly devoured during periods when he withdrew from music to effect a rehabilitation. Indeed, over subsequent years his reputation diminished to such an extent that for many he is just one more name in a long list of ex-big-band members consigned to obscurity when a line was drawn under the swing era in the early 1950s.

Yet Chaloff still remains one of the finest, arguably *the* finest, baritone saxophonist jazz has ever seen. Such recognition, however, was largely withheld during Chaloff's lifetime because of his proselytizing ways with drugs. His interpersonal relationships, both as a user and as a pusher, degenerated into chaos, damaging more people than just himself, and had the consequence of relegating him to the dubious status of a sort of nonperson in jazz. As the *Metronome Yearbook: 1956* observed: 'The most subtle, yet the most telling indication of those problems was the reaction of other musicians to him. In the caste system which jazz musicians automatically form, Serge had every right to expect consideration and respect. But it should have been evident in these last years that he has received little of either and that, in its queer way, was the final stamp of disapproval.' [38]

Today it is his tenure as the fourth brother for the duration of the Second Herd's brief existence that is responsible for any lustre Chaloff's name now evokes. In an aggregation not short of great soloists, Chaloff was featured on more recordings than any of the other distinguished Herman sidemen, had a number dedicated to him, *The goof and I*, and had his own virtuoso feature, *Man, don't be ridiculous* (Queendisc [It] Q-005). It is on this latter piece, a frantic contrafact based on the *Rhythm* changes, that Chaloff demonstrated, perhaps more than in any of the studio recordings under his own name, an astonishing technical facility that was quite without precedent on his instrument. It was not appropriated from Charlie Parker as many commentators have suggested, rather it was inspired by Parker's example, grasping more the emotional basis of Parker's playing and using it as a starting point for his own style. Chaloff, as a sideman with Herman and with his own small groups and those of others, revealed he had completely mastered bebop by the late 1940s as well as developing an immediately identifiable and personal tone. In short, since his debut with the Tommy Reynolds band in 1942, Chaloff had risen to become one of the leading musicians of his day.

Herman wound up his Second Herd at the end of 1949, but as early as 1951 Chaloff was speaking about 'getting away from the fireworks that don't really mean anything' that had been a part of his style up to that point and 'adding more colour and flexibility' to his work. [39] It was a significant statement, suggesting that he was well ahead of his time in realizing that despite the great possibilities opened up by bebop, virtuosity for virtuosity's sake could nevertheless be ultimately limiting. Indeed, Al Cohn, Chaloff's closest friend, fellow ex-Herman brother and most frequent recording companion to 1950, observed: 'It wasn't until he left the big bands that he really started to develop as a soloist.' [40]

Chaloff was an accomplished tenor saxophonist, actually beginning his professional career on the instrument with the Reynolds band. But there seems no doubt that he preferred the baritone saxophone because of the greater breadth of expression it gave him. At home in the upper register of the instrument, he produced a 'tenor'-like tone playing with all the agility of a tenor saxophonist, contrasting sound-sheet fluency with breathy, Ben Webster-like whispers. But he also revelled in plumbing the deep, dark resonating tones that lurked at the bottom of the baritone's range; during his big-band days he used to dominate saxophone sections in the way that Harry Carney led from behind. 'Serge Chaloff was one of the masters of the baritone,' recalled pianist Nat Pierce, 'he has not been credited with all he could do. He could play fully, as well as Harry Carney in the section.' [41] This power was often unleashed in unexpected and occasionally frightening bursts that gave a dangerous dimension to his playing that anticipated the techniques of tonal distortion and over-blowing that would be exploited by the avant-garde almost 15 years later.

With *Easy street* from 1954 and *Body and soul* and *What's new* from 1955, tonal organization had begun to play an important role in his improvisations, introducing 'more colour' – distortion, use of alternate fingering, dramatic vibrato – and 'flexibility' – a flawless control throughout the whole range of the saxophone. Chaloff utilized these aspects of technique to bring an emotional intensity to his playing that lifted it to a dramatic, uncompromising plane far removed from the cool young men of the West Coast or the hard-bop certainties of the East.

The album's title takes it name from a Chaloff original based on the chords of *Cherokee* and originally recorded in 1946 by a group he assembled with Ralph Burns, although *Blue Serge* is not performed on this occasion. This 1956 session produces Chaloff's finest recording; all the elements that composed his style, the 'minute particulars' that he had been working on over the years, seemed finally to coalesce into a greater whole. His playing, pyrotechnically brilliant throughout, remained in the service of content with an unceasing flow of coherently seamed ideas. What emerged was a player of unexpected contrasts; it is impossible to predict from moment to moment in what direction his ideas might take him. During *I've got the world on a string*, for example, his tiptoeing *sotto voce* exposition of the theme is suddenly brought to life with powerful bell tones that make the melody line stand out, as if in 3-D.

And while the runaway virtuosity of *Man, don't be ridiculous* remained, it was never deployed gratuitously. Frequently he used it to cram dense phrases into small spaces, such as in the middle eight of *The goof and I*. Such speed of execution would not appear in jazz again until Coltrane's *Giant steps* in 1959, Chaloff articulating each phrase with such precision that their detailed construction only reveals itself with close listening. But stunning technique was but one element among many that comprised his style. When he turned to ballads, he could be profound as well as moving. On *Stairway to the stars*, for example, he caresses the melody with Getz-like sexiness while creating a solo of great architectonic beauty that can be returned to time and again without it seeming to lose its freshness.

On *Thanks for the memory* his melodic invention is reinforced by manipulating tonal devices for greater emotional impact. His wildly exaggerated vibrato, his use of alternate fingering, producing differing densities of tonal quality on the same note, and his use of subtone at the bottom of his range (the so-called bell notes, an unremarked technical feat that few saxophonists completely master), combine to produce a riveting performance that is not simply exemplary baritone saxophone playing but jazz of the highest order. So profound is his performance that the wry humour of grafting a paraphrase of *Where or when?* onto the coda almost passes unnoticed.

Indeed, paraphrase becomes central to his performance of *Handful of stars*, where he scrupulously avoids stating the melody as written before launching into a breathtaking double-time chorus. At one point, he plumbs the baritone for a bumptious bass note and soars to the top of the instrument's range in one breath, effortlessly concealing the remarkable technical skill required for such seemingly throw-away trifles. This sheer joy at music-making seems to give his playing a life force of its own, such as his exuberant swing on *All the things you are* or his puckish melody statement on *How about you?* (Mosaic only).

While Chaloff is front and centre throughout *Blue Serge*, his accompanists also play a vital role in making this a memorable album. Despite being an ad hoc group, they perform with great unity and precision, drifting from *alla breve* into straight-ahead 4/4 and back again so smoothly they sound like a set, working unit, and their tight-swinging four-bar exchanges in *The goof and I*, for example, are a model of cooperation and competition.

Chaloff uses the resources of the group in interesting ways, varying the tonal colours of the standard sax-plus-rhythm to create ensemble textures of varying densities. The bass solo in *The goof and I*, for example, is accompanied by piano and drums, treating the bass as if it were a member of the front line, and so sustaining the momentum of the performance. Even today, bassists have not quite twigged that long, unaccompanied solos effectively slice a performance in half. Other subtle touches include Chaloff's subtone sax shadowing Vinnegar's bass solo in *I've got the world on a string* or the use of unaccompanied four-bar exchanges using each member of the quartet in turn. And though these were small details, they create variety and interest at a subliminal level that help compel our attention.

Sadly, Chaloff appeared only once more in the recording studios after *Blue Serge* and this in the role in which he has now become typecast, as a charter member of the Four Brothers. [42] Yet while his recording legacy remains pitifully small for such an enormous talent – his entire output on disc under his own name is barely enough to fill four CDs (†Mosaic MD4–147) – he nevertheless succeeded in aspiring to the ultimate challenge posed any artist in jazz, that of forging 'a mode of expression independent of any one stylistic school or period'. [43] In cutting himself off from the prevailing orthodoxy, Chaloff's playing has not dimmed or become date-stamped by the passage of years. At once playful and dangerous, Chaloff's style is a refreshing release from the claustrophobic role-model hierarchy, which, with just a few exceptions, has dominated the evolution of the saxophone in jazz. S.N.

Dave Brubeck

311 Dave Brubeck's All-Time Greatest Hits

CBS (E) 68288 (2 LPs), CBS (A) PG32761 (2 LPs)

Paul Desmond (alt); Brubeck (p); Norman Bates (bs); Joe Dodge (d). Newport, R.I., 6 July 1956.
Two-part contention

Joe Benjamin (bs), Joe Morello (d) replace Bates, Dodge. Newport, R.I., 3 July 1958.
The Duke

Gene Wright (bs) replaces Benjamin. Los Angeles, 23 April 1959.
Camptown races

Same personnel. New York City, 1 July 1959.
Take five

Same personnel. New York City, 3 May 1961.
Castilian drums · It's a raggy waltz

Same personnel. New York City, 8 June 1961.
Unsquare dance

Same personnel. New York City, 3 January 1962.
Coracao sensivel

Same personnel. New York City, 12 January 1962.
Some day my prince will come

Same personnel. New York City, 2 July 1962.
I'm in a dancing mood

Same personnel. New York City, 5 July 1962.
The trolley song

Same personnel. Carnegie Hall, New York City, 22 February 1963.
St Louis blues · Blue rondo à la Turk

Same personnel. New York City, 15 February 1965.
Let's get away from it all

Desmond absent. New York City, 22 September 1965.
My favourite things

Desmond returns. New York City, 8 December 1965.
Night and day

It has usually been argued that the best, or at any rate the least bad, music under Brubeck's name is that of his early quartet. This is to say the kind of improvising heard on such LPs as *Jazz at Oberlin* (†Original Jazz Classics [A] OJCCD046–2) and *Jazz at Pacific College* (†OJCCD047–2), which attracted much attention in the early 1950s. Rather than being a mere leftover from Brubeck's octet, the quartet grew out of it, and in an unexpected direction. The earlier ensemble played elaborate and carefully planned music, discussed under **450**, whereas the quartet was founded on the glories of spontaneity. As Brubeck chose to call himself 'a composer who plays the piano', the grounds for confusion were obvious.

The octet's work has been described, quite reasonably, as being part of 'a bop-inspired experimental trend' on the American West Coast in the middle-to-late 1940s. [44] Yet by the time the quartet's first music was recorded in 1951, all trace of bop had vanished. Influences are, indeed, hard to detect. Brubeck claimed Teddy Wilson, Art Tatum and in particular Billy Kyle as exemplars, [45] but there is no sign of this in any of his recorded playing, and he said that he strove to sound like none of them. [46] Quite implausibly, Brubeck asserted that Pete Brown had a considerable effect on Desmond! The latter's achievement is, of course, that even though faced with Charlie Parker's all-embracing innovations he was able to come up with something almost disconcertingly individual. If he was touched by anyone it was another staunchly independent personality – Lee Konitz; and Desmond does have a certain affinity with Lester Young's clarinet solos. Certainly Desmond was among the few in jazz to understand the virtues of understatement, the value of occasionally leaving important things unsaid.

In general, however, the case of the Brubeck quartet seemed like that of Erroll Garner (**263**), influencing and being influenced by nobody in jazz. Only two of his pieces ever got close to becoming part of the standard jazz repertoire, *The Duke* and *In your own sweet way*, and this was not so much due to their Brubeckian qualities as because Miles Davis recorded them. [47] Even the use of time signatures like $^5/_4$ and $^7/_4$ arose from within his band's own music – the bridge of *What is this thing called love?* in Bill Smith's arrangement for the octet, for example, is in $^7/_4$ – and such initiatives, despite a fairly widespread espousal of $^3/_4$ in jazz, had an effect only on the quartet's output, not elsewhere. There is of course nothing to say that jazz bands, or listeners, must confine themselves to the main highway, yet the Brubeck quartet's lack of orthodoxy was among the reasons for the almost uniformly bad press it received. Another factor was that the group's popularity, like that of Garner, the MJQ and, at some stages, Miles Davis, offended the congregation of the faithful. People do not object to artists deserving success – only to their getting it. Again, much of the music was too optimistic in tone for many jazz commentators, who, like most pseudo-intellectuals, can only take catastrophes seriously.

A stock answer to the annoyance caused by this band was to dismiss Brubeck as a classical musician playing *at* jazz; but this, on the evidence, will not do. Though his mother was a piano teacher and he heard much classical music from infancy, he never tackled that repertoire himself, and by his own account was unable to read music even when pursuing his rather too celebrated studies with Milhaud (1946–9). Brubeck claims to have studied counterpoint, fugue and orchestration with the latter, yet these subjects can only be mastered through working large numbers of exercises critically corrected by the teacher, and it is hard to know what he can have learned without this. A few passages, like his solo on the Oberlin *These foolish things*, suggest that he managed to pick up a little by ear, but without much focus on crucial details.

And though 'pseudo-baroque counterpoint' was a key phrase in journalistic assaults on Brubeck across the decades, we never find in his performances the specific devices of baroque contrapuntal technique used, for example, in John Lewis's fugal pieces for the MJQ (**363**). There is quite a lot of counterpoint between piano and alto saxophone on early quartet performances and at best this results in good continuity, even a convincing display of musical logic. But it is essentially, and in the circumstances appropriately, informal, as is confirmed by the fine ensemble passage on the Oberlin *Perdido* following Brubeck's dreadful solo. The bombast of this solo signalled a cause for greater concern, and there are many further examples in the quartet's early work, *Le souk* (Columbia [A] CL566, 1954) being a notorious one. Such lapses resulted in the pianist hammering away at repeated chords in a manner that was highly unrhythmic, even completely unmusical, and seemed like a comic representation of hysteria – not that everyone agreed that such playing was an instrumental equivalent to Johnny Ray's crying.

Of course, the redeeming feature of this band's music even at its most abysmal was its alto saxophonist, whose status as a great improviser still has not been unequivocally grasped, in part because of his long association with Brubeck. (For Desmond free of any pianist see **366**.) He sounds as if he would be lonely even, or especially, in a crowd, and it is apt that he resembled nobody else. The tone is singularly pure yet always expressive, the strikingly long melodic lines are sustained beyond all expectation and are beautifully developed – never being merely a question of endurance. Depending in part on arcane quotations is a delightful sense of musical fun, usually described as unduly clever by the humourless, who cannot recognize the tradition of the trickster/magician to which it relates. There is even something akin to literary wit, although this in turn is only apprehensible to those who know the lyrics of the songs he sometimes quite obliquely quotes.

These degrees of subtlety might seem remote from Brubeck, yet 1 despite the keyboard-thumping histrionics he early displayed a quite strong faculty for melodic variation, for instance on the 1949 trio version of *Blue moon* (Fantasy [A] LP3–2). And in *You go to my head* recorded at Storyville (Fantasy [A] F24727, 1952) he offers a lyrical extension of the melody fully as sensitive as Desmond's, equally free of rhetoric. What unites these two at a deeper level, though, is a general principle that Brubeck, at least, might have absorbed not from Milhaud but through hearing classical music during his youth. In most jazz improvisation one idea is followed by another, then another . . . whereas at their best Desmond and Brubeck tend repeatedly to modify, in fact to develop, a single idea. Good examples include the piano solos on the Pacific College *All the things you are* and the second one on the above *Two-part contention*. Both of Desmond's seemingly effortless solos on the latter are outstanding in this respect, as are his unedited 13 choruses on the concert version of *St Louis blues*. Obviously other jazzmen undertake this sort of motivic development, but with a few exceptions like Rollins, they usually are composers, such as Morton or Monk. It is no bad thing for music to be well argued, and in such performances the quartet's claim to stake everything on the free associations of spontaneity seem less convincing, and Brubeck's to be 'a composer who plays the piano' more relevant.

If there was a contradiction here, it pointed to a shift in the band's orientation, and although nearly the entire jazz press, including the present writer, was united in an attempt to stab Brubeck to death with our pens, the music did change; it could almost be said to have evolved. The main agents of this were Morello and Wright, who joined in 1956 and 1958 respectively, each bringing a more varied experience of jazz than could be claimed for Brubeck or Desmond. They went a considerable way to mitigate the former's rhythmic weakness and to show that the quartet's earlier bassists and drummers had been heavy-handed dilettantes. Morello in particular gave the band's output a hard, percussive edge that did much to alter its character. Brubeck's own playing changed, too, becoming clearer in outline, better organized, purposefully varied, exploring well-defined areas of the music, and moving, in his best solos, towards quite specific goals. A good illustration is the Newport account of *The Duke*, which includes one of his finest solos on record, almost completely avoiding stereotyped responses, as also does *It's a raggy waltz.*

And he composed more. The Pacific College or Oberlin concerts, say, consist entirely of improvisations on popular songs, whereas on the above CBS collection six out of 16 themes are his, with one each by Desmond and Teo Macero. Here also *The Duke* is a good example of what Brubeck was now able to do. Whatever Irving Townsend may have written in the sleeve note to the original issue, this has nothing whatever to do with Ellington stylistically but it pays worthy tribute to the famous composer in Brubeck's own manner. Again, because he now had moved on to something more personal in both playing and composing, the 'pseudo-baroque counterpoint' disappears once and for all.

While a performance like *Some day my prince will come* – with the drums in 3/4, the bass in 4/4 and the alto and piano sometimes in one, sometimes in the other – is undeniably absorbing, and successful, enough has probably been said elsewhere on the quartet's use of time signatures like 5/4, 7/4 and 9/8, including some very able comments by Brubeck himself in various old LP sleeve notes. Still, on Desmond's *Take five*, the first jazz instrumental recording allegedly to sell a million copies, it is intriguing that while Brubeck keeps the 5/4 vamp going throughout (too loudly on LP issues, better on CD), Morello gradually releases himself from this pulse and builds up some aggressive cross-rhythms. Brubeck later said that this performance 'was a little stiff' [48] and the band did later play it in a more relaxed manner, as the 1963 Carnegie Hall recording shows (CBS [Eu] 66234). *Take five*'s popularity was not explained by its 5/4 time signature but by its exasperating repetitions, a weakness it shares with otherwise quite different jazz pieces that received similarly uncritical acceptance such as Lee Morgan's *Sidewinder* and Cannonball Adderley's *Sack o' woe*. (However, for a quite different view of *Take five* see **366**).

Refreshingly different is Macero's *Coracao sensivel*, a sensuous melody that Desmond extends most resourcefully. Brubeck sustains the mood, and does so again in *Blue rondo à la Turk* until repetition – thunderously applauded – takes over. There are plenty of contributions from Desmond, for instance on *Let's get away from it all*, *Blue rondo* and, of all things, *The trolley song*, to prove that the fire evident in the early days still lived within him.

That this quartet's work lay outside the main stream of jazz does not alter the fact that works of art, large and small, should be evaluated on their own terms and for their own sake, not according to whether they were influential or not. These 16 performances are an excellent cross-section of the band's large output over a decade, the catchpenny title notwithstanding. It should not be confused with *Dave Brubeck Greatest Hits* (†CBS [Eu] CDCBS32046), with which it has eight titles in common. We have rather arbitrarily placed it at the end of this book's first section on cool jazz, for it is no more cool than it is bop or West Coast. It is simply, in varying proportions, Brubeck–Desmond–Morello–Wright music, unclassifiable stylistically. Given the overwhelmingly subjective nature of most jazz, there are worse things to be said than that.

M.H.

The Big Band Survives

Large jazz bands were so rich in musical resources that even when the swing era was over there still was a great deal to be done with them.

Woody Herman

312a **The Thundering Herds Vol. 1**
CBS (E) BPG62158, Columbia (A) C3L25 (3 LPs)

Pete Candoli, Sonny Berman, Chuck Frankhauser, Carl Warwick, Ray Wetzel (tpt); Bill Harris, Ed Kiefer, Ralph Pfeffner (tbn); Herman (clt, alt, vcl[1]); Sam Marowitz, John LaPorta (alt); Flip Phillips, Pete Mondello (ten); Skippy DeSair (bar); Ralph Burns (p, arr[2]); Billy Bauer (g); Chubby Jackson (bs); Dave Tough (d); Margie Hyams (vib). New York City, 19 February 1945.

Laura[1,2] · *Apple honey*[2] · *I wonder*[1,2]

Neal Hefti (arr[3]), Frances Wayne (vcl[4]) added; band vocal[5]. New York City, 26 February 1945.

Caldonia[1,2,3,5] · *Happiness is a thing called Joe*[2,4]

Same personnel. New York City, 1 March 1945.

Goosey gander[2] · *Northwest passage*[2] · *A kiss goodnight*[1,2] · *I've got the world on a string*[1,2]

Hefti, Conte Candoli, Ray Linn (tpt), Tony Aless (p) replace Frankhauser, Warwick, Wetzel, Burns. New York City, 10 August 1945.

The good earth[3] · *Put that ring on my finger*[1,2]

Same personnel. New York City, 20 August 1945.
Bijou[2]

Buddy Rich (d), Red Norvo (vib) replace Tough, Hyams; Irving Lewis (tpt) added. New York City, 5 September 1945.
Gee, but it's good to hold you[2,4] · *Your father's moustache*[1,3,5]

Tough (d) replaces Rich; Linn, Norvo absent. New York City, 8 September 1945.
Wild root[3]

Shorty Rogers (tpt), Mickey Folus (ten), Don Lamond (d) replace Conte Candoli, Mondello, Tough. New York City, 26 November 1945.
Blowin' up a storm[3]

312b The Thundering Herds Vol. 2

CBS (E) BPG62159, Columbia (A) C3L25 (3 LPs)

Pete Candoli, Berman, Irving Lewis, Rogers (tpt); Hefti (tpt, arr[3]); Harris, Kiefer, Pfeffner (tbn); Herman (clt, alt, vcl[1]); Marowitz, LaPorta (alt); Phillips, Folus (ten); DeSair (bar); Aless (p); Bauer (g); Jackson (bs); Lamond (d). New York City, 10 December 1945.
Let it snow![1,3]

Arnold Fishkin (bs) replaces Jackson; Frances Wayne (vcl[4]) added. New York City, 3 January 1946.
Welcome to my dream[2,4]

Conrad Gozzo, Irving Markowitz (tpt), Sam Rubinowitch (bar), Jackson (bs) replace Hefti, Irving Lewis, DeSair, Fishkin. New York City, 7 February 1946.
Panacea[1,2]

Berman (tpt); Rogers (tpt, arr[6]); Harris (tbn); Herman (clt, alt, vcl[1]); Phillips (ten); Jimmy Rowles (p); Bauer (g); Jackson (bs); Lamond (d); Norvo (vib, arr[7]). Chicago, 16 May 1946.
Steps[6,7] · *Fan it*[1,6,7]

Rogers absent. Chicago, 20 May 1946.
Igor[6,7] · *Nero's conception*[6,7] · *Lost weekend*[6,7] · *Pam*[6,7]

Gozzo, Berman, Pete Candoli, Rogers, Cappy Lewis (tpt); Harris, Kiefer, Pfeffner, Lyman Reid (tbn); Herman (clt, alt, vcl[1]); Marowitz, LaPorta (alt); Phillips, Folus (ten); Rubinowitch (bar); Rowles (p); Chuck Wayne (g); Joe Mondragon (bs); Lamond (d); Norvo (vib). Hollywood, 17 September 1946.
Sidewalks of Cuba[2]

Mary Ann McCall (vcl[8]) replaces Frances Wayne. Hollywood, 18 September 1946.
Lady McGowan's dream (parts 1 and 2)[2] · *Romance in the dark*[2,8]

Personnel as for 20 May 1946 except that Chuck Wayne (g), Mondragon (bs) replace Bauer, Jackson. Hollywood, 12 October 1946.
Someday, sweetheart[6,7] · *I surrender, dear*[6,7]

Personnel as for 17 September 1946 except that Al Porcino, Bob Peck, Chuck Peterson (tpt) replace Pete Candoli, Berman, Rogers; Reid, Folus, Norvo absent. Chicago, 10 December 1946.
Woodchoppers' ball[3]

312c The Thundering Herds Vol. 3

CBS (E) BPG62160, Columbia (A) C3L25 (3 LPs)

Personnel as for 17 September 1946 except that Burns (p) replaces Rowles. Hollywood, 19 September 1946.
Summer sequence (parts 1–3)[2]

Rowles (p) replaces Burns; Mary Ann McCall (vcl[8]) returns; Rogers (arr[6]). Hollywood, 20 September 1946.
Everywhere[2,3] · *With someone new*[2] · *Wrap your troubles in dreams*[2,8] · *Back talk*[6]

LaPorta (arr[9]); personnel as for *Woodchoppers' ball.* Chicago, 10 December 1946.
Non-alchoholic[9]

Stan Fishelson, Bernie Glow, Markowitz, Ernie Royal (tpt); Rogers (tpt, arr[6]); Bob Swift, Earl Swope, Ollie Wilson (tbn); Herman (clt, alt, vcl[1]); Marowitz (alt); Zoot Sims, Herbie Steward, Stan Getz (ten); Serge Chaloff (bar); Fred Otis (p); Gene Sargent (g); Walter Yoder (bs); Lamond (d); Burns (arr[2]). Hollywood, 19 October 1947.
I told ya I love ya, now get out[1,2]

Same personnel. Hollywood, 22 December 1947.
I've got news for you[1,6] · *Keen and peachy*[2,6]

Al Cohn (arr[10]). Hollywood, 24 December 1947.
The goof and I[10] · *Lazy lullaby*[1,2]

Jimmy Giuffre (arr[11]). Hollywood, 27 December 1947.
Four brothers[11]

Burns (p) replaces Otis. Same date.
Summer sequence (part 4)[2]

Otis (p) replaces Burns; Mary Ann McCall (vcl[8]) returns. Hollywood, 31 December 1947.
P.S. I love you[2,8]

Herman's 1945–6 ensemble, the so-called First Herd, emerged from the final version of 'the Band that Plays the Blues', which he had led since 1936. The latter always treated its materials and their sources with respect, and the more creative stance of the First and Second Herds arose out of this. Certainly there was a remarkable transformation, and, wise with our knowledge of what soon was to happen, we can, on key 1944 Herman records, hear the elements of the First Herd moving into place. As this almost implies, the band's new style was eclectic in its origins if unified in its final effect. The rhythmic foundation was along Basie rather than bop lines but considerably more radical procedures were imposed on this in both the ensemble writing and the improvisations. In fact part of the continuing appeal of this jazz may lie in a tension between conservative and progressive aspects. Usually it is held against Herman that his was not fully a bop band, although, as suggested under **256**, no large ensemble ever was, despite such valiant efforts as Gillespie's *Things to come*, dating from almost two years after the initial V-Disc *Apple honey*. [49] As early as 1942 Herman, of course, had recorded *Down under* by Gillespie, who also wrote *Woody 'n' you* for him, although that unfortunately was not recorded by this band.

The expanded harmonic usage of the First Herd had been explored by Ellington and Eddie Sauter, among others, in the 1930s, and what most directly pointed to bop in Herman's new music were such features as the linear, exhilaratingly mobile brass scoring, epitomized by the famous unison trumpet passage in *Caldonia*. Indeed, bands such as this, Kenton's (**313**) and Raeburn's (**314**), despite precedents set, again, in the 1930s, embodied a new level of ensemble virtuosity. And if the flamboyance is reminiscent of Lunceford (**138**), the feeling is less theatrical because this band plainly was out to amaze and satisfy its audience with its strictly musical capabilities. Some of the uncommon freshness of these performances stems from the musicians' youthfulness, although this leads also to such things as Pete Candoli's monstrously vulgar outburst at the end of *Apple honey*, ruining the hitherto overwhelming build-up of riffs; and he does it again in *Wild root*. It is surprising that Herman allowed even these rare lapses of taste, which are quite different from the genial humour that is an effective counterweight to the band's underlying seriousness and justifiable pride in its achievement.

Even more than on the above studio recordings is this achievement evident from air shots of the First Herd's numerous public appearances. These emphasize the continuing vitality of the band's interpretations and the large amount of improvising that went on. If this music still sounds so good, it is because it was genuinely new in its own time. And all this is a tribute to the leader, for however exceptional the individual players, it was he who chose them and all the elements which make up the collective style and held them in balance.

As so often in jazz, the finest material came from within the band. And as the above discographical details show, chiefly responsible for the unique library was Burns, who already had made his mark with such pieces as *The moose*, a brilliant solo vehicle for Dodo Marmarosa with Charlie Barnet's band (Affinity [E] AFS1012). Hefti, also, did his earliest and best jazz composing and arranging for Herman. Their greatest achievement was the creation of a series of wild yet disciplined pieces which partly reflected and partly brought into being the band's essential turbulence. These include *Goosey gander* with its mild onomatopoeics and mixture of *Shortenin' bread* and the blues, *Blowin' up a storm*, juxtaposing intimate piano and guitar passages with roaring ensembles,

Bijou, subtitled *rhumba à la jazz*, *The good earth* (retitled *Helen of Troy* on V-Disc!), *Northwest passage*, *Your father's moustache*, and, despite Pete Candoli, *Apple honey* and *Wild root*. Then there is Rogers's *Back talk*, the peak of the First Herd's integration of solo improvisation and virtuoso ensemble playing. This may be the best single recording under Herman's name, and few large bands have ever approached the brass section's final immaculate fury here.

Writing as successfully ambitious as this inevitably gave rise to a couple of larger pieces, of which *Lady McGowan's dream* is the more logical as a musical structure. *Summer sequence*, also by Burns, is less convincing in that respect, suffering from weak transitions but also containing memorable ideas and throughout, like *Lady McGowan*, beautifully written for the ensemble. Really the *Sequence* was complete in its original three sections and was often played in that form (e.g. Queen [It] Q-005, 1949). As Herman honestly admitted, the fourth part was added only because there was space to be filled on the discs and the independence of this afterthought was confirmed by its taking on a separate life of its own. First it reappeared as an instrumental piece featuring Getz and Terry Gibbs and retitled *Early autumn* (Capitol [H] 5CO52 80805, Capitol [A] M11034, 1948), then simplified into a song with words by Johnny Mercer which the band also recorded (Verve [A] MGV2030, 1952). The above original account of *Summer sequence* as a whole is best heard in conjunction with the interesting complete performance of a dozen years later (Everest [A] SD1032).

Such endeavours would have counted for little, however, without Herman's gift as a judge of talent and in particular his decisions as to which members of the Herd should solo. As it is, the improvisations fully match the larger entities of which they are part, and in Harris the band had a major original who recorded nearly all his best work under Herman. The trombonist's most acute lyrical statement is *Everywhere*, an outstanding vehicle for soloist and band which although slow and mostly quiet, is strategically varied by Hefti and Burns to make a constantly changing musical tapestry. But that is only one side of Harris, whose line can in a single improvisation pass from the murmur of seductive insinuation to full-throated manic expostulation. Herman's alto reminds us of Johnny Hodges, Phillips has listened closely to Coleman Hawkins and Lester Young, but Harris seems to have come from somewhere that we have never heard of. Every conceivable aspect of technique (including exemplary control of vibrato) is adapted to his special purposes and every kind of phrase is admissible, including some hitherto not associated with the instrument. He shared with other top-ranking jazzmen the paradoxical quality that his solos remain surprising to listen to even when one knows them by heart. And his subversive humour – frequently a guying of sentimentality – is an apt foil to the band's intensity.

If Harris was the First Herd's soloistic triumph, Berman was its tragedy – another virtuoso, out of Eldridge and Gillespie, and a potential major trumpeter but dead at 22. It is fortunate that Herman let him solo often. Note how on *Sidewalks of Cuba* he begins with a sardonic reference to Harry James's notorious *Flight of the bumble bee.* In *Fan it* Phillips takes a stop-time solo, this device being rarely employed in such music, but more representative are the sensitivity displayed on *With someone new* and the dynamism of pieces like *Northwest passage.* He again did his best recorded playing with Herman. A notable aspect of the First Herd was its finding a regular place for the vibraharp, this leading to unusual duets between Miss Hyams and Harris in *Laura* and between Phillips and Norvo in *Gee, but it's good to hold you.*

All this is admirably seconded by rhythm sections that have been underrated because of the spectacular work of the horns. But the team of Burns, Bauer, Jackson and Tough drove the band with much power and swing, and Lamond brought off the seemingly impossible feat of being a more than adequate replacement for Tough.

Like other large ensembles of its time, the First Herd was compelled to play much sentimental ephemera, but, given the band's essential character, its approach to this material was frankly ambiguous. Herman delivered these ditties of adolescent love in a musical version of 1930s crooning, the effect of this often being subverted by the rest of the performance. Note for example the sometimes ferocious interjections between Herman's vocal phrases in *I wonder,* the way the ensemble strikes out afterwards and adds an abrasive Harris solo; or Berman's solo and the shouting ensemble before Herman returns in *A kiss goodnight.* In fact some ballads include passages as violent as any of the up-tempo rampages, *Gee, it's good to hold you* for instance.

Yet Burns in particular could score ballads with a sensitivity and quiet invention comparable to Sauter's work for Goodman (**143**). The resulting mixture of warm pastel tones and the variety of texture are best heard on such items as the LPs taken from 1945 broadcasts (Fanfare [A] 22–122 and 43–143). Most exceptionally well recorded, these convey a stronger sense of the band's physical presence at any tempo and better communicate the impetus of the rhythm section. Other public performances, too, such as the 1946 Carnegie Hall *Blowin' up a storm* (MGM [A] 3043), improve on the studio versions.

Although the First Herd was nearly always an extremely musical band, its successor, which lasted for nearly two years from 1947, was even at its most exuberant more subtle. As such it cost its leader a lot of money, as did Raeburn's band and the most interesting Kenton units. Its origins were once more eclectic and the unusual reed-section instrumentation, for example, was adapted from the band of Tommy DiCarlo, who employed four tenors. Again, the tenors Herman began with, Getz, Sims and Steward, were all developing Lester Young's initiatives along different lines. However, Chaloff was the Second Herd's most original soloist as Harris had been the First's. The best indication of that here is *The goof and I*, although the point is more strongly made by the March 1948 broadcast version (Queen [It] Q-2001). Unlike Harris but like Getz, his rival in originality, Chaloff did his finest work elsewhere (e.g. **310**).

The old practice of incorporating an earlier recorded solo in an arrangement is followed by *I've got news for you*, which quotes Parker's solo on take 3 of *Dark shadows* (**258**). LaPorta's *Non-alchoholic* shows that the First Herd's mode of fast-paced aggression was not the monopoly of Burns and Hefti, even if Porcino's excesses at the close rob this performance of perfection. In fact despite its differences of emphasis the Second Herd yielded little to the First in ensemble attack, even if no new frontier was passed; after *Back talk*, that scarcely would have been possible. With Chaloff, Getz, Sims, Swope and Steward it had, if anything, a stronger group of soloists; and hear Royal's stinging contributions to *I've got news for you* and *I told ya I love ya.*

While the most outstanding of the above items give a very fair idea of the Second Herd's character and capabilities, they need to be studied along with the many recordings of broadcasts that have become available in more recent years. Notable among these are programmes from the Royal Roost, New York, in October and November 1948 on Cicala (It) 8027, Queen (It) Q-005 etc. For one thing, the soloists have more space.

Meanwhile select members of both First and Second Herds had been shown in other lights by small-combo recordings. Everything from the sessions of May and September 1946 was jointly arranged by Rogers and Norvo, several titles also being composed by them. The result was superbly performed chamber jazz which still had room for a maverick like Harris. Rowles's playing has more substance here than that of Aless with the full Herd and Wayne proved a real addition to the solo strength, for instance on *Someday, sweetheart.* But although Herman's Noone-like trills in *Nero's conception* could well have been dispensed with, these evidently happy occasions found everyone on their best form, above all Norvo in *I surrender, dear.*

Mention should also be made of a Sonny Berman LP originally put out as *Jazz Immortal 1946* on Esoteric (A), then as *Beautiful Jewish Music* on Onyx (A) 211, then under its original title again on Fresh Sounds (Sp) FSR533. This allows us to hear Chaloff, Cohn, Swope and Burns at length in a well-organized jam-session context and leaves no doubt whatever of Berman's potential. Burns's exceptional capacities at the keyboard were unavoidably put in the shade by his writing, yet *Bijou* (Fresh Sounds [Sp] FSR250, Bethlehem [A] BCP68) is a telling statement of his pianistic thinking. Perhaps the most durable of all Herman-associated small-group recordings, however, are by Berman's Big Eight (Spotlite [E] SPJ132) with a haunting Burns *Nocturne* and, once again, memorable jazz from Harris, Chaloff, Phillips, Wayne as well as Berman and Burns. Some of Rogers's arrangements for this 1946 date anticipate West Coast scores of a decade later (see **359** etc.), but music always carries the seeds of its own future.

The American Columbia number given three times in the above heading is of course a 3-LP boxed set, the contents of which, leaning heavily on the First Herd, are identical with those of the three separate British LPs. They are badly programmed and represent a rather distant phase of jazz reissuing. It is unfortunate that for many years before this book's publication there was no attempt at a systematic reissue of these great bands' output. Again, it is inexplicable that solos by Harris and Phillips should have been edited out of *Blowin' up a storm* in the above LPs. They are restored in such later issues as Affinity (E) AFS1043.

Herman's subsequent career was almost symbolized by the *Caldonia* trumpet passage being played faster and faster and meaning less and less. By 1963 it was possible for Bill Chase to lead the trumpets through it while himself playing an octave higher (Philips [A] PHS600–092). In short, Herman's bands maintained the excitement of the music discussed here but never advanced beyond it. And this was despite the discreet modernization that was carried out over the decades of his exceptionally long career, not least in the rhythm section, and despite pieces by Monk, Mingus, Coltrane and Hancock being added to the repertoire. He ended as a prisoner of his own past, rather like Kenton. M.H.

Stan Kenton

313a A Concert in Progressive Jazz

Creative World (A) ST1037

Buddy Childers, Ray Wetzel, Al Porcino, Chico Alvarez, Ken Hanna (tpt); Milt Bernhart, Eddie Bert, Harry Betts, Harry Forbes, Bart Varsalona (tbn); George Weidler, Frank Pappalardo (alt); Bob Cooper, Warner Weidler (ten); Bob Gioga (bar); Kenton (p); Laurindo Almeida (g); Eddie Safranski (bs); Shelly Manne (d); Jack Costanzo (bon); Pete Rugolo (comp, arr). Los Angeles, 24 September 1947.
Elegy for alto

Kenton (p); Almeida (g); Safranski (bs); Manne (d); Costanzo (bon); René Touzet (mar). Los Angeles, 25 September 1947.
Fugue for rhythm section

Previous full band personnel; Salvador Armenta (mar) added. Los Angeles, 20 October 1947.
Monotony

Art Pepper (alt) replaces Pappalardo. Los Angeles, 22 October 1947.
Lament · Impressionism

Carlos Vidal (con), Machito (mar), Jose Luis Mangual (timb, cw bl) added. Los Angeles, 6 December 1947.
Cuban carnival

June Christy (vcl) added; Vidal, Machito, Mangual absent. Same date.
Lonely woman

Robert Graettinger (comp, arr); Christy absent. Same date.
Thermopylae

Vidal (con), Machito (mar) added. Los Angeles, 21 December 1947.
Introduction to a Latin rhythm

Christy (vcl intrjc) added; Vidal, Machito absent. Los Angeles, 22 December 1947.
This is my theme

Wetzel, Maynard Ferguson, Shorty Rogers, John Howell, Alvarez (tpt); Bernhart, Dick Kenney, Betts, Bob Fitzpatrick (tbn); Varsalona (bs tbn); Bud Shank, Pepper (alt); Cooper, Bart Calderell (ten); Gioga (bar); Kenton (p); Ralph Blaze (g); Don Bagley (bs); Manne (d). Los Angeles, 20 March 1951.
Theme for alto

Conte Candoli, Stu Williamson, John Coppola (tpt), Bill Russo (tbn), George Roberts (bs tbn) replace Wetzel, Rogers, Alvarez, Bernhart, Varsalona; Stan Fletcher (tu), Christy (vcl) added. Los Angeles, 20 September 1951.
Come rain or come shine

313b **New Concepts of Artistry in Rhythm**

†Capitol (Eu) CDP792 865–2, *Creative World (A) ST1002

Childers, Ferguson, Candoli, Don Dennis, Reuben McFall (tpt); Bob Burgess, Frank Rosolino, Keith Moon (tbn); Russo (tbn, comp, arr[1]); Roberts (bs tbn); Lee Konitz, Vinnie Dean (alt); Richie Kamuca (ten); Bill Holman (ten, comp, arr[2]); Gioga (bar); Kenton (p, vcl intrjc[3]); Sal Salvador (g); Bagley (bs); Stan Levey (d); Johnny Richards (comp, arr[4]). Chicago, 8–9 September 1952.
Prologue[3,4]

Gerry Mulligan (comp, arr[5]). Chicago, 10 September 1952.
Portrait of a count[1] · *Young blood*[5] · *Frank speaking*[1]

Denon Kenneth Walton (bon[6]), Kay Brown (vcl[7]), Gene Roland (arr[8]) added. Chicago, 11 September 1952.
23 degrees north 82 degrees west[1,6] · *Taboo*[4] · *Lonesome train*[7,8]

Graettinger (arr[9]); Walton, Brown absent. Chicago, 15 September 1952.
Invention for guitar and trumpet[2] · *My lady*[1] · *Swing house*[5] · *You go to my head*[9] · *Improvisation (part 1)*[1]

Same personnel. Chicago, 16 September 1952.
Improvisation (part 2)[1]

Despite his presence on the jazz scene for several decades, there is no serious treatment of Kenton's music aside from discographies. No critical essay or entry in a work of reference has attempted a coherent account of his output as a whole. This is because of its sheer size, its having so many facets, and above all because of its extremely diverse quality. All artists are variable, but their production seldom fluctuates in aim and achievement as wildly as Kenton's. Entire groups of pieces may be admirable, yet they will show few links, beyond the general character of the band's sound, with other groups. Kenton's records present items travelling paths that are not only different but incompatible, even contradictory, quite without a unifying purpose. In the long term almost anything goes, provided it is in some way 'modern', and there is a kind of old-fashioned futurism here, even a vague, and long-discredited, belief in 'progress'. Yet despite this lack of focus, sometimes even because of it, there is along with much grotesquely bad music some that is excellent, even importantly original.

One reason for this is that despite its often determined attempts at concealing the fact, it is rooted, like Woody Herman's modernism, in sound earlier traditions. A start was made with harmless pieces of swingfare like *Painted rhythm* (†Mosaic [A] MD7–136) and *Eager beaver* (again Mosaic), these being catchy tunes well suited to big-band conventions, mainly composed and scored by Kenton himself. As did others, his ensemble raided its predecessors and *Intermission riff* (Mosaic) descends from Lunceford's *Yard dog mazurka* (MCA [F] 510 040), as Billy Eckstine's *Opus X* (Audio Lab [A] 1549) does from *Lunceford special* (Columbia [A] CS9515) and Gillespie's *Ow!* (**315**) from Hines's *At the El Grotto* (Official [D] 3029). (In a few, admittedly isolated, cases the traffic appears to move in the opposite direction and Lunceford's 1934 *Stratosphere* (Hep [E] 1011), for example, with harmony surprisingly modern for that time, sounds like a score Rugolo wrote for Kenton, or George Handy for Raeburn, a dozen years later.)

Obviously something more than such minor borrowings was required to shift the repertoire from swing to modern jazz; rather than just a pile of new arrangements, it needed to embody some kind of organic unity. Here the impreciseness of Kenton's ambitions proved an advantage. Lacking a well-defined sense of the several directions his ensemble could take, unable to give a purely musical lead by himself, he mainly required not arrangers offering just a skill in processing given material in whatever manner they were asked but a composer who would present a music whose self-consistency amounted to a new approach to orchestral jazz. Thus the die was cast, and composers were usually involved prominently whenever the band was producing its finest music and were noticeably absent when it was doing the opposite. Discographies show the remarkable number of excellent soloists to whom Kenton gave prominence, but he has never received credit, in the jazz world at large, for providing a platform for so many composers. And Rugolo was the first.

It would not be true to say that he gave Kenton's band its identity, yet he wrote for it music which, rather like Gil Evans's contemporaneous work for Thornhill (**375**), was quite independent of other paths then being followed. Rugolo, like Evans, offered a new way of thinking jazz orchestrally. Both made far more drastic departures from convention than, say, the arrangers (and composers) for Gillespie's band (**256b**, **315**), whose efforts usually resulted in juxtapositions of bop solos and swing ensembles rather than a new synthesis. Rugolo's originality, unlike Evans's, has not been widely recognized, and this is in part due to a purely external circumstance, the generally chaotic state of Kenton reissues. Most of the performances from the 1940s in particular have been put on LPs and CDs in random order, the best music with the worst. This heightens the extremely variable quality of the band's work and its overall lack of direction, blunting the impact of the finest pieces through sheer muddle. **313b**, from a slightly later time, is an exception, **313a** a partial one; but to deal with Rugolo's contribution properly it will be necessary to refer to other records.

Especially in the key year of 1947, many of his titles seem almost deliberately misleading. There is nothing impressionistic about *Impressionism*, for instance, still less is *Monotony* monotonous. Over the latter's constant *ostinato* bass figure there take place ensemble exchanges with many lines from single instruments – Weidler's keening alto, for example – and from variously made-up choirs of instruments. Everything derives from the four-note theme heard on the piano at the outset, and the lines overlap, become simultaneous, as intensity grows. (This bold piece of orchestral polyphony lost most of its point in Rugolo's 1958 rescoring for strings – Creative World [A] ST1033.) An outwardly simpler kind of dialogue, between Weidler, then Cooper, and the ensemble, is presented in *Impressionism*, and the theme is even simpler, its core being only three notes. This snippet is permutated by the band at various strengths with different colours. The ensemble seemingly cannot escape this basic idea and hence is static while the solos represent the opposing principle of linear growth – until near the close, when the soloists as it were persuade the band to attempt longer phrases, thereby fusing the piece's divergent tendencies. Jazz precedents for Rugolo's building fairly complex structures from very simple themes – properly, motifs – had occurred exactly where might be expected, in Ellington's work. A fine instance is the 1937 *Diminuendo and crescendo in blue* (**152a**), where brief, elemental note patterns are developed via richly detailed harmony and orchestration.

Rugolo's *Blues in riff* (†Capitol [A] 8 59965 2) of 1950 is another example of one short melodic invention providing all the material for a piece, yet his earlier *Abstraction* (†Mosaic, 1947) takes larger risks, the basic motif having only a pair of notes. At first this performance seems purely the rhythm section's affair, but the horns make pointillist (two-note, two-chord) additions much varied in colour, texture, rhythm. Weidler, in *Monotony* vein, contributes longer lines, yet the main ensemble's part is intermittent, in contrast with the rhythm section's purposeful continuity. The effect is that of two separate discourses, each contradicting but heightening the impression made by the other. Another kind of two-voiced structure is offered by the slow-burning *Mirage* (†Capitol [A] 8 59965 2, 1950), which again has a very simple motivic basis yet employs larger resources, including strings that are well written for. It builds steadily not with a mere increase of volume but through a sort of long-term calculation that is scarcely commonplace with jazz. In fact the climax arises from interaction between the two 'voices', and the fragmented falling away afterwards is particularly well managed.

Lament is more intimate, exploring the texture of guitar plus Latin percussion heard just at the start of *Cuban carnival.* In fact the often massive sounds of the horns are tellingly subdued by the quiet-voiced guitar in an at once expressive and witty reversal of the 'screaming brass' Kenton image. The sort of music produced by piano, guitar, bass, Latin and conventional percussion is developed further in *Fugue for rhythm section*, which, aside from Roscoe Mitchell's 1978 *The maze* (Chief [E] CD4), is the nearest jazz ever got to Varèse's *Ionisation (1929–31). Though it starts like one, the piece is not really a fugue, yet this is a constantly inventive study in cross-rhythms plus the mixture of percussive colours; and what a good pianist Kenton was for such items, which had no real equivalent in the outputs of other bands at that time. This point is underlined by the remarkable Chorale for piano, brass and bongos* (†Mosaic), which opens with a dialogue between sustained *legato* piano chords and the bongos' sharp, dry accents. Indeed, one of the most striking resources of the Kenton band during this period was the extreme contrast between its characteristically full textures and the hard, unsentimental rattle of Costanzo's bongos. The dialogue, using the piano's theme, is taken up by open and muted brass, then all the brass are open as this is developed. Piano and bongos join in, then add a postscript based on their opening ideas.

Inevitably some of Rugolo's scores broke less new ground, although they still occupied their own world of sound. Perhaps it would be more relevant to say that less abrasive pieces such as *Interlude* and *Collaboration* (both Mosaic) reveal his lyricism and do not go soft at the centre. (In this they differ from *Theme to the west* – also Capitol – a regular Hollywood 'concerto'.) Kenton solos throughout *Interlude* but shares *Collaboration* with Kai Winding, who ensures a more extroverted stance. *Elegy for alto* and *Theme for alto* were designed as vehicles for Weidler, the latter in 1948 though not recorded until 1951, by which time Shank was *in situ.* Some of the band's more sensuous colours are drawn forth by *Elegy*, though brass and bongos prevent the result from growing too indulgent. The Hollywood Bowl concert performance (ST1030) is slightly preferable to the one included here.

Rugolo's scoring of *Come rain or come shine* was done in 1946 yet again not recorded until 1951. Miss Christy's singing is dealt with under **329**, but the instrumental support is far more independent of the vocal line than is usual in treatments of such material, becomes daringly so in *Lonely woman* and positively violent in *Conflict* (†Capitol [A] 8 59965 2). For *This is my theme* Miss Christy abandons singing and speaks up for the adolescent American id. Kenton alluded to Richards's *Soliloquy* (again †Capitol) as 'a journey into the subconscious' but that description could be applied far more ineptly to this sub-Freudian narrative, whose humour is no less engaging for evidently being unintentional. More important is the highly inventive out-of-tempo orchestral commentary which here, as in *Lonely woman*, encloses rather than merely accompanies the voice.

That Rugolo should have had imitators producing music less personal than his own was inevitable, and Hanna's *Somnambulism* (†Mosaic) is a fair instance of the results. A processional theme with a secondary idea in staccato repeated notes is counterpointed by alto and tenor solos (Weidler, Cooper) which briefly exchange phrases yet do not distract the ensemble's slow, rather heavy forward tread. The implication perhaps is that this sleepwalker will never wake up.

Utterly different is *Thermopylae*, Graettinger's first composition for the band that was to record his main jazz works (**477**). Nothing has been discovered, up to the time of this book's publication, about his possible earlier scores for Bobby Sherwood, Jan Savitt and others, but this densely textured piece, almost oppressive in its insistence, is completely original. The opening, which recurs, with the reeds' melody in a losing battle with heavyweight brass punctuations, could be seen as a none too benevolent caricature of the call-and-response clichés of swing. There are no solos, but Weidler's plangent alto provides needed contrast, and in general the band tackles admirably writing of real and necessary complexity. In the context of the most adventurous jazz of the 1940s, even in relation to Kenton's (or Raeburn's) most advanced undertakings, *Thermopylae* is quite extraordinary. So too is the stubbornly dissonant counterpoint of Graettinger's *Modern opus* (**477**), recorded in March 1950 by the ensemble heard on **313b**. And from *You go to my head* another complex web of sound is generated, transforming this romantic ditty into another poem for the band, richly expressive yet also disquieting in its churning, dark-hued detail.

The craftsmanlike skills of a Holman are of a rather different order, yet *Invention for guitar and trumpet* is a very effective piece, not least in its successful matching of an unlikely pair of solo instruments. Although it lasts for under three minutes and the pace is fast, the final impression is of leisure and spaciousness. Ferguson is a dangerous man to trust with a solo as the result can all too often be a series of disconnected shrieks. But it is important to recognize the exceptions. *A trumpet* (**477**) remains the best vehicle he ever found, yet *Invention* has another way of offering him the right balance of freedom and limitation. A further equilibrium is maintained between Ferguson's risk-taking acrobatics and the security suggested by Salvador, lively though his flow of ideas is. The soloists are heard contrapuntally, then separately, then together again.

To conventional-minded jazz fans this orchestra, heard throughout **313b**, is the most acceptable Kenton unit because it was the one closest to the usual kind of swinging big band. Certainly it should be mentioned first if doubts are raised about his strict jazz credentials. But the most original achievements under his name lay elsewhere, in the hands of men such as Graettinger and Rugolo. Mulligan's contributions, *Young blood* and *Swing house*, illustrate the problem. These have splendid solos by Candoli, Kamuca, Konitz, yet despite passages such as the magnificent closing ensemble of *Young blood*, they essentially are updated swing and less modern than what Mulligan did elsewhere. Rogers transplanted to Kentonian ground more comfortably and both *Round robin* and *Jolly Rogers* (both †Capitol [A] 59965 2) are aggressively powerful up-tempo swingers with admirable solos from Pepper and their composer. A rather more characteristic use is made of this band's specific resources than in Mulligan's pieces. (A quite different version of *Round robin*, retitled *Conte Candoli* and featuring that trumpeter, is on †Laserlight [E] CD15770.)

In contrast with the indigestible stew of jazz and light music that he concocted in *Soliloquy*, Richards did an imaginative job with *Prologue*, which remains the nearest jazz ever got to *The Young Person's Guide to the Orchestra* by Britten (1946). Kenton takes us on a tour of his band man by man, with each briefly demonstrating his prowess. All this is contained in a continuous flow of music that, while making room for each player, unfolds as a single piece, unified yet with considerable variety. On repeated hearings one grows tired of Kenton's narrative and the sometimes embarrassing way that he delivers it. But at the end he allows the band to rise to a 'typical' Kenton climax that drowns him, thereby revealing a sense of humour not always apparent.

Nobody is drowned in Russo's excellent miniature concertos. *Portrait of a count* enfolds an extended Candoli solo, slow and lyrical, then zestfully rhythmic at up-tempo. The ensemble participates extensively, in fact in the fast section bringing the music to a climax and a halt. From this springs a tumbling cadenza by the trumpeter which leads back to the opening mood. For Candoli see also **273**. *My lady* is Russo's effective vehicle for Konitz, with only brief interjections from the band, the last admittedly volcanic. This piece ends quietly, however, with just alto and guitar – an indication of the range of gesture Russo was already using. It is interesting to hear Konitz at such length at this time out of the Tristano context. See also **293–5**, **298**, **365** and **375–6** for Konitz. *Frank speaking* features playing of typical verve by Rosolino at two tempos with contributions from the ensemble. For Rosolino see also **275**.

The band is again hard at work in Russo's *23 degrees north 82 degrees west* (the coordinates of Havana), both in an excellent contrapuntal opening ensemble and during and between solos by Rosolino and Konitz. A properly musical use is found too for Ferguson's extreme register at the close. Longer than Russo's other pieces here, *Improvisation* has in 1951 been recorded in a considerably different version by the 'Innovations' orchestra that included strings. Here there is imaginative backing to Burgess's sonorous opening solo, this leading to a substantial interlude resourcefully composed in Russo's already characteristic manner. Sharp contrast is provided by a contrapuntal, apparently improvised passage from Childers, Russo, Konitz, Holman, this resolving to a duet between Konitz and Salvador. The latter's role is only accompanimental and so the passage does not reach the level of musical density achieved by Konitz and Billy Bauer on **298**. Yet *Improvisation* stands with *My lady* as probably the altoist's best recorded statement with Kenton. (See also **321** for Russo.)

The four items on the CD version of **313b** not included on the LP are *Taboo*, *Lonesome train*, *Swing house* and *You go to my head.* M.H.

Boyd Raeburn

314 Jewels

Savoy (A) SJL2250 (2 LPs)

Tommy Allison, Alan Jeffreys, Johnny Napton, Dale Pierce (tpt); Jack Carmen, Ollie Wilson, Sy Zentner (tbn); Hal McKusick, Leonard Green (alt); Stuart Anderson, Frank Socolow (ten); Guy McReynolds (bar); George Handy (p, arr, vcl intrjc[1]); Hayden Causey (g); Ed Mihelich (bs); Jackie Mills (d); Ginnie Powell (vcl[2]); David Allyn (vcl[3]). Los Angeles, 15 October 1945.

Tonsillectomy · *Rip van Winkle*[1,2] · *Forgetful*[3] · *Yerxa*

Carl Groen, Ray Linn, Pierce, Nelson Shalladay (tpt); Hal Smith, Wilson, Britt Woodman (tbn); Harry Klee (alt, fl); Willie Schwartz (alt, clt); Ralph Lee, McReynolds (ten); Lucky Thompson (ten[4] only); Hy Mandel (bar); Raeburn (bs sx); Dodo Marmarosa (p); Dave Barbour (g); Harry Babasin (bs); Mills (d); Handy (arr[5]); Ed Finckel (arr[6]); Powell (vcl[2]); Allyn (vcl[3]). Los Angeles, 5 February 1946.

Temptation[2,5] · *Dalvatore Sally*[5] · *Boyd meets Stravinsky*[4,6] · *I only have eyes for you*[3,5]

Frank Beach, Linn, Pierce, Shalladay (tpt); Smith, Wilson, Freddie Zito (tbn); Lloyd Otto, Evan Vail (fr h); Raeburn (sop, bs sx); Klee (alt, fl); Schwartz (alt, clt); Julie Jacobs (ten, ob); Lee (ten, bsn); McReynolds (ten); Mandel (bar); Hal Schaefer (p); Tony Rizzi (g); Babasin (bs); Mills (d); Gail Laughton (hrp); Handy (arr[5]); Finckel (arr[6]); Johnny Richards (arr[7]); Powell (vcl[2]); Allyn (vcl[3]). Los Angeles, 3 June 1946.

Over the rainbow[5,7] · *Body and soul*[2,5] · *Blue echoes*[3,5] · *Little Boyd blue*[6]

Tommy Pederson (tbn), Loretta Thompson (hrp) replace Wilson, Laughton; Bill Starkey (ten, eng h), Ralph Flanagan (arr[8]) added; Klee, Jacobs absent. Los Angeles, 14 September 1946.
Hip Boyds[8] · *Man with a horn*[7] · *Prelude to the dawn*[7] · *Duck waddle*[6,7]

Bob Fowler (tpt), Burt Johnson (tbn), Max Albright (d) replace Shalladay, Zito, Mills; Ethmer Roden (alt, fl) added; McReynolds plays alt, fl. Los Angeles, 5 November 1946.
Love tales[7] · *Soft and warm*[2,7]

Conte Candoli, Buddy Colaneri, Norman Faye, Bernie Glow (tpt); Milt Bernhart, Leon Cox, Bart Varsalone (tbn); Otto, Al Richman (fr h); Buddy DeFranco (clt); Raeburn (sop, bs sx); Jerry Sanfino, Sam Spumberg (alt); Jimmy Giuffre, Shirley Thompson (ten); Mandel (bar); Ray Rossi (p); Steve Jordan (g); Joe Berisi (bs); Irv Kluger (d); Richards (arr); Powell (vcl). New York City, 14 August 1947.
The lady is a tramp · *How high the moon?* · *Trouble is a man* · *St Louis blues*

Large studio orchestra including Paul Smith (p); Harry Bluestone (vln); Richards (arr); Allyn (vcl). Los Angeles, 19 September 1949.
It never entered my mind · *Wait till you see her* · *It can't be wrong* · *When love comes*

Raeburn's absence from the first of the above personnels is symbolic. Aside from the case of William McKinney and the Cotton Pickers (**83**), there can be few cases of a band attaining so distinguished a reputation while its leader had so little influence on its music. He was a mediocre instrumentalist, no arranger, still less a composer, and no judge of talent. Such musicians as heard the bands Raeburn fronted in the 1930s recalled them as being spectacularly bad, commercial music at something like its worst. Given such a dubious background, his ensemble had to go through a large and rapid stylistic evolution in order to arrive at modern jazz, and this it did.

By 1942 Raeburn led a group most of whose library was written by Jerry Valentine and Budd Johnson, and he soon had such people as Sonny Berman, Earl Swope, Don Lamond and June Christy working for him. He took the advice of his sidemen on which arrangers and players to employ, and the band's music thus reflected the aspirations of its more progressive members. They were guided by purely musical considerations, especially by current developments in jazz, and so the band, unlike those of immediate rivals such as Kenton or Herman, had no long-term strategy for survival. In fact its life was as short and eventful as the finest of its music has remained memorable. The above Savoy 2-LP set is the best single issue of the studio recordings, but some important work by the band originated at other sessions before, between and after these. It will therefore be necessary to refer to several other discs.

The initiative lay chiefly with the composer-arrangers, who worked out an ensemble style as individual as that of any comparable large group and one to which the sidemen, specifically the soloists, responded with notable commitment. The essential Raeburn style was created by Handy (a Copland pupil), supplemented by Finckel, their efforts further developed by Richards (a Schoenberg pupil), with several others making subsidiary contributions. In the course of this drastic transformation of a soft-centred 'society' outfit the group obviously needed to go through a swing-band phase and some excellent pieces were borrowed from other leaders, notably Ellington (who invested in Raeburn's enterprise), Basie and Herman. Stinging Raeburn versions of *Tush* [50] and *High tide*, both with characteristic Thompson solos, are on †Hep (E) CD42, while *Bagdad*, an item Juan Tizol wrote for Ellington, is on Hep (E) 3. For the Basie pieces they played the original Dicky Wells and Earle Warren arrangements and Tizol's of *Bagdad*, [51] while Herman's *Blue prelude* (†Hep [E] CD42) was thoroughly reorchestrated by George Williams.

Naturally more independent in spirit, however, are the many pieces composed specifically for Raeburn, particularly by Finckel, whose association with the band started before Handy's. Finckel's idea was to make the group an updated extension of Basie's, playing what he called 'orchestrated Lester [Young]', although this is a more apt description of what he later wrote for Gene Krupa and Buddy Rich than of the scores he produced for Raeburn. Typical is *The eagle flies* (†Hep [E] CD1), an engaging up-tempo swinger with solos to match; and the completely un-Ellingtonian *Boyd meets the Duke* (First Time [A] FTR1515) shows how aggressively efficient Raeburn's ensemble became at such things. Another instance is *Boyd's nest* by Milt Kleeb (†Hep [E] CD42, with a fiercer reading on Hep 3). The power generated in scores such as *Bobby socks* (alias *Bernie's tune*) is very impressive and by the time we reach the ferocious *Little Boyd blue* or the unusual fast treatment of *Blue moon* (all on First Time), aspects of the style properly associated with Raeburn are emerging. They may be said to have done so fully with *Foolish little boy* (†Hep [E] CD42), which sounds like a Handy sophistication of *Whistle while you work* and includes some exhilarating Marmarosa piano improvisation.

By now a link-up with one of the mainstream jazz avant-gardists such as Gillespie was entirely feasible, and this duly took place in January 1945, a month before the trumpeter recorded the earliest titles on **256**. In Gillespie's composition *A night in Tunisia* (†Hep [E] CD1) they play the arrangement he earlier had made for Hines's band. The other pieces in which he is heard are Finckel's *March of the Boyds* (Musicraft) and *Barefoot Boyd with cheek* (First Time), a striking Ralph Burns score, its title a reference to Max Shulman's tale 'Barefoot boy with cheek'. Gillespie's solos typify his first maturity and he is well matched by a Raeburn band that by now is completely transformed.

A matter for no little outrage when new, this music inevitably seems less threatening when heard several decades later, yet the best of it remains of high value. Certainly it is not surprising that at the band's public appearances Handy's scores especially were listened to with close attention by such people as Pete Rugolo. A nicely judged blend of assertion and suavity, the very swinging *Tonsillectomy* was jointly written with McKusick, and has solos by him, Allison and Socolow, the two latter doing their finest work on record with Raeburn. Note the beautiful theme-based saxophone background to Allison's solo. *Yerxa* also features McKusick and Socolow, stresses the band's capacity for refinement and is full of the sensitive mixtures of tone colour that mark Handy's most representative work.

So is *Temptation*, whose subtle textures imply a perceptive awareness of Ellington without sounding remotely like him. The ensemble is more active, the figuration more varied and growing fiercer than is usual with vocal accompaniments, but like other Handy scores it shows Ginnie Powell to singular advantage. She always said that she found it hard to accommodate to his arrangements and her point is underlined by her account of *I can't believe that you're in love with me* (†Hep [E] CD42), which is crammed with dissonant and diverse modernistic gestures. The fact remains that she did her best singing in these challenging settings rather than later with Krupa, Charlie Barnet or Harry James. She was indeed a considerably better musician than most vocalists of this type, with a personal sound, individual phrasing and very clear diction. (This *Temptation* should be compared with the completely different instrumental version later written for the band by Richards, on Hep [E] 3.) Raeburn's other singer, Allyn, was far less impressive, and his crooning was almost the ensemble's only concession to popular appeal.

Perhaps the most remarkable single performance this band ever recorded, *Dalvatore Sally* is the first movement of a suite that can be heard complete on †Hep (E) 1. Again there are many fresh mixtures of brass, woodwind, saxophone and rhythm section, procedures that later arrangers never took up specifically. There is a fast middle section during which Marmarosa dialogues agilely with the band and altogether an entire small world is packed into these three minutes. The title *Boyd meets Stravinsky* was a *folie de grandeur* and as it quotes *Chant of the weed* (**123**) in its introduction, a better name would have been *Raeburn meets Redman*. Still, it is another of Finckel's rapid swingers, one having top-class Thompson and Marmarosa plus great section playing. An exuberant virtuoso performance, it contrasts interestingly with the restrained earlier version on Joyce (A) LP5010. *Body and soul* is Ginnie Powell again and in the introduction Handy oddly throws violent, disruptive figures against pastel-toned woodwind carrying the melody. Apparently the score of *Over the rainbow* was started by Handy and perhaps finished by Richards. There is a Richards-like use of harp and woodwind at the beginning, yet with Handy's sort of textural discontinuity. Indeed there is a surprisingly successful integration of swinging and rhapsodic sections, excellently handled by the ensemble.

When he took over from Handy as Raeburn's chief arranger Richards made a more consistent use of woodwind, harp and french horns. Such jazz puritans as chanced to hear the band objected to the romantically introspective english horn of *Man with a horn* and to the harp on *Prelude to the dawn*, which has lovely Schwartz alto. *Duck waddle*, written by Finckel in 1944, revised by Richards two years later, is another inappropriate title, this being a propulsive, even pungent, swinger with splendid Linn and Pederson. The latter is also to the fore in *Love tales*, which offers the rich palette of colours also shadowing Ginnie Powell in *Soft and warm*. Raeburn's last session here features her throughout at her absolute best and with the ensemble participating as energetically as ever. For instance *The lady is a tramp* is done almost as much as a vehicle for a trumpet section in dazzling form as for her. In fact there is something of interest in the band's support throughout, above all in the imaginatively detailed *St Louis blues*, which may be her finest recording.

The last four items in this set are not Raeburn's but an initiative of Richards's when he was music director of the Discovery label. His scoring is as colourfully ingenious as ever, particularly in the use of Bluestone's violin and the woodwind. But Allyn sings all the time.

Many other consistently resourceful scores by Richards are scattered among various haphazard LP issues of Raeburn's output, such as a very characteristic and quite complicated *Yesterdays* (Golden Era [A] LP5014). Outstanding is his *Cartaphilius* (†Hep [E] CD42), which actually looks forward to **377**. There are also some curiosities, like a condensation of Rimsky-Korsakov's *Scheherazade* (Hep [E] 22) done as a clarinet concerto for DeFranco! Note should also be taken of the obscure Tommy Talbot, who, presumably following the example of Shep Fields's 1941–4 band, scored a 1946 Raeburn date using french horns, woodwind and a rhythm section including Erroll Garner (Hep 22). This session produced the *Please let me forget* mentioned under **263**, an independently scored *Caravan* and a Talbot version of *C jam blues* which unfolds as an almost formal set of variations, personal in tone, yet anticipating the West Coast school's 1950s use of woodwind.

Raeburn's band continued to make occasional appearances into 1948, and at various times included Al Killian, Maynard Ferguson, Eddie Bert, Tiny Kahn and Mel Lewis, among others. More recently, with the establishment of the jazz repertoire movement, his library has been performed to audiences at last ready for the music, for example by Mike Crotty's band in Washington, with both Handy and Finckel writing new pieces. M.H.

Dizzy Gillespie

315 **The Complete RCA Victor Recordings**
†RCA-Victor (A) 07863 66528 2

Gillespie, Shad Collins (tpt); Bill Dillard (tpt, vcl); Dicky Wells (tbn); Russell Procope, Howard Johnson (alt); Robert Carroll, Teddy Hill (ten); Sam Allen (p); Richard Fullbright (bs); Bill Beason (d). New York City, 17 May 1937.
King Porter stomp · *Yours and mine* · *Blue rhythm fantasy*

Gillespie (tpt); Benny Carter (alt); Coleman Hawkins, Chew Berry (ten); Clyde Hart (p); Charlie Christian (g); Milt Hinton (b); Cozy Cole (d); Lionel Hampton (vib). New York City, 13 June 1939
Hot mallets

Gillespie (tpt); Don Byas (ten – except *Anthropology*); Al Haig (p); Bill DeArrango (g); Ray Brown (b); J. C. Heard (d); Milt Jackson (vib). New York City, 22 February 1946.
52nd Street theme (2 versions) · *A night in Tunisia* (2 versions) · *Ol' man rebop* · *Anthropology* (2 versions)

Gillespie (tpt, vcl[1]); Dave Burns, Elmon Wright, Matthew McKay (tpt); Taswell Baird, William Shepherd (tbn); John Brown, Howard Johnson (alt); James Moody, James Gayles (ten); Cecil Payne (bar); John Lewis (p); John Collins (g); Ray Brown (b); Joe Harris (d); Jackson (vib); Kenny Hagood (vcl[2]). New York City, 22 August 1947.
Ow! · *Ooop-pop-a-da*[1,2] · *Two bass hit* · *Stay on it*

Gillespie (tpt, vcl[1]); Burns, Elmon Wright, Lamar Wright Jr, Benny Bailey (tpt); Shepherd, Ted Kelly (tbn); Brown, Johnson (alt); Gayles, 'Big Nick' Nicholas (ten); Payne (bar); Lewis (p); Al McKibbon (b); Kenny Clarke (d); Chano Pozo (perc); Hagood (vcl[2]). New York City, 22/30 December 1947.
Algo bueno (Woody 'n' you) · *Cool breeze*[1,2] · *Cubana be* · *Cubana bop* · *Manteca* · *Ool-ya-koo*[1,2] · *Minor walk* · *Good bait*

Gillespie (tpt, vcl[1]); Burns, E. Wright, Willie Cook (tpt); Andy Duryea, Sam Hurt, Jesse Tarrant (tbn); Brown, Ernie Henry (alt); Gayles, Budd Johnson (ten); Payne (bar); James Forman (p); McKibbon (b); Teddy Stewart (d); Joe Harris (perc); Sabu Martinez (perc). New York City, 29 December 1948.
Guarachi guaro · *Duff capers* · *Lover, come back to me* · *I'm be boppin' too*[1]

Gillespie, Miles Davis, Fats Navarro (tpt); Kai Winding, J. J. Johnson (tbn); Buddy DeFranco (clt); Charles Parker (alt); Charlie Ventura (ten); Ernie Caceres (bar); Lennie Tristano (p); Billy Bauer (g); Eddie Safranski (b); Shelly Manne (d). New York City, 3 January 1949.
Overtime (2 versions) · *Victory ball*

Same personnel as 3 January 1949 except: Davis, Navarro, Johnson and Caceres out. New York City, 3 January 1949.
Victory ball (short version)

Same personnel as 29 December 1948 except: Benny Harris (tpt) replaces Burns; Yusef Lateef (ten) replaces Johnson; Al Gibson (bar) replaces Payne; Vince Guerra (perc) replaces Harris and Martinez; Johnny Hartman (vcl[2]). Chicago, 14 April 1949.

Swedish suite · *St Louis blues* · *I should care*[2] · *That old black magic*[2]

Same personnel as 14 April 1949 except: Joe Carrol (vcl[3]) added. Chicago, 6 May 1949.

You go to my head[2] · *Jump did-le ba*[1,3] · *Dizzier and dizzier* · *I'm be-boppin' too*[1]

Same personnel as 6 May 1949 except: J. J. Johnson, Charles Greenlea (tbn) replace Hurt, Tarrant. New York City, 6 July 1949.

Hey Pete! Le's eat mo' meat[1,3] · *Jumpin' with Symphony Sid* · *If love is trouble*[2] · *In the land of Oo-bla-dee*[3]

During the 1940s, Gillespie was one of a handful of musicians who helped redefine jazz. As one of the leading figures of the bop movement he was instrumental in moving jazz from the essentially diatonic conventions of the swing era into chromatic harmony, so enlarging the number of note choices available to the improviser. This was underpinned by new rhythmic thinking that broke free of the four- and eight-bar phrases within which pre-bop improvisers contained their solos, stressing instead angular, fragmented phrases that began and ended in unexpected places. Although bop was never destined to attract the widespread following of the swing bands, it nonetheless enjoyed considerable exposure in the music press and a fast-growing following among young urban black and white audiences, particularly in New York and the Northern cities. For these fans, the focal point of the music was Gillespie – Charlie Parker, the key figure of the era, remained in the background so far as the public was concerned, acclaimed only by musicians and an inner circle of New York enthusiasts for most of the 1940s. It was Gillespie who was bop's front man. A rare combination of clown and master musician, he was an ideal media person, someone who could be relied upon for good copy; photogenic and witty, he would always oblige with a humorous pose or a zany quotation.

Gillespie's emergence from obscure sideman to the musician widely perceived as epitomising the bop movement is charted in part on these Victor recordings by his work for Teddy Hill, playing alongside his early mentor Bill Dillard, and with a Lionel Hampton pick-up band (**161b**). These tracks, together with those on *Dizzy Gillespie: The Development of an American Artist 1940–45* (Smithsonian [A] R 004), which include examples of his work with Cab Calloway, a jam session at Monroe's, with Les Hite, Lucky Millinder, Coleman Hawkins, Billy Eckstine, Sarah Vaughan, Oscar Pettiford and his 18 All-Stars, Joe Marsala, Boyd Raeburn, Georgie Auld, the Tempo Jazzmen and with his own Sextet, chart Gillespie's acceleration from the conventions of swing-era trumpet masters such as Roy Eldridge, 'Hot Lips' Page and Henry 'Red' Allen, who helped shape his formative style, to the startling virtuoso of the 1945 Musicraft sessions (**256a**).

In 1945 Gillespie was encouraged by his manager Billy Shaw to form his own big band, which he promptly booked into a touring package with the comedians Patterson and Jackson, the vocalist June Eckstine and the Nicholas Brothers, a dancing duo. Called *The Hepsations of 1945*, they went out on a 90-day tour of the Southwest – south of the Mason–Dixon line – where, quite apart from countless incidents of blatant racial prejudice, the band were unable to find favour with Southern audiences who complained they could not dance to the band. Later in the year Gillespie made another unsuccessful foray, this time with a small band that included Parker, in an attempt to induct West Coast audiences into the rites of the new music. By 1946, however, Gillespie's fortunes were beginning to improve. Voted No. 1 Trumpet Man in the annual *Metronome* poll, in February he opened a successful residency at the Spotlite Club on 52nd Street in New York. He also contributed four sides, along with four by Coleman Hawkins, to an album produced by Leonard Feather for RCA-Victor called *New 52nd Street Jazz* (apparently Victor were not confident to use the term bop at the time).

Byas had previously played with Gillespie in a small group the trumpeter led at the Onyx Club on 52nd Street in 1944 and had appeared on record with him as a member of the Dizzy Gillespie Sextet for the Manor label in 1945. Two sides from this appear on (**249**) and the complete session appears on the Smithsonian issue referred to above. Stylistically, Byas bridged the old and the new manners. Like Coleman Hawkins, to whose style he was indebted, he related harmonically to bop while rhythmically he remained rooted in the swing era. Even so, he was a perfect foil for Gillespie and today his playing has the effect of showing the trumpeter's startling virtuosity up in sharp relief. Thelonious Monk's *52nd Street theme* was a ternary 32-bar AABA composition, using the chords of *I got rhythm* for the A sections and the chords of *Honeysuckle rose* for the B section, or middle eight. The Parker–Gillespie composition *Anthropology* was also a contrafact, this time based entirely on the underlying harmonies of *I got rhythm*, a favourite chord progression of Gillespie's which had also provided the chords for his more famous composition *Salt peanuts* (**256a**).

The Gillespie–Paparelli theme *A night in Tunisia* is one of the great bebop tunes and was recorded before the Victor session by both Sarah Vaughan and Boyd Raeburn (Smithsonian, as above) and several times later by both Gillespie and Parker. In fact, it is the latter's version on the Dial label that today springs most readily to mind (**258**), but Gillespie's original performance of his tune merits careful study. Although it uses a straightforward form, the standard ternary AABA, it is worth noting that subsequent versions do not adhere to the scheme used on this version, particularly in the use of 'interludes', or specially written sections, which follow the trumpet and tenor solos.

Intro 8 bars + A (10 bars) + A^1 (8 bars) + B (8 bars) + A^1 (8 bars)
+ interlude (12 bars) + trumpet solo (A + A^1 + B + A^1)
+ interlude (4 bars) + tenor solo (A + A^1) + vibe solo (B)
+ ensemble (A^1)

On subsequent versions of the composition, the 12-bar interlude was expanded to 16 bars and was usually employed after each improvisation. Gillespie's solo, while clearly emerging from the shadows of the swing era, was moving towards a new language in terms of accents and phrasing; indeed a multi-note motif in the final eight bars of his solo would become something of a Gillespie trademark, a testament to his burgeoning virtuosity. The remaining title from this session, *Ol' man rebop*, a contrafact on the chords of *Ol' man river*, is a catchy riff theme that includes workmanlike solos from Byas and the leader.

As 1946 progressed, bop began to be recognized as both hip and new in the music business. Gillespie's extrovert playing and behaviour was seized upon by the music press and as the year progressed he found himself something of a public figure, with articles, reviews and features about him appearing in national publications. Mort Schillinger pointed out in a lengthy profile that: 'Never before in the history of jazz has so dynamic a person as Gillespie gained the spotlight and idolization . . . few musicians have escaped the aura of Dizzy's music . . . But the fad of copying Dizzy unfortunately has not stopped with the music; followers have been trying to make themselves look and act like Dizzy to boot.' [52]

Gillespie affected a goatee beard and often wore a beret and horn-rimmed spectacles. By mid-1946 *Ebony* had advertisements for 'Bop Glasses – Real Gone Frames only $3.95' to which fans added small paper beards and a 'bop cap', a beret with a peak. By the spring of 1946 Gillespie felt confident enough to try another big band, recording for Musicraft in June that year (**256b**). In November 1946 the band set out on another tour that had echoes of the *Hepsations of 1945* debacle. This time Ella Fitzgerald lent her name and presence to the tour, but despite her popularity once again it floundered south of the Mason–Dixon line. 'They would look up to the bandstand as if we were nuts,' said the saxophonist James Moody. [53]

In the summer of 1947 Gillespie signed with Victor, but by that time Sonny Stitt, a key soloist on the Musicraft small-group sessions who had also taken all the alto solos in the big band, left, leaving his presence in the big band undocumented, his replacement the workmanlike John Brown. However, Gillespie's August 1947 session did at least bring together on record for the first time the pianist John Lewis – who was fresh out of the army and, having previously studied music at the University of New Mexico, was continuing his studies at the Manhattan School of Music – with the vibraharpist Milt Jackson and the bassist Ray Brown to begin a musical relationship that would culminate in the formation of the Modern Jazz Quartet in 1951–2.

Lewis contributed *Two bass hit*, which would reappear as *La ronde* by the MJQ (**363**); this was based on the blues in contrast to the earlier *One bass hit* (**256b**), an *I got rhythm* contrafact. *Two bass hit* contained some of Gillespie's most lucid playing on his Victor big-band tracks, together with a solo from Brown that helped establish him as an important bassist of the 'new jazz'. Gillespie's fondness for vivid ensembles was demonstrated on *Ow!* and *Oop-pop-a-da* with trumpet passages that sounded for all the world like orchestrated Gillespie solos. The former was again an *I got rhythm* contrafact while the latter, a blues, was a vehicle for Gillespie's and Hagood's bop vocalizing. On it Gillespie implied that, like Louis Armstrong, he played as he sang and sang as he played; and again like Armstrong, he laced his vocals liberally with humour. Gillespie's principal arranger was Gil Fuller, and on several arrangements it is quite possible that he collaborated with Gillespie, who also may well have had a hand in Lewis's *Two bass hit.* Tadd Dameron's *Stay on it* was acquired by Gillespie from Billy Eckstine, whose historic band had recently folded, although it in fact sounds tailor-made for Gillespie's band through Dameron's deft melodicism and muscular part-writing. It is possible that Gillespie had a hand in writing this arrangement too, since he shares composer credit.

By the time of the second Victor big-band session Gillespie had appeared with Ella Fitzgerald at Carnegie Hall on 29 September 1947, which was billed as 'A Concert of the New Jazz' and included a guest appearance by Charlie Parker. The five Parker–Gillespie small-group performances and most of Gillespie's portion of the concert appeared on *Diz 'n Bird at Carnegie Hall* (†Roost 7243). The concert was a sellout, and provided evidence that bop was beginning to take hold on the public consciousness. No longer the music of a few experimentalists in Harlem after-hours clubs, bop was fast displacing swing as the *lingua franca* of jazz. While Gillespie was blasted by the critics for trying to steal the limelight from Ella, the concert as a whole was considered an unqualified success musically, described as one of the freshest things since Ellington's January 1943 concert. Perhaps it was no coincidence that the December 1947 session would prove to be Gillespie's most productive and artistically satisfying for Victor. The central exhibit was Gillespie's collaboration with George Russell on two compositions, *Cubana be* and *Cubana bop.* These were Russell's first attempts at applying the theories he was working on that subsequently were expounded in his theoretical study *The Lydian Chromatic Concept of Tonal Organization.*

Cubana be and *Cubana bop* reflected Gillespie's increasing interest in

Afro-Cuban jazz which dated back to his time with the Cab Calloway orchestra (**148**). Gillespie owed his position in that band to its lead trumpeter, Mario Bauza, who was so impressed by the younger man's ability that he pretended to be sick one Monday night (he went to a ball game) and sent Gillespie to Calloway in his stead. [54] Bauza's ruse succeeded; Calloway was duly impressed with Gillespie's playing and when a vacancy occurred in the trumpet section he sent for him. Like Dillard in the Hill band, Bauza became a mentor for Gillespie and aroused his interest in Cuban music. By the mid-1940s, Bauza had become musical director of his brother-in-law Machito's band, and when the leader was called up for army service, Bauza began experimenting with combining Cuban music and jazz, a pioneering role for which he was given little or no credit during his lifetime. The prospect of merging Cuba's exciting rhythms with jazz's spontaneous impulses intrigued Gillespie, who often sat in with Machito's band. By 1947 Gillespie decided to add an authentic Cuban percussionist to his band, and approached Bauza to suggest someone suitable. Bauza put him in touch with Chano Pozo. 'This was a great creative period in our history,' said Gillespie later, 'and *Cubana be, Cubana bop* was one of our most adventurous pieces.' [55]

Cubana be had its origins in fragments of a big band chart of *Relaxin' at Camarillo* which Russell had contributed to the band but which never was recorded. However, *Camarillo* was performed at Carnegie Hall along with *Cubana be* and *Cubana bop*, the latter two pieces linked by an interlude featuring Pozo and renamed *Afro-Cuban drum suite*. According to Gillespie, the first piece was written by Russell, the idea for the percussion link in the middle was Pozo's and Gillespie himself was responsible for the second piece. [56] In both conception and execution these pieces were ambitious, yet today they seem strangely unfulfilling. The studio versions, played with much more confidence than at Carnegie Hall, open with a percussion interlude followed by a modally based instrumental section written by Russell that is perhaps the first use of modal writing in jazz (albeit making use of dissonance). This gives the way to a statement of an AABA theme by Gillespie and the orchestra and an embellishment of the B section. *Cubana bop* opens with percussion and chant by Pozo aided by Clarke on bongos, and an emergence of more dissonant writing and a partial reprise of the B theme. But it ultimately eschews thematic development to arrive at an oblique coda and an unexpected ending. If any numbers from Gillespie's big-band repertoire distanced his band from the prevailing big-band orthodoxy, then it was these, which still sound resolutely modern with their jagged intervals, dissonance and feral power.

In contrast, *Manteca* also employed Caribbean rhythms and again the use of static harmonies was more attributable to Latin music's *mortuno* than to modal principles. The tune's thematic construction is a variation of the standard AABA forms which dominated the band's repertoire in that it used 40-bar choruses that make use of double-length bridge sections. These choruses were separated by an 'interlude', an aspect of Gillespie's writing that had previously appeared to interesting effect on *A night in Tunisia*:

Intro (22 bars + 2 bar trumpet break + 4 bars) + A (8 bars) + A (8 bars) + B (8 bars) + B^1 (8 bars) + A (8 bars) + interlude (10 bars) + C (8 bars) + C (8 bars) + B (8 bars) + B^1 (8 bars) + A (8 bars) + coda (10 bars)

Once again the harmonies of *I got rhythm* emerge, this time on the straight-ahead swing of the second chorus, to provide the basis for Nicholas's tenor solo, which uses the A sections of Gershwin's composition. Overall the composition hangs together well, the contrasting vamp sections and the lunging swing sections making effective use of the principal of tension and release. The catchy, polyrhythmic vamp inspired by Pozo – to which Gillespie would later sing 'I'll never go back to Georgia', no doubt as a result of his experiences during his 1945 and 1946 tours – was based on just three notes, with one a b7 of the Mixolydian scale, a scale common to many Cuban compositions. As the *ostinato* builds, so does Pozo's rhythmic intensity on his conga drums, which he had tuned to the three pitches of the *ostinato*. The powerful use of staccato trumpets and Gillespie's own soaring solo all helped make *Manteca* Gillespie's most popular composition and the recording a minor hit.

Gershwin's enduring *Rhythm* changes pop up again as a basis for *Good bait*, albeit this time in modified form, since the middle eight is really the A section transposed up a fourth. Originally written for Basie by Dameron, this elegantly loping theme was first recorded by Gillespie with his All-Stars – Trummy Young (tbn); Don Byas (ten); Clyde Hart (p); Oscar Pettiford (bs); Shelly Manne (d) – in January 1945 (Smithsonian, as above). Solos are by Gillespie, Kelly on trombone, McKibbon on bass and Clarke briefly at the close, although here Pozo appears to have difficulty in breaking away from the traditional Cuban *clavé* rhythm in favour of straight-ahead jazz rhythms. *Cool breeze* was another chart Gillespie obtained from Eckstine, a blues composed and arranged by Dameron who took the idea for the theme from a counter-melody Gillespie played on *Disorder at the border* on a February 1944 Coleman Hawkins date (Smithsonian, as above). Gillespie and Hagood provide a witty scat interlude, with Gillespie working in a quote from *Ornithology* and Hagood replying with *Doing what comes naturally*. Note that the background figure Dameron wrote for *Cool breeze* would in turn form the basis of his composition *The squirrel* (**260**).

That same 1944 Hawkins session also produced a version of *Woody 'n you*, a Gillespie original that was slightly recast here as *Algo bueno* as a feature for Pozo with the band leaning towards the sound of Machito's Afro-Cubists in several places. *Minor walk* was a minor blues written by Erroll Garner's brother Linton and arranged by Gillespie, who exploits the high register of his horn in his solo with John Brown on alto adding his voice. The Fuller arrangement of *Ool-ya-koo* with its crazy bebop vocals taken together with those on *Ow!*, *Oop-pop-a-da* and *Cool breeze* represent the sort of concessions Gillespie had to make to attract a broader audience, trading on the novelty value of bop, spelling out onomatopoeically bop's rhythms in song and generally trading on the faddishness of the new music.

After the December 1947 sessions the band launched into a tour of Europe in January 1948, where the impact of its performances have been documented by performances in Sweden and in Paris. Its extended departure from New York was responsible for the 21-year-old bassist Ray Brown handing in his notice. Having just married Ella Fitzgerald on 10 December 1947, he felt he should devote himself to his wife's career. She was about to undertake a tour of Eastern cities with the saxophonist Illinois Jacquet, so Brown was replaced by Al McKibbon. In Europe, Gillespie's tour was generally mismanaged, with dates in Switzerland, the Netherlands and Czechoslovakia falling through. To add to the general confusion, Britain's Ministry of Labour overruled the Musicians' Union and forbade the band's appearance. This prevented what undoubtedly would have been a major musical event for a beleaguered jazz community which had been without live American jazz since 1935. That was when the Ministry of Labour, after lobbying by the Musicians' Union, demanded reciprocity of employment in America for British musicians, imposing a ludicrous ban that would only begin to be relaxed with an appearance by the Kenton orchestra in 1956.

During the hiatus between the December 1947 date and upcoming December 1948 session, caused by the second AFM recording ban, Parker appeared with the band at the Pershing Ballroom in August 1948. However, the resulting recordings focus chiefly on Parker's contribution and are of variable sound quality. They nevertheless reveal the band playing numbers like *Things to come*, *Ooo-bop-sha-bam*, *Manteca* and *Good bait* with an easy fluency: *The Unheard Charlie Parker Vol. 1: Bird Seed* (†Stash [A] STB2500). Perhaps the best representation of the band during this period was the concert recorded on 26 July 1948 at the Pasadena Civic Auditorium in Los Angeles by Gene Norman: *Dizzy Gillespie Big Band in Concert featuring Chano Pozo* (Gene Norman Presents [A] 23). Included were sterling versions of Gillespie's most enduring numbers which confirm the band's confident handling of their material: *Emanon*, *Ool-ya-koo*, *Round about midnight*, *Stay on it*, *Good bait*, *One bass hit*, *I can't get started* and *Manteca*. However, as 1948 drew to a close, Pozo, a key member of the band, was shot dead in the Rio

Bar on upper Fifth Avenue on 2 December 1948. When the band appeared at Carnegie Hall on Christmas Day, his replacement, Sabu Martinez, broke the skin of his conga drum, such was the ferocity of tribute to Pozo. Before his death, Pozo had collaborated with Gillespie on *Guarachi guaro*, a number orchestrated by Gerald Wilson and designed primarily as a percussion feature.

Duff capers was perhaps one of the more straightforward compositions and retained a dual affinity between impulsive bop figures and swing while giving Ernie Henry's alto prominence alongside the leader's trumpet. Gillespie's arrangement of *Lover come back to me* is a little bizarre, cast in Latin rhythms, with the trumpeter's *grandioso* statement of the theme preceding a double-tempo passage prior to the *fermata*. Presumably intended as a *tour de force*, it was poorly conceived, resulting in meaningless grandstanding. However, while Gillespie's trumpet style was resolutely extending the boundaries of jazz, very often his heart seemed in the swing era, exemplified by the sort of novelty numbers the big bands use to throw in to please the dancers, such as *I'm be-boppin' too*. Yet by now Gillespie's trumpet style had shed much of the impulsiveness he inherited from Eldridge. During the later Victor sessions he exhibits a more even control over his instrument and seemed to have overcome the occasional technical failings he had shown in his 1945 recordings. These later tracks reveal an unparalleled mastery of his instrument, embracing speed, agility and high-register control. Now he seemed able to access all the registers of his instrument with ease, creating gloriously constructed lines that, while being brief within the context of a big band, clearly marked him as the premier trumpet player in jazz.

From 18 to 24 March 1949 the band appeared in Chicago with Sarah Vaughan at the Regal Theatre, remaining in Chicago to fulfil a further engagement, where the band was recorded on 14 April. Fuller's *Swedish suite* remains resolutely in the bop idiom, but by now bands like Woody Herman were sounding far more 'modern' by smoothing over the harsh edges of bop inspired by a saxophone section applying Lester Young's melodic logic to bop's harmonic challenges. From this point on, Gillespie seemed to have difficulty in positioning his band to compete in a declining market. He seemed unwilling to move towards a less frantic expressionism, a direction clearly telegraphed by his sometime protégé Miles Davis with his *Birth of the Cool* ensemble (**376**). The May 1949 session was also recorded in Chicago when the band were working the Blue Note club after appearing in Portland, Oregon, while the July 1949 session was recorded in New York during an engagement at Bop City. On these dates Gillespie seemed to be looking backwards rather than forwards with the inclusion of ballads by Johnny Hartman on *I should care*, *You go to my head*, *If love is trouble* that are in the popular black balladeer tradition of baritones like Herb Jeffries and Billy Eckstine. Of these, Hartman was a true talent, and though he handles his material competently here, his greatest performances on record would have to wait until 7 March 1963 when he cut the excellent *John Coltrane and Johnny Hartman* (†Impulse GRD157).

Although there are moments of interest in these final Victor sessions, there are fewer of them. Budd Johnson's arrangement of *St Louis blues* begins with Parker's clarion call that opens *Parker's mood* (**257**), and the writing was sufficiently adventurous for W. C. Handy to have reputedly opposed the release of the record for 15 years. The unpromising *In the land of oo-bla-dee*, written and arranged by Mary Lou Williams, has a vocal by Carroll which it manages to survive, yielding some deft part-writing that revealed how Miss Williams, a charter member of the old Andy Kirk Orchestra in the 1930s (**77**, **132**), had moved with the times. *Hey Pete! Le's eat mo' meat* is a harbinger of Gillespie's gruesome Capitol period epitomized by such lamentable numbers as *You stole my wife you horse thief*, which sadly represented a desperate bid to reach out to a broader following as the audience for big bands (and bop) began to drift away. When the band played Little Rock, Arkansas, in 1950, for example, they played for an audience of two dozen people in a 5000-seat auditorium. By then the lethargy and lack of interest that seemed evident in the recording studio was apparent in live performance, as Barry Ulanov's review of the band in Bop City in early 1950 revealed: 'Dizzy Gillespie was a disappointment at Bop City. This was, like most of the recent music at the would-be Jazz Center of the World, not bop but only a distant echo. John was as pleasant a front for his band as ever; he played a few cadenza exercises on his trumpet; he joined Joe Carroll in scatting battles, which Joe won hands down. The band seemed lost in a riff groove in which Dizzy has set it of late and nothing really came off.' [57] In late 1950 Gillespie wound up the big band and formed a small combo. The Victor compilation ends with Gillespie's appearance in the *Metronome* all-stars band alongside Fats Navarro and Miles Davis. 'Me and Fats decided to follow Dizzy's lead and play all the shit he was playing instead of playing our own styles. It was so close to what Dizzy played *he* didn't know when he left off and when we started,' said Davis in 1989. [58] Sadly it denied posterity a unique opportunity to hear their contrasting styles, and the *Metronome* tracks add little to our understanding of Gillespie the artist.

At the time of Gillespie's first big-band recordings it was by no means clear whether bop was small-band or big-band music. Certainly Gillespie, as one of bop's founding fathers, did not think it was the special preserve of the small groups. The recorded evidence demonstrates that the complexity of the 'new music' could be just as effectively negotiated by a high head count as a low one – albeit the big band did sound a little ragged on occasion. Indeed, the dominance of the trumpets and the complexity of the frequent trumpet solos in his arrangements had considerable influence on how arrangers subsequently approached writing for a trumpet section. Although histories tell us that bop was a small-band music 'because of the music's inherent complexity', the reason seemed to have more to do with economic and logistical considerations than musical ones: the cost of arrangements, the cost of a portable public address system, the high wage roll, transportation costs, management costs, booking agents costs, the complexity of putting together tour itineraries and so on. In contrast the small ad hoc ensembles, often put together at a moment's notice for club dates, did away with the logistical and financial encumbrances of a big band and did not even require arrangements. They relied instead on a memorized repertoire of bop tunes and favourite standards that were often supplemented by a couple of original heads worked up on the job. Ultimately, it was to Gillespie's great credit he was able to preserve the authenticity of bop within a larger ensemble.

Despite the financial failure of his first two big-band ventures, the large ensemble would remain Gillespie's first love for the remainder of his life. Subsequently he led some notable aggregations, such as the one he took on a 1956 State Department tour. During his final years he led his United Nations Orchestra, a pleasantly volatile ensemble, from 1988 until a few months before his death in 1993. He never seemed to have his heart in organizing a really effective small group, with many of his sidemen joining him as unknowns and enjoying similar status when they left. With the exception of his subsequent work with Parker and a few albums for the Verve label (where it was the producer Norman Granz who created the context in which to feature Gillespie's trumpet [59]), his not inconsiderable discography is most rewardingly traversed using the occasions he led a big band. Certainly that is where many of his best latter-day solos are to be found, the man himself citing his solo on *Dizzy's blues* with his 1957 big band on *Dizzy Gillespie at Newport* (Verve [J] MV2604) as one of his best on record. [60] Yet in considering his discography as a whole, it is impossible not to conclude that Gillespie did not significantly advance his art beyond his great achievements between 1945 and 1950, which was unusual considering his status as an artist. 'To live longer than 40 years is bad manners,' said Dostoievsky's Underground Man, and it remains an uncomfortable truth that such is the way jazz history is constructed that had Gillespie become one of jazz's young martyrs, his work between 1945 to 1950 in particular would undoubtedly be valued far more than it is today. S.N.

Machito and his Afro-Cuban Orchestra

316 **Mucho Macho**
†Pablo (A) PACD 2625 712 2

Machito (cond, mar, clv, vcl); Mario Bauza, Frank Davila, Bobby Woodlen (tpt); Gene Johnson, Fred Skerritt (alt); Jose Madera (ten); Leslie Johnakins (bar); Rene Hernandez (p); Roberto Rodriguez (bs); Jose Mangual (bon); Luis Miranda (con); Ubaldo Nieto (timb); Graciela (vcl). New York City, 1948–9.

Asia minor · Un poquito de tu amor · Tumba el quinto · Jungle drums · Llora timbero · Vive como yo · Babarabatiri · Cleopatra rumba (Desert dance) · U-bla-ba-du · Elsopon · Gone city · Babalu · Vaya niña · Hall of the Mambo King · Donkey serenade · Mambo jambo · At sundown · Why do I love you? · Mambo is here to stay · Rose room · Tea for two · Finaliza un amor · The world is waiting for the sunrise · St Louis blues

Since before the turn of the century, Latin music regularly featured on the fringes of the American musical mainstream. *La Paloma* dates from around 1870, *Estrellita* was an enduring US hit from 1909; and by at least 1914 a habanera section had found its way into W. C. Handy's *St Louis blues*. And although Jelly Roll Morton always insisted a 'Spanish tinge' was an essential ingredient of jazz, the influence of Latin American music nevertheless remained little more than exotic flavouring until the 1940s. Although there had been a tango craze in the 1920s, followed by a rumba craze in the 1930s, its rhythms seldom really impinged upon jazz. That was set to change on Sunday night, 28 May 1943 at La Conga Club in midtown Manhattan.

Machito's orchestra was two years into a four-year residency at the club. Its leader had recently been claimed by the army and was several miles away, undergoing basic military training at Camp Upton, New Jersey, and the band was being fronted by Mario Bauza, their musical director. He called for *La botellera* and while the band members were pulling out their charts, the pianist Luis Varona began an improvised *montuno* to set the mood of the piece. The following day, at the band's weekly rehearsal at Park Place Ballroom at 110th Street and 5th Avenue, Bauza put together a head arrangement based on Varona's *montuno*, or piano vamp, which combined jazz phrasing and authentic Cuban rhythms. Asked what he was going to call the piece, an onlooker suggested it was as exciting as *tanga*, an African word for marijuana. *Tanga* was soon adopted as the band's theme song and was heard regularly on their broadcasts from La Conga Club on Radio WOR. For many it marked the beginning of what became known as Latin jazz.

Machito and Bauza were both born in Havana, Cuba. The extroverted Machito (Francisco Perez Gutierrez, better known as Frank Grillo) first met Bauza, a musical child prodigy, in 1926 through his sister Estella. At the time Bauza, still a teenager, played oboe and clarinet in the

Havana Philharmonic Orchestra where he had played under the baton of Leopold Stokowski. On a 1929 trip to New York, he was captivated by the city's vibrant music scene: 'It was jazz, I couldn't believe it, I heard Frankie Trumbauer and took up alto sax; I wanted to be part of it.' [61] A year later he was. He emigrated to New York and, now playing trumpet as well as sax, an unusual double that inspired Benny Carter to follow suit, gravitated from Cuban bands to jazz bands and from Hy Clak's Missourians to Chick Webb's Orchestra at the Savoy Ballroom. There he became the band's musical director before moving on to Cab Calloway's orchestra, where he was responsible for getting Dizzy Gillespie into the band. He soon assumed the musical directorship for Calloway, and introduced the band to Cuban rhythms on *Rhapsody in rumba*, *Conchita* and *Goin' conga*. 'Imagine,' Machito recalled, still slightly awed, in 1980, 'a Cuban fellow, 22 or 23 years old, directing a big black jazz band, rehearsing the musicians and okaying the arrangements. [Mario] is really is a top flight musician, an analyst.' [62]

Meanwhile Machito, who had been singing and playing maracas for a variety of Cuban bands, followed Bauza to New York in 1937. In 1940 he left Alberto Iznaga's band and formed his own ensemble; Bauza, now married to Machito's sister Estella, joined him a year later. As Machito's musical director he reorganized the band, getting rid of musicians who were unable to read music and giving assignments to the former Webb arranger Edgar Sampson and the Calloway arranger John Bartee. What Bauza set about doing was to replace the often genteel sound of a typical Latin American orchestra with a band that duplicated the power and precision of the big black swing orchestras with which he had worked in the 1930s and early 1940s.

When Machito returned from military service, Bauza's process of creating a fusion between jazz and Afro-Cuban rhythms continued, building and expanding on *Tanga.* However, it is fair to say that the innovation of combining jazz and Cuban music did not immediately take the world by storm; but it was nevertheless a first step in developing a sound that would set standards in Latin music for 20 years. It was not until the New York City DJ Fred Robbins promoted a concert of Latin jazz featuring 'Machito and his Famous Afro-Cuban Orchestra' with Stan Kenton at New York's Town Hall on 24 January 1948 that Latin jazz was finally on the road to breaking through with the public at large.

Throughout Machito's transformation from a Cuban dance band to a Latin jazz band, Gillespie and several up-and-coming members of the nascent bop movement, including Charlie Parker, regularly sat in with the band while Dexter Gordon was a featured soloist during Machito's residency at the Ebony Club in 1947. Bauza had turned Gillespie on to Afro-Cuban rhythms almost as soon they were sitting alongside one another in Calloway's trumpet section and as a consequence he would be far more at home among Latin rhythms than ever Parker was. As

Gillespie would acknowledge in his autobiography *To Be or Not to Bop* in 1981, 'Mario helped me a lot, not just by giving me an opportunity to be heard and land a good job [with Calloway], but in broadening my scope in music. Mario was the first to impress me with the importance of Afro-Cuban music.'

In fact, when Gillespie came to form his own big band in 1947, it was on Bauza's recommendation that the Afro-Cuban drummer Luciano Pozo Gonzalez, better known as Chano Pozo, joined the band, contributing such numbers as *Tin tin deo* and *Manteca.* Gillespie was now widely perceived to be at the forefront of the bop movement, and his embracing Afro-Cuban music through such compositions as the *Afro-Cuban suite* and George Russell's *Cubana be* and *Cubana bop* (**315**) led to the musical hybrid being dubbed Cubop. Equally, because Stan Kenton was one of the most popular attractions in jazz during the late 1940s, his experiments with Latin crossover music such as *Machito, Cuban period, Journey to Brazil, Bongo riff, Introduction to a Latin theme* and *Peanut vendor* played a vital role in raising the profile of the music, establishing Cubop as a serious movement far from the notion of Latin music being something agreeable but essentially light, such as the frothy offerings of a Carmen Miranda or a Xavier Cugat.

With his close affinity to the bop musicians, Machito and his orchestra were universally recognized as the authentic sound of Cubop. They recorded for the Coda, Roost and Continental labels during the late 1940s, but it was Norman Granz's Clef recordings that were the most sought after by jazz fans. *Tanga* was recorded in December 1948 for an elaborate limited edition (5000 copies) collectors' set, complete with Herman Leonard photographs and David Stone-Martin artwork that appeared in 1949 as *The Jazz Scene* (†Verve 314512661–2). [63] Of the three takes that appear on the CD reissue, two have Flip Phillips (ten) sitting in and taking an extended solo, while the third features the band. A mambo with Machito's singing a model of the *sonero*'s art, *Tanga* is a very simple head arrangement built over a repeated vamp that features both instrumental and climactic ensemble passages. Machito's arrangers usually respected a traditional Cuban two- or three-part form; the theme would be presented first, followed by a *montuno* section for improvisation by the singer or instrumentalists or both, and a section derived from the popular big bands of the day, contrasting brass and sax riffs, became known as the 'mambo' section. At the *montuno* on *Tanga*, the alto saxophonist Johnson, and to a lesser extent Phillips, have trouble negotiating the static harmonies of the vamp by applying a vertical approach to a linear concept, locking on rather unimaginatively to strong chordal tones in their improvisations. It is only on the extended, two-part version without Phillips that the band show what they can do, with Bauza's trumpet and Johnakins' baritone idiomatically more secure, giving a good idea of what audiences might have heard broadcast from the La Conga Club in 1943.

Granz also recorded Machito and his Afro-Cubans with Parker in December 1948: *No noise* (parts 1 and 2) also with Phillips as guest, and in January 1949, *Okiedoke* and *Mango Mangue*, all probably arranged by Bauza. On 11 February 1949 Granz brought Machito's band across from the Clique Club and on to the Carnegie Hall stage to perform with Parker to herald the beginning of his 1949 JATP national tour with Coleman Hawkins, Fats Navarro, Shelly Manne, Phillips, Tommy Turk, Ella Fitzgerald, Hank Jones and Ray Brown. However, while the addition of a Phillips or a Parker helped bring Machito's music to the attention of jazz audiences, Granz also wanted to capture the authentic and exciting Afro-Cuban sound of the band in its own right. In either 1948 or 1949 he set up a series of sessions that did just that.

Asia Minor, a minor key composition (of course), is the blockbuster which enabled Machito's orchestra to become a best seller in 1949. Opening with Bauza's oboe over a bass riff borrowed and modified by Gillespie on *Manteca*, this is a strong riff number over a rumba rhythm that suggests the power, drama and rhythmic excitement of Cubop. *Un poquito de tu amor* is a slow mambo (perhaps closer to a cha-cha-cha, except that the dance did not emerge until around 1953) introduced by a loping unison sax riff before an exposition of the theme by the whole band which gives way to a passage that modulates into Graciela's warm, attractive vocal. *Tumba el quinto* is also a superb example of Latin jazz, the swirling mambo rhythms, the staccato trumpets contrasted by legato saxophones, Machito's *sonero* vocal answered by chants from the band underpinned by a rhythmic excitement that added a new dimension to jazz. It is difficult to imagine the impact this music must have had on audiences in 1949; certainly these recordings capture the drama and swirling excitement, but live the band must have been sensational. *Jungle drums*, performed as a rumba, consciously evokes the Ellingtonian 'jungle' brass sound from the trumpets. Even without a trombone section, the band manage a wide range of tonal diversity in a wholly original presentation of a familiar theme in a Latin guise. *Llora timbero* is an engaging mambo with an expressive Machito vocal backed by the stabbing, insistent brass phrases that are a hallmark of Latin jazz. Again the harmonic backdrop is largely static, the song constructed over an insistent *montuno*. *Vive como yo* has a pleasing Graciela vocal, with ensemble passages by the band that would be widely imitated in the 1950s by a legion of commercial Latin bands.

However, the centrepieces of this album are the stirring orchestrations and exciting performances of *Asia minor* and *Tumba el quinto* along with numbers such as *Babarabatiri*, *Vive como yo*, *Gone city*, *Cleopatra rumba* (again with Bauza's *mysterioso* oboe) and *Vaya niña*. This is music that set the standards in Latin jazz for a generation and is as vibrant and exciting today as it was when it was recorded. The Bauza–Gillespie connection emerges on the introduction of *U-bla-ba-da*, a Latin *Oo-bop-sh'bam-a-klook-a-mop* no less, and prompts speculation about who borrowed what from whom. *Babalu*, despite earlier associations with Cugat and later Desi Arnaz, emerges as a powerful vehicle for Machito's *sonero* style. Machito claimed that he was the man who introduced the mambo to the American public and two mambos, *Mambo jambo* and *Mambo is here to stay* reflect the popularity of the dance as well as producing two fine performances from the band, with allusions to *Night in Tunisia* in the final trumpet passage on the latter.

To fit their music into the expectations of an essentially white entertainment infrastructure, Machito had his arrangers produce Latin arrangements of Tin Pan Alley standards. The results – purists notwithstanding – were far from the gruesome compromise that might be expected. *Rose room*, after a society-band pastiche, explodes into a fine feature for Johnakins's baritone; and in *Donkey serenade* shades of Alan Jones are left at the starting gate with an excellent arrangement that moves to a well-conceived climax. That other bandleaders would see the commercial potential of this concept was perhaps inevitable. The Tommy Dorsey orchestra had a big hit with *Tea for two cha cha* in the 1950s, but here it is Machito's mambo version of the standard that sticks in the memory with Hernandez's octave piano and the band's final chorus, where, as in *Donkey serenade*, they depart from the original melody to retain their own Afro-Cuban integrity and intensity.

Bauza's role, as he put it, 'behind the throne' of Machito's success obscured his very real role in transforming American music. In combining the vigorous complexity of Cuban music with the forthright power of the big bands through the use of jazz-oriented arrangers and by incorporating the musical innovations occurring within the bop movement, he set the standard for Latin jazz. One of his rare trumpet solos can be heard on *Cubop city*, an original he wrote in 1948 which was recorded by Howard McGhee and his Afro-Cuboppers (effectively the full Machito orchestra) for the Roost label (*The Original Mambo Kings – An Introduction to Afro-Cubop 1948–54* [†Verve (A) 513 876–2]). Perhaps most ambitious confluence of Afro-Cuban music and jazz came in December 1950, when Parker was the guest soloist on the five-part *Afro-Cuban jazz suite* performed by an augmented Machito orchestra.

Until Cubop, jazz had been boxed in by straight-ahead 4/4; now it had to adjust to the rhythmic complexity of new, alien time signatures, 3/8, 6/8, 3/4 and 2/4, not only in their own right but also superimposed over a basic 4/4 pulse. It sent reverberations through the jazz mainstream. Latin rhythms once regarded as a novelty began to surface in the work of leading hard boppers such as Art Blakey and Horace Silver, as much as its lesser-known musicians like Tina Brooks (**340**). Machito was the front man, the salesman who came to personify Afro-Cuban music and whose persistence in maintaining a band from 1940 until shortly before his death in 1983 provided a shop window for the music, whereas Bauza's true role behind the scenes was only beginning to be recognized at the time of his 80th birthday, in April 1991, [64] when the *New York Times* acknowledged him as one of America's most important musicians. 'Without Mr Bauza, jazz . . . wouldn't be the same, and large ground-breaking Afro-Cuban orchestral works – along with the salsa – probably wouldn't exist. Mr Bauza almost single-handedly introduced Afro-Cuban music to the United States.' [65] Sadly, Bauza had little time to enjoy his long overdue recognition. He died on 11 July 1993. [66] S.N.

Don Ellis

317 Electric Bath

†Columbia (F) COL 472620–2

Ellis, Glenn Stuart, Alan Weight, Ed Warren, Bob Harmon (tpt); Ron Myers, Dave Sanchez, Terry Woodson (tbn); Ruben Leon, Joe Roccisano (alt, fl, sop); Ira Schulman (ten, fl, picc, clt); Ron Starr (ten, fl, clt); John Magruder (bar, fl, bs clt); Mike Lang (p, clvt, el p); Ray Neapolitan (bs, sitar); Frank De La Rosa (bs); Dave Parlato (bs); Steve Bohannon (d); Chino Valdes (con, bon); Mark Stevens (tim, vib, misc perc); Alan Estes (misc perc). Hollywood, September 1967.

Indian lady · Alone · Turkish bath · Open beauty · New horizons

Initially, Ellis was recognized as an early proponent of the avant-garde. By the 1960s he had shed the big-band-sideman image he had acquired after stints with a Glenn Miller ghost band directed by Ray McKinley, Charlie Barnet, Herb Pomeroy, Sam Donahue, Claude Thornhill, Woody Herman and Maynard Ferguson as a result of his work with George Russell and Charles Mingus. He also led his own trio and co-led a quintet with the pianist Jacki Byard and had cut three small group albums that addressed improvising on tone clusters and tone rows, including *How Time Passes* (**454**), which demonstrated his concern with freedom. [67] Yet in a *down beat* feature in 1966, Ellis argued that the music of Archie Shepp, Albert Ayler and most of the artists in the ESP record catalogue were now acquiring stylized mannerisms: 'The lack of a definite pulse or melodic structural coherence, the use of myriads of fast notes with no overall direction, the at-one-time-unusual shrieks, honks and bleats have now become commonplace and clichéd.' Acknowledging that initially freedom represented 'an exciting and creative period', he predicted the music was 'degenerating into musical incoherence'. [68] Uncannily anticipating the reasons given by free musicians returning to 'the tradition' during the period of stylistic regrouping during the late 1970s and early 1980s, he was one of the first to reconsider the role of the avant-garde from within its ranks, realizing freedom was not the ultimate destiny of jazz but rather a component part of a greater whole.

In recognizing that free jazz could in itself be limiting, Ellis put forward a few ideas of his own which he felt might contribute towards a more vigorous avant-garde. They were, in a sense, a musical manifesto that he pursued until his death in December 1978. Among the elements he cited that should be present in jazz was a 'new rhythmic complexity, based on a swinging pulse with new metres . . . and new rhythms along with new intervals (pitches)'. [69] This proposition arose from his experiences with Hari Har Rao in a group they co-led called the Hindustani Jazz Sextet. This was an association which provided him with insight into Indian music, ragas and unconventional metres that he drew on to forge an individual personality for a bold new big band he put together at the Club Havana on Sunset Strip in Los Angeles. Beginning life as a rehearsal band, it was notable for the number of drummers and bassists in its ranks. Its first album, recorded at the Monterey Jazz Festival on 18 September 1966, *'Live' at Monterey* (Pacific Jazz [A] ST20112), revealed Kentonesque grandeur and a foray into *outré* time signatures that was as audacious as it was exciting, and earned one of the longest standing ovations in the history of the festival. *33 222 1 222* was a piece in 19/4, *New Nine* in 9/4 and *Concerto for Trumpet* in a modest 5/4. 'Ellis's amendment to the traditional constitution of jazz is yet another test of the music's accommodating nature, as well as a tribute to his inventiveness', said *down beat* awarding it four stars. [70]

When the Club Havana closed down, Ellis found a home for the band at a club called Bonesville in West Los Angeles. With his wife on the door taking admissions and selling 'Where's Don Ellis?' bumper stickers, word on the band gradually spread, helped by Kenton himself. His second album, *Live in 3⅔/4 Time* (Pacific Jazz [A] PJ10123), again fearlessly trod where only Dave Brubeck had ventured before, including *Freedom jazz dance* in 7/4, *Orientation* in 16/8 and *Upstart* taking the exotic signature from the album's title, in effect 11/8. What was remarkable was that despite the heavy head count, drummers bashing and bassists sawing plus additional percussion, the band actually swung in these unusual time signatures.

On both these albums it is easy to understand why Ellis was being tipped as the 'new Kenton'. On the one hand the band could justifiably claim to have brought some of the most complex time signatures to jazz and Charlie Haden once quipped that 'the only thing Don Ellis plays in 4/4 is *Take five*'. On the other hand there was a certain brassy splendour which remained under the shadow of Kenton's ensembles and was not helped by charts such as *Passacaglia and fugue* on the Monterey album from Hank Levy, who also contributed extensively to Kenton's book. However, as a result of John Hammond's urging, the band were signed by Columbia, and by the time they came to record *Electric Bath* in September 1967, they had developed a much more individual personality. Coincidental with the band's emergence was the rise of rock and the emergence of the San Francisco music scene. Psychedelic tone colours were all the rage as was the sound of the sitar, popularized by the Beatles on 1965's *Norwegian wood.* With the mystic East a source of fascination to members of the counter-culture movement, Ellis's bold young band had many elements that were attractive to rock audiences, with whom Ellis became enormously popular in the 1960s, playing rock venues such as the Fillmore.

The central exhibit that brought together the sounds of the mystic East, bold rhythms and volume associated with rock was *Indian lady*, a piece that would become something of a show-stopper in live performances. Ellis would subsequently record the piece twice more for Columbia in somewhat fragmented live versions, [71] but this original version is by far the best. The piece opens with a drone and a *rubato* statement of the five-note and four-note phrases on which the theme is based. Ellis responds with an *obbligato* manipulating quarter-tones using a four-valve trumpet he had specially customized for the purpose. The overall tonality strongly suggests Indian music until the band enter *a tempo* in a brisk $^5/_4$. The initial exposition is straightforward:

(*rubato* intro/band plus Ellis) + (*a tempo*/8 bars tbn riffs) +
A (8 bars) + A (8 bars) +A^1 (8 bars) + (9-bar interlude/stop time)
+ A (8 bars) + (4 bars tbn riffs to solos)

A modal piece, its basic form is modified as the performance progresses, the A sections appearing in rondo form between solo interludes and also in variation. Ellis takes the first solo, and for a modernist has a surprisingly broad tone. He had a very precise technique that allowed him to construct a solo of beguiling intricacy that embraced quarter-tones while retaining a focused intensity, an impression that remains even after repeated listenings. As the ensemble begins generating a powerful groove under Ellis's high notes, Lang enters to contribute a clavinet solo that sustains the swirling momentum of the ensemble passages and from this Myers emerges on trombone with a solo based on motifs and variations of the *Indian lady* theme. As the band recapitulate and embellish the original exposition, Starr on tenor contributes what can only be described as a booting solo in character with the shouting brass from which he is catapulted. Bohannon's drums provide a link to the *treble forte* brass finale of rousing intensity mediated to great effect by his inspired drumming. An equally able pianist, he created something of a stir by playing his gigs barefoot but was to die shortly after the session in a car crash. The tongue-in-cheek false ending presages a grandstand finish whose underlying humour provides the perfect release to the intensity of the performance, its easy communication of exuberance and contagious excitement contributing to one of the more memorable post-swing-era performances by a big band.

Alone was also in 5/4, but is a performance of a completely different character, a reflective 32-bar ballad which again is built around simple eight-bar sections:

8 bar intro (4 bars bs /4 bars bs clt plus tbns) + A (8 bars) + A[1] (8 bars) + A (8 bars) +A[1] (8 bars) + (2 bars) to tpt solo (cup mute)

Although the theme is played by a combination of clarinets and flutes, the writing is not so adventurous as that of Toshiko Akiyoshi's (**318**) for similar combinations, but is ingratiating for all that. Ellis contributes another excellent solo, this time using a cup mute, then, after an ensemble interlude by the brass, plays a dramatic, climatic open solo leaving the ensemble to return the performance to ground level. But if this is fairly straightforward stage-band stuff, albeit impeccably executed, then *Turkish bath* is assuredly not. The piece is introduced by a sitar, but the most arresting feature is the entrance of the reeds, which the arranger Ron Meyers voiced in quarter-tones. As in *Indian lady*, the performance centres around ensemble cohesion and the way the band get behind the insistent riffing of this modal piece. As the brass and reeds riff to a climatic descending glissando, Ellis enters, echoing the gliss with a tumbling, descending run in quarter-tones before flying high over the insistent brass riffs, which bubble and brew behind successive solos by Roccisano (on soprano), the arranger Myers on trombone and Land on clavinet. Again a false ending, leaving the rhythm section to walk the piece out to a fade.

Typical of the more ambitious time signatures the band were confronting was the 17/4 of *New horizons*, counted 5 + 5 + 7. Opening with a Maynard Fergusonesque flourish amid Kentonesque bombast, the initial flurry subsides, allowing a flute solo over an *ostinato* to establish the 17/4 groove that flows through the whole piece. The flute gives way to a brief trombone solo that provides a reminder that throughout the album the trombone section contribute some of the most compelling ensemble playing (*Indian lady*, for example), their powerful, rhythmic riffing over the simple harmonic foundations pumping the songs full of life. Lang plays a curious 'in the tradition' solo on acoustic piano and is followed by a *rubato* Ellis. Here and on *Open beauty* there are moments that prefigure Miles Davis's ruminations on *In a Silent Way* (†Columbia 450982–2) from two years later. At a time in jazz when the rock revolution was blurring the way ahead, everyone was listening to everyone else and it is inconceivable that Davis did not check out Ellis, who was, after all, signed to the same label. As the band return *a tempo* Ellis rides the gathering ensemble storm with high note *obbligatos* and asides to the written arrangement. Again he opts for the big finish, slightly overplayed after the impact of *Indian lady* and here sounding contrived. Ellis was somewhat prone to the grand gesture; it is difficult to think of an introduction in the whole of jazz that grandstands quite as much as that to *5/4 Getaway* from his 1971 *Tears of Joy* (CBS [A] GQ30927).

The Fender Rhodes piano and bowed basses set the 'space is the place' feeling for *Open beauty*, an impressionistic piece that allows Ellis to dialogue with himself via a tape loop. Confronted with his own staccato imagery being played back electronically to him, he forays into simple and complex harmonies in parallel and contrary motion setting up a shimmering dialogue of trumpet sounds that at the time seemed in tune with the electronic tone colours being imported into rock music. This sort of electronic tinkering would be exploited in live performance, giving the band an appeal beyond the jazz constituency to an audience open and responsive to the new sounds that were sweeping through popular culture during the 1960s. Within three years the band would come to embrace jazz-rock more explicitly, both in terms of rock rhythm-section patterns adapted to unusual metres and in its use of electronic devices such as echoplexes, ring modulators and, in 1970, the electric amplification and tonal manipulation of his saxophone section. This was undoubtedly a band of its time. Brash, exuberant and trading off the in-person excitement that only a big band can create, Ellis was among the first jazz musicians to realize that a rapprochement with popular culture was necessary to invigorate jazz as much as to retain its audience. The band's unusual yet insistent rhythmic patterns appealed to rock audiences, as did the exuberance and sheer volume, which Ellis was not slow to exploit – hear *Live at Fillmore*.

Ultimately, however, innovation lay in the band's ability to handle unorthodox time signatures with ease and present improvisations that were stylistically satisfying in a complex rhythmic context, such as 19/4 counted 3 + 3 + 2 + 2 + 2 + 1 + 2 + 2 + 2, rather than any innovation in their orchestrations. These still relied more on the old swing-era work ethic of perspiration generating inspiration for their effect. Within the big-band movement, fresh discoveries were rare, and appeared more often than not as revelations of old truths. With the emergence of 'rehearsal bands' around this time, often playing copies of Ellis, Kenton and Herman arrangements, big bands were seen as touchstones of craft, where like-minded craftsmen gathered to sharpen their skills and re-affirm old beliefs. Yet Ellis was right in insisting that free jazz was in danger of ending in a cul-de-sac, that the 'startlingly new and different when introduced by the originator becomes trite and hackneyed when reiterated by others' and that the avant-garde was 'in danger of becoming stagnant' by the mid-1960s.' [72] Maybe his propositions were not the answer, but they were nevertheless a fascinating diversion. Arguably, by 1970 he had suggested greater conceptual possibilities within jazz-rock than had Miles Davis: 'I've developed electronics for a big band further than anyone else, and then there was the emphasis on rhythm 'n' blues and rock. I've done all these things,' he was able to claim.' [73] S.N.

Toshiko Akiyoshi

318 Road Time

RCA Victor (A) CPL2–2242

Steven Huffstetter, Bobby Shew, Richard Cooper, Mike Price (tpt); Bill Reichenback, Jim Sawyer, Jimmy Knepper (tbn); Dick Spencer, Gary Foster (alt); Lew Tabackin (ten, fl); Tom Peterson (ten); Bill Byrne (bar); Toshiko Akiyoshi (p); Don Baldwin (b); Peter Donald (d); Kisaku Katada (kotsuzumi[1]); Yutaka Yazaki (ohtsuzumi[1]). January–February 1976, Tokyo and Osaka, Japan.

Tuning up · Warning: Success may be hazardous to your health · Henpecked old man · Soliloquy · Kogun[1] *· Since Perry/Yet another tear · Road time shuffle*

Miss Akiyoshi is the first woman in the history of jazz to have written and arranged an entire library of music for a big band and have her own ensemble to perform it. Incredibly, she has never really been given the credit she deserves, not only as one of the finest composers and arrangers in jazz, but also as an exceptionally able pianist. She formed her big band on the West Coast in 1973 and by the mid-1990s had recorded almost 20 albums, all of which had two things in common: a poor to nonexistent distribution and a level of compositional and orchestral ingenuity that made her one of perhaps two or three composer-arrangers in jazz whose name could seriously be mentioned in the company of Duke Ellington, Eddie Sauter and Gil Evans. Every album was, without exception, a minor gem of imaginatively crafted and impressively executed big-band jazz, interpreted with audible glee by her sidemen. Miss Akiyoshi first made her mark as a highly competent Bud Powell clone in Japan, impressing visiting American musicians with her ability. She was persuaded by Oscar Peterson to move to the USA to further her career. After a period of study at Berklee College of Music she began to find her own voice and became associated with Charlie Mariano, whom she later married. She played for ten months with Charles Mingus in 1965 and with an impressive variety of musicians as resident pianist at George Wein's Storyville Club, and in the bands of Johnny Richards and Clark Terry; but subsequently she led her own groups. However, despite an acclaimed solo piano performance in 1994 for the important *Maybeck Recital* series for Concord Records (†Concord CCD4635), it is as a bandleader, composer and arranger that her significance in jazz lies.

Her first big-band album, *Kogun* (RCA-Victor [A] AFL1–3019), was originally recorded for Japanese Victor and achieved such good sales that it was subsequently released in the United States. What was particularly striking was her use of polytonal effects and arching glissandos on the title track, which also included the use of Japanese *tsuzumi* drums, combining a 2/2 feel evoking Japanese folk music from the woodwinds and a straight-ahead four from the brass and rhythm section that suggested the Western idiom of jazz. Yet Miss Akiyoshi's brilliant handling of cultural collisions was just one aspect of her writing; on the same album, for example, *Henpecked old man* was based on the blues, and both these titles appear two years later in much extended form on *Road Time.* By then, *Kogun* had evolved into an impressive concert piece. It opens with traditional Japanese chants and drumming from Katada and Yazaki, [74] against the sliding pitches of Tabackin's flute. As the woodwinds enter, they emulate a *gagaku* sound, bending notes down and up with impressive control as they perform the slow, stately pentatonic theme. 'The beat is different. It's more circular, arched rather than an up or downbeat,' [75] Miss Akiyoshi explained.

After the second repeat of the opening section, Miss Akiyoshi emerges in solo against a straight-ahead four, an important change from the original studio version, giving better balance to the piece. This new interlude is based on the dorian mode over which she makes extensive use of a pentatonic scale while also prefiguring the ensemble passages that will follow, giving a pleasing sense of unity to the overall construction. Reflecting the contemporary trend for saxophonists to double on flutes, clarinets, piccolos and so forth, Miss Akiyoshi realized very early she had a valuable tonal resource, and one of the distinguishing features of her band is the dazzling colours she creates using combinations of clarinets and flutes. These feature in the instrumental section that follows her dramatic piano solo, building to a steady climax using a combination of stabbing *ostinato* figures from the woodwinds against powerful brass accents. Tabackin, among the finest flautists in jazz, follows with a flute cadenza that, while maintaining the pentatonic feel of the piece, is also packed with minute sounds from double-tonguing flutters to shrieks and quarter-tone smears that lead into a recapitulation of the original pentatonic *gagaku* melody. It is an impressive performance, combining the power and muscle traditionally associated with big bands with completely new sounds in the big-band lexicon derived from pitch bending and unusual combinations of woodwinds and brass.

Typical of Miss Akiyoshi's writing woodwind combinations are the solos in *Road time shuffle* which combine piccolo, flute, alto clarinet, clarinet, bass clarinet and trombone, all doubling the melody line. Part of her technique was to write vertically, no matter how fast the tempo. 'That way if it is played slowly, there will still be a beautiful line,' she said. [76] While contemporary writing often favours a more horizontal or linear approach to voicing harmonies, Miss Akiyoshi's lines are full of depth and inner movement. *Roadtime shuffle*, originally from the band's third album *Tales of a Courtesan (Oirantan)* (RCA-Victor [A] JPl1–0723), is a 16-bar swinger with a clever harmonic shift that still retains its ability to surprise and delight after repeated listening. The opening sections feature Spencer's hard-swinging alto followed by brass and woodwind solos, then Tabackin, the band's principal soloist, moves from the piccolo he used in ensemble to tenor sax for a typically swaggering solo. One of the (surprisingly) few tenor saxophonists to be influenced by Sonny Rollins, he developed a lunging, headlong approach and is an improviser of rarely acknowledged skill. He takes a central role on *Since Perry/Yet another tear* which opens with another unconventionally voiced woodwind *soli.* An *I got rhythm* contrafact, it is essentially a vehicle for the tenor saxophonist, whose rush of ideas climaxes with a soaring cadenza that leads into his own composition, the ballad *Yet another tear.*

Tuning up is exactly that, beginning with a concert A and moving up a tone against a firm 12-bar blues laid down by the rhythm section, leading into the exposition of Miss Akiyoshi's theme. Tabackin follows with a perfectly focused tenor solo that leads into a trombone *soli* that delineates the 12-bar changes using the basic unit of a crotchet. Reichenback's easily conversational solo precedes Foster's nimble alto that adds to the gathering excitement, climaxed by a perfectly executed trumpet *soli* and a series of exchanges between Shew and Huffstetter. After the trumpet solos, a saxophone *soli* announces a duel between Tabackin and Peterson which leads to a humorous mock-Basie coda. Shew, an exceptionally able trumpeter who somehow failed to make his mark in jazz to the extent he was surely capable, gives a further résumé of his beautiful tone and dancing lines in *Henpecked old man*, sharing the spotlight with Tabackin, Reichenback, Spencer and Byrne on a 12-bar blues that was originally put together by Miss Akiyoshi in 1964. Shew was one of the few lead trumpeters in jazz able to take on the bulk of solo work as well. [77] Here he enters towards the end of Tabackin's solo, jousting with the tenor saxophonist before launching into several neat, concisely thought-out choruses of his own. Miss Akiyoshi then reverses conventional wisdom by having Spencer, Reichenback, Byrne and finally Tabackin (again) *begin* their solos with a cadenza. Although this is a long performance, some 22 minutes, it was not an extended-form composition. It seemed only a matter of time, however, before Miss Akiyoshi ventured into this challenging format, and it came on her fourth album, *Insights* (RCA-Victor [A] AFL1–2678) from later in 1976, in the three-part *Minamata.* This heralded a series of suites on subsequent albums that were a testament to her sure handling of form and content, including: *Two faces of a nation* from *European Memoirs* (Baystate [J] RJL-8036), *Liberty suite* from *Wishing Peace* (†Ken [J] 27KEN-001), *Kourakan suite* from *Carnegie Hall Concert* (†Columbia 472925–2) and *Desert lady/Fantasy* [78] from *Desert Lady/Fantasy* (†Columbia 477800–2). These extended compositions represent an impressive body of work, and it is impossible not to conclude that she is the most successful composer and arranger to grapple with the medium in jazz, including Ellington himself.

Warning: Success may be hazardous to your health combines Miss Akiyoshi's fluent writing for woodwinds and driving brass against a rhythmic backdrop that is derived from the samba. Huffstetter contributes an engagingly intimate solo with Foster and Donald equally on the money in what is perhaps the least adventurous track of the album. *Soliloquy*, employing clever metre changes, is a relaxed interpretation that allows details of nuance in Miss Akiyoshi's writing to stand out. A frequently used device is writing the flutes with trombones, which here introduces the piece. A Tabackin flute cadenza leads into Miss Akiyoshi's statement of the theme in loping 6/8 before the ensemble takes over with a driving jazz-waltz feel and a fluent alto solo from Foster which is the centrepiece of the composition. Again the brass, as they have done throughout the album, play with great cohesion; indeed, all the sections not only have a good blend of tones, their phrasing, particularly on *sforzandos*, diminuendos, crescendos and particularly *glissandos*, is even and smooth and their attack very precise.

Miss Akiyoshi rehearsed the band meticulously every Wednesday afternoon in Los Angeles, and on several numbers the phrasing is so distinctive that it was clearly the result of much perspiration: 'In our case the music was brand new and in a lot of it was a little strange; it had smears and things like that . . . but certain things have to be played in a certain way, and the musicians weren't used to it and there was some music they didn't even want to do. They couldn't relate to it since they had never done anything like it before,' Miss Akiyoshi reflected in 1977. [79] By then, her hard work had paid off; she had created her own distinctive ensemble playing some of the most adventurously crafted arrangements in jazz. Yet her recording company RCA never seemed aware that they had on their books one of the finest post-swing-era ensembles. So with 1980's *Farewell* (RCA Victor [J] RVJ-6078) she ended her association with the label. Some albums had come out in America, some in Japan; hardly any in Europe. Her marketing by RCA was so completely random that her 1977 appearance at the Newport Jazz Festival was originally issued in Germany, whereas Volume 2 appeared only in Brazil! [80] It was the pop, rock and disco ensembles that had the promotional budgets and the marketing push. Yet today so many of these groups are now forgotten while the jazz product continues and represents a genuine long-term investment, this being something big corporations still have not come to terms with in almost a century of recorded jazz. Recording company executives still fail to realize that demand for albums of the quality Miss Akyoshi produced here will last for as long as people continue to buy jazz recordings. S.N.

Sun Ra

319 Sunrise in Different Dimensions

†Hat Hut (Sw) 6099

Michael Ray (tpt, fl h); Marshall Allen (alt, fl, ob); Noel Scott (alt, bar, fl); John Gilmore (ten, fl, clt); Kenneth Williams (ten, bar, fl); Danny Thompson (bar, fl); Sun Ra (p, org); Chris Henderson, Eric Walker (d); June Tyson (vcl). Unnamed concert hall, Switzerland, 24 February 1980.
Untitled · *Untitled* · *Untitled* · *Cocktails for two* · *Round about midnight* · *Ladybird/Half Nelson* · *Big John's special* · *Yeah man!* · *Untitled* · *Untitled* · *Untitled* · *Queer notions* · *Limehouse blues* · *King Porter stomp* · *Take the 'A' train* · *Lightnin'* · *Untitled* · *Untitled*

A nonet line-up did not, even with the armoury of some 17 instruments, at first appear a promising example of big-band survival. Even so, controversy has been a streak in Sun Ra's talismanic aura, and in jazz terms, his beginnings belong in a time significantly earlier than the bop movement's startling challenges to the wartime rage for the swing music that, through the mid-1940s and after, kept the famous big bands popular.

At a time roughly contemporary with Kenton's *Metronome riff* (**248**), a certain pianist named Sonny Blount was playing and writing for Fletcher Henderson's Club DeLisa band in Chicago. A little later the style of his own early bands, though it reached for the new, hung close to convention. Yet Blount (now Sun Ra), a man of bizarre vision, always knew what he required of his gathered musicians, was firmly independent, and developed a 'supra-terrestrial' public style wherein sound and appearance drew upon a weird treasury of space fantasy and cabbalistic ceremonial. Born, according to public record, in Birmingham, Alabama (a place he, oddly perhaps, would in 1965 celebrate musically as *Magic city* [†Evidence (A) EDC22069]), Sun Ra nominated Saturn as his birthplace. His Arkestra was from an early stage a community self-supported by the outside earnings of its members, and kept together for the most part by the extraordinary personality of its leader.

From the 1950s to the 1970s its collectivist conception of 'freemusic', with Sun Ra's keyboard and synthesizing artistry, on the Arkestra's many ambitiously organized records beguiled many of those modern jazz lovers who were little more than amused by the ritualism and fancy costumes. Although Sun Ra's organization, partly because of its brand of jazz communalism, tended to be regarded uncritically as a sort of big band, a large number of its line-ups hovered between ten or a dozen musicians and numerically large bands – like that for *Magic city*, for instance. For what is probably the most widely remembered title, *The Heliocentric Worlds of Sun Ra Vols. 1* and *2* (†ESP [A] 1014 and 1017, 1965), the personnels list eleven and eight players. Among the band roster above are men such as Allen, Gilmore and Thompson, who already had been members with Sun Ra since the Arkestra's early days, like a number of others – the baritonist Pat Patrick, the bassist Ronnie Boykins et al. – who long proved the faithfulness of the communal bond. Their jazz credentials were admirable.

Sunrise in Different Dimensions, spacious enough as it is for most of us, is one of the more earthbound of Sun Ra's scenarios. The leader himself forgoes his more decibel-magnifying contraptions, playing acoustic piano a great deal of the time. Of the 18 items in the programme, eight are *Untitled*, and these are, in general, extempore beatings and blowings by groups of odd sizes, usually piano-prompted. The ten things titled are what gives the record its value as a breathless and windswept view astern from a supersonic jazz roadster's dickey-seat.

The piano introduces the decidedly unevocative *Cocktails for two*, treated for much of its course as a piano-alto duet well loaded with romantic drama. Monk's *Round about midnight*, a classic which first 'went public' with Cootie Williams's 1944 big band (Big Band Archives [A] LP1208, Affinity [E] AFS1031) and had bop big-band treatment from Gillespie on a number of 1940s occasions, is given a fairly unreflective, brisk and sharp-edged outing here; a strong ensemble confidence grows around piano chords and interventions from Ray and Gilmore.

He-man pianistics urge the Dameron–Davis conjunction – *Ladybird/Half Nelson* – to toughening assault tactics which do not invite comparison with any particular groups' erstwhile versions. *Half Nelson* is engaging, with a notably fierce inner discipline firing the saxophone riffing, and the self-effacing hard-bopster Gilmore discountenancing all ideas of nostalgia. But nostalgia cannot be entirely held at bay for Horace Henderson's *Big John special*, which **127**'s commentary on Fletcher's 1934 rendering called an 'identifying anthem of the swing craze'. Ensemble and soloists respond with proper gusto to the leader's own swinging humour, and it seems part of the day's spirit that a small lightsome mockery of swing-band cliché is not resisted at the end. The headlong career of *Yeah man!* suits the same spirit. This rudimentary Noble Sissle number must always have seemed to be steering swing-bandery precipice-wards almost as soon as the wagon got onto the highway. The death-defying glee of it all can hardly be mistaken, or resisted.

Amid the *Untitleds* which precede *Queer notions* there occurs a stretch of electronic organ playing which conjures nothing more surely than some spectral fairground Wurlitzer selection. What, in these general circumstances, this might signify, other than the contrary thought that no Wurlitzer, however lusty – and this one is not that – could be as effective a 'big band' as an acoustic pianoforte in appropriate hands, it is hard to guess. Sun Ra's characteristic piano style reflects Cecil Taylor; but other accents spill out often enough . . . Ellington . . . Hines, perhaps . . . and other, newer fingerings too.

Queer notions proves one of the most cohesive recreations; *Limehouse blues* one of those most unrepentantly skewed at the edges. *King Porter* shimmies in, yet relishes its own possibilities to the extent of most clearly evoking not New Orleans bordello swagger but rather that transitional 1930s refurbishment of Morton's magisterially reshaped ragtime into dance music for jitterbugs (cf. **45**, **86**, **126** and **141**).

The full-tilt swing achieved for Ellington's *Lightnin'* pays some kind of tribute to a venerable company which could outswing most other bands if need were. It pays no tribute, however, to the peerless balance of sectional and individual utterances which Dukish devotees treasure still. That kind of acknowledgement was not, one supposes, the point of this exercise. The *'A' train* is 'taken' as an inebriated waltz, the entire manner of the thing practically dictated by the leader, who gives an expressive role to trumpeter Ray. During *Lightnin'* Allen's oboe protrudes similarly.

The last but one of the *Untitled* tracks has something that no chronicler of big-band jazz should overlook – a band vocal, led here by June Tyson. (Did *Metronome* ever give an award to any example of this phenomenon?) In this one Sun Ra, Tyson and Co. bring the solar system well within the range of the holiday brochure: 'On Jupiter, the skies are always blue.'

E.T.

Willem Breuker

320 Willem Breuker Kollektief in Holland

Bvhaast (H) 041/2 (2 LPs)

Boy Raaymakers, Andy Altenfelder (tpt); Willem van Manen, Bernard Hunnekink (tbn); Breuker (sop, ten, clt, bs clt, vcl[1]); Bob Driessen (alt, bar); Maarten van Norden (alt, ten); Henk de Jonge (p, acc); Arjen Gorter (bs); Rob Verdurmen (d). Amersfoort, Holland, 21–22 April, 6 May 1981.
Ouverture 'De Vuyle Wasch' · *Sur l'autoroute* · *Tango superior* . *Interruptie* · *Deining* · *Kudeta* · *Prokof* · *Invasie musiek Bob + Babe* · *To be with Louis P.* · *Pale fire* · *Hopsa, hopsa* · *Concertino No. 5 in F minor* · *Marche funèbre from 'De Vuyle Wasch'*

As a minor militia unit of the European avant-garde, the Kollektief is seen to have affinities with the Vienna Art Orchestra of Matthias Ruegg; though it may not seem quite so free in its manoeuvrings along disputed musical territory as the outfit which achieved such a stunning rapprochement with early 20th-century *fin de siècle* art music on Ruegg's *The Minimalism of Erik Satie* (†Hat Art [Sw] 6042). Yet much depends on which side of a frontier one reckons one is on, or on where one reckons the frontier to be, or on whether one desires to recognize any frontier at all.

Admittedly, the inclusion of the Breuker Kollektief in this book is an acknowledgement of a jazz link in some sense primary. Breuker, like Ruegg, is a jazz practitioner. Some of Ruegg's orchestrations are big-band jazz scores ranging along a lengthy frontier without hearing any call to cross it. Breuker organizes his ten-piece big band in ways betokening experience of the Globe Unity Orchestra in so far as the Kollektief thrives on interaction between complex ensemble strategies and free improvisation, solo and collective. Most of the solos here may now sound 'free' to an almost conventional degree. What is of greatest interest is the provenance of the band's characteristic themes – mostly from Breuker's hand, but borrowed from the folk and pop culture of the Netherlands, Germany and elsewhere, which frequently means that the rhythmic exploitations ask less from the expected jazz impetus and yet are eager to welcome shock tactics and burlesque tokens which jazz may have disowned long ago.

This is not written solemnly. One might guess that Breuker's mission is partly to remind us that jazz was once warmly hospitable to the slapstick, truck horns and tethered hyenas of the *zanni*, and that it was Jelly Roll Morton, none less, who admonished posterity that 'vibrato was nothing at the beginning but an imitation of a jackass hollering'. [81] At all events, *Willem Breuker in Holland* contains a fine ration of tempestuous musical humour.

The theatrically spirited ensemble in *Ouverture* has a *réclame* lack of restraint – like circus or bullfight paradery. After several brash shifts it is steered into a mad stomp in the course of which Hunnekink declaims raucously over jungle drums. A grandly magnified piano, which is set to reappear as a choice *deus ex machina*, dominates the jerky stampede of *Sur l'autoroute*'s beginning, but van Norden emerges as the chief soloist, running through his post-Coltrane avant-garde effects, and showing both his muscles and his fangs.

Few of us might hear *Tango superior* without a sneaked recollection of *The crave*. Morton inflated the spirit of the tango with his own kind of jazz eroticism. Here the dance becomes an engine of assault to which power is all. *Interruptie* extends the hostilities with zest, as Breuker's soprano chatters and squawks. *Deining* has a strong rocking swing; a satisfying sound, with fine work from Raaymakers, who burrows into the theme, ignoring the scanty space allowed by sweating bass and drums. There is little semblance of section scoring, and the giant piano re-enters at the end . . . or is it the end? No, we are into *Kudeta*, and Henk de Jonge, master of the clangorous keyboard, tempers the resonance and develops a notable solo with concerto echoes in it – 'Warsaw', Tchaikovsky No. 1, even a suspicion of NAAFI 'joanna' may be recognized by really old listeners. The ensemble comes back for some fearsomely placed anvil blows. Then, out of the piloted chaos of *Prokof*, van Manen soars alone to scrawl the welkin, heralding flashes of *William Tell* storm music, plus *Die Walküre*, jumping off against the clock. There is some nightclub business in *Invasie musiek Bob + Babe* passing into Breuker's deliciously ridiculous singing – a bit like M. K. Gruber when, as it were, idling, but like every scat-artiste in history when *To be with Louis P.* shifts into overdrive. Other individual jammers join the rapid fire.

Pale fire has declamatory big-band force; slithering rhythm shapes, unjazzy, you might say, until they swerve into swingtime excitement. Gorter's irresistible bass stirs the cauldron of mayhem that swirls about van Norden and Verdurmen. Wild chantings placate the paracelestial piano before *Hopsa, hopsa* becomes *mazel-tov* and *fralich*, a festivity in which *Jingle bells* and Rossini are par for the course.

The performance of Unico Wilhelm Graaf van Wassenauer's four-movement *Concertino* as an undistorted wind-band piece is mysteriously motivated. There's nothing overearnest about it, however. It sounds as if it is played for fun, with zest and skill, relaxation and precision, and as an exhortation to the good-time spirit. Pretty much like everything else in the show. Its nearest formal relative is the *Marche funèbre*, though that is spiritually darker, and made spooky by Breuker's interplanetary transmissions through a bass clarinet. The minatory rhythm of the march accelerates until the ghostly piping hits its highest register. The orchestral pilgrimage is braked by the peremptory snare drum, the piano-god looms, a last jerk of tango would have us step to a different drama, but the drum, muffled, distracts the cortège and leads it away. E.T.

Bill Russo

321 The Seven Deadly Sins

Roulette (A) S52063

Burt Collins, Johnny Glasel, Danny Stiles, Louis Mucci (tpt); Bill Elton, Don Sebesky, Mike Zwerin, Eddie Bert (tbn); Kenneth Guffey (bs tbn); Dick Meldonian (alt, clt[1]); Tony Bunopastore (alt); Don Mikiten, Larry Wilcox (ten); Tony Ferina (bar); Howard Collins (g); John Drew (bs); Ed Shaughnessy (d); Sy Barab, Avron Coleman, Lorin Bernsohn, George Knutzen (cel); Russo (comp, arr). New York City, 2 August 1960.
The seven deadly sins (theme) · *Greed* · *Lechery*[1] · *Gluttony*

Same personnel. New York City, 4 August 1960.
Anger · *Envy* · *Sloth* · *Pride* · *Epilogue*

If we set aside the special cases of Graettinger and Rugolo, Russo in several ways remained the most independent-minded composer brought forward by Kenton's band. The evidence of intellectual ferment behind the outward formality of his best works, such as the above, is more than just attractive. It is undoubtedly our loss that he spent so much time away from jazz – engaged, for example, in the series of operas which he composed during the 1960s and 1970s.

A classmate of Lee Konitz in grade school in Chicago, Russo studied alongside Konitz with Lennie Tristano and later most notably with John J. Becker, a highly interesting avant-garde composer of the Ives/Ruggles/Riegger generation. Even his earliest scores for Kenton, with whom he spent the years 1950–4, are more advanced in their musical language than the updated swing which some of the band's other writers were supplying. An instance from 1950 is *Solitaire* (†Mosaic [A] MD4–136) for solo trombone and a large ensemble including strings. Inappropriately retitled *Ennui*, this was recorded in a different but again effective version under Russo's own name the following year (Byg [F] 529154). Further of his contributions are dealt with under **313b** and others again on Mosaic also deserve attention. Recorded in 1954, some of these latter are vehicles for soloists, and others, like *Thisbe*, a striking piece for trombones and rhythm, are compositional studies pointing in a number of directions followed in Russo's subsequent work. Meanwhile *Egdon Heath* is already more substantial, as is the eventful and well-organized *Dusk*.

Previous records in this section are anthologies of separate items, whereas this and some of those which follow are concerned with large, sometimes LP-long projects. It is appropriate to start with Russo because always apparent in even his small pieces is a drive towards larger forms. This is best exemplified prior to *The Seven Deadly Sins* by his *World of Alcina* ballet music (Atlantic [A] LP1241, 1956) and the remarkable *Image of Man* (†Verve [E] 527 780–2, 1958), recorded by Konitz and a string quartet playing without vibrato. Russo's aims should not be regarded as wildly eccentric in view of the proliferation elsewhere of large-scale jazz works of extremely diverse character. Examples are Dameron's *Fontainebleau* (**280**), Coleman's *Free jazz* (**400**), Russell's *Electronic sonata* (**324**), Carisi's *Moon taj* (**385**), Coltrane's *A Love Supreme* (**424**) and Schuller's *Variants on a theme of Monk* (again **400**).

The ground plan Russo adopts for *The Seven Deadly Sins* is that of a theme and variations, naturally with one variation for each fall from grace and with *Pride* flowing into the *Epilogue* which restates the theme. It cannot be said that he gives clear musical delineation to these weaknesses. Are not the violently stabbing figures of *Pride* just as suggestive of anger, envy, even lechery? Who, listening without prior information, could undertake to distinguish between greed and gluttony, envy and anger? If there is an exception it is *Sloth*, with its imaginatively lugubrious writing for the cellos – a delicious piece of musical humour. To speak of the representational imprecision of the rest, however, is not adversely to criticize Russo but to accept a long-recognized limitation of music. Arising out of the matter of symphonic programme works, questions of what the art can hope to suggest, represent or portray of specific events, places, individuals – let alone the failings listed above – have been debated at length on many occasions and hence need not be gone into here. (Perhaps that is why Don Gold's sleeve note makes no comment on any aspect of the music whatever.)

What counts is the extraordinary range of gesture, both linear and textural, that Russo was led to produce by this work's metaphorical subject matter. As with the finest of Handy's scores for Boyd Raeburn (**314**), or Stravinsky's *Ebony concerto* for Woody Herman (**109**) for that matter, one can only regret that arrangers never took up some of the initiatives here offered. As in most of Russo's other large pieces, there is a confident handling of form, with particular skill shown in structurally important transitional passages and in the expressive use of contrasts between different styles. A good instance is the surprising combination of sounds that surrounds Elton's trombone solo in *Lechery*, giving the impression that the music, strongly suppressed, is about to explode, this being contradicted by the extreme change of mood which comes with Barab's cello solo. Some of the solos were written out but there is a fair amount of improvising and it would be as well to identify the soloists in the latter cases. These are Mucci and Mikiten in *Greed*, Elton, Barab, Meldonian (clarinet) and Mikiten in *Lechery*, Burt Collins in *Anger*, Mikiten in *Envy*, Ferina and Guffey in *Sloth*, Sebesky and Glasel in *Pride*.

Why counterpoint, one of music's more intellectual dimensions, should be chosen to symbolize gluttony it is hard to say. Yet Russo's superb writing in this movement advances considerably in richness of thought on what he did in *23 degrees north 82 degrees west* (**313b**) and was taken further still in such pieces as *Fugue for jazz orchestra* (Columbia [E] 33SX1758, 1964). Very few have managed to unite this kind of full polyphonic texture with big-band instrumentation, although the linear vitality was foreshadowed in certain of his 1951 Chicago recordings like *Pooch McGooch* and *An aesthete of Clark Street* (Byg, as above). Some of his scoring was adversely criticized for an undue reliance on brass, and several of his pieces, such as *The halls of brass* (Mosaic), do make a powerful, indeed virtuosic, use of brass sounds and textures.

In *The Seven Deadly Sins*, however, reeds and the pianoless rhythm section are given much to do, and the cellos, no doubt chosen by Russo because of their exceptionally wide range and ability to project string tone with real power, are almost everywhere present. (This is one initiative that *was* briefly taken up elsewhere, by Johnny Richards in his 1961 scores for Ben Webster [Reprise (A) S2001].) Beyond such details lies the impact of this piece as an indivisible whole, arising from the wide arch of its eight movements being perfectly sustained. There seems no point in remarking on the fact that this brilliant composition has received no comment at all in the literature of jazz while the broken-backed concoctions of certain bandleaders have continued to be heaped with unqualified praise. M.H.

Kenny Wheeler/John Dankworth

322 **Windmill Tilter**
Fontana (E) STL5494

Derek Watkins, Hank Shaw, Henry Lowther, Les Condon (tpt); Wheeler (fl h, comp, arr); Chris Pyne, Mike Gibbs (tbn); Dick Hart or Alf Reece (tu); Dankworth (alt); Ray Swinfield (alt, bar, fl); Tony Roberts (ten, bs clt); Tony Coe (ten, clt); Alan Branscombe or Bob Cornford (p); Dave Holland (bs); John Spooner (d); Tristan Fry (vib, bon). London, March 1968.
Don the dreamer · Bachelor Sam · Sancho · The cave of Montesinos · Altisidora · Don no more

Wheeler (fl h, comp, arr); Coe (ten, clt); John McLaughlin (g); Holland (bs); Spooner (d). London, March 1968.
Preamble · Sweet Dulcinea blue · Propheticape

N.B. Before *Sancho* and after *Altisidora* the quintet plays short, untitled and unbanded passages.

The programmatic jazz suite had its partially frustrated beginnings with the search of Ellington back in the 1930s for greater orchestral elbow room. [82] The success of such sequences was made possible only by the arrival of the long-playing tape and disc. When he asked Wheeler to provide the music which makes up *Windmill Tilter*, Dankworth had already composed several acclaimed suites, [83] and his *The Million Dollar Collection* (Fontana [E] TL5445) bears relation to Wheeler's work, first because the orchestra is virtually identical in its manning in each case; second because of Dankworth's role as catalyst and as director-in-the-event.

Jazz has always gone in for evocative titles and, in its rumbustious youth, liked 'special effects'. The ODJB's *Barnyard blues* (**12**) and Jelly Roll Morton's *Sidewalk blues* and *Hyena stomp* (**47a**) with their simulated animal calls and well-tempered motor horn, might almost be bracketed with those effects in Richard Strauss's symphonic poem *Don Quixote*, of which Donald Tovey wrote: 'Muted brass instruments . . . achieve in ten rehearsals what a flock of sheep achieve extempore.' [84] But programme music goes back a very long way, and has numerous patterns. Why, even the title of a short piece might be a 'programme', suggesting what the ear might expect to hear, inviting the listener; and the adversary of all extraneous programmes, 'pure music', still shows little sign of driving it from town.

The issue regarding *Windmill Tilter* is whether the actual music is better listened to in response to the programme's invitation, or, as far as is possible, unbiased by the programme. In this case the programme may be a little suspect. There is evidence that at least a proportion of Wheeler's music was written before the Don Quixote idea came to mind. No serious deceit attaches to that, of course; but, except in a few small areas, the approach to the literary sequence is sufficiently abstract for the movement titles to be regarded as ciphers. There certainly is none of what Tovey describes as 'expensive realism'. [85] Titles, however evocative, have seldom been other than expendable in any kind of music. The suite, as a form, may be regarded as the prerogative of the larger instrumental group, although there have been notable exceptions to that. One instance is John Benson Brooks's *Alabama Concerto*, recorded in 1958 by a conducted trio of well-known jazz players (†Original Jazz Classics [A] OJCCD1779). The advantages of big-band resources are used with enthusiasm in Wheeler's composition, but he also uses a quintet at nicely judged intervals, not merely for contrast, relief or compromise, but as a personal extension of possibilities.

Preamble is an airy interweaving of counterpoint by the small group before Holland rocks the orchestra into *Don the dreamer*. Wheeler in solo sounds for only a brief moment like Miles Davis, but it is neither timbre nor attack which gives this impression; it is merely a snatched phrase. Wheeler, 38 at the time, conceals his influences within a very individual style. As player and as composer, he is his own man.

After questing orchestral shapes a dialogue develops between the flugeller and various sections of the band. Holland's part is beautifully clear and authoritative, Pyne and Roberts play rather uneasy solos. The quintet returns for *Sweet Dulcinea blue* – quiet, yet purposeful solos by McLaughlin, Wheeler and Coe. *Bachelor Sam* involves the orchestra. It begins sombrely; there is more exchange between Wheeler and different sections. The Dankworthian practice of using individual reed players in a quasi-sectional role is employed here and there, and as the mood livens Wheeler and Coe swap phrases of expanding boldness.

Sancho is preceded by the quintet's small fantasy of trotting rhythms – perhaps the closest intention towards literalness in the suite. *Sancho* itself, with a ¾ basis, cheerfully celebrates a few time-beatified big-band tricks, pyramid arpeggios and so on. An altoist, probably Dankworth, solos at agreeable length, then, as the ensemble darkens tone and diversifies rhythm, Wheeler remains jaunty.

A unison of string bass with reeds sets *The cave of Montesinos* off. A satisfying aspect of the performance throughout is the clarity with which all the voices may be traced by the ear, and this even when Wheeler calls the band towards extroversion, and the interrelation of sectional pronouncements grows complex. Above all that Wheeler breathes a quiet strength. Then, more pyramids, and abrupt discords call a halt. The quintet in *Propheticape* muses out-of-measured-time until Holland leads it into swift, riding jazz. Coe, fleet and mischievous, precedes McLaughlin; then Coe and Wheeler dance in rapid unison for several bars. The somewhat peevish five-way meditation returns; then, for *Altisidora*, there comes a discreet Latin rhythm, percussive phrases interspersed with Wheeler's attenuated fragments of fanfare. In a development which needs and gets skilfully controlled dynamics, Wheeler's broad, floating lines are punctuated by ringing syllables from Fry's vibraharp.

The quintet's semidetached coda to *Altisidora* is a brief sambalike interlude, leading to a counterchange of quasi-independent thoughts. After this the theme statement of *Don no more* involves high-pitched brass above a dark tuba undertow penetrated by darting flashes from Fry and the pianist. Holland and Spooner propel things forward, and then, as the tension lessens, there is lovely section writing. The admirable Coe improvises lean alto lines at length with the rhythm section. It is his voice too that debates matters with the ensemble through slowing passages. The end comes with Wheeler's detached lament.

Wheeler's stature as a creative musician has grown over the decades. Never one to parade his gifts, he even so has lent unusual distinction to many fine sessions in various parts of the world. As he has risen to the challenge of musical change, he has made his own vivid contribution to the changes themselves. Across 25 years and more, *Windmill Tilter* sounds a fresh and remarkably nonderivative example of large-band jazz, with the quintet episodes like miniatures set within the wide canvas of the suite as a whole. It has been assessed here independently of its stated programme. The programme may seem more relevant for other listeners in the light of their knowledge of Cervantes's masterpiece. For this listener, the music is self-verifying and needs no extraneous idea to commend it.

E.T.

Martial Solal

323 Martial Solal Big Band

†Dreyfus (F) 849 230–2, Cy (F) 733 617

Tony Russo, Roger Guérin, Eric LeLann, Bernard Marchais, Patrick Artero (tpt); Patrice Petitdidier (cnt); Jacques Bolognesi, Hamid Belhocine, Christian Guizien, Glenn Ferris, Denis LeLoup (tbn); Marc Stecker, Philippe LeGris (tu); Jean-Louis Chautemps, François Jeanneau, Jean-Pierre Debarbat, Pierre Mimran, Pierre Gossez, Roger Simon, Jean-Pierre Solves, Francis Cournet, Georges Grénu (reeds, fl); Pierre Blanchard (vln); Philippe Nadal (cel); Solal (p, comp, arr); Frederic Sylvestre (g); Cesarius Alvim (bs); André Ceccarelli (d). Paris, December 1983, May 1984.
Et si c'était vrai · *Hommages* · *Piccolo*

N.B. Not all the above take part in every piece.

Though not quite the main point here, it should be noted that the problem of accommodating a creative and virtuoso improviser in a large jazz ensemble first arose with Armstrong in Henderson's band (**37**). There it was hardly central, however, because the trumpeter was not yet fully mature artistically, and the question became more acute during Coleman Hawkins's much longer tenure (**85–6**, **126**). But the most nearly relevant case, for obvious reasons, was that of Hines (**79**, **129**,

147). Solal, though, evolved his music entirely in France, indeed in Paris; he seems never to have concerned himself with American fashions, and this, perhaps remarkably, has been as true of his big-band scores as of his keyboard work. His status as a highly original pianist of great virtuosity is reasonably well known, yet his orchestral output, considerable in quantity and deriving from an obviously important aspect of his artistic personality, has received little comment outside France.

Solal began writing for large bands as early as 1956 (†Vogue [F] 74321131112), and that session employed two musicians, Guérin and Grénu, who also participate in the 1983–4 works considered here. Some of his pieces were also taken up by other leaders, for example the rather sombre *Illusion* recorded by Christian Chevalier (Columbia [F] ESDF1132). By the time the above, much later, music appeared, the path had long been an independent one. There are no flirtations with rock or electrification – except, reasonably enough, for the four string instruments, which have important roles. There is no attempt at continuing the Basie 'tradition,' which could only have resulted in just another band of the Thad Jones–Mel Lewis type. There are no moves in directions like those taken by the Jazz Composers' Orchestra, Sun Ra (**319**) or Willem Breuker (**320**). A little is perhaps owed to Don Ellis (**317**), possibly to George Russell (**324**), the writing for tuba certainly follows on from Gil Evans (**376, 382–3, 460**). But the ways piano and orchestral sounds are mixed in, for example, the second movement of *Et si c'était vrai* can have few precedents.

A crucially guiding sense of form has always been manifest in Solal's piano solos (**473**) and in his improvising with small groups (**365**), and the speed and multiplicity of events in his large-band music is a rare sort of equivalent to his keyboard virtuosity. The multistoreyed intensity of these pieces arises not from the rather full instrumentation but from the ways that Solal develops his ideas. Hear for instance his 1977 *Suite for trio* (MPS [G] 5C064–61397), which has the same kind of irregularly shifting tempos and kaleidoscopic rhythmic variety as are found in the orchestral pieces.

Choice of an issue to represent these latter came down either to the above or to a 1981 LP with the same title on Gaumont (F) 753 804. In fact both are essential, and they should be heard in conjunction with a further Solal big-band record, of André Hodeir compositions, dating from 1984 on †Carlyne (F) 008CD. The Gaumont places a somewhat greater emphasis on solos, for example by Solal in *Texte et pretexte*, by Blanchard in *Valse à trois temps*, and also on the former's sharp and very musical sense of humour. The Dreyfus CD/Cy LP was thought even more relevant to the purposes of this book, though, because of its wealth of ensemble writing. Yet Gaumont's *Suite* stands with the three-movement *Et si c'était vrai* as a considerable event in the annals of big-band music, even if there have been no signs of either being recognized as such. Both last an effortlessly sustained 20 minutes or so, and there are many correspondences; lines of musical thought flow out of, beside and across each other because imagination and technique have fused to liberate the discourse from its traditional routes. The results are sometimes reminiscent of Elliott Carter – for example the Concerto for Orchestra – and one might adapt a phrase of Woyciech Karolak's and say that Solal's is 'a symphonic way of writing for a large jazz orchestra'. [86] *Et si c'était vrai* employs a rather more advanced language than the *Suite*, however, and one that results in, among other features, a greater degree of outward discontinuity.

Basic to the character of this music, indeed, is that it shifts and changes almost constantly, and in several different ways. Energetic, sometimes violent passages unpredictably alternate with thoroughly lyrical, even quietly intimate ones not in merely external contrasts but in ways hard to explain without detailed analysis, that are motivated from within the music itself. This is also true of the relation between the written and improvised (or, as one might say, the aleatoric) parts. As is usual with most high-quality jazz of this kind, it is often hard, without seeing the scores, to decide what is predetermined and what spontaneous. Yet it can safely be said that the improvisations are never simply individual displays, but contribute, sometimes crucially, to the effect of the piece as a whole. In fact the extemporized passages to some extent go beyond filling the spaces between written parts and to some degree shape, or at least complete, the form of the work. Yet this is also a matter of Solal composing well-structured, stylistically unified pieces which grow from within. There is nothing here of the mechanical form which bedevils so much jazz – no 12-bar blues, no 32-bar AABA patterns. Each of the three works develops organically, discovers its own form, and this is seldom concealed by the music's rhythmic flow being diverted by frequently changing tempos, by its coming to rest on fermatas, by its being interrupted with the sudden eruption of cadenzas.

Besides Solal's melodic style, largely familiar from his keyboard improvisations of course, there is also a finely elaborated harmonic idiom here, more developed than is always possible on the piano. And it is often dissonant, some of the pitch combinations really being quite daring even by late-20th-century standards. At the same time use is made of big-band procedures inherited from the past – which is to say from ensembles far more highly regarded than this but often of much less musical distinction. One often feels that these devices are being employed to ironic ends, particularly in their rhythmic aspect. Yet neither this nor the diversity of writing techniques weakens the high level of integration already noted. Naturally this was a matter of interpretation as well as of composing; and sometimes it is as if we have joined the recording halfway through because the intensity, the feeling of involvement from the opening bars, are such as would normally be expected only from performances already well into their stride. The razor-sharp execution maintained almost throughout signals the dedication and amount of work that went into this record. Considering what much big-band fare is like, the musicians were lucky to have such absorbing jazz to play and improvise on, while Solal was fortunate in having such brilliant performers to do so. The rhythm section deserves especial praise for its unflagging invention and energy. M.H.

George Russell

324 The Essence of George Russell

Concept (A) CR004/5 (2 LPs), *†Soul Note (It) 121 044

Palle Boldvig, Palle Mikkelborg, Bertil Lövgren, Jan Allan (tpt); George Vernon, Gunnar Medberg (tbn); Runo Ericksson (bs tbn); Christer Boustedt, Claes Rosendahl (alt); Bernt Rosengren, Jan Garbarek (ten); Erik Nilsson (bar); Russell (comp, p); Rune Gustafsson (g); Roman Dylag (bs); Jon Christensen (d); Rupert Clemendore (con). Stockholm, 16 September 1966.
Now and then

Gustafsson (g). Stockholm, 15–16 January 1968.
Concerto for self-accompanied guitar

Lövgren, Allan, Maffy Falay, Lars Samuelsson (tpt); Stanton Davis (tpt, fl h); Olle Lind (bs tbn); Arne Domnérus (alt, clt); Rosendahl (fl, sop, alt, ten); Lennart Åberg (fl, sop, ten); Garbarek (ten); Nilsson (bs clt, bar); Russell (comp, p); Bengt Hallberg (p); Gustafsson, Terje Rypdahl (g); Georg Riedel, Arild Andersen (bs); Egil Johanssen, Christensen (d); Sabu Martinez (con); Berndt Egerbladh (vib, xyl). Stockholm, 6 October 1970.
Electronic sonata for souls loved by nature

When jazz impresses it usually does so as great riches in a small room, but the above version of the *Electronic sonata,* which lasts for just over an hour and fills three LP sides, is one of the few musically satisfying large-scale forms to have come out of jazz. As such, and unlike Mingus's tirelessly promoted and hopelessly broken-backed *Epitaph*, it has attracted no attention. It should be heard in conjuction with the earlier and later combo performances Russell set down of the piece in 1969 (Flying Dutchman [A] FDS124) and 1980 (Soul Note [It] SN1009). The use of 'sonata' in the title is unfortunate only if it is assumed this music's organization is in some way related to what is normally, and misleadingly, called sonata form or first-movement form. Russell's use of the term is justified in that it has for the past five centuries had a far wider range of stylistic and formal connotations, though it has usually been applied to multimovement instrumental compositions. The real point is that as an unfolding yet finely balanced structure the piece works, and does far more than that. This music exults in its singularity, thinks aloud, and aspires to humane ideals as great and comprehensive as can be found in jazz.

The *Sonata* consists of 15 events – Russell prefers this term to 'movement' – of which numbers 7, 13 and 14, based on material by Garbarek, were newly prepared for this orchestral version of the work. However, the above personnel details tell only part of the story, because these 15 segments of music, in which Russell says 'much is improvised, much is controlled improvisation', are as it were imposed on other music heard almost continuously from a tape. This latter is no linking background, being integral to the work. Indeed it came first and is the basis of the whole, the *Sonata* being composed in 1968, the tape prepared the previous year. This was done in the electronic-music studio of Swedish Radio and consists 'of fragments of many different styles of music, avant-garde jazz, ragas, blues, rock, serial music etc. treated electronically', recordings of African musics and passages improvised by Russell himself on a Norwegian church organ also being included. All these together represent what he saw as 'the world cultural implosion of that time', [87] and it is no mere coincidence that one is reminded of Stockhausen's *Telemusik* of 1966.

Dimensions new to jazz are given the *Sonata* by this taped music, which is both a continuum and a counterpoint, both underlining and dialoguing with the instrumental passages somewhat in the manner pioneered by Varèse's *Déserts* (1950–4) and continued in many subsequent works by other composers that combine live performance with prerecorded tapes. An event-by-event commentary is scarcely needed here, but Russell employs all strategies, generating many different levels, or intensities, of interaction between instrumental and electronic sounds, these being characterized by a quite exceptional variety of tempos and types of musical gesture. The richness and diversity of texture is still more remarkable, the effect not so much kaleidoscopic as of irregularly shifting perspectives. Sometimes the taped music emerges from behind the instruments and disappears behind them when they resume; mostly both elements audibly interact; and the tape is always there, so as the piece grows familiar it can be sensed even when it cannot be heard.

Always mentioned in connection with Russell's name, if seldom explained, is his *Lydian Chromatic Concept of Tonal Organization*, yet at least equally relevant here is his idea of what he calls vertical form. This he defines as the expression of a nonhierarchical awareness of a large number of simultaneous independent events. [88] He adds that 'the idea of vertical form is not new', and it relates to certain thoughts of the composer Stefan Wolpe, with whom Russell studied for a while. Wolpe also was concerned with simultaneity of events and hence with a music of many layers which enfolded a host of independent events going on at different places at different speeds. His most advanced pieces seem free and spontaneous while in reality being tightly organized. They avoid causal links between events by presenting opposed and dissociated images, or several versions of the same image, or juxtaposing without connection extremely different states of the same material.

Wolpe had other jazz pupils, notably John Carisi (**385**) and Eddie Sauter (**369**), and regarded jazz as an important element in musical life, especially as a way of opening out tightly controlled structures to improvisation. That is what Russell has done, and although he does not approach Wolpe's fearsomely complicated rhythms nor the elaboration of his structural processes, hugely energetic compositions such as the *Electronic sonata* do indeed have nonhierarchical forms that are full of multiple aspects of their own imagery. It demonstrates, as Russell had before and would again, that intellectual illumination and emotional catharsis are the essence of the aesthetic experience.

Extreme vigour also informs *Now and then*, the first of his Scandinavian recordings, inaugurating a period during which his development as a composer was reactivated, as is confirmed by a whole series of pieces. In *Now and then* some very free improvising, solo and especially collective, is contained by a strong framework. Were it not for the example of certain of his earlier sextet performances, one might have thought it impossible for a composer to retain a shaping control while letting his players so far off the leash. But the concept of vertical form allows this, and *Now and then*, Russell tells us, is to be regarded as his first vertical form piece. [89] Second is the *Othello* ballet suite (Soul Note [It] SN1014), third the *Electronic sonata*, fourth *Listen to the silence* (Concept [A] CR002, Soul Note [It] SN1024), fifth *Living time* for Bill Evans (CBS [A] S65010) . . .

Concerto for self-accompanied guitar is in fact for two guitars and Gustafsson duets with himself by means of overdubbing. It was written in 1962 for Barry Galbraith, who took a central role in earlier music by Russell (**379–80**) and can be heard as a fine latter-day response to the guitar duets which Eddie Lang and Lonnie Johnson had recorded 40 years earlier (**68**). Here, though, the piece's inherent unity of musical style is underlined by a unity of performance style.

Considering the unusual size and scope of the main work here, it is especially unfortunate that the lengthy accompanying notes, written in bad, sometimes incomprehensible English by a Swedish composer and musicologist, are almost no help. This was a regular feature of most issues of Russell's Scandinavian recordings. M.H.

Maria Schneider Jazz Orchestra

325 **Evanescence**
†Enja (G) ENJ 8042 2.

Tony Kadleck, Greg Gisbert, Laurie Frink, Tim Hagins (tpt, fl h); John Fedchock, Keith O'Quinn, Larry Farrell, George Flynn (tbn); Mark Vinci (alt, fl, alt fl, clt, picc); Tim Ries (alt, sop, fl, clt); Rich Perry (ten, fl); Rick Margitza (ten); Scott Robinson (bar, bs sx, bs clt, clt); Ben Monder (g); Kenny Werner (p); Jay Anderson (b); Dennis Mackrel (d); Maria Schneider (comp, cond); on *Gush* add Emidin Rivera, Bill Hayes (perc). New York City, September 1992.

Wrgly · *Evanescence* · *Gumba blue* · *Some circles* · *Green piece* · *Gush* · *My lament* · *Dance you monster to my soft song* · *Last season*

Recorded in 1992 at her own expense, *Evanescence* was not released until 1994. For a year Miss Schneider shopped the tapes around recording companies, unable to get a return on her $30,000 investment. 'The response was that I wasn't "marketable", whatever that means,' she said. 'They said I was some chick that nobody ever heard of who ran a big band.' [90] It was not until Mathias Winckelmann, owner of the Enja label, heard it, that she had a deal. 'I knew he was going to pick it up,' she continued. 'I could tell he was the sort of person who was more interested in music than marketability.' [91] On release it immediately secured two Grammy nominations (Best Large Ensemble Performance and Best Instrumental Composition for the title tune) and ushered in a major new talent for the 1990s.

Maria Schneider was born in 1960 in Windom, Minnesota, and was attracted to jazz at the age of five through Evelyn Butler, a classical musician and stride pianist with whom she studied for 13 years. Pursuing a career in music, she received a Bachelor of Music degree in theory and composition from the University of Minnesota, going on to study at the University of Miami and the Eastman School of Music, where she earned a Master of Music degree in jazz writing and contemporary media. Still aiming to extend her knowledge, she moved in 1985 to New York City, where a National Endowment for the Arts grant enabled her to study with Bob Brookmeyer, who became her mentor. She was introduced to Mel Lewis and began contributing originals to his Monday-night orchestra at the Village Vanguard. Around the same time she also met Gil Evans and for the final three years of his life (he died in 1988) she worked as his assistant, playing an important role in several challenging projects that came Evans's way, including the soundtrack for the film *The Color of Money* and arrangements for the pop singer Sting's European concert with the Gil Evans Orchestra. [92]

At the urging of Lewis, Miss Schneider formed her own band in 1989 to get her compositions heard, initially with the help of the former Woody Herman trombonist and arranger John Fedchock. After performing in New York for three years they went their separate ways, their preferred styles of music quite different. Miss Schneider eventually secured a regular home for her band on Monday nights at Visiones, a tiny, low-key supper club that specializes in Spanish-American cuisine at 125 Macdougal Street at West 3rd Street in Greenwich Village. By 1997 *The New Yorker* was able to say: 'The composer and arranger's big band has settled nicely into institutional status.' [93] The importance of regularly playing together becomes apparent early on in this album; the soloists clearly understand the material at hand and construct their improvisations around the needs of the composition, rather than launching out on their own personal muses. In Miss Schneider's orchestra it was not a question of standing up and blowing for a few choruses but a matter of finding a voice within the composition that did not alter its meaning.

Although Miss Schneider's writing has been compared to that of Gil Evans, the title track reveals how little she has taken from his style. As this composition makes clear, they like to inhabit similar moods of introspection but have different ways of expressing them. Evans's sense of colour exhibited through the use of unusual combinations of instruments has been absorbed by Miss Schneider, yet Evans tended to pare away extraneous detail until he reached the heart of a song whereas Miss Schneider favours sweeping textures. However, the most significant difference between them is an obvious one – Miss Schneider is both composer and arranger and in handling structure and development she exerted ultimate control over the destiny of the composition, while in contrast Evans dealt with other people's compositions and his writing tended to be limited to theme and variation with solos on the form of the tune. While Evans tended to deal with short compositional forms, Miss Schneider's great strength was in handling long-form compositions, something only a handful of musicians in jazz have attempted, with varying degrees of success. Miss Schneider uses ad hoc song forms linked by developmental passages that lead into second, third and even fourth subjects. Often her soloists are given forms and harmonic material on which to improvise that is quite different to the harmonies and structures of the instrumental passages.

Wrgly, a programmatic piece and one of her finest compositions, deals with three subjects, contrasting metres and tone rows, yet flows organically from one section to the next as if guided by some unseen hand. It begins with what sounds like an allusion to the Basie band playing their popular 1950s arrangement *Cute*, but, perhaps surprisingly, the voicings were inspired by the sound of Michael Brecker's EWI (electric wind instrument) from the album *Don't Try This at Home* (†Impulse MCAD 42229). Mackrel (who performed with the Basie orchestra after Basie's death) uses brushes in the introduction and behind the theme, stated by muted trumpets, which initially appears as standard stage-band fare. But brooding, contrasting voices from the trombones and saxophones introduce a second subject in a contrasting metre. In fact the initial theme, built on a tone row derived from the third subject, is at double tempo and the second subject is played at half tempo, creating a dark undertow that overwhelms the bright, breezy introduction as the composition suddenly metamorphoses into something quite different, reaching a climax with brass riffs *a tempo*.

This powerful mood gives way to a third subject, this time a tranquil episode that introduces the first soloist, Margitza, on tenor saxophone. His solo respects the new surroundings, entering in quiet contemplation, but the rhythm section's time-keeping moves from post-bop to increasingly square rhythmic patterns that suggest rock. The band re-enter in this new rhythmic mood with brass riffs derived from the first subject, climaxing in a brief passage in double tempo before Fedchock's trombone enters *a tempo* against an increasingly implicit rhythmic pulse, emphasized by the addition of percussionists, built on a vamp derived from the third subject. When Ben Monder's guitar enters, it is overdriven and close to distortion in a way that suggests Jimi Hendrix and is a significant moment in the composition. The electric tone colours take the arrangement to places where acoustic instruments cannot go, adding a new level of intensity to the performance. The climax, enacted against insistent riffs that had originally been introduced at the beginning of the composition (as a part of the secondary theme), is reached when Monder sustains a chord with the band dropping out for just one bar. In its stark simplicity the device is wholly effective; it is then left for a subdued reading of the riff figure, carried by the piano, to take the composition out.

Intended to portray a 'monster whose metamorphosis progresses from a mesmerizing vapour to an embodiment characterized by a display of multiple flailing limbs [who] in its final moments . . . vanishes', [94] *Wrgly* reveals an assured handling of ad hoc forms and developmental writing which, combined with her use of contrasting metres, give her composition an unexpected elasticity. Nothing is quite as at seems, lending an enigmatic, elusive quality to her writing. She succeeds in sustaining a sense of momentum throughout, her thematic material always appearing to be in a state of becoming as she gradually constructs a series of imaginative interconnecting episodes that stand scrutiny on their own, yet together build inevitably towards a well-conceived climax.

Gush, in contrast, is a subdued piece, almost entirely based on an F-sharp minor pedal. Except for a bar of $2/4$ as the piece moves into its second subject on repeat, it is in $4/4$ throughout, its effect made through the apparent simplicity of the writing that gives the performance depth and transparency. An eight-bar introduction introduces a minor tonality and the initial exposition of the main theme reveals an AAB scheme, with the A sections eight bars and the B section, which modulates to B minor, 12 bars. Miss Schneider has spoken of how, while studying with Brookmeyer, she was encouraged to value her feminine side in her writing, [95] and an example is a motif played by the bass clarinet at the end of the A and B sections; it is a small, graceful touch that seems to offer more in colouristic detail than such a simple device appears capable of yielding. The AAB form is repeated, but when the composition opens for solos it is on a completely different scheme. Tim Ries on soprano solos on F-sharp minor, with variations, on a CCDE structure, where C is 22 bars, D is 14 bars and E 30. This subtle shift gives a feeling of spaciousness to the piece, which is accentuated by a predominance of sustained tones in accompaniment. At the end of the E structure, the AAB form is recapitulated once to a small two-bar coda.

Throughout the album, subtlety is a hallmark of Miss Schneider's writing. It prompts equally thoughtful responses from her soloists; for example Kenny Werner on *Gumba blue*, a minor blues which takes as its melody the bass line, and *Green piece*. Margitza also features on the latter and *My lament*, which number among the album's highlights. *Green piece* is another impressive example of long-form writing that takes a simple, diatonic song, which might be sung by a child, through dark Phrygian modes and intensely felt moods that imply ecological disaster before re-emerging into the sunshine, returning the theme to a major-key centre.

Miss Schneider's skill in using shifting metres emerges in a very subtle way on *Last season*. The piece opens with a freely interpreted introduction on the piano in 3/4, a further eight bars where a 4/4 rhythm is established followed by an unusual 27-bar through-written melody that at bar 16 uses a bar of 6/8, followed by three in 4/4, then successive bars in 5/4, 6/4, 5/4, two in 4/4, and successive bars in 3/4, 5/4 and, finally, 6/4. That the tune flows easily and without artifice through such a succession of metric and harmonic changes owes much to Miss Schneider's attractively luminous melodic sense rather than to the mechanics by which it is achieved; and it is this seamless quality that sets her writing apart from the formalistic devices that so often limit the potential of the big band. When the piece opens out for solos from Hagans and Ries after a repeat of the first section, the scheme is altered to an AB form, with A and B each 16 bars. After a 22-bar transitional passage the original theme returns and moves to the coda.

In 1996 Miss Schneider followed this impressive debut with *Coming About* (†Enja [G] ENJ-9069 2), which moves from the often contemplative mood of *Evanescence* to more intensely felt emotions. Included was a notable three-part suite, *Scenes from childhood*, which seems in part an excoriation of personal demons. It was confirmation, if confirmation were needed, that here was a major talent who was able to wring something new from the then ageing institution of the big band, something only a few have been able to achieve since the demise of the big-band era in the 1940s. By 1997 her talents as a composer were being rewarded with commissions, mostly from outside the United States, including the Orchestre National de Jazz in Paris and the Metropole Orchestra in the Netherlands. Sadly, work from within her homeland was less frequent. S.N.

Some Singers

A jazz singer is one who is sufficiently creative to produce a style of his or her own, not just a collection of mannerisms or gimmicks, who can improvise and reshape songs into something that is personal and recognizably in the jazz idiom.

Sarah Vaughan

326 Sassy Swings the Tivoli (Complete Version)

†EmArcy (J) 832 788–2 (2 CDs)

Vaughan (vcl); Kirk Stuart (p); Charles Williams (bs); George Hughes (d). Copenhagen, 18–21 July 1963.

I feel pretty · *Misty* · *What is this thing called love?* (2 versions) · *Loverman* (two versions) · *Sometimes I'm happy* · *Won't you come home, Bill Bailey?* · *Tenderly* · *Sassy's blues* · *Polka dots and moonbeams* · *I cried for you* (2 versions) · *Poor butterfly* · *I could write a book* · *Time after time* · *All of me* · *I hadn't anyone till you* · *I can't give you anything but love* · *I'll be seeing you* · *Maria* · *Day in, day out* · *Fly me to the moon* · *Baubles, bangles and beads* · *The lady's in love with you* · *Honeysuckle rose* · *The more I see you* · *Say it isn't so* · *Black coffee* · *Just one of those things* · *On Green Dolphin Street* · *Over the rainbow*

Of all the sounds in jazz, the vocal is the most accessible because it contains within it the potential to be more readily understood by a wider audience than its instrumental counterparts, this being due to its 'storytelling' privilege. It is hardly surprising, therefore, that most jazz vocalists have at some point in their careers either succumbed to, or been importuned into, distinctly non-jazz environments with songs and arrangements designed for the widest possible appeal. This is certainly true of the career of Sarah Vaughan, whose discography and curriculum vitae betray no single, exclusive commitment to jazz. In many ways her voice reached beyond the arbitrary boundaries of both jazz and pop, being described by some as of operatic proportions; Gunther Schuller went the whole distance by describing her as the 'greatest vocal artist of our century, [96] a claim that he may have wished to revisit after she performed alongside Dame Kiri Te Kanawa and José Carreras in the 1980s.

What *is* beyond question, however, is that, from a technical standpoint, her voice was perhaps the finest to be applied to jazz and vernacular singing. Her range, her technique and her tone, from a cavernous baritone to a *voix céleste*, saw to that. Yet there were times when this remarkable voice was used as an end in itself, the song merely a vehicle to demonstrate her astonishing virtuosity; and there were others when her artistic integrity was surrendered to commercial expediency. What is surprising about Miss Vaughan's recorded legacy is that for all the hyperbole expended on describing her great talent, there are few albums when deeds actually match those words, and it is fair to say that her reputation was based more on her live performances. As early as 1949, just two years after her stay with Billy Eckstine, whose big band was at the vanguard of the bop movement – and whose reputation, coincidentally, is also based on live performance rather than discs – she was contracted for four years to Columbia Records. On this label she sang, for the most part, with lush orchestras arranged and conducted by the likes of Joe Lippman, Hugo Winterhalter, Paul Weston and Percy Faith.

Miss Vaughan was just under 25 when she began her recording contract with Columbia and just under 29 at its conclusion in 1953. She then moved to Mercury, where she remained until 1959, and it is interesting to note that she claims she had no limitations imposed on her until 'Quincy Jones left; [then] there was nothing'. Nevertheless, the goal of both Columbia and Mercury was a hit record; it was the same with Teddy Reig, for whose Roulette label she was contracted between spring 1960 and early 1963. Her output during all those years was biased towards such an end and she duly obliged. She had done the same in 1947 with *Tenderly* and *It's magic*, which provided the Musicraft label with their most successful releases. And she had several big sellers for Mercury, including *Make yourself more comfortable*, *How important can it be?*, *Whatever Lola wants* (which reached six on the *Hit Parade* chart), *Experience unnecessary*, *C'est la vie*, *Mr Wonderful*, *Fabulous character*, *The banana boat song*, *Passing strangers* with Billy Eckstine, and, her biggest hit of all, the million-selling *Broken hearted melody* from 1959. However, none of the arrangers Mercury used, including Quincy Jones, ever gave Capitol's Billy May or Nelson Riddle sleepless nights.

Of the relatively few out-and-out jazz performances on record during this period, *Sarah Vaughan with Clifford Brown* (†EmArcy 814 641–2) and *Swingin' Easy* (†EmArcy 514 072–2), both from 1954 for Mercury's jazz subsidiary, EmArcy, number among her finest work on record. It is significant that both these albums present her in a small-group setting, the former with a rhythm section, trumpet, tenor and flute and the latter with just a rhythm section. Not until relatively late in her recording career was her voice to be heard regularly away from larger ensembles and elaborate arrangements. However, in contrast to her performances in front of big studio orchestras, the day-to-day business of earning her living as a singer was in clubs up and down the country in front of her piano trio. She always kept a strong group together, but her first live album, *At Mr Kelly's* (†EmArcy 832 791–2) from August 1957 with

Jimmy Jones (p), Richard Davis (bs) and Roy Haynes (d), failed to capture the dynamism and sheer exuberance she generated at her best. Boasting 'all new' material on the album cover, she sang everything from lead sheets, an inhibiting factor for a singer as dramatic as Miss Vaughan, particularly in matters *volti subito*, so that she ended up tiptoeing gracefully through her material with great professional competence but little inspiration.

Six years later, on *Sassy Swings the Tivoli*, she appears as a far more confident, outgoing artist. The tessitura of her voice had changed and was now more mellow than the somewhat emotionally naïve singer of the Columbia and Mercury sessions. Buoyed by a wildly enthusiastic audience she produced performances that are as riveting as they are powerful. In her later years the charge was levelled at Miss Vaughan that she got more into her voice than she did into her material, a point not without some foundation, as some of the more rococo moments of *Sarah Vaughan Live in Japan* vols. 1 and 2 (†Mainstream MDCD701/702) from ten years later reveal. However, at the Tivoli she was backed by the uncompromising swing of the Kirk Stuart trio and is goosed into a forthright mood that is sustained throughout the album.

In her prime, when this album was recorded, Miss Vaughan was a stunningly attractive woman, and part of her presentation, or act, was to play the 'sexy chick' on stage. She used *I feel pretty* to open her performances for years; in ¾ it was a throw-away number to establish rapport with her audiences. Only when she launched into *What is this thing called love?* (Disc 1) did the gloves come off as she hits a swinging groove that is both joyous and soaring. The second version (Disc 2) lacks the focus of the earlier version yet makes for interesting comparison, particularly in those millisecond variations of emphasis in the placement of notes that make one version appear to swing more than the other. *Loverman* had been in her repertoire since at least 1945, and here she is clearly experimenting with the sound of her voice and that of her vibrato at the expense of emotional content. She approaches each of the song's stanzas with an entirely different voice: first, a clear contralto, then, closing her throat, she produces a sour sound for the next four bars, then a nasal-sounding voice, then a round operatic tone with a huge vibrato, and so on; each is a different Sarah Vaughan bearing in on the songwriter's and lyric writer's original intentions. This virtuosic approach to singing does not, as becomes clear throughout subsequent ballad interpretations such as *Tenderly*, *Polka dots and moonbeams*, *Poor butterfly* and *Maria*, make for a coherent presentation or interpretation of a song's lyrics. Instead of responding to any song's inherent 'story', she appears more interested in tonal manipulation and this has the effect of divesting the lyrics of meaning and focusing attention on her voice. This aspect of her style would become more pronounced and in her final years she made a showpiece out of *Send in the clowns*, which became, in essence, a repository for every vocal effect she had worked up.

Although at medium and fast tempos these techniques were also employed, the effect appeared less stylized on a faster-moving lyric line with less time to dwell on individual notes. Here the ear is drawn not so much to her technique as to her extraordinary rhythmic vitality. The lyrics of *Sometimes I'm happy* are dispensed with in just one chorus before she launches out into scat. Scat is vocal improvisation using phonetic sounds traditionally (but not always) similar to the instrumental sounds of jazz. The sound of scat is a mixture of consonants and vowels and most scat lines have a preponderance of phonetic consonants, particularly words which begin in a 'b' or a 'd' – voiced plosives (the sound production involves the release or 'explosion' of retained breath). Plosives are categorized by the place in the mouth where the sound is articulated; those from the front are known as bilabial plosives, from the back lingua-alveolar plosives. Miss Vaughan also extensively used sounds beginning with 's' and 'h', known as frictives because their production involves a frictionlike sound; the former a lingua-alveolar frictive and the latter a glottal frictive. [97] Thus her scat style can be said to make extensive use of bilabial and lingua-alveolar plosives and glottal and lingua-alveolar frictives, and these tonal resources were at the disposal of a remarkably sophisticated musical imagination. Although she had a range of almost three octaves, her line remained sharply focused in her middle register and seldom wandered into chest or head tones, developing and toying with one idea after another with great clarity and wit.

Because so much has been written about Miss Vaughan's 'harmonic daring', her virtuosity and how she emerged as part of the bop revolution singing with Parker and Gillespie on *Mean to me* for the Continental label in May 1945, she is generally referred to as the vocal equivalent of bop's instrumental flights of fantasy. In fact, she rarely scatted, and recorded examples of her employing scat in relation to her whole discography, are few and far between. Thus to have two examples of her scatting on one album is a rare thing indeed, and the second example on this album, *Sassy's blues*, is one of her most impressive performances in the idiom. Although the most commonly cited example is *Shulie a bop* from *Swingin' Easy*, this live performance is far better in both conception and execution, with a greater emphasis on structural unity, as back-to-back comparison will reveal. Her move into falsetto is achieved seamlessly while her tone remains as full as ever as she works towards a climax that incorporates a long, sustained note which swells and swells in tone that is topped by a stock rock-'n'-roll riff. Although Ella Fitzgerald is usually cited as the prime exhibit for driving scat performances, Miss Vaughan, when she wanted to, could turn up the heat to a point where few singers could live with her; and whereas Ella's performances always exuded a great sense of fun, the sense of a pleasure shared, there is a profundity and majesty to *Sassy's blues*, due both to the deeper texture of her voice and the structural linkage of her ideas, that puts it in a class of its own.

One rarely cited influence on Miss Vaughan's singing was Billy Eckstine, and this comes through very clearly as she makes great use of chest tones and vibrato on *Time after time.* Certainly, when she signed with Columbia she began to record more and more material patterned after the Eckstine MGMs. However, the high spots of these Tivoli performances are the medium-paced and up-tempo numbers, where she turns in a series of *tours de force* of questing brilliance that leaves the listener in no doubt that with a microphone in her hand and a rhythm section behind her, she was best served in a small-group setting. *Just one of those things* sees her riding the tonic, a cliché in lesser singers but something that brings the song alive, while on *I cried for you* there is an impish touch of humour in the final chorus. *Baubles, bangles and beads* is a good example of how well rehearsed the Kirk Stuart trio was; Stuart himself frequently plays block chords providing a very orchestral type of backdrop for the singer and it is clear he and the trio are working to quite specific arrangements. Even so, they create a lot of latitude for themselves and provide her with an expansive, highly swinging accompaniment that contributes enormously to the success of the album.

These sessions show Miss Vaughan in exuberant mood performing at the top of her form, reaching out to the audience who in turn take her into their hearts. It is the sort of two-way exchange that often inspires performers to reach creative heights that somehow appear beyond their grasp in the recording studio. But while these performances reveal her as one of the finest singers in jazz, they also reveal a flaw, her love of excessive ornamentation on slower numbers, which, while sometimes appearing engagingly eccentric, is ultimately distracting. Here artifice struggles to become art and raises a curious paradox: while practically every other singer in jazz had a reach that exceeded their grasp, Miss Vaughan was practically alone in being able to reach any note or combination of notes that she could ever dream of singing. The result, curiously, was not the heaven one might expect but a stylistic narcissism that at times might appear heroic, but could ultimately lack emotion. S.N.

Chris Connor

327 A Jazz Date with Chris Connor

†Rhino-Atlantic (A) R271747

Joe Wilder (tpt); Al Cohn (ten); Ralph Sharon (p, arr); Oscar Pettiford (bs); Osie Johnson (d); Eddie Costa (vib); Chris Connor (vcl). New York City, 16 November 1956.

Poor little rich girl · Everything I've got · All I need is you · It only happens when I dance with you

Sam Most (fl), Joe Puma (g) replace Wilder, Cohn. New York City, 17 December 1956.
Lonely town · Fancy free · Moon ray · Driftwood

Cohn, Lucky Thompson (ten) replace Most, Puma; Chano Pozo (bon), Mongo Santamaria (con) added. New York City, 19 December 1956.
My shining hour · Just squeeze me · I'm shooting high · It's a most unusual day

Stan Free (p, arr); Mundell Lowe (g); Percy Heath (bs); Ed Shaughnessy (d); Connor (vcl). New York City, 13 March 1958.
Blow, Gabriel, blow · Chinatown, my Chinatown

Bobby Jaspar (ten, fl) added. Same date.
Here lies love · The night we called it a day

Jaspar absent; George Duvivier (bs) replaces Heath. New York City, 8 April 1958.
On the first warm day · Johnny one-note

Al Epstein (eng h[1], bs clt[2]) added. Same date.
Be my all[1] · *Our love affair*[2] · *Good for nothing*[2]

Epstein absent. New York City, 23 May 1958.
Be a clown · Moonlight in Vermont · Loverman

Ever since her three short periods with Thornhill and two with Kenton, Chris Connor has been an individual, indeed original, singer. And she has long been misunderstood, including by some musicians, apparently because of her failure to conform to stereotypes of the female jazz singer. Avoidance of clichés – of attitude as well as of musical practice – is, however, an aspect of her rare character. Her preoccupation is always with the actual stuff of music, with her own particular ways of handling it, and, as with the other singers dealt with in this section, there is nothing for people seeking mere show-business slickness.

Though it inevitably changed as the long years of her career passed, Miss Connor's tone of voice was always special and memorable. But there are plenty of husky-voiced singers, and the point was how she employed that tonal quality. The use of vibrato was particularly individual, although this, too, changed over the years, as recordings demonstrate. Especially characteristic was the manner in which vibrato was introduced just before the end of a long note. And few singers are so unpredictable in their deployment of dynamics, this sometimes appearing arbitrary yet finally justified by the overall effect. It is the same with her use of displaced accents, some of these being extreme. The immediate, as it were local, impact is striking enough but appears even more so when heard in relation to the entire chorus. These factors of course were contributory to her reshaping of the given melodies: all real jazz singers do this, yet few have gone to such extremes. Sometimes entire phrases are dislocated, shifted right out of their usual place within the chorus. As Ralph Sharon commented on the sleeve of the initial LP issue, she sometimes phrases so far behind the beat as to make us think she is lost, out of contact. But that seldom happens. Often she produces entire melodies which though related to the originals, are to a remarkable extent her own.

On *Poor little rich girl* the freedom of Miss Connor's reinterpretation of the melody is emphasized by the horns' jaunty, repetitive figures. Then her departures in the almost stop-time passages are even more daring; and Cohn's solo is an excellent complement to her endeavours. Altering the notes and stretching the words naturally changes what the music is saying, and Noël Coward's song of rather facile reproof is turned into something else. In this connection Miss Connor's own 'evil gal' lyrics – going some way beyond Lorenz Hart – certainly give a new slant to *Everything I've got*, and again ensemble riffing heightens the boldness of her version of the melody. In fact the actual detail of her reshapings of such material deserves unflagging attention – as Ran Blake long ago insisted [98] – because the surprises come thick and fast, the length of this note or the placing of that so often being different from what we expect.

Almost never do these commanding manipulations sound like mere embellishment, ornament or even elaboration: rather, she recasts phrases and whole melodies from within. She actually 'phrases like a horn' in the way often claimed for jazz singers, and comparison between her different recorded versions of a given song, such as *Chinatown, my Chinatown* or *Blow, Gabriel, blow*, demonstrates how much improvisation there is in her work. This being so, Miss Connor is usually at her most intense on the kind of sessions detailed above; they prove that, contrary to what has so often been written about her, there is rarely much of the understatement of cool jazz in her singing. The first 12 of the above titles surfaced in 1958 as *A Jazz Date with Chris Connor*, the second dozen as *Chris Craft*, another 1958 issue. The latter would not have been a connoisseur's first choice to put with *A Jazz Date*, which ought to have been accompanied by the further collection of 1956 performances simply titled *Chris Connor* (Atlantic [A] 1228), partly because of her extraordinary melodic and rhythmic ventures on *I get a kick out of you* and *Almost like being in love*. In these she is supported by a quartet including John Lewis and Barry Galbraith, always splendid accompanists, who, with Pettiford and Connie Kay, provide the sort of participatory commentaries that serve a singer of jazz best.

She receives them here, too, and if she finds less than usual in *All I need is you* she still gives it her own slant, and again Cohn's *obbligato* adds something further. So do the solos by Sharon and the two by Wilder on *It only happens when I dance with you*, where she substantially alters the melody on the second time round. A by no means incidental effect of Miss Connor's approach is that she sometimes makes outstandingly foolish ditties seem as if they have something to do with real life, even forcing their words to take on a degree of meaning. Several here prove that these enhancements of value arise out of a well-calculated use of several types of ambiguity. [99] At the other extreme she discovers good songs that seem to have been missed elsewhere, such as *Driftwood* and, in the *Chris Connor* set, *When the moon was green.*

The support she gets on all except the last of the above dates provides plenty of contrast with the voice, and, particularly on the second December session with two tenors, rhythmic propulsion too. Of course, this singer generates more than enough rhythmic propulsion of her own, but in *Just squeeze me* Cohn and Thompson cushion her voice to advantageous effect. They provide good, pithy solos here and on this date's other titles, as does Costa, and there is exceptional Sharon on *It's a most unusual day.* At the previous session, instrumental commentaries are more spare. In *Moon ray* only Pettiford supports fore and aft with the others being heard only in the middle, and in *Driftwood* the same plan is followed but with the piano early and late instead of the bass. On both of these performances, where her voice is much exposed, Miss Connor's reshaping of the melodic phrases is evocative of sensitive line drawings. In Bernstein's *Lonely town,* with its resourceful Most *obbligato,* there is another finely judged rereading of a good melody, which is shown in an unexpected further light when the pace slackens.

Chiefly on *The night we called it a day* and *Here lies love* we hear intent, ever personal readings of the melodies, the former paced by Lowe, the latter by Free, with arresting moments in the codas of both. Generally the sidemen get plenty of chances, and *Blow, Gabriel, blow* is the only piece among the above 24 on which Miss Connor is heard throughout.

The next date included three rather obscure songs from Bert Howard, once Mabel Mercer's accompanist, and these are delivered in a rather too straightforward manner. Epstein's english horn counterpoint behind the voice on *Be my all* adds a welcome ingredient, yet far preferable is Lowe's beautifully nuanced and melodious guitar work, intimately entwined round the vocal phrases, on *Loverman* and *Moonlight in Vermont.*

Obviously there can be no such thing as a definitive performance of any of this material (or of any other music), but several of the above recordings almost suggest otherwise, as do earlier specimens from Miss Connor's work such as the Bethlehem *Out of This World* or much later cases like the Contemporary *Laura.* Certainly it is thoroughly misleading that the packaging of the above CD bore a label describing her as 'this 1950s jazz great'. She is one of that rather small minority of jazz musicians who went on developing and facing new challenges over a long period of years. Records like *Chris Connor Classic* (Contemporary [A] C14023), dating from 1986, reveal further aspects of an art which retained the freshness and vital capacity for change into the 1990s, a point confirmed by *As Time Goes By* (†Enja [G] ENJ7061–2). M.H.

Anita O'Day

328 The Big Band Sessions

Verve (A) VE2–2534 (2 LPs), Verve (E) 2632 083 (2 LPs)

Unidentified studio orchestra; Billy May (arr); Anita O'Day (vcl). Los Angeles, 2 April 1959.

Just one of those things · Easy to love

Jimmy Giuffre (arr) replaces May. Los Angeles, 6 April 1959.

Come rain or come shine · You're a clown · Easy come, easy go · A lover is blue

Same personnel. Los Angeles, 7 April 1959.

Gone with the wind · Hershey bar · My heart belongs to daddy

Same personnel. Los Angeles, 8 April 1959.

The way you look tonight · It had to be you

May replaces Giuffre. Los Angeles, 9 April 1959.

I get a kick out of you · Get out of town · What is this thing called love? · Night and day

Same personnel. Los Angeles, 6 June 1960.

Johnny one-note · Lover · Have you met Miss Jones?

Same personnel. Los Angeles, 8 June 1960.

Ten cents a dance

John Anderson, Al Porcino, Jack Sheldon, Ray Triscari (tpt); Stu Williamson (tpt, tbn); Louis McCreary, Dick Nash, Frank Rosolino (tbn); Joe Maini (alt, ten); Chuck Gentry (bar); Russ Freeman (p); Al Viola (g); Buddy Clark (bs); Mel Lewis (d); Larry Bunker (vib); Johnny Mandel (arr); O'Day (vcl). Los Angeles, 18 January 1961.

Travellin' light · Don't explain · I hear music · Crazy, he calls me · Lover, come back to me · If the moon turns green

Herb Pomeroy (tpt); Bob Brookmeyer, Willie Dennis (tbn); Walt Levinsky (clt, alt); Phil Woods (alt); Zoot Sims, Jerome Richardson (ten); Hank Jones (p); Barry Galbraith (g); plus others unidentified; Gary McFarland (arr); O'Day (vcl). New York City, 16 October 1961.

The ballad of the sad young men · Up state · You've come a long way from St Louis · Boogie blues · A woman alone with the blues · Night bird

As noted at the beginning of this section, the status and identity of jazz singers has always been disputed, yet one is tempted to assert that if Anita O'Day is not a jazz singer, then there are *no* jazz singers. She always appeared more secure in her identification with this music than most other vocalists and has indeed always been completely at ease in jazz settings. The most obvious early examples come from her period with Gene Krupa's band – fulfilling her role to perfection in Sy Oliver's powerful 1945 score of *Opus 1* etc. – and she was equally at home broadcasting with Tadd Dameron from the Royal Roost, recording with Roy Eldridge, Bill Harris and others in Ralph Burns's band, with Don Fagerquist, Ben Webster and others again under Russ Garcia's leadership. There were numerous other contexts, several of which found Miss O'Day, as on the above *What is this thing called love?*, holding her own in four-bar exchanges with drummers – not something that one could trust many singers in jazz to do well.

It has usually been agreed that singers are limited in the amount of jazz they can bring into their performances because they are tied to the words and hence to an at least recognizable version of the song's melody. [100] But although reflecting, when she was too young to know better, the widespread Billie Holiday influence, Miss O'Day's approach was almost radical. With a few maverick exceptions such as Leo Watson – who preceded her as an occasional vocalist with Krupa – singers had interpreted songs as they stood, with varying degrees of skill and understanding. Most still do. Yet Miss O'Day's venture was a form of quasi-instrumental expressionism to varying degrees subordinating the initial verbal and musical texts. It was still singing, of course, but this was a new way of doing it, a new kind of vocal music; and her achievement was rather more singular than has been generally appreciated.

The equipment she brought to her task began with a voice of limited compass yet very flexible. It has an immediately recognizable timbre, husky in an appealingly individual way, almost without vibrato except on long notes, where its use appears to be finely calculated. Just as personal is her diction, the syllables being articulated in such ways as always to enhance rhythmic impetus. A sense of rhythmic adventure, in particular great freedom of accentuation, is common to her various modes of performance, as is an ability to swing. Added to this basic virtue is a capacity to deliver convincing blues, as *Up state* and *Boogie blues* show.

A lot of her phrases are instrumental in character and may be drastically reshaped when they recur as well as being significantly displaced within the chorus. Sometimes a phrase or word is split into halves, or other fractions, and there is in fact a considerable use of rests. A single note or syllable may be isolated, or a whole series thus spaced out, emphasizing the rhythm section's pulse. At other points a word or syllable may be spread over several notes, its vocal colour being repeatedly changed the while. Miss O'Day's inflections of the latter sort can scarcely be discussed because they are hard to describe in a reasonable number of words, and are impossible to notate; and such nuances are almost constant in her singing. One phrase will be run into the next, or part of it, and by this stage the notes are no longer an interpretation of the words, the words becoming rather a commentary on the notes.

This being so, words may be omitted, seemingly at random, reducing the lyrics to telegraphese, and beyond the fragmentation of *It had to be you* when it gets into the fastest of its three tempos lies the occasional deliberate garbling of a song, usually at great speed and with everything subordinated to melody and rhythm, as in several of her devastations of *Tea for two*. In this climate problems of repertoire disappear and all the usual objections to pieces like the arch *You've come a long way from St Louis* or the simply embarrassing *Johnny one-note* do not apply. Everything is shaped to specifically jazzlike ends with a consistency that belies the often seemingly offhand delivery. A logical, or at least inevitable, end to these tendencies is a performance such as the wordless *Hershey bar*, a Mandel theme recorded by Stan Getz in 1950 and 1951 (**299**), which presents Miss O'Day as the pure improvising jazz scat singer.

Along with these strictly jazz endeavours she can also interpret lyrics and even original melodies with an insight beyond that of most singers who do nothing else. *I hear music* and *Come rain or come shine* are excellent instances of the sheer clarity she applies to this, although such performances have led to her being accused of an emotional aloofness which supposedly limits her art. Such charges are the result, first, of her never lapsing into sentimentality, or even into the blandness that, for some listeners, spoils much of Ella Fitzgerald's work. Second, they are the penalty of her performances sometimes having, for all their zest, a certain austerity, containing no embellishments, nothing extraneous: everything is essential. And the best answer to notions of her undue detachment lies in Miss O'Day's moving accounts of songs like Joe Albany's *You're a clown* or the stoical *Ten cents a dance.* In this latter she conveys a disenchantment that is total yet avoids overemphasis. *Don't explain* is comparable, and if a trace of Billie Holiday's influence lingers here it is appropriate because Miss Holiday is supposed to be part-composer of this plea for peace at any price. Then there is *The ballad of the sad young men*, a musical equivalent to that hallowed *New Yorker* cartoon in which one of a row of men sitting glumly in a bar says to the next; 'My desperation is quieter than the desperation of any other man in the house!' But Miss O'Day draws out the real pathos in Tommy Wolf's song in a reading which almost can stand with Gil Evans's performance on **460**.

And the 'interpretive' and more directly jazzlike poles of her output are in no sense disconnected. She often shifts from one mode to another within a single performance, fluidly incorporating scat phrases into relatively straight accounts of words and melody. These in turn fuse with the instrumental solos, as when Dennis or Maini alternate with her scatting in *Up state* and *Lover, come back to me*, a melody which latterly she revises to fine effect. Characteristic too are renderings like *Easy to love*, the second chorus of which is done as a duet with the whole band, voice and instruments pursuing different variants of the melody.

This anthology is drawn from her Verve output, now available complete on the 9-CD Mosaic (A) MD 9–188, and sensitive though Mandel's and particularly Giuffre's scores are, those by McFarland best match the singer for consistent inventiveness. *Boogie blues*, which she had been singing ever since the Krupa days, is made to sound almost new, not least because of a forthright Woods solo. McFarland each time encloses Miss O'Day in a quite elaborate framework, resourcefully varied in detail that is managed so as to complement and enhance, rather than to divert attention from, her singing. *Night bird* is perhaps the most beautiful example. M.H.

June Christy

329 The Best Thing for You

Affinity (E) AFF145, *†Capitol (E) CDP796 329-2

Frank Beach, Ray Linn, Shorty Rogers, Ray Triscari (tpt); Harry Betts, Tommy Pederson, Herbie Harper, Sy Zentner (tbn); Gus Bivona, Al Gershoff (alt); Bob Cooper, Ted Nash (ten); Bob Gioga (bar); Buddy Cole (p); Vince Terry (g); Phil Stephens (bs); Alvin Stoller (d); Pete Rugolo (arr); June Christy (vcl). Los Angeles, 17 November 1952.
My heart belongs to only you

Maynard Ferguson, Conrad Gozzo, Rogers, Jimmy Zito (tpt); Milt Bernhart, Pederson, Harper, George Roberts (tbn); Bivona, Bud Shank (alt); Cooper, Nash (ten); Chuck Gentry (bar); Geoff Clarkson (p); Barney Kessel (g); Joe Mondragon (bs); Frank Carlson (d); Rugolo (arr); Christy (vcl). Los Angeles, 14 August 1953.
Something cool

Beach, Gozzo, Linn, Triscari, Uan Rasey (tpt); Nick di Maio, Dick Noel, Pederson, Dick Reynolds (tbn); Skeets Herfurt, Willie Schwartz (alt); Fred Fallensby, Nash (ten); Gentry (bar); Paul Smith (p); Tony Rizzi (g); Mondragon (bs); Stoller (d); Rugolo (arr); Christy (vcl). Los Angeles, 27 December 1953.
The midnight sun

Ferguson, Gozzo, Rogers (tpt); Bernhart, Betts, Pederson (tbn); Harry Klee, Shank (alt); Cooper, Nash (ten); Gentry (bar); Russ Freeman (p); Howard Roberts (g); Mondragon (bs); Shelly Manne (d); Rugolo (arr); Christy (vcl). Los Angeles, 18 January 1954.
I'll take romance

Conte Candoli, Buddy Childers, Gozzo, Rogers, Zito (tpt); Betts, Bernhart, John Halliburton, Harper, Roberts (tbn); Klee, Shank (alt); Bill Holman, Jack Montrose (ten); Jimmy Giuffre (bar); Rugolo (p, arr); Laurindo Almeida (g); Mondragon (bs); Manne (d); Christy (vcl). Los Angeles, 9 May 1955.
This time the dream's on me

Pete Candoli (tpt); Betts, Harper, Noel, Roberts (tbn); Klee (fl); Bob Gordon (bar); Claude Williamson (p); Almeida (g); Harry Babasin (bs); Larry Bunker (d); unidentified string section; Rugolo (arr); Christy (vcl). Los Angeles, 26 July 1955.
Dearly beloved

3 unidentified tpt, Shank (alt, fl), Cooper (ten) added; strings absent. Los Angeles, 27 July 1955.
Until the real thing comes along

John Graas (fr h); Shank (alt); Cooper (ten); Roberts (g); Mondragon (bs); Manne (d); Bernie Mattison (vib); unidentified string section; Corky Hale (hrp); Rugolo (arr); Christy (vcl). Los Angeles, 16 January 1956.
This year's kisses

Don Fagerquist (tpt); Frank Rosolino (tbn); Vince DeRosa (fr h); Clarence Kavella (tu); Shank (alt, fl); Cooper (ten); Dave Pell (bar); Benny Aranov (p); Roberts (g); Red Mitchell (bs); Manne (d); Bunker (vib); unidentified string section; Rugolo (arr); Christy (vcl). Los Angeles, 3 January 1957.
When Sunny gets blue · The best thing for you

Bernhart, Harper, Pederson, Rosolino, George Roberts (tbn); Aranov (p); Howard Roberts (g); Mitchell (bs); Stoller (d); Mattison (vib); Rugolo (arr); Christy (vcl). Los Angeles, 2 July 1957.
Give me the simple life

Ed Leddy (tpt); Rosolino (tbn); Red Callender (tu); Shank (alt, bar, fl); Cooper (ten, arr); Freeman (p); Almeida (g); Monty Budwig (bs); Manne (d); Christy (vcl). Los Angeles, June 1958.
When lights are low · My one and only love

Childers, Fagerquist, Ollie Mitchell (tpt); Bernhart, Bob Fitzpatrick, Rosolino (tbn); Kenny Shroyer (bs tbn); Callender (tu); Shank, Paul Horn (alt, fl); Copper, Pell (ten); Gentry (bar); Freeman (p); Jim Hall (g); Mondragon (bs); Manne (d); Rugolo (arr); Christy (vcl). Los Angeles, January 1959.
How high the moon? · Easy street

Rosolino (tbn); Jim Decker (fr h); Shank, Norman Beno (alt); Buddy Collette (ten); Cooper (ten, arr); Gentry (bar); Joe Castro (p); Callender (bs); Stan Levey (d); Kathyrine Julye (hrp); Christy (vcl). Los Angeles, late 1959.
Kissin' bug

The less resounding of the two main clichés about June Christy is that she was 'the voice of Stan Kenton's orchestra'. This all too plausible formulation by Joachim Berendt [101] is quoted, usually without acknowledgement, in most pieces written about her. And is was her misfortune that unlike Anita O'Day (**328**) and Chris Connor (**327**), who immediately preceded and followed her in the band, her fame derived from relatively short periods with Kenton, these somehow detracting from the independent reputation merited by quantities of excellent work done under her own name. Misleading also was that most inept of publicists' epithets, 'the misty Miss Christy', which also dogged her for the rest of her life. The voice was alleged to be husky, breathy, and hence supposedly well suited to the cool jazz of the 1950s, especially Kenton's. Yet much of that music was not cool, least of all his.

In fact there was nothing 'misty' about Miss Christy, and the above recordings prove that she sang with both directness and sensitive feeling.

There was no hint of modish detachment, either, in the full-voiced, nearly exultant *My heart belongs to only you* or the almost conversational *Something cool,* and Berendt was more to the point with his commendation of 'the warm, human climate' of her interpretations. Further, there could be no serious question about her status as a singer of jazz in the face of performances like *How high the moon?* and *When lights are low.* A third cliché is that she was heavily influenced by Anita O'Day, and Gene Roland, who scored her first Kenton accompaniments, went so far as to claim that she was initially just an O'Day impersonator. [102] This is emphatically not confirmed even by Miss Christy's earliest recordings, done in 1945 with Kenton sidemen including Roland, such as *Mean to me* or *Get happy* (Hindsight [A] 219).

Well before the 1952–9 performances detailed in the heading were set down she was singing with considerable individuality, each phrase shaped with musical and emotional perception, due weight given to every word, the diction virtually perfect. *Easy street* and the wry *This time the dream's on me* are beautiful examples of her approach, and if *This year's kisses* is rather too jaunty, *I'll take romance* deftly alternates intimacy and exuberance, and *The midnight sun* is a small masterpiece. Occasionally there is a question to be asked about her intonation, but this weakness has been much exaggerated, and in view of her ability to negotiate aggressively dissonant and contrapuntal scores like Rugolo's *Lonely woman* (**313a**), *Conflict* (†Capitol [A] 8 59965 2) and above all Robert Graettinger's *Everything happens to me* (**477**), there can be few doubts concerning her general musicianship.

Certainly Miss Christy, with a period in Boyd Raeburn's increasingly progressive orchestra behind her, was comfortably at home with the Kenton organization, and although the above performances were recorded under her own name, the arrangements, nearly all by Rugolo, are intelligent adaptations of the Kenton method of those years. The voice is displayed to much advantage amid resourcefully varied brass, woodwind and saxophone textures, the strings being deployed quite effectively in *This year's kisses* and the coda of *When Sunny gets blue. Something cool, The midnight sun, I'll take romance* and *This time the dream's on me* are from Miss Christy's first (10-inch) LP, also titled *Something Cool.* This was rerecorded in stereo during 1960, but it is the earlier, and superior, mono recordings that are found here. The selection is in fact taken from several LPs and is excellent, yet could have been improved by the replacement of a lachrymose *Dearly beloved* and damn-fool *Kissin' bug* with *I should care, Do nothing till you hear from me, My ship* or *They can't take that away from me,* further outstanding performances from this period of the singer's career (and all on †Capitol [E] CDP792 588–2).

Congenial as these big-band settings obviously were, it needs to be remembered that Miss Christy spent much of her time working in

nightclubs, usually with just keyboard support (the superlative Jimmy Lyon in the early years). Her very interesting *Duet* disc with Kenton and no orchestra (†Capitol [A] 7 89285 2) tells us much about Kenton's music. But she ought to have been recorded systematically in such contexts. They would have given her greater freedom and it might have been enlightening to hear what she did with it. *The Intimate Miss Christy* (Capitol [A] ST1953), a 1963 programme in which she is accompanied only by guitar, bass and sometimes flute (Bud Shank), suggests considerable possibilities.
M.H.

Sheila Jordan

330 Portrait of Sheila

†Blue Note (A) CDP 7 89002 2

Jordan (vcl); Barry Galbraith (g); Steve Swallow (bs); Denzil Best (d). New Jersey, 19 September and 12 October 1962.

Falling in love with love · *If you could see me now* · *Am I blue* · *Dat dere* · *When the world was young* · *Let's face the music and dance* · *Laugh, clown, laugh* · *Who can I turn to?* · *Baltimore oriole* · *I'm a fool to want you* · *Hum drum blues* · *Willow, weep for me*

Miss Jordan was always an infinitely better singer than she was a typist, but it was only when she reached pensionable retirement that she was able finally to concentrate on singing full time. Jazz for her remained an extracurricular activity since she was left with the responsibility of raising her child, Tracy, from an unsuccessful marriage to the pianist Duke Jordan (1952–62). On her own admission she did not 'concentrate too much on singing' during that time, [103] although she had studied harmony and theory with Lennie Tristano after moving to New York in 1951. By the time she made *Portrait of Sheila* she was broadening her career, with work in Harlem and Greenwich Village and regular appearances with Jimmy Giuffre, Don Ellis and George Russell, plus part-time work as a typist for an ad agency to make ends meet. It was through Russell's enthusiasm that she made her recording debut with Blue Note, a major departure for the label's unstated policy at the time: 'I knew they didn't record singers and I knew they didn't record too many white musicians,' she reflected in 1980. [104]

Portrait of Sheila was a critical success when released in 1963. She came from nowhere to top the *down beat* International Critics' Poll that year, but response from the general public was muted. Although seeming on the verge of success, the predicted breakthrough to the public at large never came and one of the most strikingly original singers in jazz was forced to struggle on in semi-obscurity. Miss Jordan's style is uncompromising, yet she seldom uses scat. Instead, she makes extensive use of melismata, as on *Falling in love with love*, where she alternates the familiar melody with her own less expansive version, crowding several pitches into sustained tones. A small, light, somewhat custardy alto, she is nevertheless able to impart great emotional depth to the Tadd Dameron ballad *If you could see me now* or *When the world was young*, *Who can I turn to?* and *Am I blue?* This is a difficult problem for singers whose vocal demeanour tends naturally to suggest sunny days and bluebirds in the skies, and one that a singer such as Ella Fitzgerald never altogether satisfactorily resolved. Miss Jordan succeeds by making space for exposed emotion and personal sentiment plus a sharp, acidic sense of timing and phrasing.

Dat dere is very much a mother's choice of song, so accurately is a child's curiosity about life caught in the Oscar Brown Jr lyrics. 'I find doing a tune like *Dat dere* doesn't give me too many liberties. The main reason I wanted to do it is because of my little girl. Whenever I sing the tune I always feel that's exactly the way she is.' [105] *Baltimore oriole*, an unusual choice, and *Hum drum blues*, with another clever set of lyrics from Oscar Brown Jr, are negotiated with just bass and drums, prefiguring her later duos with the bassists Arild Anderson and Harvie Swartz. These are clever, intimate one-to-one performances that are as engaging as they are absorbing, harnessing the storytelling privilege of the singer, yet moving comfortably within the jazz orbit through her unexpected melodic and harmonic shifts and a serene rhythmic placement of key phrases. *Willow, weep for me*, a song that has been done to death by jazz and torch singers alike yet strangely by few jazz instrumentalists, emerges less as a nightclub crowd-pleaser than as a heartfelt lament. This is a high-risk strategy for a jazz singer, moving in the twilight world between pathos and gravitas, but one that Miss Jordan resolves throughout this album with a disarming up-front emotionalism that would become more pronounced as her career developed. This aspect of her singing surfaces again on *Laugh, clown, laugh* as an almost disturbing feature, yet projected with an abstraction that prefigured her forays into free jazz with Roswell Rudd in the 1970s. [106]

The frantic tempo of *Let's face the music and dance* reveals great poise and a willingness to employ a wide vibrato for sudden and startling effect, as in the opening bars. However, vibrato is not normally a feature of her singing, and if used at all it is generally confined to a relatively soft terminal vibrato. She made great use of subtle inflections in her voice, of varying timbres (her pronunciation of 'romance' in *Let's face the music . . .*) and intensity, turning one-syllable words into multisyllable words, sudden fall-offs, unexpected glissandos, abrupt contrasts of head tones and chest tones and brief flights into falsetto, as in the end of *Hum drum blues*. Through a mixture of personal circumstance and poor representation ('I am very poor at selling myself'), Miss Jordan's name has remained that of an underground figure in jazz for almost the length of her career. It can be only a matter for speculation how her career might have developed with the right breaks, but it is a testament to her dedication that she was still performing in the 1990s, undaunted by lack of recognition yet sounding as original as ever. S.N.

Mel Tormé

331 Mel Tormé Swings Shubert [*sic*] Alley

Verve (A) MGV2132, Verve (E) 2304 235

Al Porcino, Stu Williamson (tpt); Frank Rosolino (tbn); Vince DeRosa (fr h); Red Callender (tu); Art Pepper (alt); Bill Perkins (ten); Bill Hood (bar); Marty Paich (p, arr); Joe Mondragon (bs); Mel Lewis (d); Tormé (vcl). Los Angeles, 21 January 1960.

Too close for comfort · Once in love with Amy · Whatever Lola wants · Hello, young lovers

Same personnel. Los Angeles, 4 February 1960.

Too darn hot · A sleeping bee · All I need is the girl · Lonely town

Same personnel. Los Angeles, 11 February 1960.

The surrey with the fringe on top · On the street where you live · Just in time · That old devil moon

Our attitude regarding Tormé, perhaps more than to the other singers dealt with in this section, is likely to be affected by our attitude to his material. Rather than recasting these songs in his own image, he accepted their inherent romanticism and made jazz out of it. Our choice of the above record was somewhat arbitrary and it is hard to speak of it separately from earlier collaborations between Tormé and Paich's Dektette, as this band was called, because of the consistency of their aim and achievement. Even at a much later date there still are few collections of songs like these, in which the voice is given jazz settings that are so uncompromising and yet immaculate. The other relevant items, both from 1956, are *Lulu's Back in Town* (Bethlehem [A] BCP52, Affinity [E] AFF85) and *Tormé Sings Astaire* (BCP6013, AFF107), both, like the *Shubert* [sic] *Alley* set, being almost perfect of their kind.

Highly professional in a way that singers of this repertoire often are not, Tormé gave the impression, at least in studio performances like these, that his every nuance received careful prior thought; yet paradoxically a feeling of spontaneity is preserved. The voice has a beautiful timbre, warm and husky, and in pieces like *A sleeping bee* something of the 'velvet fog' still lingers. Slow numbers such as *Lonely town* are sung with much feeling, quick ones like *Too close for comfort* with engaging zest, and in most cases the variety of his phrasing indicates an active imagination. So do his placing of rhythmic accents, underlining of particular words, shading of the tone of his voice; other devices are impossible to categorize, but of course all these things act together.

Tormé's intonation was such that he had no fears about exposing his voice over minimal bass and drum support at the start of *Just in time* or amid the piled-up dissonances near the end of *That old devil moon.*

Except in the rather contrived treatment of *Hello, young lovers*, his alterations to melodies usually have expressive point rather than being made for incidental effect; such reshapings, like his scat singing (*On the street where you live*), are done with musicality and intelligence. Sometimes the voice resembles, or deliberately imitates, an instrument, perhaps a nimble french horn. Yet the diction is virtually perfect, and occasionally he amusingly improves the lyrics.

As much Tormé's ideas as Paich's, the instrumentation and style of writing employed here obviously derived from **376** via the Tentette items on **300**. Matters are handled in such a way that the ear is drawn to the voice and the instruments equally, and success here, as with the earlier collections, is not just a result of good singing in front of lively jazz backings. There is close interplay between the voice and the ensemble, as in *Too close for comfort*, and between the voice and individual musicians, as with Perkins on *Once in love with Amy*. There are some fine, knowingly concise improvisations, too, for example from Williamson in *On the street where you live*, Perkins in *All I need is the girl*, Rosolino in *Whatever Lola wants* and the all-out *Too darn hot* and from Pepper repeatedly. Now and then the Dektette takes over for an interlude, as in *That old devil moon*, *Once in love with Amy* and *On the street where you live*, but the variety of instrumental colour and ensemble textures remains just as impressive when Tormé is singing. And though Paich's scores occasionally shadow the voice, as in *Lonely town*, far more often there is independent movement, almost a degree of real counterpoint, between the vocal lines and the instrumental patterns. *That old devil moon* is a particularly good instance.

There are indeed plenty of subtle touches, and not the smallest pleasure of this music is that of noting Tormé's and especially Paich's glances elsewhere. Examples include the brief reference to **165**'s *Things ain't what they used to be* at the very end of *Once in love with Amy*, to **257**'s *Steeplechase* in *Too close for comfort*, to **376**'s *Godchild* in *Hello, young lovers*. Still more enigmatic is the glimpse of *Old man river* during *On the street where you live*, which also squeezes in Ellington's *I'm beginnin' to see the light*. Note also the full-blown presence of *Who's sorry now?* in *Just in time*: the band plays one melody, Tormé sings the other, and they fit together to excellent musical effect. Such 'learned' references are balanced with humour, instances being the corny tuba and finger-snapping at the start of *Once in love with Amy* and the brief yet comically grandstand finish to *Whatever Lola wants*. A quintessential specimen of American sentimentality like *The surrey with the fringe on top* seems proof against such assaults, [107] but nearly all this music swings a great deal.

Decades later Tormé carried the same youthful and romantic air. As Richard Cook put it: 'He still sounds as if he's serenading beneath a balcony instead of being up there in the bedroom.' [108] This was confirmed by *Round Midnight: A Retrospective 1956–68* (†Stash [A]

STCD4) and more particularly by his 1988 *Reunion* with the Dektette (Concord [A] CJ360). Not many singers, least of all of this repertoire, would care to undertake such a test three decades later, yet Tormé's high notes – for example – were there as sound and sure as ever. M.H.

Betty Carter

332 The Audience with Betty Carter

†Verve (A) 835684–2

Carter (vcl); John Hicks (p); Curtis Lundy (bs); Kenny Washington (d). San Francisco, 6–8 December 1979.

Sounds (Movin' on) · I think I got it now · Caribbean sea · The trolley song · Everything I have is yours · I'll buy you a star · I could write a book · Can't we talk it over/Either it's love or it isn't · Deep night · Spring can really hang you up the most · Tight · Fake · So . . . · My favourite things · Open the door (theme song)

Throughout her career Betty Carter committed herself without compromise to the art of the jazz vocal. She remained true to a set of values forged when bop was setting the musical agenda, refusing to succumb to the blandishments of commerce and remaining impervious to the conceits of record producers. This unequivocal stance while relentlessly perfecting her own wholly individual style, of shaping it while at the same time creating a context wholeheartedly in the jazz idiom in which to perform, had its price. As the end of the 1970s approached she was working in semi-obscurity to an audience she had developed by personal appearances and through her own poorly distributed Bet-Car label. A gloomy prognosis in the *Village Voice* feared she might die an unknown genius. However, by 1989, after several deserved but unsuccessful nominations she finally won a Grammy for *Look What I Got* (†Verve [A] 835661–2), recorded in 1988 for the reconstituted Verve label. With it her career took off. Betty Carter, so often overlooked in favour of more easily acceptable offerings of lesser jazz vocalists was, after 40 years in the business, in danger of becoming an overnight success.

Although only 12 years separated Miss Carter from Ella Fitzgerald and only five from Sarah Vaughan, [109] she was the logical extension of Miss Fitzgerald's stand-alone scat extemporizations and Miss Vaughan's ability to harness technique to take you to places of which a song's composer never dreamed. 'In the fifties when I was brought up, we were brought up to be different,' she once explained. 'I could not be an Ella Fitzgerald or a Sarah Vaughan and make it.' [110] As a result she developed a style quite unlike any singer in jazz. Imposing herself on her material in a way that no other singer, with the honourable exception of Leo Watson, had managed, her unique process of creative distortion refracted the melodic contours of a song like images glimpsed in a hall of mirrors. She seldom, if ever, sang the melody as written: 'The young kids I sing for have never heard the songs I sing, so the melody means nothing and the older ones know the melody and can hum it without my help.' [111] She created an aural drama that in live performance was underlined by her intensely personal choreography. As Will Friedwald pointed out, she 'combines composition (music and lyrics), arrangement, performance and improvisation into a single integrated statement . . . she works them into something more than a style, more than an approach or a point of view, but an entire musical universe.' [112]

Miss Carter's 'musical universe' proved the dramatic validity of the jazz singer's art. Yet for years jazz criticism has been hamstrung by its ambivalence to jazz singing. Respected critics such as Benny Green, Joachim Berendt and Leon Ostransky have all gone into print expressing great reservations about whether there can be such a thing as a 'jazz' singer, [113] simply because the vocal performance implies adherence to melody and lyric in a way that an instrumental solo does not. This dilemma was rationalized within conveniently partisan parameters of the 'voice as instrument' notion, a wholly inadequate aesthetic that suggests the same criteria used to judge an instrumental performance should be applied to the jazz vocal. Such limited terms of reference – it is like comparing apples with oranges – not only implies a corollary value judgement that the so-called 'jazz vocal' did not deserve to be evaluated on its own merits, but denied the fact that it was underpinned by a quite specific aesthetic of its own. Yet as Miss Carter approached the 1980s it was plain to those who would listen that she had become a walking definition of what 'jazz singing' meant. Soaring beyond the 'voice as instrument' argument that has for so long polarized jazz commentary, Alec Wilder's erudite summation of Cole Porter seemed to sum up her art perfectly, that 'of bringing a certain theatrical elegance, as well as interest and sophistication, wit and musical complexity to the popular song form'. [114] It also appeared as a good a working definition of a jazz singer as any.

Although Miss Carter first recorded under her own name in 1955 – *Social Call* (†CBS Special Products [A] A36425) – and intermittently thereafter, it was not until she signed with Roulette in the late 1960s that there was clear evidence that her style had fully coalesced. On albums such as *Finally* (†Roulette [A] CDP7953332) and *Round Midnight* (†Roulette [A] CDP7959992), both recorded live at Judson Hall in December 1969, or *Now It's My Turn* (Roulette [A] SR-5005) from 1976, all the central elements of her style were present. These included a preference for excruciatingly slow tempos contrasted with a dramatic ability to handle the fastest tempos of jazz, a highly individual vein of scat, her very personal use of melismata and her dramatic recasting of the song both rhythmically (often changing metre) and melodically. *The Audience with . . .* comes from 1979, after Roulette went the way of so many independent labels, and was originally released on her own Bet-

Car label as a double-album set (Bet-Car [A] MK1003). Although it was recorded in concert, the sound quality is excellent. With Miss Carter, a live album brought with it the almost certain guarantee of a vintage performance; in front of an audience she gave her all. 'An audience makes me think, makes me reach for things I'd never try in a recording studio,' she asserted. [115]

The centrepiece of the album is *Sounds*, a *tour de force* of scat, shifting tempos and metres that lasts 25 minutes 20 seconds. Throughout, she holds centre stage, there being no solos by her trio; she is out on the high wire. The piece opens with a piano *ostinato* which, literally, 'vamps 'til ready'. Miss Carter enters with a little scat, but the theme actually begins as she sings *Sounds* and the song's construction emerges as:

(vamp till ready) + A (28 bars) + B (10 bars) + A + B +
(open, watch cues)

After the theme statement, the form is very loosely constructed, responding to her cues, where on her direction she introduces the B section and the lyrics 'Movin' on', signalling she is moving on to another change of mood. This high-risk strategy of spontaneously reordering a piece during performance had its roots in the playing of Ahmad Jamal (**335**), who spliced interludes into songs and moved sections around as he heard them on the spot, bringing a revolutionary spontaneity to group playing.

Each new episode of *Sounds* reveals a different rhythmic climate, Miss Carter singing in four over the rhythm section's three, the rhythm section powering ahead at a stunningly fast tempo while she holds back, singing in half tempo, swinging in straight-ahead four, but throughout, each 'free-form' section deliberately contrasts the one before. The cohesion Hicks, Lundy and Washington achieve during such mesmerizing tempo changes is one of the delights of the album. Her scat is entirely her own, marked by great melodic freedom, rather like scatter-brained arabesques, using an astonishing variety of phonemes (i.e. vocal sounds) to maintain the forward momentum (swing) of her improvisations that on close study reveal melodic, rhythmic and timbral ideas of great cohesion and wit.

Miss Carter owes much to the quirky, idiosyncratic tonal distortions of Sarah Vaughan but embraces the whole panoply of phonemes from plosives through to frictives, nasals and glides articulated in every possible way. Yet she is not about trying to jam the entire alphabet into each passing measure; her spirit is free-floating, associating snippets of melody with pitch-slides, bends (which, interestingly, affect her rhythmic construction), weaving a wide range of vocal timbres that dramatically interacts with her trio. Everything she does remains firmly related to the basic pulse, even though she may have progressed to an entirely different metre to that of her rhythm-section colleagues; indeed in one section of the song Miss Carter, the piano, the bass and the drums are each playing in a different metre!

I think I got it now is performed at a profoundly slow pulse, [116] one of her specialities. While it is tempting for the lay listener to imagine that the fastest tempos provide one of the greatest challenges in jazz, it is in fact the reverse. Few musicians allow themselves such close public scrutiny at slow tempos as Miss Carter does. Here, and on *Everything I have is yours*, *Can't we talk it over?*, *Either it's love or it isn't*, *Spring can really hang you up the most* and *So* the tempo moves at such a glacier pace that any weakness in intonation, time and technique would be immediately and ruthlessly exposed. Most musicians break for the sanctuary of double time as quickly as they can; but she constantly courted disaster, moving through the emotional mood of a ballad as if in a dream, stalking the stage and abruptly freezing in some strange choreographed pose before moving on, the tempo always secure, her intonation inch-perfect. It is these challenging tensions she imposed on herself that give her performances such a sense of danger and drama.

In contrast is her imaginative treatment of the *Trolley song* with its tempo changes and changes of metre, one of the more subtle ingredients that Betty Carter the arranger – an art she learned under the saxophonist Bobby Plater's wing while a member of the Lionel Hampton band between 1948–51 – imposes on her material. After a hurtling introduction, she abruptly halves the tempo at the middle eight with a heavily ironic, and comic, 'Clang, clang went the trolley' that bears no relation to the song as written; indeed, the whole number is sung ignoring the songwriter's intentions, completely customizing it to suit the idiosyncracies of her style; not for nothing was a 1992 release called *It's Not About the Melody* (†Verve [A] 513 870). Indeed, *I could write a book*, a medium-tempo swinger, is preceded by the improvised section of scat before a highly refracted statement of the lyrics.

Miss Carter's organization of her material is consistently impressive and demanded immaculately disciplined sidemen to cope with the challenging musical environment in which she operated. Although Art Blakey has been given much praise for providing a forum for promising young musicians to reach artistic maturity, she too deserves equal praise for the important role she has played in presenting pianists such as John Hicks, Onajae Alan Gumbs, Mulgrew Miller, Stephen Scott and Cyrus Chestnut, as well as hosts of bassists and drummers, not least Kenny Washington, Winard Harper and Lewis Nash. *Deep night*, a Rudy Vallee number (!), contrasts ¾ and 4/4 and a sudden and unexpected double-tempo solo from Hicks, who also contributes fine solos on *So* and *Tight*, which, as the latter implies, demands the strictest of playing from the trio as a unit.

Perhaps the finest example of group interplay between Miss Carter and her trio is the stunning *My favourite things*. Like *Movin' on*, this is an integrated group performance, albeit with her at the helm. She and Hicks had a great affinity and mutual respect for each other's work, and the freedom he finds within the form lifts this into a performance that can be returned to and savoured time and again, each fresh listening revealing a little more inner detail and nuance in Lundy's bassline, Washington's drumming or Hick's comping. His accompaniment blossoms into a counterline to her singing – who can say which of the two lines predominates? This is a performance which soars above limiting arguments about the validity of jazz singing or the criteria whereby it is judged. It is quite simply jazz of the highest order and that is enough. To say that this is one of the finest jazz *vocal* performances on record is limiting because it is among the great contemporary albums of jazz. S.N.

Cassandra Wilson

333 **Songbook**
†JMT (G) 514026–2

Wilson (vcl); Graham Haynes (tpt); Rod Williams (p); Kenneth Davis (bs); Marc Johnson (d). New York City, May 1987.
Let's face the music and dance

Wilson (vcl); Mulgrew Miller (p). New York City, February 1987.
Sweet Lorraine

Wilson (vcl); Grachan Moncur III (tbn); Jean-Paul Bourelly (g); Lonnie Plaxico (bs); Marc Johnson (d). New York City, December 1985.
Blue in green

Wilson (vcl); James Weidman (p); Kevin Bruce Harris (bs). New York City, August 1991.
Baubles, bangles and beads

Wilson (vcl); Mulgrew Miller (p); Lonnie Plaxico (bs); Terri Lyne Carrington (d). New York City, February 1988.
I'm old-fashioned · Autumn nocturne

Wilson (vcl); Rod Williams (p); Lonnie Plaxico (bs); Marc Johnson (d). New York City, July 1989.
Whirlwind soldier

Wilson (vcl); Steve Coleman (alt); Geri Allen (synth); Kelvyn Bell (g); Kevin Bruce Harris (bs); Marvin 'Smitty' Smith (d). New York City, January 1986.
Little one, I'll miss you

Wilson (vcl); Rod Williams (p); Reggie Washington (bs); Marc Johnson (d). New York City, November 1990.
Body and soul

Wilson (vcl); Graham Haynes (tpt); Steve Coleman (alt); Geri Allen (p); Lonnie Plaxico (bs); Marc Johnson (d). New York City, March 1985.
No good-time fairies

Throughout the pluralistic 1980s into the 1990s, it is fair to say that Cassandra Wilson struggled to define her identity as a jazz singer. Unlike so many of her generation, she was not content to settle for neoclassic recapitulation, despite an impressive and critically acclaimed album of standards in 1988, *Blue Skies* (†JMT [G] 834419–2). Such was the album's impact that both the public and the critics were united in the belief that here was the continuation of a line of jazz singers that could be traced back to Billie Holiday. With a voice whose maturity belied her youth, a sure grip of the tradition and an ability to inhabit the great standards as if they were her own, Miss Wilson seemed assured of her future. But while acknowledging her debt to her predecessors, she refused to settle for what she saw as easy artistic compromise by remaining with the standards repertoire. Instead, her stated aim was to establish her own identity and move the music forward on her own terms instead of remaining rooted in the past. 'I think what we have to do is learn what we can from the masters,' she asserted in 1992. 'Copying what they do we're not really doing justice to the tradition and I think it's a kind of insult, actually. I think the whole point is to establish some kind of identity and help propel the music forward and make it speak of our needs today. When you do standards people expect you to do them *ad infinitum* and I can't do that. Things change, the music changes!' [117]

As if to underline her point, she followed *Blue Skies* with *Jumpworld* (†JMT [G] 834434–2), which was, in her own words, 'a radical departure'; an avant-funk album laced in equal parts with sci-fi conceptualizing and trenchant social commentary, it owed much to the inspiration of Steve Coleman's M-Base vamp music and even flirted with hip-hop. This shift between her own often awkward music and her startlingly beguiling way with the great American popular song confused and confounded her audiences, creating a critical ambivalence to her work that was not wholly reconciled until the mid-1990s. [118] Yet in retrospect it was hardly surprising that her creative impulses drove her beyond the sanctuary of standards repertoire and the comfortably accessible neoconservative mainstream which became so fashionable in the 1980s and early 1990s. Born in Jackson, Mississippi, she sat in with Ellis Marsalis and Earl Turbitson in New Orleans before moving to New York City, where she decided to pursue singing full time. Debuting at the Galleon in 1981 and working other uptown clubs such as Smalls and Carl's on the Corner, she was heavily into standards when she gravitated into the orbit of Steve Coleman, who, along with Greg Osby, Jean-Paul Bourelly, Graham Haynes, Marvin 'Smitty' Smith, Lonnie Plaxico and Geri Allen, was attempting to develop a modern lingua franca for jazz.

Inspired by the music of James Brown, they called their music M-Base, and this rhythmically complex, funk-based hybrid was first revealed on 1985's *Motherland Pulse* (†JMT [G] 834401–2) under Coleman's name with a band he called Five Elements. On it, Miss Wilson made a cameo appearance that impressed the producer Stefan Winter, who encouraged her to make a recording in her own right. In early 1986 she recorded *Point of View* (†JMT [G] 834404–2), which was followed by *Days Aweigh* (†JMT [G] 834412–2) in 1987, an album that clearly reflected the M-Base conception. A short period with the acclaimed free-jazz group Air followed, with Henry Threadgill warmly praising her ability, although their relationship was soon to dissolve into acrimony over the ownership of a song. Nevertheless, she became impressed with the cross-pollination of ideas that was happening in New York City at this time between the AACM and BAG collectives. 'They were the precursors of M-Base, a very similar philosophy, the philosophy of inclusion,' she explained. 'Whatever it is that's a part of your experience in music, incorporate it in your thinking. The significance is that it makes the music much broader.' [119]

This became M-Base thinking and underwrote her own musical philosophy. For a generation of young jazz musicians who had grown up listening to the Beatles, Tamla-Motown, disco and hip-hop, these musical experiences provided new elements to weave into their music. A brief return to standards working with Jim DeAngelis and Tony Sigma prompted Winter to suggest that she do a whole album devoted to 'where she came from', an album of standards. With the success of *Blue Skies*, she finally made the impact on both critics and public that her M-Base-inspired work had conspicuously failed to do. While on the one hand Miss Wilson's association with Coleman gave her a sense of artistic direction, on the other a question posed by Winter was whether that direction made the most of her undeniable talent. 'After the success of *Blue Skies*,' he recalled in 1992, 'that was the turning point in my eyes. After that it was nearly impossible to work with Cassandra, there was no communication . . . I think very often she got bad advice, what she should do and who she should work with.' [120]

The final three albums for JMT were fulfilled with no input from Winter, including *Live* (†JMT [G] 849149–2) from April 1991, which neither producer nor artist felt was a good representation of her talent. However, her penultimate album for Winter, *She Who Weeps* (†JMT [G] 834443–2), shed the arty self-consciousness of her more rhythmically oriented albums, often with clattering drum machines and chattering guitars, to create her best-focused album since *Blue Skies*. Equally, her final JMT album, *After the Beginning Again* (†JMT [G] 514001–2) and the 1992 album for the Japanese DIW label, *Dance to the Drums Again* (†DIW [J] 863), revealed a surer grip on her own original material, among which, incidentally, she always mixed at least one or two standards. Signing with the reconstituted Blue Note label at the end of 1992, *Blue Light Till Dawn* (†Blue Note [A] CDP07777) saw a change of backdrop with a predominance of acoustic instruments and a willingness to reinvent the tradition, taking two Robert Johnson tunes and adapting them impressively to the unusual instrumental combination she used.

Yet while each of her albums contained performances that by any standards were impressive, the feeling persisted of unevenness of artistic aspiration; even on her otherwise exemplary *Blue Skies* there are one or two moments that betray stylistic deference to her favourite singers (notably Betty Carter) and a slight immaturity in balancing a swing feel at the expense of meaning. However, in 1995 the producer Stefan Winter compiled this thoughtful collection of her work from his label, often using alternative takes that did not appear on the original albums. Whatever problems he experienced on a personal basis never diminished his admiration of her talent, and *Songbook* reflects this, providing a balanced retrospective which explores how he, and indeed many others who admired her abilities, perceived the strengths of her unique style, that part of her which never turned her back on the standards repertoire. For Miss Wilson, however, standards were but one aspect of her overall musical personality in which the composition and performance of her own songs assumed central significance. Winter reflects this in his selections for *Songbook*, but also includes some of her better work from within the M-Base sphere of influence.

Let's face the music is an impressive post-bop performance that features Haynes on trumpet as much as Wilson. The son of Roy, one of the great drummers in jazz, he has an off-centre lyricism and sets up a compelling duality between the improvised (his solos) and the written, and Miss Wilson's vocals. Together they create a remarkably mature performance supported by a well-integrated group and succeed in revitalizing a well-known standard with clever tempo and metre changes; the highly original introduction, for example, is extremely well executed. Miss Wilson herself has an intriguing voice; a contralto that often mesmerizingly dips into the domain of a tenor and even that of a baritone, using full chest tones which give vowels and consonants a special resonance. Often, she uses the technique of a sustained tone to begin a chorus, varying her dynamic approach to give certain words emphasis and extra meaning.

Sweet Lorraine is a duet with the pianist Mulgrew Miller and is approached with greater gravitas than the take issued on *Blue Skies*. In fact, both takes reveal a security of pitch and tempo that even the most experienced singers can fail to achieve using just piano accompaniment. *Blue in green*, the ten-bar theme from *Kind of Blue* (**393**), uses contrasting metres in Miss Wilson's initial exposition (an *alla breve* bass against a distinct four by the drums) and opens into the mellow refinement of Moncur's trombone, which, after his promising Blue Note work (**395**), unaccountably became a rarity in jazz. Although not primarily a scat singer, Miss Wilson re-enters after the solos with great poise, constructing her improvisation favouring voiced consonants that owed much to Betty Carter. She is able to handle the slow tempo of the song with great aplomb, even implying a change of metre in her line, from a four feel to a three near the end that leads into a well-executed *rubato* finish. *Baubles,* *bangles and beads* is approached from the perspective of a very slow ballad and adds an entirely new dimension to the song. This is a technique Billie Holiday occasionally used, one adding surprising depth to the lyrics. Here, Miss Wilson is intensely introspective, singing at a snail's pace with a maturity that is impressive for her age. With the skeletal duo accompaniment from Weidman's piano and Harris on bass, she is assured and confident at a tempo that provides one of jazz's great challenges as much for singers as instrumentalists.

A more traditional approach to the standards repertoire is announced by Carrington's brushwork to introduce *I'm old-fashioned*, with Miller cunningly using the 'Coltrane substitutions' at several points to add a little harmonic piquancy. *Whirlwind soldier* is one of Miss Wilson's original compositions, this one taken from *Jumpworld.* In contrast to the standards repertoire, the tune reflects contemporary pop's emphasis on lyric content rather than harmonic sophistication. This leaves her somewhat stranded with the singer's storytelling privilege which alone is not sufficient to compel our attention; the featureless melody serves to dissipate the impact of the lyrics. *Little one, I'll miss you* is in contrast a resourceful presentation of the Bunky Green original that illustrates the M-Base philosophy of 'inclusion'; here the piece is performed over a soft reggae beat, a rhythm that has curiously not been exploited more in jazz – supplied by Steve Coleman's Five Elements – and is taken from the album *On the Edge of Tomorrow* (†JMT [G] 834405–2). In this, perhaps the most successful track on the album, Miss Wilson is fed gentle counterpoint by a round-robin between Coleman's alto and Allen's synthesizer that enhances the singer's brooding calm. From another Coleman album, this time *Motherland Pulse*, his debut on the JMT label – *No good-time fairies* was the song that originally led to Miss Wilson's recording contract with Winter. An acoustic track that also gives prominence to Haynes on trumpet, it has a melody line, like that of *Whirlwind soldier*, that fails to compel. In a metre of six, the unusual rhythmic gait is contrasted by a fast-moving lyric line, but the static harmonies of the song leave the singer with much to do to create interest, something she does not entirely succeed in doing.

Miss Wilson's imaginative and haunting recasting of *Body and soul* begins with sustained tones over a piano vamp. The singer often favoured beginning a new chorus in this way and here it is incorporated as a specific feature of her introduction. She begins the exposition of the melody using the dark-brown grain in her voice which plunges into her tenor range, and although her intonation is for a fraction suspect it does not detract from her imaginative rearrangement of a tune that throughout subtly contrasts tempo and metre effectively. Equally, her treatment of *Autumn nocturne*, another alternative take from *Blue Skies*, is performed with such poise and assurance that it is impossible not to conclude that she is the most important jazz singer to have emerged in a generation. If her own originals, particularly in her earlier albums, lacked the substance of the standard repertoire, then all the while there has been a sense of an artist moving forward, of developing an individual style and finding herself. This balancing act, of reconciling tradition with her own contemporary ideas, meant she took a number of artistic left turns as her career unfolded; but if these were shown up in high relief it was because so many musicians of her generation were absorbed with virtuosic recapitulation. In contrast, she consistently worked towards a broader vision of jazz than that of the strait-laced neoclassicists, exploring her expressive power and imaginative verve in ensembles that might have offended the neoclassicists' purism, but at least was a sincere attempt to move the music on from the stasis that was beginning to grip the jazz mainstream.

S.N.

3

Consolidations and Developments

Bop Redivivus

Amid the variety of jazz styles outlined in the two preceding chapters, bop persisted and it now did so almost exclusively as a small-combo mode of expression.

Miles Davis

334a **Workin' with the Miles Davis Quintet**
†Original Jazz Classics (A) OJCCD391–2, *Prestige 7166, *Prestige PR24034

Davis (tpt); John Coltrane (ten); Red Garland (p); Paul Chambers (bs); Philly Joe Jones (d). Hackensack, N. J., 11 May and 26 October 1956.
It never entered my mind · *Four* · *In your own sweet way* · *The theme* (2 versions) · *Trane's blues* · *Ahmad's blues* · *Half Nelson*

334b **Steamin' with the Miles Davis Quintet**
†Original Jazz Classics (A) OJCCD391–2, *Prestige 7200, *Prestige PR24034

Same personnel, location and dates.
Surrey with the fringe on top · *Salt peanuts* · *Something I dreamed last night* · *Diane* · *Well, you needn't* · *When I fall in love*

334c **Relaxin' with the Miles Davis Quintet**
†Original Jazz Classics (A) OJCD190–2, *Prestige 7129, *Prestige PR24001

Same personnel, location and dates.
If I were a bell · *You're my everything* · *I could write a book* · *Oleo* · *It could happen to you* · *Woody 'n you*

334d Cookin' with the Miles Davis Quintet

†Original Jazz Classics (A) OJCCD128–2, *Prestige 7094, *Prestige PR24001

Same personnel, location and dates.
My funny Valentine · *Blues by five* · *Airegin* · *Tune up/When lights are low*

Contractual obligations provided Bob Weinstock's Prestige label with more than enough material for four albums when Davis decided to sever his connections and move to Columbia. 'The real money was in getting to the mainstream of America, and Columbia Records served the mainstream of this country,' said Davis. [1] In fact, he had begun recording for Columbia the previous year, which precipitated this remarkable windfall for Prestige when he pragmatically insisted on disposing of his outstanding commitments to the small independent in two marathon sessions before moving on. The results were in essence a documentation of the band's repertoire that it played nightly on the bandstand. There were no second takes, with the exception of *The theme* (two versions), which was literally a postscript to the May session, as if signing off as they would in live performance, after completing 14 masters in the space of a Friday afternoon and evening.

At the time Davis was widely acknowledged to be leading the hottest band in jazz and was attracting attention everywhere he performed. The group had come together in Baltimore in 1955, shortly after Charlie Parker's death, and many looked to it as the standard-bearer for the future. It was here Davis shaped his musical outlook for at least the next ten years; the lonely, plaintive harmon-muted trumpet on ballads contrasted with fast, aggressive swingers and throughout a gradual movement towards looser harmonic frameworks, already quite subtly at work in Garland's work but yet to take the leap forward it did when Bill Evans took over the piano chair in 1958.

When Garland joined Davis in 1955, he began omitting the root of the chord from the bottom of some of the voicings he used to accompany soloists, [2] a device particularly effective on dominant seventh chords. This was often employed by the pianist Ahmad Jamal, whose playing had an enormous influence on Davis, [3] who in turn urged Garland to incorporate many of the Chicago pianist's methods. Consequently, Garland started playing either the third of the chord at the bottom or sometimes the (flat) seventh, and voiced his chords nearer the middle or upper portion of the keyboard. [4] This gave a lighter feeling to his accompaniment as well as a feeling of harmonic ambiguity which suited Davis's melodic, or horizontal, style of improvising. [5] Paradoxically, this also suited Coltrane's vertical approach to improvising, presenting him with a lot of options for his chordally based style, since, for example, a rootless dominant seventh chord can sound like two chords at the same time in certain circumstances, and Coltrane took advantage of this.

A good instance of Garland's use of rootless chords can be heard in *Blues by five* (**334d**), which also provides an excellent curtain-raiser to these sessions, revealing the individual characteristics of the very different styles that made up the quintet. Note that the soloists rest on the final bar of each chorus to highlight the blues form; Coltrane, still a year away from his September 1957 *Blue Train* (†Blue Note [E] CDP746095–2) and three from April 1959's *Giant Steps* (**421**), was explosive, jagged and a little raw. Together with the equally explosive Jones on drums, the soloists consistently raised the temperature of the creative moment with their great energy and unpredictability. Chambers, with impeccable time and a huge tone, deserves credit as much for keeping the band on course as for allowing Jones the licence to punctuate his time-keeping with outrageous accents and syncopations. And in Garland, Davis had a pianist whose workmanlike swing was sufficiently uncontroversial not to clash with his more exuberant rhythm-section mates, yet capable of strong, individual solos in his own right. Together with Davis, whose playing at the time walked the boundary between introversion on slower numbers (*I dreamed last night*, *When I fall in love*) and suppressed extroversion at faster tempos (*Tune up*, *Woody 'n you*), the success of the quintet lay in the collective force of their individual musical personalities.

Until 1958, Davis used mainly blues, standards and songs by bop-oriented writers. Consequently much of what he did was in either the 12-bar or 32-bar AABA format, as these sessions demonstrate. Three numbers came from the repertoire of Ahmad Jamal, including *Surrey with the fringe on top*, *It could happen to you* and the trio version of *Ahmad's blues*. Jamal's influence was not confined to repertoire, however. It hovered over the sessions in a variety of ways, such as the distinct Jamalesque hues Garland employs on *It never entered my mind* after Davis's harmon-muted melody statement. Equally, Davis's frequent use of a two-beat style on numbers like *When lights are low* and *It could happen to you*, alternating a puckish cut-time feel with an even four, ran so counter to the prevailing hard-bop methodology that it is impossible not to think it was inspired by Jamal's approach. [6] However, Davis did not follow Jamal's version of *When lights are low*, either in 1953 when he first recorded it or for these sessions, since he dispenses with the middle eight as written, based on a cycle of fifths, and simply transposed the chords of the A section up a fourth – just like the middle eight of the composition *What's new?* And finally, Davis copies Jamal's use of vamps on *If I were a bell*, a 32-bar ABAC composition, by using a four-bar tag to end each solo that could be repeated at the improviser's discretion. Davis also supplies his own eight-bar introduction with the pianist imitating a bell, playing chimelike chords meant to represent 'ding-dong-ding-dong'.

Davis's first-choice tenor saxophonist for his group had been Sonny Rollins, whose compositions *Oleo* and *Airegin* were recorded by them both in 1954, when Davis began the first of many overtures to get Rollins to join his band. *Oleo*, a 32-bar AABA *I got rhythm* contrafact, here shows Davis, occasionally liable to fluff notes even on ballads, holding up to the brisk tempo with technical aplomb. He varies the texture of the ensemble through the simple but effective juxtaposition of instrumental combinations. Trumpet and tenor do not play the theme together as the hard-bop rule book demanded; instead Davis plays the first A section unaccompanied using his signature harmon mute (with the shank removed), the second against Chambers's walking bass, the release with full rhythm, while Coltrane states the final A section against the bass. Davis takes two choruses in the middle register of the trumpet, the A sections with a walking bass only, the release with full rhythm. Coltrane follows this scheme for his first chorus but then the full rhythm section explodes around him for the remainder of his solo, contrasting the intimacy of Davis's solo with his lusty power drive. Red Garland then provides an interesting touch with his single-note solo, which is taken, unusually, in the lower register of the piano, first with bass and then with bass and drums. Davis returns, again juxtaposing rhythm section combinations behind him, and when the theme is finally recapitulated, Davis still succeeds in defying our anticipation by playing it in unison with the piano, not the tenor. Only at the end does he finally resolve our now heightened expectation of an orthodox trumpet/tenor statement when he is briefly joined by Coltrane for a conventional recapitulation of the theme. Taken together, the unexpected instrumental combinations used to present the theme, together with a variety of shifting textures behind the solos, reveal a performance of unexpected contrast that succeeds in challenging our expectations of the typical tone colours we might expect from the instrumentation of the quintet. While our focus of interest is rightly on the soloists, the unexpected shifts in ensemble textures represents a subtle device to attract and compel our attention to the performance as a whole.

Coltrane was one of many saxophonists during the 1950s who cited the influence of Sonny Stitt on their playing. Stitt's style on tenor was both thrusting and authoritative, and this was certainly a characteristic of Coltrane's playing. However, Stitt's influence was more specific than the emotional force he brought to his improvisations. His approach to melodic organization through the use of melodic patterns [7] had an important bearing on the way Coltrane shaped his style. [8] It would progress in leaps and bounds over the next three years, but as these four albums reveal, his playing had not yet matured and could be inconsistent. However, those strangely puritan aesthetics of his later work were beginning to emerge, manifested by a combination of austerity (hard tone) and hard work (the desire to play every note of every chord). On some numbers he was full of confidence, as in his powerful *Surrey with the fringe on top* solo – despite Davis's and Garland's differing interpretations of how the melody should be played – while on others he could be tentative. A battle to end drug addiction and a period of consolidation with Thelonious Monk (**292**) were ahead of him, yet by the time of his return to Davis in 1958 he would be standing on the threshold of greatness.

Coltrane was for a while a member of the band led by Eddie 'Cleanhead' Vinson, the alto saxophonist and singer who composed *Tune up* and *Four* previously recorded by Davis in 1953 and 1954 respectively. *Four*, a 16-bar theme usually played twice, as it is here, so that it becomes, in effect, a 32-bar AA[1] song with no release, became closely associated with Davis. He recorded it again in 1958 for a noncommercial label and in 1964 for Columbia and has often been given composer credit; when Anita O'Day performed the number at the 1958 Newport Jazz Festival, for example, she announced the number as coming 'from the Miles Davis school of thought'. In fact Vinson was quite probably the composer of *The theme* as well, and all three numbers figured prominently in Davis's quintet performances during this period. *Four* has a particularly engaging theme and is interpreted freely by Davis and Coltrane. Davis's solo that follows is among his best constructed from this four-album series; developing melodic fragments, paraphrasing the theme, reaching for a climax with a brief foray into the high register, using smears and half-valve effects to bring tonal variety to his line and referring back to ideas he developed on his 1954 recording of the number. It is neatly balanced by a thoughtful contribution from Coltrane, one of the few occasions where his solo compliments rather than contrasts with the trumpeter.

Coltrane's solos often felt like a jolt of electricity following Davis's carefully manufactured epigrams. But with his ballad performances Davis clearly sought to create a mood using a consistent emotional tone with subtle rhythmic variety which he did not want broken by the saxophonist's vigorous swathes of sound. Coltrane sat out during the trumpeter's intimate harmon-muted ruminations on *When I fall in love*, *Something I dreamed of last night*, *It never entered my mind* and *My funny Valentine.* However, Davis was wise enough to realize that even in ballads, the occasional use of contrast could be both dramatic and effective, and *In your own sweet way* and *You're my everything* have Coltrane's sudden entry keeping the audience awake while neatly avoiding a similarity of concept throughout all Davis's pulseless ballads. That ballads were now becoming an important element in Davis's performances is demonstrated by his affection for *My funny Valentine*, the first of three recordings he made of the tune. Here he makes remarkable use of silence (second entry) and again uses the device of rising to a high note from his normal area of operations in his bruised but romantic middle register to create drama (as he had in his otherwise middle-register *Four* solo), something that was retained in subsequent versions of the tune.

Throughout these albums the rhythm section is a model of consistency; never less than absorbing, they are frequently exciting. Garland's comping is a model of tasteful support, gently ushering the soloists with poise and no little elegance. Chambers, who would become Davis's longest-serving sideman, was just 21 at the time of these recordings and plays with security and ease that belie his youth. Together with Jones, one of the great drummers in jazz, they are the main reason why these performances still sound so fresh and exciting today. Jones had an expansive style, not simply playing time but contributing a crisp and stimulating rhythmic commentary behind the soloists and ensembles, such as his high-density fills at cadence points and turnbacks. On *Airegin*, for example, his strong percussive support recalls Davis's 1953 sides with Blakey for the Blue Note label.

With the perspective afforded by hindsight, these recordings reveal a slight shift of emphasis to simpler chord structures as a basis for improvisation. While several songs here actually came from the bop era and others might be described as an extension of the bop era, with changes moving at one or two every bar, Davis was also bringing in new material with relatively uncomplicated changes, such as *If I were a bell*, *Bye bye blackbird*, *Diane* and *Surrey with a fringe on top*. And while tunes like the *I got rhythm* contrafacts *Oleo* and *Salt Peanuts* and other up-tempo numbers such as *Woody 'n you* and *Tune up* prompted him to play fast strings of notes in the bop manner, on Monk's bright AABA 32-bar *Well, you needn't* he solos with spare 'storytelling' eloquence that would eventually dominate his style and, as he had done on *When lights are low*, replaces the middle eight with one of his own. Equally, his choice of ballads favoured relatively uncomplicated changes where he was developing a tender, spare approach to melodic construction. This, together with the harmonic ambiguity that was beginning to creep in with Garland's occasional use of rootless voicings and polytonality, [9] was already the stage for the next sea change in his career. Within two years he would say: 'I think the movement in jazz is beginning away from the conventional string of chords and a return to emphasis on melodic rather than harmonic variation. There will be fewer chords but infinite possibilities as to what to do with them. It becomes a challenge to see how melodically inventive you are.' [10] S.N.

Ahmad Jamal

335 Ahmad's Blues

†Chess GRP18032, *Argo LP636, *Argo LP2–638

Jamal (p); Israel Crosby (bs); Vernel Fournier (d). Spotlite Club, Washington, D.C., 6 September 1958.

Ahmad's blues · It could happen to you · I wish I knew · Autumn leaves · Stompin' at the Savoy · Cheek to cheek · The girl next door · Secret love · Squatty Roo · Taboo · Autumn in New York · A girl in calico · That's all · Should I? · Seleritus · Let's fall in love

One of the problems that face jazz musicians who enjoy any degree of popularity is that they tend to be overrated at the time and underrated thereafter. Such was the fate of Ahmad Jamal. He is not alone: Benny Goodman, Dave Brubeck and Wynton Marsalis, for example, have all felt the force of the critical backlash that seems to follow any artist whose appeal extends beyond the true believers. However, Jamal's case was slightly different. When many critics dismissed his work as 'cocktail piano' after *Poinciana* rode the best-selling charts in 1958, his response, after the death of Crosby in 1962, was a series of albums that, with just one or two exceptions, appeared to prove his critics right. It was not until *Live in Cannes* (†Jazz World [Por] JWD 102–214) with Gary Burton from 1981 that he began seriously to address what had effectively been a creative void of some 20 years.

However, it is only with the perspective offered by the Okeh/Epic sides from 1951–5 and a series of albums for the Chicago-based Chess label, beginning with *The Chamber Music of the New Jazz* (Cadet LPS602) from 1955 and ending with *Ahmad Jamal at the Blackhawk* (Chess LP703) from 1961, that Jamal's talent comes into focus. Among the Okeh sides was a striking version of *Billy Boy* that caused a stir within musicians' circles. Several pianists lifted entire passages when they came to record the tune, not least Oscar Peterson and Red Garland. The latter's version appeared on the 1958 Miles Davis album *Milestones*, but this was only one of several tunes that Davis took from Jamal's repertoire, including *Old devil moon*, *Ahmad's blues*, *Will you still be mine?*, *Surrey with the fringe on top*, *Girl in calico*, *Green Dolphin Street*, *New rhumba*, *All of you*, *Autumn leaves* and *Love for sale*.

Jamal's influence on Davis's 1950s quintet and sextet (**334a/b**) was considerable; 'I live until he makes another record,' Davis once said. [11] He often took members of his band along to listen to Jamal, whose influence was all too clear on *The Musings of Miles* (Original Jazz Classics [A] OJC004) from 1955. However, though Davis's debt to Jamal's style cannot be precisely calculated, it certainly went deeper than song titles. The rhythmic lightness and melodic understatement of Jamal's trio were something he urged his own rhythm section to listen for, particularly Garland. But it was not only Garland whom Davis urged to listen to Jamal. Bill Evans, on leaving Davis, had clearly listened hard to Jamal, and his trio with Scott LaFaro and Paul Motion (**372**) was quite different from his previous work, with the dominance of the piano reduced, like Jamal's trio, to allow for a more discursive relationship between piano, bass and drums. Evans too was not beyond borrowing numbers from Jamal's repertoire, not least *The girl next door* which appears on this album.

Jamal's use of silence was particularly arresting, often letting several beats pass without playing, a high-risk technique that few improvisers used and that clearly impressed Davis. Examples here include *Stompin' at the Savoy*, where Crosby alternates between carrying the melody, when Jamal lays out, and his traditional time-keeping role, and the highly sprung yet effortless swing of *Cheek to cheek*, illustrating how Jamal would abruptly lay out, leaving the missing fragments of melody to be 'played' in the listener's subconscious. This less-is-more aesthetic which underwrote Jamal's approach to improvisation, together with his somewhat impressionistic device of tossing phrases, melodic fragments and even quotations against a steadily moving harmonic canvas, created an approach that was quite unique in jazz of the 1950s and early 1960s.

A feature of Jamal's trio was their cohesiveness, which depended on a high level of interdependence on each other's finely balanced role within the ensemble. Often Jamal would cede much space to Crosby and Fournier, who would respond with playing of great clarity and economy. On the opening of *Ahmad's blues*, for example, Fournier liberates himself from the metronomic rigidity of the hi-hat cymbal afterbeat by using just brushes and snare while Crosby marks the first beat of the bar to create a tautness that is only resolved by the succeeding passage in an even four. Indeed one of the highlights of the album is the resourcefulness of Crosby and Fournier in generating maximum swing through maximum economy; each musician is aware of precisely what was needed from moment to moment. Together they represented the epitome of high-intensity swing at low-intensity volume. 'Anybody can play loudly,' Jamal once asserted. 'It is much more difficult to play softly while swinging at that same level of intensity you can get playing *fortissimo*'. [12] The trio as a whole had a remarkably wide range of dynamic control and there is a significant difference between loud and soft that added both variety and tension to their playing: *Stompin' at the Savoy*, with its treble forte chords contrasted by sotto voce Basie-isms, and *Should I?* are just two examples of many to be found throughout this album.

Jamal frequently imposed his own forms on a tune and this clearly fascinated Davis, who through George Russell and Bill Evans was discovering modes as an alternative basis for improvisation. For example, on the second chorus of *Squatty Roo*, a ternary AABA song, he replaces the 16-bar AA section with a vamp so that his return to the B section truly makes it a 'release'. But perhaps the most striking example of imposing his own form on a song is his version of the 32-bar *Autumn leaves*, where he exploits the song's unusual AABC construction as a springboard for his own form, inserting an extended vamp for his improvisation (emulated by Herbie Hancock and Wayne Shorter in Davis's September 1964 version of the same tune on *Miles in Berlin* [CBS/Sony (A) CD62976]). What is particularly arresting, however, is how, towards the end of the second vamp (after a second return to the theme), Jamal uses a rolling chordal figure that would appear later in the year as the basis of the Miles Davis composition *All blues* on his album *Kind of Blue* (**393**).

Jamal was greatly misunderstood at the time, particularly by critics, whose forceful denouncements eroded what should have been a secure place in jazz. But the reissue of these performances, with good sound quality even though recorded live, suggests that Jamal's role in the 1950s deserves radical reappraisal: as a conceptualist, in realigning the relationship of instruments, one to another, within the standard piano trio, as a pathfinder whose practical application of vamps pointed to the use of modes as a basis for improvisation, as an innovator in spontaneously reordering song forms – a technique that can be heard in the work of musicians as diverse as Betty Carter, Keith Jarrett and Wynton Marsalis – and for his role as a catalyst who profoundly influenced Miles Davis and thus, at one remove, much jazz of the 1950s. Ultimately, however, he should surely be remembered as a leader of a quite exceptional trio, whose playing still remains an object lesson for young musicians in achieving unity, flexibility and swing with great economy and singleness of purpose. [13] S.N.

Charles Mingus

336 Mingus Mingus Mingus Mingus Mingus

†Impulse (A) MCAD5649, †Impulse (A) IMP11742

Rolf Ericson, Richard Williams (tpt); Quentin Jackson (tbn); Don Butterfield (tu); Jerome Richardson (fl, sop, bar); Dick Hafer (fl, ob, ten); Charlie Mariano (alt); Jaki Byard (p); Jay Berliner (g); Mingus (bs, p); Dannie Richmond (d). New York City, 20 January 1963.

IX love · Celia

Williams, Eddie Preston (tpt); Britt Woodman (tbn); Butterfield (tu); Eric Dolphy (fl, alt); Richardson (fl, sop, bar); Hafer (fl, clt, ten); Booker Ervin (ten); Byard (p); Mingus (bs, vcl intrjc[1]); Walter Perkins (d). New York City, 20 September 1963.

II B.S. · Mood indigo · Better get hit in yo' soul · Theme for Lester Young · Hora decubitus · Freedom[1]

This obsessively titled album directly associates two bands of similar instrumentation, one recorded early and the other latish in 1963. The 20 January date is the one that is renowned for the production of what is almost habitually described as 'Mingus's masterpiece', *The Black Saint and the Sinner Lady* (MCA [A] MCAD5649), recorded by a band which Mingus curiously publicized as his 'New Folk Band'.

'Ellingtonian in ambition and scope' is a recent description of that group, [14] and instincts of an Ellingtonian nature will undeniably be discerned in parts of *Black Saint.* Yet the making of Mingus's controversial 1963 essay in extended jazz composition is not really an achievement in the spirit of Ellington; and, indeed, whether it is indubitably conceived in the spirit, or established modus operandi, of Mingus himself may be worthy of argument.

The recreation of *Mood indigo* is, in ensemble terms, a reflection of the prototype, waxed in 1930, of the pensive octet (**91**). Reasons for judging this tribute a notable one are given below. But it will be convenient to refer here to other previously recorded themes which are recreated in both these Mingus sessions. All six of these are Mingus works. *Haitian fight song*, recorded for Debut in December 1955, for Atlantic in February 1957, then for RCA-Victor in July 1957, is somewhat reshaped here as *II B.S.*; *Celia*, first recorded in August 1957, reappears, as it were, 'in person'. *Better get hit in yo' soul* is partially a version of *Wednesday night prayer meetin'*, first recorded by a Mingus unit for United Artists in January 1959 and again for Atlantic in the February. Then, for Atlantic in May of the same year, it became *Better git it in your soul*, at a session which included *Goodbye pork pie hat*, here retitled (or specifically identified as) *Theme for Lester Young. Open letter to Duke*, which also was featured at the May 1959 meeting, itself related to Mingus's *Nouroog*, and, where the earlier of the present sessions is concerned, to *IX love*. From the aforesaid February 1959 Atlantic date came *E's flat, A's flat too*. This re-emerges as *Hora decubitus*.

Both *IX love* and *Celia* establish a fairly languorous tempo, though *Celia* contains some significant double-up sequences, reportedly Mingusian recollections of an old song called *The lady in red*. These tempo switches make their own sense, but in this recreation, as in *IX love*, the dominant expressive voice is Mariano's. His beautiful extemporizations show a confident defiance of boundaries by revealing the influences of Parker and Hodges via the alchemy of his alto style. (He also took an important role in *Black Saint*, not only on the same day but also several days later, at the leader's active behest, by means of overdubbing. Blessed instancy appears to be preserved in *Celia* and *IX love*.)

What makes the Mingus version of *Mood indigo* peculiarly distinctive is not its evocation of the Ellington original, though the performance recaptures, even enhances, what Constant Lambert once called the 'exquisitely tired . . . four in the morning' character by taking the piece distinctly slower than Duke took it. It is, without any doubt, Mingus's bass figurations that bestow a new significance. His improvisation, starting after Byard's short introduction, with skilful linear support of the first theme, provides harmonizations where in 1930 there had been only Fred Guy's banjo 'footfalls'. His solo across the bridge could be reckoned one of the man's most beguiling creations, a genuine double-bass *cantilena* which continues ruminatively while Byard restates the main theme and the wind instruments carry the mood to its close.

Better get hit in yo' soul sticks, in its familiar section, close enough the 1959 adaptation of *Wednesday night prayer meetin'*, but it adds a stirring coda – of which more in a moment. *Better get hit* . . . has (Mingus 'emphasized' to Nat Hentoff) no religious significance. He claimed to be enjoying 'the challenge of playing in 6/8 time faster than anybody had ever tried before'; enjoying a demonstration that an unusual time signature can be made to swing. Earlier record-sleeve notes contain avowals that Mingus was utilizing recollections of 'church music' for deliberate imitative effect.

Two queries: why the colloquial title spelling? Was it because the unexplained coda, which is in conventionally swinging common time – perhaps a sort of gospel $^{2}/_{4}$ – was added as a 'second movement' prompting a revised title? Or could it have been that the addition was a snatch of 'Savoy Stompers' impetus called up for comparative proof of the swingability of $^{6}/_{8}$? Explanations seem beyond reach now. The twofold item is unfailingly stimulating.

Some fine scoring crops up in each of the latter sections, and delightful brass figures provide a telling backing to Ervin's poignant tenor line in *Theme for Lester Young.* The Ervin voice was generously featured during the Mingus sessions of the late 1950s and early 1960s, a richly toned and flexible voice, a distinctly Southwestern dialect in saxophonic terms, its shaping by the blues steering it clear of the lures of Coltranism and suchlike emerging trends (hear also **341**). Dolphy's was a recently emergent voice, and he was a Coltrane associate as well as a profoundly admired Mingus sideman. The most striking records of Mingus–Dolphy collaboration are on **425**, and though Dolphy is part of the 20 September band, the solo which tends to do little more than endorse the increasing savagery of *Hora decubitus* is his principal emergence. This is an exciting venture whose near kindred, in terms of grooving impetus, are *II B.S.* and the upstart coda to *Better get hit in yo' soul.*

Mingus's instincts as composer, arranger and leader seem to have wavered pretty constantly between the need to encourage spontaneity and the lure of the durable. His published statements during the Jazz Workshop days of the mid- to late 1950s are well known. 'My whole conception . . . deals with nothing written. I "write" compositions – but only on mental score paper – then I lay out the composition part by part to the musicians. I play them the "framework" on piano so that they are all familiar with my interpretation.' [15] The reactions of his musicians were not always patient, though his method differed little from the 'head arrangements' well enough known among bands such as Basie outfits of earlier decades. But the complexity of Mingus's ideas, together with the increasingly disruptive effects of his health and behaviour, meant that preparations tended to involve much more writing, band members and specially engaged arrangers and copiers being called upon from time to time.

The leader's jazz skill at the piano, which was by no means inconsiderable (hear *Mingus Plays Piano*, †Mobile Fidelity [A] MFCD783), was at most occasions a ready agent of instruction. In addition, attention to his splendid bass continuum in *Mood indigo*, and almost equally, though evidence is not always as clearly manifested, to the way that his bass playing in such numbers as *II B.S.*, *Better get hit* and *Hora decubitus* combines steersmanship and promptive support, should emphasize how constantly his individual jazz instinct and its instrumental expression was part and parcel of his orchestral stimulus. Even his work with small groups bonds frequently enough with his collective vision. He could be as self-effacing as any bassist where a simple rhythm-section role was called for, even in his own creations. His 1962 trio collaboration with Ellington and Roach (**223**) calls for some bass subservience – though dodgy recording balance sometimes works against his contributions even there – but there are passages where the innovative composer's mind asserts itself. Ellington himself recalled that *Fleurette Africaine* had previously only been outlined at the piano during the meeting at his office, and yet it was completed in a single take with just a brief verbal description and a key signature as instruction to his accompanists: 'Mingus, with his eyes closed, fell into each and every harmonic groove, adding countermelodies as though he'd been playing the number all his life.' [16]

Mingus's bass playing was at least as relevant to his composing as his pianism or his 'mental score paper'. Without doubt, he would have acknowledged what he owed to the vistas opened out for bassists by Jimmy Blanton (who died in 1942: hear **153**); and, among those players who also are, and have been, venturesome heirs to the Blanton legacy, his orchestral extensions of the wisdoms he garnered should be held in high regard. E.T.

Wes Montgomery

337a The Complete 'Smokin' at the Half Note' Vol. 1

†Verve (J) POCJ-1816

Wynton Kelly (p); Montgomery (g); Paul Chambers (bs); Jimmy Cobb (d). Half Note, New York City, 24 June 1965.

No blues · *If you could see me now*

Same personnel. Van Gelder Studio, Englewood Cliffs, N.J., 22 September 1965.

Unit 7 · *Four on six* · *What's new?*

337b The Complete 'Smokin' at the Half Note' Vol. 2

†Verve (J) POCJ-1902

Wynton Kelly (p); Montgomery (g); Paul Chambers (bs); Jimmy Cobb (d). Half Note, New York City, June 1965.

No blues · *If you could see me now* · *Willow, weep for me* · *Impressions* · *Portrait of Jennie* · *The surrey with the fringe on top* · *Four on six* · *Misty*

The name Wes Montgomery is immediately synonymous with his 'signature' sound on electric guitar. This was due in part to the deep-bodied acoustic-electric Gibson L-5 CES closely associated with him throughout his career and played (in the late 1950s and into the 1960s) through a Fender valve amplifier. But although the guitar-amp combination produced quite a distinctive sound in its own right, Montgomery produced a far thicker tone than any other guitarist in jazz because he used the meat of his thumb instead of a plectrum. An autodidact, he picked up the guitar at the relatively late age of 19, and quickly developed a uniquely personal sound based on an unorthodox technique which simultaneously charmed and confounded his fellow guitarists.

He first made an impact with a series of recordings for Orrin Keepnews's Riverside label beginning with *The Wes Montgomery Trio* (Original Jazz Classics [A] OJC-034) from October 1959 and *The Incredible Jazz Guitar of Wes Montgomery* (OJC-036) from 12 weeks later. [17] He recorded regularly with Riverside until 1964, when he signed with Verve, whom he left in 1967 to join the A&M label where he remained until his premature death in 1968. No guitarist in jazz could afford to ignore Montgomery's recordings, whether to incorporate his patented 'parallel octave' sound – something his fellow guitarist George Benson took a stage further by playing octaves with either a major or a minor third in between, which in turn became *his* patented signature – his remarkable voice-leading passages over blocked chords, his tone or his amazingly fluent technique. If the first wave of electric guitarists can be said to have been headed by Charlie Christian, then the second great wave was headed by Montgomery.

According to many observers, his studio recordings never did him justice and certainly the live selections from the Half Note seem to offer a more valuable perspective of his playing than his previous live disc, *Full House* (OJC-106) from 1962, also with Kelly, Chambers and Cobb who were at the time moonlighting from the Miles Davis sextet. *No blues* belies its title since it is, in fact, a 12-bar blues. The head is dispensed with in one chorus and gives way to Montgomery's solo, constructed with that great regard for form which was a hallmark of his playing. Generally, his best solos moved through quite specific developmental stages in their construction. Beginning with single-note playing, he progressed to octaves, then to octaves mixed with chords, reaching towards a climax with dramatic block-chord passages. These climaxes were made even more exciting by the use of question-and-answer chords with octave punches, evoking the 'shout' choruses employed by big-band arrangers.

The use of alternating textures in strong riff patterns may have been the influence of big bands on Montgomery, who was brought up during the big-band era. He first learned the guitar copying Charlie Christian solos with Benny Goodman and his first 'name' job was with the Lionel Hampton between 1948 and early 1950, where as the only teetotaller in the band he earned the nickname of 'the Rev' from his exuberant bandmates including Charles Mingus, Milt Buckner and, for a brief spell, Fats Navarro. Montgomery, however, was not alone in modelling his solos on big-band arrangements typical of the swing era; Ella Fitzgerald's scat solos, for example, were probably influenced by the brass and saxophone environment she grew up in within the Chick Webb band. Even after she had digested bop, her scat choruses followed specific 'developmental' passages that worked towards a 'big band' climax in her 'solo', [18] frequently alternating bilabial plosives, evoking the sound of wind instruments with lingua-alveolar plosives, similarly suggesting brass instruments, in call-and-response episodes.

Montgomery's association with the Wynton Kelly Trio lasted for the summer of 1965, touring the major jazz clubs in the United States and making an appearance at the Newport Jazz Festival on the afternoon of Sunday 4 July. The live recordings date from the beginning of their working relationship, and provide a wonderful opportunity to examine the playing of Kelly, a greatly underrated talent who, on form, as here, was both an elegant soloist and, as might be expected with someone with perfect pitch, a nonpareil accompanist. [19] His trio came together in the Miles Davis quintet and sextets of 1959–63, and played with a cohesion and polish rare in jazz. This was due in no small part to the easy, buoyant swing of Chambers and the deft, assertive Cobb, who worked so well with him. Indeed, Cobb had previously toured briefly with Montgomery in an organ trio with Melvyn Rhyne in 1963 and was no stranger to the guitarist's playing, providing another reason why this group meshed together so well.

Both Montgomery and Kelly have plenty of room to stretch out on *Unit seven*, a 44-bar AABA composition where the A sections are a 12-bar blues and the B section a straightforward middle eight built around the ii-V-1 and ii-V progression. Kelly takes two precise yet swinging choruses that set the climate for Montgomery's four that follow. As he works towards his inimitable block-chord passages, the 'chains of inversions' that were such a trademark of his style, it is interesting to note his use of chromatic 'push chords', chords a semitone below the main chord which are played much like a grace note, giving impetus to his line (for example, a B7 into a C7). Once again Montgomery's strong affinity for the blues is apparent, a blues feeling permeating all his work, even his interpretations of popular standards. However, it was not an affectation the way some players consciously adopted bluesy mannerisms to sound 'funky', but rather an underlying aesthetic that coloured his whole approach to playing.

His solo on his own composition, *Four on six*, which he had previously introduced in 1960 on *The Incredible Jazz Guitar of Wes Montgomery*, is another fine example of his work. It unites all the main characteristics of his style and it is easy to see how he turned the jazz world on its collective ear with work of this quality. The overall structure of *Four on six* is simple, a 16-bar ABA^{1}C composition with each section four bars. It is preceded by a 16-bar intro, with the bass and piano in unison, playing a bass line in intervals of a fifth. Montgomery enters in bars 11 and 12 with stop chords (which will later appear as part of C). The four-bar A theme is outlined, contrasted with the B section comprising stop chords for four bars, A is repeated again, and contrasted with a different configuration of stop chords in C, leaving the final two bars as a solo break leading into the 16-bar modified blues sequence for solos, now played with a walking bass. Montgomery's seven choruses that follow show him to be the consummate storyteller, his blues-based rhythmic feel creating a solo of genuine excitement, complexity and strong melodic interest. Perhaps the most arresting aspect of his playing, not just here but on all the numbers so far discussed, is the feel of spontaneous improvisation guided by a sense of direction and cohesion. His frequent use of thematic development in his solos gave his work a feeling of balance and symmetry as did his use of developmental passages to reach a climax.

In the autumn of 1961, Montgomery played for a while with John Coltrane's group, including a performance at the Monterey Jazz Festival, which culminated in an offer from the saxophonist to become a permanent member. Montgomery declined because of other obligations, something Coltrane regretted, but a legacy of this brief period is his version of *Impressions*, with some of Montgomery's most powerful playing of the whole Half Note date; single-note lines singing effortlessly give way to an adventurous yet supple climax of octaves and block chords. In contrast were several ballad interpretations that reveal a more ingratiating style of universal appeal that would later set the stage for his crossover into easy listening jazz. Indeed, *Willow, weep for me*, *Portrait of Jennie* and *Misty* subsequently appeared on *Willow, Weep for Me* (Verve [A] V6–8765) with Wynton Kelly's piano almost totally removed from the mix and some very bland brass and woodwinds arranged by Claus Ogerman and added during the postproduction stage, reflecting the new direction the guitarist's career had taken.

Much of Montgomery's subsequent output became biased towards 'pop-jazz', a term coined specifically to deal with his brand of crossover music. With his albums appearing regularly in the *Billboard* Top 100 and a Grammy award for *Goin' Out of My Head* (Verve V6–8642), he died unexpectedly on 15 June 1968 of a heart attack at the peak of his popularity. His influence during his lifetime had been huge and it continued to grow after his death as jazz guitarists emulated his parallel-octave and double-octave playing as much as his 'impossible' block chords and voice-leading passages. His style went beyond the arbitrary boundaries of jazz and crept into film soundtracks, pop, easy listening and rock (for example Carlos Santana, Jimi Hendrix, the Grateful Dead and the Doors). Indeed, when Larry Coryell and Lee Ritenour, after years of playing crossover music, returned to their jazz roots on record, both adopted the sound and stylistic devices of Montgomery. [20] But it was in jazz his impact was most powerfully felt. His style and sound became a model for subsequent generations of guitar players and can be heard echoed in the playing of George Benson, Emily Remler, Bruce Forman, Pat Metheny, Mark Whitfield, Kevin Eubanks and a host of others. These recordings go some way to illustrate why Montgomery was so influential, the effects of which are still with us today. S.N.

Jackie McLean

338 **Bluesnik**

†Blue Note (A) B21Y-84067

Freddie Hubbard (tpt); McLean (alt); Kenny Drew (p); Doug Watkins (bs); Pete La Roca (d). Van Gelder's, N.J., 18 December 1960.

Bluesnik · Goin' away blues · Drew's blues · Cool green · Blues function · Torchin'

McLean's first session as a leader for Blue Note was *Jackie's Bag* (BLP 4051) from January 1959 and it was a measure of how the label felt about his not inconsiderable talent that just 23 months later, *Bluesnik* represented his sixth date for them. By then he had also appeared as a sideman on Blue Note albums by Walter Davis Jr, Sonny Clark, Jimmy Smith, Donald Byrd, Lee Morgan, Freddie Redd and Tina Brooks and was regarded as one of the label's up-and-coming stars. In fact, McLean had begun recording as a 19-year-old in 1951 with a Miles Davis group on *Dig* (Prestige [A] OJC-005). Also on the date was his neighbourhood idol Sonny Rollins, who had taken the young alto saxophonist under his wing. Work with Davis and another record date, this time for Blue Note in 1952, followed. From then on McLean, whom Charlie Parker once regarded as his protégé, was never far from the cutting edge of jazz during the 1950s, although his impact was lessened by addiction to narcotic drugs. 'All the Prestige things, the early Blue Note things when I was with Miles's band, I mean I was in terrible shape all during that period. I had a nervous breakdown in 1955 and went into Bellevue,' he said later. [21]

By 1955 McLean had worked with the pianist Paul Bley and was appearing at the Café Bohemia with George Wallington's group. In 1956 he became part of Charles Mingus's Jazz Workshop and began recording under his own name for Prestige and New Jazz. He later joined Art Blakey's Jazz Messengers, where he remained until 1958. He was off the scene for almost a year following two drugs busts, and a short-lived band including Ray Draper on tuba and ex-Messenger Bill Hardman fell apart since without a cabaret card he was unable to perform in nightclubs. In 1959 he took a part in Jack Gelber's *The Connection*, a play about narcotics addicts. It was during his run with the show that he signed with Blue Note. One of his recordings as a sideman for the label was an album of Redd's music written especially for the play, *Music from 'The Connection'* (†Blue Note [A] CDP0777 7 89392 2 1). Recorded in February 1960, it reveals, even more than the albums under his own name for Blue Note up to that point, [22] how he had matured as a soloist.

The most obvious characteristic of McLean's playing was a large, biting tone and a very intense delivery. Although his name had been linked to that of Parker's during his formative years, by now it was hard to detect that he had borrowed anything from the Bird other than a strong emotional affinity for the blues and certain mannerisms of tone colour, apparent as early as 1956 on such albums as *4, 5 and 6* (Prestige [A] OJC056) and *McLean's Scene* (New Jazz [A] OJC098). However, his propinquity for the blues was in the context of an altogether simpler lingua franca that was wholly his own. The velocity of his playing was far slower than Parker's, whose goal was often the juxtaposition of the greatest variety of material in the briefest possible time, and his rhythmic conception was altogether more fundamental than that of his former patron.

Bluesnik places the alto saxophonist with his long-time associate Drew, a pianist who had great sympathy for his work and with whom he played in 1949 in a neighbourhood band led by Sonny Rollins; La Roca had previously appeared on McLean's second Blue Note album, *New Soil* (BLP4013). On previous sessions he had used Donald Byrd and Blue Mitchell on trumpet but here opts for the faster company of Hubbard. The result was McLean's most satisfying album of his hard-bop period and, for many, of his career. Subsequently he made rather lumpy and indigestible forays into free jazz, heralded by *Let Freedom Ring* (Blue Note [A] BST84106). His Blue Note recordings between 1964 and 1966 suggested that the passion seemed to be ebbing from his playing, [23] and by the 1970s he was groping with crossover music.

The title track is a repeated two-bar phrase set against a 12-bar blues, split by an eight-bar vamp to create an ABA composition, although solos are on a straight 12-bar blues. McLean immediately launches into 20 successive choruses which have a breathless seat-of-the-pants urgency. The hard-bitten tone, the often angular and intense phrasing, an occasional quote (first up is *Salt peanuts*), are all propelled by a restless, rhythmic drive that was a hallmark of his hard-bop playing. What is clear is that McLean is not looking to Parker's methods of constructing a solo, but seems to owe a debt to Miles Davis and Dexter Gordon. From Davis he borrowed the modal-based lyricism and from Gordon the notion that a solo's construction, even without a melodic gift as sublime as Parker's, could be united by creative heat, which could even appear to weld together otherwise disjointed lines. 'A lot of my performances have been very emotional because I wasn't putting any work into it and I hit the stage with no practise under my belt,' he once confessed. [24]

At this brisk tempo, [25] McLean does not sound entirely comfortable. Ideas come and go, some are developed while others are left hanging in mid-air before being brushed aside by a further flurry of activity. There are 'under-the-finger' phrases that allow time for new ideas to be organized and although this solo lacks overall cogency, there are nevertheless some inspired moments. One of the endearing characteristics of his work is the emotional commitment of his playing, here heard in abundance, creating what is often referred to as the 'McLean burn'. In contrast, Hubbard stands back from the creative heat of the moment and contributes a beautifully balanced solo that makes exemplary use of the rising line to create tension and excitement. To achieve this he incorporates almost the entire practical range of his instrument, two octaves and a perfect fourth, and while his phrasing remains extremely precise, it is nevertheless melodic and lyrical.

The 'down-home' feeling on *Goin' 'way blues*, a 12-bar theme against La Roca's insistent quaver triplets, provides a manifesto of McLean's approach to a slow-tempo blues. He had shown on the title track of Sonny Clark's *Cool Struttin'* (†Blue Note [E] CDP748513–2) from 1958 and on *Funky Mama* from Donald Byrd's *Fuego* (BST84026) from 1959 that slow- and medium-tempo blues was his forte, and this is another superb example of his handling of the idiom. His tone sounds fuller, and here his ordering of ideas is far more convincing, manipulating his unique style of phrasing to far better effect than at faster tempos.

Drew's blues is an easy-swinging 12-bar blues with Drew using the tonally ambiguous *So what* voicings in his comping, which give the piece a light, airy feel. Again, at a none too frantic tempo, McLean is able to create a solo that, like the previous track, unites passion and purpose to excellent effect. What is interesting is the difference in approach to the blues idiom between McLean and Hubbard. The former is a blues player first and foremost, even able to make non-blues material sound bluesy, whereas the latter regarded the idiom more as a set of changes. Hubbard's playing, technically beyond reproach on this album, does occasionally sound emotionally distant from his material in a way that McLean's does not, creating a compelling duality that is as absorbing as it is stimulating.

Another Drew composition, the minor 12-bar blues *Cool green* with a II-V-1 turnaround, contains some of the best work of the session from both Hubbard and McLean. Proceeded by an eight-bar introduction, the bass plays in a cut-time for the first eight bars of the 12-bar theme, which is repeated twice, walking the last four and through into the solos, giving a pleasing sense of lift and buoyancy. Throughout the session, Drew performs with poise and creativity which makes it hard to understand why he never got the credit as the fine player he was. Hubbard's *Blues function* returns once more to the 12-bar idiom with an *alla breve* theme that opens into a powerfully swinging four with Hubbard entering after the theme statement and once more making use of the rising line to create tension, using simple phrases that are quietly developed through elongation, permutation and sequence.

Torchin' is anything but. A 16-bar AA^1 BA^1 theme of succeeding four sections, it shares the same harmonic base as Sonny Rollins's *Doxy* and is played in *alla breve*, except for the B section, which makes effective use of a stop-time chorus. The solos are in an even 4/4 throughout, both McLean and Hubbard clearly relaxed. Here the alto saxophonist suggests, as he does throughout the album, that he had much to contribute to the hard-bop idiom. That he was always in the vanguard of the movement, but never a force in forming that vanguard, must be put down to his personal problems during this period. By the time he conquered them, times had changed, leaving a feeling that this passionate and frequently exciting musician never realized his full potential during the 1950s and 1960s. S.N.

Booker Little

339 Victory and Sorrow
Bethlehem (A) BCP-6034

Little (tpt); Julian Priester (tbn); George Coleman (ten); Don Friedman (p); Reggie Workman (bs); Pete La Roca (d). New York City, August or September 1961.

Victory and sorrow · *Forward light* · *Looking ahead* · *If I should lose you* · *Calling softly* · *Booker's blues* · *Matilde*

'Booker was very energetic; it was if he knew he wouldn't be around for a long time so he was always hurrying, get it all done, very intense,' said the pianist Mal Waldron in 1994. [26] And certainly Little's time was brief. He was born in 1938, and entered the Chicago Conservatory in 1955 to study trumpet, piano, music theory, orchestration and composition. By October 1961 he was dead, a victim of uraemia, just as his career was gathering momentum.

Little joined the Max Roach quintet in June 1958 on the recommendation of Sonny Rollins and he made his first recordings with the drummer that month, *Max Roach + 4 on the Chicago Scene* (EmArcy [J] 195J-41). Immediately afterwards Roach revamped the band, dropping the piano to add, somewhat incongruously, Ray Draper on tuba. This new group made their formal debut at the Newport Jazz Festival on Sunday 6 July 1958. Roach was the house drummer for the evening performances, and his new group opened proceedings at 8 p.m. with an extended set, of which six numbers were issued as *Max Roach + 4 at Newport* (Mercury [J] 195J-42).

Both albums provide a fascinating glimpse of Little only weeks before he graduated from the Chicago Conservatory with a Bachelor of Music degree. Although his style is still somewhat short of artistic maturity it is immediately apparent that the young trumpeter has great assurance. While there is an occasional fluffed note or slightly imperfect intonation at the extremes of his range, *Chicago Scene* nevertheless reveals a lucid melodic conception on *My old flame* and *Shirley*. The Newport set, although of below-average recording quality, shows him with a technique sufficient to cope with Roach's preference for fast tempos on *Tune up* and *Villia*, albeit at the expense of rhythmic variety, drawing inspiration from Clifford Brown and a preference for relying on long lines of evenly accented quavers. However, on his own composition, a less frantic *Minor mood*, he showed a precise lyricism that favoured unusual intervals. Clearly here was a player of great potential.

A progress report from later in the year came with his debut as a leader on record, *Booker Little 4 & Max Roach* (†Blue Note [E] CDP784457–2). It showed greater care with both intonation and organizing his line, a more secure technique and an improved ability to incorporate unusual leaps into the overall melodic architecture of his solos. Little remained with Roach until 1959, recording with him again in September that year (EmArcy [A] MG20911) with Julian Priester (tbn) replacing the lugubrious Draper. In February 1960 he recorded an album under the leadership of Frank Strozier backed by the Miles Davis rhythm section of Wynton Kelly, Paul Chambers and Jimmy Cobb, *Waltz of the Demons* (Atlantis [A] ATS5). Together with the second album under his own name, *Booker Little* (Time [A] 2011, Bainbridge [A] BT1041) from April, his playing showed an impressive leap forward to deliver on the deferred promise of his artistic maturity. On his own album, with just piano, bass and drums, his playing was exposed to far greater scrutiny than before, yet nevertheless revealed him moving into the ranks of the foremost trumpeters in jazz. He had closed the gap between inspiration and execution and his melodic organization had been refined to the point where every note he played had a vital role in the construction of his solos. Significantly, of the six numbers that comprised *Booker Little*, five were original compositions, which revealed a refreshing desire to move away from standard song forms: *The grand valse* is a 32-bar AB song of two 16-bar sections, while *Opening statement* is an ABA song with A 14 bars and B 10 bars.

Little, a thoroughly trained musician now fast approaching the peak of his abilities, naturally gravitated towards musicians of his generation with a similarly advanced outlook. One of those with whom he formed an association was Eric Dolphy, and together they assembled a quintet for a date with Prestige on 21 December 1960. Earlier in the day Dolphy had participated on *Free Jazz* (**400**) with Ornette Coleman, and on *Far Cry* (New Jazz [A] NJLP8270) there is certainly a degree of animation in his playing that is absent from Little's, who appears pensive in comparison. Yet as he entered 1961, the young trumpeter seemed on the threshold of greatness. In March he assembled a small ensemble in the recording studios for his third album as a leader, this including Dolphy, his former boss Roach (d), Priester (tbn), Don Friedman (p) and either Ron Carter or Art Davis (bs).

Out Front (Candid [A] BR5019) was an album of originals by Little in what was the best résumé of his talents to date and was far removed from the concept of the straightforward blowing session then prevalent in hard bop. He uses unusually wide voicings, contrary to the hard-bop norm of tight unisons and thirds, there are tempo changes on *Quiet please*, contrasts of consonant and dissonant harmonies on *Strength and sanity* and changes of metre from 3/4 to 4/4 to 5/4 and into 6/4 on *Moods in free time.* Little's own playing continued to reveal a preference for slow and medium tempos and his tone had developed a pleasingly warm hue. He continued to favour legato phrasing, incorporating a slight vibrato on sustained notes, and was now introducing half-valve effects to give tonal contrast to his line. However, Little's writing here was on the whole less successful than the creation of an original context to feature his playing, exploring a variety of contrasting moods, sometimes in one composition, such as *Quiet please.*

In April Little was a member of a large ensemble assembled by John Coltrane to record *Africa/Brass* (**422**), with arrangements by Dolphy who also played saxophone on the date. Dolphy was now performing with Coltrane's quartet on an on-and-off basis that was becoming increasingly frequent, and Coltrane extended an invitation to Little, Dolphy's regular musical associate, to join his group, with a view to augmenting it to a sextet. The trumpeter played several times with the group but Coltrane was surprised when Little eventually declined the opportunity, explaining that ill health prevented him working every night. Nevertheless in July Little rehearsed for two weeks in a band he co-led with Dolphy in preparation for a two-week engagement in the Five Spot. The group was recorded by Prestige and enough material for two albums was taken down on the night of 16 July, *Eric Dolphy at the Five Spot* Vols. 1 & 2 (†VDJ [J] 1504 and 1525). With a rhythm section of Waldron (p), Richard Davis (bs) and Eddie Blackwell (d), Little's articulate solo on the brisk *Aggression* illustrated an increased command of fast tempos and on *The prophet* he moves between inside and outside playing with ease.

Victory and Sorrow was Little's fourth album as a leader and was destined to become his final appearance on disc. Recorded shortly after he cut *Percussion Bitter Sweet* (Impulse [A] S8) with Roach, it represents his most rounded musical statement to be preserved. Around the time of *Out Front*, Little had told Nat Hentoff: 'My own feelings about the direction in which jazz should go are that there should be much less stress on technical exhibitionism and much more on emotional content, on what might be termed humanity in music.' [27] This album is a significant move to realizing this manifesto. If *Out Front* could be faulted, then it was because of the conflicting musical personalities of his sidemen, which made the album appear to be pulling in different directions at once. There was an uneasy balance between Roach's dominating drumming and the outward-bound forays of Dolphy. Equally, Little's writing at times strained for effect, *Quiet please*, for example, appearing as an obstacle course of contrasting moods and tempo, albeit negotiated with great aplomb by the trumpeter. *Victory and Sorrow* addressed these shortcomings. The presence of Coleman on tenor saxophone, with whom Little had worked in Roach's quintet, is a key factor in a warmer blend within the front line, while Roach performed in service of the ensemble rather than of the self.

The title track is one of Little's finest compositions and his solo here is one reason why writers have often described him as 'the Clifford Brown of the 1960s'. The form of the composition is intriguing, beginning with a slow, unaccompanied fanfare by the front line before the exposition of the theme *a tempo*:

A (8 bars) + x (2 bars quarter tempo) + B (4 bars) + C (13 bars) +
A + x + B

Coleman's solo is cogent and to the point, but he was yet to undergo the transformation into the powerful and often commanding musician he would develop into during later years. Priester produces perhaps his finest solo of the session here, the medium-fast tempo ideally suiting his playing. Little was clearly absorbed by tempo shifts in his writing, and on *Forward flight* they become a central feature of the composition itself, although the soloists are not asked to deal with shifting tempos in their improvisation. Rather, they play off straight-ahead medium-fast changes that have solos by Priester, Coleman and Friedman, with Little not sounding at his best here.

Looking ahead continues Little's fascination with interrupting his free-flowing compositions with tempo hiccups:

A (8 bars) + B (8 bars) + C (8 bars) + D (8 bars) + x (8 bars
quarter tempo) + D (8 bars) + y (4 bars quarter tempo) +
E (8 bars to solos on ABCA)

The trumpeter's writing treats the ensemble like a miniature big band, with the trombone and tenor working as a 'section' in counterpoint to the leader's long, melodic lead lines. The C section has a pedal point, which gives an unexpected lift to the soloists, all of whom participate in what might have been, if the composition's title is anything to go by, the direction in which Little saw his music heading.

The only non-Little composition on the album is *If I should lose you*, a ballad he performs with just the rhythm section. Ballads were one of his great strengths and even on his first recording date with Roach his playing on *My old flame* is one of the album's highlights; he was clearly working to expand his handling of the idiom. His own ballad composition, *Matilde*, with a chamber-music-like approach, presents an alternative way of tackling the idiom.

Little's compositions were extremely melodic and it is surprising that they have not had wider acceptance as part of the standard repertoire of jazz. *Calling softly*, for example, emerges after the introduction as an engaging 34-bar ¾ piece:

A (8 bars) + B (12 bars) + A (8 bars) + C (6 bars, a truncated variant of B)

Booker's blues is not a blues at all, but is a 24-bar composition incorporating successive pedal points:

A (8 bars) + A^1 (8 bars) + A^2 (8 bars)

As in all Little's compositions on this album, the moods are more cogent than *Out Front*, the voicings warmer, and there is less a feeling of experimentation, rather one of focus and direction. The speed with which Little developed both as a trumpet player and composer-arranger can be charted through the four albums he made as a leader. The transition from a trumpet player of great promise with Roach to the accomplished artist on the title track of *Looking ahead* was achieved in under three years. That this was done alongside developing his writing and compositional skills suggests a musician of considerable resource. Early on he realized the importance both of mastering the formidable technical and theoretical skills required at the highest level to survive as an instrumentalist and of creating a context in which to function as a jazz musician. Within weeks of recording *Victory and Sorrow*, Little was dead. Had he lived, such a role would have surely placed him at the forefront of jazz.

S.N.

Tina Brooks

340 **True Blue**
†Blue Note (E) CDP724382897521

Brooks (ten); Freddie Hubbard (tpt); Duke Jordan (p); Sam Jones (bs); Art Taylor (d). Englewood Cliffs, N. J., 25 June 1960.
Good old soul (2 versions) · *Up tight's creek* · *Theme for Doris* · *True blue* (2 versions) · *Miss Hazel* · *Nothing ever changes my love for you*

Tina Brooks was the most enigmatic of all the Blue Note recording artists. He fleetingly surfaced on albums from the late 1950s and early 1960s by Jimmy Smith, Kenny Burrell, Jackie McLean, Freddie Redd, Freddie Hubbard (**346**) and on this album, the only one issued under his own name during his lifetime, before he disappeared. Ironically, he became best known to Blue Note collectors the world over for an album recorded in October 1960 under his own name that was *not* issued. [28] *Back to the Tracks* was one of only a few Blue Note albums to be allocated a catalogue number and have a cover designed for it without actually ever being released. Since it was advertised on some inner sleeves during the early 1960s, some fans mischievously claimed either to own a copy or, at least, to have seen one. It all added to the mystique of one of the most individual and absorbing saxophonists to emerge during the hard-bop era.

Brooks arrived in New York at the age of 12 with his family, and his first professional experiences in music were in rhythm 'n' blues with bands such as Charles Brown and Amos Milburn, the latter at various times including the likes of Elmo Hope, Johnny Griffin and Philly Joe Jones in his line-up. In the mid-1950s Brooks toured with Lionel Hampton before forming an association with the trumpeter Benny Harris to play various Harlem clubs. Later it would be Harris who recommended him to Alfred Lion of Blue Note. Lion was impressed with Brooks's style, and it is easy to hear why. His tone ran counter to the prevailing trend of hard-toned, aggressive tenor players such as Coltrane, Rollins and Griffin, all of whom recorded at various times for Lion. Brooks had what can only be described as a soulful tone on his instrument, which he combined with a lyrical approach to improvisation. He had very few pet phrases or licks; instead he relied on his ability to create and continue building melodic lines of grace and symmetry in the way that evoked, but did not copy, the horizontal approach to improvisation of Lester Young. Brooks's tone was more vocal in that there are moments in his solos that suggest the 'cry' of blues singers and the personal inflections of tone and timbre they brought to their singing; yet Brooks achieved these effects through nuance and subtlety rather than grand gesture.

True Blue was recorded six days after he had made an important contribution as an instrumentalist and as a composer-arranger to Freddie Hubbard's debut as a leader on *Open Sesame* (**346**). Hubbard again provides a perfect foil to Brooks's quietly undemonstrative but moving style. For his own album, Brooks contributed five of the six numbers and from the availability of all Brooks's work in the 1980s and 1990s, it is now clear that his compositions comprise some of the most original and distinctive to emerge from the hard-bop era. If they were perhaps not quite in the same league as those by a Thelonious Monk, a Charles

Mingus or a Tadd Dameron, they can today certainly be mentioned in the same breath as those by a Horace Silver or a Benny Golson.

A regular feature of Brooks's writing was to juxtapose a Latin section within the overall architecture of his compositions. Thus, *Good old soul*, a 38-bar AABA composition, is constructed:

Intro = 8 bars + (A = 10 bars + A = 10 bars + B = Latin 8 bars + A = 10 bars)

The introduction also includes another of Brooks's hallmarks, that of concealing the tempo of a composition by its deliberately confusing metre. Usually this is over just a few bars, but one of the features of the title track is its ambiguous tempo delineation; it appears on superficial listening to have two tempo possibilities, which become the central feature of the song. By cleverly juxtaposing metre against tempo, Brooks transforms a straightforward 12-bar blues into a wholly compelling event.

Up tight's creek, an up-tempo swinger, also introduces a Latin section, again within the basic ternary AABA song-form, this time of 32 bars:

Intro = 4 bars + (A = 8 bars + A = 8 bars + B = Latin 8 bars + A = 8 bars)

Here Hubbard is crisp, assertive, bubbling with ideas and moving from the top of his range to the bottom with deceptive ease. Brooks contributes three choruses that are in a sense a manifesto of his style: a calm, unruffled lyricism, an interlocking melodicism where each phrase seems like a logical extension of the previous one, and a very mellow tone that is bent one way and then the other to bring expressive weight to his solo.

Compositionally, the most arresting track of the album is *Theme for Doris*. An *ostinato* figure played by unison piano and bass against drum accents sets the mood for eight bars. A highly syncopated figure, it is very cleverly written since, on first hearing, it conceals the underlying tempo of the piece by its unusual metre. Brooks's tenor enters playing lead on the A theme over this rhythmically confusing figure, with Hubbard uncharacteristically reduced to sustained background figures. It is not until the emergence of the B and C sections, played as 'Latin swing', that the underlying tempo becomes clear. The ABC composition recapitulates, this time with the addition of a powerfully swinging D section, leading into a third reprise of the ABC sections, thus:

Intro = 8 bars (rhythm section/*ostinato* figure) A = 8 bars (*ostinato* continues) + B = 8 bars (Latin swing) + C = 8 bars (Latin swing) + A = 8 bars (*ostinato* returns) + B + C (both Latin swing) + D = 8 bars (hard swing) + A = 8 bars (*ostinato* returns) + B + C (both Latin swing) to solos

This is Brooks at his most assertive; his strong lead playing, which provides an unusual role reversal between trumpet and saxophone in hard bop, extends naturally into a two-bar pick-up that announces his solo, which unravels with crafty cross-references to the A, B and C themes. The ever supportive Hubbard, again with that crackling tone and an imagination brimming with ideas, ensures that the momentum of the piece is continued to the theme recapitulation.

The brisk, up-tempo swinger *Miss Hazel* is another number that includes the Brooks trademark Latin section in the theme (but, like all the previous numbers, dispenses with it for solos, which are all against a straight-ahead rhythm):

(4-bar intro) + A = 16 bars + B = 8 bars (Latin) + A = 16 bars
(to solos)

The melancholy mood of *Nothing ever changes my love for you*, with its theme statement avoiding the hard-bop norm of unisons or simple harmony parts for the front line and with Brooks weaving a counter-melody to Hubbard's theme statement during the Latin sections of the theme, prompts an affecting solo from Hubbard, expansive but nevertheless retaining the blue mood of the piece. Brooks follows Hubbard's lead, and at moments implies a double-tempo feel in his line which gives his solo a suggestion of suppressed momentum, as if he is going to burst into a sprint at any moment. The theme is once again a pleasing contrast of medium-tempo straight-ahead swing and Latin sections juxtaposed to produce a satisfying compositional whole of 56 bars, in a ternary AABA form, but of unusual construction, thus:

(Intro = 8 bars) + A = 16 bars (8 bars Latin + 4 bars swing + 4 bars Latin) + A = 16 bars (8 bars Latin + 4 bars swing + 4 bars Latin) + B = 8 bars (straight-ahead swing/solo saxophone) + A = 16 bars (8 bars Latin + 4 bars swing + 4 bars Latin) to solos.

Since *Open Sesame* from the previous week, there had been comings and goings in the rhythm section with just Sam Jones, then with Cannonball Adderley, the common denominator. The playing of Jordan, Jones and Taylor was uniformly tight, cohesive and supportive, one of the benefits of the Blue Note policy of paying for adequate rehearsal time. Yet their contributions remain subsidiary to that of the front line. However, despite the crisp, inventive solos of Jordan, it is Hubbard and Brooks who took centre stage and absorb our attention. They complemented each other perfectly, both in their solo work, the fiery trumpeter and the lyrical saxophonist, and in ensembles, where they achieved a distinctive blend, both in unison and harmony. Yet, despite the success of both albums, they also suggest unfulfilled promise.

Although Brooks recorded two further albums as a leader for Blue Note, neither was quite as resourceful as *True Blue*, or indeed issued during his lifetime. For whatever reason, Brooks turned next to Blue Mitchell and then to Johnny Coles on his subsequent recording sessions. And Hubbard, on his next session as a leader, used Hank Mobley, a dependable and capable saxophonist, but one who did not fire the trumpeter's imagination in quite the way Brooks did. Thus the recorded legacy of the Hubbard and Brooks combination was just *Open Sesame* and *True Blue*. They are of a piece, a representation of the hard-bop idiom at its best, combining highly creative solos, imaginative compositions and a touch of flair that still sparkles today. S.N.

Booker Ervin

341 The Freedom Book

†Prestige (J) VICJ-3782

Ervin (ten); Jaki Byard (p); Richard Davis (bs); Alan Dawson (d).
Englewood Cliffs, N.J., 3 December 1963.
A lunar tune · Cry me not · Grant's stand · A day to mourn · Al's in · Stella by starlight

Booker Telleferro Ervin II was one of the great jazz artists of the 1960s. Born in Denison, he belonged to the tradition of Texas tenors, earthy, powerful, full-bodied and steeped in the blues. A trombonist between the ages of eight and fourteen, he took up the tenor while performing his military service between 1949 and 1953. After two years at Berklee College of Music in Boston, he worked in a variety of bands before arriving in New York in May 1958. Six months later he had linked up with Charles Mingus, and appeared on *Jazz Portraits* (†Blue Note [E] CDP7243 8 27325 2 5) recorded live at the Nonagon Art Gallery on Second Avenue on 16 January 1959. Ervin's forthright style instantly appealed to Mingus, and after his careful, yet secure, recording debut he became a regular in the bass player's ensembles, where he gradually revealed the more expansive side of his personality, which touched base with his experiences in the Tulsa-based rhythm-'n'-blues band of Ernie Fields during 1955–6. Now Mingus's first-call tenor saxophonist, he appeared on some of the most important albums of the bass player's career, including *Mingus Ah Um*, *Mingus Dynasty*, *Mingus/Oh Yeah*, *Blues and Roots*, *Mingus, Mingus, Mingus, Mingus, Mingus* (**336**), *Pre-Bird* and the excellent *Mingus at Antibes*, where his playing perfectly contrasts with that of Eric Dolphy.

Ervin made an album each for Bethlehem, Savoy and Candid under his own name between 1960 and 1961 before signing with the Prestige label in 1963 while still with Mingus. Of the seven albums he recorded for the label under Don Schlitten's direction, it is usually agreed that the 'Book' series – *The Freedom Book*, *The Song Book*, *The Blues Book* and *The Space*

Book – represents his best work. All have in common the exemplary playing of Davis and Dawson, but it is the albums with Byard, *The Freedom Book* and *The Space Book*, that number among the most distinguished albums of the 1960s. *The Freedom Book* in particular reveals Ervin as an exceptional instrumentalist, brimming with ideas, who took his playing to the door of the avant-garde without aligning himself with it. 'I'm all for progress in modern music,' he said, 'but up to the point of the avant garde which has organization in it, which I strive for myself.' [29]

Ervin had a readily identifiable sound as much as his own way of approaching a solo. He blew with terrific strength and his technique allowed him to move around the instrument with impressive velocity. At a time when saxophonists had come under the sway of either John Coltrane or Sonny Rollins, Ervin was steadfastly his own man. He blew every note as if it might be his last, exclaiming: 'There is nothing on earth I like better than playing music,' [30] and this facet of his playing shines through clearly on *The Freedom Book*. Here he explodes with confident creativity; he knew his history and his playing refracted elements of Coleman Hawkins, Sonny Stitt, Dexter Gordon and Lester Young, but most of all it showed him to be a natural bluesman; that unmistakable cry of pain mixed with anger was just as apparent in his handling of a ballad as at fast tempos.

Recorded while appearing with Byard in Mingus's Jazz Workshop at the Five Spot Café, *The Freedom Book* was recorded in just five hours. *A lunar tune* cleverly trades off metre and tempo in a series of four-bar phrases over differing pedal points within a 32-bar structure. The tempo is startlingly fast, [31] yet Ervin remains expressive and original in structuring his ideas, varying his expressive tone colouring to give his playing a powerful, soaring quality. Byard is lucid and refuses to let the intensity slacken, producing a fluent solo that, as ever with his work, sounds simultaneously contemporaneous and in the tradition, here evoking shades of Earl Hines. *Cry me not*, a ballad written by Randy Weston, with whom Ervin toured Nigeria in 1961, is the only non-Ervin composition. Ervin responds with such emotional engagement in his playing, as he works his way into the belly of the song, that is as moving as it is unsettling. *Grant's stand*, a vital, swinging 12-bar blues, was the first number cut on the session. Very often it is the first cut that acts as a barometer of things to come on a recording date, and from the start the outlook was sunny. Ervin had the equilibrium and greased invention that could be found in the playing of the great tenor titans, and the solid, purposeful urgency of his flowing lines is matched by the stirring work of the rhythm section, who match his intensity and commitment with speed of thought and vibrant, stimulating interaction.

The playing of the rhythm section is one of the features of this album; indeed they present an integrated group concept that succeeds in creating an environment for the soloist that is as stimulating and original in its way (side-tracking for a moment the distracting argument of 'who is best') as the then established units in jazz such as Coltrane's quartet, the Davis sextet, Monk's quartet or the Evans trio. *A day to mourn* refers to the assassination of President Kennedy, a heartfelt lament over a 6/4 *ostinato* (A), contrasted by a swinging bridge in 4/4 (B):

A (4 bars) + A (4 bars) + B (16 bars) + A (4 bars) + x (2-bar tag in 6/4)

After the theme statement, solos are taken with a *rubato* feel, Davis's bass solo, for example, appears free in its fluidity. *Al's in*, which follows, is an equally impressive performance, a piece that also deliberately invokes 'outside' playing with its polytonal introduction. It finally emerges as a typically supercharged quartet performance with Dawson's drumming outstanding throughout. After such powerful performances, *Stella by starlight* appears to come as light relief – it was not issued on the original LP configuration – but with Ervin's solo he moves towards the spirit of the avant-garde as his playing abruptly veers 'outside'. This development of his style had caused club owners to shy away from him; in 1963 13 gigs were cancelled from under him because word had spread he was 'too far out'. [32] In fact his playing here is a perfect balance of freedom within form, of 'inside-outside' playing that was almost two decades ahead of its time.

It is difficult to believe, although sadly true, that this group never performed outside the recording studio. With work slowing down, Ervin moved to Europe for 19 months in 1964, returning home in June 1966. The curious paradox of his career was that while he was recognized by his peers as an original, passionate and highly swinging player, public recognition that should have been his due never came his way. He went virtually unnoticed during his lifetime and when he died, on 31 July 1970, at the age of 39, his former producer Don Schlitten firmly believed it was because of a broken heart. [33] S.N.

Art Blakey

342 Mosaic

†EMI/Blue Note (E) CDP746 523–2

Freddie Hubbard (tpt); Curtis Fuller (tbn); Wayne Shorter (ten); Cedar Walton (p); Jymie Merritt (bs); Blakey (d). Hackensack, N.J., October 1961.

Mosaic · Down under · Children of the night · Arabia · Crisis

Influential early in the days when bop was beginning to harden (see **281–91**), the Jazz Messengers started as a co-operative involving Kinny Dorham or Donald Byrd, Horace Silver, Doug Watkins and, already injecting a good deal of what was distinctive about the band, Blakey.

Silver was credited as first leader, and †EMI/Blue Note (E) 746 140–2 [34] may be regarded as the threshold of a long history, over which Blakey was to preside. The effective unveiling of the typical Messengers format under Blakey's leadership was the 1954 quintet, with Clifford Brown a new star and Silver still the pianist, which is written of under **270**. The long and distinguished succession of similar Blakey bands was to continue, with a rather arid period, recordwise, in the 1970s, right through to his death in 1990. Several of the creative spirits who, in addition to Blakey, gave the band its well-sustained flavour were able to springboard into independent renown. Among succeeding trumpeters, saxophonists and pianists there was, as happens with jazz outfits of established 'voice', a deal of cross-fertilization in both improvising manner and composition.

This 1961 line-up was one of Blakey's most distinguished. Shorter, an emerging stylist, had joined in 1959; Hubbard, not long in New York from Indianapolis, replaced Lee Morgan in 1961, gained a New Star award the same year, and soon bid fair to match Morgan's shining reputation. Fuller came, in the same year, from experience with a number of influential bands including the Art Farmer/Benny Golson Jazztet. Cedar Walton, a Jazztet associate also, a pianist once classified as 'Silver-and-small-change', [35] joined Blakey in 1961, Merritt came in 1959. Shorter was acting as the group's musical director.

As an album, *Mosaic* demonstrates the composing art of the front-line players plus Walton. Walton's introductory *Mosaic* piece is a patterned creation of some brilliance. Hubbard builds on rising 13ths across the pianist's minor vamp, and he is concerned with subtle mood-building too, abetted by Fuller's and Walton's solos. Shorter's essay is irregularly punctuated. Blakey's substantial solo builds to a cymbal crescendo and Walton's characteristic conclusion. *Down under* is Hubbard's, an unusually conceived 16 bars sliced into a series of six-bar phrases. Shorter is wide-sweeping, Fuller robustly simple, Hubbard plaintive in further ascents. Shorter's *Children of the night* alternates eight- and twelve-bar phrases in a markedly intense piece of music, the tenorist's own masterly solo makes its rhythmic design intriguing with hints of early jazz dance – mildly *démodé* echoes of Harlem, but zesty nonetheless.

There is a suggestion of venerable songstyle in *Arabia*, linked to a parallel hint of Oriental mode. It is a 32-bar theme with three-chorus improvisations from Hubbard and Shorter, and some dramatic rhythm-section work more than anything else re-emphasizes (if that is not too weak a term) the tremendous scene-setting potential of Blakey's drumming – powerful but varied too, and subtle enough to do justice to the skills of his principal creators. Fuller wrote *Arabia*, and he toys with other nostalgic suggestions as he ad libs at the close.

The able Merritt has a phrase from the composer Hubbard to introduce *Crisis*, and Walton, a much more self-possessed artist than his devaluers used to suggest, shapes the downward-tending 56 bars (16 twice repeated with an eight-bar bridge), in which there are striking inner contrasts. Merritt contributes open, lissome persuasions; and the other solos – Shorter declamatory, Fuller elegantly firm, Walton puckish – argue towards a Hubbard-led reprise which fades off towards a Blakey-marshalled future with nearly three decades yet to run. The immediate years were to see a handful of pretty successful recordings with a minimally altered Messengers group.

Following upon the early 1960s, the affairs of Blakey vis-à-vis the Messengers became a little less clearly defined. This caused a sizeable hiatus in his discography; but in the later 1970s, and through the 1980s to his death, this exceptionally personable drummer and shrewd encourager of young jazz talent would oversee much more fine jazz. Almost any good post-1970s Messengers performance might seem a true core example of hard bop as an established style; though a danger of its being judged as the preservation of a style which had outrun its best resources was present often enough. *Mosaic* may be genuine hard bop, but that does not, on best reflection, define its abiding appeal. While it might, from one perspective, show how a significant strand of hard-bop enterprise was progressing, its fecundities of personal interaction may make its insertion into a subchapter concerned with the revivifying of earlier realizations of jazz modernist seem apt enough. E.T.

ClarkTerry/Bob Brookmeyer

343 **Clark Terry – Bob Brookmeyer Quintet**
†Mainstream Records (A) MDCD728

Terry (tpt, fl h); Brookmeyer (v-tbn); Roger Kellaway (p); Bill Crow (bs); Dave Bailey (d). New York City, 1964.

Tete à tete · Pretty girl · Blue China · Hum · Blindman, blindman · Step right up · Weep · Straight, no chaser · Sometime ago · The hymn

The importance of the 'New Thing' and the work of certain key musicians of the 1960s, not least Coleman, Coltrane and Davis, have effectively conspired to wipe the ledger clean of any references to what, in comparison, might be considered the 'old thing' verities of the Clark Terry–Bob Brookmeyer Quintet. Yet the group managed to achieve an enthusiastic following in the early to mid-1960s, despite the more fashionable and widely reported events occurring elsewhere in jazz. Indeed, they were even flown across the Atlantic to guest on the now legendary *Jazz 625* TV series – 'an event unheard of outside *This is Your Life*,' appositely quipped the presenter Humphrey Lyttelton.

The paring of 'Mumbles' and 'Grumbles' brought together two highly individual musicians who had the priceless gift of an instantly recognizable sound on their respective instruments. Terry, on trumpet and more especially flugelhorn, was one of the most admired brassmen in jazz, whose technique and supreme lyricism seemed to make every note he played smile. No other brass musician has achieved such a rich, glowing tone. It was brassy, yet round and full of vibrant warmth that was sustained even on the fastest of triple-tongued or flutter-tongued passages. His use of the flugelhorn, which he adopted during his tenure in the Duke Ellington brass section (1951–9), helped popularize the instrument through his exuberant, technically impressive solos. In contrast, Brookmeyer on valve trombone was a gruff master of paraphrase and melodic development. Not quite the self-starting soloist that Terry was, he usually built up from the ground well-thought-out counter-arguments to Terry's dancing phrases.

The quintet was originally formed in the summer of 1961 at the request of the Canterino brothers, owners of New York's Half Note. Brookmeyer was vacationing from a long spell with the Gerry Mulligan Quartet and Terry was just getting established as a member of the NBC staff orchestra, fresh off the road from a long spell with Ellington and a trip to Europe with Quincy Jones's ill-fated *Free and Easy* tour. Terry was one of the first black musicians to break the notorious colour bar to land the job of a network staff musician, and the quintet was his out-of-school indulgence to keep his jazz chops up. The group was first recorded live by Verve at the Half Note in 1962, but the results were shelved because Eddie Costa's piano was out of tune. An album taken from the sessions eventually saw the light of day 11 years later as *Clark Terry & Bob Brookmeyer* (Verve [A] V6 8836), but was a disappointment as much for the poor mix as for the lack of cohesion normally associated with a set, working group.

After the death of Costa, the pianists Tommy Flanagan, Herbie Hancock and Derek Smith filled the breach until Kellaway joined in 1963. This CD, recorded three and a half years after their original formation, is a reissue of *Tonight* (Mainstream [A] S 6043, Phillips (E) TL 5265), and is the most congenial of their recordings for Bob Shad's Mainstream label. [36] In contrast to their recording for Verve, Brookmeyer, a consummate arranger, got to grips with their repertoire and provided a series of well-crafted charts for the group that go beyond the tenets of simple heads. His clever part-writing made a virtue out of the unusual all-brass front line, varying tone colours from full, round unisons to simple harmony parts. Refreshingly he avoided the head-solos-head format, a limiting concept that relegates the theme to the role of bookends to contain improvisations, by the use of contrapuntal episodes that might be written or improvised, clever little counter-melodies and riffs behind soloists and transitional themes, all of which combined to give a pleasing sense of diversity to their material.

Tete à tete, a Terry original, first appeared on the Buddy Tate album *Tate à Tate* (Swingville [A] 2014) on which Terry also played. It is a 32-bar AABA tune with the A sections based on the *I got rhythm* changes except for a pedal point sustained between bars one to four on the supertonic. The B section uses chords that are similar to the bridge of *Take the 'A' train*. Terry's two-chorus solo is a masterpiece of construction, using several simple ideas to maximum effect, not least the contrast between long note values which begin both choruses and neatly tongued arpeggiated figures which finally emerge to dominate the whole of the second middle eight. Here he uses his hallmark rising semitone leading into descending, perfectly tongued arpeggios. The rising semitone, used like a grace note, was something we associate with Clifford Brown, but it also occurs frequently in Terry's improvisations and is one of the most readily identifiable characteristics of his style; here, for example, he uses it twice in the opening four bars of his solo. The tempo is brisk, [37] but this does not impede his essentially vertical approach to improvisation. Throughout, he frequently spells out the chord tones, yet this neat, orderly approach to improvisation does not sound in the least mechanical. Terry's singing tone and precise articulation consistently makes the technically difficult sound easy.

After such a deft, light-footed solo, it might seem that Brookmeyer's contribution on valve trombone was doomed to remain earthbound. Yet he was an enormously resourceful soloist whose management of ideas was matched by his ability to execute them and he was not in the least overshadowed by the quicksilver Terry. He steadfastly held the middle ground and, although sometimes appearing straight man to the nimble trumpeter's puckish humour, often emerged as a compelling alternative with his wry, laconic approach to improvisation. Kellaway subsequently came to be valued as much as a jazz pianist as a symphonic composer, but here was a 25-year-old bursting with unorthodox ideas, fresh from the New England Conservatory. Opening his solo with a lusty, if somewhat incongruous, stride passage he serves to underline the diversity of talent that made up this unusual little group.

Tete à tete also has a rhythmic scheme that recurs during each solo. Imposing a rhythmic scheme in addition to the pre-existing harmonic and melodic form was unusual in jazz. The most obvious example of this was the quite specific rhythmic framework adhered to throughout Herbie Hancock's composition *Maiden voyage* (**353**), but this was unusual; the norm in jazz was for an interactive role in accompaniment largely left to the discretion of the rhythm section. However, Terry and Brookmeyer explore the concept of imposing various rhythmic frameworks within their compositions, from simple stop chords to certain specific rhythmic patterns at prearranged points in the arrangement. Here, every beat is played as an evenly accented crotchet, with every eighth beat accented during the first two A sections of the solos, contrasting the straight-ahead 4/4 swing that follows. This simple device, creating tension and release, gave the soloist unexpected impetus with the move to an even four and serves to underline how even a simple rhythmic device can give a performance unexpected definition.

Blue China has a rather trite 'Chinese' passage (X), but even so develops into a solid performance. Its form is unorthodox:

8-bar intro (cymbals) + X = 8-bar 'Chinese' interlude +
Y (12 bars) + Z (8 bars stop chords) + X + [Y + Z + 12 bars
stop chords + Z] to solos

Solos follow a ternary AABA format with two choruses of 12-bar blues (A+A) + 8 bars stop chords (B) + one chorus 12-bar blues (A). Note that Terry begins his solo with 12 bars of stop chords, but nevertheless adheres to the AABA scheme.

Here, the rhythmic device of stop chords is an important feature of the composition; indeed, Terry begins his solo against 12 bars of them, which, together with the ensemble passage that preceded it, makes for a passage of 40 bars in all! It is a very effective recasting of a device popular in jazz until the mid-1930s without sounding dated. A Brookmeyer composition, it again reveals his refreshingly open approach to jazz of all eras that resulted in *Traditionalism Revisited* (**458**) from 1957, an album that unselfconsciously returned to the jazz tradition for inspiration almost 30 years before it became fashionable in the 1980s.

The wonderful warm unisons on Brookmeyer's *Hum* is, like the Ellington method, a combination of quite specific musical personalities to create a new sound texture. [38] It is not simply a flugelhorn and a valve trombone in unison, but a uniquely brown tone colour which in itself becomes the specific feature of Brookmeyer's original 32-bar song. The song comprises an eight-bar theme which is repeated up a semitone three times, A A A^1 A, with A^1 effectively a variation of the original eight-bar motif. The combination of the rising line and bright tempo draws a wholly engaging performance from Terry, whose playing during this period was the finest of his long and distinguished career. [39] Brookmeyer again employs stop chords during solos, this time at A^1, followed by eight bars of evenly accented crotchets. This rhythmic scheme during the last 16 bars of each blowing chorus might have unsettled some soloists who preferred an unfettered, driving rhythm, but Terry and Brookmeyer exploit the contrasting rhythmic devices to bring a sense of tension and release within the overall architecture of their solos.

Composed by Kellaway, *Step right up* is full of interest and variety both compositionally and within the structuring of the solos. In just six minutes of music, a lot happens. During his own solo, for example, he appears to drift into an arrhythmic interlude, yet the bars are clicking by in perfect time and he returns *a tempo* smack on the money at the end of his chorus. Terry and Brookmeyer climax the piece with a series of exchanges reminiscent of Clifford Brown's *Blues Walk*, [40] where Brown and Sonny Rollins begin trading four bars, progressively halving them in value, to two bars, to one bar and to half a bar, without destroying the cogency of the improvised line. In exactly the same way, Terry and Brookmeyer's exchanges follow the same course and seem directed by one mind, so close is their empathy. In fact, this number is the finest on the album.

A genuflection in the direction of 'funky' hard bop comes with Herbie Hancock's ten-bar theme *Blindman, blindman* from his 1963 album *My Point of View* (†Blue Note [E] CDP72343829331–2). Here Terry and Brookmeyer get far more out of the song than ever did Donald Byrd or Hank Mobley on the original. At the time of the recording, Terry and Brookmeyer were members of Gerry Mulligan's Concert Jazz Band with whom the composer-arranger Gary McFarland was associated [41] and *Weep*, one of his compositions for the big band, appears here in a suitably miniaturized version. As on all the numbers on this album, not least Thelonious Monk's intriguing 12-bar *Straight, no chaser* and Parker's *Hymn*, the themes are perfectly articulated by the front line. 'I have a sort of fetish about two-horn groups that don't hit precisely together,' said Terry. 'Because there's only two it should be very compatible in the attacks, expressions and releases.' [42]

Terry and Brookmeyer combined impeccable musicianship with flair, individuality, wit and the therapeutic power of 'positive swing'. Terry's role in jazz has come to be sadly undervalued since much of his subsequent recorded output placed him in limiting mainstream situations rather than the expansive roles his great gift seemed to cry out for. [43] Too often he became the victim of unimaginative record producers who, conscious of his ability to make silk purses, tended to hand him sow's ears to work with. Yet Terry's style steadfastly resisted convenient categorization and even in the most unpromising performing situations he was always capable of creating gems. One of the finest trumpet and flugel players in jazz, he was in truly copacetic company with Brookmeyer and the album session provided an ideal context for his playing. It is interesting to note that when this album first appeared in 1965 it received a rave review in *down beat* and a four-and-a-half star rating. When it was re-released in 1972, at the height of the jazz-rock craze, a reviewer, hip to the latest trends, nevertheless repeated the rating, saying: 'Records like this are rarely made any more so the reissue of these sides is especially welcome.' [44] Almost 25 years later, that verdict still holds good.

S.N.

Bud Shank

344 New Groove

Pacific Jazz (A) PJ21, Vogue (E) LAE12288

Carmell Jones (tpt); Shank (alt[1], bar[2]); Dennis Budimir (g); Gary Peacock (bs); Mel Lewis (d). Los Angeles, May 1961.

New groove[1] · *The awakening*[2] · *White lightning*[1] · *Sultry serenade*[2] · *Well, you needn't*[1] · *Liddledabllduya*[1]

Once listed as being 'among other West Coast altoists', Shank was until recently the subject of almost no critical comment in the literature of jazz. [45] Indeed he is all too good an illustration of the fact that a person can produce sterling work over decades, yet still be ignored by those who fabricate this music's history. Clearly his main influence was Art Pepper, with whom he worked in Kenton's band, though with the intriguing combination of Parker and Konitz in the background. Shank had arrived at his own music, however, several years before the above record was made.

With the exception of Lewis, the participants had prior to the session been playing regularly with him at the Drift Inn, Malibu, California, and the music demonstrably benefits from this shared experience. This is most apparent in the work of the rhythm team, whose collective pulse is flexible yet driving, frequently shifting in emphasis as the relationship between the guitar, bass and percussion parts change. Budimir takes particular advantage of the absence of a piano to vary his role, especially in respect of the foundation provided by the always adventurous Peacock (who went on to appear with George Russell, Albert Ayler and Jimmy Giuffre). The rather marked stereo separation of the horns aids our hearing all this properly – not least the evidence of Lewis's fine sense of ensemble – and the rhythm team's response to the front line is, again, at once intricate and imaginative. This is equally true in the matter of solo improvisation. For example in the *New groove* piece itself Budimir's melodic refinement, descended from Jimmy Raney and Tal Farlow, is an appropriate foil to the assertiveness of Jones and the leader and there is much quiet invention here.

New groove takes the form of a 'blues march', a convention of that time here put to productive use. The trumpeter had plainly learned much from Clifford Brown, and his melodic directness here contrasts tellingly with the alto saxophone's virtuoso convolutions. His splendidly warm tone matches Shank's too, particularly when the latter takes up the baritone instrument for *The awakening*. Two different but related sorts of lyricism are heard in their solos, which flow into the heightened intensity of informal yet entirely apt counterpoint. There had been little composing by Shank on his previous releases but the above titles are by him, as is *White lightning*, a very fast blues. All these highly accomplished executants are relaxed at this unforgiving pace, though it is noticeable here, and again on Peacock's fleet *Liddledablldduya* (on the chords of *Love me or leave me*) that Shank's ideas are rather more tightly packed than Jones's.

Not that any of them, with all their fluency, is guilty of mere padding, but the verve and incisiveness, the emotional force and rhythmic commitment of the leader's playing does stand out. As these are precisely the virtues that West Coast jazz allegedly shunned, it should be added that *Well, you needn't* is not the sort of piece they were supposed ever to perform. In reality the entire band relates to it extremely well, and this stands with Pepper's *Rhythm-a-ning* of the previous year (†Original Jazz Classics [A] OJCCD169–2) among the best non-Monk improvisations on a Monk theme. The longest track, *Sultry serenade*, shows how well pieces associated with Ellington (it was actually composed by Tyree Glenn) survive treatments utterly different from his, in this case one in which Budimir again demonstrates the virtues of understatement.

The *New Groove* record is best heard alongside its little-known complement, Shank's *Barefoot Adventure* (Pacific Jazz [A] PJ35). This was made a few months later by the same personnel except that Bob Cooper is added on tenor saxophone and Shelly Manne replaces Lewis. Remarkably few passages are restricted by the music's being required to underline the visual images of a surfing film of the same name and all concerned put in some notable improvising. *Barefoot Adventure* ought to rank high among the few films that have given rise to excellent jazz. Luckily the contents of both these LPs, together with other Shank Pacific Jazz studio dates of 1956–9, have been reissued on Mosaic (A) MD5–180, a 7-LP 5-CD set.

When it first appeared, *New Groove* was hailed, even by those unfriendly to West Coast jazz, as a big improvement for Shank. It is a superb record, yet, viewed from a much longer perspective of years, it does not mark the advance then claimed. Its admitted eloquence does not surpass, for instance, Shank's heated declarations on two 1956 issues both called *The Bud Shank Quartet* (World Pacific [A] WP1215, Vogue [E] LAE12041 and WP1230, LAE12113). Of at least equal quality is *The Saxophone Artistry of Bud Shank* (Pacific Jazz [A] LP1213, Vogue [E] LAE12143), half of which finds him in 1955, with Bob Brookmeyer, on one of the few sessions where jazz improvising fuses properly with the use of strings – above all in the mad square-dance explosion of Brookmeyer's *Rustic hop*. Again, Shank, aided by Peacock and Chuck Flores, got more jazz into his collaborations with Laurindo Almeida such as *Latin Contrasts* (World Pacific [A] WP1281, Vogue [E] LAE12248), than can be found in the later jazz/bossa nova affairs (which are not dealt with in this volume). M.H.

Dodo Marmarosa

345 Dodo's Back

Cadet (A) UXP118, †Affinity (E) CDAFF755

Marmarosa (p); Richard Evans (bs); Marshall Thompson (d). Chicago, 9–10 May 1961.

Mellow mood · *Cottage for sale* · *April played the fiddle* · *Everything happens to me* · *On Green Dolphin Street* · *Why do I love you?* · *I thought about you* · *Me and my shadow* · *Tracy's blues* · *You call it madness*

The title given to the Affinity release, *The Chicago Sessions*, lends a not quite plausible 'historic' sense to these 1961 dates. The more familiar title, that on the original Argo LP, subtitled 'The Return of Dodo Marmarosa, a brilliant jazz pianist', may, on the other hand, have raised an optimism about him that also lacked justification. As for the past – in terms of name recordings, there had been three Los Angeles sessions, the first a quartet including Lucky Thompson and Ray Brown, the second a trio with Barney Kessel, the third a conventional trio which appears to have been Marmarosa's most substantial essay as leader before the present one and which produced a number of original compositions. (His complete recordings for Dial are on †Spotlite [E] SPJCD128.) Yet another trio, brief in programme and uncertain in date, was recorded in Pittsburgh two or three years later. Pittsburgh seems to have been his base during that period, and probably later. He was about 35 years old when, with Joe Segal's encouragement, Jack Tracy supervised this 'comeback' appearance at the Argo studios. Two further albums, one featuring Gene Ammons, came out around that time before failing health forced him back into obscurity.

Marmarosa's pianistic address reveals a satisfying variety of expression with a very lively instinct for cohesion. In this context, the possibilities of his vigorous romanticism can be more openly exploited than they could in his appearances as a combo member, though pretty strong indications of his leanings are heard in his work with Parker (**258**), Lester Young (**252**) and Wardell Gray (**268**). The pattern of each of these 1961 pieces develops along lines similar to the rest, the similarity residing chiefly in an instinct for including a variety of complementary and contrasting elements into any solo.

Mellow mood (a Marmarosa tune that was featured in his 1946 date with Lucky Thompson) has its theme stated chordally in a manner that may echo Tristano or Shearing, and continues with an invention of strong accents and timing deceits of several kinds. The thoughtful reverie of *Cottage for sale* benefits, like everything else, from the sensitivity of Evans and Thompson, the bassist's lyricism here being impressive. *April played the fiddle* moves as happily as its title suggests – a measured emphasis in the bop-shaped lines and, towards the close, some punchy drama. It is a contained strategy of phrasal, registral and dynamic inner dialogue that creates his dramatic episodes in a number of pieces, and this is marked particularly in *Me and my shadow*, with its fizzing crush accents and fetching multiplications. In the robustly moving things (*On Green Dolphin Street*, *Everything happens to me* and *Why do I love you?*), peremptory strokes, running chord lines and wry sequences of modernistic contrivances show a firm mastery of jazz thinking which, though bop experience subsumes it, does not leave abandoned those things he learned from men like Teddy Wilson and Johnny Guarnieri. See **160**, where Marmarosa's work with Artie Shaw is likened to Bud Powell's with Cootie Williams. And, on that aspect, though there may be a streak of nostalgia in the pre-bop echoes of the slow *I thought about you*, that number, with its 'breathing' control of the rhythm relations and its abrupt strategic junctures, is close to the occasional romantic 'mask' assumed by the later Powell – and there are pre-bop echoes there too.

Dodo's Back maintains individuality when compared to the works-in-re-emergence of Al Haig (**356**) and Joe Albany (e.g. SteepleChase [D] SCS1019). Though broadened in scope, Haig's bop fealty may sound more strongly, while Albany, fleetingly brilliant in the 1940s, might have achieved something akin to Marmarosa's late style had his expressive control been more reliable. The latter's enforced retreat was and remains regrettable. This record will probably be his lost music's best memorial.

E.T.

Freddie Hubbard

346 Open Sesame

†Blue Note (E) CDP784040–2

Hubbard (tpt); Tina Brooks (ten); McCoy Tyner (p); Sam Jones (bs); Clifford Jarvis (d). Englewood Cliffs, N. J., 19 June 1960.

Open sesame (2 versions) · *But beautiful* · *Gypsy blue* (2 versions) · *All or nothing at all* · *One mint julep* · *Hub's nub*

When Hubbard cut this album he had already earned a formidable reputation since arriving in New York from Indianapolis two years earlier. Alongside Philly Joe Jones, Charlie Persip, Slide Hampton and, most notably, Sonny Rollins, he had been earmarked as rising star and was currently performing with the J. J. Johnson sextet. Indeed, there is a snap and crackle to his authoritative solo on *Open sesame* that immediately announces the arrival of a major new talent in jazz. It is a moment that prompts reflection on the 1980s, a decade in which record companies actively promoted young jazz musicians performing in the hard-bop idiom. Press offices worked overtime in hyping the arrival of their new signings, and the jazz media responded with stories of coming greats. None, however, matched the authority, poise and sheer ability of Hubbard's debut here; this was the genuine article and the album is among the finest of his career. Indeed, in 1994 Jon Faddis pointed out that Hubbard himself had come to regard his earliest recordings as among his best recorded work. [46]

One of three originals Brooks contributed to the date, the title track is both interesting and resourceful in its construction: a 64-bar AABA form in the minor, with the A and B sections 16 bars each. The scheme is:

A = (X = 8 bars + X^1 = 8 bars) + A = (X + X^1) + B = (16 bars) +
A = (X + X^1)
Note: final X^1 = 6 bars + 2-bar pickup to solos on AABA.

The A section contrasts a Latin passage, X, with straight-ahead swing, X^1, while B is straight-ahead throughout, as are the solo choruses. It is typical of Brooks's best compositions, which contrasted melancholy minor moods with a dash of Latin flavouring, his solid craftsmanship lifting his themes out of the often limiting formulas of hard bop that relied on basic blues forms worked into simple heads.

Hubbard takes a long, 176-bar solo, almost three choruses, a challenge indeed for a young brass player making his recording debut. Yet he sounds far removed from the rookie debutant; his tone and attack are remarkably assured and he effortlessly sustains interest and variety despite the very brisk tempo. His ideas are ordered in the logical, highly swinging way Clifford Brown approached a solo, but his tone is far broader and his attack more aggressive, breaking his line with stabbing phrases including a high register paraphrase from *Laura*.

One of Hubbard's great strengths has always been his ballad playing, an area where few post-Gillespie brass players have been totally secure, even Clifford Brown. Yet from his very first recording, Hubbard's ability within the idiom was at once fully formed, something quite unusual in a young player. On the Brooks ballad *But beautiful* his exceptionally precise sense of time allowed him to express ideas that were both clear and concise with unsentimental lyricism. Slow tempos are a far greater challenge to an improviser than fast ones are. For a wind instrument they can show up imperfections in intonation, breath control, phrasing and articulation, consequently most instrumentalists head for the safe haven of double time as quickly as possible. Yet Hubbard resists the urge, merely hinting at the option towards the end of his solo, preferring instead to show off his warm, brown tone that could dissolve into a whisper or leap into the high register seemingly at will.

Gypsy blue, Brooks's third original for the session, is essentially a minor Latin theme over an extended 12-bar blues sequence but is presented as:

(X = 4-bar vamp) + A = 14-bar theme + (X = 4-bar vamp) +
A = 14-bar theme + (X = 4-bar vamp) to solos (minor 12-bar blues)

Once again modest materials are marshalled to telling effect. When Brooks enters he abruptly snaps into a straight-ahead four, sucking elements of the theme into his solo and making it sound a logical extension of his composition. His style ran counter to the prevailing hard-bop orthodoxy with a gentle, graceful tone and an often quite sensitive lyricism. Although he occasionally reached for an idea that seemed fractionally beyond his technical compass (such as bar 20 of his *Sesame* solo), there was nevertheless great clarity and unity of ideas in his work. 'Tina made my first record date wonderful,' said Hubbard later. 'He wrote and played beautifully.' [47]

The refreshing momentum generated on the Brooks compositions continues through *All or nothing at all*, despite its curiously detached piano introduction, an impish but irresistible two-beat version of *One mint julep* and Hubbard's own engaging *Hub's nub* with an intriguing 44-bar form of:

$$(\text{Intro: } X = 8 \text{ bars} + X^1 = 8 \text{ bars}) + (A = 12 \text{ bars} + A = 12 \text{ bars} + B = 8 \text{ bars} + A = 12 \text{ bars})$$

Solos are over the full 44-bar AABA format and Hubbard finishes the album as he began with a long, confident, yet captivating solo, this time of three choruses. Within a week, Hubbard was again in the recording studios for Blue Note, this time for a Brooks date that produced *True Blue* (**340**). Both albums were originally released in autumn 1960, and today they suggest that both Hubbard and Brooks, then 22 and 28 respectively, stood on the threshold of potentially great careers.

Somehow it was not to be; Brooks never entered a recording studio after 1961 and was not heard of again outside the Bronx, whereas Hubbard, after an initial flash of brilliance, [48] later embarked on a series of recordings for CTI and Columbia where commercial considerations rather than aesthetic merit were paramount. The results placed him in something of a quandary; as the sales mounted so did his disillusionment with their musical merit. Yet despite some eccentric and inexplicable albums in his discography, Hubbard, in 1960 as in the 1990s, always suggested that the best lay ahead of him. S.N.

Tubby Hayes

347a Down in the Village

†Redial (E) CD 588 184–2, Fontana (E) 680 998TL

Jimmy Deuchar (tpt); Hayes (ten[1], sop[2], vib[3]); Gordon Beck (p); Freddy Logan (bs); Allan Ganley (d). Ronnie Scott's, London, 17–18 May 1962.

Johnny one-note[1] · *But beautiful*[3] · *The most beautiful girl in the world*[1] · *Down in the village*[3] · *In the night*[2] · *First eleven*[1]

347b Late Spot at Scott's

†Redial [E] CD 588 183–2, Fontana (E) TL5200

Same personnel and dates.

Half a sawbuck[1] · *Angel eyes*[3] · *The sausage scraper*[1] · *My man's gone now*[1] · *Yeah!*[1]

Although he died as long ago as 1973, Hayes is still a well-remembered presence on the British jazz scene and in fact had international standing, twice recording as the leader of distinguished and otherwise all-American groups in New York. A busy professional musician from the age of 15, he was a natural virtuoso of the tenor saxophone, gifted with that instantaneous link between rapid thought and magnificent technique which is always found in major executants. Predictably he both relished the challenge of very fast tempos and always sounded at ease in them. The fluency and communicative power of his solos on pieces such as *Johnny one-note*, *First eleven* and *Yeah!* – each taken at an unforgiving pace yet with every note decisively articulated and exactly timed – perfectly represent the side of his playing that has always been emphasized. Such improvising would obviously excite jazz fans, yet his technique was never simply athletic and even under pressure he still shaped his phrases with notable sensitivity. The effect of these headlong performances can certainly be overwhelming, but more is communicated in the less extreme cases of *Half a sawbuck*, *My man's gone now* and *The sausage scraper*.

All these achievements, indeed, are rooted in a wider and deeper musicality which makes the labelling of Hayes's output as 'British hard bop' a misleading simplification. Though he will always be identified principally with the tenor, he was never merely the UK's answer to Johnny Griffin (**283**). In fact he was among the most convincing of jazz multi-instrumentalists, and his choice of additional instruments tells us a lot about his true artistic nature. He was adept on the baritone saxophone, yet it is with the flute and vibraharp that he made statements as personal as on the tenor. He had no problems in moving beyond the confines of 4/4, as is shown by the smoothly negotiated 3/4 of *In the night* and *My man's gone now* on the above records and the 9/8 of *Sasa-hivi* (Fontana [E] TL5221); another facet of his rhythmic capacities is his being able to maintain the pulse during quite long unaccompanied cadenzas, as in the middle of *100% proof* (Fontana TL5410) and at the end of *Tubbsville* (Fontana STFL562). He also had the ability to go beyond the formal limitations of the orthodox jazz of that time and improvise engagingly in a freer manner, as in his two versions of *Mexican green* (Miles Music [E] MM079). Then there is his writing, for he composed something approaching 100 themes and arranged for ensembles large and small with much resource. A concentrated illustration of his sensitivity in this area is the woodwind scoring which opens *Milestones* (TL5410).

Such a wide-ranging and individual talent implies diverse influences and besides Parker, Getz and Rollins are usually cited as early Hayes models. But whatever he learned from them had been completely assimilated before any of the records mentioned here was made. Altogether, playing with him must have been a severe challenge, not least because of his consistency, and it is this quality that makes the selection of recorded examples of his music so difficult. He made plenty of LPs during his short career that are on a similar level, yet none is better than the two detailed above. It says a good deal for British jazz of the early 1960s that, exceptional though Hayes was, the group he leads here is entirely worthy of him. Further, the whole band was on something like top form and these recordings preserve a genuinely memorable occasion.

Actually, its members seem as unconcerned about really fast tempos as their leader, and *Johnny one-note*, Hayes's *Down in the village* – an excellent theme – Deuchar's *First eleven* and Horace Silver's *Yeah!* find the ensemble at once fiery and relaxed. During this period Deuchar sometimes drew close to matching Hayes, the thrusting, exploratory trumpet playing on the above items plus *The most beautiful girl in the world* being impressive for its continuity and rhythmic life, the tone brassy yet sensitive. Often he rephrased the themes imaginatively, and more of this particular aspect of his music can be heard in his *Thou Swell* collection (Esquire [E] 330), where he improvises on popular ballads, making his solos grow out of them organically. Although he is perhaps best in *Yeah!*, there is more outstanding Deuchar on two further Hayes themes, *The sausage scraper* and *Half a sawbuck*, which also include fluent improvising from Beck. Other features include an inventive dialogue between Ganley and the ensemble which leads to that considerable rarity, a drum solo that is worth hearing.

Yet another Hayes theme is the rather Scots-sounding *In the night*, on which he plays the soprano saxophone, an instrument with which he did not persist: this performance should be compared with the later one on TL5221, where he plays the flute. The poise and thoughtfulness of his work on the vibraharp, as in *But beautiful* (from which Deuchar is absent), are striking, and further evidence of Hayes's essential sensitivity. Thoroughly effective though all the arrangements here are – and they include contributions from other hands such as Deuchar's scoring of *Johnny one-note* and Ganley's of *Angel eyes* – Hayes's flute and vibraharp work benefits from richer orchestral textures. Usually he played in conventionally instrumented settings, but it is interesting to hear him moving through the woodwind colours of *The folks that live on the hill* (STFL562). Another fine vibraharp improvisation occurs on *Bluesology* (TL5410), while for exceptional flute playing by Hayes *Raga* (TL5221) and *A night in Tunisia* (again TL5410) are suggested. M.H.

Dexter Gordon

348 Go!

†EMI/Blue Note (E) CDP746 094–2

Gordon (ten); Sonny Clark (p); Butch Warren (bs); Billy Higgins (d). Englewood Cliffs, N.J., 27 August 1962.

Cheese cake · I guess I'll hang my tears out to dry · Second balcony jump · Love for sale · Where are you? · Three o'clock in the morning

A wondrous array of ideas spins out of Gordon's *Cheese cake* improvisation, punched-out phrases and curving smears, tarrying just a little behind the pulse as the first tenor solo moves into greater fluidity. This dark-toned, sensitive musician has not forgotten his dues to Lester Young, yet his is a formed modernist vocabulary without being obviously imitative of anyone. After the terse preamble to *Second balcony jump*, he fashions and refashions new notions and, in addition to quoting *Mona Lisa* and *My heart stood still* as if they were instant inspirations of his own, he interpolates entirely original songlike snatches in a multitude of amiable conceits which never threaten linear constancy. Here is one of the most inventive soloists jazz has known; also one of the most humorous.

Was Gordon the first tenor saxophonist to latch on to bop innovations? Wardell Gray and Teddy Edwards might have contested the claim. There was a kind of contention for the honour in the later 1940s, and Gordon's dazzling jousts with Gray are well remembered. Gary Giddins regards Gordon as having developed 'the most influential new approach to the tenor' in the days of transition. [49] At all events, following serious hindrances in the 1950s, it was he who forged ahead as bop got its second wind, never too closely identified with fashionable adaptations of the mode. And although his influence fell upon different pioneers – Coltrane, Rollins – the form and spirit of the Gordon utterance remained essentially consonant with his earliest mature style. As the man who 'really did bridge the swing and bop eras', [50] he knew that a bridge has two ends. Asked in 1982 who had inspired him he listed 'Lester Young, Billie Holiday, The Duke, Jimmy Lunceford . . . Roy Eldridge . . .'; yet his natural stance faced the morrow. In the same interview, during the last decade of his life, he insisted: 'Bebop is the music of the future.' [51]

In 1943, with bop as yet unrevealed, Gordon, playing with Nat Cole (**180**), had the basis of his style well formed. It developed further, outwardly and inwardly, as he consorted with kindred spirits up to the opening of the 1950s. The years following were to contain personal setbacks but this 1962 record, and its identically manned companion *A Swinging Affair* (†EMI/Blue Note [E] CDP784 133–2), made two days later, bear vivid witness to the man's self-restitution. In quality there is little to choose between these fine sessions on the eve of his departure for Europe.

Clark, Warren and Higgins show complete rapport with Gordon and among themselves. Clark's entry in *Cheese cake* echoes the leader's enunciations and mock hesitancy, and his brittle fingering lends a touch of inwardness as counter to Gordon's extroversion.

I guess I'll hang my tears out to dry is justly best remembered of many fine ballad interpretations. Gordon traces its parts with relaxed openness, yet, as the beat establishes itself, there is no lack of life. In his second solo his sinewy sound is not at variance with the depth of his feeling. In between Clark contributes gentle, lucid, nicely poised remarks. Alert always, the pianist comes in on a clear echo of the tenor's first solo ending in *Second balcony jump*; and as Gordon is rolling out his thoughts while *Love for sale* phases from Latin to common time, Clark verifies the inspiration with memoranda of the tune and, at the same time, primes his thoughts for his own eagerly adroit solo.

There are both unforced pathos and heightened expressive tension in *Where are you?*, Gordon contriving to sound lazy and vigorous by turns, vaulting into high register, mouthing repeated notes with Lesterish technique, and, Lesterlike too, proving the value for communication of lyrical familiarity with the song as song. A medium-speed *Three o'clock in the morning* becomes a high-humoured expedition through which the quartet lopes side by side. In the course of it *Poinciana*, *The five o'clock whistle* and *Take me out to the ball game* fall into step and pay their impudent respects. The old Ted Lewis favourite has its honour restored before Clark calls a halt in a still, small *piano* voice. E.T.

Sonny Rollins

349 In Stockholm 1959

Dragon (Sd) DRLP 73

Rollins (ten); Henry Grimes (b); Pete La Roca (d). Stockholm, March 1959.

St Thomas

Same personnel. Stockholm, 4 March 1959.

There will never be another you · *Stay as sweet as you are* · *I've told every little star* · *How high the moon?* · *Oleo* · *Paul's pal*

At the time of writing, these represent the last known recordings by Rollins before what was technically his second furlough from jazz, usually given as August 1959 to November 1961. [52] When he re-emerged after his celebrated practice sessions on Williamsburg Bridge, it was as a somewhat different Rollins to the one who had played his last gig fifteen months earlier with Thelonious Monk at the Five Spot. Consequently, these recordings represent an important documentation of a pivotal point in Rollins's career. For many, the period between November 1955 and his temporary withdrawal from public performance in August 1959 represent an artistic plateau that the saxophonist appeared to struggle for the rest of his life to match. During this period he was involved in some 20 sessions for the Prestige, Blue Note and Contemporary labels, a creative high that produced, among others, *Saxophone Colossus* (**282**), *Way Out West* (Original Jazz Classics [A] OJC337), *Freedom Suite* (OJC067) [53] plus a couple of classic Blue Note dates for good measure.

By any standards it was an astonishing period of creativity that saw Rollins prising jazz improvisation from the vicelike grip of Charlie Parker's omnipresent influence. Parker left a legion of followers whose solos often sounded like one enormous glissando, but on albums such as *Worktime* (OJC007), with its versions of *There are such things* and *There's no business like show business*, Rollins demonstrated that jazz improvisation could be sustained for lengthy periods with coherence, subtlety and wit. The beacon that illuminates this period was *Saxophone Colossus*, a masterwork that made Rollins's reputation with aficionados and public alike. Yet within three years Rollins was apparently going through something of a personal and musical crisis. This, however, does not reveal itself in his recordings and might be seen as further proof, if proof were needed, of the impossibility of reading the mind's construction through the music. His only problem seemed to be in finding suitable accompanists in general and a pianist in particular. Thus for pragmatic reasons Rollins first recorded with just bass and drums on *Way Out West* in 1957. It became a recurring theme during the next two years, and a further four sessions see him in this format, the final occasion in July 1958, appearing on *Sonny Rollins/Brass – Sonny Rollins/Trio* (†Verve [A] 815 056–2).

In many ways the trio format was the ideal forum for Rollins's great talent; indeed in the case of *Freedom Suite* it produced a minor masterpiece. However, the sound of the tenor in such minimalistic surroundings was hardly new to jazz. As early as 1940, Ben Webster had emerged from Ellington's ensemble in *Conga Brava* (**153**) with just bass and drum accompaniment for his memorable 40-bar solo, albeit with the piano discreetly intervening at bars 15 and 16, 35 and 36 to mark the cadence points of Tizol's 2 x 20-bar structure. And in 1945, Don Byas recorded for the Commodore label accompanied by just Slam Stewart on bass. But for Rollins, using only bass and drums provided a context that in many ways suited his high-flying imagination best. Indeed, on *Saxophone Colossus* the pianist Tommy Flanagan seems to sense this, such is the skeletal nature of his comping behind Rollins. Primarily a vertical player, Rollins enjoyed in a trio format the freedom spontaneously to employ chord substitutions to fill in colourist detail to his line to a greater extent than he normally would do when accompanied by a conventional rhythm section. The flexibility offered by just bass and drums gave him the freedom to lead where a piano player might not be able to follow without prearrangement, giving him greater opportunity spontaneously to reorder and rearrange his performances in service of the creative moment. In later years he would specialize in effusive cadenzas, stream-of-consciousness parabolas that often competed with what had gone before with their startling audacity. The skeletal accompaniment of bass and drums placed him one remove from such total poetic licence, yet his trio recordings remain perhaps the most overlooked items in his discography, not least his Village Vanguard sessions for Blue Note in 1957 (*A Night at the Village Vanguard* Vols. 1 and 2 †Blue Note [E] CDP7 46517–2 and 46418–2). However, after his 'return' in 1961, he used the format infrequently on record, albeit leading a pianoless quartet with Jim Hall until 1962. Examples of his continuing to dabble with the tenor-bass-drums instrumentation can be heard on *What's New?* (†Bluebird [A] 07863 52572 2) and *On the Outside* (†RCA [A] ND82496), both from 1962, and *East Broadway Run Down* (†Impulse [A] IMP11612) from May 1966.

Rollins had previously been in Scandinavia in September 1958, albeit without his own rhythm section: *Sonny Rollins in Denmark* Vols. 1 and 2 (†Moon [A] MCD037–2 and 038–2). These live recordings, together with his final presabbatical album session *Sonny Rollins and the Contemporary Leaders* (Contemporary [A] S7564) from the following month, fail to suggest any slackening of creative resolve in his playing. Rather, they reveal an artist at one with his craft and certainly *In Stockholm 1959* supports this, revealing his creativity continuing unabated right up to his 16-month absence from jazz, taken, according to the saxophonist himself, to enable him to kick his habit with hard drugs. [54] As an aside, although three numbers on this album had been previously recorded, Rollins was devouring new songs by the week, and the fresh numbers here barely suggest the extraordinary variety of material in his repertoire. The sheer size of that repertoire as much as his choice of numbers was quite unparalleled in jazz at this time, frequently revealing off-the-wall titles like *Sonny boy*, *Rock-a-bye your baby*, *Toot-toot-tootsie goodbye*, *In the chapel in the moonlight*, *If you were the only girl in the world*, *Wagon wheels*, *How are things in Glocca Mora?* and *The theme from the Pathétique Symphony*.

St Thomas, recorded at the Nalem Club in Stockholm three days after his arrival in Sweden on 1 March 1959, represents the only live track. The remainder were recorded live in the studios of the Swedish Radio Company and broadcast about a year after Rollins's visit. *St Thomas*, from *Saxophone Colossus*, is a simple but hugely catchy 16-bar AABC theme of four-bar sections built around a ii-v-i progression that appears at the end of the two four-bar A sections and again at the end of the penultimate bar of C. Rollins always seemed to derive a great deal of pleasure from this number, which allowed a playful streak in his personality to surface, as in his quotation from *Camptown races*. At the time Swedish critics were hailing him a 'young and angry avant-gardist', prompting speculation on what they made of this joyful calypso. *There will never be another you* marks the opening of his radio broadcast and includes a spoken introduction by Rollins that is both genial and gracious, beginning 'Good afternoon, jazz fans . . .' In contrast, the concentrated application of his playing was often blunt, frequently varying his attack from *legato* to staccato and beginning and ending his phrases in odd places, altering the metre of his improvisation against the underlying ground beat or abruptly doubling time. He could move in and out of tempo with amazing skill; his rhythmic sense was seemingly infallible. In all his solos, he presents a series of propositions that could be spun endlessly rather than the pronouncements of an Armstrong or a Parker, which appeared to arrive etched in stone. In 1992 he acknowledged: 'I epitomize the spontaneous aspect of playing jazz. I see myself as a work in progress: I always feel my best work is yet to come.' [55]

Stay as sweet as you are is a beautiful ballad performance, and is played with the kind of aplomb Rollins reserved for slower tunes and with the kind of conviction that does not suggest he thinks his best chorus will be the next. *I've told every little star*, a number he had recorded the previous October for *The Contemporary Leaders*, provokes one of those impish Rollins performances that are often such compulsive listening. His statement of the theme includes two answering phrases done *sotto voce* off mike and are, as he intended, genuinely humorous. However, when he parts company with the theme he launches into a magnificently expansive solo, dismantling the song and reassembling it with sudden dark turns, clever substitutions and awkward rhythmic displacements. *How high the moon?*, a 32-bar ABAB tune with pleasingly logical changes based on the cycle of fifths, is initially presented as an exercise in redistributing the melody somewhat lumpily over its underlying harmonies. An off-the-cuff number to give the sound engineers an opportunity to check balances, it was not intended for broadcast. This off-duty performance evolves into an easy swinging solo with new ideas tumbling over themselves as he explores the song's familiar harmonies. Rollins's style combined both vertical and horizontal playing to a degree that was unusual in jazz, and his solos easily incorporated every chord, yet even at the fastest tempos were vibrantly melodic. The spontaneous melodies Rollins created seemed to come from an inexhaustible fund and were at least as inventive and resourceful as those to be found in the work of Charlie Parker, an important early influence. It is somehow appropriate that *How high the moon?* ends on a fade, his stream of melodic invention seeming to continue on into the ether. 'I always stress to the various people I play with that music never ends, it just continues, there is no real cut-off,' he once explained. [56]

Oleo, a Rollins original, an *I got rhythm* contrafact and a jazz classic, was originally recorded with Miles Davis in 1954 at a time when the trumpeter was making one of many concerted efforts to get Rollins to join his band. An exercise in fleet change-running, it provides a feature for La Roca, a very capable drummer who dropped out of the pack during the shuffle between jazz-rock and the pluralistic 1980s to become a lawyer. By the 1990s he was back on the New York scene as Pete Sims, leading a spirited band with the soprano-sax master Dave Liebman in its ranks. Rollins also gives some elbow room to Henry Grimes, a bass player who had been appearing with him in the trio setting since July 1958's *Sonny Rollins/Brass – Sonny Rollins/Trio.* Rollins concludes his broadcast with *Paul's Pal,* an original that first appeared on *Tenor Madness* (†Prestige [J] VDJ-1514) from May 1956, provoking comparison with how Rollins reacted with a piano trio as against just bass and drums. Perhaps the most striking difference is that Rollins sounds so much at ease with himself in the latter context. In 1959 he was one of a handful of jazz soloists who could manipulate rhythmic phrases and tonal variety in such a way that he made each chorus dance. Assured of his virtuosity and observing that his confidence seemed to have grown markedly since *Saxophone Colossus,* audiences would come to expect magic at every concert he played. He usually delivered, but there would be times later in his career when this great improviser would reveal a gulf between expectation and execution, a humanizing factor that was as frustrating as it was endearing. S.N.

Horace Silver

350 Blowin' the Blues Away

Blue Note (A) BLP4017, Blue Note (A) BST84017; Blue Note (J) GXK8036, †Blue Note (E) CDP746526–2, †Blue Note (J) CP325246

Blue Mitchell (tpt); Junior Cook (ten); Silver (p); Eugene Taylor (bs); Louis Hayes (d). Englewood Cliffs, N.J., 29, 30 August, 13 September 1959.
Blowin' the blues away · The St Vitus dance · Break city · Peace · Sister Sadie · The Baghdad blues · Melancholy mood

Four-fifths of this quintet were together for a Blue Note recording session on 15 June 1958 to back the singer Bill Henderson. By the time they cut the album *Finger Poppin'* (Blue Note [A] BST84008) on 1 February 1959, Mitchell had joined on trumpet. It completed what many people regard as the classic Horace Silver quintet. 'I think people loved that particular band,' Silver conceded in 1993. [57] The Mitchell–Cook alliance would be a fixture for five years, until shortly after a 28 January 1964 recording session, appearing on a total of seven albums with Silver. [58] Throughout this period, Silver was producing a series of well-crafted and often memorable compositions which his group delivered with audible delight and a spirit akin to that of the early Basie band.

Blowin' the Blues Away is the second Mitchell–Cook collaboration with Silver and is probably the best representation of this band, although, to be fair, all the albums they made together were remarkably consistent. Silver was a perfectionist. It may come as a surprise to fans of his effortlessly swinging ensembles that it was take 39 of the number *Juicy Lucy* and take 37 of *Come on home* that appeared on the album *Finger Poppin'*. Much careful planning went into Silver's numbers: he expected his group to rehearse regularly, to arrive promptly and to get down to business straight away. In performance, he wanted to hit a creative groove from the off, and worked with Ellington-like craftsmanship to create just the right settings for his soloists to ensure this. In a 1963 interview both Cook and Mitchell spoke of their growing ability to play meaningful passages within the confines of Silver's arrangements, [59] yet subsequently, just like so many Ellington sidemen, neither seemed capable of realizing his full potential away from their former leader.

Silver's compositions are filled with simple, catchy melodies that, while being easy to pigeonhole as 'funky hard bop', have in fact long outlasted that brief period in the 1950s and early 1960s when it was all the rage. Countless Silver compositions are now generally regarded as jazz standards; *Sister Sadie* from this album, for example, was recorded to great effect by the big bands of Buddy Rich on *Swingin' New Band* (†Pacific Jazz [A] 7243 8 35232 2 1), Woody Herman on *Woody Herman 1963* (Phillips [E] 652025BL) and Gil Evans (**383**). Silver's compositions were generally more elaborate than those of any other hard-bop group, and frequently used unusual forms. *Melancholy mood*, for example, [60] is a 28-bar AABA composition where each section is seven bars in length. Silver's arrangements were always well crafted and gave his group an unmistakable identity; as each unfolded there might be clever use of counterpoint, stirring riff figures behind soloists, use of secondary or subsidiary themes, quartal voicings for the front line, use of polytonal accompaniment, arranged bass lines that interlocked with the arrangement or were doubled by the piano and carefully arranged piano and drum punctuations.

Silver's own playing, a savvy mixture of left-handed rhythmic dissonance and right-handed bluesy consonance (a good example being his solo on the title track), had, for a while, come under the spell of Bud Powell. But he had also learned Avery Parish's *After hours* by heart, this being effectively a lexicon of public-domain blues licks. Tempering Powell's velocity with an engaging melodicism firmly rooted in the blues tradition, he created a style of powerful rhythmic vitality that sounded familiar yet was wholly his own and was widely imitated by pianists in the 1950s and 1960s. But Silver's style did not rely wholly on the congeniality of the blues; that left-handed dissonance, for example, was an acknowledged influence on Cecil Taylor. [61] And in his solo on this album's *Baghdad blues*, for example, he moves from a blues scale in the first chorus to a whole-tone scale in the second.

Silver's comping behind solos was particularly arresting. While superficially he might appear all bustling intensity, frequently he played quite specific piano riffs in contrast to the more flexible response of most pianists, who reacted to the direction taken by the soloists. Often his riffs sounded as if they might have been written out in advance, and in this respect his approach is similar to that of John Lewis with the Modern Jazz Quartet. While there may be arguments for and against this method of accompaniment, the fact remains that in Silver's hands (and Lewis's), this particular approach to accompaniment worked very effectively. As Martin Williams pointed out: 'The overall impression is one of cohesion and order . . . particularly on *Blowin' the blues away* and *Sister Sadie*, Silver uses his piano excellently . . . propelling his soloists along with background riff figures.' [62] The word 'propelling' is particularly apt, especially on the title track, which still remains one of the most stirring hard-bop performances ever recorded.

Blowin' the blues away is at a very bright tempo [63] and, as the title suggests, is a 12-bar form. The theme is preceded by a two-bar 'fanfare' in tempo and immediately it is clear a lot is happening – and very quickly. The tempo is pretty close to the limit at which a bass player can comfortably sustain four beats to the bar, while the theme, repeated twice, is built on a series of accents and cross-accents against the basic pulse. Throughout, Hayes's drumming is a model of controlled abandon, his performance adding immeasurably to the excitement of the whole. Cook takes four choruses, and on his second weaves his line around a figure Silver plays in his accompaniment that showed just how the front line used Silver's pre-written figures to their own advantage, although when the figure reappears in the second of Mitchell's five choruses he chooses to ignore it. Each solo is a model of precisely addressing the needs of the moment in a lucid, yet economical way. A highlight of the album is how both Cook and Mitchell conceived their solos as logical wholes; throughout, their playing is a model of construction; there is nothing wild-eyed about their work, nothing is gratuitous or throw-away; instead there is a focus and intensity from which aspiring young musicians can learn even today.

On *Break City* Silver takes a ten-chorus solo and it is interesting how that solo remains within the orbit of the closely voiced chords usually played around the centre of the keyboard; there are no sweeping Bud Powell runs in his playing; instead percussive melodic fragments and phrases are stirred into an intense, boiling cauldron that Cecil Taylor described as 'the real thing of Bud, with all the physicality of it, with the filth of it and the movement in the attack'. [64] Silver's left hand plays a more prominent role than that of Powell, using densely voiced chords in the lower part of the keyboard, often as accents and cross-accents, almost in the way the old bop drummers used to 'drop bombs'. Sometimes his left-hand accompaniments could be distinctly polytonal and the attack with which they were played clearly impressed Taylor. Following Silver's solo, Mitchell opens two choruses of two-bar exchanges with Cook, rising to the challenge of sustaining a cogent line between them, rather as if one horn were soloing. A highly effective device, it not only climaxes a powerful group performance but also underlines the enormous empathy they had developed, both by dint of careful preparation and hours spent together on the bandstand.

The ten-bar theme *Peace*, with its pleasing major-minor feel, again demonstrates both Cook's and Mitchell's unity of construction in their solos, this time in a ballad context. *Sister Sadie* is one of the best known of all Silver's compositions. The emphasis is on a gospel feel that for a while exemplified the back-to-the-roots ethos of hard bop during the 1950s, which, of course, ideally suited Silver's piano style. A 32-bar AABA song, it still sounds fresh today, almost certainly because of the integrity of both composition and performance. Silver cleverly uses a blues change by remaining in the tonic for the A sections, moving to the subdominant in the B section, a chord movement that evokes the I-IV change in the 12-bar blues sequence. The takes from the 29 August session were rejected and this, the second take from the 30 August session, has a swagger and confidence that is the essence of this group's best performances. After a statement of the theme, Mitchell takes just one chorus, followed by Cook's two. During the second, Mitchell and Silver introduce a hard-driving riff figure behind the A sections of Cook's improvisation. After Silver's two-chorus solo, two secondary themes are introduced, again on the A sections, leaving the B clear for improvisation. The second of the two new themes is a recapitulation of the riff figures played behind Cook, but here introduced as a theme in its own right, lending a pleasing sense of unity to the performance before a return to the original theme.

While it might be argued that the way Silver structured his material was modest, in the context of so much of hard bop it provided a refreshing alternative to the head-solos-head approach that characterized so much of the music. Hard bop was essentially rugged and powerful, and overcomplication would have detracted from its urban rawness. What Silver did was to find a balance between the competing needs of expressive freedom and compositional design and in so doing produced some of the most satisfying, enduring and often exciting music within the hard-bop idiom. S.N.

Lee Morgan

351 Leeway

†Blue Note (E) CDP7243 8 32089 2 0

Morgan (tpt); Jackie McLean (alt); Bobby Timmons (p); Paul Chambers (bs); Art Blakey (d). Englewood Cliffs, N.J., 28 April 1960.

These are soulful days · *The Lion and the Wolff* · *Midtown blues* · *Nakatini suite*

At the age of 15, Morgan was attracting the attention of name jazz musicians who played in Philadelphia, as much for his talent as for his precociousness in demanding to sit in with them. He was often heard on a Friday-afternoon show run by a disc jockey, Tommy Roberts, who presented a mixture of local talent and visiting jazzmen in town to play the clubs. By then Morgan was playing in the rock-'n'-roll band of Carl Holmes and the Jolly Rompers, along with Archie Shepp and Reggie Workman. Three years later, in 1956, he was a member of Dizzy Gillespie's State Department big band and for those who saw him, it was clear that an important young talent was on his way; Nat Hentoff has spoken of him so electrifying an audience at Birdland that all conversation in the room stopped. [65] Later in the year, a few months after his 19th birthday, he signed with Blue Note and *Lee Morgan Indeed!* (Blue Note [A] BLP1538) was recorded in November, followed by *Lee Morgan* (Blue Note BLP1541) four weeks later. He can also be heard featuring with Gillespie's big band on *That's all* from *Dizzy in Greece* (Verve [A] MV 2630) cut in 1957. Taken together, it is easy to see what all the fuss was about. He had a large tone and clean, fast articulation evoking the extrovert, joyful tradition of such trumpet players as Navarro, Gillespie and Clifford Brown rather than the lyrical, understated approach personified by a Miles Davis or an Art Farmer. Morgan was by no means subservient to precedent, however; he had his own ideas and presented them with flair – impressive stuff for a teenager.

In 1957 Morgan cut a further four albums under his own name for Blue Note, and appeared on albums by Johnny Griffin and Clifford Jordan and was particularly impressive on Coltrane's *Blue Train* (†Blue Note [E] CDP746095-2). In 1958 he left Gillespie, and in April was recorded live at Birdland at a date emceed by 'Symphony Sid' Torrin with, among others, Curtis Fuller, Hank Mobley, Billy Root and Ray Bryant, *Monday Night at Birdland* (Vogue [E] VJD565). This informal session provides a valuable progress report on the young trumpeter prior to his joining Art Blakey's Jazz Messengers the following autumn. Although *Candy* (Blue Note BLP1590) was the only album under his own name he recorded that year (he appeared, however, on Blue Note sessions by Hank Mobley, Jimmy Smith and Tina Brooks), live recordings are often more revealing than the more considered offerings made in recording studios. Here, though, they simply confirm that Morgan was as exuberant inside a recording studio as he was outside. The 20-year-old trumpeter is captured working out on a series of familiar jamming standards of hard bop – *Walkin'*, *Bags' groove*, *All the things you are* and so on – and is clearly the most creative talent on display. His bravura approach is immediately arresting as he balances technique against emotion and musical judgement. Although it has been said in these pages before, the arrival of young talent today is usually to the accompaniment of resounding hyperbole from the extremely proactive press offices of recording companies. So it is worth reflecting on this modest Monday night in Birdland, far removed from corporate brouhaha, allowing us to hear Morgan's work speaking for itself. Nobody needed to tell you that here was an important young talent because it was self-evident.

On joining Blakey, Morgan came under the shrewd stewardship of Benny Golson, the band's musical director who had joined in February 1958. He was moving Blakey away from the 'blowing session' rut that had come to characterize the Messengers since their formation in 1955. Not only did Golson attempt to mediate a balance between primacy of the ensemble and the leader's powerful drumming, he also provided distinctive compositions which had a galvanizing effect on the band as a whole. Under Golson, Blakey's band evolved into one of the drummer's most distinctive ensembles and the raw talent of Morgan was an important part of this. Under Blakey, his playing assumed greater focus without sacrificing his daredevil exuberance. 'I used to love Lee Morgan,' recalled Blakey in 1979. 'He would be up on the bandstand and if you didn't know who I was you'd swear Lee Morgan was Art Blakey . . . a lot of people thought he was cocky. No, he was just having fun.' [66]

By the time he recorded *Leeway*, his sixth album for Blue Note, Morgan had not recorded under his own name since February 1958, although he had appeared on six Messengers sessions in the interim. Blakey's drumming had an inspirational effect on the young trumpeter's playing, clearly apparent on two live albums from the end of 1958, *Art Blakey 1958 – Paris Olympia* (†Fontana 832659–2) and *Art Blakey and the Jazz Messengers – Paris 1958* (†BMG/Bluebird 74341101522), and it is no coincidence the drummer was present on Morgan's first date under his own name for two years. Two compositions are by Cal Massey, and the first, *These are soulful days*, is a minor AABA 32-bar theme, [67] with the middle eight in $3/4$ save the last bar (although all B is played in $4/4$ during the solos). Played *forte* and in unison, it is a superb representative example of the kind of hard bop defined by the Blue Note label at this time.

Recorded with just a touch of echo in the mix, haloing Morgan and McLean's dramatic theme statement against *alla breve* accompaniment by the rhythm section, the solos open with the unexpected entrance of Chambers, then with Miles Davis, walking in his powerful way for a full chorus. Timmons follows for two choruses and, although not an entirely consistent pianist, produces a well-executed, beautifully balanced statement that builds on the foundation laid by Chambers. McLean's shouting entry notches the excitement level up a few more degrees with a solo that stands alongside some of his best from this period, preparing the way for Morgan. He creeps in, if not *sotto voce*, then certainly on tiptoes, gradually building his line to climax the composition. By now he was very much his own man, full of confidence and even reckless with an occasional idea that adds a feeling of the spontaneity to the piece.

Morgan's own composition *The Lion and the Wolff*, a tribute to his two patrons at the helm of the Blue Note label, begins with a mysterioso unison piano and bass introduction with Blakey laying down a Latin feel. The theme echoes this mood of exotic mystery, but is in fact a good old 12-bar blues that snaps into a straight-ahead swinging four with McLean's entry. He is direct and dramatic, his style not given to quavers but favouring the minim as the basic unit of his melodic pronouncements, handed down large and written in stone. Morgan is at his most reckless here, trying ideas and discarding them, yet retaining cogency and a powerful blues hue to his work. *Midtown blues* is jumping 12-bar theme by McLean that leans on a romping backbeat; Morgan, over-exuberant as ever, almost tangles himself in knots but extricates himself using a repeated motif that becomes the core element of his line before experimenting with a little side-slipping towards the end of his solo. McLean echoes this air of adventure, spicing his line with an occasional sour note, and, egged on by Blakey and Morgan, produces a long solo of rising intensity with the participants' enjoyment clearly audible. Timmons begins soulfully, but ends up deferring to Wynton Kelly in one of the most enjoyable cuts of the album.

Massey's *Nakatini suite* is not a suite at all, but an expansive 66-bar composition [68] with an 18-bar middle eight, structured:

A (8 bars) + B (8 bars) + A + B + C (18 bars) + A + B

Perhaps this is the most satisfying track of the album; the soloists seem to respond to the long form with direction and purpose, with Blakey exemplifying the mood with a well-structured solo at the climax of the piece.

In all a further 16 Blue Note albums by Morgan saw the light of day, although several sessions remain unissued, and it was not until 1996 that a live date at the Lighthouse in Hermosa Beach was finally released, *Live at the Lighthouse* (†Blue Note (A) CDP 7243). However, the next date under his own name, in December 1963, produced *The Sidewinder* (Blue Note [A] BST84157) and an unexpected hit. On some of his subsequent albums commercial reality prevailed, and the thought of a further success did not seem far from Morgan's mind. There was nevertheless some fine work as well, his sometimes flashy display now moderated with emotional maturity but none quite captured the brashness and sheer enjoyment that is apparent on this session. A quintessential hard-bop player, he remained true to the idiom, even though the musical climate around him began to change as the 1960s progressed. However, here, with so much ahead of him, the sheer fun and love of music-making is contagious.

S.N.

Wayne Shorter

352 **Speak No Evil**
†Blue Note (E) CDP746 509–2

Freddie Hubbard (tpt); Shorter (ten); Herbie Hancock (p); Ron Carter (bs); Elvin Jones (d). New Jersey, 24 December 1964.
Witch Hunt · Fee-fi-fo-fum · Dance cadaverous · Speak no evil · Wild flower

Hubbard absent. Same date.
Infant Eyes

By the time of this recording, Shorter was one of the most original tenor saxophonists in jazz. A matter of weeks before he had joined Miles Davis's quintet, his route to what was universally recognized as one of the top spots in jazz being accomplished surprisingly fast and by paying relatively few dues in the bands of others. Although he had taken music and the saxophone up at the late age of 16, he nevertheless graduated from New York University with a degree in music education in 1956. After two years in the army, he moved in quick strides through Maynard Ferguson's mid-band and into Art Blakey's Jazz Messengers, where he was a fixture from 1959 to 1963. With Blakey he acquired the nickname 'the young Coltrane', but as early as his solo on his own composition *Contemplation* on Blakey's *Buhaina's Delight* (†Blue Note [E] CDP784 104–2) from November 1961, he was showing clear evidence of developing a personal style that no longer resembled his early influence. His rhythmic conception was clearly much looser than that of Coltrane, utilizing fewer notes and his playing was moving towards a floating, melodic quality that evoked classical influences such as Debussy and Satie.

Shorter was advancing on two fronts. Not only was he to distinguish himself as an instrumentalist, he would also emerge as one of the finest composers in contemporary jazz. During his brief tenure with Ferguson, where he first met the pianist Joe Zawinul, he had begun composing and arranging, something Blakey subsequently made a point of encouraging – as he did with all the young musicians who passed through his bands. From Shorter's very first recording date with the drummer on *Africaine* (Blue Note [A] BNLT1088), recorded in November 1959, *Lester left town* began a regular flow of Shorter originals that became a significant factor in defining what would generally become regarded as the finest of all the editions of the Jazz Messengers. [69]

By the time Shorter left Blakey in March 1964 – his replacement was the Chicagoan John Gilmore – he had cleansed himself of the clichés of bop and had absorbed Coltrane's lessons into a highly individual style of his own. What was striking about his work was a highly developed sense of melodic construction within his solos. Often, his improvisations appeared as logical extensions of his compositions and had such structure and cohesion of their own that some passages, if isolated, could stand as compositions in their own right. Just as in the 1930s, Lester Young and Coleman Hawkins represented two entirely different approaches to improvisation; by the time of this recording the relationship between Shorter and Coltrane was analogous. Both Young and Shorter had a highly individual approach to improvisation that favoured melodic construction above harmonic deference to every passing tone, chord extension and substitution in the manner of Hawkins and Coltrane. Equally, Shorter, whose own *Lester left town* [70] was dedicated to Young, shared much of Young's philosophy towards improvisation. Even though there was no discernible Young influence in his playing, there was, as in Young, never a feeling of gratuitous virtuosity in Shorter's work; indeed one of the hallmarks of both players was the restraint they exhibited. Young never seemed hindered by cadence points, turnarounds and bridges within a sequence of chords, something Shorter took a stage further by eliminating them from his own compositions. Yet his strong sense of melodic continuity and rhythmic independence meant that, just as Young's in the 1930s and 1940s, Shorter's style, from around the time of this recording and into the 1970s, was quite different from that of any saxophonist in jazz.

When Shorter left Blakey in March 1964 he did not immediately join Davis. During this brief career hiatus he recorded his first Blue Note date as a leader in April. *Nightdreamer* (†Blue Note [E] CDP784 173–2) brought together Lee Morgan, with whom he had once shared the front line with Blakey, with the Coltrane rhythm section of McCoy Tyner, Reggie Workman and Elvin Jones. In a band of very assertive individuals, what impressed was how the emotional climate was dominated by the strength of Shorter's compositions. Although overall Shorter had not entirely shed the strong influence of the hard-bop climate from which he had just emerged, the album highlight was the title piece, a medium-tempo jazz waltz, a composition which more than any other on the album distanced him from Papa Blakey's vision. A 16-bar AAB tune with the A sections four bars and the B section eight bars, it had an unusual harmonic construction, the hallmark of Shorter's best compositions. He frequently used combinations of extended chords in sequences that were unusual in jazz, and here, even though the feeling was overwhelmingly minor, it was often achieved through a combination of major and minor chords.

Shorter's second album, *JuJu* (Blue Note [A] BST84182), recorded four months later, placed the saxophonist in a solo role with the Coltrane rhythm section. Here, with his virtuosity less masked against the stirring interaction of Tyner, Garrison and Jones, comparisons, however odious, are inevitable with his former influence. Having seemingly purged his soul of any remaining Coltraneisms on an album that in many ways failed to represent either the overall direction of his playing or his compositional talents, he returned to the recording studios on 2 November

1964 to record *Speak No Evil.* The personnel was identical to the subsequent 24 December date except for Billy Higgins on drums. However, Shorter was unhappy with the results and all three tracks cut that day were rejected. For the successful December date, Shorter's preference for a strong assertive drummer resulted in Elvin Jones getting the call. [71]

Witch hunt begins with a clarion call to arms, a swirling 14-bar introduction introduces the 24-bar AB theme, contrasting a 16-bar modal A section with an 8-bar B section using contemporary or extended chords. The theme utilizes an interval of a fourth, which was becoming popular in contemporary jazz at this point. Shorter, Hubbard and Hancock all introduce motifs based on a fourth in their solos, which each develops with clear-eyed intelligence. Hubbard, who had also worked alongside Shorter in Blakey's Jazz Messengers from autumn 1961 until March 1964, was an ideal partner for the tenor saxophonist. They would once again work with each other with the creation of VSOP in 1976 along with Hancock, Ron Carter and Tony Williams; he would also appear on the next two Shorter dates, *The Soothsayer* (Blue Note [J] GXK 8512) and *The All Seeing Eye* (†Blue Note [E] CDP724 3829100 2 2). Hubbard was a player with the technique and imagination to respond to the challenges of Shorter's compositions and the tenor saxophonist consistently drew the very best from this occasionally unpredictable trumpeter.

A good example of how Hubbard responded to Shorter's compositions is the title track, where he contributes one of those stunning solos he seemed to produce during the 1960s that made it seem he was destined for true greatness. A 50-bar AABA composition, Shorter's theme is simplicity itself, essentially one note, the subdominant in the home key of C minor, which occupies the first eight bars followed by a two-bar modulation and a return to the one-note theme, now the dominant, for the next four bars. The 14-bar theme is then repeated, the B section is a true middle eight of eight bars of broken phrases followed by a return to the A theme. This is minimalistic stuff; 42 bars using essentially two notes was the complete antithesis of bop and hard bop. However, although the burden of complexity was removed from the front line, it was transferred to the rhythm section, where Elvin Jones's polyrhythms assume central interest, framed as it were by the static melody line.

Fee-fi-fo-fum, a 24-bar ABA composition that comprises three eight-bar sections, is another piece with a slow-moving melody line. Hubbard again reveals his lucid imagination, this time utilizing half-valve effects, and is followed by a shouting Shorter. *Dance cadaverous* is a reflection more of Shorter's penchant for intriguing song titles than a ghostly dance for the dead, apparently inspired by Sibelius's *Valse triste.* It is a long, 64-bar composition with an ABAB[1] form, comprising four 16-bar sections:

Intro (8 bars) + A (8 + 8) + B (8 + 8) + A (8 + 8) + B^1 (8 + 8^1)

A slow-moving melody line in $3/4$ predominates and both Shorter and Hubbard sound fresh – the trumpeter exploiting his beautiful tone in the lower register of the instrument – and it is difficult to believe that this is in fact the 27th take of the number. It is interesting to note that Shorter actually arranged *Valse triste* for a sextet on his upcoming *Soothsayer* session, although not to the same overall effect as *Dance cadaverous*. The rhythm-section permutations on these two sessions, drawn from the two foremost groups in jazz, also make for interesting comparison; the Hancock–Jones *Speak No Evil* combination is more successful than the subsequent Tyner–Tony Williams *Soothsayer* pairing.

The most arresting composition of the album, however, is *Wild flower*, a 32-bar AA^{1}BCAA^{1}B^{1}A piece, with each section of four bars. Since it is written in the time signature of $6/4$, the four-bar sections cover more ground than a similar composition in $4/4$. Four bars in $6/4$ produce 24 crotchet beats, whereas four bars in $4/4$ produces sixteen beats. Consequently the ear does not yearn for a traditional eight-bar phrase; Shorter's four-bar phrase lengths in $6/4$ do not sound short or truncated but flow logically and with great melodic coherence. The reappearance of the A strain in particular produces a pleasing feel of structural unity to the composition as a whole. The melody is phrased in unisons and thirds except in bars 3, 4, 12, 15 and 16, where Shorter employs his favourite interval of a fourth. Even though the take selected for release was the 12th, the group as a whole sound fresh and bursting with controlled energy. As in all the numbers on this album, Hubbard's and Shorter's scrupulous attention to dynamics and articulation is an important feature of their performance, allowing these carefully sculptured melodies to assume a melancholy serenity.

Much of the revolution that took place in the music of Miles Davis in the latter half of the 1960s was sparked by the compositions of Wayne Shorter, who joined the trumpeter's band three months before these sessions in September 1964. Up to that point, Davis had used predominantly conventional songforms. Through Shorter's influence he began favouring compositions with simple forms and static, or at least relatively slow, harmonic movement, or songs where the chord changes were implied by the improviser against a prearranged tempo (or more than one), known as 'time, no changes'. This approach allowed the rhythm section to adopt a role that was often equal to the front line in prominence, reversing the traditional front line–rhythm section relationship of bop and hard bop with rhythmically and harmonically intricate lines with the rhythm section adopting a supportive role in accompaniment. This new style adopted by the mid-to-late-1960s Davis quintet became widely influential in jazz, yet Shorter, modest and self-effacing, remained the quiet revolutionary. Although he was already working towards this major shift away from hard-bop methodology before he joined Davis, it would subsequently be to the latter that credit for this new innovation would accrue. S.N.

Herbie Hancock

353 Maiden Voyage

†EMI/Blue Note (E) CDP746 339–2

Freddie Hubbard (tpt); George Coleman (ten); Hancock (p); Ron Carter (bs); Tony Williams (d). Englewood Cliffs, N.J., August 1965.
Maiden voyage · The eye of the hurricane · Little one · Survival of the fittest · Dolphin dance

Hancock, Carter and Williams were Miles Davis's new supporting team when Hubbard joined them in August 1964 for *Empyrean Isles* (†EMI/Blue Note [E] CDP784 175–2). Between that date and the making of *Maiden Voyage*, Davis's *E.S.P.* (†CBS [A] 467 899) appeared early in 1965, a year during much of which Davis himself was incapacitated. For the present item Coleman, another Davis associate, is added to the line-up, and it should not surprise anyone that the group's music has close kinship with *E.S.P.* and the *Plugged Nickel* set (**396**) from the end of 1965. Indeed, *Little one* reinterprets a composition which Hancock contributed to *E.S.P.*

Referring to Davis recently, Francis Davis has written: 'The harmonically spacious, metrically suspended music he played . . . in the mid-sixties remains the dominant style of jazz two decades later, although no one has yet put a satisfactory label on it.' [72] The style has been remarkable for its hardihood, resurfacing even during periods which found Hancock and his ilk involved in heavily electronic music. Wynton Marsalis, fresh from Blakey's Jazz Messengers, toured with Hancock, Carter and Williams in the United States and Japan during 1981. A Tokyo session (Columbia [A] C2–38275) included *The eye of the hurricane* and the influence of this encounter may be heard in some of Marsalis's early essays as a leader in his own right, e.g. **486** and *J Mood* (†CBS [A] 57068).

All of this said, *Maiden Voyage* now seems, considering its intrinsic virtues, a classic of jazz unconstrained by its time. The darkly pulsating median beat of the title piece is a Hancock trademark. The mood is ushered in by dissonant signals from trumpet and tenor before Coleman, light-toned, hazards comments; then, gentle as Hubbard's additional musings sound, the feeling edges closer to early hard bop and the subtle clashings and illusory *rallentandos* in Hancock's solo do not evict that sense altogether. *The eye of the hurricane* is brisk, deliberate, propelled by Carter patterns complementary to Hubbard's tripping attack with its sliding witticisms and rough-edged curlicues. Hancock does not conceal his debt to Bill Evans (perhaps the most significant single influence behind this music); neither does he bury the loan in the sand of mere imitation.

After the whispering drumroll opening *Little one*, instrumental sounds drift in, curiously related; the piano lines brood, slow, almost pulseless, with Carter a sympathetic adviser. Coleman, not a match for Wayne Shorter in the earlier Davis version of the number, attractively recalls some old childhood tale, and Hubbard's interpolation is half elfin fanfare, half cradle song. There are incitements to escape, Hancock strikes evocative intervals which widen and grow stronger yet remain, somehow, essentially interior. Over soft bass-fiddle lyricism the indeterminate opening fabric is spread out once more.

Williams, among the most musically literate of drummers, leads into the punchy dance of *Survival of the fittest*, which, though it takes risks, is not as competitive as its Spencerian-Darwinian title might suggest. In contrast with earlier Hancock appearances, Hubbard is more skilful and balanced. Carter is again in marvellous evidence; games are played with metre and Williams surges through into a cannily chosen tempo. Coleman seeks, not quite ably, for a distinctive role, and then it is the pianist, tiptoeing along the drummer's rough-laid path, who develops a linear reflection that almost becomes a duet with a lonely cymbal, lulling expectations in advance of an aggressive finale which everyone concerned survives without scar.

Dolphin dance enters with the horns in songlike unison. Hubbard and Coleman utter undemonstrative statements, yet there is an immediacy that relies hardly at all upon brashness or peremptoriness. Hancock's subdued lyricism is crafted with a technique drawn from the blues.

In jazz, a volatile art, the truest modernists are usually the best traditionalists; those who honour the best traditions may be the most free. But this is no academic point. Whatever the conditioning, immediacy is what matters. 'Jazz is immediate and very adaptable,' said Hancock in a 1992 interview; and Tony Williams added; 'I'm not playing for history, I'm playing for right now.' [73] E.T.

George Coleman

354 Live at Yoshi's

†Evidence (A) ECD 22021–2

Coleman (ten); Harold Mabern (p); Ray Drummond (bs); Alvin Queen (d). Oakland and San Francisco, August 1987.

They say it's wonderful · *Good morning, heartache* · *Laig gobblin' blues* · *Io* · *Up jumped spring* · *Father* · *Soul eyes*

After 27 years in jazz, Coleman's first feature in a major music magazine came in 1980. There has been little else since then. And while lack of interest from the music press has scarcely been an impediment to producing great jazz, it is nevertheless a reflection of the lack of recognition that has dogged Coleman's career. A member of B. B. King's horn section at 17, he is widely believed to have played the alto solo on one of King's first hits, *Woke up this morning.* Shortly afterwards he moved to Chicago and, now playing tenor, he joined the Max Roach quintet, sharing the front line with Kinny Dorham, later Booker Little, and recording for Bob Shad's EmArcy label, a subsidiary of Mercury. When he replaced John Coltrane in the Miles Davis quintet in 1963, it seemed his star was in the ascendance. Appearing on four important Davis albums, *Seven Steps to Heaven* (†CBS/Sony 4669702), *In Europe* (CBS 62390), *My Funny Valentine* (CBS 85558) and *Four and More* (CBS 85560), he stayed with the trumpeter for about a year. The last two albums, recorded at the Philharmonic Hall, New York, in February 1964, showed Coleman to be a player of great promise, although an amalgam of his favourite saxophonists, including Earl Bostic, Charlie Parker, John Coltrane and Eddie 'Lockjaw' Davis. His decision to quit Davis's group a few months after the Philharmonic concert, along with Ron Carter (who rejoined Davis for a tour of the Far East a couple of months later), perplexed jazz fans thereafter aware that the profile a run with Davis might have offered appeared as a career opportunity missed. And although Coleman appeared on the Herbie Hancock album *Maiden Voyage* (**353**), an important album of the 1960s, his profile in jazz progressively waned during the succeeding years, despite recordings with Elvin Jones, Horace Silver, Cedar Walton, and an impressive duo with the Catalonian pianist Tete Montoliu, *Meditation* (Timeless [H] 110). In the 1970s and early 1980s he toured and recorded, with his octet, *Big George* (Vee Jay [J] 20YB-7015) and in 1985 he recorded with his quartet *Manhattan Panorama* (†Evidence [A] ECD 22019–2).

Throughout, Coleman had been honing and refining his talent in something approaching quiet obscurity and by the mid-1980s as he was approaching 50, his playing was in the full flower of artistic maturity. From the breadth and depth of his accumulated life's experiences his improvisations had acquired a grandeur and vitality to the extent that during that renascent decade he was among the most commanding players in jazz, a position he maintained into the 1990s. The imperious emotional force he brought to his playing in live performance is perfectly captured on *They say it's wonderful*, *Good morning heartache* and *Soul eyes*. Coleman's handling of these ballads is impressive, not only for the overall musicality of his performance, but also for his application of techniques that remain one of the most unacknowledged areas of jazz improvisation, the use of psychological principles that elicit specific emotional responses from the listener. Because of the inherent spontaneity of a jazz performance many listeners imagine that the subjective feelings that a musician stirs within them occur equally spontaneously. Indeed most jazz criticism deliberately excludes any reference to what makes an improvisation capable of arousing emotion, as if such feelings might deny the possibility of jazz as an art form but rather confirm it as an 'entertainment', redolent of the slow drag in New Orleans or of jitterbugs dancing in the aisles.

But certain musical patterns correspond with certain emotional reactions, and the best jazz improvisers will take account of these factors in structuring an improvisation, particularly to create the archetypal musical sensations of tension and release. For example, moving to high notes, contrasting 'inside' and 'outside' passages or playing a passage of notes faster than the basic unit of time can all cause the listener to experience feelings of tension. Indeed, heightening expectation (tension) and postponing resolution for a 'heroic' ending has occupied the great composers of classical music for centuries. As Hindemith has pointed out; '[A composer] knows by experience that certain patterns of tone-setting correspond with certain emotional reactions on the listener's part . . . with frequent references to those musical progressions that evoke the uncomplicated feeling-images of sadness or gaiety in an unambiguous form, he can reach a fairly close approximation to unanimity of all listeners' reactions.' [74] It is hardly surprising therefore, that many jazz musicians, in their own modest way, should take account of such principles in organizing their material so as to manipulate their audience's emotions. What is interesting about Coleman's performances here is the succinct deployment of such devices to create tension and release, and the structured way in which he approaches this, building his improvisations up from the ground in a series of stages that unfold like a journey into the very heart of the song.

Coleman's performance of *They say it's wonderful*, a 32-bar AABA standard, was inspired by the much neglected 1963 collaboration between John Coltrane and Johnny Hartman, *John Coltrane and Johnny Hartman* (†Impulse [A] GRD157). After Mabern's introduction, Coleman freely essays the Irving Berlin melody in a breathy subtone. The rhythm section, who work hand in glove with Coleman throughout the album, play a decorative two-beat with Mabern adopting a rhapsodic role in accompaniment, frequently using the sustaining pedal of the piano to give a particularly ringing quality to his playing. As Coleman's improvisation opens at the second chorus, his tone becomes appreciably steelier, and he introduces several key motifs that will appear in succeeding choruses either in variation or much embellished form. Mabern's accompaniment now changes to goading, bright, staccato chords, quite unlike conventional comping, while bass and drums hold an implacable two. Coleman, however, suggests a regular four in his line, creating an inherent tension through this duality of metre. The third chorus appears to release the tension as the rhythm section move into four, but now Coleman strongly implies double time throughout the chorus, so the expected release never comes. On the fourth chorus, the rhythm section double the tempo and the feeling of release is palpable, but as Coleman soars, Drummond hints at returning to two, continuing the rhythmic tension, which throughout has been gradually tightened like a tourniquet. Now, as Queen follows Coleman into double time, Drummond briefly joins him but then returns to a decorative two, and the contrasting metres again combine to create tension. This sort of rhythmic interplay and playing off one another can be achieved only by working regularly together and being acutely aware of each other's role in the totality of the performance.

While at one level the rhythm section remains focused on their role of creating tension through their collective rhythmic counterpoint to Coleman's soloing, the saxophonist himself is also working to intensify the performance. He employs the effectiveness of the rising line to create tension, since the more a line continues to rise, the more we anticipate change. When the change occurs, expectations are fulfilled and we experience a release, this being a technique which Coleman manipulates supremely well. He gradually reaches higher and higher into the saxophone's range, often using alternate fingering to intensify his phrases while equally making use of side-slipping (providing a contrast between consonance and dissonance) and the simple subterfuge of increasing the drama of his line by playing more notes. These devices, manipulated one against the other through each level of his solo, together with the sheer authority he brings to his improvisations produce a succession of choruses that build logically into a dramatic and memorable performance which communicates as readily with his live audience as it does through compact disc.

Good morning, heartache uses the same structured technique of building chorus by chorus and is the finest performance of the album. The song was originally written for Billie Holiday and was commissioned by Milt Gabler, then her record producer at Decca, and was specifically tailored to her nightclub image of a woman unlucky in love. A 32-bar AABA form, it is a very well-constructed song, both harmonically and melodically, with a pleasing major/minor ambivalence (it is written in the major). For almost four decades the song remained so closely associated with Holiday that it was seldom performed by jazz musicians, and only in the 1980s and 1990s did it find favour as a vehicle for improvisation, something it richly deserved with its interesting changes and extended voicings in the middle eight. Coleman's was one of the first contemporaneous versions that broke the strong subjective association with Holiday.

Coleman opens after Mabern has set him up with a tasteful four-bar introduction, the saxophonist content to play a mildly embellished version of the theme. Behind him, the pianist provides another rhapsodic backdrop with the bass and drums playing a discreet two. As Coleman launches into his improvisation on the second chorus, Mabern abruptly lays out for 16 bars (the first two AA sections), rejoining at the middle eight, but now the bass, drums and Coleman tease the listener with implied double time, albeit still remaining in the basic two. When Coleman and the rhythm section do break into double time at the beginning of the third chorus, the effect is electric. At the end of the third chorus, Coleman inserts a 16-bar transition that he uses in a particularly dramatic way. He introduces a highly embellished form of a motif he had previously been developing in the second and third chorus, repeating it over and over using double breathing so as not to pause for breath. It provides a dramatic high spot in the performance which he then seeks to top with the sheer force of his melodicism for two further choruses, reaching from bell notes to high under-the-palm shrieks. At the end of the fourth full chorus, he winds down and moves back into the original tempo in two. Playing only eight bars of A, he leads into a *rubato* finish and it is clear that this has been a *tour de force* by a master improviser.

Coleman is an exemplary blues player, and uses an elemental riff in $^5/_4$ to provide a simple head for *Laig gobblin' blues*, taking several choruses that see him side-slipping and utilizing the full range of his instrument. It also provides the first extended solo by Mabern, a much neglected pianist [75] and a long-time associate of Coleman's (they attended the same school together in Memphis). In it he employs his trademark, ringing block chords played as staccato quavers that sustain the heat of the creative moment. Both this and *Io*, a contemporary vehicle that moves effortlessly in $^7/_4$ with effective solos from Coleman, Mabern and Queen, were recorded in the studios in San Francisco after the live date. The Freddie Hubbard composition *Up jumped spring* in $^3/_4$, recorded live, provides another elegant showcase for Coleman and Mabern, each of whose solos generate a hypnotic swaying feel, while *Father*, another studio cut, is a congenial Coleman original that perhaps lacks the intensity and drive that grips his playing when performing live.

Climaxing the album is Mal Waldron's classic *Soul eyes*, which receives a warm exposition of the melody from Coleman before he builds the performance block by block until he has constructed a glittering temple, reinforcing the feeling that here was an unacknowledged latter-day master of the saxophone. The song also acts as a feature for Mabern, another player careful not to play his hand early. He was a rousing, percussive pianist capable of moments of graceful introspection, and his playing was washed with the feeling of the blues. Far from tempering his style when working alongside a dominant personality like Coleman, he ascends and descends the rungs of a song together with him, each pushing at the limits of his style in search of shared truths, a working partnership aware of each other's most intimate musical secrets. In a career that had conspicuously lacked recognition, Coleman might have felt that performances such as these merited, at the very least, a raised eyebrow from the recording industry. Musical fashion dictated otherwise, however. In an area of jazz he had spent a lifetime mastering, record companies were looking elsewhere, at young, photogenic talent, some fresh out of music college. Throughout the 1980s and into the 1990s, jazz was awash with albums by young debutants, signed by record companies eager to cash in on the success of a Wynton or Branford Marsalis. While on the one hand, unreasonable expectation was raised with the arrival of each new whizz-kid, some as young as the 14-year-old GRP signing Amani Murray, on the other jazz had still to come to terms with the fact that in wooing the future it was overlooking the present. In the rush to sign the youngest and fastest, Coleman and others like him were relegated to the sidelines and the lack of recognition that is the inevitable result of inadequate recording exposure. And although *The New Yorker* noted in 1995 that 'Coleman is a marvel; there isn't a sax player who knows his instrument better, or one who imparts so much knowledge in every marathon solo', [76] by then he had made just two more albums since *Live at Yoshi's*. S.N.

Jimmy Raney

355 The Influence

Xanadu (A) 116

Raney (g); Sam Jones (bs); Billy Higgins (d). New York City, 2 September 1975.

I love you · Body and soul · It could happen to you · Suzanne · Get out of town · There will never be another you · The end of a love affair · Dancing in the dark

For an artist of Raney's established allegiance, the revivifying of the bop agenda was bound to entail lines of expression acquired in those byways of the era where the fingerposts had been cunningly tilted. It was not merely the Tristanoesque themes for the Raney-led quintet of April 1953 (**299**) that signalled an influence which persuaded one chronicler to aver that Raney was 'to the guitar what Lee Konitz is to the alto sax'. [77] Raney, pitting his improvising voice against Getz's was producing lines that were in some sense 'symphonic'. In the alto and guitar duets noted under **298**, Billy Bauer was Konitz's foil, but it is clear from related work with Teddy Charles in the same item that Raney was a denizen of the same thought-world (*cf.* **293** as well). The persistent effect of such associations is heard with emphasis in this trio session of 1975, with the highly adaptable Jones and Higgins, who, by this time, were virtually an independent public partnership.

The lightness and flexibility of approach is lent dramatic edge as *Body and soul* opens, by guitar arpeggios, note clashes and, with the establishment of a slow pulse, by lines in octave. The mood contrasts sharply with *I love you*, preceding it and full of rapid melodies motored by Higgins's elegantly urgent brushes. Yet any sure sense of the contemplative in *Body and soul* is bothered by brittle and yet resilient blue-noted asides and punctuations. *It could happen to you* is at mid-tempo, but a mock-hesitant prologue anticipates an intimate, if not quite inward, tactical method creating an interesting tension between the rhythmic and the melodic in the guitarist's shaping of terms; flashes of bitonalities are effected too. There is a degree of experiment with temporal contrast during *Suzanne*, with Raney duetting with his dubbed *alto ego*; informal canonic effects and subtler overlappings of temporal variation. This is a typical piece of Raney lyricism, venturesomely artistic, and not averse to a little dalliance with congenial European modernisms – 'Bartókian,' says Doug Ramsey in the Xanadu sleeve note. A second guitar line is added also to a trio version of the samba-rhythmed *Get out of town* which is easy-going and deceptively simplistic in spirit.

The end of a love affair is a solo so technically skilled that suspicions might be aroused that more recording trickery was involved. There is no fixed tempo, and the registral contrasts are vivid and fascinating. Then it is a more driving, ochre-toned Raney that steers *There will never be another you* and *Dancing in the dark*, pieces rendered all the more swinging by the buoying support of the rhythm duo. Jones, not frequently noted for solo endeavour, often proves his melodic gift here, and Higgins, a gentle provocator, occupies the background so effectively that one might call his unobtrusiveness positively commanding. E.T.

Al Haig

356 **Solitaire**

Spotlite (E) SPJLP 14

Haig (p). New York City, 24–5 February 1976.

Lament · Joanne · Summertime · Bess, you is my woman now · In your own sweet way · Never let me go · Here's that rainy day · Don't you know I care?

The 20-year-old pianist supporting Gillespie and Parker on 11 May 1945 (**256a**) had formed his style adequately to the requirements of a freely transformed jazz. The piano sounds heard in those revelatory recordings – *Salt peanuts, Shaw nuff, Hot house, Loverman* – were almost as assured in execution and as apt in idiomatic dimension as the lines uttered by the men of original vision who were leading the sextet.

It would soon become a little too easy to suggest that Haig was a disciple of Bud Powell, but he was too early on the bop scene to have done other than achieve his style within that enthusiastic ferment. By his own account, a catalyst was his hearing of Gillespie playing *A night in Tunisia* around 1944. [78] He attracted Gillespie's and Parker's attention while playing at a 52nd Street club alongside Tiny Grimes, and Dizzy became a chief preceptor. He rapidly became known as a reliable bop supporter and was deservedly prominent during the bop heyday and on into the cool revisions with Miles Davis and Stan Getz. **299** includes 13 numbers from a celebrated Getz session with Haig giving the best of what he achieved in bop before his career hit problems. In *Move* and *Budo* Getz let him show his expressive mettle with a latitude which the studio format of the Davis 'tuba band' versions of 1949–50 (**376**) had not permitted; and not even the death-defying tilt of Getz's *Move* will call in question the later judgement that Haig's playing in general displayed 'grace and urbanity at whatever tempo'. [79]

It may not now be entirely possible to account for the long post-1950s hiatus during which this admired adept of the bop genre concealed his gifts in obscure quasi-jazz outfits and breadwinning solo engagements. But listening to the series of recordings which his re-emergence in the early 1970s made possible one is presented with an enigma. The splendid assurance he shows evidences a mastery of wide-ranging expressive techniques. While none of this is essentially at odds with what he achieved in the 1940s and 1950s, it is tempting to speculate about some barely suspected need to break free from a situation that was taking his stylistic aptitudes too narrowly for granted. Be that as it may, the music heard in *Solitaire*, in the earlier *Jazz Will o' the Wisp* (Counterpoint [A] CPT551, Xtra [E] 1125) and in the other Spotlite albums, *Invitation* (Spotlite [E] AH4) and *Special Brew* (Spotlite [E] LP8), is so strong in refreshed inspiration, at once unified in conception and broad-sweeping in technical resource, that it almost demands a different set of critical standards. Maybe it sits uneasily in a section titled 'Bop Redivivus'; but if it is more precisely 'Haig Redivivus' it may assist one's critical readjustment to recall that Haig acknowledged such pianists as Teddy Wilson, Count Basie and Art Tatum as important in his jazz formation; and certainly no less important to accept his acknowledgement of Bud Powell, given that Powell was a contemporary rather than a precursor and had evidently imbibed at similar fountains.

As its title should make clear, this album is entirely solo, whereas the other albums mentioned involve bassists, drummers and a guitarist. Every number contains out-of-tempo passages and each number employs, more or less, the gamut of Haig's expressive treasury. And while there is little scope for the detailed comparison of separate pieces within it, the programme, taken as a whole, in terms of melodic contrast, registral colouration, variety of chordal figures, decorative runs used strategically à la Tatum, bold overlay of tempos and so on, never for a moment lacks inventive impetus or emotional logic.

A number of pianists' compositions are chosen: Ahmad Jamal's *Lament*, which is made rich in atmosphere; Gershwin's *Summertime* and *Bess, you is my woman now*, the one deeply pondered, the other a floating celebration; Brubeck's *In your own sweet way*, which joins a debonair gait to some airy jugglery; Ellington's *Don't you know I care?*, the leisurely, slightly offhand feel of which oddly recalls Bud Powell at moments rather than Duke. *Never let me go* is, even at firmest tempo, ruminatory. *Here's that rainy day* is dark-hued but dancing, and has witticisms deftly inserted into swift runs that other players might simply have dashed off for effect. His own composition, *Joanne*, maintains a kind of wistfulness and, in its interpretation, shows its creator to be no slave to what might be called – with more readily lauded pianists in mind – an obligation to extemporize. Still merely at the hems of celebrity, Al Haig died in 1982 at the age of 58.

E.T.

Phil Woods

357 Here's To My Lady

†Chesky (A) JD3

Woods (alt, clt[1]); Tommy Flanagan (p); George Mraz (bs); Kenny Washington (d). New York City, 20–21 December 1988.

Superette · *Johnny Hodges* · *Another love song* · *Canadian sunset*[1] · *Charles Christopher* · *Butter* · *Visions of Gaudi* · *Yours is my heart alone* · *Blue and sentimental*[1] · *Origins* · *Here's to my lady* · *Waltz for Debby*[1] · *Just us*

One of the least slavish and most durable of the Parker-inspired altoists, Woods was shown to be, as jazz approached the 1990s, a blithely contemporary artist, with a vigour of imagination undiminished some 40 years beyond his jazz beginnings. After study with Tristano and at the Juilliard School, which followed a teenage hearing of Johnny Hodges confirming an early attraction to the alto saxophone, he made his first recordings with Jimmy Raney and George Wallington in the mid-1950s. A recent association with the celebrity-laden orchestra Rhythmstick, playing Benny Golson arrangements (†CTI [A] 1006–2), recalls early big-band experience with Charlie Barnet, Dizzy Gillespie and Quincy Jones; but his records made with numerous small groups contain the better evidence of his powers.

The consistency of his performance is, retrospectively and in imaginative terms, impressive. The illustrative virtue of *Here's to my lady* will be found in its affinity with the powerful work that Woods did, not only with his European Rhythm Machine of the late 1960s and early 1970s and the Little Big Band quintet/sextet of 1984–90, but also with the mid-1950s combinations of a time when his collaborations with the altoist Gene Quill were a feature of the New York scene. Flanagan provides a further personal link with a Woods–Quill session of June 1956 (†Original Jazz Classics [A] OJCCD092–2).

The programme above includes three of Woods's original themes, other originals by three of the altoist's collaborators in a contemporary group, a dedicatory piece to a former colleague composed by another altoist, four long-established themes, and a famous tune by a pianist whose approach to song interpretation seems to have influenced Woods's approach to a session in which lyricism is at a premium. For three numbers Woods turns to the instrument in which he specialized at Juilliard, the B-flat clarinet.

Tom Harrell's playful piece *Superette* has Washington gleefully tapping the dancelike measures along. Woods is beautifully in control, yet savouring the playfulness which Flanagan's gentle bop has no difficulty in matching. The reason for Woods's *Johnny Hodges* will be apparent from a remark already made, but there is no trace of imitation in the improvising, nothing Ellingtonian in the group presentation, and if this is a celebration of the alto saxophone it is undoubtedly Parker's donations that shape the celebrating style. Yet when, in *Charles Christopher*, the beam of eulogy switches to Parker, it is not only the Parker inclinations of the Woods style that are illumined. That those are richly evident will seem proper in one whose earliest encounter with Bird was also in teenage, and whose personal closeness to a peerless master of modern jazz became evident for reasons other than musical.

Jerry Dodgion is the altoist and former Quincy Jones associate whose *Butter* commemorates another Jones sideman contemporary with Woods, Quentin Jackson (1909–76), formerly a well-known Ellingtonian. *Butter* is an affective threnody for a jazz veteran, but more telling than Woods's solo is Flanagan's vivid keyboard reflection. It has to be admitted that an idiosyncratic waywardness of intonation in the altoist's upper register is exaggerated at slow tempos, and has tended towards weirdness in some of his recent sessions.

Spanish rhythm is appropriate to Harrell's *Visions of Gaudi*, but whether sufficiently appropriate to conjure the spirit of the great Catalan architect's eccentric variant of art nouveau is not too easy to say. This is a theme of stop-time rhythmic artifice. Woods blows full-toned, responding to the underlying tricks with vehement doublings of the beat. Flanagan negotiates the mock pitfalls with the same ease that marks his display of elegant shapeliness in the musical comedy foxtrot which the group makes of Lehár's *Yours is my heart alone*. For that Woods swings prodigiously, and Mraz, the unfailing melodist, solos firmly and gracefully. Similar relaxation characterizes Johnny Mercer's *Here's to my lady*, though here the mood tends to inwardness.

Washington is generally a reliable monitor of these changing moods, touching recklessness only when given his head towards the close of *Origins*, a fast, forceful, simplistic theme which also coaxes from Woods a jauntiness which had become a frequent characteristic of his playing alongside the trumpeter Harrell, the pianist Hal Galper and the trombonist Hal Crook, the last of whom composed *Origins*. (Note the admirable sequence of albums that was launched with *Integrity* (†Red [It] VPA177) of 1984 and culminated with *All Bird's Children* (†Concord [A] CCD4441) of 1990.) Galper's mid-tempo theme *Just us* has some hard-bop swagger too, but the dazzling rhythmic multiplications engaged in by both Woods and Flanagan are more reminiscent of the form and spirit of the European Rhythm Machine of a couple of decades back (e.g. Verve [G] 2304 098).

For Eddie Heywood's *Canadian sunset*, the Basie classic *Blue and sentimental* and Bill Evans's *Waltz for Debby*, Woods plays the clarinet with assured but anonymous poise. His phrasing in the Heywood number is, at least, more enterprising than Flanagan's. He calls his recreation of the Basie number 'a doff of the cap to Lester Young's clarinet playing', [80] and the Basie original, made 'notable' by Young, is commented upon under **134**. An avowed love for its composer's 'approach to playing songs' lies behind the choice of the affectionate waltz. To recall that Woods, back in 1957, recorded his own composition *Waltz for a lovely wife* (†CBS [A] PRT465027) may be merely to add needless emphasis to the kinship of spirit with Evans and his like which is so apparent in much of this later session displaying Woods's artistry. E.T.

Joe Henderson

358 Power to the People

Milestone (A) MSP 9024

Mike Lawrence (tpt); Henderson (ten); Herbie Hancock (elec p); Ron Carter (el bs); Jack DeJohnette (d). New York City, 23 May 1969.

Afro-Centric · Power to the people

Henderson (ten); Hancock (p, el p); Carter (bs); DeJohnette (d). Same date.

Black narcissus · Opus one-point-five · Isotope · Lazy Afternoon

Hancock absent. Same date.

Foresight and afterthought (An impromptu suite in three movements)

Although it took until the 1990s to find the degree of recognition that had conspicuously eluded him throughout his career, Henderson's small but meticulously crafted discography was never short of albums of substance that might have prompted an earlier celebration of his talents. Certainly as early as the 1960s, when he became a regular on the Blue Note label, there was much to commend a style that had avoided drawing directly on the almost universal influence being exerted by John Coltrane. Henderson's first Blue Note date was for the trumpeter Kinny Dorham, *Una Mas* (†Blue Note [E] CDP746 515–2), in April 1963. His own debut as a leader on the label followed two months later, again with Dorham, *Page One* (†Blue Note CDP784 140–2), and on it were two items that were destined to become jazz classics and staples of jam sessions and pick-up bands the world over, Dorham's *Blue bossa* and Henderson's *Recorda me.* Two further albums with Dorham followed, plus *Inner Urge* (†Blue Note CDP 7 84189 2), a quartet date with McCoy Tyner, and a sextet date with Lee Morgan and Curtis Fuller, *Mode for Joe* (Blue Note BST 842227) in 1966.

Henderson was also in demand by others signed to the label, appearing on albums by Grant Green, Johnny Coles, Andrew Hill, Bobby Hutcherson, Freddie Roach, Horace Silver, Duke Pearson, Freddie Hubbard,

Pete La Roca, Larry Young, McCoy Tyner, and on Lee Morgan's two best-selling albums *The Sidewinder* (Blue Note [A] BLP 84145) and *The Rumproller* (Blue Note BLP 84199). He made his final Blue Note appearance on Herbie Hancock's *The Prisoner* (Blue Note BST 84321) in April 1969, although he would later sign for the reactivated Blue Note label in 1985. Yet despite this exposure on recordings as well as touring with Horace Silver, Herbie Hancock and the jazz-rock group Blood, Sweat and Tears, his profile with the jazz public at large had, until his latter-day success on the reconstituted Verve label in the early 1990s, remained low.

Henderson's style is less vertical than that of John Coltrane, although he has played that way on occasion. Generally he is a more melodic player whose ecumenical vision has taken account of Ornette Coleman and Sonny Rollins as much as modernists beyond the field of jazz such as Bartók and Stravinsky. Henderson is a very consistent player, setting and usually achieving the highest standards for himself so that very often it is the work of his accompanists that advances the claim of one album over another. A spellbinding solo on *Round about midnight*, for example, with a Japanese rhythm section, was a highlight of *In Japan* (Milestone [A] MSP 9047), but it is *Power to the People* from this period that stands out for the fine rhythm section, Henderson's excellent compositions and, of course, some notable playing by the leader. By 1968 Henderson had signed with Orrin Keepnews's Milestone label, debuting with *The Kicker* (Milestone [A] MSP 9008) and following it shortly afterwards with the quartet album *Tetragon* (Milestone [A] MSP 9017), which showed him taking account of the work of the mid-1960s Miles Davis quintet. Indeed, one title, *R.J.*, had been previously recorded by Davis on his *E.S.P* session in January 1965 (†Columbia [A] 467899–2). On *Power to the People*, his third album for Milestone, Henderson used a rhythm section well versed in Davis's music. Carter and Hancock had been key figures with Davis in the mid-1960s, DeJohnette had replaced Tony Williams in Davis's band in December 1968, and Lawrence's playing reflected the influence of Davis's playing. A promising player, Lawrence later featured in Larry Coryell's Eleventh House in 1974–5, where he contributed some inventive work within the fusion idiom on *Larry Coryell and the Eleventh House at Montreux* (†Vanguard [F] 662181) and *Level One* (Arista [A] ARTY 113) before dying suddenly in his late 20s. [81] However, while Henderson employed the methods of Davis's mid-1960s quintet, he was nevertheless able to impose his own imprimatur within these stylistic boundaries, emerging with a convincing and wholly absorbing album in its own right.

Black narcissus is a 24-bar medium-tempo jazz waltz. It has an ABC construction, 8 + 8 + 8, and the same tranquil, floating quality Wayne Shorter's compositions brought to the Miles Davis quintet and featured on his own albums for the Blue Note label. This feeling is heightened by

Hancock's tasteful use here of the electric piano. Effectively, a melodically and harmonically static passage of eight bars is repeated a tone lower for a further eight bars and answered by the C section, which in contrast is more melodically and harmonically dynamic, allowing the rhythm section to kick. Following the rhythmic advances of the Bill Evans trio with LaFaro and Motian (**372**), subsequently expanded on by the Hancock–Carter–Williams combination with Miles Davis, rhythm sections were liberated to decorate the basic pulse rather than state it explicitly.

Henderson states the *Black narcissus* theme with a very delicate tone, hardening at the C section for dynamic effect. The contrast between the floating quality of the A and B sections and the kicking C section is preserved throughout his improvisation, an opposition of feather-light phrases and steely assertions. Hancock's ethereal electric piano is rhythmically very free in the A sections, and his use of the instrument throughout introduces pleasing tone colours, frequently voiced in fourths and synonymous with the modal feel of the A sections. *Afro-centric* is an up-tempo vehicle of 26 bars in length and is another song that uses an ABC construction, this time as 10 + 10 + 6, where interestingly the final six bars of the harmony changes once every bar but has no written melody. Effectively the A and B sections are treated as modes over which the highly syncopated theme is written. DeJohnette maintains a turbulent 'Afro' rhythm-section pattern, while Henderson approaches his improvisation with great clarity of thought; unhurried, there are no redundant phrases, but instead a series of clearly stated propositions. Lawrence acquits himself well on trumpet with a clear idea of what he wanted to achieve in his solo and succeeds in accomplishing his goal. Hancock again provides a fine example of utilizing the specific tonal qualities of the electric piano, his fleet touch ideally suited to the instrument, able to avoid the muddy textures that was often the province of lesser pianists.

Carter's composition *Opus one-point-five* again returns to the floating quality of *Black narcissus.* A ballad performance, it shows in perhaps clearer detail the interactive role of the rhythm section behind Henderson's beautiful craftsmanship with its echoes of Paul Desmond's 'dry martini' tone when he dwells in the higher registers of his instrument. Once again, Hancock, Carter and DeJohnette lend a hypnotic, almost dreamy feel to the rhythm. In contrast *Isotope* has a distinct *alla breve* feel. It is a modified 12-bar blues; its most arresting characteristic is the traditional move to the dominant being replaced instead by a flattened fifth, followed by the dominant and then a two-bar turnaround of descending minor thirds. Previously recorded by Henderson on *Inner Urge* (†Blue Note [E] CDP788 4189–2), its theme was written as a tribute to Thelonious Monk. Henderson's playing has a lyrical urgency that can be found in all his best solos; Hancock makes Monkish allusions while remaining his own man and Carter, as throughout the album, contents himself with doing precisely the right thing at precisely the right time alongside DeJohnette's mature-beyond-his-years wisdom.

The title track, another Henderson original, is in $^6/_4$. It is a simple AABA construction and sees the leader's most impassioned playing on the album. However, Henderson's is controlled passion; he never releases his grip on logic and coherence, even when splitting notes to produce overtones or moving out of key with side-slipping runs; individual detail never loses sight of architectural design. Lawrence's short solo is expansive and without fault, and precedes an exemplary Hancock workout on electric piano exploiting the wide range of contrasting tone colours that is possible with the instrument. *Lazy afternoon* is an easy swinger in a purely acoustic setting, the kind of number that he played nightly in clubs up and down the country.

In contrast *Foresight and afterthought*, in a trio setting, reveals another aspect of Henderson's performing persona. Together with *Barcelona* (Enja [G] 3037) from 1976 and also in a trio format, they create a context in which to view his highly regarded two-album set, *The State of the Tenor* (Blue Note BT 85123 and BT 85126). Recorded live for the reconstituted Blue Note label at the Village Vanguard in November 1985 (with Al Foster on drums and, coincidentally, Carter on bass), the scrupulous improviser allows his creative impulses to dictate the destination of his melodic inventions. This air of risk taking and abandon that flows through these two albums is accuarely presaged on *Foresight and afterthought* (and the free form *Barcelona*). It exposes a feeling of poetic abandon that one suspects is never far from the surface, contributing to a suppressed tempestuousness apparent even in his more considered work. A spontaneously conceived 'suite', *Foresight and afterthought* moves freely from one tonal centre to another in a way inspired by Ornette Coleman's methodology, and is in three parts. The first is at a bright tempo with Henderson toying with melodic fragments, some of which coalesce into the jagged logic that forms the opening improvisation. It is contrasted by a more overtly 'free' slow section, where he employs tonal coloration such as overblowing and overtones but without losing sight of melodic unity. The third section returns to the original brisk tempo, with Henderson's scurrying lines marked closely by DeJohnette and Carter, alert to every nuance and turn he makes. It represents some of Henderson's most dramatic playing on record, a broad spectrum that on the one hand had joined with Andrew Hill on his classic exploratory albums such as *Point of Departure* (†Blue Note [E] CDP841 672–2) and on the other could lay down a booting blues with the organist Freddie Roach on *Brown Sugar* (Blue Note [A] BST 84168). S.N.

Cool Continuations

As in the later growths of bop, cool styles continued to diversify, and in directions substantially different though still with a degree of understatement.

Shorty Rogers

359 The Complete Atlantic and EMI Jazz Recordings of Shorty Rogers

Mosaic (A) MR6–125 (6 LPs), †Mosaic (A) MD4–125 (4 CDs)

Rogers (tpt); John Graas (fr h); Gene Englund (tu); Art Pepper (alt); Jimmy Giuffre (ten); Hampton Hawes (p); Don Bagley (bs); Shelly Manne (d). Los Angeles, 8 October 1951.
Popo · Didi · Four mothers · Over the rainbow · Apropos · Sam and the lady

Rogers (fl h); Bud Shank (alt, alt fl); Jimmy Rowles (p); Harry Babasin (bs); Roy Harte (d). Los Angeles, March 1954.
Shank's pranks · Casa de luz · Lotus Bud · Left bank · Jasmine · Just a few

Rogers (tpt); Giuffre (clt, ten, bar); Pete Jolly (p); Curtis Counce (bs); Manne (d). Los Angeles, 1 March 1955.
Isn't it romantic? · Not really the blues · Martians go home · My heart stood still · Loaded · Oh, play that thing! · Bill · Twelfth Street rag · The lady in red

Same personnel. Los Angeles, 3 March 1955.
Trickleydidlier · Solarization · That's what I'm talking about · Michele's meditation

Rogers (tpt); Giuffre (clt, ten, bar); Lou Levy (p); Ralph Peña (bs); Manne (d). Los Angeles, 26 October 1955.
Barbaro · Planetarium · Martians come back · March of the Martians

Same personnel. Los Angeles, 29 October 1955.
Papouche

Same personnel. Los Angeles, 3 November 1955.
Papouche · Martians stay home · Peals · Lotus Bud · Easy · Amber leaves

Rogers (tpt, fl h); Conte Candoli, Pete Candoli, Harry Edison, Don Fagerquist (tpt); Levy (p); Peña (bs); Manne (d). Los Angeles, 6 December 1955.
Serenade to Sweets · Astral alley · Pixieland

Rogers (tpt, fl h); Bob Enevoldsen (v-tbn); Graas (fr h); Paul Sarmento (tu); Giuffre (clt, ten, bar); Shank (alt); Levy (p); Peña (bs); Manne (d). Los Angeles, 9 December 1955.
Wail of two cities · Baklava Bridge · Chant of the cosmos

Rogers (fl h); Edison (tpt); Shank (alt); Jolly (p); Barney Kessel (g); Leroy Vinnegar (bs); Manne (d). Los Angeles, 16 December 1955.
Dickie's dream · *Moten swing* · *Blues way up there* · *Blues way down there*

Rogers (fl h); Giuffre (clt, ten, bar); Herb Geller (alt); Shank (alt, bar, bs sx); Bill Holman (ten); Levy (p); Peña (bs); Manne (d). Los Angeles, 27 March 1956.
Toyland · *I dig Ed* · *Adam in New York* · *Clicking with Clax*

Same personnel. Los Angeles, 30 March 1956.
Put the goodies on · *Our song* · *Pete's meat* · *Mike's peak*

This is music from mostly a decade or so after the initial phase of modern jazz declared itself in 1945. Bop offered a new kind of sophistication, especially rhythmic, and it was apt that the above later music should do likewise though on quite different lines. Hitherto anything described as West Coast jazz signified music that simply happened to be performed in California, but Rogers's 1951 recordings are conventionally identified with the emergence of a fresh approach associated with the Pacific shores. Nearly all genuinely new developments in jazz are condemned at first and this is one of the few cases of a hasty initial judgement being sustained over many years. The main reason for this is dealt with below, although it should immediately be noted that the origins of a specifically 'West Coast jazz' and of Rogers's own style were less simple than is supposed in most of the literature.

True, as a trumpeter and partly as a writer, he emerged from the big bands, having worked for Barnet, Kenton and, earlier and more formatively, for Herman. With *Jolly Rogers* and *Round robin* (both †Capitol [A] 8 59965 2) Rogers made valuable additions to the Kenton library, but he worked out his basic orchestral method earlier through composing such pieces as *Back talk* and *Keen and peachy* (both **312c**) for Herman. His approach to smallish combos would seem to have had the same roots and can be studied in a 1946 Herman Woodchoppers date which produced *Igor*, *Nero's conception* etc. (**312b**). Rogers followed this later the same year with *Curbstone scuffle* for Sonny Berman's Big Eight (Spotlite [E] SPJ132), and here occur small hints of the ensemble style fully realized in the sessions detailed above. In fact during the years leading to the 1951 occasion he gradually hammered out a personal style through writing for other people's recordings; examples include a Terry Gibbs date for New Jazz and *Chickasaw* for Serge Chaloff's Futurama session (†Mosaic [A] MD4–147). It is noteworthy that this piece is so closely wrought, with a more effective use of instrumental colour than is usual in bop. This is also true of his *Be my guest* and *Softly the horn blows* for John Graas (MCA-Coral [A] 622188). In due course Rogers also wrote for Dave Pell, Louis Belson, Chet Baker and supposedly for the Benny Goodman group with Stan Hasselgard and Wardell Gray. [82]

Although Basie's kind of jazz was an important part of the Rogers heritage, as is confirmed by the masterly rewritings of his *Shorty Courts the Count* (RCA-Bluebird [E] 59171RB), the overtly exploratory side of his activities was also significant during the early years. Aspects of this are discussed under **432** in connection with sessions with Giuffre, Manne and Russ Freeman, and his participation in the 1953 *Collaboration West* (†Original Jazz Classics [A] OJCCD122–2) with Teddy Charles and again Giuffre is also relevant. Thus it was from this side of Rogers's work, not from the conventionalisms of big-band scoring, that arose such independent gestures in his orchestral output as *Tale of an African lobster*'s use of irregular *ostinato*s, the tellingly varied timbral densities of *Infinity promenade* (both RCA-Bluebird, as above) and the bitonality of his later *I'm gonna go fishin'*.

A not unexpected fusion of conservative and progressive elements, then, contributed to Rogers's style. Oblivious of this, the *idiots savants* of jazz commentary, recoiling from the first recordings under his name, unanimously seized on the presence of french horn and tuba as proof of an incapable bowdlerization of the Davis items dealt with under **376**. Thus, 'Shorty Rogers tried to copy the arrangements and "west coast jazz" was born with Miles as reluctant midwife.' [83] This same refusal actually to listen to the related music is echoed in countless texts, but Rogers produced nothing sounding remotely like Evans's *Moondreams*, Carisi's *Israel* etc. Rogers's scores are less dense in texture, much less dark in mood and sound, and there is nothing among the Davis pieces at all like, for instance, *Sam and the lady*. Again, both on the 1951 date and the other sessions discussed below, most of the themes and all the arrangements are by Rogers, there being nothing like the association of composers and arrangers served by Davis's nonet. Inevitably there elsewhere occurred scattered examples of belated and merely parasitic imitation of the Davis approach, specifically in using french horn and tuba, such as *Little Niles* or *Speculation* by the Jazz Lab nonet of Gigi Gryce and Donald Byrd (Columbia [A] CL998), and these did not sound like Rogers either. Both his 1951 recordings and those of Davis from 1949–50 were alike in one respect, however. This was that each body of music represented a constructive reaction against the thin, often unison, ensembles of bop and the Tristano school, even if faint echoes of earlier times may be caught in *Popo* (Gillespie's *Ool-ya-koo*) and in *Sam and the lady* (Parker's *Chasin' the Bird*). Each score recorded by Davis and by Rogers had a distinct character of its own, and although the latter's output was so widely condemned in the jazz press it is amusing how straight-ahead even the earliest items now sound.

Certainly the initial octet pieces are never actually complex, but there is real compositional skill here – rather than merely deft arranging – and they are performed with drive and often with high spirits. The best improvisations are not just cogently inventive but seem to be organically parts of the larger wholes, and virtually all the solos keep to the point, like Rogers's scores, shorn of decorative flourishes. A blues, *Popo* is typical, although the close interweaving between Pepper and Rogers in *Sam and the lady*, another blues, is more striking. The altoist still owed something to both Parker and Konitz yet was now assuming a personal identity and made a definitive statement on *Over the rainbow*. This is a vehicle for him alone, scarcely referring to the familiar melody and with sensitively scored backing from Rogers. Giuffre's *Four mothers* is one of the most forceful pieces here, with full participation by the other horns most of the time, while *Apropos* is lithe and energetic, again with considerable emphasis on the ensemble.

The tendency outlined by these six items was confirmed by two sessions Rogers led 15 months later for RCA using a very similar personnel, though with Milt Bernhart's trombone making the combo a nonet (RCA-Bluebird, as above). Outstanding are *Morpo*, yet another Rogers blues, and the rich-textured *Bunny*, this latter being a further vehicle for Pepper surpassing the memorable *Over the rainbow*. Although each piece stands perfectly well on its own, these two groups of recordings are best studied together and in conjunction with a 1957 Pepper date for Pacific Jazz (Mosaic [A] MR3–105). This with great verve reinterpreted Rogers scores from both the 1951 and 1953 sessions. The altoist's music had by then developed considerably, as is shown by the acutely expressive later account of *Bunny* and his magnificently sustained improvisation on *Popo*. There is excellent work too from Holman, Fagerquist, Manne and, at the piano, Russ Freeman, and these performances usefully show Rogers's composing in a different light.

This set's next music first appeared under Shank's name, being originally issued on the transient Nocturne label and prefiguring the quintet instrumentation adopted by a majority of the subsequent recordings. Now emerging from the shadows cast by Konitz and Pepper, the altoist was beginning to sound individual, this impression being much strengthened by the December 1955 sessions in which he took part. Shank's solo on *Casa de luz* is especially well put together but he, Rogers and Rowles are remarkably consistent, although it is regrettable that all six performances follow the same alto-flugelhorn-piano sequence for the solos. Besides, this is the one date here on which Manne was not behind the drums and while Harte is highly propulsive it has to be acknowledged that he is less imaginative. Though not the first entirely convincing use of the flute in jazz (see **388**), *Lotus Bud* is this session's best-recalled track, and Rogers's writing for the alto flute, sounding a fourth lower, is a characteristic example of his sensitivity to instrumental colour. This is emphasized by comparison with the longer 1955 version where Giuffre's clarinet reigns and, despite good counterpoint between him and Rogers plus a superior solo from Levy, the effect is less remarkable. In both cases, however, the rhythm section's firm pace prevents the music from going soft at the centre.

Rogers had taken up the flugelhorn earlier in the year of this Shank date, where he plays it exclusively, as on the 1956 sessions, and extensively on the December 1955 occasions. Its mellow tone has a wide appeal and it was in due course employed by other trumpeters, including Miles Davis. Though Rogers always exerted more influence as a composer, arranger and bandleader, his playing was now approaching a level he maintained until the late 1950s. His original models were Bunny Berigan and Harry Edison, two very different virtuosos, but his own playing ignored technical fireworks and particularly high-register histrionics. Rogers's trumpet (and flugelhorn) sound was broad, warm, avoided undue vibrato, and he kept chiefly to the middle register, most of his well-articulated phrases, and indeed whole solos, having the sort of logical structure found in his best compositions. He is one of those jazzmen who, although contained by definite executive limitations, are instantly recognizable; and he often sounds happy.

Within the context of Rogers's 1950s career as a whole these highly productive 1955–6 sessions for Atlantic are best viewed as an interlude between two alliances with RCA. The leader obviously aside, the personnel is entirely different from the Shank date, resulting in music that is more aggressive and more sharply defined in aim and character. No doubt this was partly because the group he was leading had for some while been a regular working band, one of the finest of its time, with an established repertoire. Some listeners, inverting an obvious Armstrong precedent (**48**), might like to think of it as the Cool Five, although a cool Five Pennies (**70**) would be nearer the mark. Yet these recordings do not bristle with modernities as the best of Nichols's did in their time (when they influenced the later Hot Sevens), and Lester Young is the tutelary spirit of Rogers's quintet. It is not that they ever copied his phrases but rather that they were sometimes affected by his obliqueness and reticence. There also is an interesting relationship between Young's and Giuffre's clarinet work, and Robert Gordon's description of the latter as 'warm yet ethereal' is exact. [84] Giuffre's doubling on tenor and baritone saxophones obviously added to the band's range of voices, and his contributions on the latter are quite unlike either Chaloff or, more relevantly, Mulligan.

Besides Giuffre, Jolly was, along with Manne, the player who accounted most for the group's positive impact. At first influenced by Horace Silver, the pianist was highly energetic in his own way, his solos and ensemble parts often being at once thick-textured and contrapuntal. It is instructive to hear Jolly leading this same Rogers personnel, augmented by Howard Roberts's guitar, on a session of his own just a few days after the first two Atlantic dates (RCA [A] LPM1105). Not that all this music is aggressive in the manner of Rogers's fiery exchanges of fours with Giuffre on *Loaded* or their fast, explosive treatment of *Not really the blues* (a Johnny Mandel piece originally for Herman). Proof enough of that is *Martians go home*, a meaningfully rarefied blues in which a small quantity of notes work hard. Indeed the longest track of this Mosaic set makes a notable use of space in both musical senses, that is silence plus very sparse textures. Less sparing in its use of notes is Rogers's contrary instruction to the Red Planet's inhabitants, *Martians come back*, yet there is more excellent blues playing here from all concerned and if the further contradiction of *Martians stay home* pursues the vein less emphatically, it still leaves an agreeable impression of fastidiousness.

An almost equally engaging essay in this sort of minimalism is *Oh, play that thing!* But *Twelfth Street rag* is as incongruous a choice for Rogers's kind of jazz as could be found. Euday Bowman's banal 1916 theme receives ironic emphasis in the first and last choruses but otherwise is forgotten as the quintet improvises seriously on the chords. *That's what I'm talking about* is still another blues, and one with which they used to close nightclub sets. Very blue, it is exactly the sort of music they were supposed not to be able to play. Going in quite another direction, *Michele's meditation* makes further and successful use of the *Lotus Bud* vein.

On the contrary, the five-trumpet session was disappointing. With Edison, Fagerquist, Conte Candoli and Rogers himself present, there obviously is some good improvising, but as on Ernie Wilkins's *Top Brass* and *Trumpets All Out* dates of 1955 and 1957 for Savoy, there is no attempt at exploring the medium's considerable possibilities. Apparently it was all the result of Rogers's boyhood dream of playing in a trumpet section with Edison [85] and musically speaking the matter went no further than that.

Next there was a modification of the 1951 instrumentation, with rich ensemble textures showing that Rogers's writing had become still more personal, and with admirable solos from Shank, Giuffre and especially Levy. The last 1955 session was unusual for the inclusion, among so many Rogers themes, of *Dickie's dream* and *Moten swing*. Shank and Edison are superb in the former, less forceful on the latter, but Kessel is excellent in *Moten swing* and *Blues way up there*. In fact this last and *Blues way down there* are both outstanding West Coast blues and very swinging.

Finally, for his Atlantic dates, Rogers teamed himself with a saxophone section that is not only of superlative quality but also, by virtue of its doublings, many-voiced. Indeed the colours are almost as varied as those produced by the previous year's nonet scores, and among the invention-packed solos those by Geller and Levy are particularly brilliant. The music's drive is maintained through both sessions and it is odd – or a wry comment on changing jazz fashions – that these performances had to wait 21 years before issue. Still, it is apt that the eventual LP took its name from the headlong *Clicking with Clax*.

After that Rogers went back to RCA and there were still good items to come such as *Blues express* (alias *That's right* alias *Boomsie*), memorable for the ferocious yet precise storming of its Maynard Ferguson-topped heights. But like so many jazzmen, Rogers put the best of himself into his early work and later the innovative drive, and his sense of curiosity, departed. Through the rest of the 1950s and beyond there were too many big-band records that demonstrated much skill, were beautifully played, yet were usually very dull and often based on characterless material, some of it his own. Typical was his background music for just one more Tarzan film. In fact, Hollywood got Rogers in the end. M.H.

Lars Gullin

360 Aeros Aromatic Atomica Suite

EMI (Sd) EO62–35282

Bertil Lövgren, Jan Allen, Maffy Falay (tpt); Sven Larsson (bs tbn, tu); Claes Rosendahl (picc, fl, ten); Lennart Åberg (fl, sop, ten); Erik Nilsson (fl, bs clt, bar); Arne Domnérus (clt, alt); Gullin (bar, comp); Bengt Hallberg (p); Rune Gustafsson (g); Georg Riedel (bs); Egil Johanssen (d). Stockholm, 16 March 1972.
S.H.T.

Gullin (p, comp). Stockholm, 7 November 1973.
Theme from 'Kvarteret Oron'

Lövgren, Allan, Leif Halldén (tpt); Håkan Nyqvist (tpt, fr h); Bertil Strandberg (tbn); Larsson (bs tbn, tu); Rosendahl (picc, fl, ten); Åberg (fl, sop, ten); Nilsson (fl, bs clt, bar); Domnérus (clt, alt); Bernt Rosengren (ten); Gullin (bar, comp); Hallberg (p); Gustafsson (g); Riedel (bs); Stefan Brolund (el bs, orch bells); Johanssen (d). Stockholm, 25–6 February 1976.
Aeros Aromatic Atomica Suite: The aching heart of an oak · Toka voka oka boka · Pretty miss

The above catalogue number is that of the initial issue of this material as a separate LP. However, it also appeared as part of a magnificent 7-LP boxed set, apparently unnumbered but titled *Lars Gullin: The EMI Years 1964–76*, containing almost his entire recorded output of that period. The three movements of the *Aeros Aromatic Atomica Suite* are most advantageously heard at the end of that 12-year sequence. At the same time, with the exception of *Lars Gullin at the Golden Circle* (1964–5), some of the performances on which are incomplete, almost any of the LPs in this set could have occupied this space. Which is to say that the choice of *Aeros Aromatic Atomica*, like certain other items in this book, was to an extent arbitrary. It also indicates how creative Gullin was in the last dozen years of his life. With a few exceptions on the earlier discs, all the themes are his, as are all the arrangements; with due respect to several others, all the finest improvising is his, as is the drive which informs the project from beginning to end.

With the emergence of Chaloff (**297**, **310**), Mulligan (**300**, **362**) and Pepper Adams, the 1950s were something of a golden age for the baritone saxophone. Gullin too began in the usual way for jazz, with short improvised pieces recorded on discs lasting for up to about three minutes. His exceptional powers of melodic invention soon led to his writing attractive themes that proved excellent subjects for improvisation, then arrangements of these; all this is dealt with under **306**. But he continued to grow, to write larger pieces, eventually works occupying a whole 12-inch LP – which was the natural format for jazz in his time. This might be seen as a natural evolution, yet not many jazzmen have the ability to sustain at all convincingly a large-scale structure like that of *The aching heart of an oak*, the first movement of *Aeros Aromatic Atomica*, lasting over 20 minutes. It is true that there is plenty of improvising, by several hands; but this is not mere filling, for Gullin ensures that it contributes to a real, long-range musical form.

When giving consideration to some of his 1954–5 music on an earlier page (**306**), it was suggested that his frequent solos on a given theme were like parts of a larger, concealed whole, in other words of a work in progress. Gullin's more sustained compositions, when he went beyond producing themes to improvise on and to create large structures, may be seen as attempts, often successful, to bring the hidden works implied by his improvisations into the open, and in them to add other voices to his own. His good fortune in discovering sympathetic and inventive colleagues for his 1950s recordings continued in the 1960s and 1970s with his scores for big ensembles; this is not something upon which composers of large-scale jazz pieces can always depend. And despite the greater length and more extended resources employed in these larger works, they retain the conciseness of his 1950s small-combo recordings: Gullin was almost as good a self-editor with a pen as with his baritone saxophone. To which it might be added that his baritone sound remained to the end absolutely distinctive, and it was reflected in the textures of his always individual orchestral scores.

It is probable that *Aeros Aromatic Atomica* is Gullin's finest single large work, especially the first movement. The language is rather conservative by the standards of 1976 yet it is written with great understanding of the capabilities of all the instruments and the potentialities of the people playing them. *Toka voka oka boka* is a brief interlude rather as *Theme from 'Kvarteret Oron'* (= the Uneasy Precinct) is a still briefer postlude, placed at the end of the record. But *Aeros Aromatic Atomica* is in its two chief movements a genuine suite, these substantial pieces audibly belonging together. In their themes, solos and linking passages they almost resemble the conventional sort of big-band score, except that they are larger – not just longer. The themes, also, are more coherently related one to another than is usual in such cases, and there are plenty of intriguing mixtures of instrumental colours both in the sometimes lengthy ensemble passages and behind the improvisations.

Although Gullin's solos are consistently the finest in terms of individuality, those of Rosengren are not far behind, particularly in *Pretty miss.* This is the more assertive of the two pieces, ending with emphatic statements by the full-voiced ensemble, whereas *The aching heart of an oak* drifts away in an apt quietness. Gullin's orchestral thinking rightly commands much attention, yet, quite apart from his and indeed Rosengren's improvisations, there are plenty of admirable solos by others. In *The aching heart* most of them are heard from more than once and it is Lövgren who is responsible for the first trumpet passage, Allan who plays the lyrical second. Others who solo cogently here include Hallberg, Gustafsson, Domnérus and Rosengren; Gullin appears three times. Åberg plays the soprano saxophone to memorable effect in *Pretty miss,* where Lövgren is the only trumpet soloist.

S.H.T. (= Salvo Honoris Titulo) is a bossa nova piece by Gullin where Domnérus's is the most prominent voice in the opening ensemble. The idea of a Swedish bossa nova may seem a trifle odd but Gustafsson, Domnérus, Hallberg and Domnérus again are prompted to vivid improvisations. Modestly the composer, though very evident in the ensembles, does not take a solo.

M.H.

Jan Allan

361 **Jan Allan 70**

Four Leaf Clover (Sd) FLC5035

Allan, Bertil Lövgren, Rolf Ericson, Lennart Axelsson, Weine Rentiden (tpt); Olle Holmqvist, George Vernon, Jörgen Johansson, Olle Lind (tbn); Bengt Belfrage, Sven Åke Landström (fr h); Lennart Åberg (fl, sop); Arne Domnérus (alt); Bernt Rosengren (ten); Claes Rosendahl (fl, ten); Erik Nilsson (bar); Rune Gustafsson (g); Roman Dylag (bs); Egil Johanssen (d); Rupert Clemendore (perc); Nils Lindberg (comp). Stockholm, 19 December 1968.

Polska with trumpet

Belfrage, Landström, Clemendore absent. Same date.

Ballad for trumpet · *Rolf Billberg in memoriam*

Allan (tpt); Åberg (sop[1], ten); Bobo Stensson (p); Palle Danielsson (bs); Jon Christensen (d). Stockholm, 25–6 September 1969.

Debalira · *Rapid* · *The eye of Odin*[1]

Is there such a thing as jazz that does not travel? It seems unlikely, yet this original and beautiful record has been almost continuously available, on several labels, ever since it first appeared in 1970, has won several local prizes, but is apparently quite unknown outside Scandinavia. There is no good musical reason for this, and it may be that other factors are at work that we do not yet understand. Almost certainly this record was prompted by the Miles Davis–Gil Evans collaborations like **382**, but such are the gifts of the participants, especially Allan and Lindberg, the composer of the pieces for large band, that it has a character entirely its own. When an international star like Davis is involved, it is thought necessary for him to be in the limelight virtually throughout, whereas here, although this is very much Allan's record, he can afford to make a late entry, as in *Rapid.* Moreover, there is space for other soloists, the miniature concerto format of the three scores for big ensemble alternating with three pieces for a small combo; and, as the above details show, the instrumentation of both groups is varied slightly.

The 1968 items represent a notable advance on Lindberg's earlier compositions, like the three-movement *Trisection* of 1962 (†Dragon [Sd] DRCD220), considerable though such achievements are. This music no more resembles Ellington than it does Evans, yet, very much like them, Lindberg explores the expressive scope of instrumental colour and texture. Quite another dimension is added, however, by the cadences of Swedish folk song, which, according to those with the ears to hear such things, find many an echo in Lindberg's work. The simplicity which this implies is balanced by an approach that is essentially polyphonic, this latter being one of the factors which unite the pieces for big and small ensembles even though the 1969 performances use themes from other composers. *Debalira* is by Danielsson, *Rapid* and *The eye of Odin* by Carl-Axel Dominique, and the treatments of their themes are, in a different yet related way, as ambitious as anything Lindberg does with the large band. He takes full advantage of the big ensemble's resources while maintaining an intimacy and in particular a mobility comparable to that of the quintet. The larger personnel was drawn chiefly from the Swedish Radio Jazz Group, a body of musicians well used to playing together who achieve here a most striking flexibility of ensemble as Lindberg's unusual textures flow into and out of each other.

This quality is equally apparent in the disjunct movement between trumpet and orchestra: sometimes one answers the other, but just as often they follow their own separate paths. Allan's playing has enough character and individuality in itself to be another factor binding these six movements together, and in quite specific ways. For example his frequent interplay during the orchestral performances between double-time phrases and the music's basic pulse mirrors the marked freedom with which tempo is treated in *Debalira* and *Rapid.* This in turn is reflected in the irregular yet always cogent ebb and flow of the inner tension of the music from both groups, Allan's ideas being especially unpredictable, his phrases beginning and ending unexpectedly, the effect heightened by his use of space. He was more influenced by saxophonists of the Tristano persuasion, such as Konitz and Marsh, than by other trumpeters, and along with his finely controlled technique goes a tone soft at the edges, and warm. Even when travelling through Lindberg's relatively complex scores, Allan sounds spontaneous yet entirely secure, fluent but never facile; he seems to dwell on the moment yet always to move forward, and, without exaggeration, every note counts. His chaste intensity avoids the jazz trumpeter's usual rhetoric and is, yet again, matched no less by the other members of the quintet than by Lindberg's bypassing of the long-standardized formulas of big-band writing.

Besides precluding mere virtuoso display, or almost any other sort of conventional gesture, the sophistication of all these players leads equally to the richness of the climactic orchestral passages before Allan's re-entry in *Polska with trumpet* and the expressive force with which inflections of tempo are employed in *Rapid* and *Debalira*. On the latter occur passages which are virtual duets between trumpet and bass, then tenor and bass, with the piano and drums adding secondary voices throughout (rather as guitar and bass do in *Ballad for trumpet*). Stensson leads a remarkable passage in *Debalira* also, with the bass and drums making equal-voiced contributions. The musical invention attains impressive density, and in fact throughout this record everything has to be given attention, nothing is truly subsidiary – or at least nothing can be taken for granted. Nor are there any easy ways out. After solos by Lindberg, Domnérus and Åberg as well as Allan, *Rolf Billberg in memoriam* closes in an aptly funereal mood. Not all musicians would be sufficiently independent-minded to end a *jazz* record thus; even the Davis–Evans *Miles Ahead* closes with *I don't wanna be kissed*, Ellington's *Such Sweet Thunder* with the equally inconsequential *Circle of fourths*. Lindberg's score and the soloists lament, protest at, but finally accept the great altoist's passing.

Although not free jazz exactly, the combo performances would not have gone as they do if free jazz had never existed, and seldom does anyone play a strictly accompanimental role for long. In *The eye of Odin* there is fine counterpoint between trumpet and soprano saxophone, the latter fluent, luxuriant, the former simple, almost stoical in its phrases, and both melodious. So is the bass, which, along with the piano, becomes more central as the soprano drops out. But the saxophone returns and the five-voiced texture flows on, offering some confirmation of Aquinas's dictum that 'beauty consists in a certain consonance of diverging elements'. *Rapid* is like that too, and includes another striking passage led by Stensson, whose phrases also, it seems, echo elements of folk music. This piece almost belies its title by coming nearly to a standstill in preparation for Allan's delayed entry, yet the essential complexity of all this music promptly reasserts itself, soon growing as eventful as ever, confirming the reconciliation of the supposed opposites of large and small ensembles is complete. M.H.

Gerry Mulligan

362a Presenting the Gerry Mulligan Sextet

EmArcy (A) MG36056, EmArcy (E) EJL101

Jon Eardley (tpt); Bob Brookmeyer (v-tbn); Zoot Sims (ten); Mulligan (bar); Peck Morrison (bs); Dave Bailey (d). New York City, 21 September 1955.

Bernie's tune · *Mud bug*

Same personnel. New York City, 22 September 1955.

Apple core · *Sweet and lovely*

Brookmeyer also plays p[1]. New York City, 31 October 1955.

Broadway · *Nights at the turntable* · *Everything happens to me*[1] · *The lady is a tramp*

362b Mainstream of Jazz: Gerry Mulligan and His Sextet

EmArcy (A) MG36101, EmArcy (E) EJL1259

Mulligan also plays p[2]. New York City, 22 September 1955.

Blues at the roots[2]

Bill Crow (bs) replaces Morrison. New York City, 25 January 1956.

Ain't it the truth? · *Mainstream*

Don Ferrara (tpt) replaces Eardley. New York City, 26 September 1956.

Igloo · *Elevation* · *Lollypop*

Mulligan's earliest quartet recordings (**300**) signalled his first maturity, which is as far as many jazzmen ever get, especially if they have the kind of success which he enjoyed with that group. But he was, rather like Benny Carter, an uncommonly adaptable musician, as is shown by his recordings with players like Monk or Hodges. He was able to relate meaningfully to such improvisers without any compromise to his own individuality, and the same point is made in a different way by the above sextet performances. This group represents an extension of the quartet not just in numerical terms but more significantly with regard to method and aesthetics; and the concert band he started in 1960 built on this sextet's discoveries and achievements.

The ensemble came together almost by chance, at a December 1954 concert by the quartet, with Eardley, at which Brookmeyer and Sims were guests. The recordings made on that occasion (†Pacific Jazz [A] B21K-46864) demonstrate the immediate rapport between all six players and the combo's obvious further potential. Eardley is strikingly lyrical on *Western reunion* and *I know, don't know how*, while the trombonist is outstanding in several pieces. This was, indeed, an interesting balance of musical personalities, producing, on the 1955–6 sextet dates, some of the finest cool jazz of its time. All the participants were touched by bop, yet most of them still had allegiances to Lester Young – or to what he stood for – and even to earlier figures. Mulligan's sympathies with some of the pioneers of jazz, not to mention his recordings of themes like *Varsity drag* and *Davenport blues*, were seized on by his detractors, usually in attempts to prove that he was not a 'real' modernist. Yet with the sextet as elsewhere, the content of his music is essentially modern, for example in its interplay between melancholy and more than one sort of humour, in the equivocation between irony and benevolence. His music usually amounted to a firmly positive response to the dictum that one should never copy the past but also never forget it.

In a group like the sextet we can hear and appreciate the high quality of Morrison's, then Crow's, playing especially well; and the horns soon break in collectively if there seems to be any danger of an extended bass solo. More centrally, the two-man rhythm team has no problem in carrying the four horns, and the front line together and individually make a highly productive use of the plain yet deeply swinging beat. Far from being new, this echoes the momentum of the quartet performances with Brookmeyer taken down in Paris in June 1954 (†Vogue [F] CDV651 600028 and 600152), which are longer and have greater authority than the earlier quartet recordings with Chet Baker. This continued in the quartet pieces with Eardley the following November (†Pacific Jazz [A] B21K-46860) and hence in the sextet.

Something that did survive from the quartet's earliest times, however, was Mulligan's essential economy of expression, even though we now have a fuller embodiment of his musical viewpoint and organizational abilities. There is in the sextet's performances a more explicit balance of solos, collective improvisations and arranged ensembles – usually theme statements – which obviously were prepared though probably not written down. Such fusions had been achieved at many other points in jazz, of course, but here is reflected almost equally the artistic characters of these four particular hornmen, and hence the result is unique even although the group concept is recognizable as Mulligan's alone. In fact, his improvising bands and the scores he has written for larger ensembles have over the years shared subtle shapings of inner voices, balances of different timbres, a swing that usually managed to be light as well as sometimes powerful, a relatively low volume; there was a place for understatement as well as for strong emphasis.

The frequent though not invariable absence of a piano (or guitar) obviously lightens the ensemble texture, throwing emphasis on linear, hence on contrapuntal, considerations and imposing a need for well-defined melodic thinking. This led in the initial quartet recordings to sequences of rather too precisely defined four- and eight-bar phrases, but the performances with Brookmeyer and Eardley referred to above show that this was loosening up, and the process reaches its fruition with the sextet. The omission of a harmony instrument was a more positive advantage with the sextet than the quartet because of the extra need for clarity; and the music's emotional climate was affected also, by the feeling of space. Mulligan and Brookmeyer in particular among these players show a real contrapuntal sense, as in *Nights at the turntable*, where the trombone's backing to the baritone saxophone becomes so melodious that it is almost an equal-voiced duet. Collective improvisations in three or four parts were an especial feature of the sextet, however, and these, besides existing for their own sake, had various functions. They would often back solos, provide links between them, would flow into the closing arranged theme statement or perhaps take its place, as in *Apple core*. In *Broadway* the theme chorus alternates collective and chordal passages, and sometimes, as in *Igloo*, the polyphonic texture is allowed to fragment around the pulse of bass and drums and then come together again. Also arising out of these collective improvisations was an unusual style of melodious – instead of anti-melodic – riffing.

Though Mulligan was a prolific composer, only four of the themes on the above two LPs are his, and two of these, *Bernie's tune* and *Nights at the turntable*, are from the quartet repertoire. *Elevation* goes back to his days of writing for Elliott Lawrence's band in the 1940s, and he had recorded *Everything happens to me*, *Igloo* and *Broadway* with various ad hoc groups. Others of the themes he chose for the sextet, like Buster Harding's *Ain't it the truth?* and Jerry (Hurwitz) Lloyd's *Mud bug* and again *Igloo*, were of jazz provenance. There are unusual treatments, also, of familiar ballads such as *Sweet and lovely* and *The lady is a tramp*.

The sequence of really excellent solos by all horns on this last represents a standard often attained elsewhere in these performances and underlines the difficulty of identifying the most suitable recordings for comment. It is complicated by the sextet's having taped different versions of the same pieces at different sessions for different LPs. The two issues detailed above certainly carry some of the group's best work, but other equally fine jazz can be found on other records, particularly EmArcy (J) 195J-35 and 36, titled *Mainstream of Jazz* Vols. 2 and 3. It would be unrealistic, for instance, to choose between the above *Blues at the roots* and the version on 195J-35 recorded immediately before it. Everyone in the band throughout responds to the blues idiom better than such players are supposed to.

Productive though Mulligan was in the studios, he can seldom have played better than in these sextet performances, and the recording vividly catches the reality of his sound during this period. Even the earliest quartet items show the advances he made in terms of instrumental control since his first recordings, but these with the sextet go further in regard to tonal variety, rhythmic relaxation, piquant melodic invention; and he makes a fuller use of the baritone's resources, producing a consistent tone throughout its entire register. There is never a hint of his instrument's cumbersome nature, least of all in *Ain't it the truth?*, *Igloo* or *Lollypop*. Nearly all his solos here, though, possess musical weight and they are shaped concisely. *Bernie's tune, Apple core, Elevation* and *Sweet and lovely* are further remarkable examples.

Eardley's playing is very different from that of either Baker or Brookmeyer, his predecessors in the quartet, yet accords well with Mulligan's ideas, taking full advantage of the looser frameworks. We could have done with more Eardley in the sextet, but his contributions still have a marked effect. This is partly because of his well-varied melodic ideas, his individual tone and the way he inflects it (as in *Sweet and lovely*), the clarity with which his solos are organized, and his excellent technique. Outstanding instances of his work here are *Mud bug, Bernie's tune, Ain't it the truth?* and *Broadway*. Concerning this last, he is still better in the alternative version on EmArcy (J) 195J-36, and the same LP's *Demanton* includes what may well be the finest solo he ever recorded with the sextet. Commentators have applied the word 'underrated' to nearly everyone who ever played a note of jazz, but Eardley is one of that select group of whom it is actually true. (Ferrara substitutes well on the final date, doing best in *Elevation*; but he has less original things to say.)

Following on from his playing with Mulligan's quartet, Brookmeyer here leaves even further behind the awkwardness of phrase that spoilt his early work. Characteristic is the subtle beginning of his *Igloo* solo, which as it were drifts into existence. He achieves an impressive variety of tone, a steady flow of unexpected ideas, and should be heard on *Apple core, Mud bug* and *Broadway*, among others. Sims, too, is always melodious, and completely at home in this band. His thrusting directness by no means precludes surprises, as the discontinuity of his *Mud bug* solo proves. Like Eardley and Brookmeyer, Sims's thinking closely accords with Mulligan's, and in *Mainstream* the rapidly alternating, then overlapping, then simultaneous tenor and baritone phrases are a memorable illustration of the well-developed understanding between the members of this band.

Although the piano is normally absent, the fact that both Mulligan and Brookmeyer could play it was obviously useful here. Mulligan offered a quite engaging version of 'composer-arranger's piano', long on ideas but short on executive finesse. The results in *Blues at the roots* are fully acceptable, but far more accomplished playing came from Brookmeyer. *Everything happens to me* is a good example, for it contains two splendid ballad improvisations by Mulligan linked via a Brookmeyer piano solo that holds the mood with real sensitivity. No wonder he was able to go on to record two-piano improvisations with Bill Evans, no less (†EMI/Blue Note [E] CDP827 324–2). M.H.

Modern Jazz Quartet

363 **The MJQ in Europe**
Atlantic (A) SD2–603 (2 LPs), *†Giants of Jazz (It) GOJCD0234

John Lewis (p); Percy Heath (bs); Connie Kay (d); Milt Jackson (vib). In concerts, Copenhagen, Gothenburg, Stockholm, April 1960.
Django · Bluesology · I should care · La ronde · I remember Clifford · Festival sketch · Vendôme · Odds against tomorrow · Pyramid (Blues for Junior) · It don't mean a thing if it ain't got that swing · Skating in Central Park · The cylinder · Round about midnight · Bags' groove · I'll remember April

The origins, personalities and musical attitudes of Lewis and Jackson differ in certain ways, a circumstance which has led to tensions, some of which have been fruitful musically, others of which led, after more than 20 years of close cooperation, to the disbanding of the MJQ in 1974. The common factor providing a catalyst for the formation of the group was the pianist's and the vibraharpist's membership of the Gillespie big band formed in 1946. When Jackson solos on such Gillespie recordings as *Things to come* and *Emanon* (**256b**) accompanied by just Lewis, Ray Brown and Kenny Clarke or Joe Harris, we hear the MJQ in prototype, for the quartet (with Clarke) began to function independently within the band to provide respite for the other musicians from the physical demands of Gil Fuller's arrangements.

As Jackson's New Sound Group, the four recorded for Gillespie's Dee Gee label in April 1949, their programme including *Bluesology* – still in the repertoire after the MJQ reunited in 1982. Jackson's other *opus populus*, *Bags' groove*, was recorded in a 1951 cooperation with Lou Donaldson (†EMI/Blue Note [E] CDP781 509–2). By that time Heath had replaced Brown. Kay appeared in 1954 when Jackson had recruited Horace Silver for some Prestige sessions (†Original Jazz Classics [A] OJCCD001–2). But before that the Modern Jazz Quartet title had been affixed for 1954–5 sessions (Clarke still seated) which introduced *La ronde*, *Vendôme*, *I'll remember April* and *Django* (†Original Jazz Classics [A] OJCCD125). By the summer of 1955 Kay had completed the personnel that was to persist for two decades until break-up and to re-emerge after a hiatus of about eight years.

At the time of Kay's arrival, Lewis's ideas were beginning to have a strong influence upon the group's presentation. The Jackson-led quartet (heard to best advantage in 1952 Savoy recordings) had continued in its Gillespie mode, the pianist's part still secondary to a vibraharp lead which stylistically reflected Dizzy's trumpet measures. These 1960 concerts show that Jackson's expressions hardly altered, but the shrewd combination of writing and improvisation which Lewis began to foster from the early 1950s, together with the pianist-composer's jazz dalliance with renaissance and baroque vocabularies, has become much more determinative. An occasional staidness led some to question the jazz commitment of the MJQ's creative route; yet seldom has the balance of experiment weighed too heavily against the blues influence and the exploitation of swingable themes which, in addition to an intimate ballad style, have suited the propensities of Jackson and the rhythm duo. A nice equilibrium is shown between different kinds of compositional imagination. Lewis's contributions are the celebrated *Django*; *La ronde*, a reworking of *Two bass hit*, written for Gillespie with Heath featured much as Ray Brown was in the original; *Festival sketch* – attractive in its dispersion of parts and sprightly improvisation kicked ahead by Kay's fourth-beat shots; the fugal *Vendôme*, exhibitive of the way in which order and freedom frequently make pact; *Odds against tomorrow* – bisectional, contrasting slow nostalgia with dazzling upbeat exuberance; and the latter's film-score companion, *Skating in Central Park*, its waltz time inevitably recalling Waldteufel's *Les patineurs* and in which Jackson ruminates coolly though never icily.

Jackson's *Bluesology* and *Bags' groove* are here; also his playful portrait of an ancient product of Detroit's most famous industry, Kay providing the chugging and backfiring. Additional to the two ballad interpretations there are celebrations of jazz heroes: Clifford Brown via Benny Golson, Ellington (a figure later to be honoured generously in the 1988 *For Ellington* (†East-West [A] 790 926–2), Thelonious Monk by his best-remembered reverie. Ray Brown also is recalled (he was later to become the group's manager) in his *Pyramid*, which was first recorded in 1949 as a tribute to Junior Raglin.

'Modern jazz' still meant bop in 1954, and even in the 1980s the bop instinct informed the best music of these men. Gillespie and Parker have been the twin ancestral ghosts, their voices idiosyncratically transmuted. Much as Lewis's improvising simplicity may have differed from Jackson's complexity, it was in bop that both styles were forged. Lewis's radical simplification of jazz argot was already evident when he was playing with Parker (**257**); not always so with Gillespie, who seemed to call for keyboard eclecticism. At the beginning of the aforementioned *Emanon*, Lewis plays in a manner that would have come inappropriately from him at any stage in the MJQ's career. Independently, he remains capable of a fulness of two-handed technique; but, preferring distillation to expatiation, he had led this ensemble much as the similarly serious Bunk Johnson led his (see **19, 28–30**); and, like Johnson, he encouraged community of thought and genuinely collective improvising. Popularity may have depended upon a consolidated, self-celebrating style, but careful listening reveals this music's subtle renewals. 'We are speaking of a sensitiveness which responds best to minutiae. Equality is the name we give to the whole sum.' [86] Jackson, who needed to work at adaptation early on, acknowledged the community and the subtlety. 'We got,' he once said, 'so we could breathe together.' [87] E.T.

Jimmy Giuffre

364 Western Suite

Atlantic (A) 1330

Bob Brookmeyer (v-tbn); Giuffre (clt, ten, bar); Jim Hall (g). New York City, 3 December 1958.

Blue Monk · Topsy · Western Suite: Pony express, Apaches, Saturday night dance, Big pow wow

Presumably because he never drew attention to it, Giuffre received little credit for the continuing, almost ruthless process of exploration which his music embodied. This was never a question of dramatic switches in direction of the sort noticeable in the careers of certain more efficiently publicized jazz figures, and for deplorably long periods he was not recorded at all. That was perhaps inevitable, and Giuffre should not be seen as a victim of fashion, having always shown an uncomplicated indifference to its dictates. When his music changed, it was usually a matter of subtle shifts of emphasis which, it repeatedly became evident, were led by his own inner promptings. These could produce striking results, however, as is proved by differences between the above account of *Topsy*, the outward discontinuity of whose fabric masks a tough inner unity, and the rather too suave reading Giuffre set down under Herbie Harper's leadership (Bethlehem [A] BCP1025). That only three years separate these divergent performances suggests how quickly an artist can move when following his true path.

Indeed he may cover so much ground as to leave parts of his audience behind, and some of Giuffre's most notable records, such as *The Music Man* (Atlantic [A] 1276, London [E] LTZ-K15216) and *Western Suite*, dealt with below, have remained obscure, little sought after. As is implied by **387**, where each piece has a different instrumentation from the rest, he always wrote for, and improvised in, a considerable variety of types of ensemble, yet he repeatedly gravitated to the trio format for the expression of his most radical ideas. The trio could be said to have emerged with *Fascinatin' rhythm* and *Quiet cook* on **387**, but an earlier indicator was *Abstract No. 1*, another trio performance in which Giuffre took part, on Shelly Manne's **432** of 1954. The latter of course parallels the tendency of Tristano's *Intuition* and *Digression* (**293**, 1949), as does *Free form* on Chico Hamilton's **389**. That came in 1955, as did Giuffre's own *Tangents in Jazz* (Capitol [A] T634, Afffinity [E] AFF60), in which several items, such as the at once folksy yet brisk *Finger snapper*, hint at his later trio output.

The performances just mentioned are reminders of some of the diverse backgrounds on which Giuffre's best work drew, and there were more of these. A model for the trio as a continuing entity was Debussy's Sonata for Flute, Viola and Harp of 1915, with the leader's clarinet and saxophones supplanting the flute, Hall's guitar replacing the harp and, at first, Ralph Peña's bass the viola. [88] Other sources were the kinds of music that so much affected Copland's ballets, Virgil Thomson's film scores, and these are especially apparent in the 18-minute *Western Suite*. Later Giuffre tried other bassists, including Ray Brown and, with particular success, Red Mitchell, but the version of the trio that was most adventurous in terms of his development at that stage was the one that replaced the bass with Brookmeyer's valve trombone. Thus it is possible to regard the brisker version of Giuffre's celebrated *The train and the river* done at Newport in 1958 (Raretone [It] 5013FC) with Brookmeyer as a fuller realization of its meaning than the studio recording with Peña (†Atlantic [A] 90981) of 1956.

Removing the bass made the absence of drums, unusual in the 1950s, all the more noticeable, but as Giuffre said much later, 'I couldn't find a drummer interested in playing softly, in listening, and resting.' [89] Certainly not everyone understood his aims and on, for example, the 1960 *In Person* set (Verve [A] MGV8387), Buell Neidlinger (bass) and Billy Osborne (drums) repeatedly begin well, yet as each performance unfolds they lose touch with their leader's unobvious requirements and the music to some extent comes apart. In contrast, Hall from the beginning sensed what was needed and swung fluently via plentiful, exactly placed accents set in what sometimes were actual harplike phrases which elsewhere acted as bass lines. Because of his instrument, Hall symbolized the (absent) rhythm section in this trio, but the drive to swing was just as integral to Brookmeyer's and Giuffre's musical thought and so they did not need a piano, bass and drums to push them.

That a late work of Debussy should have been an exemplar is unsurprising in view of the structural role of instrumental colour in his music finding a ready, if indirect, echo in Giuffre, with whom composing and improvisation were often organized round specific textures and patterns of sound. Which is to say that normal signposts such as chorus length, harmonic cadences and a steady tempo might be promptly abandoned in accord with the developing mood or atmosphere of a performance. This is partly why any two or more accounts of a given piece can be so different, as will be found if the above *Pony express*, opening movement of *Western Suite*, is compared with the Newport version (Raretone, as above) and the television one (Fresh Sounds [Sp] FSR405). Such a piece, in its several readings, typifies this edition of the trio with stops, starts, changes of pace, interludes, out-of-tempo passages, as equally does *Saturday night dance*, the straight-ahead third movement, a jazz-inflected 6/8 square dance-like outing.

It helped that Brookmeyer and Hall were composers like Giuffre, both in the functional jazz sense of being 'theme writers' and in having produced larger pieces, their grasp of form-building processes contributing much. Yet although they gave freely of themselves, bringing forth hitherto unsuspected aspects of their seemingly fully rounded musical personalities, this is essentially a composer's record, as are many of Giuffre's others. This is not because a multi-movement suite is included but rather because the music is almost Webernian in its cherishing of each precisely located sound. Here and there the outward simplicity can seem nearly ostentatious, yet this music's expressive resonance goes far beyond its deliberately restricted volume and range of gesture. In accord with the mysterious process whereby a specific body of music seems to change as the years pass, there now appears to be a much greater variety of expression, of emotional content, here than when these pieces were new, and a greater directness too.

Indeed, melody is the basic premise, sometimes two or more of them sounding together and influencing each other's growth. From this linear complex as much as from instrumental colour does form arise. There are many 'solos', for instance from Brookmeyer in *Topsy* or Giuffre, on clarinet, in *Blue Monk*, but the other two participants usually still contribute and are expressing themselves as much as the soloist. Perhaps we should speak of one player or another 'leading' a given passage, except that sometimes all three are 'leading' simultaneously. Again, the feeling of spaciousness which this music imparts belies the relative shortness of the pieces: *Topsy*, the nearest we get to a traditionalist item, has the longest performance at 11 minutes 28 seconds. This sense of space is anything but a matter of restraint, being instead the result of each player listening intently and leaving plenty of room for the other two. The result is a seeming contradiction, compositionally organized improvisation of a very high order. It is a special case of free jazz, as free as anything that Ornette Coleman or Cecil Taylor were then doing or would do in the immediately succeeding years but moving towards an utterly different goal, radical yet sounding as if it were outside time.

Themes such as *Topsy* and *Blue Monk* enable us through their familiarity to grasp this band's processes of deconstruction and reconstruction, thus helping us to follow them in Giuffre's own pieces. This music's density arises from its melodic economy, which in turn results from his careful – though not too careful – methods of motivic development. These, no matter how outwardly different their styles, place him fairly close to Monk, as is indicated not only with *Blue Monk* but also during *We see* from the *In Person* set. With each musician there is a central concentration on essentials, and Giuffre, like Monk, is always ready both with the right note and the right silence. The *Western Suite* LP was recorded just before this edition of the trio broke up, and the above performances benefit from its having been, along with its companion pieces, in the band's repertoire, and regularly played, for several months. It should be heard in conjunction with *Travelling Light* (Atlantic [A]

1282, London [E] LTZ-K15137), done almost a year earlier, just after the group was formed.

A whispering barker who offered amazing reductions, Giuffre introduced not just a fresh sound but a kind of sensibility new to jazz. His search for melodic, rhythmic and harmonic freedom contained by a sense of form that was strong yet flexible, always open to further possibilities, continued far beyond this point. There was never any leaping forward to embrace the ego-projections that all too many artists mistake for the future, but a certain kind of ultimate was reached by the trio's longest-lasting edition, with Paul Bley and Steve Swallow, in their *Free Fall* LP of 1962 (Columbia [A] CL1964). Of this Giuffre much later said: 'There's no time, no key, no metre.' Yet even beyond that lay, for instance, the uncommonly sensitive use of electronic resources on records he made in the 1970s and 1980s. Given the way that jazz is usually written about, he will perhaps always be rated a minor figure because he is not perceived as having influenced anyone much. The fact that this Brookmeyer–Hall version of the trio provided an acknowledged model for John Zorn's **464** warns us off premature conclusions on that score, however. And the finest of this music is as stubbornly individual, as instantly recognizable, as that of anyone at all in jazz, and this is amply confirmed by *The Complete Capitol and Atlantic Recordings of Jimmy Giuffre* on †Mosaic (A) MD6–176. M.H.

Lee Konitz–Martial Solal

365 Four Keys
MPS (G) 68241

Konitz (alt); Solal (p); John Scofield (g); Niels-Henning Orsted Pedersen (bs). Villingen, Germany, May 1979.

Brain stream · *Not scheduled* · *Grapes* · *Retro active* · *Energy* · *Satar* · *Four keys*

Some interpreters have described Tristano's experimental *Intuition* and *Digression* (**293**) as anticipations of the free jazz which emerged some ten years after those essays were taped. The notion is debatable. It can hardly be agreed that 'It took nearly a decade to catch up with Tristano's achievements', [90] since the existence in, say, Ornette Coleman's music of any sense of belated continuity with anyone else's experiments is quite without evidence. Barry Ulanov was perceptive enough, on the morrow of the *Intuition* session, to hear this apparent departure into freedom as 'The inevitable development of . . . Tristano's years of . . . experiment', and wisely enough, he left the music's futurity uncontemplated. [91]

Konitz recalling, 30 years afterwards, the May evening when four unpremeditated group extemporizations were recorded, [92] decides to try a little catching-up as a kind of adjunct to what otherwise is a programme reflecting differently harvested insights. How successful the attempt is can only be judged within the whole session's context.

That context is varied and lively, displaying the fruits of wide jazz experience. Solal and Konitz are contemporaries. When Konitz was still on the Tristano proving ground, the pianist was starting to run the gamut of jazz cooperation in Paris – Bechet to J. J. Johnson. His unclassifiable, adroit, cosmopolitan, pawky style has been one of the delights of the recent scene. The young virtuosos Scofield and Pedersen, prodigies in teenage, have been widely and modernistically active since the 1960s, and they wed immense, confident skill to swift imagination. Konitz, in spite of a chain of associations, still seems the ploughman of a solitary stylistic furrow; and though his tone and temper have toughened enough for him to meet these enthusiasts on fair terms he sounds a little self-effacing in their company.

In short, a world of change separates these four from the sextet of Konitz, Marsh, Tristano, Bauer, Fishkin and Best which assaulted the horizon in May 1949. And most of what is played here is of a different order, which is not to say that the informing spirit is other. There is, indeed, a remarkable improvisatory freedom, though it dances attendance on firm group discipline. There is no 'stream of consciousness' looseness about *Brain stream*. The bonded lines of alto and guitar are precise, though suited to the flexible rocking beat, and Solal's rapid spurts and multiplications are the more exciting because their tricksiness is always under control. Even when the pianist, in *Retro active* and *Energy*, steals clashing, scrambling shapes from Cecil Taylor, he snips the fringes of wildness from them. Yet there is evidence here, and it is by no means the only bit, that this liberty of association has been made possible by two decades of post-Coleman, post-Taylor freedom – extreme in some of its manifestations – which was the milieu of not one of these men but has left its stamp upon their proceedings.

The effect is not, of course, to any marked extent upon individual lines and tonal characteristics. Konitz, altered fellow though he is, recalls the cool grace of old – if not its astringency – in *Grapes*, and Scofield's following statement has, in its rhythmic emphases, something of the same elegance. The guitarist swings more warmly in *Not scheduled*, a sequence with no stated theme in which Pedersen solos agilely with Scofield's chordal punctuation, and Konitz, using stronger tone and shorted phrases, shows more than ever he did in the past that he has heeded Charlie Parker. *Satar* is a series of tempoless solos – Konitz fully toned, Scofield ranging the registers, Pedersen guitarlike and tipping the highest harmonics, Solal loitering, trying and discarding quasi-fugal subjects.

After *Satar* comes *Four keys*, also bestowing the album title as though it provided the *raison d'être* of the occasion. It does fulfil to a notable degree Konitz's earlier mentioned wish: no theme, no time signature, each man improvising freely in a different key from the others. It is a recollection of the '49ers' rather than a recreation of their experiment. It is different because the men – even Konitz himself – are different, and it does nothing to remove the old dilemma. *Intuition*, listened to after *Four keys*, sounds gentler, its chance relationships rather more clearly defined, but the effect is essentially the same, as is the question. Where can such music go, except on and on in its involuted fashion? *Intuition* avoided the question by gliding to a stop. *Four keys* seems to answer ironically by allowing itself to be faded out mechanically.

Still, the attempt at recreation is laudable. The companions of Konitz bring thoughtful aptitude to this belated tribute to a group that once posed a question well worth posing. For a suggestion as to how that old experiment may have influenced other, more fruitful departures, see **379–80**.

Energy, which precedes *Satar*, may have some kinship with *Four keys* but it is more in character with the rest of the session. After Solal's Quasimodo caper across small bass footholds, Scofield and then Konitz enter and a freely devised exchange gradually intensifies. Pedersen abets them in a variety of ways throughout until the music subsides with a sense of curious logic. If there are overlappings of tonality here, they are not the sort imposed in advance, but grow organically out of the interchange. One feels that, for a moment, some real 'free' alternative to the ritual clamour of post-*Ascension* anarchy has been glimpsed. Yet the paradox of separation *and* interaction is something that has been heard throughout the record. It is this which makes the whole meeting such a hopeful experience, something hinted at already by Konitz and Solal's duets of 1977 (Horo [It] HDP17/18) and confirmed by their later encounter (MPS [G] 15577, 1980). E.T.

Paul Desmond

366 Live

Horizon (A) A&M SP-850

Desmond (alt); Ed Bickert (g); Don Thompson (bs); Jerry Fuller (d). Toronto, 25, 27, 30, 31 October, 1 November 1975.

Wendy · *Wave* · *Things ain't what they used to be* · *Nancy* · *Manha de Carnival* · *Here's that rainy day* · *My funny Valentine* · *Take five*

'There is so much interior room within the limitations of harmonic and melodic playing,' Desmond once said, 'you don't have to cancel out all the rules to make progress. In some ways, it's more of a challenge to refine one thing and find something in it that hasn't been done before.' [93] That challenge began on record with Dave Brubeck in 1950–1 [94] and continued until shortly before his death in 1977, when he guested on the title track of Chet Baker's album *You Can't Go Home Again* (†A&M CDA0805). However, it was during his tenure as a charter member of Brubeck's quartet from 1951 to 1967 that he built his reputation (**311**). By the end of the 1950s the group had risen to become the most popular attraction in jazz and Desmond its most famous sideman.

From the beginning, Desmond possessed a personal and highly original voice on his instrument with a light, dry tone often conveniently rationalized as an extension of the Frankie Trambauer–Lester Young lineage, but without doing it justice. For all its 'dryness', by the time of his solo on *These foolish things* from Dave Brubeck's 1953 recording of *Jazz at Oberlin* (†Original Jazz Classics [A] OJC-046 and †Fantasy [A] FCD60013) it was also full and round and remarkably even throughout the three octaves of the saxophone. More importantly, he was one of the very few improvisers whose playing could be said to be wholly his own; without precedent, his style was subservient only to the broadest of category: cool. Like that of Konitz and Pepper, Desmond's playing owed nothing to the omnipresent influence of Parker, at its zenith in the late 1940s and early 1950s. Yet even within this tiny counter-current, Desmond's style was unique and widely admired by musicians as diverse as Gerry Mulligan and Anthony Braxton. [95] 'There are so many imitators of Parker and to me Paul is one of the few true individuals on his instrument,' Brubeck once asserted. [96]

A particularly melodic player, Desmond had an unhurried lyricism which served to disguise how daringly polytonal his ideas could be when jousting with Brubeck's rumbustious piano playing. His intonation throughout the whole range of the saxophone was inch-perfect, allowing him abruptly to switch from one octave to another, answering, paraphrasing and commenting on his solo in different registers of his instrument, often in implied counterpoint, yet without loss of balance or symmetry to his line. An example is his fine solo on *Balcony rock* from Brubeck's *Jazz Goes to College* (†Columbia [A] 465682 2). He was one of the first saxophonists to explore *and* control the extreme range of the saxophone; [97] even today his use of high notes impress with their fullness of tone, their ease of execution and their tasteful use within the overall concept of his work.

Despite the critical brickbats levelled at the Brubeck–Desmond alliance, their relationship was one of genuine empathy. Brubeck's style, still largely misunderstood, as much by critics [98] as fans (but not by a Milhaud or a Cecil Taylor), underwent a remarkable transformation as soon as the alto saxophonist stepped up to the microphone. Desmond wanted a quite specific musical climate in which to conduct business, speaking of his aversion to accompanists who 'wait for you to leave a hole and play some tricky little thing that sounds great for them but hangs up your line of thought'. [99] He insisted on the minimum of musical interaction with his accompanists, something Brubeck respected and in so doing revealed, in contrast to his solo work, a remarkably sensitive side to his playing.

While Desmond always honoured Brubeck's wish that he did not make recordings under his own name using a pianist, a consistent feature of his work away from Brubeck was his preference for passive rhythm sections. It was as much a feature of his work with the guitarist Jim Hall [100] as his albums on the CTI and A&M labels. He was one of the few outsiders allowed to sit in with the MJQ, and *The Only Recorded Performance of Paul Desmond with the Modern Jazz Quartet* (†Finesse Records [A] FINLP6050) reveals him totally at home amid the group's unobtrusive and uncomplicated accompaniment. 'I guess we always thought about things the same way,' explained Lewis. [101] Indeed, Connie Kay from the MJQ was a regular on Desmond's sessions with Jim Hall, beginning in 1959 on Warner Bros and continuing through four albums for RCA Victor, with the MJQ bassist Percy Heath appearing on the first and last dates.

Desmond wanted time and space to unravel his long, melodic solos, each a miniature gem of the improviser's art, and was careful not to be blown off course by the intrusion of other people's ideas into his private musical universe. His solos were typically based on the basic unit of a quaver; semiquavers were always used sparingly, thus a Desmond solo never sounded rushed. He favoured smooth, unaccented lines and approached chord sequences horizontally, never seeming to become enmeshed in the harmonic thickets of a song. He was a player whose work could truly be said to be poetic in conception and he was one of a select few improvisers in jazz who could sustain a cogent flow of melodically original ideas over several choruses while remaining free from repetition, cliché, rhetoric, bombast, habit or pattern-running.

In 1973, six years after he left Brubeck, Desmond was persuaded out of semi-retirement to play at the Half Note in New York. It was a first step into a more active jazz life that saw him travelling from time to time to Toronto where he performed with the guitarist Bickert, who appeared, along with Ron Carter and Kay, on *Pure Desmond* (†Epic [A] ZK64767). In the autumn of 1975, Desmond played a two-week engagement at Toronto's Bourbon Street with a Canadian group led by Bickert who were wholly attuned to the saxophonist's style, which was based on the time-honoured aesthetics of proportion, balance and symmetry. Bickert, whom Desmond described as 'unique', [102] provided the saxophonist with precisely the sort of accompaniment he needed, a delicate balancing act avoiding the predictable while providing a discreet, supportive presence behind the soloist. Desmond, who once, tongue in cheek, claimed to have won an award for quietness, had long realized that intensity need not be synonymous with volume. His solo on *Wendy*, an original 32-bar ABAC composition, is assembled in a way similar to constructing a house of cards. Each fragile phrase is laid out, one on top of the other, the melodic continuity of his ideas wholly dependent on the relationship of what has preceded it. It creates a beguiling tension in that the further his solo progresses, the greater the chance that the next card he lays might bring the whole crashing to the ground. It never happens, of course; instead he assembles a series of quietly beautiful ideas that are the essence of his art.

On much of Desmond's recorded work under his own name it is noticeable that away from the friction of Brubeck's playing he was a significantly more passive player, concentrating on his sound for its own sake. 'If you're playing slow and melodically, which I prefer,' he once said, '. . . I try to get a pure sound on every note I hit, with the overtones implicit in that note.' [103] Here, this concern seems at the forefront of his mind on *My funny Valentine*, where he seems to savour every note he plays as it emerges over the slow-moving harmonic backdrop. Yet the extra edge a live audience often brings to a performance did not allow him to dwell too long and hard on this aspect of his playing. *Things ain't what they used to be*, a number he played at the White House in 1969 for Duke Ellington's 70th birthday celebration, stunned the Duke, and everyone else, with his perfect take-off of Johnny Hodges. It is here played with engaging modesty and a freshness that is the eternal mark of quality. Desmond's blues might be cool, but they are his own; indeed, it is difficult to think of any other musician in jazz whose playing steadfastly refused to draw on that stockpile of bluesy licks built up by musicians over the years which somehow seem to find their way into most solos in the 12-bar idiom. His solo begins with an approximate paraphrase of the theme, albeit in reverse, and as his solo progresses he implies a 'three' feel against the prevailing metre of $4/4$. The second chorus opens with an allusion to *I won't dance*, moving to an exploitation of the rising line to increase tension. As subsequent choruses unfold, Desmond reveals a mastery of 'playing silence' – a careful use of space between his phrases which lends overall form to the solo as a whole.

Other than Tchaikovsky's use of $5/4$ in the second movement of the *Pathétique* Symphony, Desmond's enduring *Take five* is probably the most famous use of the compound time signature in Western music. In practical terms, $5/4$ tends to be divided into two simple metres, either $2/4$ plus $3/4$, or as here, $3/4$ plus $2/4$. However, it is often overlooked that the *Take five* theme represents a perfect example of Desmond's originality of melodic construction. The song is a standard 32-bar AABA tune in the minor, with the A sections based on a simple two-chord vamp. Against this static harmonic backdrop, it is the integrity of Desmond's line that attracts and intrigues us. In contrast to a show tune written with a vocalist in mind, this is a melody which is wholly instrumental in conception and unfolds much like an improvised solo – and that is part of its great attraction. Although sounding spontaneously conceived, there is nevertheless great symmetry in his line that compels our attention so that the ear is drawn to the theme rather than to the neutral harmonic movement in the accompaniment, which passes by almost unnoticed.

Desmond was one of the few improvisers who preferred improvising on long-form songs; indeed, his discography with Brubeck contains several examples, not least a memorable version of the 68-bar *The way you look tonight.* [104] Here *Wave*, a 44-bar AABA song constructed with the A sections of 12 bars and a traditional middle eight, becomes a perfect vehicle for his lyricism with its theme extending through the unusually wide interval of a 12th. And while *Manha da Carnival* is not a long-form composition, it nevertheless reveals his preference for songs that are a little different to the norm; here the form comprises an A and a B section of 16 bars each, plus a four-bar tag (not used during the improvisation)

A great romantic, Desmond filled his discography with countless superior standards. Here, *Nancy* and *Here's that rainy day* are transformed so completely that his melodic ideas seem to stand out in sharp relief against their familiar melodies; yet despite the distance he travels from the songwriter's original intent, he nevertheless succeeds in remaining entangled in the emotional meaning of the songs. They are excellent examples of his noncombative, yet wholly engaging style, which was a major alternative to every other saxophonist in jazz, as this collection shows. [105]

It is a matter of regret, however, that he kept his steely side under wraps. Although Brubeck, in several interviews, has mentioned how Desmond disliked fast tempos, his playing *Perdido*, *The way you look tonight* and *How high the moon?* from *Jazz at Oberlin* reveal him pushing towards the fastest tempos in jazz. [106] Here his playing is more declamatory and sounds for all the world as if he were in a cutting contest where he is the only competitor. His ideas are just as articulate and melodic as ever, but played with an intensity that is entirely absent at slower tempos and represent an area of his performing personality that was never fully explored on record. Here then, perhaps, is the only criticism that can be laid at this remarkable player's feet. Constantly inhabiting slow and slow-medium tempos can ultimately be limiting as creating one mood and sustaining it means by definition it excludes as much as it includes. It is to Desmond's credit, however, that what he did include consistently merits our attention. S.N.

Rolf Billberg

367 We'll Be Together Again

Odeon (Sd) EO54–34830

Jan Allan (tpt); Billberg (alt); Rune Gustafsson (g); Roman Dylag (bs); Rune Carlsson (d). Skellefeld, Sweden, 23 February 1965.

Ablution · *We'll be together again* · *Fobic* · *Nursery rhyme*

Allan Botschinsky (fl h); Billberg (alt); Ole Molin (g); Niels-Henning Orsted Pedersen (bs); Carlsson (d). Malmö, Sweden, 16 April 1966.
Sound-Lee · *Darn that dream* · *Palo Alto*

Billberg is one of a considerable number of non-American jazzmen whose reputations ought to have spread much further beyond their own countries than they actually have. This Swedish alto saxophonist largely has been ignored by reference works, and if any remarks have been made elsewhere in jazz commentary they seldom have gone beyond a perfunctory dismissal of him as a mere copyist of Lee Konitz. The latter heard things differently and is quoted in the notes accompanying the above record as saying that at most Billberg sounded 'like a distant cousin'.

As with other players of comparable tendency, Lester Young was in the background with his rhythmic relaxation, soft-edged rather than dry tone, and emphasis on melody – though Billberg's lines are more energetically convoluted than his ever were. Nearer the foreground, indeed, were Konitz and Parker, the former more immediately evident from the use here of Tristano's *Ablution* theme (on the chords of *All the things you are*), Konitz's *Sound-Lee* (on *Too marvellous for words*) and *Palo Alto* (*Strike up the band*). A more overt intensity was imposed on the Youngian foundation, and while this could be said of other saxophonists of that time, Billberg made something especially personal out of it, hence his presence in this book.

If the 'cool' label that is usually given to such musicians implies a degree of emotional detachment from their work, then it was never relevant to Billberg, and the above recordings are the best of those issued under his name to make this point. The fine detail of his solos on *Darn that dream* and *We'll be together again* is a translation of strong emotion: hear in particular the beautifully expressive interplay between the basic pulse and double time in the latter, his fluency here being as good an illustration as any of his technical mastery and the use to which he put it. *Darn that dream*, having the effect of a slow, pensive dance, is the occasion for two especially moving alto solos, the second reaching its moments of greatest concentration in the concluding unaccompanied cadenza. For contrast observe the impulsively displaced accents of his solo on *Nursery rhyme*, another Konitz theme which in its rhythmic life is more like an exultant up-tempo hymn than a nursery rhyme. Billberg has another soaring passage in *Sound-Lee* and there is a constant feeling of discovery in his work, *Ablution* being another fine instance. With fast tempos as much as slow one searches in vain for the stock responses that are the chief substance of all too much so-called improvisation, and the variety of shape, duration and stress of his solos on *Palo Alto* and, again, *Sound-Lee* should be noted.

Also deserving attention is the exceptional continuity maintained throughout the alternation of four-bar passages from Billberg and Allan in *Nursery rhyme*. This is just one illustration of the stylistic unity of the two extremely well-matched teams employed here. The music is taken from broadcasts, the later one taking place well inside the final year of Billberg's short life (1930–66), and both groups benefit from strikingly flexible pianoless rhythm sections and bassists who propel the up-tempo pieces aggressively. On following solos by the horns Gustafsson never lets the tension down, his invention being as tightly packed as theirs. Molin is as good an accompanimental player as Gustafsson but less engaging as a soloist. Carlsson's drumming is effective yet normally restrained, though he becomes quite boppish during the alto and guitar solos on *Fobic* (a stimulating theme by the leader) and in some other places.

Strategies to some extent shift from one piece to another, but counterpoint, which seems almost inherent to this style, keeps breaking out, most memorably between Allan and Billberg on *We'll be together again*; and the differences between these passages are enough indication of their spontaneity. The bass line, too, sometimes becomes a melodic rather than simply an accompanimental voice, as during Allan's solo on *Nursery rhyme*.

This book's main comments on Allan appear under **361**, but it should be noted that the above sessions reveal interesting differences between him and Botschinsky within the same idiom. Allan's phrases are more taut, thrusting, disjunct, particularly in *Nursery rhyme*, while Botschinsky is slightly more traditional in stance, outwardly calmer, providing a more direct contrast with Billberg – though he becomes more assertive in *Palo Alto*. For Botschinsky and Billberg in more extrovert moods, their performances with Ib Glindemann's vigorous large band should be heard, especially the 1957 concert recordings (Olufsen [D] DOC6001). These make a quite enlightening comparison with the intimate, though lively, atmosphere of the dates considered here. Billberg should also be heard with Lars Gullin (e.g. †Dragon [Sd] DRCD264), with whom he had a particularly fruitful partnership, with Nils Lindberg (e.g. DRCD220) etc. M.H.

Stan Getz

368 West Coast Jazz

Verve (A) MGV8028, Columbia (E) 33CX10018

Conte Candoli (tpt); Getz (ten); Lou Levy (p); Leroy Vinnegar (bs); Shelly Manne (d). Los Angeles, 15 August 1955.

East of the sun · Four · Suddenly it's spring . A night in Tunisia · Summertime · Shine

369 Focus on Stan Getz

Verve (E) SVSP29/30 (2 LPs)

Getz (ten); Levy (p); Vinnegar (bs); Stan Levey (d). Hollywood, 24 November 1956.

Blues for Mary Jane · *There'll never be another you* · *You're blasé* · *Too close for comfort* · *Like someone in love* · *How about you?*

Same personnel. Hollywood, 2 August 1957.

Smiles · *Three little words* · *Time after time* · *This can't be love*

Getz (ten); string orchestra including Beaux Arts String Quartet (Gerald Tarack, Alan Martin [vln], Jacob Glick [vla], Bruce Rogers [cel]); John Neves (bs); Roy Haynes (d); Eddie Sauter (comp); Hershy Kay (cond). New York City, 14 July 1961.

I'm late · *Her* · *Pan* · *I remember when*

Same personnel. New York City, 28 July 1961.

Night rider · *Once upon a time* · *A summer afternoon*

The 1956 items originally appeared as *The Steamer*, those of 1961 as *Focus*; the latter are on †Verve (E) 521 419–2.

Though he was among the most famous of all jazz musicians, Getz's popularity was never held against him by his fellow players as was that of Goodman or Brubeck. Highly subjective factors are involved in such cases but Getz's wide acceptance was evidently a matter of a strong and individual melodic sense, a beautiful tone – and a certain rhythmic conservatism. Yet these did not all come together and certainly did not stay the same. Like most youthful musicians, he was affected by what went on around him and there are a few early records which suggest the examples of Georgie Auld and, most surprisingly, of Dexter Gordon. Lester Young was his real model, however, and Getz was the most original of the many tenor saxophonists of his generation who followed that route.

But what does such a comment mean? Among the necessary elements of a good style are lucidity, elegance and individuality. Lucidity does not imply universal intelligibility. Getz was the most lucid of saxophonists, yet not the simplest. His popularity has already been noted, but such wide acceptance did not always mean that the audience comprehended. Certainly the nature of his debt to his great predecessor is widely misunderstood. Getz adopted various fairly superficial aspects of early Lester Young but he put these to substantially different uses, and this for two, if not three, reasons. Young was concerned with the presentation and organic development of a given melody: he even believed that to improvise on it properly one needed to know the words. The result would be essentially lyrical, yet rarely would the melody be altogether transcended. The approach of his supposed disciple, however, was strictly expressionistic, the melody having little value in itself, being merely a vehicle, entirely subject to Getz's personal expression.

This is what we should expect, given that each was an entirely different sort of character: Getz had nothing whatever of Young's vulnerability either as a man or as a musician. Further, notwithstanding all that has been written about Getz's melodiousness and the warmth and luminous quality of his tone, he was also among the great virtuosos of jazz, a point confirmed by most of the above recordings and by one of them in particular. Young was a fine executant in his prime, but he never had Getz's sheer mastery of the instrument which enabled him to throw off exceedingly difficult passages with apparent ease. And Getz, while he continued to make new departures in his own playing, nowhere approached Young as probably the greatest innovator in the jazz language between Armstrong and Parker.

At the time he made the **299** recordings Getz often played with tempestuous enthusiasm, with vehement attack, the liberties taken in shaping his sometimes fairly asymmetrical phrases being fired by an ability to continue making fresh melodic discoveries in familiar harmonic situations. In fact his melodic vein seemed inexhaustible and yet, while very rarely faltering, was never glib. Sensitivity to tone colour was also extremely important, and his sound, very pure in the early years, gave ultra-sharp definition to his rhythmic as well as melodic ideas. A firm pulse was needed to heighten the effect of Getz's subtle rhythmic inflections and the truth is that he reconciled spontaneity and perfect finish to a degree that must always be rare in jazz. There can be no more vivid example of this, and of his technical mastery, than *Shine*. This builds on earlier achievements such as 1949's *Crazy chords*, an extremely fast blues improvisation going through all 12 major keys which at that time represented a new level of virtuosity for the tenor saxophone. In terms of beat and articulation the sheer flexibility of Getz's phrases on *Shine* is astonishing, and this remains one of the great recorded *tours de force* of tenor playing. Quite apart from being delivered at such an unforgiving speed, it is marked by unflaggingly intelligent melodic invention and no little wit. The deftness and elegance have to this day remained unsurpassed, yet the main point of this inspired flight is its expressiveness. With due respect to Candoli and Levy, anything would sound redundant after the leader's 16 choruses, and it is worth adding that he starts swinging before the rhythm section has entered, something he could always do, other instances being *How about you?*, *Blues for Mary Jane* and *There'll never be another you.*

Getz and Levy were first together in Herman's 1948 Herd and then with Vinnegar and Manne on a 1955 Lionel Hampton session, during which the tenor played for once in an almost completely unrepresentative manner. Far better were various 1955–9 dates which brought Getz and Levy together, the latter gradually developing a melodic vocabulary which complemented the former's particularly well. On *East of the sun* both of them, like Candoli, quickly get away from the original melody and cultivate immaculate thoughts of their own. Getz returns for a brief further exploration at the end before a fairly oblique restatement. In *Four* they all dig more deeply, as one might hope on a jazz theme, though it must be said that Getz in particular again pursues his own ideas rather than extending Eddie Vinson's theme. Candoli is fine here, yet his best improvising with this sort of group is discussed under **273**. On *Suddenly it's spring* Getz puts forward a great variety of phrases while still displaying lucid melodic continuity and he is even more striking in his second *Summertime* solo than during his first. For *A night in Tunisia* they reverse the established tenor-trumpet-piano order of the improvisations and to good effect, Getz's being the most memorable. A comparable flow of invention is maintained on *Blues for Mary Jane* and his second solo is again the more remarkable. Both here and in *How about you?* he makes an imaginative use of the ancient stop-time device which has been ignored by modernists in general. *You're blasé* is a brief mood piece, but on *Too close for comfort*, *Like someone in love* and especially *There'll never be another you*, admirably seconded by Levy, he attains an extraordinary melodic purity with each thought vital and, it seems, newly minted.

After spending considerable time in Europe, especially Scandinavia, Getz went back to America in 1961. *Focus* was to some extent a comeback album and was a sizeable variant on the jazz musician's usual type of 'with strings' outing. Sauter employed these instruments in rather simple ways in comparison with what they can do, yet the music's ambitions are such that it was inevitably derided as 'pretentious' in the expected quarters. For example his writing was described as 'derivative of Bartók' [107] even though there is no stylistic resemblance at all. However, the seven movements of *Focus* did represent an unusual venture and, even allowing for Getz's musicianship, it is remarkable that they came off so well, particularly in view of his later admitting that prior to recording this work he 'had never seen 5/4, 6/4, 9/8 and so forth'. [108]

The main point was that he needed to establish a different kind of relationship with his context from the normal interplay with piano, bass and percussion found in the above 1955–7 performances and countless others. There the chief issue was continuity, whereas especially in *I'm late – I'm late* it is at least outward discontinuity, for tenor and strings keep interrupting each other. Yet the whole makes perfect sense, and while the variety of gesture in Getz's usual improvisations was already remarkable, it is here even greater. There is exceptional rhythmic freedom on the parts of both tenor and strings, with each sometimes following quite different pulses. Indeed they rather often juxtapose very diverse phrases which fit together excellently; and after Sauter and Getz the main hero is Haynes. The sleeve note by Dom Cerulli for the initial LP issue suggested that *I'm late – I'm late* 'immediately calls to mind' the Mad Hatter rushing to that tea party in Wonderland, though it is uncertain whether this was merely his notion or was actually something

Sauter, or even Getz, had thought of.

Tenor and strings are less disjunct in *Her* and the latter could almost be said to accompany the former, although sometimes they venture a line of their own and even take the lead occasionally with Getz content to lend support. On *Pan* tenor and strings again pursue quite different paths in the outer sections and while they are closer together in mood during the slower middle section they still play very different notes. The central *I remember when* is more conventional, fairly close to the usual tenor-with-strings texture, though with Getz making statements that are very irregular and mainly short. *Night rider* is more astringent, with tenor and strings following substantially different routes but complementing each other. They are especially divergent rhythmically here, yet *Once upon a time*, ranging between the sombre and the jaunty, has the most diverse contents of any of these pieces so far as types of phrase from both tenor and strings are concerned. However, it is *A summer afternoon* that is at the furthest extreme from *I'm late – I'm late.* In fact Getz states and extends a melody more continuously here than anywhere else in this work and in place of any sort of contradiction the strings at last offer an enhancing commentary.

He was heard on the soundtrack of the film *Mickey One*, composed by Sauter in 1965, and the following year he recorded with the Boston Pops Orchestra along with Gary Burton and Jim Hall in material provided by Alec Wilder and others, even including Sauter. But the results completely lacked purpose or direction, and *Focus* stands out as a uniquely successful venture within the whole of Getz's vast discography. Yet his music, while remaining conservative rhythmically, continued evolving beyond the point represented by the above records, the melodic vocabulary growing even richer, his tone still more expressive. There is a sense, however, in which *Focus* stands for Getz's finest hours in a recording studio. M.H.

Zoot Sims

370 Blues for Two

Pablo (E) 2310 879, †Original Jazz Classics (A) OJCCD635

Sims (ten, sop[1]); Joe Pass (g). New York City, 2 March, 23 June 1982.
Blues for two · Dindi · Pennies from heaven[1] *· Poor butterfly · Black and blue · I hadn't anyone till you · Takeoff · Remember*

Over the 35 years following his first departure from Woody Herman's Second Herd (**312c**), Sims developed into possibly the most consistent of the former Four Brothers team. A tenacious reputation as a Lester Young follower is challenged by evidence of serious attention to Ben Webster in pre-Herman days (as witness his work for a Joe Bushkin–Bill Harris group in 1944 [Mosaic (A) MR23–128]); by an avowed admiration for Sonny Stitt; and by a mutually influential partnership with Al

Cohn which further assisted the growth of a very personal style. Interestingly enough, it has sometimes been in his playing of the blues – for example the 1951 *Zoot swings the blues* (Original Jazz Classics [A] OJC242) – that the Young influence has seemed stronger. It is not absent, quite, from *Blues for two*, at the start of this admirable duet album, but there are instances here of habits of tonal inflection which are totally personal to Sims.

In this blues Pass, from the outset, is content with a subsidiary part, strumming with rich guitar tone as Sims discourses on the age-old message, wedding strength and delicacy. Pass has a virtuosic reputation – the 'Art Tatum of the guitar' he has over-enthusiastically been dubbed. What he contributes to these sessions is an exercise in accompaniment. 'Just play the way you feel like,' Sims encouraged a questioning Pass. [109] 'Often it is the musicians with whom Pass has recorded that gave some albums a particular bias.' This is one such, 'a welcome contrast to his frantic virtuosity' in certain other contexts. [110]

After the strolling rhythm of the blues, Pass leads *Dindi* into a slow, almost tentative expression of Jobim's charming song melody. Sims is meditative, soliloquial in relation to the guitarist's functionalism; but then, as if to prove the tempo irrelevant, Pass comes into his solo like a spirited tortoise overhauling a philosophical hare. Suddenly Pass seems to abet Sims's flexibility. In *Pennies from heaven* Sims, playing soprano, leans closer to Pass's mode, his slender tone suggesting a comparison with the sound of Steve Lacy (**475**). This, the longest track, is very special, Zoot drawing an individual renewal of jazz thought out of precursions popularly regarded as premodernist. There is a clarity of both skill and intention in Pass's solo insertion which relates it, along with other things here, to his work in the 1978 *Virtuoso No. 3* (Pablo [E] 2310 805), to themes like *Minor detail* and *Pasta blues.* There may be a degree of self-effacement to this kind of backing, but there are delightful subtleties and dazzling sinuosities even in the slow *Poor butterfly* and *Black and blue* wherein he combines tricksiness with deference and varies his dynamics with a shrewdly restricted compass.

Only a few years Sims's junior, Pass had serious narcotics dependency to overcome before he could resume, in 1961–2, a musical career begun in swing bands with a style drawn from Charlie Christian and the first stirrings of bop. Regenerate, he shone as the most accomplished performer on Arnold Ross's *Sounds of Synanon* (Fontana [E] 688 139, Pacific Jazz [A] PJ48), and wide recognition came quickly. In his frequent work without rhythm backing he has developed his instrument's flexibility, contriving simulated bass-line counterpoint to his ongoing chordal and melodic inventions. *I hadn't anyone till you*, with plangent, contrasting deep bass lines and high-register chordal effects, demonstrates how pianistic this style can sound (but conjuring Ellis Larkins, perhaps, rather than Tatum). Upon this pleasing background Sims lays plainer, drier lines with a touch of deliberation. The track is a delight.

Wasting no time upon pointed elaborations, Sims, unaccompanied, swings in his original *Takeoff* with that gift for an essential jazz zest which calls to mind his answer to a question about the nature of jazz: 'I've never had to ask myself.' [111] As the accompanying 'keyboard' illusions become spikier, the more expressions grow a little gruffer, edging towards rifflike figures. The number finishes simply by finishing: total relaxation, total unanimity. *Remember* invites and gets a wry wistfulness from both partners, Sims lazily blowing offhand trills and retarded phrases, Pass easing his patterns with a sunny acuteness. E.T.

Chet Baker

371 The Last Great Concert Vols. 1 and 2

†Enja (G) 607422

Baker (tpt); NDR Big Band, Dieter Glawisching (cond); L. Axelsson, H. Habermann, B. Lanese, M. Moch (tpt); W. Ahlers, P. Plato, M. Grossmann, E. Christmann (tbn); H. Geller, A. Boether, E. Wurster, H. Ende, K. Nagurski (saxes); W. Norris (p); J. Schroder (g); L. Lindholm (bs); A. Tanggaard (d); W. Schluter (vib). Hanover, Germany, 28 April 1988.

All blues · Well, you needn't · Django · Look for the silver lining · Sippin' at Bell's

Baker (tpt); Radio Orchestra Hanover, Dieter Glawisching (cond); W. Laatz, L. Kosak, H. Bosse, H. Schmidt, V. Schell, Ch. Heinrich, M. Blazejewska-Woller, A. Schleinschock, H. Yashima, W. Schadow, H. Jahreis, V. Mutschler, W. Krohne, Ch. Bruening, F. Haus, U. Fietkau, J. Meyer, E. Cieslinski (vln); D. Penkov, Ch. Pohl, G. Moos, M. Ben Dor, M. Brockhaus, H.-V. Koff (vla); H. Beckendorf, H. Jeroscheiwitz, W. Ebert, F. Dolling (cel); J. Norman, M. Gunther, A. Karow (bs); S. S. Raabe, S. Bleir (fl); D. Luhrmann, K. Matsubara (ob); J. Peitz, K. Kirschvink (clt); K. O. Hartman, W. Rudiger (bsn); J.-W. Wierness, H. Nicki, H. Schaefer, U. V. Stemm (fr h). Same date and place.

I fall in love too easily · I get along without you very well · There's a small hotel · Tenderly

Baker (tpt); Radio Orchestra Hanover, Dieter Glawisching (cond); plus Walter Norris (p). Same date and place.

I fall in love too easily

Baker (tpt); Radio Orchestra Hanover, Dieter Glawisching (cond); plus Walter Norris (p); John Schroder (g). Same date and place.

My funny Valentine · Summertime

Baker (tpt); Walter Norris (p); John Schroder (g); Lucas Lindholme (bs); Aage Tanggaard (d). Same date and place.

In your own sweet way

Baker (tpt); Herb Geller (alt); Walter Norris (p); John Schroder (g); Lucas Lindholme (bs); Aage Tanggaard (d). Same date and place.
Conception

In 1953 Baker was voted 'New Star' in the *down beat* critics' poll and he topped the 1953 and 1954 *down beat* readers' polls and the 1954 and 1955 *Metronome* readers' polls. He seemed at the threshold of a very promising career. However, when he left for a European tour with his quartet in September 1955 he was addicted to narcotic drugs. On his return in April 1956 he was busted several times, spending time in the federal narcotics hospital in Lexington, Kentucky, and on Riker's Island in New York. In July 1959 he returned to Europe, spending 17 months in an Italian jail for possession. Shortly after a proposed film appearance with Susan Hayward fell through in England, he was caught again for possession and deported to France. Making his way to Germany, he was eventually caught again for drugs offences and, after 40 days in hospital, he was deported back to the United States on 3 March 1964.

On his return, his lifestyle deteriorated further and to turn a buck he recorded anything that came his way, including a Glenn Miller tribute with the Mariachi Brass and a grisly set of songs written by Steve Allen. The final indignity came in 1968, while he was living on the West Coast, when he had his teeth knocked out at the behest of a drug dealer. This spectacular nosedive into Skid Row meant a slow and painful return to playing throughout the 1970s which included a reunion with Gerry Mulligan in Carnegie Hall in 1974: *Gerry Mulligan/Chet Baker Carnegie Hall Concert* (†Epic [A] 450554–2). Addiction, sadly, proved to be a recurring problem throughout his life, but another, the writer Mike Zwerin observed, was that the world was not, 'and may never be ready to accept a red-neck jazz musician'. [112]

Baker gradually re-established a reputation, albeit as the one of most precarious bookings on the jazz-club circuit. Some nights he could barely play his trumpet and his singing voice was reduced to a whisper, but, as *The Times* pointed out, 'his innate musicianship could still achieve small miracles of wounded grace'. [113] His style would be simultaneously moving and unsettling, a musical confessional that was as honest as his life was corrupt. However, throughout the 1970s and 1980s there were was no shortage of small, independent record labels willing to take an inexpensive chance on recording him, leaving a trail of countless musical fixes in the wake of his peripatetic lifestyle.

Much of his recorded output during this period were controlled exercises in Baker's professional introspection and none challenged in any meaningful way his earliest work with the Mulligan quartet in 1952–3 (**300**) or the quartet he led with Russ Freeman on piano in 1953–5, the recordings which had secured his reputation in jazz. Indeed, on his first appearance in New York after his return in 1964, aspects of Miles Davis's spare, haunting style, a personal favourite, were more apparent than ever in his playing, [114] something that was often readily discernible for the rest of his career. Yet the disparity between his 'notorious' reputation as stereotype jazz musician, a ne'er-do-well womanizer who did drink and drugs, and the fragile beauty of his art was a powerful drawing card throughout Europe. If he gave a bad performance it was interpreted as life reflected in art, if he gave a good performance it was seen as art reinforced by life, and during his final years he could do no wrong. When his trumpet playing appeared shaky, he turned to his vocalizing, also something of a variable commodity, and, it must be said, something of an acquired taste (much like the acting of James Dean, to whom the trumpet player has often been likened in his early years). He appeared in glossy magazines and Sunday newspaper supplements, his much-photographed face reflecting the ravages inflicted by his life, his performances the subject of much overromanticized commentary.

However, though Baker often did enough to suggest great reserves of emotional power in his performances, there are no recordings that suggest he ever fulfilled his early promise. The unassuming charm and often beguiling low-keyed ardour of his early work was now an elusive thing, but when it did surface it was not so much a promise fulfilled as a validation of his status as a jazz legend, albeit with all the romantic allure of a star fallen from grace. That Baker could rise to the occasion is amply demonstrated on these recordings, a unique concert at the Funkhaus in Hanover produced, broadcast and recorded by the NDR. Throughout, Baker was on stage with two large orchestras, performing a programme of numbers he selected himself. The arrangements were specially commissioned for the concert from Heinz Muhlbradt and Bernard Ebbinghouse and both orchestras rehearsed them over a two-day period. It was a remarkable affair and a reflection of how much jazz is valued on continental Europe; the thought that such a concert might have been produced for radio or television in the United Kingdom, [115] or indeed in the United States, is laughable.

From his opening solo on *All blues*, the NDR executives must have breathed a collective sigh of relief; the trumpeter is clearly on form, his ideas are lucid and cogent and his small tone is as warm and round as at any part of his career. As Baker made his entrance on stage to applause from the audience, Norris, an expatriate American whose performance credits include Ornette Coleman and the Thad Jones–Mel Lewis Jazz Orchestra, [116] opened with the piano vamp Bill Evans used on the original Miles Davis recording (**393**). The mood is low-key and the big band play with utilitarian tact behind Baker, who negotiates his way through unfamiliar surroundings with caution, pointedly ignoring any references to Miles Davis in his solo and claiming the song for himself. His version of *My funny Valentine* must surely be the finest from his long career and certainly the longest at a shade over nine minutes. Baker opens with a *rubato* exposition of the melody accompanied by Norris and Schroder, quite the most beautiful, yet fragile, moment of the whole concert. Norris changes key and the strings enter, somehow preserving the moment to allow Baker's artisan vocal to move the song into a fresh dimension. There is a stirring modesty in Ebbinghouse's arrangement, the collective ambitions of the strings a perfect contrast to Baker's broken-wing attempts at vocal flight.

Well, you needn't is taken at a medium tempo with the big band, and the string orchestra swings *Summertime* with similar ease and grace behind an animated Baker, with Norris and Schroder inserting quietly tactful solo episodes of their own in the latter. A small group places Baker in more familiar surroundings for Brubeck's *In your own sweet way*, and surrounded by sympathetic accompaniment the trumpeter continues to deliver at a remarkable level of lyricism again inviting comparison with his best recorded work. He never once gave the impression of faltering, coasting or of the doubtful intonation that often showed up in the sprawling discography of his later years. Instead he seems to draw on a remarkable fund of ideas which he projects with a soft, hazy focus and elegant poise. *Django* had been imaginatively recast for a large ensemble before, not least by Gil Evans and Don Sebesky, and although the arrangement is tailored for Baker, he shares honours with the big band who rise up around him, seemingly aware that the trumpeter is giving a once-in-a-lifetime performance.

If Baker's vocal perfectly suited the moment on *Funny Valentine*, then it is perhaps less successful on *I fall in love too easily* and *I get along without you very well*, the latter with an expansive Norris solo. The voice of his youth that once had 'the innocent sweetness that made girls fall out of their saddle Oxfords' now skirted dangerously close to artifice in late middle age. A couple of Miles Davis-isms appear in his melody statement of *Look for the silver lining*, but as they recede behind him, the balance and timing of his improvisation are couched with a logic that did not fail him once during the whole concert. *Conception*, using the small group, has a stirring contribution by Herb Geller, who appeared on Baker's fifth date as a leader in December 1953, and he almost matches Baker's own fleet solo. *There's a small hotel* retreats into the quietly contemplative; *Tenderly* starts slowly and builds with solos from Norris and Schroder that complement another convincing performance by the trumpeter. The brisk *Sippin' at Bell's* by the big band is a leaping performance with a another highly articulate solo from the 60-year-old Geller.

The producer, Kurt Giese, has pointed out that Baker was so late for the first rehearsal the string orchestra had packed up and gone home when he arrived, so he ran down the numbers to recordings using headphones. [117] He was even more cavalier at the big-band rehearsals, when to save his lip he merely sat and listened, and the small-group pieces were simply discussed. But as he had kept demonstrating throughout his life, Baker was an autodidact with a startling musical gift, a gift he took for granted and abused, yet very real for all that, as these concert performances make plain. Baker wound up proceedings with a *rubato* rendition of *My funny Valentine* with just piano and guitar. It had become his favourite setting in later years; 'The whole atmosphere is much softer, everything is much clearer. You can hear everything . . . drums cover up stuff.' [118]

When these recordings were originally released, they went to number 5 on the *Billboard* and *Cashbox* jazz charts, a remarkable achievement as much for Baker, who had been out of sight and out of mind of Stateside audiences for years, as it was for a small, imported, independent German label. The critical acclaim was almost unanimous: 'Baker's full throated horn never sounded better' (*Time*), 'Chet at the top of his form' (*Jazz Times*), 'The best of Chet's twilight years' (*Musician*) were among the many accolades that came the album's way. Undoubtedly it is a major item in the trumpet player's discography and once again he appeared convincingly set on the comeback trail. Two weeks later he was dead: Chet Baker had almost made it, again. S.N.

Bill Evans

372 Portrait in Jazz

Riverside (A) VDJ1506, †Original Jazz Classics (A) OJCCD088–2

Evans (p); Scott LaFaro (bs); Paul Motian (d). New York City, 28 December 1959.

Come rain or come shine · Autumn leaves · Witchcraft · When I fall in love · Peri's scope · What is this thing called love? · Spring is here · Someday my prince will come · Blue in green

When bop came, Evans was a boy musician already engaged with jazz. He was to develop his individuality almost free of direct bop contacts, consorting with similarly nonconformist people like Konitz, Giuffre, George Russell and Mingus, and significantly assisting Miles Davis further to transcend his bop formation. His technical versatility coped triumphantly with Russell's Lydian chromaticism (**380**, **478**), and with Mingus's unusual keys in *East coasting* and *Conversation* (Bethlehem [A] BCP6019). However, in those contexts he was still markedly influenced by aspects of Tristano's piano style and was still as much an adaptable as an innovatory pianist.

His brief re-association with Davis in the spring of 1959 brought evidence of stylistic consolidation; so the *Kind of Blue* sessions (**393**), involving for Evans a concentration upon modal venture more intense and personal than his 1956 engagement with Russell, probably formed a clearer preparation for *Portrait in Jazz* than his earlier Riverside trio albums, *New Jazz Conceptions* (Original Jazz Classics [A] OJC035) and *Everybody Digs Bill Evans* (OJC068). *Blue in green* is the obvious link, but this performance is emphatic of a new kind of cooperation, moving beyond the former trios towards the shared improvisation which supplies the touchstone for assaying every piece here. Evans had a determinative hand in *Blues in green* and, interpreting it wholly in trio terms, he is freer to vary mood, stressing the cadences of melancholy but interpolating tougher accents at midpoint. The ways by which Motian and LaFaro respond to his new mixture of freedom and discipline are well instanced here and elsewhere; fascinatingly so in the obliqueness of contours in *Come rain or come shine* with its departures from strict time. The collective liberty, made possible for Evans by his companions' openness, will be carried forward a little further in *Explorations* (†Original Jazz Classics [A] OJCCD037–2), but already here it is enhanced by elements of the keyboard style; notably by a manual coordination which results during *Witchcraft* in a sophisticated exploiting of contrary motion, a virtuosity less eye-opening than Cecil Taylor's (**384**) only because it is understated dynamically.

LaFaro's mental and executive dexterity occasionally outdoes Evans in stretching beyond established harmonic ideas, as in *Some day my prince will come*, where the bassist tucks himself away in a remote corner of the theme's native tonality. The various rhythmic superimpositions of that same number are far more subtle than Brubeck's famous wedding of 3/4 and 4/4 – a clash of beat rather than of rhythm (**311**). Indeed, advanced imagination and skill, in relation to rhythm and harmony, are often used so undemonstratively throughout this session that careful attention may be needed to grasp all their achievements; particularly so in places where the music is most clearly meditative (*When I fall in love*) and when evoking an impression of stillness and space might seem the chief desire. There the reshufflings of thematic phrases can appear surprisingly complex, and Motian's effective tricks with pulse and texture can be, as it were, observed in slow motion.

When the music releases these players' ability to swing at ease, the variety is no less challenging. A jaunty *Autumn leaves* has Evans using sudden doublings and also judicious pauses, LaFaro distancing himself from the melody and Motian providing contrast on his own account with sparsely scattered brushstrokes. In *What is this thing called love?* and in his songlike original *Peri's scope* the pianist shows how those gamut-running percussive monologues which dominated his work with Russell can be adapted to a greater sensitivity of relationship.

The Original Jazz Classics CD includes alternative versions of *Autumn leaves* and *Blue in green*. What differences these reveal are subtle (except that the previously unreleased take of *Blue in green* is slower than its mate), and their main significance is their further proof that, when inspired minds consort, to speak of search or discovery is to misjudge the immediacy of the occurrence.

Forward-looking as this music appeared in 1959, it established a pattern which would not alter greatly over two decades. Demands upon concentrated listening would still be made, but sympathetic ears, familiarized, probably heeded them less; and they were never to be lightened by obvious levity or by facile daring. Wit there would continue to be in plenty, something akin to that 'tough reasonableness beneath the lyric grace' which T. S. Eliot discerned in the Caroline poets [119] – romantic and yet intellectually tenacious; but seldom as rarefied or as genteel as even some well-disposed commentators have allowed themselves to suggest.

A serious figure, Evans once said that 'words are the children of reason', incapable of explaining either his jazz or the Zen to which he was attracted. [120] He seems also to have learned that meditation and rumination are quite different things, and he proved frequently that meditation can swing. Words can at least celebrate his jazz, even though they will never explain this or any other creative wisdom. E.T.

Bill Evans

373a Waltz for Debby

†Original Jazz Classics (A) OJC20 210–2

Evans (p); Scott LaFaro (bs); Paul Motian (d). New York 25 June 1961.
My foolish heart · *Waltz for Debby* (2 versions) · *Detour ahead* (2 versions) · *My romance* (2 versions) · *Some other time* · *Milestones* · *Porgy (I loves you, Porgy)*

373b Sunday at the Village Vanguard

†Original Jazz Classics (A) OJC20 140–2

Personnel and recording date as above.
Gloria's step (2 versions) · *My man's gone now* · *Solar* · *Alice in Wonderland* (2 versions) · *All of you* (2 versions) · *Jade visions* (2 versions)

The Evans–LaFaro–Motian combination first came together on the bandstand of New York's Basin Street East not long after Evans finished an 11-month spell with Miles Davis in the autumn of 1958. Work for the new trio was infrequent, however, and their first recording together was as part of a Tony Scott group that recorded *Sung Heroes* (Sunnyside [A] SSC1015) in October 1959. The following month the new trio played four consecutive weeks at the Showplace in Greenwich Village. 'That gave us some basis to record,' said Evans. [121] *Portrait in Jazz* (**372**), the pianist's third album under his own name and the first with his now regular group, was recorded the following month, and *Explorations* (OJCCD [A] 037–2) followed in February 1961.

These albums showed a somewhat forthright Evans, with a concept that had its roots in Bud Powell's approach to improvisation. Most immediately apparent was how Evans had adopted a similar manner of comping to Powell (albeit often more harmonically ambiguous with rootless left-hand voicings) and a tendency towards the somewhat staccato phrasing favoured by Powell. Motian recalled his initial working relationship with LaFaro within the trio: 'I had a hard time getting with LaFaro at the very beginning, 'cause I wasn't used to the way he played – they said in those days, "This guy sounds like a guitar player!" We didn't click right away, it wasn't like, "Ah, magic!" Personally we were good friends; remember he hadn't been playing that long, either, just a couple of years to that point. It took a little time, but we hooked up, hooked up for good. We each made adjustments, maybe, but we didn't talk about it. We didn't even rehearse much. Playing, okay, but rehearsals, no.' [122]

Although *Witchcraft* and *Autumn leaves* on **372** suggest a loosening of the rhythmic conventions of hard bop, a less forthright, rhythmically more interactive approach is actually more apparent on *The Legendary Bill Evans Trio: The Complete 1960 Birdland Sessions* (Cool n' Blue [A] C&B CD106). Recorded live between March and May 1960 at the famous 'Jazz Corner of the World', it predates the Vanguard sessions by almost a year. Robust versions of *Autumn leaves* and Tadd Dameron's *Our delight*, both at brisk tempos, reveal an accomplished pianist presenting exceptionally coherent, lyrical improvisations. As a result of his previous musical experiences with George Russell (**380**) and Davis (**393**), Evans had moved towards voicing certain chord sequences in terms of modes. [123] Since his tenure with Davis, he had also begun extensively refining the harmonically ambiguous voicings the trumpeter so admired in the playing of Ahmad Jamal. With intricate voice-leading passages over blocked, 'locked-handed' chords (which would become something of a signature), Evans gives no indication of the kind of introspection or, perhaps more accurately, preference for slow and medium tempos, which he would increasingly come to favour. On the contrary, his playing displays great poise and fluency at fast tempos. On the slower *Beautiful love*, however, we have a clear indication of what was to come, with Evans leaving space for LaFaro to interact with harmonic and rhythmic asides, presenting the burden of explicit timekeeping to Motian. Again, Evans makes use of reharmonized passages and harmonically equivocal voicings. That he was clearly moving to a more reflective style of playing becomes clearer on *Come rain or come shine* and *Blue in green* which anticipate the emotional climate of the Vanguard sessions and show how he had largely cleansed himself of the long, smooth quaver lines that owed much to his personal favourites Tristano, Konitz and Powell. Evans was using a more *legato* style which favoured sustained chords at these slower tempos, and the diverse elements of his style were coalescing into a wholly original approach to the jazz piano. Although the faster tempos revealed his accomplished technique, [124] overall it was now being gloved in the service of a more expressive, romantic melodic style.

Equally, his trio as a whole was moving to a more sophisticated rhythmic conception that represented a watershed for the jazz rhythm section. Jamal had demonstrated that intensity need not equate with *treble forte* and that in certain circumstances *pianissimo* and silence could be effective – even dramatic. Jamal also encouraged his bass player Israel Crosby and his drummer Vernell Fournier to interact to a degree then quite unusual within a piano-bass-drums unit of the late 1950s. [125] These quite specific elements of Jamal's style were rare, if not unique, in jazz at the time, though Evans would have been well aware of them since Davis had urged both Evans and his predecessor Red Garland to listen to Jamal, even taking them along to hear the Chicago pianist whenever he could. With his own trio, Evans explored these aspects of Jamal's approach with a much greater awareness of carefully nuanced melodic detail.

Through the familiarity of regular performance and inspired musicianship, the trio suggested that if everybody kept time in their head, then the need to express it explicitly in terms of the then conventional rhythmic approach derived from bop and hard-bop models was unnecessary, allowing them the flexibility to react and comment on each other's playing. By the time of the Vanguard recordings they had made such significant advances in this direction that it now suggested a meeting of like minds. Although Motian could be a forthright drummer [126] as much as LaFaro could lay down a powerfully driving four beats to the bar, [127] they were now exploring an area of interaction suggesting a floating three-way conversation with Evans at the hub, mediating the ebb and flow of ideas with discretion and courtesy. Although occasionally they observed the conventions of the tradition from which they had emerged, the main thrust of their performances together would emancipate the jazz rhythm section from the hard driving, straight-ahead style then prevalent in jazz.

What the Vanguard recordings reveal above all else is how the disparate elements of Evans's previous musical experiences had coalesced into a wholly individual style and how the forum of his trio had been shaped to create an effective context for his playing. His repertoire now favoured a mixture of standards and originals that were both reflective and tranquil, sometimes evoking the pastoral moods and chordal textures of Delius, a personal favourite. His touch, or tone, was exquisite; delicate, yet never fragile, full, yet never harsh; and he was one of the few pianists in jazz to make extensive use of the piano's pedals as a means of heightening his expressivity. In short, Evans was now ready to make his first truly definitive statement as an artist.

The culmination of the advances Evans had made in his own playing and of the group empathy the trio had evolved is exemplified by *Solar*, a

12-bar theme, although not using blues changes. Evans interprets the theme very freely, with LaFaro playing a prominent role, as much as a time-keeper as a second voice commenting in contrapuntal duetlike figures. Evans's solo is given over, for the most part, to single-note right-hand lines in the middle register of the piano with – a hallmark of his playing – his delightful use of perfectly fingered quaver triplets. LaFaro, mixing time-keeping with counterpoint, often in the higher register of his instrument, plays a prominent role in accompaniment, intertwining his ideas with Evans's line, with Evans adding subtle comping figures with his left hand in accompaniment to his increasing interaction with LaFaro. The degree to which the bassist had defined a new role for his instrument was clearly a radical readjustment of interrelationship of piano and bass within the three-man rhythm section. Throughout, Motian holds this animated discourse together by playing relatively straight time.

On *Gloria's step*, an original by LaFaro, this two-way conversation is extended to include Motian, whose conception of time is more fluid than his role in *Solar*. The song itself is unusual, a 20-bar AB song where the A and B sections are 10 bars each, the theme is again interpreted very freely by Evans. It is perhaps worth highlighting at this point what an exceptionally refined sense of time he possessed that allowed such temporal freedom within form. This sense of time was vital to his work; he excelled at the slowest tempos in jazz, and it still surprises some fans (and some critics) to learn that slow tempos are far harder to master than the fast. Evans was one of the few instrumentalists in jazz who made slow tempos a specific feature of his performances, previously only Billie Holiday and Davis spring readily to mind in this respect.

My foolish heart is one of the major exhibits of these sessions. The tempo is *largo/larghetto*, [128] which would be considered slow for classical music, never mind jazz. The inherent drama of the piece lies in the trio's collective handling of such a mesmerizingly slow pulse. Here, explicit statement of the beat occurs most commonly at cadence points, when the trio fleetingly unite to provide aural reference points before moving forward in a series of languid sighs among clusters of notes that seem to hang in the air just long enough to illuminate Evans's unique voicings; indeed this is truly music that breathes, each player intensely aware of their precise role one to another and in moving the music forward.

In contrast, *My romance*, a 32-bar ABAC composition, which was later used as a feature for the drummer in subsequent editions of the trio, is here free from percussive onslaught and is taken at quite a bright clip [129] and although *presto*, this is somewhat disguised by the use of *alla breve*, or cut time. As Evans develops his solo, he creates a pleasing contrast by moving from a cut-time feel to 4/4 and gradually the ear begins to demand an even four from LaFaro, which is finally resolved late in Evans's solo, giving a sense of lift and of climax.

Evans liked melodies with unusual structures such as *My romance* and his own compositions refused to conform to the usual show-type-tune construction of the standard 32-bar AABA format. [130] In this respect *Waltz for Debby* is perhaps the most interesting of all of his compositions. [131] The piece begins with an exposition of the melody in pure $^{3}/_{4}$. The tempo is very brisk for a waltz, [132] but since LaFaro plays only the first beat of the bar, one's initial perception of the tempo is that it appears more languid. [133] This sets up a pleasing contrast between tempo and metre; in fact it may surprise some listeners to learn that the tune is 80 bars long. It has an AA^1BC construction, where the A and B sections are 16 bars each and the C section is 32 bars. Strictly speaking, the C section comprises the first 10 bars of A, a further 10 bars that in essence are a variation of A, and finally 12 bars that resolve the melody.

However, Evans elides the final 12-bar section of C to 10 bars and uses it as a transitional passage to move into $^{4}/_{4}$. This is achieved so subtly that many listeners are unaware of what has happened and think the whole performance remains in waltz time. This is because LaFaro plays a highly embellished *alla breve* time in $^{4}/_{4}$, which echoes the compound time feel of the main body of the theme spread over the previous 68 bars leading up to the transitional 10-bar passage. At the end of bar 78 of the now modified first chorus, there is a subtle shift in the harmonic backdrop for soloing as the form changes to a 40-bar ABC construction with A and C 16 bars each plus a B section of 8 bars. The harmonic movement of the revised ABC section is distinguished by a frequent use of ii-V progressions, probably the most definitive chord movement in the mainstream of jazz. Evans takes three choruses on the revised form, followed by LaFaro and a return to the main 80-bar theme in $^{3}/_{4}$. It is a wonderful piece of Evans magic, with smooth transitions between form and metre, revealing a wealth of inner detail in the role and relationship of each member of the trio that showed the group to be one of the most exciting in jazz.

On *All of you*, LaFaro again plays in highly decorative *alla breve* and although the tempo is a bright *presto* [134] there is no feeling of haste. Typically he plays on the first and third beats of the bar, while Evans accents the second and fourth. However, the degree of interaction LaFaro employed with Evans would simply not be possible with a pianist whose lines filled all available space like a Powell or an Oscar Peterson; indeed at this tempo the tendency of both pianists would have been to insist on a driving four beats to the bar from the bass player, leaving no room for the sort of loose, flexible interaction that LaFaro employed here. LaFaro's virtuoso style of playing became widely adopted by a whole school of modern jazz bass players and still remains a benchmark of excellence in jazz today. Equally, Motian's playing complemented the fluid feeling of interaction between Evans and LaFaro by reacting sensitively and inventively to their playing, often adopting the role of colourist as much as time-keeper. The coda is a circular four-bar sequence whose origins reside with Ahmad Jamal's version of the number.

Evans makes reference to his tenure as a sideman with Miles Davis in his only recorded version of *Milestones*, the modal classic from the album of the same name, here used as a feature to showcase LaFaro's virtuosity. *Jade visions*, the second of two LaFaro originals on these recordings, is in 9/8 and is an example of the delicate, floating romanticism that became associated with this historic group. In all there is some two and a half hours of music that in both concept and execution remain perfectly realized, with a freshness that has not succumbed to the passage of time.

'We knew we were doing something that was different, new, good and valid,' said Motian in 1986. 'It was like three people being one voice instead of a piano with bass and drums accompaniment. We talked about that. And at the end of our Vanguard gig, when we recorded, we were talking about how we really reached a peak, we got to be sure to work more, play more. But Scott died that 4 July weekend, the same year.' [135]

Throughout, Evans had set new standards for piano jazz and exemplified what he called 'the science of building a line', a challenge that occupied him throughout his life. Here it is pursued with such focus that one is reminded of his liner notes for the original issue of the Davis album *Kind of Blue* (**393**), where he likened the improviser to a Japanese brush painter, such is the calm deliberation with which he defines his art. 'This conviction that direct deed is the most meaningful reflection, I believe, has prompted the evolution of the extremely severe and unique disciplines of the jazz or improvising musician.' And although there is a joy and spontaneity in Evans's playing, as much as quiet reflection, he was also the most disciplined of artists who achieved a clarity of expression that with these performances elevated him into the company of the master improvisers in jazz. They are recordings that are significant for either of two reasons: the emergence of an important and original voice in jazz or the revolutionary approach to the jazz rhythm section. The fact that both occur simultaneously underlines the importance of these albums. S.N.

Adam Makowicz

374 Naughty Baby

†RCA-Novus (E) 30222N

Makowicz (p); Charlie Haden (bs); Al Foster (d). New York City, 25–7 June 1987.

Somebody loves me · *Fascinatin' rhythm* · *Naughty baby* · *Bess, oh where's my Bess?* · *My man's gone now*

Dave Holland (bs) added. Same place and dates.
They all laughed · *Prelude No. 2* · *Maybe* · *Embraceable you* · *Rhapsody in blue* · *Summertime*

Given the unique position of Art Tatum (**181–3**, **217–9**, **254**), it was most unlikely that anybody would appear whose pianistic mastery was as extensive and individual as his, let alone that the person concerned should have been born in Czechoslovakia and long domiciled in Poland before going to the United States. Yet that is what happened. Normally jazz commentary makes little contact with the music itself, and just as Tatum's magnificent technique was the sole aspect of his work to receive much attention in print, so, once the fact that Makowicz commanded a parallel virtuosity had registered, it was automatically concluded that they must sound alike. True, his 1973 solo account of *Cherokee* (Pool Jazz [G] IRS942 115) could more readily be taken as a tribute to the earlier master than Peterson's avowed salute in *Someone to watch over me* (**470**), but even there Makowicz does things which do not in the least resemble his alleged mentor. There is a much later piece actually called *Tatum on my mind* (†Concord [A] CCD4541) recorded in 1992, but that does not sound like him either. A further point of dissimilarity is that from 1972 onwards Makowicz became much concerned with composition: seven of the themes on his 1983 †Sheffield Lab (A) CD21 are his, as are all eight on the 1986 †Sonet (Sd) one (SNTCD983). It must be acknowledged that he reckons Tatum and Keith Jarrett (!) his chief jazz influences – other sources being European composers of the romantic period. Yet as the above improvisations on Gershwin particularly well demonstrate, Makowicz's sound world includes substantial elements new to jazz. In fact the opposite assertion that 'his style is an amalgam of several earlier giants' [136] is as futile as attempts to reduce him to a mere Tatum imitator.

If Makowicz's attitude to touch, sonority and texture represents an approach different from that of any comparable piano virtuoso, a telling influence appears to have been his involvement with electronic keyboards. This began in 1970 and was pursued in bands led by Michal Urbaniak and co-led with Tomasz Stánko (the latter one of the earliest significant European free-jazz groups). Sometimes the effect on Makowicz's acoustic piano work is quite explicit, as with the sudden crystalline upper-register flourish in *Naughty baby* just after the theme has begun its restatement. And highly expressive though his music is, Makowicz's execution has a clarity so unfailing as to suggest a more than human precision. This is heightened by a consciousness of dynamics more acute than we find in most jazz, operating in terms both of the piano and of the group as a whole. Makowicz's variety of touch, like that of Bill Evans, is altogether exceptional in jazz pianism, ranging through almost infinite degrees from notes and chords struck with the sharpest (most rapid) attack imaginable to others that barely murmur.

These are deployed in keyboard textures and figurations of comparable diversity. Makowicz recorded extensively before going to America in 1977 but in improvisations such as those detailed above, in an extension of his earlier, more patterned virtuosity, the lines are threaded into quite unpredictable formations. Indeed, his resources are such that one can seldom have much idea of what is coming next. The variety of textural density is especially impressive, above all when he accelerates from one extreme to another – from dreamy, transcendental intimacy, let us say, to stormy restlessness, or vice versa. Obviously this acts on both a large and a small scale, in treatments of whole pieces such as the ruminative though never merely decorative *Embraceable you* and the surging *Somebody loves me*, and, equally, in the brilliant use of double time within a single phrase found in the latter piece. In both cases Gershwin's melodies and harmonies hover ghostlike behind, or in the midst of, Makowicz's, Haden's and sometimes the whole ensemble's elaborations. He can also change a theme so as to go completely against its initial character, as in *They all laughed*. Perhaps *Summertime*, which stomps with seeming decisiveness, appears to be a still better example, yet, because we are allowed to remain aware of its original status as a lullaby, this distils a rather ambiguous passion. In striking contrast to such apparent vigour is the sheer lyrical beauty of *My man's gone now* and *Bess, oh where's my Bess?*, the other excerpts from *Porgy and Bess*, although even here the slow-moving yet still mercurial spontaneity has about it something enigmatic.

This arises not only from Makowicz's own kaleidoscopic improvising but also out of the ensemble aspects of this music. He feels no need to be always at the centre of the stage and his quality as a team player was settled by 1971 recordings with Urbaniak (Pool Jazz [G] IRS942 113). His particular style of involvement in the overall texture of performances began decisively to emerge on records two years later, in his Fender keyboard duets with the percussionist Czeslaw Bartkowski (Pool Jazz [G] IRS942 115). This resulted in something very different from the heavily soloistic character of so much piano virtuosity, and even if a little was learned from the Scott LaFaro edition of Evans's trio (**372–3**), Makowicz employed trio format and extensions thereof to far more variously inventive ends than Tatum.

These are best heard as developments of Makowicz's ensemble approach, in particular of the complications which arise from emphasizing the inner voices of textures. Obviously he is drawn to the fuller enlargements of trio instrumentation, as with the two percussionists plus bass of the Sheffield Lab CD and two bassists plus drummer here. These several musicians rarely have subsidiary roles but are much on the move, complementing with alacrity the frequent complexity of Makowicz's own contributions. The use of two basses may remind us of Martial Solal's

1971 recordings (†RCA [F] PD7079–2), yet Makowicz repeatedly brings new ensemble situations into being, rich in implications while transparent in texture. And, again unlike so many other virtuosos, he is always ready to make room for others and to devise quirkily stimulating accompaniments for them, be it Haden's extended solos here or the assertive brilliance of Phil Woods in several pieces on the Sheffield Lab CD.

Although more involved implications often lurk beneath the music's surface, Makowicz can also be simple, as in *Prelude No. 2* before the massive concluding tremolos. (These make a cheap, melodramatic effect in the hands of most pianists, but if executed with a perfectly even touch, as here, the result is quite different. For a still better instance of Makowicz's use of this device, hear *Seamless dream* on the Sonet CD.) In *Maybe* and *Naughty baby* the expression is mainly delicate, yet a flight of virtuosity may arise suddenly, almost as an aside, while *Embraceable you* is the opposite case, its bravura constantly producing fresh blossoms of melody, the mounting intensity, climax and resolution generated entirely from within the music. But nowhere does the individuality of expression arise solely from complexity of method, as the toccata-like *Fascinatin' rhythm* shows. This is close to a straightforward trio performance, at least at first; but as it unfolds this gesture towards conventionality serves to emphasize the personal nature of Makowicz's ideas in themselves and of the pianistic forms in which he casts them. In *Prelude No. 2* and *Rhapsody in blue* – which latter is not a performance, even a free one, of the piece Gershwin wrote but a collective improvisation on some of its themes – although Makowicz is chiefly pursuing thoughts of his own we do glimpse some brief yet fascinating revisions and expansions of some of the composer's original keyboard layouts. On the contrary, if anything explicit survives from Makowicz's early classical training it is the element of *fioritura*, which, as in *They all laughed* and *Somebody loves me*, does rather distantly echo Liszt and Chopin. M.H.

4

Other Currents

New Textures

In groups large and small, and in a considerable diversity of styles, jazz continued to develop new instrumental textures, not only for colouristic purposes but to increase still further its range of expression.

Claude Thornhill

375 **The Real Birth of the Cool**
†CBS/Sony (J) 25DP5321, CBS/Sony (J) SOPC57104, *Affinity (E) AFSD1040 (2 LPs)

Rusty Dedrick, Conrad Gozzo, Bob Sprentall (tpt); Tasso Harris, Bob Jenny (tbn); Irving Fazola (clt); Dale Brown, George Paulson (clt, alt); John Nelson, Hammond Rusen (clt, ten); Ted Goddard (clt, bar); Thornhill (p); Chuck Robinson (g); Harvey Cell (bs); Gene Leeman (d). New York City, 10 March 1941.
Snowfall

Dedrick, Louis Mucci, Jake Koven, Clarence Willard (tpt); Harris, Jenny (tbn); Ray Schmidt, Sandy Siegelstein (fr h); Bob Walters (clt); Jack Ferrier, Goddard (clt, alt); Nelson, Carl Swift (clt, ten); Chet Pardee (clt, bs clt, bar); Thornhill (p); Barry Galbraith (g); Iggy Shevack (bs); Billy Exiner (d). New York City, 17 July 1946.
Arab dance

Bernie Savid (tpt), Tak Tavorian, Jerry Rosa (tbn), Harold Yelten (fr h), Joe Aglora, Jack Dulong (clt, ten), Barney Spieler (bs) replace Dedrick, Harris, Jenny, Schmidt, Nelson Swift, Shevack; Fran Warren (vcl) added. New York City, 11 November 1946.
I get the blues when it rains · *A Sunday kind of love*

Dedrick, Emil Terry (tpt), Walt Welscher (fr h), John Hefty (clt, ten), Walt Bettman (clt, bs clt, bar) replace Savid, Koven, Yelten, Aglora, Pardee. New York City, 10 March 1947.
We knew it all the time

Eddie Zandy, Mucci, Terry (tpt); John Torick, Allan Langstaff (tbn); Welscher, Siegelstein (fr h); Harold Weskel (tu); James Gemus, Vic Harris, Ed Stang (picc, fl); Bill Glover (fl, alt); Danny Polo (clt, alt); Mario Rollo (clt, ten); Micky Folus (bs clt, ten); Bill Bushey (clt, bs clt, bar); Thornhill (p); Galbraith (g); Joe Schulman (bs); Exiner (d). New York City, 4 June 1947.

Early autumn

Takvorian (tbn), Bill Barber (tu), Les Clark (clt, alt) replace Torick, Weskel, Glover. New York City, 30 June 1947.

La Paloma

Personnel and recording date unknown.

La Paloma

Lee Konitz (alt) replaces Clark. Date unknown.

Anthropology · *Sorta kinda*

Personnel and recording date unknown.

The old castle

Paul Cohen (tpt) replaces Terry. New York City, 17 October 1947.

Robbin's nest

Red Rodney (tpt) replaces Cohen. New York City, 26 November 1947.

Loverman · *Polka dots and moonbeams* · *Happy stranger* · *Donna Lee*

Same personnel. New York City, 17 December 1947.

Yardbird suite · *Let's call it a day*

N.B. The Affinity 2-LP set is titled *Tapestries.* Mussorgsky's *The old castle* is a movement from his *Pictures at an Exhibition* and is wrongly titled *The troubadour* on nearly all issues.

Viewing the emergence of Konitz at the end of the 1940s, Barry Ulanov saw the young altoist joining the Thornhill orchestra and, with it, leaving Chicago in August 1947 as 'a year's sojourn with the sweet nothings of that polished organization [which] left him in New York, where he joined forces with Tristano'. [1] In one dismissive clause the commentator sums up what many in the jazz audience may at that time have thought about Thornhill's musical produce. That Ulanov should have known better than to generalize is evident from his patent knowledge, not only of the contribution of Gil Evans to the library but also of the latter's contemporary association with Miles Davis and Gerry Mulligan. To be sure, there was a number of drifting reveries in the Thornhill repertoire, but some of these pieces have to be assessed with a degree of ambiguity, as will be suggested below.

Evans's work for Thornhill began in 1941–2 with arrangements of popular compositions of Brahms, Schumann, Grieg and Dvořák which probably expressed something beyond the then popular mischief of 'swinging the classics'. Certainly by the time he tackled Tchaikovsky's *Arab dance* in 1946, his self-tutored orchestrating skill and his ability to make the most of an instrumentation which now included french horns lent a touch of 'seriousness' to the transformation; though even here he may be feeling his way, nodding vigorously to Eddie Sauter-like swing scoring and careering into a climactic quotation from Ellington's 1940 *Ko-ko* (**153**) as if in exuberant laudation of a personal source of inspiration. In the sections of the dance which are recognizably his own, his achievement in orchestral colouration shows an instinct for the commingling of sounds which most swing arrangers would have emphasized in contrasting lines.

La Paloma in two versions, differing chiefly in length, has aspects looking forward to the 1957 *Blues for Pablo* (†Columbia [E] CK65121 and hear also **382**, **460**) and to evocations of the Spanish spirit more advanced still. Already there are forecasts of greater daring – sudden brassy climaxes subsiding into quiet harmonies edged by the dryness of horns, the contrast achieved during the trumpet solo. By June 1947 a tuba had been added to the brass, but this, though it was a harbinger of later alliances, seems to have been used by Evans as much for middle-register enrichment as for depth-lending *basso* – a balance sought by Evans and other other arrangers for Bill Barber's role in the music of Davis's **376**.

Mussorgsky's *The old castle*, a movement from his *Pictures at an Exhibition*, a suite originally for piano solo, is best known in Ravel's splendid orchestration. With piccolo, flute and guitar leading in a snatch of the linking *Promenade*, Evans introduces a recreation which, although it uses the rhythmic sinews and tonal emphases of jazz, has nothing of the self-consciousness of swing-style 'poking fun at the longhairs'. That Evans was intimately familiar with Ravel's score is certain, and he had learned from it; yet his recomposition is all the more remarkable because encompassed by the limitations of what was, while unusually augmented, a dance-band instrumentation. The treatment is vividly original.

The intrinsic value of much of this work should be unmistakable, but all that is characteristic has long been assessed in the light of Evans's post-Thornhill activity. The broader orchestral palette of the 'classical' recreations and some of the accompanimental scores is related naturally to *Porgy and Bess* (**382**) and its kindred sessions, though its importance to any evaluation of the Davis nonet should be marked. Yet before the Thornhill–Davis link is examined more closely, the oddness of the title given to this whole item and the one attached to **376** ought to be mentioned. The inauguration of the 'cool' style in jazz remains a debatable matter, though in the period we are considering, the example of the tenorist Stan Getz loomed larger among enthusiastic scene-watchers (**297**, **299**, **312**). Thornhill's version of *Early autumn* was recorded a year ahead of the Herman–Burns arrangement with Getz's glowing subtemperature solo and has no element of coolness, however that might be defined. In any case, what 'the cool' is taken to mean may be a red herring across this particular trail. The influential link between the

Thornhill orchestra of 1946–7 and the Davis band of 1948–50 is more likely to appear structural than temperamental, a matter less of moods than of makings.

The most obvious single link with the nonet is forged by the solos of Konitz in *Anthropology* and *Yardbird suite*, but that link is really fortuitous, even though the Parkerish note flurry which the altoist is required to execute at the start of his otherwise typically fragile *Yardbird suite* statement does amusingly point up the contrast between the tensions of bop and the search for cool relaxation. Evans's scoring of these two Parker numbers and of Davis's *Donna Lee* does not quite solve the problem of how to translate an essentially small-group form into larger orchestral terms. *Yardbird suite* approaches success the most closely, but there are in the other pieces intricate unison witticisms and ensemble variations, elements which were soon to find a better fulfilment in the more boppish offerings of Davis's marvellous 'tuba band'. That fulfilment was *not* a fortuity. Evans had approached Davis for the lead sheet of *Donna Lee* before making the Thornhill arrangement and in turn Davis requested Evans's score of *Robbin's nest*. [2] The consequence of that small mutuality developed into a lengthy strand of collaborative jazz.

As for the cloudy driftings, these slowed gently towards immobility (*vide Loverman* and *Polka dots and moonbeams*, where the breathings of the ensemble become at times almost a sustained snore). And the earlier hinted ambiguity rests in Evans's own attitude to such essays. His subtle gifts proved perhaps *too* suitable to the refinement of slow numbers with an imaginativeness of which Thornhill's own *Snowfall* arrangement fell distinctly short. Such demands eventually proved far too tedious and he quit the band. But it was, by strange alchemy, out of this dubious musical territory that a unique jazz masterpiece was to emerge, Evans's *Träumerei* for nine Davis-led instruments, *Moondreams*, a jewel of sternly concentrated experience. E.T.

Miles Davis

376 The Complete Birth of the Cool

†Capitol (E) CDP792 862–2

Davis (tpt); Kai Winding (tbn); Junior Collins (fr h); Bill Barber (tu); Lee Konitz (alt); Gerry Mulligan (bar); Al Haig (p); Joe Schulman (bs); Max Roach (d). New York City, 21 January 1949.

Jeru · Move · Godchild · Budo

J. J. Johnson (tbn), Sandy Siegelstein (fr h), John Lewis (p), Nelson Boyd (bs), Kenny Clarke (d) replace Winding, Collins, Haig, Schulman, Roach. New York City, 22 April 1949.

Venus de Milo · Rouge · Boplicity · Israel

Gunther Schuller (fr h), Al McKibbon (bs), Roach (d) replace Siegelstein, Boyd, Clarke; Kenny Hagood (vcl[1]) added. New York City, 9 March 1950.
Deception · *Rocker* · *Moondreams* · *Darn that dream*[1]

The music of the Davis nonet has long been thought of as a reaction against the passionate expressions associated with Parker, Gillespie and Bud Powell. Yet to understand the genesis and character of this music it needs to be remembered that it was created while bop was still in the ascendant. Though the dating of performances is confused, it is clear that in the period of the nonet's Royal Roost debut Davis was negotiating the intricacies of the bop trumpet style with skill and vigour in the Parker quintet at the same venue. A lot of his solo work for the emergent nonet was in manner similar. This was in the late summer of 1948 when Davis's regular association with Parker was coming to an end. That the trumpeter had been searching for an amended mode of expression is evidenced by an encounter in 1947, mentioned under **375**, when he exchanged material with Gil Evans and, more tellingly, by a May 1947 recording (with Parker, Lewis, Boyd and Roach) of *Milestones*, a Davis composition out of character with Parker's usual approach, in which his tenor assists a mellower ensemble sound, and Davis and Lewis solo in a manner closer to their work for the nonet. If the nonet provided a re-evaluation of bop, Davis's personal re-evaluation began well over a year before the nonet was formed, and *Milestones* (an apt double pun) indicated a turning point. [3]

A parallel reassessment began with arrangers and composers utilizing the resources of large groups. Lewis's and George Russell's writings for Gillespie provide cases in point (**315**), as do Mulligan's arrangements in the mid-1940s for Krupa and later for Thornhill, plus Evans's Thornhill scores. This kind of organization, often adapting small-band achievements, was, in turn, to influence small-group experiments.

Talk about trends and movements in jazz is, often enough, a fairly subjective weighing of facts. Objectivity can more confidently be applied to the processes preceding and encompassing the studio recordings of the nonet; for we know something, if in sparse detail, about the consultation of musicians who rallied to Evans's genial ensign in the earlier months of 1948. Mulligan, Evans, Lewis and John Carisi seem to have been leading schemers, linking their personal ideas to a hope of transposing aspects of the Thornhill–Evans sound, using much reduced instrumental forces. Three elements in Evans's scores were suggestive: recomposition of themes from European romantics, exploitation of harmonic colouration in slow numbers, and arrangements of Parker and Davis tunes.

Davis seems to have entered fairly late into this consultative arena, proving a keen and forceful additional catalyst, not least because he sensed here a means of furthering his own musical aspirations. These aspirations were as important a tributary of the nonet's music as was the one provided by Evans's influence. The direct contribution of other members of the Evans coterie is indicated by the composing/arranging roster: Mulligan – *Jeru*, *Venus de Milo*, *Rocker*, George Wallington's *Godchild* and perhaps Van Heusen's *Darn that dream*; Lewis – *Rouge*, Denzil Best's *Move* and perhaps Powell's *Hallucination* retitled *Budo* by Davis – although this also might have been scored by Mulligan; Carisi – *Israel*; Evans – his own and Davis's *Boplicity* and Chummy McGregor's *Moondreams* (some have credited *Darn that dream* to Evans also); Davis possibly took George Shearing's *Conception* and arranged it as *Deception*, although this too may have been from Mulligan.

With a band less than half the size of Thornhill's, the impression of Evans's characteristic timbres could only be suggestive. His use of woodwind could barely be hinted at by the saxophones, so much depended on the deployment of horn and tuba if a proper small-band 'voice' was to be discovered. Lengthy analysis would be needed here to show the numerous ways in which all the wind voices are organized in ensemble – for instance how even the deeper instruments range through the registers, and how many timbral phases and levels tend to Davis's consistently middle-register lines. Approaches to chord and counterpoint differ somewhat according to the mind of each arranger, Mulligan's contrapuntal methods contrast with, for example, Lewis's. Compare the more tentative polyphonic implications at the beginning of *Venus de Milo* with the firm countersubject of *Move*. Harmonic substance is, predictably, rich. The rhythmically disciplined chordal scoring in *Move*, *Godchild*, *Venus de Milo*, *Budo*, *Rouge* and elsewhere shows the influence of Evans's bop recreations, while in Evans's arrangements of *Boplicity* and *Moondreams* the harmonic lines seem closer to his ballad and 'classical' charts. Melodic elements in the various arrangements usually simplify bop shapes to a marked degree, but sometimes do this (particularly in Mulligan's writing) by falling back upon familiar swing clichés.

The *Darn that dream* arrangement regards Hagood's suave tones in quasi-instrumental terms, allowing them to suggest their own orchestral support. (Even if Mulligan's claim to this particular work has justice, Evans's prints might be discerned upon the score, as, indeed, they may be upon much else in the repertoire.

Ensemble passages have tended to hold more interest for commentators than have the nonet's soloists, Davis's essays perhaps excepted; but, at least in the studio recordings, solos are integral to each conception, and ensemble and improviser complement each other in a number of ways. Davis is the most memorable soloist. His long, leisured *Godchild* improvisation begins with a favoured quotation from Jerome Kern's *Bill*, and its relative coolness sets the mode for other solos, though in *Move* and *Budo* he hews closer to the briskness of bop. Mulligan and Konitz are always interesting, even for their occasional shortcomings. Their tendency towards stiffness, like that of the trombonists, possibly has something to do with the atmosphere of the recording sessions, which (though supposedly seeking a new stylistic relaxation) have been described as 'tense, hectic and filled with headaches for all concerned'. [4]

Roach's breaks and solos are apposite and well integrated, and Lewis's shapely solo in *Rouge* expresses the manner so much more congenial to him than the imitations of Haig or Powell that he was often required to devise when playing for Parker. Haig figures in the first session, taking the place which Lewis filled in the Roost versions of *Move* and *Budo*. His rhythmic support differs from Lewis's in emphasis, and he never solos.

The two pinnacles of the nonet's achievement are *Israel* and *Moondreams*. Carisi's *Israel* is a remarkable transformation of the 12-bar blues, its investigation of Dorian steps making possible exciting phases of bitonality; and it anticipates departures which Russell and Davis were later to make, as well as Carisi's own programmatic works heard on **385**, where Evans's presence is also felt.

The dry but progressively expansive texture of *Moondreams* effectively dispels the sentimentalism of McGregor's song. Whatever solos there are are firmly integral and premeditated, and help to create a singular mood, presaged in jazz (apart from earlier Evans essays) perhaps only by Strayhorn's *Passion flower* (**165**). Of all the nonet's numbers, *Israel* and *Moondreams* must have seemed the most disconcerting to early hearers, and almost five decades on they still carry their sensation of enigma.

A few words about befores and afters. If the nonet had entered the Capitol studio during the Royal Roost engagement instead of having to wait several months, with problems of reconvenement, and if the limits of 78-rpm registration had not been imposed, the results might have been different. Transcriptions of Roost broadcasts made in September 1948 (†Bandstand [E] BDCD1512) preserve a more vigorous ensemble spirit, well in control of the formal shapes of *Godchild*, *Moondreams*, *Budo* and *Move* and of the additional *S'il vous plaît* (composed and scored by Lewis) and *Why do I love you?* (arranged by Evans). Davis's men on hand are Collins, Barber, Konitz, Mulligan, Lewis, McKibbon and Roach, with Mike Zwerin as trombonist. Most pieces are lengthened by extended solos. Davis's *Godchild* solo begins and continues quite differently from the well-known one. Of odd interest is the way in which Konitz and Mulligan improvise jointly on *Move*, prophesying a Mulligan manner that was to be developed in the following decade.

A 1950 version of *Deception/Conception*, recorded at Birdland with Davis, Johnson, Stan Getz, Tadd Dameron, Gene Ramey and Roach, anticipates by one month the Capitol performance in which Johnson reproduces his solos ideas (†Suiza [It] JZCD313). A Mulligan score of *Godchild* recorded by Thornhill in the spring of 1948 (Hep [E] 17) with Siegelstein, Barber, Konitz and Mulligan on board sounds evident pre-echoes of both Royal Roost and Capitol. The Tentette's *Rocker* (**300**) shows Mulligan carrying his inventive enthusiasm forward, as also in his Concert Band 1961 reading of *Israel* (Verve [A] MGV8415), and Carisi himself led an octet version of that piece in 1956 (†RCA [E] ND86471).

No set of recordings during Davis's long and varied career had a more important impact on jazz thinking than this of the nonet. And, cooperative as the genesis of the music may have been, the directive credit must be Davis's. Mulligan in 1971, thanking his 'lucky stars' for having been involved, said of Davis; 'He took the initiative and put the theories to work. He called the rehearsals, hired the halls, called the players and generally cracked the whip.' [5] The multifarious aftereffects of the nonet's example are not to be facilely discerned, and certainly not by a listing of re-creations of the repertoire. But in mid-1991 Mulligan approached Davis to tell him of his hope of recording the nonet pieces anew. Miles died before this could come to pass, but Lewis and Barber were able to join the baritonist at the end of January 1992, along with Wallace Roney (tpt), Dave Bargeron (tbn), John Clark (fr h), Phil Woods (alt), Dean Johnson (bs), Ron Vincent (d); and Mel Tormé to sing *Darn that dream*. There should be no hesitation in lauding this project. Mulligan was one of the strongest of the original conspirators and knew as well as any partner, and better than some, what made these creations live. What might be called 'the settling of old scores', though faithful, is too inwardly virile to appear merely reverential. The solos belong to their makers and to the new day, and there are admirable ones among them, especially from Mulligan, Lewis and Phil Woods. This venture (†GRP [A] GRD9679) re-presents past things in a way that is as personal for the new men as for the veterans. Not the least of its virtues may be that it will help to save the veterans among listeners who may be tempted to view the original nonet as held in the stasis of nostalgia. E.T.

Johnny Richards

377 **Annotations of the Muses**
Legende (A) LP1401

Joe Wilder (tpt); John Barrow (fr h); Julius Baker (fl); Robert Bloom (ob); Vincent Abato (clt); Harold Goltzer (bsn); Johnny Smith (g); Jack Lesberg (bs); Sol Gubin (d); Richards (comp, arr). New York City, early 1955.
Annotations of the Muses: Calliope · Clio · Erato · Euterpe · Melpomene · Polymnia · Terpsichore · Thalia · Urania

Reputedly the only jazz musician ever to dedicate a piece to Ghengis Khan (First Heard [E] FH45), Richards was never in good odour with the pseudo-highbrows of jazz. They strongly disapproved of such things as *The Rites of Diablo* (Roulette [A] 52008, 1958) with its innovative placing of choral voices in the big-band context, later taken up by Don Ellis. Usually Richards's works have a particularly strong rhythmic orientation, for example the six-movement *Cuban Fire* for Stan Kenton (†Capitol [E] CDP796 260–2, 1956), which centres on a fuller integration of Latin rhythms and big-band scoring than has often been achieved. Better still, and in fact one of the most satisfying records Kenton ever made, is *Adventures in Time* (†Capitol [E] CDP855 454–2), a main point of which is the fluent use of uneven time signatures such as 5/4 and 7/4.

Unlike most jazz composers, Richards was at his best in large-scale works, especially when he could plan a session or group of sessions as a whole. All too many jazz 'suites' and supposedly long 'compositions', including some by band leaders of far greater renown, are merely assemblages of random short pieces which display few essential – which is to say musical – links, if any. Probably Richards's finest single work, *Annotations of the Muses*, is the opposite case, though it should at once be noted that its completely unified fabric could be woven only at a cost which other jazz composers have likewise had to pay. As in such pieces as Ellington's *Reminiscing in tempo* (**131b**) or Dameron's *Fontainebleau* (**280**), there is very little improvisation, this amounting to no more than a couple of solos each by Wilder and Smith.

No background to the title of this work or to those of its individual movements is offered by the sleeve note so it ought to be stated here that in Greek mythology the muses were the goddesses of the arts – as they were then conceived – and were the daughters of Zeus and Mnemosyne. In the order in which Richards takes them they were: Calliope, who presided over eloquence and epic poetry, Clio over history, Erato over erotic poetry and elegy, Euterpe over music, Melpomene over tragedy, Polymnia over lyric poetry, Terpsichore over choral dance and song, Thalia over comedy and Urania over astronomy. Except occasionally in the most general sense, as with the elegiac warmth that informs the *Erato* movement, Richards is wise enough not to attempt to portray, barely to suggest, these areas of responsibility. What is important is that this mythological subject matter led him to a quite remarkable variety of invention on melodic, rhythmic and harmonic planes, and just as much in terms of orchestration, the range of instrumental colours, textures and blendings being extraordinary. And not only blendings, for Richards often writes in such a way that rather than fusing together, the instruments stand off from each other. Given the work's frequently rich counterpoint, this is crucial.

He is much aided in this by using the well-differentiated components of a classical wind quintet as his basic resource, adding to them only a trumpet and a pianoless rhythm section. An element in the music's organization is interplay between the wind quintet as a separate entity and the ensemble as a whole, though it should be stressed that this is only one of a considerable number of stratagems used. Doing without set chorus lengths or repeating chord sequences, the work is freely composed yet maintains formal lucidity throughout. Questions about the jazz or classical origins of the many techniques of writing employed never arise because this music flows with apparently unforced naturalness through its diverse moods and several climates of expression.

Each movement has a distinct character but they are linked in three larger sections. In fact these nine pieces for nine instruments are arranged in three groups of three. Smith in places acts as an intermediary, joining together movements or sections thereof, occasionally leading, often accompanying. Gubin's timpani are sometimes prominent also, but essentially *Annotations* is a great extension and purification of several aspects of Richards's work for Raeburn (**314**), and was to a degree anticipated by specific pieces such as *Cartaphilius* (†Hep [E] CD42). Another possible influence was Tommy Talbot's group of 1946 scores for Raeburn using woodwind, french horns and a rhythm section, and an earlier precedent was the Alec Wilder octet with flute, english horn, clarinet, bass clarinet and bassoon which supported Mildred Bailey on some of her 1939–40 recordings.

Although not inherent in the programmatic titles, it is a sign of the quality of Richards's imaginative response to them that these nine movements, rather than seeming like stages in a journey as in a true suite, appear to radiate from one central experience, their great variety notwithstanding. Indirect proof of this was given when he made a later recording of the *Terpsichore* movement by itself (Capitol [A] T981, 1958). Removed from its context, this made very little impression and its character was virtually destroyed by transfer to conventional big-band instrumentation. A further, if slightly paradoxical, indication of this work's unity as much as of its diversity is the frequency of its shifting into and out of tempo, the range of tempos indeed being exceptional. This draws attention to the fine performance it receives. Richards evidently chose his men well, for the playing is full of subtle nuance, and although this is music of very unusual character, its interpreters demonstrably understand it completely.

The fact that it was issued on Legende, a minor Roost subsidiary, has obviously not helped this work, but it is supposed to be part of the task of critics and historians to find out about obscure yet valuable endeavours. In fact, the literature of jazz appears to be innocent of any reference to *Annotations of the Muses*. Richards's score stands as a small but absolutely distinctive monument, however, and one that will continue quietly to demand the attention it deserves. M.H.

Teddy Charles

378 Tentet
Atlantic (A) 790 983–1, †Atlantic (A) 790 983–2

Art Farmer (tpt); Gigi Gryce (alt); J. R. Monterose (ten); George Barrow (bar); Don Butterfield (tu); Mal Waldron (p); Jimmy Raney (g); Teddy Kotick (b); Joe Harris (d); Charles (vib). New York City, 6 January 1956.
The quiet time · *Nature boy*

Same personnel. New York City, 11 January 1956.
Green blues · *You go to my head*

Same personnel except Sol Schlinger (bar) for Barrow. New York City, 17 January 1956.
Vibrations · *The Emperor* · *Lydian M-1*

Art Farmer (tpt); Eddie Bert (tbn); Jim Buffington (fr h); Butterfield (tu); Hal Stein (alt); Bob Newman (ten); Barrow (bar); Hall Overton (p); Raney (g); Addison Farmer (bs); Ed Shaughnessy (d); Charles (vib).
New York City, 23 October 1956.
A word from Bird

Bert, Buffington absent. Same date.
Show time

Charles refused to be diverted into hard bop or cool, the two main stylistic strands that dominated 1950s jazz, preferring instead to run with a small group of New York-based musicians who were exploring ways of extending the music's boundaries. Since these musicians tended to work away from the more widely reported events of the decade, their significance in anticipating changes in jazz, sometimes years in advance of the event, has, with the passage of time, come to be overlooked. In a sense, the work of such musicians as Charles, George Russell, Charles Mingus, Hall Overton, Teo Macero and Jimmy Giuffre might more accurately be represented as a part of an avant-garde movement within 1950s jazz, although today such a term has come to be associated with the more readily identifiable 'free jazz' movement of the 1960s. Should a study of the 1950s experimenters ever be completed – of whom Charles was an important figure – a generous amount of realigning of accepted moves would surely follow.

For example, while potted histories have it that Miles Davis brought the jazz world modes with *Milestones* in 1958, there are countless examples of modalism that predate this. George Russell's introduction to *Cubano be* for Gillespie in 1947 (**315**) was probably the first example of modalism in jazz, and by the 1950s its use, if not widespread, could be found on several albums. These included *Collaboration West* (†Original Jazz Classics [A] OJCCD122–2) by Charles and Shorty Rogers from 1954, *Chico Hamilton Quintet* (**389**) from 1955 on the number *Free form*, George Russell's consistent application through much of **379–80** in 1956 and on and his impressive *Lydian M-1* in this album. Equally, the move from the constraints of prearranged harmony had continued to beguile many musicians long before Ornette Coleman's emergence on the California scene in 1958. While Tristano's *Intuition* and *Digression* (**293**) are usually cited as the first voyages into free, similar experiments continued throughout the 1950s, including those of Cecil Taylor (**418**), Dick Twardzik (see also under **418**), Charles Mingus, most notably with his recording of *What love* (*The Complete Candid Recordings of Charles Mingus* Mosaic [A] MR4–111), and Shelly Manne with Giuffre and Rogers in 1954 on **432.** Note also a rarely cited performance by Shelly Manne with André Previn and Leroy Vinnegar on *Oh happy day* from *Modern Jazz Performances of Songs from Li'l Abner* (Contemporary [A] C3533) from 1957.

In 1954 Charles himself had ventured into freedom with Rogers and Giuffre on *Collaboration West*, and his composition and arrangement for the album detailed above, *The Emperor*, begins and ends on a note of 'free' jazz organized around a tonal centre. As with the arrival of bop in the mid-1940s, the innovations of both freedom and modalism of the 1960s should perhaps be viewed less as revolution, more as evolution. Charles had arrived in New York in the 1940s to study at Juilliard, but also found work on 52nd Street. His first professional work came with Benny Goodman, Artie Shaw, Buddy DeFranco (**293**) and Chubby Jackson. But by the 1950s he became involved in the more experimental ensembles of Overton, Raney and Macero, and recording with Miles Davis, Mingus and Wardell Gray (**268**) among others. He also began a career as a record producer during this period, launching the New Directions series for Prestige, and with it such artists as John Coltrane, Waldron, Rogers, Giuffre and Phil Woods. At the same time he was recording the cutting edge of jazz in the 1950s, he was also producing and accompanying rhythm-'n'-blues artists and pop singers for King Records. As his talents as a composer and arranger grew, he was in demand for countless albums and gigs around New York, where he worked regularly with Mingus. He also became an executive producer for Bethlehem records, producing, composing or performing on over 40 albums for that label. However, with the rise of rock he became disenchanted, retired from music and, purchasing a charter boat, moved to the Caribbean, where he built a successful sailing business.

If by the 1990s Charles was only intermittently involved in jazz through occasional gigs and festival appearances, his position remains secure through recordings such as *Tentet*, which, although emerging from the margins of jazz in the 1950s, nevertheless sought to expand the basic vocabulary of bop through sound musical principles and practice. *Vibrations*, composed and arranged by Waldron, is an ambitious piece of contrasting tempos and rhythmic figures. In a sense it is a miniature concerto for a small jazz ensemble and soloist with two contrasting themes that are developed and expanded against tempo and rhythmic variation. Waldron places Gryce, his principal soloist, in a variety of situations, a cappella, against a specific written rhythmic pattern, against a straight-ahead four and against an ensemble playing rhythmic figures without the rhythm section.

In contrast is Giuffre's *The quiet time*, a skilful piece of orchestration using a basic 32-bar AABA structure. The exposition of the theme is followed in fragmented variation before moving into Charles' solo, played with engaging energy, particularly during the stop-time passage. After the initial promise of *Four brothers* for the 1947 Herman orchestra (**312c**), the skill Giuffre demonstrates in writing for larger ensembles was incrementally lost to jazz as his involvement in his own trios and quartets grew (**364**). Charles's own *The emperor* includes two episodes of free playing and polytonal writing, yet such restless modernism was based on the oldest of vehicles for improvisation, the chord structure of *Sweet Georgia Brown* – albeit drastically reharmonized. Between the somewhat jarring fanfares that announce each soloist, Monterose, Raney, Charles and Farmer in turn produce solos that are substantially shaped by the new chord substitutions.

Less frantic but equally absorbing is Charles's second contribution to the album, an arrangement that in its reharmonization of *Nature boy* suggests some of the dense orchestral colours of Gil Evans. It introduces moments of unexpected tension through fragments of 'outside' playing and Raney, as he did on *The emperor*, epitomizes the approach of each soloist on these sessions: they move within the carefully proscribed limits of the arranger's intentions, subservient to the needs of the moment rather than simply 'blowing'. On Evans's own arrangement of *You go to my head* he reveals his great gift for recomposition, realigning the melody into a personal nocturne that is less self-consciously experimental, his bisecting counter-melodies a stone's throw from his famous rising french-horn line on Miles Davis's *Summertime* (**382**).

In contrast, the least successful track is Charles's own *Green blues*, primarily through its surrender to dance-bandisms in its ensemble writing. Cutting away the introduction, tags and transitions, it is a basic 32-bar AABA structure that, while provoking a reliable solo from Monterose, sounds easily the most dated of the charts presented here. Amends were made, however, with *Blue greens*, a quartet track by Charles, Overton, Mingus and Shaughnessy recorded in November 1956. In any case, the value of *Tentet* today lies in the variety of musical approaches employed by Charles's small ensemble which, as Max Harrison has pointed out, 'anticipated procedures which would come to have central significance in later jazz'. [6] It also illustrates how the canonical method of jazz writing, of a 'masterpieces only' approach to history, has tended to conceal a broader picture of jazz as a work in progress. Whatever the shock announcing the new that periodically swept jazz, it was less the revelations of one great man than histories might have us believe. Such exemplars are usually claimed as figures around whom events can be constructed, but under closer examination they appear more as representatives of a gathering consensus.

The diversity of approach found on the *Tentet* sessions was taken further at Charles's next Atlantic date in October 1956. This produced *A word from Bird* and *Show time*, which initially appeared on an LP titled after the former track but are now added to this CD reissue of the *Tentet* material. Although fine solos from Stein, Charles and Art Farmer are included, the weightiest thoughts on *A word from Bird* occur in the many ensemble passages, which include some dramatic gestures at more than one tempo. This piece goes beyond anything from the January sessions apart from *Lydian M-1*. Stein's solo at first shadows some of the alto phrases on the original *Parker's mood* (**257**) and this acknowledges Charles's ultimate source of inspiration. *Show time*, composed by Bob Brookmeyer, is shorter, simpler, more conventional. Inventive solos by Charles, Stein, Art Farmer and Raney get artfully varied ensemble backing. S.N.

Hal McKusick

379 The Jazz Workshop

RCA-Victor (A) LPM1366, †RCA/Bluebird (Eu) ND86471

McKusick (alt); Barry Galbraith (g); Milt Hinton (bs); Osie Johnson (d); George Russell (d[1]). New York City, 3 March 1956.

Lydian lullaby (Russell) · *Ain't nothin' but a memory now* (Al Cohn) · *The day John Brown was hanged*[1] (Russell)

Art Farmer (tpt); Jimmy Cleveland (tbn); McKusick (alt); Gene Allen (bar); Galbraith (g); Jimmy Raney (rhythm g); Hinton (bs); Johnson (d); Russell (tambourine[2]). New York City, 3 April 1956.

Blues for Pablo[2] (Gil Evans) · *Alto cumulus* (Manny Albam) · *Jambangle* (Gil Evans)

Sol Schlinger (bar) replaces Allen. New York City, 4 April 1956.

Tommy Hawk (Johnny Mandel) · *Miss Clara* (Russell) · *One score and eight horns ago* (Jimmy Giuffre)

Farmer (tpt); McKusick (alt); Galbraith (g); Teddy Kotick (bs); Johnson (d). New York City, 31 December 1956.

Just leave it alone (Giuffre) · *The blues train* (Giuffre)

The CD reissue was titled *Jazz Workshop: The Arrangers.*

George Russell

380 The Jazz Workshop

RCA-Victor (A) LPM2534, †RCA/Bluebird (Eu) ND86467

Farmer (tpt); McKusick (alt); Bill Evans (p); Galbraith (g); Hinton (bs); Joe Harris (d). New York City, 31 March 1956.

Ezz-thetic · *Jack's blues* · *Ye hypocrite, ye Beelzebub* · *Livingstone, I presume*

Paul Motian (d) replaces Harris. New York City, 17 October 1956.
Round Johnny rondo · *Night sound* · *Concerto for Billy the Kid* · *Witch hunt*

Kotick (bs), Johnson (d[3]) replace Hinton, Motian; Russell (chromatic d[4]) added. New York City, 21 December 1956.
Fellow delegates[3,4] · *Ballad of Hix Blewitt* · *Knights of the steamtable* · *The sad sergeant*

Reaching New York during the ascendancy of bop, Russell reacted to the music of Parker and Gillespie with enthusiasm, but his first preserved work, *Cubana be/bop* (**315**), though it was a collaboration with Gillespie, already showed hints of a dissatisfaction with normal bop steersmanship which had not so evidently touched, for example, John Lewis's writing for Gillespie's large band. Like Gil Evans and John Carisi, who, with other innovative minds, had argued out their frustrations at the end of the 1940s (see **376**), Russell went on to create music which ran counter to the more popular modernism, allying himself to nonconformist movements along the penumbral rims of bop. It may be of more than coincidental significance that the first recording of *Ezz-thetic* was made in 1951 by a sextet of which four members were associates of Lennie Tristano – Konitz, Mosca, Bauer and Fishkin (**298**) – and that the 1949 *Bird in Igor's yard* (an engagement of Parkerism to borrowed stresses from *The Rite of Spring*, **293**) was realized by a DeFranco band including Konitz and a number of notable 'cool' Hermanites, one of whom, Earl Swope, had also played with Tristano.

Tristano in later life stressed the spontaneity of jazz creation, playing down the importance of composition; [7] and yet the nature of Russell's workshop productions (including the items for McKusick) appears to grow from an attitude to jazz not dissimilar to Tristano's, because the latter's early work gave considerable importance to formal cohesion as well as challenging the restriction of chordal sequences. Even the so-called 'free' improvisations recorded in 1949 (*Intuition* and *Digression*, **293**) are so clearly conditioned by preliminary experience of structural discipline that it seems hardly surprising that some early hearers believed them to be wholly composed; and they now sound anticipatory much more of the methods which Russell developed than of the later free jazz of Ornette Coleman and Cecil Taylor.

The recording dates of these two workshop collections interlock, and the earliest Russell pieces are by the McKusick group. *Lydian lullaby* starts and finishes with cyclic alto and guitar lines in rapid $^6/_8$, the sustaining vigour of the longer slow section depending upon the constantly shifting appositions of the two leading voices. The title contains a reference to the way in which Russell's thinking had progressed.

That one can enjoy these Russell pieces intelligently without having mastered the intricacies of his 'Lydian concept' is patent. That one can go on enjoying them, and finding their capacity for challenge undiminished, is doubtless due in some measure to the freedom which the exploration of modal bases had won for Russell and his men. Once linear variation had been led from chordal to scalar infrastructure and had discovered the 'escape hatches' provided by the odd steps characteristic of certain modes, greater daring was possible in movement between different key centres and the use of polytonality. The outworkings of Russell's theory might be fearsome in their complexity, especially when combined with his polyrhythmic innovations. In fact, the lullaby and the John Brown piece make fairly modest use of polytonality, the most startling instance occurring in the latter where alto lines, uttered simultaneously in what seems an alien key, lend to the guitar's recollections of the simple 'John Brown's body', an unexpected aspect of desolation, even of menace.

More often than not, Lydian disclosures are employed by Russell evocatively, rather than, as it were, academically, and he seems almost as keen as Ellington to convey mood and scene. The contrast of melancholy with bizarre cavorting in the John Brown drama even has a literary parallel, provided by the composer: 'The day John Brown was hanged,/ Some did a dance,/ Some wailed the blues . . .' – lines which, in themselves, indicate the spirit which always overrides the newer formalisms. However daringly convoluted and rhythmically diversified the music may become – as in *Ye hypocrite, ye Beelzebub* and *Livingstone, I presume* – Russell's love of black song and jazz dance traditions sounds paramount. His enthusiasm for the roots of jazz and his grasp of the advances already made by jazz creators within a diatonic framework save him from academicism, even though his respect for certain European modernisms is evident too. There are somersaulting figures in *Ezz-thetic* and elsewhere that sound, for all their outlandish fashioning, as vivacious and as sprucely suited as many a John Kirby ensemble variation, for Russell's irrepressible, self-guying sense of fun (later reflected in such titles as *Lydiot* and *Pan-daddy*) is frequently exhibited.

It is this jocosity as much as the adventurousness of his means that makes his music so defiant of verbal analysis. When one has pointed to the skilfully marshalled harmonies of *Miss Clara*, the twin effects of cohesion and independence in *Jack's blues* and *Night sound*, the thematic diversity of *Round Johnny rondo*, the polychromatic texture of *Witch hunt*, the swirling geometries of *Ye hypocrite* and *Livingstone, I presume* and the Bartókian percussiveness of *Fellow delegates*, one has really made little advance upon indicating nothing at all, so rich is the variety everywhere encountered. It would be as difficult to do justice to the imaginative aptitude of Russell's musicians, who move from reading to improvisation with an ease which belies the scores' fiendish requirements. It is not only the splendid agilities of Farmer, McKusick and Galbraith that are to be noted; there are also the contributions to colour and texture made variously by Cleveland, Allen, Schlinger and the rhythm teams.

Bill Evans is the most prominent and possibly the most memorable soloist, introducing that headlong percussive style of line-building that was to emerge again in the Brandeis *All about Rosie* (**478**). The impetus of this owes a lot to Bud Powell, yet the manner of it can be added to McKusick's Konitz-like sound for a strengthening of the Tristano link; and this will hardly be doubted by anyone who has also heard the older pianist's *Momentum* (Elektra-Musician [E] 96–0264–1), recorded in the same period. (Evans is the 'Billy' of *Concerto for Billy the Kid.*)

(All the recordings under consideration here are monaural, but the above CD reissue inserts previously unavailable alternative takes of *Ballad of Hix Blewitt* and *Concerto for Billy the Kid* in slightly sharp stereo. A heightened immediacy is noticeable, yet the burst of delighted laughter preserved at the end of the second alternative is, perhaps, as potent a token of the occasion's verve as is the added vividness of the sound.)

Russell is often, and for obvious reasons, bracketed with Gil Evans, so it is instructive to have two of Evans's very few actual compositions in the second McKusick session. These readings of *Blues for Pablo* and *Jambangle* will, understandably, be listened to comparatively, since Evans's own later realizations of these pieces have become better known. *Jambangle* is the less consequential, its 'traditionalism' looking back no further than swing and the boogie woogie craze, but its carefree amble is engaging. *Blues for Pablo,* in McKusick's version, suggests a dual comparison, for while its sound is rather intimate, set beside the echoing spaciousness of the famous 1957 Evans–Davis adaptation, McKusick's sounding of the flamenco holler soon to be appropriated by Davis has an eerie similarity to the wayward threnodies of *The day John Brown was hanged.*

Smaller interest attaches to McKusick's other scores. They are able enough as examples of contemporary group tendencies, though one feels that more might have been made of some of them. Giuffre's pieces are fairly typical of his writing at the time. *The blues train*'s evocations are perhaps a little over-obvious and the canonic effects in *One score* show better imagination. Galbraith shines vividly in Cohn's offering, and McKusick's solo in the same item shows how differently effected his lines are from the expiations of Konitz. Albam's *Alto cumulus* provides a good instance of the manner in which the octet uses its spread of timbres. Mandel's *Tommy Hawk* poses no challenges, yet Farmer's lines seem less free than his responses to Russell's firm demands. In several of these performances the use of the group's deeper resources recalls, superficially, the sound of the Davis nonet (**376**), making it difficult, at times, to persuade oneself that no tuba is present. E.T.

Kenny Graham

381a Kenny Graham's Afro-Cubists Vol. 1: Mango Walk

Esquire (E) 308

Jo Hunter (tpt); Graham (ten, comp, arr); Jack Honeybourne (p); Roy Plummer (g); Cliff Bell (bs); Dickie Devere (d); Leonado (Leonard Wilkins) (mar); Ginger Johnson (bon); Bob Caxton (con). London, 10 February 1951.

Mango walk · Pina colada

Ralph Dollimore (p) replaces Honeybourne; Johnson absent. London, 4 June 1951.

Chloe · Over the rainbow · Skylon · Dome of discovery

Stan Wasser (bs), Don Lawson (d), Jon Havana (mar) replace Bell, Devere, Leonado; Johnson returns. London, 13 February 1952.

Mike fright · Pip squeak · Kenny's jig · Cuban canon

Terry Brown (tpt), Bruce Swain (bs), Devere (d), Leonado (mar), Billy Olu Sholanke (bon), Tommy Oduesso (con) replace Hunter, Wasser, Lawson, Havana, Johnson, Caxton; Plummer absent. London, 8 October 1952.

Boom · Barbados · The king's horses · Peanut vendor

Hunter (tpt), Sammy Stokes (bs), Phil Seamen (d) replace Brown, Swain, Devere; Derek Humble, Pete King, Joe Temperley (ten), Oscar Birch (bar) added; Sholanke switches from bon to con; Leonado absent. London, 5 February 1953.

I'll remember April · Jump for Joe

381b Kenny Graham's Afro-Cubists Vol. 2 The Caribbean Suite

Esquire (E) 329

Same personnel and date as for the last two items.

Jump for Joe (alternative version) · *A night in Tunisia · Take the 'A' train*

Norman Fantham, Eddie Mordue, Wally Moffatt (ten), Joe Muddell (bs) replace Humble, King, Temperley, Stokes; Lati Pedro (mar) added. London, 29 April 1953.

Flamingo · Keni b'sindika · Afro-kadabra

Temperley (ten), Don Honeywill (bar), Dill Jones (p), Stokes (bs) replace Moffatt, Birch, Dollimore, Muddell; Judy Johnson (vcl, mar), Donaldo (bon), Plummer (g) added; Sholanke, Pedro absent. London, 23 October 1953.

Bongo chant · Saga boy · Tempo medio lento · Beguine

Mordue plays clt on[1]; Plummer absent. London, 27 October 1953.

Mango walk[1] · *Dance of the zombies · Wha' happen, sah? · Haitian ritual*

The Afro-Cubists . . . it sounds like a dutiful European echo of the Afro-Cuban, or cubop, venture by Parker (**266**), Gillespie (**315**) or particularly

Machito (**316**). Other apparent models suggest themselves, like the James Moody–Chano Pozo group that waxed for Blue Note in 1948 (*Cu-ba*, *Tin tin deo* etc.), and perhaps even Charlie Ventura's rather frightful 'Bop for the People' outfit. True, the Afro-Cubists did record Ventura's 1948 *Pina colada*, which then had wide currency via American Forces Network radio programmes. But Graham, even on his first session, turned it into something considerably more interesting than the composer's original 78-rpm version on the National label. In fact, rather as Joe Harriott some years later developed his own sort of free jazz independently of Ornette Coleman's initiatives (**404**), so Graham's music was the result of personal insights.

During the years immediately after World War II he made a living performing in dance bands, and these, in Britain at least, used to devote part of each evening to Latin American dances. Most of the band left the stage for this, but Graham, having few opportunities for improvisation, would stay and quietly play jazz along with the maracas, congas etc. These were probably reproducing no very authentic echo of the music of the Caribbean archipelago, much of which had more of Africa in it than survived in the United States. Yet Graham found that his kind of post-Minton's phrasing accommodated well to the patterns of Latin American percussion, which scarcely was surprising in view of the polyrhythmic nature of bop. He decided to form a band to develop his discoveries and to further his ambitions as a composer and arranger.

Although the fact is nowhere hinted at by the conspicuously brief Graham entry in *The New Grove Dictionary of Jazz* – hastily scribbled by someone ignorant of his entire output – he founded what almost certainly was the first regular working British jazz group, apart from the Johnny Dankworth Seven, with a real claim to originality in a modern idiom. It lasted for slightly less than two years, 1951–2, later reforming for Esquire recording sessions, a few club dates, an occasional broadcast. The present writer first heard the Afro-Cubists in 1951, when they opened Studio 51, a club which in the early 1950s became the major London venue for modern jazz (even if the all-knowing *Grove* claims it was 'opened around 1956 by Ken Colyer' [*sic*!])

Graham's contacts in London's West Indian community led him to several outstanding rhythm players, some of whom were in fact Africans who had come to Britain with various dancing troupes. The contributions of such musicians combined with first Devere's and then Seamen's bop drumming – then exceptional by European standards – not only provided Graham with a rhythm section livelier than any other on the UK scene of that time but also with rhythmic counterpoint as meaningfully complex as almost anything heard on recordings by the American boppers with Machito mentioned under **316**. Indeed, the personnel details suggest the band would be rhythm-heavy and the fact that it rarely was, either on records or in person, is a tribute not only to the players but also to Graham's skills in composing, arranging, and in the less easily defined craft of bandleading.

All the writing was of course by him, and along with his own original pieces he adopted some excellent jazz themes by others, these including choices particularly apt in relation to what the band was aiming to do, such as Parker's *Barbados* and Gillespie's *A night in Tunisia.* Also quite suitable were Gene Roland's *Jump for Joe,* Strayhorn's *Take the 'A' train* and just one theme by Dollimore, a good one, *Dome of discovery.* Unavoidably there was a scattering of Tin Pan Alley products like *Over the rainbow, Flamingo* and one seemingly jazz-proof item, *The king's horses.* Even here, though, there was no feeling of Latin American percussion being merely grafted on to a jazz front line, or vice versa.

The two 1951 sessions were rather badly recorded, [8] yet *Mango walk* is otherwise a briefly effective sampling of the band's characteristic sounds and textures, with pithy tenor and trumpet solos. *Pina colada* is the first of several recordings with a percussion-only interlude, such passages being essentially studies in cross-rhythms. Echoes of the bop ensemble style are recognizable in what Hunter and Graham play together but they are transformed by the rhythm and to a lesser extent by Plummer's contributions. The guitar did not have much of a place in post-Christian bop, yet it did in Tristano's nonconformist version of that music, and Plummer had clearly listened to Billy Bauer.

Further transformations took place at the next session, for which Dollimore, a much stronger jazz player, took over at the piano. *Chloe* and *Over the rainbow* were thoroughly, and boppishly, recast by Graham and the former especially was firmly separated from its phoney exoticism. Both offer the identical sequence of solos – guitar, tenor, trumpet, piano – but with *Chloe* a further 32 bars are given to four-bar exchanges between Graham, Hunter and a fiercely inventive Devere. The two original themes, Dollimore's *Dome of discovery* and the leader's *Skylon,* were named after the two most striking temporary buildings on the London site of the Festival of Britain in 1951. The *Dome* has a 16-bar nonrepeating theme finally shifting from $4/4$ to $3/4$. Solos are of 32 bars length, in $4/4$ yet introduced in each case by four bars of $3/4$ taken from the end of the theme. *Skylon* has a comparable device with its four-bar theme over $12/8$ rhythm. Here the solos are 16 bars each, with the theme restated before each solo, and, as in *Kenny's jig* and *Keni b'sindika,* a kind of rondo effect is produced which signifies Graham's desire both to unify each performance and to mitigate the unthinking theme-solos-theme routine of so much jazz. In both *Skylon* and *Dome of discovery,* too, there is no mere repeat of the theme at the close but an ensemble coda based partly on new ideas.

Best of the *Dome* solos is its composer's, reconciling elements of Powell and Tristano, whereas Hunter does best on *Skylon.* Scarcely reflecting his introverted personality, the latter's clear, ringing tone and agile phrasing clearly took Gillespie as their model, yet Hunter had plenty of thoughts of his own and noticeably made no attempt at imitation on Gillespie's *A night in Tunisia*. These and most of the subsequent performances were obviously curtailed by 78-rpm limitations, yet they still give an idea of the assertive fire with which the band played at its public engagements.

The next session was an especially fine one in terms of ensemble performance and highly confident solos giving expression to various aspects of the Afro-Cubists' idiom, with Graham providing three strongly characterized themes plus one joke. And we can now hear the guitar properly. Admittedly the three-part counterpoint of *Cuban canon* is short-lived, as is the way of such things in jazz, yet there is a sequence of steadily inventive solos climaxed by fours between Graham, Hunter and the drummer; and when the canon returns at the close it seems no anticlimax. *Kenny's jig* turns out to be the *Kerry dance*, presumably sanctified for jazz use by Tatum's frequent quotations and here boppishly rephrased.

Next came the single date without Hunter, who is sorely missed. Charles Trenet's *Boom* was an eccentric choice, *Barbados* an almost inevitable one, yet Brown is in neither case adequate and further tension is let out of the latter by a dull bass solo. This is not a successful performance, and nor is *Peanut vendor*. Yet *The king's horses* works despite all expectations. A lugubrious opening fanfare and military drumming suggest the worst, but Graham's rephrasing of the leaden melody changes its character with disconcerting completeness, and admirable solos by him and Dollimore follow.

By the 1953 dates the Afro-Cubists had been forced to disband, yet this meant that Graham had more time to devote to his composing. As much was symbolized by his expansion of the front line to six instruments, although these added no fresh individual voices and the solos still came from Hunter, Dollimore and the leader. The February 1953 titles were notably less Afro-Cubist than the rest and the conga drumming counts for little during *I'll remember April*, an excellent Graham vehicle. Sholanke is more evident in *Jump for Joe*, however, and it is satisfying to listen to Hunter soloing against rich saxophone harmonies. Though *A night in Tunisia* was a natural choice, its presentation is a considerable revision of bop rhythmic practice. Surprising also is *Take the 'A' train*, which is divested of what its composer termed 'the Ellington effect'. Indeed the start and finish are quite original, signalling that this train is no happy-go-lucky local, and it is a pity another bass solo causes the music to sag between Graham's and Hunter's fine passages.

Again, the treatment of *Flamingo* has no obvious model, and this is true also of the saxophone writing in general, which owes nothing to Herman's 'four brothers' methods (**312**). All the remaining compositions are by Graham, starting with *Keni b'sindika*, which title sounds vaguely

African. In fact Brian Davis's sleeve note tells us it is back-slang for cannabis, and that this had to be changed – to ginger beer! – for the purposes of a broadcast for the then highly moral BBC. Also recorded at this session was *Afro-kadabra*, Graham's longest composition thus far and initially issued as one side of a 10-inch LP. It has a questioning, melancholy opening from the tenor which is supported by the other saxophones. Hunter presents the same idea in a different way and he is joined by Graham. Next the rhythm section is added, followed by the saxophones with a repeated figure which sounds quite threatening. Over this trumpet and tenor imitate one another and then follow outstanding solos from each.

A real sense of occasion is evident and both Graham and Hunter are at their absolute best in what are perhaps the most inspired improvisations they ever recorded. There are sustained chords by the saxophones alone, and then the rhythm section joins them, this leading to another trumpet and tenor duet very different in mood from the first. Next come brief gestures by the trumpet-led ensemble which simplify into isolated chords before a long interlude for percussion alone which at last fades. A brief gesture by the horns restarts the rhythm section, which this time dialogues with the horns before again fading. This formal scheme is not exactly ambitious even for a piece lasting for less than ten minutes, yet the atmosphere is well sustained.

The fact remains, however, that Graham, like some far greater musicians such as Ellington, was at his most inventive with even shorter movements such as those of his *Caribbean Suite*, recorded at the last two dates. Even so, the ideas of *Mango walk* deserved to be extended to greater length than they are here or in the 1951 version, although this is a much superior performance. The saxophones are especially well employed throughout this suite, in *Saga boy, Beguine* and the *Zombies* piece above all. This last is memorable both for its melody and its suggestion of menace. Indeed both here and in *Wha' happen, sah?* Graham's orchestration is particularly inventive and personal, and in the latter both he and Hunter again solo at their best. Effective also is the wordless voice threading its way through the aggressive rhythm section textures and the horns' declarations in *Tempo medio lento*. A vehicle for Plummer, *Beguine* is perhaps the Graham melody which is hardest to forget, and the guitar murmurs it across rich ensemble textures. *Haitian ritual* is a memorable expression of the drama that is never far below the surface of this kind of music and it makes a fitting end.

In composing this work, which lasts a fraction over 23 minutes, Graham faced a considerable test and one that he passed with much credit. Each movement has its own character yet all eight are clearly related, and not just because of the percussion instruments and the continuity of colours and rhythmic formulas associated with them. Plenty of more famous jazz musicians have achieved less. On Esquire's original

10-inch LP the movements were linked by a rather unfortunate spoken narration from Dennis Preston, but that has been eliminated from the above version.

Though once briefly attracting attention at a journalistic level, Graham, like Hunter, Dollimore and Devere, is scarcely remembered now, the sole evidence of his bandleading venture being the survival of a few long-deleted LPs. He plays very well on most of these recordings. Quite apart from the special case of *Afro-kadabra*, his is the best of the four solos on *Over the rainbow*, and listen to his aggressive contribution to *Bongo chant*, not to mention *The king's horses*, *Take the 'A' train* and the gentler *Flamingo* and *I'll remember April.* Yet the tenor was never his strongest suit. After absorbing the predictable early influences of Hawkins, Webster and Chew Berry, he settled into what may be termed Wardell Gray's extension of the Lester Young style. Graham was consistently more creative in his composing, as these recordings demonstrate. He wrote arrangements for Ted Heath and Humphrey Lyttelton, and produced a certain amount of film music. But the uncomprehending *Grove* entry and Graham's being ignored by other reference works tell their own story, and it is no small criticism of the jazz world that he got so few chances in later years. M.H.

Miles Davis–Gil Evans

382 Porgy and Bess

†Columbia (E) CK65141

Davis (tpt, fl h); Ernie Royal, Johnny Coles, Bernie Glow, Louis Mucci (tpt); Joe Bennett, Frank Rehak, Jimmy Cleveland (tbn); Dick Hixon (bs tbn); Willie Ruff, Julius Watkins, Gunther Schuller (fr h); Bill Barber (tu); Cannonball Adderley (alt); Phil Bodner, Romeo Penque (fl); Danny Bank (bs clt); Paul Chambers (bs); Philly Joe Jones (d); Evans (arr, cond). New York City, 22 July 1958.

My man's gone now · *Gone, gone, gone*

Jimmy Cobb (d) replaces Jones. New York City, 29 July 1958.

Here come de Honey Man · *Bess, you is my woman now* · *It ain't necessarily so* · *Fisherman, strawberry and devil crab*

Jerome Richardson (fl) replaces Bodner. New York City, 4 August 1958.

Prayer (Oh Doctor Jesus) · *Bess, oh where's my Bess?* · *Buzzard song*

Same personnel. New York City, 14 August 1958.

Summertime · *There's a boat that's leaving soon for New York* · *I loves you, Porgy*

Central in the great trilogy of Davis–Evans suites, *Porgy and Bess* seems rather more comprehensively a celebration of Davis's expressive talents than *Miles Ahead* and is, together with that precedent, much more wholeheartedly a jazz exercise than *Sketches of Spain.* Their complete 1957–62 Columbia studio recordings, with many alternative takes, are on †Columbia [A] 67397-S1, a set of six CDs. The startling, brassy big-city yell which opens this treatment of Gershwin's music and introduces *The buzzard song* signals a realism that will be as destructive of mere nostalgia as the seductive visions of New York, sardonically interposed in the opera, were destructive of the idyll of Catfish Row. The realism is that of jazz itself, a spirit which Gershwin never fully imbibed; and jazz is, indefeasibly, big-city music. Here, even the recollections of rural love and piety have their disturbing edge of irony, never letting tenderness escape entirely unmocked.

It is true that Gershwin's romanticism could be hard-edged, but just how differently Evans and Davis draw out the dramatic implications of his music is instanced by *Summertime*, where the striding tempo never acknowledges that the original aria was a lullaby, and the harmonic support to Davis's stark solo dismisses – as does that to *Bess, you is my woman now* – all memory of the composer's predictable constructions. Similarly the deeply solemn chords, drifting, slowing, which accompany Davis in the atemporal *Gone, gone, gone* have nothing of yearning in them, only stern-faced resignation. Even *Prayer* sounds a tone of cynicism, the solo horn full of blues, the snatching brass comments and writhing woodwind forming a cold ascending chant. In *Bess, oh where's my Bess?* and *My man's gone now* the phases of ensemble sound are multifold, not only in the shifting exploits of instrumental colouration but also in unpredictable flirtations with tempo change. The increasing tentativeness of *Bess* finds strange resolution in an organum cadence; *My man's gone* succeeds Davis's breathy rehearsal of black song styles with bursts of exultant brass, yet ends in mazy inconclusiveness.

So divergent is all this from Gershwin's own musical conception – appropriate as that may have been to his purpose – that the judgement passed upon some of Evans's Thornhill scores, to wit 'We find the craft of dance band arranging transformed virtually into an art of recomposition', may seem apposite here, though it is a little too formal in its implications since improvisation is as important to these transmutations as is writing. [9] Sophisticated and demanding as much of Evans's scoring may be, its underlying motive, closely linked to the soloist's peculiar strain of inventiveness, is really no different from the motive of any genuine jazz reinterpretation. Maybe 'imagined anew,' a clause used by Stravinsky in recalling his instrumental translations of Gesualdo madrigals, is better than 'recomposed'. [10] At all events, the sense of experiment, even the alleged difficulties caused for some participants by the writing and directing procedures, far from detracting from the marvel of this overall achievement, actually heighten the realization that here is a jazz event of exceptional significance. The music, enlivened by variant stresses of urgency, gathers its own special identity.

In *It ain't necessarily so* interest centres on Davis's intricate, swinging improvising, the orchestration seeming designed in part to frame expressions developed in the Davis small groups of immediately preceding times. The activities of Cobb and Chambers obviously assist this effect, which is even more marked during *Summertime*. *Gone*, apparently a friendly intruder lacking clear Gershwin credentials, has brilliant episodes of big-band jazz and gliding dissonances led by the flugelhorn. It gives prominence to Philly Joe Jones, who meshes so closely into Davis's fast solo that he almost transforms it into a duet.

The mood typified by the reticent ensemble and muted soliloquy of *I loves you, Porgy* and the dreamy exhalations of *Fisherman, strawberry and devil crab* shows that the cloudiness which, by 1948, had induced boredom in Evans (see **375**) could again have its uses when combined with the astringencies of an inspired soloist. It may be that this sort of ambivalence, inwardly reflected in several of Davis's *adagio* statements, carries us closer to the soul of the opera than does anything else in this suite. Even though the good-time bounce of *There's a boat that's leaving soon for New York* eventually overtakes, with its metropolitan insolence, the harrowed poetry of Catfish Row, the last word is a questioning, quiet chord fading into a silence of uncertainty. E.T.

Gil Evans

383 Out of the Cool

†Impulse (A) IMP11862

John Coles, Phil Sunkel (tpt); Jimmy Knepper, Keg Johnson, Tony Studd (tbn); Bill Barber (tu); Ed Caine (alt, fl, picc); Budd Johnson (ten, sop); Bob Tricario (bsn, fl); Evans (p, arr); Ray Crawford (g); Ron Carter (bs); Elvin Jones, Charlie Persip (d, perc). New York City, 18 November 1960.
Where flamingos fly · Sunken treasure

Same personnel. New York City, 30 November 1960.
Stratusphunk · Sister Sadie

Same except Ray Beckstein (alt, fl, picc) replaces Caine. New York City, 10 December 1960.
La Nevada

Same personnel. New York City, 15 December 1960.
Bilbao song

When Helen Merrill recorded *Dream of You* (†EmArcy [J] EJD-3026) in June 1956, she insisted on Evans doing the arrangements. The producer Bob Shad strongly resisted the idea, not because Evans's talent or imagination were in dispute, but because of his reputation in other respects. 'Gil was very, very slow in the studio,' Miss Merrill explained, 'costs would go up enormously because Gil would often still be working on his arrangements and rehearsing the band on studio time.' [11] She insisted on Evans, however, and in the end Shad relented, albeit predicting a very expensive recording session. He was right, which further harmed Evans's reputation among recording-company executives.

Although this is seldom commented upon, Evans had worked with vocalists throughout his career; with Skinnay Ennis as early as 1938, later contributing to the Bing Crosby radio show. And in mid-1948, when the Claude Thornhill band broke up, he had gone on the road with Peggy Lee. With Miss Merrill, he produced wonderful little cameos of his art and perhaps here, rather than on **466** from two years later, does he intimate the direction of *Out of the Cool*, recorded incidentally ten months after *Sketches of Spain* with Miles Davis.

Miss Merrill selected all but two of the songs for *Dream of You*, Evans suggesting *I've never seen* and *Where flamingos fly*. The latter reappears on the record detailed above four years later and it is interesting to compare the two versions of John Benson Brooks's theme, whose four-note ascending riff is borrowed from Prokofiev's *Romeo and Juliet*. Clearly the instrumental version owes much to the original vocal one. Although the tempo is slower, much of Evans's detail is retained, such as the percussive effects in the release, the use of woodwinds to provide the haunting backdrop and the repeated piano *ostinato*. Much also has been refined and simplified, creating perhaps the most haunting of all the *Out of the Cool* tracks with Knepper's trombone taking the 'vocal' role. Playing with the minimum of embellishment, it is his stark, languid exposition of the melody against Evans's shimmering heat haze that remains in the memory.

The band which Evans assembled for these dates had just played six weeks together at New York's Jazz Gallery, and although Evans recalled that they subsequently recorded *Out of the Cool* in 'one afternoon', [12] the problems of trading individual creativity against commercial expediency remained, since the album was actually completed over four sessions, the two December dates yielding just one completed take each. For cost-conscious recording companies, Evans's failure to stay within budget meant that his discography is remarkably small for such an imaginative rethinker of orchestral jazz. Indeed it was only his phoning Creed Taylor to say he was in need of work that led, via an album of arrangements written for the vocalist Astrud Gilberto, to *The Individualism of Gil Evans* (†Verve [A] 833 804–2), which, taken with the above record, represents the pinnacle of his work under his own name.

La Nevada is based on a vamp, opening with a piano *ostinato* with the former Ahmad Jamal guitarist Crawford's comping taking a central role. Harmon-muted trumpets enter briefly with a sustained four-bar phrase based on three notes before the piano outlines a new four-bar phrase which is taken up by the trombones and then embellished by the ensemble, with woodwinds doubling the melody three octaves higher. Coles was a Miles Davis-influenced trumpeter and an Evans favourite, whose appearances on record with him began in the late 1950s (**460**) and continued to 1971's *Where Flamingos Fly* (†A&M [A] CD0831), and he takes the first of the extended solos that follow. His soft, round tone was strongly evocative of Davis's flugelhorn on *Miles Ahead* (†CBS/Sony [J] 32DP511), perhaps the most important of all the Davis–Evans collaborations. Coles's presence is a reminder of one commentator's wry assertion that everything Evans wrote was with Miles Davis in mind.

Studd, on a more optimistic note against a background coalition of bacchanalian trombone *glissandos* and stabbing harmon-muted trumpets, creates little melodic motifs which are developed and expanded before Johnson, in no-nonsense mood, plunges into an exposition of his swing-era roots at the expense of the inherent mood of the piece. It is left to Carter and Crawford to reconstruct the original disposition of the piece with gentle ellipses and paraphrases of the original theme during their solos. Crawford, often capable of refreshing originality, is a forgotten figure today but in 1961 before he moved to the West Coast, disenchanted with his career, he recorded *Smooth Groove* (†Candid [A] CCD79028) which confirmed why both Jamal and Evans regarded his talent so highly. As his solo closes, the ensemble returns for a brief reprise of the four-bar theme and with it the realization that a minimum of material has been marshalled to maximum effect.

Bilbao is a natural extension of the floating clouds of sound that were so much a part of the Thornhill orchestra. Kurt Weill's theme moves slowly into view played by unison trumpet, flute and saxophones under a soprano lead, bending tones to give a timeless, haunting feel, something that is reinforced by the cadence-free ending that suggests the piece carries on indefinitely in the ether. The theme, melodically neutral in that it is a series of repeated motifs, is less important than the mood created, first by the bass, then by the ensemble. Evans's writing, although harmonically rich, is very spare because there is hardly any counterpoint, just a theme statement and a reiteration by the ensemble that on the last repeat is modified by sustained saxophone tones, an effect widely imitated by other arrangers.

Russell's *Stratusphunk* is a 12-bar blues where the interval of a sixth predominates in the theme's construction in the way that it does in, for example, Monk's *Mysterioso* (**292**). After a discordant brass fanfare, the bass trombone outlines a walking bass line and as the contrabass takes over, the saxophones slap-tongue the theme. This is taken up by harmon-muted trumpets against the return of the bass trombone doubling the walking bass line with the acoustic bass. Crawford contributes a typically well-thought-out solo, refusing to take up the implied double-time gauntlet thrown down by the rhythm section. The ensemble gradually builds in accompaniment using brass voicings with a flute lead that anticipate figures used by Evans on another Russell blues, *Blues in orbit*. [13] As the ensemble density suddenly thins, Crawford and the trombones improvise textures against the ensemble riffs which build to a climax, resolved by a short solo by Coles before the theme is passed around the sections and the ensemble reprise the introductory figures.

Sunken treasure is, like *Bilbao*, a mood piece featuring Coles in a role that again evokes the Evans–Davis collaborations. In it, Evans gives his ensemble a brief passage which is repeated over and over until cued, this being another example of using a minimum of orchestration to maximum effect.

Horace Silver's *Sister Sadie* is something of an anomaly in the context of these sessions, looking back to Evans's **460**. It was withheld from the original and subsequent album reissues, appearing on LP only in 1978; this reissue marks its first time on CD. A hard-blowing cover of Silver's simple combo arrangement, it makes an uneasy companion to these orchestral tone poems whose significance lies in the balance between the written and the improvised. While the solos are central to Evans's thinking, the textures with which they are surrounded are frequently fluid enough to be moulded by the creative moment. Sometimes he gives his musicians little more than a melodic snippet to construct engaging and frequently profound edifices. *La Nevada*, for example, is erected from the leanest of written material, but under Evans's careful stewardship a major performance emerges. Such a creation, taking up a full day's studio time, was painstakingly worked up to the horror of budget-conscious recording executives looking for a greater return for a day's work than one tune. It remains ironic that within a few years, pop and rock groups often spent as much as a year in a recording studio to produce albums that today are forgotten. In contrast, Evans could produce something imperishable in a single day. S.N.

Cecil Taylor

384 The World of Cecil Taylor
Candid (A) 9006, †Candid (A) CCD79006

Archie Shepp (ten[1]); Taylor (p); Buell Neidlinger (bs); Dennis Charles (d). New York City, 19 November 1960.
Air[1] · *This nearly was mine* · *Port of call* · *E.B.* · *Lazy afternoon*[1]

'Gil Evans'

385 Into the Hot
MCA/Impulse (A) 29034, †MCA/Impulse (A) MCAD39104

John Carisi (tpt, comp); Doc Severinson (tpt); Urbie Green (tbn); Jim Buffington (fr h); Harvey Philips (tu); Phil Woods, Gene Quill (alt); Eddie Costa (p, vib); Barry Galbraith (g); Milt Hinton (bs); Osie Johnson (d). New York City, 14 September 1961.
Angkor Wat

Clark Terry (tpt), Bob Brookmeyer (v-tbn), Art Davis (bs) replace Severinson, Buffington, Hinton. New York City, 6 October 1961.
Barry's tune

Ted Curson (tpt); Roswell Rudd (tbn); Jimmy Lyons (alt); Shepp (ten); Taylor (p); Henry Grimes (bs); Sunny Murray (d). New York City, 10 October 1961.
Pots · Bulbs · Mixed

As for 6 October except that Joe Wilder (tpt) replaces Terry. New York City, 31 October 1961.
Moon Taj

Taylor's recordings, up to and including these 1960–1 dates, furnish a persuasive impression of a musician of original vision gathering resources into style, influences into identity, idiosyncrasies into personality. The resources were finely developed when he emerged as a leader, informed by jazz experience and meticulous academic study. The early pianistic influences were various, yet never so obtrusive in relation to his own inventive gifts as to render his playing greatly dependent. The idiosyncrasies laced the concoctions of his mid-1950s sessions in ways that were, perhaps, merely startling; but here, developed and integrated, they have become appropriate ingredients of a strongly fermented brew which sometimes explodes with demoniacal force.

Air opens with a savage drum tattoo followed by fraught piano chords even more vehemently struck. As the atemporal prologue continues, Taylor demonstrates a thoroughly personal executive device in which notes are hit abruptly and yet with a light pedal sustenance, an effect of naïveté, even of hesitancy, which is clearly intentional – a ruminative contrast to his fiery *sforzando* complexities. There was little of either rumination or conflagration in the music of his 1957 Newport Festival appearance (Verve [A] MGV8238, Columbia [E] 33CX10102), though that had moved further than the 1956 *Jazz Advance* (†EMI/Blue Note [E] CDP784 462–2) towards disjunctiveness. In the Newport *Johnny come lately* and *Nona's blues* the influence of an admired Horace Silver manner is strong, the innovations being mainly harmonic – chords nudged at the outskirts of key – and, in the long and intricate layout of *Tune 2*, thematic. The linear improvising there cannot quite prepare the ear for the tumbling and leaping treble torrents challenging conventional rhythmic processes in *Air* and virtually overturning them in the ferocity of *E.B.*, a set piece for Taylor's devotion to percussiveness – the piano as drum choir.

The vocabulary of this pianist's work in both the Candid and Impulse sessions, shaped as it all is by his uninhibited approach to tonality, is taken largely from the lexicon of jazz. There is as much of native instinct as of intellect in his playing. Not for him the academic avenues to atonality; and, indeed, though he may frequently achieve de facto atonality, he has insisted that his musical thought is tonal – an approach similar to Dolphy's but, with pianistic and ensemble means, leading to much more diversified results. Diversity required discipline. The close interrelation of pianist and drummer, beautifully achieved during *Port of call*, typifies the kind of cooperation Taylor has from both Charles and Neidlinger, and shows how vigorously their ideas had grown along with his. Charles, for most of the faster episodes, swings into a Blakey-prompted momentum against which Taylor pits his dislocations of rhythm; but the exciting, vivid, light stickwork which complements the brittle keyboard filaments in *Air* is only one of several suggestions that Charles was, at this stage, a more suitable drummer for Taylor than the younger Sunny Murray, soon to become a Taylor regular. Neidlinger is well attuned to the leader's imagination, and as apt for Taylor as Charlie Haden was for Ornette Coleman. Of the wind players, Shepp, who generally is allowed to follow his own stylistic star, is certainly the most interesting, echoing Coltrane in his gliding elisions and heeding Coleman in the forming of his linear notions. The horns play a more subordinate role on the Impulse date, and in both sessions it is Taylor's vision that illuminates most of what happens.

By now, whatever may have applied earlier, not much can be credited to extraneous influence. He transforms a few blues clichés in *Port of call*, can be as earthy as barrelhouse during *Lazy afternoon*, and the recognizable bits of *This nearly was mine* are coaxed on by mannerisms for which he would quite happily hold Brubeck responsible. The repetitive treble tumblings may recall Mal Waldron's terrier-with-rat methods or Coltrane's nimbler scalar weft, but their obliquities are personally attained, differently employed. The amazing independence of right and left hands makes possible frequent bitonal, birhythmic products. Against his concern for overall structure and unity of expression, there is a sense of continuum, as if the music could end anywhere or never end at all. As with the diffidently rocking phrase that ends both *Port of call* and *Pots*, conclusion usually depends upon Taylor's finding of some fortuitous aptness in the continuum at which to subside without fuss.

Given Taylor's (not original) notion of the piano as a potential orchestra, and given his consequent methods, his more recent successes as a monolithically powerful solo star have come as no surprise. In terms of ensemble cooperation the best examples here are probably *Lazy afternoon*, where the evocative half-steps of the melody prompt a treatment very different from that imposed on the Kern standard and Shepp's part is closely integrated; and the programmatic *Mixed*.

(The five items of the 1960 Candid issue are reasonably representative of the period. A boxed set – (*The Complete Candid Recordings of Cecil Taylor and Buell Neidlinger*, †Mosaic [A] MD4–127) – includes this material and expands it by adding previously issued titles from the same date and unissued and formerly available things from two other Candid releases, *Cecil Taylor All-Stars* and *New York R & B*, taking in a further October 1960 session plus dates in January 1961 with various alternative versions included. The third of the Candid items involves a group of musicians comparable to that Taylor uses for *Into the Hot.* In this present volume **418–20** jointly deal with issues from the period 1973–81.)

Carisi's jazz career had a fugitive air. With big-band experience and a writing ability applicable to several types of music, he admired the orchestral gifts of Gil Evans, Gerry Mulligan and George Russell. He collaborated with the first two on the Davis nonet repertoire, producing in 1949 one of the gems of that enterprise, the Dorian blues *Israel* (**376**). In the same year he wrote *Lestorian mode* for a Brew Moore septet which included Mulligan. In 1956 he recorded versions of *Israel, Lesterian mode, Barry's tune, Hip's* and *Springsville* (this last a year before it was recorded by Evans and Davis); and these may be heard on †RCA/Bluebird (E) ND86471.

With the concentrated brilliance of the Davis *Israel* in memory, one approached these works of Carisi's with keen expectations. Yet perhaps with a paucity of Carisi material it turns out that *Israel* – and the conceptually relative *Lestorian mode* – have loomed too large as touchstones. The works considered here are differently conceived and must make their own impression. There is advanced musical thought in *Moon Taj* and *Angkor Wat,* and their hints at the breadth of Carisi's thought are tantalizing. Modal ideas may still be heard, integrally used towards the end of *Angkor Wat,* and incidentally elsewhere as servants of mood. The arrangement of *Barry's tune* is a skilful rejuvenation of swing, similar in impetus to *Springsville* but without the latter's minatory shadows. The mood is infectious and Galbraith plays beautifully. Canonic patterns in the theme statement nod in Russell's direction.

It denotes integrity of purpose that, though the two other Carisi pieces were inspired by an Oriental cultural tour, they employ no Eastern musical effects, mock or genuine. *Moon Taj* begins with a jazz-inflected exploitation of *Klangfarbenmelodie* technique, and this seems a clear indication that the composer's intentions move beyond modalism in the direction of serialism. And yet the cast of the music also suggests a mild tug-of-war between tonal and atonal elements. Even though one ends up with the feeling that tonality has prevailed, there seems sufficient evidence that Carisi's conception springs essentially from things learned from the serialist Stefan Wolpe concurrently with his work for Moore and Davis. An intriguing conjunction of things determines the outward character; atonalism makes a pact with a romanticism gained through an Evans-like use of unresolved, or only partially resolved, dissonance warmed by brilliantly blended instrumental timbres.

The bouncier tempo of *Angkor Wat* (named for ruined temples in the Cambodian jungle) and its more liberal deployment of solo improvisation cheat anticipations of exoticism. There is a two-bar phrase used hypnotically under Green's solo and skewed slightly to bitonal effect as piano and guitar devise a kind of duet; but only in the closing bars does the music draw near to that unifying of disparities which was so compelling in *Israel* and renders *Moon Taj*, along with *Angkor Wat*, the finest of what little music we had from Carisi.

It will be clear that although there was a musical relationship between Carisi and Gil Evans, and though the title of the LP (and subsequent CD) of music by Taylor and Carisi obviously derives from Evans's *Out of the Cool* (**383**), the latter was not directly involved with any of these performances. Simply, there was a typical record-company muddle too complicated to explain here whereby the record sleeve, with the title and Evans's name and picture on it, was printed ahead of the music being recorded. E.T.

Bob Cooper

386 Shifting Winds

Capitol (A) T613, Affinity (E) AFF59

Stu Williamson (tpt, v-tbn); Bob Enevoldsen (v-tbn, bs clt, ten); Bud Shank (fl, alt, ten); Jimmy Giuffre (clt, ten, bar); Cooper (ob, eng h, ten); Claude Williamson (p); Max Bennett (bs); Stan Levey (d). Los Angeles, 26 April 1955.

Strike up the band · Hot boy · Sunset · It don't mean a thing

John Graas (fr h), Joe Mondragon (bs), Shelly Manne (d) replace Stu Williamson, Bennett, Levey. Los Angeles, 13 June 1955.

It's de-lovely · Deep in a dream · Hallelujah · Drawing lines

Ralph Peña (bs) replaces Mondragon. Los Angeles, 14 June 1955.

Round about midnight · Tongue twister · All or nothing at all

Cooper's resource as a composer and arranger has led to his receiving little attention as a soloist, yet these sessions prove, if indirectly, how closely the two sides of his activity could be related. That his writing should have taken precedence is not surprising if we recall the amount he did over several decades, under such a wide variety of circumstances and in association with such diverse musicians. Yet despite the size of his output he always, except in a few merely banausic commercial tasks, had something freshly his own to contribute. To gain a proper idea of Cooper's achievement as a composer and arranger is hard because so many of his pieces were recorded under the names of others. Consider, though, such well-buried treasure as *Jazz Structures*, his LP-long suite (Philips [A] PHS600–012) issued under Howard Rumsey's aegis, the *Divertimento for Brass and Percussion* done for a 10-inch Shelly Manne disc (Contemporary [A] C2511, Vogue [E] LDC143), or the several ingenious scores he provided for the *Bud Shank and Three Trombones* date (Pacific Jazz [A] LP14, Vogue [E] LAE12143).

For another sort of contrast try *Double or Nothing* (Liberty [A] LRP3045), briefly circulated under Rumsey's name. For this Charlie Persip led a quintet from Gillespie's band which joined in various combinations with the Lighthouse outfit. It is instructive to hear Benny

Golson and Cooper improvise side by side in *Moto* and *Wildwood*, the former's ideas descending from Coleman Hawkins via Don Byas, the latter's arising from Lester Young. Both swing strongly, blending new thoughts with established practice, and as a soloist Cooper is of the same ilk as Zoot Sims, Al Cohn, Brew Moore. In parallel with this, however, his writing for these 1955 sessions, nearly all of which finds him at his most inventive, extends into another dimension some of his great mentor's aesthetic innovations. It can scarcely be coincidental that as a tenor saxophonist Cooper is idiomatically closest to Young on *Deep in a dream*, where the pastel tones of his score convey real tenderness, intensifying the mood of the song which is this music's starting point. French horn and bass clarinet more than pull their weight, and although writing like this is remote from anything we normally would associate with Young, the character of his slowest ballad performances is such that it is not quite idle to wonder how he might have responded to such a setting, which, like several of the other pieces here, speculates more formally on some of the meanings of his improvisational discoveries.

Following a respectable jazz tradition, though, Cooper seldom goes along with the spirit of his given material to quite that extent. This is not just a matter of such things as his interesting reharmonization of *It's de-lovely*, which has unusual ensemble textures, but of the way he divests the 64-bar *All or nothing at all* of its doleful overtones with a bright tempo and effective countermelody. Of the same order is his imaginative rewriting of *The way you look tonight* for a sextet date of a year earlier (Capitol [A] HL6501, Affinity [E] AFF65), which can be recommended for examples of Cooper's soloing and writing in a more conventional setting than this. On these 1955 sessions a main point is the amount of instrumental doubling the wind players do; or rather what is important is what Cooper does with this capacity.

Monk's *Round about midnight* offers a more serious challenge than any melody of Kern or Porter, and Cooper responds more radically. From the opening french and english horn calls a singular atmosphere is created, and the scoring is notable for the way the instruments are alternatively made to stand off from, and blend with, each other. There is excellent counterpoint between Shank's flute and the english horn, and again the bass clarinet and french horn add significantly to the result. We should not allow the relative novelty of Cooper's instrument to distract us from the beauty of his melodic invention here. In the light of what happens on **388**, these sessions could have done with more of his english horn and oboe, although the latter is to the fore in *Hot boy*. This title is a corruption of the French 'hautbois' and has a wry aptness because the scoring, which makes the small band sound quite large because of the rich effect of several independent lines, does generate a glowing warmth. The catchy theme, aided by a separate and simultaneous line from Stu Williamson's muted trumpet, brings out the jazz side of the oboe's character and there are formal niceties such as the restatement of this theme starting before Giuffre's baritone solo has finished. The tenor solo is presumably Shank's. *Tongue twister* is another fertile theme of Cooper's, easily justifying its receiving the longest performance here. Back on alto, Shank has a particularly characteristic solo, as does Claude Williamson, who contributes work of a high standard throughout yet is especially fine in this piece. *Tongue twister* includes, as does *Strike up the band*, a passage of collective improvisation that tellingly contrasts with the session's general sequence of ensemble and solos.

Most personal of Cooper's themes here, though, are *Sunset* and above all *Drawing lines*, which lives up to its name with melodious writing for flute, oboe, bass clarinet and french horn that is subtle in its shapes and colouring. As *Drawing lines* is, indeed, the best piece in the collection, there is something almost perverse in its being slowly faded. Here as elsewhere, Cooper scores bridge passages between solos so as to reassert, and even extend, the specific character of the theme statements. Probably the opposite extreme from *Drawing lines* is marked by *Strike up the band*, which, apart from an unexpected slow introduction and bluesy coda and a passage of collective improvisation, is mainly a vehicle for Cooper's up-tempo soloing and is less engaging than the rest of this music. He takes most of the tenor solos on these dates, of course, and elsewhere makes a far more positive impression. Four men play the tenor at various points and in *It don't mean a thing* we can savour the unemphatic yet clear-cut differences between Shank, Enevoldsen and the leader. Putting three tenors and a baritone on this suggests a glance towards the baritonist's *Four brothers* (**312c**). *Hallelujah* is another occasion for a sequence of up-tempo solos, but Cooper writes for the french horn in such a way that it gives a distinctive aspect to the linking ensembles. In fact he astutely takes account of each wind instrument's special capabilities. M.H.

Jimmy Giuffre

387 The Jimmy Giuffre Clarinet

Atlantic (A) 1238, †Atlantic (A) 90144

Giuffre (clt, foot-tapping). Los Angeles, 21 March 1956.
So low

Jimmy Rowles (cls) added. Same date.
Deep purple

Buddy Collette (fl); Bud Shank (alt fl); Giuffre (clt); Harry Klee (bs clt); Shelly Manne (d). Same date.
The sidepipers

Collette (alt clt); Giuffre (clt); Klee (bs clt). Same date.
The sheepherder

Giuffre (clt); Rowles (p); Manne (d). Same date.
Fascinatin' rhythm

Bob Cooper (ob); Dave Pell (eng h); Giuffre (clt); Maury Berman (bsn); Ralph Peña (bs). Los Angeles, 22 March 1956.
My funny Valentine

Giuffre (clt); Peña (bs); Stan Levey (d). Same date.
Quiet cook

Harry Edison, Shorty Rogers, Jack Sheldon (tpt); Giuffre (clt); Cooper, Pell (ten); Berman (bar); Peña (bs); Levey (d). Same date.
Down home

Jazz Phrasing and Interpretation is the title of a manual 'for classroom and private work' copyrighted in 1969 by Giuffre. [14] Very thorough, with copious examples in staff notation, it is designated 'a personal approach', so it can be an informative companion for part-reading listeners to *The Jimmy Giuffre Clarinet*. Notable is the author's identification of certain 'effects' – the 'bebop effect', the 'slide-slur', the short and sustained 'pick-up', the 'blues-folk attack' with its 'bwee effect' and so on.

Didactic expression of his own jazz approach will seem easiest for a musician of fairly simple aims. Giuffre's 'simplicity', though refreshing, is deceptive. He has not been one of the great expanders of the language; his success is as a distiller of essences, a revealer of essential relationships. Behind his painstaking book lies not only long jazz experience but also academic distinction and intense study of compositional techniques. In the temporal superimpositions of *My funny Valentine* and the elegantly prepared multitonal colloquy of *The sheepherder* one hears evidence of extra-jazz knowledge. But that these pieces are sure candidates for essential jazz is clearly never due to some overladen 'jazz effect'. Jazz wisdom is at the heart of them, expressed with a complete absence of overstatement. Spaces given to Manne's expressive brushwork in *The sidepipers* (and he is allowed the last whisper to himself) are important tokens of the number's character. The instrumental parts in that, and in the other two pieces mentioned, are brilliantly allotted and disposed by Giuffre. In the minor-key pastoral of *The sheepherder* the clarinet lines become determinant of the interchange of voices; and the composer's wit is shown by 'lazy' suspensions of time and in the closing bars where the harmonic tendency appears to predict a *tierce de Picardie* yet leads instead to a wry intensification of the minor mood.

There is a no doubt unintentional likeness in the opening accompaniment of *My funny Valentine* to part of Randy Weston's *Little Niles*, and the phrase establishes both the meditative nature and the ambiguous time concept of a treatment in which the clarinet statements are stretched over an accompanimental doubling of the basic tempo.

The title *So low* is a multiple pun. Giuffre's tapping foot provides self-accompaniment, he seldom strays outside his instrument's lower register, and the 'blues-folk effect' makes the old jazz epithet 'low down' seem peculiarly apt. The forlornness of the voice calls to mind his instruction regarding vibrato: 'should be wide – almost a quarter-tone waver at times . . . slow, irregular, never constant.' He speaks only of long notes, and this rather desolate musing is typical chiefly of his 'blues-folk' essays of which *The train and the river* (first recorded in 1956, †Atlantic [A] 90981) is the most famous example.

The splendid keyboard gifts of Rowles are displayed in *Deep purple*, where the partly improvised and partly premeditated interplay of clarinet and celesta make for one of the most imaginative versions of this song ever recorded; and in *Fascinatin' rhythm*, with Rowles (piano), Manne and Giuffre exhibiting their unfailing knack of reaching the heart and spirit of a theme, and the swift jugglings of relative statements joined to a kind of reticence ensuring that no effect is overextended. *Quiet cook*, introducing Peña and Levey, the former a bassist of agile imagination, the latter a rather less thoughtful drummer than Manne, is a rapid trio number in which determination and freedom are beautifully combined.

The nonet plays in *Down home* an example of Giuffre's better-known ensemble style. Compared to the woodwind scores, some of these ensemble phrases are conventional, but everything is marshalled according to a typical Giuffre strategy. The debate of trumpets, predictably vivid, seems something of an intrusion in this record's programme; however, at the very end the clarinettist strolls down home alone, vibrato wide, 'bwee effect' prominent, foot patting in echoless solitude. (However, the interestingly different account of *Down home* on Giuffre's Fresh Sounds [Sp] FSR405 should also be heard.) E.T.

Howard Rumsey

388 Lighthouse All-Stars Vol. 4: Flute 'n' Oboe

†Original Jazz Classics (A) OJCCD154–2, Vogue (E) LAC12146

Bud Shank (fl, alt fl); Bob Cooper (ob, eng h); Claude Williamson (p); Rumsey (bs); Max Roach (d). Los Angeles, 25–6 February 1954.
Albatross · Aquarium · Bags' groove · Happy town · A night in Tunisia · Hermosa summer · Warm winds · Still life

Buddy Collette (fl), Sonny Clark (p), Stan Levey (d) replace Shank, Williamson, Roach. Los Angeles, 25 September 1956.
A bit of Basie · Blue sands · Waikikian · Swing house

Although these and many other recordings show him to have been a competent bassist, Rumsey was musically speaking a negligible figure, yet one of a number of such who have a place in the jazz story because they created situations in which others could give of their best, and, as in this case, do something both worthwhile and unusual. The appearance, in West Coast jazz especially, of flute, oboe, french horn etc. gave rise to many comic expressions of outrage when the music was new, usually on the dogmatic grounds that these were somehow intrinsically unsuitable vehicles for jazz, even although there were precedents in all instances.

True, not all the precedents made a good case for the jazz potential of these instruments, an obvious example being Wayman Carver's flute playing with the Chick Webb band. In, say, *Down home rag* (**125**) the flute is employed with two clarinets as a sort of 'classical' interlude, this providing a vivid illustration of how not to do it. Far more jazzlike is the flute solo by Harry Klee in Ray Linn's *Caravan* (†Hep [E] CD1) of 1945–6 and it was a little later, in the 1950s, that serious use of this instrument, and indeed of the oboe, started in jazz.

Shank and Cooper began doubling on flute and oboe respectively with Kenton's Innovations in Modern Music Orchestra (**477**) and were trying duets along the lines of the above recordings by 1953. The point was a thoroughgoing exploitation of flutes, oboe and english horn as the chief means of solo expression instead of their occasional employment for novelty effects. Despite this, most of the themes, apart from the well-established *Bags' groove*, *Swing house* and *A night in Tunisia*, were specially composed for these sessions, and the ensemble passages have considerable, if unobtrusive, diversity. This is partly a matter of Shank and Cooper sometimes playing alto flute (pitched a fourth lower than the ordinary flute) and english horn (in effect an alto oboe, pitched a fifth lower) respectively and these producing subtle differences of tone colour. But it is more important that there is a good deal of non-imitative counterpoint, as in Cooper's *Still life* and *Waikikian*, where flute and oboe glide together in close formation like polyphonic serpents. From the ensemble viewpoint this record is best heard in conjunction with Lyle Murphy's *Gone with the Woodwinds* (Contemporary [A] C3506, Vogue [E] LAC12135), a 1955 collection whose music combines flutes with a full range of saxophones and clarinets, including the rare contrabass clarinet, in all manner of richly varied, dark-hued mixtures which even decades later have been little employed. [15]

Whatever their contrapuntal virtues, *Waikikikan* and *Still life*, along with *Hermosa summer* and *Warm winds*, both also Cooper themes, embody a kind of sunny lyricism which, be it from this or any other source, has found little favour with sourpuss jazz commentators. The results are beautiful, just the same. Related yet different is a piece like Collette's *Blue sands* (the above account of which should be compared with that on **389**), this being an attractive instance of the sort of 'Eastern' exotica which jazzmen have gone in for ever since the 1920s. [16] This instrumentation, with Cooper playing his english horn, emphasizes, too, the exotic aspect of Gillespie's *A night in Tunisia*, bypassed in most straight jazz performances. *Bags' groove* is likewise better suited to these tone colours than might have been expected, and in both cases Roach makes a particularly fine contribution – although he drums with masterly restraint throughout, his quiet propulsion, well matched on the 1956 date by Levey, is a considerable factor in the musical achievement of these occasions.

Something of a stylistic exercise is Collette's *A bit of Basie*, which here produces a result quite different from Pepper's splendid reading on **461**, yet with just as well defined a character. This derives chiefly from the crossing of earthy blues elements with the Rumsey group's woodwind refinements, although space is found for humour too, as in Cooper's amusing variant of Lester Young's *Taxi war dance* quotation of *Old man river* (**135a**). *Warm winds* contains an especially conclusive demonstration of the oboe's capacity as a jazz instrument, Cooper's articulation being remarkable. [17] Yet Shank's is still more so, given the nature of the flute, and it must have been his tone and phrasing, more than those of any other player, which first convinced many listeners of the instrument's serious jazz capabilities. Shank's very fast *Happy town* is another memorable instance of his and Cooper's alacrity.

It should be added that Collette's playing is fully comparable to Shank's, and he went on to employ the whole family, from piccolo to bass flute, in his 1958 *Swingin' Shepherds* collection (EmArcy [A] 36133). Shank's and Cooper's use of flutes, oboe and english horn in more formal circumstances may be studied on **386**. The permanent establishment of these instruments in jazz was of course part of a general expansion of that music's colouristic and textural scope in the 1950s, typified by the french horn on **308** and the cello on **389.** This in turn was part of an increase in the expressive resources of jazz which can never be simply a matter of expanded melodic, rhythmic and harmonic vocabularies. M.H.

Chico Hamilton

389 The Chico Hamilton Quintet

Pacific Jazz (A) PJ1209, Vogue (E) LAE12039

Buddy Collette (alt, ten, fl, clt); Jim Hall (g); Fred Katz (cel); Carson Smith (bs); Hamilton (d). Long Beach, Ca., 4–5 August 1955.

Spectacular · Buddy boo · I want to be happy · Walkin' Carson blues

Same personnel. Los Angeles, 23 August 1955.

A nice day · My funny Valentine · Blue sands · The morning after · The sage

All editions of this band were routinely denounced as 'twee', but that judgement serves least well for its beginnings. Returning decades later, many listeners may be surprised at how 'down home' a lot of the music sounds. That will partly be in comparison with much that happened later, of course; yet a performance like *Walkin' Carson blues* ought to have settled most of the inevitable questions about the group's credentials. Certainly there is more straight jazz here than most scribes could hear when these recordings first appeared, and this is a good demonstration of the point that all critical assessments are provisional, whatever many practitioners of that craft fondly imagine to the contrary.

Making his first records in 1941 (with Slim Gaillard, alas), Hamilton brought a wide range of professional experience to this refined and, even by 1950s West Coast standards, decidedly adventurous band. An excellent drummer along Jo Jones lines, he actually studied with Lee Young, but Jones was always his great exemplar personally as well as musically, [18] and a slightly later quintet piece is named after him (Pacific Jazz [A] PJ1225, 1956). Hamilton attracted international attention as a member of Mulligan's quartet (**300**) and as leader of this – again pianoless – quintet. As good leaders must, he provided opportunities for outstanding young players when they were little known, starting with Collette and Hall, whom many people first heard with this group. Later came Eric Dolphy, Ron Carter, Dennis Budimir, Arthur Blythe, John Abercrombie, Paul Horn – and, regrettably, Charles Lloyd. Hamilton also from time to time brought in such as Clark Terry, Charlie Mariano, Harold Land and Ray Nance. [19]

Some of the tendencies which came to the fore in the quintet had already been suggested by Hamilton's 1953–4 trio sessions with Howard Roberts and George Duvivier (World Pacific [A] WP1220, Vogue [E] LAE12077), with both of whom he had worked when they all were accompanists to Lena Horne. He first played with Collette during their high-school years, he had worked alongside Katz during the Lena Horne period (Katz as pianist), and Smith was a fellow member of the original Mulligan quartet. Hence four members of the Hamilton quintet knew each other's playing well, and this goes some way to explain an integration of ensemble that is impressive particularly in view of the unusual instrumentation. Hall is quoted in the sleeve note to the initial American LP issue as saying that thoroughly worked-out arrangements were necessary because of the cello: 'It's the cello that pulls us together.' Which is to say that the instrument was a factor in keeping them off the beaten track. In the same place Collette makes the point that many of their pieces were based on ideas that emerged during improvisation. This is true of many good bands, of course, though it must have helped that nearly everyone in the group composed and arranged.

With Collette's several voices, Hall's post-Christian guitar work, Hamilton's thoughtful exploration of percussion timbres, and the alliance of cello and bass, this band presented uncommonly fresh resources of colour and texture. Whether riding the riffs of *Buddy boo* – a blues very different from the *Walkin' Carson* piece – or during the solo, followed by a duet with the clarinet, at the start of *A nice day* or later, in tempo, dialoguing with the guitar, Katz's cello was an especially new, disquietingly romantic voice to many no-nonsense jazz listeners. It was nowhere more so than in *My funny Valentine*, whose glowing warmth makes it as ardent as the following year's version by Giuffre (**387**). How aptly cello and electric guitar partner each other here! This is a notable instance of the kind of unlikely yet highly effective instrumental combination that jazz has so often uncovered. Its expressive impact is a telling rejoinder to one of the more fatuous objections to the use of the cello and even the flute in such music. This was that they represented a 'surrender' to European influences, as if (a) they were not being employed to perfectly explicit jazz ends and (b) European influences had not acted on jazz from an early stage.

It made good sense to record Hamilton's group both in the studio and in public – the earlier titles being taken down at the Strollers' Club, Long Beach, California. This presents the band as it were from contrasting angles, bringing out different aspects of their approach; besides, in the club the microphones picked up the profoundly symbolic noise of the cash register. As if in defiance of the commercial verities, *Free form* makes a decided thrust into the future, though echoing the obvious Tristano (**293**), Manne (**432**) and other initiatives. The drums participate almost as a front-line voice and the ensemble passages are richly detailed, sometimes virtually in five real parts. One or another is usually the most prominent, however, and this lead shifts from one musician to another; although we may respectfully doubt whether they were aware of the precedent, this is something like the lead-passing in latter-day New Orleans ensembles. And this polyphonic aspect persists elsewhere. It runs from simple cases such as the cello counterpointing the flute in *The morning after*, although even this leads to a three-part texture with Hall joining in and Hamilton double-timing. Something comparable happens in *I want to be happy*, where there are short bursts of $3/4$.

In apt contrast, *Walkin' Carson blues* offers a straight sequence of solos, the most affecting from Collette and Hall. Several of these pieces, though, are sensitively developed as satisfying wholes. Despite its misleading title, Hall's very swinging *Spectacular* is a good example with its alternation of heavy and light ensembles, fine guitar solos, duetting between tenor and guitar, and striking textures, including behind the solos. A pity the *pizzicato* duet between cello and bass was not more sustained. Collette's *Blue sands*, another instance of the 'Oriental' vein in jazz, likewise shows this group at its most resourceful, with Hall's flamenco echoes and Hamilton's mallets. This should be heard in conjunction with the reading on **388**. [20] A different sort of lyricism from that of *Blue sands*, or of *My funny Valentine*, is caught by Katz's *The sage*, which has a pastoral *simplesse* that is rare in jazz. After hearing these and comparable recordings by Hamilton's quintet, it is depressing to reflect that he later replaced the cello with a trombone – four trombones on one 1976 date – and subsided into conventionality. However, the complete Pacific Jazz recordings of the quintet are on †Mosaic (A) MD6–175. M.H.

World Saxophone Quartet

390 Dances and Ballads

Elektra Nonesuch (E) 79164–4

Julius Hamphill (alt, sop, fl); Oliver Lake (alt, sop); David Murray (ten, bs clt); Hamiett Bluiett (bar, alt clt). New York City, April 1987.
Sweet D · For Lester · Belly up · Cool red · Hattie Wall · Adjacent · West African snap · Full, deep and mellow · Dance until dawn (For Little Anthony) · Fast life

In the sphere of chamber music, saxophone ensembles have never attracted much enthusiasm, to some extent because of these instruments' rather bland 'straight' tonal quality. Even in a jazz context the perils are not too easily removed, although the techniques required to compensate for the lack of a rhythm section can cause a greater danger of sameness. Jazz distortions of tone – particularly of the post-Ayler kind – widen the tonal possibilities, and it is because of its exploitation of these, as well as by the augmentation of the sound spectrum by the use of woodwinds, that the WSQ has made something quite distinctive and worthy of development out of what started as a fortuitous, occasional association. The fact that in all but two of these numbers the WSQ performs strictly to its name – saxophones only – may testify to its healthy defiance of the mode's hazards.

Moving well beyond the preliminary rummagings of their first recording, *Point of No Return* (Moers Music [G] 01034), *Dances and Ballads* builds upon the consolidations of techniques to be heard in *Revue* and *Steppin'* (Black Saint [It] BSR0056 and BSR0027), and *The WSQ plays Ellington* (Elektra Nonesuch [E] 979137–1). What came out of the wry flirtations of the last-named album has its effect at several points in the present programme; and, allowing for the wryness mentioned, this emerges interestingly in the trundled baritone undercurrent to staccato chords as Bluiett's *Hattie Wall* (the group's signature) gets under way, and in the 'Dukish' harmonies which support Bluiett in his other composition, *Full, deep and mellow*, and Murray in his own *For Lester.* These recollections evidently owe something to Bluiett's predilections – though, truth to tell, his frequent cellar steppings recall the Adrian Rollini of, say, *Honolulu blues* (**72**) more than they do Harry Carney.

The more personal expressive routes of the quartet have been fairly clearly defined; for example, complicatedly spaced and harmonized melodic designs supported by dogged rifflike figurations; solos and duets, either accompanied by partially arranged sequences, or not accompanied at all; stretches of savagely tangled collectivities which contrast with more open combinations of individually improvised series. Most ear-catching are the unexpected ways in which premeditation and extemporaneity interact. An apparent desire for both freedom and exactitude has injected a paradoxical degree of control into all but the wildest free-for-alls. Not that this is automatically enriching – everyone knows what habit did to the Dixieland collective – yet, conversely, the harmonic resources of the composed passages and a certain skill in planned rhythmic discontinuity seem related to elements discovered in spontaneity.

The continuing occasionality of the group's appearances may account for the fact that individual dialects are seldom submerged. Hemphill's predominant style is revealingly compared with Murray's in *Hattie Wall*, showing how the former is, at that jolly pace, rather more indebted to Dolphy than the latter is to Ayler or Coltrane. Lake's alto in the Jamaican-sounding *West African snap* is much less angular than Hemphill's choppy soprano in that number. Hemphill and Murray exchange quieter thoughts during *Adjacent*; and in *For Lester*, where flute and alto clarinet emphasize abrasive intervals, Murray plays a lovely memorial reflection which, in its susurrating edges, gives a subsidiary nod to Ben Webster.

Dance until dawn is a meander of elusive pulse which utilizes all the voices (Murray, the composer, on bass clarinet this time) in almost random fragmentation, dryly atonal. It is Bluiett's role on baritone that gives the piece much of its character as it develops gradually out of the balladlike spirals of its beginning into an extended, languorous dance with suggestions of some old ballroom marathon. (The dedication may indicate something different.)

Clear time signatures are fitful overall – a strong feeling of 5/4 at the start of *Belly up*, whose untethered, suspended exchanges drift over an energetic ground-bass grunt; and a hint of 6/8 launching *Fast life*, which is mostly a gale of abstract expressionism. Various tempos are overlaid in *Sweet D*, yet the tenor-baritone tramp eventually touches tedium. One may still doubt whether the WSQ members can carry their concept much further, but there is much here to extol, allurements more than sufficient to draw one back to this advanced yet tradition-conscious music. E.T.

Billy Bang

391 Outline No. 12

†Celluloid (A) CEL5004

Charles Tyler (clt); Henri Warner (alt clt); David Murray (bs clt); Frank Lowe (sop); Wilbur Morris (bs); Sunny Murray, John 'Kbuwana' Fuller (d); Bang (vln, comp); Jason Hwang, Joseph Hailes (vln); Khan Jamal (vib); Butch Morris (cond). New York City, July 1982.

Seeing together · Conception · Outline No. 12

There is more of a violin tradition in jazz than is always realized, one that reaches back to earlier yet related musics. By the same token, this instrument has more of a presence in free jazz than is sometimes apparent. This is demonstrated by the contributions of Leroy Jenkins, Zbigniew Seifert, Alan Silva, Jean-Luc Ponty, Didier Lockwood, Egerton Tidmarsh, Ramsey Ameen (for his playing with Cecil Taylor, see **419**) and others for whom this book has no space. But these names are enough to indicate that routes away from the violin's classical associations have long existed, although Bang put the matter quite touchingly when he said that the instrument 'wasn't from my neighbourhood, and wasn't welcome there'. [21]

Born William Walker in Mobile, Alabama, Bang emerged into jazz during the 1970s on the New York loft scene. He did promising work, along with James Emery (guitar) and John Lindberg (bass), in the New York String Trio, showing that he had the beginnings of a personal voice. Bang was in other enterprising groups such as the Jazz Doctors (and in Forbidden Planet, a thoroughly uninteresting one), but it hints at the nature of his talent that his finest work has been recorded under his own name. Which is to say that much of its character arises out of his specific qualities as a composing bandleader. Bang's playing, and that of the other participants here, so nearly matches his writing that part of the music's intensity derives from the precision of its execution. This in turn leads to the point that he was already well acquainted with the players chosen for these performances and wrote with their musical personalities well in mind. It is the clearest sign of Bang's achievement of his aims that one seldom is sure exactly what was improvised and what composed.

The instrumentation was obviously decided on only after much thought and gives rise to many unusual textures and (rather austere) colours. Although Bang has said that he strives for simplicity in everything he plays, [22] this is rather hard to believe in the face of such music as the above, and there are some ensemble passages – the opening theme of *Seeing together*, for example – which suggest the kind of thing Stravinsky might have written if he had taken the trouble really to understand jazz. Even so, it is unusual for a composer of jazz to congratulate the conductor, as Bang did Butch Morris in connection with these performances, on a faithful interpretation of the scores. Various types and degrees of freedom come under varying levels of control here, though, and the conductor has a vital role, almost for the first time in jazz. The ensembles, written or otherwise, are heterophonic rather than contrapuntal, and are fascinating in their freshness and diversity. Though usually brief, these ensemble passages, thematic or otherwise, are crucial in shaping the three performances as unified wholes. Bang employs them to direct free improvisations – solo, duet, collective – through distinct yet clearly related phases, viewing a given musical situation from several angles.

Less immediately evocative than, say, *Bien-Hoa blues* on the later *Valve No. 10* (†Soul Note [It] 121 186), the music of the *Outline No. 12* collection is abstract in comparison, hard-edged but always purposefully so. At the same time each piece has a separate and well-defined character. Thus *Seeing together* opens with an almost extravagantly rhythmic theme played by the ensemble, launching a solo from Bang which, occasional punctuations aside, is unaccompanied, covers a wide area of the violin's capabilities, and is very aggressive. Indeed this sounds like a quite deliberate contradiction of the image of the instrument that still lingers in jazz circles and it is almost as abrasive as some passages in Bartók. There follows a duet between Murray and Jamal, with the former employing a rather Dolphy-like vocabulary yet also matching Bang for invention. Use of the vibraharp here should be compared with the marimba's role on *The Fire from Within* (†Soul Note [It] SN1086), another record with an unusual instrumentation.

Next Murray has exchanges with the percussionists and, with Bang leading, there follows another ensemble, high, intense, sour – in fact so high as to remind us of two comparable passages in Ayler's 1965 *Spirits Rejoice* (†ESP [A] 1020–2), on which Tyler took part. This swerves into something different again, with Bang, David Murray and Jamal playing brief, isolated phrases suggesting that the music could fall apart. But there is instead another ensemble outburst which ushers in another solo by the leader. He continues to impress with a wide variety of phrase shapes which cover most of the violin's register and include some multiple stoppings. Bang alternates with thematic interjections from the ensemble until the latter makes an abrupt end.

Coltrane is always mentioned in connection with this violinist, yet it seems more relevant to suggest that he combined aspects of Leroy Jenkins's classically founded approach with Ornette Coleman's almost alarmingly spontaneous methods with the instrument. This has proved no break on his individuality (as Coltrane might have done), as is demonstrated by the eponymous *Outline No. 12*, where, after two dirge-like clarinet chords, his improvising, if less incisive than on *Seeing together*, is just as expressive, and even rhapsodic. Wilber Morris provides a very active bass line in support, vocalized to match the violin's inflections, and the vibraharp softly murmurs in the background. Hwang and Hailes join in *pizzicato* with the drums sounding quietly and the vibraharp now more prominent, then the bass clarinet. After several flourishes the soprano saxophone engages in a duet with the percussion, Lowe's style being post-Ayler in some respects. The clarinets dolefully echo their opening gesture and the violins make a brief thematic statement. This is answered by the clarinets in very heterophonic mode until the violins answer with superimposed chords. Then clarinets, now in parallel motion, and violins alternate, overlap, and finally the strings impose an ending. [23]

More complicated and substantially longer, *Conception* brings the whole ensemble's resources more consistently into play. After an introduction calling on all forces, the violins state a first theme but clarinets and vibraharp soon join in more or less antiphonally, although by no means is this a conventional call-and-response pattern. The violins continue to hold the main thread while bass and drums replace the clarinets. These soon return, however, and there are polyphonic passages for the full ensemble with each instrument going its own way. In fact this becomes a long collective improvisation, with sometimes the string bass and sometimes the bass clarinet taking the bottom line. Next a trio of soprano, vibraharp and percussion is heard from, although the leader soon takes the saxophone's place and the string bass adds a fourth voice. Gradually Bang assumes the lead, mainly with support from Wilber Morris, but the others return, if in more subdued mood. They yield to a vibraharp solo with just occasional drum and string punctuations, this being followed in turn by the clarinets and string bass, the soprano soon being added, although the bass continues as more or less the main voice. The violins return thoughtfully but the clarinets are imposed on them and the strings in response grow more heterophonic. This leads to a duet between Bang and David Murray, with quiet punctuation by percussion and the other violins, but a further outline is scarcely needed of this richly developed and detailed tapestry, which is plainly the main achievement on this disc and a major event of Bang's recording career.

Though he is a virtuoso and naturally allots himself adequate space, he is also more willing to take a back seat than other contemporary bandleaders who could be mentioned. And Bang is a real composer, none of these pieces seeming, despite a considerable emphasis on texture, in the least episodic. The fact that he played drums at one stage probably helped, even if that was only with Arlo Guthrie. It might have been enlightening to read Bang's notes which accompany this record, but the sort of design genius all too often turned loose on CD packaging decreed that they should be printed in a minute, highly eccentric typeface which makes them illegible. M.H.

George Lewis

392 **Homage to Charles Parker**

†Black Saint (It) BSR0029

Lewis (tbn, electronics[1]); Douglas Ewart (bs clt, alt, cym); Anthony Davis (p); Richard Teitelbaum (polymoog, multimoog, micromoog synth). Milan, 1979.

Homage to Charles Parker[1] · *Blues*

Some may wonder, over 40 years after his death, whether so crucially involved a jazzmaker as Parker, an artist whose voice and creative language we normally suppose can only be recaptured from and preserved in the jazz records he left behind, could have entertained any conception of a 'jazz beyond jazz'. There can be little doubt that he could. He extended jazz expression himself, and was never musically insular. During the one and only 'blindfold test' he ever underwent with Leonard Feather (*Metronome* in the summer of 1948, reprinted in *down beat* 11 March 1965) he enthused over Kenton's *Monotony* (**313a**) and over the 'real marvellous alto work' of the almost forgotten George Weidler in Kenton's *Elegy for alto* (also on **313a**), acknowledged 'music at its best' in Stravinsky's *The Song of the Nightingale*, and refused to 'classify music in words . . . Personally, I just like to call it music, and music is what I like.' Which is a remark to keep in mind when Lewis, one of the most spectacularly talented of the trombonists in the jazz of the last quarter-century, jibs at regarding himself as a jazz musician. It will be less than easy for those who hear his zestful contributions to John Zorn's jazz 'revisitations' in *News for Lulu* (**464**) to take such diffidence seriously. But the diffidence is shared by contemporaries of Lewis's, Henry Threadgill (**436**), Anthony Braxton (**467**), Lewis's mentor Muhal Richard Abrams (**435**), and the men who are the trombonist's companions here for an attempt to probe beyond the formalities of Parker's triumphant jazz, and make music that will in some manner signify the inner reality of the great artist's persona.

After a resourceful boyhood study of the trombone, Lewis joined Abrams's association for the Advancement of Creative Musicians in 1971. He also played with a group led by the slightly older Ewart, a Jamaican whose jazz progress had been creatively challenged by Eric Dolphy's multi-instrumentalism. Ewart was also an Abrams associate. To the visionary principles of the AACM the pianist Davis also became allied during the 1970s; moreover the free jazz of Advent, an ensemble including Lewis, was part of the experimental period which, as well as touching the thought of the present recording, edged these musicians further towards the bridge-crossing of such outfits as the octet Episteme which spanned post-bop freedom and European (e.g. serial) techniques. This was territory increasingly dominated by Braxton, a pretty frequent soulmate of Lewis then and later.

Those who would rather hear the jazz-conscious virtuosos of those days celebrating the Parker jazz spirit than turning to what Lewis – in a rather profitless liner note – refers to as 'a new appraisal of world music after Parker's life' might listen to the vivid free-jazz playground Braxton and Lewis made of *Ornithology* back in June 1976 (*Elements of Surprise*, Moers Music [G] 01036 – very different from another Braxton reading on **467**). But *Homage to Charles Parker* and the closely allied *Blues* depend for their character upon the much more formal musical philosophy associated with the pianist Davis. Though welcoming post-Coleman liberation, Davis found a new concern for creativeness in exploring the formalities not only of the European avant-garde but of Oriental expressive strands as well. What made the Parker and pre-Parker jazz sustain its creative freedoms without dumping every time-honoured convention was, in the 1970s and 1980s, under review by men of Davis's mind, without their being ensnared by either nostalgia or false mimicry. 'The harmonic dimensions are coming back. I hear almost everything I play as being tonal . . . I think that improvisation is one compositional tool within the framework of a given piece.'

It might be glibness to suggest that the latter notion, if not its sober verbiage, is at least as old as Jelly Roll Morton in jazz thought. The balance of 'improvisation' counterpoises the balance of 'composition' more significantly in the fascinating rumination of the *Homage* than it can easily be judged to do in *Blues*.

Blues is an extended and 'unrhythmed' exchange that would have been impossible to devise without the musical vocabulary of 'primitive' jazz. The form of the blues is at no point ever resolved, but the spectre of the form is there throughout; from the bass clarinet of Ewart and Lewis's trombone pedal notes which begin the piece, to a colloquy of reed and brass voices, into which are drawn Davis and some fairly sparse moogisms from Teitelbaum. The sensations are fragmentary – and probably carefully premeditated – except for a critical moment at which a freeish bout of collective confabulation develops briefly.

Homage to Charles Parker emerges through penumbral atmospherics of synthesizer overlay, growing from near silence to make itself varyingly essential to the composition's mood. It is notable, considering this electronic background, how vital to the nature of the *Homage* are the extended extemporizations of Ewart – on cymbal, then on alto, with a jazz freedom that is lively and inventive despite its gentle tone; Davis – in a meandering meditation which, while attractive, lacks jazz accent; and Lewis – whose smooth loquacity manages to answer Davis's fancies with a jazz accent that will not, need not, be deflected.

Metres are variable throughout, and, as is often deemed suitable for homages, the mood tends to be sombre. Considering what Lewis and Braxton made of *Ornithology*, let alone what Bird countless times made of *High society* and *The Kerry dance*, it is feasible for jazz genuflections to be fun, even some, it may be, that are heading for the beyond. E.T.

Modality and Its Implications

One definition of modal jazz might be: few chords, lots of space. Davis's *So what* was a straightforward AABA tune, but if taking more than one chorus, a soloist found himself playing on one chord for 24 bars (the last eight-bar A section plus the first 16 of AA), a radical change from some bop themes which presented the improviser with a new chord twice in a single bar! Modality offered new challenges, not least in focusing on scales, or modes, related to a chord rather than on the chord itself. It caused a seismic shift in improvisation, away from thinking vertically (the chord) to horizontally (the scale).

Miles Davis

393 Kind of Blue

†Columbia (E) CK64935

Davis (tpt); Cannonball Adderley (alt[1]); John Coltrane (ten); Bill Evans (p); Paul Chambers (bs); Jimmy Cobb (d). New York City, 2 March 1959.
So what?[1] · *Blue in green*

Wynton Kelly (p) replaces Evans. Same date.
Freddie Freeloader[1]

Bill Evans (p) replaces Kelly. New York City, 22 April 1959.
All blues[1] · *Flamenco sketches*[1]

Despite what others had already done, George Russell (**380**) in particular, and despite Davis's own initiative of a decade earlier in realizing John Carisi's Dorian blues, *Israel*, this album, *Kind of Blue*, is still confidently cited as a point of promise in the establishing of a sort of modal aptitude in jazz. How much was this a formal programme where Davis was concerned? How much was it, as has been suggested (**376**) with regard to his part in the building of the 1948–50 nonet, a personal means of 'furthering his own musical aspirations', without necessary attention to pace-setting?

For John Litweiler's chapter on 'Modal Jazz' in *The Freedom Principle*, the typesetter has, for both contents and headings, spelled modal as 'model'. Let it be agreed that *Kind of Blue* is *model* jazz [24] – in the sense that, as jazz per se, it is revelatory, as the liveliest arts always will be, and invites emulation.

All through the decade succeeding the nonet recordings, in his small groups, and in collaborations with Gil Evans, Davis had been looking to ways of improvising that were freer of the demands or incitements of conventional harmonic structure; pared down, uncluttered, enabled in terms of plainly melodic innovation. This was a path from which he would not seriously swerve, even in his *affaire* with jazz-rock fusion. Litweiler reckons that by the mid-1960s, with the *Plugged Nickel* sessions (**396**) and *Miles Smiles* (†Columbia [A] 471 004–2), 'the modal idiom had begun to disintegrate'. [25] This revives the question: was it fully a modal idiom in the first place? – that is, at these two 1959 sessions?

Kind of Blue is a splendid jazz achievement which can be heard without feeling that the question has become quite irrelevant. The role played by the sextet's rhythm team is hardly advanced, stylistically, beyond that of the Davis groups of the mid-1950s (**334**) and the period when Coltrane joined in. That role, though immaculately encompassed, is largely supportive. As against that judgement, the part Chambers plays in the Dorian-related *So what?* is a rather formal hint at greater flexibilities for a rhythm section yet to be gathered; and the role of Bill Evans in the entire matter appears to have gone well beyond the merely supportive. Davis was officially credited with the composition of all five numbers, but it has been claimed for Evans that he composed *Blue in green* and *Flamenco sketches* and that he himself claimed credit for arranging every piece. His detailed involvement must now remain problematical; but, as Jack Chambers has written, 'clearly Evans was not invited to participate . . . just for old times' sake. He was deeply, if unofficially, involved in them.' [26] See also the second paragraph of **372**.

Davis's sophisticated simplicity establishes the wistfulness of *Blue in green*, which in fact has Evans's mind-prints all over it. The pianist's accompaniment of the trumpet's airy tunes demonstrates that no theory lurks here that might discourage harmonic colouration. How to be magisterial without vying for laurels is near the essence of Evans's art. In solo both Evans and Coltrane aspire to Davis's weaving lyricism. *So what?* opens at a very lazy tempo, but quickens to an irresistible swing as Davis's celebrated solo unfolds. Evans's chordal subtleties alleviate the bass/drum tendency to the somewhat mechanical impetus that marked the work of Chambers and Philly Joe Jones on **334**. That tendency is even more marked in *Freddie Freeloader*, closer to the riding, theory-free jazz of three or four years earlier, and much more congenial to Kelly than it might have been to Evans. As with Russell's workshop creations (**380**), the listener needs some exterior pointer to the formalities involved. They will not seem obvious to habitual jazz perception; and, indeed, as is said in this book's entry on Russell in 1956, the music can be enjoyed intelligently 'without having mastered the intricacies of the . . . concept'. There is a swing to the rocking 6/8 of *All blues* which might discourage discernment of its sixfold patterns, described by one critic as 'a good example of primitive jazz serialism'. [27]

Coltrane's solos in *All blues* and *So what?* are fascinating, and foresee a passage through modality that would bring him eventually to wilder, more ritualistic things. Adderley, though reliable in arranged passages – as in *All blues* – is otherwise hardly the man for such an occasion. In *So what?* he stabs in emulation of Coltrane's vigorous, staggered clauses, and his quick reversion to neo-bop type may not seem of much consequence. His marked uneasiness with the cool blues form of *Flamenco sketches* seems rather surprising, for whatever scalar or linear innovations these may be, they seem closer to folk-music elements than to modes of classical origin.

However, Adderley's inadequacy is negative confirmation that something adventurous was afoot. And Davis's rather offhand improvisatory ease suggests that his approach to these experiments relied more upon his own musings and probings – less deliberately formulated than his claim to authorship implies, and, perhaps, is positive evidence that the preparatory shaping work really was Bill Evans's.

So what? was to be featured subsequently both by Davis groups and by others. The *Plugged Nickel* version (**396**) shows how the theme could be ushered almost roughly into free music territory. For the erstwhile hierarch of modality, Russell, Davis's 1959 solo became all that mattered of *So what?* In June 1983 he recorded a transcription for brass section by Gotz Tangerding with jazz-rock underpinning (†Blue Note [E] CDP746 391–2). Such solos as associated themselves with this liberally embalmed sanctity showed little evidence of modal – or model – imagination. E.T.

John McLaughlin

394 Extrapolation

†Polydor (E) 841598

John Surman (bar, sop); McLaughlin (g); Brian Odges (bs); Tony Oxley (d). London, January 1969.

Extrapolation · *It's funny* · *Arjen's bag* · *Pete the poet* · *This is for us to share* · *Spectrum* · *Really to know* · *Two for two*

Here is a beautifully consistent sequence of jazz excellences inspired and led by a musician whose career in the music has not displayed anything like the same quality of homogeneity despite his immense virtuosity and the sincerity of his philosophical and artistic vision. *Extrapolation* is one of the most original, most prophetic albums produced by a British jazz group in the late 1960s and early 1970s. 'It was a virtual summary,' Ian Carr wrote, 'of current small-group playing techniques [and] anticipated the jazz-rock movement of the 1970s.' [28] Carr's further judgement that it revealed McLaughlin as 'a sublimely original guitar stylist' might approach justification on the basis of this album and related sessions; but John Litweiler is of the opinion that 'Miles Davis's 1969 records [were] the first demonstration of McLaughlin's extraordinary ability to recall and reproduce others' licks in a discontinuous fashion [and] he became the loudest of freak-out players'. [29] The guitarist's contributions to the Davis albums *In a Silent Way* (†CBS [E] 450982–2) and *Bitches' Brew* (†CBS [E] 460 602–2), both from the same year as *Extrapolation* – hear him in Davis's brief acknowledgement of his gifts, a number titled 'John McLaughlin', on *Bitches' Brew* for example – are useful comparisons in assessing his potentialities at that time, and doubtless confirm him as a co-founder of the 'fusion' of jazz with the idioms of rock which loomed as the 1970s hove into view.

Memories that recall *Extrapolation*'s first appearance will link it closely to the Davis albums mentioned – in particular to *In a Silent Way* – but the relation may not now be as compelling as it seemed at the time. Of these four musicians, McLaughlin was the only active link to Davis; and though this was his session – his first as leader – and much as his compositions may reflect his keen instinct for what Davis was discovering, the real magic of what his group creates here springs as much out of the individual creative instincts of Surman, Odges and Oxley as it does out of the particular empathy with his notions that the leader was able to inspire in them.

The Odges–Oxley lead-in to *Extrapolation* has long been familiar enough to call to mind the Haden–Higgins entrée to Ornette Coleman's *Lonely woman* (**400**), and, although the inner conception may similarly be quite different, the unison fleetnesses of Surman and McLaughlin may not seem stylistically too far removed from the Cherry–Coleman voicing of *Eventually* (also **400**). That is perhaps a facile way of acknowledging that Surman and Oxley in particular, and McLaughlin too, through an earlier liaison with Gunter Hempel were still very much conditioned by a free-jazz immersion. Soloing, Surman, as was his contemporary wont, echoes a few swinging surges from the 1930s – the Savoy Sultans, perhaps? (**136**) And, let it be faced, the rock patterns that were tempting some jazz group leaders then usually had their genesis in the swing era. McLaughlin's rapid electric fragments spill a similar message; but in this opening number which celebrates what jazz was toting towards new territories, it is not unreasonable to admit that the little-remembered Odges lays fair claim to the most impressive heroism – but his inspiration is rather less easy to define. He is interestingly teamed with Surman and McLaughlin over Oxley's brilliant commentary during *It's funny*, which is a thematic close cousin to Mingus's *Goodbye, pork-pie hat*. Odges rocks and rides through *Arjen's bag*, dedicated to a Dutch bass player. Another dedicatee is Pete Brown, a poet associated with *New Departures* magazie and prominent in the local jazz poetry scene; Charles Fox described his 'stage personality' as 'almost as amiable as Louis Armstrong's'. [30] *Pete the poet* is aptly jocose, Surman and McLaughlin playing with contrasting and complementary possibilities, and Oxley contributing a solo for which McLaughlin's epithet for Brown – 'amazing' – can only be reiterated.

In *This is for us to share* ('Dedicated to my true love'), as in his Iberian hints for *Arjen's bag*, the guitarist uses his acoustic instrument to impressive effect. There is a remarkable sense of freedom, and the overall effect depends much upon Oxley's underlay of percussive sounds. Some of McLaughlin's strongest electric pronouncements are in the dazzling swing of *Spectrum*. The guitar-baritone unisons, here and elsewhere, are as typical as anything can be of the attractions of this whole corpus of delights. *Binky's beam* is for the bassist Binky McKenzie. Surman's lyricism develops into savage declamation. There are accents in the guitar-led extensions of this piece which carry hints from ancient blues/ gospel accompaniments. The brief *Really to know* starts with a ¾ guitar venture which progresses into striding passages. *Two for two* is skilled ensemble freedom, and McLaughlin's vigorous flamenco flurries sound formal within it. Surman's baritone surges aloft before a deepening of mood sidesteps into *Peace piece* – rather less than two minutes' worth of quiet after musings from the guitar.

However McLaughlin's leadership may be categorized in retrospect, 'fusion' is no word for it. Wiser reflection will consider the variety of 'current small-group playing techniques' which this quartet was able to draw upon, and should remember the very adventurous though differently framed work which, for example, the Oxley Quintet was achieving in *The Baptized Traveller* (RCA-Victor [E] SF82115, 1969) and Surman's groups in *How Many Clouds Can You See?* (Deram [E] SML-R1045, 1970) alongside the early productions of the Spontaneous Music Ensemble and other free music continuations. Linked though it was to these things through its participants, *Extrapolation* can be distinguished from them as it can from the music of Ian Carr's soon-to-be-founded Nucleus and especially from the fused architectures of the Mahavishnu's *Inner Mounting Flame* (†Columbia [E] CK31067, 1971). Clearly, it can stand up for its own vivid identity. Suggesting pigeonholes is mischievous when eyries commend themselves more readily. E.T.

Grachan Moncur III

395 Some Other Stuff

†Blue Note (E) CDP7243 8 32092 2 4

Moncur (tbn); Wayne Shorter (ten); Herbie Hancock (p); Cecil McBee (b); Anthony Williams (d). Englewood Cliffs, New Jersey, 6 July 1964.
Gnostic · Thandiwa · The twins · Nomadic

An admirer of J. J. Johnson, Moncur put in road time with Ray Charles (1959–62) and the Benny Golson–Art Farmer Jazztet where he filled the trombone chair originally occupied by Curtis Fuller. With the Jazztet he cut *Here and Now* (Mercury MG [A] 20698) in March 1962 and *Another Git Together* (Mercury [J] EXPR-1002) three months later. On the latter he contributed *Space station*, a brisk jazz waltz, but it was his cleanly executed J. J.-influenced solo on *Reggie* that caught the ear. In 1963 he settled in New York and within a six-week period in spring 1963 he had appeared on Herbie Hancock's *My Point of View* (Blue Note [A] BST84126) and an unreleased Horace Silver session and was invited to join Jackie McLean's group. He was inside Rudy Van Gelder's recording studio almost immediately with McLean to cut *One Step Beyond* (Blue Note [A] BST84137). Five months later he recorded again with McLean, *Destination Out* (†Blue Note [E] CDP7243 8 32087 2 2), contributing three original compositions. This, together with his solo work on tracks such as *Riff raff*, convinced Alfred Lion to give him his own date. In November 1963 he made his debut as a leader on record with *Evolution* (Blue Note [A] BST84153) using McLean, Bobby Hutcherson (vib), then a member of McLean's group, Bob Cranshaw (b) and the former McLean employee Tony Williams, who a couple of months beforehand had joined Miles Davis. Still in McLean's orbit, that album is to a certain extent a continuation of the freer approach to improvisation the saxophonist had adopted in *Destination Out*.

Eight months later McLean wound up his group to work on the West Coast as a single. Moncur's next job was performing his own music behind the James Baldwin play *Blues for Mr Charlie* on Broadway and it was during this period he cut *Some Other Stuff*, his second, and last, album as a leader for Blue Note. *Gnostic* is organised around a three-note motif and opens with Moncur's simple theme and extemporization. His solo is built around this simple theme and is against a harmonically free, time-no-changes accompaniment in $^{12}/_{8}$ that is dominated by Hancock's insistent accompanying figures. Moncur's tone is full and round in contrast to the anguished cry of Shorter's solo that prompts a more fluid accompaniment from Hancock, whose role is crucial to the success of the piece. Hancock's own solo is played with a freedom that contrasts his insistent accompanying figures, splashing sound clusters and jagged runs against the slow repeating pulse of McBee and Williams before a return to the stark theme.

Thandiwa is linked to the *Gnostic* motif that appears in modified form of the B section of the 24-bar ABAB song. The A section contrasts a highly syncopated figure with a smooth, cautious B section that leads into the powerfully swinging solos, opening with Shorter, who shows the ground he had opened up between himself and Coltrane. His harmonically fluid, highly individual phrasing makes for compulsive listening; consistently thoughtful, he would rather cross the street than fall prey to predictability or cliché. As he begins to wind up his solo, the finest on the album, he begins to toy with time and is immediately followed by the big ears of the Hancock–McBee–Williams rhythm section, giving a fascinating preview of the remarkable catch-as-catch-can interplay that would be a hallmark of Shorter's work some 12 weeks later when he joined Hancock and Williams in the Miles Davis quintet. In contrast, Moncur's approach is governed by the three-note motif from the A section which is also used as the pick-up for Hancock's solo, a mixture of gentle lyricism and extended chords that takes the piece out amid fistfuls of notes and skittering arabesques.

The simple schoolyard chant of *Twins* has much in common with the sometimes sarcastic melodic themes that Albert Ayler might introduce. 'I wanted to get a picture of two young, mischievous boys,' Moncur explained. [31] Introduced by a bass *ostinato* in the basic unit of a crotchet for 12 bars and two beats, the theme is a repeated eight-bar phrase in tempo before launching into a rhythmically free Moncur solo using elements of the 'chant' based on a pedal point implied by *ostinato* and theme. Using largely sequence, repetition and permutation, he reinforces his line by returning to it towards the end of his solo. In comparison to Shorter and Hancock, whose instruments allow a wider range of scalar/chordal options through their inherent fluidity, he nevertheless maintains his composure and confidence in melodic organization, using few notes to maximum effect. Shorter follows, again developing blood-brother-like rapport with Hancock and Williams, whose handling of freer forms represents musicianship of a high order. Hancock, both in solo and ensemble, throws the efforts of those around him in sharp focus.

In live concerts drum solos earn massive applause, and this presumably encourages drummers to stretch out on record. Atmosphere and the visual correlative clearly play a part in audience enthusiasm, but that does not entirely explain why such a fine drummer as Tony Williams does not sustain interest over the seven minutes and 41 seconds of *Nomadic.* Perhaps it is the close proximity of a record collection vying for audition that makes the listener restless over long feats of unrelenting rhythmic pummelling, interdependent limb control and much else that goes into a drum solo. The only instrumental interventions are short descending phrases played by Shorter and Moncur as Williams falls into the trap that most older and wiser drummers learn from experience, that of keeping solos short and to the point on record. Indeed, 25 years later, Williams hardly ever soloed in the series of hard-bop albums he made with his own group for the reconstituted Blue Note label in the 1980s and early 1990s.

Moncur's use of harmonically free structures side by side with compositions of prearranged harmonies was nevertheless an extension and broadening of the bop heritage from which he emerged. It remains a source of regret that this was his final album as a leader for Blue Note. His contact with the label was thereafter intermittent: a session with Wayne Shorter in 1965, two with Jackie McLean in 1967 and an unreleased Lee Morgan session from 1971. Although he has remained active in jazz, his potential on record at least has remained sadly unfulfilled. S.N.

Miles Davis

396 Live at the Plugged Nickel

Columbia (A) C2 38266 (2 LPs), CBS (E) 88606 (2 LPs)

Davis (tpt); Wayne Shorter (ten); Herbie Hancock (p); Ron Carter (bs); Tony Williams (d). The Plugged Nickel, Chicago, 22 December 1965.
Round about midnight

Same personnel. 23 December 1965.
Walkin' · *Agitation* · *On Green Dolphin Street* · *So what?* · *The theme* · *Stella by starlight* · *All blues* · *Yesterdays*

This issue, appearing ten years after the music's taping, came as a revelation even to those who were familiar with the innovations of *E.S.P.* (†CBS [E] 467 899) recorded at the beginning of 1965 before Davis succumbed to illness. *Agitation*, the only fresh number here, is only the most obvious link with the studio-recorded *E.S.P.*, but this club recording needs to be heard with reference to earlier concert sets and particularly to this quintet's Berlin appearance of September 1964 (CBS [G]

62976), when Shorter was new to the group. The Berlin *Walkin'* and *So what?* set out at speeds as furious as those at the Plugged Nickel and there were hints, as things proceeded, at the free experiments with time and tonality which later become so constant. Whereas in the Berlin *Walkin'* Davis had played less defiantly, pausing to invent catchy tunes and including a not untypical phrase which was to be the seed of *Agitation*, in Chicago he blurs the delineation of choruses and sustains a challenge to tonality which is more advanced. Even so, the Chicago solo bears an odd relation to both modality and freedom; certainly striding well ahead of the modality which could prompt Davis to sidestep into polytonality in only one chorus out of 13 in a Stockholm *Walkin'* of 1960 (Dragon [Sd] DRLP90/91), yet paying heed more to Davis's own daemon than to any prompting from Don Cherry's free jazz.

If at these sessions 'free vistas . . . become possibilities', [32] the key is not in the advance-through-abandonment of Coleman and Cherry but still in the response to scalar patterns in *Kind of Blue* (**393**). Furthermore, the 1965 liberations of measure and syntax have been attained by the quintet's own route of progress. In *So what?* Shorter, who by now has moved out of Coltrane's shadow into the light of his own discoveries, sounds abrasive after the diffident airiness of his solos in *Agitation* and *On Green Dolphin Street*; and, at the end of a monstrously bullying exhibition by Williams, Hancock's lines dart like eels in the receding surf.

In *Walkin'* tenorist and pianist swap jerky clauses of developing length, keeping a deceptive degree of thematic control – deceptive because the seeming abandonment even of the rudimentary designs of themes such as this one is part of a deliberately variable attitude towards 'chord changes' that was beginning to be evident in Berlin.

Agitation scarcely merits notice as a theme. Its title indicates the intended character of solos and exchanges, and may appear to suit much of what happens during other numbers. But the imaginative control is much firmer than casual listening suggests. Shorter's masterly grasp of time warp in his animated *Stella by starlight* narrative is a case in point; and Davis's solo in the same piece is well steered. The scrappy conversation between Shorter and Hancock in *Agitation*, suspended in near silence, contrasts with the peevish sparring of these two in *All blues* where, like Davis in his grimly mischievous solo, they might be thought intent on getting grievances out of their systems. But this is art, not mere catharsis. Davis allows his young men ample scope to work out their intensity of ideas.

The argument with time is continual, never resolved in any way that demands capitulation to convention or slackening of intellectual stamina. In *Round about midnight*, one of the most challenging tracks, a sardonic Davis gathers pulse out of initial maziness; Shorter shapes and reshapes plagihedral figures against crashing, tempo-swallowing percussion. In

Yesterdays too, we are reminded of the beat only spasmodically as Davis searches plaintively for some old Gil Evans backing and gets instead sparse soliloquial comments from Hancock and Shorter. The tempo slows almost to a stop; then, after impetus is resumed, Shorter and Davis devise a cockeyed scrabble of Mulliganish counterpoint.

Williams is more consistent than he had been in Berlin, and his control of basic tempos and background textures gives him an axial role. As for the splendid Carter, self-effacement does not succeed in hiding considerable inventive skill and vigour. As one returns to this strangely bothersome and, in the end, unanalysable marvel of a record, the aptness and variety of the bassist's abetments become increasingly apparent as a contribution to music-making which is both spontaneous and intense – rewarding in new ways at every hearing.

Out of due time, one has realized how, midway through a decade which began in modalism and closed at the rim of electric rock, Davis's music asked fierce questions of both past and future. They did open vistas for they were not impossible questions. Nevertheless, when, after Davis had resumed work following further illness, *Miles Smiles* (Columbia [A] CL2601, CBS [E] 85561) was made in October 1966, different speculations were finding voice; and by the early 1970s Davis, Shorter, Hancock and Williams would be immersed in things which sounded, superficially at least, much more conservative. E.T.

Phil Woods

397 At the Frankfurt Jazz Festival

Embryo (A) SD530

Woods (alt); Gordon Beck (p, el p); Henri Texier (bs); Daniel Humair (d). Frankfurt Jazz Festival, 1969.

Freedom jazz dance · Ode à Jean-Louis · Joshua · The meeting

From March 1968 to December 1972, Phil Woods lived in France. He had turned his back on a secure career in the studios of New York working on film and TV soundtracks and advertising jingles to pursue a career in jazz. His reputation as a first-rate lead alto saxophonist as much as a supremely gifted improviser in the Charlie Parker school was built working with a quintet he co-led with his fellow altoist Gene Quill, which produced three albums, and in the big bands of Dizzy Gillespie, Quincy Jones, Oliver Nelson and Benny Goodman. With Jones he created a widely admired solo on *The midnight sun never sets* and virtually defined the Leonard Feather blues *I remember Bird* with Oliver Nelson.

On 28 March 1968 he opened at the Cameleon, a small Paris club, with two Swiss musicians, George Gruntz on piano and Henri Texier on bass, and a Frenchman, Daniel Humair, on drums. That marked the birth of the European Rhythm Machine, Woods's first full-time band of his own. After an appearance at the Newport Jazz Festival in July 1969

Gruntz left and was replaced by the Englishman Beck, a fluent pianist who had enhanced his reputation with a spell in the Tubby Hayes quintet (**347**). When the new line-up appeared at the Frankfurt Jazz Festival later in the year, it was clear that the saxophonist had made a radical departure from the certainties of the post-Parker bop tradition within which his style had orbited in America.

From the chromaticism of bop, Woods embraced the areas of rhythmic freedom explored by Herbie Hancock, Ron Carter and Tony Williams in the mid-1960s while members of the Miles Davis quintet. Woods and the Rhythm Machine developed a similar rapport, enabling them to change tempos, textures and moods seemingly spontaneously during their performances. Suddenly solos might dissolve into abstraction before emerging as a half-tempo rumination and then abruptly powering forward at the original, whirlwind tempo, or subvert into a rock passage. In short, the group had collectively adopted a very pliable approach to time which could be spontaneously changed according to the mood of the moment.

At Frankfurt the alto saxophonist was captured at a creative peak; his soaring playing ignited the rhythm section and left his audience gasping. Although subsequent creative heights found their way on to record, such as his 1976 *Cheek to cheek* solo from the Grammy-winning *Live from the Showboat* (RCA [F] PL02202), his performance here reveals the greatest range and diversity of his playing on record. *Freedom jazz dance*, an Eddie Harris composition making extensive use of the interval of a fourth, is taken at a blistering 288 beats per minute. There is no exposition of the theme at the beginning, Woods launching immediately into his solo. At once the listener is aware that here is a saxophonist of the highest order, displaying a technical fluency that allows an unhurried feeling despite the fast tempo, a cogent ordering of ideas, including a contrast in certain passages between the metre of the solo against the underlying rhythm, an ease in moving from one tempo to another, a fluent use of chromatic substitutions, a secure tone throughout the instrument's register, a variety of attacks and tonal manipulation including the use of a growl and alternate fingering and a utilization of the whole range of the instrument (two octaves and a fourth) to encompass a wide range of expression.

Woods uses various motifs, some based on the interval of a fourth, which swirl through his rush of ideas and give a feeling of unity and direction to his solo. And this is not gratuitous virtuosity, his solo as a whole being very expressive and evolving logically to its climax, rounded out by a fragment of the Harris theme. Beck follows on acoustic piano, a musician then as now hugely undervalued. His solo has a very fluid approach to time, gradually dissolving into an unaccompanied *rubato* passage that flirts with atonal areas of sound which suggest Cecil Taylor before launching into a driving medium swing. Woods re-enters at this new tempo, his concise yet articulate lyricism leading into a Humair solo. The former Swingle Singers drummer is far removed from the 'plodding' approach Americans often associated with European drummers; indeed a specific feature of the European Rhythm Machine is how distinctly free from such stereotypical preconceptions they sound. As Humair reaches a crescendo, Woods abruptly enters at the very bright original tempo, stating the 16-bar theme in full for the first time before allowing the mood to relax and segue into a slower *Ode à Jean-Louis.*

The new theme employs a squarer approach to rhythm, close to patterns associated with rock, but incorporating the equally fluid approach to time of *Freedom jazz dance.* Woods still commands our attention with the sheer density of ideas that pack his solo, his tone full and round, which he intensifies with a growl to emphasize certain phrases. Beck is featured with a long solo, and it is clear that he was well abreast of advances contemporary jazz piano had made at the hands of Bill Evans, Herbie Hancock and Chick Corea. His fleet and personal style translated well on to the Fender Rhodes piano and his playing here suggests he was probably the most able of all the pianists associated with Woods's groups.

Joshua, like *Freedom jazz dance*, was a number associated with the 1960s Miles Davis repertoire. He recorded the number three times in 1963–4, on *Seven Steps to Heaven* (CBS [A] 62170), *At Antibes* (CBS [F] 62390) and *Four and More* (CBS [A] 5560). The first version was set down in the studio and provides the most precise execution of a very interesting composition. It uses an AABA form for the theme statement, where the A sections are 12 bars long and the B section eight bars long which is split between four bars in $^3/_4$ and four in $^4/_4$. Although the A sections are 12 bars, they are not a blues but are dominated by the tonality of a IIm7 chord for eight bars, effectively the Dorian mode. For solos, however, the form changes to AABBBA and the B section, utilizing a cycle of fourths, is altered to six bars of $^3/_4$ and only two of $^4/_4$. Thus with its unusually long 60-bar chorus for improvisation, the contrast between static harmony (A section) and fast harmonic motion (B section) and the alternation between $^3/_4$ and $^4/_4$ time (B section), *Joshua* presents a very challenging vehicle for improvisation.

Woods, with Beck at the electric piano, begins with free-ranging exposition of the theme at a medium-slow tempo that touches on free and rock that he ends on a sustained note, allowing the bass and drums to re-enter, setting a staggeringly fast tempo. [33] After the statement of the theme at the faster tempo he launches into a solo that demonstrates just why he is held in such high regard by saxophonists the world over. Perhaps the most striking feature of his playing is how the cogency of his ideas remains intact at a tempo at which few musicians could contemplate participating without losing coherence. Idea follows idea and they are explored across the whole range of his instrument, even using 'false fingering' to produce notes above the normal range of the alto, something that rarely occurred in his earlier – or indeed, his later – work. Towards the end of his solo, a brilliant, unaccompanied cadenza leads into a furious chorus that ebbs into quarter tempo and returns *a tempo* for Beck's solo. Now at the acoustic piano, Beck is equally undeterred by the whirlwind pace, his work maintaining the poise and composure that used to distinguish Teddy Wilson's playing almost four decades earlier. Gradually the precise ordering of his ideas blurs into 'outside' episodes and a very free approach to tempo before abruptly returning to terra firma. Woods then comes back for a series of exchanges with Humair that lead into an impressive drum solo, full of interesting 'percussive' sounds not usually associated with the standard kit. Woods re-enters, winding up with a recapitulation of the theme. *Joshua* represents the climax of the album, a true tour de force with every member of the group contributing in equal measure to a highly successful performance that is appropriately acknowledged by the large audience.

The final track, a Beck original called *The meeting*, is a good old-fashioned 12-bar blues, played with a strong backbeat which, although showing the group *au courant* with the rock revolution happening around them, today seems less rock per se than simply employing squarer rhythm-section patterns. Beck at the electric piano shows he can lay down a funky backdrop and sounds suitably mean and low-down during his solo, while Woods relishes his opportunity to sound soulful and lets his hair down with a rumbustious outing full of blusey hues: flat thirds, fifths and sevenths. This is the group having fun, and it shows.

The European Rhythm Machine lasted until December 1972, when Woods eventually returned to the United States. There he flirted with an electronic rock group on the West Coast for ten months before returning to the East Coast, where his solo on Billy Joel's *I love you just the way you are* reminded the world that Phil Woods was back in town. His subsequent groups, normally with his long-time associates Bill Goodwin and Steve Gilmore, were, however, for the most part somewhat conservative and more in the post-Parker tradition in comparison to the six albums he made with the Rhythm Machine, of which this is an outstanding example.

Here he set new standards for the post-bop alto in jazz, standards which, by and large, remain unsurpassed even today. 'In the beginning there was Johnny Hodges and Benny Carter,' said Woods in 1975. 'On the second day there came along Charlie Parker. The third day produced Paul Desmond, the fourth Julian Adderley. The fifth day gave us Phil Woods, while the sixth gave us Ornette Coleman. Will there be a seventh? Is anyone out there strong enough?' [34] Almost three decades later we are still waiting for an answer. S.N.

Chick Corea

398 Now He Sings, Now He Sobs

†Blue Note (E) CDP790055–2

Chick Corea (p); Miroslav Vitous (bs); Roy Haynes (d). New York City, 14, 19 and 27 March 1968.

Matrix · My one and only love · Now he beats the drum – now he stops · Bossa · Now he sings – now he sobs · Steps – what was · Fragments · Windows · Pannonica · Samba yantra · I don't know · The law of falling and catching up · Gemini

The Italian-American home into which Corea was born in 1941 was filled with music. His father, Armando Corea, had a dance band and at an early age his son was exposed to the European tradition as much as the bop masters. Pursing formal classical studies with Salvatore Sullo, Corea began playing jazz gigs around his home town of Boston while still in high school. When he arrived in New York in the early 1960s, he had developed an impressive technique that was backed by a thorough musical education. He enrolled in Columbia University intending to pursue an academic career but dropped out, wanting to play jazz. After a brief period of indecision he returned to Boston to prepare for an audition for Juilliard, and, although accepted, he stayed for only two months before finally deciding his future lay in jazz. On the New York scene he first worked with the Latin bands of Willie Bobo, Mongo Santamaria and Cal Tjader, and in 1965 he recorded *Standing Ovation at Newport* with Herbie Mann (Atlantic [A] 1445). However, his first appearance on a straight-ahead jazz album was with the trumpeter Blue Mitchell, whom he joined after the trumpeter left Horace Silver, following two weekend engagements at Birdland in March 1964, to form his own band with the tenor saxophonist Junior Cook. On *The Thing to Do* (Blue Note [A] BST84178) from July 1964, Corea contributes *Chick's tune*, based on the chords of *You stepped out of a dream*, which combined an attractive melody with the prevailing hard-bop certainties.

Corea's playing with Mitchell revealed his careful attention to Bud Powell and Horace Silver, but he would quickly add more contemporary influences, particularly the modal chord voicings of Bill Evans (he would later compose *Waltz for Bill Evans* in 1969 as a tribute [35]) and McCoy Tyner. On Mitchell's *Down with It* (Blue Note [A] BST84214) from 1965 and on two tracks on *Boss Horn* from 1966 (Blue Note [A] BST84257) it is apparent that the diverse strands he was absorbing were now coalescing into a coherent style. Corea's original *Tones for Joan's bones* which appeared on the latter album was a sophisticated ABCAD structure with contrasting sections and provided the title cut for his debut album as a leader on Herbie Mann's Vortex label, also from 1966. [36]

By now Corea was incorporating the influence of the French impressionists, combining Debussyesque washes of colour with darting runs, bittersweet dissonances and sudden changes of tempo. Evidence that he had evolved a fresh, original style by the time he was invited to join Stan Getz's quartet (as Gary Burton's replacement) in early 1967 is clearly apparent on *Sweet Rain* (†Verve [A] 815 054–2), recorded 30 March that year. Here, Corea emerges as a talent to watch. He contributes two originals, *Litha*, which makes use of fourths in the melody line (these are a particular characteristic of McCoy Tyner's work and the composition is inspired by Coltrane) and *Windows*, which is another interesting ad hoc form presenting a 48-bar structure thus:

A (8 bars) + B (8 bars) + C (8 bars) + D (8 bars) + E (16 bars)

Corea's imaginative flair for composition, producing highly original, challenging song-forms for improvising, has seldom been recognized, but nevertheless over the years he has contributed a small body of impressive compositions to jazz.

After touring extensively with Getz in 1967, Corea worked as an accompanist to Sarah Vaughan in 1968 when he recorded *Now He Sings, Now He Sobs.* This presented an extremely fresh approach to the piano trio and numbers among the finest in the genre. Corea's accompanists were among the most accomplished in jazz; Haynes had been a member of Getz's quartet during Corea's tenure with the saxophonist, and Vitous had played with Corea in Donald Byrd's group, an association documented on Byrd's *The Creeper* (Blue Note [A] BN LT-1096) from October 1967. [37] *Matrix* is a modified 12-bar blues where the tonality of the IV chord in bar five of the progression and the II chord in bar nine is restrained. The theme, a refraction of Monk-like phrasing (another Corea favourite), is stated with great rhythmic freedom within the 12-bar cycle. During his 16-chorus solo he frequently makes use of long, unbroken lines that extend as long as six bars (specifically, in choruses 4, 5, 10, 13 and 15) which are contrasted with short bluesy figures (particularly in choruses 6 and 11). Throughout, he makes frequent use the pentatonic scale and often plays 'outside' the changes, in fast, twinkling side-slipping runs or by deliberately using dissonance to build tension. It sets the tone for the album, where loose, freely stated ideas are exchanged by the group whose horizons are the limits of their imagination.

Although Corea was an admirer of Bill Evans, he did not use silence to the extent that Evans had, and there is less interaction among the group than the give-and-take to be found in *The Village Vanguard Concerts* (**373**); and Vitous functioned in a more orthodox time-keeping role. Yet Corea's highly developed sense of rhythmic freedom permitted a feeling of discourse even if the rhythms implied or stated were often quite specific. *Now he beats the drum – now he stops* begins with a reflective interlude largely built around a tonal centre and contains interesting chord voicings that suggest contemporary classical music. It then opens into a medium-tempo freely improvised piece that appears to possess harmonic complexity even though the base is not; throughout the album Corea's rootless voicings suggest harmonic ambiguity with his extensive use of slash chords.

The title track is another well-constructed Corea original. It opens with a marchlike introduction in 4/4 that leads into a jazz waltz and the exposition of the melody. Like much of Corea's work it is full of interesting touches:

Intro (4/4): X (13 bars)+ X^1 (first four bars of X) + transition
(3/4 to end): Y (8 bars) + A (16 bars) + B (20 bars) + A (16 bars) +
B^1 (first 12 bars of B) + solos

His solo was taken over a simplified 16-bar sequence of chords quite different from the harmonies for the theme, albeit preserving the dominant B-minor tonality. Corea's extemporization grows organically out of the theme; indeed, the mixture of improvised and written blend into a seamless whole. Agile and spirited, his playing often implied a double-time feel with his rush of ideas; he had a crisp touch with a very smooth, even execution. Vitous responds with agile, imaginative bass lines and Haynes, a veteran of Charlie Parker, Lester Young and John Coltrane groups, reveals his enormous versatility within the context of this highly contemporary performance.

Steps – what was begins as an extemporization out of tempo, drawing on Debussy-like washes and dissonant splashes before launching into a 'time no changes' passage at a brisk tempo which contains some of Corea's most inspired playing of the session. Little wonder that this made such an impression on musicians when the album was released. This passage leads into a long solo for Haynes, beginning on cymbals and then gradually incorporating his whole kit before returning to cymbals to prepare for the entrance of piano and bass. In contrast to the first passage, they unite on a preset composition that would reappear in October 1972 as *Spain* from the album *Light as a Feather* (Polydor [E] 2310247), one of Corea's most famous pieces. In this early incarnation, melody and form have been settled on, although a more formal presentation of the melody would come later. Corea's attraction to spontaneous group interaction is revealed on *Fragments*, *The law of falling and catching up* and *Gemini*, the last-named alternating between episodes by the pianist and by Vitous which veer into abstraction, a precursor of a musical direction that would claim his attention from 1968 to 1971.

The configuration of the original LP issue was *Matrix*, *Now he beats the drum – now he stops*, *Now he sings – now he sobs*, *Steps – what was* and *The law of falling and catching up.* As can be seen, a considerable amount of material went unreleased until the CD appeared in 1988. This 'new' material serves only to underline what an exemplary group this was, with arresting performances of, among others, Corea's *Windows* and Monk's *Pannonica*. The unusual construction of *Windows* has already been discussed.

Corea's use of ¾ time reflects the influence of Bill Evans, whose use of that metre helped usher it into the repertoire of many contemporary jazz musicians. The exposition of the theme is stated very freely without a repeat before Corea moved gracefully into an improvisation full of rich melodic motifs and shimmering flourishes. His left hand was never intrusive, frequently using figures voiced in fourths (as he does throughout the album). In giving prominence to his fleet right hand, he favoured the higher end of the piano which together with his light touch added to the feeling of bright, sparkling improvisation. *Pannonica* reflects Corea's love of Monk's music and it is interesting to note that when this trio was reconvened after a recording hiatus of 13 years, they produced a double album with one LP devoted to Monk's music and the other to spontaneous interaction, *Trio Music* (ECM [G] 1232/33).

On *Pannonica*, an AABA tune with three eight-bar sections and a quirky extra bar in the final A section to make it 33 bars long, Corea does not allow Monk's personality to overwhelm his playing in the way many pianists seem to do by playing in Monk's style. Instead, he honours the spirit of Monk's composition by improvising on the theme, taking motifs, inverting and reversing them and developing them without straying beyond his own musical personality, but wittily signals we are in Monk territory by a sparse use of Monkian dissonance.

When *Now He Sings, Now He Sobs* was released, it set a standard among contemporary musicians with its free-flowing, yet highly disciplined performances; indeed, many pianists learned the album note for note, such was its influence. Six months after recording it, Corea was invited to join Miles Davis's group after the group's regular pianist Herbie Hancock failed to return on time after taking a honeymoon in South America. Corea's tenure with Davis lasted two years and his first recording with Davis was to finish off *Filles de Kilimanjaro* (**441**), an album which he had begun with Hancock the previous June. After leaving Davis, Corea formed a piano trio (later joined by Anthony Braxton on saxes) to explore spontaneous interaction. This he abruptly ended and during a brief spell with Getz formed an acoustic ensemble called Return to Forever. The eponymously titled album again highlighted Corea's compositional gifts, [38] but after one more album by the group, Corea launched himself into a glossy version of jazz-rock with involved hi-tech runs and a certain pomposity using orchestral devices inspired by classical music. Corea anticipated what became known as fusion, a highly commercial jazz-influenced variant of pop music. In later years he sought a free pardon back into acoustic jazz – his album of duets with Gary Burton from 1979 is certainly recommended [39] – but he has fundamentally remained, since the mid-1970s, a brilliant musician content to let his great talent languish in pursuit of commercial ends. S.N.

McCoy Tyner

399 Atlantis

†Milestone [A] MCD55002–2

Azar Lawrence (ten, sop); McCoy Tyner (p); Joony Booth (bs); Wilby Fletcher (d); Guilherme Franco (perc). San Francisco, 31 August–1 September 1974.

Atlantis · In a sentimental mood · Makin' out · My one and only love · Pursuit · Love samba

Tyner's role as the voice of reason which united the competing parts of John Coltrane's classic quartet of 1960–65 catapulted the former Benny Golson–Art Farmer Jazztet pianist to international recognition. During his period with Coltrane he introduced a fresh approach to piano jazz with a way of comping that was new to this music. Instead of the model commonly adopted by pianists who had evolved from Bud Powell, Tyner's approach was more aggressive and, particularly in modal numbers or those based on a pedal point, he employed insistent, repeated rhythmic patterns of open-voiced chords that were often made up of a chord voiced in fifths in the left hand and one voiced in fourths in the right. His extensive use of quartal voicings came to characterize his 'voice' within the quartet, their open, unresolved sound (as opposed to conventional triads) lending an air of harmonic ambiguity that suited Coltrane's style. Yet his work as a leader in his own right for Impulse and Blue Note revealed a more considered, less energetic player. This is illustrated by his 5 July 1963 performance on *McCoy Tyner Live at Newport* (†Impulse [J] AS48), with a pick-up group under his own leadership, contrasted by his performance two days later at the same festival as a member of Coltrane's quartet on *Newport '63* (†Impulse [A] GRP 11282).

Tyner recorded six albums as a leader for Blue Note, beginning with *The Real McCoy* (Blue Note [A] BST84264) in 1967, [40] and it is now clear that on these albums, his style, although extremely influential while with Coltrane, was still to coalesce fully. 'I was really riding a tremendous wave when I was with John; it was my school, my university,' he pointed out. 'I developed a lot working with him, but it took a while after I left him to get settled and find a perspective. When I left it was like coming down off a mountain top. I had to settle down. I recorded standards (*Time for Tyner* [Blue Note (A) BST84307]) and it was a different kind of feeling. An artist has to reflect what he feels at a given time and that is how I felt after that peak experience.' [41]

His departure from Coltrane's quartet coincided with the rise of rock music, which had the effect of dramatically squeezing work opportunities in jazz. Like many at this time he was forced to take day jobs to make ends meet, including taxi driving, as well as working as an accompanist for Ike and Tina Turner and Jimmy Witherspoon. But after over five years of struggle on the periphery of the music business, the producer Orrin Keepnews signed him to Milestone Records. His first album for the label, *Sahara* (†Original Jazz Classics [A] OJCCD 311–2), recorded in January/February 1972, re-established his career, winning the 1973 *down beat* critics' poll as Record of the Year and receiving two Grammy nominations, as Best Jazz Performance by a Soloist and Best Jazz Performance by a Group. Recorded with a quartet comprising Sonny Fortune (sop, alt, fl), Calvin Hill (bs) and Alphonse Mouzon (d), the album is notable for its long (23 minutes) title track and Tyner's abstracted alleluia, *A prayer for my family.* What is immediately apparent, however, is a seeming transformation in Tyner's playing.

His virtuosity was less masked, but it was the ends to which he put it that was so arresting. He made greater use of polytonality and of dissonance and had taken account of Cecil Taylor. There was a greater drive in his playing and he favoured crashing cadence points and rumbling *ostinato*s. His playing was less linear than on his Blue Note albums, the emphasis more on clusters of sounds contrasted by long, greased runs of semiquavers. The force of his attack made his quartal voicings appear dense, shimmering structures – indeed, overall his playing had become darker, denser, more intense. It was if the elements that characterized his playing with Coltrane had been magnified to the power of ten.

With *Sahara* Tyner suddenly emerged as a piano visionary, something that became clear on *Song for My Lady* (Milestone [A] 9044) from 1973 and *Song of the New World* (Milestone 9049) from the same year with a large ensemble that included strings. In May 1973 Fortune left and was replaced by Azar Lawrence, a 22-year-old former Ike Turner tenor saxophonist fresh from the Elvin Jones quartet, while Joony Booth, who had been playing with Tony Williams, came in on bass for Hill, who had departed shortly after *Song for My Lady.* It was with this revamped quartet line-up that Tyner played the 1973 Montreux Jazz Festival on Saturday 7 July.

Enlightenment (†Milestone [A] MCD55001–2) documents the occasion, and revealed the full visceral impact of his playing in a way that his previous three studio recordings, all nevertheless important, did not. On *Enlightenment* Tyner emerges with a voice that in terms of its emotional force and spirituality could now be said to equal that of Coltrane. One of the highlights of the album, *Walk spirit, talk spirit,* captures his group taking flight. A long, discursive solo from Booth leads into Tyner's dramatic entry, a repeated two-bar *ostinato* that is the basis of the composition over which Lawrence, a still immature Coltrane-influenced saxophonist, plays a repeated four-bar melody that leads into a crashing cadence point and a return to the theme. Lawrence solos first, capable and energetic, but it is Tyner who captures our imagination.

Like Coltrane, he begins his solo at an intensity that was almost superhuman and succeeds in sustaining and actually increasing the energy and forward momentum of his ideas logically and cohesively, his dense, swarming virtuosity making extensive use of side-slipping, chromatic runs and crashing *ostinatos*. The rhythm section drop out on cue and he spins a feverish Cecil Taylor-like interlude. Although he seems to veer into free time, the two-bar *ostinato* continues to play in perfect time in Tyner's mind, the elaborate fantasia he spins being a surreal counterpoint to a pulse imagined rather than stated. Suddenly Tyner restates the two-bar motif, and re-entering the song *a tempo* he takes the piece to its conclusion. Hitherto there had been nothing in Tyner's discography to suggest the frightening intensity of his playing. 'I felt very good that night,' he said, 'the people came to listen and they gave me something back that was necessary to make the music a success.' [42]

During the last two weeks of August 1974, he was booked into the Keystone Korner, Todd Barkan's legendary San Francisco jazz club which finally closed in 1983, and *Atlantis* was recorded during Labor Day weekend. By now, Tyner had let Mouzon go, replacing him with Wilby Fletcher who had in turn been replaced by Billy Hart, who, with the addition of the Brazilian percussionist Guilherme Franco and an augmented front line, appeared on *Sama Layuca* (Milestone [A] M9056). However, Fletcher continued to keep in touch with the leader, closing his experience deficit (he was only 19 years old when he first joined Tyner) by working with Charles Earland. When Hart left, Fletcher returned and the quintet quickly shook down into an impressive working unit. By now, Tyner's stock in jazz had soared. All his Milestone albums had been critically acclaimed and at the time of the Keystone engagement, playing to overflow crowds, he was *down beat*'s critics' choice for the second year in succession. A contemporaneous review of the engagement observed: 'The depth of the audience's response cannot be measured by the decibels of their applause as much as the looks on their faces. It is safe to say the crowd was spellbound rather than attentive, transported, rather than moved.' [43]

It is important to realize that at this time his music was being enacted out against a background of jazz-rock and, with attention centred elsewhere, his playing during this period has tended to be overlooked. While practically every pianist in jazz was plugging in during the early 1970s and going electric, Tyner remained steadfastly acoustic, able to make a Steinway roar without amplification. *Atlantis* followed the successful format of *Walk spirit, talk spirit* – a discursive introduction, this time by the percussionist Franco and Tyner, a statement of the theme over a fingered bass by the pianist in unison with Booth, a Lawrence solo, more assured and with greater momentum and variety in his line than his work on *Enlightenment*, and then the swirling power of Tyner's piano. His high-tensile attack, his sound-sheet arpeggios and thunderous pedal points with his hands pounding the keyboard from shoulder height, his high-register lines that carved out unpredictable paths, were now among the most exhilarating experiences in jazz. Although the piece is based on the hypnotic bass *ostinato*, he makes extensive use of side-slipping, or side-stepping as it sometimes called, adding great tension to his playing. The static harmonies of modal tunes and those based on an *ostinato* or pedal point respond well to dissonance, providing a contrast the ear welcomes and which Tyner masterfully exploits. Here too, was a better empathy between the group, perhaps even mutual respect; internally intricate and exotic, outwardly forceful and unrelenting.

His solo interpretation of *In a sentimental mood* illustrates with great clarity the advances he had made in his playing since his Blue Note days. He was no stranger to reharmonizing the standards repertoire, and Coltrane's *Body and soul* from *Coltrane's Sound* (Atlantic [A] SD1419), for example, is a seldom commented upon masterpiece of reharmonization from 1960. As personal a statement by Coltrane as his playing, the middle eight is perhaps the best-known part of the saxophonist's treatment of the tune, where he substitutes changes similar to *Giant steps* which move the key centres around in major thirds. Coltrane's poetic licence in adapting Johnny Green's ballad clearly suggested a huge range of possibilities to Tyner, who was then learning his craft. Similarly, he uses considerable licence himself as he personalizes *In a sentimental mood*, demonstrating the wide-ranging theoretical knowledge needed to master the substitute changes.

During the exposition of the melody, Tyner also showed his mastery of playing 'outside' the chords, effectively bitonal, using two tonalities at the same time. This could easily sound as if he was playing a bunch of wrong notes, but his imperious authority makes his note choices outside the written harmony sound 'right'. He had already demonstrated his mastery of inside/outside playing during his Blue Note period on numbers such as *Passion dance* from *The Real McCoy*, and this technique now emerges as a key element of his style. Often he played sequences that began within the harmonies, went outside them, then returned. Most commonly he achieved the 'outside' feel by playing a semitone away from the song's tonality, which, while achieving a dissonant effect, allows the ear to relate to the underlying harmonic base and conceive logic in the dissonance. Equally, Tyner's darting chromatic runs offered a further sense of harmonic ambiguity since chromatic scales belong to every chord yet to none. Overall, *In a sentimental mood* is a genuine *tour de force* and revealed why he had emerged as one of the most influential pianists in contemporary jazz.

Makin' out and *Pursuit* continue his high-energy workouts, with the latter, in terms of form, rhythm and tempo, cohering far more cogently than the former. *My one and only love*, a piano-tenor-percussion ballad, is as much a feature for Lawrence as it was for Tyner. 'I hired Azar because he was exciting at that time,' said the pianist. 'I thought he had some potential. But in general I was a little sensitive about people trying to sound like Coltrane, that's why I had a lot of alto players in my band up to then.' [44] Lawrence was never to fulfil the potential Tyner saw in him, however, and after leaving the group in 1976 he dropped out of jazz. Tyner's *Love samba* is far more muscular than the title suggests, a well-written theme presented with layers of polyrhythmic interaction that produced a solo of equal polyrhythmic density from the leader and, along with *My one and only love*, also provoked some of Lawrence's best work on the album.

Throughout the 1970s Tyner continued an exemplary run of albums. When Lawrence left he was replaced by John Blake on the violin and, at various times, the saxophonists Joe Ford, George Adams and Gary Bartz. [45] Tyner's emergence as a major soloist during the 1970s continues to be overshadowed by the rise of jazz-rock and even today, potted jazz histories tend to lump Tyner in with the Coltrane quartet and pursue his career no further. [46] Yet the completeness of his pianistic concept by the time of *Enlightenment* set him apart. 'Few musicians in the history of jazz have radically changed its practise, its daily working vocabulary . . . [as] McCoy Tyner,' noted the *New York Times.* [47] Just as importantly, he not only forged an instantly recognizable style but envisaged a challenging context to focus his virtuosity. Unusually, he did not initially see the piano trio as a forum to express his great talent, preferring instead to work with ensembles from a quartet to, on record at least, large ensembles with desks of violins, violas, cellos, brass and saxophones. It was not until May 1984 that he formed his own trio, which became his preferred working group into the late 1990s. During this period, however, the intensity and emotional force of his playing slackened and he often deferred to the able, yet by no means equal, musicians alongside him. Nevertheless, a trilogy of solo albums for the reconstituted Blue Note label between 1988 and 1991 [48] represented another peak in an often overlooked career. S.N.

5

Out into the Open

Free Jazz

Once thought of as a fundamental break with the past, this can now be heard as having roots that reach back further than jazz itself.

Ornette Coleman

400 **Beauty Is a Rare Thing**
†Rhino-Atlantic (A) R271410 (6 CDs, boxed)

Don Cherry (cnt); Coleman (alt); Charlie Haden (bs); Billy Higgins (d). Hollywood, 22 May 1959.
Focus on sanity · Chronology · Peace · Congeniality · Lonely woman · Monk and the nun · Just for you · Eventually

Same personnel. Hollywood, 8 October 1959.
Una muy bonita · Bird food · Change of the century · Music always · The face of the bass

Same personnel. Hollywood, 9 October 1959.
Forerunner · Free · The circle with a hole in the middle · Ramblin'

Ed Blackwell (d) replaces Higgins. New York City, 19 July 1960.
Little symphony · The tribes of New York · Kaleidoscope · Rise and shine · Mr and Mrs People · Blues connotation · I heard it on the radio · P.S. unless one has · Revolving doors

Same personnel. New York City, 26 July 1960.
Brings gladness · Joy of a toy · To us · Humpty Dumpty · The fifth of Beethoven · Motive for its use · Moon inhabitants · The legend of bebop · Some other · Embraceable you · All

Same personnel. New York City, 2 August 1960.
Folk tale · Poise · Beauty is a rare thing

Freddie Hubbard (tpt), Eric Dolphy (bs clt), Scott LaFaro (bs), Higgins (d) added. New York City, 21 December 1960.
First take · Free jazz

Hubbard, Dolphy, Haden, Higgins absent. New York City, 31 January 1961.
Proof readers · W.R.U. · Check up · T. & T. · C. & D. · R.P.D.D. · The alchemy of Scott LaFaro

Jimmy Garrison (bs) replaces LaFaro; Coleman plays ten. New York City, 22 March 1961.
Eos

Same personnel. New York City, 27 March 1961.
Enfant · Ecars · Cross breeding · Harlem's Manhattan · Mapa

Coleman (alt); Jim Hall (g); Alvin Brehm, La Faro (bs); Sticks Evans (d); Charles Libove, Roland Vamos (vln); Harry Zaratzian (vla); Joseph Tekula (cel); Gunther Schuller (comp). New York City, 19 December 1961.
Abstraction

Robert DiDomenica (fl); Dolphy (fl, bs clt, alt); Coleman (alt); Bill Evans (p); Hall (g); George Duvivier, LaFaro (bs); Sticks Evans (d); Eddie Costa (vib); Libove, Vamos (vln); Zaratzian (vla); Tekula (cel); Schuller (comp). New York City, 20 December 1961.
Variants on a theme of Monk

Coleman was greeted with the hostile response that is usual for all centrally influential jazz figures, yet his music no more demanded a total upheaval of his audiences' listening habits and expectations than had that of Parker or Armstrong. Cecil Taylor put the matter excellently a few years after Coleman's arrival: 'This is not a question of "freedom" as opposed to "non-freedom" but rather a question of recognizing different ideas and expressions of order.' [1] And in fact his earliest playing seems to have been in a rather traditional, indeed pre-bop, style, done in various Southwestern rhythm-'n'-blues outfits such as those led by Pee Wee Crayton and Clarence Samuels.

Coleman had taken up the alto at 14 to be in a school band which also included such later professional associates as Dewey Redman and Charles Moffet. His additionally learning the tenor saxophone was prompted by the unrecorded Red Connors, in whose band he for a time also played. There he learned about aspects of bop and was introduced to Charlie Parker's music. In due course he read on his own several harmony and other theoretical textbooks and gradually evolved a style founded on his own intuitions and on the Southwestern country blues and folk forms, and shaped by his extremely personal interpretations, or misreadings, of the various musical texts to which he had access. Like some of his later associates, such as Paul Bley, he never approved of the term 'free jazz' – even though it became the title of one of his LPs. And like some other creative American loners, such as Harry Partch and Conlon Nancarrow, he had a system: 'Once I found I could make mistakes I knew I was on to something.'

Rather than Coleman's early records being bolts from the blue which they still appear in the selective light of historical memory, they, like some other recordings crucial to this music's history, crystallized certain hitherto scattered tendencies, fortifying them with the hand of genius. In one obvious sense he was a modern primitive, his work a response to, or reaction against, the sophistication jazz had acquired by the end of the 1950s; hence his shock value when people first became aware of him. Jazz had long thrived on assimilating techniques from elsewhere but Coleman was the first major figure to move in the opposite direction, to simplify things; and yet in his music the art continued to grow organically. It might be suggested that, somewhat like the Douanier Rousseau in another time and place, Coleman with his mixture of naïveté and skill fulfilled a necessary myth of spontaneity, of invention liberated from conventional restraints.

All the same, there were precedents of a certain kind for what he did, such as Tristano's unplanned and unrehearsed ensemble performances (**293**) and Mingus's reaching towards extended form in collective improvisation (Affinity [E] AFF750). It seems unlikely that Coleman was aware of such endeavours, and certainly they did not influence him. Rather they were 'in the air' of jazz as comparable portents had been prior to the emergence of bop. Hence he was, again, less radical than was at one time supposed and yet the hostility of musicians in particular was in one sense predictable. Coleman rejected, to a large degree bypassed, their carefully acquired sophistication and the Southern accent of his blues music reminded them of things of which they did not, until rather later, wish to be reminded. The bitterness of Miles Davis's comments seems all the odder in view of his own efforts to break away from 'running the changes', but presumably they expressed nothing more than professional jealousy generated by the amount of press attention Coleman received when he first played in New York. The commentators who witnessed that engagement at the old Five Spot, very few of whom deserved to be described as critics, had to pretend to their readers, to themselves, and above all to each other, that they completely understood what was happening in the music although few of them did, and decades later some of them still do not. Yet what Coleman had done was simple, even inevitable.

In his hands, and soon afterwards in Ayler's (**407**, **408**, **409**), some aspects of 'the New Thing', as free jazz was at first called, were closer to the blues than certain immediately preceding styles had been. Coleman in particular, given his rhythm-'n'-blues background in the 1940s, always made an extensive use of blue notes and blues melodic formulas independent of functional harmony. Although it took most of us nearly as long to appreciate the large element of the blues in Coleman's music as it had in Parker's case, this was in fact crucial and eventually helped to bridge the gap between free jazz and other styles, showing how they were related. Good examples were the Oliver Nelson–Eric Dolphy *Screamin'* *the Blues* (†Original Jazz Classics [A] OJCCD080) and the Mingus–Dolphy **425**, both of 1960. Six tracks on Coleman's initial Contemporary LP of 1958 (*Something Else!* †Original Jazz Classics [A] OJCCD163) use blues forms and another instance, *Tears inside* from his second, of the following year, employs the 12-bar form but with pauses between each four-bar phrase (OJCCD342).

Despite his often opaque verbal and written comments, especially on his later harmolodic notions, he did at least once convey his ideas clearly outside music: 'Emphasis is placed on the melodic line rather than on the chord structure of a composition. The tonality of a piece emerges from what is played . . . we are not restricted by bar divisions or chords or even the melodic line. You might think there would be confusion, but there isn't . . . Jimmy Dorsey, Pete Brown, Johnny Hodges and Parker all left something of themselves with me . . . By working with pitch and reaching for the sound of the human voice I found satisfaction and adequate expression.' [2] He was above all articulate on wanting the alto saxophone to sound like the human voice, this being precisely what disturbed many about his music, [3] although it has become commonplace more recently to say that it is now hard to understand why his work caused such vast indignation.

This was understandable in that Coleman made a fuller and more systematic use not only of the blue notes and blues melodic formulas referred to above but also of all the other off-pitch notes and other sounds, the bent, vocalized and otherwise inflected sounds – with which all listeners ought already to have been familiar from the jazz tradition. His liberation from the chord sequences basic to most jazz hitherto carried with it, as he said in the quotation above, a leaving-behind of standard phrase and chorus structure and any concept of formal melodic variation. But his essentially 'horizontal' approach had already been extensively investigated by Lester Young and more recently by Miles Davis, who in **393** replaced chords with modes. Some would say that whereas Davis and Coltrane concentrated on such aspects of free jazz as were assimilable by the main stream – modality, approximate harmonies etc. – Coleman leaned towards those that were less so, such as variable pitch, free metre, collective improvisation. Certainly he reinterpreted jazz rhythm, beat and the concept of swing on freer, more asymmetrical lines. The results were highly mobile in tonality, rhythmic continuity and form, and hence unpredictable in their freedom and flexibility. His playing was modal in a rather different sense from that of Coltrane or Davis, being rooted in older, simpler – virtually pre-jazz – black folk idioms.

Links with bop are quite evident on the Contemporary sessions and on the performances later released on the Inner City and Improvising Artists labels – at least, they are evident now, but were much less so when the music was new. In this connection one has always had problems with Coleman regarding the presence of a piano, even though

Walter Norris plays excellently on the first Contemporary date, as did Paul Bley on Improvising Artists and Inner City. Given his attitude to pitch and to harmony, it is not surprising that the instrument seems to inhibit him, and it was the same decades later with Geri Allen (†Harmolodic/Verve [A] 531 657–2) and with Joachim Kühn (†Harmolodic/Verve [A] 537 789–2). Yet those who said there was no link between Coleman's themes and his improvisations on them were badly mistaken. In the first place his themes are real melodies rather than tunes picked out of the notes of a dense harmonic sequence. Indeed he sometimes gives the impression that he hears rhythm as melody, as some of the earliest jazzmen seem to have done. And in fact his improvisations are actually better related to the themes than most, deriving from the melody rather than, like so many others, from any underlying chords. Of course, the more imaginative soloists had long played around the chords rather than merely *on* them, and Coleman Hawkins appears to have been the most prominent among those who established the practice of elaborating the given harmonies of a theme. This was taken further by Parker's generation and with such musicians even the most chord-based solo had a melodic logic of its own not deriving from the harmonies.

After the initial rejections duly chronicled in the biographical treatments, of which John Litweiler's is easily the best (see Bibliography), Coleman gathered around him a few players who had similar ideas to his own. These included Bobby Bradford (trumpet), Blackwell, a member of the New Orleans bop underground, then Cherry, Haden and Higgins. These last three, as the above personnels show, in due course became the first Coleman Quartet, with Blackwell in 1960 replacing Higgins. Theirs was essentially an ensemble music, and this was not properly understood by the recording engineers responsible for the Contemporary and other early sessions. It made a constant use of spontaneous collective interplay through the ensemble despite the apparent subservience of bass and drums. Early listeners tended to hear it as jazz for virtuoso soloist with rhythm accompaniment – but that was not Coleman's perspective. In respect of the above performances he said: 'No one player has the lead. Anyone can come out with it at any time.' [4] In fact that is a counsel of perfection – one that we should keep in mind – because Coleman so often dominates. Beside him, other jazz improvisations, though not Ayler's, offer too little resistance to closure, too little purposeful uncertainty and hence too little information; impulses within the musical material are gratified without obstacle or deviation, and parametric relationships are conformant. Coleman's solos make us feel, even now, the uncertainty of the improbable while convincing us, finally, of its aptness. They occupy a rich terrain of functional ambiguity, and such functional ambiguity, where contradictory potentials are embedded in the same structure, are a formidable condition of great music.

Hence, though his themes may be of small dimensions they compress numerous melodic, rhythmic and even harmonic ideas so that they can serve as sources of extended improvisations, and it was the existence of this large body of music in manuscript that led to Coleman's first contact with Contemporary. Certainly the above quartet performances were the result of much work and thought over a number of years (whereas *Free jazz* was to a considerable extent a leap in the dark). By the time of his 1958 sessions for Contemporary, his style was completely formed, even if it was only with the Atlantic dates that it was fully demonstrated. His normal procedures were thoroughly established and he was in possession of an entirely consistent and worked-out idea of what jazz is and how it can be played. These factors were embodied in the large body of music already referred to and with the exceptions of the two versions of *Free jazz* from December 1960 nothing on the sessions detailed above, with the partial exception of *Mapa*, sounds even slightly experimental. It was not for nothing that, his brilliant improvisations notwithstanding, Coleman said: 'I've always thought of myself as a composer who also performs music.' [5] So far as it went, the pianoless second Contemporary album was exactly what should be expected as leading to the Atlantics and hence its title, *Tomorrow Is the Question*, was apt.

As it happened, the first Atlantic date came a little over two months after the last for Contemporary, yet the main happening of that next year for Coleman was his debut, at 29, in New York, taking place on 17 November 1959. This may be seriously described as one of the crucial events in jazz history, but although his music and the method adopted by his band were securely settled, everyone, as noted above, was shocked. That was because, aside from a few close musical associates, nobody had observed any of the steps in his development. This explains the band's sounding far more radical than was actually the case. It made nine seminal LPs for Atlantic and then Coleman's work moved in several other closely related directions. Some of his later music receives comment on other pages, which is as it should be; yet none of it has had the musical impact of the Atlantics, which must be compared to that of Armstrong's Hot Fives and Sevens (**48**) and Parker's Savoys and Dials (**257–8**). But for all its ground-breaking status, Coleman's 1959–61 music has probably remained, as Richard Cook suggested, the least known from major jazz recording sessions. [6]

This boxed set was perhaps designed to redress that balance and it sets in strict chronological order everything from dates that often were split between the initial LPs. It restores to their proper place the various further takes which had appeared on later albums and adds six previously unheard items, amounting to about 45 minutes of music plus two pieces for larger combos in which Coleman took part from the Gunther Schuller *Jazz Abstractions* LP (Atlantic [A] 587 043).

When considering the individual performances, it is best to start before the Atlantic sessions, if only to mention *Lorraine* from the second

Contemporary LP – one of a series of remarkable dirges which also included *Lonely woman* and *Sadness* (ESP 1962, Polydor 1965). *Tears inside*, likewise from the 1959 Contemporary disc, is also notable. This was the first Coleman theme to be recorded by another saxophonist, namely Art Pepper, who improvised a magnificent solo on it, which receives comment under **461**. The fact that a major jazzman of long-established reputation could do this so promptly ought to have given pause to those many who dismissed Coleman as merely a fake.

Admittedly his solo in *Focus on sanity*, the first item recorded for Atlantic, embodied a new degree of rhythmic freedom, and it also goes for a discontinuity rather different from his usual sort of thematic improvisation found in *Forerunner* or the very unified *Free* solo. [7] There is a slight hint of Rollins in the astringent intelligence of his solos on *Chronology* and *Congeniality* from that initial Atlantic date. His improvisation on the latter is a fascinating tissue of sequential ideas, some directly arising out of the theme, which occur not only in sequence but recur in echo patterns in a most interesting extension of the AABA song pattern. Hear for example the idea which begins in his 56th bar: this is derived from the theme and its later appearances serve to shape the solo overall and to close it. [8] His solo on the Atlantic *Ramblin'* has remained one of his greatest blues improvisations and here again it seems to grow out of a single phrase which may evolve, die, be reborn; in such cases he apparently thinks through every aspect of an idea, and some who have played with him have remarked that he never plays any two consecutive notes at the same volume; so the accents are richly varied. It should be compared with his 13-chorus solo on the version of a year before (Improvising Artists [A] IAI373852) which, as John Litweiler has suggested, provides 'a heretofore missing link between Charlie Christian and Charlie Parker'. [9] Like several other tracks, the Atlantic *Ramblin'* has something of the feeling of a Southwestern hoe-down and the bass solo is almost bluegrass. This was a particularly well-realized concept which, once more, ought to have given those who ridiculed Coleman reason to think again. In one sense its follow-up is Charles Tyler's *Saga of the outlaws* (Nessa [A] N16).

Again, in *R.P.D.D.* Coleman's ten-minute solo begins by stating an idea which he then modifies, alters, modifies again from every imaginable angle until it gives rise to a new idea or until its thorough exploration suggests a contrary idea, either of which will be similarly developed, varied and extended in a chain of logically (or at least coherently) handled musical phrases. He improvises almost throughout this piece in a *tour de force* which actually suggests that his invention is inexhaustible. Coleman takes another long solo in *The alchemy of Scott LaFaro*, then Cherry is heard, then a long contrapuntal duet between the two of them with bass and drums silent until near the end. *W.R.U.* includes an eight-minute solo from Coleman, the most remarkable from this session and, like those on *C. & D.* and *R.P.D.D.*, following his method of motivic development. On *Blues connotation* the notes of the theme are constantly displaced and the leader plays with especial force and determination while extending it with much logic and in a thoroughly pantonal way; this is an enthralling performance. *P.S. unless one has* is an alternative version and on it Coleman is even fiercer, seemingly in response to Blackwell's commentary – one could hardly call it an accompaniment. This is also true for this occasion's *Kaleidoscope* except that that is even more violent.

Even when Coleman and Cherry play a theme 'in unison' their voices are distinct. The latter's performances have a rough-hewn aspect which rather suits the former's music and their ensemble work is strikingly accurate even on the second Contemporary disc; nobody else in free jazz ever did this kind of thing so well as they. The partnership was more nearly equal on the 1959 Contemporary dates than it became on Atlantic, where Coleman's stature became ever more apparent; yet later in the Atlantic sequence the emphasis shifted back towards Cherry again. To put this another way, the microphone balance tends to favour Coleman, and to favour the horns very much over bass and drums. They frankly were lucky to have found each other, and Cherry was on 19 of Coleman's first 21 recording dates; then they came together again for recording purposes in 1969, 1971, 1972, 1976, 1977, 1987 and for personal appearances up to 1993.

Cherry usually played a pocket cornet, though for reasons best known to himself he invariably called it a pocket trumpet. In later years he sometimes employed a full-sized cornet, for example on **402** and *Symphony for Improvisers* (Blue Note [A] BLP84247). On the performances detailed above, his style appears to derive chiefly from Coleman, yet he said he had been affected by Navarro, [10] Miles Davis, Harry Edison, Mexican trumpet styles, as in *Una muy bonita*, and the sound of the conch trumpet. He had been well on the way to mastery of hard bop when he met Coleman, took on the challenge of his music and could in due course make statements in it that were entirely his own, not only on these Atlantic sessions but also with Rollins in 1962 (†RCA-Bluebird [A] ND82496) and Ayler in 1964 (**408**). Though Cherry may often seem to be in Coleman's shadow, there is a fair number of the above performances on which this is clearly not the case, such as *The alchemy of Scott LaFaro*, *P.S. unless one has* and *Mr and Mrs People*, despite this last including an especially decisive alto solo.

It could be said that *Lonely woman* is summarized by the short bass solo at the end. Besides the close musical relationship between Coleman and Cherry, it is also clear that Coleman and Haden are fired by mutual inspiration. Coleman instructed Haden in his music before the October–November 1958 Hillcrest Club engagement which came between the two Contemporary LPs, so Haden was altogether inside it by the time of the Atlantic dates in particular. Hence comparison with LaFaro is instructive. The latter is just as musical and more overtly virtuosic, yet his response to Coleman's improvisations, though very prompt, is not so instinctive as Haden's, and certainly they sounded altogether different. Haden, for whom *The face of the bass* is something of a vehicle, worked mainly in the middle and low registers, LaFaro in the upper, and running a highly melodic counterpoint to the horn lines. Garrison on the tenor dates was another case. Coleman's music was not greatly changed by his playing the larger horn but Garrison's solos are far less interesting than Haden's or LaFaro's: he belonged elsewhere (see **423–4**).

A good illustration of how LaFaro's different relationship to this music from that of Haden (or Garrison) affected several other aspects of the situation is provided by *Proof readers*. There are long solos from Coleman and Cherry here, and a shorter, yet highly articulate one by LaFaro. In *W.R.U.*, the longest track of this particular session, he is eloquent, at times almost vehement. On this track Cherry for once solos first – the fragmentation of what he plays is more apparent than real – followed by a long and glorious flight by Coleman, then Blackwell. In *C. & D.* it is LaFaro who takes the long opening solo, followed by a contrapuntal theme, then Coleman, Cherry and Blackwell in turn. *T. & T.* is chiefly a vehicle for Blackwell with brief flourishes fore and aft from the horns and bass. Lazily melodious, *Check up* sounds like a theme by somebody other than Coleman but the band responds with improvisations which are characteristic yet leisurely. Certainly it was a mistake for commentators to claim that it made no difference upon what themes they improvised.

Perhaps the title is a coincidence, but the theme of *Bird food* is rather boppish, as is that of *Chronology*; Cherry's solo on the latter has, too, some hints of his earlier hard-bop affiliations. Similar comments apply to *Monk and the nun* and to Coleman's solo, not least its double-timing. In the case of *The legend of bebop* the theme might be a satire on bop, yet not the solos. In fact Coleman's would be a good one with which to begin listening to him, being mostly a slow-motion demonstration of the way he improvises. [11]

That last track closes with a quite long, particularly fine ensemble and *I heard it over the radio* includes a comparable passage, as does *Brings goodness*. Such spontaneous collective interplay, at an intimate level, goes far to explain the freedom and unpredictability of this music's discourse, its mobility in terms of tonality, rhythmic continuity and form. In this connection *Beauty is a rare thing* is deeply impressive, quasi-orchestral, and rightly gave its title to this whole set. In one sense an experiment, in that all four players improvise independently of each other, especially in rhythmic terms, *Mapa* too is one of the great collective improvisations in recorded jazz. But it seems probable that it was *Beauty is a rare thing* that prompted *Free jazz* a few months later. Certainly with *Beauty is a rare thing* behind him, Coleman turned his music in a number of slightly different directions: towards *Free jazz*, to the session with LaFaro, to the date on which he played tenor, to the encounter with Schuller.

Obviously the tenor saxophone lent more power and tonal richness to Coleman's work, though he continued his normal processes of motivic development, as in *Ecars* for instance. In *Enfant* Cherry continues the main idea of his leader's solo to splendid effect, yet it was *Cross breeding* which gave rise to one of Coleman's, or anyone else's, greatest recorded improvisations, a lot of it unaccompanied but without any loss of rhythmic impetus.

Some have claimed that for the 'double quartet' experiment of *Free jazz* Coleman originally wanted Bobby Bradford rather than Hubbard, and it is true that Dolphy, LaFaro and particularly Hubbard sound more tonally oriented than the rest. What we find here are not so much solos as exchanges between a lead voice and comments from the others as seemed apt. The written themes and the order of the 'solos' were the only premeditated elements in this often turbulent, sometimes joyous performance. There are effective contrasts between Hubbard and Dolphy on one side and Coleman and Cherry on the other; and one should again note LaFaro's extraordinary virtuosity as against Haden's lyrical directness. The most remarkable single passage is that led by Coleman, an unfettered stream of melody. On the shorter trial run, *First take*, there is more real collective improvisation, some good solos, and it ends with extensive bass and drum outings. This was issued only in 1971 but *Free jazz* was, for obvious reasons, probably the largest single influence on free jazz during the 1960s.

Both in *Abstraction* and *Variants on a theme of Monk* the diamond-clear stillness of Schuller's string writing deliciously gathers tension from the jazz solos and each piece has countless fascinations, such as the way, in the *Monk variants*, the improvisations overlap, or Coleman's amazing revision of the theme early in his solo. That theme is *Criss cross* and the 15 minute and 22 second performance, in parallel with Hodeir's recompositions (**455**), uncovers all sorts of relationships, exploits all manner of developmental possibilities that could only be hinted at in Monk's own brief recording on **292**. Yet Coleman and Schuller added much that was their own, and the fact that an untutored 'natural' jazzman and a serialist composer could work together so productively showed how useless it was to assess such pieces – and this is perhaps even more true of *Abstraction* – exclusively as jazz or exclusively as straight music. They proved once again that the old dividing lines no longer operated. [12]

The fact that men who in their turn had been major innovators in the language of jazz, such as Gillespie, Davis and Monk, reacted so uncomprehendingly to Coleman is a sad comment on human nature rather than merely on jazz politics. Did he perhaps, with his country-blues tunes and parade-band accents, stand in a similar relationship to other avant-gardists as Monk had once stood to the boppers? Even when

Coleman's ideas seemed traditional, he employed them as parts of a freely varied and developing discourse. And there is a sense, as with Ayler, in which one never does get used to the finest of his improvisations, their power and originality striking one afresh on each hearing; and this is as true now as when these recordings were new. His playing operated through subtleties of reaction, of timing, of nuance, of colour that were not exactly unfamiliar in jazz but had not been used in his way, or to that extent, before. Coleman's work remained an extraordinary creative fusion of jazz, blues, modal, atonal and even microtonal music. That he was so influential was partly because, rather than contradicting more conventional jazz, he added further dimensions, as bop had added to swing. Hence his effect was great not just on avant-gardists but also on non-free players. M.H.

Ornette Coleman

401a **At the Golden Circle Vol. 1**

†Blue Note (A) BCT84224

Coleman (alt); David Izenson (bs); Charles Moffett (d). Golden Circle, Stockholm, 3–4 December 1965.

Faces and places · *European echoes* · *Dee Dee* · *Dawn*

401b **At the Golden Circle Vol. 2**

†Blue Note (A) BCT84225

As above, except that on the first title Coleman plays vln and tpt.

Snowflakes and sunshine · *Morning song* · *The riddle* · *Antiques*

Coleman's long career in music might be seen as a campaign against the frustration of being a devoted visionary individual. From one point of view, his ability, despite early rejections, to gather kindred spirits to his quest for a 'collective conception of sound' might be thought impressive and admirable; yet it may seem remarkable also that, while the collective expression of his groups has evolved, over some 40 years, from bop line-up through 'new wave' and Third Stream groups of several sizes and shapes, to the 'harmolodic' rock-fusion of Prime Time, Coleman's personal style of playing and composing has advanced only in executive skill.

Reminiscing during the 1992 BBC2 TV series 'Birdland', he admitted that in his youthful – and frequently abortive – dalliances with some of his jazz 'idols' he had played 'as I play now, at this point in time'. [13] With any set of companions, and according to whatever avowal of musical principle, his personal concept has dominated, even when his wish might have been other than that. Playing *Spelling the alphabet* in the 'Birdland' set, amid the unrelenting Prime Time clangour, Coleman's lines upon alto, trumpet and fiddle differ but little in mode from those which can be heard on the trio masterpieces considered below. If he in the 1990s is a 'harmolodist', then he was demonstrably one the moment he launched into the whinnying complaint of his *Alpha* solo back in 1958 with his rhythm section bopping doggedly ahead (†Original Jazz Classics [A] OJCCD163). The constancy of the style bespeaks the inevitability of the theory.

For his admirers the constancy also means that, without paradox, Coleman's early music on record remains as eccentrically captivating as ever, and, in the case of these mid-1960s trio sessions, as revealing of his imaginative quest. The Stockholm concerts need to be set in context. The recording debut of this trio was a New York Town Hall concert at the end of 1962 (ESP [A] 1006). A two-year retirement, during which Coleman studied the trumpet and violin, ensued; then it was in late August 1965 that the trio per se was recorded at the Fairfield Hall, Croydon, the first significant demonstration of the leader's new-found instrumental skills (Polydor [E] 623246/7). In programmatic terms, the Stockholm recording is usefully compared to the Croydon one; but for uncommon insight into the cast of Coleman's mind at the time, particularly in relation to the stimulus provided by Izenson's freshly creative approach to bass playing, an ear might be lent to November 1965 recordings made in Paris (Affinity [E] AFFD102). These were for a film titled *Who's Crazy?* and the discontinuous episodes were apparently improvised by the trio in instant response to the screening of parts of the film. The titles given to the episodes were probably not Coleman's. They include *The misused blues (The lovers and the alchemist)*, *Better get yourself another self*, *The duel* and so on, which may indicate visual responses. At all events, this is a quite different kind of musical experience from the concert programmes, comparative maybe only to the lengthy improvisation of *The ark* in the 1952 Town Hall performance, and dramatically different from that in so far as Coleman's violin and trumpet are brought into the process.

Blue Note recorded the trio on the final two evenings of its two-week appearance at the Golden Circle. *Faces and places* is the valedictory piece, and has an exultancy which, one senses, is not merely due to end-of-engagement relief. In the numbers registered on the first evening, Coleman plays alto only. *Antiques* has a fairly complex minor-key alto line supported by rocking *pizzicato* simplicities and fairly delicate cymbal patterns. The minor theme returns at length after Coleman's investigation has borne it some way beyond any lure of tonality. The support is rather unwavering; less so in the melancholy complaint of *Morning song*, during which Izenson's bow initiates strands of counterpoint and Moffett juggles tempos with mild similarities to the dizzying time changes that emerged in the *Who's Crazy?* laboratory. These is more bass-alto counterpoint in *Dawn*, a piece no less morose of mood than *Morning song*.

European echoes, from the second session, is lifted directly from the *Who's Crazy?* tailpiece. It is a mock-cautious waltz beyond whose main-line Coleman tracks a variety of wills-o'-the-wisp that dart back from the days and nights of his original declaration of universal independence. *The riddle* releases whirling alto over wildly threshing drums. This kind of saxophone extemporizing is this fellow's indisputable expressive territory – a jazz gaucho's lassoing of brainwaves with totally personal lightning aplomb; jazz with not a shadow of dubiety, and exhilaratingly skilful. In this, as in the magnificent sequential *Dee dee*, Moffett and Izenson find opportunities for contrast. In those several places where their rhythm-section skills support the leader's more 'old-style' swinging essays it is instructive to mark how little Coleman's preferences were yet moving beyond contemporary hard-bop methods.

This leaves the singularity, where this record is concerned, of *Snowflakes and sunshine* which sets off with Coleman sawing away at some satanic hoe-down with Izenson's *arco* abetment no whit less demonic. Many of the 'string-duet' patches from *Who's Crazy?* may be recalled, but it would be too glib to see this number as closest to the cinema sequence, for there are numerous other similarities elsewhere. It is worth comparing *Snowflakes and sunshine* with *Falling stars* from the Croydon concert. In both those pieces Coleman's undoubted, if idiosyncratic, facility on both the fiddle and trumpet is revealed beyond question to any capable of analysing it upon its own merits. In an extravaganza not lacking temptations to wayward organization, it is chiefly Moffett who preserves the jazz feel, suggesting the right kind of backing for some sustained trumpet passages which approximate to Coleman's saxophonic dialect to a striking degree.

Jazz was, unfortunately, not to hear much more from Izenson, though among Coleman's many bassists he was arguably the most provocative in artistic terms. Moffett was not the best of the Coleman drummers – Higgins and Blackwell may vie for that title – but he was a musically minded supporter, often imaginative at critical moments. He, too, did not apparently survive these years long in professional music.

Excellent examples of Coleman's most celebrated quartet – with Cherry, Haden and Higgins in 1959 – are dealt with under **400**. April 1968 saw a quartet with the tenorist Dewey Redman, Jimmy Garrison (bass) and Elvin Jones (drums) record *New York Is Now* (†Blue Note [E] CDP784287) and *Love Call* (CDP784356), probably the best of the pre-Prime Time groups, and conceptually linked to the 1965 trio. Opinions will vary as to how much of the Prime Time output is essential jazz listening, but see **438**.

The unchanging nature of Coleman's own style has enabled him to recall friends of his Atlantic days successfully to the studios for revivals that have no hint of 'traditionalist' nostalgia about them. Note for example *In All Languages* from February 1987 (†Caravan of Dreams [A] CDPCD85008), which has Coleman, Cherry, Haden and Higgins on some tracks and a Prime Time aggregation on the rest. Certain Coleman themes are interpreted by each group independently. E.T.

Don Cherry

402 Complete Communion

Blue Note (A) BST84226

Cherry (cnt); Leandro 'Gato' Barbieri (ten); Henry Grimes (bs); Ed Blackwell (d). Englewood Cliffs, N.J., 24 December 1965.

Complete communion (Complete communion/And now/Golden heart/ Remembrance) · Elephantasy (Elephantasy/Our feeling/Bishmallah/Wind, sand and stars)

It was for a fairly short space that Cherry, with his 'squashed trumpet with bent mouthpiece' [14] and his occasionally slightly diffident soloing style, took the risk of being regarded as a poker-faced jester at the court of King Coleman. In addition to the fact that by about 1962 he was seeking fresh jazz partnerships – among which his brilliant association with Ayler is particularly notable (**408**) – he quite early sought the kind of escape route which Coleman, in a recollection of remote frustrations, once described as quitting 'the music business for the music world'. [15] From a period roughly coeval with the above recording, Cherry was long resourceful in presenting himself more and more as a 'world musician', schooling himself and others in intercultural musical understandings and skills. 'Primal music' became and remained his aim. [16]

But we should be grateful that 'primal music' allowed for real jazz ventures from time to time, some of which, like the 1970s quartet Old and New Dreams (**410**), were to hearken vividly back to a very Coleman-esque 'music world'. **406** treats of complementary 1963 sessions.

One of Cherry's companions here renews the Coleman connection – the drummer Blackwell, a musician with a New Orleans background, who joined Coleman after rhythm-'n'-blues service. The Philadelphian Grimes became 'schooled' in post-bop jazz and was significantly teamed with Cecil Taylor (**385**) and Sonny Rollins (*On the Outside* †RCA-Bluebird [A] ND82496) prior to the present recording.

Cherry's tenorist 'Gato' Barbieri's origin points up the post-1945 'world music' development of jazz itself. Charlie Parker's music led this Argentinian to eschew the traditions of his homeland. A thorough submersion in jazz avant-garde procedures followed a European encounter with Cherry, and his playing here marks a stage in his development towards the screaming abstraction of the 1967 *In Search of the Mystery* (ESP [A] 1049), a kind of terminal climax to his jazz aspirations, beyond which, returning to his South American roots, he too sought into primal music via 'Latin' pathways. In *Complete Communion* and *Elephantasy* his voice and vocabulary are fairly redolent of Coleman's and Ayler's but several degrees short of the devotedly abstract.

Cherry's own verbal preamble to these related suites-in-miniature stresses their emotive-imaginative connotation. The musical aim in the first sequence is that performance should enable each contributory sound somehow to encapsulate 'the overall oneness which makes up our complete communion'. The 'phantasy' of the second sequence relates, it seems, to 'direct emotion' so 'loosely controlled' that the listener's imagination may play its part too. [17] Which is well enough, but this music can very ably deliver its own communication, which does not differ in any essential from the venturesome message that struck through way back when jazz music shook off the illusion that it was meant to be no more mind-engaging than good-time fun.

What groups of this sort were learning from Coleman's pianoless groups, additionally to controversial approaches to tonality and phrasal/sequential regulation, was the importance of the fullest and freest interplay of 'voices'. At the start of the first subsection, a certain formality touches the exchange of fanfares and dancing episodes, and there is some extremely swinging rhythm. The sense of pretty careful rehearsal persists despite some wild tone distortions from Barbieri and super-agile *obbligatos* from Grimes. There are 'careful' unisons for the horns, and some responses that sound strategic, as it were. These are characteristics affecting the work overall. *And now* develops some of the dance patterns with a steadying of pace. Barbieri's is a cagily poignant voice above hoisting *pizzicatos* from the bassist, who later resumes the dancing in partnership with a delicately stepping Blackwell. Deceleration creates an impressive spaciousness for *Golden heart.* The agilities of Grimes and Blackwell increase within this splendid leeway, yet the voices of Cherry and Barbieri do not conceal a degree of forethought which touches even the latter's avant-gardist punctuation of lyricism with irascible or despairing noise. What things cornet and tenor do together here are gentle for the most part. *Remembrance* unwraps a fresh rhythm, striding, accelerating; and there is a return to themes from the first section, reprise and reconsideration, before the music slows once more.

More lively but well-anticipated unisons and exchanges happen in the medium tempo of *Elephantasy*'s opening scene. Cherry ranges freely, even 'atonally', as Grimes maintains his apt monotony and Blackwell his shrewd punctuations. Barbieri mixes unmelodic blurtings with placatory snatches of tunefulness. The echoing exchanges of *Our feelings* are altogether more casual-seeming. Lingering lines develop with suddenness into impressions of swift progress which encourage Barbieri into an Aylerish diatribe ahead of a reintroduction of propriety by Cherry who then contributes a whimsically melodic solo. The Orientalisms of *Bishmallah* involve intensely skilful jugglings by drums and bass with a provocative sense of unusual time signatures. Barbieri's soloing is wild, but he is called to order by cornet clarities. The bowed work of Grimes touches virtuosity and is, at times, so mischievous that one suspects he is taking Barbieri's side against the leader's passion for imagination that is strung on sturdy threads of musical order. The ending of the record is a brief *Elephantasy* reprise, but that arrives only after a descent from *Wind, sand and stars*, a title for high-born adventure. A cornet-tenor unison ups the tempo into a complex layering of time patterns. There is a dazzling demonstration of Blackwell's multivoiced imagination which is well catered for within the fine variety of vigorous give-and-take, rebellious ardour, and peaceable colloquy achieved by this band. Its music may be described with unctionless pen as mind-engaging jazz. Some of it is good-time fun as well. E.T.

Sonny Simmons

403 Manhattan Egos

Arhoolie (A) 8003

Barbara Donald (tpt); Simmons (alt, eng h[1]); Juma (bs, con[2]); Paul Smith (d); Voodoo Bembe (con[3]). Los Angeles, September 1967.

Coltrane in paradise[2,3] · *The prober* · *Manhattan egos* · *Seven dances of Salami*[1] · *Visions*

In his first jazz occasions the altoist Simmons was a 'West Coaster'. As the 1960s progressed, following the stir caused by Coleman's 1959–61 Atlantic recordings (**400**), the earliest made in Hollywood, the Californian jazz avant-garde was sparse and wide-scattered. Yet there were notable agents to be heard. Simmons, who had taken up the saxophone round 1950, was, by the middle of the 'Ornette decade', a member of the altoist and flautist Prince Lasha's quartet and recording with them (e.g. *Firebirds*, †Original Jazz Classics [A] OJCCD182–2). Earlier on, Simmons met Barbara Donald in San Diego, and she, a former pianist and classicist turned trumpeter, had thriven on a love of Clifford Brown and Fats Navarro. Collaborating with Simmons, and having listened to Don Cherry, she gained proficiency, and a certain eloquence, in the tongue of a new age. By the year of *Manhattan Egos* newer things were afoot. Recent general comment upon the heyday of Simmons–Lasha has tended to overstress the Coleman effect; but already sounds and accents like those of Albert Ayler and Pharoah Sanders were prompting rejiggings of jazz imagination, including ensemble conception.

Simmons starts off this programme with a title which reminds us that Coltrane's committal of *Ascension* (†Impulse [A] GRP21132) happened in 1965 and that the life of that noted charismatic tenorist had ended in the summer of 1967. In between *Giant Steps* (**421**) and *Africa Brass* (**422**), Coltrane used celebrated Coleman associates of the day – Cherry, Haden, Blackwell – in an attempt to adapt his current complex dialect to the freedoms of the quartet's recent work (*The Avant Garde*, †Atlantic [A] 90041), but with scant persuasiveness. It may be more apt to suggest that what was most affecting Simmons's tough alto style was the more personal development by which Coltrane the hard-bop chrysalis became the 'New Thing' butterfly of *A Love Supreme* (**424**) and *Meditations* (†MCA [A] MCAD39139).

Juma's *arco* monotone underlines a brassy *moderato* unison of horns as *Coltrane in paradise* begins. Expression alters almost immediately to an agitated bridge passage, also unison, but closer to a sort of demo chant. Miss Donald solos over *pizzicato* bass. From here the tempo ceases to be relevant, swallowed with a gluttonish aptitude by Juma's and Smith's consequent and joint colourfully percussive extemporization. The altoist's ranging annunciation, always forceful yet admirably focussed timbrally, makes frequent use of his instrument's lowest sounds, and in some of his more agitated forays effectively contrasts the colours of his registral extremes.

In *The prober* Simmons's stylistic variety allows a surprisingly diffident lyricism to surface in a bandying of ideas with Miss Donald. In *Manhattan egos* the patterned unisons shape to an angular, airily cynical balladry, with the bassist plucking rich sounds below. Rapid bowing comes later, when, after a long, unremitting quartet collective, Simmons appears to be searching for possibilities of respite – in expressive terms, it can be thought – but the cessation comes with abruptness just as the songlike unison has been reprised briefly. *Visions*, an illusionist prank, is in fast time and forcibly so, although a few pauses and spurts deliberately occur. The theme-line unison smacks of bop at its most mockingly cockeyed, yet of Charlie Parker – an avowed idol – Simmons lets slip not one hint. Smith gets his best solo chance, and when alto and trumpet improvise, bassist and drummer assist in the deceit of suspending the ear between fast tempo and tempolessness. The dance sequence, *Seven dances of Salami*, in which Simmons plays the english horn and there is a good deal of atmospheric drumming and chanting, has no jazz character, but perhaps represents an ambition of Orientalism which has stirred in many a jazz reed player in stylistic periods that have not yet all reached moribundity.

Regrettably Simmons's best-remembered career was brief. For whatever reasons, he lapsed into obscurity and never capitalized on the interest aroused by his handful of 1960s records. A recently issued CD, *Backwoods Suite* (†West Wind [A] 2074), recorded in January 1982 under his own name, has some compelling blowing from the altoist, but the stylistic feel is by no means a reassurance of continuity. For those so far unable to hear the music of one who, having been significantly active in years when free jazz moved into the open but who slipped back into hidden places far too soon, *Staying on the Watch* (†ESP [A] 1030) and *Music from the Spheres* (†ESP [A] 1043), which includes the capable lady trumpeter in the line-up, might still be commercially available. E.T.

Joe Harriott

404 Free Form

Jazzland (E) JLP949S

Shake Keane (tpt, fl h); Harriott (alt); Pat Smythe (p); Coleridge Goode (bs); Phil Seamen (d). London, November 1960.

Formation · *Coda* · *Abstract* · *Impression* · *Parallel* · *Straight lines* · *Calypso sketches* · *Tempo*

Harriott made three LPs for Jazzland, of which *Free Form* was the third. Keane replaced Hank Shaw for the second, which contained no clear hint of radical ideas. Smythe's replacing of Harry South seems to have been of marked importance for the working out of Harriott's thoughts of 'abstraction' in what is the first recording which might support Ian Carr's assertion that Harriott was 'the father of European free jazz'. [18] (New thoughts had been stirring for a while. Jack Cooke recalled 'being in the old Marquee one Friday night in 1958 when Joe and Dizzy Reece were trying with some success to get out of the idea of playing on chords and into the kind of free melodic playing that Ornette Coleman was just beginning to put on record, though at that time none of us had heard him, or hardly even heard of him'. [19])

The timing of these ventures led to comparisons with Coleman, but these tell nothing about the genesis of *Free Form*. Harriott contemplated an abstract approach while recuperating from tuberculosis. 'What we are doing,' he explained later, 'has form . . . the themes are structural, our approach to it is abstract. We make no use at all of bar lines, and there is no set harmony or series of chords, but there is an interplay of musical form and we do keep a steady four in the rhythm section.' [20] This does not say everything, but it is refreshingly intelligible beside the 'music of feeling' definition offered by some other more famous innovators.

'Interplay of musical form' is an important clause, and it is here that the significance of preparation asks to be remarked. Companions were picked who latched quickly on to the leader's aims, and a lot of rehearsing was done. The formal themes, though carefully worked out, themselves have a pronounced air of freshness. There is a fund of musical wit in *Coda*'s wiry whimsicality; *Formation* is partly jazz fanfare, partly staccato tiptoeing, and has a section where the beat suspends itself on a different plane; the acrobatic *Parallel* has an accelerating bridge passage; and in everything there is a marvellous ease of ensemble. *Impression*, prefaced by drifting broken unisons and dissonances, is the piece in which freedom more notably triumphs over structure – 'the most "advanced" thing,' says Harriott.

The rhythm section, far from militating against the rhythmic and harmonic disjunction of the horns, frequently contributes aptness and added variety. Goode, a distinguished veteran of British swing and bop, suits each mood with unconventional intervals, and the inestimable

Seamen is alert in support to every shift of temporal emphasis and solos in ways that are lucidly stimulating and, in one place, prophetic as – in *Coda* – he predicts uncannily the playing of Blackwell in the 1961 *T. & T.* (**400**). Coleman abandoned use of the piano early, but for Harriott's concept Smythe is indispensable, in both accompaniment and solo, injecting a rich stream of perceptions, never getting in anyone's way harmonically (the prime risk), and far outstripping Walter Norris's contributions to Coleman's *Something Else!* (†Original Jazz Classics [A] OJCCD163).

Keane's effectiveness is tasted near the beginning of *Formation* when he and Harriott swap spurted comments over Smythe's fierce chords; and most of the excitement of original discovery is heard in the free argument between trumpet – or flugelhorn – and alto in every piece. It is part of the exercise that solos can be interrupted at will, the interloper either adding comment or urging changes in expression or direction. Harriott's fine solo after the ambiguous opening of *Tempo* meets contrast in Keane's legato ascents and in Smythe's cross-beat enterprise. Then it is Harriott who provides spasmodic antitheses to Keane's dazzling lines. Some of Keane's best flugel work is in *Calypso sketches* where, after butting in on Harriott's magnificent early improvisation, he also uses the plunger mute with quite personal mannerism and skilful delicacy. *Straight lines* (ironically titled, perhaps) has artfully interlocked lines by Smythe and the altoist plus a solo from the latter which acknowledges a debt to Parker yet adapts bop accents in individual ways. (It may not help much to know that another Harriott favourite was Charlie Ventura.) The distant, muted flugel acknowledgements of Goode's *Straight lines* donation and the exuberant Keane–Seamen foray in the same number are moments of unpredicted collusion typifying the magic of this music. All sorts of similar encounters and particular regard to rhythmic variability can be savoured in *Abstract.*

Ian Carr's assessment of Harriott as a free-music pioneer for Europe comes from one eminently capable of offering such a judgement; but, in retrospect, it may seem overgenerous in implication and is to be read in the ironic light of nonacceptance and enforced capitulation. Harriott died in 1973, starved of both adequate income and due appreciation, but apart from an *Abstract doodle* duetted with Smythe in 1967, his dedication to free jazz had begun to wane (at least, in recordings) by 1963. *Abstract* (Columbia [E] ESX1477, 1962) is well up to the standards set by *Free Form*; *Movement* (Columbia [E] ESX1627, 1963) contains evidences that innovation was hard to maintain, and its inclusion of *Revival*, a piece which Harriott had recorded with Chris Barber's Dixieland group in 1961, seems hardly appropriate. Other than outward discouragements, regression may partly be due to Harriott's tireless interest in a variety of jazz styles and other kinds of improvisatory music. A result of that eclecticism was his collaboration with the Indian musician

John Mayer (**484**); yet the number of those entering similar liaisons more recently who would own Hariott's precedence may be as small as the number of European free musicians who now remember his 'glorious quintet' (Carr) with anything approaching reverence. There are bits of *Abstract* and *Impression* which presage later experiments by John Stevens's Spontaneous Music Ensemble and the Tony Oxley Quintet, but one suspects that the similarities are accidental. E.T.

George Russell

405 Ezz-thetics

†Original Jazz Classics (A) OJCCD070

Don Ellis (tpt); Dave Baker (tbn); Eric Dolphy (alt[1], bs clt[2]); Russell (p, comp); Steve Swallow (bs); Joe Hunt (d). New York City, 8 May 1961.
Ezz-thetic[1] · *Nardis*[2] · *Lydiot*[1] · *Thoughts*[2] · *Honesty*[1] · *Round about midnight*[1]

Even among the sadly restricted clientage that regards Russell with anything close to genuine admiration these days, there may be those who view him as an inhabitant of a particular branch of the jazz avant-garde, that is as a revolutionary to the jazz of the past. His own words, penned to introduce his October 1960 sextet record *Stratusphunk* (†Original Jazz Classics [A] OJCCD232), spell out a different assessment: 'I think my music can best be summed up in terms of my belief that any valid new movement in jazz must be firmly rooted in the past . . . our objective as a band . . . [is] to build on established jazz; to further it by making broader use of all the materials that are available to us; to create new concepts in the areas of rhythm, tone and form through both composition and improvisation – but always to build and evolve from the best and most valid aspects of what has preceded us.' [21]

Rather than taking a cue from the current, more unruly 'new thing' innovations, Russell – complaining the while about 'the new players' . . . overevaluated sense of their ability to become instant composers' [22] – used his variously manned sextet to build with vigorous energy upon his Workshop ventures of the mid-1950s (**379, 380**).

The personnel for *Ezz-thetics* differs from that for *Stratusphunk* in the replacement of the trumpeter Al Kiger by Ellis, of the tenorist Dave Young by Dolphy and of the bassist Chuck Israels by Swallow. Ellis was an experimenter of a different stamp to Russell: his wry 1960 tourney with durational, temporal and metric conventions on *How Time Passes* is dealt with under **454**, his massively challenging big-band neologies under **317**. Dolphy's well-known claim, 'I play notes that would not ordinarily be said to be in a given key, but I hear them as proper,' demonstrably renders him a prime collaborator with a composer-leader whose Lydian concept other contemporary soloists found liberating. With his 'I hear them as proper' Dolphy seems to echo that other Russell – the miraculously eccentric Pee Wee – avowing: 'We hear something and say "That chord just has to be there," whether it's according to Hoyle or not' (see **209**). George Russell would hardly reckon himself a 'traditionalist'; yet neither did Morton, Oliver, Bechet or Armstrong. His jazz activity, largely as composer and arranger, was sparked by discovering Monk's music and working in association with Gillespie, and his cooperation with musicians of such stylistic tendencies assisted important shifts of creative thinking.

The music of his sextets of the 1960s, if compared to that of his Workshop ventures, may appear closer in overall design to the freer conjunctions of direction and initiation, of leading-idea-cum-spontaneous-response typical of any bop or hard-bop combo. The zest of most of these performances is invigorating to the listener familiar with what Russell means by 'the past' of jazz. *Ezz-thetic* (a theme dedicated to the boxer Ezzard Charles) was an early (1949) statement of scalar or modal scoring imagination remembered for characteristic launchings by Parker and Konitz. Taken fast here, it loses nothing at all of its spiky sinuosity or virile humour. An important part of the invigoration is due to the way in which the headlong extended solos of Baker, Ellis and Dolphy anticipate the 'open moment' of unsupported measures of improvising occurring around mid-career. The somewhat theatrical *Honesty* has frequent out-of-tempo spaces during the continuity of solos, including that of Swallow, thus lending a dual meaning to 'extemporization'.

A leisurely speed suits Miles Davis's mock-Oriental *Nardis*, the shortest of these performances, in which each solo – Ellis's muted, Dolphy's in the upper register of his bass clarinet – are gently, mock-laggardly lyrical. Russell's supportive pianistics in his sextet dates has sometimes been patronized with faint plaudits by commentators who might have lent a more discerning ear. His style in this famous session will hardly bear comparison with the inventiveness of Bill Evans in the Workshop ventures, yet his one extended solo, which heads the roster in the moderately paced *Lydiot*, is a minor marvel of witty investigation of the modal theme. He surely was the aptest pianist for this gathering, Monklike in many of his instincts, and as unerringly supportive as a composer and leader of his standing would be likely to be. At a nice juncture during this *Lydiot* solo he has the three horns execute the tremolo which is one of his own favourite, and most simply effective, accompanist's clichés.

Thoughts seems to consist of cracker-barrel jazz reminiscence, its theme leisurely at base but allowing various patterns of tempo-doubling, some of them fragmentary in a manner that may recall part of Morton's 1926 *Cannonball blues* (**47a**) without jeopardizing any claim to modernity. Dolphy's other bass-clarinet solo, brisk and meditative at once, happens in the course of this. Each of Russell's participants is sufficiently at ease with the leader's requirements to encompass them with a very personal spontaneity. Swallow and Hunt are excellent; this was, reportedly, the but recently active Swallow's first recording date.

Monk had been a sort of godfather to Russell's real beginnings, so presumably the inclusion of *Round about midnight* in this programme seems an act of devotion. Leaving stylistic innovations a little to one side, useful comparisons might be made between Russell's sextet dates and Monk's celebrated Blue Note groups dealt with under **292** – bop stepping beyond bop. Interpretation of the well-known nocturne is assigned largely to Dolphy, whose lovely alto improvisation is introduced and concluded by creepy noises committed by others. This entirety invites the kind of comments that are ventured regarding Dolphy elsewhere in this volume. Well chosen as this splendid musician undoubtedly was, he stands out from most of the other sidemen as an innovative thinker. This *Round about midnight* is, to most intents and purposes, *his* conception. Another recruited sideman whose intuitive faculties exceeded mere understanding of Russell's 'pantonal' vision at the time was Don Cherry, who in 1965, when his habitual manner still retained close links with the days with Coleman, played his cornet with Russell at a Stuttgart concert where the name of the leader's *femme de ménage*, Lydia, figured in at least four of the titles, and played – according to Michael James, who wrote up *The George Russell Sextet at Beethoven Hall* (Polydor [E] 583 706) back in 1969 – 'as if to the manner born'. [23] E.T.

The New York Contemporary Five

406a Live at the Jazzhus Montmartre Vol. 1
Sonet (D) SLP36

Don Cherry (cnt); John Tchicai (alt); Archie Shepp (ten); Don Moore (bs); J. C. Moses (d). Jazzhus Montmartre, Copenhagen, 15 October 1963.
Cisum · *Crepuscule with Nellie* · *O.C.* · *When will the blues leave?* · *The funeral* · *Mik*

406b Live at the Jazzhus Montmartre Vol. 2
Sonet (D) SLP51

Same personnel and date.
Consequences · *Monk's mood* · *Emotions* · *Wo wo* · *Trio*

These celebrated Jazzhus recordings were made at a juncture in post-Coleman jazz development at which Ornette himself had decided, after his 1962 trio concert at New York Town Hall (see **401**), to withdraw from the scene awhile and Sonny Rollins had re-emerged after seclusion and registered an indeterminate interest in Colemanesque freedom which led to a not notably productive meeting of minds with Cherry in 1962–3 (*On the Outside*, †RCA-Bluebird [A] ND82496). Shepp, a more traditionally minded new-wave saxist, learned lessons about thematic improvisation which may reflect the pre-sabbatical as much as the re-emergent

Rollins. His lusty tone and whimsical tendencies acknowledge an older pre-bop tenor style also. Yet Shepp is as remembered as a new-wave pioneer as is Cherry. Already, he had recorded with Cecil Taylor in 1960 (**384**).

A crucial partnership in the run-up to the formation of the New York Contemporary Five was that involving Shepp and the trumpeter Bill Dixon, a thoughtful and dedicated musician. Moore also was part of that group, and Tchicai was to join it, quitting his native Copenhagen during 1963. The NYCF's birth was a consequence of the shared musical thought processes of Shepp, Dixon, Tchicai and Moore, plus Roswell Rudd, who did not become a NYCF member, though his influence is acknowledged in certain parts of its programme. There is some justice in the sleeve-note comment that 'the work of the quintet is not so much of a pioneering as of a consolidating kind'. The performing career of the quintet appears to have been mostly European. It toured continental venues during autumn 1963, and this Copenhagen engagement, fixed by Tchicai, ended the group's Scandinavian visit and shortly preceded its effectual break-up.

Cisum, a reversal of 'music', is Cherry's idea, with some shaping contributions from Dixon. It is, at first, a wild bestrewing of rapid fanfares, loose notes and uninhibited drumming. J. C. Moses, who had taken over from the Shepp–Dixon quartet's drummer, maintains immense toughness all through, sustains a gruelling tempo, and takes the final solo with sharp eggings-on from Cherry. In the midst of all this Tchicai does little more than repeat simple motifs and Shepp, with a quotation that could well be a genial signal to a distant Rollins, toys slitheringly with a phrase from *Sonny boy*.

Cherry had been active with Coleman's quartet till the end of 1961. For the NYCF he had adapted a couple of themes learned with Coleman, which he, Cherry, titled and for which Dixon had given arranging help. These are *O.C.* and *Emotions*; and there is also *When will the blues leave?* from an early Cherry recording with Coleman of March 1958 (†Original Jazz Classics [A] OJCCD163). *O.C.* is a driving blues theme recorded here for the first time. Tchicai and Shepp respond to the theme in differing accents of sturdiness, Shepp's the more belligerently thoughtful; Cherry's extended piece of lyricism is eminently avant-garde without quite concealing expressive twists from earlier styles. Solos again provide the substance of *When will the blues leave?* – nine choruses from Cherry and eleven each from Tchicai and Shepp. Coleman's motif is strong, and the development of it benefits from the firm support of Moore and Moses plus some whimsically *passé* riffing by the saxophonists.

Shepp's *The funeral* is suitably measured, and in mood might be considered a forecast of his penchant for jazz expressions of racial complaint, such as *Le matin des noirs* recorded at the Newport Festival of 1965. The ensemble introduction of Shepp's intensely topical dirge for

Medgar Evers, who had been murdered by a white racist in June 1963, was devised by Dixon.

The conceptual highlights of these combined albums are *Mik* and *Trio*. *Mik*, a Tchicai–Dixon collaboration, is a simple minor blues of moderate pace. Basicality is reprieved by the soloists, who depart from the restrictions of the chord pattern. Tchacai's most liberated imagination takes flight here in lines that are clear-toned and seem both deliberately pondered and lissomely steered. Moses, with fine skill, maintains the balance of this, though the further contributions of Cherry and Shepp adjust the 'spirituality' of the mood to a certain degree. The Tchicai–Dixon *Wo wo*, a brisk 14-bar number, has a bit of sledgehammering from the drummer, a little less eloquence from the altoist, yet a gentler Cherry. Shepp, in droll intention, sounds to be inventing quotations for want of hitting on real ones.

Trio, Dixon's own creation, is, in devised form, more ambitious than anything else in the repertoire. It employs elements of modalism and is in ¾ time. Moore, who had played on the Shepp–Dixon group's earlier record of *Trio*, introduces this version with delightful ease. The ensemble statement precedes some dramatic extravagances by Cherry, and here again there is some rudimentary riffing from Shepp and Tchicai. The latter's personal witnessing is interrupted by some collective mayhem; Shepp solos above more riffs; then, as Moses bumps out the ¾ mischievously, Shepp yells 'Five! Five!' at him and the metre becomes 5/4 accordingly. But ¾ is retrieved for a Moore–Moses duet, another fine Moore solo, and a vicious and tensely marshalled finale. The curiously balanced genius of the NYCF is displayed memorably. Last to be heard is a tiny snatch of George Russell's *Ezz-thetic* – the quintet's band-call.

Last to be said in this writing is that, to these ears, the performances of *Crepuscule with Nellie* and *Monk's mood* (prepared, we are told, by Roswell Rudd) are about as inventive a tribute to a great jazz master as T. S. Monk's own pawky 1957 arrangement of W. H. Monk's *Eventide* ('Abide with me') for Ray Copeland, Gigi Gryce and Coleman Hawkins was a convincing evocation of a mid-Victorian hymnodist at sunset (†Original Jazz Classics [A] OJCCD084). E.T.

Albert Ayler

407 Spiritual Unity

†ESP [G] 1002–2

Ayler (ten); Gary Peacock (bs); Sunny Murray (d). New York City, 10 July 1964.

Ghosts (2 versions) · *The Wizard* · *Spirits*

The years of 1964 and 1965 were Ayler's most productive. This had much to do with the sympathetic accompaniment of Peacock and Murray, who by early 1966 were no longer working with the saxophonist, who never found suitable replacements. This unique trio – one of the finest modern jazz groups – was formed shortly after Ayler's move to New York City after a European trip in the winter of 1962–3. That trip had produced an iconoclastic assault on standards with *My Name is Albert Ayler* (†Black Lion [E] BLCD760211) from January 1963 with a memorable version of *Summertime.* Although Ayler had previously recorded with a group of unsympathetic Swedish musicians in October 1962 for a limited edition LP, *My Name is Albert Ayler* is generally regarded as the emergence of an entirely new approach to both playing the tenor saxophone and to jazz improvisation.

Eschewing the conventional jazz swing feel, Ayler followed the harmonies of a song only loosely. His saxophone tone took inspiration from Sidney Bechet, as much for its fullness as for its domineering role within the jazz ensemble, and he employed an extremely broad vibrato, like Bechet's, which was a highly unusual departure for a 'New Thing' player. Typically he hurled himself into his improvisations, seldom playing with restraint for very long, and his work was often violent. Speed was a very important element in his playing, and his lines ran the entire range of the saxophone and upwards for at least one additional octave, this being achieved through false fingering and manipulating the mouthpiece. Interjecting vocalized inflections, high squeals and rhythm-'n'-blues honks amid his technically very demanding intensity, Ayler was both original and controversial in his playing. The most startling instrumentalist to emerge from the free-jazz movement of the 1960s, he has, since his unexplained death at the age of 34 in November 1970, been one of its most influential players.

Ayler would record *Ghosts* several times – in September 1964 in Copenhagen, in Paris in 1966, in February 1968 on *Love Cry* (†GRP/Impulse [A] 11082) and as *New ghosts* on *New Grass* (Impulse [A] A9175). But this first version on *Spiritual Unity,* with its simmering fervour, earmarked Ayler as one of the most original and innovative tenor saxophonists of his generation. A religious man, he exhibited in his playing, it has been pointed out, 'an affinity with the music of the fundamentalist black churches in its unrestrained emotional content'. [24] This may be a convenient rationalization with hindsight, yet it is hard to disentangle the notion that the emotional destiny of his playing was in some way governed by an element of evangelical fervour.

Underpinning his sometimes outrageous style was a firm grounding in the blues. One of his first jobs was with Chicago blues-harmonica player Little Walter, whose amplified passion and use of bent pitches may have inspired Ayler's approach to tone. Certainly the drummer Milford Graves has spoken of how well versed Ayler was in 'the tradition', and that he could 'really play honky-tonk'. [25] Yet *Ghosts* begins conventionally enough, a somewhat garbled introduction, a simple diatonic four-bar phrase answered by an equally simple variation and a repeat of the original motif. The whole piece is based on the elemental harmony of the repeating four-bar form. Many of Ayler's compositions were thematic fragments like this, often of a march or hymnlike cast. As he plays the theme, he makes it sound profoundly sinister and alarming, and as he embellishes the simple, arpeggiated melodic motif, it becomes a basis for his extemporization. His phrases, sometimes lengthy and tenacious, crash naturally through bar lines and end when he runs out of steam. There is plenty of bathos in an Ayler solo, proud phrases contrasted by ribbons of sound with notes pressed so close together that they sound like *glissandos* which lead nowhere and have no resolution.

Indeed, Ayler has had a considerable influence on avant-garde string players and these skittering asides, slightly off microphone, explain why. Although his relationship to the four-bar form appears fluid, his feeling for time is remarkably secure, however oblique his phrasing, however liquid his accompaniment appears at any given moment. The basic structure on which he builds his solo appears to provide the obstacle his inspiration needs. Peacock, a bass player in the mould of Scott LaFaro, avoids an explicit statement of time in his solo before Ayler returns with the theme. Murray, although implying tempo, only sporadically states it. His playing, largely free of a specific time-keeping role, was that of colourist, employing unpredictable sounds and patterns in volatile commentary. Together, Peacock and Murray provided an undercurrent of activity that echoed Ayler's own freedom within form.

The Wizard, a more agitated variation of *Ghosts*, uses the repeating four-bar harmonic base, but Ayler's approach, briefly alluding to the *Ghost* motif, almost immediately disappears into disjunction and distortion that goes beyond conventional phrasing and phrase lengths with his slippery tonality to produce a statement of unsettling melodic fragmentation and free-jazz excitement. The second variation of *Ghosts* is in the agitated manner of *The Wizard*, and is perhaps the most intense version, with complexity and speed key elements of Ayler's solos that, with his fondness for arbitrary overstatement, meant individual notes lost their identity. Thus the emphasis settles upon texture and colours rather than melodic substance, and highlights how Ayler's conception of a jazz solo presented a radical alternative in jazz. *Spirits*, a slow dirge played with Ayler's characteristically broad vibrato, allowed his improvisational freedom to shape its form, his *legato* phrasing swirling through seemingly unbroken ascending and descending ribbons of indeterminate note choices. 'I like to play something people can hum,' he once explained. 'From simple melodies to complicated textures to simplicity again and then back to the more dense, more complicated sounds.' [26]

Ayler's influence on jazz may not have been as great as Ornette Coleman's or John Coltrane's, but it is often overlooked that he was a close friend of the latter, who was instrumental in getting him a recording contract with the Impulse label in 1966. And it should be noted that Ayler's playing was absorbed into Coltrane's own conception and thus consumed at one remove by every saxophonist who followed in Coltrane's tracks. Yet Ayler was also the first saxophonist to make a definite step towards a post-Coltrane movement, as in the work of his contemporary Charles Tyler, a more linear soloist who used Ayler's methods, and David Murray, who emerged in the late 1970s revealing the extent to which he had learned Ayler's techniques and how masterfully he could deploy them, as in his first album, *Low Class Conspiracy* (Adelphi [A] 5002). Further, the Lower East Side experimentalist John Zorn passed through an Ayler phase during his 'noise-making' period, and in Europe, the sheer speed of Ayler's playing is echoed in the work of Evan Parker. And the rude power of his work is an important element in the playing of Peter Brötzmann. Indeed, there are few saxophonists in the 'European Free' school who do not reflect at least some aspects of Ayler's playing.

S.N.

Albert Ayler

408 Vibrations

†Black Lion/Freedom (E) 741000

Don Cherry (cnt); Ayler (alt, ten); Gary Peacock (bs); Sunny Murray (d). Copenhagen, 14 September 1964.

Ghosts (2 versions) · *Children* · *Holy spirit* · *Vibrations* · *Mothers*

Ayler was nobody's jazz disciple. The chronicler of Ornette Coleman's adventures has claimed that Ayler 'was a successor . . . who pushed aspects of Coleman's discoveries to extremes'. [27] But no voice heard in jazz has been more singular than Ayler's, or more facilely misapprehended. The voice is unmistakable in its startling intonation and sometimes fearsome force. How much did its acquisition have to do with a genuine quest for style? And to what extent is Ayler's music to be assessed within the purview of 'free' or 'post-Coleman' jazz? The trail that led to his conception of himself as a 'spiritual artist', [28] if investigated, assists an evaluation of his relation to any jazz tradition only fitfully. Boyhood links to black church music, and a reported mastery of bop techniques, remain enigmatic, even though some hearers have discerned echoes of 'primitive' jazz, and even though some boppish shreds clung to his first recorded evidence of personal mode (*The First Recordings*, †Sonet [D] SNTCD604). That maverick session from late 1962 showed some regard, in programme choice, for jazz exemplars, yet the already vicious, calculated ugliness of sound in his tenor expostulations might be thought to steal some of its bleak rawness from the overtones of amplified rhythm-'n'-blues saxes, harmonicas and guitars. Ayler had been a teenage rhythm-'n'-blues sideman on the alto back in Cleveland and it is an open question whether his return to a blend of gospel and rhythm-'n'-blues near the end of his life was a jazz visionary's sad capitulation or a repayment of old debts by a man still capable of artistic choice.

This *Vibrations* programme, recorded, like the Sonet issue, in Copenhagen but with more congenial companions, has appeared in various guises, otherwise titled *Ghosts* and *Mothers and Children*. Like the incongruously programmed, strangely manned yet revelatory *My Name Is Albert Ayler* (Fantasy [A] 86016, Fontana [E] 688 603ZL), recorded the previous year, this album finds Ayler still probing half-excavated ideas and benefiting greatly from the empathy of Cherry, Peacock and Murray. That musical camaraderie may seem partially to answer the question about Ayler's relation to free jazz – Ayler and Murray also had worked with Cecil Taylor in Europe. However, the association with a Cherry who was at the point of making his own post-Coleman foray beyond the possible 'restrictions' of too close a jazz identification must have been one of Ayler's happier options. The telling, unaleatory melodic alliance between the two leading voices in the 'foggy dew' ruralism of *Ghosts* – not the only Ayler creation which merited Cherry's description of him as 'a total folk musician' [29] – is one of the session's most instructive features. The second, much lengthier, version of *Ghosts* is approached obliquely at first. It has some jokey disjunctions from Ayler, along with those kinds of grossly sustained bellowing which, offensive as they seemed, continued to be part of this player's way of pursuing a strain of Stygian lyricism.

That paradox is also present in the tenor assaults in *Vibrations*, where the shades of the unexpressed beauty which this jazz mystic professed to seek have to be discovered within an extended sequence of new-wave exhibitionism, arguably close kin to Coleman's *Free jazz* (**400**), passages where self-challenge too easily leads toward the species of artistic *hara-kiri* which was to prove irresistible to Coltrane and *his* kindred. To Ayler's tirades Cherry adds little other than exclamation marks, but the full quartet is busily involved. Peacock's work is, as elsewhere, more sensitive and poetic than that of anyone other than Murray. It is Murray who stuns *Vibration*'s wildness with one peremptory cymbal smash.

Holy spirit begins as apocalyptic dirge-making, and already poses the 'jazz primitivism' question. The tempo-negating undertow of drums and bass nurtures patterns alternative to the soliloquies and unisons of brassy alto and serenely poised cornet. Lullaby and domestic balladry seem to inspire Ayler's tunes for *Children* and *Mothers*. Cherry's keen knowledge of Ayler's intentions is marked in *Children*. His close commentary, in a mode less speech-inflected than that of his Coleman solos, helps in developing some attractive duet passages. In *Mothers*, having bumbled and nattered beneath Ayler's querulous lamplit serenade, he counters that theme with another built of clear, loftily sustained notes; a tune quite different, and, for what it seems to matter, not jazz in any known style. After that Peacock reintroduces Ayler's tune in the cellar beneath the parlour; but the leader's mock-maudlin piety has the final say.

Ayler's collaboration with Cherry is the first high point in his recording career. How far it goes in establishing his jazz status is not easy to measure, despite its undeniable fascinations. The later groups involving Ayler's brother Donald and the violinist Michel Sampson pose the enigma quite differently. The sextet to be heard in **409** provides an intriguing set of examples for consideration. For those, *Vibrations* should seem the right kind of preamble, showing this saxophonist as a natural – though not intellectualist – analyser of sounds, and at the same time an ecstatic eager to claw his way inside some sensed essence of a music which had been his milieu and his formation. The last thing to doubt, at any stage, is the man's sincerity. E.T.

Albert Ayler

409 The Village Concerts

ABC-Impulse (A) AS9336/2 (2 LPs)

Donald Ayler (tpt); Albert Ayler (ten); Michel Sampson (vln); Bill Folwell, Henry Grimes (bs); Beaver Harris (d). New York City, 18 December 1966.

Spirits rejoice · *Divine peacemaker*

Albert Ayler (ten); probably Call Cobbs (p); presumably Folwell (bs). Same date.

Angels

Joel Freedman (cel) added; Alan Silva (bs) replaces Grimes. New York City, 26 February 1967.

Light in darkness · *Heavenly home* · *Spiritual rebirth* · *Infinite spirit* · *Omega the alpha*

There is a small number of artists whose work remains difficult, even extremely difficult, despite the passage of many years. Albert Ayler has remained the chief example of this in jazz and he was perhaps the last major figure in that music the best of whose output conveys a real sense of danger, a seemingly authentic whiff of hemlock. Even now, almost 30 years after his death, he is more written about than listened to, and his obscurity of intention and meaning can almost be described as organic. This is not just a result of the isolation of an artist in a stupid world but, on the contrary, arises from an entirely conscious, fully intended, incomprehensibility in the music. This is not a mystical obscurity – whatever we care to make of the religious slant of many of his titles – but an obscurity that ruthlessly makes the greatest demands on listeners and does so with all the aggression of a self-confident, consciously creative man who violently widens the gulf between himself and his audience.

Often listeners feel assaulted by Ayler's earlier music because everything he did was so extreme. Its confrontational aspects were such that, in worthy attempts to get on terms, many influences were read into it.

Echoes were supposedly detected of raw country blues, of old marching bands, of European folk ensembles, of New Orleans dirges, of gospel hollers and several other kinds of black American religious music along with hints of allegedly African survivals. Of course the music's extreme fervour ought to have been our main clue, its missionary zeal indicating that it was all very much Ayler's personal inspiration, the fruit of a daring and highly individual mind and heart, of promptings less manic than shamanic. Certainly there is nothing here like a quest for a fulfilment which never comes, such as we hear in Coltrane.

And yet the influences Ayler *did* claim were so respectable as almost to arouse suspicion, among them Lester Young and in particular Bechet. At the same time bop, normally considered more complex than anything Young or especially Bechet played, 'was like humming along with Mitch Miller; it was *too* simple'. [30] Did this merely imply a different set of priorities from the usual ones, or did Ayler aim to go further back in order to come forward again in a quite different way?

Although there are isolated instances of his playing blues, he never seemed much interested in that idiom. Instead he used elemental themes or motifs – they might at this stage more suitably be termed signals – which suggested bugle calls and the like, which certainly reached back beyond Bolden. Ayler appeared, whatever his talk about Bechet or Young, to refer to nothing in earlier jazz history and to offer music that was entirely new, entirely modern, entirely him. The wild vibrato would have sounded absurd from almost anyone else but not from Ayler because of his deadly seriousness. This invokes melancholy, even tragedy, and an absolutely single-minded force. Chaos seems always threatening, yet what is so disturbing is less that than the fact that he is so much in control, is so entirely coherent. Only a master of the saxophone could hope consistently to produce such a vast sound and use it, particularly including all the multiphonics, with such command. And only a great master of what still was evidently jazz could so drastically reshape its essentials *ab ovo*.

Any idea of going back to the beginning and starting again may contrast oddly with his dismissal in the *down beat* interview quoted above of bop as '*too* simple'. But on that same occasion he also claimed: 'I want to play songs like I used to sing when I was real small. Folk melodies that all people would understand. I'd use these melodies as a start and have different simple melodies going in and out of a piece. From simple melody to complicated textures to simplicity again and then back to the more dense, the most complex sounds.' This concept of reconciling complexity with extreme simplicity is striking, yet the fact is that much of what Ayler played during the early and middle 1960s seemed, in its livid power, like a belated aural equivalent to Edvard Munch's *The Scream* of 1895. Perhaps, however, as one of William Golding's characters says, 'the way towards simplicity is through outrage'. [31]

True, Ayler's career was short, yet his music's turbulence was such that it went through considerable changes. Two of its earlier phases are dealt with in the preceding entries and magnificent though trio recitals like **407** are – Jack Cooke wrote of this music's 'remarkable purity of style and intention' [32] – Ayler's work often benefits from the participation of other horns. An especially good example is *New York Eye and Ear Control* (†ESP [A] 1016–2), where he is partnered by Don Cherry (cornet), Roswell Rudd (trombone) and John Tchicai (alto). Indeed it may be that the most conventionally satisfying of Ayler's music was what he recorded in company with Cherry in the latter half of 1964 (**408**). Already with Ornette Coleman (**400**) Cherry had proved himself a sensitive, if occasionally quizzical, respondent, but in 1965 he was replaced by Albert's younger brother Donald, a limited and, in particular, a much less inventive player. Luckily the music was again changing its emphases and this in some ways compensated.

In contrast with the brief and ascetic motives upon which most earlier improvisations had been founded, thematic material became more important and occupied considerably more space. Thus among the performances dealt with here the first theme of *Spirits rejoice* is close to *La Marseillaise*; *Omega is the alpha* relates, in travesty, to a Christmas carol; *Our prayer* similarly to a 19th-centry American Thanksgiving hymn; and the first theme of *Truth is marching in* is close to Stephen Foster. These and similar passages were played in a remarkably straightforward manner even if not quite 'like a Salvation Army band on LSD'. [33] Presumably these were the 'simple melodies' of which Ayler had spoken to *down beat*, although it was also possible that this material, just like the earlier, briefer motifs, was designed by its very commonplaceness to throw emphasis on the many other elements in the music. By the time of the 1966 performances recorded at Slug's (Base [It] 3031 and 3032) Ayler's pieces had become tapestries of extremely varied music, ranging from heterophonic representations of ensemble frenzy to rather sedate marches. The following Paris and Lörrach sessions (Hat Art [Sw] 2009) were similar, except that on the latter Folwell contributed a more aggressive bass part than Lewis Worrell had at Slug's.

While there was a natural tendency to think of Coleman's violin playing of the previous year (**401b**), Sampson, first heard on the Slug's recordings, seemed a most improbable addition to a band like Ayler's. His role proved to be significant, however, and was soon extended. The performances detailed above are best heard in conjunction with others from the same two sessions variously issued as *Albert Ayler in Greenwich Village* (Impulse [A] IMPL5021), *The Awakening* (Impulse [A] AS9155) and under other titles. In fact some of these tracks will be considered first.

Truth is marching in starts with a marchlike theme on the trumpet with counterpoint from the tenor employing very diverse figuration over stormy basses and drums with the latter growing more so. The violin emerges briefly before a second march theme is initiated by the tenor with the trumpet following. Then the tenor goes into some very free playing, as extreme as anything Albert Ayler ever recorded. Next the second march theme is heard again more briefly, leading to a free, seemingly quite random, trumpet solo. The march theme is then heard once more before the violin takes the foreground with basses and drums very active. Yet again the march theme surfaces before there is a very free collective improvisation leading to a last appearance of the march theme before a long-drawn-out coda during which the music gradually winds down. Several of the performances are rather like that but *Our prayer* is quite simple. It has a hymnlike theme by Donald Ayler against which his brother throws more than one sort of counterpoint with very full support from basses and drums.

Longest of these interpretations is *Spirits rejoice*, the resemblance of whose first theme to Rouget de Lisle's familiar patriotic melody has already been remarked. This is repeated and followed by a fairly gentle tenor solo and a return to the quasi-French melody, followed by another marchlike theme, which gives way to an apparently random trumpet solo: what the basses and drums are doing simultaneously is considerably more interesting. Later there is another tenor solo very different from the first, two fine violin solos and a long excursion by the bassists, one bowed and one *pizzicato*. Between these various episodes one or another of the themes recurs, ending with the caricatured *Marseillaise* and another extended coda. *Divine peacemaker* reverts to a brisk bugle-call type of theme, followed by another slower, not exactly marchlike idea. The trumpet and tenor weave around this latter in various relaxed ways before returning to the first theme at its original tempo. There follows an anything-goes trumpet solo and one from Sampson with the basses once again prominent. Next the second theme leads into a particularly free tenor solo, much of it in very high register over very animated drumming.

From the same date came *Angels*, which may be the most puzzling item Ayler ever recorded. Even after the most persistent listening over many years it seems impossible to discover any musical relationship between Ayler's acerbic phrases and Cobbs's lushly romantic rhetoric. One remains as defiantly unsuited to the other as can be imagined, and this is a performance whose intent appears thoroughly misconceived. In acute contrast, *For John Coltrane*, from the 1967 occasion, may be the most overtly beautiful piece Ayler left us. The trumpet is blessedly absent and Ayler switches to alto not, as has been suggested, because fearful of Coltrane's prowess as a tenor saxophonist but clearly because the character of the music is better suited to the lighter-voiced instrument. Certainly there is no link with any aspect of Coltrane's music. Some might, on the contrary, hear this piece as a nightmare re-enactment of Parker with strings (**266a**), but Ayler's tone is much smoother than usual, as this piece demands. The string music, with long violin and cello solos, is quite astringent, however, and although chords are obviously produced, both the discourse and the texture are essentially linear – whereas in *Angels* the piano's harmony seems a real obstacle to comprehension.

Although Donald Ayler returns for the remaining performances, he is little evident on several of them and they are notable mainly for his elder brother and for various deployments of the apparently inexhaustible resources of four string instruments. Thus *Heavenly home* has much plangent tenor amid the string network, followed by a long passage for strings alone. The tenor then returns but more repetitively and is again supplanted by the strings, notably Sampson. In *Spiritual rebirth*, as in several other pieces, the tempo is freely inflected. Sampson is once more prominent in seeming opposition to Albert Ayler, who improvises around the simple opening motives. For *Infinite spirit* the tenor again improvises on the rather straightforward initial ideas against the violin, slowly growing more demonstrative. On *Change has come* the Aylers are less obsessively march-inclined but there is much free playing from both, although with the strings quite prominent. So they are again during *Light in darkness* and into their rich texture the Aylers insert short, repetitive, even insistent, motifs on which they improvise freely, yet with returns to the initial material. The tenor once more gets into extremely high register and there is a further at-random trumpet solo, enclosed, as was the tenor solo, in a thick network of basses and drums. There is also a virtuosic passage from Sampson and further numerous statements of the march ideas.

Nor is *Omega is the alpha* so very different, with short, repetitive phrases from the horns that we have often heard before in these performances. Of the trumpet solo especially all one can say by now is that Donald was lucky, as we are unlucky, that Albert was prepared to tolerate him. The satisfactory and unsatisfactory aspects of this phase of Albert Ayler's music will have been evident in the above paragraphs. It did seem, however, despite the crudity and evident incomprehension of Donald Ayler, that a new way of making jazz was being hammered out beyond what had been achieved with Cherry in 1964. A year later Dan Morgenstern described Ayler's new band as sounding like 'a rhythm-'n'-blues outfit gone beserk' [34] and this proved all too prophetic. A further year after the sessions discussed here Ayler issued *New Grass* (Impulse [A] AS9175), which offered the crudest sort of rhythm 'n' blues. He still resembled himself in terms of sound, yet the heavily square soul rhythm defeated him, reducing his ideas to something utterly predictable. The so-called *Last Album* (Impulse [A] AS9208), luckily misnamed, was even worse, and taken together these must be two of the most banal issues ever put out under the name of a great jazz musician. It is true that, like others before him and since, Ayler had been compelled to perform such nonsense to gain his earliest professional experience during his teens. But to play, and record, dross like this at a much later stage in his career, after he had won international fame, was a monstrous regression from all he had stood for.

Fortunately it showed signs of being corrected before the end of his life. In 1970 he for the last time escaped to Europe, where he always had met with greater understanding than at home. In the south of France he recorded performances from several concerts which, particularly in *Holy family* and *In heart only* (Shandar [F] SR10000), find his originality fully preserved. It may be that, no matter how depressing, the reversion to rhythm 'n' blues was a passing aberration and that his jazz career would have been resumed. Alas, his tragically early death came before the end of the year.

Even decades later, on listening to Ayler's courageous, bewitched, desperate music we are haunted by the strange and disquieting impression that we are out on the very limits of the expressible, out on the last dangerous fringes where the ice of what we normally call art is so thin that we can almost see through into the depths below, into the mysterious thing-in-itself from which we abstract the all-too-human conventions of music. What he did in his best moments seemed like a further attempt at exploding the language of music so that it might eventually approximate to the mind's complexity. To those who say that language, even musical language, is a social contract which cannot be broken without loss of communication, Ayler would maybe have replied that his aim was less communication than communion in the apprehension of mystery. M.H.

Old and New Dreams

410 **Playing**
ECM (G) 1205

Don Cherry (tpt, p, vcl); Dewey Redman (ten, mus); Charlie Haden (bs); Ed Blackwell (d). Bregenz, Austria, June 1980.
Happy house · Mopti · New dream · Rushour · Broken shadows · Playing

Old and New Dreams, a title that came from their first album in 1976, united four profound musicians inextricably linked to the evolution of the music of Ornette Coleman. However, their individual careers also reveal a multiplicity of interrelationships. Haden, Blackwell and Cherry date back to some of the earliest Coleman combinations, Redman a little later, while Haden performed for several years as a member of the Keith Jarrett quartet alongside Redman. Also, both Cherry and Redman were members of Haden's Liberation Music Orchestra in its earliest manifestation in 1969 and its 1980s reincarnations, and in the 1970s they both recorded with Haden for the Horizon label.

Such long-standing camaraderie produced a collective empathy that often eludes reunions, however well-intentioned. Yet this was a reunion with a difference. From the start it was clear that this was not a gathering set on rediscovering themselves in the past, but rather in the future. In 1978 the band began accepting dates in both the United States and Europe and recorded *Old and New Dreams* (ECM [G] 1154) in 1979, expanding on a small core of Coleman compositions with their own originals. At the time Coleman himself was pursuing electronic endeavours but since 1962 his public performances had been intermittent, so that a generation of jazz fans had grown up without hearing his music in its purest form. When, in 1979, Old and New Dreams performed a concert at New York's Town Hall, there were whoops of recognition at Coleman's themes and standing ovations, a remarkable volte-face from the controversial reception that greeted his music at the Five Spot 20 years before.

Recorded live during their 1980 tour of Europe, *Playing* opens with a genial version of Coleman's *Happy house*, a composition which all the participants had jointly recorded with the saxophonist during his *Science Fiction* sessions in 1971 but which had not seen release until 1982 on his album *Broken Dreams* (Columbia [A] FC 38029). A brief exchange between the ensemble and Blackwell's sophisticated drumming introduces Redman's conceptually bright solo. Playing it close to the chest to begin, he gradually becomes expansive and lyrical, ordering his ideas with calm and cunning. Technically secure, precisely articulated and rhythmically fluid, he makes it easy to overlook the backdrop provided by Blackwell and Haden. The bassist's harmonic contribution to Coleman's music has long been taken for granted, but he was an essential ingredient in the *sound* of that innovator's work, maintaining a reference point that swung the music in a way that subsequent bass players never seemed quite able to do. Twenty years on he had grown both in stature and ability, meshing with Blackwell's deceptively simple patterns to nudge the soloist into the unexpected. But despite the level of sympathetic interaction, there is a sense of discovery and urgency that flows through this music, a creative compulsion to make music of the moment. Cherry, who used a French Meha pocket trumpet, achieves an unexpectedly broad tone from his tiny instrument as he chisels melodic fragments into unexpected shapes and sizes. After Haden's solo is acknowledged with cheerful gusto by the audience, Cherry and Redman unite in simultaneous dialogue before Blackwell provides the icing: a drum solo that is not self-indulgent but sustains the creative flow before Cherry and Redman resume the fragmented exchanges that mark a return to the theme.

Cherry's original composition *Mopti* reflected his increasing interest in world music, ethnomusicology and multiculturalism since leaving Coleman in 1961. He chants an eight-bar motif over a two-bar vamp accompanying himself on the piano, and as the melody is taken up by

Redman, Cherry returns to the trumpet. They both toss variations back and forth, with Redman the predominant voice over Blackwell's appropriately exotic rhythm. After a reiteration of the chant between trumpet and saxophone, Blackwell emerges in a central role with a hypnotic solo that leads back to a recapitulation and variation of the theme by trumpet and saxophone, and finally by piano and saxophone. *New dream*, an exercise in contrasting metres, opens with a dirgelike motif followed by an abrupt, boppish answering phrase and has a curious limping swing that provokes anguished, on-the-edge solos from Redman and Cherry. The concise melody of *Happy house* is here exchanged for prickly introspection and angular responses to the tense, three-legged rhythm-section patterns of Haden and Blackwell.

A bop fanfare loosely based on the opening bars of *The theme* heralds Redman's *Rushour*, a motif that can be occasionally glimpsed in the vortex of ideas during his solo and is used in its original incarnation to mark the transition from soloist to soloist. Cherry, surreal in his placement of notes that are both long and carefully considered, stretches phrases that move slowly over the frenetic tempo beneath him before abruptly changing metre and dissolving into squalls of quavers and semiquavers. *Broken shadows* is a Coleman dirge that moves to Blackwell's stately tom-tom rhythm. Cherry again trades metre against rhythm in a curious yet captivating left-of-centre solo. Redman's musette, with its pinched Middle Eastern tone, sways to Haden's occasional *arco* interventions, a mood echoed in his solo before Cherry and Redman, now on tenor, duet in other-worldly harmonies. Haden returns, and *segues* into *Playing*, a dirge of anxious textures, random associations and elongated noodles. Haden's knotty solo of around-the-bridge harmonics and percussive asides allows Cherry to rethink the mood. He enters full of hard-bop flourishes and under-the-finger arabesques that seem to cohere to the logic of chance yet achieve a spontaneity of shape and design. Redman briefly considers a response but instead adds an aside before Blackwell gently winds the performance down.

As in his period with Coleman, it is Haden's independent logic that binds these performances together. His quick ears respond to the direction of the music, pushing, challenging and supporting those around him. In a band of equals he was perhaps a little more equal than the others, and his support play with Blackwell, a consummate section mate who was rooted in the traditionalism of New Orleans, clarifies the logic of Cherry and Redman. This is more 'inside' than 'outside' free, yet Cherry and Redman delight in adding arresting twists to their ideas, splintering bop licks and fracturing old-timey blues hues into intensely personal statements. Often they choose the physical and the intuitive over intellectuality and refinement, yet they never descend into blind emotion. Exploding rote thinking, they show how the energy playing of the late 1960s and 1970s had already begun to sound anachronistic. S.N.

John Carter

411 Castles of Ghana

Gramavision (A) 18–8603–1

Baikida Carroll (tpt, vcl); Bobby Bradford (cnt); Benny Powell (tbn); Carter (clt, vcl); Marty Ehrlich (bs clt); Terry Jenoure (vln); Richard Davis (bs); Andrew Cyrille (d). New York City, November 1985.

Castles of Ghana · *Evening prayer* · *Conversations* · *The fallen prince* · *Theme of desperation* · *Capture* · *Postlude*

Carter was born in Fort Worth, Texas, just six months before one of his earliest associates, Ornette Coleman. But while Coleman and other young musicians from Fort Worth, such as Dewey Redman, Charles Moffett and Price Lasha, went on to national recognition, Carter and the legendary Red Connors, whom Coleman described as the greatest saxophonist he ever heard, remained at home. In Carter's case it was to pursue a career in academia; a scholastic prodigy, he graduated from high school at 15, had a BA in music by the time he was 19 and an MA at 26. Most of his life was spent teaching in the public school system, first at Fort Worth, then in Los Angeles.

His jazz career developed intermittently until he formed an association with the trumpeter Bobby Bradford in 1964, Bradford having been recommended to Carter by Coleman. Bradford had actually preceded Don Cherry in Coleman's ensembles, an association that went unrecorded. In 1967, Carter conducted Coleman's concert with a symphony orchestra at UCLA. However, recording opportunities with Bradford were few, although they did record for Bob Thiele's Flying Dutchman label in 1969, *West Coast Hot* (†Novus [A] ND83107), following it with another three albums culminating in 1972's *Secrets* (Revelation [A] 18). Carter continued to pursue a career within the education system, touring during his vacations and making the occasional recording, but in 1982, at the age of 53 and with his family grown up, he decided to follow his muse in the none too secure world of jazz.

Carter was a clarinet virtuoso, his technique and expressionism perfected apart from the round of one-night stands, nightclubs, festivals and concerts that is the lot of the professional jazz musician. His tone was full and – like that of Jimmy Hamilton, who played in Carter's Clarinet Summit during the 1980s – even and clear through all registers from his woody *chalumeau* to a full altissimo range, where through false fingering he extended the range of the clarinet beyond that normally associated with the instrument. Carter suddenly emerged as one of the finest clarinettists in jazz and in 1980 he recorded *Night Fire* (Black Saint [It] BSR0047) with a quintet including Bradford and the flautist James

Newton. This included an extended composition, *Night fire – an American folk suite*, a partly programmatic piece, the night fire being a visitation by the Klu Klux Klan on a black family. It was a precursor to his highly ambitious cycle *Roots and Folklore: Episodes in the Development of American Folk Music*, which would absorb him through the 1980s. This comprised five suites, each represented by a separate album: *Dauwhe* (Black Saint [It] BSR0057), *Castles of Ghana* (as above), *Dance of the Love Ghosts* (†Gramavision [A] 18–8704–2), *Fields* (†Gramavision 18–8907–2) and *Shadows on a Wall* (†Gramavision R279422–2). Taken together, the *Roots and Folklore* cycle numbers among the finest extended compositions in jazz; indeed, it is difficult not to conclude that with the passage of time, it will become recognized as the pre-eminent post-Ellington extended work in jazz.

Throughout the cycle Carter largely retains the same nucleus of seven players who appeared on *Castles of Ghana.* However, from *Dance of the Love Ghosts* onwards Fred Hopkins came in as bassist instead of Davis, and Don Preston was added on keyboards. This was the first time Carter recorded with a keyboard, and thus the group was expanded into an octet, which was often further augmented by additional instrumentalists, percussionists or vocalists. Even so, it meant Carter was able to maintain the Ellington proposition of writing and composing for a basic ensemble of specific voices, exploiting their distinct musical personalities individually and in combination.

The cycle begins in Africa, where the spirited people depicted in *Dauwhe* are captured and become a part of the slave trade. *Castles of Ghana* takes it title from the many forts and castles along the Ghanaian shores, some dating back to the fourth century, which were used as holding stations for African captives awaiting shipment to the New World. Subsequent suites deal with deportation, slavery, emancipation and the urbanization of the Afro-American. *Castles of Ghana* opens with a repeated motif on tom-toms by Cyrille and a series of brass cadences before Carter's flutter-tongue interlude introduces an ensemble passage of Ellingtonian depth belying such a (relatively) small head count. Its brooding tone sets the scene for solos by Carroll, Ehrlich, Powell – using a plunger mute à la Tricky Sam – and Jenoure, who all hold to a basic tonal centre rather than to any specific changes. They work out over Carter's subdued mutterings, a constantly bubbling witches' cauldron brewed in the shadows of Davis's and Cyrille's hard-edged vamp. The final ensemble passage freely envelops the chattering voices of the ensemble, a collective polyphony of confusion and pain that speaks of the human drama being enacted within the castle dungeons.

Evening prayer, based on a pedal point, is a soliloquy of great depth and almost unbearable sadness. Its mood is broken by Cyrille's introduction to the strident, moody *Conversations*, which features a dizzying duet between Carter and Ehrlich. They begin with unison bop fragments but end in the extremes of instrumental colour before the ensemble announces a return to order. The realization that slavery meant an end to centuries-old traditions is depicted by *The fallen prince*, with Powell, on open horn, cast in a central role of essaying the wounded grace of a noble warrior being swept into an alien culture. Jenoure adds melancholy with sympathetic asides before adding his weight an octave higher towards the end. *Theme of desperation*, a duet between Jenoure and Carter, rises and falls in unusual intervals as the violinist is joined by a falsetto voice and faraway chimes of doom.

The suite's *tour de force* is *Capture*, again built around a tonal centre, opening with strident riffs and counter-riffs marshalled by Cyrille's backbeat. Carter's rhapsodic clarinet, progressing ever higher and higher to notes unvisited by previous exponents of this most difficult of woodwinds, enters in an unaccompanied *rubato* episode. As he draws the episode to a close, Cyrille and Davis, whose mutual empathy is one of the highlights of the album, enter at fleet tempo with Carter to the fore, in headlong dash to evade abduction. Long 'organ' chords emphasize the drama, before Bradford, a most lyrical improviser, and Ehrlich become part of the high tension of the chase. Carroll surfaces at the end of Ehrlich's bass-clarinet solo, and remains in fractured duet until the return of Carter. But escape is impossible, capture inevitable. Suddenly a voice, over distant drums, intones the *Postlude*: 'The journey facing these captives will prove to be truly arduous, a journey that would, before its completion, interrupt and redirect the dynamics of human existence on our planet.'

Castles of Ghana in particular, and the *Roots and Folklore: Episodes in the Development of American Folk Music* cycle in general, demonstrate how great taste and imagination are, in John Litweiler's words, axiomatic to 'the freedom principle'. Throughout there is not a redundant phrase or gratuitous flourish; Carter's writing is incisive, programatically rich and vital, possessing an insight that matches the scale of the task he set himself. Perhaps more important, he created a series of compositions in which both he and his soloists respond with spontaneity, a sense of self-discovery and a refreshing vitality that all lie at the heart of great jazz.

S.N.

Peter Brötzmann

412 Machine Gun

†FMP (G) CD24

Brötzmann (ten, bar); Willem Breuker (ten, bs clt); Evan Parker (ten); Fred van Hove (p); Peter Kowald, Buschi Niebergall (bs); Han Bennink (d). Bremen, May 1968.

Machine gun (2 versions) · *Responsible* (2 versions) · *Music for Han Bennink*

It was perhaps inevitable that in the United States free jazz became inextricably linked with the civil-rights movement of the 1960s. Many young musicians felt that by freeing themselves from bar lines, harmony and rhythm they were participating both literally and metaphorically in the black crusade for freedom and social justice. For many, free jazz became an anthem that screamed rejection of racial inequality, and there is no doubt that much of the ethos of 'New Thing' thinking was bound up in the social climate from which it emerged. Yet by the end of the 1960s free jazz in America was floundering, its intense deconstruction of established methodology unable to find an audience of sufficient size to adequately support it. But while free jazz was eventually forced underground in America, by the middle of the 1960s it had taken hold in Europe, becoming the only example of a genre of jazz to develop and expand beyond American shores to assume its own specific identity that was equal – many would argue superior – to its American counterpart. Indeed, by the mid-1970s some of the key European free-jazzers, such as Brötzmann, Albert Mangelsdorff, Evan Parker and Derek Bailey, were actually beginning to influence American free jazz.

While European free jazz did not have the strong ideological undercurrent of its American counterpart, it nevertheless was rooted in 1960s counter-culture. With the emergence of the so-called generation gap, it seemed to many that a major division in society was opening up. Traditional values and the political beliefs of an older generation which had been the cement of society were either being swept aside or openly questioned. An entire youth culture that embraced rock music, clothes, drugs and, with the advent of the pill, free love, was emerging with new ideals and a shared belief they could change the corporate state without violence. They firmly believed a new consensus would emerge to undo the iniquities of the past. This loose coalition of protesters represented a counter-culture that was united in its adoption of anti-establishment rhetoric and the questioning of society's basic values but not much else. For a while it seemed enough. In May 1968 student rioting in Paris almost succeeded in destabilizing de Gaulle's government. *Machine Gun* is very much a product of those heady times. As much as free jazz was harnessed as a music of civil-rights protest in America, in Europe it was suffused with a strong undercurrent of social protest to the extent that it is impossible not to think of *Machine Gun* as anything other than one enormous fart in the face of the establishment, or at the very least, established values.

As coruscating as it is alienating, *Machine Gun* remains an important statement from the emerging pan-European free-jazz movement. Uniting players from five countries, the Netherlands, the UK, Belgium, Sweden and West Germany, it announced an approach to freedom quite different to American models. In 1972, Kowald described their approach as 'Kaputt-play', the main objective of which was to 'do without the musical influence of most Americans'. [35] Despite the intensity of free-jazz excitement on albums such as Coleman's *Free Jazz* (**400**), its logical successor, Ayler's *New York Eye and Ear Control* (†ESP [A] 1016–2) – itself an important predecessor to Coltrane's *Ascension* (†Impulse [A] GRD2–113) – their relationship, however arcane, to the jazz tradition was never lost. With *Machine Gun* there is no such comforting umbilical; it simply arrives as a fully formed manifestation of the Godzilla principle, the appeal of the strong and ugly. Brötzmann's own playing was allied to the abandonment of technique and he used such devices as overblowing, biting the reed and growling through the instrument to add to a continuously high level of intensity in his playing that was in turn matched by the more formal approaches of Parker and Breuker. Brötzmann's approach to improvisation was fundamentally different from that of American jazz musicians, and was aptly summed up in an interview in *Cadence* magazine: 'I think this over-weighting of technical possibilities is simply the wrong way . . . It is too much related to technique and that Americans are very open to . . . music has never been a matter of technique, at least the music I consider as being important.' [36]

While it could be argued that simply relying on intensity was in itself limiting, since the alternatives are creating either less or even greater intensity, *Machine Gun* actually marshals this device well. Quite possibly the title is read as a programmatic instruction by the improvisers, who respond with appropriately machine-gun-like phrasing and emphasis on the lower instrumental registers. Based on a pedal point, the saxophones open with a devastating staccato foray before a solo interlude that is rent apart by communal shrieks of terrifying dimensions discharged on cue. Van Hove's swirling 'outside' solo which follows gradually gives way to the two basses in call-and-response repartee. Bennink is superb throughout, discharging his duties with controlled madness, but the most dramatic moment emerges at the end of the bass solos with a palpable rise in tension as the horns hubble and bubble in the background before launching into further combat. As the intensity of the moment rises, with Brötzmann blowing himself every shade between pink and purple, a crazy blues riff emerges to break the tension and move the piece to conclusion. This is very scary stuff. Music is not supposed to sound like this, bereft of beauty and eloquence and determined to offend, yet here, paradoxically, lies its fascination.

If the subsequent takes of *Responsible* and *Music for Han Bennink* yield less than the title track, it is because the initial punishing experience of *Machine gun* came close to exhausting the meaning of what followed. These tracks impose the burden of creative listening on its audience since, like all free jazz, it is all about a range of abstract possibilities that do not submit to orthodox musicological explanation. *Machine gun* is music that attracts and repels (and attracts again) through extremes of imagistic contradictions: is this the music of 'dangerous aliens or boisterous kids, wild animals or wayward pets'? [37] Or is this a simple juxtaposition of the primitive/intellectual homology, like Robert Louis Stephenson's Mr Hyde, who threatens to overwhelm his creator, Dr Jekyll; in other words, is this jazz eating itself? S.N.

Tomasz Stańko

413 Music for K

Pool Jazz (G) IRS942112

Stańko (tpt); Zbigniew Seifert (alt); Janusz Muniak (ten); Bronislaw Suchanek (bs); Janusz Stefanski (d). Warsaw, 8–10 January 1970.

The ambusher · *Infinitely small* · *Cry* · *Music for K*

No matter what the discographies say, no flute or soprano saxophone is heard from Muniak on any of the above.

Stańko was a maverick, being very Polish yet always a figure apart in the jazz of his country. But he was, with Krzysztof Komeda (Trcinski) and Zbigniew Namyslowski (**415**), one of the three most significant influences on Polish jazz over a long period, and besides their separate endeavours their partnerships were important. Stańko studied the trumpet at the High School for Music in Cracow and one is tempted to suggest that whereas the main influence on his playing was Miles Davis, Ornette Coleman had the shaping effect on his approach to jazz. He usually described himself as a 'free jazz musician' and certainly, always having preferred open to closed forms, he took to Coleman's initiatives more readily than did most people in European (or American) jazz, later saying that study of the early Atlantics (**400**) was crucial for his first band. [38] Yet Stańko also asserted in the same *Jazz Forum* interview that Joachim Berendt's description of him as 'a white Ornette Coleman' was 'stupid'. The opinion was indeed a rather misleading simplification because at latest by the 1970s Stańko's music was enriched in terms of harmony, rhythm and structure by well-integrated contributions from several other contemporary styles.

Having first heard jazz at a 1958 Brubeck concert, Stańko formed his initial band, which he called the Jazz Darings, with Adam Makowicz in 1962. Many years later he said that ensemble played hard bop and it was only after Makowicz's piano was replaced by Muniak's tenor saxophone that it started to perform in something like Coleman's way. Even then Stańko improvised with a wealth of expression and variety of tone that have increased over the years; he never sounded like anyone else. He also played for Komeda and a bit later with Andrzej Trzaskowski. Probably his closest links were with Komeda, who was, quite apart from his jazz output, the most significant European film composer of the 1960s. For the quintet Komeda led in that decade, which besides Stańko had Michal Urbaniak (tenor) and sometimes Namyslowski, he wrote some highly individual themes. Stańko's contributions to the band's performances brought out the mood and in particular the drama of Komeda's pieces, as in *Svantetic* and *Astigmatic* (†Power Bros [P] 00125). There were extensive tours of Czechoslovakia, Scandinavia and what was then Yugoslavia, besides appearances at major jazz events in Germany (Berlin, Nuremberg, Baden-Baden, Donaueschingen).

In due course the Stańko Quintet was formed and the above was their initial record, first issued on Muza (P). It stands among the best free jazz, European or otherwise, of its time, yet there are several other discs made over the next few years which are of very similar quality. Among them are *Purple Sun* (Calig [G] CAL30610), *Twet* (Muza [P] SXL1138), *Balladyna* (ECM [G] 1070) and *Almost Green* (Leo [Fi] 008). Much later Stańko opined that music is pure abstraction, but neither this jazz, nor even several of its titles, suggest any such thing. *The ambusher* opens with a quite complex multivoiced ensemble and then after the briefest of pauses there is a solo from Seifert which is very free in its high-pressure invention. Bass and drums make an energetic response to this, playing as it were beside the altoist rather than behind him. Next there is a drum solo, better than many such and even with some quiet moments. Gradually the ensemble returns, surrounding Stefanski's continuing solo rather than accompanying it. Finally the opening themes are heard again.

A less unruly ensemble starts *Infinitely small* and Stańko is more prominent. Then he improvises at length with plenty of ideas and strikingly free in organization. Next, quiet chords from the saxophones prompt him to continue more thoughtfully. Then an ardent mood arises and alternates with the more restrained feeling until the latter takes final possession of the music as Stańko continues to solo. *Cry* begins with the leader and Suchanek at work against saxophone chords which are keening rather than merely thoughtful. The reeds become more insistent as Stefanski joins in and Stańko improvises more extravagantly. Next he joins his voice to those of Seifert and Muniak as the drums become furiously active. Another direction is set as after a brief solemn moment Seifert is heard against very busy drums and bass. As he continues, the drums grow fiercer before falling silent and leaving Seifert playing by himself. The end comes with a short, sombre chordal ensemble led by Stańko.

Finally comes *Music for K*, which is justifiably the longest piece here and is of course Stańko's tribute to Komeda. It opens with another fairly dense collective improvisation, slightly Aylerish in tone and gesture. Then a more restricted ensemble passage leads to an even quieter theme from Stańko over warm saxophone chords. Next there is an improvisation by Seifert that is free in construction and slowly grows almost wild as the bass and drums become more active. Stańko and Muniak enter and the music for a short while again becomes complex. Then there is a rather long unaccompanied solo from Suchanek, followed by more striking thoughts from Seifert during which bass and drums again respond fiercely. Stańko and Muniak re-enter but Seifert for a while retains the leading voice in the collective improvisation. After a pause there is a quiet bass passage over still horn chords before Stańko solos over sustained saxophone harmonies. As he continues, Seifert and Muniak become far more mobile, even slightly Aylerish. Stańko's playing grows even more adventurous as the reeds and Suchanek and Stefanski take over with increasing animation. This leads to a drum solo and a collective improvisation with which this inexplicably shapely performance closes. Except that after a pause there is a brief snatch of the main *Ambusher* themes, to which there seems no point.

Music for K should be heard in conjunction with Urbaniak's *Tribute to Komeda* (MPS [G] MC21657) in which Stańko, Seifert and several others were involved. All the music noted here, though Stańko's especially, shifts in its emphasis and direction repeatedly yet remains firmly in contact with the defining elements of jazz.

Naturally Stańko's career has continued, with work for Chico Freeman, James Spaulding, Jack DeJohnette among others, and in 1988 he was in Cecil Taylor's big band (†FMP [G] CD8/9). Before that, in 1980, he became one of the very few trumpeters to give concerts unaccompanied, including in India at the Taj Mahal and the Karla Caves (Leo [Fi] 011). Given his uncommonly wide range of tonal resources, this venture is less outlandish than it may at first appear. And he has further expanded his activities in several directions, for example from 1985 with his Freelectronic group (*Montreux Performance* †ITM [Sw] 1423CD, 1987). Indeed Stańko remained productive into the 1990s, as with *Bluish* (†Power Bros [P] 00113CD, 1991) and *Leosia* with Bobo Stenson and Tony Oxley (†ECM [G] 531 693–2, 1996). M.H.

Bernt Rosengren

414 Notes from Underground

Harvest (Sd) E154–34958/9 (2 LPs)

Rosengren (alt, ten); Tommy Koverhult (ten); Torbjörn Hultcrantz (bs); Leif Wennerström (d). Stockholm, 17 September 1973.
Gluck · Splash

Rosengren (p). Stockholm, 18 September 1973.
Markitta blues

Koverhult (fl), Hultcrantz (bs), Wennerström (d) added. Same date.
In the ocean

Rosengren switches to ten, fl, Koverhult to ten. Same date.
Iana has been surprised in the night

Maffy Falay (tpt); Bertil Strandberg (tbn); Rosengren (ten); Koverhult (ten, sop); Gunnar Bergsten (bar); Bobo Stenson (p); Hultcrantz, Björn Alke (bs); Wennerström (d); Okay Temiz (perc); Bengt Berger (tabla). Stockholm, 24 September 1973.
Gerda

Alke absent. Same date.
Fly me to the sun

Strandberg, Bergsten absent. Stockholm, 25 September 1973.
Theme from Rachmaninoff Piano Concerto No. 2

Salih Baysal (vcl, vln); Falay (darbuka); Temiz (perc). Same date.
Meyhane

Rosengren (tarragot) added. Same date.
Hakim hanim

Falay (tpt); Strandberg (tbn); Rosengren (alt, ten); Koverhult (ten); Bergsten (bar); Stenson (p); Hultcrantz, Alke (bs); Wennerström (d); Temiz (perc); Berger (tabla). Same date.
Some changes I · *Some changes II* · *Some changes V*

Berger absent. Same date.
Some changes VI · *Markitta blues* · *Psalm*

Rosengren appeared on the Swedish jazz scene in 1957 at the age of 19 as a member of the hard-bop quintet Jazz Club 57 which recorded a few notably spry pieces for the Sonet label. He was perhaps affected initially by Chicago saxophonists like Gene Ammons, but was lucky enough, or creative enough, to avoid Coltrane's stifling influence and quite soon arrived at a style of his own. This he continued to develop over many years and he must for a considerable time have been among the finest tenor saxophonists in Europe as well as becoming a remarkable flautist. Alas, this continuing musical growth was little rewarded in terms of public recognition, though Rosengren stubbornly continued to make outstanding records, among which the above may be the best.

Certainly matters started well, the first major career event, for example, being his membership of Marshall Brown's International Youth Band, a large ensemble of European jazzmen which performed at the 1958 Newport Festival and recorded for Columbia. Further prominence came with Rosengren's soloing in the soundtrack music which Krzysztof Komeda composed for Roman Polanski's 1962 Polish film *Knife in the Water.* By then he already had recorded with Benny Bailey in 1959 (and would do so again in 1976), with Lars Werner in 1960, appeared with Komeda and the Romanian Jancy Korossy at the Polish Jazz Jamboree of 1961, recording a few titles with each of them for Muza. In 1964 he was on an Idrees Sulieman Columbia date and the following year recorded with Staffan Abelsen and the Swedish Radio Jazz group, a big band. Rosengren was in several other ambitious and demanding ensembles over the years, most notably those led by George Russell (**324**), Lars Gullin (**360**), Don Cherry and Palle Mikkelborg.

In 1967, however, he assumed leadership of a quartet with the unlikely instrumentation of two tenors, bass, drums – and no piano or guitar. The other members were Koverhult, Hultcrantz and Wennerström, and they remained together for about a decade, recording for several labels.

This is the core ensemble of the sessions detailed above and it is instructive to compare the results with the 1971 version of Rosengren's little band on Gazell (Sd) GMG1226. The collective title given for these 1973 dates stems from Dostoievsky and the phrase 'all man actually needs is independent will, at all costs and whatever the consequences', quoted on the sleeve, occurs in his *Notes from Underground* (1864). Yet that had merely an externally shaping influence, the music arising from deep within the jazz tradition, especially from the main participants having worked together for a number of years. And the quality of the results was such that it was decided to issue this as two LPs rather than the initially intended one.

It is helpful to listen to the basic quartet first, on *Gluck* and *Splash*. Whether in tenor solos or duets, the former is strikingly free music, giving a clear indication of the differences and similarities between Rosengren and Koverhult. The leader is the more imaginative, and if one thinks of any of the American masters it is not Coleman, certainly not Coltrane, but Ayler – who of course had made his first recordings in Stockholm. That was in 1962, however, and Ayler seems to have been no more than a marginal influence on Rosengren, though still colouring a phrase here, an inflection there. This is the more so in *Splash*, one of the set's most remarkable tracks, much of it a duet between the two tenors. Rosengren's greater originality is confirmed by his second solo here. On *Iana has been surprised in the night* he plays mainly the flute and sounds faintly Oriental. This is not altogether surprising as this melody was of Bulgarian folk origin, though fully translated into jazz by Rosengren's arrangement. A different quartet instrumentation is tried for *In the ocean* with the leader proving a serviceable pianist and Koverhult an excellent if rather consistently busy flautist. Bass and drums are very active here also, and this is by no means a soft-centred piece.

In an interview given many years later, Rosengren claimed that he did not compose much. [39] This may have been true by then, yet ten of the above themes are his. It seems the more surprising, therefore, that he based one of these performances on the opening theme of Rachmaninoff's most popular work, an absurdly inappropriate choice. Yet once distortions of the Russian master's noble melody are left behind there is powerful improvising from both saxophones and then by Stenson, who in several of these pieces is almost as impressive as Rosengren. But whereas this resorting to Rachmaninoff was a lapse of taste, a bad one, the inclusion of two Turkish songs, still couched in their original idiom, was purely a mistake. The sleeve note tries to excuse *Meyhane* and *Hakim hanim* by saying their presence was 'thanks to Rosengren's openheartedness and generosity'; he plays a brief introduction to the second on a taragot, a wooden wind instrument with a reed, generally associated with Hungarian music. Yet these songs are completely irrelevant to the rest of the music on these discs and they belong elsewhere. Perhaps

Stenson was to some extent responsible for the inclusion of these Turkish songs and the jazz adaptation of the Bulgarian piece because his group Rena Rama, formed in 1971, was among the first to incorporate folk elements, particularly from Romania and India. It was also during the 1970s that Stenson founded the Oriental Wind ensemble with the Turkish drummer Temiz. Falay was also Turkish, though he spent most of his time further north, in Germany and particularly Sweden. Rosengren recorded with Falay's Sveda group in 1972–3 on Caprice and Sonet.

The larger personnels of these Harvest sessions were drawn chiefly from the ensembles just mentioned, though Falay is rarely prominent and neither Temiz nor Berger ever has anything significant to add. *Gerda* is by Wennerström and is more overtly disciplined than several of these pieces, the start, finish and links between solos provided by ensemble passages unflaggingly driven by the composer. Here the solos are by Koverhult, Rosengren and then Strandberg, whereas *Fly me to the sun* opens with Stenson thoughtfully alone, followed by the ensemble improvising collectively until there is another fine piano solo. And Stenson is again to the fore in *Some changes I*, which is rather more conventionally organized – the title is to be taken literally. Koverhult's solo here is probably his best on these discs, yet, despite brief, excellent Rosengren, this is Stenson's track. There is more robust Koverhult on *Some changes II* and the leader here emerges more decisively. Stenson is again highly inventive and even Falay is heard to more purpose than usual. Freer than either of these performances is *Some changes V*, which is mainly a highly detailed collective improvisation, with the two tenors most strongly in contention. *Some changes VI* sounds as if it, too, is going to be chiefly ensemble and so it proves, though with the individual voices gradually attaining an unusual freedom of movement and even richer textures than on the previous track. This is probably the most original jazz on these two discs.

By comparison, *Psalm* and the ensemble version of *Markitta blues* seem almost traditional, though in a thoroughly good sense. Both indeed are attractive yet in a different way from the other major pieces here, it sounding in each case almost as if the band is reading an arrangement. Rosengren's solo piano account of *Markitta blues* is of more than Webernian brevity (53 seconds) and requires no special comment.

Having in 1977 broken up the quartet on which the above music is founded, Rosengren put himself at the head of a big band playing chiefly his arrangements which for some years worked irregularly in various Swedish dance halls and recorded for Caprice, Dragon and Steeple-Chase. Also in 1977 he recorded a session with the Jones–Lewis band for Four Leaf Clover, and he was on fairly numerous other dates besides the ones mentioned above, for example with Rolf Ericson, Sabu Martinez, Eje Thelin and with the Norwegian guitarist Thorgeio Stubo.

Rosengren also recorded several times with another guitarist, Doug Raney, for SteepleChase and Criss Cross, yet none of this or other activity won him quite the regard which his best music deserved. M.H.

Zbigniew Namyslowski

415 **Polish Jazz Vol. 4**
†Polski Nagrania (P) PNCD027

Namyslowski (alt); Adam Makowicz (p); Janusz Kozlowski (bs); Czeslaw Bartkowski (d). Warsaw, 14 January 1966.
Seven-four bars · Frances the terror

Namyslowski (alt, cel, p); Tomasz Szukalski (ten, fl, bs clt); Stanislaw Cieslak (tbn); Pawel Jarzebski (bs); Kazimierz Jorkiez (d). Warsaw, February 1973.
Wine feast[1] *· No dough, no kicks · First take · Ballad on the roost · Teddy bears*
[1]band vocal.

Namyslowski (alt); Szukalski (alt, ten); Wojciech Karolak (el p); Jarzebski (bs); Bartkowski (d). Warsaw, March 1975.
Kujawiak goes funky · Gesowska · Appenzeller's dance

Namyslowski (alt); Kuba Stankiewicz (p); Dariusz Oleszkiewicz (bs); Jerzy Glod (d); Jose Torres (perc). Warsaw, 1987.
Who can I turn to? · Very sad bossa nova

At first it was intended that this position be occupied by Namyslowski's *Wine Feast* LP in its German reissue (Pooljazz [G] IRS942114), originally on Muza (P). That should still be heard for the sake of *Gogoszary, Not less than five percent* and *Taj Mahal* (which ends with the opening *Wine feast* theme), the items omitted here, because of the close partnership between the players, especially Namyslowski and Szukalski. This 1973 date has perhaps the freest improvising recorded under Namyslowski's name and was, by the standards of Polish jazz, a best seller. But this CD, though its contents are not ideally chosen, was preferred because it covers more than 20 years.

Contrary to the reference books, Namyslowski was not born in Warsaw but in a train on the way to Vilnius, the Polish capital being, on 9 September 1939, under bombardment from Nazi aeroplanes. His youth was spent in Vilnius and Cracow, starting work on the piano at four, the cello at twelve. He returned to Warsaw in 1954 and studied at the High School for Music. Becoming interested in jazz, he acquired fluency on the trombone and flute and, in 1960, the alto saxophone. His professional debut, a double one, came at the second Sopot Jazz Festival of 1957, when he played the trombone in Janusz Zabieglinski's All Stars, a Dixieland group, and the cello in Krzysztof Sadowski's Modern Combo. He was also a member, as trombonist, of Jerzy Matuszkiewicz's Hot Club Melomani in the historic first jazz concert in the Warsaw Philharmonic Hall during March 1958. That same year he performed with the

Polish All Stars in Denmark, the first time a Polish jazz band appeared in the West.

Namyslowski continued playing the trombone in bands of this sort for a few years, recording for Muza with Bogdan Styczynski's Modern Dixielanders in 1959 and with the New Orleans Stompers (obviously the Polish, not the German, Italian or Swiss bands of that name) as late as 1961. It is a curiosity of his early career that his reputation as Poland's leading traditionalist trombone player overlapped with his much greater fame as one of that country's most adventurous modernists.

He already had decided to concentrate on the alto in 1960, when he started the Jazz Rockers. That was an unfortunate name in view of the character of their music, and Namyslowski was soon a member of Andrzej Trzaskowski's Jazz Wreckers, actually a hard-bop outfit but another misleading title. This latter toured Europe and the United States in 1962, their two months in the States representing the first time Polish jazz was heard in America, though, typically, they were not asked to record. Namyslowski's own quartet, however, was the earliest Polish jazz band to make a record in the West, in London for Decca in 1964 (Decca [E] LK4644). By then the group was quite well established, having recorded for Muza in 1961 with Krzysztof Sadowski (piano), Adam Skorupka (string bass) and Andrzej Zielinski (drums). Michal Urbaniak (tenor) was added for a session taken down at the Warsaw Philharmonic Hall the following year. Also in 1962 the altoist recorded with Krzysztof Komeda (Trcinski), which he would do again in 1965 and 1967. Tomasz Stańko (**413**) was also involved on some of these occasions, the results probably standing as the best strictly jazz sessions recorded under Komeda's name, not least for Namyslowski's solos on *Astigmatic* and *Svantetic* from the middle date (†Power Bros [P] 00125).

Again in 1965 Namyslowski, along with Makowicz, was on the sophisticated Novi Vocal Quintet's first recordings, in Warsaw, and recorded with them again in 1968 and 1973. Long before that, though, his quartet had toured Europe, visiting not only Britain but many other countries, including what was then the USSR, and going on to India, Australia and New Zealand. Namyslowski not only played on film soundtracks but also composed for films, radio and TV, and was at one time a member of the Polish Radio Jazz Studio Band. To judge from an interview given in 1963, he soon was clear about the futility of copying anyone in this music, especially the Americans and above all Brubeck – who was extremely popular in Poland from the time of his first visit there in 1958. Much later he expressed great admiration for Pepper, Parker, Rollins, Coltrane, Coleman and Arthur Blythe yet was emphatic that he did not 'try to imitate them or play in their styles', [40] and everything he has recorded on the alto bears this out.

Certainly influences from America are at best marginal on any of the music carried by the above CD. Namyslowski's work is part of the main jazz tradition above all in the sense that he sounds like nobody except himself. His improvising and compositions are highly emotional, heavily coloured by folk music of Poland, the Balkans and even India. As might be expected from this latter concern, he also has taken an interest in idioms with a partial relationship to jazz, such as soul and funk, though he always preserves his version of the jazz language. Along with this has appeared a preoccupation with periodically getting away from $^{4}/_{4}$ into such metres as $^{5}/_{4}$, $^{7}/_{4}$ and $^{15}/_{8}$, deriving not from Brubeck but from Polish and more generally other Eastern European folk music.

Others in jazz from that part of the world have employed these irregular metres, of course, a good example being Urbaniak's 1974 *New York batsa*. But Namyslowski, like György Szabados (**416** below), has been persistent, and besides the above *Seven-four bars* there is the earlier *Five-four bars* from his quartet's 1963 Muza LP done at a Warsaw Philharmonic Hall concert and *Piatawka* from their London LP. This again is in $^{5}/_{4}$ and in the *Jazz Forum* interview referred to above, Namyslowski explained in some detail how differently this is organized from *Take five* (**311**). It may be added that *Kujawiak goes funky* is in $^{17}/_{8}$ and there is the 1980 *Seven-eleven* on the earlier of his two Air Condition LPs.

Namyslowski's personal breakthrough came with the 1963 Warsaw Jazz Jamboree, his quartet then having Wlodzimierz Gulgowski (piano), Tadeusz Wojcik (bass) and Bartkowski (drums), as on their Decca LP. On that record, as on the above compilation, all the themes, with the obvious exception, are the leader's, and it must be noted that, communicative though his music has always been, his compositions make considerable demands on the players in terms of rhythm, sound, harmony and form, and have become more so in pieces later than those discussed here. Yet tone is perhaps the most personal element of all and these performances offer many vivid instances of the superiority of music over prose. The inflections of instrumental sound which so characterize Namyslowski's improvising are so rich in meanings as to be quite impossible even to suggest in words.

These various points are evident during his long opening solo on *Seven-four bars*, first lightly accompanied and then more insistently. It is full of ideas as quickly identifiable as the saxophone tone, and the executive technique is masterly. Makowicz was not yet the great and highly original pianist of **374** and other records from that period, and the left-hand vamp unduly restricts his treble ideas. *Frances the terror* starts with a duet between Namyslowski and Kozlowski leading to the theme from the whole quartet in a quite elaborate and aggressive statement. Makowicz improvises first and sounds much freer than on the previous track, more suggestive of what he would do later. Like him, Namyslowski is heard at two tempos, with Bartkowski more active at the faster pace. The leader plays unaccompanied for a while, then duets freely with

Makowicz; then bass and drums return and the initial manner of performance is resumed. Finally an energetic outburst from Bartkowski leads back to the theme.

The intertwining of sounds on the *Wine feast* date is often subtle so that, even though only five players are involved, it is not always easy to know who is playing what. For example there is a passage with Namyslowski on cello, Szukalski on tenor and Jarzebski on bass, and a long duet between cello and bass with drums. *Wine feast* is a continuous piece in several sections, some overlapping, some at different tempos. And there is a brief band vocal near the end which is unmentioned on the above CD or on the Pooljazz or Muza LPs or in any discography. There is a comparable mystery regarding the flute solo on *First take*, nowhere acknowledged in the supporting literature. Namyslowski plays this instrument but he is at the piano throughout the flute passage, which therefore is presumably by Szukalski. Again there are some interesting mixtures of tone colour in *First take*, for instance with bass clarinet and string bass supporting the trombone. Later Namyslowski switches to almost aggressive alto playing, there is a long, virtuosic bass passage and then the alto again but now from Szukalski because Namyslowski has returned to the piano; alto and piano grow increasingly agitated, not to mention bass and drums.

Ensemble thinking dominates the 1973 session even during the solos, but the 1975 date has the participants more exposed. The leader is heard to particular advantage in his improvisation on *Kujawiak goes funky*, though he does not sound very different from on the 1966 titles. Better use of the electric piano is made here than in most jazz contexts and Karolak has a long and excellent solo. Namyslowski is heard at length again too, sounding rhapsodic, in contrast with Szukalski, on tenor, who is altogether abrasive. *Appenzeller's dance* is a rather obsessive affair, yet at last the repetitions fade and Namyslowski solos in a relaxed, melodious way, latterly joined by Szukalski on alto, this being a change from the turmoil.

A further shift is marked by the last pair of titles and *Who can I turn to?* might easily have seemed redundant after all the foregoing music. Luckily Namyslowski soon invents melodies of his own which are better, and far more complex, than Anthony Newley's banal original. The most uncomplicatedly happy piece on this record is *Very sad bossa nova*, and the title presumably is a simple instance of the Polish sense of humour.

M.H.

György Szabados

416 The Wedding

Hungaroton (Hun) SLPX17475

Szabados (p, zither[1]); Sandor Vajda (bs); Imre Köszegi (d); Lajos Horvath (vln, bs). Budapest, 1973.
Miracle[1] · *The interrogation of Irma Szabo*

Same personnel. Budapest, 1974.
The wedding · *Duo for piano and violin*

Szabados was already giving concerts of free jazz in Budapest during the 1962–3 season, which was early for Eastern Europe. His music came in several respects to make a new departure for jazz, especially in Europe and above all in Hungary. While taking some of its cues from initiatives in both jazz and modern classical music from much further west, it also unambiguously drew on some aspects of Hungarian folklore.

This last source was surprising in that Szabados, in a 1987 interview, had stated that he at one time objected to Hungarian folk music, then incessantly heard over the radio, seeing it as the music of the communist establishment. Yet, although strongly drawn to jazz, he felt that it could no more express what was going on in Hungary than could the older classical music. He had come to jazz during the 1950s and started by imitating bop and cool styles but felt that 'jazz at that time was too strictly defined in rhythmic terms.' [41]

So perhaps the local folk music could be a source of authentically Hungarian jazz? 'We began to work quite freely, and our musical instincts brought new solutions. I was lucky to come up with a rhythmic language which combined Hungarian musical feeling and jazz. My starting point was folk singing, not instrumental music. All kinds of music come from singing and the ancient character of Hungarian music is mainly a *parlando-rubato* type of singing which apparently lacks a defined rhythm. But deep down it has some kind of rhythm: intuition and feeling make it move in such a way that . . . it is asymmetric.' [42]

Certainly the result, as on the record detailed above, is work of great expressive intensity, arising out of harmony that is sometimes rather complex by jazz standards and out of the asymmetric rhythms to which Szabados refers. These latter are in any case familiar from Bartók's and Kodály's adaptations of features of Hungarian, Romanian and related folk idioms. By utilizing in terms of style and form such musical means, Szabados has indeed opened up a fresh realm for jazz in Hungary and elsewhere, one that grows out of his own folk music yet also has connections with the avant-garde of classical music.

Quite another factor is that he is a pianist of exceptional powers even by the highest contemporary standards, and it is our loss that he has recorded so little. [43] Despite the contributions of the other players, his virtuosity affects almost every moment of this music, not only in terms of his pianistic mastery but also with regard to his fluency in deploying East European odd-numbered rhythm patterns.

Although there is no pictorial element in this music, *Miracle* was prompted by a visit to Lourdes made by the quartet while touring France, when that focus of pilgrimage reminded them, rather surprisingly, of the atmosphere of the Transylvanian mountains. It begins with drums, then bass, then piano and finally violin. Szabados broadly unfolds a beautiful Hungarian folk song against bells sounded by Köszegi which recur near the end and this is contrasted with a second, psalmlike theme; both are characterized by the *parlando-rubato* to which Szabados refers above. It soon appears that he and Horvath are pursuing different lines of thought and the fabric of the music is coloured by what Bartók termed polymodal chromaticism. Vajda and Köszegi too are rather independently active and there is a curious high-register bowed bass solo accompanied by Szabados on the zither, a very rare use of that instrument in jazz. Then the piano and violin abruptly return, the latter briefly sounding quite Gypsylike but soon yielding second place to the rising tide of the leader's by now almost explosive virtuosity. It is patent that the main thrust of the argument lies with the piano during this passage yet one does regret, here and in several other places, that the recording balance does not favour the violin more, especially as bass and drums are also very active.

Each of these performances takes an essentially dramatic stance, though in contrast with much else here *The interrogation of Irma Szabo* opens with its melody picked out almost simplistically by Horvath, Szabados and Vajda. This theme is a Transylvanian folk song about a mother who killed her child and its treatment quickly grows agitated, with the violin holding to wide-arched melodic phrases while piano, bass and drums go their own ways. Considerable density of texture is generated and yet the lines of thought can still be quite clearly followed. After this fast and furious storm a sort of calm returns with the initial folk melody picked out in detached notes by violin, piano and bass.

Szabados and Horvath have *Duo for piano and violin* to themselves and remind us that while it occurs frequently in classical music the teaming of violin with piano is rare in jazz. [44] Horvath spins a wide-ranging and astringent melodic line while Szabados makes comments which at first are discontinuous, seemingly fragmented. But there is a fine piano solo at the centre of this performance, and later, after Horvath has returned, the leader becomes almost frantically active, as he is in *The wedding*. The latter seems a wholly inappropriate title for a piece which, having opened with a notably sombre, though very accomplished, bass solo, quickly rises to almost frightening intensity. Again, however, the quartet textures hold a balance between density of incident and lucidity of musical discourse.

East European asymmetric rhythms are again prominent in *The wed-*

ding as a furiously complicated improvisation unfolds – or rather is detonated. Engaged with the whole keyboard, Szabados is essentially in the lead with Horvath, though not Vajda nor Köszegi, as a subsidiary voice. The intensity of expression becomes almost overwhelming and the music, rather than becoming spent or running down, in the end just fades.

One is reminded of Schoenberg's comment that an interpretation of notated music ought to sound as if improvised while an improvisation should be so decisive as to sound as if notated. Repeatedly these often impassioned performances evoke the latter half of that dictum. [45]

M.H.

David S. Ware

417 Great Bliss Vol. 1
†Silkheart (A) SHCD127

Ware (ten, fl, saxello, stritch); Matthew Shipp (p); William Parker (bs); Marc Edwards (d, perc, timp). New York City, 8–10 January 1990.

Forward motion · *Angular* · *Bliss theme* · *Cadenza* · *Sound bound* · *Mind time* · *Saxelloscape one* · *Thirds*

By the time this recording was made, free jazz had been around for more than 30 years. It is a sobering thought that in the 1940s, the advocates of a style then some 30 years old – New Orleans jazz – were derisively labelled 'mouldy figs'. What was once a shocking music to polite society in 1917, when the first jazz record was released, was by 1947 being castigated as backward and corny. It was something that the zealous reformers behind every shock that announced the new are, to a lesser or greater degree, forced to confront. However radical the schism with the past, there comes a point when the shock ceases to be a shock and the new is no longer new. This was perhaps felt more in 'the New Thing' than elsewhere in jazz since the initial reactionary zeal became hard to sustain once the barricades of the revolutionary 1960s had been dismantled. As the 1970s progressed, the fervour of the 1960s gave way to excess and ultimately tedium, culminating in the overindulgences of the New York loft scene at the end of the decade where, by more or less common consent, things had gone too far. Meaning was being sacrificed in the name of the avant-garde, freedom had become a licence for musical apostasy.

Some sort of reaction seemed inevitable, and had in fact been building up throughout the 1970s, most notably in Chicago's Association for the Advancement of Creative Musicians. Their policy of 'inclusiveness' sparked a return to 'the tradition' as a means to revitalize and moderate their music that anticipated the 1980s stylistic regroupings. However, not all musicians associated with free jazz chose to realign their music in this way. A few attempted to face the problem of sustaining the avant-gardist's creative impulses without submitting to rationalization, confronting the challenge of retaining the crusading spirit of the 1960s innovators without surrendering to the pitfalls of excess. Such answers did not offer themselves readily, yet by the end of the 1980s Ware and his fellow tenor saxophonist Charles Gayle were at the forefront of improvisers who had built on the spirit of the past without being claimed by what had become the overworked devices of the 1960s 'noise-makers' – squeakaphonics and sundry textural devices that all too often were a retreat into either parody or superficiality.

Ware and Gayle combined a high degree of instrumental facility and idiomatic originality with a deep understanding of the improviser's art. While the technically dexterous Gayle, on albums such as the trio *Kingdom Come* (†Knitting Factory Works [A] 157) with Sunny Murray, and with a quartet on *Raining Fire* (†Silkheart [A] 137) and *Translations* (†Silkheart [A] 134), tended to favour a shifting personnel, Ware, robust and perhaps the more dangerous of the two, preferred a set, working group. After spending time with Cecil Taylor in the 1970s, two long stints with the drummer Andrew Cyrille, as a member of Raphe Malik's trio and in groups led by Beaver Harris, Ware realized the importance of creating an effective context in which to present his playing.

His first group was with just bass and drums, and *Passage to Music* (Silkheart [A] 113) from 1988 documented this period. But a year later he added Shipp, who was then just 29. Both volumes of *Great Bliss*, and *Flight of i* (†DIW Columbia [A] 52956) from 1991, reveal how quickly the new quartet developed, creating fresh standards in ensemble cross-talk – their integration of timpani on *Sound bound*, for example – within the standard horn plus rhythm quartet that were both imaginative and contemporary. The *Great Bliss* project was prepared over three months in both rehearsal and on the bandstand, and the group played for five days straight before heading into the recording studio. They arrived focused yet adventurous, their abstractions striking at the very kernel of improvised music.

A player of great authority and power, Ware convincingly built on the legacy of the great 1960s free improvisers – there were sometimes flashes attributable to Ayler, to Kirk, or to the rugged mien of mid-period Coltrane – building a style that while reflecting these influences was not enmeshed by precedent. There is great discipline in what he plays which often draws on the impact of 'playing' silences. On *Sound bound*, for example, there is a six-second respite nine minutes into the piece which in the often frenetic nature of free music other musicians might have crowded out. Also, he does not deny the privileged position occupied by the cyclical form of prearranged harmonies as the dominant basis for improvisation in jazz; numbers such as *Bliss theme* and *Thirds* reveal his awareness that structure, too, can provide the obstacle needed to fire inspiration. *Forward Motion*, a dark, brooding piece against jackhammer chords from Shipp and a swirling counterpoint of brushes and bass, remains locked in one key. Ware's angular flute flurries sweep over the ensemble before Shipp moves regally in and out of key, retaining the rhythmic contours of his accompaniment during his solo. Parker's and Edwards's democratic interaction gives way to a solo from each, Parker's full of loping figures, Edwards's skittish and fleet, before Ware returns to mediate the ensemble's collective impulses and draw the number to a close. *Angular* has Ware on saxello, an instrument close in tone to a soprano saxophone. Alternating periods of turbulence with oases of calm, the opening section includes a duet between Ware and Shipp of such interlocking aplomb that it is impossible to say whose is the leading instrument. *Great bliss* is a 14-bar theme that features Ware's voluminous tenor sound which slips in and out of the changes during his solo, creating moments of compelling tension and release.

Cadenza is a workout on the stritch, an alto saxophone of altered shape originally conceived as an instrument for marching bands in the 1930s. Ware gets a deep, powerful tone and if glimpses of Roland Kirk surface briefly, the passion he brings to his playing ensures that the influence of the late multi-instrumentalist is kept at arm's length. Always allowing space in his lines to give his sharp-eared accompanists opportunities to interact with his playing, the piece begins with brusque exchanges between soloist, striding in huge intervals up and down his horn, and the ensemble, a series of cadenzas contrasted by brash, percussive ensemble interludes. *Sound bound* begins with a dramatic timpani roll that alternates with cymbal splashes before Ware's strident saxello rises to dominate a percussively charged accompaniment, with Edwards using his full range of effects from kit to timpani to cymbals and cowbell in what is perhaps the most staunchly individual piece of the collection.

Saxelloscape one is an unaccompanied saxello solo which exploits the tonal resources of the instrument through bends, overblowing and sound-sheet arpeggios that float threateningly free from melody. On *Thirds* Ware returns to the tenor saxophone in a structured piece which, as the title implies, makes use of the interval of a third in the tune's construction. Ware's clearly articulated playing, often strikingly fast, develops the theme, decorates and varies it and expands phrases that relate to it with musicianly patience that made virtuosic display unnecessary as he lavishes care in exploring microscopic corners of the composition. Throughout, Edwards plays a highly sympathetic role in accompaniment, his playing owing much to Andrew Cyrille's 'conversational rhythms', rhythms that approach speechlike patterns, often locked in intimate dialogue with Ware.

The extent to which Ware's music diverged from the comfortably accessible mainstream of the 1990s appeared in even sharper relief when laid beside the neoconservative movement. It is perhaps ironic that by 1989, the writer Gene Santoro was branding Wynton Marsalis a 'contemporary mouldy fig', [46] a charge that would be heard with increasing regularity as the 1990s progressed. Marsalis's music and that of the neoconservatives remained essentially governed by precedent, and in arguing that their music was free from the taint of commercialism, the 'chaos' of the avant-garde or Eurocentrism, they were echoing precisely the arguments of the New Orleans traditionalists in the 1940s in defending their stance. The fate of the traditionalists was to be bypassed in time, their music reduced to a repertory function, much as the music of the 1980s and 1990s neoconservatives appears today. In contrast, Ware, although active in an area of music that chronologically was not much more than some 10 or 15 years younger than hard bop, nevertheless succeeded in remaining contemporaneous by obeying a basic tenet, that great art is meant to disturb, not to reassure. S.N.

Cecil Taylor

In terms of sheer keyboard technique, Taylor was not far behind Tatum, but the end to which he employed this technique was a radical alternative not only to Tatum but to anything else heard in jazz. Using bop as his starting point rather than his destination, and drawing on his early studies of Bartók, Stravinsky and Elliott Carter, he created an intense, demanding style that changed the vocabulary of jazz improvisation.

Cecil Taylor

418 **Looking Ahead**
Contemporary (A) 7562, Boplicity (E) COP030, †Contemporary (J) VDJ1633

Taylor (p); Buell Neidlinger (bs); Dennis Charles (d); Earl Griffith (vib). New York City, 9 June 1958.

Luyah! The glorious step · African violets · Of what · Wallering · Toll · Excursions on a wobbly rail

The path Cecil Taylor trod over the years was never easy. There is nothing accessible or even attractive in his music; he speaks in dense, nonharmonic tongues and multinoted cascades, and throughout his long career he has encountered resistance to meeting him on his own terms and on his own artistic ground. Describing his appearance at the 1958 Great South Bay Jazz Festival, Whitney Balliett said that the audience 'fidgeted, whispered and wandered nervously in and out of the tent, as if the ground beneath had suddenly become unbearably hot'. [47] It was the sort of response that has greeted his playing throughout his career.

Taylor studied music at the New England Conservatory in Boston in 1952–5, and during this period he began to pull together the diverse strands of influence from which his style would ultimately evolve. He turned to European classical models as much as the jazz tradition, to

Bartók, Stravinsky, Stockhausen, Ives and Berio as well as Ellington, Monk, Brubeck, Silver, Waller and Walter Bishop Jr. Active on the Boston music scene at the time were such players as Serge Chaloff, Charlie Mariano, Herb Pomeroy and Nat Pierce, all of whom Taylor mentions in his reminiscences of these early years. [48] But in the context of his ultimate style the major influence on his playing must surely have been Richard Twardzik: 'There was this white cat, Dick Twardzik,' Taylor recalled. 'He was like the white pianist power up there [in Boston].' [49]

Twardzik (1931–55), a former pupil of Margaret Chaloff, a faculty member of the New England Conservatory, [50] was highly active on the Boston music scene at the time Taylor was a student there. The recorded evidence of his playing in 1954 reveals a pianist with a highly original conception. In September he recorded a piece of his own, *The fable of Mabel*, with a Serge Chaloff group. [51] It is an ambitious, though not wholly successful, composition involving changes of mood and tempo. However, what is striking on all three available takes is Twardzik's radical piano solo. It clearly anticipates the direction of Taylor's own playing – which would not appear on record for over a year. [52] Twardzik's 36-bar solo uses stabbing dissonance and is preceded by a brief interlude of simultaneous free improvisation. In terms of both conception and execution, Twardzik's work is clearly the product of a mind whose thinking was well in advance of the jazz mainstream.

In December 1954 Twardzik recorded seven numbers in his own right for Dick Bock's Pacific Jazz label. [53] It is his playing on two original compositions that catch the ear. Both *A crutch for the crab* and *Albuquerque social swim* use dissonance, dense textures and spiky, fragmented phrasing that today sound more radical for their time than Taylor's own work both on *Jazz Advance* and the album discussed here. What succour or inspiration Taylor gained from Twardzik's playing can only be a matter of speculation. But it is clear that from the beginning he was not working in a vacuum; certainly in his reminiscences Taylor appears keen to point out that Twardzik 'thoroughly approved of the goings-on' when he heard him play. [54]

Like Twardzik's recordings, Taylor's playing on *Looking Ahead* is based on composition and chord changes. Both players attempt to cut themselves loose from the prevailing orthodoxy with often jarring remonstrations, although when Taylor tries to swing, it must be said, it was without lilt or buoyancy. Initially, fracturing chord changes with angular dissonance provided Taylor's 'point of departure' from convention. However, his voyages into atonality were always underpinned by a strict sense of form (or 'structures' as he liked to call them), of which *Toll* is a good example. The slower 'blowing' choruses are sandwiched between a bright 32-bar introduction and a *rubato* coda which lingers on the border of abandoning pre-set tempo; in between the band members are introduced in turn: bass, bass and vibes, bass vibes and drums and so on in various permutations. Taylor's excursions into abstraction, however, were here quite modest by the standards of his later work, yet they here reveal him trying to resolve what he described as 'the problem . . . [of] reorganization of ingredients to discover surprise', adding, 'harmonic changes provided yesterday's dynamism.' [55]

The allusions to stride piano in the introduction of *Wallering*, a Taylor original dedicated to Fats Waller, sound more like Waller-through-Monk. But as Taylor's solo unfolds, it highlights what a logical step it was from Monk's methods of fragmenting the melodic line, something Taylor does throughout the album, to abandoning melody entirely in favour of abstraction. This is illustrated by a trio performance of *Of what* which demonstrably points to his mature style. Despite the regular pulse employed by Charles, Taylor's ideas slip free of regular tempo and of any discernible underlying harmony, making his subsequent step, of abandoning both tempo and pre-set chord changes, inevitable.

Looking Ahead is a valuable cipher to decode Taylor's abstract world. It shows how he moved from within the tradition to develop his personal musical language, and although he would later appear as a one-man avant-garde, with a style seemingly free from precedent and wholly his own, it does appear on the basis of recorded evidence he had listened hard to Twardzik during his period of study in Boston. By the time of his Candid recordings between 1960 and 1961 [56] his playing had become significantly more radical; but it is clear that his style was a logical extension of the jazz piano tradition which could be traced back to the first great jazz piano virtuoso, James P. Johnson. That is something of which Taylor himself was well aware: 'Tradition is not a prison,' he asserted, 'I'm constantly aware of that . . . I can see how the lifeblood of jazz has been changing through the years. I can see myself in relation to it . . . you cannot claim that the energies of the past have no relationship to whatever you are engaged in now . . . when I get in the hole for ideas it's one of the sources I go to . . . I feel very much part of (the tradition).' [57] S.N.

Cecil Taylor

419 Unit

New World Records (A) NW201

Raphe Malik (tpt); Jimmy Lyons (alt); Ramsey Ameen (vln); Taylor (p); Sirone (bs); Ronald Shannon Jackson (d). New York City, 3–6 April 1978.

Idut · Serdab · Holiday en masque

As (**418**) reveals, Taylor's first recordings show him basing his improvisations, for the most part, on chord changes, while playing 'time' with a conventional rhythm section. By the beginning of the 1960s, however, his playing underwent a considerable sea change. With the death of his father in 1961, a traumatic event in his life that also removed the degree of financial security he enjoyed up to that point, his music increasingly broke free of both harmonic restrictions imposed by chord changes and pre-set tempo. Eschewing swing, his technique – his 'ten drummers' – was in service of texture and abstract colouration, forming an uncompromising style pitched well over the head of the casual jazz follower. More and more his improvisations relied on spur-of-the-moment inspiration. His work became increasingly complex, highly percussive and full of energy and turbulence. As Ekkehard Jost observed: 'By getting away from the steady beat (then one of the *sine qua nons* of jazz) Taylor's music took on a more strongly pronounced jazz character than before.' [58]

His music soon became a *casus belli* among commentators, from extreme praise on the one hand to the English writer Benny Green on the other, who doubted whether it was music at all, let alone jazz. Taylor continued undeterred by the controversy, joining the faculty of the University of Wisconsin in 1971, where he taught black music to the largest registered class in the history of the institution. He spent 1972–3 with Jimmy Lyons as artists in residence in Antioch College and during the 1970s his music gradually began to find acceptance within the establishment. In 1973 he was awarded a Guggenheim Fellowship and in 1977 he received an Honorary Doctorate of Music from the New England Conservatory. When the above recording was made, in 1978, he had reached what many consider the peak of his career. During the next five years he would record a series of albums that are among the most acclaimed in his discography, of which *Unit* numbers among his finest achievements. Performed by his sextet which existed for the first part of 1978, *Unit*, together with *3 Phasis* (New World [A] NW303), an hour-long composition, and *Live in the Black Forest* (PA/USA [A] 7053), is one of the finest of all Taylor's group recordings.

Recorded after four days of intense rehearsal, the aural flagellation of *Holiday en masque*, 29 minutes and 41 seconds of densely textured cacophony constantly refracted by speed and dynamics, slowly reveals, on repeated listening, many varicoloured events. Swirling motifs appear and abruptly dissolve, stormy duets emerge and subside, and even riffs make momentary appearances. The ebb and flow of these energetic squalls do, for the most part, replace tempo and in parts Taylor's improvisation is genuinely atonal, something that is not as common as might be thought in free jazz. Frequently even the most 'far out' improvisations, collective or solo, are organized around tonal centres, either specific keys or modes, a characteristic of Ornette Coleman's playing, for instance.

Serdab has the widest area of colouration; an almost pastoral beginning gives way to Taylor's furious, tumultuous inventions: an improviser's job, he once explained, was to 'organize sounds' utilizing a 'compression of energy'. [59] Throughout, the exceptional give-and-take among ensemble members, particularly his exchanges with Lyons, ably bonded by the rigorous empathy of Jackson, set standards of sympathetic yet wholly spontaneous interaction, with Taylor's hyperactive piano dictating events, building one platform of colouration before moving on to the next. Indeed, Taylor once described his role within a group context as a 'catalyst feeding material'. [60] This is clearly apparent in his role during *Idut.* He seems to propel and shift players along specific musical paths as the intensity is varied with different combinations of instruments working out on ideas which Taylor feeds from the keyboard. Gradually it is the pianist who emerges from the ensemble textures to end the piece with some surprisingly pretty, delicate reflections.

Despite the success of *Unit,* many argued that Taylor's music is essentially a piano soloist's art, that the problems of his sidemen in creating improvisations of worth alongside the density, speed and explosive dynamics of the pianist's style are too great to be surmounted. However, this is only partly true; Taylor's art is both conceptual and philosophical and his performances with an ensemble or as a soloist simply serve to reveal different aspects of his vision. A certain amount of conflict is needed for his music to achieve depth, and this can be achieved from within as from without. S.N.

Cecil Taylor

420 In Florescence

†A&M (A) 395286–2

Taylor (p, voice); William Parker (bs, voice); Gregg Bendian (d, perc, voice). New York City, 8 June 1989.

J. Pethro visiting the abyss · Saita · For Steve McCall · In florescence · Ell moving track · Sirenes 1/3 · Anast in crisis mouthful of fresh cut flowers · Charles and thee · Entity · Leaf taken horn · Chal Chuiatlichue goddess of green flowing waters · Morning of departure · Feng shui

In Florescence finds Taylor in the most basic jazz unit of all, the piano trio. But while it might be the most basic and, indeed, the most common configuration in jazz, there is nothing remotely like Taylor's trio. He is his own point of reference, his own North Star to guide himself by, and his own musical tradition. Taylor truly marches to the sound of a different drummer. This was his first album for an American label for over a decade, and is representative of his live performances during the early 1990s; vocalized noises, ritualistic chants and poetic verse, sometimes spontaneously conceived, sometimes not, and intoned in his slightly querulous voice. Although its effect in live performance in the 1990s could be startling, poetry and jazz had forged a link almost 40 years before, in 1950s San Francisco, where Beat poets like Lawrence Ferlinghetti, Gregory Corso and Allen Ginsberg spontaneously invented verse to jazz composition. Taylor himself was moving closer to the idiom towards the end of the 1980s, recording six of his poems – oblique, dense and occasionally baffling soliloquies – in 1987 as *Chinampas* (Leo [E]). Gradually in live performance, poetry often came to set the scene for the piano improvisation that followed. 'I currently view the presentation of music from a very ritualistic point of view,' he explained. 'The voice, the chanting, the poems and the movement are all things I have been working up throughout my whole career.' [61]

Since 1980's *Fly! Fly! Fly! Fly! Fly!* (PA/USA [A] 7108), many of Taylor's live performances and recordings began working towards musical episodes of smaller duration and although there were exceptions to this, as the decade progressed he gradually appeared to favour more condensed statements, highly concentrated bursts of energy and turbulence contrasted by periods of meditation. It suggested that Taylor was now balancing his rampaging approach to the keyboard by moments of quiet, reflective playing, consciously impelling his music with grace as much as bombast. This album, therefore, is a good reflection of Taylor's live performances between the late 1980s and early 1990s. Recorded during the summer of 1989 amid a busy schedule of concerts in Boston and New York, all 14 tracks are of relatively short duration, with *Pethro visiting the abyss* the longest at a fraction over seven minutes, in contrast to some of his more ambitious improvisations in the past that might have stretched to almost an hour.

J, a tribute to Taylor's long-term collaborator Jimmy Lyons (1933–86), begins with an attention-getting vocalized noise, as disconcerting on record as in live performance, and one of Taylor's cryptic quotations before launching into angular phrases of remorse for his dear departed friend and colleague. Taylor's unaccompanied *Ell moving track* is a miniaturized example of how he built tension, often left unresolved, which in the past might have taken over 30 minutes to climax. It shows him taking a basic idea, expanding and developing it until it becomes something new, and then starting the whole process over again. In many ways this encapsulates Taylor's basic modus operandi. Many of his ideas grew organically within this simple theme-and-variation method, which, for all the complexity of the variations, could often appear like the same image viewed in a series of distorting mirrors. However, this basic principle of theme and variation, together with his use of call and response, very often lay at the heart of his work: the left- and right-handed octaves in dialogue on *Charles and thee*, for example, punctuated by groundswells of crazy-chord clusters. 'Everyone has their own way of organizing sound,' explained Taylor after the session. [62]

Parker, a fixture in Taylor's ensembles for much of the 1980s, and Bendian, then new to his group, worked with great imagination to embellish their leader's work, and, like the conventional role for bass and drums within the piano trio, underscore rather than intercede. It is Taylor who holds the focus of our attention, while Parker and Bendian produce a wholly sympathetic climate for his sometimes startling imagination. The beginning of *Chal Chuiatlichue goddess of green flowing waters*, for example, begins with a long period of accompaniment to Taylor's strangulated cries, sounding for all the world as if a badly behaved child has been taken behind a screen and is having his limbs removed without anaesthetic as some sort of bizarre punishment. Episodes such as this added to Taylor's mystique as a 'performance artist', earning him a following beyond the jazz constituency, enabling him to aspire to his own modest goal of earning a salary equivalent to that of 'a chamber music player'.

Arguably the finest jazz piano technician since Tatum, Taylor played by his own conventions to create an intensely personal language that represents a major alternative to anything else in jazz. Whereas Tatum harnessed creative energy in service of conventional harmony and rhythm, Taylor uses it to fracture and disrupt our expectations at every level of music-making, in terms of harmony, rhythm and melody. Steadfastly recondite, his unorthodox ear masks a strange and eerie lyricism, as in a section of the title track that actually seems to rock, touching base with rhythm 'n' blues. But no matter how the often bewildering yet compelling musical disjunction of his style is interpreted, it is a fact that Taylor's music remains more the province of critical acuity than public patronage, even after over 40 years in jazz. S.N.

From Inside to Outside

The predictability of a sequence of chords can be broken by playing outside the changes. It adds drama and surprise, yet playing outside can mean several things, including playing a semitone or a tritone away from the home key, or playing in a remote key; or it could mean literally playing free, or atonally. Now not only did musicians have to master playing inside changes, they had to learn how to play effectively outside them as well.

John Coltrane

421 **Giant Steps**
†Atlantic (E) 781 337–2

Coltrane (ten); Tommy Flanagan (p); Paul Chambers (bs); Art Taylor (d). New York City, 4 May 1959.
Cousin Mary · Spiral

Same personnel. New York City, 5 May 1959.
Countdown · Syeeda's song flute · Mr P.C. · Giant steps

Wynton Kelly (p), Jimmy Cobb (d) replace Flanagan, Taylor. New York City, 2 December 1959.
Naima

422 Africa Brass
†MCA (E) MCAD42001

Booker Little, Freddie Hubbard (tpt); Charles Greenlea, Julian Priester (eu); Jim Buffington, Julius Watkins, Don Corrada, Robert Northern, Robert Swissheim (fr h); Coltrane (sop, ten); Eric Dolphy (fl, bs clt, alt, arr); Pat Patrick, Garvin Bushell (reeds); McCoy Tyner (p); Reggie Workman (bs); Elvin Jones (d). Englewood Cliffs, N.J., 23 May 1961.
Greensleeves

Hubbard, Greenlea, Bushell absent; Britt Woodman (tbn), Carl Bowman (eu), Bill Barber (tu), Art Davis (bs) added. Englewood Cliffs, N.J., 7 June 1961.
Africa · *Blues minor*

Romanticism and anti-romanticism vie for space in these celebrated records. The themes of *Naima* and *Spiral* are affectively songlike; even *Giant steps* has something of that character. Heard in relation to the improvisations which accompany them, they indicate a contrariety in Coltrane's thinking. Charlie Parker's tunes fit his improvisatory thought because they are, as it were, simplifications of it. Coltrane's unrelenting torrents of extemporization are at odds with his composed themes in most of these numbers – almost as if the themes had some separate justification. Strong as the tunes are melodically, their romanticism even seems a little dated now. They are not unrelated to certain things which emerged in hard bop, and it ought certainly to be to their credit that they also recall some of Monk's more affective melodies. (Listen to Coltrane stating the melody of *Ruby, my dear* with Monk on Riverside/Jazzland [E] JLPS946.)

Perhaps the saxophonist needed to maintain this contrast between different sorts of emotional forthrightness. Some of his compositions had deeply felt personal associations (*Naima* remained his particular favourite) which explain their intensity. What matters here to the improvising Coltrane is the themes' usual harmonic simplicity, rather than any melodic reference, since the simplicity can liberate a complexity of line which has gained in fluidity when compared to what he was playing a few years previously. The new expressiveness, consistent as it is in its way, alters the forward-racing sequential development of hard-bop improvising and seems to be aiming at comprehensiveness of thought at almost every stage of its movement. There is still hard-bop influence in the very exciting *Giant steps* solo, but the transit of consecutive ideas is giving way to an Olympian wholeness of concept, assisted by those notorious (and lamely named) 'sheets of sound' – arrhythmic jets and cataracts of semiquavers no longer, as often before, interpolative, but so integrated as to become newly determinative of style. This works best where the basic matter is harmonically simple, as in *Syeeda's song flute* (named for a small daughter's tonette kazoo), where the saxophone suggests a modal conception with cross-rhythmic runs and spiralling figures juxtaposed.

In much of this playing there is an adamant consistency of tone which might tend to tedium; but the fleet spinnings of the brief *Countdown* are lightly voiced, as are the tenor statements of *Naima* (a dedication to Syeeda's mother) where the improvisation is all in a piano interlude and, for once, it is the tune and only the tune that counts for the tenorist.

In the minor-keyed *Cousin Mary* prophetic bursts of incantation are heard. But here there is more variety of phrase than in *Giant steps*, rather more heed to the possibilities of expansion, remarkable episodes of rhythmic variation. Flanagan's exploratory solo is adventure quite different from Coltrane's, and, as in *Spiral*, the pianist links his boppish lyricisms more confidently than had been managed in *Giant steps*. There are bass solos in nearly every piece: they are in a fairly conventional way, but are not helped by rather airily recorded tone quality. Taylor, who supports intelligently throughout the May sessions, gets his best chance in the fast *Mr P.C.*, where the rhythm team, with 'Mr P.C.' plucking athletically, is superb – but in his exchanges with Coltrane towards the end the drummer is almost caught out of tempo.

In *Africa Brass*, his first date for Impulse, Coltrane introduces Elvin Jones, who was to record with him until, with *Cosmic Music* of 1966, he gave place to Rashied Ali. Jones's intricate, powerfully searching yet always lucid style suited exactly the ways in which Coltrane's imagination was heading. The musicality of his work is nicely shown when, in his solo near the end of *Africa*, he echoes the orchestral vamp and, from its stark rudiments, develops dual lines of stickwork upon tuned skins. The origins of the vamp itself, which Dolphy's orchestration eases through various dynamic levels, can be heard in the left hand of Tyner's support of Coltrane's thematic invocation. The tenor tune has not quite abandoned euphony but what follows on its heels – snarling tremolos, wild yells, antimelodic shapes reiterated – betokens change and the gradual death of the romantic instinct. The solo of that other enduring companion, Tyner, proceeds lightsomely with wry melodies returning, as Coltrane's solo does, constantly to the region of the minor tonic. Tyner, too, was closely in sympathy with the leader's aspirations. His debts to Bud Powell, Monk and Tatum were being repaid only in small change, and his own style was well formed by this stage.

Africa may aim at greater sophistication, but its effects do not remove it very far, at least in orchestral terms, from Ellingtonia's kindred dreams. The work of the two bassists is notable, some of the high-register *arco* lending eerie atmospherics. From Africanism to a tune credited by some to Henry VIII is a broad stride, and it seems at first that, in *Greensleeves*, Coltrane has stepped back to lyrical nostalgia; but after a gentle reading of the tune there is stern incantation, helped again by the frugal harmony. Even so, there is more variation of tone, and delicacy does make other returns. Tyner comes in with 'locked hands' to introduce a solo whose imagination matches that in *Africa*. The fragments of orchestration use dissonance in a Gil Evansish manner. Then, fierce and high, Coltrane pits himself against brassy monotony until the theme re-emerges.

A family likeness to *Bags' groove* marks the riff of *Blues minor* but this is a less politely mannered relative. The wild force of the tenor solos could discourage analysis but in them there is much to be observed regarding Coltrane's approach both to the 12-bar unit and to the traditional chord sequence. They are up among his finest recorded solos, certainly equal to the best on these two discs. In between them Tyner spins thoughtful lines, contrasting their relaxation to the saxophonist's fire. Though much of *Blues minor* is in effect a quartet performance, the entire ensemble has interesting opportunities, and Dolphy's score does wonders with the embryonic notions given to him. E.T.

John Coltrane

423 Newport '63

†Impulse (A) GRP11282

Coltrane (ten); McCoy Tyner (p); Jimmy Garrison (bs); Roy Haynes (d). Newport, Rhode Island, 7 July 1963.

I want to talk about you · *My favourite things* · *Impressions*

Same except Reggie Workman (bs) in for Garrison; add Eric Dolphy (alt). New York City, 2 November 1961.

Chasin' another Trane

The Coltrane quartet closed the 1963 Newport Jazz Festival on the evening of 7 July. They had been preceded by the Jimmy Smith trio, who had brought the audience to fever pitch, almost prompting a riot with a set that one contemporary review described as appealing to 'the baser teenage emotions'. His four blues numbers so excited the youngsters in the audience that they were standing on their chairs yelling and dancing in the aisles, needing Willis Conover's skills as an MC to quieten them down and restore order. It was not the sort of situation in which any performer would relish taking the stage. It says much for the sheer emotional force of Coltrane's playing that by the end of his first number he had erased the memory of what had gone before and had his audience's undivided attention. Coltrane had been playing *I want to talk about you* since his 1958 recording of the tune on *Soultrane* (Original Jazz Classics [A] OJC-021) with the pianist Red Garland's trio, and he would record the Billy Eckstine composition again on *Live at Birdland* (†Impulse [A] IMP11982) in November

1963. While Coltrane had acquired considerable notoriety for his sound-sheet technique and his formidable theoretical knowledge – for example, moving key centres around by major thirds on his composition *Giant steps* (**421**) was a revolutionary step forward in jazz in 1959, a point seldom mentioned – it was often overlooked that he was one of the strongest and most convincing ballad players jazz has ever known. [63]

The great respect with which he treated the idiom could well have come from his period with the Johnny Hodges septet in 1953–4. A consistent characteristic of his approach to ballads was an austere romanticism, rendering the statement of the melody with little or no ornamentation. He employed a full tone and played with a warmth that was less obvious on faster numbers. In other words, Coltrane seemed to be concentrating on producing a beautiful sound when playing ballads, a value he shared with Hodges.

Unlike Coltrane's advanced and highly sophisticated reharmonization of *Body and soul* on 1960's *Coltrane's Sound* (Atlantic [A] 587 039), his harmonic approach to *I want to talk about you* was relatively conventional. What is memorable about this performance is the intensity of his playing, part self-inquisition, part spiritual quest; even during a ballad he conveyed the same sense of urgency that was apparent at faster tempos. Coltrane splits his performance into three parts; the first is an exposition of the melody, followed by his improvisation and the third is a cadenza that accounts for three minutes 23 seconds of the eight-minute performance. During it he explores melodic motifs from the song, shimmering fragments that appear and reappear amid the multiplicity of scales and patterns that made up his basic vocabulary.

From April to October 1963, Coltrane was without his regular drummer, Elvin Jones, whose drug addiction had resulted in a conviction and incarceration at Lexington, Kentucky. The drummer Coltrane most frequently turned to was Roy Haynes, who, although still under 40, had played with some of the greatest saxophonists in jazz, including Charlie Parker, Lester Young and Stan Getz. Less rhythmically complex than Jones, Haynes was nevertheless a consummate drummer who adequately filled the most demanding drum chair in all of jazz. Like Jones, Haynes interacted with Coltrane's playing, and on *My favourite things* plays a prominent role in accompaniment. First recorded by Coltrane in 1960 (*My Favourite Things*, †Atlantic [A] 7567 81346–2), the choice of tune was a conscious attempt to expose his playing to a wider audience. After playing Cannonball Adderley's version of *Jive samba* over and over for a whole day on a diner jukebox, he realized how a modest hit recording could transform the career of a jazz artist and he acted accordingly. *My favourite things* became the minor hit he had hoped for and became something of a signature in live performance.

He plays it as a medium-tempo waltz. The structure of the tune is

AAB, but Coltrane plays only the A sections, assigning the B section to function as a coda. After a fanfarelike introduction, a clarion call to his fans, who would erupt with delight on hearing it, he plays the melody accompanied by the regular changes, but opens up a new section for improvisation based on an E-minor ninth/F#-minor ninth vamp. [64] This minor tonality together with a swaying ¾ rhythm lent a hypnotic, meditative feel to the piece and during his solo Coltrane imports a wide variety of scalar options incorporated from his vast repertoire of diminished, Indian, Eastern and pentatonic scales. This, together with his use of the soprano saxophone, which many people found close to the sound of Middle Eastern instruments, lent an mysterious, incantatory, Oriental ambience to the performance, prompting some critics mistakenly to assert that Coltrane was introducing ragas to jazz, or that his improvisation was 'raga-like'. [65] The A theme is repeated halfway through his solo and again as a lead-in to Tyner's solo, for whom the piece becomes an extended feature.

Tyner achieved a fresh approach to the modern jazz piano, influenced by the block chording of Red Garland, the advanced voicings of Bill Evans, the aggression of Horace Silver and the linear style of Bud Powell. An exceptionally forceful player, he occupied a pivotal role in Coltrane's quartet, holding together the competing claims of drums and saxophone. His comping style, often using a fifth in the bass and overlaid with right-hand chords voiced in fourths, became widely imitated. These ringing chords were not played in the bop manner, but formed a constant rhythmic undercurrent that was in contrast to the sparse form of bop accompaniment pioneered by Bud Powell. The pianist Steve Kuhn, who preceded Tyner in the quartet, has said the traditional bop style of comping simply did not work with Coltrane and that he was at a loss to provide the answer. When he heard Tyner with the group, he realized that this was the style of accompaniment for which Coltrane had been searching. [66] Tyner sustains his seesawing chords throughout his solo, overlaid by fast single-note lines and the dramatic use of side-slipping. It is interesting to contrast this highly personal style of playing with Tyner's appearance at Newport just two days earlier, this time in a trio with Bob Cranshaw on bass and Mickey Roker on drums, *McCoy Tyner Live at Newport* (†Impulse [J] AS48). Here, backing his guests Clark Terry and Charlie Mariano, his playing largely reverts to the bop-based style he previously employed while a member of the Art Farmer–Benny Golson Jazztet before joining Coltrane in 1960.

Impressions is a contrafact of Miles Davis's *So What?*, a 32-bar AABA modal composition with the A sections based on the D Dorian mode and the B section a semitone higher in Eb Dorian. The inspiration for the tune probably comes from Ahmad Jamal's version of Morton Gould's *Pavanne*, taken from the second movement of *2nd American Symphonette.* About halfway through Jamal's version, recorded on 25 October 1955,

[67] the guitarist Ray Crawford can be heard playing the secondary theme, an eight-bar melody that would become *Impressions*, and then repeating it up a semitone for another eight bars, prefiguring precisely the A and B sections of Coltrane's composition.

Coltrane would have been aware of Jamal's playing during his tenure with Miles Davis in 1955–7 and 1958–60, since Davis was something of a proselytizer for Jamal's keyboard approach. Coltrane takes the tune at a very bright tempo and employs a relentless pattern-running approach to begin his solo, exemplified by his approach to the harmonically complex *Giant steps*. The first four choruses of improvisation are with Tyner, Garrison and Haynes and his playing presents notes in groups of repeated patterns. Even though the harmonic base was simple, Coltrane devised ways of creating harmonic complexity through chord-stacking, bombarding the listener with vertically dense passages of such coherence that it appeared he was playing a set of changes. But when Tyner lays out, and then shortly afterwards Garrison, his playing becomes progressively fragmented, alternating jagged motifs with multiphonics and periods of turbulence that anticipate his free improvisations during the final years of his life. Janus-like, he seems to be looking backwards at his past achievements and forward to the new areas of music then being opened up by the 'New Thing' improvisers.

By way of comparison to Coltrane's approach to improvising with just drum accompaniment, *Chasin' another Trane*, a previously unissued take from the 2 and 3 November 1961 sessions that produced *Live at the Village Vanguard* (†MCA/Impulse [A] MCAD39136), again has Haynes in place of Jones. Although the liner notes claim there is no piano, one is plainly audible for the exposition of the theme. When Coltrane launches into his improvisation, his sequential use of patterns reveals a closer relationship to his 'vertical' *Giant steps* approach, then only 18 months behind him, achieving harmonic complexity through stacking or superimposing chords and scales on top of each other.

Dolphy, who appeared regularly with Coltrane from September 1961 to March 1962, was a daring and unconventional improviser who played with an audacity that both extended the boundaries of the alto saxophone and influenced the development of the avant-garde of the 1960s. He extended the alto range by at least an octave – and, by extension, its emotional scope – and controlled it with considerable fluency. With Coltrane he explored the possibilities of extended improvisation on alto, flute and bass clarinet, but in contrast to his use of bass clarinet on *Live at the Village Vanguard*, he appears on alto here. Solo transcriptions of Dolphy's solos often reveal quite conventional note choices presented in unconventional ways, through asymmetrical phrasing or a startling juxtapositioning of intervals that makes them appear as dangerous as the dissonant harmonies he also employed. [68] Like Coltrane, he used irregular groupings of notes and even today there is an exciting avant-garde edge to his playing that is wholly compelling. His greater willingness to use angular phrases and greater variation in his rhythmic approach effectively contrasts Coltrane's detailed excursions into exploring chord inversions and exotic scales in more conventional patterns. Although subsequently it might have appeared that a differing rationale lay behind Coltrane's *Crescent* (†Impulse [A] IMP12002) and Dolphy's *Out to Lunch* (**428**), recorded within a few weeks of each other in 1964, in fact Coltrane's playing on his Newport set and a few months later on *Live at Birdland* reveals a greater willingness to employ Dolphy's methods of phrasing; a use of wide intervals across the range of the saxophone, a greater fragmentation in his line and more frequent use of the extreme ranges of his saxophone that would surface more obviously in the freedom of his post-*Ascension* period. [69] S.N.

John Coltrane

424 A Love Supreme

†Impulse (A) GRD155

Coltrane (ten); McCoy Tyner (p); Jimmy Garrison (bs); Elvin Jones (d). New York City, 9 December 1964.

Part 1: Acknowledgement · *Part 2: Resolution* · *Part 3: Pursuance* · *Part 4: Psalm*

Although Bob Thiele does not mention it in his autobiography, [70] the unexpectedly high sales of Coltrane's *A Love Supreme* played a major role in ensuring the financial viability of the Impulse record label. It was by far Coltrane's most popular record, going 'gold' (sales of half a million) by 1970, appealing to listeners beyond the jazz constituency with its combination of spirituality, intensity and serenity. Its sales were further helped in 1973 with the release of the best-selling album *Love, Devotion and Surrender* (Columbia [A] KC32034) by Carlos Santana and John McLaughlin, which featured the 'Love supreme' motif from *Acknowledgement*, bringing Coltrane's music to the wider attention of rock audiences. 'Peace and love' was the byword of the era, and college students roamed the campuses chanting the 'Love supreme' invocation. In California, a church was dedicated to Coltrane, whose followers believed he had been spoken to by God before the recording session and considered him a saint. By the 1990s, *A Love Supreme* had achieved sales of a million worldwide, yet in no way was it compromised by commercial considerations. In fact, quite the reverse, since Coltrane modestly intended the album to be his 'gift to God'. The inner album-sleeve notes included a long poetic dedication and a letter to the 'Dear listener' that spoke of the saxophonist's 'spiritual awakening' in 1957, and on the outer sleeve Coltrane's image was portrayed in pensive mood to underline the deep seriousness he attached to the project.

A Love Supreme is thus an album that evokes strong symbolism as much as it does emotion. Even today, the spiritual connotation looms so large that it threatens to overwhelm its musical significance in Coltrane's career. Yet it is the culmination of what most observers refer to as Coltrane's 'modal' period. Coltrane's career can be broadly divided into three phases: his 'change-running' period up to 1959's *Giant Steps* (**421**), his 'modal' period from 1960 to 1965 with his 'classic' quartet of Tyner, Garrison and Jones, and his 'final' or 'free' period from 1965 until his death in 1967. The final period, although still employing modal pieces, was characterized more by free-form pieces, simultaneous collective improvisation as on such albums as *Ascension*, *Meditations*, *Expression* and *Live in Seattle*, the use of technique for technique's sake (high-register playing, multiphonics and dense, abstract, high-intensity flurries) and a greater involvement with Eastern musical concepts. However, it was through his first two periods that he made his most significant contributions to jazz, and his modal period had perhaps the furthest-reaching influence, both in jazz and rock music.

Coltrane's modal period began when he was introduced to modes by Miles Davis on the *Milestones* and *Kind of Blue* (**393**) sessions, although subsequently it was Coltrane who emphasized the use of modes more than Davis. By 1961 Coltrane had himself recorded a *So What?* [71] contrafact he called *Impressions* and his modal treatment of such songs as *My favourite things*, *Greensleeves* (**422**), *Out of this world* and *Chim chim cheree* had become closely identified with him in live performance. In his *Lydian Chromatic Concept* George Russell defined a mode as 'the complete circulation of a (major) scale begun and completed in any one of its tones'. [72] This definition implies that a mode has a specific relationship to a key. However, Coltrane's approach to modal improvisation was only loosely based on the overall tonality suggested by the parent key.

In the strictest musical sense, Coltrane's playing was not modal at all, but the principles he adopted in improvising over modes have become so widely used by both jazz and rock musicians that it is the universally accepted approach to 'modal' playing. Coltrane showed that his infatuation with harmonic complexity did not end with *Giant Steps*. Even over the static harmony of a modal base (or sometimes pedal-point drones) he continued to create harmonic complexity using a variety of different scales including diminished, whole-tone, diminished whole-tone, pentatonic plus exotic scales derived from Spain and India and Nicholas Slonimsky's *Thesaurus of Scales and Melodic Patterns*. [73] These scales in turn implied new chords and harmonies and these often distantly related chords were stacked on top of each other, creating the feeling of harmonic complexity over static modal harmony. Sometimes his use of scales was so systematic that it sounded as if he was referring to an underlying set of changes, such was the sense of direction he employed in their use. Equally his solos might be governed by using three-, four- and five-note motifs to organize the basis of his solos, as in the 5 November 1961 version of *Impressions* where he worked a simple melodic idea through a myriad of permutations. This approach can also be heard on such numbers as *Chasin' the Trane* and *My favourite things.*

A Love Supreme is a four-part modal album that utilizes three tones in a four-note motif in sequences, permutation and repetition to organize all four compositions and provide the raw material on which his solos were based. *Acknowledgement* is a free-form modal tune that suggests some degree of preplanning, such as a simple sketch outlining the direction he wished to follow during its course. It opens with a cadenza using three notes (not the 'Love supreme' motif) over a sustained chord built on intervals of a fourth and fifth followed by the 'Love supreme' *ostinato* played by Garrison in the minor. [74] Coltrane then introduces what appears to be an eight-bar melody based on elements of the 'Love supreme' motif together with elements of the *Pursuance* motif from later in the album. This eight-bar section is repeated with small variations, and for the moment the structure hovers around a sixteen-bar A + A^1 form. In his solo Coltrane initially acknowledges this sixteen-bar structure but gradually distances himself from it, working over the 'Love supreme' and *Pursuance* motifs (a variation of 'Love supreme' [75]), giving us glimpses of the tonal materials he will use in Part 3. He then returns to the original four-note 'Love supreme' motif which he moves through all 12 keys, and which we take to be a metaphor for universality, to introduce a vocal incantation of 'a love su-preme', which is repeated 19 times. This motif and the pentatonic scale it implies, F, A flat, B flat, C, E flat, provides much of the harmonic material through the entire album. The significance of the 19 incantations is explained by J. C. Thomas, one of Coltrane's earlier biographers: 'One means alone, nine stands for universal. One creative man alone, either with or against the universe, but definitely of the universal consciousness. One plus nine equals ten. And, in addition, according to the Kabbala, there are ten manifestations of God.' [76]

During the final section of *Acknowledgement*, Coltrane somewhat lumpily modulates into the key of E flat, presumably because *Part 2: Resolution* is in that key. This piece is based on an eight-bar theme which is repeated three times, giving a 24-bar AAA form followed by an improvised release of 16 bars on the same mode, followed by a reprise of the AAA section. Coltrane's entry after a 16-bar introduction by Garrison deserves comment since it is at a level of intensity most musicians would reserve to climax their solos. This was typical of Coltrane's approach to improvisation, however. The intensity during his solos could reach almost superhuman levels and undoubtedly contributed to his mystique, the notion that his music was possessed of some sort of spiritual force. Beginning a solo at such a level has inherent problems, however, primarily that of sustaining and even building on what has gone before.

Coltrane's exposition of the *Resolution* theme is followed by a solo from Tyner, already an aggressive player whose ringing, dramatically voiced chords, often combining intervals of fifths with fourths, pile-driving pedal points and shimmering right-handed runs, would mark him as one of the pillars of the contemporary jazz piano in the 1970s. Coltrane's improvisation reveals him able to raise the intensity level from his assertive theme statement by increasing the density of his line through the simple device of playing more notes, his use of high notes (his range went some seven semitones above the natural range of the instrument), and through slurs, rips and glissandos. He calls on these devices again on *Pursuance*, which, although a minor 12-bar blues, makes extensive use of modal harmonies. Jones, whose drumming was quite different to anything in jazz, provides the introduction. Although he plays in a basic metre of four, his style is associated with his ability to superimpose a metre of three over four, giving a loose polyrhythmic feeling to his playing, since his fills and accompaniment were often in units of three instead of two or four. These basic units would be distributed around his kit through his remarkable independent coordination of his arms and feet, as if each limb was a separate drummer, so that even his basic time-keeping might sound like several different rhythms played independently.

Coltrane plays two choruses of the theme, which immediately sounds familiar since he had revealed the *Pursuance* motif earlier in *Acknowledgement.* Tyner's solo follows, using some of Coltrane's methodology as a basis for improvisation. He explores and permutates the *Pursuance* motif and introduces several side-slipping runs to increase tension. At the end of the solo his open-voiced, ringing chords provide the perfect launching pad for the saxophonist's solo. Typically, Coltrane's entry is full of energy, and throughout his 18 choruses it is sustained and intensified. Like Tyner's solo beforehand, his is harmonically very free, side-slipping to remote keys towards the end for additional drama. Once again, the *Pursuance* motif figures prominently and for at least the first three choruses it is possible to keep track of it within Coltrane's swirling lines, which are governed by the pentatonic scale derived from the bass *ostinato* in *Acknowledgement*, which is retained through most of his solo (except, of course, during side-slipping, which on one occasion took almost a whole chorus). *Pursuance* ends as it began, with a Jones drum solo which winds down to allow the stately entrance of Garrison.

In his liner notes, Coltrane describes *Psalm* as 'a musical narration of the theme, A Love Supreme, which is written in the context'. In it he 'narrates' his poem, which is reproduced on the album sleeve, playing a note at a time on his saxophone to represent each syllable of the text. This recitation is performed with great solemnity, and clearly represented an act of spiritual commitment by Coltrane to God. It is performed over a rhythmically free background using bass drone, piano and Jones on timpani, and the effect is that of a free-form ballad. This is punctuated by a phrase equivalent to 'Thank you, God' with a minor third or fifth descending to the tonic for 'God'. As he finishes his instrumentalized poem, his saxophone clearly enunciates 'Amen'. As he did at slower tempos, Coltrane relinquishes his steely tone in favour of a softer, rounder and more expressive sound. Although during his 'change-running' period Coltrane could be a lyrical player, his playing after 1960 had a pronounced lyrical quality even at fast tempos, and his ballad playing on albums such as *Ballads* (†Impulse (A) GRD 156) and *John Coltrane and Johnny Hartman* (†Impulse (A) GRD 15) could be masterful. As he approaches the end of his solo a note of desperation creeps into his tone, perhaps that his supplication be heard by the Almighty. Somewhat mysteriously, a second saxophone can be heard at the end, a reminder that the piece was rerecorded the following day with Archie Shepp added to the ensemble.

Coltrane recorded only two albums in 1964, *A Love Supreme* and *Crescent.* Both project a serenity that was sharply at odds with his next occasion in the recording studios, to record *Ascension* on 28 June 1965. Once again he uses a musical motif to organize his material, this time of five notes, but the improvisations were totally free of pre-set harmonies, just like Ornette Coleman's *Free Jazz* (**400**) from five years before. A new phase of his music was underway that would occupy him until his death.

Each of Coltrane's periods had a great impact on jazz. His influence was almost as if Charlie Parker had appeared in jazz three times, such was the effect of his innovations and methodology within each phase. Not only did Coltrane revolutionize jazz instrumentally, he did it harmonically and rhythmically as well, and its effects are still being felt today. S.N.

Charles Mingus

425 Charles Mingus Presents Charles Mingus

†Candid (A) CCD79005

Ted Curson (tpt); Eric Dolphy (bs clt, alt); Mingus (bs, vcl intrjc); Dannie Richmond (d). New York City, October 1960.

Folk forms No. 1 · Original Faubus fables · What love · All the things you could be now if Sigmund Freud's wife was your mother

For most of 1960, in several ways an acutely innovatory year for jazz, Mingus's companions in this quartet had been engaged with him at a small Greenwich Village club, the Showplace. Live recordings made at Antibes, in the south of France, in the summer of that year but unreleased until after Mingus's death in 1979 preserve earlier outings for some of the material made famous by this Candid set (†Atlantic [A] 90532–2).

Despite admirable work by Curson and Richmond, it is Dolphy's response to the restless free-compositional ideas of the leader that, along with those ideas and the constantly inspiriting bass playing, have given this record classic status in the annals of postwar jazz.

A jaunty bass introduction announces *Folk forms No. 1.* Alto and trumpet present the minor-oriented theme in unison. Provocative acts of dialogue involving Mingus, Curson and Dolphy develop along a familiarly Mingusian trajectory into some fairly combatant ensemble improvising, the tangle of which unravels itself into what seems a rangy relative of the 'New Thing' libertarianism to which certain other groups were giving rein. The savage rant against 'Nazi-USA' racist politics in *Original Faubus fables* is also lent an appropriately minor feel. Dolphy's insulting alto tone may be thought of as more effective, dramatically, than the ridiculing taunts vocally interjected by Mingus; similarly Curson's vivid stabbings of disdain. Dolphy fashions oblique riffs with Mingus often breaking into double tempo; and Dolphy's principal solo revives his earlier sardonic vocalizations, 'fusions of satire and agony', [77] which most convincingly achieve the contempt which this essay in fierce satire calls for. Nothing quite as expressive as this was reached in the version of the *Fables* heard on *Mingus Ah Um* (CBS [E] 5552346), though, for some hearers, the larger ensemble used for that 1959 interpretation possibly reached other nuances of drama lying beyond the quartet's spectrum.

What love, in origin an early Mingus abridgement of *What is this thing called love?* which allowed for vagaries of tempo, has, in this version, long been celebrated for a designed-to-be-overheard private conversation between Mingus's bass and Dolphy's bass clarinet. This is an exchange of instrumental vocalism in an almost comprehensible dialect prompted by Mingus's annoyance at the likelihood that Dolphy was to quit his employ and evoking excuses, apologies, justifications, what else? . . . in response. Apparently this became a feature of Showplace sets much earlier in the year and was certainly performed at Antibes. If it touches the grotesque, it should be noticed how it emerges with a kind of established logic from what precedes it in the piece, in particular from Dolphy's marvellously expressive bass-clarinet lines, so engagingly supported by Mingus and Richmond. Whatever elements of temperamental rawness and self-guying humour may be heard in it, it may in proper context be regarded as a typically conceived jazz duet. After *What love's* songline is reprised a lone ascending bass figure escapes the earth's gravity in an exasperated squeak.

What you could be now . . . has a wry fury in some of its speedier solos and exchanges that would appear to come close to a free-music sort of abandon until one identifies the extent to which the expression dallies with bop. Curson, as in his *What love* solo, even veers a little towards a romantic lyricism. Dolphy, responding to the way in which wild rhythms depart and return, contrasts virtuosic celerities, which owe a great deal to Charlie Parker, with swooping adagios in a voice which is almost wholly his own. Parker was almost certainly Dolphy's most profound jazz inspiration. Mingus told of finding him practising by improvising along with one of Parker's records. At the same time it was his restless imagination and wide musical ambition that fuelled his quest for a language that would, as it were, honour Parker by ingenious trans-shapings of his stylistic parlance.

No 'school' can categorize Dolphy, however widely he may have allied his skills to contemporary groups. Many a later solo employs a very personal form of modalism within the development of a more self-expressive phraseology. His chief and only partially fulfilled need was to play 'his own music'. After the 1964 album *Out to Lunch* (**426**), the chance of again seeking opportunities in Europe was provided by Mingus. The recorded evidence of several Mingus concerts in the spring of 1964, their format sprawling, their personnel stylistically rather diffuse, does not suggest a context really congenial to Dolphy's urgent pursuit. He played well when his moments arrived but a few post-Mingus dates such as **427**, with a very sympathetic European rhythm team, allow us to hear him nearer to the independence he wanted, but with his early death imminent as well.

In a posthumous recollection Mingus described the relationship he had with Dolphy in the period this Candid album represents. 'He had such a big sound, as big as Charlie Parker's, I mean . . . Inside that sound was a great capacity to talk in his music about the most basic feelings. We used to do that, you know . . . actually talk in our playing'. [78]

Missing from the album is a version from the same date of Harold Arlen's *Stormy weather* which contains some of Mingus's most sensitive playing. It can be heard in a Candid miscellany, †Candid 79033. Dolphy's alto statement of the tune is, one might suggest, near to his 'basic feelings' voice, but he extends it into an improvisation of stunning linear shapeliness, and here it is the deliberative Dolphy speaking. There is no doubt that this voice was as basic as the other, and would necessarily remain so in a jazz conception as comprehensive as his. E.T.

Eric Dolphy

426 Out to Lunch

†Blue Note (E) CDP746 524–2

Freddie Hubbard (tpt); Dolphy (alt[1], fl[2], bs clt[3]); Richard Davis (bs); Tony Williams (d); Bobby Hutcherson (vib). New York City, 25 February 1964.

Hat and beard[1] · *Something sweet, something tender*[3] · *Gazzeloni*[2] · *Out to lunch*[1] · *Straight up and down*[1]

Eric Dolphy

427 Last Date

†EmArcy (G) 510 124

Dolphy (alt[1], fl[2], bs clt[3]); Mischa Mengelberg (p); Jacques Schols (bs); Han Bennink (d). Hilversum, 2 June 1964.
Epistrophy[3] · *South Street exit*[2] · *The madrig speaks, the panther walks*[1] · *Hypochristmutreefuzz*[3] · *You don't know what love is*[2] · *Miss Ann*[1]

These two celebrated recording sessions were made during the last year of Dolphy's life. Testimony to the time and circumstances of *Last Date* is provided in the recollection of the Dutch critic Michiel de Ruyter appended to a reprint of Nat Hentoff's sleeve note to the original 1964 release. This was, in cold fact, not the last recording Dolphy made; there were to be other sessions before his death in Berlin on 29 June 1964.

Out to Lunch seems Dolphy's greatest critical success. In 1987 a British magazine asked 35 jazz commentators to vote on what were supposed to be the 100 top jazz albums of the modern (post-Parker) era; half a dozen LPs involving Dolphy qualified, and *Out to Lunch* topped the top 12. Such upshots are, often enough, treated with caution: jazz writers, certainly, are pretty wary of polls. *Last Date* was unlikely to figure since it had long been deleted at the time of the poll. [79] Jazz polls are soon forgotten and fine music has a better chance of being treasured, though *Last Date* had to wait.

Gazzeloni, named after an admired flautist of the non-jazz vanguard, is one indication of the breadth of Dolphy's musical vista. Gunther Schuller recalled that Dolphy 'loved and wanted to understand all music . . . his appetite . . . voracious yet discriminating . . . extending from jazz to the classical avant-garde', encompassing 'older jazz . . . the sonic surfaces of Xenakis, the quaint chaos of Ives, the serial intricacies of Babbitt . . . the experiments of the "new thing".' [80] He also was drawn to Oriental scales and timbres, to the music of the Congo Pygmies and to the call of birds. Yet the music we hear from this very remarkable multi-instrumentalist is, however taxing to classification of style, undoubtedly jazz.

Despite his skill, Dolphy's ability to encompass his often outlandish imaginations has been doubted by some writers, and assessments of his progress have been contradictory. Some of this has to do with the problem of guessing whether he belonged with hard bop, with the modal movement, or with post-Ornette 'freedom'. He cooperated willingly enough in many contexts – too willingly, some may judge; even so, he was his own man chiefly and without question and was, as an avant-gardist, both pre- and post-Coleman, and on his own terms.

Out to Lunch shows advance upon *Outward Bound*, the first Dolphy-led recording (†Original Jazz Classics [A] OJCCD022). Compare the Hubbard and Dolphy of that recording not only with the same men here but also as December 1960 partners in Coleman's **400**. *Gazzeloni* reminds one of the opinion some have held that Dolphy's slowest advance towards technical mastery was on the flute. He was often thought to be playing out of tune when executing his more complicated elaborations, and those who thought such accusations justified would apply them to parts of *Gazzeloni*. Yet private recordings of explorations upon the flute made in November 1960 (†Blue Note [E] B21Y-48041) leave little doubt that Dolphy possessed the legitimate means to negotiate the most demanding conceptions as well as to slant his timbral dialects into wry areas when searching wit prompted. Compare also two versions of *Glad to be unhappy*, one on *Outward Bound* and the other at a Copenhagen concert (Prestige [A] PR24027), the first with scarcely a hint of a microtone, the second sure to offend the feeble-eared. Both were recorded in 1960. In addition, the firm agility of his December 1958 treatment of *Beyond the blue horizon* (†Giants of Jazz [It] CD53164AAD) bespeaks a fluting ability more than adequate to the advanced bop inventiveness of his then current aspirations.

However, there is more to *Gazzeloni* than fluting, and the more is what makes this the most satisfactory of all Dolphy's preserved sessions. He may have played longer, more personally exploratory and passionate solos in other settings; but where drawing his companions freely into the spirit of his own conceptions is concerned, maybe only his second album, *Out There* (†Original Jazz Classics [A] OJCCD023), also pianoless and with Ron Carter's beautifully disposed cello, offers rivalry.

Hubbard was an early, not always likely-seeming mate, and Davis was the Five Spot bassist. The latter and Hutcherson had played alongside Dolphy during 1963 and in March of that year Schuller's *Densities* with Dolphy on the B-flat clarinet and Davis at the bass was recorded at Carnegie Hall (†Enja [G] 5045). Davis's 'I knew what was inside his music; I was familiar with it and how he put it together' is shown to be no idle claim. [81] It is often the vigour of Davis's intuition that steers this ensemble from within. Initiation within overall direction marks this kind of free jazz. Its discipline rests upon Dolphy's personality and preparation, and is the fruit of his care in choosing men with complementary gifts. Expectedly, the ringing voice of Hutcherson's instrument puts a kind of atmospheric stamp on the music from the start. (How firmly did a recollection of Warren Chiasson's vibraharp part in *Densities* touch Dolphy's thoughts ahead of this session?)

There are constant variations of tempo-rhythm relationship, sorts of rhythmic improvisation upon known or felt tempos that are stated only fitfully; procedures to be compared with certain adventures at Chicago's Plugged Nickel (**396**) in which Tony Williams, a year and a half after Dolphy's death, would fill a role more varied yet no more apt than the one asked of him here. The drummer shows considerable delicacy and flexibility. Listen to him during the fascinating layering of accents which grows in *Hat and beard.* His propulsive work also is arresting enough, but the familiar concept of 'leading horns with rhythm support' has little part here. There are places in *Out to lunch* where Davis prompts forward movement by hinting at a basic beat; and at the end of that number it is some very specialized drumming from Williams that nudges the ensemble back into the barmy parade swagger of the theme.

The multitonal sauntering of the bass clarinet early in the sectional *Something sweet, something tender* shows, incidentally, how much of Coleman Hawkins could surface in Dolphy's rhythmic instincts; yet more importantly it suggests in a speed kinder than that of some of his alto solos the radial pattern suggested in the evolving of his improvisations' jagged lines seeming to move outwards through circles of intervallic relationships until their only possible course of return runs through the fortunate crisis of having to meet themselves coming back.

Though Hubbard sometimes sounded out of place in *Free jazz* (**400**), this music suits him well. In *Out to lunch* he scatters quicksilver notions and joins vibraharp and bass in an aerial game of tag. And how appropriate seems his skein of melodic prettiness to the squiffy carousal of *Straight up and down.*

Dolphy had minor popular recognition and insufficient professional reward in his short life. Fortunately for his surviving admirers, the wistfulness of his spoken words included during *Last Date*, though preserved from a separate interview – 'When you hear music, when it's over it's gone in the air. You can never capture it again' – is happily contradicted in a practical if not an ideally verifiable manner by the existence of these recordings, as also of a large proportion of the recordings dealt with in this book. The reappearance in the lists of *Last Date* restores yet another treasure from this admirably creative spirit's brutally axed career. Whereas in *Out to Lunch* every number was a Dolphy composition, in *Last Date*, a more conventionally conceived session, three out of six are Dolphy's, the other three are attributable to Monk, Mengelberg and the songwriting team of Raye and DePaul.

Epistrophy is introduced, if that is the word, by overblown shrieks and pedal grunts from the bass clarinet, presumably not only to demonstrate the instrument's range. Dolphy plays energetically, stating the theme at a somewhat leaden mid-tempo. Once the not particularly fetching theme line has been traced, the bass clarinet's registral colours are exploited and punctuated by some more of those uncomplimentary squawks. In his solo Mengelberg, a widely inventive musician with a good deal of humour in his improvising, searches after, without quite encompassing, that flamboyant élan which reinterpretations of Monk's puckish brainwaves call for. He is, however, an excellent stylist for the date (and elsewhere: see **465**, **468**). Dolphy's alto sounds both declamatory and exploratory, the voice of an artist whose passionate expressions took sustenance from a reservoir of jazz thoughtfulness.

The flute in *South Street exit* is close-linked to the flautist's hard-bop encounters and might be compared to his early work for Chico Hamilton as above. Dolphy's other flute feature reaches a different grade of achievement. *You don't know what love is* deserves nomination as the finest track on the album and maybe as Dolphy's finest employment of the flute. His improvisation is a remarkable celebration of the instrument, and though there is a well-sustained elegance in much of it, there is also sufficient of the man's characteristic colouration and artful vocalization to challenge those who have thought the flute too pastoral an implement to sustain a place in the jazzman's armoury. Schols's deep bowings sustain the proper mood for both exposition and reprise.

Mengelberg's *Hypochristmutreefuzz* is a fast, writhing hard-bop-plus creation. The pianist takes an extended first solo. Dolphy's bass clarinet is played with a savage sort of elation, ranting splendidly in the instrument's upper reaches. There is an appropriately bright stabbing at harmonic contrasts from both pianist and bassist.

Of the two numbers for which Dolphy chooses alto, the bi-metric *The madrig speaks, the panther walks* (formerly titled *Mandrake*) is the more accomplished exposition of his ingeniously probing style. *Miss Ann* is celebrated jauntily. Dolphy's alto phrasing is lacklustre at first, though it is enlivened some way short of the piece's precipitate ending. Mengelberg's contribution to this item plods rather wearily too. Perhaps a brisker pace should have been set. (An earlier performance of *Miss Ann* with Herbie Hancock and others, heard on an uninformative Israeli LP pressing [Unique Jazz U10], is taken at a notably increased speed which does make for greater relaxation. [82])

Dolphy stayed in Europe at the close of Mingus's tour in the late spring of 1964. He planned to rejoin his fiancée, Joyce Mordecai, in Paris on 3 June. At the end of May he rehearsed with Mengelberg, Schols and Bennink. Over that weekend there were a number of concerts, including one at the Amsterdam Concertgebouw, by this transitory quartet and then after this recording he left for Paris. At the end of June, news came of his death in Berlin from a heart attack provoked by diabetes. A gentle, generous and unassuming man, Dolphy was also an ardent jazz artist whose playing and composing kept vividly alive a spirit of creative dissatisfaction to fascinate those who heard him and who hear him still. E.T.

Oliver Nelson

428 Blues and the Abstract Truth

†Impulse (E) IMP1154–2, †Impulse (A) GRP9335

Freddie Hubbard (tpt); Eric Dolphy (alt, fl); Nelson (alt, ten); George Barrow (bar[1]); Bill Evans (p); Paul Chambers (bs); Roy Haynes (d). New York City, 23 February 1961.

Stolen moments · Hoe down · Yearnin' · Butch and Butch[1] *· Teenie's blues*

This was one of six small groups Nelson led between September 1960 and February 1961. Three of the resultant issues, the above plus †Original Jazz Classics (A) OJCCD080 and OJCCD099, have Dolphy in the personnel. This activity ran concurrently with Ornette Coleman's pathfinding work for Atlantic, a coincidence which in stylistic terms would be of small significance save for the fact that a little over a year before, both Dolphy and Hubbard had performed with some dedication as members of the Coleman double quartet in *Free jazz* (**400**). On that occasion Hubbard sounded rather like a friendly earthling on Mars, stabbing at a Martian dialect yet veering towards his home tongue. Dolphy, though not too evidently a free-jazzman, sounded much more adaptable. It might be contentious to suggest that Hubbard's 'home tongue' can be heard here with Nelson. His playing under Dolphy's leadership on **426** typifies the imaginative range of his vocabulary: Clifford Brown (**270**) and Booker Little (**339**) were his trumpeting exemplars and he had learned from Dolphy's idiomatic discoveries as well.

Nelson's line-up, perhaps a slightly odd association, proves an inspired selection in view of his aims for this and comparable sessions. 'The compositions on this recording,' he says, 'present a phase of my development up to the present time as a jazz writer.' He names the blues in its 12-bar form and songs typified by *I got rhythm* 'being 32 measures in length . . . for all the compositions on this album.' Thematic motifs, melodic notions and deliberate metric divisions augment those formal basics here and there. Thus *Stolen moments*, for example, is a minor blues derivation stretched over 16 bars which are divided, for the theme, as 8 + 6 + 3, the divisions innerly contrasted rhythmically and melodically. The solos between theme statement and reprise add further contrast by following the C-minor blues progression, Hubbard's agile hard-bop excursion becomes rapidly repetitive towards its end as if responding to the theme's repetitive six-bar division. Dolphy's expressive flute sounds his ongoing search for some preternatural lyricism hiding in the air above his head. Nelson – dispatched by some wayward acoustic to a distant corner of the studio – also is reflectively repetitive on tenor and a little more inventively so than Hubbard. Evans's lovely single-line tracery is naturally lyrical but not at all ethereal.

Hoe down, an admired antiphonal jollity, presents an intro of 4 bars followed by five 8-bar sections: AABAA. 'The two notes at the very beginning of the tune are responsible for the melody itself, and it turns into a statement and response kind of thing which lasts for 44 measures,' Nelson wrote. [83] Solos follow a 32-bar AABA pattern 'for the sake of variety,' Nelson adds. Hubbard scampers in after the theme, gaining impetus by way of tricksy fragmentations. Dolphy, on alto, swirls robustly and the distant leader drives more virilely still. After eight acute bars from Haynes the bucolic theme returns. An exercise for saxophone, recalled by its student deviser, is the basis of the self-fermenting *Cascades*. Hubbard solos using a strategy of phrase-building as complex as the theme itself, gyrating deceptively through its chord sequence. Evans enters softly, building to a confident intensity through thoughtful speculations into dancing chordal figures. And an Evans double 12-bar chorus introduces the C-major blues *Yearnin'*. A first ensemble employing 16 bars is followed by a second of 12 bars, then by an emotional Dolphy and an aggressive Hubbard. Evans counters force with quiet yet elaborate shapes developing into blues patterns sounding a bit more conventional. *Butch and Butch*, an unrestructured blues showing fealty to almost unrestructured bop, has its line stated first by Hubbard and Dolphy, who repeat it immediately with added depths supplied by Nelson's tenor and Barrow's baritone. Of the ensuing solos, the leader's spins whereas Dolphy gains his post-Parker coherence in a recycling of riven shards of melody, then Evans closes the rota with jazz of calm directness.

Nelson restricts the harmonic progressions of the blues in the final number, *Teenie's blues*, the line of which he and Dolphy play in alto duet, executing its strange, mockingly diminished intervals in appropriate tones. Dolphy expostulates, multiplying and dividing weird, half-familiar snatches with reedy hints of the vocalization that had already so beguiled Mingus (**425**). In his yonderness, Nelson seizes Dolphy's final phrase as a rung to climb into an exalted fierceness. Evans weaves a pellucid variation that even he has rarely surpassed, solemn and light-hearted at once. With that already mature modernist Haynes brushing gently, Chambers, a man of like pedigree and skill, who has ushered in *Teenie's blues* with two choruses of walking bass, takes a couple more to demonstrate what a compelling improviser he could be. He was currently demonstrating the selfsame eloquence with the Miles Davis sextet, and beyond that employment he had but a few years to live. Chambers and Haynes were the perfect bassist and drummer for this famous gathering.

E.T.

Bobby Hutcherson

429 Dialogue

†Blue Note (E) CDP746 537–2, Blue Note (A) BST84198

Freddie Hubbard (tpt); Sam Rivers (ten, sop, bs clt, fl); Andrew Hill (p); Richard Davis (bs); Joe Chambers (d); Hutcherson (vib). Englewood Cliffs, N.J., 3 April 1965.

Catta · Idle while · Les noirs marchent · Dialogue · Ghetto lights

Dialogue may well still be regarded over 30 years after its making as one of Hutcherson's most significant productions, allowing that the significance resides very much in association and in the temper of the time. The previous year had seen the magnificent collaboration with Dolphy, Hubbard and Davis in *Out to Lunch* (**426**). The summer of 1965 saw the vibraharpist's Newport appearance with Archie Shepp which produced *Le matin est noir* and the other Shepp episodes (†Impulse [A] GRP11052) and which, though probably ambivalent in a 'New Thing' context, pinpointed Hutcherson's emergence as a jazz contender even more clearly than the Dolphy endeavour. Certainly the mid-1960s were Hutcherson's time for 'new star' renown, poll winning, and tilting in the lists as jazz cheered fresh champions of innovation.

Things said under **426–7** about the difficulty of identifying Dolphy's music in stylistic terms may apply to a good deal of the more questing mid-1960s jazz sessions. Not a little of current hard-bop production grew obsessional and touched sterility. Yet the challenges of post-Ornette free music were not easily responded to in such a context until artists of the calibre of Dolphy, Hubbard, Hill (**431**) and of the youngsters Miles Davis was gathering to himself began to explore fresh regions of tonality, daring the unresolvable, as Hill may have seemed to be doing in his 1963 *Black Fire* (†Blue Note [A] 84151).

Hutcherson's leadership gives an air of dramatic vividness to these proceedings and he plays with great beauty and executive control; but the chief conceptual hand is Hill's. This pianist conceived the first, third and fifth numbers, Chambers the other two. Yet listing such credits and acknowledging Hutcherson, Hubbard and Rivers as the foremost voices by no means tells the whole story of this session's music. However subtly, Hill's directive influence may be felt throughout, his role may be to a degree self-effacing, and he arranges for, or permits, the emergence of other formative and directive leadings and promptings within the group, particularly in the more experimental pieces.

Commentators have made too much of Hill's Haitian infancy (in fact he grew up in Chicago and learned his jazz there), but his title *Catta* – a Port au Prince dialect – is his own acknowledgement of origin; and the number is a forceful mambo tethered by Hill's characteristic patterns, a statement of atmosphere and identity and notable for Rivers's tenor declamations. Gentler upon the flute, and paired with Hubbard, Rivers makes the tune of Chambers's *Idle while* (a lovely title pun for nostalgic air travellers) seem inconsequential and this episode of ¾ time pastoral is chiefly memorable for the playing of Davis, reminding us how telling his ensemble role in **426** had been.

Idle while and *Dialogue* are testimony to the musical vision of Chambers, a drummer whose importance as a collaborator in the jazz of these men and this period is not made blatantly evident by his playing here, which could be taken as merely sensitive and workmanlike. He wrote for Hutcherson on other occasions and among the leaders he has worked with Jimmy Giuffre is mentioned as a formative spur.

Having said that, it should be evident that where both *Les noirs marchent* and *Dialogue* are concerned, ordinary notions of composition tell little about the conceptual process. Though *Les noirs marchent* takes a sombreness from Hill's initial march theme and though *Dialogue* seems generally lighter in mood, the inner relationships of each performance are determined by a freedom to improvise collectively which might on the surface of things seem as radical in possibility as the freedom of *Free jazz* (**400**) or even of Coltrane's *Ascension* (†Impulse [A] GRD21132–2). And yet the freedom claimed was in order to make discoveries possible within a diatonically related interplay of voices, not to stray into do-it-yourself atonality or mystagogic anarchy. This is, as one has said, 'demanding listening', [84] but it is not at all inaccessible; and as a matter of fact the spaces and shapes created are more congenial than daunting. Their tendency towards simple 'impressionism' may be counted a failing by some listeners.

Some kind of deliberation seems evident in the way particular voices influence the internal balances, suggesting different phases of character. The flute seems a Puckish, fifelike strand in the development of Hill's *marche* scenario, the bass clarinet an unusually disturbing interlocutor in *Dialogue*. Hutcherson may take a rather more forthright role in parts of the latter, but in both the dialogic numbers and elsewhere too Davis gives the impression of having intuitions not quite as clearly recognized by the rest – not even by Hill, though he seems a man sufficiently confident of his powers to keep his own counsel when that suits his strategy.

Consorting with Shepp and Dolphy at the times concerned, Hutcherson may rather hastily have been numbered among the breakers of tradition. Better perspectives prevail now. Francis Davis lately adjudged the importance of the music 'made in the middle-1960s . . . for Blue Note . . . with . . . like-minded musicians who included the vibraharpist Bobby Hutcherson' to be 'an insistence on moderation at a time when a revolution was going on elsewhere in jazz'. [85] Moderation was not timorousness, as the present album shows clearly enough. The further research of bop's potentialities could bypass the expressive hang-ups of hard bop; but the triumphs of either iconoclasm or fusion caused some of these hopefuls to appear to lose their nerve for a time. Hutcherson even became a Milt Jackson 'clone' in John Lewis's New Jazz Quartet in 1982 (RCA [F] PL45729) after cheerless endeavours through almost a decade. But as the 1980s nudged the 1990s he produced new work which proved that his jazz vision could be as lively as ever (as in Landmark [A] LM1517, LM1529). E.T.

Dave Holland

430 Conference of the Birds

ECM (G) 1027.

Anthony Braxton (alt, sop, fl); Sam Rivers (ten, fl); Holland (bs); Barry Altschul (d, perc, mrm). New York City, 30 November 1972.
Four winds · *Q & A* · *Conference of the birds* · *Interception* · *Now here (Nowhere)* · *See-saw*

When Ornette Coleman ushered in an era of free jazz, his emotionally affecting, often swinging brand of melodic freedom gave way to a broader consensus that favoured high energy, dense textures and rhythmic turbulence rather than Coleman's rhythmic and melodic inclinations. By 1964 Sunny Murray had broken the 'time barrier' and many improvisers were drawn increasingly towards the anguished pyrotechnics of social protest. Perhaps this was inevitable in the context of the times. A corollary was emerging between the growing civil-rights movement that gave expression to political awareness and rejection of racial injustice and young black musicians who felt by freeing themselves from bar lines, harmony and rhythm they were participating, both literally and metaphorically, in the crusade for freedom and social justice.

For many, free jazz became the anthem that screamed rejection of racial inequality, Archie Shepp for one proclaiming: 'We are not angry men. We are enraged . . . I can't see any separation between my music and my life. I play pretty much race music.' [86] This inevitably posed problems of critical evaluation, free jazz sometimes weighing more heavily on critics' consciences than on their pleasure centres and a certain critical discretion preceded valour lest posterity marked the denigrator of a new Picasso or Joyce. The problem was that freedom, used as vehicle for social protest and racial indignation, was often mistaken for musical merit. It was a time, as Marshall McLuhan observed, when 'art was anything you could get away with'. For several years free jazz remained impaled on the barriers of sociopolitical issues, part rhetoric, part artifice. But as the music gradually became disentangled from the social fabric in which it had become embroiled, musicians began separating its individual strands and re-examining the component parts that made up the whole.

When *Conference of the Birds* was recorded in 1972, free jazz was moving underground in the face of the advance of jazz-rock. The album represented a reunion of Holland, Altschul and Braxton, who had previously been members of Chick Corea's group Circle a year earlier. Holland's ascent into the ranks of the top jazz performers had been as unexpected as it was sudden. Plucked as a 22-year-old from the relative obscurity of the interval band at Ronnie Scott's jazz club by Miles Davis, he found himself in the recording studios four weeks later completing the two final tracks of *Filles de Kilimanjaro* (**441**) which presaged a two-year stint with the trumpeter. However, at the end of Davis's 1970 tour of Europe, both Holland and Corea left to pursue the ideals of acoustic freedom rather than laying down vamp figures to underpin Davis's electronic music. Initially they formed a trio with Altschul, later augmented by Braxton, *Circle – Paris Concert* (ECM [G] 1018/19). However, Corea had come under the sway of Lafayette Ron Hubbard, the scientologist, and one tenet among many of his controversial teachings held that art should concern itself with communication rather than aesthetics. When Corea rather abruptly abandoned Circle, it was in favour of music that took account of this dubious aesthetic or, as Corea explained, creating music that might 'achieve a better balance between technique and communication'. [87] *Conference of the Birds*, its title taken from a 13th-century epic poem of that name by Fariduddin Attar, emerged under Holland's sage mediation using the basic Circle line-up with Rivers standing in for Corea. Holland's originals for this album had been previously performed by a group he led for a New York concert that included Randy and Mike Brecker on trumpet and tenor respectively, the pianist and guitarist Ralph Towner and Altschul. [88] Braxton and Rivers, however, were chosen for the recording as better able to respond to the opportunist disjunctions offered within Holland's compositions. *Conference of the Birds* emerged as a definitive statement of swinging free expression. It was, in essence, a return to the rugged discipline of early 1960s free improvising by working off melodic foundations using the 'time, no changes' principle to achieve greater control over that elusive quarry, freedom.

Four winds has a boppish 20-bar theme and is the only 'closed form' piece on the album where the form of the song is repeated over and over at the end of each chorus in the time-honoured method of playing over 'changes'. Holland and Altschul mix walking rhythms and subtle exchanges to allow Rivers's tenor and Braxton's soprano to work within the structure of the piece. Ingenious and direct, they present an important alternative to the endless, often ugly, free-for-alls that had become the norm in free jazz. There is no run-of-the-mill overblowing here.

The remaining pieces are 'open form', where the theme is stated at the beginning or near the beginning of the piece to set tempo, key and mood, and the improvisers are free to develop their improvisation in any direction they chose. Holland and Altschul then have the burden of spontaneously ordering their accompaniment to follow the improvisers' impulse. Altschul begins *Q & A* with a series of percussive effects without metre to introduce conversational flurries argued by Braxton's alto and Rivers's flute against Holland's spiky asides. Rhythms may change, but Altschul and Holland retain the infectious quality of a LaFaro and Motion or a Haden and Higgins. A point of common agreement emerges as the conversants unite briefly on a theme fragment before joining in collective voice to pursue abstract figures that refuse to coalesce in melodic logic.

This fragmented discourse returns in chastened camaraderie on the title track inspired, said Holland, by the morning chorus: 'Around four or five o'clock in the morning, just as the day began, birds would gather one by one and sing together declaring its freedom in song.' [89] Braxton on soprano and Rivers on flute enter in cautious twitter, uniting to state the theme in solemn incantation before blurring into simultaneous improvisation. As the dialogue recedes, Altschul on marimba toils in service of the creative moment; evocative without being programmatic, he moves with measured tread towards a recapitulation of the theme which, in its quiet way, frames the dawn.

The resolutely woody sound of Holland's bass dominates *Interception*, with its headlong dash into the fastest tempos that Rivers, now on tenor, can muster. Holland, in his background role, comments on and answers Rivers's querulous turbulence before moving into a solo that sustains rhythmic momentum while seemingly moving free from a time-keeper's shackles. One of the finest bassists in jazz, he has tone, technique and imagination that resonate with the overtones of tradition – great bass players such as Blanton, Brown, Pettiford and Mingus – yet his playing is so melodic and personal he could almost be singing. Braxton toys with high-velocity runs, then stumbles into the knotty undergrowth, his tone anxious and harsh as he moves among the thickets. Altschul's drum solo beckons the fragmented theme as the group collide in unison voice before their hasty departure.

Now here (Nowhere) is in contrast pensive; Braxton's tone being almost classical as he is joined in fractured harmony by Rivers. Together they advance in solemn dialogue, inventing phrases that drape around each other warmly, like woolly scarves on a cold day. Holland, more light-footed, playfully moves in and out of the shadows of their strange harmonies. The mood is broken by *See-saw*, a return to a boplike head that launches Braxton on a perilously balanced excursion, his uneasy sense of swing given strong propulsion at Holland and Altshul's insistence. A brief return to the head presages Rivers's strong solo; moving with the limping grace that characterized his work on *Miles in Tokyo* (CBS/Sony [J] 18AP 2064), he gathers momentum before cascading into strident confusion as the coda looms like an admonishing road sign emerging from the gathering gloom. S.N.

Andrew Hill

431 Shades

Soul Note (It) 12113–1, †Soul Note (It) 12113–2

Clifford Jordan (ten[1]); Hill (p); Rufus Reid (bs); Ben Riley (d). Milan, 3–4 July 1986.

Monk's glimpse[1] · *Trippin'* · *Chilly Mac*[1] · *Ball Square* · *Domani* · *La Verne*[1]

A 1965 review of Hill's 1964 *Judgement* (Blue Note [A] BLP4159) considered the possibility of regarding the emergent artist as 'the Horace Silver of the avant-garde'; [90] another writer, greeting Hill's 1989 return to Blue Note, called him 'essentially . . . a hard bopper (albeit a highly idiosyncratic one)'. [91] Thirty years after *Black Fire*, his first record on Blue Note (BCT84151), the old stylistic enigma seems to remain. The earlier critic regarded the Silver comparison as 'glib', but that others made it cannot be denied, and the dates and the styles of Hill's collaborators perhaps lend a shade of excuse. If listeners still have to make up their minds about this man in the present, the fitfulness of his performing and recording career can partly be blamed for that. But there may be other reasons, not quite so easily stated, which touch upon the present condition of jazz development. At all events, if, to employ staple terms, the Hill of the 1980s and 1990s is 'essentially a hard bopper', the brilliant linear fragmentation of *Rob it Mohe* (Soul Note [It] SN1010, 1980) and the Joplinistic self-challenges of *Verona rag* (†Soul Note 121110, 1986) should prove how 'idiosyncratic' a specimen he is. That *Shades* is placed here, in a sequence of items ranging from 1959 to 1987, may be symptomatic of the elusiveness of critical certainty. It was recorded on the two days preceding the *Verona rag* album, but its close kinship with the Hill groups of two decades earlier will be manifest, especially in a comparison of the pianist's own expressive solo and supporting style. The consistency of his keyboard work is evidenced even in the more assertive context of *Dance with Death* (Blue Note [A] LT1030, 1968), where the band writing yielded more to prevailing modes, and even Hill's solo in *Fish 'n' rice* ventured a few solid Silverian accents.

Only the title of *Monk's glimpse* makes Hill's admiration of a hero obvious. The fingering is light, fleet, more gently waggish than Monk. Reid donates firm motion with sustained lyricism, and Riley uses his sticks with nice, brittle precision. Jordan, a tough contender once, plays with delicacy in linear terms and with just the right sonic weight. The tenorist is absent from *Tripping* and *Ball Square. Tripping* establishes its shapes by degrees, discovering an Afro-Latin undercurrent that is developed in relaxation by Riley and courted and challenged by an allusive and oblique keyboard phraseology which manages to seem death-defying without suggesting that control is in real danger. Jordan swings into the start of *Chilly Mac*, slithering elegantly and swapping brisk fours with Riley. Hill enters for a humorous sequence of mimic uncertainties, alongside which both Jordan and Reid echo the pianist's fashion to some extent. Riley is splendid.

Ball Square is either a serious joke or a whimsical pomposity, alternating skipping $^4/_4$ with surging, dramatic $^3/_4$ *rubato*. Riley is granted much space and uses it with unfailing élan. In some ways this is quite a formal piece, yet the jazz instinct worries liberations out of the temporal pattern. Reid inserts cheeky *arco* whinings into the *rubato* bits. The lightsome swiftness of *Domani* is spiced with deceptive pauses, and decelerations and dynamics are deployed deceptively too. Hill's solo is the most interestingly sustained of the album – errant movements in the right hand with judiciously yet very freely related codes in the left, displaying his manner of idea-tracing at some length, particularly as these are linked to his organization of group music and showing how he retains the kind of freedom he wants within a group strategy without endangering a very carefully balanced cooperation. Jordan's contribution is well in character, jazz full of arresting notions, fugitive messages, and some exciting swing.

La Verne is a soft balladlike number. Steady-stepping rhythm work supports Jordan, and Reid's role is important. The tune has affective repetitions which Hill's piano commentary bypasses until he feels the need to recall them obliquely, joining Reid in glimpsing the subject's profile from a number of vantages. Nothing is sought here beyond the easy equipoise of gentle thoughts.

It might be thought that Hill's work with groups is more accessible and better contained than his recent, rather extensive solo albums and broadcasts. Other recent meetings comparable to *Shades* are rare, but *Eternal Spirit* (†Blue Note [A] 792 051), which also has Reid and Riley, should prove an interesting link with that older liaison at **429** because the other participant there is Bobby Hutcherson. Some of the solo sessions may recall another comparison of old, but very little in either **384–5** or **418–20** is likely to lure any but the rashest of slick labellers into calling Andrew Hill the 'Cecil Taylor of hard bop redivivus'. E.T.

The Combo Explodes

Reflecting combinations of new and existing knowledge, the sound of the jazz combo could be gloriously unpredictable. The whole jazz tradition and beyond provided the jumping-off point to moving into the future, the only precondition being adventure.

Shelly Manne

432 **The Two and the Three**
†Original Jazz Classics (A) OJCCD172–2, Vogue (E) LAC12276

Shorty Rogers (tpt); Jimmy Giuffre (clt[1], ten[2], bar[3]); Manne (d). Los Angeles, 10 September 1954.
Flip[1] · *Autumn in New York*[2,3] · *Pas de trois*[1,2] · *Three on a row*[3] · *Steeplechase*[2] · *Abstract No. 1*[1,2,3]

Russ Freeman (p); Manne (d). Los Angeles, 14 September 1954.
The sound effects Manne · *Everything happens to me* · *Billie's bounce* · *With a song in my heart* · *A slight minority* · *Speak easy*

Having left Kenton for the last time in 1951, Manne settled in Los Angeles and became heavily and permanently involved with studio work for films and television as a composer as well as drummer. Yet right till the end of his life he never lost his zest for jazz and regularly led small jazz combos in and out of the recording studio, and even successfully ran his own nightclub, Shelly's Manne-Hole (1960–74). Obviously a musician of exceptional versatility, he was able not only to contribute to the sort of extensions of the jazz idiom which characterized the West Coast school of the 1950s (**386–9**, **450–1**, **453** etc.) but also to initiate some of these, as in the case of the above 1954 sessions.

This jazz has ample intrinsic value of its own, yet the fact that the participants had been playing together in a considerable variety of musical situations over several years and had comparable imaginative flexibility was an important element in the character of its success. The promptness and subtlety with which they could respond to each other's ideas enabled them to avoid established patterns of solos with subsidiary accompaniment in favour of various kinds of linear simultaneity. Hence portents of the future emerged in both sets of performances, and this tells us something about the ways in which the musical language of jazz changes and grows. In view of the subsequent achievements of free jazz, a degree of historical imagination may be needed in listening to these pieces, however, and Freeman's and Manne's both soloing at once in *Speak easy* now inevitably sounds less daring than it did several decades ago.

Perhaps, too, antiphony between the three players in Manne's *Flip* teeters over into counterpoint in a manner that is still delicious, but the counterpoint remains of a fairly conventional type. In contrast, *Abstract No. 1* stands as a real intimation of later procedures and because jazz at such moments shows 'the continuity, logic, unity and inner necessity which characterize all true art', [92] it needs to be heard in context with such comparable ventures as Tristano's 1949 *Intuition* and *Digression* (**293**), Macero's *Explorations* of 1953 (†Debut [A] 12 DCD4402) and *Neally* 1955 (**479**). Following earlier experiments independent of the rhythm section by Giuffre and Rogers in the setting of the latter's Giants combo, *Abstract No. 1* was a collective improvisation without theme or chord sequence. It stands, with its interlocking of melodic and rhythmic planes, as free jazz in all but name and is, like several other performances such as those just mentioned, a striking demonstration that a potential for such playing already existed within the music.

And not far behind is *Autumn in New York*, where the sheer independence of Rogers's and Giuffre's lines still seems, in the most impressive passages, quite remarkable in its polyphonic freedom and spontaneity. There are some particularly expressive Giuffre phrases and Manne registers a protest against the usual sort of drum solo, whose noise and emptiness exert such an irresistible appeal to jazz fans. Following the acutely linear stance of Giuffre and Rogers here, he attempts in his down-tempo solo what can only be termed a melodic approach in the *Klangfarbenmelodie* sense. This applies to much of his drumming on both dates in fact, and looks forward, not always tentatively, to the innovations of such different free-jazz drummers as Sunny Murray and Milford Graves.

Already distant from the essentially traditional big-band music he wrote for Herman (**312**), Giuffre in *Pas de trois* now goes beyond his *Alternation*, recorded with Manne, Rogers and others the previous year (Contemporary [A] C2511), moving towards the substantially more fluid music heard from him on **387** and in the many editions of his Trio (e.g. **364**). *Pas de trois* is a rondo which, raising the bid of *Flip*'s canonic imitation in two parts, treats three themes as three-part canons. To grasp these one has to understand that the drums are again regarded as melodic instruments, and this, given Manne's range of nuance, is not unreasonable. There are telling divergences between the tightly patterned ensemble passages and the freedom of the solos, and this is also true of Rogers's *Three on a row*. This is a fully competent essay in serial technique, elementary yet a necessary beginning, pointing to the Coleman–Schuller *Abstraction* (**400**) and beyond that to work by Mack (**456**), Blatný (**457**) and others. Rogers's 12-note row is heard a dozen times and a few of its potentialities, compositional and otherwise, are uncovered. Perhaps the tempo changes are too frequent in a piece that is closely organized but lasts only a fraction over five minutes. There is an interesting and unexpected coda.

It scarcely needs adding that both *Autumn in New York* and *With a song in my heart* are divested of their sentimental and fatuous Tin Pan Alley associations. The latter especially is made to yield all kinds of rhythmic complexities that might have seemed foreign to its nature, this being a typical example of the paradoxical relation between jazz and some of the material on which it draws. An intent, densely textured reworking of the blues, *Billie's bounce* is here shaped by a particularly articulate reading of the theme's rhythmic potentialities, while *Steeple-*

chase gives rise, like *Flip*, to exultant dialogues between trumpet and drums, tenor and drums. Both Parker themes are here lent emphases very different from those implied by their initial, seemingly quintessential, bop character.

It might have been expected that the medium of piano and percussion would be exploited more often in jazz recordings, and not merely to use the drums as accompaniment as in, say, the 1944 Commodore titles by George Zack and George Wettling or Jess Stacy and Specs Powell. The 'extreme' situation of the above session drew out the linear and percussive facets of Freeman's playing in such a way as to make him a virtually ideal partner in what are largely percussion duets. Muscular and incisive, his work here de-emphasizes the sensuous impact of harmony, stressing line rather than mass. Indeed he was quoted on the original LP sleeve note as saying that he liked 'to think in lines as much as possible' and to use his 'left hand for another melody as well as rhythmically . . . I want a line or two lines going in my right hand and at least one line in my left hand, the lines working out contrapuntally and also being in different rhythms without losing the swing.'

Actually, there is a witty reversal of roles between drums and piano in the first chorus of *The sound effects Manne*, a Freeman theme of 32 bars taken as 16 + 16. And with regard to Manne assuming melodic responsibilities, observe how he gets a different sound from his drum kit in each of his three solos here. As noted, the implications of these dozen performances were taken much further in many other places, not least in some of the Solal MPS dates such as **365** and *Zo-Ko-So* (†MPS [G] 843 107–2), which latter has the instrumentation of 'The Three'. M.H.

The Art Ensemble of Chicago

433 Urban Bushmen

ECM (G) 1211/12 (2 LPs)

Lester Bowie (tpt, bass d, long horn, vcl); Joseph Jarman (sopranino, sop, alt, ten, bs sx, clt, bs clt, picc, fl, alt fl, conch shell, vib, cls, gongs, tom-toms, whistles, bells, siren, bass pan d, vcl); Roscoe Mitchell (sop, alt, ten, bar, bs sx, picc, fl, bon, con, clt, bamboo fl, gongs, glock, whistles, bells, pans, vcl); Malachi Favors Maghostut (bs, perc, melodica, bass pan, vcl); Famoudou Don Moye ('sun perc', trap d, bendir, bike horns, whistles, con, djimbo, djun-djun, donno timp, chekere, conch shell, long horn, elephant horn, gongs, cym, chimes, wdb, belafon, cans, bass pan d, vcl). Munich, May 1980.

Promenade · Côte Bamako I · Bush magic · Urban magic · March · Warm night blues stroll · Down the walkway · RM express · Sun precondition two · Theme for Sco · Soweto messenger · Bushman triumphant · Entering the city · Announcement of victory · New York is full of lonely people · Ancestral meditation · Uncle · Peter and Judith · Promenade · Côte Bamako II · Odwalla/Theme

Rather portentous notions about sociology, ethnic awareness and sound in its relation to silence have sometimes affected comment upon the music of the Art Ensemble and its formative predecessor, the Roscoe Mitchell sextet. The best of this music seems, though it occasionally wishes to convey rather solemn messages, markedly relaxed, free of theoretical posturing, tricksy, and more concerned with exploring a broad range of music than with proving a philosophy. Or, at least, that is how it sounds. Bowie's attraction to the music-making of Mitchell and company evidently had less in common with Jarman's later thoughts of 'salvation through music' and 'the speechless ones, those urban heroes/heroines of darkness' than it had with a simple recognition that this association brought him opportunity of escape from rhythm-'n'-blues-band territory into 'playing jazz full time'. [93]

There is no denying that several parts of *Urban Bushmen* draw inspiration from beyond jazz; yet the Ensemble's eclecticism must stem from the hopeful listening of Jarman and Mitchell to Coleman, Ayler and the Coltrane of *Ascension*, and from their discovery that even the roots of jazz had strange roots of their own. Immediate promptings are equally telling, of course. 'Great Black Music – Ancient to the Future', yet another, this time more mouth-filling, attempt to rename jazz, touches willy-nilly on ideas listed in the first sentence above, and on more. Besides, if one were not simply to hear the music but at the same time to see the painted faces and hieratic vestments, the formidable array of wind instruments, the movement between the gong stand, the bell racks ('like sculptured icons in motion . . . the drums of every size, the entire semicircular "machine"' [94]), one would undoubtedly have to report a different experience. Only the sounds are preserved. Like the sounds of opera divorced from the theatre, of liturgical music divorced from the church, they concentrate all their signals upon the ear and must be thus assessed.

The heart of the *Côte Bamako* items beats furiously in the ritual drumming, punctuated by whistle signals which are certainly African; but it would suit the manner in which the music frequently heeds the ambivalence of the LP's title that they might simultaneously be police whistles. In the second *Côte Bamako* the drumming prevails only gradually over a mixture of chanting, shouting, traffic noises and free improvisation which are evocative in ambiguous ways. *Bush music* and *Urban magic* compound the paradox, the first pitting Favors's jazz-informed bass against scatterings of percussion sound; the second interrupting a march of blurted trumpet syllables, timpani and siren with a magnified pythonic voice which might either be bush divination or a public-address loudspeaker heard at a distance. Other things are less equivocal. *Warm night blues stroll* develops from a closely miked bass walk into a sequence of free-jazz collectives with splendid work from Favors, Bowie and Moye. *RM express* is jazz drumming throughout. *New York is full of lonely people* reshuffles recollections of the 1969 *People in sorrow* (Nessa [A] 3) which achieved a kind of poetic realism through which every sound could be the evocation of a thing or experience, the signal of some particular scene or space; an exactness of art which at certain stages centred its attention so closely to the reality evoked that, for example, the child's voice complaining about the rats in the walls became the focus, naïve yet true, of the framing artistry.

Bowie's role is much more extended in this later piece, the dry intervals of disregarded speech are exclusively in the trumpet voice. If there is enigma in *Ancestral meditation*, it is found chiefly at the beginning where it is for some time uncertain whether anything is happening at all. Silence is allowed its 'word' – or is it *quite* silence? Sounds grow almost imperceptibly out of the looming syllable of throbbing conch shells, sounds less variegated than those which gradually overlay the tamboura-like monotone in *Peter and Judith*, and the meditation is cut off by the street dirge from another channel of ancestry which introduces *Uncle*, a saga of extemporaneous techniques which contains some of Mitchell's and Jarman's lengthiest and most exciting saxophone work on the record. The *Odwalla* theme is a jazz celebration in twisted minor-key riff patterns which gives everyone a change to savour the kind of jazz exuberance which has lately predominated in the repertoire of Bowie's *Brass Fantasy*. The musicians are presented to the audience by another pythonic voice, and the concert ends.

Urban Bushmen is perhaps the best compendium of the Art Ensemble's range of unconventional visions, more consistent in achievement than later recordings – for instance *The Third Decade* on ECM (G) 1273 – in which they sometimes yield to the temptation luring artists who have captured devotees by their inspirations into assuming a right to test them at great length by their obsessions. In a crowded panorama it is not easy to single out individuals for praise, but after several hearings it is the playing of Bowie and Favors that satisfies most in retrospect. E.T.

David Murray

434 Ming

Black Saint (It) BSR0045

Olu Dara (tpt); Lawrence 'Butch' Morris (cnt); George Lewis (tbn); Henry Threadgill (alt); Murray (ten, bs clt); Anthony Davis (p); Wilbur Morris (b); Steve McCall (d). New York, 25 and 28 July 1980.
The fast life · The hill · Ming · Jasvan · Dewey's circle

Murray gained attention towards the end of the 1970s as a post-Ayler traditionalist working within the structured environment of the World Saxophone Quartet and through a series of ad hoc 'out-to-lunch' blowing dates with small ensembles. From the beginning of his career, Murray recorded prolifically and if his first album, *Low Class Conspiracy* (Adelphi), revealed a tendency to fall back on borrowings from Ayler and various AACM (see **435**) and BAG artists, subsequent albums such as *Live at the Lower Manhattan Ocean Club* Vols. 1 and 2 India Navigation [A] IN1032 and 1044) and *Last of the Hipmen* (Red Record [It] VPA129) did nothing to dispel the impression of a somewhat *déjà vu* third-generation 'new' music. His best work up to this point had been with the World Saxophone Quartet (**390**), whose fast company prodded him beyond emulation mode to reveal more of himself.

As the 1980s approached, Murray began to moderate his kamikaze approach to improvisation; as a member of James 'Blood' Ulmer's Music Revelation Ensemble and Jack DeJohnette's Special Edition, he began to seek more form and structure in solos, moving away from squeakaphonics towards such pillars of saxophone rectitude as Paul Gonsalves, Ben Webster and Coleman Hawkins, declaring: 'The music has to start swinging again. People don't want music they have to suffer through.' [95] Aside from directing his energies into expanding his emotional and technical control of the saxophone, he also sought to develop a context for his playing rather than the blowing dates and solo recitals that had characterized his work to that point. Initially he wanted to form a big band along the lines of the ensemble he presented at a series of concerts at New York's Public Theatre and Howard University in 1978, but was thwarted by economics. Instead he formed an octet that succeeded in creating a series of emotionally mature statements that are among the most enduring from the 1980s.

Initially the group was built around the AACM trio Air of Threadgill, Morris and McCall, to which was added an impressive roster of instrumentalists associated with the avant-garde, including the brassmen Morris, Dara and Lewis and the pianist Anthony Davis. *Ming* is the first of three important statements by Murray's octet; the others being *Home* (Black Saint [It] BSR 0055) and *Murray's Steps* (Black Saint [It] BSR 0065), either of which might have been discussed here. [96] The opening track, *The fast life*, alternates a fanfarelike theme with a vamp at a very brisk tempo. [97] The sections are of irregular length and often vary, so it is possible that the move from one section to the other is done on cue. Solos are over a pedal point which is interpreted very freely by the improvisers. After the exposition of the themes, the ensemble dissolves into a free section, but remains in time, from which Murray emerges with a solo that reflects the evangelical fervour of his late 1970s period, reaching into the saxophone's hysterical range, those freakishly high notes just before sound disappears into a dog whistle. Butch Morris is, in comparison, much more lyrical, content to operate from the middle range of his instrument. Perhaps the most striking solo of the piece is that by Davis, a virtuoso player, who makes use of extensive side-slipping, polytonality and irregular metre. His own work with his group Episteme is, in comparison, much more subdued, moving improvisation within formal, pre-set structures that merge European classical and Asian traditions. Here his work is explosive, moving to the very doorstep of Cecil Taylor's personal universe. McCall leads into the final section with a solo that seems to push the beat in several ways at once, the ensemble cohesion loose and polyphonic, the textures vivid and unforgettable.

Murray had recorded *The hill* in both solo and quartet versions, but this version, fully fleshed out and more contemplative, leads in slowly with a simmering duet between Morris's *arco* bass and Murray's bass clarinet, with McCall implying a pulse rather than an explicit beat. Gradually the whole ensemble move into the gathering turbulence which gradually builds into a cauldron of interlocking lines, some confused, some jagged and some simple, bubbling *ostinato*s topped by Threadgill elegantly cutting through the groundswell before a stark fanfare announces the completion of the odyssey. *Ming* is a sumptuous Ellington-through-Mingus ballad dedicated to Murray's wife, with a graceful Lewis solo evoking the richness of Lawrence Brown. *Jasvan* swings with optimistic fervour in ¾, Murray providing the outline theme which is then expressed freely by the collective, giving the impression of several bristling lines at work simultaneously. Once again Lewis is featured, his long, flowing lines and resourceful imagination setting the stage for equally melodic 'inside' solos from Murray, Morris, Threadgill, Daru (muted), Davis and Wilbur Morris. In contrast to his solo on *The fast life*, Davis reveals a mastery of the tenets of swing, his lines full of poise and purpose revealing a well-rounded musician.

The exceptionally engaging *Dewey's circle* employs the good old-fashioned backbeat that gets the ensemble rocking, and although this is primarily an Olu Daru tribute to Armstrong, one of the arresting points of the performance comes during passages of ensemble improvisation, touching base with New Orleans polyphony and a wild Mingus brawl. There is a rambunctious edge to this music, which achieved an autonomous character that was at the heart of its effectiveness. By mixing avant-garde rawness with a variety of approaches that spanned the vast legacy of jazz, Murray's music rang with truth as much as it redefined the tradition. In many ways it represented a counter-culture to 1980s neotraditionalism simply by redefining tradition rather than merging with it. S.N.

Muhal Richard Abrams

435 Colours in Thirty-third

†Black Saint (It) BSR1091

John Purcell (sop, ten, bs clt); John Blake (vln[1]); Abrams (p); Fred Hopkins (bs); Dave Holland (cel[2], bs); Andrew Cyrille (d). New York City, 19 December 1986.

Drumman Cyrille · *Miss Richards* · *Munktmunk* · *Soprano song*[1] · *Piano-cello song*[2] · *Colours in thirty-third*[1,2] · *Introspection*[1,2]

Abrams's work is almost certainly less celebrated than that of numerous men who came under his influence and drew invaluable practical support from the Association for the Advancement of Creative Musicians, of which Abrams was a founder in 1960s Chicago. Among these beneficiaries are the members of the Art Ensemble of Chicago (**433**), Henry Threadgill (**436**), Anthony Braxton (**467**) and George Lewis (**392**, **464**). Abrams is as considerable a musician as any of these; of immense importance for the understanding of the intense experimental and didactic purposes which towards the close of the 1960s increasingly aimed at 'forging an orchestral syntax for what used to be called free jazz'. [98]

Cyrille's early influences were separate from Abrams's large 'Experimental Band' and the AACM both in stylistic ambition and in locale. The briskly timed *Drumman Cyrille* has telling evidence of the drummer's kinship with Abrams's ideas. As Cecil Taylor's percussionist in the years up to 1979, he had been a key participant in Taylor's experiment in redefining jazz in ways increasingly shaped by percussive sounds and techniques. Abrams moved to New York in 1979 and recorded with Cyrille about that time. The drummer's natural aptitude for Abrams's kind of musical balance was evidenced in *Chambea* from Abrams's 1981 album *Blues Forever* (†Black Saint [It] BSR0061) and this both in a brilliant free-time solo and in ensemble drumming which is almost entirely predesigned.

Drumman Cyrille is not a special feature for the drummer. It has a whimsical subject celebrating the ensemble and all its angular parts are intriguingly interrelated. Cyrille's solo tails a melodic *pizzicato* from Hopkins, and his drumming is fast, lightsome and beautifully varied. Purcell's alto has full-toned richness but his phrases sound a bit workmanlike. The whimsy returns at the end. *Miss Richards* is a gentle trio. Purcell ranges the bass clarinet's registers, making it sound altolike and occasionally piccololike in its upper reaches. Hopkins supports unassumingly with sustained tones emphasizing a pastoral mood. Abrams's part has a sombre edge as he calls upon the romantically indolent colourings preserved in his wide stylistic repertoire. In *Drumman Cyrille* his solo sounds very much like the headlong single-note rapidities strung together by a previous jazz pedagogue, Lennie Tristano (**293**, **294**) and emulated by Bill Evans in certain of George Russell's renowned flashes of jazz histrionics (**380**, **478**).

The oblique unisons of the march *Munktmunk* are just a little less agitated than those of the first piece. Cyrille maintains military regularity most of the time, but Hopkins, much less bound by rhythm chores, makes his part increasingly relevant to ensemble proceedings. There are stretches of tentative collectivism and here Purcell's tenor is effective. The leader's keyboard peroration is magisterial and deliberately unjazzy some of the time. *Soprano song* has a cursorial theme line which piano and soprano present in fleet unison. Then follow solos heeding a fairly strict code of variation in relation to the stated subject. Blake's violin enters the fray here with well-turned and potent measures. It is nicely in spirit with the soprano's lines which Purcell gives a churlish sort of edge. Hopkins and Cyrille work with immense panache in the initially strutting title piece. Strong work from everyone, Blake and Holland included, makes this perhaps the most successful piece of all. Alto and fiddle solos precede some of Abrams's most pugnacious pianism, running lines which race into free-time complexity in a manner which appears revelatory both of this man's orchestral instincts and of the 'syntax' he aims at. Toward the end Hopkins, who has with Cyrille accompanied the others with marvellously swinging élan, is left completely on his own to fashion a solo which lapses quite naturally into meditative irregularity without sounding in any way ambiguous. Sparely arranged ensemble swiftness resumes briefly with Abrams confirming a few already suspected brainwaves.

The breadth of the AACM didactic would certainly include study of musical creativity beyond jazz. *Piano-cello song*, Holland's and Abrams's duet, is evidence of this ecumenism. Imaginatively fashioned, beautifully played, it is not by any current stretch of the imagination jazz. But *Introspection*, with its strategy of composing with a non-jazz sense of space and movement for a fully engaged ensemble of jazz-conditioned players, is enough of an unexpected sort of hybrid to seem much more persuasive than the duet.

A possible comment might be that *Introspection* is, among its fugitive kin, a slightly better success than several of Abrams's attempts at redefining jazz per se. One can often guess, approvingly, at what he aims for; less often is one sure that he has arrived at it. This is well regarded as one of his finest recordings to date. *Colours in Thirty-third*, with its tantalizing games of variety in similarity and tightrope-walking along narrow frontiers, is close to essential listening. The Muhal is said to be a reluctant interviewee, better pleased to let his music and musicians do his explaining. As all but the proudest commentator should say – so be it! E.T.

Henry Threadgill

436 The Henry Threadgill Sextet: You Know the Number

RCA (F) PL83013

Rasul Sadik (tpt); Frank Lacy (tbn); Threadgill (alt, bs fl); Diedre Murray (cel); Fred Hopkins (bs); Pheeroan Ak Laff, Reggie Nicholson (d, perc). New York City, 12–13 October 1986.

Bermuda blues · *Silver and gold, baby, silver and gold* · *Theme from Thomas Cole* · *Good times* · *To be announced* · *Paille Street* · *Those who eat cookies*

For 'sextet', read 'septet' or, if you like, 'Threadgill plus sextet', although the latter would mislead. Threadgill, though master of the project, functions as part of the troupe and has taken the creative levelling – 'up' and 'down' – of instrumental functions within the post-hard-bop combination into new fields of experiment. In the 1960s he was a hard bopster in Chicago along with fellows who like him would later, with Rafael Garret and Muhal Richard Abrams, play with the so-called Experimental Band, a rehearsal outfit, and share in the formation of the Association for the Advancement of Creative Musicians.

His appearance as David Murray's altoist on **434** and on that octet's 1982 *Murray's Steps* (†Black Saint [It] BSR0065) is typical of the company he was keeping, and of a shared commitment toward original concentrations shaped of possibilities which a decade of post-Coltrane freedom had occasionally allowed to career into thickets of self-indulgence. But it is on his gifts as an innovative leader that Threadgill's 1980s repute should be assessed. Innovation in ensemble sound begins, of course, with instrumentation, and the line-up of two brass, two strings, two drummers and one mildly multivoiced reedsman is marshalled in ways that prove Threadgill a marvellous colourist as well as an acute transmuter of styles.

There should be no doubt in any listener's mind that his and his well-knit ensemble's work is firmly in the jazz continuum – though Threadgill himself is insouciant about categories. Yes, there are episodes now and then whose dialect smacks of the slightly Germanic strutting which is the liking of the Breuker Kollektief (**320**) and such. An album cover photograph that poses the musicians on a bandstand is agreeably apt. One senses a delight in a multifarious band tradition which, far older than jazz, has fed jazz growth and can remind the new jazz of international parallels; but the soil of the Threadgill rooting is rich in a fecundity as American as Morton's or Ellington's inspiration. (A healthy reminder when the rock culture permits the most unlikely sets of performers to pose as 'bands'!)

The typical inner balances of the ensemble in *To be announced*, where the horns' stuttering unisons and more shifting alliances vie excitingly with an analogous quasi-ensemble of drumming and *pizzicato* string playing, reflect a strand of Threadgill's formation in the 1970s when his interest was strongly drawn towards percussive techniques. In addition to off-beat, indeed almost folksy experimentation with reconstituted junkyard findings, he began to approach band composition from a percussionist's point of view. 'Writing from the drums,' he has called this. 'I'm writing music . . . as if I were a drummer. Sometimes I go from the bass, but right now I'm involved in writing from the drums.' [99] That thinking of this kind, in addition to furthering the abolition of rhythm-section apartheid, aids a new kind of jazz-ensemble strategy will be clear from the items in *You Know the Number* and other of Threadgill's 1980s albums. 'It changes the whole frame of reference in terms of what accompaniment is all about . . . It kind of kills accompaniment and puts everything on an equal footing. And that's what I'm after.' The *pizzicato* of Hopkins and Miss Murray, with drumming from Ak Laff and Nicholson, leads in *Bermuda blues* which has a non-blueslike tune – more like a work song for the liberated – declaimed by the three horns. In the development of this Hopkins, who with Threadgill and the drummer Steve McCall made up the 1970s trio Air, shows how closely attuned he is to the leader's notions. Piquant viol voice introduces the threnodic *Silver and gold, baby, silver and gold*, its complaint led affectingly by the altoist and as affectingly harmonized for the other instruments with bass *arco*. The cellist steers the interior parts; but her most open opportunity happens in *Paille Street*, a composition heard on the 1979 album *Air Lore*, where it was slotted between Morton and Joplin numbers. It is a moody commemoration of Threadgill's one-time penchant for funereal themes.

Theme from Thomas Cole has Lacy and Hopkins in unison and Sadik committing a tactic of contradiction. Lacy becomes prominent prior to the precipitous close, after the ensemble, challenging the ear to distinguish between debate and debacle, has demonstrated one aspect at least of a satisfying ability to realize syntheses of free improvisation with orchestration. The formal aspects can be both rigorous and wily, and this hot, swivelling theme itself suggests some of the wiliness.

Good times generates tremendous dancing excitement. The propulsive property of the riff is unearthed by horns and strings while the drummers' magnificent forays trundle and threaten. Again anarchy is geared to the ensemble form-drama. Lacy cries savagely with a vividness matched by Sadik's high-register aviation. Beyond the crude fanfares and mocking staccatos that climax *To be announced* lies pale *Paille Street*; and then *Those who eat cookies*, marchlike, in a procession more rapid, more flashingly heraldic than anything preceding. The protrusive voices, a blurting Threadgill and a squalling Sadik in the main, leap out of a restless thresh whose brash repetitions of old, nameless jazz tags eventually taper down to delicate bass and cello pluckings.

Precedent to *You Know the Number*, the album *Just the Facts and Pass the Bucket* was a rather less compulsive 1983 airing for the same instrumental grouping with certain different musicians. (The excellent Diedre Murray would remain characteristically important to the phonetics of the band.) Later came *Easily Slip into Another World* (†RCA [A] 83025, 1987) and *Rag, Bush and All* (†RCA [A] 83052, 1988), each with some personnel variants. Given that Threadgill appears to have changed tack and albums appearing after 1988 have new instrumental combinations, it seems reasonable to regard this as a sequence with its own particular character, to which **436** is a choice introduction. Threadgill's safari into the future is, however, something of which it is well worth keeping track. E.T.

Pharoah Sanders

437 Live

Theresa (A) TR116

Sanders (ten, vcl); John Hicks (p); Walter Booker (bs); Idris Muhammad (d). San Francisco, 12 April 1982.

You've got to have freedom · Easy to remember

Same personnel. Santa Cruz, 20 April 1982.

Blues for Santa Cruz · Pharomba

John Zorn, at a period when he was experimenting in public with the various noises he could make with saxophone mouthpieces, both with and without buckets of water, explained that what he was doing took its inspiration from the 'sound-players' of the 1960s. This borrowing of Ekkehard Jost's famous phrase referred to such musicians as Shepp, Ayler and Pharoah Sanders. In 1965 it represented the front-line trenches of the 'New Thing', where critique brought up in less revolutionary times was asked to make one final push in the name of the superiority of the avant-garde. Those who pulled through wore their battle scars with pride, particularly in Europe, which became a willing host to free jazz; and since the 1960s it has represented one of the few areas of jazz to be significantly developed and extended beyond the borders of the United States. Abstraction, energy and 'spontaneous interaction' that often abandoned harmony or rhythm or both, became valued as the ultimate form of jazz expressionism. For many, the subsequent evolution of jazz seemed anticlimactic in comparison and post-free developments were viewed with great suspicion as the 1980s approached and the hard-earned terrain of freedom was incrementally reclaimed by the forces of melody, harmony and rhythm.

But while European freedom, with its arcane preoccupation with the radical and, one might unkindly add, the marginal, gathered momentum, in the United States the 'New Thing' eventually ran its course, retrenching in a series of artists' collectives. Sanders, one of the main players associated with energy and abstraction, subsequently came to wonder what Coltrane saw in his playing, and, viewing his work as immature, set off in an entirely new direction. What he and others, including Shepp, realized was that after almost 20 years of levelling the block, the time had come for rebuilding, and by the end of the 1970s musicians began exploring ways of reconciling the putative opposites of 'inside' and 'outside' playing. Sanders's arrival at this confluence was by a long and hard path. His high-energy approach at the end of the 1960s with Leon Thomas and Sonny Sharrock and a group that included the pianist Lonnie Liston Smith saw him being hailed as Coltrane's heir and the very future of jazz. But his subsequent series of albums on the Impulse label, which included hypnotic *ostinatos*, religious chants, tinkling bells and invocations, were overwhelmed by developments elsewhere in jazz.

He made no recordings under his own name between 1974 and 1980, although he flirted with disco music in the late 1970s with Norman Connors. [100] However, in the early 1980s he returned to active performance and recording with a sharply focused aesthetic that reconciled 'late-period Coltrane' within the broader context of the totality of his playing experiences that included blues and rhythm 'n' blues, the tranquil moments of karma from his Impulse period and bop.

The result was a series of highly praised albums for the Theresa label, of which *Live* is perhaps the most dramatic and striking. The reason is the exceptional empathy he developed with his nonpareil rhythm section of Hicks, Booker and Muhammed during the course of a two-week tour of the West Coast when this album was recorded. *You've got to have freedom* is based on a repeated two-bar vamp that explodes into life with Sanders outlining the two-bar riff in multiphonic shrieks. Multiphonics is playing two or more notes simultaneously – effectively playing chords on the saxophone – and the urgency of his clarion cry is echoed by the rhythm section. As so often happens, live performance can create an adrenaline-charged atmosphere that can never be reproduced in the recording studio. This is one of the few records that capture the sheer energy-as-a-life-giving-force that can be experienced on so many of Coltrane's live albums. Hicks, at his best an expansive and totally riveting soloist, who can be curiously reticent when recording under his own name, here contributes one of his more memorable moments on disc. Like McCoy Tyner's, his fingering technique is exceptionally powerful, yet without sacrificing the darting speed associated with Bud Powell. As his left hand outlines the basic two-bar riff, his right utilizes all the resources of the keyboard with beautifully balanced runs that swirl in and out of the basic rhythm, gradually developing quite specific counter-rhythms which, together with his use of chord extensions, create a subtle polyphony that adds to the mounting tension, which is only resolved by Sanders's re-entry. His solo is one of contrast; the subtle tone he employed on the Impulse titles with lambastes of 'energy' riffing. Throughout Booker and Muhammad are exceptionally alert, Booker employing double-stop glissandos while Muhammad superbly anticipates Hicks's block-chorded accompaniment with dramatic accents.

The group return to terra firma with *Easy to remember*, which reveals Sanders as a profound interpreter of ballads. The grave beauty of his tone is not captured live to the extent that it was in the studio, as on *Central Park West* from *Rejoice* (†Evidence [A] ECD22020–2) for example; but it is nevertheless sufficient to invest his performance with a majestic grace to which few contemporary saxophonists aspire. For his part, Hicks, a wonderfully energetic pianist, had by this point in his career found an equally expressive voice at slow tempos and provides a wholly sympathetic foil for the saxophonist's introspection. *Blues for Santa Cruz* not only shows how resilient the 12-bar structure has been to survive in jazz for so long, but also confirms that it has continually provided an inspiring basis for improvisation with jazz musicians from all eras and styles. Hicks opens at a medium tempo, with Booker's line a model of taste and construction which he sustains on every chorus. Sanders enters with a simple riff which he then takes apart and reconstructs in a variety of ways, gradually building to a powerful climax that touches base with his rhythm-'n'-blues days; this is powerful stuff, moving from vertical patterns at the beginning of his solo and climaxing the performance with swathes of horizontal lines that lead into the initial riff. Without letting the tension of the performance slacken, Hicks sustains the groove with magnificent sweeping runs charging through several choruses that bristle with energy and ideas. A brief respite comes during Booker's solo, before a final Sanders backlash where he contributes a few choruses of blues-shouting in a voice that seems, like his chants in *You've got to have freedom*, about to split into a vocal multiphonic.

Pharomba is a ten-bar AB tune which contrasts a six-bar A section against a rumba rhythm with a four-bar straight-ahead B section. Here Sanders is more reflective, his solo returning to his bop roots and his tone full and round, yet with the curiously sour edge he invokes as his phrasing gathers in intensity, making full use of the contrasting rhythmic sections of the song's construction. Once again Hicks's crisp poise sustains, then builds on the momentum of Sanders's solo; he is a greatly underrated soloist, whose fine playing can be heard on albums by Betty Carter (**332**), Arthur Blythe and David Murray among others. [101]

Sanders's growth as an artist, from his 'sound-making' shrieks and his own acknowledgement that chords did not interest him, to a player working within the constraints of harmony, melody and rhythm, in many ways mirrors the realignment of the avant-garde with the jazz mainstream that occurred during the early 1980s as 'free' became one element among many in an artist's performing personality. Here, the juxtaposition of the raw, primal screams of *You've got to have freedom* within the context of his more conventional playing gives the music an exciting edge, the possibility that his playing could erupt with such power and energy at any moment creating an inherent tension, which Sanders exploited to the full, so that when he unleashed another burst at the end of his solo the drama is framed, the tension resolved. This rambunctious music and the acknowledgement that rhythm still provided a compelling threat to rationality was part of a general realization among free players that to avoid rhythmic impulse was to wilfully ignore the source of its effectiveness. S.N.

Ornette Coleman

438 Of Human Feelings

Antilles AN2001

Coleman (alt); Bern Nix, Charlie Ellerbee (el g); Rudy McDaniel (Jamaaladeen Tacuma) (el bs); Denardo Coleman, Calvin Weston (d). New York, 25 April 1979.

Sleep talk · *Jump street* · *Him and her* · *Air ship* · *What is the name of that song?* · *Job mob* · *Love words* · *Times Square*

In December 1962 Ornette Coleman staged a concert at New York's Town Hall, capping the evening, to everybody's surprise, with a performance featuring a rhythm-'n'-blues group, that included a technically accomplished drummer and a virtuoso bassist. On the one hand he was returning to his rhythm-'n'-blues upbringing in road bands in Texas, but on the other he was seeking an allegory of the past, present and future of jazz. It was a concept that he did not forget. Yet three and a half years after his 1959 Five Spot debut he had all but retired from performing and recording, only to return in 1965 to reveal an artisan skill on trumpet and violin and to feature the rudimentary drumming of his nine-year-old son Denardo. Subsequently he incrementally added to his reputation for controversy with an excursion into chamber music at his famous British concert on 29 August 1967 and with a magnum opus, the puzzling *Skies of America*, from 1972. By that time the achievements of his early work with Don Cherry, Charlie Haden and Billy Higgins and, later, Ed Blackwell (**400**) were beginning to be absorbed into jazz.

While Coleman worked only intermittently in the early 1970s, the main thrust of free jazz had passed to an unlikely source, Miles Davis. Having put down free jazz in general and Coleman in particular, in a U-turn to end all U-turns Davis led an electronic free-jazz ensemble that included Chick Corea at the piano between 1970 and 1971. Away from the recording studios, Davis was exploring free jazz with a vengeance, a music of random associations, fragmented ideas and swirling textures where rock rhythms were bent in and out of shape like images glimpsed in a hall of mirrors. Many writers dubbed it 'space jazz', a term that derived from the music of György Ligeti and the way that composer used bleeps, chirps and oscillating sounds on the soundtrack of the motion picture *2001.* Less charitably, the term was also used to denote music to get 'spaced out' to. In any event, Davis was far from pandering to teenage tastes; this was hardly music for Adorno's 'humming millions' [102] and was as remote from the expectations of jazz fans in one direction as it was for rock fans in another, resulting in a complete paradox, with jazz fans thinking it was rock and rock fans imagining it was jazz. Davis's free jazz-rock added another dialect to the multi-tongued music in which Coleman had by then become something of an occasional participant.

In 1975 Coleman appeared to wipe the slate clean and start all over again. In his first recording since 1972's *Skies of America* (Columbia [A] 31562), [103] Coleman assembled an electronic band of unknowns to espouse yet another dialect, harmolodics. *Dancing in Your Head* (†A&M [A] CDA0807), from December 1975, although released in the summer of 1977, collapsed the melody of *The good life*, a bluesy theme from *Skies of America*, into a near nursery-rhyme chant renamed *Theme from a symphony*. Once again, however, Coleman refused to play *en règle*; the backdrop against which he was now performing, a squabble of competing electronic voices in different keys and metres, was dominated by funky rhythm-section patterns.

Today the very vitality and vigour of Coleman's electronic music appears to overshadow the ambient shapelessness of Miles Davis's electric free-jazz experiments such as *Black Beauty* (†CBS Sony [J] 28AP 21556), *Double Image* (Moon Records [It] MLP010/11), *Live at Fillmore* (CBS [A] CG30038) and, later in 1975, his pre-furlough albums *Pangaea* (†CBS/Sony 4670872) and *Agharta* (†CBS/Sony 4678972). These reflected the trumpeter's progressive disenchantment with jazz – and he too took a leave of absence from performing and recording, from 1975 to 1981. In contrast, Coleman's music, despite its inscrutability, seemed to realize his 1962 Town Hall dream. Significantly, Coleman's saxophone dominated. The simple head of *Theme from a symphony* was repeated over and over and was followed by a long, intense solo that perhaps more than any other revealed his close links with the blues in its earthy realism and emotional force. 'People have started asking me if I'm really a rhythm-'n'-blues player,' said Coleman in 1981, 'and I always say, why, sure. To me rhythm is the oxygen that sits under the notes and moves them along and blues is the colouring of those notes, how they're interpreted in an emotional way.' [104]

Body Meta (Artists House [A] AH1), recorded at the same time as *Dancing in Your Head*, lacked the latter's jarring focus, sounding perhaps more like a work in progress, albeit exploring more moods. Although these electronic albums at the time appeared as a radical departure from his acoustic work, Coleman had in fact had allowed an electric guitar across the threshold in the early 1970s in the person of Jim Hall (*Broken Dreams*, Columbia [A] FC 38029), but that album was not released until 1982. Consequently the radical realignment of his music appeared fully formed and without precedent when it was originally released in the 1970s. Yet Coleman's approach to improvising had changed little; indeed, the explicit rhythmic pulse in his music could even be traced back to 1961's *T & T* (**400**).

Although much has been made of his harmolodic theories, when Coleman himself attempted to explain its principles it was impossible to decipher what he meant. [105] Total understanding and comprehension of these or of harmolodic music itself, remained tantalizingly beyond one's grasp. But what these albums made clear was the primacy of melody (Coleman's saxophone) over rhythm. Since any system of cadences was abandoned in favour of polymodality, several simultaneous tonal centres of independent counterpoint allowed Coleman's melodic brief to roam free on the impulse of the moment, the rhythm section converging around him in a way that forsook traditional harmonic thinking, acting instead like a drum choir. His melodic sense was never constrained by the mode or tonal centre he was in at a given moment, yet, as *Theme from a symphony* – both takes – demonstrated, a sense of thematic organization and development was ever present in his playing, something that could be traced back to his first recordings. Supposedly the antithesis of free jazz, it suggested that some of the conclusions that have been drawn from his playing were in need of revision.

With the release of *Of Human Feelings*, Coleman presented a far more cogent statement than was realized in either *Dancing in Your Head* or *Body Meta*. Here was a visceral intensity that was just as focused as any of his acoustic recordings. It was Coleman's claim that anyone in the band was free to solo or play rhythm at any time, and this took the form of free collective improvisation. As early as 1960, in the liner notes to *Free Jazz* (**400**), Coleman had said: 'The most important thing was for us to play together all at the same time, without getting in each other's way and also have enough room for each player to ad-lib alone.' Almost 20 years later the principles remained the same, albeit regrouped around a funky backbeat. Coleman, the major soloist and voice of reason within the ensemble, had his band reacting with greater clarity to his playing than on the previous two albums and, as he intended, his music communicated. *Love words* made it clear that no limitations were imposed on the use of polymodality, the heart of harmolodics. Coleman, having set mood and tempo, launches out on an extended improvisation that appears free of predetermined harmonic relationships against a backdrop suggesting West African rhythmic complexity in its dense textures and a collective spirit of improvisation that could be traced back to New Orleans jazz. *Sleep talk* seems to have been derived from the opening bassoon solo in Stravinsky's *The Rite of Spring*, and emerges as a genial excursion that can be returned to time and again. Early Coleman laments such as *Lonely woman* and *Sadness* are echoed in the first section of *What is the name of that song?* before being claimed by a contrasting funky section. *Times Square* is an atonal strut, a surreal excursion into a 22nd-century dance music, a testament to Coleman's race to keep one step ahead of history. Yet, as always in Coleman's playing, the blues remained at the heart of his music; *Jump street* is a blues with a bridge.

Coleman's music with Prime Time continued into the 1990s, and another good representation of his style, plus a return to earlier acoustic triumphs with Cherry, Haden and Billy Higgins, can be found on 1987's *In All Languages* (†Dreams [A] 008). Suggestions that he may have been aiming for a more accessible variation of his electronic music came with 1987's *Virgin Beauty* (Columbia Portrait [A] PRT4611931), which had Grateful Dead's Jerry Garcia drafted in on guitar and an overt rock mix to his music. Interestingly, 1995's *Tone Dialling* (†Verve [A] 527 483–2) contained vocals, but even this could not conceal the raw, avant edge to the group. It suggested that even free jazz had not been able to disengage itself from the entertainment infrastructure within which jazz was still constrained, despite the stance of the bop pioneers – not least Charlie Parker, whom Coleman deeply admired – of creating a music more concerned with artistic excellence than commercial consideration. It seemed that the high aspirations of cutting the music free from the consumption of mass audiences had now turned full circle and with it the great irony that the greatest free-jazz musician, within the conventions of his own integrity, was in search of, if not a mass audience, then a much larger constituency than was customarily associated with free music. What was remarkable for this area of music was that, in his own way, Coleman succeeded, losing some adherents but gaining more en route. S.N.

Pat Metheny/Ornette Coleman

439 **Song X**
†Geffen Records (A) 924 096–2

Coleman (alt, vln); Metheny (g, g-synth); Charlie Haden (bs); Jack DeJohnette (d); Denardo Coleman (d, perc). New York City, 12–14 December 1985.
Song X · *Mob job* · *Endangered species* · *Video games* · *Kathelin Gray* · *Trigonometry* · *Long time no see*

Metheny (g, g-synth); Haden (b). Same date.
Song X duo

While the Pat Metheny Group consciously projected a commercially accessible appeal that went beyond the jazz constituency, it also concealed Metheny's intense commitment to jazz, fulfilled in a variety of absorbing associations, none more so than this with Coleman. Metheny's love of Coleman's music began in childhood and was a recurring theme on his more uncompromising jazz albums, which always included at least one Coleman composition, something that dated back to his debut as a leader on record, *Bright Size Life* (†ECM 1073) from December 1975, with *Round trip/Broadway blues*. One of the finest guitarists in jazz, Metheny was a child prodigy and was teaching guitar at the University of Miami at 17 and was a faculty member of Berklee College of Music at 19. He was with Gary Burton during 1974–6 and as his career gathered momentum, financial security was assured with the success of the Pat Metheny Group. However, in 1980 he recorded a highly regarded double album with an impressive cast which included Dewey Redman, Mike Brecker, Haden and DeJohnette, *80/81* (ECM [G] 1180/81). It marked his initial association on record with the bassist Haden, a key member of Coleman's early groups, and was renewed on the trio album *Rejoicing* (†ECM 817 795–2), where they were joined by the drummer Billy Higgins. On it, Metheny included three Coleman compositions, but it was his handling of his original composition, *The calling*, that revealed a steely edge to his playing which evoked Jimi Hendrix through James 'Blood' Ulmer. While his more temperate listeners were left somewhat shell-shocked, it prefigured his playing two years later on *Song X*.

Metheny's meeting with Coleman was aided and abetted by Haden, who saw in the ingenious guitarist and the inscrutable saxophonist two views of a similar vision. Although Coleman's harmolodic partisanship had embraced electronic tone colours and pumping body rhythms since *Dancing in Your Head* (A&M [A] CDA 0807), his music had received little exposure on record. *Of Human Feelings* from 1979 (**438**), which Coleman claimed to be the first digitally recorded album in jazz, was only the third representation of his new direction prior to *Song X*. Yet none of his electronic albums had, or would have, the same coruscating edge, the same sense of danger or drama as his meeting with Metheny, who together with Haden and DeJohnette brought to Coleman's music the skills, reflexes, technique and imagination of virtuosos in a way that Coleman's Prime Time musicians did not. Despite this, when *Song X* was released in 1986 it was to instant controversy: 'One of the events of the 1980s,' claimed *The Illustrated Encyclopaedia of Jazz*; 'Practically unlistenable,' *The Times* asserted. But in spite of the critical response, it sold some 200,000 copies in the first year of its release, quite astonishing sales for an avant-garde album; and it won the *down beat* readers' poll as Jazz Album of the Year. It suggested that Coleman might be the *vox populi* of free jazz; indeed, since his Five Spot debut in 1959 he quite probably always had been.

On every track of *Song X* Metheny used a Roland GR303 guitar linked to a Synclavier II, a synthesizer with polyphonic sampling capabilities. On the title track, he uses this facility to echo Coleman's alto in tumultuous canon, sounding like two saxes in dialogue. DeJohnette and Haden run away at a crazy tempo, with Metheny shadowing the jagged fragments of Coleman's solo with spiderlike arpeggios in ragged counterpoint. Metheny's solo is in contrast lyrical, refusing to be drawn into the eye of the rhythmic mêlée before Coleman re-enters, his awkward, scurrying phrases bobbing wildly on the froth of the turbulent rhythmic undercurrent before the theme, part cry of anguish and part angry shout, silences the growing drama. In contrast, the jaunty four-to-the-bar lyricism of *Mob job* reaches back to Coleman's early Atlantic sides (**400**).

Even his violin playing, in its early manifestations something more than an acquired taste, moves with a hard-edged angular logic. *Endangered species*, a name later adopted by the group when it went out on tour, is perhaps the most exciting of the album. With a relentless fury that would later become the calling card of John Zorn's group Spy vs. Spy's *Play the Music of Ornette Coleman* (†Elektra Musician 960 844–2) from 1988, the music teems with inner detail yet appears as a primal roar. Metheny's guitar synthesizer emulates violin sounds through most of the piece, and duets in unholy fury with Coleman in a series of collective crescendos before the saxophonist launches a soaring solo, rising clear of the seething undercurrent created by DeJohnette and Metheny's head-to-head duet. The piece is essentially an ensemble drama of ever increasing polyrhythmic resolve conducted by the harmolodic master's intercessorial alto, which mediates rhythmic density, contributes fractured counterpoint and decides the direction of his ensemble. Suddenly he allows the holocaust to relent as DeJohnette and Denardo Coleman slug it out in percussive duet before the theme, in ever growing intensity, returns, swells and finally dies in an arching *rubato*, allowing an episode of percussive afterthoughts to tumble back to earth.

The complexities of sound Metheny is able to draw from his guitar are exemplified by *Video games*, a simple eight-bar theme essayed twice in duet with Coleman before Metheny, using the hiccuping rhythm of the theme as the organizing principle, draws on strange and otherworldly voices that move with increasing complexity through his solo. Coleman abruptly emerges in the sunlight, accompanied by just bass and drums, and immediately suggests the stern majesty that thrust him to centre stage in 1959. That sense of *déjà vu* surfaces in *Kathelin Gray* and *Trigonometry*. The former, a stately duet that revolves around a basic metre of three, features Coleman's full, haunting alto-saxophone tone which refuses to stray too far from the melody in its limping melodicism, with Metheny's voice haloed in simple unison. The latter, a sprightly bop line, has Coleman in elegant mood but somehow forbidding in his poetic lyricism. Metheny, who throughout his career supressed the impulse of mechanical patterns in favour of a well-pruned melodicism, sits well alongside the Coleman of yesterday, today and tomorrow.

The second version of *Song X* is a duo between Coleman and Metheny, who move in concentric circles of harmolodic enquiry with allusions to earthy Delta blues and bop, a recurring element in solos throughout the album; on Coleman's compositions such as *Bird food* his love of Parker was closer than most commentators care to admit. *Long time no see* begins on a rock rhythm-section pattern before dissolving into an opaque head and a restless four under Metheny's clipped lyricism and, surprisingly, an oblique allusion near the end of his solo to the well-known Italian song *Santa Lucia.* Coleman progresses in a series of seemingly unrelated melodic episodes but an unexpected rain of rim shots from Denardo prompts a pithy snatch from *It don't mean a thing* from his father that brings them to a quick end. Metheny re-enters in close-order dialogue as jagged phrases are bounced at Haden and suddenly coalesce into the lumpy theme.

After the recording, Metheny suggested that both in preparation for the session and during the subsequent tour he and Coleman took the music further out than the music represented here, a direction Max Harrison has speculated might be suggested in *Endangered species*. [106] It reveals a breadth to Metheny's talent that otherwise might have lain in the shadow of the Pat Metheny Group and perhaps was an acknowledgement of something he knew all along, that, as Anthony Blanche observed in *Brideshead Revisited*, 'Charm can be fatal to works of art.' S.N.

Last Exit

440 The Noise of Trouble – Live in Tokyo

Enemy (G) EMY103

Akira Sakata (alt, clt); Sonny Sharrock (g); Peter Brötzmann (ten, bar, taragato); Bill Laswell (el bs); Ronald Shannon Jackson (d). Tokyo, 2 October 1986.
Straw dog · You got me rockin' · Take cover · Ma Rainey · Crack butter · Pig cheese · Panzer be-bop · Base metal · Blind Willie · Needless balls · Civil war test

As above, but add Herbie Hancock (p). Same date.
Help me, Mo, I'm blind

When Ornette Coleman unexpectedly embraced electronic tone colours in the mid-1970s, his pan-modal message was taken up by his former sidemen James 'Blood' Ulmer and Jackson, who, with their own ensembles, offered a new spin on the saxophonist's harmolodic rainbow. Ulmer had Coleman himself making a rare appearance as a sideman on his first album as a leader, *Tales of Captain Black* (Artists House [A] AH7) from December 1978, a quartet date that was filled out by members from Coleman's own group. Ulmer was yet to move out of his former leader's shadow. His two subsequent albums, *Are You Glad to Be in America?* (Rough Trade Records [A] Rough 16) and *No Wave* (Moers Music [H] 01072), made by a quartet with David Murray on saxophone collectively called the Music Revelation Ensemble, proved to be stepping stones to a major-label contract with Columbia. In contrast, Jackson's path was more uncompromising. He was the only musician to record with both Ornette Coleman *and* Cecil Taylor, and his curriculum vitae included spells with Betty Carter, Joe Henderson, Jackie McLean and Kinny Dorham. Forming a group called the Decoding Society which became a forum for his hyperactive rhythmic intensity, he mixed electronic and acoustic instruments, rock rhythms and freedom, gritty textures and tightly arranged lines. The nine albums they recorded between 1980 and 1990 were, however, for all their initial angularity and on-the-edge ensemble work, over-reliant on Jackson's powerful rhythmic personality. Even Vernon Reid on guitar and Melvin Gibbs on bass, who both appeared on the earlier albums, seemed unable to command attention in the way their leader did, something for which even the most tightly knit ensemble playing could not compensate.

Jackson's most convincing post-Coleman work came when his creative impulses were matched by an equally commanding musical personality. As a member of Power Tools with Bill Frisell and Melvin Gibbs, he released *Strange Meeting* (Antilles [A] AN 8715) in January 1987. Then Jackson stepped back from the claustrophobic in-fighting of Decoding Society as he and Frisell gave each other space to breathe, a musical stand-off that allowed their mutual creativity to grow in stature. Even more dramatic was Jackson's work with Last Exit, a tornado of a band that represented perhaps the most exciting merger of the crude and complex in jazz. The guitarist Sonny Sharrock, the German saxophonist Peter Brötzmann and the bassist and producer Bill Laswell, who was responsible for mixing the proto-rap Lightin' Rod single *Doriella Du-Fontaine* (a spontaneous jam between Jimi Hendrix, Buddy Miles and Jalal of the Last Poets), took the raw energy of Hendrix, something that Miles Davis had attempted to exploit on *Jack Johnson* (**444**), and expanded it onto a broader canvas. This crowded vision was driven by Jackson's cavalry charges which gave shape to a modernist vision of angst as meaning and ugliness as an aspect of authenticity.

Last Exit broke from calm modernist rationality with their postmodernistic superimposition of past forms upon each other, creating a collage of fragmented musical traditions from the vernacular of rock's heavy metal to the free vistas of avant-garde jazz to create something independent and autonomous. But fragmentation and pluralism pose problems of communication. Modernism accepts a relationship between the message and the signifier. Postmodernism accepts a rather different theory, of 'continually breaking apart and re-attaching in new combinations', [107] so that contemplation of a central theme is no longer the (modernist) issue, but rather recognizing the deconstructionist impulse to look inside one 'text' for another, of dissolving one 'text' into another, or building one 'text' into another. Collage/montage is the primary form of postmodernist discourse; indeed the collision and superimposition of different ontological worlds is a major characteristic of postmodern art. Postmodernism suggests, therefore, that we cannot aspire to any unified representation of the world, which in turn produces a preoccupation with the 'signifier' rather than the 'signified', with participation, performance or happening a central focus rather than an authoritative finished art object. This reduction of experience to 'a series of pure and unrelated presents' is central to the music of Last Exit.

The collage of the past and the present in the mini-suite *Straw dog – You got me rockin' – Take cover – Ma Rainey – Crack butter*, from Jimmy

Reed to Ma Rainey, from heavy metal to Delta blues, from avant-garde jazz to punk rock, functions in the shadow of Hendrix's more deconstructionist urges. These reference points speed by in a dizzying fury of sound; there is the joy and terror of Sharrock's guitar – he once said: 'I've been trying to find a way for the terror and the beauty to live together in one song' [108] – and his is a central force amid the interweaving, or collage, of diverse musical elements. Intensity is achieved as much through the sheer force of the music as by the use of seemingly unrelated 'presents' in time. Yet their use is less through a sense of historical continuity so much as postmodernism's incredible ability to plunder history and absorb whatever it finds there as some aspect of the present. This produces a loss of historical continuity with the tradition, which in turn becomes the leitmotif of the album. Its coruscating effect is more dramatic than the Paris studio date that produced their first album, the eponymously titled *Last Exit* (Enemy [G] EMY101), which equally poses problems in terms of orthodox critical judgement. There is a sense, as Barthes has proposed, of judging the spectacle in terms of how spectacular it is, and in this context it is difficult to imagine postmodernist mores being evinced within the ambit of jazz in more spectacular fashion than by Last Exit.

Although Brötzmann's saxophone advocates less revolutionary impulses than on *Machine Gun* (**412**), Sharrock's guitar is focused, and his blistering speed combined with his use of raw noise suggests both the openness of jazz and the power of rock. Together with Jackson and Laswell, they create an environment where deconstruction can flourish, and, defying explanatory logic, produce a triumph of effect over cause. Yet within the context of jazz, this is ultimately a plunge into a maelstrom of ephemerality, a triumph of surface values over emotional depth. This rigorous emotional fundamentalism works within symbolic structures that draw from the jazz avant-garde as it does from art rock, heavy metal, Jimi Hendrix and punk rock, providing a sense of dislocation and mystery. But even though Swift has cautioned mistaking the wondrous dark for the wondrous deep, one product of postmodernism is that the greater the ephemerality, the more pressing the need to discover or manufacture some kind of truth that might be contained within.

Yet Last Exit, in writing off traditional and historically acquired values, are paradoxically limited by them as well. Their emotional focus is narrow, dwelling on and appealing to one aspect of the human psyche, the appeal of the strong and the ugly. Within such parameters, emotionality becomes a function of fundamental values, and in abandoning the system of cadences built around the well-tempered scale, they are limited to degrees of light or shade; to become more or less ugly, to become more or less loud, to favour more or less abstraction, to become more or less implicit rhythmically. Such loss of temporality and the search for instantaneous impact was marked by a parallel loss of depth, since such impact has no sustaining power over a period of time. Its only recourse was in increasing the intensity of the overall effect, a device to be used with caution lest it appear a contrivance. But if at a purely artistic level, Last Exit poses questions of postmodernism's resignation to bottomless fragmentation – a question it generally refuses to contemplate – then within the arena of 1980s jazz it indicated the futility of the neoclassic attempts to bridge the gap between culture and high culture.

The problem that confronted Wynton Marsalis and his followers and their obdurate rationality within the tradition was the difficulty in exceeding the achievements of their predecessors in the 1950s and 1960s, despite claims, however well meaning, that precisely those achievements should not be forgotten. Ultimately, the young neoclassicists failed to redefine their chosen art in its own terms, since their work existed only as a reconstruction of the past in terms of the present, devoid, most crucially, of the elements that had made the original music subversive and compelling in the first place. Their music, of course, had value as a representation of what jazz used to be, but could not compete with the original recordings it drew its inspiration from, ultimately posing the question of whether it was art at all or merely an artifact analogous to a poster reproduction of a Picasso or a van Gogh. Equally, the problem this posed for the development of jazz was not contemplated, or indeed even addressed, since if jazz was to exist as a repertory function, it implied the music had ceased to be an evolving art form. Yet critical opinion, in general, refused to acknowledge this. It was as if Tom Keating had taken over the fine-art mainstream and was being celebrated for his forgeries of the Italian masters simply because a body of opinion preferred forged Italian masters to what was happening elsewhere in art. Clearly this flip-flop of creative values could never stand up to any sort of serious aesthetic scrutiny, yet remained a problem with which the jazz establishment generally refused to grapple.

In contrast, Last Exit demonstrated that the tradition was there to be used, and, despite the postmodernistic zeal with which they plundered it, they used it to define and redefine their music. Such imagery itself became a focus for innovation, a rallying point for less celebrated areas of jazz to establish its own identity. More importantly, at another level, it represented a vigorous reawakening of the pioneering fervour of the avant-garde, strangely mute through most of the 1980s. For if there is one thing that jazz has always needed, it is a flourishing avant-garde, if only to keep the mainstream honest; and here perhaps was Last Exit's ultimate success. S.N.

Where the Roads Crossed

By the late 1960s the audience jazz traditionally enjoyed among college students had been claimed by the sudden and unexpected rise of popular music and culture triggered by the popularity of the Beatles. Jazz clubs were either closing down or converting into establishments called discotheques. While not exactly casting jazz into outer darkness, the 1960s pop explosion did at least relegate jazz to the commercial twilight, prompting jazz with its usual pragmatism, to set about finding a rapprochement with its distant yet upstart cousin.

Miles Davis

441 Filles de Kilimanjaro
Columbia (A) CS9750

Miles Davis (tpt); Wayne Shorter (ten); Herbie Hancock (p); Ron Carter (bs); Tony Williams (d). New York City, 19–21 June 1968.
Tout de Suite · Petits Machins (Little Stuff) · Filles de Kilimanjaro

Davis (tpt); Shorter (ten); Chick Corea (p); David Holland (bs); Williams (d). New York City, 24 September 1968.
Frelon brun (Brown hornet) · Mademoiselle Mabry (Miss Mabry)

Wayne Shorter joined the Miles Davis quintet in September 1964, the catalyst to what would subsequently become Davis's most creative and artistically satisfying period in a long career that did not lack for musical incident. Before Shorter's arrival, Davis had been playing to a script that had evolved since the 1950s, a mixture of standards (such as *Autumn leaves, My funny Valentine, Stella by starlight*), blues (such as *Straight, no chaser, Walkin'*) and original jazz compositions (such as *So what?, Joshua* and *Oleo*). With the exception of *Joshua* (see **397** Phil Woods), these songs honoured the system of cadences common within popular song forms such as AABA and AB. However, Shorter's writing style soon had a profound effect in changing the sound of the Davis quintet, contributing numbers that featured unusual combinations of harmonies – he was one of the few jazz musicians in the 1960s to use sustained b9 chords, or 'sus chords', then a relatively new sound in jazz harmony – and subtle, undramatic themes that seldom used bridges, turnarounds or common cadences [109] found within popular song-forms.

In January 1965 Davis recorded *E.S.P.* (Columbia [A] CS9150) and the impact of Shorter's writing style is immediately apparent on the group. Davis recorded seven original compositions, and although only two are from Shorter, it is clear that Carter, Hancock and Davis, who contributed the balance, quickly adapted to the musical direction Shorter proposed. The music on this album is quite different from any of Davis's previous work, and what is immediately apparent is how quickly the band had distanced itself from the popular song-form since Shorter's arrival. [110] Shorter's compositions favoured simple schemes, such as the all-A, 16-bar themes of *E.S.P.*, and, from later albums, *Iris, Nefertiti* and *Dolores* (all from *The Complete Columbia Studio Recordings of the Miles Davis Quintet 1965–68* [†Columbia/Legacy (A) AC6K 67398]). [111]

A characteristic of Shorter's compositions for Davis became how the burden of complexity was passed from the front line to the rhythm section. In bop and hard bop, complex themes were the province of the front line, while the accompaniment provided by piano, bass and drums followed established conventions of clarity and simplicity. What Shorter proposed was the reverse of this; themes of sustained tones, often with a dreamy feel to them, which appeared to float over a high degree of turbulence generated by the rhythm section. [112] In realigning the traditional roles of melody and rhythm instruments, Shorter's style lent itself to rhythmic variation and metric ambiguity, moving away the four-to-the-bar conventions of hard bop, with ride rhythms and the hi-hat snapping shut on the two and the four. On *Dolores*, for example, a 38-bar piece, the melody is played over and over allowing great licence to Davis's drummer, Williams, for whom the piece is virtually a feature; and on such numbers as *Eighty-one*, *Stuff* and *Vonetta*, Williams introduces square rhythmic patterns that were an unmistakable signpost along the road to a confluence between jazz and rock.

Between *E.S.P.* and *Filles de Kilimanjaro* came four albums that explore with increasing sureness Shorter's style of composing which allowed – indeed encouraged – a more horizontal approach to improvisation. It marked a further departure from the conventions of hard bop; indeed, it is impossible not to think of Davis's music after *Kind of Blue* as a musical odyssey in search of forms ever more challenging to hard-bop orthodoxy. The Shorter composition *Masqualero*, for example, clearly illustrates the gradual dissolution of hard bop's certainties into something more abstract, more experimental. Comprising an ABA form with modal harmonies, its thematic scheme is made up of elliptic melodic motifs that are some distance from the unambiguous melodies characteristic of the American popular song. *Filles de Kilimanjaro* represents the culmination of this period of experimentation with some of the most assured playing from Davis's classic quintet – Shorter, Hancock, Carter, Williams – just before it broke up. It also reveals how Davis was aligning his music to make an accommodation with popular culture, something he was under considerable pressure to do from his label chief Clive Davis, and it represents a bridge between his acoustic and electric work.

The sudden and unexpected rise of rock music in the 1960s had put unprecedented pressure on the jazz-music business. Clubs were closing, work opportunities diminishing and recording companies were becoming less and less interested in the sort of return sales of jazz albums were producing in the face of the enormously profitable sales from rock music. Even the word 'jazz' had widely become perceived as an impediment to sales. Indeed, *Filles de Kilimanjaro* is described on the front album cover as 'Directions in Music by Miles Davis', apparently because Miles had urged Clive Davis not to call his music 'jazz' in the hope of encouraging more sales. Recorded against a backdrop of unprecedented social and musical change, *Filles de Kilimanjaro* is one of the great, but seldom acknowledged, albums in Davis's discography. On it he gives prominence to the tone colours then associated with popular culture through the use of an electric piano (he had previously and unsuccessfully tried to integrate a guitar into his quintet using Bucky Pizzarelli, Joe Beck and George Benson) and rhythmic patterns that suggest and imply the 'square' feel of rock music. While in the past rock's rhythms had surfaced in his music, as early as 1964's live *My funny Valentine*, they appeared more as an element of rhythmic colouration than central to the music's purpose. But in May 1968, Davis had recorded *Stuff* for the album *Miles in the Sky* (Columbia [A] CS9628) which presented an unambiguous merger of jazz improvisation with rock rhythms.

The June sessions yielded further steps along the road to a confluence between jazz and rock. *Petits Machins* is in fact *Eleven*, a Gil Evans composition in $^{11}/_4$, used on his 1970s masterpiece *Svengali* (Atlantic [A] SD1643). Evans was apparently a shadowy and largely unacknowledged presence at all the 1968 Davis sessions; according to Bob Belden's annotations for *The Complete Columbia Studio Recordings of the Miles Davis Quintet 1965–68*, Evans's voice is clearly discernible on Davis's rehearsal tapes from this period. [113] What is immediately striking is the opening phrases of Davis's solo after the fanfarelike theme, which formed the basis of the theme for *Jean Pierre* on his first major post-furlough album, *We Want Miles* (CBS [A] 88579) from 1982, a melodic motif that became one of the most imitated riffs of the 1980s. While the rhythmic climate here is not jazz-rock, it is also not hard bop; Williams sets up a turbulent commentary that continues to suggest Davis's desire to distance himself from the latter idiom. Both Shorter and Hancock, on electric piano, further give testimony to this intention with solos of jumpy, angular construction that is some way from the hard-bop norm before Davis returns with a recapitulation, not of Evans's theme but of the *Jean Pierre* fragment, which suggests he sensed potential in the riff even then.

Tout de suite had already been tried out, unsuccessfully, at the *Miles in the Sky* session the previous month. This time a longer form is used, again with Hancock on electric piano and with Carter on electric bass. The tune opens with loping figures in $^{3}/_4$, with Hancock's piano playing a prominent role in accompaniment, making use of uncharacteristic (for the Davis quintet at least) bluesy phrasing in the manner of the then popular 'soul-jazz' exemplified by the group led by a former Davis sideman, Cannonball Adderley. As in so much of the quintet's recorded output during the tenure of Williams, the emotional climate is governed as much by his drumming as by the leader's trumpet. This number in particular responds to the drummer's careful shading and attention to the density of his accompaniment; during the initial exposition of the theme his playing is almost transparent until Hancock enters at double tempo. As Davis enters for his solo, Williams maintains a careful balance between wide-eared accompaniment and forceful dialogue with his leader's trumpet, a discourse that virtually becomes a duet during Shorter's solo that follows. Again, during Hancock's solo, Williams seems to possess advance knowledge of the pianist's line, framing phrases, underlining phrases and commenting and cross-accenting almost everything Hancock plays, before the introduction of a blues riff cues the slower (half-tempo) main theme.

Gil Evans would later point out in words and music how he and Davis had incorporated the chords of Jimi Hendrix's *The wind cries Mary* into the title track of the album. [114] By then both Davis and Evans had become admirers of the guitarist's playing and musical conception, something that would become central to the trumpeter's vision of how he wanted to position his version of electric jazz. The rhythmic climate on *Filles de Kilimanjaro* is polymetric, Williams's square rhythm-section patterns set against a broken *ostinato* electric-bass line from Carter suggests a metre of three against four in some places. The solos are based on a pedal point, something that would become a characteristic of much of Davis's subsequent foray into electric jazz. Once again, in his choice of an elliptical theme and square rhythm-section patterns, he maintains his distance from hard-bop orthodoxy.

By the time of the September sessions, Carter's busy career as a session musician, which had in the past made him miss out-of-town tours with the band, finally claimed him, and after a brief run with the bassist Miroslav Vitous, Davis introduced a young musician he had heard in Ronnie Scott's Club in London, Dave Holland. When Hancock failed to return on time from a honeymoon in South America, he was summarily dismissed, replaced by Chick Corea, then an accompanist to Sarah Vaughan. On *Frelon brun*, the rhythmic climate Williams generates is now unmistakably adapting rock rhythm patterns to the free-flowing impulses of the improvisers. The theme sounds uncharacteristically close to the funky soul-jazz that was a house speciality of Blue Note records, but quickly disappears to offer a vehicle for the soloists over a more equivocal rhythmic climate. Yet Williams is never boxed in by the ubiquitous backbeat, his rhythmic approach drifting in and out of areas of turbulence and rhythmic colouration behind Davis, Shorter especially, and Corea.

That Davis was now moving into rock territory is best demonstrated by *Mademoiselle Mabry*, which at some 16 minutes is the longest track of the album and demonstrates a considerable step towards an accommodation with the dominant popular culture of the time. A subtle abstraction of 'soft' soul music, which had little to do with James Brown or Aretha Franklin but was the hip new sounds running through black music exemplified by Isaac Hayes or Donny Hathaway, this sees his music uniquely balanced. On the one side is the weight of the hard-bop/

post-bop tradition, still clearly a part of his music. On the other there is an acknowledgement that change was not only inevitable, it was necessary. Yet there was one further hurdle to surmount. In popular music, volume was an important aspect of the music's authenticity. Initially, jazz musicians sought to control rock music by adapting its rhythms, attempting to make it conform with their notion of primitivism. But control is incompatible with rock's energy, and to avoid its primitivism was to fail to acknowledge its source of energy. While jazz musicians, including Davis, would initially find the concept of high volume a denial of subtlety, it would soon become clear that if a specific genre of jazz-rock were to emerge, then in its quest for authenticity jazz was going to have to voyage deeper into rock territory and confront the electronic sounds that were so much a part of that music's construction. S.N.

Tony Williams

442 Emergency!

†Verve (A) 539 117–2

Larry Young (org); John McLaughlin (g); Williams (d). New York City, 26 and 28 May 1969.

Emergency · *Beyond games* · *Where* · *Vashkar* · *Via the spectrum road* · *Spectrum* · *Sangria for three* · *Something spiritual*

Although Miles Davis is indelibly marked in the ledger as having ushered in jazz-rock, in reality he merely sanctioned a move that had been bubbling beneath the surface after the eruption of popular culture following the arrival of the Beatles in America on 7 February 1964. In their wake came a period in pop history known as 'the British Invasion', when the American charts were overwhelmed by British groups and singers. By 1966 the Beatles had toured America twice more and with a billion-dollar gross for the music industry looming, Beatlemania was already giving way to something more experimental, less categorizable, called rock. Columbia, a label that had relied on a strict middle-of-the-road policy dictated by the once seemingly ubiquitous Mitch Miller, began aggressively signing flamboyant new rock stars to their roster at the instigation of their new boss Clive Davis. They were not alone in reacting to the prevailing market forces. As the music industry found itself riding a huge boom, there was an excitement in the air that was not driven by purely financial considerations. The whole culture within recording companies was changing: new, young entrepreneurs surrounded by retinues of young assistants were bringing new ideas to an industry whose conception of popular music was still centred on the Brill Building and the business etiquette of the 1950s.

The effect of the sudden and unexpected rise of rock on jazz was initially predictable. Jazz musicians, club owners, promoters, magazines and record producers were united in thinking it was just another passing phase, like the twist or the locomotion, and would soon burn itself out. But it didn't. By the mid-1960s a large section of the audience on which jazz had come to rely during the 1950s and early 1960s, college and university students, had been swept up by the counter-culture movement: 'Either you get someone old enough to be their father or a bunch of angry guys pouring frustration, protest and hate messages out of their horns. That's not the message these kids want to hear,' said one booking agent. [115]

By 1968 the once thriving New York jazz-club scene had shrunk to just five clubs, while bastions of jazz respectability such as Duke Ellington, Count Basie and Ella Fitzgerald found themselves recording covers of Beatles hits. Even 'New Thing' saxophonist Albert Ayler made use of rock rhythms and soul singers on *New Grass* (Impulse [A] A-9175), and Gerry Mulligan summed up the mood of change with an album called *If You Can't Beat Them, Join Them* (Limelight [A] LML4013). With jazz suffering something of an identity crisis, many music commentators began to advance the prognosis that the end was in sight, that the music had run its course: *Melody Maker* contained a 'Requiem for a jazz we loved and knew so well', *Rouge* magazine headlined 'Jazz is dead . . . Folk is dead . . . Long live rock!' while *down beat* magazine, a solid and reliable chronicler of the winds of change that had blown through jazz since 1934, pronounced 'Jazz as we know it is dead!' on its 5 October 1967 front cover.

Many musicians, disenchanted with the rapidly diminishing work opportunities in clubs and on recordings, moved to Europe; among them were Phil Woods, Stan Getz, Ben Webster, Art Farmer, Johnny Griffin, Benny Bailey, Leo Wright, Carmel Jones, Stuff Smith, Kenny Drew, Jimmy Woode, Mal Waldron, Anthony Braxton and several key members of Chicago's AACM. Others found themselves having to supplement their earnings with non-jazz activities; for example, McCoy Tyner and Pete La Roca drove taxi cabs, and Steve Kuhn played in society dance orchestras. Jazz has always been inexorably linked to the social backdrop against which its dramas are enacted and although jazz histories patriotically underplay the detrimental effect rock had on jazz during the 1960s, it has to be said while rock did not wholly cast jazz into exterior darkness, it at the very least relegated it into the commercial twilight. [116]

The 1960s was the 'We' decade, a decade when 'we' would 'overcome', characterized by a strong current of social nonconformity among the young who found cause against the bomb, the Vietnam War and a whole lot else. For young jazz musicians, the revolution in popular culture was hardly something they could ignore. They were a part of it, their friends were a part of it, and it was going on all around them in high schools and on college and university campuses. There was an excitement in the air about being caught up in something that had captured the imagination of the youth across the Western world. 'The closest Western Civilization has come to unity since the Congress in Vienna in 1815 was the week *Sgt Pepper* was released,' said *Rolling Stone*. [117] A hit single from it, *Lucy in the sky with diamonds*, could be reduced to the acronym LSD and institutionalized a hallucinogenic drug in 1960s pop music. Pop culture was swept with unusual connections and new ideas. LSD, 'capable of transforming the mundane into the sensational', arguably led to a greater sensibility to colour and design and certainly had an important influence on 1960s media style and advertising. Traditional taboos were being broken at every level, from dress codes to free love. In such a climate, combining jazz and rock seemed like the most logical connection to make of all.

There had certainly been enormous speculation about the possibilities of this in the press, from *Time* magazine to *down beat*, with its editor, Dan Morgernstern, pointing out in 1968: 'A particularist, exclusive, non-proselytizing attitude ill behoves jazz in its present predicament, which briefly stated needs a bigger audience. If rock offers a bridge, jazz would be foolish not to cross it.' [118] As early as 1966, the British group Cream had suggested what a union between rock and jazz might actually sound like with extended, well-executed blues-based improvisations from the guitarist Eric Clapton and a degree of interactive playing from the former jazz musicians Jack Bruce on bass and Ginger Baker on drums; indeed, when the group first toured America there was confusion in the music press whether it was actually a jazz group or a rock group because of the quality and length of their improvisations. In America, the group Free Spirits, with Larry Coryell, attempted a combination of jazz improvisation and rock rhythms in 1966, but it was the Count's Rock Band, a union of Coryell, the saxophonist Steve Marcus and the pianist Mike Nock, that combined freedom, rock grooves and Coltrane-influenced modal playing to convincingly suggest the aesthetic possibilities inherent in jazz-rock. Gary Burton's quartet was equally impressive in a chamber group setting, while on the West Coast, John Handy's quintet, inspired by Coltrane, launched into jazz-rock grooves in places like San Francisco's rock palace, the Fillmore. Even more successful was the Charles Lloyd quartet, with the pianist Keith Jarrett, the bassist Ron McLure and the drummer Jack DeJohnette, who suggested quite unequivocally that rock could provide a genuine source of energy and inspiration for jazz, as did perhaps the finest of all the 'pre-Miles' jazz-rock groups, Mike Nock's Fourth Way.

For these musicians, combining jazz and rock was not seen as a sellout but a way of expanding the music in a new direction, as bop or free jazz had done in the past. Equally important, it was a way for younger jazz musicians of finding a voice in jazz that did not cut them off from the exciting culture of *their* generation. For Tony Williams, who was just 17 when he joined the Miles Davis quintet in May 1963, playing in the foremost group in jazz and redefining the role of the drummer, and indeed, the whole rhythm section, might have engaged him while on the bandstand, but his off-duty listening was to contemporary pop culture. 'I was the only musician in 1964 to have a Beatles poster on my wall in the apartment where I lived in, Miles lived upstairs from me and . . . I remember I told Miles in '64 or '65 that we ought to play a concert opposite the Beatles, but he didn't understand it then . . . I remember hearing Gary Burton's band . . . and then I would listen to Charles Lloyd's group and I would say if they could do it, so could I.' [119]

Clearly, when Williams decided to leave Davis, he was going to create a group that was in tune with the changing times and reflected his generation's musical tastes. Finally, after staying with Davis for just under six years, he decided to go out on his own in March 1969. Approaching the guitarist Sonny Sharrock to join him, he was bluntly turned down, Sharrock saying he didn't want to play rock 'n' roll. Instead, Williams turned to the British guitarist John McLaughlin, who had jammed with DeJohnette and Chick Corea in London and earned the reputation as a forward-thinking musician with a formidable technique. McLaughlin left London to join Williams on 3 February 1969 and on arriving in New York was immediately taken up to Count Basie's club in Harlem to jam. Anybody who was anybody happened to be in the club that night, including Larry Coryell, the Cannonball Adderley group and Miles Davis. As soon as Davis heard McLaughlin he invited him to join his own group, but McLaughlin declined, citing his commitment to Tony Williams. Nevertheless he would become a key sideman on Davis's recordings over the next two years, almost immediately appearing on Davis's *In a Silent Way* (†Columbia [A] 450982–2), recorded 18 February 1969.

Twelve weeks later McLaughlin was in the recording studios again, this time as a member of Tony Williams's new group, Lifetime. Where Davis's *In a Silent Way* appeared tentative in combining jazz and rock, the mood seemingly mediated by the album title, Williams produced a roar the like of which had never before been heard in jazz. Here was apodeictic testimony that jazz and rock could be combined in new and interesting ways. For a moment at least, it seemed as if Williams had glimpsed the future and it was to him rather than Davis that destiny was beckoning. At the time, no one in jazz had harnessed the dynamics of electricity to such coruscating effect as Lifetime. Significantly, each member of the band had jammed with Jimi Hendrix in his Electric Ladyland Studios a matter of weeks before the session. Hendrix, whose impact on jazz has barely been acknowledged, was a musical force whose guitar playing revealed hitherto unglimpsed horizons. In the same way that a Cecil Taylor redefined the piano or a John Coltrane redefined the saxophone, Hendrix redefined the electric guitar.

Hendrix achieved this by treating the guitar as an electric instrument, not as an amplified acoustic one. An autodidact, he balanced energy and ingenuity, using techniques of his own invention to achieve distortion, feedback, sustain and hammering-on that together with his impressive technical skills represented an assault on convention. To rock audiences he was a rock guitarist, but there was so much more to his playing that was picked up by open-eared jazz musicians such as Gil Evans, Miles Davis, Steve Lacy, Larry Coryell and a whole generation of guitar players that followed, such as Bill Frisell, David Tronzo and Jean-Paul Bourelly. Hendrix's influence on Miles Davis was profound, and thus at one remove he helped shape the direction of much electronic jazz into the 1990s.

Lifetime plunged into the sonic electronic spaces opened up by Hendrix in terms of feedback, distortion and sustain and applied it to many of the ideas that McLaughlin had developed on the 16 January 1969 session in London that had produced *Extrapolation* (**394**). Rhythmically and harmonically fluid, McLaughlin's English group applied their free-flowing impulses to the 'time, no changes' principle of improvising, where the composition existed to set tempo, key and mood, leaving the choice of chord changes to the spontaneous interaction of improviser and accompanists.

Emergency! used these principles, but is reinforced with the energy and electricity associated with rock. Indeed, *Spectrum* came directly from the *Extrapolation* session, and even if rhythmically Williams's playing approached rock rhythms from the perspective of post-bop, there was no doubt that jazz was never going to be the same after this record. Williams allows free rein to his creative impulses; impassioned and fiery, he seemed intent on distancing himself from his work with Davis. The title track moves from a fast, repeated four-bar figure to a slow, spacey half-tempo improvisation by McLaughlin. With a reprise of the theme, Williams's drumming occupied square rhythmic patterns, but reverts to post-bop for the slower tempo of Young's improvisation which is climaxed on a note of free jazz. Once again the four-bar figure returns with the original, faster tempo and Williams again returns to the square rhythmic patterns to the audible delight of Young and McLaughlin. On Carla Bley's hypnotic *Vashkar*, Young's role as colourist, providing the basic textures for the incendiary flights of Williams and McLaughlin, comes into clearer focus – here was the glue that held everything together, the ingredient that prevented it from disappearing over the edge.

In many ways, Lifetime were a logical continuation of Cream, a band that Williams is on record as having admired. This probably explains the appearance of vocals on *Where?* by the drummer and *Via the spectrum road* by the whole band, but as in Cream, the voice was soon overwhelmed by the instrumental content of the performance. In any event, Lifetime's approach was far closer to the edge than the blues-based improvisations of Cream (who had made their final public appearance a year earlier, on 26 October 1968). Broadcast tapes that exist of Lifetime, probably from the New York club Slugs, show the band making no concessions at all to commercial expediency. [120] Often Williams made no reference to rock rhythms, which remained just one rhythmic device among many in his remarkable arsenal of drumming skills. Like the best tracks on *Emergency!*, these broadcast tapes reveal bold, uncompromising jazz, full of complex interaction and sophisticated soloing that often dispensed with pre-written harmony and sometimes ventured into abstraction.

With Lifetime, McLaughlin made his reputation as the most widely admired guitarist in jazz and became the most imitated since Wes Montgomery. His playing contained none of the relaxed syncopation of the Charlie Christian–Tal Farlow–Jimmy Raney–Herb Ellis–Wes Montgomery lineage; he represented a point of departure for a style that had remained essentially unaltered since Christian's recordings with Benny Goodman in 1939–41 (**159**). McLaughlin's solos were often stunningly executed strings of semiquavers contrasted with sustained tones that were sometimes distorted for dramatic impact. In fact, McLaughlin had more in common with 1960s John Coltrane than any guitarist who had preceded him. Young was an organ virtuoso who had equally applied the lessons of Coltrane to the keyboard and brought the modernist grammar of contemporary jazz to an instrument which had been dominated by the 'preaching', blues-drenched style of Jimmy Smith and his followers. Young had distinguished himself with a string of impressive albums on the Blue Note label [121] which marked him the most influential jazz organist of his generation and the one that followed. With McLaughlin's high amplifier settings enabling him to bring to jazz the electronic effects pioneered by Hendrix, and Young's Hammond played at equal levels of intensity, combined with Williams's dynamic drumming, which even in the acoustic surroundings of the Miles Davis quintet was no stranger to volume, Lifetime wrote themselves into jazz history with their uncompromising vision of jazz and rock.

In 1970, the Cream bassist Jack Bruce was added to the line-up, but McLaughlin was later moved to say: 'Everything except the music was incredibly bad [with Lifetime]; management, economics, administration, organization . . . incredibly bad.' [122] The band produced one more album, *Turn It Over* (†Verve [A] 539 118–2), [123] before breaking up in April 1971. Throughout the 1970s Williams struggled to position his music in jazz. Subsequent versions of Lifetime were a pale shadow of what he had achieved with McLaughlin and he seemed more secure in retracing his footsteps with former members of the Miles Davis quintet in a group called VSOP than confronting the future. Perhaps he had achieved too much too young. S.N.

Mahavishnu Orchestra

443 Birds of Fire
†Columbia (A) CK 31996

John McLaughlin (g); Jerry Goodman (vln); Jan Hammer (kybd); Rick Laird (b); Billy Cobham (d). New York City, September/October 1972.
Birds of fire · Miles beyond · Celestial terrestrial commuters · Sapphire bullets of pure love · Thousand island park · Hope · One word · Sanctuary · Open country joy · Resolution

The stepping stone between McLaughlin's work with Tony Williams's Lifetime (**442**) and his own group, the Mahavishnu orchestra, was the album *My Goals Beyond* (†Rykodisc [A] RCD101051), recorded in March 1971, around the time Lifetime were breaking up. Since February 1969 McLaughlin had been a regular on Miles Davis's recording sessions and an occasional participant on live dates, such as the Hill Auditorium date at Ann Arbor in February 1970 and the dates in December that year that appeared as a part of *Live-Evil* (†Columbia/Legacy [A] C2K65135). It was at the latter date that the trumpeter encouraged McLaughlin to form his own band. McLaughlin gave the notion serious thought and decided to go ahead with the help of Davis's then manager, Nat Weiss.

My Goals Beyond was an album of two parts. Side one comprised eight tracks of unaccompanied guitar that was a precursor to hundreds of similar solo guitar records in jazz. Side two contained two long tracks of unplugged ethnofusion that was a forerunner of McLaughlin's mid-1970s experiments with Shakti and brought together the saxophonist Dave Liebman, the bassist Charlie Haden, the percussionists Mahalakshmi, Airto and Badal Roy, and, significantly, the former Flock violinist Jerry Goodman, and the drummer Billy Cobham, star of the group Dreams. McLaughlin had earmarked Goodman and Cobham as possible sidemen for a new electric ensemble he proposed forming and the date provided the opportunity to put his ideas to them and invite them both to join him. On the recommendation of the bassist Miroslav Vitous, McLaughlin approached Sarah Vaughan's pianist Jan Hammer and turned to his fellow expatriate Rick Laird, just off the road after two years playing bass with the Buddy Rich Big Band.

The Mahavishnu orchestra opened in Greenwich Village's Gaslight au Go Go in July 1971 and immediately caused a sensation. A month later they were in the recording studios to cut *Inner Mounting Flame* (†Columbia [A] CK 31067). With the benefit of hindsight, Tony Williams's *Emergency!* now seems like a wake-up call when put alongside the power and virtuosity of the Mahavishnu Orchestra, whose short existence created a kind of future shock in jazz from which it still has not quite recovered. Many listeners who heard the Mahavishnu orchestra live were genuinely awestruck with the band's impact and contemporaneous reviewers struggled to find words to describe the experience: 'The resultant power is almost frightening . . . [their] coherence and control comes as a shaft of light upon the muddied and confused,' said *Melody Maker*. [124] The album generated a great deal of attention in both jazz and in rock and reached 89 on the *Billboard* chart. Although the ensemble cohesion is not quite what it would later become, McLaughlin was nevertheless aiming for a kind of freedom within form, where through concentrated rehearsal the complexity of the music became second nature to the group, so their starting point was elevated to a new level, a level unencumbered by the technicalities of the music.

What is immediately apparent is the intensity of the Mahavishnu orchestra's precise, yet discursive ensemble passages alternated with flat-out improvisation. McLaughlin's own playing immediately became the benchmark by which all other guitarists were judged, in jazz and rock. He employed long lines of semiquavers that brought to mind Coltrane's sound-sheet intensity which he punctuated with dramatic sustained tones. By the time of the recording there had been plenty of long, loud guitar solos in rock and plenty of long guitar solos in jazz, but nothing to equal McLaughlin's speed allied to his melodic and harmonic resourcefulness. The base of this music had much in common with Coltrane's approach to Indian music. McLaughlin, like Coltrane, had studied Indian culture and Indian music and both incorporated Eastern scales and modes into their playing. McLaughlin's compositions also used asymmetrical metres which owed nothing to the $^4/_4$ backbeat of rock or the straight-ahead swing of jazz, but had more in common with Indian music – *Dawn*, for example, moves from $^7/_4$ to $^{14}/_8$.

An important aspect of Mahavishnu was how McLaughlin incorporated volume as an aspect of authenticity. The high volumes associated with rock music are capable of provoking a certain visceral response that contributes to the physical, rather than emotional, appeal of the music, and after working with steadily increasing volume levels with Lifetime, he realized that volume offered a new dimension that had not been fully exploited in jazz: 'I was into loud music, I wanted to play loud. [Mahavishnu] was a powerful band,' he would later say. [125] Yet a rise in volume does not go hand in hand with a parallel rise in intensity. As rock musicians had discovered, and particularly the influential guitarist Jimi Hendrix, to achieve intensity at loud volumes it is necessary to alter the timbre of the music, usually through distortion. Here the guitar, violin and keyboards employed distortion in wave form and in pitch, usually through wah-wah attachments and distortion boxes.

McLaughlin might not have been the first guitarist to adopt the metallic edge associated with rock, introduced gradually into his playing from around the time of *Experiments with Pops* (Major Minor [E] MMLP21) made in England with the pianist Gordon Beck in 1967, but he was by far the most influential. By the time of *Birds of Fire*, recorded some 12 weeks after *On the Corner* (†Columbia [A] 474371–2), his last recording with Miles Davis until the 1980s, Mahavishnu had shaken down into an impressive force in the burgeoning jazz-rock movement. Musicians were no longer looking to Davis but to McLaughlin's band. For all his importance to jazz-rock, Davis's albums, such as his important *Bitches Brew* (Columbia [A] S64011), were often turgid and congested.

Mahavishnu adapted to the new electronic technology and, in so doing, built their ensemble sound around the specific characteristics of electric instruments. Indeed, there are moments of who's-doing-what confusion in trying to discern whether it is a guitar, an amplified violin or a keyboard-generated sound at certain moments in their performances. Their intricate ensemble playing and powerful soloing were underpinned by the virtuoso drumming of Cobham, who, while with Mahavishnu, was to become to 1970s drumming what Tony Williams had been to the 1960s. Like McLaughlin on the guitar, Cobham became the new benchmark of excellence. He had a thorough grounding in the rudiments of drumming and had developed a fast, precise technique. A feature of his playing were fleet, cleanly executed paradiddles and variations of paradiddles in unusual groupings of notes such as 7, 11, 13 and 17, spread around an expanded kit that included an array of tuned tom-toms and two bass drums that produced spectacular and widely imitated fills.

One of the features of *Birds of Fire* is the high level of interaction between McLaughlin and Cobham which appeared to be mutually inspirational. The title track is one of the great moments of early jazz-rock; the ominous gong that announces the piece followed by the entrance of McLaughlin's overdriven guitar in $^{18}/_{8}$, then the statement of the theme in unison with Goodman against the obsessive arpeggiated figures from Hammer's keyboards, all given greater impact by Cobham's dramatic drum accompaniment. A year later their performance inspired the arranger Don Sebesky to combine *Birds of fire* with extracts from Stravinsky's *The Firebird*, a juxtaposition that might have worked well but was poorly executed, on *Giant Box* (†Epic [A] EPC 450564–2).

The band's appeal was in its intense virtuosity, which even today conveys something of the shock of the new that so impressed audiences at the time. Thus the tracks that attract today are ones like *Celestial terrestrial commuters*, with its absorbing exchanges between McLaughlin, Goodman and Hammer, *One word*, which explodes into life on the back of a Cobham single-stroke roll on his snare and uses a chase interlude between McLaughlin, Goodman and Hammer to lead into a drum feature; the slow, majestic, arching arpeggios of *Hope*; and the equally ominous *Resolution*. In fact, the device of soloists trading solos with each other came from the earliest of jazz, but the manner in which it was executed, with such brio and *élan*, made many episodes appear as one continuous solo, adding to the intensity of the performance. Although today Mahavishnu are remembered for power harnessed to virtuosity, they developed quite a broad range of expression; the contrasting, quaint sections featuring Goodman which bracket the powerful middle section of *Open country joy*, the peaceful yet mysterious power the swirls and eddies throughout *Sanctuary* or McLaughlin's use of an acoustic guitar on *Thousand island park*.

Birds of Fire, much to McLaughlin's surprise, became a hit album, reaching 15 on the *Billboard* chart. This sudden success created stress lines between the divergent personalities in the band and after just one more album, the live *Between Nothingness and Eternity* (†Columbia [A] CDCBS32114), recorded in August 1973, [126] the band finally broke up after a concert in Detroit on 29 December 1973. 'The Inner Mounting Flame Goes Out,' quipped *down beat*. [127] Yet during their short existence, their impact had been enormous, as Joe Zawinul of Weather Report would later observe: 'John McLaughlin was an incredible big part of jazz-rock. He had a very powerful band, but the guitar was the trip. Here you had a *master* guitar player and the Mahavishnu Orchestra with all these ingredients in it – with Billy Cobham at the heart – I mean, no rock band ever played like that! They were into another music, a new language of jazz. They were a fantastic band, huge energy, they killed everybody.' [128]

McLaughlin continued the Mahavishnu concept with subsequent versions of the band until 1975 and again between 1984 and 1986, but none captured the moment quite like their first two albums. Yet although no one realized it at the time, the original Mahavishnu spelled the beginning of the end of jazz-rock. What began as something very exciting that looked like becoming a leap into the future ended up with countless bands copying the superficial aspects of McLaughlin's ideas and style, not least speed of execution and highly technical ensemble passages. Chick Corea, who was leading a very creditable acoustic group flirting with rock and samba rhythms called Return to Forever, was one of many musicians inspired by Mahavishnu. By his own admission his electric version of Return to Forever was consciously modelled on the Mahavishnu orchestra, but Corea commandeered its superficial aspects in his desire to 'communicate' with audiences. It produced a music where high-tech riffs and gratuitous virtuosity were exploited and became an end in themselves. [129] Corea's popularity in turn inspired a further legion of copyists and very quickly an emasculated musical form called fusion emerged, where the dominant elements that combined with jazz improvisation came not from the creative side of rock music but from the glossy hooks of pop.

Actively marketed by the major recording companies, this music found its way onto the FM airwaves, and soon its characteristics were specially constructed with the requirements of radio-station programmers in mind. This commodification of jazz-rock into something bland and noisome was not the end of jazz-rock, however. Once the Rubicon had been crossed and electric instrumentation and a new rhythmic basis had been introduced into the music, jazz was at last able to break free of the hard-bop stranglehold and variations of the straight-ahead rhythms of the foxtrot and the quickstep from the early 1920s that had formed the basis of jazz rhythm for over 50 years. Suddenly there was a vast palette of electronic tone colours and new rhythms to explore, not just rock-inspired rhythms but a range from funk to rhythm 'n' blues and a myriad of world rhythms. And through the 1980s and into the 1990s, often out of sight of the easily accessible and somewhat self-righteous acoustic hard-bop mainstream, some of the most interesting jazz to be heard combined these elements in new and interesting ways. What jazz-rock had begun could not be stopped. S.N.

Miles Davis

444 Jack Johnson

CBS (A) 70089; †CBS/Sony (A) 471003 2

Davis (tpt); Steve Grossman (sop); Herbie Hancock (kybd); John McLaughlin (g); Michael Henderson (el bs); Billy Cobham (d). Note: Sonny Sharrock (g) claimed to have been on this session and a second guitar is on occasion audible. New York City, 7 April 1970.
Right off · *Yesternow*

With the sales of his recordings dwindling in the late 1960s, Davis was coming under increasing pressure from Clive Davis, the president of Columbia Records, to make some sort of rapprochement with rock music. He began flirting with the idea on a December 1967 recording session when the guitarist Joe Beck sat in with his band; but it is usually agreed that *In a Silent Way* (†CBS [A] 450982–2) from February 1969 marked his formal entry into jazz-rock. Six months later he recorded *Bitches Brew* (†CBS [A] 460602–2) and the die was cast. Reaching 35 on the *Billboard* chart and with sales of 450,000 in the first year, it demonstrated both the commercial and aesthetic feasibility of jazz-rock and was a significant step in moving jazz into a new era. However, by the end of 1969 the saxophonist Wayne Shorter had left the band after five years to be replaced by Grossman, a 19-year-old from Brooklyn. In the context of Davis's past groups, he was a somewhat lightweight stand-in. However, in the new electric environment, saxophone solos were no longer the *raison d'être* of Davis's music as they were in the days of Coltrane, Adderley and Shorter; indeed, even Davis's own playing had veered sharply in favour of fragmentation and coloration amid the tribal chatter of electronic sounds. His old narrative certainties were now reduced to often jagged motifs, frequently distorted and electrified through a guitar wah-wah attachment.

But having entered rock territory, Davis gave every sign of having no clear idea where to position his music. The post-*Bitches Brew* period is one of experimentation as his studio sessions through November 1969 into March 1970 reveal. The fact the results were not released at the time, appearing on composite albums released several years after the event, [130] suggests that Davis and his producer Teo Macero where unhappy with the results. A variety of ideas were tried out and musicians were simply thrown together in the hope that creative sparks might fly to provide some answers. In November 1969 the then fashionable sitar appeared on *Great expectations*; in January 1970 Billy Cobham, the drum star from the jazz-rock group Dreams, was paired with Jack DeJohnette on three tracks; in February 1970 *Willie Nelson*, with its rather delicate country-rock beat, was a tribute to the country-and-western star, and *Duran* flirted with a highly mobile bass line and stabbing chords of James Brown's funk.

But despite his interest in the music of James Brown – 'I listen to James Brown and those little bands on the South Side. They swing their asses off' [131] – the bass lines in his own music remained pedestrian in comparison with Brown's music during much of this period. What he did seem to take from Brown was his on-the-spot method of composition, as in Brown's 1967's *Get it together*, where in the second part of the tune Brown reorders the density of the composition and instructs the baritone sax and brass to contribute riffs, or *Soul power* from 1971, where he provides a musical cue to move from a vamp of indeterminate length to a structured bridge. This kind of hands-on musical direction would become a feature of Davis's live performances, achieved by minimal nods and gestures to alter the texture of the music or cue a tempo or key change, another soloist or even a new composition entirely.

Davis's indecision continued into March 1970, with Macero trying to add a little interest to *Go ahead John* by adding a tape loop halfway through the piece at the post-production stage, so making Davis's solo appear as if he is in dialogue with himself. 'One thing about Miles and his music, about working with Miles,' explained Macero, 'you can experiment as much as you wish. You can take his music, you can cut it up, you can put filters in, you can do anything you want to.' [132] While the *sound* of Davis's ensemble was well and truly different from anything that had gone before, another striking deviation in his music was a concerted application of post-production techniques by Macero. It marked the beginning of a new philosophy in the recording of jazz, which until then had preserved the primacy of improvisation by largely recording in real time.

In popular music the notion that an album should sound like a 'captured' live performance had increasingly given way to elaborate production techniques in the studio. Most famously, Phil Spector's creation of a 'wall of sound' was nothing like anything you ever heard in a concert hall. It was a source of inspiration to the Beach Boys' Brian

Wilson, who produced *Pet Sounds* in 1966, revealing the Beach Boys as a group whose real potential lay in the recording studio. When Paul McCartney heard it, his reaction was 'How do we follow this?' The answer to this apparently rhetorical question was *Sgt Pepper's Lonely Hearts Club Band* in 1967, a recording that took nine months of careful editing to piece together in the studio by the Beatles and their producer George Martin. It was in stark contrast to the 16 hours of real-time recording that had resulted in their first album, *Please Please Me*. From that point on, pop and rock artists no longer tried to capture the sound of a live performance in the studio, but tried to figure out how they could reproduce the sounds they conjured up in the studio during live performance.

Davis had previously utilized post-production techniques during the recording of *Miles Ahead* (†Columbia [A] CXK67397) in 1957, which utilized an exceedingly large number of edited or spliced takes, overdubs and post-production work to produce a classic. Equally, *Porgy and Bess* (**382**) and *Sketches of Spain* (†Columbia [A] CXK67397) contain much after-the-fact rationalization. Such studio creations demand to be heard on their own terms, for what they are, rather than what they are patently not, a 'captured' live performance. After all, the most important thing about art is not the means used to achieve an end, but the end achieved. Generally, however, while the fast-developing studio technology was readily harnessed by the rock and pop musicians – and here Jimi Hendrix also deserves credit, his *Axis: Bold as Love* from 1967 was received as 'a miracle of four-track recording' – these techniques were yet to be exploited fully in jazz, which gave every appearance of having learned nothing from 50 years of record-making. In contrast, Davis, without too many preconceived notions, was nudging his talented sidemen towards finding a route into jazz-rock by allowing the tapes to run during long and often rambling jam sessions and handing the results to Teo Macero to edit and reassemble into a coherent performance.

The uncertainty of his post-*Bitches Brew* period was finally resolved in April 1970 when he decided to confront the music of Jimi Hendrix head on. His boast in *Rolling Stone* that he could 'put together a better rock and roll band than Jimi Hendrix' was as much macho challenge as a statement of intent. [133] Davis was particularly impressed by Hendrix's music, recognizing in the guitarist a unique talent who was a sound innovator. Hendrix revealed an emotional range far greater than any contemporary guitarist. His playing exerted a profound but seldom acknowledged influence on Davis's music. Davis had met Hendrix several times – Hendrix later became responsible for the break-up of Davis's marriage to Betty Mabry – and had jammed with him informally at his home. Indeed, Gil Evans has pointed out how the Hendrix influence was making itself felt on Davis's music as early as *Filles de Kilimanjaro* (**441**).

Jack Johnson marks the point where Davis confronted Hendrix's music in terms of power and visceral impact. It could be argued that Hendrix's influence lurked within the matrix of sound in *Bitches Brew*, but until this point this 'energy' was not a consistent factor in his studio work in a way that post-*Jack Johnson* it would be. The album presents the soundtrack music from the producer Jim Jacob's film of the same name and was pieced together in post-production by Macero, and, as on Davis's other film soundtrack albums *Ascenseur pour l'échafaud* (Mercury [E] 644701) from 1957 and *Siesta* (†Warner Bros [A] 925655–2) from 1987, there were moments that were subservient to visual rather than musical logic.

However, viewed in the context of the music Davis was playing at the time he recorded *Jack Johnson*, the album represented a sharp departure in the organization and structure of his ensemble. Three days after the session he recorded his first live album since the Plugged Nickel engagement in 1965 (**396**) with his regular band and the result, *Black Beauty: Miles Davis at Fillmore West* (CBS/Sony [J] 28AP 2155 6), saw his ensemble moving towards textural density at the expense of melodic and harmonic exploration. Notes did not seem to matter except in their overall contribution to the jungle density; musicians played through the music, not on top of it. What Davis was playing was neither low-brow nor high-brow but directed completely over the heads of his audiences, who, for the most part, accepted it with perplexed patience. Away from the recording studios, he was exploring free jazz with a vengeance, a music of random associations, fragmented ideas and swirling textures where rock rhythms were bent in and out of shape like images glimpsed in a hall of mirrors.

Although *Black Beauty* might have suggested otherwise, *Jack Johnson* showed that Davis had by no means abandoned the lyricism of his acoustic period. His solo on *Right off* is as impressive as any in his long career, framed by a raw electronic energy inspired by Hendrix. Today the controlled abandon of both Davis and McLaughlin seems more memorable than the often subdued approach of his earlier jazz-rock albums, or the free-form electronic shock therapy that would culminate in his pre-sabbatical offerings *Agharta* (CBS-Sony [J] SOPJ 92–93) and *Pangaea* (CBS-Sony [J] SOPZ 96–97) from 1975, which were in themselves Davis's most sonic abstractions of Hendrix's music.

Right off began innocuously enough, as McLaughlin recalled: 'We were in the studio, Herbie Hancock, Michael Henderson, Billy Cobham and me. Miles was talking with Teo Macero in the control room for a long time. I got a little bored and I started to play this shuffle, a kind of boogie in E with some funny chords. The others picked it up and locked in. The next thing, the door opened, and Miles runs in with his trumpet and we played for about 20 minutes. It was a large part of the record yet it came out of nowhere.' [134] McLaughlin's guitar was recorded forward in the sound mix and his powerful opening chords announce a solo that, while being untypical of his style in that it is mainly chorded, threatens to dwarf anything that follows. Around bar 50 he begins to set the stage for Davis's entry, dropping in volume, and from around bar 60 he begins a climactic build-up to frame Davis's entry at bar 75, a masterpiece of impromptu construction that presented the trumpet player with a perfect launching pad for his solo.

Davis makes the most of what he has been given, and his commanding entry here is one of the great moments of jazz-rock. Like all his finest solos, it has memorable structure and poise. But it is quite unlike his work with acoustic ensembles; instead of introspection and control, his playing was more outgoing and full of tension, often contrasting staccato passages with fast sweeping runs that incorporated the high register of his instrument. The drama of Davis's entry is enhanced by McLaughlin's modulation from E major to B flat, and the bassist Michael Henderson, then playing with Stevie Wonder's group, Wonderlove, missing the key change, staying in the original key for 12 further bars until he realizes his error, creates a clash of tonalities that adds to drama of the moment at hand. It is a reminder of the informality of these studio jam sessions and the extent to which Davis had become a one-take artist in that he did not seek to correct the mistake by going for another take, convinced that the spontaneity of the moment could not subsequently be recaptured.

Right off lasts for some 26 minutes, but it is McLaughlin and Davis who command our attention with their relentless and ultimately triumphant purpose. Davis's solo, full of power and aggression, insists uncompromisingly on his right to endure; indeed, the trumpeter later said he had a boxer's movements in mind during the recording. [135] It is worth noting that McLaughlin's role in accompaniment plays a significant role in helping shape the ultimate destiny of the trumpeter's line; his use of side-slipping, for example, encourages Davis to follow suit, temporarily moving into remote tonalities, and this interaction between guitar and trumpet becomes a feature of this track. In fact McLaughlin's role, as both catalyst and *agent provocateur*, is as absorbing and exhilarating as that of any of Davis's acoustic collaborators from earlier eras and gives a strong indication why Davis rated him so highly. [136] After 11 minutes the rhythm fades for an interlude of Davis's harmon-muted trumpet in tempo. This gives way to bass and drums and Grossman's soprano sax. The only dull patch is Hancock's keyboard solo at the 15-minute mark, where he gives the impression of being a fan of the Tornados. With the return of McLaughin's insistent guitar riffs, something of the original drama of the opening passages returns, with further solos by Hancock, Grossman and McLaughlin leaning heavily on the wang-bar.

The remaining track, *Yesternow*, typifies Davis's approach to jazz-rock, relying on the cut-and-paste post-production techniques extensively employed by Marcero. 'From the time the musicians start playing, we take down every note of music,' the producer explained in 1974. 'I make masters of everything. I may have 15 reels of Miles and cut those reels down . . . so that the front becomes the back, the back becomes the middle, the middle something else. It's a creative process being producer with Miles.' [137] A forlorn and pensive workout against a static harmonic backdrop, *Yesternow* comprises at least five separate episodes spliced together, including an extract from *Shhh/Peaceful* from three years before with a totally different personnel. All are essentially free-form pieces with no pre-set chord changes, relying on a simple vamp and the musicians' integrity to produce *simpatico* background coloration and Davis's direction of the musical traffic in ordering soloists. However, this method of on-the-spot composing often meant that many pieces sounded like works in progress rather than the finished article, and this is the case here. 'If you leave the room to answer a phone call and return ten minutes later you won't have missed much,' said the *Rolling Stone* review of the album. [138] As each section fades in and fades out, the actor Brock Peters's voice, representing that of Jack Johnson, is whistled up to say how the world would never forget he was black. It was a comment that had equal resonance in Davis's life.

Although it is Davis who is largely given credit for moving jazz into an era of jazz-rock, with the passage of time his own work in the idiom has come to be overshadowed by the musicians who passed through his bands, such as Zawinul, Shorter, McLaughlin, Hancock and Corea. To paraphrase Gertrude Stein on Hemingway, Davis did it first and others came along and did it better. However, as the 1970s progressed, the idiom at its most commercial became progressively narcissistic, glorying more in self-indulgent displays of empty virtuosity than in content. In contrast, the greater proportion of *Right off* represents one of the enduring moments of jazz-rock. It possesses an elemental rawness that was all but bleached out of the jazz-rock genre by the end of the decade. The virtuosity of McLaughlin is masked while Davis's playing, often a fragile and delicately introspective thing, is here expansive, powerful and as at home with the music as ever he was with a performance of *My funny Valentine*.

Once again he had succeeded in creating a context where he was able to sound profound, and although no one knew it at the time, it was his final act of musical prestidigitation which had kept him ahead of the game since *Birth of the Cool* (**376**). When he returned from a five-year hiatus in 1980, his days of musical innovation were long behind him. Picking up where *Jack Johnson* left had off years before, he leaned on his guitarist Mike Stern to lay down post-Hendrix textures for his new band. Commentators bridled but audiences simply expanded their definition of jazz to accommodate him; in the 1980s people turned out to a Davis concert not so much for the music as to consume the physical presence of a true jazz legend before it was too late. S.N.

Weather Report

445a **I Sing the Body Electric**

†Columbia (A) 468207 2

Wilmer Wise (piccolo tpt); Wayne Shorter (ten, sop); Andrew White (eng h); Hubert Laws (fl); Joe Zawinul (kybd); Miroslav Vitous (bs); Eric Gravatt (d); Dom Um Romao (perc); Yolande Bavan, Joshie Armstrong, Chapman Roberts (voices). New York City, late 1971.
Unknown soldier

Shorter (sop, ten); White (eng h); Zawinul (kybd); Ralph Towner (g); Vitous (bs); Gravatt (d); Romao (perc). New York City, late 1971.
The moors

Shorter (sop); Zawinul (kybd); Vitous (bs); Gravatt (d); Romao (perc). New York City, late 1971.
Crystal

Shorter (ten, sop); White (eng h); Zawinul (kybd); Vitous (bs); Gravatt (d); Romao (perc). New York City, late 1971.
Second Sunday in August

Shorter (ten, sop); Zawinul (kybd); Vitous (bs); Gravatt (d); Romao (perc). Tokyo, 13 January 1972.
Medley: Vertical invader, T.H., Dr Honoris Causa · Surucucú · Directions

445b **Mysterious Traveller**

†Columbia (A) 471860 2

Shorter (ten, sop); Zawinul (kybd, voc, perc); Alphonso Johnson (bs); Ishmael Wilburn, Skip Hadden (d); Romano (perc). New York City, *c.* 1974.
Nubian sundance

Shorter (ten, sop); Zawinul (kybd); Vitous, Johnson (bs); Wilburn (d); Romao (perc). New York City, *c.* 1974.
American tango

Shorter (ten, sop); Zawinul (kybd); Johnson (bs); Hadden (d); Romao (perc). New York City, *c.* 1974.
Cucumber slumber · Mysterious traveller

Shorter (sop); Zawinul (p, kybd). New York City, *c.* 1974.
Blackthorn rose

Shorter (sop); Zawinul (kybd); Johnson (bs); Romao (d, perc). New York City, *c.* 1974.
Scarlet Woman

Zawinul (p, org, kybd); Don Ashworth (woodwinds); Isacoff (tabala, finger cymbals); Romao (perc). New York City, *c.* 1974.
Jungle book

Zawinul and Shorter first met in the summer of 1959, at a time when both were members of the Maynard Ferguson band. Shorter's stay was briefest, he moved across to Art Blakey's Jazz Messengers after just four weeks. Zawinul left a few months later and spent almost two years accompanying Dinah Washington; he appears on her hit record *What a difference a day makes*. By then he was an accomplished musician; as a child in Vienna he had studied piano under Valerie Zschorney, a pupil of Weingartner who had in turn been taught by Liszt. In Europe Zawinul had played in several bands, including those of his mentor Friedrich Gulda, where he played trumpet, bass trumpet, clarinet and saxophones. Realizing that the prevailing climate in Europe in the late 1950s meant that to establish a reputation in jazz it was necessary to move to America, he obtained a Berklee scholarship, but attended only a few lectures before being invited to join Ferguson's band as a pianist. He can be heard on *A Message from Birdland* (collected on *The Complete Roulette Recordings of the Maynard Ferguson Orchestra* [Mosaic (A) MD10–156]), recorded live on 17 June 1959. Later in the year Zawinul made his debut as a leader on record for the cut-price Strand label, with George Tucker on bass and Frankie Dunlop on drums, with the addition of Ray Barreto on conga on some tracks: *The Beginning* (†Fresh Sounds [Sp] FSRCD 142).

These albums reveal Zawinul to be a fluent and technically assured pianist who, while taking inspiration from Bud Powell, was yet to project a specific identity of his own. After his tenure with Miss Washington, he joined Cannonball Adderley's quintet and during the ensuing ten years he consciously shed his playing of cliché and developed an aversion to the obvious, both rhythmically and harmonically. He used unexpected silence to produce a restrained yet biting lyricism, and by the time he left Adderley he had contributed several songs to the saxophonist's repertoire, not least *Mercy, mercy, mercy*, Adderley's major hit of the 1960s from the album *Mercy, Mercy, Mercy: Live at The Club* (Capitol T [E] 2663), and the title tracks to the albums *74 Miles Away* (Capitol [E] ST2822) and *Country Preacher* (†Capitol [E] CDP7243 8 3045 2 8). On *Why Am I Treated So Bad?* (Capitol [A] ST2617), he contributed two pieces, *One for Newk*, a piano feature, and the ballad *Yvette*. These albums find Zawinul making a transition from acoustic to electric piano and on an instrument that can so easily swallow a player's identity, he created a specific tonal identity by screwing down the tone bars of the Fender Rhodes piano to inhibit their resonance, producing a more percussive sound, which he further modified by creative use of distortion through overdriving the amplifier.

Meanwhile Shorter, after distinguishing himself as a member of Blakey's Jazz Messengers 1959–63, both as a post-Coltrane soloist and a composer, wrote himself into jazz history as a member of the Miles Davis quintet from September 1964 to December 1970. By now he was widely acclaimed as one of the most original saxophonists in jazz (**352**). Compositionally, he had transformed the musical outlook of the Davis quintet (**396**) by moving away from the Broadway songbook, the blues and jazz standards to originals from inside the band, primarily his own, but also from Hancock, Carter and Davis, who took their cue from Shorter's particular writing style with subtle, undramatic themes that allowed greater freedom for the rhythm section.

The first musical meeting between Zawinul and Shorter since their Ferguson days came on 18–20 February 1969, a recording date under Miles Davis's leadership. On it, Zawinul ended by acting as Davis's musical director, contributing *In a silent way* which gave its name to the resultant album (†Columbia/Legacy [A] 450982–2). Subsequently, Zawinul became a regular on Davis's studio albums over the next two years, contributing such compositions as *Orange lady*, *Directions* and *Pharaoh's dance* and appearing on *Bitches Brew* (†Columbia/Legacy [A] 460602 2), *Circle in the Round* (†Columbia/Legacy [A] 467898 2), *Live-Evil* (†Columbia/Legacy [A] C2K 65135) and *Big Fun* (Columbia [A] PG 32866). [139]

Shorter left Davis in Christmas 1970, some four months after Zawinul left Adderley. In the summer of 1969 Shorter recorded *Super Nova* (†Blue Note [A] CDP 7 84332 2), which used three of his original compositions Miles Davis had earlier used on the album *Water Babies* (Columbia [A] PC 34396), recorded in June 1967 (but not released until 1976). Meanwhile, the bassist Miroslav Vitous's *Infinite Search* (Atlantic [A] SD 1622) – later rereleased as *Mountain in the Clouds* – from November 1969 presented an arresting version of Eddie Harris's *Freedom jazz dance*. Common to both albums were the guitarist John McLaughlin and the drummer Jack DeJohnette.

In late 1970, Zawinul recorded his fourth album as a leader, *Zawinul* (†Atlantic [A] 7567–81375–2), a series of impressionistic tone poems that made ingenious use of electronic tone-colours with a line-up that included Shorter and Vitous. [140] On it, *In a silent way* is peformed as the composer intended, rather than the version with Miles Davis which abandoned Zawinul's pre-set harmonies in favour of performing on the tonic. [141] Here it emerged as an impressive programmatic tone poem, a lament to his lost youth as a shepherd boy in Austria. Also on the album was Zawinul's *Double image* (previously recorded by Davis on *Live-Evil* [142]) and an impressive *Dr Honoris Causa*, which Zawinul would later rescore for symphony orchestra as *Gypsy* almost 25 years later on his *Stories of the Danube* (†Phillips [E] 454 143–2).

These albums suggested a commonality of musical direction that prompted Zawinul, Shorter and Vitous to form a band of their own. A certain amount of indecision followed as to what line-up the band should adopt, or indeed what they should call themselves. Finally deciding on the name Weather Report, they settled for a surprisingly conventional line-up of tenor, piano, bass and drums with additional percussion. However, the music they produced was anything but conventional.

Their first album, *Weather Report* (†Columbia Legacy [A] 468212–2), had no electronic instruments and was recorded in three days during March 1971. It pulled together many of the techniques that could be heard evolving in the 1965–8 Miles Davis quintet and on their recent albums under their own names. *Eurydice* was free from conventional metric and harmonic structure with a metre that was intentionally vague or constantly shifting. *Milky way* was a tone poem that harnessed the natural acoustic resonance of a piano in a highly individual way. *Seventh arrow* and *Umbrella* were collective improvisations, and *Orange lady* evoked the work of Debussy and Ravel with their beguiling tone colours. In the context of its time, *Weather Report* was a highly individual album and step on the way to several of the advanced musical concepts the band would pursue on subsequent albums. Although it won the Album of the Year category in *down beat* magazine and Japan's *Swing Journal*, Zawinul was not wholly satisfied with the results.

I Sing the Body Electric was Weather Report's second album, and comprised material recorded in the studios in late 1971 on one side of the original vinyl release, and extracts from a live recording made during a Japanese tour in early 1972 on the other. The key exhibit among the studio tracks was *The unknown soldier.* According to Zawinul, it is about his recollections as a youth of war-torn Europe in the 1940s and his images of the Third Reich. [143] It is another composition that would later reappear on Zawinul's symphony *Stories of the Danube* and here, in its original form, it opens with the kit drummer playing brisk time figures on the ride cymbal presaging the exposition of an angular, haunting first subject using bowed bass, piano and voices. After a recapitulation by Shorter's soprano and White's english horn, an interlude of interjections by bass and percussion over a pedal point leads into a fragmented transitional passage outlined by White that in turn leads into the second subject. This is followed by a programmatic interlude with 'military' snare-drum figures and voices emulating the wail of air-raid sirens, which give way to a freely improvised passage with Shorter in a dominant role against percussive machine-gun-like sounds and electronically generated sounds simulating bomb blasts. The return of the original subject, in fragmented form, against the insistent time of the kit drummer's ride cymbal allows elements of the first and second subjects to congregate before a haunting episode by White, using long tones, leads to a fade.

The moors made use of a long, freely improvised introduction by Ralph Towner on 12-string acoustic guitar. 'When he came into the studio, he was nervous,' Zawinul recalled. 'So I said to the engineer when he tuned up "Don't put the red light on, I better get him early." He played for about 20 minutes, practised, and said "I'm ready," and I said, "That's very nice, but Ralph, are you ready now to pack up your guitar because it's done!" And that was the introduction to *The moors.* It was great, I think.' [144] After Towner's a cappella introduction, the rhythm section establishes tempo with Shorter stating an elongated *legato* melody whose accompaniment varies in density and turbulence, and it is the contrast between the soprano's melancholy purpose and the rhythmic variety that compels our attention. Like *The moors*, *Crystal* is largely a collective improvisation of great restraint and taste. On it, Zawinul uses electric piano with a wah-wah attachment, which he uses to produce a series of other-worldly sounds behind Shorter's soprano improvisations that emerge so organically they sound pre-composed. *Second Sunday in August* is rhythmically more vigorous than either *The moors* or *Crystal* and uses a pre-written theme stated in unison with White's english horn.

The Japanese concert was taken from a 2-CD set called *Live in Tokyo* (†Sony [J] SRCS 7174–5), originally only available in Japan. The portion that appears on *I Sing the Body Electric* comprises an edited version of the opening medley (26 minutes 10 seconds pared down to 10 minutes 10 seconds) together with *Surucucú* and *Directions*, which were themselves originally part of a longer medley that included *Lost* and *Early minor*. The whole ethos of the band was given over to collective improvisation, or, as Zawinul once put it, 'Everyone solos, no one solos.' The emancipation of the group from the predetermined roles of hard bop and post-bop which had begun on *Weather Report* was now complete. Whereas the earlier album had been an entirely acoustic album, Zawinul now uses a Fender Rhodes with a ring modulator with a wah-wah attachment. The difference is striking: *Orange lady*, *Tears*, *Seventh arrow* and *Eurydice* from *Weather Report* are transformed into aggressive and abrasive statements featuring episodes of spontaneous interaction that might be described as electric free jazz.

As Zawinul, Shorter or Vitous states a brief melody, those around him respond in highly interactive ways. 'Melodies had shorter motifs,' Zawinul pointed out. 'A lot of them sounded improvised but they were written to sound that way.' On *Medley*, the sounds in *Surucucú* and *Directions* take their meaning from their relationship one to another rather than from their place in the musical whole. The soloist/accompanist roles of bop had been abandoned completely and often there was no distinction between the melody carrier and the accompanist. This is music where the elements of storytelling (the soloist), architecture (form and structure) and resolution (chord sequence) are replaced by a field of interconnecting intensity generated collectively by the whole band.

A soloist might stand out briefly, but the remainder of the group felt free to comment or pick up and elaborate the motif; at any moment the music could be polytonal, polyphonic and polyrhythmic, a linear relationship of interconnecting events that did not have to satisfy conventional form and structure with their systems of cadences, modulations and resolutions. The form was open-ended, the structure was what it was at any given moment. Rhythm, unlike its function in the popular song, is not bound up in harmonic narrative, it remains apart, creating its own tensions and coloration. Everyone in the band was capable of reacting melodically by creating sounds that added to the overall concept of the composition. Elevated to an equal role alongside saxophone and keyboards, Vitous, an improviser first and a bass player second, operated in a manner originally suggested by Scott LaFaro, commenting rhythmically, harmonically and melodically on the ever changing events around him.

Although Weather Report is customarily referred to as a jazz-rock group, their first two albums had nothing in common with the genre, and *I Sing the Body Electric* emerged as an ambitious experimental album. It says much for Columbia's *grand fromage* Clive Davis that he supported such a group as this, which, although unique, was still establishing a direction for its music. Remarkably, the album actually figured at 147 on the *Billboard* chart, such was the more ecumenical musical climate of the times, which was also seeing ambitious, if ultimately pretentious, experimentation in the field of rock music. Indeed, it was difficult to imagine any major record company marketing such bold, serious contemporary music as *I Sing the Body Electric* in the often grey, conservative 1980s or 1990s.

Before Weather Report, there had been very few recordings where individual improvisation was of secondary importance to collective improvisation. Broadly speaking, few artists exceeded the quality of their work in noncollective contexts. In contrast, Weather Report stand out as highly successful exponents of this approach – to all intent and purposes, this was electrified avant-garde. However, Zawinul did not see a future for the band in pursuing a collective identity, no matter how successfully the band might have functioned from time to time within this idiom. 'We had no focus,' said Zawinul. 'The music was nice, sometimes creative, sometimes incredibly creative, but if we were not totally on, nothing! I didn't want that, I didn't want to search.' The kind of direction he envisaged was suggested on *Second Sunday in August.* Here was a brief hint of the future, with a rhythmically robust role for the bass, and a combination of written and improvised material that imposed a greater sense of direction which seemed to channel the creative impulses of the group in a specific direction. From this point on, by Zawinul's own confession, he began to assert a more decisive role as leader and the results were immediately felt on their next album, *Sweetnighter* (†Columbia/Legacy [A] 485102–2) from 1973. His own tunes began to predominate and he began to arrange other band members' compositions, including Shorter's. 'I wanted the band to play stronger rhythmically,' said Zawinul. 'I wanted a groove.'

To get the groove Zawinul aspired to, he augmented the group with the drummer Herschel Dwellingham and Andrew White who played broken, or funky, lines on electric bass, thus representing a significant departure from the approach that had liberated the acoustic Vitous from a basic time-keeping function. It reflected Zawinul's growing disenchantment with his co-founder. 'Miroslav could play, believe me, he's hell of a musician, but he should have been a guitar player. He never had what I call a "bass" concept.' Vitous was shown the door and for *Sweetnighter* Alphonoso Johnson, previously with Woody Herman and Chuck Mangione, came in on electric bass, with Vitous appearing on only one piece, *American tango*, to which he contributed just the introduction. On this album Zawinul used a Moog synthesizer for the first time, an instrument developed by Dr Robert A. Moog in the late 1950s. However, unlike many albums from the 1970s when the instrument became popular, Zawinul avoided the obviousness inherent in many electronically generated sounds manufactured by the instrument, seeking instead electronic tones that had an acoustic resonance. By the time the group came to record *Mysterious Traveller*, Zawinul had expanded his keyboard set-up with two Arp 2600 synthesizers. He had also moved from New York to the West Coast, which in musical terms meant a new recording studio in Devonshire Sound in North Hollywood, where with the recording engineer Ron Malo he began to explore, to a far greater extent than before, the possibilities offered by the recording studios.

In classical music, the English producer Walter Legge and others had long ago argued that a recording was superior to a live performance, if only because a performer could attempt take after take over hours, days, weeks or even months before admitting only the best of those performances into the public domain. More importantly, Legge realized that a kind of perfection could be achieved in the studio by manipulating the truth, such as the dubbing-in by Elizabeth Schwarzkopf of certain high notes of Kirsten Flagstad's *Isolde.*

By the mid-1960s the development of multitrack recording made it possible to store different instruments recorded on different dates and in the final mix-down add, rerecord and alter the relationship one to another of these tracks. With his move to the West Coast, Zawinul became increasingly absorbed in the potential offered by the recording studio and the fast-developing technology to increase the dynamic and expressive range of Weather Report. *Mysterious Traveller* sees his first concerted effort to begin to take advantage of contemporary studio techniques. *Nubian sundance* is a joyful celebration that announces that the band has redefined itself again and contains a complex layer of rhythmic patterns using two drummers (Wilburn and Hadden) and two percussionists (Zawinul and Romao), whose polyrhythmic groove was built up through patient multitracking. The piece was built around a recording of an extended piano improvisation by Zawinul on piano, based on an *ostinato* in F major with motifs and orchestral effects introduced through multitracking to produce a constantly changing canvas of sound that at one point has Zawinul's voice mixed into synthesizer riffs to provide colour. It opens as if in a concert hall waiting to hear Weather Report perform; the sound of the audience absorbed in conversation gives way to a roar of the crowd as the band hit the first notes. It is an effective idea that Zawinul would return to again as the opening (in slightly varied form to produce a programmatic sound impression of an ethnic marketplace) on the title track of *Black Market* (†Columbia/Legacy [A] 468210–2).

The difference Johnson on bass made to the band is underlined by his own composition *Cucumber slumber*, which achieves an effective groove, a term that has been about in jazz for years, but in electric jazz began to assume a quite specific meaning. On a 'groove' number, the unity of rhythmic expression is achieved through economy of purpose. A groove demands you 'listen with your body', its effectiveness almost entirely mediated by the physical effect the music has on the listener – whether they feel compelled to pop their fingers, tap their feet or get up and dance. Engaging with the music in this way is in contrast to 'listening with the mind', contemplating it in a way that denies a bodily response as the mind absorbs its technical complexity. The groove is a rhythm-focused experience of African origin that appeals to the subjective dancer within us all. On both this and the opening track, the role of Shorter as epigrammatic colourist and soloist is vital to the group's authenticity. Although Zawinul was now de facto leader, Shorter nevertheless exerted a powerful creative influence on the band. 'No Wayne, no Weather Report,' was how Zawinul put it. 'We was always partners in crime, you know? He wanted it like that, one guy doesn't make a great group, it's like a soccer team. Without Wayne it would never have happened in the first place.'

Shorter contributed the title track, which opens with the electronically generated white noise favoured by movie-makers to suggest extraterrestrials. Zawinul enters on acoustic piano and sets up a repetitive figure that is heard throughout the first section of the piece. As bass and drums join him, a secondary subject, a brief descending phrase, is reintroduced periodically by way of contrast. A key change introduces Shorter's solo, and a new, less syncopated rhythmic subject on electric keyboards emerges, which remains until the coda, where by way of recapitulation the white noise suggestive of extraterrestrials returns. Once again, this is a groove piece, the central subject Shorter's tenor-saxophone solo. Across a hypnotic, swaying pulse, brief motifs are exchanged by Shorter and Zawinul which still retain the impromptu, colouristic feel that characterized their work on the Japanese concert portion of *I Sing the Body Electric*.

That Shorter and Zawinul had not abandoned this earlier spontaneous interplay is evidenced on *Blackthorn rose*, an improvised duet that in live performance continued to be a feature of the band until they disbanded in 1986. So close was their interplay, so melodic and well crafted their exchanges, that their improvisations assumed the symmetry of a previously written piece. *American tango*, on which Zawinul shared compositional credit with Vitous as 'a going-away present', is a stately, dramatic theme over broken bass figures that gives way to Shorter's brief solo and a return to the theme, over increasingly intense rhythmic activity, before a faded ending suggests that listeners were outsiders to a party only just beginning. *Scarlet woman* continues the slower mood of *Tango* with similarly dramatic, repetitive figures sculpted out of near-silent, gently pulsating rhythms suggested by Romao and Johnson.

Jungle book, like *Nubian sundance*, originated as a Zawinul piano improvisation and was built up through multitracking in the studio and at Zawinul's home studio. It includes a subtle fabric of wordless vocal choirs and exotic programmatic interludes over an undulating rhythmic tapestry built up through a variety of unusual percussion, including clay drums, tamboura, kalimba, maracas, tabala, finger cymbals and cabassa. As a whole, *Mysterious Traveller* opened up the potential of the studio-as-instrument for Weather Report, something that would be increasingly capitalized on in forthcoming albums. If 1975's *Tale Spinnin'* was an overindulgence, succumbing to a myriad of electronic effects, the band's move to bold new ad hoc forms on *Black Market* and *Heavy Weather* (†Columbia/Legacy [A] CK65108) benefited from the greater colouristic detail made possible by combinations of electronic instruments through multitracking.

Weather Report's journey from the free-form, collective improvisation on the concert section of *I Sing the Body Electric* to the ad hoc song forms of *Mysterious Traveller* produced the often impressionistic and programmatic soundscapes Zawinul originally envisaged on *Zawinul*. Subsequently, the group's discography would come to reflect an even broader range, from classical influences of the French impressionists to free jazz, from world music to bop, from big-band music to chamber music, from collective improvisation to tightly written ad hoc song forms. Despite their being routinely described as a 'jazz-rock' group, their stylistic outlook was extremely broad and any success the band enjoyed was clearly earned on their own terms that did not succumb to commercial artifice. Overall, Weather Report's significance in jazz has continued to grow since they disbanded in 1986, with the gradual acknowledgement that Zawinul and Shorter created a body of work that, outside of Duke Ellington's music, numbers among the most diverse in jazz. S.N.

Neil Ardley

446 **Kaleidoscope of Rainbows**
Gull (E) GULP1018, †Line (G) LICD900 351

Ian Carr (tpt, fl h); Bob Bertles, Barbara Thompson (fl, sop, alt); Brian Smith (fl, alt fl, sop, ten); Tony Coe (clt, bs clt, ten); Geoff Castle, Dave Macrae (el p, syn); Ardley (syn, comp, dir); Ken Shaw (g); Paul Buckmaster (cel); Roger Sutton (bs g, el bs); Roger Sellers (d); Trevor Tomkins (vib, perc). London, 1976.

Prologue · *Rainbow 1* · *Rainbow 2* · *Rainbow 3* · *Rainbow 4* · *Rainbow 5* · *Rainbow 6* · *Rainbow 7* · *Epilogue*

Stan Sulzman replaces Barbara Thompson on *Rainbow 2* and John Taylor replaces Dave Macrae on *Rainbows 6* and *7*.

Kaleidoscope of Rainbows is the final part of a trilogy, the other segments of which are *Greek Variations* (1969) and *A Symphony of Amaranths* (1971), and they are most advantageously heard in sequence. Quite apart from his listing Stravinsky, Ellington and Gil Evans as his main influences, the fact that the middle panel of his trilogy is dedicated to the two latter already tells us a lot about Ardley as a musician. In his quiet way he was almost subversive, for each of these pieces draws much out of little: before our ears small seeds grow into substantial trees, and such economy, not to mention such logical ordering of musical material, is highly unusual in the jazz sphere, where verbosity all too often reigns. Inevitably, some people have argued that the results, particularly because of the care and detailed planning in relating written and improvised aspects, mean that the results are 'not jazz'. [145] Yet the precedents for what Ardley in fact did are obvious in Ellington and before that in Morton; and in any case only authentic jazz musicians could give idiomatic performances of these works.

Greek Variations illustrates both the sort of compositional control exercised by Ardley and the amount of freedom he gave his musicians. Employing a nine-piece jazz ensemble plus string quintet, this piece is a sequence of variations on a Greek folk song and as these unfold they gradually shift further away from that source and provide a progressively freer basis for improvisation. The nature of the compositional craft involved is such that while thoroughly exploiting the potential of the chosen material, the soloists' scope is nowhere inhibited. Indeed the fact that one element can be heard as enhancing the other is precisely what makes this an important achievement in jazz composition. Similar comments are invited by *A Symphony of Amaranths*, which uses a large orchestra including string sextet. In the *Variations* there is improvisation both on Greek scales and on the intervals of the folk song, this practice being taken further, in another direction, by *A Symphony*. Here the initials of the two dedicatees, GE and DE, with some help from ACGB (because the Arts Council of Great Britain helped finance the recording), provided motifs and chords that are sources of both composing and the improvising it enfolds.

Elemental building blocks are also at the root of *Kaleidoscope of Rainbows*, yet the fact these derive from Balinese music indicates that here is another piece that follows a path of its own. In its initial version this was first heard in 1974, was scored for a large band of conventional instrumentation, and was companioned by a group of dances for two cellos. *Biformal from Bali* was the collective title of these two works, but Ardley recomposed the *Rainbows*, incorporating some of the cello material and now employing a smaller and more flexible ensemble of acoustic instruments but with some electricity used by pianos, synthesizers, guitar and bass. At that stage the piece occupied a whole concert, but it is here recorded in a shortened version, though still lasting almost 55 minutes.

The fundamental musical elements in *Kaleidoscope of Rainbows* are simple Balinese scales of five notes, one, known as *pelog*, being the characteristic scale of Indonesia while the other, *slendro*, is a pentatonic scale occurring throughout Eastern music. These are employed as the sources of a variety of patterns. Each pattern has a certain combination of colours – a specific colour of rhythm, another of order in its composition, and of feeling in the improvising to which it gives rise. This work matches the range of colours, if not quite of textures, found in *Amaranths*. Colour patterns are made from the hues of the rainbow and it is as if aural rainbows – the notes of the scales or the instruments of the ensemble or of some particular rhythm – are chopped into fragments and swirled repeatedly as in a kaleidoscope, resulting in ever new patchworks of sounds. It was originally intended to record this piece in quadraphonic sound so that the sounds of the instruments would in effect gyrate around the listener before settling into slow and stately, yet still moving, patterns. The results do not seem Balinese, the ensemble could hardly sound less like a gamelan, and there is no trace of 'ethnic exploitation'. At the same time, though the music does sound very much Ardley's, there is a lot of improvisation in the textures, some of this following Balinese manners of procedure while evidently being perfectly natural to the players.

In *Prologue* the musicians enter one by one, each going through a series of overlapping fragments using *pelog* notes but in different rhythms. Then *Rainbow 1* is a dialogue of linear phrases, again employing *pelog* notes. Almost from the first moment one's impression is of motion, of colour: the textures are tightly packed, yet everything dances. While there is much repetition of small rapid patterns, here the result is quite different from the products of minimalism – that village idiot among contemporary schools of composition. Rather is there a unified variety of endeavour from all the players, not least because although the basic tempo is held, emphasis in other respects changes, with various small ensembles of instruments briefly emerging and leading into quite other kinds of event, including a fairly wild Carr solo. Note also the slowly fading coda.

The becalmed *Rainbow 2* could scarcely be more different from most of *Rainbow 1*, singing quietly to itself with beautiful choirs of voices, for example flute, soprano saxophone, alto flute and bass clarinet. Another striking contrast is provided by the energetic *Rainbow 3* with its rapid-fire gestures. The shortest of these movements, this is a collective improvisation developed over several performances in public before the recording. After such activity, *Rainbow 4*, apart from its opening repeated-note ideas, restores calm, though in a way quite different from *Rainbow 2*. Included is a lovely rhapsodic soprano saxophone solo from Barbara Thompson. *Rainbow 5* is quick again, or rather it at first sets a relatively slow melody against a much faster accompaniment. Later Coe is exceedingly agile with his clarinet, offering a more daring, even abandoned, echo of the birdlike flight of *Rainbow 4*'s soprano-saxophone solo. A particularly atmospheric piece, *Rainbow 6* is conjured out of initial trills and tremolos, which recur at the end. It is made up of diverse elements which seem, deliberately, never to come altogether into focus. There is no particular solo voice and the music is somehow diffused within the ensemble. This is shaped by the work's most original thinking and it is perhaps unsurprising that *Rainbow 7*, the longest movement, is in comparison less interesting despite good solo playing by Castle, Smith, Shaw and Bertles.

In *Epilogue* the themes reappear one by one over the opening bass figure, this being reminiscent of the varied recapitulation of the finale to *Greek Variations*. These lead in *Kaleidoscope of Rainbows* to a briefly rhetorical ending, which confirms the impression made by *Rainbow 7* that there is a certain lessening of inspiration as this work approaches its close. It remains, however, Ardley's finest single work. Attention should also be given to earlier pieces recorded by the New Jazz Orchestra, notably *Western reunion* (1968), as well as to Ardley's later multimovement works *Will Power* (1974) and *Harmony of the Spheres* (1979). Ardley's subsequent greatly diminished involvement with music is much to be regretted, and one cannot help wondering what further he might have achieved in more favourable circumstances. M.H.

John Abercrombie

447 Night

ECM (G) 1272

Mike Brecker (ten); Abercrombie (g); Jan Hammer (key); Jack DeJohnette (d). New York City, April 1984.

Ethereggae · Night · 3 east · Look around · Believe you me · Four on one

Abercrombie's association with DeJohnette and Hammer dates back to 1974 and his impetuously driven album *Timeless* (ECM [G] 21047), his debut as a leader on records. A modernistic slant on the organ trios of the fifties and sixties, Abercrombie succeeded in pulling the tenets of jazz and rock guitar together under one roof. It marked the beginning of a fruitful association with DeJohnette that saw the formation, with Dave Holland on bass, of the Gateway trio in 1975 that produced *Gateway* (†ECM [G] 1061) and *Gateway 2* (ECM [G] 1105) in 1978. That same year Abercrombie joined DeJohnette's New Directions group for two years, appearing on two albums by the group. Subsequently, the Gateway trio, a cooperative venture but effectively a forum to feature Abercrombie's playing, reconvened to tour and record in the 1990s. *Homecoming* (†ECM [G] 1562) and *In the Moment* (†ECM [G] 1574) stated a persuasive case for inclusion in these pages, with their memorable and adventuresome approach to open form-improvisation.

Night reunited the original *Timeless* trio with the addition of Brecker on tenor saxophone, and was among the first recordings in the 1980s to suggest that the by now discredited jazz-rock movement of the 1970s, which had ground to a standstill through a combination of commercial excess and, to use Charles Shaar Murray's apposite phrase, 'cornball monumentalism', could yet have the potential to move to horizons unglimpsed in the previous decade. As Max Harrison has pointed out, free jazz appeared on the verge of creating a whole new musical language in the 1960s, but appeared to falter through a failure of will. History repeated itself in the 1970s as jazz-rock briefly suggested the promise of doing the same; Tony Williams's *Emergency!* (**442**) and recordings that built on it, like Miles Davis' *Agharta* (†Columbia [A] 4678972), suggested the potential of evolving into something that might eventually define itself as a wholly independent genre quite apart from the sound and conventions of anything that had gone before. Second time round, however, such ambitions were stifled by commercialism.

Yet the potential inherent in broadening the range of jazz expression through electricity (new tone colours) and metre (new rhythms) remained persuasive even as jazz-rock mutated into a peculiar species of jazz-inflected pop music that eventually took up residence on FM radio. As this music grew to fill the viewfinder, it began to obscure the very real achievements of the original jazz-rock pioneers. All too quickly an accommodation, or perhaps a fusion, first with rhythm 'n' blues and then with funk, overwhelmed any potential for artistic growth in favour of commercial exploitation. Any early promise of an expanded musical vocabulary was sacrificed in favour of expanded markets and shaping the music for the broadest possible market appeal, or, more accurately, the lowest common denominator.

The original premise on which jazz-rock had been founded, on risk, danger and exploration, was nevertheless clear to many of the musicians who participated in the first wave of jazz-rock. Brecker had been a key component of one of the most widely admired of all the early jazz-rock groups, Dreams, a band that never succeeded in translating their musical potential onto record, and he had subsequently played with Billy Cobham and the Brecker Brothers. Jan Hammer had been with the original Mahavishnu Orchestra. DeJohnette had performed with the Charles Lloyd quartet and with Miles Davis. Abercrombie had also been a member of Dreams, and of Billy Cobham's group. To these musicians, the original premise of jazz-rock was not one that succumbed to rampant virtuosity and the cute hooks of pop music.

As the 1970s had progressed, it became increasingly clear, most notably through the recordings of Miles Davis and Weather Report, that the 'big beat' of good old-fashioned rock music was never enough; indeed, this had never seriously been part of the equation. As jazz reached out to popular culture for reinvigoration, as it had in the past (most notably by importing popular Broadway standards as a way of expanding its expressive range), the possibilities suggested by rock music set in motion a search for ways to integrate the new electronic tone colours within the compositional and expressive palette of jazz as much as a quest to adapt new rhythms (to jazz, at least) as a way of invigorating a rhythmic scheme whose essential elements had remained virtually unchanged since 1917.

This case is stated emphatically on *Ethereggae* using the Jamaican reggae rhythm that was itself a fusion of *mento* and rhythm 'n' blues, which formed the basis of late-1960s classic reggae. The dramatic electronic tone colours that open the piece, a booming, four-note fanfare that is repeated ominously six times, gives way to a secondary subject with a subtly taut reggae rhythm. As Hammer launches into his solo using ear-catching, pre-MIDI electronics, the rhythm becomes more explicitly stated, but in DeJohnette's hands it appears colourful, suited to embellishment, with a fluidity that becomes more apparent during Brecker's entrance and solo. A reprise of the ominous opening motifs provides the background for Abercrombie's solo, which climaxes the piece. The title track is a conduit for the three expressive voices, Abercrombie on acoustic guitar, Brecker and Hammer (on acoustic piano), which suggests New Age without becoming bathetic, but is nonetheless striking for its emotional rigour.

3 east opens in post-bop mood; Hammer's repeated organ riffs leading to Brecker's statement of the fractured melody and Abercrombie's inscrutable guitar, straining to make every note count. Abercrombie's playing, ennobled by his strong rapport with DeJohnette, becomes a flowing abstraction of the theme and is held together by powerful logic that governs his note choices. When Brecker enters, his solo of rising intensity becomes almost a duet with DeJohnette. The climax is reached, and abruptly after a brief theme statement, the tune is over. *Look Around* confronts the 'big beat' of rock in a piece of changing moods; Abercrombie and Hammer in hushed give-and-take, DeJohnette and Brecker with a contrasting section of rhythmic intrigue. Abercrombie's solo engages with his influences – Montgomery, Kessel – before moving from the quiet refuge of contemplation to a contrasting mood of spiky assertion. Brecker enters, allowing a pastoral mood to define his playing as he considers the potential the flexible form of the composition offers him before steadily moving towards cueing the explicit, square rhythmic patterns derived from the contrasting section of the introduction, where his impassioned lyricism is lifted and driven by DeJohnette's inventive exertions.

Hammer succeeds in evoking memories of the Mahavishnu Orchestra with his insistent, haunting accompaniment to Abercrombie and Brecker as they state the suspended, floating theme of *Believe you me*; DeJohnette creates a swirling backdrop of shifting percussive colours in the same way Tony Williams filled the spaces around him with sound in the Miles Davis quintet. This rhythmic field of intensity generated behind the often shimmering electronic sounds has a timeless quality that is in contrast to the bop-inspired head of *Four on one.* Here the players respond to the requirements of the complexities of the style in a free-flowing, open-form piece that appears at odds with the generic ambiguity of the earlier compositions. Everyone gets a chance for exclamatory declaration, having deferred to the specific moods demanded by earlier numbers such as *Ethereggae* and *Believe you me* with their roots in jazz-rock. It was on these numbers in particular that Abercrombie suggested the possibility of moving forward to something that offered a greater range of musical and rhythmic possibilities in contrast to the generic boundaries restricted by tradition that for an increasing number of musicians in the 1980s and 1990s would come to offer the sanctuary of certainty. S.N.

John Scofield

448 **Blue Matter**
Gramavision (A) 18–8702–1

Scofield, Hiram Bullock (g); Mitchell Forman (key); Gary Grainger (b); Dennis Chambers (d); Don Alias (perc). New York City, September 1986.
Blue matter · *Now she's blonde* · *Make me*
Hiram Bullock absent. Same date.
Trim · *Heaven hill* · *So you say* · *The nag* · *Time marches on*

When Scofield joined Miles Davis's band in 1982, his impact was considerable. It is widely agreed that the three albums on which he subsequently appeared with Davis, *Star People* (Columbia [A] 38657), *Decoy* (Columbia [A] 38991) and *You're Under Arrest* (Columbia [A] 40023), are the best in the trumpeter's post-furlough discography. By then, Scofield was a widely experienced musician, having recorded with musicians as diverse as Gerry Mulligan and Jay McShann, Lee Konitz and Charles Mingus, Billy Cobham and Dave Liebman. He had also appeared as a leader in his own right with a quartet (1977–8) and a trio, with Steve Swallow on bass and Adam Nussbaum on drums, which he formed in 1980 and led until his stint with Davis. Scofield's approach to the guitar, although he had extensive experience in jazz-rock during the 1970s, actually evolved from his love of Jim Hall and the 1960s soul-jazz tradition of musicians like Wes Montgomery and Grant Green.

During his tenure with Davis, Scofield had recorded *Electric Outlet* (Gramavision [A] 8405). When he left he briefly fronted a pick-up group which recorded *Still Warm* (Gramavision [A] 18–8508–1). However, *Blue Matter* represents his first regular post-Miles ensemble. It became one of the more memorable bands of a largely renascent decade, primarily through the personal chemistry that combined Scofield's twisted blues lyricism with the forceful and dramatic playing of Sebastian on bass and Chambers on drums. The latter had spent almost ten years laying down the funk in George Clinton's Parliament/Funkadelic ensembles but was a far more rounded jazz drummer than the somewhat eccentric surroundings from which he emerged might suggest. Sebastian had played with the group Pockets, but he was an accomplished bassist in a wide variety of settings.

As with *Still Warm*, Scofield did not cut his ties with Davis's music; *Blue matter*, for example, has a loping bass figure for ten bars that immediately evokes the trumpeter prowling around the stage. It is contrasted by a powerful eight-bar B section of funk featuring Chambers's startling semiquaver bass drum figures, [146] before returning to a now embellished *mysterioso* opening section. Throughout, Scofield's hornlike *legato* lines, which seem to wrench meaning from his guitar, announce the coming of age of one of the major soloists to emerge in the 1980s.

Often, Scofield's compositions are deceptively simple. *Time marches on* begins as a feature for bass against sustained chords for eight bars. The second section, B, is introduced for a further eight bars, which lead into the solo section of eight bars that is repeated over and over. On cue the band return to the B section and then move to the coda, a transition from $4/4$ to $15/16$ time. The mechanics, although simple, are less interesting than what the musicians make of them, bringing it alive with an almost desperately combative edge. Each tune has a specific groove designed to evoke a specific feel; *Heaven hill* is an gospel ballad, full of blue hues and bent notes, and is in essence a study of Scofield's economical lyricism. *So you say* is an intense refraction of a calypso that, like all Scofield's music, uncoils in mysterious ways, a combination of jazz's technique and the visceral attack of rock's touchstone, the electric guitar.

Scofield's skill in highlighting the most compelling elements of each musical form without surrendering his intensely personal guitar signature, as identifiable as the thumbprint sound of previous eras of jazz musicians such as a Johnny Hodges or a Benny Carter, was combined with a sophisticated harmonic knowledge of guitar voicings often voiced in terms of modes. The loping theme of *Now she's blonde*, seemingly composed out of blues fragments assimilated during his stay with Miles, assumes a life of its own; his solo, angular and rigorously edited, emerges as a series of epigrams and elliptical asides that together could stand on their own as another song, such was its gritty compositional logic.

The nag is pure groove, whose effectiveness is almost entirely mediated by the physical effect the music has on the listener, whether they feel compelled to engage with the music by tapping a foot or popping their fingers. This is entirely different to listening with the mind, contemplating the music in a way that denies bodily response while the mind absorbs the music's complexities. The groove has its origins in African drum choirs, where the body becomes engaged with the rhythm in a way it does not in European music. What Scofield succeeds in doing is reaching a compromise between the two: by presenting complex ideas within a strong rhythmic framework, he demands you listen with both the body and with the mind.

Scofield's presence on the touring circuits in the mid-1980s, as well as the remarkable popularity of his former boss Miles Davis, helped rejuvenate interest in electric jazz which proposed new life for what had become one of jazz's weariest identities. With this group and with his subsequent band, a quartet with the saxophonist Joe Lovano, and indeed with later groups, he demonstrated that his conceptualism would not stand still, an important lesson he attributed to Miles Davis. 'I seem to have ended up having really good bands and moving on to something else,' he said in 1998. 'I think I'm a junkie for getting people together, getting that creative rush and as soon as the spark dies, moving on to try something else.' [147] By 1996 Scofield had topped the influential *down beat* critics' poll for four straight years, an important alternative to the emergence of an acoustic mainstream who played in the adopted voices of jazz's older and posthumous heroes. By refusing to be trapped in the past he suggested the potential of jazz was far from exhausted in a way that those clinging to a rigorously acoustic paradigm of the music, rooted in 1950s hard bop, failed to do. S.N.

Marc Johnson

449 **Bass Desires**

†ECM (G) 1299

John Scofield, Bill Frisell (g); Johnson (b); Peter Erskine (d). New York City, May 1985.

Samurai hee-haw · *Resolution* · *Black is the colour of my true love's hair* · *Bass desires* · *A wishing doll* · *Mojo highway* · *Thanks again*

By the time of this recording, Johnson, who was born in 1953, had a broad range of experience under his belt. When he entered the North

Texas State University at the age of 19, he was already working professionally as a member of the Fort Worth Symphony. A recording made with his fellow student and pianist Lyle Mays with the university's One o'Clock Lab Band earned a Grammy nomination. On graduation Johnson joined the Woody Herman orchestra, where he appeared on three albums before joining Bill Evans in 1978 and remaining with him until the pianist's death in 1980. Since Johnson was following in the shoes of such distinguished bassists as Scott LaFaro and Eddie Gomez, the eyes of the jazz world were on him and Johnson did not disappoint. On albums such as the two-volume *Paris Concert* (Elektra/Musician [A] 60164–1 and 60311–1) and the 6-CD set *Turn Out the Stars* (†Warner Bros [A] 945925–2), he revealed an eloquent tone, a facility throughout the whole range of his instrument, and although less mercurial than his predecessors, he was nevertheless a virtuoso musician whose playing did not lack for imagination or fluency.

After working with Stan Getz, the Mel Lewis Jazz Orchestra, JoAnne Brackeen, Bob Brookmeyer, Philly Joe Jones and John Lewis in an acoustic environment, Johnson decided to explore the potential offered by an electric ensemble. In the mid-1970s he had been impressed by a two-guitar set-up with Pat Metheny and Mick Goodrick in a group led by Gary Burton, and in the 1980s he was again drawn to the concept through the playing of John Scofield and Mike Stern, first in a group led by the bassist Peter Warren and later in the then current Miles Davis group. When he came to try the concept out himself, he originally turned to John Abercrombie and Scofield, but pressure of work prevented Abercrombie from joining the band. Johnson then turned to Bill Frisell, recording the group in a New York club in January 1984. After sending the tapes to Manfred Eicher of ECM records in Munich, he was offered an opportunity to record the band. Bass Desires was born, although from the start it was destined to be an occasional project, since his in-demand sidemen were all developing careers as leaders in their own right.

Johnson's warm bass sets the tone for the group and throughout, his rapport with Erskine emerges as an album highlight. Their special empathy was such that other leaders, including Gary Burton and John Abercrombie, hired them as a unit on their own albums. The wittily titled opening track *Samurai hee-haw* brings a little of what Johnson has called that 'Mid-West vibe' – he is from Nebraska – saying: 'I wanted those open harmonic and melodic feelings.' [148] Indeed, this feeling chimes with the Colorado-born Frisell, whose meditations on Americana would increasingly colour his outlook, creating a style where the sounds of rock, jazz and country existed in almost perfect synchronicity. Frisell's playing style was the most original guitar sound to emerge in vernacular music since that of Jimi Hendrix, who had clearly provided him with a source of inspiration to create his own version of sonic legerdemain. Utilizing controlled feedback and a wide range of signal-processing effects such as delay, chorus and fuzz, Frisell expanded the range of the electric guitar into the realms of impressionistic sound-on-sound pastiches. From the sound of plain old overdriven guitar to ethereal, heavenly-host choirs, Frisell pulled the apparently opposing poles of Hendrix and Jim Hall under one roof to create a wholly unique approach to the electric guitar that perfectly complemented Scofield's anguished brevity.

The album's longest track and its centrepiece is a shimmering version of Coltrane's *Resolution*, from *A Love Supreme* (**424**), a composition that in its original form repeated the basic eight-bar theme three times to give, in essence, a 24-bar AAA structure. Here, it begins à la Coltrane, with a bass solo, prior to the exposition theme which is illuminated in contemporary tone colours by the two guitars in dizzying duet. The eight-bar theme is repeated twice, with a 16-bar interlude before a final repeat of the eight-bar theme that provides a springboard for Scofield's solo. The loose, jangling finesse of his line, with side-slipping glances into distant keys, is in contrast to the tight rhythmic hold he exerted on *Blue Matter* (**448**). Such rhythmic flexibility characterizes all the great players, irrespective of what instrument they play, and is something Scofield deploys to telling effect throughout the album as he responds to the needs of the moment.

He is contrasted by the sonic revelry of Frisell's statement, which was a virtual textbook of postmodern guitar playing. While the ambient colour washes he provides at the end of this piece, and throughout *Black is the colour of my true love's hair*, might owe something to Brian Eno run through the prism of Frisell's imagination, these sounds emerge as intensely personal statements rather than imitation that flatters its source. On the latter piece, taken at a slow tempo, the rhythm is suspended and periods pass without any implicit statement of the beat before Frisell outlines and embellishes the theme of this traditional lament. Erskine does not play time, colouring the haunting atmosphere with dustings of cymbal tones. As Frisell's line becomes fragmented, with spiky punctuations and anguished asides, the mood darkens. Despite the feeling of suspended animation, the emotional force of the performance remains in the memory long after the piece has floated by.

Erskine's composition gives the album its name, a dialogue between Frisell and Scofield against the walking bass and insistent post-bop drumming of Erskine. Yet while Johnson may be playing four-to-the-bar with Erskine's rhythms underlining the rhythmic climate the guitarists play in a different metre, creating several layers of sound, rhythmic interest and contrast. *A wishing doll*, an unusual choice written by Elmer Bernstein and David Mack, returns to Frisell's eerie moonscapes with Scofield outlining arpeggios in deferential accompaniment as Frisell wrings un-guitarlike sounds from his instrument – a violin, a flute – as the melody appears and disappears like the great white whale.

Mojo highway suggests an abstracted reggae, a voodoo groove of brooding mood and is one of the most powerful tracks on the album. Frisell's playing here, when placed alongside his contributions to *Black is the colour of my true love's hair* and *A wishing doll*, reveals how much he broadened the expressive range of the guitar post-Hendrix. *Thanks again* is another piece at a slow, loping tempo that Bass Desires seemed to inhabit effortlessly.

After just one more album, *Second Sight* (†ECM [G] 1351), another much admired work, Bass Desires were gone. The fast-accelerating careers of all the participants made pursuing the project more and more difficult to fit into their conflicting schedules. Not until 1998 did Johnson reactivate the two-guitar format, this time with Frisell and Pat Metheny with Joey Baron on drums. *The Sound of Summer Running* (†Verve [A] 539 299–2) turned out to be worth the wait. However, in the mid-1980s, Bass Desires provided eloquent testimony to the less-is-more aesthethic and was a potent reminder that electric jazz, despite a period of excess and overindulgence in the latter half of the 1970s and the rise of the fusion movement in the 1980s and 1990s, continued to offer jazz a fruitful avenue for further exploration and development. S.N.

6

Alternatives to Freedom

Paths Not Followed

Jazz has a seemingly innate tendency to increase its expressive range and its variety of techniques, but the music dealt with below embodies potentially major developments that were not followed up.

Dave Brubeck

450 The Dave Brubeck Octet
†Original Jazz Classics (A) OJCCD101–2

Dick Collins (tpt); Bob Collins (tbn); Bob Cummings, Paul Desmond (alt); Dave VanKreidt (ten, comp[1], arr[2]); Bill Smith (clt, bar, comp[3], arr[4]); Brubeck (p, comp[5], arr[6]); Ron Crotty (bs); Cal Tjader (d); Jack Weeks (arr[7]). In or around San Francisco, 1948–9.
How high the moon? · *I hear a rhapsody*[2] · *Laura*[6] · *Playland at the beach*[5,6] · *Serenades suite*[1,2] · *The prisoner's song*[7] · *Rondo*[5,6] · *Schizophrenic scherzo*[3,4] · *You go to my head* · *Closing theme*[5,6]

Bob Cummings absent. San Francisco, July 1950.
Love walked in[2] · *Indiana*[4] · *What is this thing called love?*[4] · *The way you look tonight*[6] · *September in the rain*[2] · *Prelude*[1,2] · *Fugue on bop themes*[1,2] · *Let's fall in love*[2]

Jazz commentators who knew them more by reputation than by personal encounter tended for a long while to lack inquisitiveness about these unique recordings. They have deserved better regard for a number of reasons: i) for their hints of how some West Coasters were reacting to bop and its relatives; ii) for their strange – perhaps uncanny – seismograph of tremors from the earliest Miles Davis Capitol nonet recordings (**376**); iii) for the light they shed upon the early aspirations of a jazz star later to become immensely popular; and iv) for their anticipations of Third Stream.

The earlier group is actually a nonet and, in several items, appears to function as a septet, disengaging the rhythm section. *How high the moon?* is a weak joke, little worthy of attention. An anonymous interlocutor, outdoing Symphony Sid in glib *non sequiturs*, links half a dozen interpretations of the tune according to well-known jazz – or near-jazz – styles.

I hear a rhapsody introduces VanKreidt's jazz-arranging manner and his capable tenor style; there are bop-prompted harmonies, efficiently handled, and, from Brubeck, a solo much more acceptable than the admixture of concerto-style romanticism and loud boorishness with which the pianist leads his own score of *Laura*. No arranger is named for *You go to my head*: a brief 3/4 superimposition may suggest Brubeck, but Smith, whose clarinet is prominent throughout, introduces a similar device during his version of *What is this thing called love?*, written in 1946 and with the bridge in 7/4. In any case the three main arrangers do not differ in any significant factor.

The other pieces, most of them very brief, show various aspects of the leading minds' flirtations with European forms. VanKreidt's *Serenades suite* wittily revives an 18th-century alfresco tradition. It is totally scored and, in general, adapts modern shapes in its counterpoint. Only the third movement gestures, briefly, towards jazz inflection. Movement four plays skilfully with rapid fugal patterns, rather less classically formed than those in Brubeck's *Playland at the beach*, which has also a clodhopping *ländler* interlude.

Smith's *Schizophrenic scherzo*, perhaps the most enterprising of all these 'serious' numbers, uses jazz phraseology in quasi-fugal patterns and is confidently slanted towards polytonality. Weeks's minuscule transformation of *The prisoner's song*, like these other experiments, uses the wind instruments only, and it may call to mind a Stravinsky on the edge of serialism. Yet brevity makes assessment difficult. *Serenades suite* is, at four and a half minutes, the longest essay by far but Smith's use of two and a half minutes is judicious enough to make his study in schizophrenia a notably more compelling augury of Third Stream amalgamations.

Rondo by Brubeck is, in retrospect, a predictable exercise and, like all his later forays of classical inspiration, it betrays innocence of the expressive techniques which tempered formalism in the days of baroque. In *Rondo* bass and drums are used sparsely, and not to provide rhythmic contrast.

Bearing in mind the month of the 1950 session, one is puzzled by Brubeck's claim that he had not heard of the Davis nonet prior to the octet's dissolution. [1] The possibility of his, or at least of other octet members, having known of the first few nonet issues seems strong on aural evidence; also consider the fact that *Move* and *Budo* were put out on 78 rpm 'within a month' of the January 1949 recording, *Jeru* and *Godchild* in April of that year, *Israel* and *Boplicity* in October. [2] The musical evidence of July 1950 is intriguing. VanKreidt's *Love walked in* and *Let's fall in love* achieve rhythmic syntax and harmonic texture which seem too close to the nonet's procedures to have been hit upon independently. Mulligan's ideas in particular may have been heeded. In *September in the rain* the same arranger's response is more free-ranging, encouraging longer, more intricate solos, and yet it closes in borrowed ethos. Smith's approach in *What is this thing called love?* is more personal, and its scoring is affected by Smith's own doubling on clarinet and baritone. It is hard to imagine that Brubeck's *The way you look tonight* was scored without an ear being lent to the nonet. The piano solo's use of the quotation from Kern's *Bill*, which opens Davis's *Godchild* solo, is an odd coincidence. But then Brubeck was suiting a Kern quotation to another Kern tune, and Davis, who sometimes slotted the *Bill* tag into other settings, [3] was not!

Smith's mutation of *Indiana* also frames lengthier solos but its ensembles echo the nonet, especially in their rhythmic punctuations. The relationship of ensemble to soloists is, in all these song scores, roughly in the Davis pattern. It must be added that other elements, in counterpoint, in melodic and rhythmic imagination, and in tonal colouration, mean that octet is saved from being merely a Davis facsimile.

VanKreidt's fast *Fugue on bop themes* may be the most thoroughgoing and effective use of fugue ever recorded by a jazz composer. Though it uses a classical form very skilfully, it is completely jazz, its adaptation of Parker-like subjects and its boppish inflections are well in character, and every member of the group fully engaged. In 1957 VanKreidt was to join the Brubeck quartet for a programme including his dreamy *Prelude* and a tribute to an honoured master, Darius Milhaud, in *Darien mode* [4] – a reminder that the teachings of Milhaud, and of Schoenberg and Roger Sessions, fuelled the ambitions of this critically neglected band's leading members. E.T.

Red Norvo

451 Music to Listen to Red Norvo By

Contemporary (A) C3534, †Original Jazz Classics (A) OJCCD155-2

Buddy Collette (fl); Bill Smith (clt); Barney Kessel; (g); Red Mitchell (bs); Shelly Manne (d); Norvo (vib). Los Angeles, 26 January, 9 February, 3 March 1957.

Poème · Red sails · The red broom · Rubricity · Paying the dues blues · Divertimento

In the fabulous story of jazz, a music which in terms of a wider musical history must be deemed an entirely modern phenomenon, itself endowed with innate perceptions of historical change, Norvo has figured as a space-time traveller with a renewable season ticket valid for several forms of transport. From when he started out at the beginning of the 1930s, it became clear (hear **199**, whose items cover 1933–8) that he was, by any perceptive criteria, a jazz modernist who would remain vitally curious about the possibilities of his music. The paradox of this hides in his striking ability to maintain a style of playing – on vibraharp and occasionally marimba – that established its aptitude within stylistically developing ensembles over a number of decades. While keeping his expressions appropriate to various swing-period groups, he allied himself, as **255** shows, with the early stirrings of bop. The trio sessions at **247** are also regarded as typical of transitional exploration.

The personnel above will suggest a number of links with West Coast groups recorded during the 1950s. Smith has a close involvement with **450**, and the fact that Jack Montrose is the composer of *Poème* may suggest comparisons with **303**. There may be other 'native' jazz ligatures as well, but most are subtle. The music of this gathering creates its own unusual character.

The fascinating yet never mystifying complexity of this music – a remarkable exhibition, in fact, of the composer-arranger's art – commends it as a minor jazz classic, while at the same time making it a prime candidate for this section with its emphasis on virtual singularity. What seems like a curious misconception of this session's overall aim appears in the suggestion of one reviewer that success was chiefly due to 'the effervescent rhythm section of Kessel, Mitchell and Manne, who inspire Collette and Norvo to produce excellent solos'. [5] How far off the mark that falls is demonstrated immediately as Manne, playing timpani, foreshadows the theme of *Poème*, a technique he is to repeat later. And Kessel's frequent solos, along with Mitchell's less frequent ones, are by no means the only evidences that the roles of these men, howsoever effervescent, are by no means tied to a functional subsection. There are times, during Kessel's *Red sails*, Lennie Niehaus's *Paying the dues blues* and elsewhere, when a swinging impetus calls for rather more conventional rhythm, but even then such passages are part of a varied episodal context, and the three men are seldom called upon to function strictly in team. This is partly practical acknowledgement of the greater flexibility being achieved in contemporary ensembles; but it must be repeated that this Norvo group is characteristic largely of itself. Improvisational spontaneity is outweighed by the use of scores, the intricacy of which encourages the contrast of several extended solos and, in addition, requires the gifts of men who can maintain the impression of the spontaneous effect most of the time.

Norvo and Kessel are the chief soloists in *Poème*, but, as in most solos on this disc, their excursions do not proceed far unaccompanied by contrapuntal and chordal figures. The sombre theme of Norvo's *Red broom* starts with an interweaving of clarinet and flute. Norvo's solo has accompaniment from those two instruments as well as from other pairings as it proceeds. Kessel, who intervenes, continues with Norvo in support. The variety of ensemble figures is complex beyond brief analysis. Silences play a significant part in *Red broom*, also in *Rubricity* and in parts of *Divertimento.* In the more evidently swinging expeditions, such as *Paying the dues blues* and *Red sails*, there are deft swing- or bop-style unison lines, and a lot of support figures, even when executed by only a couple of instruments, seem to imitate big-band expressions as if from a kind of giant-killer stance. The lightness of all 'voicings' underscores the joke here.

Rubricity, a slow air by Duane Tatro (**453**), introduced melodically by Manne's timpani, has a dreamy quality not unlike *Poème.* Silences are deployed to enhance an enigmatic mood, and as Norvo improvises, spaced chords punctuate a deliberate measure which has grown out of initial indeterminacy. Collette's broad-toned flute statement swaps blither figures with the vibraphonist's rather dry lines.

Divertimento is a four-movement composition by the widely talented Smith, active as a composer beyond the limits of jazz and a teacher at the University of Southern California round the time of this recording. The style of this suite does not differ significantly from that of the other numbers, which suggests that Smith's was a major guiding hand for the entire session. Neither the comedy of *Schizophrenic scherzo* nor the cool loitering of *What is this thing called love?*, recorded with Brubeck's innovatory groups of several years before (**450**), predict the manner of this 1957 music.

Moving through i) a strategy of skewed melodic diversions at mid-tempo, during which Collette is given his head briefly before Norvo assumes a quiet lead into ii) a sombre conversation enlivened somewhat by sinewy Smith–Collette exchanges, Smith, while he often puts Norvo at centre stage, also sets down contour lines and 'chairs' varying question-and-answer 'sessions'. Mitchell and Manne kick off and close a jaunty foray iii) in the midst of which Norvo invents freely, then he and Collette together ride some vigorous harmonic writing. With the tempo upped a little iv) Smith toys with a variety of antiphonal forms – Norvo answering the reeds, Smith and Kessel running counter to Collette, Norvo riffing merrily as other characters cultivate mildly pyrotechnical shapes, Collette and Smith fuguing . . . and so on . . .

A writer cannot hope to get beyond the merest impression of the richness of these remarkable jazz creations, and would be a fool to suggest what the real reason might be that this quite fascinating path was not followed. It has the power to fascinate still, and its preservation is a just cause. E.T.

Gil Melle

452 Primitive Modern

Prestige (A) PRLP7040, †Original Jazz Classics (A) OJCCD1712-2

Melle (bar, comp); Joe Cinderella (g); Bill Phipps (bs); Ed Thigpen (d). New York City, 20 April 1956.

Adventure swing · *Mark one* · *Dedicatory piece for the geophysical year 1957*

Same personnel. New York City, 1 July 1956.

Dominica · *Ballet time* · *Ironworks*

This is perhaps the most rewarding of the series of records, full of intriguing ideas that suggested all kinds of further potentialities, which Melle set down for Blue Note and Prestige in the 1950s. Combing the jazz press of that time leaves the impression that, apart from an occasional offhand record review, they attracted no attention whatever. Melle's jazz now inevitably sounds conservative beside much of what has happened since, yet a feeling of adventure, of significant exploration, survives. Its fusing of exuberant fantasy with precise detail should have met a kinder fate than to have been nearly lost in the swamp of discographical fact. Hence some attention will be paid here to certain of his other records.

In Melle's somewhat rambling notes for *Primitive Modern* he claims that 'modern jazz at it's [*sic*] best is a wedding of the classics with the more modern developments native to jazz', and he also speaks of 'the perfect admixture of classical techniques with jazz emotion and beat'. Yet this music offers no real parallel with the Schullerian Third Stream, and though adaptations of techniques from elsewhere have been made throughout the history of jazz, Melle's work exemplifies rather the extension of its musical language via growth from within. His output is 'primitively modern', however, in the sense that the bass and drums swing quite hard to compensate for the generally more complicated roles of the baritone and guitar. This comes off well because the balance of complexity and simplicity shifts flexibly, the roles occasionally being almost reversed.

Given the unusual demands made by a lot of this music, the quartet is remarkably sure-footed, sounding as if they have done much work together. There is a particularly close understanding between Melle and Cinderella. These are, indeed, tightly integrated performances, refined yet sometimes fierce, with much polyrhythm and a wide range of dynamics, the differences between the guitar's and the baritone's registers being an especial aid to balanced textures. The absence of a piano has the usual effect of lightening the ensemble's sound and promoting flexibility. [6]

One message of the *Primitive Modern* and *Quadrama* (Prestige [A] PRLP7097) quartet records is that Melle's jazz thrived best on limitations, benefiting from the taut discipline of exactly focused musical explorations. In noteworthy contrast, the *Gil's Guests* sessions (Original Jazz Classics [A] OJC1753) tended to produce just strings of solos, albeit very good ones, because of the need to accommodate Art Farmer, Hal McKusick, Kinny Dorham, Julius Watkins and other extra players. An exception is *Ghengis*, and this leads to other points.

Melle's list of influences is striking, with not only Parker and Konitz on the jazz side but also King Oliver and Herbie Nicholls. He gives Bartók as his chief classical exemplar, yet is insistent, the remarks quoted above almost to the contrary, that any devices and procedures coming from that kind of source must be fully assimilated into jazz. He is as good as his word, and *Soudan*, also from *Gil's Guests*, though it had Bartók's harmonization of a Wallachian folk melody as its starting-point, is wholly a jazz piece. Likewise for *Ghengis*, which is more specifically programmatic than most jazz. Its main theme imitates the contours of Eurasian folk song, but although Melle says this item was prompted by Bartók's String Quartet No. 4, the music contains no detectable allusions to that score. Other of Melle's themes, such as the *Block Island* line, benefit, as does *Ghengis*, from the added tone colours of the *Gil's Guests* set, and as examples of his and Cinderella's work on records are so few, even the more casual of this collection's settings are precious.

And even amid the dissonant counterpoint and bitonality of the quartet performances, some part of its repertoire is fairly straightforward. A good instance is *Rush hour in Hong Kong* (not the Abram Chasins piano piece) from the *Quadrama* sessions. Two Ellington titles from the same source do not sound like anything heard *chez le Duc*, yet a slow, if fairly dramatic, ballad of Melle's, *Jacqueline*, has some pretence to conventionality. In fact, despite the somewhat complex ambitions of Melle's more characteristic music, its acerbity and occasionally strident emphasis, it is often, in both his themes and in his and Cinderella's solos, appealingly melodious – so much so that one might have thought this would lead to its wider acceptance. Cinderella achieved the considerable distinction of being ignored by even more books on jazz than Melle himself. As improvisations like the one on *It don't mean a thing*, from the *Quadrama* dates, establish, his work is as compelling in its rhythmic life and tireless melodic invention as that of any guitarist discussed in this book.

The fact remains that a leader who puts *Dominica* first on a record is unconcerned with immediate popularity. Melle calls this 'a jazz dirge' and there are ample precedents for such a thing, for example from the Young Tuxedo Brass Band on **18**. The tempo picks up at some points and there is fine three-part writing for baritone, guitar and bowed bass, the voices greatly varying in prominence from one moment to another. The modal and speedy *Adventure swing* includes a brilliant guitar solo with the leader murmuring to excellent effect in the background; then the roles are reversed. Melle at first played the tenor, and *Cyclotron* from

1953 (Blue Note [A] BLP5020) is a good instance of his work on that instrument, although he was recording with the baritone by the following year. He certainly achieves a more characteristic expression on the latter, his dark tone and supple phrases not sounding like anyone else. Typical is the way both his ideas and Cinderella's are tightly packed, not least in the exchange of four-bar phrases between them and Thigpen before the *Adventure swing* theme is recapitulated.

Said to incorporate North African drum patterns at some points, the *Dedicatory piece* offers a more equal-voiced duet between guitar and baritone. The guitar then takes the lead but Melle remains too active for this to be called a guitar solo. There is another highly inventive sequence of fours leading back to the two-voiced theme. *Mark one* is a bit more conventional at first, though Cinderella and Melle are soon weaving counterpoint together, and there is another superb guitar solo. Sometimes a chord sequence underlies the solos which is different from the one harmonizing the theme. Melle writes: 'Many times a progression which lends itself well to the theme falls short in providing an incentive-creating foundation for improvisation.' Apparently the earliest instance of this was his *October* of 1953 (Blue Note, as above) and the important example here is *Ironworks*, in which the theme's difficult harmonization is turned into something still more demanding for the solos – at a very fast tempo. Another fiery guitar solo results, and Melle reminds us that, quite apart from his ideas, he is an extremely accomplished executant.

As if in confirmation of a point made above, *Ballet time* is so melodious that we could say it is positively tuneful. And here is possibly Melle's finest solo, shapely and lucid in its unfolding, and Cinderella, lightly accompanied by the others, is again productive of graceful, memorable ideas, his solo as beautifully sustained as his leader's. During the 1970s Melle went into electronic music, but a piece such as *Ballet time* makes the neglect of his early work seem not so much disappointing as positively mysterious. M.H.

Duane Tatro

453 Jazz for Moderns

Contemporary (A) C3514, †Original Jazz Classics (A) OJCCD1878–2

Stu Williamson (tpt); Bob Enevoldsen (v-tbn); Joe Eger (fr h); Lennie Niehaus (alt); Bill Holman (ten); Jimmy Giuffre (bar); Ralph Peña (bs); Shelly Manne (d); Tatro (comp). Los Angeles, 13 September 1954.
Backlash · *Multiplicity* · *Turbulence* · *Folly*

Vince de Rosa (fr h) and Bob Gordon (bar) replace Eger, Giuffre. Los Angeles, 4 April 1955.
Outpost · *Maybe next year* · *Conversation piece* · *Low clearance*

Joe Maini (alt) and Giuffre (bar) replace Niehaus, Gordon. Los Angeles, 1 November 1955.
Dollar day · Easy terms · Minor incident

If, as Nabokov claims, human life is a series of footnotes to a vast obscure unfinished masterpiece, then perhaps Duane Tatro's career in jazz might be described as a footnote to a footnote in the obscurest part of the masterpiece. This is his only jazz recording, although Red Norvo and Art Pepper recorded compositions by him that are dealt with under **(455)** and **(467)**. As his name is only once mentioned in the standard reference works on jazz, the 1955 edition of *The New Encyclopedia of Jazz*, some biographical detail seems to be appropriate. [7] Tatro was born in Van Nuys, California, on 18 May 1927, but his family moved to Iowa when he was one. His father was something of an inventor in the electronics field and had a factory there. During a summer vacation job in a restaurant in the Waterloo district he was entranced by the sounds of the big bands, including those of Larry Clinton, Woody Herman, Tommy Dorsey and Glenn Miller, in a dance hall adjacent to the restaurant. Resolving to become involved in music, he supplemented his small income with gardening jobs to save up for a clarinet, which was eventually bought with the help of his father. By the time he moved to tenor saxophone, the family had returned to Los Angeles. With America entering the war in late 1941, Tatro found himself sufficiently accomplished to play professionally in USO (United Service Organization) groups, joining the Musicians' Union at 15. His first full-time job was in a band led by Mel Tormé, which led to a call from Stan Kenton when he was still only 16. Despite family protests that he finish high school, Tatro played with Kenton around Los Angeles and recorded with the band on Armed Forces Radio Service transcriptions but not commercially. When Kenton took over Skinnay Ennis's spot on the Bob Hope Show, Tatro went out on tour with the package for the duration of the mismatched pairing, 39 weeks. Then, when a disenchanted Kenton moved his operation to New York, the young saxophonist was finally prevailed upon to return to high school and complete his education.

During the remainder of his time at high school, he took occasional dance-band jobs, usually taking the jazz solos. He was drafted in 1945 and completed a radar course in Chicago, but as the war ended he found himself transferred to a band at Great Lakes Naval Station where he came into contact with some of the top musicians who had been drafted into the navy. Indeed, Great Lakes was where Artie Shaw had been stationed just before going overseas with his famous 'Rangers' navy band a couple of years earlier. It was here Tatro's interest was stimulated in composing and arranging. Out of the navy, he played with Joe Venuti and Dick Pierce while studying music at the University of Southern California and it was during this time he composed several of the numbers on this disc. Subsequently he took advantage of the GI Bill to study music at the École Normale de Musique in Paris. There he studied composition with Darius Milhaud and Arthur Honegger, counterpoint with Honegger's wife Andrée Vaurabourg – who had previously taught Boulez – and conducting with Jean Fournier. During his two-and-a-half-year stay in France he formed a jazz band that performed at weekends and during holidays; occasionally they played with visiting Americans, including Rex Stewart in Paris and Roy Eldridge in Tunisia.

In 1951 Tatro returned home and returned to USC again, studying in the day and working in an electronics firm at night. In 1953 an introduction to Contemporary Records and Lester Koenig resulted in a commission for four pieces, but because of the demands on his time these were not recorded until September 1954. Four more pieces were commissioned and completed more promptly, and were recorded at the April 1955 sessions. These in turn led to another three commissions, recorded at the final November 1955 date. After his period in USC he entered the electronics business full-time, but he had now begun writing for the Burbank Symphony in his spare time. This led to an introduction into the movie business where he began ghost-writing soundtrack music. Soon he was back working in music full time, and began concentrating on television music, writing for any number of well-known series, including *M.A.S.H.*, *Streets of San Francisco*, *Dynasty*, *Love Boat*, *Mission Impossible* and *Barnaby Jones*. By the middle of the 1990s this work had fallen back, but in semiretirement he continued to work as a composer of classical music.

Looking back on his career from the perspective of the 1990s, Tatro said he continued to be proud of *Jazz for Moderns*, pointing out that he had a completely free hand in what he wrote and that Lester Koenig imposed no commercial pressures on him whatsoever. The result was an album of singular character and high quality that sounds very much of its time and place – one cannot imagine many recording companies taking a chance on a project such as this in any other place or at any other time. The album's title, *Jazz for Moderns*, is clearly a catch-all device; obviously Koenig did not quite know what to call this unique recording. Although there are several characteristics associated with the 'West Coast sound' of the period – the light, subdued 'Lester Young'-inspired sound of the saxes, the relaxed feel the musicians succeed in communicating – this does not determine the music's character as it does on countless Contemporary or Pacific Jazz albums. Rather, the music is mediated by the strength of Tatro's writing and these smoothly flowing performances, almost perversely emphasize the music's challenging ideas.

The concept governing Tatro's writing was to apply classical-music devices, and in particular 20th-century classical music, to jazz. *Easy terms*, for example, is an exercise in polyphonic writing where every voice has a destiny of its own, which is in sharp contrast to the homophonic writing on *Dollar day*, where the harmonic voicings are subservient to the dominant melody line. Each composition is of a piece in that it is through-composed and in this departure from conventional jazz writing lies the main interest of this album. Tatro's elimination of piano and guitar – 'the idea was in vogue then and I was particularly affected by the Gerry Mulligan quartet,' he explained – is central to the way the music's detail is focused, giving great clarity to the movement of inner voicings.

With the exception of *Dollar day* Tatro uses the standard 32-bar choruses throughout, although this can be misleading, since the whole point of the majority of the compositions was to remove the compositions from the province of a cyclical chord progression and let the developmental nature of the music dictate the movement of the underlying harmonies. Thus no key signature is used on the score, the destiny of the current key being shown by accidentals along the way. For this reason, none of the soloists plays off 'changes' in the conventional sense; they are simply given a guide to the underlying harmony or a scale on which to base their solo, or both, to guide their improvisation. The bass line is pre-written to ensure that the chord voicings are precisely congruent with the composer's intentions and thus has great harmonic significance within the context of the orchestration as much as its rhythmic function. Some pieces, such as *Low clearance*, are entirely written, yet the sympathetic reading the musicians give to these challenging charts makes them appear spontaneously conceived. As Max Harrison points out, it is misleading to follow the jazz custom and speak of these pieces as being 'composed and arranged' by Tatro. Every one is a genuine composition whose instrumentation seems to have come hand in hand with his thematic ideas; and with so many ideas being expressed in a short space of time – only *Easy terms* exceeds four minutes – it prompted Harrison to observe that the writing is analogous to the spirit of Webern in its sheer concentration of ideas, although of course there is not the slightest stylistic resemblance. [8] When this was put to Tatro, he responded by saying he was very conscious of Webern at the time.

Backlash is a modal piece, which, along with the Shorty Rogers/Teddy Charles album *Collaboration: West* (†Original Jazz Classics [A] OJCCD122–2) from the year before, places it among the first experiments using modes (rather than pedal points) in jazz. Williamson and Enevoldsen in duet play an insistent, repeating motif that is the theme, with the valve trombone moving in contrary motion to the trumpet. After eight bars, Tatro introduces a counter-melody by the saxes, Niehaus offers a brief, flowing solo, and the ensemble returns to dwell on the thematic motif and counter-melody in subtle variation to the tune's conclusion. *Multiplicity* presents a greater degree of developmental writing intended to move away from the tonic key to remoter harmonies and sthen return again to the tonic. This is achieved by presenting the theme and variations with careful counterpoint against a pre-written Enevoldsen solo, a further juxtaposition of the motifs with Holman's brief solo appearing as a logical development of the whole. *Minor incident* allows Holman greater scope of expression within a framework of gradually evolving part-writing as the roles of melody and counterpoint are tossed back and forth between often unison saxes to brass, a round robin that appears to be capable of evolving for ever.

Turbulence was the first piece to be recorded and is the shortest. It opens with a theme built on a 12-note row, a sequence that Tatro says was difficult to arrive at so it would both swing and 'lay on the instruments'. The bridge reverses the row, the saxes stating it in retrograde form, proceeding from the last note to the first. Overall, however, serial technique is not adhered to strictly and the underlying harmonies are based on a series of tonal centres. *Low clearance* evokes memories of the *Birth of the Cool* band with its smooth contrapuntal writing and Williamson's Miles-like solo that disguises a polychordal middle eight. *Folly* actually takes polychordal writing a stage further, since the whole piece is written over a polychordal structure and includes flashes of Niehaus and Giuffre. *Dollar day* is the only non-32-bar tune, although it has an AABA structure of 12 + 12 + 16 + 12. In this homophonic piece, Tatro writes across the whole ensemble with wide sound blocks that enclose Niehaus's discourse with the ensemble which contrasts the specific polyphony of *Easy terms*. The album's longest track, a fraction over four minutes, it opens with Peña's relentlessly swinging bass that leads into a statement of the theme by unison saxes which is taken up by the brass then developed by the whole ensemble before Niehaus, for whom this is virtually a feature, takes up a dominant position in the ensemble, first with his solo and then as a leading voice.

Outpost appears as a duet between Williamson and Giuffre, but is another example of Tatro's use of contrary motion; the trumpet plays the melody which is mirrored by the baritone, but although both start on the same note, when the trumpet goes up a certain interval the baritone goes down the same interval. Trumpet and baritone then take the leading lines in the deftly written variation of the theme; sometimes in unison, in counterpoint and in harmony. *Maybe next year*, an affecting ballad, later recorded by Art Pepper, is given to Niehaus for the exposition against sustained 'organ' chords from the ensemble. Surprisingly, the solo is handed to Giuffre's gruff baritone in unexpected contrast to the alto's gliding lyricism, before the ensemble develop the thematic material to a recapitulation of the theme by Niehaus. *Conversation piece* makes extensive use of the interval of a fourth, then an unusual interval in jazz. Although it became fashionable in the 1960s, here its extended use, requiring Niehaus to incorporate it into his solo, was daring for its time.

When *Jazz for Moderns* was first released, critics and musicians were not quite sure what to make of it. *down beat* was concerned whether it swung – it did – and when it was introduced in Leonard Feather's 'Blindfold Test' some musicians had difficulty relating to it. However, in Britain, *Melody Maker* greeted the album with enthusiasm. Today it is difficult to see what the controversy was over; modes are now an everyday thing, as are tonal centres, while the contemporary pianist must now know how to voice 'slash' chords, producing polytonality that scarcely excites comment. Tatro's harmonies – criticized at the time in almost the same way *Ein musikalischer Spass* once raised eyebrows – sound less 'modern' in current times. He reminds us how little developmental writing – effectively the 'theme and variations' or sonata form – has been employed in jazz. This series of sonatinas, such as *Multiplicity*, where the subject is developed, juxtaposed and restated in keys quite remote from the tonic before returning once more to the home key, should be considered as individual entities in their own right, rather than a theme plus a series of choruses. That this was achieved without pretension, with genuine jazz feeling and with improvisation integrated into their overall scheme, represents a small but very secure achievement within the West Coast movement. On the strength of this album, Leonard Feather described Tatro as 'one of the best equipped and most stimulating writers among those who have tried to take jazz into atonal fields while retaining its basic rhythmic qualities'. [9] When this album was originally released in 1956 it was designated Volume 1 of a two-volume set. That the pressures of business and family life prevented him following up and expanding on this real achievement in jazz must be a source of regret. S.N.

Don Ellis

454 How Time Passes

Candid (A) 8004, †Candid (A) CCD79004

Ellis (tpt, p[1]); Jacki Byard (p, alt[2], vcl intrjc[3]); Ron Carter (bs); Charlie Persip (d). New York City, 4–5 October 1960.

How time passes[1,2] · *A simplex one* · *Waste*[3] · *Improvisational suite No. 1*[2] · *Sallie*

In such few discussions of Ellis's work as have so far appeared, it usually is noted that he was linked with Ornette Coleman and Cecil Taylor as a proponent of the new jazz of the 1960s, but it is normally added that he followed a less radical and free-form method. This was not actually so, as is indicated by the above record and his *New Ideas* collection (†Original Jazz Classics [A] OJCCD431–2) of 1961, which employs the same team plus Al Francis on vibraharp. Rather, it was a matter of a different sort of radicalism, equally valid; and the fact is that the greater impact of his subsequent big band (**317**) obscured the specific character of his earliest recorded ventures.

Ellis's beginnings seemed conventional enough, with a degree in composition from Boston University plus time spent in the Glenn Miller orchestra directed by Ray McKinley, with Charlie Barnet, Sam Donohue, Claude Thornhill, Woody Herman, Maynard Ferguson, Lionel Hampton and others. Against such a background his many innovations stand off in sharp relief, and they were of two kinds, instrumental and organizational, the latter being the more significant. In comparison with far-reaching developments on the saxophone and in drumming, the new jazz of that time offered few departures in trumpet playing. It therefore was the more to Ellis's credit that he extended what already was a virtuoso technique in several directions.

His first promptings so far as this instrument was concerned were from Gillespie with Navarro and Clark Terry as secondary influences. The effect of these exemplars was greatly modified, however, by electrical amplification, ring-modulated tonal distortion, the use of a phase-shifter, etc., roughly paralleling Miles Davis's resorting to fuzz box and wah-wah pedal. Following the initiative of the Czech musician Jaromir Hnilička (**457**), Ellis also took up the four-valve quarter-tone trumpet (later sometimes played by the whole trumpet section of his big band), and this particular resource led to an involvement with alternative tuning systems which also was a consequence of his interest in the works of Harry Partch. In such a context Ellis's study of Indian classical music with Hari Har Rao is no surprise, and they founded the Hindustani Jazz sextet, one of the first groups to fuse aspects of jazz and Indian procedures (though see **484**). From this in turn arose the emphasis on long and complex metres which so marked his big band's output.

Clearly this was a lively mind, possessed of great musical curiosity, and, as might be expected, Ellis was as much concerned with the larger world of music as with jazz, and sought reconciliations between the two parallel to his endeavours with Indian music and jazz. All of which could have led to the worst sort of eclecticism without the unifying effect of a personal aesthetic vision. This he developed early, and at just about the time the above session was recorded, Gunther Schuller wrote that Ellis had 'already found his own voice, which seems to consist of a fascinating blend of jazz and contemporary classical influences. In fact, his playing represents one of the few true syntheses of jazz and classical elements, without the slightest self-consciousness and without any loss of the excitement and raw spontaneity that the best jazz has always had.' [10]

To this end he sometimes employed a variant of the aleatoric procedures introduced by John Cage, for example in *Despair to hope* from the *New Ideas* session and to a lesser extent on the above *Waste*, during which each soloist is free to choose his own tempo for every chorus he leads. This relates to Ellis's desire, which he shared with Byard among others, to expand not only the melodic and harmonic vocabularies of jazz but most especially to bring greater freedom to the roles of tempo and metre, these being dimensions in which jazz had then achieved much less variety than in other areas. Particularly relevant here is the eponymous *How time passes*, which takes up certain of Stockhausen's early thoughts about the nature of musical time. [11] Remarkable here is the success with which all four players maintain an entirely coherent, indeed fluent, discourse in the face of an almost constantly shifting tempo. This should be compared with the two accounts of Hodeir's *Osymetrios* on **455**.

At the opposite extreme from indeterminacy stand the serial tendencies which shape *Improvisational suite No. 1.* In this Ellis said his aim was to produce 'an extended piece which would be almost totally improvised, which would sound new and fresh each time, and which would present a variety of moods and levels of density and intensity but would be highly unified structurally'. And the resources of the serial method are such that these goals are not so contradictory as they appear. Typically, the *Suite*'s beginnings were empirical rather than doctrinaire and lay in explorations conducted in several Greenwich Village, New York, coffee bars where Ellis led a trio, L'Avant Trio, which sometimes included Al Francis. The trumpeter also took part in the summer of 1960 in a number of rehearsals by a group jointly led by John Benson Brooks and Don Heckman that was likewise experimenting with 12-tone writing in jazz and ways of improvising on tone rows. [12]

The *Suite* does not adhere to its tone row as strictly as do the somewhat later works of Davis Mack (**456**) and Pavel Blatný (**457**), but it uses it to unify a quite lengthy series of free associations. That is to say the 12 pitches of the row and the order in which Ellis placed them are signposts, this at some stages leading the soloists into definite atonality and at others into relatively tonal improvising. In so far as it consists of a sequence of well-contrasted sections rather than a group of separate movements, the *Suite* is not well named, but its alternation of free cadenzas and passages at regular tempos is always highly effective.

First the row is announced by Ellis in a pair of two-bar phrases in $^3/_2$, this receiving an answer from Byard, pondering on the identical pitches. Ellis then restates the series, beginning on the fourth note and adding the first three at the end of his phrase. This is answered by Byard, who has now switched to the alto, and by Carter. Next the 12 notes are distributed singly among trumpet, piano and bass, pointillist fashion, with percussive comments added. There follows a four-bar harmonized passage topped by the trumpet again stating the row in its original form while the bass plays the retrograde version. A fast section alternating between free and regular pulses follows, this being more tonal in feeling than earlier passages. There is a bass cadenza with a brief percussive interruption complete with timpani portamentos and then a section which is conventionally swinging except that the harmonies derive from the row's original and retrograde inversion forms. Harmon-muted, Ellis takes a quite long solo and then Byard does likewise but out of tempo, this taking us into a duet between Ellis (now cup-muted) and Carter employing the row in several forms.

There follows what Ellis called the 'boogie' section, in which his solo gradually slips out of tempo, leading to exchanges between trumpet and alto in which each follows a different version of the row. This is perhaps the work's most intense passage, but eventually it fades and a drum solo draws the other instruments back into the music's flow, leading to a climax with fragments of the row scattered among trumpet, piano and bass. After this, a somewhat abbreviated version of the harmonized passage heard earlier brings the *Suite* to an end. Each episode is strikingly different from the rest, with quite frequent unaccompanied passages for each instrument, yet the whole, lasting just over 22 minutes, remains mysteriously unified.

There is an equal emphasis on material and treatment in the other pieces – all of which are by Ellis except Byard's *Waste*. There is a fine piano solo here, and another on *A simplex one*, both using a broad range of resources that well accords with this music's ambitions, suggested in this latter case by an involved underlying harmonic sequence. In *Sallie* the rather luxuriant keyboard arpeggios contrast tellingly with Ellis's tightly muted precision. This piece, a sort of modal ballad, represents the music's otherwise often hidden lyrical aspect and its directly melodic invention, although this is almost equally evident, at a faster tempo, in *A simplex one*. Ellis and Byard both improvise with impressive fluency on *Waste*, and in *A simplex one* and *How time passes* the leader invokes Henri de Regnier's 'bright shout of the trumpet'. As suggested above, Ellis was never less than an outstanding player, and this music, like **317**, should leave us in no doubt that he was a great deal more.

And yet it still does not appear to have been grasped how severe a loss his death in 1978 was to jazz, least of all in the land of its birth. Indeed, the man who supervised the session which produced this great record found it convenient some years later to describe it as 'very antiseptic' and to claim that he did not know why he had recorded it. [13] Such are the penalties for a jazz musician who falls out of fashion. In reality several of these pieces, like further items in the *New Ideas* set, especially *Despair to hope*, arrive at overall forms considerably more free and varied, which is to say more genuinely unpredictable, than most of those found elsewhere in what in those years was called 'the New Thing'. M.H.

André Hodeir

455 Jazz et Jazz/Les Tripes au Soleil

†Fontana (F) 836 070–2, *Philips (A) PHM200–073

Roger Guérin (tpt); Emmanuel Soudieux (bs); Richie Frost (d) – electronically modified; Hodeir (comp, etc). Paris, 1952.
Martial Solal (p) added. Paris, 1960.
Jazz et jazz

Studio orch. inc. Guérin (tpt), Pierre Gossez (alt), Mimi Perrin Vocal Group inc. Christiane Legrand; Hodeir (comp, cond). Paris, 1959.
Les Tripes au Soleil · Danse · Spiritual · Le désert · Blues

Guérin (tpt); Nat Peck (tbn); Georges Grenu (ten); Solal (p); Pierre Michelot (bs); Kenny Clarke (d); Hodeir (comp, arr). Paris, autumn 1960.
Trope à Saint-Trop · Osymetrios I · Osymetrios II

Le Jazz Groupe de Paris: Christian Bellest (tpt), Gossez (alt), Armand Migiani (bar), Jean Pierre Drouet (vib, perc), LeGrand (vcl) added; André Paquinet (tbn), Christian Garros (d) replace Peck, Clarke; Solal absent. Paris, autumn 1960.
Jazz cantata (I A shout – The inviolable dream, II A sketch – Memory of itself, III A scat – Multiple and solitary, IV An aballad – Does it know its desire? V A horn – Living another life, VI A chord – The nocturnal wait, VII A vocalizing – Already it lives its death)

Peck (tbn), Hubert Rostaing (alt) replace Paquinet, Gossez; Legrand absent. Paris, autumn 1960.
Le palais idéal (Necessity, Obsession, The journey, Masks, Mirrors, Solitude, The tomb)

Raymond Guiot (fl); Solal (p); Michelot (bs); Clarke (d). Paris, autumn 1960.
Flautando

Aside from Gunther Schuller (**400**, **478**), Hodeir is the sole writer of a substantial body of jazz criticism, including some of the best, also to attain distinction as a composer. To a much greater extent in the latter than in the former case do the music and the criticism, the artist and the thinker, complement each other. Hodeir's compositions are of course self-sufficient, yet there is a sense in which one line of activity helps explain the other, and this relationship awaits full examination elsewhere. The above performances are best heard in conjunction with others recorded in the several preceding years in Paris and New York by his Jazz Groupe de Paris and other ensembles for the Swing, Vega, Philips and Savoy labels. If the above collection, mainly from 1960, was chosen for inclusion here, this is because it best conveys the variety of emotional climates this music occupies. As much should be obvious from a single hearing, and the technical skill informing these pieces should be almost as apparent. The order of the tracks on the Philips LP was altered for the Fontana CD in accord with Hodeir's wishes; and the *Tripes au Soleil* items were added because of the extra time available on a CD.

All too often those who attempt to write jazz adopt hit-or-miss procedures, but Hodeir displays a comprehensive mastery of compositional techniques, some of them applied to this music for the first time. Among other highly specific features which shape the material and its development should be noted a strong feeling for melodic climax and a well-varied use of melodic and harmonic fourths and fifths, including flattened fifths, a kaleidoscopic sense of modulation and a restrained use of bichordalism, a leaning towards themes in minor keys and to no-metre floating effects. Never dragged in merely to demonstrate that Hodeir knows about them, these and other means are selected rigorously because they match his expressive ends. And the sheer technical dexterity notwithstanding, he has the restraint, and sophistication, never to overcrowd. There is in fact a decisiveness about this writing which can make several of these works appear simpler than actually they are, and this despite Hodeir's music sometimes implying almost as much as it states. Moreover, each point is made so concisely that, like the few other real jazz composers, he says more that is original in a piece lasting a few minutes than will be found in, for example, many longer and far more pretentious works.

In the initial reception given Hodeir's music, the point was seldom grasped that although emotion rather than skill is the ultimate source of music, the application of new techniques can give rise to new structures. The mirror forms of the two *Esquisses* are clear instances. And new forms lead to new content (unless it is the other way round) because the *way* a composer says something is partly *what* he says. Here the most vivid example is the *Jazz cantata*, whose independence, even after all these years, still comes as a shock to most first-time listeners. Such pieces followed on, by just a few years, roughly comparable ventures by the MJQ (**363**) elsewhere. Hodeir shared that ensemble's liking for entries in imitation but went much further, arriving via inversion, retrograde, augmentation, diminution, almost Webernian use of hocket, etc., at a more rigorous counterpoint, often canonic.

These pieces of Hodeir's also followed on, by just a few years, from his writing that 'the problem of the relationship between theme, arrangement and solo' was 'the most formidable problem the modern jazzman has to solve'. [14] Such a formulation obviously helps to define his own perception of jazz at that time. How did his own music, with its impressive marshalling of resources, answer this? Did he preserve the spontaneity that is supposed to be characteristic of good jazz? Did he want to? There are, after all, several written-out solos in these pieces, as detailed below. Was there too much predetermination, so that the performers were inhibited by this music's real complexity and reduced just to coldly reading their parts? In truth, he was lucky in his performers, and Le Jazz Groupe de Paris was at this time, as Wendell Otey suggested, 'his *alter ego*', [15] and fully inside his music. This is confirmed by the perfect sympathy with which the written-out solos are delivered and by countless nuances elsewhere – and by the fact that completely unnotated elements such as the bongos' *obbligato* to the third movement of *Le palais idéal* are wholly in accord with this music's spirit.

As much can be said of *Jazz et jazz*, another joining of the fixed and the free. This remains in certain respects the boldest of Hodeir's solutions to 'the problem of the relationship between theme, arrangement and solo', and was the earliest in origin. The basic sound material was recorded by Guérin, Soudieux and Frost and then modified by Hodeir in the studios of Radio France by the usual *musique concrète* techniques of filtering, acceleration, inversion etc. Later Solal's fluent and remarkably apt improvisation was imposed on the result, and one can only regret that there were not more such initiatives.

If this *Jazz et jazz* confrontation is the furthest the contents of this CD depart from the conventions of jazz, then the four excerpts from the soundtrack of Claude Bernard-Aubert's 1959 French–Italian production *Les Tripes au Soleil* draw closest. Outwardly they make normal use of big-band resources, yet this is deceptive. Graced with excellent solos by Gossez and Guérin, *Danse* is the most direct of these pieces and the only one that is purely instrumental, wordless voices having important, and different, roles in the others. In fact the vocal group predominates in the mellifluous *Spiritual*, and, though Hodeir would be unlikely to take it as a compliment, this movement reminds one of the last of Milhaud's *Six Symphonies pour Petit Orchestre* of 1923, which likewise is mainly for wordless voices. *Le désert* is the most striking of these items, largely because of inventive brass writing, although the climax and resolution are won through Christiane Legrand's soprano vocal line. This piece should be compared with the extended version titled *Le désert recommencé* recorded by Solal's big band in 1984 (†Carlyne [F] 008CD). *Blues* expectedly employs a more traditional language, yet does so with distinction. There are well placed solos from Gossez and Guérin, and telling use is made of vibraharp, bongos and voices. Most important, this little score evolves continuously instead of repeatedly going round a 12-bar circle.

Although tremolos, terminal downward smears and the like occur in *Le palais idéal*, the above four items are the only ones here to employ the devices of 'hot' expression such as vibrato, portamentos and tonal distortions, Hodeir's chiefly being cool jazz in the 1950s sense. As such it demonstrates that there are of course plenty of other ways of producing musical tension, including angular melodic lines, dissonance, contrapuntal and rhythmic complexity and more or less elaborate developmental procedures. Most of these occur in the remaining music considered here, although the first three relate to the blues, *Trope à Saint-Trop* most closely. This emphasizes repeated notes at different positions within the bar and includes notable solos by Guérin and Solal. *Osymetrios I* and *II*, substantially different orderings of the same piece, stress blues feeling much less, and, as those adept at anagrams might discover, this is a recomposition of Monk's *Mysterioso* (**292**). It is far indeed from being a nostalgic restatement of faded hopes, and both versions show that even when Hodeir takes an idea from elsewhere, he makes it entirely his own.

This is repeatedly demonstrated by *Kenny Clarke Plays André Hodeir* (Philips [F] 834 542), for which he in 1956 arranged, or again virtually recomposed, themes by Ellington, Dameron, Miles Davis, Mulligan and others. Each account of *Osymetrios* shifts through 'metric modulations' (shades of Elliott Carter!) between two different tempos, opposing yet related, this being achieved principally through masterly playing by Clarke and Michelot. However, the soloists, Guérin, Solal and again Michelot and Clarke, also cope extremely well in an unfamiliar situation. Solal, who later produced several of the finest recorded improvisations on demanding Monk themes, [16] is heard twice in *Osymetrios I* and in exchanges with Clarke in *II*, a solo by the latter ending this last.

After this considerable diversity of instrumental combinations we arrive at Le Jazz Groupe de Paris, which performs the remaining pieces and whose last recordings these, alas, are. The basic instrumentation of three brass, three reeds and three rhythm was the same as that of Dameron's 1953 Atlantic City band except that the piano is here replaced by a vibraharp. This lightened the weight of the rhythm section and promoted flexibility. Although only the *Tripes au Soleil* pieces are from an actual soundtrack, all the music in this collection, with the exceptions of *Jazz et jazz* and *Flautando*, was originally connected with the cinema, and this gives more than a hint of how much more receptive to jazz the French film industry was than others. Enemies of modern jazz naturally seized on this link as evidence of the music's purely 'background' character, although much that has been composed for the screen, by Prokofiev, Bliss, Virgil Thomson and others, has gone on to lead a separate existence of its own. And anything less like background music than Hodeir's *Jazz cantata* would be hard to imagine.

Indeed, it was too radical to be understood at the time, yet its origins lie in music for Michel Fano's 1958 film *Chute de Pierres: Danger de Mort* (just as *Trope à Saint-Trop* and *Osymetrios* were heard, in very different versions, in *Saint-Tropez Blues*, a 1960 French–Italian production directed by Marcel Moussy). Fully written out, the *Jazz cantata*'s seven movements receive a superlative performance, above all from Christiane Legrand, whose exacting part is not so much scat as written in an 'imaginary language'. It lies unusually high for jazz singing, yet is delivered with stinging drive. She is not heard in all the movements for there is a considerable variety of instrumental as well as vocal gesture, with important roles for the vibraharp in the beautiful fourth movement

[17] and for muted trumpet in the fifth. The voice's most frequent and immediate companion, however, is the alto saxophone and its part, like that of the singer, is written so as to sound like an improvisation. Some interesting counterpoint between the two is a result. [18]

Again entirely written out and likewise in seven movements, *Le palais idéal* is the longest piece here. The title refers to a ceramic edifice, a miniature building, in the south of France made entirely by hand by a man named Chaval, a postman whom the surrealists thought to be a genius. Quaint enough to be pointed out to tourists, it is still visited for its strange naïve sculpture and was the subject of a 1957–8 film by Ado Kyrou. Le Jazz Groupe de Paris is heard on the soundtrack of this, but the music included on the above CD and LP was newly recorded in 1960. The first and last movements are closely related and are based on rather fanfarelike ideas. In the second and third movements and even more in the fourth the ensemble is broken up into different and frequently changing groups of instruments. In the sixth movement the two vibraharp solos, most sensitively interpreted by Drouet, form the work's climax.

And we end with the blues. *Flautando* is for five flutes, three in C and two alto flutes in G. Via multitracking Guiot plays them all, achieving a superb quality of ensemble with himself, particularly as Hodeir's writing for these instruments is extremely demanding. Indeed, there is a musically beneficial tension between the mellifluous sound of the flutes and the adventurous, extremely varied phraseology of that writing, underlined by the diverse ways the ensemble is employed. For a 'commentary' on this piece, hear *Transplantation I* as recorded by Solal (Carlyne, as above).

Beyond *Le palais idéal* and these other works lie *Anna Livia Plurabelle* (Carlyne [F] CAR005 and Label Bleue as below, 1966) and *Bitter Ending* (Epic [A] 80544, 1972), the *Jazz cantata*, especially, pointing directly to them. Up to the time of this book's publication these two major works of Hodeir's have remained far less well known than they should be, although *Anna Livia Plurabelle* was recorded again in 1993 (†Label Bleue [F] LBLC6563) and had some further performances. Attacks on the boundaries of jazz are never welcome, of course, but our continuing ignorance does us no credit.

Perhaps it goes some way to explain Hodeir's pursuing this line no further, just as he wrote no more jazz criticism after the publication of the widely misunderstood *Worlds of Jazz* (see Bibliography), also in 1972. Matters go best for a jazz composer when he has a regular ensemble to hand, like Ellington, or like John Lewis with the MJQ. But Hodeir had that with Le Jazz Groupe de Paris, and produced, like Ellington, Lewis, George Russell and a very few others, a consistent and developing body of work – one that conveys an excellent idea of the upper reaches of jazz activity in Paris at the time, which is to say during the years immediately following the death of Charlie Parker. Certainly on listening to the above still-hodiernal pieces it is hard to believe that he had said all that he had to say. M.H.

David Mack

456 New Directions

Columbia (E) 33SX1670, Sirenus (A) 1007

Shake Keane (tpt, fl h); Gordon Lewin (clt, ten); Ralph Bruce (sop); Al Baum (alt); Jim Easton (bar); Don Lowes (p); Coleridge Goode (bs); Joe Gibbons (d); Eric Allen (perc); Mack (comp). London, 20 March 1964.

Johnnie's door · Altona · Chiquita moderne · Cameo · Clockwork boogie · Tonette · Half-tone poem · Ralph's mead · Dreamy fugue

Pavel Blatný

457 Third Stream Compositions

Supraphon (Cz) 015 0528

Richard Kubarnát, Jan Capoun, Václav Hybš, Vitězslav Horák, Jaromir Hnilička (tpt); Pavel Vitoch (bs tpt); Ladislav Pickert, Artur Hollitzer, Miroslav Koželuh, Bedřich Beránek (tbn); Karel Krautgartner, Miroslav Klazar (clt, alt); Jaromir Honzák (sop); Milan Ulrich (ten); Kamil Hála (p); Luděk Hulan (bs); Ivan Dominák (d); Blatný (comp). Prague, 11–15 November 1968.

Concerto for jazz orchestra: Passacaglia, Models for Karel, Rhythms and timbres · Für Graz · Pour Ellis · 24.7.67 · Study for quarter-tone trumpet and orchestra

Atonality and then serial technique arose in jazz rather as they had earlier in European and American classical music. That is to say atonality emerged as a result of the steadily increasing chromaticism of the musical language. This led to a breakdown of functional harmony and the formal processes, large and small, associated with it, and 12-note technique surfaced, first in Europe, as one of several possible strategies intended to arrive at a new method of imparting structure to music. This was a process of natural growth rather than an abrupt innovation, and while serial technique was pioneered by Schoenberg, Hauer, Webern, we discover in work of other contemporaneous composers such as Reger, Scriabin, Roslavets unordered sets often of fewer than 12 elements.

Jazz once seemed a quintessentially tonal music, its vitality in the 20th century apparently amounting to a resurgence of tonality in the face of its decline in the most adventurous Western art music. Yet in jazz too chromaticism became a rising tide, even if belatedly in comparison with European and American classical works. The process is typified at an advanced stage by Stadler's harmonizations of *Air conditioning* or *Ba-lue bolivar ba-lues-are* on **462**. As a result of this growing chromaticism atonality appeared piecemeal fashion in jazz as it had elsewhere, this eventually leading to various degrees of serialism. Thus Tristano's *Intui-*

tion (**293**) was noted by the German composer Wolfgang Fortner as showing tendencies towards the 12-note method. [19]

Some initial jazz use of tone rows was fragmentary and inconsequential. For instance the 12-note row in the first eight bars of the bass of Brubeck's *The Duke* (**311**) is not employed in a serialist manner at all. But soon rows were used in, and as, actual themes, examples including DeFranco's *12-tone blues*, Giuffre's *Densities I*, Harold Farberman's *. . . then silence* and Wally Cirillo's *Trans-season*. Coltrane's *Miles mode* (alias *Red planet*) goes a little further, employing both a row and its retrograde, and Rogers's *Three on a row* (**432**) goes further still, stating its row a dozen times and uncovering a few of the compositional potentialities. Most such pieces, however, having used a 12-note series as their theme, reverted to conventional harmony as the basis for improvisation. Thus Bill Evans's *Twelve-tone tune* states its row three times, with some octave transpositions, then goes on to harmony which, though personal and distinguished, is tonally quite straightforward, employing the familiar cycle-of-fifths idea.

A fuller use of serial technique had already been made in jazz composition, for instance Mátyás Seiber's *Jazzolettes* of 1929 and 1933, in the second of which the trumpet leads off with a 12-note series that is at once inverted by the trombone. Far more ambitious is the use of serialism found in Babbitt's complex *All set* (**478**), and note should also be made of Daniel Schnyder's *A call from outer space* in his ECM collection *Decoding the Message.* Going even further than Babbitt is Lalo Schifrin in *The ritual of sound*, which in a way that has remained extremely unusual for jazz imparts serial organization not only to pitches but to all other parameters. [20]

Not surprisingly, though, jazz musicians have usually chosen to make a more restricted use of 12-note procedures, as in Ellis's *Improvisational suite No. 1* discussed under **454**, where the row is employed to unify a rather lengthy sequence of free associations. Stricter, if of shorter duration, are the uses made of a tone row in Macero's *Adventure* and again in *24+ 18+* (both **479**). Special and different cases are represented by Don Banks's *Settings from Roget* (1966, unrecorded), especially the first two pieces, [21] and Schuller's *Abstraction*, dealt with under **400**, which combines elaborate serial organization with free improvisation by Ornette Coleman. This is a reminder of the point repeatedly made by Sidney Finkelstein that jazz has always been a mixture of languages. [22]

No matter how pointedly these diverse and fairly numerous instances may have been ignored in jazz histories and works of reference, they provide ample precedents for Mack and Blatný to employ 12-note procedures in jazz composition and particularly in improvisation rather more extensively. [23] In both groups of performances ensembles predominate but there are serial improvisations in all cases. On *Ralph's mead*, for example, Bruce and Keane are heard quite briefly, yet what they play accords entirely with the score's tone row. Keane's serial improvisation aside, ensembles are again to the fore in *Johnnie's door* but in *Cameo* there are longer solos, by trumpet and clarinet. During *Chiquita moderne* Mack fuses jazz and Latin American idioms while maintaining 12-note principles, including in Keane's solo. He capped this by introducing *ostinatos* whose repetitions for once do not weaken the prevailing atonality because of the strength of the overall serial organization.

However, *Tonette* may be Mack's strongest piece, not least in that it includes a passage of subdued collective extemporization that still adheres to the tone row. Obviously a very high standard of musicianship is needed to produce 12-note solos at all and to bring off collective improvisation is extraordinary, even allowing for the partial precedents of Macero's 1955 *Adventure* and *24+ 18+*. Also in *Tonette* Keane plays a free-form solo – holding, that is, to neither tone row nor chords – against a dodecaphonic background. The parallels with Banks, Schuller et al. are clear. Mack's remaining serial piece was the gentle *Half-tone poem*, and he concentrates here on the sorts of mellow sound that he felt had all too often been neglected in 12-tone writing. Certainly it is rewarding to listen to Keane's flugelhorn riding smoothly over the murmuring saxophones. And here as in Mack's other scores – and indeed Blatný's – there is an unrelenting attention to every detail.

His attainment was that he created a music which, though remaining jazz, dispenses with tonal harmony and is based on a proper employment of serial methods. Yet the extent of this should not be exaggerated. What Mack and later Blatný did with 12-tone technique was elementary beside what Schoenberg and his pupils had done, let alone what composers such as Babbitt and then Boulez would do. But serial practices are truly used by Mack, and some of his bandsmen were able to improvise, if at no great length, on tone rows, and their employment of these meant that every bar of their solos was closely related to the composed material, the 12-note series of each piece indissolubly binding together the whole performance. A further advantage of Mack's compositions, as of Blatný's, is that the listener is no longer aware of the string-of-choruses format which is an inescapable feature of so much jazz.

That might seem enough of an achievement, yet soon further advances were being made by Blatný, a figure who has remained obscure in jazz chronicles. Besides Janáček, his father's teacher, Blatný noted Stravinsky and Martinů as early influences. During several years prior to writing the pieces considered here, Blatný composed extended symphonic works, chamber pieces, vocal and dramatic items. Later he wrote further orchestral and chamber pieces that were intended for classical players yet increasingly used elements of jazz. The next stage was composing for combinations of jazz and classical musicians, and then finally, as in the works detailed above, for jazzmen only. These latter pieces are serially organized but retain, as Blatný wrote in 1968, 'the sound of jazz musicians' unrestricted expression'. [24] They are excellently performed by the Czech Radio Jazz Orchestra, founded in 1960, which under Krautgartner's name performed two Stravinsky items on **109**.

Passacaglia, dating from 1962, and *Pour Ellis*, which belongs to 1966 and is canonic, combine old polyphonic structures with the 12-note method. *Models for Krautgartner* (1963) and *24.7.67*, whose date of composition is as would be expected, employ something of the preacher-and-congregation format which occurs in some of Blatný's earlier pieces. In *Passacaglia* the 12-note series is also the theme of a sequence of variations, with each a variation on its predecessor. The series/theme is first heard from the double bass, then with the piano added. There follow several variations and then the 12-note series is heard again, this time from the trumpets and trombones, who play it as isolated points of sound. More variations follow and then the saxophones offer a tiny melodic fragment derived from the series.

In due course there is a clarinet solo and this leads to a climax in which the series is shared between five players. There is a short further development and then the series is heard in vertical form, first with six notes, then nine, finally all twelve. It reappears melodically, first on the trombone and then completed by the double bass, this leading to a further round of variations, shortened and in reverse order. In the coda the series is heard once again vertically from the whole orchestra playing quietly, and then the piece ends with a trumpet flourish using half the series and a chord from the piano employing the other six notes.

The above indicates that *Passacaglia* is a highly concentrated piece in which much happens in a few minutes, and it is unnecessary to outline the remaining items in such detail. It should be noted, however, that all include solos that appear to be improvised, most obviously in *Models for Krautgartner*, where the soloist is heard on both clarinet and alto saxophone. There is also a brief yet intense passage of collective improvisation, as there is in *24.7.67.* There is more colour in *Rhythms and timbres* (1964) than elsewhere and the gestures are sometimes more extreme. Latterly quite complicated, this is remarkably free of the conventions of big-band writing and is highly original in its acerbic way. By the time we reach *Für Graz* (1965) it is necessary to acknowledge that Blatný's range of expression is considerably wider than Mack's, particularly with regard to the music's asymmetry and discontinuity. Like *Pour Ellis* and *24.7.67*, this is another crowded canvas, and *Für Graz* includes fine trumpet and piano solos. The latter seems reminiscent of Monk, although this is probably coincidental. Other notable solos are from Honzák in *Pour Ellis* and by Hnilička in the 1964 *Study.* This last is again extremely eventful and not just because of the overt concerto aspect or the soloist's trumpet quarter-tones. The writing for big band is again highly unusual and one can only wish that some of Blatný's initiatives had been taken up by other arrangers.

Whether the use of 12-note techniques in jazz by Mack and Blatný could ever have led to a mainstream development comparable to free jazz can only be a matter for conjecture. It was possibly yet another case of jazz, in too much of a hurry as usual, rushing past a possible major field of growth because Mack and Blatný, almost needless to say, were never given a chance of taking their work further. M.H.

Revisitations

These recordings, made over many years, did not arise, as was sometimes eagerly suggested, from the notion that there was something wrong with the present of jazz but from the fact that it had such a rich inheritance. This music had rushed through its resources and past potential avenues of development all too quickly and some re-examination was at various times overdue.

Bob Brookmeyer

458 Traditionalism Revisited

World Pacific (A) PJ1233, Affinity (E) AFF127

Brookmeyer (v-tbn[1], p[2]); Jimmy Giuffre (clt[3], ten[4], bar[5]); Jim Hall (g); Joe Benjamin (bs); Dave Bailey (d). Hollywood, 13 July 1957.
Louisiana[1,4] · *Santa Claus blues*[2,3] · *Some sweet day*[1,4] · *Don't be that way*[1,2,5] · *Sweet like this*[1,3]

Giuffre absent. Same place and date.
Jada[1]

Giuffre returns; Ralph Peña (bs) replaces Benjamin. Hollywood, 16 July 1957.
Truckin'[2] · *Honeysuckle rose*[1,2]

Was there ever – particularly in 1957 – a 'traditionalism' to revisit? Everyone honoured here – Oliver, Armstrong, Beiderbecke, Waller, Edgar Sampson – undoubtedly regarded himself as a modernist. 'Trad' in the mid-1950s was itself a visitation upon the body of jazz, and anyone looking for an acceptable traditionalism might well have discerned it not among the archaeologists but in the style of music which Brookmeyer himself, along with Mulligan, Giuffre and others, was helping to develop.

Given that there is no attempt (other than briefly in *Sweet like this* and *Some sweet day*) to recreate older voices and styles, it may be of significance that shortly before these dates a *Guide to Jazz* had been compiled on LP by Hugues Panassié. This included three of the numbers listed above so it may have provided a trigger for Brookmeyer. His most pointed tribute to his forebears occurs in *Sweet like this*, where Oliver's and Dave Nelson's trumpet solos are rehearsed note for note by trombone and clarinet, the different instrumental timbres colouring the effect interestingly. 'Older voices and styles'? Literally, yes; but the ensuing improvisations of Brookmeyer and Giuffre, each in his own character, may indicate how little had really changed between 1929 and 1957, at least in essential expression. The ensemble elements which now date the Oliver track are happily forgotten here (cf. **82**).

The tempo of Oliver's original is matched exactly. Most of *Some sweet day* moves markedly faster than Armstrong's 1933 recording (also in the Panassié compilation – on RCA-Victor [A] LPM1393 and cf. **115**), though there are echoes of the model in the slow trombone prologue and in the swinging finale. The zest and immediacy of fine solos by the two horns and Hall are, as in most of this album, the best sort of acknowledgement of the masters' legacy. Listening to the Armstrong of 1933 or 1924 (*Santa Claus blues*), one does not bother oneself with the speculation that he might be recreating or initiating a tradition.

The other Panassié inclusion is Lionel Hampton's *Don't be that way*, which has several Ellingtonian participants. Brookmeyer's tempo approximates to that of the 1938 recording but the revisitors' interpretation owes little else to Hampton. The choice of Giuffre's baritone could be a respectful nod to the composer, Sampson, who plays a brief solo on that instrument with Hampton; yet the much younger man's adaptation of his own blues-affected clarinet style to the bigger horn does find him digging back beyond Sampson's Hawkins-affected accents seeking deeper roots – but for his own purposes and without pose.

Rhythm support through both sessions is excellent and unassuming, Peña proving himself a more subtle bassist than Benjamin; and Brookmeyer's occasional piano is simple and lively, showing some signs of Ellington influence in the lightsome *Truckin'*. In part of *Honeysuckle rose* he contrives to play his two instruments in duet, not an everyday feat in jazz, old or new.

The stomping last chorus of *Louisiana* shouts the group's distinct personality, and there is a quality of timelessness. Still, perhaps the 'historic' inspiration of this piece's choice can be heard not in the late 1920s performances of Beiderbecke (**63**, **65**) or Ellington (**90**) but in Basie's 1940 version (**135b**). Fragments of Lester Young's nudging morse code, cleverly inserted by Giuffre and Brookmeyer into the first ensemble chorus, and Giuffre's tenor solo, even though the latter celebrates a more relaxed Young than the man who so mightily contended with Andy Gibson's (or perhaps Tadd Dameron's) minatory section writing, seem to make the source evident.

N.B. The first session included an additional number, *The Sheik of Araby*, issued on Playboy (A) PB1959. *Slow freight* and *Brook's blues*, additional to the second date, appeared on Crown (A) CLP5318. E.T.

Sam Most

459 Most Plays Bird and Bud, Monk and Miles

Bethlehem (A) BCP75, Fresh Sounds (Sp) FSR2039

Chuck Harmon, Doug Mettome, Ed Reider, Al Stewart, Don Stratton (tpt); Jim Dahl, Bill Elton, Frank Rehak (tbn); Most (fl, clt); Dick Meldonian, Davey Schildkraut (alt); Ed Wasserman (ten); Marty Flax (bar); Bob Dorough (p); Oscar Pettiford (bs); Paul Motian (d). New York City, 6 March 1957.

Blue Bird · *Round about midnight* · *Strictly confidential* · *Serpent's tooth*

Mettome (tpt); Most (fl, clt); Schildkraut (alt); Dorough (p); Tommy Potter (bs); Motian (d). New York City, 7 March 1957.

Celia · *Confirmation* · *Half Nelson* · *In walked Bud*

The few bop-oriented musicians who gained anything close to celebrity on the B-flat clarinet, if popularly remembered at all, need less than a hand's fingers to be counted – DeFranco, Giuffre, Tony Scott, possibly Bill Smith. The evidence of the present recording suggests strongly that Most deserves a finger, even though celebrity as a clarinettist eluded him in the days that mattered. (More than one supposedly reputable jazz guide published in recent decades has not listed him in any category at all.)

From 1959 to 1961 Most played in a group led by Buddy Rich which toured Asian centres as an adjunct to the Joey Adams Vaudeville Show (Americana on display under the sponsorship of the Eisenhower administration). His flute playing began in that period to attract more attention. He introduced a technique of humming in unison with his flute lines, the origination of which he claimed for himself in defiance of Roland Kirk, who demonstrated a similar skill around the same time. Most's fluting on a 1953 record, *Undercurrent blues* (Prestige [A] EP1322), has been claimed as his establishing as 'the first bop flautist'. [25] In the same year a Debut (A) LP included a clarinet extravaganza, *Notes to you*, which one hears now as a spurt of jazz derring-do and as a possible counter to the remark credited to Tony Scott on quitting the US jazz scene at the end of the 1950s: 'The clarinet died, and I hate funerals.' [26] Recent times have found the man concentrating upon the flute rather than the clarinet and alto, but this recording, in addition to its avowed celebration of Parker, Powell, Monk and Davis, preserves the work of a musician who appears to disbelieve all portents of the clarinet's demise.

The 15-piece orchestra which interprets Most's forthright scores of one title each of the four masters to whom he is paying respect is manned by musicians who were in their teens, or just emerging from them, when bop first appeared. Potter, the bassist of the second date, is decidedly the veteran at these occasions. But it is possible to say that there is no younger participant who had not been pretty well soaked in the flowings of bop from the very beginnings of his active musical life. So, if they can properly be said to be revisitors, what they revisit is a part of their own developing sense of style a decade before. They deal in addition with quite recently devised themes; e.g. Davis's *Serpent's tooth*, recorded for Prestige for possibly the only previous time in 1953. Powell's *Celia*, perhaps named for his daughter and not to be confused with Mingus's opus of the same title (**336**), was recorded but once by the pianist at a February 1949 Norman Granz session which also introduced *Strictly confidential*. The latter number was to be recorded on one other occasion in the early 1960s. [27]

Most's *Strictly confidential* is a splendidly relaxed big-band arrangement providing imaginative backgrounds to some excellent soloing. Most's straight-toned and mild-mannered introduction is followed by an exposition of Powell's jaunty AABA tune that divides its 'paragraphs' between A) trumpets, A) reeds, B) trombones and A) contrapuntal ensemble. Pettiford's spaciously patterned bass support to all this is magisterial. Relaxed ensemble figures back the solos of Schildkraut, Flax, Wasserman, Dahl, Rehak and Mettome. Most's improvisation is, like his companions', thoroughly in the bop tongue, and assuredly it is no simple matter to recall a better example of straightforward bop 'big-bandery' than this almost unassumingly launched celebration of the great pianist's fugitive melody.

The second date tackles Parker's *Confirmation*, Powell's *Celia*, Monk's *In walked Bud* and Davis's *Half Nelson*. The handling of the Monk piece has a punchy virility giving the well-marshalled feel of a larger group. Schildkraut's Parkerish agilities are noised in the deeper tenorlike regions of his alto. Deliberate contrasts in the parts of his improvisation are considerable proofs of this then recent Kenton sideman's practical admiration for Bird. Dorough, who reportedly (**264**) played at some of Parker's 'apartment sessions', produces one of his most impressive solos, a single-line improvisation with firm inner vigour, during *Half Nelson*. More impressive still is the dazzling way in which Most ranges in the clarinet's high register through the changes of this same Davis piece.

It is unarguable that, as a clarinettist, Most is confidently his own man, and that in his choice and presentation of what is a rather unusual programme of recollection he displays authoritative gifts. There are few places, if any, where this might seem less evident. *Serpent's tooth* has an exciting band score which in its earlier part virtually becomes a duet for clarinet and ensemble. The swing is unfailing, decidedly helped by the boldness of Most's almost piercing continuity of line.

The score for *Round about midnight* effectively sets off the 'after dark' sombreness of the $^4/_4$ exposition and reprise of the tune – graced by Most's *chalumeau* statements – by doubling the beat for the central choruses, with powerful brass comments egging forward Most's passionate high-register variations. Splendid pacemaking skill here from Pettiford and Motian, who do the same in different circumstances as Most gently states the melody of *Blue Bird.* The bassist's ranging line is facilitated by this subtle arrangement which begins peaceably but reaches a climax, after fine solos from Rehak, Wasserman, and Mettome, with some percussively hortatory variations for the reeds and then brass. Placid *chalumeau* restores calm at the close.

As a technician Most may lack the elegant fluidity of phrasing that distinguishes DeFranco's playing. Still, his mastery of his instrument is impeccable and the skills of his fingering technique are evident, particularly as they relate – quite fascinatingly sometimes – to his improvising thought. Whether Most's apparent abandonment of the clarinet only a short space after these 1957 recordings is judged regrettable will depend on judgements of his subsequent career which cannot be made the business of this entry. But it *is* relevant to remark that his musicianship in achieving these recreations – or continuations – of a particular phase of jazz-making must be judged in the light of his instincts both as a clarinettist and as an arranger and director. Those instincts can be judged extraordinary, and what results from them possesses virtues which resound clearly beyond Most's immediate celebratory intentions towards admired masters. E.T.

Gil Evans

460 Pacific Standard Time

†EMI/Pacific Jazz (E) CDP746 856–2 (2 CDs), Blue Note (A) BN-LA461-H2 (2 LPs)

Louis Mucci, Ernie Royal, Johnny Coles (tpt); Joe Bennett, Frank Rehak, Tom Mitchell (tbn); Julius Watkins (fr h); Harvey Philips (tu); Cannonball Adderley (alt); Jerry Sanfino (reeds); Evans (arr, p); Chuck Wayne (g); Paul Chambers (bs); Art Blakey (d). New York City, 9 April 1958.
St Louis blues · King Porter stomp · Round about midnight · Lester leaps in

Bill Barber (tu), Phil Bodner (reeds), Philly Joe Jones (d) replace Philips, Sanfino, Blakey. New York City, 2 May 1958.
Willow tree

Blakey (d) replaces Jones. New York City, 21 May 1958.
Struttin' with some barbeque

Clyde Reasinger (tpt) replaces Royal. New York City, 26 May 1958.
Manteca · Bird feathers

Mucci, Coles, Allen Smith (tpt); Bill Elton, Curtis Fuller, Dick Lieb (tbn); Robert Northern (fr h); Barber (tu); Al Block (reeds); Steve Lacy (sop); Evans (arr, p); Wayne (g); Dick Carter (bs); Dennis Charles (d). New York City, January 1959.
Davenport blues · Straight, no chaser · Django

Mucci, Coles, Danny Stiles (tpt); Jimmy Cleveland, Fuller, Rod Levitt (tbn); Earl Chapin (fr h); Barber (tu); Budd Johnson (clt, ten); Lacy (sop); Ed Caine (reeds); Evans (arr, p); Ray Crawford (g); Tommy Potter (bs); Elvin Jones (d). New York City, 5 February 1959.
Chant of the weed · *Ballad of the sad young men* · *Joy spring* · *Theme*

The above group of sessions first appeared as two separate LPs, the 1958 occasions as *New Bottle, Old Wine*, those of the following year as *Great Jazz Standards*. And from the start there was minor confusion about the earlier dates, signalled by their labels carrying the title 'Old Bottle, New Wine'. As Evans confirmed 20 years later, [28] the latter was obviously the title originally intended, for he gave the old bottles strikingly unfamiliar contents; and then did it again with the 1959 sessions.

This music was interleaved with his three great collaborations with Miles Davis. The *Old Bottle* dates came between *Miles Ahead* and *Porgy and Bess* (**382**), the latter being followed by *Great Jazz Standards*, which led to *Sketches of Spain*, the whole clearly being a period of intense creativity for Evans. Comparisons between these two related bodies of work are in many ways instructive but in one respect puzzling. Why is it that although employing top New York session men in both sequences he obtained far better ensemble performances on the sessions under his own name than on those with Davis? It is as well he did so, for the lines of these scores are chiselled with a cool and reasoned accuracy that never tones down the luminous glow of his orchestral writing. Even in passages whose gesture may soberly be described as fantastic, the truthfulness of Evans's musical temperament fuses the diverse thematic elements more than just convincingly, offering a positive comment on the essential continuity of jazz history. That everything in the writing is finished and precise in aims and achievement is indeed reflected in magnificent playing, for example the stinging lead trumpet work of Mucci and Royal. There is even fine playing in the service of humour, as when initial statement of a theme by a virtuoso trumpeter, Armstrong's *Struttin' with some barbeque*, is given to the tuba: this is no small improvement on comparable passages from King Oliver such as in *Frankie and Johnny* (**82**).

As is plain from his recorded output as a whole, Evans never accepted notional separation between jazz and other musics, and even less the parochial dividing lines supposedly ruled across the jazz terrain. It is therefore unsurprising that he should undertake a highly condensed history of jazz, from *St Louis blues* to *Bird feathers*, with *Great Jazz Standards* as a supplement. And rather than being like decaying statues in a deserted museum, his chosen themes, some of them quite old, are shown to be as vital as ever. The historical perspective which guided this choice makes a telling contrast with what seemed the rather deliberately random selection of items which made up *Miles Ahead*. And Evans's ignoring the limitations of style, form and expression seemingly implicit in these 15 themes is paralleled by his choice of personnel, which for instance results in Budd Johnson and Steve Lacy playing in harmony together. In this world, too, it is perfectly apt to have a modern trumpeter such as Coles solo on Beiderbecke's *Davenport blues*; and the integration of diverse soloists with such varied themes further implements Evans's view of the wholeness of the musical continuum.

Unlike Evans's first major outing with Davis, here most of the pieces are not linked together in a continuous musical fabric, *King Porter stomp* is joined to *St Louis blues*, *Struttin' with some barbeque* to *Willow tree*, *Manteca* to *Round about midnight*, and that is all. Yet for reasons suggested above, the effect is one of continuity, of unity at a deeper level. In fact right back to the Thornhill days (**375**) Evans's method was always his own. It is notable especially for a richly chromatic, though always tonally oriented, harmonic language and for almost proverbially inexhaustible blendings of instrumental timbres.

These timbres were never mere colouristic effects but, as with Ellington, are indissolubly related to the harmony. The varied timbral mixtures are sometimes expressed in opaque, almost clusterlike voicings which may alternate with rich polyphonic textures. The vivid imagination infusing this music is manifest in an altogether exceptional level of invention, so that, indeed, 'colour itself becomes action'. [29] Even the most watchfully critical ear could detect few of the standard procedures of orchestration: there are no easy ways out here, every detail being newly experienced, each note sounding freshly minted. Some passages indeed are of extraordinary beauty, so real in their glowing colour, so unreal in their phantomlike mystery. Certain of the slow pieces, notably *Willow tree* and *Round about midnight*, have the irrational passivity of dreams.

Although Adderley predominates at the 1958 sessions, there is no question of his being, as was Davis elsewhere, the only soloist. Rather like Ellington with his sidemen, Evans made Adderley sound better than he ever did elsewhere and did so on the basis of only a short acquaintance. When this music was new and not yet properly understood it was suggested that the altoist's contribution was marked by a 'disassociation from the context of the arrangements'. [30] But the truth can now be heard to be the opposite, and Adderley is clearly on his mettle, and in his best moments, as on *Lester leaps in* or *Manteca*, we catch just a hint of what the once proposed collaboration between Evans and Parker might have been like. In fact these were auspicious occasions altogether, with both Cleveland and Lacy improvising more decisively here than they did for Evans on his 1957 Prestige dates (†Original Jazz Classics [A] OJCCD346–2). And the work of several other soloists, including Coles, Rehack, Johnson, Wayne, Crawford, Chambers and Blakey, gives this music the advantage of a whole range of further insights.

Besides these solos there is considerably more of Evans the pianist on the above recordings than hitherto. It is revealing to hear him express himself with ideas specific to the 'black and white' medium of the piano rather than through the colours available to a large ensemble. He evidently found a direct involvement with performances helpful and he continued to play a certain amount, on the piano and various electronic keyboard instruments, on records and at public appearances, though seldom as much as on these 1958–9 sessions.

The opening notes of *St Louis blues* are Adderley's and this piece first unfolds as a dialogue between him and the ensemble. Evans draws from the latter a remarkable variety of gestures, sounds and textures in response to the altoist's elaborately decorated account of Handy's themes. Latterly the rhythm section comes forward, mainly in the person of Evans with the guitar murmuring behind him. This passage turns into a coda which is quieter and cooler but, thanks to Wayne and Chambers, just as active rhythmically; and it serves as preparation for Adderley's return with *King Porter stomp*. Morton's thematic material is addressed with uncommon flexibility and the ensemble is less subservient to the altoist, with Evans deploying an even greater diversity of textures, sounds and gestures. More specifically he here extends the sort of thematic variations and developments that he had begun including in his Thornhill scores ten and more years earlier (**375**).

Although the often rumbunctious Fats Waller composed *Willow tree*, it is here the cue for pastel tones and some particularly sensitive piano work. After the tuba has finished its statement of the *Struttin' with some barbeque* theme there is a Rehak solo followed by the trumpets bringing the theme back as a prelude to a long Adderley solo. This the ensemble interrupts with several ideas of its own before there is an alto-saxophone coda over low, long-sustained brass tones. *Lester leaps in*, with its sequence of solos from Adderley, Wayne and Rehak followed by a dialogue between Blakey and the horns, might have seemed more conventional were it not for the blistering theme statements and other ensemble passages so vividly conceived, so brilliantly executed. And there is a condensed recapitulation, differently orchestrated from before, then a coda leading into *Round about midnight*. This includes the leader's main solo of the 1958 sessions, enhanced by the ensemble rather as he once had Thornhill's playing enhanced. At this stage in Evans's development slow performances like this and *Willow tree* suggest an almost Proustian melancholy and elegiac striving for lost time, and the feeling is heightened by the illusionist manner in which one piece can fade into another.

Under *Midnight*'s concluding piano trill Chambers enters with the main thematic idea of *Manteca* while the flute glides in with the middle eight's melody. But soon there is a blazing assertion of Gillespie's theme and then it is Adderley all the way, urged on by the ensemble in an extraordinary propulsive manner yet with moves unpredictably varied. In contrast *Bird feathers* begins and ends with a minimalist gesture, this theme's rhythmic framework, its essence, being heard from Blakey's brushes. This is then clothed with pitches, first with a bop-styled unison around which the rest of the ensemble grows. Adderley's entry was surely a deliberate evocation of Parker. After his first solo the ensemble returns with some very independent figurations before Rehak, Coles and again Blakey are heard from. But Evans has further ideas boldly derived from Parker's theme and the ensemble expounds these at length. There is a Chambers bowed solo accompanied by Wayne and Blakey before the altoist re-enters. The other horns repeat several times the dying fall of a phrase from Parker's 1953 *Chi chi* as Adderley scurries past, and the *Bird feathers* theme itself reappears in a differently instrumented echo of the bop unison sound. Finally everything winds down to Blakey's brushes with the skeleton of the theme.

On *Davenport blues* Evans again draws from a musician one of his finest recorded performances, for Coles solos almost throughout this. There are just brief comments from the piano, and Evans as usual sets the trumpeter's phrases amid beautiful and much varied textures. Rather than any increased tension in Coles's line, it is the ensemble that brings this piece to its climax. *Straight, no chaser* has a seductive introduction with the piano in the lead, and we are reminded that humour, a strictly musical humour, is often a factor in Monk's music. The theme is stated in an assertive ensemble unison, especially telling here because of the jazz feeling which unites all these players. Solos from Coles and Lacy follow, with the latter really getting inside the theme. They are heard with the rhythm section alone but the ensemble at last joins in behind Cleveland. There is a duet between Evans and Carter; indeed it is Evans who, at the piano, has the most cogent ideas on Monk's theme. And that theme's restatement offers the track's most original ensemble passage, still employing the unison idea yet putting it in a far more complex setting, a real piece of *kolorischer Orchesterbrillanz*.

Though noncommittally named *Theme* here, this melodic snippet, apparently by Evans, later appeared as *La Nevada* (**383**). His piano is again in the lead but Johnson is the main soloist, on tenor, and that instrument's characteristic directness is set off against quite complex brass figures. There is a guitar solo by Crawford which retains its intimacy despite Evans's punctuations and Jones's busy drums. These grow busier and finally break out into a solo that is the best possible contrast to Johnson and the brass. The final choruses use a climactic effect comparable to *Straight, no chaser*, thickening the harmonies so that great tension is generated, and then released. Tactics are different for *Joy spring*, where Clifford Brown's theme is conjured out of the material which precedes it. This has aptly been called 'a sort of theme and variations in reverse'. [31] Cleveland finds a vehicle in *Ballad of the sad* *young men*, and Evans sets restlessly shifting mixtures of instrumental sound behind him; listen for example to the unexpected way the flute is used.

Most sophisticated of Evans's 15 themes is *Chant of the weed*, though first recorded in 1931, early days for jazz composition. Here it is done in part as a miniature concerto for Johnson, who is heard on clarinet, and his assertive playing made a considerable impression at a time when the instrument was in the midst of a long period of neglect as a solo voice in jazz. His warm and confident phrases cut across Redman's abrupt whole-tone lines to excellent effect. Comparisons with earlier recordings of Evans's themes are not quite the point here, yet it is worth saying that the nervous agitation of Redman's initial version (**123**) is here supplanted by a wry humour, and while some of the scoring is a knowing evocation of bands of the early 1930s, other passages put a modern gloss on that kind of writing.

There is finally an intriguing account of *Django*, a piece that the present writer has never especially liked but which is here lent a new kind of intimacy, the full ensemble being employed with much restraint. Note the *obbligato* between flute and french horn, the interplay between soprano and piano over guitar, Lacy improvising while Coles improvises, the passage where the drums seem to be trying to put everyone into double time yet the ensemble resists. During Evans's second solo the bass figure integral to Lewis's composition briefly fades in, and Coles emerges amid the ensemble to develop a solo against repeated but varied figures that remorselessly build tension. The trumpeter is momentarily drowned yet returns calmly, with the bass; and to end the ensemble allows us a glimpse of the theme.

As noted, this music came during a period of high creativity for Evans and there were to be further substantial instances of the *elegantia, splendor et proprietas* of his finest work. *Out of the Cool* (**383**) came next, and there was the Ampex LP and the sessions that were eventually issued as *The Individualism of Gil Evans* (†Verve [A] 833 804–2). But subsequently there was a steep falling-off, as is suggested by setting the above *King Porter stomp* or even *The meaning of the blues* (from *Miles Ahead*) beside the readings on RCA's 1975 *There Comes a Time*. Finally, as with George Russell, there was the sad ending of an involvement with rock, and Evans's final music was consequently as overpraised as it was undercomposed.

M.H.

Art Pepper

461 Smack Up

†Original Jazz Classics (A) OJCCD176, Boplicity (E) COP031

Jack Sheldon (tpt); Pepper (alt); Pete Jolly (p); James Bond (bs); Frank Butler (d). Los Angeles, 24–5 October 1960.

Smack up · *Las Cuevas de Mario* · *A bit of Basie* · *How can you lose?* · *Maybe next year* · *Tears inside*

Sheldon must have seemed a hopeful companion for Pepper at a session indicative of a greater re-establishment of the altoist's powers. The two had fronted the 1956 quintet for *The Return of Art Pepper* (Jazz-West [A] JWLP10) shortly after Pepper's first serious absence from music; and Sheldon's had been an engagingly fresh voice, fresher, arguably, than Pepper's own, which sounded a slightly defiant revival of the style of his early Discovery recordings. Other essays of that same year on Jazz-West and Playboy, with Chet Baker and others, showed increasing strength and new rhythmic development. Jolly was the pianist on most of those occasions. It seems that the hearing of current records by Coltrane had helped to spark Pepper's self-rediscovery, [32] and a milestone in the process (though Coltrane's mark was not upon it) was the justly lauded Pepper–Marty Paich collaboration *Art Pepper plus Eleven* (Boplicity [E] COP007), on which Sheldon played all the trumpet solos. That was a more obvious sequence of revisitations but here the process is more subtle, a salute to persons, perhaps, rather than to the atmospherics of jazz history-making.

Not one of the tunes was exactly famous at the time of the session. Harold Land's *Smack up* appeared only three years previously. Pepper speeds it up markedly, and it is not easy to decide whether the choppiness of some of the altoist's lines is a new development or part of a quirky attempt to 'bop up' the theme. But his notes dance, and so do Sheldon's, supple, firmly tongued, packed with wit. Jolly, who in 1956 had sounded an average supporter, sparkles throughout, interestingly anticipating the mannerisms of Roger Kellaway. Looking back to his Lighthouse days with Conte Candoli, Pepper revives a 5/4 blues of his own. The character of *Las Cuevas de Mario* is established partly by the persistent figure set down by the piano, with the steadfast support of Pepper's older *compadre* Butler, and partly by the angular tune shaped in unisons and colliding seconds by trumpet and saxophone. Pepper's soloing is aptly plaintive: staccato flurries may indicate newer lessons learned.

Buddy Collette's *A bit of Basie* also has Hermosa Beach connections – a Lighthouse All-Stars origin. A swinging urgency helps in making Bond's virtues more evident. The bassist takes a good solo before Pepper and Butler exchange breaks. Then, anyone wishing to test the theory that Benny Carter was one of Pepper's chief influences might attend to the treatment of an expectedly tuneful Carter creation, *How can you lose?*

To this listener, the younger saxophonist's expression is very much his own, however much at home he may be with the music of a former employer. Penetrating in thought and tone, Pepper seems to relish the unpredictabilities of Duane Tatro's adventurous *Maybe next year*, and the urge to go searching touches Jolly as well as he plays his best solo on the record with fitful augmentations of tempo and increasing confidence within the unusual chords. (Hear **453** for Tatro's own treatment of this theme.)

The final piece is the most intriguing of the lot. With Ornette Coleman still in the course of introducing his free music, and with controversy raging on every side, Pepper thoughtfully, unsensationally looks into Coleman's second Contemporary LP to choose a theme which, while it has Ornette's prints all over it, is an only fractionally adjusted 12-bar sequence, described by Don Cherry as 'an old folk-type blues in the Jesse Fuller vein'. [33] Pepper was ever a keen player of the blues, and became an even more devoted one towards the end of his life. As the ambivalent *Tears inside* struts along, the members of the quintet respond to the sprite of modernity not by stylish emulations but by a demonstration that jazz drawing on its deepest wells cannot be superseded. They all shine but Pepper's solo is the marvel of it all, gathering a variety of skewed repetitions into a pattern of deceptive power, power which, despite the tempo, has a core of calmness. Amid a furore of critical words is made a wise *musical* comment – yet not a solemn one. With a puckishness as Parkerish as it is Colemanesque, a little snatch of *Silver threads among the gold* is inserted into the design.

Little more than a year later Pepper was foul of the narcotics laws again, and that would be far from the end of the matter. A year before his death in 1982 this incredible survivor of woes still believed that he could grow creatively. [34] His voice certainly had changed. The effect wrought upon him by Coltrane during the 1960s has been as hard as any other suggested influence to recognize with certainty. Towards the end his ability to absorb himself in the blues could lead to music of almost unbearable pathos. There may also have been an ineradicable nostalgia in him, for he loved to visit his musical past, recreating, for example, *Las Cuevas de Mario* in a 1977 club set (Contemporary [A] 7643), and *Mambo de la Pinta* from his 1956 *Return* LP for a studio session also during 1977 (Boplicity [E] COP019).

The holes in his career, added to the plethora of recordings in his last decade, make Pepper a difficult artist to assess in the round. Though hard to delineate, his stature now seems considerable, and the record detailed above reveals his gift clearly at an important and memorable stage. E.T.

Heiner Stadler

462 A Tribute to Monk and Bird

†Tomato (A) 269 630–2 (2 CDs), Affinity (E) AFFD187 (2 LPs)

Thad Jones (cnt, fl h[1]); George Lewis (tbn); George Adams (ten, fl[2]); Stanley Cowell (p); Reggie Workman (bs); Lenny White (d); Stadler (arr). New York City, 17–19, 25 January 1978.

Air conditioning · Au privave · Straight, no chaser

Warren Smith (timp) added. Same dates.

Mysterioso · Perhaps[1,2]

Cecil Bridgewater (tpt) replaces Jones. Same dates.

Ba-lue bolivar ba-lues-are

Anyone who believes that jazz can no longer shock with the force of a completely independent identity, that nothing remains to be discovered, should hear these performances. Though taken down in 1978, they have remained, in Boulez's phrase, 'violently of the present'. [35] The obscurity of Stadler, a Pole born in 1942, trained in Hamburg, and a New York resident from 1965, can be seen, in the ever fashion-conscious world of jazz, as no small compliment to him. It may in part have been due to the absence of picturesque biographical information, but more to the point it enabled him, as a comparable situation enabled Monk during his most productive years, to do his best work undisturbed. Indeed, Monk provides Stadler, as does Parker, with some of his starting points, for he explores the further potentialities of three themes by each of them, this being done with particular thoroughness in the cases of Monk's *Straight, no chaser* and *Ba-lue bolivar ba-lues-are*.

Parker's *Air conditioning* furnishes an excellent illustration of how a theme with sufficient inner strength and self-consistency can be taken to pieces and put together again in a variety of more complex ways. The performance opens, almost ironically, with a unison statement of the theme in C major, and there are solos by all hands. But Stadler reworks Parker's line polytonally, this being very apparent from the backgrounds to the improvisations: it results in their becoming disrelated from the theme's basic harmonization. Again, he has each player begin his solo before the preceding musician has stopped, this producing a layered, overlapping effect that is telling and unusual. After the horn solos there is some real, which is to say unpatterned, collective improvising which leads to *ostinato* figures in dissonant counterpoint whose flavour will at once be recognizable to those few who know Stadler's other work. A piano solo arises out of this passage and Cowell's improvisation, like those from Workman and White that follow, is relatively free yet does follow guidelines provided by Stadler. Finally Parker's theme reappears in its original form on the horns, but even when this recording has grown familiar its return has a genuine impact far removed from the perfunctory gesture that many such recapitulations make. This is because of what has happened since we last heard it in this pristine state, much of the wonder and exuberance of its hidden musical potential having been searched out by Stadler's processes. These amount to recomposition instead of merely of arrangement, and such results being obtained while giving each member of the band his head in solos.

A different yet audibly related set of procedures can be observed working on a larger scale in *Ba-lue bolivar ba-lues-are*. The melody is harmonized polytonally but there is a collective, and really free, improvisation between each phrase. Stadler points out that this already developing theme statement introduces block chords using all 12 pitches, the implications of which are most skilfully maintained in subsequent three-part writing for the horns. An example is the background to Cowell's solo, which is in fact a harmonization of Monk's own solo on his initial Riverside recording. This satisfyingly dense-textured passage is eventually called into question by the rhythm section's satirical references to rock 'n' roll and the horns' quoting from Richard Strauss's *Till Eulenspiegels lustige Streiche*, a symphonic portrait of a very accomplished joker.

Far more ought to be said about these two extraordinary performances, which reconcile a saturated complexity of musical detail with a shining truth and beauty of utterance. But there is no space here for more analytical findings or to say much about the four remaining pieces. Certain features must be noted, however, such as the very chromatic treatment of Parker's *Au privave*, done as a vehicle for Lewis's trombone playing. This is virtuosic not in the sense that he offers an elaborate yet empty display but rather that he brings off musically demanding assignments with grace, seeming ease, and acute expressiveness. Adams gives us Parker's theme first, against a bass line in another key, then Lewis plays phrases based on the theme before going into a free solo. What the score asks him to do is to 'Play in approximately half-tempo but never precisely. Play either slower or faster and combine the various half-tempo levels by means of *ritardandos* and *accelerandos*; short excursions into the original medium-fast tempo should be played throughout your solo.' Lewis makes it all sound perfectly natural, and while he is doing so the other horns back him with phrases which follow their own separate schemes of speedings-up and slowings-down. Add to this the rhythm section's steady pulse and the effect is that of a kaleidoscope shifting at several tempos at once.

Stadler also fragments the other Monk themes, in the case of *Mysterioso* using its separate parts as a framework for a duet improvisation by White and Smith. Here the other chief soloist is the bassist and again the written, and polytonal, figurations behind him speed up and slow down unpredictably. Workman's solo is almost a compendium of the bass techniques usable in jazz, building to a magnificent statement – and this is the view of one normally put to sleep by bass solos. In *Straight, no chaser* the theme's phrases are, on its announcement, once more separated by collective improvisations. When it is heard in continuous form it is as a polytonal canon, with Jones, Lewis and Adams starting on different beats in different keys. Jones goes on to a superb improvisation, well able to stand beside his work on the Riverside *Five by Monk by Five* sessions of 1959. Like his solo on *Air conditioning* and contributions to the other Stadler performances, this reminds us what a curious musician he was, producing large quantities of routine work for Basie and in the band he co-led with Mel Lewis and then, once in a very long while, coming up with something so inspired as to suggest that he was meant to be one of the major figures of this music. And shortly after these dates Jones was responsible for a further demonstration of the potency of Stadler's ideas when he took part in a session led by his brother Hank, the fruits of which appeared as *Groovin' High* (Muse [A] MR5169). For this he wrote a version of *Anthropology* which made use in jagged ensemble passages of certain of Stadler's procedures, with bitonality heightening the essential character of the Parker–Gillespie theme. It was enough to raise this track to an entirely different level from the rest of that routine LP.

Not in terms of style or specific method but as thoroughgoing explorations, Stadler's treatments of these half-dozen Parker and Monk themes are reminiscent of Hodeir's compositional revaluations of several Monk pieces (for instance *Osymetrios I* and *II* on **455**) and Schuller's *Variants on a theme by Monk* (**400**). Stadler goes beyond them, however, in the sense that he transforms these hitherto separate themes into a unified family of pieces. Yet while these performances together form the best point of entry into his rich and strange world, conveying the voice of emergent self-knowledge, a better idea of his stature is naturally gained from recordings of his own compositions. Besides the *Retrospection* set (†Tomato [A] 269 652–2), whose centrepiece is the remarkable half-hour *Clusterity*, these include the aptly titled *Brains on Fire* (Labor [A] LRS7001/2) and *Jazz Alchemy* (LRS7006) collections.

All these tumbled into the well of uncomprehending silence that awaits so many real achievements, and this is partly a question of Stadler's music being even more recalcitrant of analysis and description than most. More important, however, is that composing of such intensity can never be imitative. As in Russell's *Jazz Workshop* pieces (**380**), there is nothing predigested for weak musical stomachs, everything being newly minted. There is no pigeonhole into which Stadler's works can be made to disappear: they are not part of any movement, embody no theory, and are simply themselves. But they exist, and will continue to demand attention as lone monuments. Stadler's time will come later, perhaps much later. M.H.

Roswell Rudd

463 Regeneration

†Soul Note (It) 121054

Rudd (tbn); Steve Lacy (sop); Mischa Mengelberg (p); Kent Carter (bs); Han Bennink (d). Milan, 25–6 June 1982.

Blue chopsticks · 2300 skidoo · Twelve bars · Monk's mood · Friday the 13th · Epistrophy

Early in 1960, teetering on the brim of the jazz avant-garde, Rudd encountered Herbie Nichols, who died in 1963 of leukemia and was not of the avant-garde. His quite exhilarating playing and composing pianism (*The Complete Blue Note Recordings of Herbie Nichols*, Mosaic [A] MR5–118) is related to the 'mainstream' jazz which coexisted with bop in the 1940s, and although some still speculate that a development of the prophetic tensions dancing through his music might have become a creative bypass for others not committed to 1960s free music, nothing is now clearer than that Nichols himself missed the opportunity (and may have lacked the will) to exploit his gifts beyond a sphere that remained almost intimately personal.

Rudd rapidly became an associate of free jazzmen but Nichols had become a musical mentor for him and remains an inspiration. This *Regeneration* session belongs to the maintenance of a mode of expression whose best masters death has claimed and who yet continue to make invaluable donations toward the enhancement of living jazz. It was in the year of Nichols's death that the New York Contemporary Five recorded unelaborated sketches of Thelonious Monk compositions which had been devised by Rudd and which presumably bear some relation to the trombonist's work with Lacy and Dennis Charles in a group whose devotion to Monk's music sometimes dominated most of its activity. In any review of Lacy's career his extended *affaire* with Monk's music is unavoidable. His solo recreations are sampled at **475**, but much of his exploration of an innovator so central to the modern movement in jazz has, like Rudd's, been aimed at redressing an expressive balance. It could be argued that the pianistic presence in the majority of Monk's most celebrated recordings, impressive as it is to those who rejoice in his stature, also has militated to an extent against any fully satisfactory independent realization of his compositions in ensemble terms, without the absence of his own hands, and of the 'private, self-contained nature of his music, its strange mineral toughness' [36] wrecking the attempt.

Deliciously quirky in its personality as Nichols's playing was, his compositions cannot, in any way similar to Monk's, be tethered to an established 'presence'. Rudd has long been dedicated to honouring Nichols. The very make-up of this splendid quintet, considering the associations of the members – and the kind of cooperative freedom afforded them by Rudd – makes the best kind of honouring of the music of these two composers an open possibility. This is not the revisitation of a tradition: it is a tradition (if that is what one wishes to call it) alive and kicking, and one that never really went away.

As *Blue chopsticks* sets off with Nichols's little cockeyed introduction of one-measure-and-a-bit of impish childishness, the theme's lines are unisoned by Rudd and Lacy. The vigour of the ensuing solo improvisations is immensely enhanced by Carter's bass support, sinewy and lissom. Lacy skates across the metre, recreating melody, Rudd, equally melodistic yet more earthily gaited, rasps out his phrases. The possibility that Mengelberg may steer the Nichols spirit closer to Monk is not too easy to affirm. His style has undoubtedly embraced some unusual complexities – used effectively in accompaniment – and the boppisms are fewer than they used to be. He ushers in *2300 skidoo* with heavily sustained ornamental chords and the quintet plays this wry tune noticeably slower than its composer did back in 1955. Both Lacy and Rudd brood somewhat, and the pianist is both searching and skimming, and inserting impudent punctuations on Carter's plangent bass shapes as though they were the turning pages of a book.

An edge of ribaldry touches *Twelve bars* and it is not easy to say here how much the composer's intentions are reflected in a parading sort of tune which Bennink introduces with military rolls and Rudd punctuates with tailgate smears. It is rather like a show tune from a burlesque musical based on some Eugene O'Neill comedy. Mengelberg, in a fetching solo, takes the chance to sound rather more like the critic musing trenchantly in the stalls on the antics of the posturers on the stage. The balance of moods is the quintet's, though; and it could well have been the composer's as well.

Monk's mood has a slow pace and its basic scoring differs from Rudd's 1963 realisation (**406b**) not only in the boldness of the trombone and soprano tone colour but also in the daring, and not obviously Monk-conjuring, keyboard contrasts provided by Mengelberg. A highlight of the number is a gentle soprano variation with linear contrasts balanced with casual legerdemain. Rudd shoulders the turning wheel of *Friday the 13th*'s subordinate theme and Lacy handles the hardly less repetitive upper melody. Much of what follows is like some half-deliberate conspiracy against the straightforwardness of the bluesy monotony. Rudd utters a statement which is far less melodic exploration than a chain of elemental wails and groans, and beneath this Mengelberg traces a commentary of well-turned keyboard witticisms. Rudd strains mockingly for a tune, coming up with a quotation from *Why don't you do right?* as Lacy sidles across the rim of the wheel into a low-register musing. Sensations become heightened as a loose exchange develops which gains a mock-revolutionary waggishness out of being never quite collective and never quite spontaneous. Mengelberg plays a sustained and beautifully fashioned solo with unobtrusive backing from Carter and Bennink. Rudd shuffles some layers of familiar repetition which resolve themselves as Lacy joins him in the reprise. The longest of these numbers, *Friday the 13th* is the one richest in the kind of artful whimsy and inventive crosscurrent that would have suited Monk's mind.

Episthrophy is the briefest offering, a simple memoir with a Latin shimmer to it, closing in a genial, unaggressive scramble. Everyone is in brilliant form for this justly lauded Rudd session and Rudd himself steers his participants with exactly the right balance of authority and respect. Cataloguing the excellencies of Bennink and Carter might have become tedious if attempted, but those excellencies really are as constant and as vital to this ageless jazz as those of anyone else involved. E.T.

John Zorn

464a News for Lulu
†Hat Art (Sw) CD6005

Zorn (alt); George Lewis (tbn); Bill Frisell (g). Lucerne, 28 August 1987.
K.D.'s motion · *Funk in deep freeze* · *Melanie* · *Melody for C* · *Lotus blossom* · *Eastern incident* · *Peckin' time* · *Blues blues blues* · *Blue minor* (2 versions) · *This I dig of you* · *Venita's dance* · *News for Lulu* · *Olé* · *Sonny's crib* · *Hank's other tune* · *Windmill*

Same personnel. Willisau, 30 August 1987.
News for Lulu · *Funk in deep freeze* · *Windmill*

464b More News for Lulu
†Hat Art (Sw) CD6055

Same personnel. Basel, 18 January 1989.
Eastern incident · *Lotus blossom* · *Melanie* · *Olé* · *Blue minor* · *Peckin' time* · *Blues blues blues* · *Melody for C*

Same personnel. Paris, 19 January 1989.
Blue minor · *Hank's other tune* · *News for Lulu* · *Gare Guillemins* · *Minor swing* · *K.D.'s motion* · *Funk in deep freeze*

This may appear a surprising venture for a thoroughgoing postmodernist such as Zorn. Yet a central plank of postmodernism in one of its aspects is selecting material entirely from the past while avoiding the simple-mindedness of revivalism. Those wishing to bring back the New Orleans or swing ('mainstream') styles, and even latter-day proponents of phases of jazz such as bop, have tried to reproduce their chosen style unmindful of the original musicians having created it without preconceptions, let alone purist obsessions. Zorn and his friends do not make that kind of mistake. A further point about postmodernism in the phase with which we are concerned here is that it is by definition a mode of criticism, a de facto commentary on its own history. As has been noted at various stages in this book, jazz has been in too much of a hurry, rushing through its resources, failing properly to explore avenues of potential major growth, and a major benefit of postmodernism is that it allows the music to go back and take another look.

The above performances are especially good examples of this, for themes recorded for Blue Note by Kinny Dorham, Hank Mobley, Sonny Clark and Freddie Redd are improvised upon with a much greater variety of expression than might have been thought possible from their earlier rather dour 1950s and 1960s hard-bop presentations. Indeed, these themes are treated in utterly new ways, are shown in startlingly fresh lights. Yet the material is treated with unblinking respect, quite without irony, and is shown to be fully alive. These new treatments take the form of largely equal-voiced collective improvisations, and besides being almost unflaggingly contrapuntal they are highly concentrated and far briefer than the hard-bop originals: at 6 minutes 40 seconds the Basel account of Redd's *Melanie* is the longest. Zorn's line-up is altogether different from that of Blue Note and comparable blowing dates, in which Lewis's and Frisell's instruments rarely were heard. Yet they were affected by other precedents, sometimes pointing in directions quite different from that of the hard bop material. Thus Zorn acknowledged the influence of Giuffre's trio with the same instrumentation (**364** etc.), which was another jazz band well able to get along without a rhythm section. [37]

Far more central than matters of instrumentation, however, was the fact that the language of jazz had changed so much since these themes were first recorded. Indeed this is a highly developed music in which every nuance carries weight, these being intent, closely knit ensemble improvisations whose combination of fire and finesse results in a great diversity of sounds and textures. And prominent though Frisell and Lewis are, this music very much carries Zorn's stamp, is shaped by his skill as a bandleader and very flexible instrumentalist, by his record collector's knowledge, and especially by the wide emotional response apparent from several of his other projects. If the atmosphere is so different from that of the blowing sessions at which these themes were first heard, it is partly because their every aspect, melodic, rhythmic and harmonic, was sought out, instead of their being used just as austere tests of very sustained improvising staying close to the original chord sequences.

And just as Zorn has taken a stance on his alto fundamentally different from that of the hard-bop tenors, so his two companions have been just as questioning in their approaches. Frisell's seems the more modest role, yet as one becomes familiar with these performances it grows evident how vital he is. He has described his music as 'Jim Hall filtered through Jimi Hendrix', [38] and although that is a simplification, it does suggest his particular concern with texture. To this we may add his concentration on the precise shaping of short but sometimes complex melodic ideas.

This chimes extremely well amid what is undertaken on the above sessions, although Frisell has played an impressive variety of music. So too has Lewis, even if he, likewise, is no quick-change artist. He can encompass the sort of technically adventurous free playing done with Douglas Ewart (†Black Saint [It] 120 026) in 1979, meet the stringent compositional demands of Heiner Stadler on **462**, and his own on **392** (where he *uses* the microphone instead of merely letting it overhear the instruments); he once sat, briefly, in Basie's machine, and he has even collaborated with Derek Bailey. When teamed with Zorn and Frisell he takes a poised, mostly structured approach to melody, rhythm and harmony, and does so with apparently complete freedom, matching his leader's diversity of phrase and sound. All three can play lyrically yet also with a fury that seems almost destructive of the musical fabric.

As is clear from the above heading, the initial studio session in Lucerne was followed two days later by an appearance at the Willisau Jazz Festival, also in Switzerland, and then by concerts in Basel and Paris 16 months further on. These latter performances were often somewhat brisker, always a bit longer, but more importantly they were at least as good as the Lucerne occasion, and it is rare for such a success to be repeated or even improved upon. In fact throughout these 35 drastic reinterpretations the players' concentration never slackens, their attention does not waver, and this is remarkable.

Zorn had earlier tackled Clark pieces on *Voodoo* (†Black Saint [It] BSP1019–2) and that experience was no doubt valuable. Each piece begins with a head arrangement and it is apparent from the repeat performances that these are set quite formally. They might almost be described as conventional, so far as the instrumentation allows. Beyond that, however, there is much improvisation, this being especially clear with Mobley's *Funk in deep freeze*, Clark's *News for Lulu* and *Blue minor*, where there are three or four versions. During the studio account of *Funk* it is sometimes as if the lead is not held by any one instrument but rather is suspended between the three of them. In the second reading, from Willisau, the guitar is more prominent – as it often is in the concert performances – and Frisell ventures pretty far towards 'noise' in the positive Varèse sense. Zorn is often melodious in something like the traditional manner here, though elsewhere he, too, can go to extremes. Lewis does this in a different way from his companions, with explosive, even wild, double-time outbursts, as in the Paris account of *K.D.'s motion* and Mobley's *This I dig of you*. Sometimes the contrapuntal manoeuvres flow easily, yet never too easily; and everything is delivered with zest. Again, it often happens that there is tension between the rather homespun melodiousness of the hard-bop themes and their densely eventful new settings, shifting constantly, always unstable. On the studio version of *News for Lulu*, note the extreme differences between the alto and trombone lines: given the divergence between the characters of the two instruments this is not surprising, but the parts constantly intermingle, separate, unite, separate.

Extreme differences between the simultaneous lines are evident in the first studio version of *Blue minor*, while the second is rather more extravagant in expression. The Basel concert performance starts with almost a minute and a half of fragmented sounds followed by the head arrangement of the theme, then some guitar extremism. In contrast the Paris reading of *Blue minor* goes straight into the theme and beyond that is an imaginative variant of what they had played the previous day. (For Clark's own recording, hear **285**.) Despite all the disjunct counterpoint there are passages that almost could be termed 'solos' because although both the other instruments remain active, one attains exceptional prominence for a time. A good instance of 'solos' in this sense is the concert performance of *K.D.'s motion* by Dorham. During this reading Zorn deploys almost every sound of which the alto is capable, but always with complete musical sense, with, indeed, resolute coherence. The two interpretations of Redd's *Melanie* are particularly good examples of the differences between studio and concert approaches. Whereas the former plunges straight into the theme, the latter has over a minute of guitar introduction ending with suggestions of Redd's tune. The two performances of Clark's *Melody for C* make an interesting study also, with fine counterpoint between Zorn and Lewis, though with Frisell a real presence also in the studio version. In Basel the alto is more in the lead during the counterpoint; the guitar assumes greater prominence and eventually goes into an exhilarating country-music-gone-mad solo with Lewis and Zorn aiding and abetting.

The studio performance of Dorham's *Lotus blossom* is more fragmentary than most and Zorn produces almost a bop alto solo over a trombone bass line. There is nothing fragmented about the concert occasion, an especially adventurous one with some altogether meaningful guitar 'noise' at the close. It is rather the same with the Basel account of Clark's *Eastern incident*, where this time the extremism is from Zorn although there is a sustained quiet ending here. In *Blues blues blues*, a Redd piece, the studio performance is rather cut and dried, the freedom of gesture notwithstanding, and greater spontaneity was evident at Basel and a seemingly complete independence of the parts, an apparently total flexibility of discourse. The best of this music, and *Venita's dance* by Dorham and Mobley's *Peckin' time* are further instances, has the sort of common-effort complication that has always been one of the most engaging features of collective improvisation in jazz.

For obvious reasons, 'Big' John Patton's *Minor swing* and even Mischa Mengelberg's *Gare Guillemins* have no place here and their inclusion in the Paris concert was a mistake. This minor error goes no distance, however, to explain why Zorn has been so pointedly ignored by supposedly major works of reference like *The New Grove Dictionary of Jazz.*

Again, when Sonny Clark (with Coltrane) recorded it in 1957, the title *News for Lulu* was no doubt innocent of associations with Wedekind's plays, Berg's opera or two of Pabst's films. But Louise Brooks starred in these latter and the link is exploited by Hat Art's packaging. Each booklet gives us the benefit of devastating shots of Miss Brooks doing her *Vénus toute entière à sa proie attachée* stuff in Pabst's *Die Büchse der Pandora* and *Das Tagebuch einer Verlorenen.* What this has to do either with hard bop or with Zorn's kind of jazz is quite another matter. M.H.

Mischa Mengelberg

465 **Change of Season (Music of Herbie Nichols)**
†Soul Note (It) SN1104CD

Steve Lacy (sop); George Lewis (tbn); Misha Mengelberg (p); Arjen Gorter (bs); Han Bennik (d). Milan, 2–3 July 1984.
House party starting · The happenings · Step tempest · Hangover triangle · Change of season · Spinning song · Terpsichore

Despite much encomia citing the compositions of the late Herbie Nichols (1919–63) as among the finest in jazz, few musicians have recorded them or even incorporated them into their repertoires. One reason might be that suggested by Nichols's biographer A. B. Spellman, that they are 'too subtle for the casual listener and too demanding for the lazy improviser'. [39] The enigmatic Nichols, a highly educated man and a student of both classical and jazz music, made few appearances on disc: two 78s for the Hi-Lo label with Chocolate Williams and his Chocolateers in March 1952, two 10-inch LPs, one 12-inch LP for Blue Note [40] and one album for Bethlehem. Yet this slim recorded evidence is enough to reveal a pianist of unique vision and style. But Nichols, a brilliant visionary whose music was quirky yet swinging, dense yet engaging, and who wrote over 100 jazz originals plus operas, theatre pieces, classical music, prose and poetry, was forced to endure years of obscurity in the trite world of neo-Dixieland. He rather shrewdly observed: 'You either have to be an Uncle Tom or a drug addict to make it in jazz, and I'm not either one.'

Not the least irony in a life that included many was the fact that his most famous composition, *Lady sings the blues*, a staple of Billie Holiday's during her final years, brought him no recognition at all. Another was that his work found its most devoted interpreters in the free-jazz movement, most notably through his friend and associate, the trombonist Roswell Rudd, and the soprano saxophonist Steve Lacy, both of whom also shared a mutual fascination with the music of Thelonious Monk, a pianist and composer who had much in common with Nichols. 'We grew up on this music and finally, after all these years, we can begin to play it like it was our own,' said Rudd. [41] Lacy and Rudd collaborated on *Regeneration* (**463**), exploring the music of both Monk and Nichols. On this subsequent album, with George Lewis standing in for Rudd and Gorter for Kent Carter, the level of constancy never flags, setting Nichols's intriguing themes off in technicolour relief from the original piano-trio recordings.

The unusual combination of soprano and trombone dates back to Lacy and Rudd's collaboration in the early 1960s when they formed a quartet to play music from Monk's repertoire. Although they recorded for both Verve and Columbia, the results were not released and the only memento of their association was a 1975 bootleg album recorded in a Greenwich Village coffee house in 1963. Here, the Lacy and Lewis combination produces delightfully dark and mysterious textures, with Lewis's technique allowing him to execute the often complex curlicues of Nichols's compositions in tandem with the more agile soprano without any loss of tonal density or velocity. Although Mengelberg and Bennink both had been primarily associated with the somewhat wilder end of the European avant-garde, the fact that they could find common cause in the work of a post-bebop structuralist was consistent with a reconciliation of the avant-garde with the jazz mainstream that occurred at the end of the 1970s, a recognition, finally, that freedom in itself could be limiting. 'It all started sounding the same,' said Lacy. 'It wasn't free any more.' [42]

House party starting is typical of Nichols's work. An engaging theme of angular resolution is spread over eight bars, then contrasted with an eight-bar variation, and the two segments are repeated. A middle eight is introduced before a return to the original eight-bar theme and variation. The form, over 56 bars, is deceptive. The middle eight makes it appear on a superficial listening that we are in the familiar terrain of the standard 32-bar popular song, but instead we have seven, and not four, eight-bar sections: $A + A^1 + A + A^1 + B + A + A^1$. (The designation A^1 has been used simply because the second theme is so close spiritually to the A theme, but it could just as easily be designated as ABABCAB.)

Lacy and Lewis complement each perfectly. Lacy is the rigorous craftsman with every phrase displayed with care and patience, Lewis a sometimes wild adventurer, threatening to go 'outside', aided and abetted by Mengelberg. It is this sense of danger that gives these performances an edge that a po-faced repertory reconstruction misses. This sense of taking the tunes in sudden and unexpected directions allows the music to breathe the fresh air of creativity rather than ending up as a musty re-creation.

The happenings is a theme of contrasts, an eight-bar phrase against a four-bar phrase. The 12-bar theme has a peculiar dark logic; it is repeated twice before Lewis enters with a raunchy, swashbuckling solo that stands the theme on its head and gradually departs from the song-writer's original sentiments. In contrast is the sprightly *Step tempest*, a 32-bar AABA song camouflaged by an eight-bar intro and a six-bar tag during the original exposition: (intro 8 bars) + A + A + B + A + (tag 6 bars). The quirky theme is echoed by the soloists, Lewis whimsical, pushing against the seams of the song, Lacy ever enquiring, probing to see what lurks beneath the song's surface, Mengelberg angular behind Lacy, yet allowing Bennink to comment vociferously on his right-handed excursions. *Hangover triangle*, an anguished, scurrying theme, has one of the best Mengelberg solos, shortened to allow Bennink to probe the deeper consciousness of his thoughts. It sets the scene for the abbreviated contributions of Lewis and Lacy before Bennink is finally given the licence he had been seeking to break out into the open spaces before the recapitulation of the theme closes the edgy and uncomfortable mood.

The dirgelike title track provokes a considered response from Mengelberg, who seems effortlessly able simultaneously to evoke both Monk and Nichols in his playing while finding room for his own private reflections. This is the sort of tempo that Lacy loves, so much of his best work is done in a mood of quiet reflection, and for a moment Lewis seems lost for words, echoing the moment and keeping his mischievousness at bay to be ready for the *Spinning song.* An unpredictably dark 40-bar structure, it contains feints and surprises in the final 16 bars: A (8 bars) + A (8 bars) + B (8 bars) + C (16 bars). Although the song seems to be shaping up for a familiar 32-bar AABA structure, C turns out to be an extended variation of the A motif developed and expanded over 16 bars. It is a clever touch and the soloists respond with some of their own unpredictable wisdom, with Mengelberg quietly revealing a great sympathy for form and structure in his elegantly constructed solo and unexpected piano tag at the end.

The finest piece of the album is *Terpsichore*; its swirling rhythms provoke a 'school's out' feel across the whole band, with Bennink leading the charge from the school playground. Lewis goes at it with brio, contributing his best solo of the date, closely marked by Bennink, whose jumpy and nervous time-keeping becomes a shared conspiracy with all the soloists, yet maintains the dark, unpredictable density that underpins Nichols's best work. Lacy invites more interaction from the rhythm section and, like any great interpreter, gives the impression that the song belongs to him. It does not, of course, but the point is made. Nichols's compositions remain a potent challenge to anyone with the conceptual vigour to work within their constraints, a series of checks and balances that provide the obstacles to stimulate inspiration. S.N.

James Newton

466 **The African Flower**
Blue Note (A) BT85109

Newton (fl); Olu Dara (cnt); Arthur Blythe (alt); John Blake (vln); Sir Roland Hanna (p); Rick Rozie (bs); Billy Hart (d); Anthony Brown (perc); Jay Hoggard (vib). New York City, 24–5 June 1985.
Black and tan fantasy · Virgin jungle · Fleurette Africaine · Passion flower

As above except Pheeroan Ak Laff (d) for Hart. Same dates.
Cottontail · Virgin jungle

As above but add Milt Grayson (vcl). Same dates.
Strange feeling

It is perhaps ironic that this collection of Ellington and Strayhorn songs should be led by a musician whose instrument played a very small part in the 'Ellington effect'. However, Newton, a flute virtuoso, here succeeds in personalizing the Ellington tradition through stylistic and timbral juxtaposition as much as careful allusion to the past. Although a large proportion of his discography is given over to Third Stream ventures with Anthony Davis on albums such as *I've Known Rivers* (Gramavision [A] GR8201), with his own ensembles on albums including *The Mystery School* (India Navigation [A] IN1046) and *Water Mystery* (Gramavision 18–8407), Newton is an enormously flexible musician. He has recorded in solo, most notably *Axum* (ECM [G] 1214), in duet with piano, with a piano and cello, with a woodwind quintet, with a string quartet and with conventional jazz rhythm sections. As his appearance at the famous 'Young Lions' concert at Carnegie Hall on 30 June 1982 revealed (*The Young Lions* [Elektra Musician (A) 96–0196–1]), he appeared in a variety of settings effortlessly adapting to ensembles as diverse as those led by Anthony Davis, Hamiet Bluiett, Chico Freeman and Wynton Marsalis.

However, Newton's interest in Ellington's music is a strand that runs through several of his albums, such as *One for Strayhorn* and *Star-crossed lovers* on *Water Mystery, Portrait of David Murray* and *Portrait of Pheeroan Ak Laff* inspired by Ellington's musical cameos of Bert Williams, Bill Robinson and Willie 'the Lion' Smith on 1982's *Portraits* (India Navigation [A] IN1051), and his faithful rendering of Strayhorn's *Daydream* on 1983's *James Newton* (Gramavision GR8205).

The African Flower brings the variety of approaches Newton had adopted to Ellington's music on other albums into sharp focus; the one constant is change and is the theme that underwrites the shifting textures and timbres he blends in exploring each composition. That the album nevertheless retains a strong stylistic identity is a tribute to Newton's strong musical personality. *Black and tan fantasy* traces the outline of Ellington's original 1927 recordings (**87**, **89**, **91**) using the following scheme:

Introduction (8 bars) + A (12 bars) + B (8 bars) + B (8 bars) to solos (12-bar blues)

Hanna's sombre introduction follows in Ellington's footsteps but although Dara echoes Bubber Miley on the A section, he does not imitate him. Newton, however, plays the B strain with such purity that he provides an even more haunting release than the original, with Rozie's walking bass providing dynamic forward motion. Dara's talking solo is followed by an introspective Hanna but Newton introduces an element of the unexpected with flute/vocal shrieks evoking Rahsaan Roland Kirk, flutter tonguing, slides and pitch bends that present an effective and unexpected recasting of Ellington's familiar composition. The piece ends, as did Ellington's, with the Chopin *Funeral march* quotation, borrowed from Jelly Roll Morton's 1926 *Dead man blues* (**47a**), where it sounded more apt.

Virgin jungle begins with a programmatic episode evoking the mysteries that lurk within a tropical rainforest before Hoggard and Rozie introduce a vamp that is retained below the 20-bar theme. After another 'jungle' episode, this time in tempo, the theme returns before the composition is opened up for solos. Hoggard's flying mallets precede an arresting Blake solo that with its jagged melodicism barely gives a sideways glance to Ray Nance. Newton, who follows, develops a typical statement that reveals the broad range of stylistic influences he has absorbed. Moving from melodic/rhythmic fragments to wide-interval leaps that suggest the music of Bela Bartók (a Newton favourite), who is often less concerned with melody per se than with the intervals he employs, Newton also uses pitch bends, slides and vocal/flute parabolas. Blythe is less esoteric but Dara is concerned only with tonal distortion, Rorschach blots of sound flung against the rhythm section's vamp for us to interpret as we will. There are hints of Schoenberg running through *Strange feeling*, particularly in the opening section. It forms a perfect contrast to the unexpected entrance of Milt Grayson, who sang the number on Ellington's 1961 recording. Here his delivery is far more authoritative, his full baritone enunciating the lyrics with elaborate precision against the 'strange' Schoenbergian backdrop created by Newton in an imaginative casting of the song.

Newton often listened to Japanese folk music, something that he explored on *Water Mystery*, and there is a shakuhachian clarity to his playing on *Fleurette Africaine*, his full, round tone and clean, elegant lines overshadowing Hoggard and Blake who follow. *Cottontail*, Ellington's classic recasting of Gershwin's *I got rhythm*, is taken at a bright tempo with Blythe piling chorus upon chorus in the manner of Gonsalves, his rich tone adding a personal ingredient to his playing of which Ellington would surely have approved. Hanna and Hoggard move from fours to dialogue with one another; Newton enters with just bass and drums accompaniment before Hanna and Hoggard discreetly comp behind him to complete the workout. *Sophisticated lady*, one of Ellington's most elegant compositions, which is rather undeservedly taken for granted in the jazz repertoire, provides a vehicle for Newton's unaccompanied solo. Perhaps surprisingly, his improvisation does not employ the variety of extended techniques for tonal manipulation that he often calls upon in his solos, but relies on its haunting tone, gentle vibrato and occasional pitch manipulation or glissando to underline his melodicism. *Passion flower* features Blythe's full, round tone in a direct salute to one of his former influences. This performance is more about fitting the various musical personalities together without straining to make them mesh; Hanna and Newton handle the improvisations, leaving Blythe to caress the melody with Hoggard, Blake and Dara providing a discreet backdrop.

Like Mingus, another favourite, Newton probed Ellington's songs for a point of access to express his own musical personality. For while standards like *It don't mean a thing (If it ain't got that swing)*, *C jam blues*, *Satin doll* or even *Cottontail* had long been part of the lingua franca of jazz, there is a vast litany of songs that have only ever been recorded by Ellington, this suggesting they are only suitable for big-band performance. Yet Newton's achievement here was a demonstration that it is possible to disentangle those compositions from single, specific orchestral performances and re-inhabit them in terms of another artist's creativity. S.N.

Anthony Braxton

467a In the Tradition Vol. 1

†SteepleChase (D) SCCD31015

Braxton (bs clt, contra bs clt, alt); Tete Montoliu (p); Niels-Henning Orsted Pedersen (bs); Albert 'Tootie' Heath (d). Copenhagen, 29 May 1974.

Marshmallow · *Goodbye, porkpie hat* · *Just friends* · *Ornithology* · *Lush life*

467b In the Tradition Vol. 2

†SteepleChase (D) SCCD31045

Same personnel. Same date.

What's new? · *Duet* · *Body and soul* · *Marshmallow* (second version) · *Donna Lee* · *My funny Valentine* · *Half Nelson*

There are elements of both the shaman and the clinician in Braxton, yet he was at first as admirer of 1950s rock 'n' roll. His view of music was changed drastically by hearing Ahmad Jamal (**335**) and then Paul Desmond (**311, 366**). The latter's work prompted him to take up the alto saxophone – he was already playing the clarinet in his high school band. Braxton became as much a composer as an instrumentalist and claims to have employed mathematical relationships and diagrams as bases for both composing and improvisation. He was among the first black free-jazz musicians to acknowledge debts contracted elsewhere, not only with Jamal and Desmond but also with Konitz, Tristano and the classical-music avant-garde. Indeed, his musical curiosity has proved tireless and he continues to search for new outlets and to do the unexpected.

Braxton studied at the Chicago School of Music, then harmony and composition at Chicago Music College, also philosophy at Roosevelt University. He became a fluent player on all the saxophones and clarinets, including what may be termed the most extreme members of both families, such as the contrabass clarinet on the recordings detailed above. He proved to be a particularly excellent free-jazz altoist, his performances on this instrument showing him to be at the centre of the jazz tradition. His tone is often highly vocalized, yet a flow of strictly musical invention is always paramount; in fact this richness can seem excessive, with almost every conceivable sort of melodic phrase and rhythmic pattern brought into play, usually with the emphasis on line rather than colour. The consistency of Braxton's style is remarkable considering that he has absorbed musical ideas from a wider range of sources than almost anyone else in jazz, from the most advanced contemporary composers down, as stated above, to rock 'n' roll; and he made something of his own out of it all. Indeed, Braxton combined sophisticated enthusiasm with a certain innocence, and added a genuinely musical sense of humour.

He became involved with the Association for the Advancement of Creative Musicians, a Chicago cooperative for avant-garde jazz, and he made his first record in 1968. This was *Three Compositions of New Music* (Delmark [A] DS415) with Leo Smith and Leroy Jenkins, whose chief media were trumpet and violin but who appeared here, as did Braxton, as multi-instrumentalists. *For Alto Saxophone* dates from the same year (Delmark [A] DS420/1), although it was not issued until 1971. It then became, in terms of avant garde Chicago jazz, something of a best seller and won a prize in Japan. There were precedents for such unaccompanied saxophone improvisations from Coleman Hawkins, Konitz and Rollins, and Braxton had started to extend unsupported solo playing considerably further in 1966 and both gave concerts and recorded in this mode on several instruments over a period of years. With Smith and Jenkins he formed the Creative Construction Company, which journeyed to Paris in 1969 and recorded extensively both there and in London, sometimes with additional players.

During this period, too, Braxton started an informal association with Chick Corea to study scores by Schoenberg, Boulez, Stockhausen and Xenakis. He then became a member of Corea's band of that time, Circle, which also had Dave Holland (**430**) and Barry Altschul and recorded for Blue Note and ECM in 1970–1. Later Braxton led his own quartet, first with Holland and Altschul plus a brass player who would be either Kenny Wheeler (**322**) or George Lewis (**392, 462, 464**). At the same time he was composing a vast quantity of music, seemingly for every medium from unaccompanied solos to pieces for multiple orchestras.

An example of this last is *Composition 82* of 1978, which is in fact designed for four orchestras playing simultaneously (Arista [A] A3L8900) and occupies three LPs. At first such monumentality was seen as only a beginning, and Braxton intended that *Composition 82* would be followed by pieces for six, eight, ten orchestras, each in a different city and linked by satellite; then 100 orchestras. He even envisioned linking orchestras on several planets, in several solar systems, finally in several galaxies; and all this by 1995! Inevitably some have managed to hear his music as wilfully intellectualized and such people have of course missed its considerable element of humour. And there have been wilder comments, from his being told to 'stop Messiaen about' [43] to the suggestion: 'If a mad scientist ever drank a potion he had concocted to formulate a jazz musician, he would undoubtedly transform into Anthony Braxton.' [44]

Given this extravagance, including certain statements of his own, it is necessary to insist that even the concert music for multiple orchestras in no way negated his ability to play jazz, and he in fact had started with an intelligent adaptation of later Coltrane to the alto saxophone. The above session implies, however, that Braxton recognized the necessity, in a jazz context, of proving himself as an improviser both on standard ballads like *Body and soul* and on themes by established jazzmen such as *Ornithology* and *Marshmallow*. Indeed with this programme he links up, even in the ballads, with several major currents of the music's history. Thus *Just friends* is associated with Parker (**266a**), one of whose themes *Ornithology* of course is (**258**). *Body and soul* can hardly fail to be connected with Coleman Hawkins (**192**) or *What's new?* with Billy Butterfield and Bob Crosby's band. *Lush life* is the one Strayhorn melody that was never attributed to Ellington, and though many people associate *My funny Valentine* with Miles Davis, there are several other distinguished versions, for instance by Konitz with Kenton (†Mosaic [A] MD4–136), by the Mulligan Quartet (**300**) and by Giuffre (**387**). *Donna Lee* and *Half Nelson* are Davis themes (**257**), *Goodbye, porkpie hat* is Mingus's tribute to Lester Young, and *Marshmallow* is by Warne Marsh, a Tristano pupil and associate.

Regarding the two versions of *Marshmallow* it has been asserted, aptly enough, that 'Braxton's subtley disorientating lines suggest Marsh's own playing as reinterpreted by Eric Dolphy', [45] while he is just as fiercely convoluted on *What's new?*, as if urgently seeking out all the melodic implications of the chord sequence. Both performances are almost continuous explosions of ideas, whereas at first *Body and soul* appears to be getting a smoother ride, especially when Braxton is supported by Pedersen only. Yet with Montoliu and Heath added it all becomes rather more hectic and the melodic extensions are most imaginative. Braxton returns for a second solo which eventually leads to a version of the melody very different from that with which proceedings opened.

In *My funny Valentine* he invokes Konitz in tone and some of his phrases. *Half Nelson* is incomplete, so we enter and leave the performance in midstream. On the other Davis theme, *Donna Lee*, Braxton takes to his contrabass clarinet, and strange it sounds on so aggressively swinging a piece of bop. During the fours with Heath this sounds like the music for a dance by some gigantic prehistoric monster. Both *Duet* and *Goodbye, porkpie hat* are by contrabass clarinet and Pedersen's tirelessly mobile string bass, yet they are little more than brief, bold exercises in eccentricity.

Passages in both accounts of *Marshmallow* are by Braxton (on alto) and Pedersen alone, but when Montoliu enters he matches his leader's fluency and, though admirable elsewhere, is particularly brilliant in this piece, sounding less disciplined and more fragmentary than hitherto, especially on the previously unissued alternative take.

Excursions like this aside, however, Braxton continued to move in several directions at once and to pass such remarks as 'Only in jazz is "thinking" a dirty word'. [46] In fact he went on blurring the supposed dividing lines between contemporary jazz and the classical avant-garde. He said that he saw his compositions as being like three-dimensional paintings, and much of his output is Third Stream music in the best sense, although that term is seldom applied to him. M.H.

Franz Koglmann

468 L'Heure Bleue

†Hat Art (Sw) CD6093

Koglmann (fl h); Mischa Mengelberg (p). Boswil, Switzerland, 20–21 March 1991.

My old flame · Baite · Slow fox · Nachts

Koglmann (tpt, fl h); Tony Coe (clt, ten); Burkhard Stangl (g); Klaus Koch (bs). Vienna, 15–17 April 1991.

Leopard lady · Moondreams · Monoblue · Night and day · It isn't easy · L'heure bleue · For Bix · Black beauty

To begin with Koglmann's music seemed to be partly a matter of collage, of ideas strung together. [47] But in due course these became interwoven; and quotation grew into subtle allusion. Probably his first mature statement was made in the music of *Ich* (†Hat Art [Sw] CD6033), which appeared in 1986. This was the first record made by what he calls his Pipetet, which may be described as a jazz chamber orchestra; and the compositions were all his. In contrast *About Yesterday's Ezzthetics* (CD6003, 1987) is by a quintet with Steve Lacy and Mario Arcari and has themes by Russell, Monk and Gillespie among others, on which it takes a strikingly personal view. Indeed, Koglmann's uses of 'old' jazz material are somewhat reminiscent of the role of quotations in the work of the German composer Bernd Alois Zimmermann, variously dislocating our sense of history, even our perception of time.

Thus the title piece of the *Use of Memory* collection (CD6078, 1990) is subtitled 'Bix, Miles and Chet', Beiderbecke, Davis and Baker having had some effect on Koglmann's own trumpet and flugelhorn playing. This piece is based on elements from a Baker solo on what is supposed to be Davis's *Tune up*, although, as acknowledged elsewhere in this volume, the theme is actually by Eddie Vinson. At the same time this performance demonstrates that this composition is less remote from *Clarinet marmalade* (**64**) than we tend to assume. The result is as disconcerting as Koglmann plainly intended it to be, and is a warning not to make too literal a reading of the jazz story. Some of his pieces may be taken as studies in fractured meanings, their covert allusions and even explicit citations being purposefully distorted, their impact then being further shifted by the new contexts in which they find themselves.

Essentially this is music about music. Performances like Hawkins's of *Body and soul* (**192**) or Parker's of *Embraceable you* (**258**) are less about the melodies by Green and Gershwin than they are commentaries on the stages jazz improvising had reached at the times they were recorded. And Koglmann and his players go further. A piece such as Russell's *Ezz-thetic* no longer sounds, on the 1987 CD, as it did when Davis and Konitz first recorded it in 1951 (**298**), any more than *Black beauty* among the 1991 performances detailed above is still redolent of the late 1920s when Ellington several times recorded it (**87**, **90**, **91**). Koglmann leaves both, like all other such pieces on his various CDs, sounding unequivocally modern and hinting that the past is more present than it used to be: to misquote a CD title given above, this music has entirely to do with today's aesthetics.

And the situation is beneficially complicated by the fact that the other root of Koglmann's work, along with American jazz, is European modernism. Practices from this latter tradition help shape his own compositions as well as his handling of transatlantic items. And yet on the European as on the American side he has contracted serious debts to no specific figure nor to any particular style, theory or period. Evidently he sees jazz especially as a continuum in both time and space, as an international musical language whose entire history and resources are still available and relevant. This is an entirely postmodernist attitude.

Nevertheless Koglmann's music is highly personal and to say that is to make several claims. Remembering its substantial elements of European modernism, does it convey a specifically European viewpoint on jazz? Is there such a thing? Does it matter? Certainly to a European listener most of these performances sound Viennese, and this remains so even when American materials are used and jazzmen from outside his usual circle participate, such as Lacy, Paul Bley, Coe, Ran Blake, Konitz or Mengelberg. Jazz seems even then to be refracted through Koglmann's Viennese chamber-music sensibility. It is never merely a question of clothing an inherited jazz vocabulary in fresh sounds and textures, for he is concerned at a deeper level with relationships between jazz and other musics, and between various sorts of jazz, hence his reference for example to 'cool jazz processed through the experiences of free jazz'. [48] Indeed, Koglmann appears especially concerned with relationships between background and foreground in music.

He began the Pipetet in 1983 with half classical and half jazz performers, but matters soon became more complicated. The personnel has naturally varied, yet Koglmann's regular players have become well acquainted with the musical landscape he has created, in particular with its sometimes abrupt but deep-laid shifts of emphasis and direction, which are on some occasions like cinematic transitions while on others one situation may gradually fade into another. Just as important for a jazz composer, he has developed great intuitive insight into his musicians' capabilities and further potentialities. And though he is an excellent trumpeter and flugelhornist, it may be said of Koglmann, as of certain other distinguished practitioners in this field, that his real instrument is his band.

However specific the aims and achievements of any particular piece, the viewpoint of his music as a whole is expansive, its emotional generosity paralleled by stylistic diversity. In the Pipetet or the smaller groups tenderness may be juxtaposed with aggression, humour with expressions of agony, violence with vulnerability. He has said that 'working with the Pipetet is like painting in oils and works for the smaller groups are like watercolours or sketches'. [49] And it is true that asymmetry and discontinuity – those prime features of European modernism – are more pronounced among the Pipetet's larger instrumental groupings. It is also true that two of his most representative collections, *A White Line* (CD6048, 1989) and the following year's *The Use of Memory*, employ the Pipetet throughout. But *Ich* uses, besides the Pipetet, quartet, trio, duo and one unaccompanied solo. *Orte der Geometrie* (CD6018, 1988) has, along with the Pipetet, two different trios and two different quintets; *About Yesterday's Ezzthetics* employs a quintet as noted; and *L'Heure Bleue* has quartet and duo.

Plainly there was no easy answer to choosing just one record to characterize Koglmann's multifaceted music and the final selection was to some degree arbitrary. With such an artist the wisest course is to hear the entire recorded output, and hence several items have been mentioned here. Some of his work is substantially different from what is heard on the *L'Heure Bleue* disc but counterpoint is of the essence in this music and there is obviously greater linear freedom in small improvising combos. There are five pieces here from outside the Koglmann world and perhaps *Moondreams* is the most familiar. Predictably, this has Gil

Evans's score for Miles Davis's nonet as its starting point (**376**) and ingeniously deploys a reduced instrumentation while recreating the nocturnal atmosphere which Evans lent to what originally was a commonplace popular song. It is in effect a recomposition of a recomposition and exemplifies two of Koglmann's fairly regular procedures. His account of *My funny Valentine* in the *Ich* collection derives from Baker's reading with the Mulligan quartet (**300**) and is here an improvisation on an improvisation. Similarly *Moondreams* recalls the modernistically skeletal recasting of *At the jazz band ball* for trumpet, oboe and guitar in *A White Line* which echoes the spirit of Beiderbecke's zestful 1927 performance (**63**). While doing so, this last, in parallel with Koglmann's interpretations of *My funny Valentine* and *Moondreams*, offers numerous changes in detail, confirming that new messages are conveyed which transmute the original framework from within.

The approach is considerably freer, however, in *Baite*, a theme by the forgotten trumpeter Tony Fruscella, and in *Black beauty*, there being little attempt to preserve the spirit, or much of the letter, of any previous recordings. The former is one of the duets with Mengelberg, about whom further comment appears under **463** and **465**. This pianist may be described as a Dutchman of Ukrainian descent whose father, Karel, and great-uncle Willem were symphonic conductors, the latter very distinguished in his time. Besides studying at the Royal Conservatoire in The Hague, Mengelberg won various jazz prizes, was on what were almost Dolphy's last recordings in 1964 (**427**) and in the following year appeared at the Newport Festival. In 1967 he was among the founders of Instant Composers' Pool, which sponsored concerts and recordings by members of the Dutch avant-garde, and formed a durable partnership with Han Bennink which receives some documentation under **463** and **465.** In the middle of *Baite* he takes a particularly thoughtful piano solo and otherwise supports Koglmann with much quiet dissonance. Aside from an occasional expressionistic outburst (as in *Flakes* on *About Yesterday's Ezzthetics*), the latter produces an attractively mellow sound and much of his playing, as here, is marked by a rather disjointed lyricism.

Black beauty is one of several pieces that benefit from Coe's tirelessly agile yet also eloquent clarinet work. A main point about what Koglmann refers to as the Monoblue Quartet, though, is the remarkable flexibility of its internal balance and hence of its textures, these resulting in the music's perspective shifting frequently as first one instrument, then another, takes the lead. This is especially evident during *Leopard lady*, and of almost equal interest to the solos of Koglmann, Coe, Stangl and Koch is what is often going on simultaneously. In Coe's elaborate clarinet solo in *Monoblue* there is again a detailed commentary from guitar and bass; in fact Koch is the only one on the quartet sessions to take solos that are truly unaccompanied. This reading of *Monoblue*, by the way, should be compared with the very different one on *The Use of Memory*, just as this *Slow fox* ought to be set beside the one in *Orte der Geometrie.* They demonstrate what divergent conclusions Koglmann can draw from the same ideas on different occasions.

The melody of *Night and day*, a very strong one and not easy to lose, is fragmented and distributed around the shifting little ensemble in Stangl's arrangement, with some phrases extended, others condensed. Texture, colour, line and rhythm are everything here. *Blue angel*, a Stangl composition, has quietly exploratory ideas for trumpet and tenor simultaneously, and then the guitarist picks up the tempo and there is a fine Coe tenor solo. There is plenty of unobtrusive humour in Koglmann's music and it particularly emerges in *It isn't easy*, where the guitar is led to make rock-'n'-roll noises. The fact that these are contained in an otherwise extremely musical performance heightens the effect.

Among other themes by Koglmann which ought to be mentioned are *L'heure bleue*, [50] *For Bix* and *Nachts.* The first two are gently melodious pieces rather similar in mood and fairly similar in treatment, though with *L'heure bleue* giving rise to greater complexity with trumpet, clarinet and guitar lines crossing and recrossing constantly. Coe's playing is especially beautiful here at the close. *For Bix* might be heard as a distant, essentially modern echo of Beiderbecke's Gang recordings (**63**). Regarding the earlier version of *Slow fox*, Koglmann has said that he 'aimed at the intrusion of what may be called a somewhat lascivious American dance music into a pan-German Bayreuth. A theme reminiscent of the chief motif of *Parsifal*, a dull brass tumble, encounters two slow fox themes played by the saxophones. The subliminal eroticism of these themes and a hidden Americanism à la Paul Whiteman clash with the Wagnerian spirit of the fascist regime. A very controversial musical event which finds no happy end, of course.' [51]

The duo with Mengelberg must obviously be skeletal in comparison, although the pianist is very active against his leader's sensitively chosen long notes. Perhaps *Nachts* is the most adventurous of the duets, however, in aesthetic and expressive terms if not with regard to technical organization. It is also the quietest and the slowest, and Koglmann's phrases seem valedictory. M.H.

Conversations with Themselves

These might be called private investigations, cases of lone jazzmen exploiting the language of their music in ways that are scarcely possible when several play together.

Bill Evans

469 Conversations with Myself

†Verve (A) 8219 884–2, †Verve (E) 521 409–2

Evans (p). New York City, January–February 1963.

Round about midnight · How about you? · Love theme from 'Spartacus' · Blue Monk · Hey there! · Stella by starlight · Just you, just me · N.Y.C.'s no lark

Evans's recognition as a major jazz figure was entirely just yet also rather surprising, given the subtlety with which his music operates on all levels. It is less of a shock that the above, which is one of the most extraordinary recorded feats in the annals of jazz improvising, has in most places been accepted only with heavy reservations. He first made an impression, among fellow musicians and connoisseurs, with brilliant recordings such as *Concerto for Billy the Kid* (**380**) and *All about Rosie* (**478**), going on to become the most influential figure in jazz pianism between Bud Powell and McCoy Tyner (**399**). Evans was inevitably affected by Powell, but also by Tristano, and he seems never to have had many bop clichés to lose in the course of discovering his singular path. Maturing away from New York probably helped, and it may even go some way to explain his affinity with one of the oldest identifying elements in jazz, namely this music's tradition of collective improvising.

Essentially polyphonic in his approach, Evans sought three-way musical conversations and found them to memorable effect in the 1959–61 trio with LaFaro and Motian (**372**), one of the great combos in jazz history. This developed several new ways for a rhythm section to operate while obviously being far more than just a rhythm section. In fact the kind of thinking which shapes the above 1963 performances was already implicit in that original trio's procedures. Such music is often delicate yet never fragile, soft-focused but intellectually acute, and Evans had already contributed valuably to highly individualized work by Russell (**380**, 1956), Mingus (*East Coasting*, †Charley [E] CD19, 1957) and Davis (**393**, 1959).

It may be that *Conversations with Myself* was Evans's most personal response, a typically creative one, to the early death of LaFaro, his most sympathetic musical partner. There were of course other answers to the gap which the bassist left, such as the 1962 *Undercurrent* sessions with Jim Hall (†Blue Note [E] CDP790 583–2), and these should be heard in conjunction with Evans's earlier piano duets with Brookmeyer (†EMI [E] CDP827 324–2, 1959) and with Bley in the *Chromatic universe* and *Lydiot* movements of Russell's *Jazz in the Space Age* (Affinity [E] AFF152, 1960). In these pairings one improviser fed the other with ideas rather as the members of Evans's trio had, and this sort of process obviously was audible elsewhere, in Giuffre's various trios (**364**, **387**), Hamilton's quintet (**389**) etc. But in this venture of early 1963 Evans did it all himself.

Three pianos are heard and he played each one; an initial keyboard part having been recorded, electronics allowed two others to be added. To conceive and execute three separate parts which together – and only together – form a single whole, to record one part while listening to what had gone before and keeping in mind what was to follow, demanded a detailed clarity of musical thinking that remains well beyond the reach of most jazzmen. Which is not to say that precedents were altogether lacking: hear Victor Feldman's 1951 London session, various Tristano recordings dealt with under **294**, and note that even a supposed traditionalist such as Bechet made use of the multitracking process (**225**). Despite which, it was still found necessary, when *Conversations with Myself* was first issued in 1963, to print on the LP sleeve a 500-word statement by Evans explaining why the results should not be dismissed as artificial, unnatural, a form of cheating. [52] Now that far more elaborate techniques and processes have been developed in electronics and employed in several types of music, this issue is presumably a dead one. However, it should be noted that this record is an early and particularly clear example of how technology can present the imaginative artist with further opportunities, in Evans's case an extension of the inherently polyphonic nature of his most characteristic vein of musical thinking.

Clearly this music cannot be spoken of as collectively improvised, yet one might think of it as resulting from a form of accumulative improvising. At once so emotional and so thoughtful, Evans's work here exists in a counterpoint of textures where perhaps one piano might strongly hold the foreground supported by another in the middle distance while a third murmurs on the horizon, with the instruments frequently changing roles. The stratagems whereby all this is shaped and directed would respond to far deeper analysis than is possible here. But even a casual hearer should be impressed by the freedom with which each piece moves, despite the obvious constraints, especially the delicacy with which the tempos are inflected. As with the LaFaro–Motion trio, this music shifts to a strongly felt internalized pulse rather than to one laid down explicitly from outside.

As would be expected from the polyphonic character of these eight performances, there is no question of placing four- or eight-bar phrases end to end. Still less is there any feeling of his merely stringing ideas together just as they occur to him. Evans perhaps gained his sense of the long line from Tristano and he adeptly relates one part of a long, unfurling phrase to another. An important but somewhat neglected factor here is his frequent and entirely unsystematized use of metrical displacement, this being a main agent of the rhythmic impetus that is at the core of his work. [53] A phrase, or the essentials of it, will be transformed repeatedly on melodic, harmonic or rhythmic levels, the tension gently building and finally resolved. One has the impression, perhaps here more than anywhere else in his recorded output, of a self-editing process going on continually as he improvises.

Certainly nobody could be less the fey impressionist than Evans, and although a high level of harmonic consciousness was as essential for this project as an acute rhythmic sense, there has been some confusion about the origins of his style. Many commentators have referred, despite their considerably different harmonic practice, to Debussy and Ravel, and Satie has been still more ineptly dragged in. Evans's music, and above all the tone he draws from the piano, appears to come from a region that other jazzmen may have sought yet almost never found. Several times on these eight tracks he gives us the quintessence of the melody without necessarily playing all its notes. Sometimes we have the feeling that his theme statements – not just the restatements – emerge from the improvisation rather than the other way round. And though it is often at a low dynamic level, Evans's playing has a much wider range of nuance than is common in jazz, and this is exploited most especially in *Conversations with Myself*, where the colours and shadings are always on the move. No wonder the engineers had the tape running at 30 i.p.s. instead of the usual 15.

Refinements of the kind referred to here are most often found in ballad performances like that of the *Spartacus* love theme, although some of these, *How about you?* for instance, are notably energetic. And though it is scarcely the most interesting of Monk's themes, *Blue Monk* serves notice that Evans was more at home with the blues idiom than we might suppose. Indeed it is notable that there are two pieces here by Monk for he was, as a pianist, at the furthest extreme from the refined Evans. As it is, *Round about midnight* is intriguingly divested of its usual nocturnal atmosphere. The most original inspiration here, though, is *N.Y.C.'s no lark*, a title which is an anagram on the name of Sonny Clark, a pianist whom Evans, generously but implausibly, listed among his influences. Here are found the most creative use of the three-piano medium and the most independent musical gestures. Perhaps Evans should have used more of his own material on these sessions. While never an obvious reflection of the asphalt jungle, *N.Y.C.'s no lark* has an intensity that leaves behind it a chill feeling of desolation.

Such work might seem enough of an achievement for anyone, yet, unlike most jazz musicians, Evans continued growing beyond this high point even though the pleasures of understatement continued to be lost on many of those who thought they were listening. To compare the versions of, say, *Nardis*, *My romance* or *Re: person I knew* from his late Paris recordings of 1979 with his various earlier performances on disc is, or should be, to understand why he expressed such admiration for 'people who have developed long and hard, especially through introspection and a lot of dedication'. [54] Equally, and despite wide imitation,

Evans's music has remained perfectly inimitable, has continued to hold long-term devotees and to yield up further secrets.

No matter how far he went, though, it continued to seem as if he was playing just for the individual listener. And nowhere more than in *Conversations with Myself* are we aware of the abiding paradoxes of Evans's music, of his depth and finished surface, his originality and immediate appeal, his public privacy, of the rare expressive freedom and potency of his insinuating *rubato*. At once lyrical and acerbic, expansive and precise, this music conveys the seeming timelessness that is the essence of intoxication. In his transformations of banal ditties there was a Merlin-like capacity for magical revelation and his finest records can still take us down to the ultimate still centre of his music with an evocative power that haunts and unsettles. M.H.

Oscar Peterson

470 My Favourite Instrument

†MPS (G) 821 843, Prestige (A) 7595

Peterson (p). Villengen, Germany, April 1968.
Someone to watch over me · *Perdido* · *Body and soul* · *Who can I turn to?* · *Bye bye, blackbird* · *I should care* · *Lulu's back in town* · *Little girl blue* · *Take the 'A' train*

Peterson has been too well publicized for it to be necessary even to outline the circumstances under which these and the associated recordings were made. But something must be said about his earlier work to put the Villengen performances into perspective and show why they compelled a partial reassessment. Hitherto Peterson had been recorded in huge quantity, quite undiscriminatingly, and it is not surprising that he made a like response.

His greatest strengths were knowledge and skill. In parallel with mastering all aspects of keyboard technique, he absorbed everything from the more conservative areas of piano jazz. Regarding the latter, his essentially traditionalist stance is clearly manifest on the rhythmic level: he plays almost as if bop never happened. Concerning the former, Peterson's true virtuosity separates him from the large majority of jazz pianists, who obtain their results despite generally quite uneven keyboard accomplishment. The exceptional range of executive and conceptual resources he commanded was normally employed, however, without discrimination, and one got the impression that if he continued any given solo long enough, he would throw in every one of his usual figurations quite irrespective of on what theme he was supposed to be improvising. Haphazard structures of greater or lesser complexity were imposed without regard to the actual character and real potential of his subject matter, and it was as if he had no particular idea of what sort of music he wanted to play. In such a negative climate digital dexterity, the mere crowding-in of as many notes as possible, was bound to become a dominant factor. It amounted to playing the piano rather than making music, finally to having played so much piano that he seemingly no longer bothered to listen. [55]

Despite all of which, Peterson remained instantly recognizable, and this hinted at artistic powers that long stayed almost dormant. A strong personal voice might be suggested, fleetingly, by the ways he selected and put together elements from his uncommonly large vocabulary. And placed in a fresh context any musical device or procedure can take on a new meaning. But fresh contexts, let alone new meanings, were scarcely going to arise from the incessant touring and apparently nonstop recording that filled most of the 20 years before Peterson reached Hans Brunner-Schwer's recording studio in the Black Forest.

A few wiser heads among jazz writers [56] had long urged that he should absent himself from success in all its seductive guises, particularly from such absurdities as the busy-doing-nothing concerts of Jazz at the Philharmonic, and should explore the depths of his talent and find out, musically speaking, who he was. That is effectively what Peterson did at Villengen, above all in the solo recordings. Of the *My Favourite Instrument* collection he said: 'It was the first album where I was completely free, and in which I did what I felt like. I chose the tempos, the keys I wanted to play in. If I wanted to change keys in the middle of a piece there was no problem because I was alone at the piano, alone with nobody to give me problems.' [57] Considering the hundreds of records on which he by then had played, that is quite a statement, and he could have added that this was also the first time he had control of repertoire, tape editing, the choice of takes to be issued etc.

The interlocking of knowledge and technique in such conditions gives these improvisations a rare feeling of balanced completeness, and this background unity gives rise to an impressive foreground diversity in their expressive and musical character. Each has a distinct emotional ambience and formal organization of its own, and from this it follows that each piece feels just the right length. Two minutes is perfectly apt for *Lulu*'s briefly bouncing good cheer, as is six minutes for the velvety calm of *Little girl blue*. The sensitivity of this many-faceted music cannot easily be suggested in words, but, whether in the lyrical feeling which shapes *I should care* or the wistfulness of *Bye bye, blackbird*'s opening, there are shades of emotion not even remotely implied in the huge accumulation of his earlier work. At last, one feels, Peterson stands revealed as himself. But exaggerated claims should still be avoided, for there is nothing, even here, that represents an addition to the language of jazz.

It still is reasonable to claim, however, that the diversity of expression of this and the other Black Forest music [58] is wider than that of all Peterson's other recordings put together. Significant aspects of this are the breadth of its dynamic range and variety of tempos, both, again, previously unheard in his output. Indeed, references to technique should not, in this instance, be taken as alluding to digital dexterity alone, although the integration of bravura into the overall shape of performances such as *Body and soul* or *Perdido* is unusually successful. Equally central to this music's effect is the richness and warmth of tone that Peterson obtains. Even allowing for a recording exceptional for its time and the use of a particularly fine instrument, this is another real achievement and most unusual in jazz piano playing. It could scarcely be in greater contrast with the hard, unnuanced touch evident on all too many of his other recordings.

In eight of these nine solos, form and content are matched with an exactness that must always be rare in improvised music, while spontaneity is reconciled with what evidently were the fruits of long consideration. True, *Someone to watch over me*, apparently done as a tribute to Tatum, has some frantic moments, as if he is striving too hard to prove . . . Well, it is obvious what he is trying to prove, but if this be compared with the older man's version on **254** it becomes plain how different these two pianists are. Tatum's performance is more organic, its structure both concise and subtle, while Peterson's contrasts of texture and motion are too deliberate. This is not felt in the equally virtuosic *Perdido*, *Take the 'A' train* or *Body and soul*, and the theme statement of the last-named quickly passes through several phases, the melody being shown as it were from different angles. The same process is heard on a larger scale in *Perdido*, which, though excellently developed as a single entity, flows through several episodes that are distinct yet arise out of one another.

It is encouraging that in the main body of *Bye bye, blackbird* Peterson's highly rhythmic treatment never spills over into histrionics, and during *I should care* his usual armoury of keyboard devices is forgotten. *Little girl blue* goes further, and one is tempted to say that here the piano is forgotten and only music remains. After this it is impossible not to wonder how much Peterson might have achieved if the limelight had not held him so relentlessly, and perhaps if he had been possessed by rather less technique. With the quiet, almost private sounds of *Little girl blue* this record should have closed, but a loud final bang was deemed essential so there follows a virtuosic, though concentrated, account of *Take the 'A' train.* It is superb, yet, after *Little girl blue*, superfluous.

M.H.

Albert Mangelsdorff

471 **Trombirds**
MPS (G) 68.069

Mangelsdorff (tbn). Frankfurt, September–December 1972.
Blues of a cellar lark · Trombirds · Yellow hammer · Introducing Marc Suetterlin · Espontaneo · Sing a simple song for change

'He was wonderful in the way he employed his conscious and unconscious art . . . and he brought into play the full gamut of his wonderful voice, a voice – what shall I say – not of an organ or of a trumpet, but rather of a trombone, the instrument possessing above all others the power to express the . . . range of emotions encompassed by the human voice – and with greater amplitude.' [59]

James Weldon Johnson's impression of a black preacher he once heard in Kansas City may invoke also memories and speculations about the varied guises of the trombone through jazz history, from the unabashed publicity of New Orleans tailgate and plungered Harlem expostulations to the distinctly more arcane developments of trombonism among the descendants of Edwards, Ory, Nanton and Mole in much more recent times. Revolutions in instrumental technique – in particular the ways in which exploitations of the harmonic series, multiphonics and such natural acoustical possibilities, to say nothing of electronic manipulations – have done much to outwit the ear within normal comparison. Flutelike sounds have issued from bass viols, flutes have sounded trumpet vocalizations and so on.

Multiphonics is a wind-instrument technique and the German trombonist Albert Mangelsdorff is a prime hero of multiphonics. In a record like *Trombirds*, multiphonics is the touchstone not merely of jazz advance but also of a novel perspective on the jazz past, a method of readapting the tradition. The artistic formation of this admirable musician responded at an early stage to Tristano and Konitz, notably to the 1949 experiments in abstract group improvisation (**293**). By the early 1960s he was an established star of European jazz and was taking a forward-looking interest in elements of European and Asian musical culture with a view to expanding the boundaries of his own jazz expression. The 1964 *Now Jazz Ramwong* (reissued lately on L+R [G] 41007) exhibited some of the fruits of that search for wider bounds, as well as exemplifying the free-jazz aptitudes of a fine quartet.

Trombirds is one of a number of solo albums, *Solo* (MPS [G] 15556) and *Tromboneliness* (MPS [G] 68.129) being others from the early 1970s. It has been unusual for the trombone to be quite solitary in any kind of music. Mangelsdorff has made it possible for his instrument to invent its own company. For Joachim Berendt, the world's foremost Mangelsdorff enthusiast and champion, the trombonist described his multiphonics process: 'You play a note and you sing another, usually higher note. In the interval between the played and sung notes overtones are created which become so audible that you end up with real chords – sometimes up to four notes. There are intervals that are easy to make and then there are others that are very difficult – all that has to do with how far you can control your voice.' [60]

The *Technik* is highly impressive. The chordlike passages heard here in *Blues of a cellar lark*, *Yellow hammer* and *Sing a simple melody for change* are novel in jazz terms but, especially in the last-named piece, sound weirdly evocative of ancient polyphony – the Lutheran chorale, it may be, or the Renaissance brass ensembles, some of whose fanfares and sonatas have been recorded, for example by Joshua Rifkin and Philip Jones. [61] Granted, the evocation is rudimentary to a degree, but it seems also to be intentional. In the fascinating second section of *Sing a simple song for change*, the closeted relation of horn sound, sung tone and 'triggered' overtones is so tautly manoeuvred that the consequence sounds both studied and excitingly dramatic.

Nearly every trombone effect ever thought of, save mute distortion, finds a place in *Trombirds*, a barbaric string of dirty notes, whoops, cries of excitement and alarm, arching leaps and flutterings, soft tonguings of intimate subtlety, and robust horn tones gathering echoing reverberations. Multiphonics and pedal notes are used as punctuations in a situation which owns no recognizable syntax; and the same holds true during *Espontaneo*, which is overlong and chiefly distinguished by a rich trombone cantilena giving way periodically to strange shaken chords with flutelike fringes.

At the start of *Blues of a cellar lark* the genesis of the 'one-man chord' is demonstrated in an octave unison of horn and voice. Several contrasting effects are laced into a long marchlike monologue; yet better examples of the brooding Mangelsdorff harmony, including its use in staccato, are in *Yellow hammer*, whose leaner tunes scatter their intervals in oddball fervour, their rhythm seemingly stolen from the well-known mendicant pleas of *Emberiza citrinella* – the bird itself.

Introducing Marc Suetterlin is jokey piece of multitracking in which two Mangelsdorffs interweave with supposed trumpet sounds on a speeded tape. When asked the identity of Marc Suetterlin, the trombonist replies: 'Das ist der neue Trompeter, der da spielt.' In other words, 'look no further'. [62] E.T.

Clare Fischer

472 Jazz Song

Revelation (A) REV31

Fischer (p). California, 9 May 1973.

Spring is here · *Suerte* · *Here's that rainy day* · *Moonmist* · *Autumn lines* · *Love locked out* · *You've changed* · *Serenidade* · *Just friends*

There is a sense of intimacy, even of privacy, about this music, coupled with an equally clear sense of generosity shaping its interpretative means. This is the work of a musician, perhaps insufficiently celebrated, whose best expressions have borne the marks of a possibly inborn skill in elemental arrangement, 'orchestral' even when displayed in solo of small-group situations.

It is fair to acknowledge that Fischer's actual orchestration skills have been exhibited on record with bands involving a number of musicians of celebrity somewhat wider than his own; also, he is not unknown for his work with the organ and, more recently, with electronic keyboards. But it is as a pianist of singular imagination that he best deserves to be regarded. The comprehensiveness of his musical interests has been remarked by Gary Foster, who first encountered this breadth of intellect a decade before the above disc was made. 'Many have [such] encyclopaedic knowledge . . . Clare can touch a keyboard and put his hands on all of it.' [63]

That claim's veracity receives no adverse challenge from the above performances. The spread of a sympathy evinced in striking harmonic daring reveals itself even in the quite brief readings of *Spring is here*, *Here's that rainy day* and *You've changed.* The power of liberating fresh possibilities is shown in *Suerte*, Fischer's own composition, with minatory bass shadows and eye-opening colouration in the vivid treble. The treatment of Ellington's *Moonmist* is described under **216** as a 'remarkable pianistic evocation of the textures of the Ellington band'. Fischer relishes the twists of this tune – tailor-made for the style of Johnny Hodges when it was first performed – and, in addition to his own chordal emulations of ensemble colour, there are a few entirely pianistic tremolandos direct from Harlem – echoes of a master far older than Fischer's more immediate stylistic mentors.

Autumn lines is exceptional and fiercely personal. Yes, it may reflect some of the procedures of Tristano and Bill Evans, yet its conception moves beyond such example, conducting a mildly assertive tune at mid-tempo through various thickets of challenge – matching, harmonizing, contrasting, complementing, counterpointing – towards an ending that manages somehow to reconcile diffidence to defiance. It is hard to think of any recorded jazz performance that achieves a comparable effect, and it is the chief treasure of this richly conceived programme.

Autumn lines and *Moonmist* would themselves justify the inclusion of *Jazz Song* in this section, but similar essays in self-challenge enliven almost every piece here. Fischer's *Serenidade* drifts slowly through airy, complex textures, and it may be that here, as in *You've changed* (another Fischer tune), which is mainly in free time, the emphasis on an exploration of emotions puts the music in some small danger of never quite establishing its musical rationale – though there are, in *You've changed*, some paradoxical strengths. In the sunny mid-tempo of *Just friends*, finely spun single note lines almost manage to intertwine with themselves before oblique contrapuntal figurations fortify a questing mood. There are wry unisons and harmonies before the amiable tune, reappearing, meanders to a conclusion.

Although an elusive item now, *Jazz Song* can hardly be too highly recommended to lovers of modern piano jazz. It is, of course, not the only example of Fischer's felicitous talent worthy of renewed availability.

A handful of recordings featuring his more eclectic cooperative works have recently been obtainable, but his several fine productions for Revelation Records appear to have slipped into limbo. With his unique pianistic combination of gravitas and restless curiosity, he is manifestly unworthy of such disregard. E.T.

Martial Solal

473 Bluesine

Soul Note (It) SN1060

Solal (p, comp[1]). Milan, 20 May 1983.

The end of a love affair · *Bluesine*[1] · *Lover* · *I'll remember April* · *Moins de 36*[1] · *Round about midnight* · *Yardbird suite* · *14 Septembre*[1] · *Have you met Miss Jones?*

Solal's earliest recordings, done for Swing (F) during 1953–6, established that he was a fine jazz musician almost from the start. A first maturity was signalled around 1960 with such items as *Darn that dream* (Pathé [F] 172731), an exuberant outburst tempered initially by a canny use of silence yet embodying an irresistible stream of ideas and suggesting a positive rapture in playing the piano. Later, although Solal's execution retained all its physical vigour, this impact became less overt, inner drive being conveyed more obliquely, although the music, almost paradoxically, remained urgently communicative. Clearly this situation echoed the ways in which Solal's thinking developed, these in turn reflected by the gradual enrichment of his resources. What happened was that the flow of invention shaping his earlier performances spread in every direction and at all levels in his work.

Such growth can be demonstrated by setting early swing improvisations beside later ones on the same themes, the 1954 *Poinciana* (†Vogue [F] 743 211 1514–2) against the 1978 version (MPS [G] 0068.221), for example, or the 1956 recordings of *Fascinatin' rhythm*, *Caravan* and *Have you met Miss Jones?* (all †Vogue [F] 743 211 1515–2) beside the interpretations of respectively 1975 (MPS [G] 68.116) and 1983 (PDU [It] A7039) and as above. [64] Such comparisons make two points, firstly the extent to which Solal's horizons widened during that long period, and secondly the organic nature of the process.

It is easy to be misled on the former of these because a certain percentage of material – the melodies and the original chord sequences – was always approached with notable indirectness, and the manner in which *Lover* or *I'll remember April* were played at the Milan session detailed above represented a long-standing tradition within Solal's music. This perhaps reached its furthest extreme in the 1977 *'Swonderful* and *Cherokee* (MPS [G] 68.201), which barely hint at the improvisations' basic subject matter. And the tendency reached back past the *Loverman* of 1960 (Pathé, as above) to the 1953 *Dinah* (†Vogue [F] 743 211

1514–2). Occasionally a treatment would specifically contradict the original character of a piece and impose a new one of its own, as in *Stompin' at the Savoy* (†MPS [G] 843 107–2, 1965), where a rather commonplace swing-band novelty is transformed into a distinguished Debussy-slanted jazz etude. [65] Similarly the above *Yardbird suite* becomes a highly sophisticated stomp, full of tricky steps that are not quite what they seem. The obliqueness of Solal's improvised comments on his chosen themes grew as his melodic, harmonic and rhythmic vocabularies enlarged and fused more deeply, and also as the refinement and subtlety of his playing increased. It became ever more possible for him to imply his thoughts rather than to state them directly.

The results were fantasias of extraordinary richness and unified variety of resource leavened with much wit, the musical wit of a virtuoso who could stand almost any improvisational situation on its head. They gave rise to countless finely discriminated contrasts of figuration, rhythm, harmony, with ideas proliferating out of, in parallel with, and across each other. Yet through all this is maintained an unrelenting clarity of texture and intention, despite frequently unforgiving tempos. Sometimes a familiar melody seems to emerge almost by chance from the incessantly agitated kaleidoscope of Solal's multi-storeyed invention and yet, as here with *The end of a love affair*, the shape of a given melody is discovered at last to have imparted form to the improvisation as a whole. Further, that form is seen to derive in part from crucial changes made during the initial presentation of the melody and its harmonic and rhythmic fabric. In such circumstances new things – items like *14 Septembre* and *Moins de 36* – are made familiar and familiar things are made new, as with the above *Round about midnight*, one of the most expressive accounts of a Monk theme not by Monk himself. [66]

We find here degrees of freedom and spontaneity that are supposedly a matter of course in jazz yet are in fact quite rare. By another paradox the element of surprise adheres to these performances even after many hearings, although the frequently shifting tempos and sheer rhythmic diversity may be perplexing. For sufficiently imaginative listeners, however, the flexibility of outline of these improvisations can be an attraction in itself. A piece such as *Have you met Miss Jones?* or the sometimes turbulent *14 Septembre* might unfold through several phases, not chorus by chorus but in a considerably more irregular and unpatterned manner. This multilayered intensity parallels the kind of collective improvisation in which Solal engages with Hans Koller and Attila Zoller on *Zo-Ko-So* (†MPS [G] 843 107–2) of 1965 and on the later **365**, where imagination and technique combine to liberate the three or four instruments from their traditional roles in rather the way individual lines are set free within his full yet meticulously nuanced keyboard textures.

There are also links with his most advanced writing for large band (**323**), and, given the organic relationship between the various parts of his development, this is not surprising. Obviously the piano was always Solal's most immediate path to expression, his most direct way of organizing musical ideas, and his work can remind us of the play of a master gambler in whose hands nearly all cards become aces. Certainly his imagination is freest when he is alone, and he never actually required the stimulus of other performers. Yet his way of thinking can often be most readily grasped when other instruments take part, be they few or many, and experience of the music he has made elsewhere should enable us to focus more sharply on the teeming detail of his piano solos.

Despite, or perhaps because of, Solal's having an almost infinite number of ways of approaching, stating and extending any idea, his main concern in each phase of his activity has been to initiate, develop and resolve exploratory musical arguments. This has shielded him from both the empty display to which many virtuosos are prone and from the cliché-ridden procedures that have stifled so much big-band writing. Indeed, given the unifying principles of Solal's output, it should be studied as a whole, the above *End of a love affair*, *Have you met Miss Jones?* and *Lover* heard with *Green Dolphin Street*, *Stars fell on Alabama* and *Nice work if you can get it* (MPS [G] 68.116), the above *I'll remember April* with the versions on Poljazz (P) SX0696 and MPS (G) 0068.221 etc. Excellent composer though he is, it naturally is revealing to hear him improvise on material from elsewhere just because he alters it so much. And such pieces as those just mentioned offer an advantageous route into Solal's music, being far removed from the climate of so many jazz treatments of sentimental ballads.

In fact his magnificent series of solo and trio discs, running from the 1963 Salle Gaveau concert (Columbia [F] FPX2221) to the above 1983 Milan occasion (to which should be joined a Lugano date of later that year [PDU (It) A7039] and such trio recordings as *Triangle* with Marc Johnson [bs] and Peter Erskine [d] of 1995 on †JMS [F] JMS076-2 and *Just Friends* with Gary Peacock [bs] and Paul Motian [d] of 1997 on †Dreyfus [F] FDM36592), emphasize such material even if a fair number of Solal's own themes are included plus a sprinkling of Ellington, Parker, Monk, Reinhardt and Miles Davis. Any of these records can stand with Hines's Chiaroscuro session (**220**), the Tatum Capitols (**254**) and *The New Tristano* (**294**) among the peaks of recorded piano jazz. Choice among them for this book was therefore somewhat arbitrary, and the above Soul Note date was selected partly because it captures many aspects of Solal's music vividly, partly because three of his own themes are included, and partly because one of them, *Bluesine*, exemplifies the blues playing, by turns abrasive and tender, that is a significant, though never central, part of his idiom. M.H.

John Surman

474 A Biography of the Rev. Absalom Dawe

†ECM (G) 523 749–2, ECM (G) 1528

Surman (bar, sop, alt clt, bs clt, kybd). Oslo, October 1995.
First light · Countless journeys · A monastic calling · Druid's circle · 'Twas but piety · Three aspects · The long narrow road · The wayfarer · The far corners · An image

The virtual pre-eminence of Surman as a multitracking converser with himself will hardly be in dispute. It is not easy to be precise about the stage in this remarkable musician's career at which his taste for hyperactive soliloquy began to develop. The end of the 1960s heard the electrophonic experimenters of European jazz-rock discovering controversial voices. Surman's most notable recording of 1969 was as a contributor to John McLaughlin's *Extrapolation* (**394**), which history links with jazz-rock fusion on the ground of McLaughlin's contemporary but independent notoriety as a plugged-in performer. The guitar–baritone unison strategies and the precipitate energy of *Spectrum* may have helped to make misjudgement likely, but the ambitions of *Extrapolation* were closer to the kind of avant-garde jazz that Surman was to record in the next decade or so with sympathetic companions of the 'school' associated at the time with Mike Westbrook, Graham Collier and their like. Probably the most advanced baritone saxophonist of that period – having extended the instrument's capabilities more by heeding Eric Dolphy's extensions of bass-clarinet technique than anything heard from other baritonists – Surman remained close to post-Coleman, post-Ayler, post-Coltrane expressionist blowing, frequently capable of giving vent to 'elephantine tear-ups'. [67] Yet there was enough in the free swinging jazz of the quartet with which he toured the UK in 1969 [68] of an older and persisting jazz tongue to encourage those admirers who may have mistrusted the lures of rock and its electronic connotations to hope that Surman would neither waver musically nor emigrate physically.

Emigration was, at least, already actively under consideration. Whether the man wavered in jazz terms may be debated. The 1978 *Sonatinas*, a collaboration with Stan Tracey, seems to have been a crucial experiment in combining instrumental improvising with synthesizer patterns, to an extent spontaneously with all elements, and to an extent planning patterns and deciding how they might subsequently be augmented in ways that combined predetermination with spontaneity. 'Electronics,' Surman commented, 'are used to help "colour" the sound of the basic improvisations and put them into a slightly different perspective.' [69] One year after *Sonatinas* Surman produced the multitracked solo *Upon Reflection* (soprano, baritone, bass clarinet, synthesizer – †ECM [G] 1148); at the end of 1984 came *Withholding Pattern* (soprano, baritone, bass clarinet, recorder, piano, synthesizer – †ECM [G] 1295); *Private*

City (partly a ballet score – †ECM [G] 1366) and *Road to St Ives* (†ECM [G] 1418) appeared in 1987 and 1990, using comparable resources.

An interest in tokens of a British tradition which had nourished his own artistic development prior to, or aside from, jazz strongly affects these programmatic works. There is a refreshing spontaneity to several of the contributory movements, but also a growing sense of isolation. In *Upon Reflection* and *Private City* the synthesized backing patterns tend to sound mechanical, militating against instrumental lyricism.

The Absalom Dawe celebrated here is Surman's great-great-grandfather, a Dorsetshire bootmaker and preacher who, according to family tradition, was Thomas Hardy's model for Robert Penny, shoemaker, a character in *Under the Greenwood Tree* (1872). The attribution is doubtful, but Surman evidently felt the Hardy-linked fancy as a spur to creative imagination. 'A specifically "rural" character was coming out in the music I was writing,' he has explained, 'as has often been the case with the pieces I've addressed in the solo albums – as well as certain "monastic" aspects. These aspects combined seemed to make it appropriate to offer the record to the country preacher in the family.' [70] What Surman knows about Absalom's career probably is sketchy. No matter. The preaching bootmaker – an itinerant, the musical legendarian seems to imply – becomes this lyrical tale-teller's model for a heraldic wayfarer, the skirts of whose tunic tangle with strands of ancient mystic piety, monastic, even pagan, which conceivably were anathema to the Victorian piety of the flesh-and-blood Absalom.

The deep, vaguely pulsating, chantlike, monotonal backdrop to *A monastic calling* superfically implies an Oriental sound-realm; yet it is, in spite of its immediate sense of irrelation, restful rather than sinister. The melody-tracing voice – Surman's baritone saxophone – is also darkly hued, and the methods of tonguing and tone-sustenance reflect jazz technique in intriguing ways. The baritone's is the major voice, but, towards the close, a high, quavering clarinet voice sounds against the Stygian backing. *Druid's circle* has an accompaniment devised with baritone sax and bass clarinet while the minor-keyed melody lines are voiced by the soprano sax, lilting, at moments almost lurching, while the deep underlying pattern shifts, challenging its own insistencies.

For the opening solo, *First light*, Surman uses his bass clarinet totally without accompaniment, displaying impressive executive skill in ranging the registers in defiance of the hazards which haunt the paths of ascent and descent for any unwary player of this instrument. The creative effect of this skill is built of simple lines and decorative turns, fecund enough in exceptional contrasts to make recognition of its modal bases tantalizing. *Countless journeys*, suggestive of preacher Dawe's itinerant lifestyle, makes a wistful soprano-sax melody thread across organlike keyboard chords. Swirling circularities of line promote an illusion of progress exterior to time – liberated pieties make possible the journeys' freedom, yet somehow the chapel's precious conventions, heard in those organ tones, will not be left behind altogether. The return of the bass clarinet, shaking off the accompaniment toward the end, reintroduces the sense of migration between differing zones of musical expressiveness.

Uneasiness felt about the changes heard in Surman's own expressive voice by any who suspect a once admired jazz pioneer of some sort of desertion will be assuaged more effectively by the present record than by some of the earlier issues in this lengthening solo sequence. That he has searched for a new voice carrying his jazz experience into newly congenial thematic adventures is not to be denied. 'When I set out there was a quest among musicians to find a voice that was instantly recognizable . . . It's taken me all my life to find something that's different. Don't ask me how I did it . . . it took time, and I'm still searching.' [71] Certainly in this latest solo odyssey there sounds to be a more confident stylistic consistency, and a finer cohesion between the different parts of the thematic continuum. Better variety of expression too.

The soprano's inward musing that affects most was of *'Twas but piety*, atemporal and uninterrupted by any other voice until the organ tones briefly sound again, has a great deal of subtle jazz expressiveness in it. *Three aspects*, also mainly atemporal and voiced by soprano, alto clarinet and baritone, gives some evidence of how a jazz expressiveness can be achieved by wry intervallic contrast rather than by either multiphonics or the older kinds of vocalization. *The long narrow road* is travelled by the bass clarinet alone – surely one of the most captivating voices we have become accustomed to after a newer breed of jazz reedmen made it familiar. Surman spins circular patterns in the horn's upper storey, and contrasts pale piping sounds with woody profundities.

The wayfarer, at almost nine and a half minutes the longest track, is one of the most fascinating in the martialling of sounds. The accompanying keyboard figures are sustained in high register and a mysterious submarine effect is achieved by the counterpoint of woodwind interlocutions, reedy voices winding and weaving together until they fill the sound space entirely. By contrast, *The far corners* explores less populated regions. The soprano sax's rising and falling melody, with its tripping ornamentation, may seek a familiarity that would make the listener a confidant, but here the electronics are engaged to surround the single improvising voice with echoes and reverberations. Familiarity edges towards mystification; yet this possibly is the most beautifully imagined track.

Darkly upsweeping sounds possess the six and a half minutes of *An image*; ascents which might be desperate – or maybe imperious – prayers and the horns' orisons vie with each other, and are windswept by echo effects to the extent that the ear begins even to seek meanings in the reverberations themselves.

Questioning the categorization of his music as quintessentially English, Surman has said; 'I certainly don't make any conscious attempt to pursue "Englishness" . . . and never have. I wouldn't necessarily argue with the characterization, though I think it's a bit unhelpful. It's just the way I've turned out, the way I play . . . I think I'm a melodic player really. I don't have any particularly sophisticated harmonic or rhythmic ideas. What I've got to offer are a few of these melodies which I twist and turn around on.' [72] Neither was *that* particularly helpful. No more so than the reply Zoot Sims once gave to the question 'What is jazz?': 'It's just a tone . . . what you do to a melody . . . how you bend it.' [73]

The best answers will, of course, be heard in the music itself. Surman's long *affaire* with electronics and multitracking has been something of a self-rediscovery for him; a courtship which, given his earlier and more recent liaisons with fellow musicians, has enabled him to make intuitive forays along the pitfall-strewn lovers' lane where composer and improviser meet. This *Biography of Absalom Dawe* demonstrates the unusual inspirations which this closeted discipline of music-making both assists and challenges. E.T.

Steve Lacy

475 **Only Monk**
†Soul Note (It) SN1160–2, Soul Note (It) SN1160

Lacy (sop). Milan, 29–31 July 1985.
Evidence · Humph · Eronel · Pannonica · Little rootie-tootie · Mysterioso · Work · Light blue · Who knows?

Lacy's personal inventiveness has frequently seemed content to conceal itself within a dedication to celebrating the inspirations of others. His introduction to jazz drew him first to pre-bop fare. A reconstruction, with the pianist Mal Waldron, of *The mooche* in 1990 (†RCA-Novus [A] PD83098) is a tribute to Ellington via Bechet, whose 1941 version of this piece (**226**) probably influenced Lacy's taking up the soprano saxophone. Beyond such preferences there is justice in a recent description of Lacy as 'perhaps the key figure in the European free jazz movement in the 1980s'. [74] Certainly no avant-garde sopranoist has matched his enterprise. Coltrane may have been drawn to the soprano by Lacy's choice but Lacy once averred: 'Coltrane plays his way, so I don't have to play that way.' [75] Indeed, his technical approach to this notoriously undocile instrument differs markedly from the approach of those who have admired Bechet's forcefulness or Hodges's romanticism. Bechet tended to use the soprano as a weapon of aggression; Lacy uses it, characteristically, more like a surgical instrument. These beautiful Monk studies demonstrate his pensive craftsmanship in forms of interpretation and reimagination that are no more slavish to Monk in their melodic or rhythmic thought than they are strict in matters of tempo. This is the art of an unbound jazz soliloquist.

Important modernist mentors were Cecil Taylor and Gil Evans, and Lacy began 'delving' (his word) into Thelonious Monk's musical ideas around 1956. Then he played with Monk's quintet for 16 weeks during 1960, receiving some of his most transforming creative influences; so for more than 30 years now he has virtually been obsessed by Monk and could be called his foremost champion and interpreter. Monk tunes, drawn, as it were, calligraphically in space by a saxophonist's 'stylus', is an odd enough notion in itself since the very 'Monkishness' of the music has such pianistic affiliations. The pianist Georgio Gaslini's widely admired tribute (Soul Note [It] SN1020) might seem more appropriate, except that Gaslini's basic musicality is less clearly hinged to Monk's doorpost. The truth of that assertion is accessible only to a listener's attentiveness, an attentiveness that may need some degree of familiarity with Monk's own recordings of the compositions here chosen. At the same time, the perception that 'this is pure soprano saxophone music' [76] will be wisely remembered, as will the realization that Lacy's procedures of exposition, which relate phrase to phrase with cumulative effect, tease out meanings in ways that are saxophonic and innate to that species of voice. For this means that *Only Monk*, like its companion album *More Monk* (†Soul Note [It] 121 210), can be admired for qualities that are decidedly intrinsic.

Most of the titles are early Monk pieces. Max Harrison's notes to this Soul Note release provide an invaluable key: '*Humph*, which has a 32-bar AABA structure, dates from a 1947 Blue Note session. A fairly typical bop variant of *I got rhythm*, Monk took it in B flat. Lacy puts it in A flat. The original version was fast and that is implied here through the play of accents; towards the close the line takes on a two-voiced character. Another 32-bar AABA, Monk recorded *Eronel* for Blue Note in 1951. This more smoothly moving theme, in G, brings out Lacy's lyricism and is a fine instance of melodic growth. A curiosity, *Pannonica*, recorded by Monk for Riverside in 1956, has a 33-bar AABA* structure in C. Lacy makes an imaginative use of the chief four-note thematic motive.

'In A flat, *Little rootie-tootie* returns to the normality of a 32-bar AABA chorus. Again based on *I got rhythm*, Monk recorded it for Prestige in 1952. It is a train piece, and Lacy imitates the steam-whistle with a "dirty" tone on repeated notes. *Mysterioso* is our old friend the 12-bar blues in B flat. Lacy begins with a deliberately uneven articulation of the famous walking sixths, and ends in the stratosphere. He shows excellent continuity in *Work*, yet another 32-bar AABA, this time in G. Monk did this for Prestige in 1954, *Light blue* for Riverside in '58. The latter has a 16-bar chorus divided AAlAAl and is in C. Lacy makes it a study in the soprano saxophone's pure-toned upper register. *Who knows?* is 32 bars again, AA1BA in F. It was first heard on a 1947 Monk Blue Note session. Lacy's variety of melodic shapes here suggests that he is trying to achieve as much contrast as possible with the eighth notes of the theme.' [77]

The programme of Lacy's first 'name' record date in 1957 included *Work.* Later he thought the inclusion 'premature and quite wrong . . . I didn't understand it,' though he admits that Monk himself thought well of the record. It may be heard currently as Original Jazz Classics (A) OJC130. Within a year of that his quartet recorded a seven-tune Monk programme on what is now OJC063, and the long flirtation, started then, is not finished at the time of writing. It by no means says everything about Lacy's achievement, which is multifarious enough, but it tells deep things about his essential formation. E.T.

Paul Bley

476 Tears

†Owl (F) 34

Bley (p). Paris, 19 May 1983.

Tears · Ostinato · Music matador · Walkman · Flame · Hardly · Head over heels · Solo rose · For Roy E.

One of the most profoundly musical of jazz creators, Paul Bley is almost impossible to categorize; little attempt has been made to divine his modes of thinking, even though he, an articulate fellow, has shown himself quite prepared to talk about his motives. Yet he has tended to make seemingly contrary assertions. Becoming known almost exactly at the point at which free jazz was assaulting our shibboleths, and becoming a close associate of some of its foremost players, he asserted, as early as 1964: 'I'm against freedom.' Later, making it undeniable by his precise and vigilant technique, particularly in his solo albums, that his attitude toward improvising was to think of it virtually in compositional terms, he told the commentator upon a session he recorded in the summer of 1987: 'I'm anti-composition.' [78]

Neither of these statements can be taken at face value. The rest of his 1987 sentence was: 'Most of this album is in fact improvised and was done in one take,' [79] which counters the 1964 claim. The 'anti-composition' assertion is countered by the fact that he has encouraged others to compose (in normally accepted ways), notably his former wife Carla (née Borg), as well as by this additional clause, restating a paradox endlessly echoed through the critical talkways of jazz analysis: 'Improvising is real-time composition.' [80] Listening without reservations, even any he might have suggested himself, to what he actually plays, is the only sure way of coming to terms with a series of avant-garde jazz inventions which, although never more than mildly and tactically assertive, is nevertheless full of subtleties of jazz-conditioned temperament.

Tears, one of Bley's relatively few totally solo albums, will reveal only a segment of the breadth of his jazz capabilities. The emphasis of its programme is, in almost every number, on his virtually extemporaneous utterance. Only one is, it seems, not entirely devised by him. That exception is *Music matador*, a product of the 1960s partnership of the altoists Prince Lasha and Sonny Simmons (**403**); every other piece is credited to Bley.

Plucking of the piano's bass strings starts the title piece, an affective manipulation, but momentary only. *Solo rose* will reintroduce it. The rest of *Tears*, which establishes the laconic, leisurely pace of the whole programme, is not notably sad music, however emotive some of its registral separations and conjunctions may seem. *Ostinato*, expectedly, has more suggestive pattern-building. Lines in mid- and high register alternate in playful counterpoint. What *ostinato* used to mean in piano jazz is not clearly recalled; the only 'obstinacy' being in the bitonality of the overall thinking.

The typically fragmentary recollections of *Music matador* explore the phraseology of hard-bop 'funkiness', yet Bley alters the mode by dispersion of the clichés. *Walkman* is half vagrant, half inventive of clues to its own more purposive, tantalizingly melodic intentions. *Flame* gets nearer to familiar lyricism with its flickering, songlike spinnings, which are set against shadowy tones. *Hardly* has dark emphases too, and its less than two minutes of quest close with an evocation of ennui.

Clauses of melody in *Head over heels* evolve into chordal patterns which suggest, but shrewdly avoid, conventional resolution. *Solo rose* opens with deep string resonances, moving beyond this impressionism to brightly struck bop-oriented phrases. Dissonance grows in persistence, lightened by a filigree of half-hinted blue notes. *For Roy E.* heeds what seems to hint from some source outside the pianist's unresting imagination – warmer syllables and rich bass tones, possibilities of assonance that have been persistently elusive elsewhere. The piece ends with an echo of some old song of acceptance with every touch of enigma gone.

These interior conversations are so exploratory, so self-challenging and so open to the new and liberating that repeated hearing of them will need fresh ways of responsive analysis to reflect their meanings. No fixed metres are used, sometimes fugitive fragments of metre are set against each other, silences may seem as vital as utterances; and it is obvious from the character of Bley's pianistic technique that his option for this miniaturistic approach is as valid and as demanding in free-music terms as the tempestuous 'orchestralism' preferred by some other notable avant-garde pianists.

Hearing Bley's work with groups of various forms and dates will help rather more than this solitary expression to reveal the span of his jazz perceptions, which is admirable. He has been known, at times, to tax the responsive acumen of some accompanists. Those who, rather than being compliant, adopt an inventive daring as uncompromising as his can be – like the drummer Paul Motian in the splendid *Notes* (†Soul Note [It] SN1190) – not only best compliment his innovations but also elicit even richer notions from him. E.T.

7

On the Frontiers

It might be said that these frontiers are seldom crossed, yet jazz has always dialogued with other, sometimes very different, musics and it here does so with considerable advantage.

Stan Kenton

477 **Stan Kenton Plays Bob Graettinger**
†Capitol (A) 7243 8 32084 2 5

Buddy Childers, Ray Wetzel, Al Porcino, Chico Alvarez, Ken Hanna (tpt); Milt Bernhart, Eddie Bert, Harry Betts, Harry Forbes (tbn); Bart Varsalona (bs tbn); George Weidler, Art Pepper (alt); Bob Cooper, Warren Weidler (ten); Bob Gioga (bar); Kenton (p); Laurindo Almeida (g); Eddie Safranski (bs); Shelly Manne (d); Graettinger (comp). New York City, 6 December 1947.
Thermopylae

Childers (tpt); Johnny Mandel (bs tpt); Billy Byers (tbn); Pepper (alt); Cooper (ten); Irv Roth (bar); Hal Shaefer (p); Joe Mondragon (bs); Don Lamond (d); Jasper Hornyak (vln); Cesare Pascarella (cel); June Christy (vcl); Graettinger (arr). Hollywood, 28 March 1949.
Everything happens to me

Childers, Maynard Ferguson, Shorty Rogers, Alvarez, Don Paladino (tpt); Bernhart, Betts, Bob Fitzpatrick, Bill Russo (tbn); Varsalona (bs tbn); John Graas, Lloyd Otto (fr h); Gene Englund (tu); Bud Shank (alt, fl); Pepper (alt, clt); Cooper (ten, ob, eng h); Bart Cardarell (ten, bsn); Gioga (bar, bs clt); George Kast, Lew Elias, Jim Cathcart, Earl Cornwell, Anthony Doria, Jim Holmes, Alex Law, Herbert Offner, Carl Ottobrino, Dave Schackne (vln); Stan Harris, Leonard Selic, Sam Singer (vla); Gregory Bemko, Zachary Bock, Jack Wulfe (cel); Kenton (p); Almeida (g); Don Bagley (bs); Manne (d); Carlos Vidal (con); Graettinger (comp). Hollywood, 4 February 1950.
Incident in jazz

Kast, Elias, Cathcart, Doria, Holmes, Law, Offner, Ottobrino, Schackne (vln); Harris, Selic, Singer (vla); Bemko, Bock, Mary Jane Gillan (cel); Graettinger (comp). Hollywood, 24 August 1950.
House of strings

John Howell, Ferguson, Conte Candoli, Stu Williamson, John Coppola (tpt); Betts, Fitzpatrick, Russo, Dick Kenney (tbn); George Roberts (bs tbn); Graas, Otto, George Price (fr h); Stan Fletcher (tu); Shank (alt, fl); Pepper (alt, clt); Cooper (ten, ob, eng h); Cardarell (ten, bsn); Gioga (bar, bs clt); Law, Cornwell, Phil Davidson, Maurice Konkel, Barton Gray, Seb Mercurio, Danny Napolitano, Dwight Mumma, Charlie Scarle, Ben Zimberoff (vln); Paul Israel, Aaron Shapiro, Dave Smiley (vla); Bemko, Bock, Gillan (cel); Kenton (p); Ralph Blaze (g); Abe Luboff, Bagley (bs); Manne (d); Graettinger (comp). Hollywood, 5, 7 December 1951.
A horn · City of Glass – Entrance into the City, The structures, Dance before the mirror, Reflections

Childers, Clyde Reasinger, Candoli, Don Dennis, Ruben McFall (tpt); Fitzpatrick, Russo, John Halliburton, Gerald Finch (tbn); Roberts (bs tbn); Graas, Otto (fr h); Dick Meldonian, Lennie Niehaus (alt); Bill Holman, Lee Elliot (ten); Gioga (bar); Kenton (p); Sal Salvador (g); Bagley (bs); Frank Capp (d); Graettinger (comp). Hollywood, 19 March 1952.
Modern opus

Graas, Otto (fr h); Shank (alt, fl); Niehaus (alt, ob); Meldonian (alt, clt); Cooper (ten, eng h); Cardarell (ten, bsn); Gioga (bar, bs clt); Bagley (bs); Capp (d); Graettinger (comp). Hollywood, 20 March 1952.
A cello

Childers, Ferguson, Conte Candoli, Dennis, McFall (tpt); Bob Burgess, Frank Rosolino, Russo, Keith Moon (tbn); Roberts (bs tbn); Vinnie Dean, Lee Konitz (alt); Holman, Richie Kamuca (ten); Gioga (bar); Kenton (p); Salvador (g); Bagley (bs); Stan Levey (d); Graettinger (comp). Chicago, 15 September 1952.
You go to my head

Pete Candoli (tpt), Graas, Otto (fr h) added. Hollywood, 11 February 1953.
A trumpet · An orchestra

Graas (fr h); Shank (alt, fl); Herb Geller (alt); Cooper (ten, ob, eng h); Cardarell (ten, clt, bsn); John Rotella (bar); Graettinger (comp). Hollywood, 28 May 1953.
A thought

Graas absent. Same date.
Some saxophones

Kenton's avowed jazz progressivism was largely unmatched by any consistent headway in expression. A dual aspiration towards commercial popularity and outré musical significance made for unpredictable leaps of style, some of them backwards. If certain critics have come to judge Kenton with rather more tolerance than used to be their wont, they have usually done so by considering his output piecemeal and finding this product or that appealing not as some token of overall development but rather on the music's immediate terms. It remains difficult to relate some of the 'rehabilitated' items to wider and more consistent evidences of jazz development; and nowhere is this dilemma more marked than in the work of Kenton's most enigmatic collaborator, Robert Graettinger.

Graettinger's professional beginnings seem to have been fairly conventional. A Californian who died in 1957 at the age of 33, he studied the saxophone when a child, then, as a teenager, took a job with Bobby Sherwood's 1940s band as player and writer. He worked similarly with Johnny Richards, Jan Savitt and Benny Carter before plumping for composing full time. In 1947 Kenton began to commission scores from him and first *Thermopylae* was recorded, a powerful fierceness darkly celebrating urgent conflict. It is really a fairly straightforward 'progressive' jazz orchestration and its modern rhythms might as well be a savage threnody for Texans as for Spartans – the Alamo being proverbially the Thermopylae of America. Yet Graettinger's vision was ready to scatter its imaginings beyond the rims of jazz.

His arrangement of *Everything happens to me* for Miss Christy and the Kenton band was performed by them live, but only recorded, as here, with Cooper directing a smaller group of Kenton associates with the chart adapted by Graettinger for reduced forces. Miss Christy's interpretation meets both contrast and dry empathy in the accompaniment's oblique chordal variation on this song.

Incident in jazz (earlier titled *An incident in sound*) is rooted, similarly to *Thermopylae*, in Kentonian self-improvement, jazzy certainly, and marked, as was much big-band jazz of the time, by violent section contrasts and stark dynamic switchings. The string section occasionally sails in like a ceremonial barque amid firing warships, sounding no more avant garde than had Artie Shaw's added strings a decade earlier (**145**). In this kind of writing Graettinger probably was putting Kenton's likings – including a symphonic romanticism as real as Shaw's – before his own ambition. That ambition is to the fore, though, in *House of strings* where, without wind and percussion, violins, violas and cellos are able to predict their role in more controversial creations yet to come.

The two song arrangements, *Everything happens to me* and *You go to my head*, each a standard frequently chosen by jazz-makers, form a particular facet of Graettinger's output and the writing invites comparison with some contemporary orchestration and recomposition – say those of Gil Evans, John Carisi, Bill Smith, Dave VanKreidt . . . The ensemble treatment of *You go to my head* is sinewy, cynical, and even sardonic. The trombones of Burgess and Russo defend the tune's honour just a little less successfully than June Christy stood up for her song.

But it is the honouring of an unusual and challenging inventiveness that most concerns us here. *Modern opus* is a fascinating, totally ensemble interweaving of – as it were – irresolute contrapuntal strands; questions seeking answers or questions that answer themselves without realizing it? This is a well-crafted attempt at creating a new kind of jazz-accented instrumental conversation, but perhaps it stymies itself by too marked a reliance upon well-established European contrapuntal techniques. At all events it is not – though recorded only shortly after it – clear kin to *City of Glass.*

The LP which formerly contained *City of Glass* plus the remaining items here was Creative World (A) ST1006 and was earlier on Capitol. At the time of issue and for a long while thereafter, the music faced critical extremes of evaluation. Reassessment of Graettinger's contributions, as of the Kentonian love of wildness and dissonance, may have been assisted by subsequent experience of Third Stream and free jazz, though one self-consciously avant-garde commentator found 'sheer pomposity' in Graettinger and found confirmation in *City of Glass* 'that [the composer's] true talent lay outside the field of jazz'. [1] On the basis of hearing – prior to theorizing – one may suggest that *City of Glass* confirms nothing of the kind, even though it might suggest an aspiration beyond jazz as usually defined. What Graettinger himself would have confirmed remains a mystery. Tantalizingly little is known about the workings of his mind, but he left us a dazzling monument to his own enigma.

Faced with the problem of relating Graettinger's most ambitious product to jazz (even his own jazz and the music of other writers during Kenton's 'Innovations in Modern Music' period) one may end up echoing the critic who says of *City of Glass*: 'It is just itself, and that is enough.' [2] Yet that assertion, though prompted by grateful approval, may seem a static verdict on music which, from the first menacing, scything string writing of *Entrance into the city* voices invitation to a journey. So densely packed are all these movements with incident, coincidence, allusion, illusion, unexpected pursuits and departures, that the journey might have to be paced and paced again many times before all its twists and its vistas can be recognized, let alone adequately responded to.

That a composer himself may not fully fathom the nature and purport of his work when it is presented for performance is testimony to the vitality of creative perception. The act of composition may, particularly as in the present instance, continue in rehearsal and in prepared performance. After Graettinger, the self-unsparing hermit, had toiled over *City of Glass* for a year, he gave the band, along with carefully scored parts, graphic charts of a kind of symbolic geometry. He sought unities by way of particularities as he built from a consideration of each individual musical part, patiently instructing each participant. One can learn almost as much from this information as from the suite's programmatic titles. (Always unwilling to talk about his music, Graettinger was reluctant to title his pieces and some were given names only after they were recorded, probably by Kenton.) One listens with greater care and wonder to the perpetual interplay of instrumental groups and fleeting solo sounds, with the intense drama of the string writing in *Entrance into the city*; the 'hocketed' pyramid arpeggios, minatory kettledrums and torrents of *pizzicato* in *The structures*; the steady yet not slavishly metronomed thresh of *Dance before the mirror* as it approaches a distorted reflection of fleet jazz familiarities – a brass echo from Ellington's *Harlem airshaft*, saxophones in a cockeyed variant of some Benny Carter variation. The consonant strands which contrast with shifting hues and the question-posing strings are answered by desperate convocations of brass that in the ambiguously named *Reflections* terminate with a tension that seems to find resolution in a sharing of uncertainty. Is the city, after all this, really there? It seems to dissolve, reappear, and dissolve again in its own glassy reflections of itself. Are Graettinger's thronging paradoxes facets of the magical paradox of Tennyson's *Camelot*, 'Built to music and therefore never built at all, and therefore built forever'? [3]

'It is just itself'? To be sure, no shrewd historian will confidently read prophecies into *City of Glass*, not precise ones at all events. Occasional similarities may be found in subsequent (even in contemporary or antecedent) musics. Nothing is proven by these. As to its place in jazz history, any claim must be backed by its being received as a part, albeit a transcendent part, of the Kentonian corpus. It may be argued that it was only in such a progressive/innovative sequence that this hybrid inspiration could prove itself. But it demands judgement largely on its own implicit terms, and by responsive and unprejudiced imaginations.

An orchestra, akin to *A trumpet*'s raucous conclusion, could be its composer's personal celebration of the orchestra which possibly inspired and certainly first interpreted his ambitious compositions; a celebration ironic, it may be, because those distributed, occasionally ascending arpeggios are but a disturbed revival of techniques as old as early vintage Whiteman, Henderson, Ellington . . . *A cello* is a small concerto for Bemko, whose lines, like Ferguson's pyrotechnics in *A trumpet*, determine rather than vie with challenge and response. Spasmodic jazz comments grow into a modernistic stomp, egging the cellist into scarcely controlled frenzy, and by this his hegemony is overturned. Still, he has the quiet final word.

A horn is something different again. Here the elusive tonalities of the soloist, Graas (*cf.* **308**), are constantly heckled by voices which are less angular than his only to the extent that they are more fragmentary. *Some saxophones* and *A thought* in their occasion and execution point up the haphazard recording history of the *This Modern World* suite, as well as the arbitrariness of its formal gathering. These two performances differ from the orchestral modernities not least in the circumstance that Graettinger was in complete control of the session (Kenton's band being on tour at the time), but more significantly in their intimacy of form.

The atonality which the saxophone piece shares with its shrill session-mate is coloured by jazz-conditioned inflections.

In June 1993 the Ebony Band, a well-established Dutch outfit, was conducted by Gunther Schuller, that long-time bestrider of musical disciplines, in concerts preponderated by Graettinger works. These thoughtful readings have value in including two versions of *City of Glass*, that is the score dated 1951, which is dealt with above, and the one dated 1947, which Kenton performed publicly about that time but never recorded. Thus is established the extent to which Graettinger recomposed the later version for a recording with significantly more participants. Included also are other pieces Kenton did not record, namely *Graettinger No. 3*, *Untitled* and arrangements of *April in Paris* and *Laura*. These are all on †Channel Crossings (H) CCS6394. Further, in 1996 the Ebony Band under its founder Werner Herbers gave two Amsterdam concerts of hitherto unknown Graettinger scores; these are on †Channel Crossings (H) CCS13198. E.T.

Milton Babbitt/Teddy Charles/Duke Ellington/Jimmy Giuffre/J. J. Johnson/John Lewis/Teo Macero/Charles Mingus/Bob Prince/George Russell/Gunther Schuller/Harold Shapero

478 Outstanding Jazz Compositions of the 20th Century

†Columbia (A) COL475 639–2 (2 CDs), Columbia (A) C28–831 (2 LPs)

Art Farmer (tpt); Eddie Bert (tbn); Don Butterfield (tu); John LaPorta (clt, alt); Macero (ten, comp); George Barrow (bar); Mal Waldron (p); Wendell Marshall (bs); Ed Shaughnessy (d); Orlando di Girolamo (acc); Ernest Anderson (vcl). New York City, 9 September 1955.
Sounds of May

Nick Travis, Al Stewart, Phil Sunkel, Jon Eardley (tpt); Bert (tbn); Butterfield (tu); Phil Woods (alt); Frank Socolow, Eddie Wasserman (ten); Sol Schlinger (bar); Harvey Leonard (p); Teddy Kotick (bs); Joe Harris (d); Prince (vib, comp). New York City, 4 January 1956.
Avakianas Brasileiras

John Ware, Melvin Broiles, Carmine Fornarotto, Bernie Glow, Arthur Statter, Joe Wilder (tpt); Miles Davis (tpt, fl h); John Clark, J. J. Johnson, Urbie Green (tbn); Joseph Singer, Ray Alonge, Arthur Sussman, Jim Buffington (fr h); John Swallow, Ronald Ricketts (bar h); Bill Barber (tu); Milt Hinton (bs); Osie Johnson (d); Dick Horowitz (perc); Lewis (comp); Schuller (cond). New York City, 20 October 1956.
Three little feelings

Horowitz absent; J. J. Johnson (comp). New York City, 23 October 1956.
Poem for brass

Davis, Hinton, Osie Johnson absent; Horowitz returns; Giuffre (comp). Same date.
Pharaoh

Louis Mucci, Farmer (tpt); Jimmy Knepper (tbn); Buffington (fr h); LaPorta (clt, alt); Hal McKusick (alt, ten); Robert DiDomenica (fl); Manuel Zegler (bsn); Bill Evans (p); Barry Galbraith (g); Joe Benjamin (bs); Ted Sommer (d); Charles (vib); Margaret Ross (hrp); Giuffre (comp); Schuller (cond). New York City, 10 June 1957.
Suspensions

Macero (bar) added; Fred Zimmerman (bs) replaces Benjamin; Mingus (comp, vcl intrjc[1]); Babbitt (comp[2]); Schuller (cond). New York City, 18 June 1957.
Revelations[1] · *All set*[2]

Russell (comp, cond[3]); Schuller (comp[4], cond[5]); Shapero (comp[6]). New York City, 20 June 1957.
All about Rosie[3] · *Transformation*[4,5] · *On green mountain*[5,6]

Donald Byrd (tpt); Bob Brookmeyer (v-tbn); McKusick (alt); Socolow (ten); Waldron (p); George Duvivier (bs); Shaughnessy (d); Charles (vib, comp). New York City, 20 April 1959.
Swingin' goatsherd blues

Cat Anderson, Harold Baker, Fats Ford, Willie Cook, Clark Terry, Ray Nance (tpt); Quentin Jackson, Britt Woodman, John Sanders (tbn); Russell Procope (clt, alt); Jimmy Hamilton (clt, ten); Johnny Hodges (alt); Paul Gonsalves (ten); Harry Carney (bar); Ellington (p, comp); Jimmy Woode, Benjamin (bs); Sam Woodyard, Jimmy Johnson (d). New York City, 8 September 1959.
Idiom '59

Though by no means its only sign of virtue, this is the kind of music that has never found much favour with jazz fans, still less with those who write for them. Such people approve the rigid application of labels and categories nearly as much as they enjoy anecdotes about their favourite musicians' heroic deeds. Yet with the exception of *Idiom '59* all these pieces are successful explorations in that they both seek and find, crossing notional frontiers to excellent purpose.

And despite a frosty reception, even a contemptuous silence, [4] nearly all these recordings have repeatedly been reissued. *Sounds of May* and *Avakianas Brasileiras* first appeared on the Macero/Prince *What's New?* LP, while the three items for brass and percussion, two of them with Davis as soloist, formed half of a *Music for Brass* LP, the remaining space being occupied by Schuller's Symphony for Brass and Percussion, the whole issued by Columbia for the Jazz and Classical Music Society. Giuffre's *Suspensions* and Schuller's *Transformation* were commissioned, along with the Babbitt, Russell, Mingus and Shapero pieces, for the fourth Festival of the Creative Arts at Brandeis University, 1–15 June

1957, and these six pieces were recorded in New York during or immediately after the festival, making up an LP imaginatively titled *Modern Jazz Concert*.

A different case is *Swingin' goatsherd blues*, from the Macero–Charles *Something New, Something Blue* LP, an enterprising collection of compositions plus recompositions of traditional material by Macero, Charles, Bill Russo and Manny Albam which has otherwise sunk without trace. *Idiom '59* on the contrary has appeared and will doubtless go on appearing in various Ellington compilations. Alas, it is the least adventurous piece here, and the compilers would have done better to replace it with the remaining titles from Prince's *Avakianas Brasileiras* session. No music is added to the further CD reissue, although the extra space could have been filled with the other tracks from Macero's *Sounds of May* date. Luckily these are on **479** and *Sounds of May* is discussed there. To all of which it might be added firstly that on the most recent LP and CD reissues the personnels are incomplete and all dates are omitted. Secondly that a title for this collection with greater historical point would have been *Outstanding Jazz Compositions of the 1950s*, because the departures made in this music were particularly characteristic of that decade, one of the most fruitful periods in jazz history.

More recently there has been a single-CD reissue titled *The Birth of the Third Stream* (†Columbia [A] 485 103–2) which has further confused the matter. It includes both Giuffre pieces and the Johnson, Lewis, Mingus and Russell scores but its major item is the Schuller Symphony, a fine work, yet one that, whatever the composer maintains in the notes, has nothing whatever to do with jazz.

Speaking of titles, *Avakianas Brasileiras* derives from Villa-Lobos's *Bachianas Brasileiras* and in it Prince deftly crosses hard, bright sonorities characterized by toccatalike figures with Latin American rhythms. Despite the reeds' presence, and even a vigorous Woods solo, brass and percussion dominate. Such rhythms are often used by jazzmen in obvious ways but here they are further crossed with dissonant counterpoint and innovative scoring which artfully varies the weight and density of the textures. Indeed, this brief piece is tightly packed with meaningful incident and is one of several items that should have been included in the *Birth of the Third Stream* CD.

At least equally independent of jazz conventions is Giuffre's highly contrapuntal *Pharaoh*, which employs more dissonance in a freer manner within less predictable textures than the other pieces for brass ensemble and is more concentrated in its expression. Fairly remote aspects of American music are invoked, such as works by Ives and Ruggles, most especially the leaping sevenths and ninths, pounding timpani and grinding dischords of the latter's *Sun treader.* Like Lewis's *Three little feelings* in relation to his work for the MJQ (**363**), *Pharaoh* calls forth a different side of Giuffre's musical personality from that shaping his prolific small-group output (**364**, **387**). *Suspensions*, on the contrary, though also fully written out, convincingly extends his combo procedures in compositional terms. It seems frankly sectional yet in fact is closely argued, foreground diversity growing out of background unity, and the percussion, instead of marking any imposed beat, participates in the music's contrapuntal flow.

Three little feelings is enough to inspire regret that Lewis did not do more work away from the MJQ and remains among his best pieces. Obviously with this large brass ensemble a broader dynamic range and a more explicit force are possible but the main points here are an alternative route for his sense of formal adventure and a different expression for his lyricism. Indeed, some of this music's impact derives from the use of a large ensemble to convey intimate, subtle thoughts, the mood being romantic yet the ideas terse. In the first movement, for example, there is a quick statement of the thematic material, with three germinal minor-keyed motifs appearing as unison lines and then one on top of another. Timpani and cymbals are briefly ominous but this feeling is dispelled by a short J. J. Johnson passage and Davis enters with one of the three motifs, a four-note pattern emphasizing the flattened fifth. His first improvisation grows out of this, simple and economical, perfectly in keeping with the musical atmosphere by now built up. An outburst from the ensemble is driven by Osie Johnson and when this quietens down there is a shorter sequence by Davis before the quiet ending.

The central movement is quiet, thoughtful, and Davis almost has it to himself, though what he plays is much enhanced by the ensemble and there is here a glimpse of his collaborations with Gil Evans which began the following year (for instance **382**). In one passage trombones and baritone horns alternate as the harmony stands still and Davis wanders, forlorn but never without momentum, across this hauntingly poignant terrain. Note the richness of Barber's tuba sound, both moving independently and blending with Hinton's bass. Back in a minor key, the third movement's most striking gesture is a french-horn call beautifully intoned by Buffington, though a variant of one of the opening piece's motifs soon appears, leading to J. J. Johnson's 40-bar solo. His jaunty episode provides exactly the shift of emphasis the music needs at this point, yet the horn call is the finale's main thematic material and is often present in one form or another during a movement that is particularly well integrated. Brass and percussion dialogue as the climax is approached and then tension evaporates and the initial call returns, now on four french horns. [5]

J. J. Johnson's *Poem for brass* is titled *Jazz suite for brass* on some reissues and it is notable that the great trombone virtuoso offers more conservative writing and generates the most consistently full textures among these brass-ensemble compositions, though he to some extent uses percussion to set movements going. *Poem* has a rather dignified beginning, with differently voiced mixtures of brass hinting at the theme. The first movement proper has a surprisingly quick tempo with further mixtures, now of open and muted sounds, predominating until Davis enters. He improvises over this constantly active texture, sometimes almost being caught up into it. Then the composer solos, making references to the theme more explicit than Davis's, and this movement ends rather abruptly. Next, at a slower pace, the four french horns, led by Singer, and the tuba play some rich parallel chords, this leading to another section which has Wilder's trumpet in unsentimental ballad mood.

The continuity is not really convincing in this movement but J. J. does much better in his finale, which has a separate title, *Metre and metal*. This is kicked off by Osie Johnson's cymbals and these alternate with diverse brass combinations, Glow being prominent. Then the argument is broken off, only brief chordal passages remaining until abruptly the six trumpets state the subject of a fugue which forms the main body of this movement. The fugue is started by Barber with other groups of instruments being promptly drawn in, the texture filling out until Johnson has five real parts going in conventional yet excellent counterpoint. Latterly founded on Hinton's very propulsive bass, this makes perfect collective sense in both linear and harmonic terms. Finally the fugal subject's potential has been exhausted and this is signalled by four separate outbursts derived from the first two movements' ideas. These make an entirely satisfying close – and hear John Ware's high, rounded C sharp at the very end, this being recorded in the closing minutes of a gruelling session.

There is magnificent playing also in the remaining pieces for the Brandeis Festival, where the commissions went to three jazzmen, Giuffre, Mingus, Russell, and three straight composers, Babbitt, Schuller, Shapero, although it should be added that the three latter had been active in spheres close to jazz. Thus Babbitt, one of the century's great composers and certainly one of the most original America has produced, became interested in jazz very young, partly through hearing Bix Beiderbecke records. He learned the clarinet and alto saxophone and 'played every kind of pop music. I played and arranged for 17 different bands. I played gigs on Saturday nights when I was ten with New Orleans musicians who came through Jackson,' Mississippi, where he grew up. [6] Babbitt also wrote popular songs and in 1946 a musical, *Fabulous Voyage*. Schuller was of course involved with jazz as composer and performer throughout his career almost as much as with straight music, and Shapero, a fluent improviser on the piano, wrote dance-band arrangements early on.

All six pieces were intended to partake in whatever proportions each composer liked of both jazz and classical tendencies, and the only limitation was that imposed by the instrumentation of the festival orchestra. To judge from the variety of sounds, colours, textures generated by these half-dozen performances this was not a severe restraint, and if one piece demonstrates this most vividly it is Babbitt's *All set*. This is best listened to at first as a nine-instrument collective improvisation even though it is the exact opposite, its composer being what he calls a maximalist (as opposed to minimalist). The constant ferment of line, colour, rhythm here in which nothing returns and no detail is repeated so that everything is completely unpredictable to the listener is the paradoxical result of everything being predetermined.

Babbitt in the 1940s started extending Schoenberg's method of 12-tone composition into a highly influential system, serializing not only pitches but also durations, timbres, dynamics, the end product being the sort of highly complex network of inner relationships found here. Everything is significant, and with sufficient rehearings the correspondences unifying the whole slowly move into focus. Equally, *All set*, the only one of the Brandeis pieces to be throughout in 4/4, abstracts melodic, rhythmic, even harmonic elements from the advanced jazz of the 1940s, namely bop, and makes some interestingly different uses of Babbitt's serial procedures from those found in his other works. [7] It is one of several pieces that should have supplanted the Schuller Symphony in the *Birth of the Third Stream* CD.

Mingus's aims and procedures are at the furthest extreme from those of Babbitt and the continuity, even the coherence, of *Revelations* depends not on the sort of compositional method that results with *All set* in what sounds like a kind of systematic spontaneity but is of an emotional order. In this sense Mingus takes greater risks than the other composers here, and his approach often works sufficiently well for him. *Revelations* certainly relates to what he had been doing with his regular group in 1956–7, although it also has affinities with *Half-mast inhibition* and *The chill of death*, fully written-out big-band pieces of early date but only recorded in 1960 and 1971 respectively.

A darkly coloured statement from the lower instruments establishes a characteristically brooding atmosphere as *Revelations* begins, yet unaccompanied solos from Buffington, Mucci and Knepper convey a sense of other possibilities. The opening returns, however, and grows threatening, but Mingus vents a theatrical, self-conscious cry of 'Oh yes, my lord' and a piano solo in 3/4 follows. This is influenced by, though not dependent upon the clichés of, black church music. It relaxes the tension and for a time the music takes on a fairly romantic feeling before growing more energetic. The 4/4 pulse returns and over a two-chord vamp there are two minutes of collective improvisation in which everybody joins. This is the climax and it resolves back to the opening. Mingus is not yet finished, however, and another improvisation follows until the music fades into the void. [8]

Like the contributions from Babbitt and Russell, Schuller's *Transfor-*

mation exhibits a compositional skill that makes some 'pure' jazz extended pieces seem naïve. Yet while bringing together aspects of straight music and jazz as they were in the late 1950s, Schuller perhaps differentiated the two entities more sharply than was by then necessary, particularly if he believed, as his notes for the original LP issue suggest, that both were in a 'continuing process of amalgamation'. The piece is founded on the passacaglia concept that lies in the background of so much jazz, in this case expressed not in a repeated bass figure or sequence of chords but as a row of single held notes, changing in pitch and each heard on a different instrument from the last. Into this, fragments of jazz are injected, these being at first tiny yet growing in size until they predominate and finally take the piece over. At that point the linear embodiment of the passacaglia idea is telescoped into its vertical form as a sustained chord, and when this breaks off Evans, Charles and the rhythm team begin to improvise music that is strictly jazz. Behind this a riff is soon heard from the horns, very softly at first but growing in strength and setting up opposition to the other instruments. Next the rhythmic continuity is broken and passages of straight and jazz rhythm quickly alternate as the piece reaches its climax and sudden end.

The passacaglia concept takes a quite different direction in Shapero's *On green mountain*. A composer early commended by Stravinsky and Copland, he did not fulfil his initial promise, turning out a diminishing number of discouragingly backward-looking works (such as the Symphony in Classical Style). He probably was invited to take part in this project only because he was on the Brandeis faculty, and it was characteristic that he turned to the past for his starting point. The fact remains that *On green mountain* achieves all its aims and has remained enjoyable listening over the years; no wonder that Shapero orchestrated this optimistic piece in 1981.

For theme he decided on the second of Monteverdi's *Zefiro torna* pieces, the one from 1632 which is itself a chaconne or passacaglia. As in other creative jazz treatments of the classics, such as those of Gil Evans, Shapero does not merely apply jazz phrasing from the outside to *Zefiro torna* but reworks the material in quite fresh terms; indeed what happens might be seen as a reversion to 16th-century paraphrase and parody techniques. The first 12 bars of Monteverdi's melody and bass are retained and harmonized richly for vibraharp, piano, guitar and bass. This is preceded by an introduction and followed by a transition that leads into the improvisations, the whole being a sensitive passage of instrumentation. For the solos *Zefiro torna* is rearranged in a 32-bar AABA pattern at double the original speed. To start Farmer was requested to stay close to the melody for eight bars, decorate it for eight, and then commit himself increasingly to free improvisation. This he does splendidly and we then hear from Galbraith and LaPorta before a jubilant climax is reached with the trumpeter's return. Shapero next revises the melody and we hear it on the hard and soft tones of muted trombone and french horn against a bluesy counter-melody from McKusick. Knepper has a good open solo and the composer effectively lowers the tension prior to the return of the opening tempo by interrupting the music's pulse with brief irregular bursts of silence. To say that this piece sends one back to Monteverdi's original is obviously the best sort of compliment to both Shapero and the players.

If Babbitt's *All set* is the most rewarding work here from the classical side of the supposed dividing line, then Russell's is the finest from the jazz side. In fact it goes back to before jazz, deriving, he said, from 'a motive taken from an Alabama black children's song-game entitled *Rosie, little Rosie*'. [9] There is much going on in this piece but it must be noted that Russell employs a superimposition of riffs fairly similar to that found in, say, Basie's *One o'clock jump* (**134**). In a manner perhaps learned from Stravinsky, however, he chooses phrases of unequal length which, as the music proceeds, overlap in different relationships to each other and to the beat. That is, tension accrues through conflict between the basic pulse and the rhythmic units of the phrases. In the first movement a cogent musical argument, shifting between $^2/_2$ and $^3/_2$, is carried through via repetition and sequence, this rising to a logical and abrupt climax and ending.

A similar process, moving through several tonal areas, can be experienced in slow motion in the central movement, which retains the spirit of the blues without the form. The organization of these two movements demonstrates real mastery in jazz composition and offers perfectly convincing instances of written-out jazz polyphony. As examples of his work discussed elsewhere in the book show, Russell can also provide stimulating bases for improvisation and the very quick finale, along with solos by LaPorta, Farmer, Charles and McKusick, includes an unforgettable one from Evans. All these Brandeis commissions benefit from superlative performances, yet none more so than this last movement of Russell's.

Another thing they have in common is that they all use the common practice of jazz not as an end in itself but as a point of departure. In this latter connection it is instructive to hear them in conjunction with the alternative versions mentioned above, not least the Gerry Mulligan Concert Band's account of *All about Rosie* (Verve [A] 2332 097).

As a postscript comes Charles's *Swingin' goatsherd blues*, a title echoing that of Moe Koffman's briefly famous 1958 *Swingin' shepherd blues*. It does indeed swing excellently, if not with the vehement impetus of *Rosie*'s finale. There is an intelligent ensemble use of the vibraharp, but this is mainly a vehicle for solos from Brookmeyer, Charles, McKusick, Byrd and Socolow. Given the context, Russo's *East Hampton blues* would have been a more apt selection from the original Macero–Charles LP.

M.H.

Teo Macero

479 Time Plus Seven

Finnadar (Sd) SR9024

Art Farmer (tpt); Eddie Bert (tbn); Don Butterfield (tu); John LaPorta (clt, alt); Macero (ten, comp); George Barrow (bar); Wendell Marshall (bs); Ed Shaughnessy (d); Orlando di Girolamo (acc); Howard Shanet (cond). New York City, 9 September 1955.
Neally · Adventure · TC's groove

Farmer, Bert, Butterfield, Barrow absent. Same date.
Heart on my sleeve

Mal Waldron (p) added. Same date.
24+ 18+

Ernest Anderson (vcl) added. Same date.
Sounds of May

Medium-sized ensemble including strings conducted by Macero (comp). New York City, 1963.
Time Plus Seven – Seven · Equals · Time · Plus

Thad Jones, Joe Newman (tpt); Jerome Richardson (alt); Dick Katz (p); Richard Davis (bs); Macero (comp) and others unidentified. New York City, 22 March 1965.
Pressure

Considering the richness of the above in terms of expression and technique, and of other pieces written by Macero, it is somewhat comic that he is known in the jazz world almost exclusively as the supervisor of numerous Miles Davis recording sessions. True, his link to Teddy Charles, for example in the Prestige Jazz Quintet, is remembered, as is his on-and-off association with Mingus (during 1953–7). In fact a later record of his, dating from 1983, is titled *Impressions of Charles Mingus* (Palo Alto [A] PA8046). Macero also had charge of recording dates by Monk, Brubeck and others, yet, despite his tenor and baritone playing – which he took up again in the 1980s – his chief significance, even if largely unrecognized, is as a composer. Thus his *Fusion* was heard from the New York Philharmonic under Bernstein in 1958. It may surprise many to learn how prolific he has been in this sphere, although he has written music for radio, TV, films, for ballet, symphony orchestra, chamber ensembles etc. Some of this output is heavily tinged with jazz, yet much of it has ambitions which reach far beyond that category. Just as his presence on some of the Brandeis tracks of **478** is probably the best indication of his sympathies as a player, so the above compilation, spanning a decade, gives a quite vivid demonstration of his jazz affinities in composition.

The most advantageous item with which to start is *Neally*, because this to some degree summarizes the compositional techniques deployed in the five following pieces. Obliquely echoing Mulligan's scoring of *Godchild* on **376**, this swings in an almost old-fashioned manner while being highly contrapuntal. The polyphony is both written by Macero and improvised by all members of the ensemble and the stylistic continuity between these two extremes is by no means the least organizational success here and in some of the other pieces. There were of course scattered precedents for such free collective extemporization, among them Tristano's *Intuition* and *Digression* (**293**) of 1949, Macero's own 1953 *Explorations* (†Debut [A] 12CD4402) and Manne's *Abstract No. 1* of a year later (**432**). The impact of nonimitative counterpoint in some passages of *Neally* and the other 1955 performances is intensified by Macero's use of several tempos at once, of shifting bar lines, of a diversity of cross-rhythms. There was even room for improvised solos from Bert and the leader, and all this might seem to imply serious overcrowding in pieces mostly lasting under five minutes. Yet such a thought represents an a posteriori reaction and in reality one procedure flows into and out of another in what is surely a genuine compositional achievement.

Counterpoint is again to the fore in *Sounds of May*, which, subsequent to the making of this recording, created a memorable impression on the soundtrack of Aram Avakian's film *End of the Road.* It is the longest of all these pieces and via multitracking Anderson produces vocal polyphony in up to eight parts. This follows the precedent of Macero's *Explorations*, in which by the same means he is heard on two alto and three tenor saxophones. Anderson's vocal lines are in *Sounds of May* combined with other forms of sound manipulation only then starting to become familiar in electronic music. Macero explained that he fused these vocal lines with 'overtones of the piano, jazz ensembles (both small and large), changing the speed of the original tape – regular to half-speed and then combining the half-speed copy with the original track – and finally overdubbing a single alto saxophone line to most of the composition'. [10] Another hint from the European avant-garde, this time about indeterminate procedures, was taken up in *Adventure*, which also happens to be orchestrated in a particularly inventive way. It includes successful attempts by Macero to extemporize on a tone row (see **456–7**) and there is a collective improvisation of unusual density, with each player working on a different chord sequence. Almost of necessity this piece is atonal and follows a slow–medium–slow pattern with new material, instead of a recapitulation, heard at the return of the slow tempo.

With *TC's groove*, a score prompted by some of Teddy Charles's musical preoccupations, extemporized solos are firmly embedded in a contrapuntal framework and the whole presents an argument of great cogency. At the same time this lithely graceful piece includes, along with another excellent Bert improvisation, some references, surely ironic, to baroque phraseology. Quite different from the stringency evident here is the jazz ballad mode suggested by *Heart on my sleeve*, although this title proves to be another piece of irony. The conventional ballad phrases are lengthened, the harmonic vocabulary enlarged, the instrumental textures deepened and subsidiary counterpoint creates shadows beneath a surface that could otherwise have seemed too placid. Macero features himself here, his tone light and airy like post–Lester Young tenor saxophonists such as Herbie Steward though with far more interesting ideas. As hinted by its title, *24+ 18+* is founded on two 12-note rows and two 9-note rows and the harmonies are of course derived from these rows. Given the (mainly) Schoenbergian origin of the serial method, it is apt that the expressionistic violence already implicit in *Adventure* should erupt here in jagged discontinuity. Even more than the five other pieces, *24+ 18+* is an extraordinary anticipation of the climate and the aesthetic preoccupations of some of the jazz of a decade and more later.

Yet this is partly deceptive because there are many compositional initiatives and ways of challenging the improviser in these scores that were not taken up elsewhere. Also bypassed was a Macero innovation concerning the instruments used. The piano accordion has always been regarded as virtually an anti-jazz device and the demonstration of its actual viability on this record (and in the *Sunday* movement of Kenny Graham's 1956 *Suncat Suite* – MGM [E] MGMC764) has been ignored in the literature of jazz commentary. Quite apart from the solos in *Sounds of May* and *Heart on my sleeve*, the accordion is here fully a member of the ensemble, nimbly filling a number of roles and contributing various types of figuration. On this showing di Girolamo was a flexible and imaginative player, and it seems unfortunate that he was not heard from again.

However, Macero's rich musical capacities continued to develop in other directions and the four movements of his *Time Plus Seven* ballet score are characteristic. These were commissioned by the Rebecca Harkness Dance Company and are superbly performed here, especially the percussion and high-lying brass parts. It is too bad the players cannot be identified. Mostly this is very tense music, the first movement, *Seven*, in particular; and somehow evocative of a sequence of malicious geometrical equations. (Was Anna Sokolow's choreography like this?) Certainly hieratic gestures are invoked by the jagged fanfarelike phrases, and dominant though brass and percussion are, the strings are fully integrated. *Equals* is slower yet more insistent with its repeated figures, and although saxophones are here quite prominent, Macero still writes plenty of high, stinging brass parts. *Time* has a more complicated outline, for its quick repeated patterns soon diversify into several things happening at once; and the closing *Plus* draws together all the threads of discontinuity, asymmetry, dissonance, innovative scoring. It is almost a paradox – though with precedents in Ellington (**131b**, **152a**), Dameron (**280**) and elsewhere – that although the improvised solo has no place here, except marginally in *Time*, this score is a fine achievement in jazz composition.

Behind the fragmentary personnel which is all that can be given for *Pressure* may be glimpsed Orchestra USA. The musical director of this large ensemble was John Lewis, who commissioned Macero's piece, first performed at Carnegie Hall in January 1965. It again finds him a pilgrim in the wilderness of tonal disruption as this score, in two parts, played without a break, is thoroughly atonal. And once more the atmosphere is brooding, almost threatening. Solo instruments occasionally emerge tentatively but are soon overwhelmed. The textures are elaborate yet rather static in their effect and the import of this hermetic music is nothing if not mysterious. Macero's compositions are in general so hard to trace that there is no knowing how he followed this up. M.H.

Friedrich Gulda

480 Music for Four Soloists and Band

Saba (G) 15097ST, Polydor (E) 583 709

Gulda (p, comp). Villengen, Germany, 20 July 1965.
Prelude and fugue

Freddie Hubbard, Stan Roderick, Kenny Wheeler (tpt); Robert Politzer (fl h); J. J. Johnson, Erich Kleinschuster (tbn); Harry Roche (v-tbn); Rudolf Josel (bs tbn); Alfie Reece (tbn, tu); Tubby Hayes (fl, ten); Sahib Shihab (fl, bar); Rolf Kühn (clt, ten); Herb Geller (alt); Gulda (p, comp); Pierre Cavalli (g); Ron Carter (bs); Mel Lewis (d). Vienna, 13–14 September 1965.
Music for four soloists and band no. 1 · Minuet

Had Gulda confined himself to jazz he would long since have been acknowledged as one of the most gifted pianists known to this music. But he also had a major reputation as a classical interpreter, and, because of the sense of inferiority which most writers on jazz feel towards the masterpieces of the European tradition, acknowledgement of his achievements in jazz has been sullenly withheld. Born in 1930, he was early recognized as one of the most gifted classical pianists of his generation, above all in Beethoven. It is notable, however, that the German music critic Joachim Kaiser wrote of Gulda's early performances of the classics having an 'improvisatory and dynamic élan'. [11] Gulda felt that the European repertoire did not have enough to say to him and his contemporaries.

He was of course very young when he first expressed that opinion, but he held to it and later tried to develop it into something more systematic – see his notes for *The Long Road to Freedom* (BASF/MPS [G] 28–20872) of 1971. More legitimately, and like Glenn Gould, another of the most interesting classical pianists of that generation, Gulda never found the life of a concert artist attractive. As Burnett James wrote during the same period, 'jazz has more than once seemed like the Golden Road to Samarkand' [12] to those who believe they can escape from the supposed limitations of the classics into the freedom of the much simpler music that is jazz. And at a rather simplistic level one may note the recording of Mozart's Concerto for Two Pianos K.365 by Gulda and Chick Corea with the Concertgebouw Orchestra under Nikolaus Harnoncourt (†Teldec [G] 842 961ZK). If there is no reason why Corea should not play music like this if he feels inclined, then Gulda need not avoid jazz.

His debut in this field came in 1956 at the Newport Jazz Festival and at Birdland, New York. His sextet included Idrees Sulieman, Jimmy Cleveland, Phil Woods, Seldon Powell, and its recordings (RCA-Victor [A] LPM1355 and 1398), some taken at the club and some done in the studio, include several successes. Perhaps most striking is Gulda's own *Dark glow*, with excellent playing from Woods, although there is no denying the brilliance of the trio performance of *A night in Tunisia* or the leader's ability to improvise with complete and notably aggressive fluency. This is confirmed by a sextet version of *Dodo*, another Gulda theme, and his playing on *Bernie's tune* is astonishing. These and several other 1956 titles ought to have settled any question about Gulda's strictly jazz capacities and the point should have been driven home by the finale of *Music for piano and band no. 2*, where, even if this movement is too brief in relation to the work as a whole, his playing is demonic.

This piece is an immediate predecessor of the *Music for four soloists and band no. 1* on the record detailed above. As Gulda acknowledged, it is a kind of piano concerto, with some more phenomenal playing by him but also with a rather too emphatic rhetoric at some points. The slow central movement is far better and remains among the finest things Gulda did in jazz, both for the orchestral writing and for his own playing. If it had been a matter of this movement and the same date's *The veiled old land* only, this record (Columbia [A] CL2251, CBS [E] BPG62513) would probably have been the selection for our book, yet *Music for four soloists and band no. 1* is a more rounded achievement, perhaps because of the need to cater for three other improvisers as well as himself. In fact, *The veiled old land* accommodated so many soloists, heard at length in a fully convincing large-scale form, as to be the best augury for *Music for four soloists and band no. 1*.

That was in 1964. The following year, before making the above record, Gulda, somewhat belatedly, set down his first collection of jazz solo and trio performances. *Ineffable* (Columbia [A] CL2346) includes the quite amazing *Quartet*, an odd name for an unaccompanied piece but one that is at Tatum's (and Makowicz's) level pianistically, and several other pieces which are jazz of a very high quality. With the stage thus set, Gulda went on to what may well be his finest single achievement in jazz, though it should be heard in conjunction with the following year's *Music for four soloists and band no. 2* (Preiser [Au] SPR3141) with Art Farmer, J. J. Johnson and Cannonball Adderley, the later *Variations for two pianos and band* (MPS [G] 88034–2) of 1972 etc.

There are miniature precedents such as Ellington's *Battle of swing* (**152a**) for the concerto grosso aspect of *Music for four soloists and band no. 1* in which the *concertino* consists of Hubbard, Johnson, Shihab and Gulda with the band (which includes some distinguished names) acting as ripieno. The soloists respond with a steady flow of highly personal invention, and Shihab, who normally is to be preferred on alto (e.g. **280**), here plays finer baritone than on most of his other records. Gulda's writing nowhere hinders them but a weakness is the undistinguished nature of the thematic ideas, which are a matter of the commonplaces of jazz phraseology and quite failing to match the composer's invention at the piano. The skill with which these commonplaces are handled, though, is another matter, and in the first movement Gulda adapts sonata form to jazz and jazz to sonata form, while the second movement is a set of variations, the third a rondo. Because he understands how these – essentially simple – structures work this piece is sustained with a continuing impact which, it has to be said yet again, is simply not found in most attempts at extended composition by musicians whose jazz credentials are thought to be far deeper-rooted than Gulda's. Also excellent, if rather conservative, is the orchestration, and the whole is beautifully performed, the piece obviously having been rehearsed intelligently and at length – something which cannot be taken for granted with most latter-day big-band recordings.

The couplings are somewhat disappointing, the *Minuet* being graceful and accomplished mood music, the *Prelude and fugue* something like the movements of Hindemith's *1922* suite (**108**), especially the *Shimmy* and *Ragtime*. The *Minuet* is identified on the sleeve as being part of a suite, *Les Hommages*, while the *Prelude and fugue* are so described in some discographies (e.g. Bruyninckx) but not on the sleeve; the fact that one movement is orchestral and the other for solo piano may have led to confusion; the other movements of this suite have not been named, nor apparently recorded.

Gulda continued working on his jazz to good effect for a number of years, as is confirmed by the impressively original *Meditation III* of 1970 (MPS [G] 68059) and even by the considerably later and perhaps rather too schematic *Variations* of 1984 (†Philips [E] 412 115–2). Joachim Kaiser wrote that Gulda was 'a Hamlet who wants to play Ionesco', and in the end he perhaps succeeded. But he continued to suffer from the prejudices of stuffier elements in the classical and especially the jazz worlds. Such few opportunities as one had of listening to him in the classics in later years left a melancholy impression of great qualities gone to seed. Playing Ionesco exacts no small price. M.H.

Ran Blake

481 Film Noir

Arista Novus (A) AN3019

Blake (p, comp) variously with Ted Curson (tpt), John Hazilla, John Heiss (fl), Hankus Netsky (ob), Daryl Lowery (alt) and others. New York City, 1980.

Spiral staircase · Eve · Garden of delight · Key Largo · Pinky · A streetcar named Desire · Touch of evil · Le boucher · The pawnbroker · Doktor Mabuse · Blue gardenia

'Dark arrangements of movie memories' is one critic's summary of Blake's impressionism and it would be hard to better it. [13] The titles are best regarded as musical creations whose *raison d'être* is spurred by specific recollections. This is not 'film music', neither does Blake seek to apotheosize the role of the old movie-house pianist (an ambition which seems to have obsessed the English pianist John Ogdon in his final years). Like poetry in Wordsworth's famous assessment, Blake's music 'takes its origin from emotion recollected in tranquillity' even when tranquillity is not the impression the music conveys. The 'movie memories' are, in the nature of the case, both personal and selective. Close familiarity with the remembered dramatic images will not therefore be essential for the listener who can attune to Blake's manners. However, a quick résumé will help to tether both the artist's purpose and this commentary upon them.

'Dark arrangements' may be apposite for other than directly emotive reasons; in most cases the films are black and white prints. In the order provided in the heading we have: i) archetypal old-dark-house thriller with psychopathic killer, and tension enhanced by fiendish thunderstorm; ii) quasi-Freudian tale of the seduction by a *femme fatale* of a young writer in Venice; iii) family of a young amnesiac practise artful deceit upon him for selfish gain; iv) atmospheric drama of war veteran's contention with gangsters among the Florida Keys; v) study of the emotional problems of 'near-white' girl; vi) celebrated Tennessee Williams drama about domestic sexual terrorism in New Orleans; vii) Wellesian crime piece, narcotics investigations plus a murder in Mexico – coldly melodramatic; viii) love threatened for young French small-town tradesman, courting local schoolmistress, but falling under suspicion of multiple murder; ix) closely observed study of New York Jew haunted by memories of prison-camp experience; x) criminal mastermind aims at world domination with strategy of hypnotism and blackmail, a melodramatic scrutiny of megalomania; xi) girl wakes in strange apartment, after drunken binge, to find dead man beside her. Critical assessment of Blake's music itself follows in corresponding sequence.

Spiral staircase: piano and guitar effect ascending and descending footsteps, approach and retreat. The rhythmic 'feel' is distinctly jazzy, with hints of piano blues. Flute notes, sustained and mysterious, introduce a sense of stillness and space in contrast to the restlessness. Tempos are ambiguous. In an atemporal interlude the oboe muses on the darkness of threat; there are staccato piano signals, and the footfalls return, accelerated by the guitar, braked by the piano. (The storm is not acknowledged.) *Eve* is mainly pianistic. There are various effects of dynamic sustenance and, in the creative sequence, sensuous but shadowy messages. Blake and Curson plays a flickering game of tag for *Garden of delight*, a brilliant duet of rapid echoes seeking consonance but finding only a semblance of it in exhausted resignation at the close.

Key Largo has passages which emphasize Blake's allegiance to Monk. There are paradoxically gentle heraldic proclamations to start with. Bass and drums assist a mildly riding, song-haunted meditation which gathers to itself a vivid overlay of Monkish abrasiveness. *Pinky*: a minor-keyed reflection is disturbed by savage tone clusters. A flute darts above the troubled piano current which moves, quite soon, into a melancholy lyricism. Tension mounts again with a tenebrous counterpoint of piano bass and string bass with agitated scatterings from the drummer's brushes. The flute's songlike snatches seem to urge hopefulness, but the pianist stabs away peevishly at dismaying echoes and shadows.

The trolleyman's clang is the apt prelude to *A streetcar named Desire*. A guitar tremolando sounds rather more like a train whistle and much of the mechanical rhythmic substructure ensuing sounds trainlike too. Blake slows things for a catena of angular melodies over deep chords, growing into a fruitless dialogue of piano and alto over track rhythms speeding up to a manic pitch.

A Latin rhythm expectedly heralds the impression of *Touch of evil*. The pianist lashes several instruments into combination. Flashings are heard of trumpet, oboe, guitar, altos. There are mocking discords, staccato plucking, a siren is simulated. Blake, attacking the keyboard, might well be Cecil Taylor. The original dance pattern re-emerges. There are hand-played drum figures. Ensemble enterprise distinguishes *The pawnbroker* as well. Zipping keyboard arpeggios whip up zestful quickstep jazz with unison lines, riffs and briefly held crescendos. Bass, alto and piano improvisations disintegrate into ensemble *tuttis* of bursting terror; but the swing music reappears, infectious, well marshalled, ending in peremptory fashion.

Doktor Mabuse is greeted by ghostly piano caveats, typical space-creating contrasts between extreme keyboard registers. There is skilful and similarly varied work from the drummer. *Blue Gardenia* is recalled in an atemporal conversation between piano and alto evoking strangeness, like waking consciousness. Anxiety is conjured by wayward saxophone intonation and threatening piano signals. Then comes a beautifully contemplative passage, Blake groping for some kind of romantic warmth and little by little arriving in what may be a variation on some remembered song. Fresh uncertainty terminates a duet in which Lowery caricatures Benny Carter's coolest suavities.

Behind Blake's role as a professional academic lie several decades of varied performing experience. Virtually an autodidact, he has been able to mix classical experience with, for example, black gospel strains, and has, in close kinship with Gunther Schuller and others, furthered the cause of jazz education. He offers his own definition of Third Stream as 'an improvised synthesis of ethnic cabaret or Afro-American music with what had been called for the last few years European avant garde'. [14] That definition will not necessarily illumine all the 'dark memories' discussed above, but it helps to indicate Blake's imaginative dwelling, which has been hospitable in jazz terms to influence from Monk, George Russell, Max Roach, Ray Charles et al. He has cooperated closely with the singer Jeanne Lee, not only in public and recorded performance, since the late 1950s, but also in musical education as a fellow member of the New England Conservatory (cf. *You Stepped Out of a Cloud* on †Owl [F] 055).

There is no speck of the dust of academicism upon the making of *Film Noir*. From recollection of full-length originals he has created vignettes of a fine creative liveliness, and if their inclusion in this chapter seems to emphasize Blake's ventures as a frontiersman, let it also be emphasized that the frontier which has most forcefully habituated this insufficiently celebrated musician is that old one which we still persist in calling jazz.

E.T.

Modern Jazz Quartet/New York Chamber Symphony Orchestra

482 Three Windows

†Warner (A) 254 833–2, WEA (A) 254 833–1

John Lewis (p, comp, cond); Percy Heath (bs); Connie Kay (d); Milt Jackson (vib); strings of the New York Chamber Symphony Orchestra. New York City, 16–20 March 1987.

Three windows · Kansas City breaks · Encounter in Cagnes · Django · A day in Dubrovnik

Precisely because its performances embody such refined internal balance, the MJQ, like the classical string quartet, has always invited augmentation. Hence the early recordings with Giuffre, Rollins, Almeida, the Swingle Singers and, more relevant here, the Beaux Arts String Quartet and Stuttgart Symphony Orchestra. Indeed, it could be said that the results of the above meeting with the strings of the New York Chamber Symphony Orchestra are something towards which Lewis in particular had been moving for many years, perhaps ever since his *Period suite* was set down in Paris with restricted forces in 1950 (†Jazz Time [F] 251 288–2).

The first decisive move, however, was the recording of five Lewis compositions by the ten-piece ensemble of the Modern Jazz Society in 1955 (Verve [F] 823 089–1). There followed in 1958 and 1960 sessions in Stuttgart with members of that city's symphony orchestra, the earlier conducted by Lewis (RCA [F] PM42476), the later chiefly by Schuller (Atlantic [A] SD1359). The RCA disc consisted entirely of Lewis pieces, the solos being from Ronnie Ross (baritone saxophone), Gerald Weinkopf (flute) and the composer; while Atlantic offered mainly pieces by others, including Werner Heider's *Divertimento*, Schuller's *Concertino* and André Hodeir's remarkable *Around the blues*. The improvising is here by the MJQ, which is also prominently featured on WEA although there also are occasional violin solos by Syoko Aki and Ronald Oakland of the New York Chamber Symphony Orchestra.

Here Lewis has fruitfully reconciled the MJQ's individuality with the claims of a substantially larger group, a thoroughly idiomatic context being found for the combo's expanded, if rather cool, bop style. Partly this arises out of the quartet's specific ensemble methods, out of the way, for example, that Lewis accompanies Jackson not with the usual noncommittal detached chords but with frequent counter-melodies, these combining with Heath's freely ranging bass parts to create an imaginative contrapuntal ambience. While there are brilliant improvisations by its separate members, the MJQ is not here a detached, purely soloistic entity out in front of the body of strings but readily dissolves into this music's broad-textured fabric. Equally the orchestra participates in the quartet's expected fugal entries and nonimitative jazz polyphony, scarcely ever lapsing into mere background support: hear the *ostinato* figure under Jackson's second *Django* solo and the developmental way it is modified. If the stylistic integration is far superior to anything achieved on RCA or Atlantic – or to the collaboration between Sauter and Getz on **369** – this is because the space of a generation had elapsed. By the late 1980s string players were more at ease with the demands of jazz and sounded more natural in it: note the violins' role in *Kansas City breaks.*

Perhaps the 'Third Stream' label might still adhere to this lively enterprise even if that line of endeavour was, as Richard Williams said, 'finally damned up by critical invective'. [15] The MJQ was similarly condemned by the herd of orthodox jazz commentators, yet such are the ironical revenges sometimes exacted by history that here, and in several other places, it is rewarded for having become one of the longest-surviving, as well as one of the finest, small groups in the whole jazz story. Rather does this fusing of apparent opposites produce music that is classical in the wider sense, being strong and elegant, moderate and noble, sophisticated, simple and on occasion witty.

Presented with the opportunities afforded by this fairly new situation, Lewis does far more than rehash old scores. Quite apart from their places in the MJQ's concert repertoire, *Django* is found on the Modern Jazz

Society programme, *Three windows* on that of *European Windows*, and yet they sound like new, which is almost what they are. The way brusque string gestures challenge Jackson's tentative reminiscence of the *Django* theme signals that old material is here treated with greater daring and now inhabits a different climate of feeling. In earlier readings the theme could be taken as a lament on Reinhardt's premature death and the solos (not based on the same harmonies) as reflecting aspects of his life, not least his sheer musical inventiveness. This WEA recomposition, though prompted by the spirit, not the letter, of Gil Evans's treatment on **460**, is more oblique and complex, bringing to light hitherto unsuspected aspects of the theme. And it contains no padding. This performance is a mere 57 seconds longer than the initial 1954 recording (†Original Jazz Classics [A] OJCCD057–2), while *Three windows* is here 8 minutes and 13 seconds as against the 6 minutes 43 seconds of 1957 (†Atlantic/WEA K781340–2). The latter can still be described as a triple fugue, yet although the themes are as before, this is virtually a new composition on them, showing Lewis's ideas from quite unexpected angles. The exposition now has six voices and *The golden striker* is heard from Jackson and is answered by the first violins; *Cortège* is announced by Heath and answered by the violas; and *The rose truc* is played by Lewis and answered by the cellos. These themes of course recur and each is developed in an improvised episode by the soloist who announced it and in dialogue with the strings.

It might, and indeed should, be a matter for astonishment that Jackson and Lewis still had as much to say on this material 33 years after the MJQ began working regularly together. In fact this is an exceptional case of artistic self-renewal, and there are striking bass solos also on *Kansas City breaks* and *Django*. Yet they respond with particular esprit, Jackson above all, to the challenges of the newer material, especially *A day in Dubrovnik*. This and *Encounter in Cagnes* make the European references long expected of Lewis and suggest what Paul Klee might have termed imaginary landscapes. Dubrovnik is a beautiful Renaissance city on the Adriatic characterized by the white marble of its main buildings, and the three movements evoke it in afternoon, evening and morning. This is a matter of atmospheres and the finale does have an air of morning bustle, while in the central movement the strings appealingly heighten Jackson's and Lewis's different sorts of lyricism. But music retains its real limitations so far as representing the material world is concerned and the story that Lewis, in the accompanying notes, attaches to *Encounter in Cagnes* could never be deduced from the music. As in a certain Schoenberg case, this is music for a film that was never made.

After such foreign excursions, *Kansas City breaks* is an instance of what Lewis called long ago 'going back into the gold mine', [16] which is to say to the resources of the American folk tradition. Yet while doing so this piece also makes a particularly full use of strings! The above performance should be compared with Lewis's 1982 sextet version (Finesse [A] FW38187). His solos, here and on *Three windows* and *A day in Dubrovnik*, tend to be series of artfully linked aphorisms, and it is no paradox to say that he remains the outstanding blues pianist he always was. Alas, the fact that he makes no use of the clichés of that idiom has done his reputation in that direction no good. Of Jackson one can only say that he is shown here to have kept the finely nuanced expressive power of his virtuosity in full bloom. M.H.

Chris McGregor

483 Brotherhood of the Breath

RCA Neon (E) NE2

Mongezi Feza (pkt tpt, Indian fl[1]); Marc Charig (cnt); Harry Beckett (tpt); Malcolm Griffiths, Nick Evans (tbn); Dudu Pukwana (alt); Mike Osborne (alt, clt); Ronnie Beer (ten, Indian fl[1]); Alan Skidmore (ten, sop); McGregor (p, African xylo[1]); Harry Miller (bs); Louis Moholo (d). London, *c.* 1970.
Mra · Davashe's dream · Andromeda · Night poem[1] *· Union special*
John Surman (bar, sop) added. Same date.
The bride

Union special, this programme's goonish coda, presents the South African regime as a self-dementing musical-hall turn. It was a 1964 invitation to the Antibes Jazz Festival that spurred McGregor, a white South African pianist playing with black colleagues, to escape apartheid and take his bop-inspired *kwela* group, the Blue Notes (with Feza, Pukwana, Moholo, Nick Moyake [tenor] and Johnny Dyani [bass]), to Europe. The impact of this band, and of their larger successor, the Brotherhood of the Breath, upon a rising generation of jazz musicians, British and continental, was striking and its reverberations were still felt at the start of the 1990s. The Brotherhood, yoking African and European sidemen, worked fitfully for almost 20 years; they were received enthusiastically in concert, but recorded all too infrequently. There were some piano recordings in McGregor's unique percussive style – 'The piano is my favourite drum' [17] – and the Blue Notes reassembled briefly in 1978. The last recording by the Brotherhood appeared in 1988, less than two years before the pianist's death at 53. He was a leader of considerable physical and mental vigour which, though original, may have missed full unity of purpose.

This 1970 production preserves his best aspirations quite excitingly, yet it may also show why a wished-for amalgam of jazz and music of the *kwela* type remained frustrated. The orchestral manner of *Davashe's dream* shows admiration for Ellington without sounding at all like pastiche. This leisurely arrangement's materials are not quite conventional but what singularity they may have does not seem particularly African; and yet this very elusiveness, met elsewhere too, may indicate a fusion achieved subliminally. Beckett's bubbling, popping, squeaking solo is more personal than Skidmore's Shepp-like snarling during the same piece. Surman's ample reflections in *The bride* upon a Coltrane but recently dead are the most satisfying improvisation and the one whose conception of jazz freedom seems most nearly to suit McGregor's purposes in utilizing the *kwela* spirit as jazz in-formation. African music generally appears jealous of its traditional formalisms and there is formalism in the popular urban dance musics which have drawn upon that variety of matter which the pianist Abdullah Ibrahim (Dollar Brand) referred to as 'the carnival music, the traditional colour music, the Malayan strains, the rural lament'. [18] Basic to the McGregor dream were memories of the melodic, antiphonal Xhosa music of his native Transkei, the communal spirit of which so deeply impressed him.

The brilliant sectional interplay in *Mra*, *The bride* and, perhaps especially, *Andromeda* is a marvel, full of colour, the strength of the trombones setting off the brittle dance of the trumpets and cornet and the coquettishness of the reeds. Vivacious piano music both shepherds movement and acts a quasi-sectional part. The possible hazards of rhythms often tethered to an on-beat instinct are usually overcome by a fine exuberance.

McGregor's 1960s encounter with free jazz – including a personal meeting with Albert Ayler – and his involving of British enthusiasts of the 'New Thing' may have been in conflict with his firm (and reasonable) conviction that improvisation is not the be-all and end-all of jazz. It is hard to hear the skilful indisciplines of Beckett and Skidmore as appropriate here. But what style of solo expression *would* have suited the situation? The question cannot have bothered McGregor overmuch – though an increasing emphasis on 'free' elements was later to alienate some of his original African members. The immoderately extended free-for-all of *Night poem* has fairly interesting phases of shifting intensity, but it is chiefly of interest because of the temporal and tonal reference continuously sounded by McGregor on a xylophone – probably the West African balaphon.

This African flirtation has little to do with that old ghostly courtship of jazz, based on suppositions of ancestral influence. Musically, the ancestry can only be partially proved anyway, and, as was shown in Volume 1, any bequests came from West Africa. For over a quarter of a century southern Africa has provided various attempts at cultural fusion. McGregor's may not even have been the most 'successful' of these, though it seems to have avoided the tediums of others' cultic, quasi-political excesses. In his recording of 1988 one hears some jazz nostalgia in both solos and scores, some degree of capitulation to the ancient wizards of Harlem. The *kwela* feeling persists chiefly in the brittle drum and *bala* echoes of the piano.

The Brotherhood's celebrations ought to remain available to a future jazz audience and the pianist's solo messages, recorded in Paris during 1977, may prove equally worthy of rediscovery (*Piano Song*, Musica [F] MUS3019, 3023 and *In His Good Time*, Ogun [E] OG521). E.T.

John Mayer–Joe Harriott

484 **Indo-Jazz Fusions**
Columbia (E) SCX6122, †Redial (E) 538 048–2

Shake Keane (tpt, fl h); Harriott (alt); Chris Taylor (fl); Pat Smythe (p); Diwan Motihar (sit); Chandrahas Paigankar (tem); Coleridge Goode (bs); Keshav Sathe (tab); Alan Ganley (d); Mayer (comp, vln, hpschd). London, 3–4 September 1966.
Partita · Multani · Gana · Acka raga · Subject

This closes our 'On the Frontiers' chapter, yet could almost as plausibly have figured in the 'Paths Not Followed' section of 'Alternatives to Freedom'. The kind of exoticism represented here offered a viable alternative to free jazz in the 1960s even though, for reasons that had little to do with music, free jazz received nearly all the attention. Some moves towards alliances between jazz and musics from outside Western culture were genuine and resulted in memorable work. But others were a matter of attitudinizing prompted by the same nonmusical considerations, without the slightest real convergence between different paths, be they African or whatever. [19] If the efforts of Mayer and Harriott produced music of permanent value, it was not just because jazz and Indian classical music both had long-standing traditions of improvisation. More constructive was a precise focus on the similarities and differences between their techniques and procedures.

There had been earlier, if unsustained, endeavours, such as Victor Feldman's now largely forgotten *Kashmir* and *Pakistan*, recorded in London in 1954 (Esquire [E] 327) after a period spent in India. More immediately related, however, was the work of Hari Har Rao and Don Ellis, of Ravi Shankar and Paul Horn, among others, and also relevant, though moving in another direction, were such compositions as Peter Maxwell Davies's *Stedman doubles*. Here one easily can detect something of the alap's slow unfolding, the developmental processes of a classical raga improvisation, and the tala-like rhythmic groupings. These are well integrated into Davies's personal idiom, although other non-European elements are present at one remove through the influence of Messiaen. The significance of such a piece here is that the materials of *Indo-Jazz Fusions*, perhaps most specifically in the *Partita*, are based chiefly on Indian resources – ragas, talas etc. – which are then shaped by Mayer's command of European compositional procedures and techniques, the resulting framework being filled with jazz and Indian improvisation. What we find, therefore, is not so much a fusion of styles as of methods, of modes of musical discourse, the balance of the synthesis favouring sometimes Indian values, as in *Multani*, sometimes Western, as in *Gana*.

Obviously this was not a chance collection of individuals assembled purely to make a record but an ensemble that worked regularly over a considerable period, performing in public and making other records. Hence a lot of earlier music, live and on disc, lay behind the achievement of these five pieces. Although the group was referred to as the Harriott–Mayer Double Quintet, because it brought together five Indian and five jazz players, the sequence of instruments is mixed in the above discographical heading because that is how they are usually heard in the music. This is, indeed, very much the work of a tightly knit ensemble, as is that, again almost completely forgotten, which Harriott recorded under his own name (**404**) with its emphasis on constant interaction. Perhaps his partnership with Mayer could be said to raise the same bid considerably higher, the frictions of the ten-piece ensemble's taut and kaleidoscopic internal responses being a vital agent in the extension of musical ideas. A theoretical disadvantage was the differing strengths of the instruments, but that was taken care of by discreet amplification at the group's public appearances, as it is here by a particularly sensitive recording balance.

Glowing colours and textures new to jazz arose from this richly vital music, but of greater importance was that the alliance between Indian improvisational and European compositional elements gave it an internal continuity all too often lacking in jazz. As Ronald Atkins wrote of *Multani* when this music was new: 'It has the indefinite, almost mystical, solemnity you sometimes get with Indian music, yet the tensile undercurrent is always felt.' [20] This is even more so with *Partita*, the longest piece, where, as the title suggests, the structural outline is baroque, and there are obvious affinities between baroque music and the 'endless passacaglia' of pre-Ornette Coleman jazz. At the time of this recording such parallels might even have seemed a little too apparent, those being the days of Jacques Loussier's ghastly Play Bach ensemble.

In effect *Partita* is a suite in three linked movements, the first of these using the Tilak-Shyam raga, which is introduced by Motihar's sitar, and the tala is Mattay–tal, with nine beats in the pattern 4.3.2. Once these are established, there comes the first of what Mayer called 'thematic fragments'. Fully written out, these crystallize some of the melodic and rhythmic potentialities of the ragas and talas, and provide concrete starting points for improvisation. Following solos from Harriott, Keane and Smythe, the second movement begins when Sathe changes from Mattay-tal to the four even beats of Kerwa-tal. Mayer's violin solo uses the Bahar raga, then for the third movement Ganley's bongos continue Kerwa-tal while Goode outlines the Bahar raga below. This is soon actually stated by the sitar and leads to a contrapuntal thematic fragment. Solos by Harriott and Keane are followed by another fragment, a variant of that of the first movement. After a sitar solo there is a remarkable collective improvisation by Keane, Harriott and Smythe, the Bahar raga still serving as the basis, and the end comes with the contrapuntal fragment, which slowly fades.

It could be argued that there is not enough jazz rhythm from the tabla and that Indian rhythmic patterns are heard on the jazz drums only where Mayer wrote them into the score. Yet here as in its public performances the ensemble generates its own kind of driving forward motion, and this was new. Though it is in many respects the most 'Indian' of these pieces, *Multani* is a good illustration of this. After Sathe and Ganley have set up two different rhythms there is an intriguing duet between violin and sitar based on the Multani raga. Then Motihar actually states the Multani notes and the tabla returns with Ek-tal – 12 beats – over which Ganley superimposes a 24-beat pattern. Taylor plays a solo based on the sitar and violin duet, leading to a thematic fragment that is followed by solos from nearly everybody, including a duet by tabla and jazz drums. The thematic fragment returns and the players fade out one by one until only Paigankar is left.

Simpler is *Gana*, which uses Jhap-tal, which has ten beats in a 2.3.2.3 sequence, and Yamani raga. It actually suggests faint echoes of Brubeck (**311**) and Harriott's playing carries a more than faint echo of Desmond (**366**)! *Acka raga*, from which Keane and Harriott are absent, is a free composition of Mayer's, employing no specific raga or tala, and is chiefly a vehicle for the sitar. Finally, *Subject* is the one piece not exclusively by Mayer, being founded on a Harriott composition whose theme is scored antiphonally between the Indian and jazz instruments. A contrasting theme by Mayer appears on the harpsichord and the sitar enters with the unusual Vilasakham raga; a rhythm of three against seven is established using Rupak-tal (seven beats as 3.2.2). A thematic fragment fades to a tambura drone which introduces a free-jazz collective improvisation on the Surat raga. The final result is somewhat reminiscent of Coleman, or more relevantly of Harriott's own abstract music, and his modal solo here is the best passage of relatively straight jazz on this record. Besides having great instrumental skill, he was an original, passionate and highly imaginative improviser. Nor was he the only one here. Keane, for instance, was a real lyricist.

A peak though it was, this record clearly pointed to further potentialities, and if there was a major aspect that Harriott and Mayer had neglected when the group broke up, it was what might be termed the manipulation of the music's time scale. The rate of the unfolding of events and the whole concept of form in Indian music is not of a sequence of closed – that is *en*closed – events or periods, but the forms, on both short and long time scales, are open, defining themselves as they unfold in a way that not only concentrates one's attention on each individual pitch and rhythm relationship with maximum intensity but also bends, or even suspends, perception of the 'passing' of time. The proper integration of this into the double quintet's output would presumably have changed everything, and would surely have taken many years. Long-term developments are very much the exception in jazz and it is regrettable that Mayer and Harriott were unable to pursue the matter further. It meant that yet again jazz missed an opportunity for growth.

M.H.

8

Fracturing into Postmodernism

With no major figure in sight of the sort who had providentially arrived in jazz to codify the diatonic, chromatic, free and rock-influenced eras, the task of moving the music forward passed to a diversity of individual contributors who refused to march in step with a somewhat self-righteous mainstream.

Arthur Blythe

485 **Illusions**
CBS (A) 36589

Blythe (alt); John Hicks (p); Fred Hopkins (bs); Steve McCall (d). New York City, 1980.
Miss Nancy · My son Ra · As of yet

Blythe (alt); James 'Blood' Ulmer (g); Abdul Wadud (cel); Bob Stewart (tu); Bobby Battle (d). New York City, 1980.
Bush baby · Illusions · Carespin' with Mamie

Blythe was 34 when he moved from the West Coast to New York in 1974, a relatively late age to attempt establishing a reputation in jazz. He had, however, been playing the alto saxophone since the age of nine and at 23 he had come under the guiding influence of Horace Tapscott, performing regularly in Tapscott's Los Angeles-based Pan-African Arkestra which rehearsed in UGMAA House near Figuroa. Although he had only recorded once with Tapscott in 1969, *The Giant is Awakening* (reissued as *West Coast Hot*, †Novus [A] ND83107), by the time he left for the Big Apple he was a well-rounded musician who had developed a highly personal voice on the alto. Lucid and passionate, he had that most valuable of possessions, an individual and instantly recognizable tone which had taken its early inspiration from the likes of Johnny Hodges, Earl Bostic and Tab Smith. When he arrived in New York he initially found work as a security guard for a porno parlour to raise money for his wife and three children to join him. He also found work with Charles Tyler, David Murray and Ted

Daniels before being invited to join Chico Hamilton's group. Hamilton considered him the finest saxophonist he had had since Eric Dolphy, and when Gil Evans heard Blythe he offered him several tours and recording opportunities with his band. With Evans he was placed in the role of a 'preaching' alto, initially alongside Dave Sanborn on numbers like *Priestess* (*Priestess*, Antilles [A] AN1010), and then in his own right. His firm, rich tone rising powerfully over the band on *Variations on Misery* from *Live at the Public Theater Vol. 1* (Blackhawk [A] BKH525), was equally identifiable within the ensemble: *Jelly rolls*, *Up from the skies*.

Blythe's reputation was further enhanced in New York's loft scene and the avant-garde cutting contests that were a feature of the 1970s, which in turn led to record dates with Chico Freeman, Azar Lawrence and Julius Hemphill. His first recordings under his own name, *The Grip* (India Navigation [A] IN1029) and *Metamorphosis* (India Navigation [A] IN1038), were two parts of a concert given at the Brook, New York City, in February 1977. Using an unorthodox line-up of alto, trumpet, cello, tuba, drums and percussion, Blythe shows startling authority. Firmly grounded in the blues and even during the occasional atonal detour, he managed to convey the impression of swing, a powerful duality in his playing that simultaneously referred to the jazz tradition as much as to the experimentalism of the 1960s and 1970s. By 1979 and after a further album under his own name, *Bush Baby* (Adelphi [A] 5008) with a pared down line-up of just alto, tuba and percussion, he landed a record deal with CBS. His first album, *Lennox Avenue Breakdown* (CBS [A] 83350), was made with James Newton, James 'Blood' Ulmer, Bob Stewart, Guillermo Franco, Cecil McBee and Jack DeJohnette. It was an impressive, if eclectic, major-label debut, from the joyous *Down San Diego way* to the inside/outside title track, prompting a fellow musician to observe that Blythe had the ability to play the entire history of jazz in one phrase. This album has become recognized as a minor, if neglected, classic, and Blythe found a perfect front-line partner in the then unknown flute virtuoso James Newton, who employed stunning microtonal pitch-bending techniques and multiphonics to give colour to his highly imaginative improvisations (see also **466**).

Blythe's arrival on the highly competitive New York scene coincided with a period when many musicians associated with free jazz were seeking areas of common ground with the jazz mainstream, seeking restraint after almost two decades of reactionary fervour that had ended by becoming reactionary tedium. Blythe emerged as a central figure during this period of realignment, an avant-traditionalist whose playing seemed at home in a variety of settings. Exemplifying this period of rapprochement, Blythe's 1979 *In the Tradition* (CBS [A] 84152), with an orthodox line-up of alto, piano, bass and drums, turned to compositions by Fats Waller, Duke Ellington and John Coltrane. Unfortunately the abysmal sound quality and the so-so playing of the pianist Stanley Cowell prevented it becoming universally acknowledged as one of the more important albums of the period. By 1980, however, Blythe had formed an association with the pianist John Hicks, an inspirational pianist in the McCoy Tyner mould.

Reflecting a desire to avoid being pigeonholed in one specific area of jazz, *Illusions* is split between Blythe's two main working bands, his 'In the Tradition' quartet and his 'guitar' band, loosely based on the line-up he had presented on *Metamorphosis* and *The Grip*, comprising guitar, cello, tuba and drums. On *Illusions* Blythe's inspiration is fired as much by Ulmer in the guitar band as by Hicks with his 'In the Tradition' quartet. The 'guitar' band relies as much on hypnotic vamps laid down by Stewart and the explicit rhythmic drive from Battle's drums as on Ulmer's and Wadud's fractured coloration. *Bush baby* uses a very square rhythmic pattern that reaches back to New Orleans marching bands as much as it looks sideways to rock. Blythe plays the theme with that ever-present bite in his tone over the funky vamp, his solo dynamic and authoritative, compensating for the static harmonic movement of the composition. Ulmer is clipped, phrases distorted by his wah-wah pedal, and is effective and economic. In contrast, the title track is like a demented bebop head inspired by the *Salt peanuts* riff and with Stewart doing his best to swing in a fast four; Ulmer is again concise and crafty while Blythe flies. Wadud uses all manner of tonal distortions from his instrument to produce a freaky, eerie backdrop. *Carespin' with Mamie* places him in a more central role, carrying the melody with Blythe. This produces an ensemble sound that is more typical of the group, which subsequently produced *Ellaborations* (Columbia [A] FC38163) 1982, *Light Blue* (CBS [A] 25937), an album of Monk compositions from 1983, and four tracks for 1981's *Blythe Spirit* (CBS [A] 85194). On these albums the group's sound seems inspired by the West Coast group of John Handy from the 1970s which combined violin and guitar with the alto of their leader to produce a distinctive tonal combination: *Monterey Jazz Festival* (CBS [E] BPG62678) and *The Second John Handy Album* (CBS [E] BPG 62881).

The Blythe–Hicks collaboration, however, provides the album's high spot and reveals a partnership of great potential, showing Air's rhythm section of Hopkins and McCall in a quite different light from their work with Henry Threadgill. The insistent octave leaps by unison bass and piano in the introduction of *Miss Nancy* precede Blythe's angular theme, stated with passion by the saxophonist, which leads into a swirling solo of breathtaking intensity. It is a 40-bar AABCA composition, whose alternating vamps and pre-written harmonies help give the improvisations a quite distinctive shape. As Blythe's solo reaches a climax, using steely yet full-toned high notes, it is difficult to imagine where theperformance is going to go other than to anticlimax. However, Hicks follows with a swirling solo of equal drama that sustains the creative heat for Blythe to return with a brief solo and take the number out. It is a memorable, almost awesome, performance and numbers among the most exciting moments of recorded jazz during late 1970s and early 1980s. The dirgelike introduction to *My son Ra* reveals Blythe's sumptuous tone at the lower end of his instrument; a composition built on a repeated bass *ostinato*, it provokes both saxophonist and pianist into introspective but heartfelt solos. *As of yet* enters at a very bright tempo, the theme contrasting short boplike phrases with longer sustained tones. A 24-bar ABC composition of three eight-bar sections, the quite distinct melodic fragments of each section form the basis of Blythe's improvisation as he respects the melodic characteristics of the A, B and C sections in his solo. Hicks in contrast plays off the changes, producing a propulsive, surging solo bristling with inner energy.

It seems unusual that Blythe did not exploit his creative empathy with Hicks and their potential for dynamic derring-do further. They continued their association on record with a couple of tracks on *Blythe Spirit* and 1986's *Da-Da* (CBS [A] 26888), but it was not until 1988 that he gave a whole album over to their ebullient partnership on the satisfying 'In the Tradition'-with-strings *Basic Blythe* (†CBS [A] 460677–2). By then the optimism that his signing with Columbia produced in 1979 had been long eclipsed by Wynton Marsalis, who joined the label in 1981 and soon achieved the breakthrough to public acclaim that had earlier been predicted for the saxophonist. It can only be a matter of speculation what effect Blythe might have had on the renascent 1980s if he had given more major-label exposure to his piano quartet rather than the guitar band. In any event, the Blythe–Hicks association was still going strong on 1993's *Retroflection* (†Enja [G] ENJ8046–2); older and wiser, perhaps Blythe sometimes gave a thought to what might have been. S.N.

Wynton Marsalis

486 Live at Blues Alley

CBS (A) 461109

Marsalis (tpt); Marcus Roberts (p); Robert Hurst (bs); Jeff Watts (d). Washington, D.C., 19–20 December 1986.

Knozz-Moe-King (4 versions) · Just friends · Juan · Cherokee · Delfeayo's dilemma · Chambers of Tain · Juan · Au privave · Do you know what it means to miss New Orleans? · Juan · Autumn leaves · Skain's domain · Much later

Since the canonization of jazz artists has traditionally been the main thrust of jazz writing, the 1980s demanded a figure of consensus to emerge around whom post-jazz-rock fusion (or post-1970s) developments could be constructed. In the past, major figures were been claimed to codify the diatonic, chromatic, harmonically free and rock-influenced eras of jazz.

Wynton Marsalis stepped into this continuum. A trumpet player with a penchant for sharp opinions and Cassius Clay I-am-the-greatest-isms – 'Everyone was saying jazz was dead, but when they heard me they knew I was taking care of business' – Marsalis by the mid-1980s had become the most visible figure in jazz. The first person to win simultaneous Grammies for a classical recording, *Trumpet Concertos* (CBS [A] IM-37846), a collection of trumpet concertos by Haydn, Hummel and Leopold Mozart, and a jazz recording, his quintet's recording of *Think of One* (CBS [A] 25354), in 1983, he was assigned the high-powered publicist Marilyn Laverty, whose clients included the rock star Bruce Springsteen, to build his name. Soon he was figuring in Sunday colour supplements, style magazines and dominating the musical press, a cynosure for a born-again jazz, a star whose artistry, unusually, came to play a secondary role to his youthful image. His success encouraged record companies to sign similar wunderkinder, creating a bandwagon effect that had the welcome effect of focusing media attention on jazz and raising its public profile. Adopting Marsalis's visual signature of sartorial elegance and using the adopted voices of some of jazz's older and sometimes posthumous heroes, this new neoconservative movement represented a major area of recording activity in jazz during the 1980s and 1990s.

The product the neoconservatives offered can be stated simply – a return to the harmonic and melodic values of the hard-bop and post-bop improvisers of the 1950s and early 1960s, with special interest reserved for the Miles Davis acoustic quintet of the 1960s. However, in Marsalis's case, Ellington and Armstrong also became fascinations. Clearly, this was a watershed of some kind. It was an attack on jazz for growing old – the neoconservatives were, after all, youthful – and it was an attack on jazz for having lost touch with its audience in the case of free jazz and for losing touch with the acoustic 'tradition' in the case of jazz-rock fusion. In essence neoconservatism presented a return to internalist principals of unity and coherence or a post-romantic concept of thematic and organic unity.

From *Wynton Marsalis* (CBS [A] 85404), his first album as a leader, made while he was still a member of Art Blakey's Jazz Messengers in 1982, Marsalis progressed with an almost icy determination to live up to the extravagant praise heaped upon him. While his integrity and dedication to the jazz idiom were never in doubt, *Think of One* from 1983, *Hot House Flowers* (CBS [A] 26145) from 1984 and *Black Codes (From the Underground)* (CBS [A] 26686) from 1985 were perhaps too scrupulous at the expense of emotion and for some reason unable to catch the kind of sparkle and *joie de vivre* he demonstrated during his solo on *Wilpan's walk* from Chico Freeman's *Destiny's Dance* (Contemporary [A] 14008). Throughout this early period, Marsalis's direction was inspired by areas of music explored by the Miles Davis quintet of the 1960s with Wayne Shorter, Herbie Hancock, Ron Carter and Tony Williams; indeed, on

Wynton Marsalis he recorded *RJ*, a Carter composition that appeared on Davis's 1965 album *E.S.P.* (CBS [A] 62577). This first Marsalis group reached an astonishing fluency incorporating metric and rhythmic shifts with an ease that passed over the heads of many in their audiences and most of the critics. They also utilized the 'time, no changes' style that the Davis group had brought to such perfection as a basis for improvisation, compositions whose function was to set tempo, key and often mood as well, leaving the choice of chord changes to the spontaneous instincts of the improviser.

In March 1985, this talented young group, whose succeeding albums always managed to suggest their best album was just around the corner, broke up without actually delivering on their great promise. Three months later Marsalis formed a new group with the young piano virtuoso Marcus Roberts, retaining only Hurst and Watts from his former group. All were still in their mid-to-early twenties. Their first album *J Mood* (CBS [A] 57068) from December 1985 was another dazzling, albeit austere affair; the 27-bar *Skain's domain*, for example, was disposed of with almost clinical precision. A year later they recorded *Live at Blues Alley* and at last Marsalis appeared to have reconciled his virtuosity with an altogether more exuberant vision that did not smack of the intricate, almost painstaking search for perfection of his earlier work. These live performances reveal Marsalis inclined to chance his arm by playing at the limit of his imagination and technique, something that had previously not occurred to the degree he exhibits here, and it is this feeling of risk-taking that adds a humanizing factor that had been missing from much of his previous work. Perhaps more importantly, he used the past as inspiration rather than succour, reaching within himself and exposing more of the inner man than any of his previous albums or to 1999 at least, his subsequent recordings.

From the album *J Mood* came the compositions *Much later* and an exciting *Skain's domain*, and from the last quintet album, *Black Codes*, came *Delfeayo's dilemma* and *Chambers of Tain*, which now surged with spontaneity, excitement and sophisticated rhythmic interaction. Marsalis, deeply conscious of his position in a trumpet lineage that could be traced back to King Oliver and Buddy Bolden, strove to keep his playing free from cliché or stylistic precedent. 'I know what my position in jazz is,' he once asserted. 'All the great players have told me, Art Blakey told me, Dizzy Gillespie told me and I know when I spoke to Miles Davis.' [1] He was well aware that a familiar lick or a phrase rather too closely associated with a Dizzy Gillespie, a Fats Navarro, a Clifford Brown or a Freddie Hubbard would, under the intense media spotlight he attracted, immediately brand him a 'copyist', something he strove to avoid. And if this meant, on occasion, a somewhat otherworldly lyricism, at least it was Wynton Marsalis.

During the several versions of *Knozz-Moe-King*, an open-ended 'time, no changes' piece originally recorded on the album *Think of One*, he splashes motifs subservient to rhythmic rather than melodic logic like arabesques against the stirring interaction of Roberts, Hurst and Watts. And if this brief foray into abstract idealism did not make for solos of great structural or melodic unity, his rhythmic and tonal intensity did have a gusto that was quite compelling; '*Knozz-Moe-King*, you can't get any freer than that in terms of the structure of the music,' he said in 1991. 'It's the most liberated I've ever been.' [2]

In contrast, *Cherokee* and *Autumn leaves*, both recorded earlier in the year on *Marsalis Standard Time* Vol. 1 (†CBS/Sony [A] 4687132), show great poise and assurance in the way he orders his thoughts, even if a rather angular melodic construction sounds as if he were trying to invent blues clichés for the end of the 21st century. In contrast, *Just friends* was surprisingly conservative, played with a cup mute throughout, which had the effect of emotionally distancing him from his material. However, on *Do you know what it means to miss New Orleans?*, originally written for Billie Holiday and Louis Armstrong for the 1946 film *New Orleans*, a melodrama set in 1917 at the time Storyville was closed down, he gave notice that he was about to turn his back on the conspicuous advances his music had made, and begin a long route march into the past to confront and explore the methodology of early New Orleans jazz. It is interesting to note that Roberts, perhaps the finest young player to emerge from the Marsalis orbit and whose playing throughout *Live at Blues Alley* was every bit as exciting, contemporary and stimulating as that of his leader, would also retreat into the past as he developed his own career on the Novus/BMG label. By his sixth album, *If I Could Be with You* (†Novus [A] 012141 63149 2), he was confronting the methods of the Harlem stride pianists of the 1920s on *Carolina shout*, and ragtime with Scott Joplin's *Maple leaf rag*.

Ultimately, neoconservatism had the effect of draining a potentially subversive music of its distinctive energy and truth by framing it within tried and tested methods of articulation and presentation. Steeped in certainties which failed to acknowledge that uncertainty was a precondition for adventure, the listener was denied the right of surprise. While the repossession of a comfortably accessible mainstream marked its musicians as different among their own generation, most of whom were into other music such as pop, soul, rock, hip-hop and rap, in the context of jazz as a whole it appeared as narrow elitism that re-encapsulated a surprisingly circumscribed range of sounds, styles and attitudes. History has shown that any return to a past 'tradition', whether it be in art, literature, music or life, usually limits horizons rather than extends them. It also brings the risk of a totalitarianism, a regime of semantics, definitions and boundaries. Movements define themselves by that which they exclude, thus the outsiders – the free-jazzers, the jazz-rockers and non-tradition-based experimenters – became exponents of 'non-jazz'.

As a cultural symbol, Marsalis represented stability in a decentered pastiche of postmodernism. In an age of increasing corporate control over cultural production, neoconservatism, like jazz-rock fusion in the 1970s, was given considerable momentum by the advertising and promotional budgets of major recording companies. This had the effect of artificially recentring the growth of a significant area of jazz around virtuosic recapitulation, a quantifiable, marketable and easily understood product. After all, marketing strategies as much as canon formation gather around unified concepts. The result was a pall of conformity that descended over jazz in the late 1980s and 1990s as a succession of young, fleet-fingered improvisers were touted by their record companies, often at the expense of middle-aged masters and experimental jazz. Hitherto, jazz had historically been expressed as an evolving whole, a work in progress, its real potential expressed as a flight *from* the status quo. The neoconservative's return to a tradition-centred synthesis of earlier styles was, of course, precisely the reverse of this. It was a flight *back to* the status quo, which Marsalis was careful to present in the broader context as a part of America's cultural heritage. In many ways he became a leading figure in elevating the perception of jazz as an art music, which, as Scott DeVeaux has pointed out, was 'indigenous to black culture and reflecting black values [and] following the same pattern of institutionalization in conservatories and repertory groups and demanding of its musicians an empathetic response to aesthetic sensibilities of the past'. [3]

In 1987, Marsalis began a musical odyssey back to New Orleans, the city of his birth. It was a journey that also took in the music of Duke Ellington ('Ellington's band, directly influenced by New Orleans jazz, Barney Bigard, pure New Orleans,' he proclaimed [4]). He subsequently rationalized his musical vision, a vision that seemed more secure in the past than the future, by claiming that since jazz was barely 100 years old, it was, compared to European music, modern and thus what he was playing, by extrapolation, was also modern. As the 1990s progressed it became clear that as long as he stayed so close to the shore, he would be discovering no new horizons. It left *Live at Blues Alley* as a career highlight and one of the major achievements of the young neoconservatives during the renascent 1980s. S.N.

Quest

487 **Quest**

Palo Alto Records (A) PA8061

David Liebman (sop, alt fl); Richie Beirach (p); George Mraz (bs); Al Foster (d). New York City, 28–9 December 1981.

Dr Jekyll and Mr Hyde · *Wisteria* · *Softly as in a morning sunrise* · *Elm* · *Napanoch* · *Lonely woman*

Liebman was the last major saxophonist to appear with Miles Davis before the trumpeter wound up his band in 1975 through illness, drug addiction and alcoholism. He had first played with Davis on the album *On the Corner* (†Columbia [A] 4743712) in August 1972 while still a member of the Elvin Jones group. The following month he recorded *Elvin Jones: Live at the Lighthouse* Vols. 1 and 2 (†Blue Note [A] CDP7 84447–2 and 84448–2) alongside his fellow tenor saxophonist Steve Grossman, one of the first recordings to document the new wave of saxophone players moulded in the John Coltrane tradition who were establishing his vocabulary as a standard in much the same way as musicians who had earlier followed in the wake of Charlie Parker. The year 1972 also saw Liebman's debut as a leader on records with the Open Sky Trio which had Frank Tusa on bass and Bobby Moses on drums. *Open Sky* (PM [A] PMR001) and *Spirit in the Sky* (PM [A] PMR003), recorded for Gene Perla's PM label from 1973, show a more considered, rounded musician than the fire-breathing tenor saxophonist on *Live at the Lighthouse.* On saxophones and flutes, Liebman and his group explored several idioms including the free music of Coltrane, the free bop of Ornette Coleman, world music and rock-oriented pieces. In January 1973 Liebman was invited to join Davis's ensemble on a full-time basis, when the trumpeter reformed his band after a lay-off following a car crash. Liebman subsequently appeared on *Get Up with It* (†Columbia [F] 485256) from 1973–4, *Miles Davis en Concert Olympia 11 July 1973* (†Europe 1 [F] 710460) and *Dark Magus* (†Columbia/Legacy [A] C2K65137) from March 1974. In June 1974 Liebman left Davis after a tour of Brazil. 'Playing with Miles gave me worldwide exposure and entry into the arena where one could have a solo career, groups and a recording contract,' he said later. 'Musically, I was as ready as I could be.' [5]

The previous year Liebman had recorded an album with a group he called Lookout Farm and the release of the eponymously titled album was timed to coincide with the group's debut at the Village Vanguard on 6 June 1974. *Lookout Farm* (ECM [G] 1039) included a core group of Richie Beirach on keyboards, Frank Tusa on bass and Jeff Williams on drums, with several guest musicians, including John Abercrombie on guitar and Badal Roy on tabalas, and was one of the better, if largely forgotten, albums from the 1970s. Liebman immediately impressed with his inclusive world-music viewpoint, the group's performances attracting high praise: 'A music unusually potent in its spirituality and intensity and in its textural and rhythmic design.' [6] Although subsequent albums by the group, *Drum Ode* (ECM [G] 1046) and *Sweet Hands* (Horizon [A] SP702), did not quite measure up to their debut album, they were nevertheless worthy representations of an ensemble that had arrived at an individual identity while also marking the beginning of a long association between Liebman and the pianist Richie Beirach.

Liebman and Beirach subsequently recorded two albums of duets, *Forgotten Fantasies* (Horizon [A] SP709) 1975 and *Omerta* (Trio [J] PAP141) 1978, which were notable as much for their mutual empathy as their technical fluency. This understanding provided a solid foundation for a larger ensemble with the addition of the trumpeter Randy Brecker, the bassist Tusa and the drummer Al Foster – with whom Liebman had worked while with Davis. *Pendulum* (Artists House [A] AH8) was recorded live at the Village Vanguard in February 1978 and consists of just three numbers, the title track by Beirach taking up side one, and *Picadilly Lilly* (sic), a Liebman original, and Wayne Shorter's modified blues in 6/8, *Footprints*, on side two. The idiom is straight-ahead post-bop, the climate is modal, *Pendulum* an extended workout on an F-sharp pedal which tests the players harmonic ingenuity by forcing them to freely superimpose their own harmonic sequences over the pedal point to give their improvisation a sense of direction. Although subsequently Liebman decided to form a guitar-based group with John Scofield, *Pendulum* marked the origins of the group Quest, a quartet he assembled in 1981.

Apart from the absence of Brecker, the only other change from the *Pendulum* line-up was the accomplished bass virtuoso George Mraz in for Tusa. *Napanoch*, a Liebman original, is taken at a very bright tempo [7] that in itself presents a challenge to the improviser. It is a binary AB tune of two 16-bar sections; the A section had previously been recorded on *Sweet Hands*, with Liebman on tenor, before his decision to concentrate exclusively on the soprano saxophone. This move was in part inspired by a desire to rethink his approach to improvisation away from Coltrane's dominating sound and influence. Liebman did not return to the larger B-flat instrument until 1997. After a 16-bar introduction by Beirach, the A section is essentially four repeats of an alternately resolving four-bar phrase, while the B section is another four-bar phrase repeated four times, the third and fourth times an octave lower with the addition of passing tones. Solos are over the F-sharp tonality of the A section (the B section is not used for improvisation), and Liebman immediately impresses with the rhythmic momentum he generates and the number and frequency of ideas and motifs that swirl through his playing. He utilizes the whole range of his instrument, introducing rhythmic variation into his line with unusual groupings of notes and varying his attack by playing either behind or in front of the ground beat. His angular lyricism is highlighted by a vocal tone that could sometimes sound like a cry or a wail reminiscent of Middle Eastern music. In combination with his hard swinging lines and intricate pattern building is a sophisticated harmonic sense that was not allowed to overwhelm the melodic stance of his improvisation. Beirach responds supportively to Liebman's line, never leading in his comping but creating a responsive context for the soloist to flourish. His own solo quickly dispenses with the explicit pulse of the rhythm section, and becomes a *colla parte* statement with colouring from Foster. Beirach's ruminations are in complete contrast to the headlong urgency of Liebman's solo, but as the pianist reaches a climax with chord piled upon chord, the saxophonist makes his re-entry with one of his vocalized wails that lead into a reprise of the head.

Ornette Coleman's *Lonely woman* is played quite differently from the original (**400**). Liebman's fascination with Third World music inspired his mythic approach to the song, which he plays on alto flute. Outlining the main melody of the piece, omitting the bridge, there is no explicit pulse and his haunting approach to the melody is interpreted in a very free *colla voce* style, the melody in of itself inspiring his improvisation, extending and developing the theme in a way that seems to grow organically out of the original. Beirach's composition *Elm*, dedicated to the late Polish violinist Zbigiew Seifert, is introduced by the pianist with an introspective interlude that takes its inspiration from Keith Jarrett's solo explorations where the natural acoustic resonance of the instrument adds a brooding air of tranquil introspection. Beirach then introduces the melody *a tempo*, shaded and shadowed by Mraz and Foster. The 16-bar theme is reiterated by Beirach and Liebman and unison, before Beirach solos in requiemlike mood. Mraz's solo reveals a fluent lyricism before Liebman enters with melodic motifs in keeping with the emotions previously expressed but gradually reveals more anguished tensions with shrieks and sighs from his instrument. The melody returns and moves into the coda, with Mraz on bowed bass joining Liebman in a final melody statement that in its move to angular resolution is elided to 15 bars.

Dr Jekyll and Mr Hyde is the drummer Al Foster's portrait of Miles Davis, with a repeated four-bar phrase against an insistent riff that gives way to Beirach, who begins his solo free from pulse and moulds seemingly abstract phrases into a cogent whole as the pulse finds its expression in a Latin-like rhythm quite removed from that used during the exposition of the theme. Liebman, too, begins his solo freely and as the pulse begins to be felt it re-emerges in the bright, Latinesque feel that Beirach revealed. In fact, the fluid, expansive handling of time by Beirach, Mraz and Foster is a consistent delight of the album. *Wisteria* is a ballad in ¾ composed by Mraz, which features his post–Scott LaFaro solo style. The exuberant *Softly as in a morning sunrise*, highly chromaticized – most notably in the middle eight – becomes a vehicle that displays Liebman and Beirach's fluency within the post-bop idiom, their playing maintaining the fundamental key structure without specific references to the changes for long periods during their solos.

One of the most accomplished musicians of his generation, Liebman consistently recorded for a variety of small labels during the 1980s and 1990s. The high standards he maintained is a testament to his musicianship as he forged a highly individual voice on soprano saxophone. Although recognition was not forthcoming, he revealed himself as one of the great saxophonists in jazz. As an aside, *Tribute to John Coltrane* (†King [J] K32Y 6212), recorded at the tenth 'Live Under the Sky' concert on 26 July 1987 in Japan, pitted Liebman against Wayne Shorter in a head-to-head on *Mr P. C.*, a minor blues associated with Coltrane. This is an old-fashioned gladiator's duel, each player lifting the other to heights of invention spurred on by an enthusiastic crowd and a superb rhythm section of Beirach, Eddie Gomez on bass and Jack DeJohnette on drums. While we will never hear the duels between say, a Coleman Hawkins and a Lester Young which are the stuff of jazz legend, we do have Shorter and Liebman fighting it out for the victor's spoils. Honours are shared evenly and while the old-fashioned 'cutting contests' as a measure of a player's stature are usually discredited in these politically correct times, this document does give us cause to pause and reflect for a moment on how such an accomplished musician as Liebman succeeded in eluding recognition. S.N.

Steps Ahead

488 Steps Ahead

Elecktra Musician (A) 96–0168–1

Michael Brecker (ten); Eliane Elias (p); Eddie Gomez (bs); Peter Erskine (d); Mike Mainieri (vib). New York City, 1983.

Pools · *Islands* · *Loxodrome* · *Both sides of the coin* · *Skyward bound* · *Northern cross* · *Trio (An improvisation)*

Originally known as Steps, this band was convened in 1979 with Don Grolnick at the piano and Steve Gadd on drums alongside Brecker, Mainieri and Gomez. Assembled for a run of dates at Seventh Avenue South, the Manhattan jazz club owned by Michael and Randy Brecker, all the participants had known each other since the late 1960s. Brecker and Grolnick had played together in a memorable jazz-rock group called Dreams, and in turn had frequently jammed with Mainieri and Gadd at the all-night jam sessions held at Gnu Music, Mainieri's music-publishing offices, from where emerged the White Elephant Band, a rehearsal big band that grappled with combining jazz and rock. Gomez, as a member of the Bill Evans trio, had been known to all the musicians since 1968. From the start Steps was a band formed by good friends for the shared pleasure of hearing each other play. Their easy rapport readily communicated and although they never advertised their gigs, they soon developed something of a following. When two Japanese recording executives heard them they were invited to Japan to perform and record. When they played their own original compositions, most notably by Grolnick and Mainieri, something of an informal jam-session feel permeated their music, prompting Mainieri to dub their music 'contemporary bebop'. Their first album, *Step by Step* (Better Days [J] YF 7020-N), was recorded on 8–10 December 1980 and was followed by a 2-LP set, *Smokin' in the Pit* (Better Days [J] YB 7010/7011-ND), recorded live at Roppongi Pit Inn, Tokyo, on 14–16 December 1980.

What is immediately apparent is the compelling rhythmic drive generated by Gadd and Gomez, with sympathetic comping from Grolnick and Mainieri, whose discretion prevented them from treading on each other's toes. The stand-out soloist was Brecker, whose ability to build tension and release and manipulate a rising line to an impressive climax made him the focal point of these albums. Yet when the band returned to New York, the participants, all in-demand studio musicians, went their separate ways. A further call from Japan to tour and record brought the band back together, but prior commitments ruled out Gadd, who was replaced by Erskine. The resulting album, *Paradox* (Better Days [J] YF 7044-N), recorded live at Seventh Avenue South in September 1981, revealed a more scrupulous attention to articulation and ensemble dynamics as the band collectively worked towards establishing an identity of its own, rather than the looser, more fluid feel of the earlier albums. However, *Take a walk* gave vent to their more freewheeling sensibilities with Brecker raising the temperature with a solo that linked passion, harmonic adventure and technique to telling effect.

During their subsequent tour of Japan the band decided to stay together but the pressures of touring prompted the departure of Brecker's close friend Don Grolnick in 1982, to be replaced by the Brazilian pianist Eliane Elias. [8] At around this time the band secured a US recording contract, but on discovering that a bar band in the South had registered the name Steps, they were forced to change their name to Steps Ahead. Their eponymously titled album was quickly dubbed 'the new acoustic fusion', the 'always new' of music marketing concealing the fact that the band had now developed a collective identity quite different from any other group in jazz. *Pools*, a Grolnick composition, captures the elegant poise the group succeeded in projecting. [9] The form uses a simple AAB structure, with the A sections 20 bars and the B section 14 bars. The initial exposition of the theme is given to Gomez, whose virtuoso lyricism belies the unusual step of bass carrying the melody, a minimalistic, fragmented theme in the minor against sustained chords from piano and vibes. The drums carry the rhythm, a relaxed, yet funky beat that conceals a surprisingly brisk tempo. [10] When the A section is repeated, Brecker joins Gomez in unison, but for the B section their roles diverge with Brecker carrying the melody and Gomez moving between a melodic role and simple, yet precise rhythmic counterpoint that is part of the tune's arrangement. The chorus is repeated, albeit this time with Brecker and Gomez now playing both A sections in unison.

For solos, the scheme departs from the AAB structure, modulating to a repeated four-bar vamp. Brecker, Gomez, Mainieri and Brecker follow in sequence and it is their clarity, technical fluency and lyrical construction that capture our attention. Both Brecker and Mainieri, in their own individual ways, provide excellent examples of clear, yet complex responses to playing over a simple harmonic structure. Both are masters of a contemporary post-bop vocabulary that makes use of substitutions, tritone substitution, side-slipping, motivic development, angular intervallic lines, chromatic runs, and polyrhythmic phrases that are all deployed with compositional care within the overall shape of their solos. Brecker, in particular, succeeds in displaying great structural unity while at the same time giving the impression he is flying by the seat of his pants. Despite the complexity of his execution, the ordering of his ideas makes ultimate destiny of the solo never appear in doubt.

These solos are acted out against suspended chord riffs from piano and vibes which provide space for Gomez and Erskine freely to interact in increasing rhythmic complexity echoing the rising intensity of the soloists as they work towards a climax – indeed, at some points Erskine moves from mere accompaniment to play a prominent role in dialogue with the soloist, adding significantly to the unfolding drama of the moment. Both Brecker and Mainieri execute uncommon groupings of notes in clusters of five, seven and even nine notes that lend a feeling of rhythmic freedom to their playing, sound-sheet arpeggiated figures with their five-over-four, seven-over-four and nine-over-four feel adding polyrhythmic contrast within the motion of their solos.

A significant aspect of the group's rhythmic approach is their refusal to comply with the traditional jazz swing feel; while *Pools* is in 4/4 they do not adhere to the rhythmic plan that had served jazz since Jelly Roll Morton's day; the dotted quaver and semiquaver [11] followed by a crotchet with the bass playing four beats to the bar and the drummer accenting the second and the fourth beats that had been retained, with modifications, through the bop and hard-bop eras but by the 1980s (and certainly the 1990s) had come to sound very tired and, indeed, old hat. In short, it was a rhythmic scheme that spoke louder to audiences familiar with older eras of jazz than to contemporary ears. Steps Ahead, whose members had thorough-going backgrounds in straight-ahead jazz – Mainieri was a musical director for Buddy Rich, Brecker had played with Horace Silver, Gomez served a long tenure as Bill Evans's bassist of choice and Erskine had come up through the bands of Stan Kenton and Maynard Ferguson – saw no allegiance to the old-fashioned rhythmic scheme. They had done it before, it no longer presented a challenge. It was time to move on.

In the 1960s Wayne Shorter had been instrumental in reversing the burden of complexity between front line and rhythm section within the Miles Davis quintet of 1965–8, giving the front line slow-moving parts that did not have bridges and complex turnarounds, so posing a drastic alternative to the harmonically complex construction of bebop-influenced numbers. It gave the rhythm section, freed from providing a metronomic 'jazz-swing' pulse, latitude to create rhythmic interest that had hitherto been the province of the front line. Steps Ahead were a part of this continuum, and only on the Gomez composition *Loxodrome* was a 'jazz-swing' pulse employed.

While *Loxodrome* may submit to rhythmic convention, structurally it presents an advanced contemporary vehicle for improvisation. Thirty-five bars in length, it presents six bars of pre-written melody, followed by eight bars of improvisation over a pedal point, [12] six bars of melody and another eight bars of improvisation, again over a pedal point, which is finally resolved by seven bars of pre-written melody. The intention is to allow the improviser to elaborate on the pre-written theme, so blurring the disjunction between the written and the improvised. The emphasis is on a slow-moving melody line with a predominance of long note values, and of the three written episodes, none is repeated during the solos, which are based on the harmonic structure of the 35-bar form retaining the two episodes of pedal-point harmony.

The introduction is actually a rubato exposition of the tune played by Brecker, with the length of the two 'open' sections left to the discretion of the improviser and in this initial rendering, Gomez marks each passing chord change with a single or embellished notes. However, on the repeat, *a tempo*, Gomez plays a walking bass line and the tune's 35-bar structure is adhered to with Brecker now 'filling' the open eight-bar sections. Miss Elias, confident and poised, is followed by Gomez, whose startling articulation was a feature of the Bill Evans trio (1966–77). He is followed by Brecker, whose style owes much to the strong influence of John Coltrane but who had by now evolved a distinct voice of his own. Building and extending on Coltrane's harmonic methods, Brecker evolved a fluent chromaticism and strong lyrical drive that by the 1980s elevated him into the most influential saxophonist since his alma mater. On the other tracks, Steps Ahead employ a variety of rhythmic approaches, such as the Latin-inspired rhythms of *Northern cross* and *Both sides of the coin*. The latter composition, written by Brecker, also poses a number of interesting challenges for the improviser.

Here, the tempo is bright [13] and the main subject includes several wide intervallic leaps characteristic of bop compositions with a contrasting secondary subject that effectively produces a *rondo* form. Thus after an eight-bar introduction – the first appearance of theme A – we have theme A and its answering theme B, where A is eight bars and B is 14 bars. This binary AB section is repeated and leads into a secondary binary subject CD, comprising two eight-bar sections, which are also repeated. The C section, with its long note values, is contrasted by the broken phrases of D. This is followed by a return of the AB section and a reiteration of A before leading into the solo. Thus a *rondo* scheme emerges as:

Intro 8 bars (theme A) + (A + B) + (A + B) + (C + D) +
(C + D) + (A + B) + A to solo

This produces a pleasing symmetry of contrasting, but complementary, sections that are given luminosity by the imaginative drumming of Erskine. Brecker's solo, however, is taken on an entirely different form and harmonic sequence to the *rondo* form above. He uses a 16-bar E section played with a half-time feel which is repeated, followed by a 16-bar F section *a tempo*, but using a samba rhythm. Brecker takes three choruses over this new EEF form before returning to the coda, CD repeated once, before the A theme returns to underline its dominance over the subsidiary C and D themes – and, tacitly, the B theme as well:

C + D + C + D + A (repeated till fade)

In their diligent application to sophisticated ad hoc song-forms, Steps Ahead offered something fresh in the early 1980s. Their musical intention was mediated by a consistency of approach, drawing on Shorter's writing style for the Davis 1965–8 quintet, rhythms that moved beyond the 'jazz-swing' feel that took account of the best rhythmic innovations within jazz-rock and the increased harmonic sophistication brought to jazz by Coltrane, Evans, Tyner and Brecker himself. *Islands*, *Skyward bound* and the spontaneous interaction of *Trio* equally suggest a group that seemed to have established itself as a one-of-its-kind ensemble whose members in realizing their collective potential, also showed great promise for the future. Such challenging compositional forms seemed beyond the grasp of most critics, however, Mainieri wearily observing: 'They just couldn't work out what we were doing; one critic said, "It would be great to hear them play the blues, that would help." But I've played the blues for 30 years – who wants to keep playing the blues? We were trying to come up with new music.' [14] S.N.

Jack DeJohnette

489 Album Album
†ECM (G) 823 467–2

DeJohnette (d, p); John Purcell (alt, sop); David Murray (ten); Howard Johnson (tu, bs); Rufus Reid (bs, el bs). New York City, June 1984.
Ahmad the terrible · *Monk's mood* · *Festival* · *New Orleans strut* · *Third World anthem* · *Zoot suite*

DeJohnette's continually evolving Special Edition was one of the most important ensembles of the early 1980s. Their albums, from 1979's *Special Edition* (ECM [G] 1152) to 1987's *Irresistible Forces* (MCA Impulse [A] MCA5992), were a commentary on jazz away from the acoustic mainstream. Although one of the music's finest drummers,

DeJohnette created an ensemble that relied as much on his compositional, organizational and arranging skills as it did on the musicians he featured. The group's first album from 1979 included David Murray and Arthur Blythe, its second and third, from 1980 and 1981, Chico Freeman and John Purcell, the looser sensibilities of both these ensembles reflecting the late-1970s realignment of the avant-garde with the hard-bop and post-bop mainstream. DeJohnette's sure handling of form and content made possible a free-flowing rapprochement of compositional design and improvisational freedom that perfectly suited Murray and Blythe, former loft-scene combatives, while Freeman, who emerged from the AACM, and Purcell, a thoroughly skilled graduate of Manhattan School of Music, reflected a more serene approach to improvisation.

With *Album Album*, the fourth from Special Edition, DeJohnette exerted tighter compositional control with deft, effective writing for his ensemble that rejecting open-ended blowing and focused on creating a balance between ensemble ingenuity and improvisational wisdom. 'An audience's attention isn't what it was when Coltrane was playing,' DeJohnette said, reflecting on 1980s channel zapping and sound-bite politicians. 'Now we're almost back to . . . two- and three-minute cuts. It makes you concentrate, consolidate yourself.' [15] Firmly rooted within the jazz tradition, he paid tribute to the Chicago pianist Ahmad Jamal, who had so inspired him as a youngster along with Israel Crosby and Vernell Fournier, with his original composition *Ahmad the terrible*. [16] The theme comprises a loping out-of-tempo A passage, conducted by Johnette, followed by three repeated eight-bar B sections in succession, a reprise of the A section plus four-bar tag; Purcell captures the mood of reverence with a perfectly judged soprano solo before DeJohnette's impressive piano interlude, added by multitracking afterwards. A piano graduate from the American Conservatory of Music, DeJohnette demonstrated a sound technique on the instrument and his solo is a reminder that the rising line still remains the most effective way of building emotional tension in jazz. In 1985 he would record *The Jack DeJohnette Piano Album* (Landmark [A] LLP11504), which somewhat undeservedly suffered critical indifference. However, it stands up well today, particularly in the light of a subsequent avalanche of albums from younger musicians whose fashionable currency ensured disproportionate praise. Murray follows, adding to the soaring feeling by reaching for Ayleresque notes in the upper reaches of his instrument before the theme returns to complete one of the more impressive performances of the 1980s.

The only title not arranged and composed by DeJohnette is *Monk's mood*, arranged by Johnson. It is reminiscent of *Pastel rhapsody* and *Ebony* on previous Special Edition albums. [17] Here the band refract Ellington through the World Saxophone Quartet (**390**), a tone poem with both DeJohnette, on sustaining electronic keyboards, and Reid's arco and pizzicato bass, layered into the close sax harmonies to produce a full, resonant section sound with wonderful detail in the movement of the inner voicings. The theme and written variations are initially played *a cappella*, but as Reid and DeJohnette, now on drums, move into a time-keeping role, the written gives way to the improvised as Johnson's baritone sax emerges before a recapitulation of theme and variations, marking this as much an ensemble feature as a solo vehicle that is played with relish and affection by the ensemble, who thoroughly subordinate themselves to the overall architecture of the music.

Festival emerges as a joyful romp in cut time and is an interesting juxtaposition of four-bar and two-bar phrases:

A (four bars) + A^1 + A^2 + A^3 + (1 bar drums) + B (two bars) +
C (two bars) + C + C + C + D (two bars) + D + D + D +
A (four bars) + A^2 + A^3 + (4 bars drums) + B (two bars) +
C (two bars) + C + C^1 + C^2 + (two-bar C vamp for 8 bars) to
collective improvisation
(Note: last eight bars of C vamp collective improvisation)

Although the overall scheme looks somewhat congested, it flows simply and seamlessly into its climax, a collective improvisation by the ensemble that looks back to the loose polyphony of early New Orleans jazz as much as to the free collective improvisations of the 1960s and 1970s, albeit now organized around specific rhythmic and tonal centres of the two-bar vamp set up during the last eight bars of the final C section. Perhaps one of the most overlooked byproducts of the free-jazz movement was that it broke, even more than modal compositions, the reliance of jazz on the structural hegemony of the American popular song. Here, clearly, DeJohnette feels no allegiance to the typical ternary and binary forms that had for so long underpinned jazz composition. He contrasts sections of simple chantlike variations over four bars (the A sections) against two-bar phrases (the C and D sections), linking them, except on one occasion, with the transitional B section preceded by a drum break. As the rhythmic undertow gathers in intensity against the insistent riffing, the 'festival' begins as the 'chants' give way to individual voices in celebration – the collective improvisation. Just as the Broadway composers worked with the requirements of a lyricist in mind, here the jazz composer concerns himself with creating a context for his improvisers; the contrast could not be more pronounced.

New Orleans strut captures the essence of Delta City's music scene, simultaneously touching base with marching bands and the Neville Brothers with its funky push-me-pull-you beat of deceptive complexity yet exciting vitality. It is a 32-bar ABAB composition with a wealth of detail in the exposition, with weaving, swirling contrapuntal figures from DeJohnette's electronic keyboards and Johnson's baritone. Purcell enters with a tense, crackling solo that preaches in Arthur Blythe's powerful style, followed by the dervishlike intensity of Murray, who dwells as much in the orthodox register of the saxophone as he does among his whistling harmonics. The complex *Third World anthem* has Johnson switching from baritone to tuba in places, often doubling Reid's bass line, an emphatic underpin that contrasts the intricate flow of DeJohnette's impressive drumming. Indeed, throughout the album it is Johnson's presence on either baritone or tuba that gives a feeling of depth to the ensemble that previous, and subsequent, versions of Special Edition lacked.

Zoot suite had been previously recorded on *Special Edition* (ECM (G) 1152), but here emerges much refined and polished, with saxophone passages that evoke the self-propelling intensity of the World Saxophone Quartet, of which, incidentally, Murray was a charter member. Yet despite the timbral similarities, there is an integrity to the performance that remains consistent throughout the whole album. DeJohnette exerts greater control, both from behind his drum kit and through his writing providing the formal structures within which the soloists are empowered to seek individual freedom. And once again it is Murray's work that catches the ear, a refreshing voice challenging the certainties of 1980s neoclassicism with his wild abandon.

One of the great drummers in jazz, DeJohnette epitomizes the changing role of the drummer originally signalled by Max Roach in the late 1940s and 1950s, who moved the drummer from a time-keeping role to that of a percussionist working within compositional structures providing colourist detail as much rhythmic impetus. Roach's speed and independent polyrhythmic coordination marked a conceptual as much as a philosophical change in jazz drumming, which moved with increasing sophistication through Elvin Jones to Tony Williams to DeJohnette. Representing the very highest level of drum technique married to almost perfect taste, DeJohnette's style has continued to evolve and develop to an extent that Roach's and Williams's did not, as his playing in a series of exceptionally varied performing situations throughout the 1980s and into the 1990s demonstrated. [18] Ultimately, however, *Album Album* is a tribute to DeJohnette's complete musicianship, for although there are no drum solos – only brief breaks – the unifying factor in this remarkably varied collection of compositions is as much the vibrant luminosity of his drumming as his ability to create a wholly effective context for his playing through his compositional and arranging skills. S.N.

Michael Brecker

490 Michael Brecker

†Impulse (A) MCAD5980

Michael Brecker (ten, EWI); Kenny Kirkland (p, kybd); Charlie Haden (bs); Pat Metheny (g); Jack DeJohnette (d). New York City, 1987.

Sea glass · Syzygy · Choices · Nothing personal · The cost of living · Original Rays · My one and only love

Until Brecker emerged from the commercial recording studios as a member of Steps Ahead (**488**) in the early 1980s, his reputation in jazz was based primarily on his work with the pioneering jazz-rock group Dreams (1970–1), in various editions of drummer Billy Cobham's jazz-rock band in the early 1970s, as a member of the Horace Silver Quintet (1973–4) and as a co-leader of the often commercially slanted Brecker Brothers group. Yet although this was the first album under his own name, by 1987 he already had the reputation as the most influential saxophonist since John Coltrane. That a musician without a recording contract of his own should have such an effect on other musicians was hardly new: Louis Armstrong while still with King Oliver, Bix Beiderbecke while still with the Wolverines, Coleman Hawkins while with Fletcher Henderson and Charlie Christian (who *never* recorded under his own name) with Benny Goodman spring most readily to mind. But by the 1980s it was unusual that a major talent like Brecker, who by the time of this recording was 38, should have eluded making recordings under his own name until so late into his career.

Almost as soon as he arrived in New York as a 19-year-old freshman from Indiana State University, Brecker was hailed by the *Village Voice* as 'one of the best young saxophonists anywhere'. [19] Recorded evidence bore this out; his recording debut as a 20-year-old on his brother Randy's album *Score* (†Blue Note [A] 0777 7 81202 2) from 1969 reveals a confident mastery of the hard bop idiom, and his solos the following year in the jazz-rock idiom on the album *Dreams* (†Columbia/Legacy [A] CK47906) – most notably *Dream suite* – demonstrated a thoroughgoing intimacy with the then new genre. By the early 1970s he was promptly fast-tracked into lucrative recording-session work, yet he was always careful to keep a foot in the jazz camp and his powerful feature with the Brecker Brothers band from 1977, *Funky sea, funky dew* from *Heavy Metal Be-bop* (†One Way Records [A] OW31447) and his straight-ahead solo on *Invitation* from *You Can't Live Without It* (Chiaroscuro [A] 185) under the guitarist Jack Wilkens's leadership from the same year, are indicative of artistic growth while also suggesting a potential that was far from realized. While his work with Steps has already been discussed (**488**), albums such Chick Corea's *Three Quartets* (Warner Bros [A] WB56908) from February 1981 and Pat Metheny's *80/81* (ECM [G] 1180–81) from May 1980 continued to flag up Brecker's formidable improvising talent. Indeed, *80/81* enjoyed considerable critical acclaim, including the *Preis der Deutschen Schallplatten Kritik* (German Record Reviewers' Prize) in 1981, with Brecker earning praise in a group he would reassemble six years later for *Michael Brecker* (albeit with Kirkland replacing the saxophonist Dewey Redman).

Brecker made no secret of his love of John Coltrane's playing: 'I am a tremendously Coltrane-influenced player . . . I consider him one of the greatest musicians this century; he changed the instrument and his music transcended not only musicians but artists in every area of art.' [20] Certainly there is no question that Brecker's playing betrays a stylistic allegiance to Coltrane, such as using the scale built a semitone above the root of a dominant seventh chord or his regular use of 'the Coltrane scale', a diminished-wholetone scale also known as a super-locrian scale. However, Brecker absorbed Coltrane's use of harmony and of scales to the point where his own solos were minor marvels of sophisticated reharmonization, revealing a fluent chromaticism of a very high order. Another Coltrane characteristic was his use of pentatonic scale patterns, which is something of a feature of Brecker's playing. Yet this was not stylistic imitation in the way Illinois Jacquet emulated Lester Young. Brecker was a highly creative musician in his own right with a lucid melodic imagination, a firm, resonant tone that remained in perfect tune across three octaves and an exceptional technique which permitted ease of execution at the most furious of tempos. His solo on Coltrane's *Impressions* from 1995, for example, while guesting with McCoy Tyner's trio on *Infinity* (†Impulse [A] IMP11712), is ten choruses in length, and during 320 bars of intense up-tempo improvisation his inventive use of motifs and patterns and his melodic development allow for little repetition, except when it serves a functional purpose. Indeed many instances of apparent repetition under closer scrutiny reveal a motif or pattern subtly altered from that which had been played before. This unusually focused invention deserves mention since during the improvisatory process, musicians frequently reach back into their subconscious, to habit, personal clichés and aquired patterns while fresh ideas are being organized. Brecker's extensive harmonic vocabulary is in evidence through a frequent use of substitute chords over the static modal harmonies to create a 'harmonic rhythm' that gave his line momentum, such as the four separate but related harmonies implied during the long 14-bar phrase in the fifth chorus. [21] The climax of his solo comes during the final five bars, where he runs a complex motif through descending semitones. The sheer *brio* with which this solo was executed demonstrates how Brecker's assimilation of Coltrane's methods was put to creative purpose, not simply imitating, but in building and expanding on what had gone before.

The one change of personnel from Pat Metheny's *80/81*, reassembled for *Michael Brecker*, was, as noted, Kirkland, who, although without the distinguished credentials of his leader or of Metheny, Haden and DeJohnette, could nevertheless claim work with Dave Liebman, Michal Urbaniak, Miroslav Vitous, Elvin Jones, Terumaso Hino and Wynton Marsalis. *Sea glass* opens with the haunting electronic tone colours of Kirkland's keyboards suggesting a ¾ pulse, with Brecker's exposition of the theme implying a rubato feel (it is not) above DeJohnette's cymbal cascades. As DeJohnette and Haden move into a flowing three, Brecker's incandescent solo begins with long *legato* lines which give way to an increasing density of notes manipulated through a rising line to climax in the high registers of his instrument. This gradual increase of intensity and density while reaching further and further up the range of his saxophone imposes a feeling of symmetry to his improvisation, despite the static harmonic movement. A feature of Brecker's playing is the dramatic power which he generates through such methods, often reaching above the normal range of the saxophone using altered/overtone fingerings. Sometimes it appears as if he is overblowing to achieve a 'New Thing' intensity; he is not, although he does exploit the full dynamic range of the saxophone, from *ppp* to a powerful *fff*. Something of a hallmark of his playing is his alteration of the density of sustained notes while, through alternate fingering or partially closing the bell-tone keys (B-flat-C-C-sharp), giving his solos an element of *vox humana*.

Syzygy begins as a tenor–drums duet, DeJohnette responding with great creativity to the rhythmic groupings of notes within Brecker's inventions before a statement of the theme that combines both written and improvised sections. Kirkland launches into his solo with sprightly right-hand figures and a minimum of (left-hand) comping but he too is conscious of moving to a logical climax, increasing density of his line against more pronounced left-hand voicings. Brecker's solo is on an EWI, an electric wind instrument that triggers sampled electronic sounds yet permits them to be bent and shaped to the same extent as a saxophone tone. His use of this instrument was less a tribute to its value as such, more the musical challenge it represented to replicate his virtuosity when his then current band, Steps Ahead, embraced electronic tone colours. It is a less satisfying instrument than the saxophone, something that is shown in sharp relief by his performance on the Mike Stern composition *Choices*.

Utilizing a slow-moving melody line contrasted by a staccato motif for bass and piano, *Choices* achieves a polymetric effect. DeJohnette plays in cut time, a loping *alla breve* feel, while the melody actually seems to pass by at half the speed implied by DeJohnette's drumming. The form is AAB, with the A sections 30 bars each and the B section 20 bars, although because it is in cut time the form actually feels like sections of 15 and 10 bars each. Throughout, the bass and piano reiterate an insistent staccato motif, the piano not comping but occasionally adding decorative figures. On the B section, the pre-writtern rhythmic figures are not present during the first 12 bars, allowing for a looser rhythmic feel to be projected by Haden and DeJohnette, but they return, embellished freely by DeJohnette, for the final eight bars. This prearranged rhythmic structure is preserved through solos by Brecker and Kirkland that follow, in much the same way as a specific rhythmic structure is maintained throughout Herbie Hancock's *Maiden voyage* (**353**).

The Don Grolnick composition *Nothing personal* is among the most interesting compositions of the album. Grolnick's tunes are almost without exception deceptively simple pieces that achieve great clarity of expression; his 1990 album *The Weaver of Dreams* (†Blue Note [A] CDP794591–2), which also included this item, and *Nighttown* (†Blue Note [A] CDP798689–2) from 1992, which included *The cost of living*, are two excellent albums of contemporary mainstream playing with a poise and elegance that is the province of the finest jazz. 'One of the beauties of Don's writing was that he was able to write simple but profound melodies where every note had equal weight; if you changed one note it would wreck the tune. That's something I still haven't accomplished in my own writing,' Brecker observed in 1998. [22] *Nothing personal* is a through-composed 24-bar piece, all A so to speak, opening on a G-minor vamp until the theme is cued. The tempo is brisk, [23] but utilizes a pre-written bass figure in cut time that reveals the broken phrases of the theme in stark relief. Within the overall 24-bar structure the penultimate four bars are given over to improvisation, before a return of the pre-written bass motif for the final four bars. The pre-written bass line is preserved for the first chorus of each solo, but then 'walks' for subsequent choruses. Metheny, a lucid melodist who gloved his brilliant technique in service of the material at hand, briefly flowers before Brecker moves to centre stage with a solo of precisely articulated logic, developing motifs through the range of his saxophone before a climax of sustained tones.

The cost of living, another Grolnick composition, and a riveting *a cappella* opening to *My one and only love* reveal Brecker's strong, elegant ballad playing where his enormous harmonic knowledge and rhythmic mastery combine to produce two exemplary performances of contemporary saxophone playing, with Metheny caught up in the emotion of the moment on the latter, contributing an especially moving and graceful solo. *Original Rays*, named after the famous New York pizza chain, is a feature for the EWI. Brecker's level of virtuosity on this hybrid instrument, which also permits chords, is mesmerizing. Brecker was once moved to observe that playing it made him sound like 'a sax section from Mars'. There is certainly an otherworldly feel about Brecker's *a cappella* introduction, something that became a feature of his live performances, captured on the bootleg album *The Cost of Living* (†Jazz Door [A] D1260). An abrupt switch to tenor *a tempo* and the short solo that follows is as dramatic as it is unexpected before giving way to another well-defined Metheny solo. Brecker's second tenor solo that follows, with its graceful, effortless execution as his lines gather in intensity, provides one of the album's memorable moments as he works towards a perfectly judged climax. Again he utilizes various levels of rhythmic density in his line, beginning with notes of long duration contrasted by sections of short rhythmic values, then mixing both phrases lengths, frequently executing very short note values – groups of five, seven and nine notes – with longer tones. The way these elements are balanced, manipulated through a rising line with a discursive use of chromaticism, together with the internal tensions created through motivic development and Brecker's variation in tonal density combine to create a dramatic improvisation. It is a moment among many on the album that reveal a player who not only was one of the most important soloists to emerge in the 1980s and 1990s, but is a figure of such stature that he numbers among the rollcall of the finest saxophonists to have appeared in jazz. S.N.

Myra Melford

491 **Jump**

†Enemy (G) 115–2

Myra Melford (p); Lindsey Horner (bs); Reggie Nicholson (d). New York City, June 1990.

Jump · *Some kind of blues* · *Frank Lloyd Wright goes West to rest* · *The world wears away* · *Sun on the sound* · *Once again* · *Only in change*

While there was no shortage of talented young pianists during the 1980s and 1990s, the Thelonious Monk Piano Competition being eloquent testimony of that, originality was at a premium. The problem was that if young musicians failed to join the massed ranks of the hard-bop foot soldiers, or, as one musician put it, joined 'the invasion of the body snatchers', [24] they almost automatically forfeited major label interest in their talent and, since the jazz media operate as a sort of service industry to the majors, the valuable press coverage that went with it. As was becoming clear by the end of the 1980s, few young musicians seemed prepared to move beyond the safe and accessible mainstream because of the security of tenure it provided.

There was, of course, no shortage of young musicians able to function effectively in this renascent environment. By the 1980s, many leading universities in America offered a variety of graduate and postgraduate courses in jazz. For jazz to be taught, it had to be explainable, analysable, categorizable and, as Mark Levine has observed, 'do-able'. [25] The style where the principles of jazz harmony and improvisation converged in a way that submitted itself most readily to these requirements was centred on the hard-bop and post-bop mainstream of the 1950s and 1960s. Yet Dave Liebman has pointed out that hard bop is 'the callisthenics of improvisation', [26] its practices now so institutionalized that they should be used to limber up for the musical challenges ahead, a starting-off point for jumping into the future, rather than as an end in itself.

In general, the majors were unlikely to sign a jazz artist in the 1980s and 1990s unless a specfic marketing and developmental plan could be constructed around them. Of prime importance was the perceived potential for sales, not only to the established audience for jazz but also for crossing over into the 18–25-year-old market traditionally associated with the highest net disposable income. Clearly this thinking favoured younger musicians, preferably photogenic, who had the potential to appeal to audiences of their peers, critics eager to validate 'new trends' and an audience identified within a well-defined demographic keen to applaud a 'coming jazz great'. Thus record-company promotion was configured around the 'always new', a marketing scheme around which the recording business was constructed. It coincided with a period when there was an almost inexhaustible flow of young musicians graduating from colleges and universities performing within a clearly discernible style that could be precisely targeted at specific audiences, often through airplay on 'jazz' radio. And here again, the music had to have specific characteristics to fit in with the overall musical format chosen by stations that favoured the acoustic mainstream. In such a world, the chances of an 'esoteric' (that is to say individual) recording getting airtime was remote, since this was seen as bad for ratings.

What was extraordinary about the hard-bop renaissance of the 1980s and 1990s was that it lasted longer than the original style had done in the 1950s and 1960s. This was primarily because the style lent itself to commercialization by record companies. It was flexible enough to allow a variety of performers to function within its clearly defined boundaries without destroying the specific, readily understood and categorizable musical characteristics essential for marketing it. Within such a musical framework, if sales of artist A slowed down, a new, younger artist B would be signed in his place, launched as 'the next coming great'. Thus the status quo had the potential to be renewed, not by musical innovation essential for any art form's growth, but through the cult of personality, with each fresh young signing signalling a renewal not of the music, but of a marketing cycle.

Yet despite individual voices being marginalized by the machinations of commerce, jazz has never been without experimenters, musicians who marched to the sound of a different drum while others marked time. It was these musicians, who regarded jazz as a developing art form and saw in the music unlimited possibilities for growth and personal expression. Myra Melford, born on 5 January 1957, was one such experimenter. She began studying piano under Irwin Helfer, who, in addition to the classical repertoire of Bach, Mozart and Beethoven, exposed his young pupils to 20th-century European composers such as

Kabalevsky and taught them to play boogie-woogie piano in the manner of the Chicago school. In college she was introduced to the music of Cecil Taylor (**384**, **419–20**) and Muhal Richard Abrams (**435**), but it was not until she attended a concert in her home town of Evanston, Illinois, given by Leroy Jenkins, Amina Claudine Meyers and Pheeroan Ak Laff that she was motivated to pursue a career in jazz. 'I thought, This is what I really want to do, I want to find my own way of playing the piano and writing music and here is a precedent for it. So this was really my turning point and since then I have pretty well pursued it steadily,' she explained in 1996. [27]

Graduating with a BA from Evergreen State College in Olympia, Washington State, she continued her studies at the Cornish Institute's Jazz Department in Seattle with Art Lande and Gary Peacock. Moving to New York City in the mid-1980s, she studied under Henry Threadgill and Don Pullen, while receiving considerable encouragement from Cecil Taylor to find her own individual voice. Although she credits Threadgill as a big influence on her composing, she also maintained great interest in Eastern European composers, including Lutoslawski, and in folk music. Work in ensembles led by Threadgill, Butch Morris, Joseph Jarman, Oliver Lake, Bernadette Speach, Juliana Kohl and Leroy Jenkins provided a context for her style to evolve, and in 1990 she was offered a short tour of Europe sponsored by Michael Dorf's Knitting Factory, which prompted the formation of her trio with Horner (also associated with Tim Berne, Marty Erhlich and Bill Frisell) and Nicholson (of Chicago's AACM and bands led by Amina Claudine Meyers, Threadgill and Ed Wilkerson).

Jump was recorded shortly after returning from their Knitting Factory tour and represents Miss Melford's debut as a leader on record. For the next few years this trio would become her main forum for expression, until she formed a quintet that included Dave Douglas (**492**) on trumpet and Marty Ehrlich on woodwinds to further her compositional ambitions. And although she continued to work with her trio throughout the decade, on *Jump* there is a flush of enthusiasm that occasionally makes itself felt in music-making upon the discovery of mutual empathy. There is a rawness here that would subsequently give way to more sensitive group interaction on *Now & Now* (†Enemy [G] 131–2) from 1992 and *Alive in the House of Saints* (†Hat Art [Sw] CD6136) from 1993 – Miss Melford's favourite trio album. Nevertheless, *Jump* is a wholly engaging debut, with an electricity that adds to the drama.

The title track reveals Miss Melford's love of explicit rhythms, energetic improvisation and, during her *scherzando* introduction, flashes of folk and blues. The theme is built on a hypnotic, quirky vamp figure that leads into her solo, intense and driving, working from a capsule of an idea and gradually expanding until it leaps the length of the keyboard, climaxing in splashing, side-slipping runs. It leads into solos by Nicholson and Horner, returning to the vamp figure and a perfectly executed retard in the coda. The composition uses a square rhythmic pattern associated with rock, yet clearly this was not a rock performance, nor was this a rock number, it was simply a rhythmic pattern that suited the mood of the composition and Miss Melford's presentation of it. With *Some kind of blues* it becomes clear that she enjoys the rhythmically unexpected. Instead of employing a walking bass and a drummer playing on the two and the four against conventional ride rhythms, which otherwise might appear an appropriate accompaniment, Horner and Nicholson combine to create a sinister rolling rhythm combining a bass *ostinato* and ominous tom-tom patterns. It is a rhythmic context that gradually creates a dark undercurrent of mystery until finally the trio surge into double time, using an orthodox walking-bass line and ride patterns from Nicholson's cymbals. Throughout, Miss Melford creates the climate of the blues with bluesy figures and plagal cadences without casting them in the traditional harmonic framework of the blues progression.

Frank Lloyd Wright goes West to rest is a vigorous piece full of shimmering abstraction and angular, precisely fingered runs that weave in, out and around of her inherent romantic sensibility. No matter how recondite her ideas become, there is a pleasing sense of symmetry and resolution in the construction of her solos, a shifting, shimmering interconnecting web of styles that allows glimpses of boogie-woogie, contemporary classical elements and freedom, often inspired by Cecil Taylor. "My goal is to try and synthesize and integrate all the different musics I love and have been exposed to into my own personal style," she explained. [28] *The world wears away*, a Horner composition, the only one not by the leader, features the bassist after an unexpected key change after the initial exposition of a simple, contemplative melodic figure. *Sun on the sound* is another well-defined piece, taken at a brisk tempo; she delights at playing against the beat and taking her powerfully fingered improvisation further and further 'outside'. What starts off as a surging bop tune becomes an encounter with free improvisation with resourceful use of the piano's pedals and ends with a vigorous, yet serene penultimate section with a bowed bass solo. This is carefully thought-out music-making which delights in changing rhythms and colours and even permits another, final, mood swing, this time introduced by a simple bass vamp that leads to an unexpected close.

Once again begins with Miss Melford suggesting a piano drone and during her improvisation she introduces a remarkable *sforzando* effect, where her chords rise in volume and abruptly decay, a fascinating trademark that is used sparingly on other tracks. *Only in change*, a dirgelike dedication to the memory of M. A. Melford, permits the most closely realised emergence of her classical influences with a quasi-pastoral episode, the bass bowed in counterpoint during the opening sequence before the melancholy mood gives way to plagal cadences, leading into a blues-inflected hymn of tribute. Throughout, her music is remarkably well defined, revealing a compositional logic that lends great shape to her improvisations, an aspect of her musical persona that would be more formally realized with her writing for her quintet. In this context, however, something of the exploratory vigour of her playing would be sacrificed in service of her compositions. Yet with her trio Miss Melford emerged with a recognizably unique, distinctive style, whose playing, often vital and challenging, was never less than absorbing. S.N.

Dave Douglas

492 Stargazer

†Arabesque Jazz [A] AJO132.

Dave Douglas (tpt); Josh Roseman (tbn); Chris Speed (ten, clt); Uri Cane (p); James Genus (bs); Joey Baron (d). New York, 30 December 1996.
Spring ahead · *Goldfish* · *Stargazer* · *Four sleepers* · *On the Milky Way express* · *Pug nose* · *Dark sky* · *Intuitive science* · *Diana*

Douglas made his recording debut as a 23-year-old in 1986 with the pianist John Espositio's group Second Sight, *Flying with the Comet* (Sunjump Records [A] SJR01), and keeping track of his subsequent discography was no easy task. By 1999 he had participated in some 90 recording sessions in a wide variety of performing contexts, including those with Anthony Braxton, Suzanne Vega, Vincent Herring and Fred Hersch. But he was more frequently to be heard within the orbit of New York's 'downtown' experimenters such as John Zorn, Don Byron, Myra Melford, Mark Dresser and Uri Caine. Perhaps unsurprisingly, the *New Yorker* referred to Douglas as 'the downtown trumpeter of choice', hailing his 'open-vista imagination and eclecticism'. [29] By then, it seemed clear that he was among the most important musicians to emerge in the 1990s, with a breadth of imagination to produce defiantly uncategorizable music. Quite apart from his frequently distinguished contributions as a sideman, his own work included a string ensemble that interpreted works by Webern and Stravinsky on *Parallel Worlds* (†Soul Note [It] 121226–2), his own compositions and those of others on *Five* (†Soul Note [It] 121276), experiments with electronics and extended collective improvisation on *Sanctuary* (†Avant [J] Avan 066) and with his Tiny Bell Trio explorations of music influenced by Eastern European and Romanian folk music – *Tiny Bell Trio* (†Songlines [Can] SGL1504–2) and *Constellations* (†hat Art [Sw] CD6173).

He also led a 'reeds and brass' ensemble, which debuted on record in 1994 with *In Our Lifetime* (†New World/Countercurrents [A] 80471–2), exploring music inspired by Booker Little in general and *Victory and Sorrow* (**339**) in particular. Although only three compositions were by Little, Douglas's solo on *Forward flight* successfully evoked the essence of the underappreciated trumpeter without mimicry, providing the *leitmotif* for the nine pieces written by Douglas himself. It revealed his skill as a composer and arranger, his compositions radiating a refreshing impromptu feel within the context of Little's work to propel the spirit of his music into the 1990s. The title track was perhaps the most successful piece on the album; robust, pluralistic and full of shifting interior detail, it failed to surrender its secrets on first hearing; accessible but uncompromising, Douglas's ensemble revealed an ability to compel and intrigue without their contemporary viewpoint overwhelming the stance of Little's original vision.

The same ensemble was brought together two years later for *Stargazer*, an album-length statement celebrating the music of Wayne Shorter. Here Douglas regarded Shorter's music in more exuberant mood than he did Little's, the late trumpeter's penchant for evoking blue moods on non-blues material inspiring Douglas towards a melancholy impressionism on some tracks. In contrast *Stargazer* revealed greater poise and a deft handling of ensemble textures that elevated interaction to levels of elation while old-fashioned polish achieved on the bandstand since their previous album created a compelling unanimity of expression. Of the nine pieces on the album, three were by Shorter himself, *On the Milky Way express* from 1995's *High Life* (†Verve [A] 529 224–2), *Pug nose* from 1959's *Introducing Wayne Shorter* (VeeJay [A] 363) and *Diana* from the 1974 album *Native Dancer* (†Columbia/Legacy [A] 467095–2). Of Shorter's music, Douglas would say: 'His intense melodic gift, rhythmic ingenuity, harmonic sophistication and sublime sense of structure are some of the elements in his music that have particularly touched me. There is also an ever-present warmth and humanity in his music which I find mirrored in his writings and his approach to life and art. His music seems to ask us to abandon our hang-ups and preoccupations with stylistic limitations and other barriers to direct communication.' [30]

Guided by these precepts, *Stargazer* unfolds in unexpected ways. Douglas, who studied music at Berklee College of Music, the New England Conservatory and New York University, accumulated a solid theoretical foundation from which to develop his writing. His accomplishment was in balancing unexpected contrasts; *On the Milky Way express*, for example, began life on Shorter's 1995 album with Rachel Z's feline synth lines over a funky rhythm section. Douglas transforms it in a way that shows deference to Shorter's larger ensemble albums, such as 1965's *The All Seeing Eye* (†Blue Note [A] CDP7243 8 29100–2), while still managing to avoid straining for contemporaneous effect. *Spring ahead* has a twisting lead line Douglas executes with aplomb in the ensembles before emerging with a solo of balance, cohesion and lyricism. Favouring vertical lines that include unusual note choices, he reveals fluency and some off-the-wall logic associated with the late Don Cherry.

Within the ensemble, Douglas contrasts written and improvised sections, yet while retaining a fluidity between the two, makes use of opposing tonal densities of the arranged and the spontaneous from which Caine emerges to flourish briefly.

Goldfish opens with Douglas outlining a melancholy ballad that seems forever poised on the edge of collective improvisation, suggesting an option for his soloists to exploit. Roseman prefers a metronomic pulse and to go his own way, but Douglas's agitated line prompts Baron to interact, then Caine and Genus, before returning to time. Caine, a pianist who, like Douglas, is able to operate in a variety of musical contexts yet retain his specific musical personality, contributes a wide-ranging solo from lumpy, broken time beginnings to a fluent climax that leads into a carefully arranged, lengthy coda. *Pug nose* is perhaps the only song that evokes most closely the Blue Note Shorter but *Dark sky* and *Intuitive science* retain Douglas's conceptual grip through the originality of his writing. *Diana*, like *Dark sky*, explores ensemble textures using the unusual combination of clarinet and trombone, or clarinet, trumpet and trombone, to create otherworldly voicings. Throughout, Douglas does not succumb to head-solos-head formats: each piece is a carefully constructed balance between the written and the improvised, with the trumpeter's lead lines imposing unexpected dynamics upon the ensemble.

Douglas's ownership of ideas too individualistic to point to any convenient stylistic demarcation revealed that once again the enemy of the creative artist was 'categorization'. Although known as a 'downtown' musician, how could such a term meaningfully fit all the styles he played, or even the individual styles of the musicians that represented his music? Douglas, however, seemed less troubled by how his work was pigeonholed. He seemed to acknowledge that waiting for recognition took time, but in a world where critical opinion was increasingly formed by marketing strategies, he was, for the time being, a voice shouting from the margins. Undismayed, he kept his work ethic undiminished, claiming in 1998 that 'all music is such a joy to me. It's finding new things in music that really turns me on.' [31] S.N.

Clusone Trio

493 Love Henry

†Gramavision (A) GCD79517

Michael Moore (alt, clt, mel, pan fl); Ernst Reijseger (cel); Han Bennink (d, perc, p, voice). Frankfurt, 13 July 1996.

Introduction · Medley 1: Red hot/When I lost you/White hot/It's you/White spots/Cuckoo in the clock/Uninhabited island/Red spots/Bilbao song · Medley 2: Restless in pieces/Love Henry/In the company of angels · Medley 3: Tempo comodo/Moeder aller Oorlogen/White Christmas/Give me your tired, your poor · Medley 4: Ao Velho Pedro/Marie Pompoen · Goodbye

Machine Gun (**412**) may not have been the first album by European 'free' improvisers to move away from the American model of jazz and attempt to establish their own specific identity, but it remains the most famous and most memorable, a landmark album that has come to represent a seismic shift in the thinking of the European free movement. But while the UK, Germany, Denmark, Norway and Sweden all produced important musicians who contributed valuable recordings that established European free as the first major movement in jazz to become wholly independent of the American influences that spawned it, it was the Dutch jazz scene that came to epitomize the diverse ways in which 'freedom' could be managed. Gaining momentum in the late 1960s, Dutch musicians embraced political issues, blurred the boundary between theatre and music, replaced the seriousness of the American avant-garde with humour and parody, embraced classical influences such as Terry Riley and Charles Ives and drew on a variety of cultural influences, not only from across Europe but also from cultures that reached back into Dutch colonial history. The separateness of the Dutch jazz scene and how it evolved its distinctive voice was worthy of a book in itself, and in 1998 *New Dutch Swing* by Kevin Whitehead, a sprawling but nevertheless engrossing document, charted its evolution and illuminated the resolute individuality of players like Willem Breuker, Han Bennink and Maarten Altena, who in 1978 had proclaimed his independence from American jazz.

Bennink was one of the most important figures on the Dutch jazz scene. His first recording was with Eric Dolphy and in the 1960s he was the first-choice drummer for many touring American musicians, including Sonny Rollins, Dexter Gordon and Hank Mobley. At the same time he was immersing himself in the European improvised-music scene and was quickly recognized as one of its most original exponents. He was one of the first drummers to assemble a drum kit from all manner of 'found' percussion (i.e. almost anything from hub caps to kitchen pans that could be banged, shaken or rattled), and his recordings include work with Cecil Taylor, Derek Bailey and Peter Brötzmann. But it was his involvement with the Clusone Trio (sometimes Clusone 3) that revealed a perfect context in which to feature his talents, not least to provide a forum that gave vent to his reputation as a 'performance' artist. His association with Michael Moore began in 1980, when the saxophonist was visiting Holland from his native America. A graduate of the New England Conservatory, Moore moved to the Netherlands permanently in 1982, observing: 'In America there's more pressure to be conformist and players who were once pioneers of new music can work a lot more if they play tunes in a traditional way. In Europe there's a larger audience that grew up listening to guys like Han over a 25-year period, and they appreciate not hearing the same thing every time.' [32]

The group was initially conceived as a quartet, with the cellist Ernst

Reijseger, to play a festival in Clusone, Italy, in 1988, but the pianist Guus Janssen subsequently withdrew to concentrate on composing. The name Clusone stayed, however, and gradually the trio began attracting more and more work together. Reijseger, who had begun applying himself to improvised music while still a teenager and had worked with Gerry Hemingway, Derek Bailey, Trilok Gurtu, Misha Mengelberg (**465**) and Louis Sclavis, was a virtuoso with what Kevin Whitehead has called 'striking strengths and weaknesses'. [33] Their first album, *Clusone Trio* (†Ramboy [H] 01), recorded at concerts in 1990 and 1991, included several Moore originals and what he called that trio's 'South American bag' – tunes by Paulo Moura and Hermeto Pascoal – originals by Frankey Douglas, Mengelberg and Herbie Nichols, and an extended collective exploration that ultimately resolved into *Girl talk.* Their second album, *Soft Lights and Sweet Music* (†Hat Art [Sw] 6153) 1993, was an audacious deconstruction of the Irving Berlin songbook. In 1994 came *I Am an Indian* (†Gramavision [A] GCD79505), taped at five European and Canadian concerts during the summer of 1993. Included were two further Berlin songs (the title track and *The song is ended*), and originals from South America, Moore, Mengelberg, Nichols, Duke Ellington, Bud Powell and Dewey Redman, and several absorbing collective improvisations.

In effect, *Love Henry* continues the story of the trio's development and was recorded at the 27th German Jazz Festival at Frankfurt in July 1996. The rapport the group had developed is apparent on *Medley 1*, several disparate compositions that were allowed to *segue* one into another forming a continuous piece of music. 'Medley' hardly seems an appropriate term, since the group had made such an art of fluidly moving from prearranged material into collectively improvised episodes and back again, perhaps wildly swinging, spontaneously interacting or in paraphrase of what had gone before. Opening with a swinging discourse on Lee Konitz's *It's you,* the brisk tempo gradually fragments into the collective improvisation *White spots.* Gradually, Moore, an unusually precise and cogent melodist, alludes to *Cuckoo in the clock*, the Johnny Mercer tune he once recorded with Benny Goodman's orchestra in 1939.

While the harmonies Clusone use are often intentionally vague or drastically simplified to allow the improviser maximum licence, the episode of improvisation that follows seems to be on the melody of the Mercer tune (rather than the chordal structure) that resolves into a statement of the melody and a shouted 'Cuckoo' from Bennink correlated by visual theatre (if the response of the crowd is anything to go by). Such gestures, Matei Calinescu has pointed out, are typical, even expected, of avant-garde art, which is often imbued with 'intellectual playfulness, iconoclasm, a cult of unseriousness'. [34] Moore then introduces his own composition *Uninhabited island* and, with a return of the manic tempo, Reijseger is reluctant to part with the *Cuckoo* motif as the band reunite around *Bilbao song*, one of the highpoints of Gil Evans's *Out of the Cool* (**383**).

What impresses is the way the individual members congregate around a song, then apparently arrive at a disjunction before breaking into a seemingly endless musical odyssey that brings together so many elements of music-making, yet ultimately relies on intuition and impulse to make it work. Rhythmically, Bennink can appear dominant, overbearing, yet within an instant, a wall of sound can dissolve in quiet, discrete brush-work. Reijseger in live performance is not beyond hitching the cello up on his knee to strum like a guitar, or use the lower register of the instrument to 'walk', contrabass-like, in the sometimes vicious periods of straight-ahead swing that Bennink seems to delight in. Using a bow, Reijseger can become locked in counterpoint with Moore, or respond in sometimes astringent paraphrase to saxophone or clarinet; his role is flexible and changing moment to moment. Moore, whose purity of tone and precise articulation frequently cast him in the role of straight man to his often disruptive companions, represents the calm in the eye of the hurricane. But the trio is also about shifting allegiances, Moore and Reijseger or Moore and Bennink, as much as it is a communal enterprise and it is this give-and-take that is used to suggest the broad frame of references from which the band work, including references to Indian music, European folk, Strauss and even the pomp and circumstance of marching-band music.

This freewheeling musical extemporization could change in intensity or density, mood or direction, rhythmically and melodically at any of the performers' whims, creating a new avant-garde that has undertaken a theoretical appropriation of jazz's historical avant-garde of the 1960s and in effect overlaid it with the gestures and pluralism of European culture. Any of the group were free to set up a motif or suggest a cue to take the music in a new direction. For this to work successfully, the group operated on a shared belief about what worked and what did not; certainly throughout the album there are moments, even episodes, that are less successful than others. This is, of course, a problem of mixing absolute improvisation with prearranged forms, structures and compositions; it is akin to a high-wire act, at its best it can be dangerous and absorbing mainly because the musicians themselves sense much the same thing. Yet if it does not work the music sweeps on, the hushed, three-way discourse suggested in 1961 by the Bill Evans trio inflated into the realms of argument and counter-argument, rhetoric and bombast. Like much Dutch music, it broadened the emotional range of jazz through humour, parody and visual theatre, elements conspicuously avoided in the American model. This was not music that could be taught in colleges or universities but came from the life experiences of three imaginative improvisers unlimited by stylistic convention. S.N.

Paul Motian Trio

494 At the Village Vanguard
†JMT [G] 514028–2

Joe Lovano (ten); Bill Frisell (g); Paul Motian (d). New York, June 1995.
You took the words right out of my heart · Abacus · Folk song for Rosie · The owl of Cranston · Miles to Wrentham · Yahllah · The sunflower · Circle dance

The death of Scott LaFaro on 6 July 1961, shortly after recording the matinee and evening sessions at the Village Vanguard on Sunday 25 June 1961 with the Bill Evans Trio (**373**), saw Evans devastated. While on the one hand LaFaro's death had thrown into stark relief what the trio had achieved, on the other it brought home the infinite possibilities that might have been within their grasp had he lived, a prospect that threw Evans into depression. 'Bill stopped playing for a while,' explained Paul Motian in 1986. 'I took some other gigs. Around that time things started changing in New York. Albert Ayler was here, Paul Bley, the Jazz Composers Guild started – I wanted to be a part of that.' [35]

When Evans reformed his trio at the end of 1961, with Chuck Israels in LaFaro's place, Motian returned to his former role, but was looking over his shoulder to the burgeoning free-jazz scene he had just experienced. In December 1963, he recorded his final album with Evans, *Trio 64* (†Verve [A] 539058–2). The two years with Evans after LaFaro's death had left him restive: 'The stuff with Bill seemed at a standstill. We were doing the same stuff over and over. I quit Bill, in California, when we were on the road. I'll never forgive myself for that, but at the time I couldn't make it anymore. We were at Shelly Manne's club, with Chuck Israels. The first night was great. The second night was a little not so great and the third night . . . everyone was telling me I was too loud, so I played softer and softer until I felt I wasn't even playing. I got pissed and I quit. Bill said, "Please don't do this."' [36] Motian, as history records, did 'do this', and Evans refused to speak to him for the next 15 years.

Motian returned to the new-music scene in New York, and within days had joined a band with a two-tenor front line of Albert Ayler and John Gilmore, plus Paul Bley on piano and Gary Peacock on bass. He also deputized on several occasions for his friend Elvin Jones in the John Coltrane quartet. 'Once I was up there I had just one thing in my mind, which was *not* to sound like Elvin. Coltrane said to me, "Hey, how about if I have two drummers in my band?" I said, "I don't know, man." I was scared. They were so hot. Mingus would show up, hold his hands above his head and bow down low in front of the bandstand going *Salaam, salaam.* He was speaking for all of us.' [37]

Keith Jarrett was the next leader to benefit from Motian's drumming, and the changes in Motian's style, from the sensitive percussionist/

drummer with Evans to the more forthright, spur-of-the-moment impulsivness that responded to the free structures of Jarrett's music, can be heard on *Keith Jarrett: The Impulse Years 1973–4* (†Impulse [A] IMPD5237) and *Keith Jarrett: Mysteries: The Impulse Years 1975–6* (†Impulse [A] IMPD4189). Jarrett's range was wide, calling on Motian to respond with traditional time-keeping, abstract coloration, Third World rhythms and sometimes semi-rock-influenced rhythms. Of that group, with Charlie Haden on bass and Dewey Redman on tenor saxophone, Jarrett would later say: 'They each thought their job was to do exactly what they wanted to, and in that context I was always aware of allowing as much freedom as possible for each person to do that.' [38]

It was through his association with Jarrett's quartet, a group that finally broke up in 1976, that Motian was offered a recording contract by ECM's Manfred Eicher. His six-album association with the company as a leader in his own right began with 1973's *Conception Vessel* (ECM [G] 1028), which applied a diversity of approaches, Jarrett on one track, a trio with guitarist Sam Brown and bassist Charlie Haden on another, an ad hoc group with Leroy Jenkins, Haden and Becky Friend, and so on. By 1975, *Tribute* (ECM [G] 1048), with a two-guitar line-up comprising Brown and Paul Metzke, failed to suggest that Motian had defined his artistic vision. What was in evidence, however, was a willingness to put distance between the airy persuasiveness he had adopted with Evans, described as 'a model for drummers working within a similar settings [that] contributed to the emancipation of the rhythm section', [39] by adopting a rugged, bustling intensity that interacted with those around him, yet played a dominant role in the foreground. In short, his style was becoming less one of accompaniment, more one of moving towards an equal voice within his ensembles.

An association with the tenor saxophonist Charles Brackeen produced *Dance* (ECM [G] 1108) in 1978 and *Le Voyage* (ECM [G] 1138) the following year, after which he decided to form a new ensemble built around a guitar. A recommendation from Pat Metheny introduced him in 1980 to the work of Bill Frisell, who became part of an enlarged ensemble with Ed Schuller on bass and with two tenor saxophones – precisely the front line of the first group he joined after leaving Evans involving Ayler. Initially Motian's new band had Mark Goldsbury and Jim Pepper on tenor sax, but in 1981 Joe Lovano replaced Goldsbury. They made their debut on record with 1982's *Psalm* (ECM [G] 1222), mixing Motian's preference for introspective moods with free bop and abstraction that employed free-tempo tension and release.

Motian persisted with his enlarged ensemble into the 1980s. *The Story of Maryam* (Soul Note [It] 1074) from 1984 again revealed a sombre yet well-integrated unit, but with *It Should Have Happened a Long Time Ago* (ECM [G] 1283) from 1985, Motian experimented with a trio, using just Frisell and Lovano. Although other quintet albums would follow –

1985's *Jack of Clubs* (Soul Note [It] 1124) and 1988's *Misterioso* (Soul Note [It] 21174) – it seemed clear that the trio format allowed for a greater degree of flexibility and mobility, hinting at a less dour, more expansive vision that did not entirely rest with Motian's gnomelike compositions. It allowed attention to focus on Frisell, who for most of the albums failed to suggest the conventional sound of the guitar at all. One of the most original musicians to emerge during the 1980s, he took the most played instrument in the world and managed to wring something wholly new from it. By pulling together the hitherto opposing poles of Jim Hall and Jimi Hendrix, he produced an incredible range of otherworldly sounds that at once provided a distinctive backdrop as well as a unique solo voice within the ensemble. Frisell, unlike most jazz guitarists, did not treat the guitar as an amplified acoustic instrument, but as an electronic instrument in itself, an important distinction that coloured his whole musical outlook. In 1983 Frisell began recording in his own right for ECM, debuting as a leader with *In Line* (ECM [G] 1241), followed by *Rambler* (ECM [G] 1287) in 1985, which included the trumpeter Kenny Wheeler, and *Lookout for Hope* (ECM [G] 1350) in 1988, before signing with Elektra Nonesuch in 1989.

By the time the saxophonist Joe Lovano joined Motian, he had already accumulated a wealth of experience. Taught to play by his saxophonist father, he furthered his studies by enrolling at Berklee College of Music in the autumn of 1971. Moving to New York in 1974, he worked with the bands of Jack McDuff and Lonnie Liston Smith, cutting his first record that year, moving on to perform with the pianist Albert Dailey and Chet Baker before in 1976 joining the Woody Herman big band, where he remained for three years. In 1980 he joined the Mel Lewis Jazz Orchestra, and in 1981 he also began working with Motian. By the time of his debut as a leader on records in 1985 on *Tones, Shapes and Colours* (Soul Note [It] 1132), with the rhythm section of the Mel Lewis Jazz Orchestra, he was 33 and an enormously experienced musician who had composed three of the six numbers on the album. 'I've been a part of a lot of beautiful records and recording sessions, great bands, so your experience grows and grows, so when you start putting your own music together it comes from everything you do. If you're a 20-year-old cat who has never played with any great leaders, you're going to have a struggle being a leader yourself.' [40]

After recording *It Should Have Happened a Long Time Ago*, Motian became more and more attracted to the trio concept, explaining in 1986: 'I had this thing in the back of my mind, this thing about the saxophone and guitar and drums, without a bass. I never had the nerve to pull it off or try it. Then I did try it, and I liked it it, it worked out. Now I'm working mostly with the trio . . . it's so simple with the trio, the transportation aspect, the money.' [41] In 1987, the trio again appeared on record with *One Time Out* (Soul Note [I] 121 224–1) before signing with Stefan Winter's JMT label in 1988. With Winter, the band produced a series of albums that are among the most impressive bodies of work in jazz during the late 1980s and 1990s. Beginning with *Monk in Motian* (†JMT [G] 834 421–2) from 1988, which had the pianist Geri Allen guesting on *Ruby my dear* and *Off minor* and Dewey Redman guesting on *Straight, no chaser* and *Epistrophy*, the band found increasing definition with the three-volume set *On Broadway* (†JMT [G] 834 430–2, 834 440–2 and 849 157–2) from 1989, dealing with Broadway standards refracted within the group's free-ranging impulses.

For *Bill Evans* (†JMT [G] 834 445–2), the group's tribute to Bill Evans from 1990 which used nine of his compositions, the former Evans bassist Marc Johnson (a friend of Lovano's from their days with Woody Herman) was added in a deliberate attempt to limit the harmonic licence of Lovano's and Frisell's absorbing flights. *In Tokyo* (†JMT [G] 849 154–2) and *Trioism* (†JMT [G] 514 012–2) from 1994, the latter with Dewey Redman guesting on one track, continued the series of sharply defined yet unpredictable albums. 'When I play with Bill I'm trying to discover what he's talking about,' said Lovano. 'I want to make him play with me. That's a challenge. That's improvising. I think lyrically and with space; that's my conception. If want to play within a free form, I don't want to lose the rhythm, I want to create the rhythm and create the harmony – I want to get personal with it and make it happen. Keith Jarrett is a big influence on me as far as he shapes his music, how he plays standard songs and makes his ideas come through within any form – that's free jazz! And I feel like that concept plays a big part in my writing and my whole attitude.' [42]

In January 1995 Lovano had a full-page feature in the *New York Times*: 'Not since Stan Getz has a white tenor sax player been taken seriously as a prime exponent of the instrument,' it read. 'On the tenor his voice is readily identifiable, affecting without being especially pretty.' [43] Equally, Frisell was receiving plaudits that spoke of his position as one of the important musicians of his generation: 'For over ten years Bill Frisell has quietly been the most brilliant and unique voice to come along in jazz guitar since Wes Montgomery,' said *Stereophile.* [44] Yet despite their fast-accelerating careers – Frisell with his work for the Elektra Musician label and Lovano with his work for the reconstituted Blue Note label – both found the challenge of Motian's group a mutually stimulating experience. In June 1995 the group reassembled for a week at the Village Vanguard, and the material was sufficient for more than one album. However, nothing was immediately forthcoming after the release of *At the Village Vanguard* (†JMT [A] 514028–2) since Polygram pulled out of a distribution deal with JMT, causing the company to be wound up. It was not until 1997 when Winter formed a new label, Winter & Winter, that further material was released from their Vanguard sessions as *The Paul Motian Trio: Sound of Love* (†W&W [G] 910 008–2).

You took the words right out of my heart is the only non-Motian composition of the album. Lovano outlines the melody with Frisell in fractured counterpoint, while Motian opts for broken rhythms, sometimes on his cymbals and sometimes on his snare. Frisell takes the first solo, respecting the harmonies of the tune, in the way a Joe Pass or a Tal Farlow might begin his solo, part chorded, part melody. Lovano enters without disturbing the harmonies and gradually Frisell's comping moves into counterpoint, with Motian careful not to disturb the balance of the voices in dialogue that leads into a recapitulation of the melody. *Abacus* reveals how the group had worked through Ornette Coleman's concepts of the early 1960s and made them their own. Lovano states a brief melody that becomes the basis of the improvisations that follow. The form is free, but the mood and direction of both Frisell's solo and Lovano's more consciously melodic meditation are dictated by the particular intervals of the original melody that reappear as uniting motifs, often fragments in inversion that act to unite the two quite distinct solos.

Folk song for Rosie is a dirgelike lament of the kind Motian frequently favoured, apparently inspired by Armenian folk music, the music of his forebears. Lovano and Frisell state the melody in unison, with Frisell adding passing tones and chords in spare accompaniment. Frisell continues the mood of introspection with chords evoking a beautiful kind of sadness, and Lovano follows, playing in essence a counter-melody to the now unstated melody line, remaining in the diatonic axis implied by the song. Both unite in solemn mood until Frisell's guitar slowly shimmers into silence. *The owl of Cranston* is more vigorous, again with an Ornette Coleman–like theme that provides the basis of Frisell's improvisation, a fantasy of awkward intervals suggested by the tune which prompts Lovano to enter with abandon, his tumbling lines meshing with Frisell's guitar so that they are less two voices exploring the harmonies suggested by the angular theme than complementing voices teeming with inner movement. 'The music is fresh every time we play,' Lovano asserted in 1998. 'We're three completely different people, different personalities, different concepts. But when we play together, we listen to each other and react to each other, trying to shape the music, whether we're playing Monk, or standards or something Billie Holiday did or Paul's music or one of my tunes or Bill's. We're listening to each other, trying to shape from our personalities together.' [45]

5 miles to Wrentham is a short dirgelike melody, full of sighing cadences and pathos in which each musician immerses himself, exploring each microscopic corner of the song with an infinity of patience, gradually coaxing new shapes and new ideas to emerge. *Yahllah* continues the mood until Frisell suddenly and surprisingly moves into a minor tonality that changes the direction of the song. His playing could suggest great sentimentality without being sentimental, honesty without naïveté, yet suddenly change the mood to drama and menace. Lovano's solo, utilizing narrative and motivic development, is colourful yet subtle, astringent in the airy spaces offered him by drums and guitar. *The sunflower* begins with Lovano and Frisell stating a Coleman-like melody, with Motian responding with tangential bursts and crashes that lead into the improvisation section which sees a cautious rumbustiousness filling Frisell and Motian as they crowd in on Lovano's line, forcing him in new directions and into lumpy melodicism. He then asserts a new melodic motif, taking the song in a new direction with Motian and Frisell immediately responding. This is seat-of-the-pants improvisation, everyone reacting with hairs-on-end spontaneity; Frisell digs deep into his array of otherworldly sounds in his improvisation, lush chords that swell and decay, full of filigree metallic notes that sound like electronic chaff. As this free-form creativity assumes a life of its own, Lovano and Motian join in fevered duet, Motian in agitated rhythm probing Lovano's increasing dialogue with himself, asking questions and posing an array of possibilities in reply.

Less frenetic, *Circle dance* readmits melodic improvisation, a circular eight-bar melody that goes around in ever dizzying circles until centrifugal force drives improvisation away from the centre. Motian's trio was no place for the faint-hearted; it left no place to hide with its demanding unpredictability. As Frisell explained: 'With Paul, 90 per cent of the material is his own. Some of it is conventional chords and melodies, played in time, but elsewhere the harmonies are complicated and the time isn't strict. He's got tunes that are fast and loud, but not strict 4/4 – the phrases breathe. Then there are tunes we play as compositions, then go totally berserk on, which are based on a scale.' [46] Certainly, the trio's work during the 1980s and 1990s provided a welcome antidote to the climate of conformity that swept through jazz; challenging, yet full of fascinating detail, each member of the trio with depth and resource to create substantial music while responding to the ebb and flow of the creative moment. Whether they were interpreting Monk tunes, Bill Evans tunes, the standards repertoire or letting their free-flowing impulses respond to Motian's compositions, the group set high standards of consistency, collectively creating a distinct original voice that stood apart in the climate of its time. S.N.

Bobby Previte

495 **Empty Suits**
†Gramavision [A] GV 79447–2

Marty Ehrlich (alt); Robin Eubanks (tbn); Carol Emanuel (hrp); Steve Gaboury (org, p, kybd); Jerome Harris (bs, g); Allan Jaffe (g); Elliott Sharp (g); Skip Krevens (ped st g); Bobby Previte (d, perc, mar, kybd, g, vcl); Roberta Baum (vcl); Davis Shea (tabla). New York, May 1990.
Across state lines · Flying buttress · Gaboo · Break the cups · Great wall · Pichl · Across state lines (reprise) · A door flies open

Previte was initially associated with the musicians and composers of New York's 'downtown' music scene in the mid-1980s. A drummer of range and resource, he was as at home playing in the 'Blue Note groove' of the 1950s and 1960s on *The Sonny Clark Memorial Quartet: Voodoo* (†Black Saint [It] BSR0109) as he was on some of John Zorn's more recondite 'games' albums, such as *Cobra* (†Hat Art [Sw] 60401). With the appearance of Zorn's *The Big Gundown* (†Nonesuch/Icon [A] 7559 79139–2) from 1985 and *Spillane* (Elektra Nonesuch [A] 979172–1) from 1987, two large-scale productions dedicated to the music of Ennio Morricone and the film noir figure Mike Hammer respectively, attention began to focus on the downtowners who hitherto had eluded the gaze of the critics because the sheer diversity of experimental ensembles defied convenient categorization.

While Previte's drumming could be heard on both these albums, whose personnel in many ways was an early 'who's who' of the downtown scene, Previte was also establishing himself as a composer and bandleader in his own right. In 1986 his soundtrack for the video *Bought and Sold*, a sinister, dark, all-engulfing musical fog, was issued as *Dull Bang, Gushing Sound, Human Shriek* (Dossier [G] ST 7532). His debut as a bandleader per se had come the previous year with *Bump the Renaissance* (Sound Aspects [G] SAS008), with an unusual acoustic quintet whose front line comprised a tenor sax and french horn. Together with 1987's *Pushing the Envelope* (Gramavision [A] 18–8711–1), they revealed a preference for dark, mysterious tone colours contrasted by carefully conceived rhythmic structures, suggesting a kind of chamber music of the film noir.

In 1988 Previte radically realigned his musical thinking, his broader musical ambitions matched by the greater tonal resources offered by Hammond organ, keyboards, harmonica, trombone, tuba, guitar, banjo, pedal-steel guitar, harp, accordion, marimba, acoustic and electronic percussion, voice – everything, it seemed, except the kitchen sink – on *Claude's Late Morning* (Gramavision [A] 18–8811–1). Artistically, it numbered among the most satisfying albums of the 1980s, revealing Previte's growing maturity as a composer and his sure handling of form and content revealed in the almost obsessional care he took to balance tempo, texture and mood. At this point Previte decided to separate his writing for acoustic instruments from his pan-textural writing which involved unusual combinations of instruments, forming his group Weather Clear, Track Fast for his acoustic endeavours and a new group, Empty Suits, for his 'electric' compositions. In October 1990, *Empty Suits* was released featuring his new band of the same name. 'Now that adherence to a museum curator's idea of authenticity has become the rallying cry, Previte's music argues for divergence and freedom to ransack the tradition,' observed *down beat.* [47]

As his earlier albums, Previte was careful to slot individual soloists into the overall compositional design of his music, explaining: 'The way the playing is integrated into the theme is where I'm at, rather than the head – solo – head philosophy.' [48] Improvisers were charged with moving within the same concentric circle suggested by the composition rather than launchimg out on an improvisation based on the harmonies of the song that might or might not relate to the compositional matter at hand. Yet it was not just the relationship of the solo to the composition that set Previte's music apart; it was the postmodernistic zeal which extended the boundaries of jazz. A regular performer at the Knitting Factory, Previte assimilated the currents running through contemporary music, and these, as well as his own expansive musical vision, are clearly apparent on *Empty Suits*. Although the tone colours are electric and the rhythms implicit, this was music that made its own space within jazz's postmodern diaspora, moving the music forward and redefining it in the process.

Across state lines opens with an African drum rhythm that is preserved throughout the piece. From this hypnotic rhythm the primary theme gradually takes shape among competing voices before Harris's guitar, dramatic and using the tone colours of rock, rises as Ehrlich's alto is briefly glimpsed. The theme then emerges in extemporized form, before Ehrlich's alto commands our attention against a haunting vocal chant that seems to illuminate the piece. Throughout, instruments emerge and recede in deference to the overall architecture of the piece. *Flying buttress* opens with orthodox, straight-ahead drum rhythms from Previte, yet the piece is anything but straight ahead. A fractured bass line emerges in contrast to the metre of the drums, yet as cadence points rise and subside, also in a contrasting metre, Previte's unequal battle with straight-ahead rhythms continues until an episode of discontinuity, a swirling spiral from which the piece takes its meaning before Eubanks restores order and the bass guitar enunciates its fragmentary rhythmic comment against Previte's straight-ahead insistence.

Gaboo has its roots in Previte's love of King Sunny Adé's Afropop, with Miss Baum's plaintive theme in tongues contrasted by Miss Emanuel's harp and Jaffee's guitar. Other influences running through Previte's music include mid-Eastern microtones in *Break the cups*, again featuring Miss Baum's voice – this time impressively emulating Middle Eastern 'wailing' – and solos from Gaboury and Eubanks. Note also the free jazz impulses of *Great wall*, written with the composer John Adams in mind and featuring Gaboury on acoustic piano, and the minimalistic *Pichl*, featuring the full, round purity of Eubanks's controlled lyricism. The reprise of *Across state lines* permits a further exposition of the thematic material displayed on the earlier track, this time allowing Eubanks to emerge in more forthright mood with a wah-wah solo. *A door flies open* confronts the sounds of contemporary pop with turntable scratching and Previte's electronic drums. Yet despite the obviousness of popular culture, the piece emerges with Previte's unmistakable thumbprint on it, with vocal chants and the Duane Eddy-ish guitar which surfaced on *Across state lines*, a device originally used on *Claude's Late Morning.* As voices, chants, guitar motifs and rhythm coalesce, Previte's organization of a variety of tonal resources moves in unexpected directions – a squabble of competing voices becomes the backdrop for a guitar solo, for example – as gradually Previte as composer moves forward to claim the foreground.

By imposing stylistic continuity on his soloists, Previte is tacitly accepting the technical mastery of his musicians as a given. Instead he presents them with the challenge of fitting into the compositional schemes he devises so that solos emerge organically from their surroundings; indeed some solos appear to be a part of the composition itself. This highly personal music exerts a tenet that gradually seemed to have been squeezed out of jazz during the 1980s and 1990s – individualism. It was something prized and respected by the early jazz musicians and something that the music turned its back on at its peril, because if the neoconservative renaissance showed us anything, it was a surfeit of imitators taking refuge behind the 'jazz tradition'. Yet Previte and his musicians could all operate comfortably within the axis of tradition (Eubanks, for example, was formerly with Art Blakey and his Jazz Messengers), but regurgitating the past glories of jazz was not what jazz is about. It is about taking the music to its limits in new and interesting ways, in shifting the balance between composition and improvisation and perhaps even redefining jazz in the process, even if it was at the expense of public recognition. S.N.

John Zorn

496 Naked City

†Elektra Nonesuch (A) 979238–2

John Zorn (alt); Bill Frisell (g); Wayne Horvitz (kybd); Fred Frith (bs); Joey Baron (d); Yamatsuka Eye (vcl). New York, 1989.

Batman · The Sicilian clan · You will be shot · Latin Quarter · A shot in the dark · Reanimator · Snagglepuss · I want to live · Lonely woman · Ingeneous ejeculation · Blood duster · Hammerhead · Demon sanctuary · Obeah man · Ujaku · Fuck the facts · Speedball · Chinatown · Punk china doll · N.Y. flat top box · Saigon pickup · The James Bond theme · Den of sins · Contempt · Graveyard shift · Inside straight

By the mid-1990s, Zorn was celebrated as a conceptualist, a composer of both jazz and classical music – in particular for the Kronos Quartet – and as bandleader/saxophonist of a bewildering range of ensembles. He was the most famous of that loose confederation of musicians that had become known as making up the 'downtown' music scene in New York City, yet such celebrity he did enjoy, which was by no means universal within jazz, was hard earned. Zorn's early experiments in sound, such as blowing saxophone mouthpieces in buckets of water to produce duck calls, prompted what he would call 'unspeakable abuse' from critics who openly doubted whether he could play a saxophone. He could, of course. While studying music at Webster College, St Louis, he once wrote a thesis on the cartoon music of Carl W. Stallings, whom he considered the creator of the 'great avant-garde music of the 1940s'; and he went on to study composition at the UN School in Manhattan under Leonardo Balada. However, he had come under the influence of the Black Artists Group while in St Louis, in particular Oliver Lake, who had taught at his college and whom he credited for helping him break free of the classical canon and the influence of composers he had been studying that included Elliott Carter, Charles Ives, Edgard Varèse, John Cage and Stockhausen. Inspired by the work of Anthony Braxton, Roscoe Mitchell and Leo Smith, he began exploring the 'sound-makers' of the 1960s 'New Thing' – Ayler, Coltrane and Pharoah Sanders. During a ferocious period of experimentation that followed, Zorn began to formulate his approach to improvisation and composition, the latter coloured by his study of Stravinsky, Webern and Varèse alongside that of Stalling. What he seemed to be working towards was methods by which he decentred the process of improvisation and composition by abrupt *segue*. This began to emerge in 'game' pieces such as *Cobra*, *Hsü Feng* and *Ruan Lingyu*, 'narrative' pieces like *Hue Die* or *Qúê Trân*, and 'file card' compositions which were constructed in time, moment by moment, like *Godard* and *Forbidden Fruit*.

The collision of ideas through abrupt *segue* that became a characteristic of Zorn's work had its roots in his love of Stalling's music: 'Cartoon music is a very strong influence in the way I put together the disparate elements of my pieces,' he explained. 'Stravinsky and Carl Stalling, who was the composer responsible for the soundtracks of the great Warner Bros. cartoons of the 1940s, were successful at that. Their mastery of block structure completely changed the way I see the world.' [49] After a myriad of self-produced solo and concept albums on obscure and almost-impossible-to-find labels, Zorn's identity as both a soloist and a composer was beginning to coalesce. In particular it was the postmodernistic zeal with which his compositions were assembled, ushering completely new sounds into jazz: blues, surf guitars, film noir moods, country music and short, sharp shocks of rebarbative noise followed one upon another in streams of vivid fleeting images. Sometimes the references could reach information overload in a provocative representation of late-20th-century life. Zorn likened this process of abrupt *segue*, something he called 'jump cuts', to channel-zapping on television, a reflection of modern youth's compressed attention span. It was postmodernism with a vengeance, and nothing like it had been heard in jazz before.

Postmodernism was a term first applied to architecture which soon found wider application in the arts. Swimming in the currents of disunity and fragmentation (Nietzsche especially emphasized the chaos of modern life and its intractability before modern thought), postmodern cultural artefacts are, by virtue of the eclecticism of their conception and the anarchy of their subject matter, immensely varied. However, collage, pioneered by modernists, is a technique that postmodernism has made its own, a juxtaposition of seemingly incongruous elements creating a matrix of internal relations where there is never one fixed configuration, thus destroying the traditional organic unity of a work of art. In literature, a similar practice occurs in the superimposition of different worlds in many postmodern novels, while in jazz, the postmodern jazz musician expropriated and transformed practices, fragments and 'signifiers' of different, sometimes alien, musics and cultures and relocated them within their own expressionism. In particular, postmodernism did not try to legitimize itself by reference to the past – a feature of the music of the hard-bop revival in the 1980s and 1990s.

Postmodernism produced a myriad of highly personal styles and innovations which did not accede to commodification in the way the specific characteristics of previous styles of jazz had done. Marketing strategies as much as canon formation gather around unified concepts such as 'New Orleans', 'Chicago', 'swing', 'bop', 'cool' or 'West Coast', 'hard bop', 'free', 'jazz-rock' and so on. The sheer stylistic diversity of postmodernism meant that collectively, it resisted convenient categorization so its impact was restricted to the recognition an individual player might achieve, rather than the collective force a community of similarly oriented and competing artists who had produced a single coherent style might generate, as had happened in the past. Then, as each new 'style' emerged, it allowed for the validating of one artist over another and these competing claims of 'greatness' have traditionally formed the music's empowerment over fans and historians alike.

In contrast, the postmodern proposition was that the essentially teleological model of coherent evolution had now passed to a diversity of individual contributors who refused to congregate around the security of established canons, but instead conceived and performed their own, often highly individual, interpretations of jazz, drawing on a variety of sources sometimes from beyond the music. It was this coruscating juxtaposition of so many references, Information Age soundbytes from alien cultures decontextualized by juxtaposition, that created 'the new'. Above all, it was the speed and variety of references that sped by in competing clamour; it was if, as the *New York Times* put it, 'someone [was] spinning a radio dial across . . . soundtrack themes, bluesy hard bop, speedy hardcore, metallic funk, squealing free jazz, metallic funk and movie music'. [50]

While the postmodern situation might have meant the absence of the emergence of a single dominant style so essential for music marketing and media validation, the possibilities it offered the individual performer by not being locked into conventions of expectation imposed by stylistic precedent were boundless. It was a situation that produced some of the most creative music in jazz since the early 1970s, with Zorn among a new, contemporary avant-garde. His bold experiments, like the great experiments in jazz before him, forced the establishment to throw up their arms and demand: 'Is this jazz?' To answer such an apparently rhetorical question, Michael Dorf's 'What is Jazz?' concert series began in 1988 alongside the JVC New York Jazz Festival in protest at the culture of conservatism that had overtaken jazz. Dorf ran New York's Knitting Factory – to all intents and purposes the latter-day Minton's of contemporary jazz – and by 1996 he had made his point with the What is Jazz? Festival, the *New York Times* reporting: 'Every year the What is Jazz? Festival has taken on weight, while the JVC Jazz Festival has become increasingly irrelevant.' [51] Yet general acceptance of the postmodern situation in jazz was less widespread, the conservative mainstream remaining in the ascendant.

Zorn was one of the first artists to be hired by Dorf when he opened the Knitting Factory in February 1987 at its original location at 47 East Houston Street in New York City (in 1994 it moved to 74 Leonard Street), and was responsible for the first line outside its doors. By then his early notoriety had given way to a kind of respectability when his album *The Big Gundown* (†Nonesuch/Icon [A] 7559–79139–2) from 1985, featuring boldly reworked movie themes by the spaghetti-Western composer Ennio Morricone, was voted a Top Ten *Pop* Record of 1986 by the *New York Times.* It was followed by *Spillane* (Elektra Nonesuch [A] 979172–1) in 1987, a homage to the B-movie genre in general and the Mike Hammer character in particular, originally recorded under the working title of *Once Upon a Time in East Village.* With this album, Zorn claimed a new legitimacy for the downtown experimenters. The composition *Two lane highway,* in essence an Ellington-style mini 'concerto', was shaped by Zorn for the bluesman Albert Collins to reveal the range of his performing persona in the manner of a *Concerto for Cootie.* The central exhibit, however, was the title track which explored the moody soundtracks associated with the film noir, complete with programmatic episodes which suggested the to-and-fro of windscreen wipers, car chases and other elements associated with the classic screen gumshoe. A piece lasting 25 minutes, it included 60 'jump cuts' or abrupt *segues* into contrasting moods.

With *Naked City,* Zorn pared down the sweeping extravaganza of *Spillane* to its essence. The album is dotted with nine musical fragments of ferocious ear-slaughter (between 8 and 43 seconds), an affirmation of the 'New Thing' sound-makers of the 1960s, which in refusing to yield to conventional meaning was experienced as a shock by the listener. These short bursts of 'sound', such as *Obeah man, Ujaku, Fuck the facts* and *Speedball,* and longer compositions such as *Saigon pickup* and *Inside straight* are analogous to another aspect of postmodernism, time-space compression. The frenetic writings of Baudrillard and Virilio are analogous in literature in the way they replicate time-space compression with their own flamboyant rhetoric, or the cinema's use of time-space compression in *Blade Runner*, a science-fiction film with postmodern themes portraying the conflict of people living in different time scales seeing and experiencing the world very differently as a result. Time-space compression is what Zorn achieves with his own 'noisy' or 'flamboyant' bursts of unfathomable sound – how long do they last? Is it seconds or minutes or even hours?

In contrast, jump-cutting was used to programmatic ends in *Latin Quarter*, bringing to mind Ellington's description of what he was trying to portray in *Harlem air shaft*: 'You hear fights, you smell dinner, you hear people making love, you hear intimate gossip floating down, you hear the radio; an airshaft is one great loudspeaker.' [52] It is as if Zorn is trying to portray similar images during a walk through the Latin Quarter, capturing the competing sounds as you walk past a restaurant, a deli, a liquor store. *Lonely woman* engages directly with the postmodernist techniques of superimposition of different worlds that bear no relation to one another; here the bass line from the Henry Mancini theme for the television series *Peter Gunn* is 'superimposed' as art comfortably coexists with kitsch. As Andreas Huyssen has pointed out, this was typical of what happened in certain films of the 1970s, such as the work of Rainer Werner Fassbinder, when 'artists increasingly drew on popular or mass cultural forms and genres, overlaying them with modernist and/or avant gardist strategies'. [53] It was a point not lost on Zorn, an avid movie buff. Finally, during the coda he is unable to resist an allusion from a world far removed from Coleman's acoustic period on Contemporary Records from which *Lonely woman* is taken – Coleman's electric period and a reference to the theme *Dancing in your head.*

These pieces rub shoulders with movie themes that include Morricone's *The Sicilian clan* from *The Godfather*, Henry Mancini's *A shot in the dark* from the comedy film starring Peter Sellers, Johnny Mandel's *I want to live!* from the Oscar-winning Robert Wise film, Jerry Goldsmith's *Chinatown* – a latter-day film noir, John Barry's *The James Bond theme* and Georges Delerue's *Contempt* from the 1963 film *Le Mépris* directed by Jean-Luc Godard. Zorn's own *Batman* theme spurns the grand narrative of *Spillane* with its simplified rhetorical representation of TV culture and attempts to carve out one world, a favourite world, from an infinity of possible worlds that are daily shown on television.

When Zorn formed the group for an engagement at the Knitting Factory in the summer of 1989, the highly professional way in which he developed a repertoire for the band astounded the club owner Michael Dorf. 'The five days and nights Naked City played and rehearsed were amazing,' he said. 'John came in at 10am and passed out a booklet of songs he had prepared for everyone. By 8pm the group had learned 25 songs and played them for a standing room only crowd in our new [performance] space. The next morning the band came in, John gave them 15 new songs and by showtime they had those down and played some of the old material. This went on for each day. In five days they had a whole repertory and went on a European tour as if they had been together for years.' [54]

The seeming ease with which the band assembled their repertoire is perhaps less surprising when the musicians Zorn chose are examined more closely. Bill Frisell had studied music at the University of Northern Colorado and at Berklee College and had become involved in the European improvised-music scene, recording with Eberhard Weber and as a member of Jan Garbarek's group for the ECM label, where he subsequently made his debut as a leader on records, cutting three albums for that label. Through a recommendation from his former tutor at Berklee, Pat Metheny, Frisell joined an ensemble led by the drummer Paul Motian in 1980, forming an enduring relationship that lasted well into the 1990s while at the same time developing a successful solo career. The keyboardist Wayne Horvitz was also a leader in his own right, recording two classic 'downtown' albums: *This New Generation* (†Elektra Musician [A] 960759–2) from 1987 and *Bring Yr Camera* (†Elektra Musician [A] 960799–2) from 1988 with his group the President. He was also co-leader, along with his wife Robin Holcomb, of the New York Composers Orchestra. The bassist Fred Frith was formerly with the experimental/avant-garde rock group Henry Cow, while Joey Baron was a ubiquitous figure on the downtown scene – a member of Bill Frisell's band, and bands led by Hank Roberts, Tim Berne and with his own ensembles. His playing credits included work with the Toshiko Akyoshi Big Band, Carmen McRae, Dizzy Gillespie and with the Los Angeles Philharmonic.

Postmodernism sees itself for the most part as a chaotic movement attempting to overcome the supposed ills of modernism either by caricaturing it or isolating aspects of it. Possibly it could be argued that postmodernism takes things too far in its emphasis on the text rather than the work, its preference for aesthetics over ethics, its often wilful deconstruction. This argument may be given force by subsequent Naked City albums: *Heretic* (†Avant [J] 001), *Radio* (†Avant [J] 003) and the unsuccessful *Absinthe* (†Avant [J] 004) which add little to the original, startling debut that suggested we should revel in fragmentation as a part of the modern world. But at least in this, Zorn, and, indeed, the downtown movement, could be said to be reflecting the contemporary milieu in which they operated more accurately than most musicians in jazz, who were concerned with celebrating the past and actually masking or concealing developments in the present through their reduction of jazz to a repertoire function. Jazz is, after all, a modernist music, and in modernism the present is only valid in terms of the potentialities of the future. Change, therefore is not only inevitable, it is essential. And it is perhaps here the most telling argument in favour of Zorn's work is to be found, in that all jazz is a reflection of its times because contemporary culture has always created the context from which we extract meaning from the music since culture does not operate in isolation from society. From that standpoint, every age is judged to aspire to cultural maturity, not by being, but by becoming. If, then, the only thing certain about postmodernism is uncertainty, then we should pay attention to the social forces that produced such a condition, for these are the forces that shaped Zorn's music. S.N.

Arcana

497 **Arc of the Testimony**
†Axiom (A) 314524431–2

Graham Haynes (cnt); Pharoah Sanders (ten); Byard Lancaster (bs clt); Nicky Skopelitis (el g); Bill Laswell (el bs; SFX); Tony Williams (d). New York City, early 1997.
Gone tomorrow

Skopelitis, Buckethead (el g); Laswell (el bs; SFX); Williams (d). New York City, early 1997.
Illuminator

Haynes (cnt); Lancaster (alt, bs clt); Skopelitis (el g); Laswell (el bs; SFX); Williams (d). New York City, early 1997.
Into the circle

Skopelitis, Buckethead (el g); Laswell (el bs; SFX); Williams (d). New York City, early 1997.
Returning

Lancaster (alt, bs clt); Skopelitis (el g); Laswell (el bs; SFX); Williams (d). New York City, early 1997.
Calling out the blue light

Skopelitis, Buckethead (el g); Laswell (el bs; SFX); Williams (d). New York City, early 1997.
Circles of hell

Skopelitis (el g); Laswell (el bs; SFX); Williams (d). New York City, early 1997.
Wheeless on a dark river

Laswell (el bs; SFX); Williams (d). New York City, early 1997.
The earth below

When Tony Williams wound up his trailblazing group Lifetime (**442**) in April 1971, jazz would never be the same again. Neither would Williams. Unsure how to position his music, he allowed subsequent albums to reveal commercial compromise and their conspicuous lack of success, either artistically or financially, caused him to withdraw from jazz. He resurfaced in 1972 as a member of a Stan Getz group that produced *Captain Marvel* (†Columbia [F] 468412–2), among the more memorable albums in Getz's discography, but little was heard of him until he reactivated Lifetime in 1975. Yet the brilliant drummer of the classic 1960s Miles Davis groups, the terrifying percussionist mediating the *Sturm und Drang* of the original Lifetime now seemed content to keep time behind a competent but dispassionate ensemble intent on ingratiating themselves with record buyers. Williams had achieved too much too soon with Davis, and *The Joy of Flying* from 1979 simply made clear what had been obvious since April 1971, his inability to create an effective context for his playing. He only appeared comfortable in the group VSOP, a reunion of the 1965–8 Miles Davis quintet *sans* the leader, usually with Freddie Hubbard on trumpet, which toured the festival circuits in the late 1970s and early 1980s. But with the return to the hard-bop standard in the mid-1980s following the success of Wynton Marsalis – who was in fact a member of the 1981 and 1983 editions of VSOP alongside Williams – the drummer's identity crisis was solved.

Here was music he was weaned on, originality was no longer at a premium, only to play with the right degree of gravitas in an idiom that had all but been exhausted 30 years before. Subsequently Williams turned back the clock, formed his own group which operated from within the hard-bop nexus – ironically with the Miles Davis clone Wallace Roney – and was instantly fashionable. It all seemed a far cry from the teenager who wrote himself into jazz history with some of the finest and most innovative drumming the jazz world had witnessed, underlining the one great truth about jazz that if a musician is not seen as a revolutionary, then he is seen as a conservative.

On the reactivated Blue Note label, a steady stream of albums followed that suggested that Williams might become a latter-day Art Blakey, nurturing new talent and bringing them to the attention of the jazz world in general. But signs that Williams was keen to revisit the ranks of the crusading avant-garde came when the bassist Laswell approached him with some ideas for recordings after their mutual involvement in a pop-music recording. Their first project together was the bassist Jonas Hellborg's *The Word* (†Axiom [A] 422–848 374), produced by Laswell, who subsequently borrowed the name Arcana from the No Wave composer and instrumentalist John Zorn to describe his projects with Williams on which he performed *and* produced. The first Arcana date was an early 1996 meeting with the British guitarist Derek Bailey, on which Zorn acted as executive producer. *The Last Wave* (†DIW [J] 903) was cited by *The Wire* as 'one of the year's most sensational moments'.

Here was an onrush of astonishing sound that was a logical continuum of the progressive and multitextural jazz-rock fusion proposed by the original Lifetime, which had been such a departure, in terms of raw energy, sound and volume, from anything else in jazz. 'I had talked to Tony about creating another environment where we could produce that kind of energy again in a setting where he could play more aggressively and more expressively in an area that's not formatted in the usual jazz way,' Laswell explained. [55] The arcane visionary Bailey instantly created a climate where Williams's drumming sounded dangerous again, rather than merely virtuosic as it had within the hard-bop environment. No longer did he seem a player without a context; instead, in a collision of willpower and freely associating idealism, both guitarist and drummer were forced to match each other's movements in fields of competing energy as Williams attempted to impose rhythmic strategies on Bailey's dark, often frightening world.

Arc of the Testimony continued Williams's voyage of exploration beyond Lifetime which surged towards new ways of assembling and constructing music. Laswell as both bassist and producer took a leading role in shaping the direction of this music; his tough-minded connoisseurship of music past and present was linked to the endless possibilities of using the recording studio as an instrument through his extensive knowledge of contemporary studio techniques. *Arc of the Testimony* is music empowered by the sonic energy of *Emergency!* (**441**), but also reaches out to new horizons. Laswell explains how this was conceived: 'We discussed the idea of improvising and then occasionally building a structure where other instruments would play repetitively and he would solo on top of a bass or a guitar, for example, and to be as aggressive and expressive as possible and not to hold back anything. The idea was to let go and to take chances and to go as far as he possibly could. I think that was the energy and the interaction and the sound that made Lifetime special.' [56]

Gone tomorrow introduces ambient sweeps with Williams playing orthodox 'jazz' time on his ride cymbal and Haynes's cornet playing a wistful, thoughtful melody. Laswell's bass introduces a note of foreboding and presages a Sanders interlude that remains in deference to the mood Haynes had created. Throughout, Williams's 'jazz' time appears unresolved since the bass is playing a counter-melody on the first beat of an implied bar structure of 4/4. Rhythm and time seem suspended, floating slowly to some unseen destination; as fast as Williams rows, the eerie cortege seems unwilling to move faster. A disconcerting note is stuck with the reappearance of Sanders, whose militant playing catches Williams's interest and tempts him to engage in discourse. Yet the floating, dreamlike feel continues in spite of the improvisational drama now being enacted, with Sanders recalling his 'sound-making' days alongside Coltrane that flew in the face of the every-note-counts legacy of bop.

Illuminator draws sustenance from heavy metal, albeit stripped down to its essential components – power chords and rhythm – with Williams's volcanic rock rhythms well up in the mix. The forward momentum is irresistible until suddenly the tune dissolves into disruptive creativity in contrast to heavy metal's roar of doom. Abruptly this pattern of contrast becomes the leitmotif of the piece; disturbing disjunctions that are gradually woven into a fabric of shimmering electronics and rhythm. *Into the circle* reintroduces ambient sound sweeps for Haynes to continue his intimate confessionals, with Williams's cymbal *obbligato* giving way to more specific, frenetic time-keeping against Laswell's languid melodic contours. The forbidding sound of heavy metal re-emerges in the background as the textures thicken and the rhythm gradually becomes biased towards rock. The former Sun Ra alto saxophonist Lancaster becomes a shadowy presence in the face of a strengthening backbeat and the gathering storm of electricity that threatens to overwhelm the reflective sonic territory introduced by Haynes, but although the increasing tension inherent in the pain of dissonance is exploited, it is never realized.

In the same way Williams's drumming gave new direction to Bailey's abstract squalls, then on *Returning*, a murky spontaneous electronic jam that recalls the drummer's love of Hendrix, rhythm gives shape to the composition so that it becomes an expressive articulation rather than an attempt to bludgeon. Despite the intensity, the whole is executed with measured virtuosity and barbaric daring. *Calling out the blue light*, along with *Gone tomorrow*, appear as the most ambitious tracks. Both are spontaneously composed and rely on the improvisers' impulses to give meaning to the fleeting structures that appear and disappear amid the ambient sound sweeps that lend an unexpected pastoral quality, despite the swirling rhythmic counterpoint that moves between drum solo and accompaniment. *Circles of hell* opens with Williams's 'jazz' time, which is in contrast to the crack-of-doom guitar chords that unleash Sanders and Williams's frenetic dialogue. The malevolent chords return, a partial guitar freak-out, before a more thoughtful Sanders re-enters asking Williams to re-engage in every day reality, which duly becomes a texture of gathering intensity as guitars, bass and other electronically generated sounds are enveloped into the swirling, cascading eye of the storm. *Wheeless on a dark river* allows Laswell to show his prowess on bass after ambient reflections from the SFX. Power chords and abstractions from Skopelitis allow a dialogue between bass and drums to conflict before galactic synthesizer washes bring the piece to conclusion. In effect, this item acts as a sort of prelude to *The earth below*, essentially a solo feature for Williams against dark core electronic exotica.

Laswell in his role as guerrilla producer has a remarkable discography that attests to his successful marshalling of others' talents, most notably from the jazz perspective under the collective Material, which were fascinating postmodern soundscapes that confronted diverse traditions by the imaginative array of talent he assembled. The musicians, all strong and possibly eccentric individuals, of which Williams was no exception, included Henry Threadgill, Olu Dara, Wayne Shorter, Trilok

Gurtu, Sonny Sharock, Herbie Hancock and Archie Shepp from the world of jazz and Bernie Worell, Maceo Parker, Sly Dunbar & Robbie Shakespeare, Bootsy Collins and the Last Poets from Black Music. By astutely mixing these strong musical personalities from diverse musical backgrounds on albums such as *Third Power* (†Axiom [A] 422 848 417–2), *Hallucination Engine* (†Axiom [A] 314 518 351–2) and *Memory Serves* (†Charly [E] CPCD8285), Laswell created a swirling mix of music, technology and rhythm that was attractive to several younger musicians looking for a route away from renascent fashion that dominated the 1980s and 1990s, including Graham Haynes on *Tones for the 21st Century* (†Antilles [A] 537692–2) from 1987 and the rhythmically more explicit *Khmer* (ECM [G] 1560 537 798–2) by Nils Petter Molvaer from 1998.

Laswell's production concepts offered Williams a route into the future by relieving him of the problems of conceptualizing a context in which to function as a musician, allowing him to concentrate on his drumming. These imaginative electronic soundscapes, combined with the visceral improvising of Sanders, Lancaster and Skopelitis contrasted with Haynes's plaintive cornet suggestive of Williams's honourable past (Miles Davis), simultaneously gazed into the future and transplanted the drummer into a musical environment that was virtually free from convenient categorization – the enemy of creativity.

In a sense, here was the lesson that Miles Davis had understood and others ignored at their peril. Williams, in choosing to play with a conventional rhythm section of piano, bass and drums through most of the 1980s and 1990s, placed himself in permanent competition with his great recordings of the past. Davis had showed that by astutely changing the backdrop against which he functioned as a musician, he forced his audience to deal with his art on its own terms and not what it had been. Davis knew he could never return to past certainties, indeed, he had no interest in creating an accompaniment to the rest of his life with tunes like *Walkin'* (**271**), *My funny Valentine* or *Footprints*; he more than anyone in jazz consistently demonstrated that the destiny of the music lay unglimpsed beyond the horizon. He had shown that by taking the precept of jazz-rock to its limits in 1975 with *Agharta* (†Columbia/Legacy [A] 467897–2) and *Pangaea* (†Columbia/Legacy [A] 467087–2) it was possible to at least partially realize the elusive goal of developing a new musical dialect, independent of other genres of music. But this electronic odyssey claimed few followers and when he returned to jazz after a six-year furlough in 1981, his musical agenda lacked the ambition of his distinguished past. Arcana reawakened the possibilities of creating such a musical dialect, this time by combining the impulses of acoustic free jazz with the coruscating use of electricity. Williams, reinvented as a drummer of the crusading avant-garde and as dynamic as he had ever been, suggested that the future promised much. It was not to be. He died during what should have been a routine gallstone operation on 23 February 1997. S.N.

Jan Garbarek

498 All Those Born with Wings

†ECM [G] 1324

Jan Garbarek (ten, sop, fl, kybd, perc). Oslo, August 1986.

1st piece · *2nd piece* · *3rd piece* · *4th piece* · *5th piece* · *6th piece*

Garbarek's music projected the stark imagery of nature near the northern lights: 'I can't say what extent growing up in Norway would influence you, but I imagine deep down it must have some influence. There are very dramatic changes of the seasons and the landscape is also dramatic.' [57] Garbarek's work represented an ordered calm in the often frantic world of jazz; rigorous and highly disciplined, he created an evocative tranquillity strongly rooted in Nordic folk forms that gave prominence to his saxophone *tone* as the main expressive force. Garbarek created a context where his haunting saxophone appeared to commune with nature, an effect heightened on the album *Dis* (ECM [G] 1093) by his use of a wind harp. *All Those Born with Wings* was Garbarek's 12th album as a leader, although this album-length statement was made without his then regular ensemble of David Torn on guitar, Eberhard Weber on bass and Michael Di Pasqua on drums. Playing all the instruments himself, he created what was in essence predominantly homophonic sketches combining sampled and acoustic timbres often encountered in folk forms, with electronic keyboards, saxophones and flute all merged into musical cohesion by patient multitracking. Although each piece is identified, none is titled but each is unmistakably impressionistic, suggestive of the brooding forests and dramatic landscapes of Garbarek's homeland. Each piece is self-contained, making no attempt to relate to another, each an evocative textural framework for a series of saxophone meditations that are sombre in mood, yet are unmistakable manifestations of a Nordic tone within jazz.

1st piece is a sound tapestry created over a hammered dulcimer *ostinato* with Garbarek's soprano creating bird-call-like effects; strings take over then with the return of the dulcimer *ostinato*, an 18-note folklike theme is repeated over and over, with soprano overdubs evoking startled bird cries rising up above the forest's ceiling. *2nd piece* begins with dramatic synthesized drum beat; soprano and tenor join in an *a cappella* duet, a kind of Middle Eastern fanfare that leads through a series of ritualistic wails into a carnival dance. *3rd piece* evokes the mood most of us reserve for staring out of the window on a rainy day. Synthesizers intone an *ostinato* figure and in the distance, at first barely discernible through the early morning mists, emerges an outline of a soprano saxophone counter-melody. The moody atmosphere hangs heavily in the air; as in all Garbarek pieces, he reaches towards areas that are mystic in their subjective allure, working within a self-limited harmonic and rhythmic palette to create an evocative tranquillity rich in impressionistic detail. *4th piece* begins on piano, perhaps some half-remembered folk tune from Garbarek's past that is then given voice through his haunting soprano saxophone.

5th piece, the longest of the suite at something around 13 minutes, begins with a sequential motif of repeated arpeggiated figures on an acoustic guitar that provides a backdrop for Garbarek's haunting tenor. Like Gullin (**306**, **360**), Garbarek in his choice of notes can often evoke Nordic folklore without directly quoting from it. Then, as if in some troubled dream, his discourse becomes agitated. Suddenly the security of the acoustic guitar is gone. As on a forest path when the mists descend, the way ahead becomes unclear; the lone saxophone voice cries out in the still air, hallowed in atmospheric echo; it is a lost voice deep in the forest, its fate uncertain. The only responses are echoes, bouncing back to him through the mists. As the cry becomes more and more distant, it finally becomes lost among nature's sounds – the wind stirring in the trees, the cry of some far-off animal.

Accessibly desolate, *6th piece* is imbued, like much of the album, with a studied hush and hallowed introspection. Garbarek's long, shimmering and occasionally vaporous soprano lines float slowly over the undulating valley bottom far below. Throughout *All Those Born with Wings* he articulates a view prevalent in European jazz that saw the technical display of virtuosity as both excessive and in poor taste. By moving in an equal and opposite direction he evokes a kind of 'virtuous' boredom through a preponderance of subdued rhythmic and linear events which, under Eicher's careful production, assumed great emotional force.

For some, however, Garbarek's music posed problems of 'authenticity': did an indigenous American music shaped by the Afro-American experience become less meaningful when played by a non-American, and specifically, a non-American who imported elements of his own culture into the music? Such a response was reminiscent of the reaction to Charles Ives's Symphony No. 2, which he completed in 1901 or 1902 when the dominant culture in America was predominantly derived from Europe. Then critics considered it lowbrow to introduce themes suggesting gospel music and Stephen Foster into the 'European' symphonic tradition. Now we are concerned with the reverse; themes suggesting a European element introduced into an American music tradition. In both instances resistance to change was framed in terms of an idealized past violated by the crass and insensitive pluralism of the present. Yet progress is impossible without change – indeed, the essence of jazz has been realized in the process of change itself. Today, however, without a dominant figure who providentially appeared in the past to provide the catalyst for change, jazz has increasingly turned in on itself. As Scott

DeVeaux has pointed out, there is 'a revolution under way in jazz that lies not in an internal crisis of style, but the debate over the looming new orthodoxy: jazz as "American classical music"'. [58]

With the 1990s New York scene given over in the main to neoconservatism and major recording companies fulfilling their commitment to jazz via the neoconservatives or fusion, a belief was being widely expressed among European musicians that the evolutionary zeal that had carried American jazz forward for almost a century had now burned itself out, and the task of carrying the music forward had crossed the Atlantic to the Netherlands, Germany, Scandinavia, Italy, Spain and Britain. [59] As American jazz paused in the 1980s and 1990s to move towards 'an alternative conservatory style for the training of young musicians' and 'an artistic heritage to be held up as an exemplar of American or African-American culture', [60] it seemed apparent that academicism was breeding revivalism and eyes turned elsewhere in search of the evolutionary continuum. The momentum for innovation, the sine qua non of modernism, which had been held in check for almost two decades, was now irresistible – not least as evidence that the music was continuing to evolve as an art form. Hand in hand with American jazz's preoccupation with its past came a failure to acknowledge the music had become so big that it had finally outgrown its country of birth and that its stewardship was no longer an exclusive American preserve. S.N.

Edward Vesala

499 Lumi

†ECM [G] 1339

Esko Heikkinen (tpt, picc tpt); Pentti Lahti (alt, bar); Jorma Tapio (alt, clt, bs clt, fl); Tapani Rinne (ten, sop, clt, bs clt); Kari Heinilä (ten, sop, fl); Tom Bildo (tbn, tu); Iro Haarla (p); Raoul Björkenheim (g); Taito Vaino (acc); Häkä (bs); Edward Vesala (d). Helsinki, June 1986.

The wind · Frozen melody · Calypso bulbosa · Third moon · Lumi · Camel walk · Fingo · Early messenger · Together

One of the key musicians in the burgeoning Finnish free-jazz scene of the late 1960s and early 1970s with the likes of Juhani Aaltonen, Eero Koivistoinen and Pekka Sarmanto, Vesala came to international attention in 1973 as a member of Jan Garbarek's trio on *Triptykon* (ECM [G] 1029), which stands as the saxophonist's most abstract statement on record. Subsequently, Vesala toured extensively as a co-leader of the Tomasz Stańko–Edward Vesala quartet which wound up in 1978 after recording five albums. While these experiences gave rein to his freer impulses, Vesala also played blues, rock, tango, classical and film music. He began his career with two years' study at the Sibelius Academy, concentrating on music theory and orchestral percussion, and as he established himself as a drummer he developed a parallel reputation as a composer in a variety of multimedia projects. His music for theatre included settings of the Finnish national epic *Kalevala*, which drew on very old folk ballads and his experiences growing up in the remote forests of eastern Finland, where he became conscious of Finnish folk music's magical/religious function and the role music and myth played in the lives of the rural community. In 1974 he recorded *Nan Madol* (ECM [G] 1077), comprising six of his compositions for an 11-piece keyboard-less ensemble that included a harp, violin, trumpet, trombone, flute and saxophones. It presented a mixture of brooding Scandinavian melancholia, freely improvised episodes and sinister folk-dance imagery which established him as one of a handful of European jazz composers to make sense of his cultural heritage within the competing ideologies of jazz expressionism.

Satu (ECM [G] 1088) from 1977 continued Vesala's restless experimentation with a larger ensemble, this time built around the Vesala/Stańko quartet with some impassioned playing from the guitarist Terje Rypdal. Vesala entered the 1980s heading his Sound & Fury music workshops, part percussion clinics and part music school, from which emerged his experimental ensemble Sound & Fury. *Lumi*, from 1986, represents their first album together with a line-up that included some of Finland's finest jazz musicians. The saxophonist Pentti Lahti was the only musician retained from the *Nan Madol* line-up, and like Vesala he had been a fixture on the Finnish scene since the early 1970s combining music education and performing. A Berklee College of Music graduate, Raoul Björkenheim composed music for the Helsinki Philharmonic Orchestra and the Finnish Radio Symphony Orchestra, had worked with Bill Laswell and after two years with Sound & Fury formed his own group Krakatau, establishing his reputation as one of Finland's foremost young jazz musicians. The saxophonist Tapani Rinne would also earn a reputation as one of Finland's leading jazz musicians after his period with Sound & Fury, going on to record several albums under his own name which made imaginative use of electronic tone colours.

Lumi has a slightly modified line-up from *Nan Madol* with one fewer woodwind, allowing Taito Vainio to come in on accordion while Vesala's wife, Iro Haarla, doubled on acoustic piano and harp. *The wind* had appeared on that earlier album and unravels with precise majesty after Miss Haarla's piano introduction. Flutes and bass clarinet repeat a series of descending phrases that move through moments of dissonance until the trumpet assumes the lead role to command the solemn reverie. There are no solos per se, instruments emerge briefly and fade back into the unfathomable depths of the interconnecting events of Vesala's carefully written ensemble passages. Like *The wind*, *Frozen melody* takes its inspiration from nature, a melodic motif repeated with varying instrumental densities; first one saxophone, then more than one with trumpet, until the trumpet leads the gently sighing ensemble to fade. It reveals Vesala's disdain for the predictable forms common in bebop and hard bop, instead favouring an egalitarian vision of minimalism with its obsessively repeated folkloric theme.

Calypso bulbosa is an exotic rhythmic piece pitting combinations of acoustic instruments against overdriven guitar with individual instrumental voices glimpsed as they emerge and recede among the competing tonal densities before abruptly cutting into an episode with falsetto voices intoning their respective instrumental parts. Vesala's relentless non-calypso rhythm is restrained but exuberant, resisting a more competitive role in accompaniment, such as his explosive playing on *Triptykon.* Perhaps because of his work in providing film soundtrack music, there is a vividly pictorial quality to *Third moon, mysterioso* woodwinds hanging in the air over Vesala's suspended rhythm; a brief vignette but texturally complex for all that, the sort of piece Vesala calls 'a small door opening into another world'. [61] The title track is in many ways the album's centrepiece, a composition that attempts to blur the distinction between the life lived and the art that is derived from it, and, perhaps more than any other track on the album, it shows Vesala's ability to create a singular introspective mood while revealing a striking variety of internal tensions and shifting timbres. Although featuring the tenor saxophonist Rinne, he is careful not to betray the emotions expressed by the ensemble mediated by Vesala's baleful drum tattoos.

Vesala's wide-ranging vision includes an appreciation of Middle Eastern and Far Eastern cultures, and *Camel walk* has a wah-wah guitar rhythm setting the mood of the piece while emulating the sound of turntable scratching. This colourful backdrop allows for a greater degree of solo expressionism than the more carefully considered mood pieces and Björkenheim's guitar follows brief interludes by Lahti on alto and Rinne on tenor before the ensemble engage in an absorbing exchange of cross-accents. *Fingo* reflects Finland's century-long love affair with the tango with no ironic distance intended. Featuring Vainio on accordion, it presents another small, if surreal, door that 'opens into another world'. *Early messenger* is a vivid piece of impressionism recalling animal cries drifting across a frozen lake, with the ensemble gradually cloaking their calls like an early evening mist. *Together* is a dirgelike piece that suddenly yields unexpected detail; the controlled vibrato of the flute choir, the majestic dynamic control of Heikkinen's trumpet and Bildo's trombone, Vesala as an epigrammatic colourist and Björkenheim's overdriven yet hauntingly rhapsodic guitar. References to the American jazz tradition lurk within his music, such as veiled allusions to Gil Evans's shimmering textures, but they are cast within a broader framework that uses the sounds of rock and of Finnish folk forms with no apparent disjunction.

Vesala's music eschews homogenized forms to embrace a multiplicity of possibilities. His primary concerns are with emotional expressivity – 'If you want to make music, do it with a 100 per cent conviction or don't bother at all' – over mechanical prolixity, his profound melodic sensibilities allowing veiled allusion to appear as subtle tautology rather than wilful eclecticism, creating a series of richly impressionistic tone poems that evoked the bleak beauty of his homeland's landscapes. As he observed the American jazz renaissance during the 1980s he became disturbed at what he saw as glib revivalism whose surface slickness, he believed, masked the music's loss of faith. He became exasperated with critics who 'just run with the trends', excusing mediocrity and the blatantly slick. Arguing that jazz had become an empty shell, he felt it morally honest to say so, and see what could be done about it. It was an argument reinforced by the originality of his own writing, which showed in sharp relief the values that the safe, accessible mainstream had lost. Those values, Vesala claimed, were emotional and spiritual qualities which had been sacrificed to ingratiate the music with a larger audience and with that most emasculating of levellers, the radio. His opposition to this perceived emotional sterility was voiced most forthrightly on his next album, *Ode to the Death of Jazz* (ECM [G] 1413) recorded in 1989, a denouncement of the status quo that he felt had come to prevail in jazz: 'This music is first of all about feeling and the transmission of *feeling*. This empty echoing of old styles – I think it's tragic. If that is what the jazz tradition has become then what about the tradition of creativity, innovation, spirituality, individuality and personality?' [62] S.N.

Peter Apfelbaum and the Hieroglyphics Ensemble

500 **Signs of Life**
†Antilles [A] 422 848 634–2

Bill Ortiz (tpt); Jeff Cressman, James Harvey (tbn, perc); Norbert Stachel (sop, ten, bar, bs sx, fl, bs fl); Paul Hanson (alt, ten, bsn); Peter Apfelbaum (ten, sop, p, kybd, perc); Tony Jones (ten); Peck Almond (bar, tpt, clt, perc); Will Bernard (g); Stan Franks (g); Jai Uttal (g, har, vcl, perc); Bo Freeman (bs, vcl); David Belove (b[1]); Josh Jones (d, perc); Deszon X Claiborne (d); Robert Huffman (perc); Scheherazade Stone (vcl[2]). Marin County California, 23–6 November 1990.

Candles and stones · Walk to the mountain (and tell the story of love's thunderclapping eyes) · Grounding · The last door · The world is gifted[2] *· Chant #11 · Forwarding Part 1/Forwarding Part 2*[1] *· Samantha Smith · Folk song #7 · Waiting*

If free jazz in the early 1960s declared an impatience with straight-ahead jazz time-keeping and excursions into jazz-rock in the late 1960s and early 1970s did away with it entirely, jazz nevertheless seemed reluctant to part with what Captain Beefheart once called 'Momma heartbeat', the bass playing four beats to the bar, the drummer accenting the second and fourth beats and the pianist comping in a style derived from Bud Powell. Since Armstrong moved away from alla breve to point to the modern conception of swing in the 1920s, many of the so-called innovations in drumming patterns claimed by historians now appear more as modifications and embellishments to a basic straight-ahead drumming style which even in the 1980s and 1990s remained the favoured form of time-keeping on the majority of jazz recordings, reflecting the climate of retrospection of this period (which was heightened by a return to the practice of the head–solos–head formula). It prompted Apfelbaum to observe in 1996: 'When I hear a jazz group I get the impulse to run up to the stage and say, "Listen, you don't have to do that anymore. There's been all these discoveries. Haven't you heard?"' [63]

Yet since the beginnings of jazz, its earliest practitioners argued for rhythmic diversity, the habanera section in W. C. Handy's *St Louis blues*, for example, and Jelly Roll Morton's insistence on the 'Spanish tinge'. In the main, however, jazz resisted the potential inherent in broadening its rhythmic base and while Ellington's huge repertoire included 'exotic' numbers, it was not until the influence of Dizzy Gillespie's former mentor Mario Bauza was felt in Gillespie's late-1940s band (**315**) that Cuban rhythms impacted meaningfully on jazz, a theme taken up by other bandleaders, including Stan Kenton. But in general musical influences from other cultures were slow to seep into jazz, and it was not until the early 1960s that John Coltrane, prompted by his exploration of Nicolas Slonimsky's *Thesaurus of Scales and Melodic Patterns*, revealed an interest in the music of India. And though Stan Getz brought Brazilian rhythms to jazz, it was the jazz-rock revolution in the late 1960s and early 1970s that offered potentially the most radical rhythmic realignment to confront jazz. [64]

Initially the adoption of rock rhythms proposed a new backdrop for jazz improvisation, not least because in straight-ahead time-keeping the cymbals carried the basic rhythmic pulse while in rock it went back to the drums because at the higher volume levels of electronic instruments cymbals allowed little definition to any subdivisions of the beat. For a while it seemed that drummers had finally been released from straight-ahead time-keeping. With the young collegiate audiences haemorrhaging to rock music in the 1960s, the straight-ahead style of drumming was associated with the values of a previous generation, in short, the style of music their parents grew up with. 'Dig that cat's craaazy beat!' cried one young rock fan as he passed a jazz club as his friends collapse to the pavement crippled by mirth.

By the 1980s, however, the free-jazz blood-letting in New York lofts, often to tiny audiences of fellow musicians and true believers, and the commercial excesses of a mutation of jazz-rock known as fusion led many young musicians to believe that jazz had taken a series of wrong turns during the preceding decade. They reasoned that only by returning to a point in jazz history before these perceived aberrations, in essence a return to the hard-bop mainstream, could the sanctity of jazz as an art form be preserved. This may have produced a model of jazz that could enter colleges and universities, but it was a version framed to satisfy pedagogical imperatives – a tangible value system within an (albeit skilfully) contrived historical narrative. It failed to allow for, indeed refused to acknowledge, the subsequent, post-1970s evolution of jazz.

Perhaps the most important thing about the jazz-rock revolution of the late 1960s and early 1970s was that once the Rubicon had been crossed by appropriating elements of another musical culture (rock) in terms of both its sounds and its rhythms to wholly reshape the established, accepted notion of jazz, it set in sway a hunt for further combinations of sounds and rhythms in which to resituate the practices and conventions of jazz improvisation. If anything characterized jazz away from the safe, accessible mainstream during the 1980s and 1990s, it was its eclecticism. Such a vision of jazz had already been glimpsed by Apfelbaum when he was in Berkeley High School in the 1970s. A multi-instrumentalist and teenage prodigy, he formed a group he called the Hieroglyphics Ensemble in 1977 to perform his own compositions which ambitiously blended reggae, salsa and jazz. Moving to New York (1978–82), he became a member of Karl Berger's Woodstock Workshop Orchestra, toured Europe with Don Cherry and became a member of Carla Bley's band. However, he failed to establish himself on the New York scene as a saxophonist, his main instrument, and returned to California. The Hieroglyphics Ensemble was only occasionally reactivated, but after some rave reviews, recognition by the Grateful Dead bassist Phil Lesh culminated in the band receiving the group's Rex Foundation Award for Creative Excellence. In 1988, while the band were actively seeking a recording contract, Apfelbaum was commissioned to write a suite for the Hieroglyphics Ensemble to be performed at San Francisco's Jazz in the City Festival.

Apfelbaum invited the trumpeter Don Cherry to perform the piece with his ensemble, who promptly adopted the band for a tour of Europe and Japan, dubbing it his Multikulti Band. When Cherry was signed by the reactivated A&M label, he in turn invited Apfelbaum's ensemble to appear on his album *Multikulti* (†A&M 395323–2). The full Hieroglyphics Ensemble appeared on *Until the rain comes* and *Divinity-tree*, while Apfelbaum and two of the Hieroglyphics appeared on *Rhumba multikulti.* Apfelbaum also appeared in a Cherry ensemble for *Dedication to Thomas Mapfumo.* On those with the full ensemble, it was clear that here was something unique in jazz, an ensemble that espoused Cherry's abiding interest in music of other cultures which he had earlier essayed in the groups Codona and Nu. However, the potential impact of the Hieroglyphics Ensemble was dissipated through a combination of poor miking, resulting in a lack of detail, and an absurdly low gain level that diminished the internal dynamics of the band. This proved crucial on *Divinity-*

tree, where Apfelbaum revealed a technique of writing he called the 'rhythm block' method, whereby 'each of the wind instruments plays a separate melodic line in "rhythmic unison" with the others, within a rhythmic pattern usually lasting eight or sixteen bars'. [65]

This method of voicing across the whole ensemble was especially striking against the Afro-salsa rhythms in which the band delighted. Yet, Apfelbaum pointed out; 'At no point in the process of writing my compositions has there been a conscious decision to incorporate African elements, or any other cultural stylistic elements, for that matter. I just write and adjust the shape of it all. My vocabulary reflects the fact I started life as a drummer, was trained in jazz theory, blues, gospel music as a sub-teenager, was inundated with African and Latin music as a teenager and became involved in group improvisation on a regular basis, listened to a lot of 20th century classical music, worked in rhythm 'n' blues, reggae, blues, Latin, African, jazz, funk, Middle Eastern and Indian bands and for as long as I can remember, I've been fascinated by how sounds fit together.' [66] In fitting these rhythmic pieces together, the band created a level of rhythmic complexity that existed in several layers – percussion, bass, drums and guitars weaving quite different, yet specific, rhythms to create a texture that owed allegiance to jazz, Africa, Cuba and Jamaica (reggae), a polyrhythmic complexity that was often greater than the sum of its component rhythmic structures. This dense, hypnotic and metrically ambiguous rhythm prompted one leading jazz trumpeter, on hearing the band perform at a jazz festival, to enquire what the time signature was on a particular a number. He was apparently amazed to learn the piece in question was written in 4/4.

In 1990, Apfelbaum secured the elusive record deal he had been after and his debut album as a leader, *Signs of Life*, opened with the Grammy-nominated mini-suite *Candles and stones*. Its four contrasting sections are performed without a break, seeking to create the kind of organic flow found in successful improvisation. Three of the sections reveal a distinct African influence: the opening 'call' played by two soprano saxophones was in the style of Yoruba praise-singing, which typically begins with an *a cappella* fanfare before the rhythm instruments join in. The following section presented the guitars and bass playing a repeated phrase using a scale found in Gnawa music of Morocco and Bambara music of Mali and are embellished by a Moroccan *sintir* and the Malian *doussou n'gouni* which are tuned accordingly. Later, a horn riff emerges that is a literal adaptation of the rhythm 'rumba Obatala', which is of Afro-Cuban origin and typically played on Bata drums. Here, the horn writing uses Apfelbaum's 'rhythm block' writing to create an exciting interlude with phrases tossed between saxes and brass. The third section, in 6/8 time, resolves around a central phrase produced by the sound of the three guitars and bass each accenting a different place within a repeated two-bar pattern. The three percussionists use their own patterns, but also accent and highlight one of the guitar parts in a way that gradually builds tension. Finally, the fourth section, in a brisk $^5/_8$, is written over a cycle of changing chords that contrasts the relatively static harmonies of the preceding sections, and introduces the balanced lyricism of Peck Almond's trumpet. Apfelbaum has pointed out how the cycles of chords in this section indirectly reflected the influence of Cecil Taylor, who taught him the value of creating one's own chords and chord progressions.

Walk to the mountain (and tell the story of love's thunderclapping eyes) had been adopted by Cherry's Multikulti band as a signature piece. Here, like *Candles and stones*, it utilizes an African rhythm tapestry approach, and a harmonic cycle that is repeated over and over to create a feeling of an African 'big beat'. The piece unfolds with a rhythmic vamp under the composed horn parts that give way to Uttal's solo on harmonium, an unexpected oasis of calm among the chattering cross-rhythms. Then follows Apfelbaum's solo on tenor, demonstrating an imperious melodic majesty as he rises above the matrix of sound before a reprise of the earlier horn section. *Grounding* opens with a moving, overdriven guitar solo by Bernard, for whom the piece is virtually a feature, followed by a bassoon solo by Paul Hanson. Here the rhythm is less ambiguous – a good, hearty old backbeat, no less.

The last door is built on another of Apfelbaum's well-constructed cycles of chords, here of chorus length over a $^7/_8$ rhythm pattern. After Harvey's exposition of the melody on trombone, Norbert Stachel on bass flute introduces a distinct Middle Eastern mood, a theme taken up by Hanson on tenor and enhanced by Uttal's wordless vocal solo which has Apfelbaum, on a megaphone, intoning 'Take the last door to get out' in the background. The final chorus by Bernard is an exotic, overdriven fantasy that ends the piece.

The longest item on the album, and also its centrepiece, is *The Forwarding, Parts 1 and 2.* Originally it was parts 4 and 5 respectively of the suite *Notes from the Rosetta Stone*, commissioned in 1988 by the San Francisco Jazz Festival with Don Cherry as guest soloist; the revised title comes from the Rastafarian concept that one always goes 'forward' in an 'upfull' and enlightened existence, never 'backward'. It opens with a reggae-style guitar and bass with Apfelbaum's keyboard interjections, which lead into the engaging initial subject played by the full ensemble. Cressman on trombone enters with just bass and percussion accompaniment presenting an effective contrast to the earlier dense, swirling rhythms. Abruptly the guitars enter to reinforce the reggae feel and the band offer accompanying riffs. Franks on guitar follows with an imaginative and well-constructed solo that leads into *Part 2.* Suddenly the rhythm changes and for his only time on record Apfelbaum uses a walking bass line in $^4/_4$. This has the effect of revealing the polyrhythmic 'layering' as the ear moves towards the familiar four of the bass, allowing the guitars and percussion, each with their own singular parts to play, to stand revealed in clear, interlocking detail. Apfelbaum's security as a leader is such that he featured another tenor saxophonist, Jones, a musician whom he had known from 1974 and whom he considered 'one of the most original saxophonists playing today'. [67] The spirit of his playing moves his fellow band members to join him in simultaneous improvisation as the intensity rises against powerful brass riffs. As the full ensemble enter, Apfelbaum's 'rhythm block' style is again apparent as they move into a new, second subject. Here the swirling drama of the Hieroglyphics is captured before Peck Almond enters with another of his poised trumpet solos, this time tightly harmon-muted. The swirling rhythm of the piece drives on through Stachel's baritone solo against the gradually rising intensity of the ensemble; the bass still walking in 4/4 but it is now the ensemble's dramatic cross-rhythms that catch the ear; they have locked in time and disguise the metre. After the solos and a reprise of the horn parts, the band falls silent, leaving only the percussionists. Here the African rhythmic foundation that had sounded so beguiling within the rhythmic layering of the band is finally exposed and is revealed as an ancient West African *Comparsa* rhythm, which is given a traditional rendering.

Apfelbaum, who aligns his thinking with those whom he calls 'restructuralists' such as Henry Threadgill, Roscoe Mitchell, Anthony Braxton, Steve Coleman, Dave Douglas, Karl Berger, Ed Wilkerson, Tim Berne, Avro Moses, Carla Bley, Warren Smith, Julius Hemphill, John Zorn and Anthony Davis, who, in the aftermath of the explosion of musical structure in the 1960s, began putting the pieces back together in different and interesting ways. Yet Apfelbaum never lost sight of the fact that the contemporary dance rhythms in the 1980s and 1990s also yielded potential for creative development. Certainly these remarkably diverse elements can be found in his work; from freedom to rock, from reggae to salsa, from open to closed form, the Hieroglyphics Ensemble appeared a perfect vehicle to express Apfelbaum's musical vision. Although the band's second album, *Jodoji Brightness* (†Antilles 314 512 320–2) from 1992, returned to the freer expressionism of the 1960s and 1970s on several tracks, the combination of arresting ensemble textures, well-written compositions and thoughtful improvisation which characterized his first album were again present, especially on the 'rhythm block' style of *Chant #9*. But overall, this album did not come up to the standard of his startling debut. Sadly, Apfelbaum was dropped from the label when the company was taken over by Polygram and, without the profile of national releases, he began to struggle to find work for his band.

This remarkable ensemble, which in its time saw the future straight-ahead jazz starlets Benny Green, Craig Handy and Joshua Redman pass through its ranks, began to break up. Jai Uttal formed the Pagan Love

Orchestra, which often featured Apfelbaum offering a distinct Indian slant on jazz with albums such as *Monkey* (†Triloka 320194–2). The guitarist Will Bernard was signed by the label that dropped Apfelbaum, recording *Medicine Hat* (†Antilles 539 325–2), and formed the group Pothole, releasing *Dirty Picnic* (†Institution INT 3504–2). Josh Jones formed Hueman Flavor and the Josh Jones Latin Ensemble and worked with David Murray, Arthur Blythe and Steve Coleman, while the drummer Deszon X. Claiborne became a regular in the blues singer Charles Brown's ensemble. Finally, Apfelbaum was forced to reduce the size of his band to a sextet, and recorded *Luminous Charms* (†Gramavision GCD 79511) in 1996. A powerful statement by a wholly original band, it lacked, of course, the impact of the Hieroglyphics Ensemble, but it did give more exposure to the leader's lyrical saxophone, his lean intensity more focused, as was the level of logic and intrigue of his compositions. However, at the threshold of the new millennium, *Signs of Life* appeared as one of the finest recordings since the jazz-rock revolution at the end of the 1960s by showing the potential of jazz to reinvent itself in a cogent, unified and original way. His music sounded like a peek into a multicultural world beyond our own that somehow made so much jazz of the 1970s, 1980s and 1990s sound dated. Perhaps more important, it revealed not only a compelling vision of jazz in the present, but with the onset of the millennium, what jazz might yet become. S.N.

Notes

Chapter One

[1] In recent years there have been some rather polemical assertions about where Newman actually made these recordings. See as an example James Patrick's 'Al Tinney, Monroe's Uptown House, and the Emergence of Modern Jazz in Harlem' in *Annual Review of Jazz Studies 2*. But as Guy is known to have had charge of the house band at Minton's during 1941, the presumed year of these recordings, and Tinney to have held a similar position at Monroe's, it seems reasonable to suggest that those on which the former is present originated at Minton's, those with the latter at Monroe's. (The CD reissue ascribes the recordings exclusively to Minton's.)

[2] In *Talking Jazz* compiled by Max Jones (London, Macmillan, 1987), p. 197.

[3] A performance of *Cherokee* allegedly recorded by Parker at Monroe's appears on **250** but, compared with the other music here, this sounds too neatly played for such casual circumstances. The alternative supposition, that this is part of a broadcast by Jay McShann's band from the Savoy Ballroom (where they opened on 9 January 1942), is more likely.

[4] *down beat*, 7 March 1956.

[5] *Toward Jazz*, p. 130 (see Bibliography).

[6] Under the Muslim name Sadik Hakim, which he had taken some years before, Thornton made this claim in 'You Can't Fight City Hall', *Melody Maker*, 19 June 1971, repeating it a decade later in 'My Experiences with Bird and Pres', *Coda*, December 1981, and in several other places. Disputes over the provenance of such items are not uncommon. For example *Sax-o-be-bop* (on *I got rhythm*), though always attributed to Young, is identical with *Frolic Sam* recorded by Barney Bigard and with Goodman's *Pound ridge*.

[7] To which it might be added that *Stuffy* on **195** is perhaps by Monk.

[8] These recordings should not be confused with the 1959–62 material done with Jimmy Cleveland, Benny Golson, Eddie Costa *et al.* and reissued as *Bean and the Boys.* There are several other records titled *Bean and the Boys*, some of them on the Bean label.

[9] Steve Kuhn, quoted by Martin Williams in *down beat*, 8 February 1968.

[10] Martin Williams: *Jazz Heritage* (New York, Oxford University Press, 1985), p. 187.

[11] Hear for example *Mean to me*, *What more can a woman do?* and *I'd rather have a memory than a dream* (Continental [A] CLP16004).

[12] Thus in 1989 Martin Williams could still republish a 1962 article in which he said that it seemed to him 'quite reasonable to say that, at his death, Navarro was still doing Gillespie, with touches of Parker, Young and others', *Jazz in Its Time* (New York, Oxford University Press), p. 44.

[13] James Lincoln Collier: *The Making of Jazz* (see Bibliography), p. 400.

[14] Bill Crow, *The Jazz Review*, December 1958.

[15] *Music and Musicians*, September 1982.

[16] A random selection from among thousands of examples: 'The bleak and barren bop days when pianists substituted an unrhythmic claw to replace the nimble left hand provided by God', Percy Traill, *Jazz Journal*, December 1977, p. 43.

[17] However, the first recordings Powell made after moving to Europe in 1959, at a concert, were by a quintet using the Modernists' instrumentation, with Clark Terry and Barney Wilen (Giganti dal Jazz [It] 8). These were followed by sextet performances with Lee Morgan, Wilen and Wayne Shorter, of two of the Modernists' pieces, *Dance of the infidels* and *Bouncing with Bud* (Fontana [F] 680 207).

[18] Typically, Martin Williams in *Jazz Heritage* (*op. cit.*), p. 57.

[19] For informative comments on the harmonic usage of *McGhee special*, see Schuller's *The Swing Era* (see Bibliography), pp. 361–4.

[20] Note also some comments from *down beat* on a 1944 performance of this piece with Georgie Auld's band quoted in Gitler: *Jazz Masters of the Forties* (see Bibliography), p. 95.

[21] Quoted in Chambers: *Milestones* (see Bibliography), pp. 79ff.

[22] Giddins: *Celebrating Bird* (see Bibliography), p. 98.

[23] Giddins: *op. cit.*, p. 98.

[24] Liner note to *The Complete Charlie Parker on Verve* (†Verve 837149–2) by Phil Schaap, pp. 32–3.

[25] *Bird: The Legend of Charlie Parker* by Robert Reisner (see Bibliography), p. 174, letter from Doris Parker dated 31 December 1956.

[26] Liner note to *The Complete Charlie Parker on Verve* (†Verve 837149–2) by Phil Schaap.

[27] Conversation with SN, February 1994.

[28] A partial list in no particular order might include Jack Noren, Cornelius Thomas, Neil Michel, Billy Graham, Sylvester Payne, Zutty Singleton, Jimmy Pratt, Marquis Foster, Morey Feld.

[29] Conversation with SN, February 1994.

[30] Liner note to *The Complete Charlie Parker on Verve* (†Verve 837149–2).

[31] *Ibid.*

[32] Quite what to make of the fact *Tico tico* was a favourite of Parker's or, indeed, that a favourite saxophonist of his was Jimmy Dorsey, is another matter entirely.

[33] Liner note to *The Complete Charlie Parker on Verve* (†Verve 837149–2).

[34] A point I am grateful to Max Harrison for suggesting to me.

[35] Interview with SN, 1 July 1981.

[36] Orrin Keepnews's highly appropriate observation on the CD reissue.

[37] Well off the scale of a standard metronome, crotchet = 280 (minim = 140).

[38] Again well off the scale, and another very fast one, this time crotchet = 308.

[39] *Melody Maker*, 17 June 1961.

[40] Examples at once volatile and emphatic, occupying ground between Johnson's deft sobriety and Bill Harris's riotous assertions, include Winding's own *Mervel falls in* (Xanadu [A] 124, 1945), Al Haig's *Hot halavah* (Spotlite [E] SPJ139, 1948) and Stan Getz's *Sweet miss* (SPJ143, 1949).

[41] Quoted in Gitler: *Jazz Masters of the Forties* (see Bibliography), p. 143.

[42] Barry McRae: *The Jazz Cataclysm* (London, Dent, 1967), p. 23.

[43] *Ibid.*

[44] Jack Cooke in Harrison (ed.): *Modern Jazz: The Essential Records 1945–70* (see Bibliography), pp. 68–9.

[45] *Miles: The Autobiography* (see Bibliography), p. 178.

[46] This is said although Mingus mistook him for Parker in a Feather blindfold test, quoted in Gitler: *Jazz Masters of the Forties* (see Bibliography), p. 41.

[47] Nat Hentoff: 'Miles Davis – Last Trump', *Esquire*, March 1959.

[48] Starting with Mingus's highly coloured account in *down beat*, 30 November 1955.

[49] For Davis's own, seemingly disingenuous account of this date, see p. 177 of his *Autobiography* (*op. cit.*); he neither confirms nor denies that Monk was his choice for pianist.

[50] Nat Hentoff: 'An Afternoon with Miles Davis', *Jazz Review*, December 1958.

[51] Richard Hadlock: *Jazz Masters of the Twenties* (London, Macmillan, 1965), p. 60.

[52] From a *down beat* interview conducted by Nat Hentoff and quoted by Burt Korall in the sleeve note of HMV (E) CLP1237.

[53] Charles Fox, Peter Gammond, Alun Morgan: *Jazz on Record* (London, Hutchinson, 1960), p. 304.

[54] Robert Gordon: *Jazz West Coast* (see Bibliography) should be noted as an honourable exception.

[55] *down beat*, 8 September 1977, p. 43.

[56] *Jazz Journal International*, February 1984, p. 8.

[57] Interview with SN, 13 May 1993.

[58] *down beat*, January 1988, p. 23.

[59] Farmer also appeared with Mulligan on two other films, *I Want to Live* and *The Subterraneans*.

[60] Martin Williams: *Jazz in Its Time* (*op. cit.*), p. 43.

[61] A fuller account of *Fontainebleau* can be found in Max Harrison: *A Jazz Retrospect* (see Bibliography).

[62] *Thad Jones–Billy Mitchell Quintet* (Dee Gee [A] 4009) was issued as an EP. The pianist was probably Terry Pollard. The Mitchell group with Jones may have also earlier recorded a couple of singles backing the singer Sonny Wilson.

[63] *down beat*, 9 May 1963, p. 16.

[64] Highly recommended is *The Complete Solid State Recordings of the Thad Jones/Mel Lewis Orchestra* (†Mosaic [A] MD5–151).

[65] 'Sonny Rollins and the Challenge of Thematic Improvisation', *Jazz Review*, November 1958; reprinted in Schuller's *Musings* (see Bibliography).

[66] A. J. McCarthy (ed.): *Jazz on Record* (see Bibliography), p. 116.

[67] 'The phrases [Arthur Blythe] plays come from the most decorative material of essentially undecorative hard bop saxmen like Johnny Griffin', John Litweiler: *The Freedom Principle* (see Bibliography), p. 293.

[68] John Mehegan: 'Jazz Pianists 4 – Hampton Hawes', *down beat*, 25 July 1957.

[69] Quoted in Feather: *The Encyclopaedia of Jazz in the Sixties* (see Bibliography), p. 21. Rollins is here commenting on Coleman's *Folk tale* (**400**).

[70] *Miles: The Autobiography* (see Bibliography), pp. 93, 102–3.

[71] Alun Morgan: 'Duke Jordan – an Introduction and Discography', *Jazz Monthly*, January 1957, pp. 26ff.

[72] Henri Renaud's notes to *I Remember Bebop* (recorded 1977), as part of which Jordan plays two compositions by Tadd Dameron.

[73] A. J. McCarthy (ed.): *Jazz on Record* (see Bibliography), p. 164.

[74] 1945–6 appearances by Bolton with Buddy Johnson are on †Archive of Jazz (A) 380 125–2.

Chapter Two

[1] See Lawrence Koch: 'Thelonious Monk – Compositional Techniques' in *Annual Review of Jazz Studies 3*.

[2] Sleeve note to *Thelonious Monk in Person*, Milestone (A) M47033.

[3] Ran Blake: 'Round about Monk – the Music' in *The Wire*, December 1984.

[4] It is thought he may have composed *Bye-ya* (†Original Jazz Classics [A] OJCCD010) as early as 1942.

[5] A dozen years later *Jazz 1959*, the *Metronome* yearbook, could still describe Monk as 'picturesquely inept'. (This same tome also confided that Mingus's music was 'filled with bleeding, brooding and blessing'!)

[6] Quoted twice in Martin Williams: *Jazz Heritage* (New York, Oxford University Press, 1985), pp. 61, 206.

[7] Leonard Feather: *The Encyclopaedia of Jazz in the Seventies*, 1976 edition (see Bibliography), p. 31.

[8] Barry Ulanov: *A History of Jazz in America* (see Bibliography), p. 383.

[9] Quoted in Ira Gitler: *Jazz Masters of the Forties* (see Bibliography), p. 235.

[10] Gunther Schuller: *The Swing Era* (see Bibliography), p. 841.

[11] Gitler: *op. cit.*, pp. 233, 237.

[12] Typical is Martin Williams's assertion: 'The work of Lennie Tristano and his pupils and the "cool" post-Lester Young tenormen shows, I think, that if attempts to impose innovations in harmony and melodic line are not intrinsically bound to innovations in rhythm they risk distorting some secret but innate balance in the nature of jazz' (Williams: *The Jazz Tradition* [see Bibliography], p. 162). Far from being peculiar to jazz, this 'secret but innate balance' between melody, harmony and rhythm is common to all Western music of any significance.

[13] *down beat*, 16 May 1956.

[14] For detailed comment on *Line up* see R. Beirach in *Keyboard*, July 1985.

[15] André Hodeir: *Jazz – Its Evolution and Essence* (see Bibliography), p. 119.

[16] Ulanov: *op. cit.*, p. 377.

[17] Hodeir: *op. cit.*, p. 121.

[18] Hodeir: *op. cit.*, p. 120.

[19] Hodeir: *op. cit.*, p. 270.

[20] *Godchild, Venus de Milo, Rocker, Jeru* and *Darn that dream.*

[21] *Jazz Masters of the Fifties* by Joe Goldberg (see Bibliography), p. 12.

[22] For example, in *down beat*, 17 January 1963, p. 20.

[23] *Ibid.*

[24] *Milwaukee Journal*, 23 September 1973. Quoted in *West Coast Jazz* by Ted Gioia (see Bibliography).

[25] *Jazz Masters of the Fifties* by Joe Goldberg (see Bibliography), p. 21.

[26] *down beat*, 17 January 1963, p. 20.

[27] *Time*, 2 February 1953: 'Mulligan's kind of sound is just about unique in the jazz field: his quartet uses neither piano or guitar.'

[28] Raymond Horricks: review in *Jazz Monthly*, April 1958, p. 13.

[29] Made in Robert Gordon: *Jazz West Coast* (see Bibliography), p. 131.

[30] Hear for example the three versions of *You go to my head* on vol. 2 of this Dragon series, DRLP75.

[31] Taped at a Stockholm concert in April 1955, these have the same personnel as the previous January's date with the valuable addition of Rolf Billberg (†Dragon [Sd] DRCD224). For Billberg also hear **367**.

[32] For another angle on Gullin's music, hear the 1983 recordings by Konitz with Lars Sjösten's octet, entirely of Gullin themes and mainly in his scorings (†Dragon [Sd] DRCD250). Quite apart from Konitz's beautiful contributions, the younger Swedish musicians give a more contemporary accent to Gullin's pieces, telling us new things about them, above all that they have remained viable over the years.

[33] Hear Gullin's 1959–60 recordings of 15 of his pieces in vol. 4 of these Dragon reissues, †DRCD264.

[34] In the sleeve note to Decca (A) DL79226.

[35] *Bird – Original Motion Picture Soundtrack*, CBS 461002 1.

[36] *A Jazz Retrospect* by Max Harrison (see Bibliography), p. 168.

[37] Liner note, Contemporary (A) 3518.

[38] *Metronome Yearbook: 1956*, Metronome Publications, New York, 1955.

[39] *down beat*, 14 December 1951, pp. 3–5.

[40] Interview with Al Cohn by SN, 10 February 1982.

[41] *The World of Count Basie* by Stanley F. Dance, Sidgwick & Jackson, London, 1980, p. 237.

[42] *The Four Brothers: Together Again!* RCA/BMG 74321 13040 2, recorded 11 February 1957.

[43] *A Jazz Retrospect* by Max Harrison (see Bibliography), p. 165.

[44] Brian Priestley: *Mingus* (see Bibliography), p. 40.

[45] With the exception noted in (48), the several references in this entry to Brubeck's own views derive from Len Lyons: *The Great Jazz Pianists* (New York, Quill, 1983), pp. 104–12.

[46] Certainly we do not have to take with undue seriousness Desmond's claim that in their early days Brubeck's playing 'made Cecil Taylor sound like Lester Lanin'. *down beat*, 15 September 1960, p. 16.

[47] Concerning *In your own sweet way* it should be noted a) that this is a 34-bar AABA song, the final A section being elided to ten bars and b) that when Davis recorded it he squared it up to 32 bars but added a vamp section of eight bars, this perhaps a result of Ahmad Jamal's influence. It seems a pity, incidentally, that Davis missed Brubeck's *Balcony rock*.

[48] Doug Ramsey: *Jazz Matters* (see Bibliography), p. 142.

[49] Locating the earliest recorded attempt at fitting at least some features of the incipient new idiom to large ensembles is not easy. Herman's initial *Apple honey* (August 1944) was preceded by Jerry Valentine's score of *I stay in the mood for you* (April 1944) for Billy Eckstine, with boppish unisons from the brass and a Gillespie solo. And there might have been comparable essays by the unrecorded Earl Hines band of the previous year which included Gillespie and Parker and for which Valentine also arranged. Further back still lie such details as the proto-boppish brass unisons of Eddie Sauter's 1940 *Coconut grove* for Benny Goodman.

[50] For a performance of *Tush* by the 1944 Basie band (with Clyde Hart at the piano), hear **196**.

[51] *Bagdad* was Tizol's name for this piece but Ellington retitled it *Casa blanca* though never recording it himself. No doubt executed according to Ellington's detailed instructions, the orchestration is definitely Tizol's, a set of parts surviving in his writing. A more recent performance, by the Smithsonian Jazz Repertoire Ensemble under Gunther Schuller, is on Smithsonian (A) NO24.

[52] Quoted in *down beat*, vol. 31, no. 20.

[53] *To Be or Not to Bop* by Dizzy Gillespie with Al Frasier (see Bibliography).

[54] Interview with Mario Bauza by SN, 28 May 1991.

[55] *Swing to Bop* by Ira Gitler (see Bibliography), p. 292.

[56] *Ibid.*

[57] *Metronome*, April 1950.

[58] Miles Davis with Quincy Troupe: *Miles: The Autobiography* (see Bibliography), p. 115.

[59] Such as the absorbing *Sonny Side Up* (†Verve 521 426–2), with Gillespie vying for solo honours with Sonny Rollins and Sonny Stitt.

[60] Mark Gridley: *Jazz Styles: History and Analysis* (see Bibliography), p. 375.

[61] Interview with SN, June 1992.

[62] *down beat*, December 1980, p. 27.

[63] *Tanga* also appears on *The Original Mambo Kings – An Introduction to*

Afro-Cubop 1948–54 (†Verve [A] 513 876–2) which, together with *Mucho Macho*, forms an excellent gateway into Latin jazz.

[64] A much edited feature on Bauza's career by SN following an extensive interview in 1992 appeared in *Jazz – The Magazine*, issue 23, March 1994.

[65] *New York Times*, 26 April 1991.

[66] His valedictory shot was three excellent albums for the Messidor label with his Afro-Cuban Jazz Orchestra, *Tanga* (†Messidor 15819–2), *My Time Is Now* (†Messidor 15824–2) and *944 Columbus* (†Messidor 15828–2).

[67] *How Time Passes* (**454**) from 1960, *New Ideas* (Prestige/New Jazz [A] 8257) from 1961; *Essence* (Pacific Jazz [A] PJ-55) from 1962.

[68] *down beat*, 30 June 1966, p. 21.

[69] *Ibid.*

[70] *down beat*, 20 April 1967, p. 36.

[71] *Autumn* (†Columbia [F] COL 472622–2) and *Live at Fillmore* (CBS 66261).

[72] *down beat*, 30 June 1966, p. 21.

[73] *down beat*, 16 April 1970, p. 17.

[74] Since there were no *tsuzumi* players in Los Angeles when the original *Kogun* was cut (RCA [A] AFL1–3019), Miss Akiyoshi had tapes flown over from Japan and added segments to the master.

[75] *down beat*, August 1980, p. 15.

[76] *Ibid.*

[77] An earlier example of Shew's style was the wonderful parabolic solo at the climax of Buddy Rich's *Big swing face* (*Big Swing Face*, Pacific Jazz [A] ST-20177).

[78] *Desert lady* was written (but not arranged) by Lew Tabackin; *Fantasy* was written and arranged by Miss Akiyoshi. The aim was to produce two programmatic pieces that evolve naturally, one into the other.

[79] *down beat*, 20 October 1977, p. 15.

[80] *Live at Newport* (RCA Victor [G] PL 40821) and *Live at Newport II* (RCA Victor [Br] 104.4145).

[81] Alan Lomax: *Mister Jelly Roll* (New York, Duell, 1950), p. 66.

[82] Max Harrison: 'Some Reflections on Ellington's Longer Works' in Mark Tucker (ed.): *The Duke Ellington Reader* (New York, Oxford University Press, 1993), pp. 387–94.

[83] For example, *What the Dickens?* (Fontana [E] TL5203, Fontana [A] 27525), *Zodiac Variations* (Fontana [E] TL52229, Fontana [A] 27543).

[84] Donald Tovey: 'Programme Music' in *The Forms of Music* (New York, Oxford University Press, 1956), p. 167.

[85] *Op. cit.*

[86] Andrzej Trzaskowski in *Jazz Forum 81* (1983) in the course of a review of the Gaumont LP.

[87] These several quotations are from the sleeve note to the 1980 version of the *Sonata* (Soul Note [It] SN1009).

[88] In the sleeve note to *Vertical Form VI* (Soul Note [It] SN1019).

[89] *Op. cit.*

[90] Interview with SN, 15 January 1998.

[91] Interview with SN, 15 January 1998.

[92] Sting's appearance with Evans at the Umbria Jazz Festival attracted a crowd of 30,000 and was broadcast live on Italian television.

[93] The *New Yorker*, 6 January 1997, p. 12.

[94] Liner note to *Evanescence.*

[95] *Ibid.*

[96] Schuller: *Musings* (see Bibliography), p. 103.

[97] The words 'labial' and 'labio' refer to the lips, 'lingua' to the tongue, 'glottal' to the throat and 'alveolar' to the gum ridge.

[98] *down beat*, 28 May 1970, p. 28.

[99] Though Miss Connor manages to be as musical as ever on it, the frightful Rodgers and Hart *Johnny one-note* is different. Its words recalls H. G. Wells's description of those inhabitants of the Moon who are news disseminators, 'almost trumpet-faced . . . with vocal organs that could well-nigh wake the dead'. (*The First Men in the Moon*, London, Newnes, 1901.)

[100] James Lincoln Collier states the conventional view: 'The singer must at least approximate the tune to keep the lyric intact' – *The Making of Jazz* (see Bibliography), p. 304.

[101] Joachim Berendt: *The Jazz Book* (see Bibliography), p. 312.

[102] Quoted by Stan Wooley in *Jazz Journal*, October 1987, pp. 18–19.

[103] *down beat*, 9 May 1963, pp. 14–15.

[104] *down beat*, November 1980, p. 21.

[105] *down beat*, 9 May 1963, p. 15.

[106] For example, *Flexible Flyer* (Arista Freedom [A] 1006), *Numatick Swing Band* (JCOA [A] 1007).

[107] Hear what Sonny Rollins does with this piece, however, on **286**!

[108] *The Wire*, March 1989.

[109] Miss Carter was not born in 1930, as all reference books say, but in 1929 – interview with her by SN, 2 October 1992. Ella Fitzgerald was not born in 1918, as all reference books say, but in 1917 – see Stuart Nicholson: *Ella Fitzgerald* (New York, Scribner's, 1994).

[110] Interview with Miss Carter, *ibid.*

[111] *Ibid.*

[112] Will Friedwald: *Jazz Singing* (New York, Scribner's, 1990), p. 402.

[113] Benny Green: 'The truth is that there is no such thing as a jazz singer' – *Drums in My Ears* (London, Davis-Poynter, 1973), p. 133; Joachim Berendt: 'Jazz singing . . . is more effective the closer it approximates the instrumental use of the voice' – *The Jazz Book* (see Bibliography), p. 374; Leroy Ostransky: 'Jazz singing will eventually, and properly, come under the classification of folk music studies' – *Understanding Jazz* (Englewood Cliffs, NJ, Prentice Hall, 1977), p. 281.

[114] Alec Wilder: *American Popular Song* (New York, Oxford University Press, 1972), p. 252.

[115] Interview with Miss Carter by SN, 2 October 1992.

[116] Crotchet = *c.* 40.

[117] Interview with Miss Wilson by SN, 12 November 1992, from which extracts formed part of his feature on her in *Jazz Express*, January 1993.

[118] For example the *New York Times*, 4 July 1995.

[119] *Ibid.*

[120] Interview by SN, 10 November 1992.

Chapter Three

[1] Miles Davis: *Miles: The Autobiography* (see Bibliography), p. 195.

[2] Feeding soloists chords is known as 'comping'.

[3] See **335** which also discusses Jamal's influence on Miles Davis.

[4] A device less effective on major seventh and minor seventh chords.

[5] An example of how Davis could attach greater importance to his melodic line rather than the underlying harmonies can be heard on his *She rote* solo with Charlie Parker (**266a**).

[6] Listen to how Jamal shapes *I wish I knew* (**335**) after the *ostinato* passages for an idea of how Davis listened and learned from Jamal's style, contrasting a jaunty 2/4 and 4/4 against an understated presentation of the melody, something Davis clearly picked up on.

[7] See **266** for a more detailed examination of this. Coltrane also owed a debt to Dexter Gordon, which he had not entirely shed at the time of these sessions.

[8] This is something that can be heard in Coltrane's *Oleo* solo, and it becomes even clearer when played back-to-back with Stitt's *Sonnymoon* (**279**), which shares the same harmonic base.

[9] The most obvious examples of polytonality being the last chord of *Four* and *If I were a bell.*

[10] Quoted in *down beat*, 6 April 1967, p. 19.

[11] Liner note to **335**, pp. 3, 4.

[12] *down beat*, January 1981, p. 53.

[13] Thanks to Todd Coolman for checking my final draft and his timely suggestions.

[14] Richard Cook and Brian Morton: *The Penguin Guide to Jazz on CD* (see Bibliography), p. 895.

[15] Mingus's own sleeve note to *Pithecanthropus Erectus* (Atlantic [A] 58731).

[16] Brian Priestley: *Mingus* (see Bibliography), p. 137. The helpfulness of this work is gratefully acknowledged here.

[17] Montgomery's first recordings under his own name were for Richard Bock's Pacific Jazz label. With the exception of *Finger pickin'*, the single title recorded on 30 December 1957, all the remaining titles were reissued on *Far Wes* (Pacific Jazz †CDP7944752) in 1990.

[18] Dealt with in greater detail in *Ella Fitzgerald* by SN, New York, Scribner's, 1994.

[19] One reason for choosing these selections over Montgomery's fine work on Riverside is Kelly's excellent performances on both the live and the studio tracks.

[20] Larry Coryell's *Comin' Home* (Muse [A] MR5303) and *Equipoise* (Muse MR5319) and Ritenour's *Stolen Moments* (†GRP 96512–2). The last-named contains some stunning playing in the Montgomery idiom.

[21] Liner note to *The Complete Blue Note 1964–66 Jackie McLean Sessions* (†Mosaic (A) MD4–150).

[22] *Jackie's Bag* (Blue Note [A] BLP4051) January 1959, *New Soil* (BLP4013) May 1959, *Swing, Swang, Swinging* (BLP4024) October 1959 and *Capuchin Swing* (BLP4038) April 1960.

[23] *The Complete Blue Note 1964–66 Jackie McLean Sessions*, see note 21.

[24] Valerie Wilmer: *Jazz People* (London, Quartet,1977), p. 119.

[25] Crotchet = *c.* 264.

[26] Interview with SN, 26 February 1994.

[27] Liner note to *Out Front* (Candid [A] BR5019).

[28] *Back to the Tracks* (and *True Blue*) appeared on *The Complete Blue Note Recordings of the Tina Brooks Quintets* (Mosaic [A] MR4–106).

[29] *down beat*, 7 March 1968, p. 24.

[30] Liner note to *The Song Book* (†Prestige [A] OJCCD-779–2).

[31] Crotchet = 352.

[32] *down beat*, 7 March 1968, p. 24.

[33] *down beat*, 28 February 1974, p. 27.

[34] *Horace Silver and the Jazz Messengers*, November 1954, with Silver, Dorham, Mobley, Watkins and Blakey.

[35] A. J. McCarthy (ed.): *Jazz on Record* (see Bibliography), p. 350.

[36] But their two subsequent albums, *The Power of Positive Swinging*

(†Mainstream [A] MDCD723) and *Gingerbread* (MDCD711), also come recommended.

[37] Crotchet = 248.

[38] The unique combination of Terry and Brookmeyer's *tone* cannot be stressed enough. In the late 1970s–early 1980s, for example, Woody Shaw led a quintet with Steve Turre on trombone, yet this first-rate group did not approach the ensemble textures of the Terry–Brookmeyer ensemble.

[39] Witness *Oscar Peterson Trio + One-Clark Terry* (†EmArcy [A] 818840–2) from 17 August 1964 and their live performance of some of the material from the session at Théâtre des Champs Elysées, Paris, on 20 March 1965 (†Europe 1 [F] 710446).

[40] Brown is at his best in the alternative take on *More Study in Brown* (†EmArcy [A] 814 637–2).

[41] Terry also appeared on McFarland's 1962 big-band album *How to Succeed in Business Without Really Trying.*

[42] *down beat*, 20 January 1972, p. 30.

[43] Only in the 1980s did he again produce two albums worthy of his great talent, in a duo with the bassist Red Mitchell: *Clark Terry–Red Mitchell* and *To the Duke and Basie* (both Enja).

[44] *down beat*, 30 March 1972, p. 24.

[45] In recent years, however, Shank has figured in several volumes on West Coast jazz (see Bibliography).

[46] *down beat*, 23 May 1974, p. 30.

[47] Liner note to *The Complete Blue Note recordings of the Tina Brooks Quintets* (Mosaic [A] MR4–106).

[48] Hubbard's best work is certainly worth looking out, however, and besides albums mentioned elsewhere in this book where he appears as sideman, a brief list might include Herbie Hancock's *Empyrean Isles* (Blue Note [A] BST 84175), much of his work with Eric Dolphy, Art Blakey and his three VSOP albums with Wayne Shorter and the former Miles Davis rhythm section of Hancock, Carter and Williams (all Columbia). Although further recordings under his own name for the Blue Note label were solid rather than indispensable, he contributed a widely admired solo to Quincy Jones's *Killer Joe* on *Walking in Space* (†A & M [A] CDA0801) in 1969. In later years he showed he could still cut the mustard with *Sweet return* (Atlantic [A] 780108–1) 1983 and *Live at Fat Tuesday's* († Limelight [A] 844 280–2) from 1991, both the sort of albums of which his discography is depressingly short.

[49] Gary Giddins: *Riding on a Blue Note* (see Bibliography), p. 250.

[50] John Litweiler: *The Freedom Principle* (see Bibliography), p. 105.

[51] Interview track on *Dexter Gordon: American Classic* (Elektra Musician [E] MUSK52392) 1982.

[52] The first was between October 1954 and November 1955 and was spent in Chicago.

[53] One of the few albums with which Rollins was satisfied; interview with SN in March 1992, *Jazz Express*, April 1992, p. 7.

[54] *Black Music & Jazz Review*, July 1980, p. 20.

[55] Interview with SN in March 1992. *Jazz Express*, April 1992, p. 7.

[56] *Ibid.*, p. 6.

[57] Interview with SN, 13 May 1993, published in part in *Jazz Express*, October 1993.

[58] Other than the two Silver albums mentioned in the text on which Mitchell and Cook appear together, the remaining albums are: *Horace-scope* (Blue Note [A] BST84042) from 8–9 July 1960; *Doin' the Thing at the Village Gate* (BLP4076) from 19–20 May 1961; *The Tokyo Blues* (BST84325) from 13 July 1962 and *Silver's Serenade* (BST84131) from 7–8 May 1963. Mitchell and Cook also appear on *Calcutta cutie*, recorded on 31 October 1963 and issued on the album *Song for My Father* (BST84185). All the titles from this 31 October session were later issued as Blue Note (J) CP32–5213 together with two tracks from their final 28 January 1964 session.

[59] *down beat*, 20 June 1963, p. 20.

[60] Previously recorded on *Further Explorations* (Blue Note [A] BLP1589).

[61] A. B. Spellman: *Four Lives in the Bebop Business* (see Bibliography), p. 62.

[62] Martin Williams: *The Jazz Tradition* (see Bibliography), p. 200.

[63] Interestingly well in excess of the fastest tempos indicated on a metronome of crotchet = 208, probably *c.* 238 beats per minute.

[64] Spellman: *Four Lives in the Bebop Business* (see Bibliography), p. 62.

[65] Liner note to **351**.

[66] *down beat*, November 1979, p. 22.

[67] Not a 24-bar theme as claimed by the sleeve note.

[68] Not a 64-bar theme as claimed by the sleeve note.

[69] Shorter's growth as a composer as much as a saxophonist with Blakey is well charted on both the Blue Note and Riverside labels. For example, in 1960 alone, the Messengers released eight albums, collected on *The Complete Blue Note Recordings of Art Blakey's 1960 Jazz Messengers* (†Mosaic [A] MD6–141). Some of Shorter's more memorable compositions during his tenure with the Messengers include: *The chess players, Sakeena's vision, Free for all, Hammerhead, Mr Jin, Children of the night* (**342**), *The summit, Sincerely Diana, Backstage Sally, Contemplation, Sleeping dancers sleep on, Noise in the attic, Roots and herbs, The back sliders, Look at the birdie, Master mind, Sweet 'n' sour, This is for Albert, One by one* and *Ping-pong.*

[70] Recorded by Stan Getz and twice by Art Blakey.

[71] Shorter's choice of drummers on his remaining Blue Note albums (before the Blue Note Liberty/United Artists era of 1967–79) were Tony Williams and the underappreciated Joe Chambers.

[72] Francis Davis: *Outcats* (see Bibliography), p. 91.

[73] 'Birdland', BBC TV, 11 September 1992.

[74] Paul Hindemith, *A Composer's World* (New York, Anchor Books, 1961), pp. 42 and 51.

[75] An oversight corrected in 1995 by Sony with Mabern's fine album *The Leading Man* (†Columbia [A] 477288–2).

[76] *The New Yorker*, 31 July 1995, p. 16.

[77] Leonard Feather: *The Encyclopaedia of Jazz in the Seventies* (see Bibliography), p. 392.

[78] 'The Reminiscences of Al Haig to John Shaw' in *Jazz Journal*, March 1978, p. 4.

[79] Max Harrison in Oliver, Harrison, Bolcom: *The New Grove Gospel, Blues and Jazz* (see Bibliography), p. 295.

[80] Liner note to **357**.

[81] See also his posthumous release of original compositions under his own name: *Nightwind* (Optimism Incorporated [A] OP-3104).

[82] The claim that Rogers contributed to the repertoire of Goodman's combo is advanced in the booklet accompanying this Mosaic set but he is nowhere mentioned in Russell Connor's *Benny Goodman: Listen to His Legacy* (Metuchen, NJ, Scarecrow Press, 1988).

[83] Brian Priestley in *Jazz fm* 9, p. 33.

[84] Robert Gordon: *Jazz West Coast* (see Bibliography), p. 128.

[85] Gordon, *op. cit.*, pp. 128–9.

[86] Charles Williams: 'A Dialogue on Hierarchy' in *The Image of the City* (London, 1958), p. 127.

[87] Milt Jackson's interview with Charles Fox broadcast by the BBC in 1987.

[88] This was revealed in a conversation between Giuffre and Brian Morton on BBC Radio 3, 17 June 1991.

[89] *The Wire*, March 1989.

[90] Alun Morgan in the sleeve note to *Jazz of the Forties: Bebop into Cool* (Capitol [E] T20578).

[91] Barry Ulanov: *A History of Jazz in America* (see Bibliography), p. 385.

[92] 'Not logically, but perhaps understandably, Capitol was bewildered by and uncertain about what it heard. As a result, two of the sides (*sic*) were erased from the recording tape, and, of the remaining two, those chosen as the best of the four, only one was released – and that two years after it was recorded. And yet these adventures in musical

intuition are among the high points of jazz.' Barry Ulanov, *op. cit.*, p. 385.

[93] *down beat*, 9 September 1965, p. 25.

[94] *The Octet* (**450**). The precise date has never been pinned down; it is generally thought to be *c.* 1950, although Brubeck suggests as early as 1946.

[95] *down beat*, 25 March 1976, p. 20; Braxton memorized complete choruses of Desmond's work.

[96] *All in Good Time* by Marion McPartland. (New York, Oxford University Press, 1987), p. 63.

[97] Above and including high F sharp on the alto.

[98] But not the perceptive critic Ted Gioia in *West Coast Jazz* (see Bibliography), pp. 86–99.

[99] Joe Goldberg: *Jazz Masters of the Fifties* (see Bibliography), p. 160.

[100] *The Complete Recordings of the Paul Desmond Quartet with Jim Hall* (†Mosaic [A] MD4–120).

[101] Liner note to *The Only Recorded Performance of Paul Desmond with the Modern Jazz Quartet* (Finesse Records [A] FINLP6050).

[102] Liner note to **366**.

[103] *down beat*, 25 March 1976, p. 19.

[104] *Jazz at Oberlin.*

[105] A further six numbers recorded at these sessions appeared in 1992 as *Paul Desmond Quartet: Like Someone in Love* (Telarc [A] CD83319), including *Just squeeze me* and *Nuages* which had appeared on *Pure Desmond.*

[106] All off the scale of a standard metronome (*prestissimo* 208); *How high the moon?*, for example, about crotchet = 310–20.

[107] Martin Williams: *Jazz Heritage* (New York, Oxford University Press, 1985), p. 77. Bartók's influence here is like Milhaud's on Brubeck in that it can be heard by those who do not know the composer's work yet not by those that do. For good measure Williams in the same sentence adds that Sauter 'offered a sort of advanced David Rose writing with some of the schmaltz drained off'! For jazz which does heed Bartók, without of course imitating him, try Gil Melle's **452**.

[108] Max Jones: *Talking Jazz* (London, Macmillan, 1987), p. 46.

[109] See Pass's liner note to **370.**

[110] Stuart Nicholson: *Jazz: The Modern Resurgence* (see Bibliography), p. 88.

[111] Sims interviewed by Ira Gitler, *down beat*, 13 April 1961.

[112] Mike Zwerin: *Close Enough for Jazz* (London, Quartet, 1983).

[113] *The Times*, 16 May 1988.

[114] *down beat* review of his appearance at the Cork n' Bib, Westbury, NY, 21 May 1964, p. 30.

[115] Ostensibly a 'public service' broadcasting station, the BBC fulfil this remit to their entire satisfaction. Just as the chancellors of the Exchequer Lawson and Lamont shadowed the German mark prior to the UK's ill-fated entry into the ERM, the BBC 'shadow' the independent television stations in a ratings war, prior to 'privatization' which they have decided will occur at some undetermined point in the future. Thus their concept of 'public service' broadcasting appears to consist of wall-to-wall game shows, situation comedies and soaps.

[116] Also recommended is his solo recital as part of the Concord record label's Maybeck series (†CCD 4457), the trio *Love Every Moment* (†Concord CCD4534) as *Sunburst* (†Concord CCD4486) with Joe Henderson (ten).

[117] Liner note to Enja (G) 607422.

[118] *down beat*, October 1981, p. 25.

[119] T. S. Eliot: *Selected Prose* (London, Faber, 1953). p. 121.

[120] *down beat*, 8 December 1960.

[121] *down beat*, October 1979, p. 20.

[122] *down beat*, May 1986, p. 24.

[123] See Evans's recordings with Russell on **380**.

[124] For example, *All about Rosie* with George Russell (**478**) from 1957 or a rare example of Evans's more expansive side with his own trio: *Bill Evans–Montreux II* (†CBS Associated [A] ZK45219) from 1970.

[125] See **351**, of several examples throughout this album, *Stompin' at the Savoy*.

[126] Such as his playing on albums like Al Cohn–Zoot Sims Quartet, *Live at the Half Note* (Liberty [J] LBJ60057) or Lee Konitz, *Live at the Half Note* (†Verve [A] 521659–2).

[127] *Crow's nest*, for example, on *Stan Getz Meets Cal Tjader* (†OJCCD [A] 275–2).

[128] Crotchet = 60. There are few examples of jazz performed within this tempo range, although perhaps the most famous example is Billie Holiday's *Strange fruit* , crotchet = 56.

[129] Crotchet = 174.

[130] For example, of two of his better-known compositions, *Very early* is a 48-bar AAB song, and *Re: person I know* is a 32-bar AA song.

[131] Evans enjoyed waltzes to an extent that was unusual among jazz musicians. *Alice in Wonderland* from these sessions was also a waltz. Among the other waltzes he recorded were *Up with the lark, Someday my prince will come, Tenderly, I'm all smiles, Elsa, Very early, B minor waltz, My man's gone now, Love theme from 'Spartacus'* (**469**), *How my heart sings* and *Skating in Central Park.*

[132] Crotchet = 184.

[133] The melody is expressed freely but appears in the range of andante; *c.* crotchet = 78.

[134] Crotchet = 184.

[135] *down beat*, May 1986, p. 24.

[136] Leonard Feather in the *Los Angeles Times*, 21 February 1980.

Chapter Four

[1] Ulanov: *A History of Jazz in America* (see Bibliography), p. 391.

[2] Chambers: *Milestones I* (see Bibliography), p. 97.

[3] In 1958 Davis titled a quite different theme *Milestones*.

[4] Quoted in the sleeve note to Capitol (E) T1971.

[5] See the booklet accompanying the CD of GRP (A) GRD9679.

[6] Max Harrison: *A Jazz Retrospect* (see Bibliography), p. 45.

[7] 'Lennie Tristano talks to Gudrun Endress', *Jazz Monthly*, February 1966.

[8] The sound of these six tracks was fairly well cleaned up for reissue as part of the 4-CD *Bebop in Britain* (†Charly [E] CDESQ100–4).

[9] Harrison: *op. cit.*, p. 133.

[10] Stravinsky and Robert Craft: *Expositions and Developments* (London, Faber, 1962), p. 105.

[11] Interview with Helen Merrill by SN, 24 November 1994.

[12] *down beat*, 23 February 1967, p. 15.

[13] *Svengali* (†Act [A] 9207–2) 1973.

[14] Giuffre: *Jazz Phrasing and Interpretation* (New York, 1969).

[15] This neglected record also includes some of Previn's very best jazz piano work.

[16] For example Armstrong's *Indian cradle song* (**80**), Ellington's *Arabian lover* (**88**).

[17] In all the years since perhaps only Mario Arcari, on several records with Franz Koglmann's Pipetet – *About Yesterday's Ezzthetics* (†Hat Hut [Sw] CD6003), *Orte der Geometrie* (CD6018), *Ich* (CD6033), *A White Line* (CD6048) and *The Use of Memory* (CD6078) – can be said to have gone beyond Cooper in realizing the oboe's jazz potential.

[18] See *Jazz Monthly*, September 1972.

[19] Not to mention Vance 'Mad Dog' Tenort.

[20] The Hamilton account of *Blue sands* was reduced to background music for John Carradine reading something called 'Night Song for Sleepless People' (World Pacific [A] WP1244).

[21] Francis Davis: *In the Moment* (see Bibliography), p. 68.

[22] *Ibid.*, p. 69.

[23] A short thematic section of *Outline No. 12* is notated in David Such:

Avant Garde Musicians Performing Out There (Iowa City, Iowa University Press, 1993), pp. 72–3.

[24] John Litweiler: *The Freedom Principle* (see Bibliography), pp. 6, 125.

[25] *Ibid.*, p. 125.

[26] Chambers: *op. cit.*, p. 305.

[27] Harrison: *op. cit.*, p. 99.

[28] Carr, Fairweather, Priestley: *Jazz: The Essential Companion* (see Bibliography), p. 313.

[29] Litweiler: *op. cit.*, p. 233.

[30] Charles Fox: 'Jazz and Poetry – a Concert Report', *Jazz Monthly*, February 1962.

[31] Liner note to this CD.

[32] Litweiler: *op. cit.*, p. 125: 'The Free vistas of Ornette Coleman and Don Cherry became possibilities for this quintet.'

[33] Crotchet = *c.* 340.

[34] *down beat*, 18 December 1979, p. 58.

[35] *Chick Corea: Early Days* (†Denon [J] 33C38–7969).

[36] *Tones for Joan's Bones* (Vortex [A] 2004).

[37] *The Creeper*, incidentally, includes the first appearance of Corea's composition *Samba yantra*, which appears on this album as one of the bonus tracks not on the original LP configuration.

[38] *Return to Forever* (†ECM [G] 1022) February 1972.

[39] *In Concert, Zürich, October 28, 1979* (ECM [G] 1182/83).

[40] Followed by *Tender Moments* (Blue Note [A] BST84275) from 1967, *Time for Tyner* (Blue Note BST84307) from 1968, *Expansions* (Blue Note BST84338) from 1968, *Extensions* (Blue Note LA006) from 1970 and *Asante* (Blue Note LA223-G) also from 1970. Several unissued selections from various sessions were gathered together and subsequently issued as *Cosmos* (Blue Note BN460).

[41] Interview with SN, 11 October 1997.

[42] *Jazz Forum*, provenance unknown, courtesy National Sound Archive, British Library, London.

[43] *down beat*, 21 November 1974, p. 29.

[44] Liner note to †Milestone MCD55002–2.

[45] Particularly recommended are *The Greeting* (Milestone [A] M9085), a live date with his sextet at the Great American Music Hall from March 1978, and *Horizon* (Milestone M9094), a studio date from 1979 with his septet that many number among Tyner's best recorded work.

[46] A recent example is *The Chronicle of Jazz* by Mervyn Cooke (London, Thames and Hudson, 1997), which, save for a passing mention as a member of Coltrane's quartet, failed to chronicle one of the most important and influential pianists of contemporary times.

[47] *New York Times*, 14 March 1996.

[48] *Revelations* (†Blue Note [A] CDO791651–2) from 1988, *Things Ain't What They Used to Be* (†Blue Note CDP793588–2) from 1989, with three duet tracks with John Scofield and two duet tracks with George Adams, and *Soliloquy* (†Blue Note CDP796429–2) from 1991.

Chapter Five

[1] *down beat*, 25 February 1965, p. 17.

[2] Burt Korall: 'Coleman Finally Wins Through', *Melody Maker*, 6 August 1960, p. 13.

[3] Nat Hentoff: 'Biggest Noise in Jazz', *Esquire*, March 1961, pp. 82–7.

[4] Quoted in the booklet accompanying this reissue.

[5] Rockwell: *All American Music* (see Bibliography), p. 190.

[6] *The Wire*, April 1994, p. 52.

[7] This solo is notated in Litweiler: *Ornette Coleman: The Harmolodic Life* (see Bibliography).

[8] This solo is notated in Coleman: *A Collection of Compositions* (New York, M.J.Q. Music, 1961).

[9] Litweiler: *The Freedom Principle* (see Bibliography), p. 35.

[10] Cherry was quoted as saying that Navarro was 'the only trumpeter I cared to copy' in Harvey Peker: 'Tomorrow Is the Question', *Jazz Journal*, November 1962, pp. 8–10.

[11] On p. 105 of Jerry Coker: *Listening to Jazz* (Englewood Cliffs, NI, Prentice Hall, 1978), Coleman is unaccountably listed as one who 'became famous through trying to duplicate Parker's style'. Is this a harmless joke?

[12] Certainly the reservations once advanced by the present writer on p. 101 of *A Jazz Retrospect* (see Bibliography) no longer seem tenable. For some account of the serial structure of *Abstraction*, see Ciro Scotto's entry on Schuller in Brian Morton (ed.): *Contemporary Composers* (Chicago, St James Press, 1992), pp. 825–30.

[13] The BBC2 'Birdland' TV programme featuring Coleman with Prime Time was broadcast on 16 October 1992. Coleman's remarks were transcribed from that programme.

[14] John Litweiler's description in *The Freedom Principle* (see Bibliography), p. 289.

[15] Coleman interviewed on 'Birdland', BBC2 TV, 16 October 1992.

[16] Quoted from Ian Carr's entry on Cherry in Carr, Fairweather, Priestley: *Jazz: The Essential Companion* (see Bibliography), p. 88.

[17] From the sleeve note to this record.

[18] Ian Carr's entry on Harriott in Carr, Fairweather, Priestley: *Jazz: The Essential Companion* (see Bibliography), p. 217.

[19] Jack Cooke, *Jazz Monthly*, June 1968, p. 18.

[20] Harriott's comments in the sleeve note to this LP.

[21] From the sleeve note to Riverside (A) RLP9341.

[22] 'Random Thoughts from George Russell', *down beat*, 29 July 1965, p. 9.

[23] Michael James, *Jazz Monthly*, January 1969, p. 26.

[24] Michael J. Budds: *Jazz in the Sixties* (Iowa City, University of Iowa Press, 1990), p. 138.

[25] Valerie Wilmer: *As Serious as Your Life* (London, Alison & Busby, 1977), p. 96.

[26] *down beat*, 1 April 1970, p. 14.

[27] John Litweiler: *Ornette Coleman: The Harmolodic Life* (see Bibliography), p. 1.

[28] Nat Hentoff: 'The Truth Is Marching In,' *down beat*, 25 February 1965.

[29] Richard Cook: 'Trumpet to Timbuktu,' *The Wire*, September 1990.

[30] *down beat*, 17 November 1966.

[31] *Darkness Visible* (London, Faber, 1979), p. 167.

[32] *Modern Jazz: The Essential Records 1945–70* (see Bibliography), pp. 118–19.

[33] Anonymous writer quoted in Litweiler: *The Freedom Principle* (see Bibliography), p. 163.

[34] *down beat*, 15 July 1965.

[35] *Jazz Podium*, December 1972, pp. 22–5.

[36] *Cadence*, October 1978, p. 22.

[37] Dick Hebdige, *Subculture: The Meaning of Style* (New York, Methuen, 1979), p. 97.

[38] In an interview with Stephen Graham, *Jazz Forum* no. 133 (1992).

[39] To Keith Knox, *Jazz Forum* no. 106 (1987).

[40] In an interview with Pawel Brodowski, *Jazz Forum* no. 73 (1981).

[41] *Jazz Forum* no. 109 (1987).

[42] *Ibid.*

[43] Other Szabados recordings which should have attention are *Adyton* (Krem [H] SLPX17724) 1981 and *Szabraxtondos* (Krem [H] SLPX17909) 1984, the latter with Anthony Braxton.

[44] For a 1993 example, far better recorded than this, hear JMS (F) JMS067–2 by Didier Lockwood and Martial Solal.

[45] Also relevant are the Swiss pianist Michel Wintsch's 1994 jazz improvisations on actual Bartók compositions on †Unit (Sw) UTR4072CD.

[46] Gene Santoro: *Dancing in Your Head* (New York, Oxford University Press, 1994), p. 244.

[47] *down beat*, 25 February 1965, p. 17

[48] A. B. Spellman: *Four Lives in the Bebop Business* (see Bibliography).

[49] *Ibid.*

[50] Margaret Chaloff (1896–1977) was the mother of the baritone saxist Serge Chaloff. At various times she was also on the faculties of Brandeis and Boston universities and the Berklee School of Music. Her students included Leonard Bernstein, George Shearing, Alan Hovhaness, Toshiko Akiyoshi, Steve Kuhn, Herbie Hancock, Chick Corea, Keith Jarrett and Mulgrew Miller.

[51] *The Complete Serge Chaloff Sessions* (†Mosaic [A] MD4–147).

[52] *Jazz Advance* (Blue Note [A] B21Y84462), December 1955.

[53] *Pacific Jazz II Collection* (CDP791616–2).

[54] A. B. Spellman: *Four Lives in the Bebop Business* (see Bibliography).

[55] *Ibid.*

[56] *The Complete Candid Recordings of Cecil Taylor and Buell Neidlinger* (†Mosaic [A] MD4–127).

[57] Quoted in *down beat*, 25 February 1965, p. 18.

[58] Ekkehard Jost: *Free Jazz* (see Bibliography).

[59] Joe Goldberg: *Jazz Masters of the Fifties* (see Bibliography).

[60] Liner note to this record.

[61] Liner note to this record.

[62] *Ibid.*

[63] A facet he explored convincingly on *Ballads* (†Impulse [A] GRD 156) and *John Coltrane and Johnny Hartman* (†Impulse [A] GRD157).

[64] Compatible with an E Dorian scale.

[65] Of several, Martin Gayford in the *Daily Telegraph*, July 1996.

[66] Interview with SN, June 1989.

[67] For the album *Poinciana* (Portrait [A] RJ 44394).

[68] For example, the three transcriptions by Ken Rattenbury in Raymond Horricks: *The Importance of Being Eric Dolphy* (Tunbridge Wells, Costello, 1989), pp. 56–73.

[69] Both takes of *Ascension* can be found on *The Major Works of John Coltrane* (†Impulse [A] GRP21132).

[70] Bob Thiele and Bob Golden: *What a Wonderful World* (New York, Oxford University Press, 1995).

[71] The first track on *Kind of Blue* (**393**); see also Ahmad Jamal (**335**).

[72] Concept Publishing Company, New York, 1959, p. iv.

[73] Coleman-Ross Company Inc., New York, 1947.

[74] A Love Su-preme = F, A flat, F, B flat.

[75] *Pursuance* is based on C, E flat, F retaining the minor third and fourth relationship of the 'Love Supreme' motif.

[76] J. C. Thomas: *Chasin' the Trane* (London, Elm Tree Books, 1976), p. 134.

[77] John Litweiler: *The Freedom Principle* (see Bibliography), p. 64.

[78] Mingus quoted in Nat Hentoff's 1964 sleeve note to *Last Date* (**427**).

[79] *The Wire*, October 1987, p. 33.

[80] *down beat*, 27 August 1964, part of an obituary on Dolphy.

[81] *Ibid.*

[82] E. Armour (tpt); H. Hancock (p); R. Davis (bs); E Bateman (d): *Miss Ann*, *Left alone* and *G.W.* No location or date given.

[83] Nelson in his liner note to this record.

[84] Max Harrison in *Jazz on Record* (ed. McCarthy, see Bibliography), p. 146.

[85] Francis Davis: *Outcats* (see Bibliography), p. 245.

[86] Quoted in Gene Lees: *Cats of Any Color* (New York, Oxford University Press, 1995), p. 196.

[87] *down beat*, 28 March 1974, p. 15.

[88] *down beat*, 9 October 1975, p. 12.

[89] Liner notes to this record.

[90] Jack Cooke in *Jazz Monthly*, March 1965, p. 10.

[91] David Rosenthal quoted by SN in *Jazz: The Modern Resurgence* (see Bibliography), p. 85.

[92] Joachim Berendt: *The Jazz Book* (see Bibliography), p. 3. It is worth adding this writer's following words: 'This development constitutes a whole – and those who single out one phase and view it as either uniquely valid or as an aberration destroy this wholeness of conception. They distort that unity of large-scale evolution without which one can speak of fashions but not of styles.'

[93] See Jarman's remarks on the sleeve of ECM (G) 1211/2; Bowie's recollections were from an interview accompanying a British TV broadcast of his *Brass Fantasy* at Bath in 1988.

[94] Jarman as above.

[95] *down beat*, June 1963, p. 24.

[96] Other octet albums include *New Life* (†Black Saint [It] BSR 0100CD) and *Hope Scope* (†Black Saint [It] 120139–2).

[97] Crotchet = *c.* 276.

[98] Francis Davis: *op. cit.*, p. 199.

[99] Unpublished interview with Tom Panken cited in Litweiler: *The Freedom Principle* (see Bibliography), p. 193.

[100] *Love Will Find a Way* by Norman Connors (Arista) from 1978.

[101] For example, his truly inspired playing on *The Audience and Betty Carter* (**329**), with Arthur Blythe, *Illusions* (Columbia [A] 36583) or *In the Tradition* (Columbia [A] 84152) and, with David Murray, *The*

David Murray Quartet (Black Saint [It] BSR0075) or *Ming's Samba* (Portrait [A] R44432).

[102] T. W. Adorno: *Introduction to the Sociology of Music* (Seabury, New York, 1976), pp. 61–2.

[103] This should be qualified by pointing out that Coleman recorded approximately three albums' worth of material with Berber musicians he met in Joujouka, Morocco, in January 1973, although only one track, *Midnight sunrise*, has been released to date; it can be found on *Dancing in Your Head* (†A&M [A] CDA 0807).

[104] *New York Times*, 24 June 1981.

[105] *down beat*, March 1984, p. 54.

[106] *Journal of the International Association of Jazz Record Collectors*, October 1988.

[107] David Harvey: *The Condition of Postmodernity* (Oxford, Basil Blackwell, 1989).

[108] *New York Times*, 31 May 1994.

[109] Most notably the ii-V-I progression.

[110] This would not be readily apparent in live performance, however, where Davis tended to stick with a tried and tested repertoire, albeit submitting the songs to considerable interpretive freedom.

[111] This set also includes *Eighty-one*, *Stuff*, *Vonetta* and *Masqualero* cited in the text.

[112] It is worth noting that James Brown was introducing similar innovations into soul music at around this time which became equally influential in the forum of popular music and would also seep into jazz-rock.

[113] Liner notes to *The Complete Columbia Studio Recordings of the Miles Davis Quintet 1965–68* (Columbia/Legacy AC6K 67398), p. 98.

[114] Wayne Enstice and Paul Rubin: *Jazz Spoken Here: Conversations with Twenty-Two Musicians* (Baton Rouge, Louisiana State University Press, 1992), p. 145.

[115] Quoted in the liner note to Charles Lloyd, *Love-In* (Atlantic [A] 588077).

[116] This is something I try to explore in greater detail in *Jazz Rock: A History* (Schirmers, New York, 1998).

[117] Jim Miller (ed.): *The Rolling Stone Illustrated History of Rock and Roll* (London, Picador, 1981), p. 185.

[118] *down beat Yearbook 1968*, p. 13.

[119] *down beat*, 29 January 1969, pp. 16–17.

[120] Thanks to Paul Wilson, National Sound Archive, London.

[121] Gathered on *The Complete Blue Note Recordings of Larry Young* (†Mosaic [A] MD6–137).

[122] *Melody Maker*, 15 January 1972, p. 28.

[123] The Williams albums *Emergency!*, *Turn It Over*, *Ego* and *The Old Bums Rush* were anthologized in 1997 on *The Tony Williams Lifetime–Spectrum: The Anthology* (†Verve [A] 537 075–2).

[124] *Melody Maker*, 1 April 1972, p. 28.

[125] *Record Collector*, date unknown, p. 108.

[126] Other than bootlegs, mostly of poor quality, as of October 1997 the three Columbia albums still remain the only documentation of this important band. However, McLaughlin has tapes of a performance in 1971 in Cleveland where he has said, 'It's so *on* it's frighening!' (*The Wire*, March 1996, p. 32), which he tried to get released to no avail. Also Columbia have in their vaults two further live dates, one at the Felt Forum in New York City from 3 March 1973 and the other at the Ahmanson Theatre, Los Angeles, from 29 April 1973. They also have an unissued studio date recorded in London from June/July 1973.

[127] *down beat*, 14 February 1974, pp. 9.

[128] Interview with SN, 2 October 1996.

[129] This aspect is dealt with in greater detail in *Jazz-Rock: A History* by SN (Schirmers, New York, 1998).

[130] *Big Fun*, *Circle in the Round* and *Directions*.

[131] *Rolling Stone*, 13 December 1969, p. 23.

[132] *down beat*, 18 July 1974, p. 20.

[133] *Rolling Stone*, 25 June 1970, p. 10.

[134] *The Wire*, July 1988, p. 37.

[135] Jack Johnson was world heavyweight boxing champion in 1908.

[136] McLaughlin was twice asked by Davis to join his ensemble as a regular member, first almost as soon as he arrived in America to join Tony Williams's Lifetime in February 1969 and again after completing the live recordings for *Live-Evil* (Columbia Legacy [A] C2K 65135) in December 1970. Even though McLaughlin declined, during the interim he appeared live with Davis on occasions and was a regular presence on Davis's recordings from *In a Silent Way* (1969) to *On the Corner* (1972).

[137] *down beat*, 18 July 1974, pp. 13, 15.

[138] *Rolling Stone*, 8 July 1970, p. 37.

[139] It is interesting to note that a similar trend in popular music had been instigated in the music of James Brown, inspired by the arrival of the bassist 'Bootsy' Collins in Brown's ensemble in 1969.

[140] Zawinul's second album, *Money in the Pocket*, and his third album, *The Rise and Fall of the Third Stream* were subsequently reissued together on CD: *The Rise and Fall of the Third Stream* (†Atlantic 8122–71675–2).

[141] It was not until 1998 that an unedited version of *In a silent way*

appeared that gave a far better view of the song than the drastic cut and paste job of the producer Teo Macero for the original album issue. Bill Laswell's production of the song from the original session tapes on *Panthalassa: The Music of Miles Davis 1969–1974* (†Columbia KK 67909-S1) was an excellent after-the-fact rationalization, and revealed that Davis did, in fact, stay closer to Zawinul's intentions than had hitherto been imagined.

[142] *Double image* was also the title song of an important Davis bootleg album that fills in a key area of Davis's career that went unrecorded by Columbia (Moon Records [It] MLP 010/11–1).

[143] Interview with SN, 6 April 1998.

[144] Interview with SN, 2 October 1996. All subsequent quotations by Zawinul emanate from this source.

[145] Thus 'his methods of composition are more related in terms of structure and thematic development to the "straight" music tradition than to jazz. The more he writes, the larger become the ensembles he writes for and the smaller the improvised sections. In fact it looks as if his tendency is away from improvisation altogether and towards totally written works.' (Ian Carr: *Music Outside: Contemporary Jazz in Britain*, London, Latimer New Dimensions, 1973, p. 6.)

[146] Made possible by a double bass drum pedal for a single bass drum.

[147] Interview with SN, 19 March 1998.

[148] Interview with SN, 14 January 1998.

Chapter Six

[1] Brubeck quoted in Charles Fox, Peter Gammond, Alun Morgan: *Jazz on Record* (London, Hutchinson, 1960), p. 65, and repeated by Brubeck with greater emphasis in Lyons: *The Great Jazz Pianists* (New York, Quill, 1983), pp. 110–11.

[2] Chambers: *Milestones I* (see Bibliography), pp. 110–11, 114.

[3] E.g. in a Paris 1949 version of *Allen's alley* (CBS (A) 82100).

[4] *Reunion*, (†Original Jazz Classics (A) OJCCD150).

[5] A. J. McCarthy (ed.): *Jazz on Record* (see Bibliography), pp. 217–18.

[6] This instrumentation, first used on records by Melle in 1954 (Blue Note [A] BLP5054), was employed that same year by Lars Gullin (**306**) rather than 'a year later' as Melle claims in his notes.

[7] I am grateful for the use of Max Harrison's comprehensive notes on both biography and performance in the preparation of this piece and for a long discussion with Duane Tatro on 18 September 1996.

[8] Max Harrison's performance notes.

[9] Leonard Feather: *The New Encylopedia of Jazz* (New York, Horizon Press, 1955), p. 436.

[10] *The Jazz Review*, November 1960.

[11] Stockhausen's essay, also titled 'How Time Passes', appeared in the third issue of *Die Reihe*, a periodical devoted to developments in contemporary music edited by Stockhausen and Herbert Eimert (Theodore Presser, Bryn Mawr, PA, 1959).

[12] For more detailed comment on this group, see Don Heckman's articles in *down beat* of 2 January 1964 and 30 June 1966.

[13] Nat Hentoff, quoted in the booklet accompanying *The Complete Candid Recordings of Cecil Taylor and Buell Neidlinger* (Mosaic [A] MR6–127).

[14] Hodeir: *Jazz: Its Evolution and Essence* (see Bibliography), p. 278.

[15] Wendell Otey: 'Hodeir Through His Own Glass', *Jazz: a Quarterly of American Music*, Spring 1959, p. 106.

[16] This book's main discussions of Solal are under **323**, **365**, **473**.

[17] Concerning the title of this movement, 'an aballad', 'a' is meant to invert the meaning of the term, on the model of 'atheist', 'atonal' etc.

[18] For Hodeir's own comments on his *Jazz cantata* (and on two of the *Tripes au Soleil* pieces) see his 'Trois Analyses', *Les Cahiers du Jazz* no.7 (1962).

[19] This is referred to by Joachim Berendt in *The Jazz Book* (see Bibliography), p. 147.

[20] Brief comments on this by Schifrin are quoted in Whitney Balliett: *Such Sweet Thunder* (New York, Bobbs-Merrill, 1966), pp. 63–4.

[21] See Banks's 'Converging Streams', *Musical Times*, June 1970.

[22] Finkelstein: *Jazz: A People's Music* (see Bibliography), *passim.*

[23] The slightly later endeavours in composition and especially in improvisation of John Benson Brooks and Don Heckman should also be mentioned. Alas, these were recorded in an extremely unsatisfactory manner. *Avant Slant* (Decca [A] DL75018), subtitled 'A 12-Tone Collage', mixes segments of their music with excerpts from poetry, radio broadcasts, pop tunes etc. in ways that make it impossible to decide what they had achieved and whether there was a further potential.

[24] In the sleeve note to this Supraphon LP.

[25] Chris Sheridan entry on Most in *The New Grove Dictionary of Jazz* (see Bibliography), p. 809.

[26] *Notes to you* appeared in 1965 as an item in an LP anthology, *Modern Jazz Hall of Fame* (Allegro [E] ALL73). Scott's remark is quoted in the entry on Scott in Carr, Fairweather, Priestley: *Jazz: The Essential Companion* (see Bibliography), p. 444.

[27] *In Miles Davis Chronicle: the Complete Prestige Recordings 1951–56* (†Prestige [A] 1028); Powell's Celia is in *The Complete Bud Powell* (†Verve [A] 314 521 669–2).

[28] In a conversation between Evans and Charles Fox broadcast on BBC Radio 3, 28 August 1978.

[29] The words are Wagner's: see T. W. Adorno: *In Search of Wagner* (New York, Schocken Books, 1981), p. 71.

[30] Don Heckman: 'Gil Evans on his own', *Jazz Review*, March–April 1960, pp. 14–17.

[31] Heckman, *op. cit.*

[32] Alun Morgan: 'Art Pepper–Marty Paich Inc', *Jazz Monthly*, November 1960, p. 7.

[33] Quoted in the sleeve note to *Tomorrow Is the Question* (†Original Jazz Classics [A] OJCCD342).

[34] D. N. Pepperell: 'Art Pepper', *The Wire*, June 1986, p. 26.

[35] Pierre Boulez: *Relèves d'Apprenti* (Paris, Seuil, 1966).

[36] Harrison: *A Jazz Retrospect* (see Bibliography), p. 31.

[37] See Zorn in *The Wire*, March 1989, p. 36.

[38] Quoted by Chris Parker in *Jazz the Magazine* no. 18, p. 20.

[39] From his liner note to this CD.

[40] Nichols's output for Blue Note, 30 tunes and 18 alternatives, are gathered on *The Complete Blue Note Recordings of Herbie Nichols* (Mosaic [A] MR5–118). The Hi-Lo 78s, five tunes and two alternatives, are collected on Savoy Jazz (E) WL70829.

[41] Liner note to Soul Note (It) SN1054.

[42] Quoted in *Jazz: The Modern Resurgence* (see Bibliography) by SN.

[43] John Storm Roberts in *Melody Maker*, 7 February 1976, p. 47.

[44] Kevin Lynch in *Coda*, February 1978, p. 18.

[45] John Litweiler: *The Freedom Principle* (see Bibliography), p. 274.

[46] This was in a conversation recorded on †Leo (E) CDLR204/5.

[47] Koglmann's beginnings are perhaps best represented by *Schlaf Schlemmer, Schlaf Magritte* (†Hat Art [Sw] CD6108) 1984, though he started with *Flaps* (Pipe Records [Au] 151) dating from 1973 and including Steve Lacy in its personnel, and *Opium/For Franz* (Pipe Records 152) 1976, which has Bill Dixon and Lacy.

[48] This is quoted in a booklet titled *Franz Koglmann Pipetet* published by the Wiener Musik Galerie, Vienna, to mark the tenth anniversary of the founding of the Pipetet in 1993, p. 22.

[49] *Op cit.*, p. 6.

[50] We cannot be sure of Koglmann's intentions regarding the title of this CD or of the individual composition. L'Heure Bleue was a Guerlain perfume that always seemed part of the distinctive odour of French cafés between the wars, along with cigarette smoke, garlic, hot chocolate, cognac and water. Equally *L'heure bleue* was the title of a tune by Mischa Spoliansky first heard in a late-1920s Berlin revue which

introduced Marlene Dietrich in a small part. Incidentally Stangl's *Blue angel* was, according to the disc container, 'inspired by M.D.'.

[51] Quoted in the Pipetet booklet, p. 27.

[52] Tristano had to defend himself against similar charges and his comments in *down beat*, 16 May 1956, are still worth attention.

[53] See Ann Beatty: 'Bill Evans: Portrait of His Life as a Jazz Pianist and Musical Analysis of his Style' in *Jazz Research Papers 1986*, ed. Charles Brown (National Association of Jazz Educators, Manhattan, Kansas, 1986), pp. 37–48. Despite its title, this consists almost entirely of an account of Evans's procedures in metrical displacement with numerous music examples and comments from the pianist himself.

[54] Quoted by Martin Williams in 'Honoring Bill Evans', *Jazz Heritage* (New York, Oxford University Press, 1985), p. 62.

[55] For an unusual exposé of Peterson's routine work, try Pete Rugolo's 1956 orchestration of a sequence of the pianist's improvised choruses in *Oscar and Pete's blues* (EmArcy [A] MG36082). Heard thus, they sound even emptier than usual.

[56] E.g. Burnett James: *Essays on Jazz* (see Bibliography), p. 136.

[57] *Jazz Hot*, April 1973.

[58] Peterson's complete Villengen recordings are brought together on †MPS (G) 513 830–2, a 4-CD boxed set.

[59] James Weldon Johnson: *God's Trombones: Some Negro Sermons in Verse* (London, Allen & Unwin, 1929), p. 16.

[60] Quoted by Ian Carr in Carr, Fairweather, Priestley: *Jazz: The Essential Companion* (see Bibliography), p. 321.

[61] *Baroque Fanfares and Sonatas for Brass* (Nonesuch (A) H71145).

[62] See Claus Schreiner's sleeve note to **471**.

[63] Gary Foster quoted in the sleeve note to **472.**

[64] In the case of *Caravan*, note also the intermediate stages represented by the 1966 and 1967 versions on respectively Columbia (F) CTX40323 and Muza (P) XLO445.

[65] Compare this with the 1978 version on MPS (G) 0068 221.

[66] Solal's deepening perception of the meaning and potentialities of this piece can be traced through earlier performances on Pathé (F) 172731 (1960), RCA-Victor (A) LPM2777 (1963) and PDU (It) A6019 (1974). Note also his improvising on Monk's *Bemsha swing* both within André Hodeir's scoring (Philips [F] 834 542–1, 1956) and in the duet version with Niels-Henning Orsted Pedersen (MPS [G] 68.110, 1976).

[67] Roger Cotterrell: 'John Surman at the LSE,' *Jazz Monthly*, July 1969, p. 18.

[68] Mike Osborne (alt), Surman (bar, sop), Henry Miller (bs), Alan Jackson (d).

[69] Sleeve note to Steam (E) LPSJ106.

[70] Surman interviewed by SN, *The Wire*, October 1995, p. 22.

[71] Unattributed sleeve note to ECM (G) 1528, †ECM 523 749.

[72] *Ibid.*

[73] Zoot Sims interviewed by Ira Gitler on 'Ornette Coleman and Third Stream', *down beat*, 13 April 1961.

[74] Stuart Nicholson: *Jazz: The Modern Resurgence* (see Bibliography), p. 106.

[75] 'Steve Lacy talks to Max Harrison', *Jazz Monthly*, March 1966, p. 7.

[76] Sleeve note for **475**.

[77] *Ibid.*

[78] Erik Weidemann's sleeve note to Bley's *Touching* (Fontana [E] 688 608).

[79] W. Royal Stokes's sleeve note to Bley's *Notes* (Soul Note [It] 121 190).

[80] Erik Weidemann, *op. cit.*

Chapter Seven

[1] Barry McCrae: *The Jazz Cataclysm* (London, Dent, 1967), p. 2.

[2] Max Harrison: 'Stan Kenton – the Innovations Band,' *Jazz Journal*, April–May 1979.

[3] Tennyson: *Idylls of the King*, 'Gareth and Lynette', line 272.

[4] For example, according to Jack Chambers (*Milestones I*, p. 242 – see Bibliography), no review of the *Music for Brass* LP ever appeared in North America.

[5] This performance is best heard along with the 1963 version of *Three little feelings* by Orchestra USA (Colpix [A] CLP448).

[6] Babbitt, quoted in the booklet by Martin Brody and Dennis Miller accompanying Robert Taub's recording of Babbitt's complete solo piano music (Harmonia Mundi [A] HMC5160).

[7] For the beginnings of an analysis of *All set* see Louis Gottlieb: 'The Brandeis Festival Album', *Jazz: A Quarterly of American Music*, Spring 1959. This essay also contains remarks on the other Brandeis pieces except Giuffre's *Suspensions*. For another performance of *All set*, hear the Contemporary Chamber Players (Nonesuch [A] H713303).

[8] *Revelations* is subtitled 'First movement' and seems to have remained incomplete. Brian Priestley has suggested that two other Mingus pieces, *Diane* and *Farwells*, might have been intended as second and third movements (*Mingus*, p. 106 – see Bibliography). But when *Revelations* was performed by the New York Philharmonic under Schuller (see *down beat*, 7 September 1978) these were not included.

[9] Quoted in the sleeve note to the original LP issue (Columbia [A] WL127).

[10] Macero's sleeve note to **479**.

[11] Joachim Kaiser: *Grosse Pianisten in unserer Zeit* (Munich, 1965).

[12] *Jazz Monthly*, February 1973.

[13] John Litweiler: *The Freedom Principle* (see Bibliography), pp. 288–9.

[14] Quoted by Ian Carr in Carr, Fairweather, Priestley: *Jazz: The Essential Companion* (see Bibliography), p. 45.

[15] *The Times*, 22 August 1987.

[16] *down beat*, 20 February 1957.

[17] See Graham Lock: 'Chris McGregor – An African Way of Swing', *The Wire*, February 1985, pp. 40–3.

[18] Quoted by Brian Priestley in the sleeve note to *This Is Dollar Brand* (Black Lion [E] BLP30139).

[19] More detailed comments on this will be found on pp. 319–22 of Paul Oliver, Max Harrison, William Bolcom: *The New Grove Gospel, Blues and Jazz* (see Bibliography).

[20] *Jazz Monthly*, May 1967.

Chapter Eight

[1] Interview with Wynton Marsalis by SN, 19 October 1991. See also *Wynton Marsalis: Uptown Ruler* by SN, *Jazz FM Magazine*, issue 10.

[2] *Ibid.*

[3] Scott DeVeaux: 'Constructing the Tradition' in O'Meally (ed.): *The Jazz Cadence of American Culture* (Columbia University Press, New York, 1998), p. 504.

[4] Interview with Wynton Marsalis by SN, 19 October 1991.

[5] David Liebman: *Self Portrait of a Jazz Artist* (Advance Music, Rottenburg, Germany, 1988), p. 51.

[6] *down beat*, 23 October 1975, p. 40.

[7] Crotchet = 284.

[8] Miss Elias would go on to secure a recording contract in her own right with the reconstituted Blue Note label and marry Michael Brecker's brother Randy.

[9] An elegant poise which appealed to the young musicians in Woody Herman's Herd, who adapted the composition for big band on *Woody Herman: 50th Anniversary Tour* (Concord [A] CJ302).

[10] Crotchet = 174.

[11] Although this rhythm is traditionally shown by arrangers as a dotted quaver–semiquaver, it is actually articulated in common practice as a quaver triplet with the first two quavers tied, so the first (tied) note has two-thirds the value of a crotchet, the second, one-third the value.

[12] Actually, a B-flat 7 sus flat 9 chord, although Gomez does treat this as a pedal from time to time during the improvisations.

[13] The piece in 4/4 but has a distinct cut-time feel, minim = 118.

[14] Interview with SN, 14 January 1997. Quoted in Stuart Nicholson: *Jazz-Rock: A History* (see Bibliography), p. 244. It is interesting to note that the critical ambivalence to which Mainieri refers was not shared by European audiences, who greeted the band with great enthusiasm, as the video *Steps Ahead: Live in Copenhagen* (Titania Television) revealed.

[15] Quoted in *Jazz: The Modern Resurgence* by SN (see Bibliography), p. 182.

[16] Subsequently arranged for his memorable big band by the late Julius Hemphill.

[17] *Pastel rhapsody* on *Tin Can Alley* (ECM [G] 1189) and *Ebony* on *Inflation Blues* (ECM [G] 1244).

[18] For example, with Pat Metheny and Ornette Coleman on *Song X* (**439**); with the Keith Jarrett 'Standards' trio; and on albums by John Abercrombie, Sonny Rollins, Betty Carter, Michael Brecker among others, all requiring a compellingly different approach.

[19] Quoted in *down beat*, 7 January 1971, p. 23.

[20] Interview with SN, 15 May 1998.

[21] The phrase begins at the end of bar four.

[22] Interview with SN, 15 May 1998.

[23] Crotchet = 240.

[24] Steve Bernstein to SN, 11 August 1998. The full quote: 'The young jazz scene now is a bunch of guys playing hard-bop songs and other people's solos. The whole concept is like robbing the dead.'

[25] Mark Levine: *The Jazz Theory Book* (see Bibliography), p. vii.

[26] David Liebman: *Self Portrait of a Jazz Artist* (Advance Music, Rottenburg, Germany, 1988), p. 51.

[27] Interview with SN, 5 November 1996.

[28] *Ibid.*

[29] *New Yorker*, 19 January 1998, p. 13.

[30] Liner note to *Stargazer* (Arabesque Jazz [A] AJ0132).

[31] *down beat*, August 1998, p. 50.

[32] Record-company press release to accompany the Clusone Trio's album *I Am an Indian* (†Gramavision [A] CD79505).

[33] Kevin Whitehead: *The New Dutch Swing* (Billboard Books, New York 1998), p. 164.

[34] Matei Calinescu: *Five Faces of Modernity: Modernism, Avant Garde, Decadence, Kitsch, Postmodernism* (Duke University Press, Durham, 1987), p. 125.

[35] *down beat*, May 1986, p. 24.

[36] *Ibid.*

[37] *The Wire*, March 1986, p. 7.

[38] Liner note to *Keith Jarrett: The Impulse Years 1973–4* (†Impulse [A] IMPD5237), p. 7.

[39] Mark C. Gridley: *Jazz Styles* (see Bibliography), p. 255.

[40] Interview with SN, 12 July 1992.

[41] *down beat*, May 1986, p. 57.

[42] Interview with SN, 12 July 1992.

[43] *New York Times*, 15 January 1995, p. 28H.

[44] Press quote in publicity for *Live! Bill Frisell* (†Rykodisc GCD79504).

[45] *down beat*, January 1998, pp. 17–18.

[46] Stuart Nicholson: *Jazz: The 1980s Resurgence* (see Bibliography), p. 273.

[47] *down beat*, February 1991, p. 31.

[48] Interview with SN, quoted in Stuart Nicholson: *Jazz: The 1980s Resurgence* (see Bibliography), p. 271.

[49] Insert note to *John Zorn: Spillane* (Elektra Nonesuch [A] 979172–1).

[50] *New York Times*, 27 February 1989.

[51] *New York Times*, 16 June 1996.

[52] Liner note to *At His Very Best: Duke Ellington and His Orchestra* (RCA Victor [E] RD27133).

[53] Andreas Huyssen: *After the Great Divide* (Indiana University Press, Bloomington, 1986), p. 101.

[54] Michael Dorf: *Knitting Music* (Knitting Factory Works, New York, 1992), p. 45.

[55] Bill Laswell interviewed by SN for BBC Radio 3, transmitted 30 May 1998.

[56] *Ibid.*

[57] *down beat*, July 1986, p. 26.

[58] Scott DeVeaux: 'Constructing the Tradition' in O'Meally (ed.): *The Jazz Cadence of American Culture* (Columbia University Press, New York, 1998).

[59] My own interviews for the *Observer* between 1996–9 with John Surman, Bobo Stenson, Gary Crosby, Louis Sclavis, Mike Westbrook, Ian Carr, Gerard Presencer and Kenny Wheeler among others all suggest that this belief is widely held among European musicians.

[60] Scott DeVeaux, *op. cit.*

[61] Notes accompanying *Invisible Storm* (ECM [G] 1461), 1992.

[62] Liner note to *Ode to the Death of Jazz* (ECM [G] 1413).

[63] *San Francisco Weekly*, 12–18 June 1996.

[64] Here I refer to quantifiable rhythmic patterns. Certainly free jazz was radical, but it often avoided rhythm altogether, the role of the drummer becoming more of a colourist, responding to the ebb and flow of the improviser's impulse using nonstandard rhythms, often on 'found' instruments that might include hub caps, bells or even sheets of metal. When time-keeping was present, it often took the form of an abstraction of the orthodox time-keeping practices of the jazz mainstream.

[65] Letter from Peter Apfelbaum to SN, 20 December 1996.

[66] *Ibid.*

[67] *Ibid.*

Bibliography

R – reprint; / – edition.

Encyclopaedias and Biographical Dictionaries

G. Testoni and others: *Enciclopedia del jazz* (Milan, 1953, rev and enlarged 2/1954)

W. Laade, W. Ziefle and D. Zimmerle: *Jazz Lexikon* (Stuttgart, Germany, 1953)

L. Feather: *Encyclopaedia of Jazz* (New York, 1955, rev and enlarged 2/1960/*R* 1984)

S. Longstreet and A. Dauer: *Knaurs Jazz Lexikon* (Munich, Germany, 1957)

L. Feather: *Encyclopaedia of Jazz in the Sixties* (New York, 1966/*R* 1986)

F. Tenot and P. Carles: *Dictionnaire du jazz* (Paris, 1967)

C. Bohländer and K. Holler: *Reclams Jazzführer* (Stuttgart, Germany, 1970, rev and enlarged 2/1977)

R. Kinkle: *Complete Encyclopaedia of Popular Music and Jazz 1900–50* (Westport, CT, 1974)

L. Feather and I. Gitler: *The Encyclopaedia of Jazz in the Seventies* (New York, 1976/*R* 1987)

I. Carr, D. Fairweather and B. Priestley: *Jazz: The Essential Companion* (London, 1987)

B. Kernfeld (ed.): *The New Grove Dictionary of Jazz* (2 vols.) (London, 1988)

Analytical and Historical Surveys

B. Ulanov: *A History of Jazz in America* (New York, 1952/*R* 1972)

L. Malson: *Les Maîtres du Jazz* (Paris, 1952, rev 6/1972)

A. Dauer: *Der Jazz: seine Ursprünge und seine Entwicklung* (Kassel, Germany, 1958, 3/1977)

N. Hentoff and A. McCarthy (eds.): *Jazz: New Perspectives on the History of Jazz* (New York, 1959/*R* 1974)
W. Mellers: *Music in a New Found Land: Themes and Developments in the History of American Music* (London, 1964/*R* 1988)
J. Goldberg: *Jazz Masters of the Fifties* (New York, 1965/*R* 1980)
J. Wilson: *Jazz: The Transition Years 1940–60* (New York, 1966)
I. Gitler: *Jazz Masters of the Forties* (New York, 1966/*R* 1983)
W. Mellers: *Caliban Reborn: Renewal in 20th-Century Music* (London, 1968)
D. Baker: *Jazz Styles and Analysis: A History of the Jazz Trombone via Recorded Solos* (Chicago, 1973)
A. Polillo: *Jazz: le vicenda e i protagonisti della musica afro-americana* (Milan, 1975, rev 2/1983)
J. Coker: *The Jazz Idiom* (Englewood Cliffs, NJ, 1975)
M. Gridley: *Jazz Styles: History and Analysis* (Englewood Cliffs, NJ, 1978, rev and enlarged 5/1994)
J. Collier: *The Making of Jazz: A Comprehensive History* (Boston, 1978)
B. Herzog zu Mecklenburg: *Stilformen des modernen Jazz: vom Swing zum Free Jazz* (Baden-Baden, Germany, 1979)
J. Berendt: *The Jazz Book: From New Orleans to Fusion and Beyond* (Westport, CT, 1982)
B. Taylor: *Jazz Piano: History and Development* (Dubuque, IA, 1982)
M. Weiss: *Jazz Styles and Analysis* (Chicago, 1982)
J. Rockwell: *All American Music: Composition in the late 20th Century* (New York, 1983)
I. Gitler: *Swing to Bop: An Oral History of the Transition in Jazz in the 1940s* (New York, 1985)
P. Oliver, M. Harrison and W. Bolcom: *The New Grove Gospel, Blues and Jazz* (London, 1986)
P. van der Merwe: *Origins of the Popular Style* (London, 1989)
G. Schuller: *The Swing Era: The Development of Jazz 1930–45* (New York, 1989)
S. Nicholson: *Jazz: The Modern Resurgence* (London, 1990)
T. Gioia: *The History of Jazz* (New York, 1998)

Record Guides

J. Wilson: *The Collector's Jazz: Modern* (Philadelphia, 1959)
A. McCarthy and others: *Jazz on Record: A Critical Guide to the First 50 Years 1917–1967* (London, 1968)
M. Cullaz: *Guide des disques de jazz* (Paris, 1971)
M. Harrison and others: *Modern Jazz: The Essential Records 1945–70* (London, 1975)
M. Harrison, C. Fox and E. Thacker: *The Essential Jazz Records Vol. 1: Ragtime to Swing* (London, 1984)
R. Cook and B. Morton: *The Penguin Guide to Jazz on CD, LP and Cassette* (London, 1992)

Criticism

S. Finkelstein: *Jazz: A People's Music* (New York, 1948/*R* 1975)
J. Berendt: *Der Jazz: eine zeitkritische Studie* (Stuttgart, Germany, 1950)
A. Hodeir: *Jazz: Its Evolution and Essence* (London, 1956/*R* 1975)
J. Berendt: *Variationen über Jazz* (Munich, Germany, 1956)
M. Williams (ed.): *The Art of Jazz: Essays on the Nature and Development of Jazz* (New York, 1959/*R* 1979 as *The Art of Jazz: Ragtime to Bebop*)
L. Ostransky: *The Anatomy of Jazz* (Seattle, 1960)
M. James: *Ten Modern Jazzmen* (London, 1960)
N. Hentoff: *The Jazz Life* (New York, 1961/*R* 1975)
B. James: *Essays on Jazz* (London, 1961/*R* 1985)
A. Dauer: *Jazz, die magische Musik* (Bremen, Germany, 1961)
M. Williams (ed.): *Jazz Panorama* (New York, 1962/*R* 1979)
B. Green: *The Reluctant Art* (London, 1962)
A. Hodeir: *Toward Jazz* (New York, 1962/*R* 1976)
C. Fox: *Jazz in Perspective* (London, 1969)
M. Williams: *The Jazz Tradition* (New York, 1970, rev 2/1983)
A. Hodeir: *The Worlds of Jazz* (New York, 1972)
M. Harrison: *A Jazz Retrospect* (London, 1976/*R* 1977/*R* 1991)
J. Berendt: *Ein Fenster aus Jazz: Essays, Portraits, Reflexionen* (Frankfurt, Germany, 1977)
G. Endress: *Jazz Podium: Musiker über sich selbst* (Stuttgart, Germany, 1980)
B. Noglik: *Jazzwerkstatt international* (Berlin, 1981 2/1983)
G. Giddins: *Riding on a Blue Note: Jazz and American Pop* (New York, 1981)
G. Giddins: *Rhythm-a-ning: Jazz Tradition and Innovation in the 1980s* (New York, 1985)
F. Davis: *In the Moment: Jazz in the 1980s* (New York, 1986)
G. Schuller: *Musings: The Musical Worlds of Gunther Schuller* (New York, 1986)
D. Ramsey: *Jazz Matters* (Fayetteville, AR, 1989)
F. Davis: *Outcats: Jazz Composers, Instrumentalists and Singers* (New York, 1990)
G. Giddins: *Faces in the Crowd: Players and Writers* (New York, 1992)
G. Santoro: *Dancing in Your Head* (New York, 1993)
G. Santoro: *Stir It Up: Music Mixes from Roots to Jazz* (New York, 1997)
F. Davis: *Bebop and Nothingness: Jazz and Pop at the End of the Century* (New York, 1996)
R. Gottlieb (ed.): *Reading Jazz* (New York, 1997)

In Theory

G. Russell: *The Lydian Chromatic Concept of Tonal Organization* (New York, 1953)
W. Russo: *Composing for the Jazz Orchestra* (Chicago, 1961)
P. McShay: *Seven Theories of Jazz* (St Louis, MO, 1965)

W. Russo: *Jazz Composition and Orchestration* (Chicago, 1968, rev 2/1975)
K. Stanton: *Jazz Theory: A Creative Approach* (New York, 1982)
A. Jaffe: *Jazz Theory* (Dubuque, IA, 1983)
M. Levine: *The Jazz Theory Book* (Petaluma, CA, 1995)

Improvisation

J. Mehegan: *Jazz Improvisation* Vols. 1–4 (New York, 1959–65)
J. Coker: *Improvising Jazz* (Englewood Cliffs, NJ, 1964)
D. Baker: *Advanced Improvisation* (Chicago, 1971, rev 1979)
D. Noll: *Zur Improvisation im deutschen Free Jazz: Untersuchungen zur Asthetik frei improvisierter Klangflächen* (Hamburg, Germany, 1977)
B. Dobbins: *The Contemporary Jazz Pianist: A Comprehensive Approach to Keyboard Improvisation* (Jamestown, RI, 1978, 2/1984)
D. Bailey: *Improvisation: Its Nature and Practice in Music* (Ashbourne, England, 1980)
D. Zinn: *The Structure and Analysis of the Modern Improvised Line* (New York, 1981)
B. Benward and J. Wildman: *Jazz Improvisation in Theory and Practice* (Dubuque, IA, 1984)

Studies of Particular Styles

N. Griffin: *To Be or Not to Bop* (New York, 1948)
L. Feather: *Inside Be-bop* (New York, 1949/*R* 1977 as *Inside Jazz*)
R. Russell: *Jazz Style in Kansas City and the Southwest* (Los Angeles, 1971/*R* 1983, rev 2/1973)
J. Roberts: *Black Music of Two Worlds* (New York, 1972)
I. Carr: *Music Outside: Contemporary Jazz in Britain* (London, 1973)
E. Jost: *Free Jazz* (Graz, Austria, 1974)
J. Viera: *Der Free Jazz: Formen und Modelle* (Vienna, 1974)
H. Kumpf: *Postserielle Musik und Free Jazz* (Herrenberg, Germany, 1975, rev 2/1981)
M. Budds: *Jazz in the Sixties: the Expansion of Musical Resources and Techniques* (Iowa City, IA, 1978, rev 1990)
R. Brinknian (ed.): *Avantgarde Jazz: Tendenzen zwischen Tonalität und Atonalität* (Mainz, Germany, 1978)
J. Roberts: *The Latin Tinge: The Impact of Latin-American Music on the US* (New York, 1979)
M. Luzzi: *Uomini e avantguardie jazz* (Milan, 1980)
S. Starr: *Red and Hot: The Fate of Jazz in the Soviet Union 1917–80* (New York, 1983)
J. Litweiler: *The Freedom Principle: Jazz after 1958* (New York, 1984)
H. Hellhund: *Cool Jazz: Grundzüge seiner Entstehlung und Entwicklung* (Mainz, Germany, 1985)
R. Gordon: *Jazz West Coast* (New York, 1986)

K. Eklund: *Jazz West 1945–85: The A-Z Guide to West Coast Jazz* (Carmel, CA, 1986)
T. Gioia: *West Coast Jazz* (New York, 1992)
D. Oliphant (ed.): *The Bebop Revolution in Words and Music* (Austin, TX, 1994)
L. Erenberg: *Swingin' the Dream* [big bands] (Chicago, 1998)
S. DeVeaux: *The Birth of Bebop* (New York, 1998)
S. Nicholson: *Jazz Rock: A History* (New York, 1998)

Studies of Individual Musicians

M. James: *Dizzy Gillespie* (London, 1959, repr in *Kings of Jazz*, ed. S. Green, New York, 1978)
N. Hentoff: *John Lewis* (New York, 1960)
M. Harrison: *Charlie Parker* (London, 1960, repr in *Kings of Jazz*, ed. S. Green, New York, 1978)
V. Franchini: *Lester Young* (Milan, 1961)
M. James: *Miles Davis* (London, 1961, repr in *Kings of Jazz*, ed. S. Green, New York, 1978)
R. Reisner: *Bird: The Legend of Charlie Parker* (New York, 1962/*R* 1975)
A. Spellman: *Four Lives in the Bebop Business* [Ornette Coleman, Cecil Taylor, Herbie Nichols, Jackie McLean] (New York, 1966/*R* 1970 as *Black Music: Four Lives*)
R. Russell: *Bird Lives: The High Life and Hard Times of Charlie Parker* (New York, 1973)
V. Simosko and B. Tepperman: *Eric Dolphy: A Musical Biography and Discography* (Washington, DC, 1974)
F. Kerschbaumer: *Miles Davis: stilkritische Untersuchungen zur musikalischen Entwicklung seines Personalstils* (Graz, Austria, 1978)
D. Baker: *J. J. Johnson, Trombone* (New York, 1979)
D. Baker: *The Jazz Style of Sonny Rollins: A Musical and Historical Perspective* (Lebanon, IN, 1980)
D. Baker: *The Jazz Style of Miles Davis: A Musical and Historical Perspective* (Lebanon, IN, 1980)
D. Baker: *The Jazz Style of John Coltrane: A Musical and Historical Perspective* (Lebanon, IN, 1980)
B. Priestley: *Charles Mingus: A Critical Biography* (London, 1982)
D. Baker: *The Jazz Style of Clifford Brown: A Musical and Historical Perspective* (Hialeah, FL, 1982)
D. Baker: *The Jazz Style of Fats Navarro: A Musical and Historical Perspective* (Hialeah, FL, 1982)
E. Nisenson: *Round about Midnight: A Portrait of Miles Davis* (New York, 1982)
G. Filtgen and M. Ausserbauer: *John Coltrane: sein Leben, seine Musik, seine Schallplatten* (Gauting, Germany, 1983)
J. Chambers: *Milestones I: The Music and Times of Miles Davis to 1960*

(Toronto, 1983); *Milestones II: The Music and Times of Miles Davis since 1960* (Toronto, 1985)
M. Hames: *Albert Ayler, Sunny Murray, Cecil Taylor on Disc and Tape* (Ferndown, England, 1983)
C. Blancq: *Sonny Rollins: The Journey of a Jazzman* (Boston, 1983)
M. Luzzi: *Charles Mingus* (Rome, 1983)
P. Wiessmüller: *Miles Davis: sein Leben, seine Musik, seine Schallplatten* (Gauting, Germany, 1984)
H. Weber and G. Filtgen: *Charles Mingus: sein Leben, seine Musik, seine Schallplatten* (Gauting, Germany, 1984)
B. Priestley: *Charlie Parker* (Tunbridge Wells, England, 1984)
D. Gelly: *Lester Young* (Tunbridge Wells, England, 1985)
C. Fox: *Sit Down and Listen: The Story of Max Roach* (London, 1985)
L. Porter: *Lester Young* (Boston, 1985)
A. Agostinelli: *Don Ellis: A Man for Our Time 1934–78* (Providence, RI, 1986)
A. Bassi: *Giorgio Gaslini* (Milan, 1986)
S. Voce: *Woody Herman* (Tunbridge Wells, England, 1986)
K. Knox and G. Lindqvist: *Jazz Amour Affair: en bok om Lars Gullin* (Stockholm, 1986)
F. Paudras: *La Danse des Infidèles* [Bud Powell] (Paris, 1986)
B. Priestley: *John Coltrane* (Tunbridge Wells, England, 1987)
J. Woelfer: *Dizzy Gillespie: sein Leben, seine Musik, seine Schallplatten* (Waakirchen, Germany, 1987)
T. Fitterling: *Thelonious Monk: seine Leben, seine Musik, seine Schallplatten* (Waakirchen, Germany, 1987)
G. Giddins: *Celebrating Bird: The Triumph of Charlie Parker* (New York, 1988)
G. Lees: *Oscar Peterson: The Will to Swing* (Toronto, 1988)
L. Koch: *Yardbird Suite: A Compendium of the Music and Life of Charlie Parker* (Bowling Green, Ohio, 1988)
M. Miller: *Cool Blues: Charlie Parker in Canada 1953* (London, Ontario, 1989)
M. Hennessey: *Klook: The Story of Kenny Clarke* (London, 1990)
L. Porter: *A Lester Young Reader* (Washington, DC, 1992)
J. Reilly: *The Harmony of Bill Evans* (New York, 1992)
J. Litweiler: *Ornette Coleman: A Harmolodic Life* (New York, 1993)
S. Nicholson: *Ella Fitzgerald* (London, New York, 1993)
R. Williams: *The Man in the Green Shirt* [Miles Davis] (London, 1993)
J. Ponzio and F. Postif: *Blue Monk: Portrait de Thelonious* (Arles, France, 1996)
S. Nicholson: *Billie Holiday* (London, Boston, 1995)
C. Woideck: *Charlie Parker: His Music and Life* (Ann Arbor, MI, 1996)
H. Martin: *Charlie Parker and Thematic Improvisation* (Lanham, MD, 1996)
J. Szwed: *Space is the Place: The Lives and Times of Sun Ra* (New York, 1997)
T. Fitterling: *Thelonious Monk: His Life and Music* (Berkeley, CA, 1997)
C. Woideck (ed.): *The Charlie Parker Companion* (New York, 1998)

B. Kirchner (ed.): *A Miles Davis Reader* (Washington, DC, 1998)
I. Carr: *Miles Davis: The Definitive Biography* (London, 1998)
C. Woideck (ed.): *The John Coltrane Companion* (New York, 1998)
G. Carner (ed.): *The Miles Davis Companion* (New York, 1998)
P. Pettinger: *How My Heart Sings* [Bill Evans] (New York, 1998)

Musicians' Memoirs

C. *Beneath the Underdog* (New York, 1971)
H. Hawes: *Raise Up Off Me* (New York, 1974)
A. and L. Pepper: *Straight Life* (New York, 1979)
D. Gillespie and A. Fraser: *To Be or Not to Bop* (Garden City, 1979)
A. O'Day: *High Times, Hard Times* (New York, 1981)
M. Davis and Q. Troupe: *Miles: The Autobiography* (New York, 1989)
S. Nicholson: *Reminiscing in Tempo – A Portrait of Duke Ellington* (London, Boston, 1999)

Index of Album Titles

References are to numbered LPs/CDs in the text, *not* to page numbers.

Index of Track Titles

References are to numbered LPs/CDs in the text, *not* to page numbers.

Index of Individual Musicians

References are to numbered LPs/CDs in the text, *not* to page numbers.